SNAKES

of the

UNITED STATES _and_ CANADA

SNAKES
of the
UNITED STATES *and* CANADA

CARL H. ERNST • EVELYN M. ERNST

SMITHSONIAN BOOKS   Washington and London

Copy Editor: Bonnie J. Harmon
Production Editor: E. Anne Bolen
Designer: Janice Wheeler

Library of Congress Cataloging-in-Publication Data
Ernst, Carl H.
    Snakes of the United States and Canada / Carl H. Ernst and
Evelyn M. Ernst.
        p.   cm.
    Includes bibliographical references (p.)
    ISBN 1-58834-019-8 (alk. paper)
    1. Snakes—United States.   2. Snakes—Canada.   I. Ernst,
Evelyn M.   II. Title.
QL666.06 E763 2003
597.96′097—dc21   2002026924

British Library Cataloguing-in-Publication Data is available

Manufactured in China
10 09 08 07 06 05 04 03   5 4 3 2 1

To our daughters and sons-in-law,

Lydia and Paul Dengel,

and Carol and David Robertson

Contents

Elapidae: Elapid Snakes

Viperidae: Viperid Snakes

Acknowledgments

Several persons have contributed in various ways to the publication of this book. R. D. Bartlett, William S. Brown, David M. Carroll, Ronald J. Crombie, James R. Dixon, Thomas H. Fritts, J. Whitfield Gibbons, Steve W. Gotte, James H. Harding, Jeffrey E. Lovich, Robert E. Lovich, Roy W. McDiarmid, Tony Mills, Robert P. Reynolds, Javier A. Rodriquez-Robles, Jay C. Shaffer, Lee M. Talbot, Cameron Young, and George R. Zug gave advice and encouragement. Our students Thomas S. Akre, Timothy P. Boucher, Timothy R. Brophy, Terry R. Creque, Sandra D'Alessandro, Kerry A. Hansknecht, Traci D. Hartsell, Arndt F. Laemmerzahl, John M. Orr, Carol M. Robertson, Shiela Tuttle, James C. Wilgenbusch, and Thomas P. Wilson helped in the field. Bernice Barbour and the Barbour family allowed us to use photographs by the late Roger W. Barbour, and other photographs or specimens were supplied by R. D. Bartlett, Christopher W. Brown, Donald J. Fisher, Steve W. Gotte, Robert W. Hansen, James H. Harding, Christopher R. Harrison, William Leonard, Jeffrey E. Lovich, Robert E. Lovich, Barry W. Mansell, Peter G. May, Liam McGranaghan, Brad R. Moon, Norman J. Scott, Jr., Cecil R. Schwalbe, John H. Tashjian, Thomas P. Wilson, and George R. Zug.

Introduction

Of all the vertebrate animals on earth, snakes are probably among the most easily recognized but least understood. Everyone knows what they look like and usually has some story of a personal encounter or one that they have heard. As these tales get told and retold, they often become so distorted they are either completely false or almost so. With so many "tales" being told, it is not surprising that people often misunderstand and fear these magnificent creatures. There are two probable reasons for their fears. First, some snakes are dangerous, and their bites can cause severe systemic damage or death. In North America, such snakes are in the minority and are seldom encountered unless one is looking for them. Without doubt, our snake fauna should be respected, just as most wild animals should be given their space. But the level of fear that many exhibit toward snakes is completely unwarranted. A second reason that many people may fear snakes is probably related to their portrayal as a symbol of evil, or as Satan's helper, in many historical, mythological, or religious writings. We take the view that the sins of humans are their own, and making snakes into scapegoats will hardly improve our moral standing. This book attempts to present a balanced picture of the lives of snakes, to tell an honest picture that, we believe, will dispel fears of these fascinating reptiles.

Taxonomy

Snakes, along with lizards and amphisbaenians, belong to the reptile subclass Lepidosauria and the order Squamata, sharing the key taxonomic trait of a modified diapsid skull—that is, a skull that evolved by having a ventral bar that closed the lower temporal opening, leaving only one temporal opening. Snakes are differentiated taxonomically by being classified as the suborder Serpentes, whereas lizards and amphisbaenians belong to the suborder Lacertilia. Presently, there are over 2,600 species of living snakes in the world.

Origins

Snakes have inhabited the earth since the Cretaceous Period. The oldest snake fossils are two vertebrae from the Early Cretaceous of Spain that are over 120 million years old. While certainly being from a snake, they are incomplete and cannot be identified as originating from any particular species. However, the snake *Lapparentophis duffrennei* is known to have lived in the Sahara Desert of Algeria during the Early Cretaceous about 96–100 million years ago. Unfortunately, its three vertebrae offer no clue as to the origin of snakes. The species is considered unique, and it has been assigned to its own family, Lapparentophiidae. Two unrelated snake genera, *Simoliophis* and *Pouitella* are known from the Mid- to Late Cretaceous. Although none of these ancient snakes seems directly related to modern snakes, the beginnings of several modern snake groups are known to have occurred in the Cretaceous— the boas (Boidae), pipesnakes (Aniliidae), and the extinct dinilysids (Dinilysiidae). Snakes also made their first appearance in North America in the Late Cretaceous with several pipesnakes and a possible sandboa in Canada and the United States. After the Cretaceous, snakes evolved into several families, and by the end of the Pleistocene, some 11,000 years ago, the modern North American snake fauna was in place (Ernst and Zug 1996; Holman 2000). It is possible that snakes evolved either from lizards or mosasaurs. Long-bodied fossils from the Middle Cretaceous, *Pachyrhachis* and *Haasiophis*, have some snakelike characters but retain hind-limb elements (Greene and Cundall 2000; Tchernov et al. 2000), so the origin of snakes is still unresolved.

Modern Snake Fauna of North America

The snake fauna of the United States and Canada is a diverse one, consisting of six families: Boidae (boas), Leptotyphlopidae (slender blindsnakes), Typhlopidae (blindsnakes), Colubridae (colubrid snakes), Viperidae (pit vipers), and Elapidae (coral snakes). Within these families are 52 genera and 131 species: Leptotyphlopidae (1 genus, 2 species), Typhlopidae (1 genus, 1 species), Boidae (2 genera, 3 species), Colubridae (42 genera, 105 species), Elapidae (3 genera, 3 species), and Viperidae (3 genera, 17 species). Most species are native to North America, but two have been introduced—the Boa constrictor *(Boa constrictor)* and Brahminy blindsnake *(Ramphotyphlops braminus)*. Most species are terrestrial, but seven genera contain semiaquatic species *(Agkistrodon, Clonophis, Farancia, Nerodia, Regina, Seminatrix, Thamnophis),* and the Elapidae contains a marine species *(Pelamis platurus).*

Although exotic species of snakes (former pets that have become feral) are sometimes found in the wilds of North America, until now only the two introduced species mentioned above have established populations. There is, however, the potential for a third foreign species to become part of the fauna of the United States (at least in Florida and Hawaii; Fritts 1984). This is the mildly venomous, rear-fanged, brown tree snake *(Boiga irregularis),* a ravenous predator on birds and other small vertebrates, which, after it was introduced onto Guam, decimated the island's bird and lizard populations, and even entered houses and bit babies. Several individuals of this snake have been found stowed away in military cargo shipped from Guam to Hawaii (Thomas H. Fritts, pers. comm.), and one was found in crated household goods shipped from Guam to Texas (McCoid et al. 1994). While introduction of *Boa constrictor* and *Ramphotyphlops braminus* has caused little disturbance to our native fauna, it would be different if the highly destructive *Boiga irregularis* were to gain a foothold in the United States. Vigilance must be kept to prevent this from happening.

Characteristics

Although they have undergone considerable adaptation to different habitats and lifestyles, all snakes share certain characteristics. They are elongated reptiles with no apparent limbs, although remnants of limb girdles are present in several of the oldest families (Boidae, Pythonidae, Leptotyphlopidae, Typhlopidae). No sternum is present, so all ribs are floating. Their skulls consist of three functional units: a bony braincase (cranium) that surrounds and protects the brain and also provides points for attachment of muscles and the various jaw bones; sensory capsules attached to the cranium, which contain the nose, eyes, and ears; and the jaw apparatus. The jaw apparatus on each side of the head consists of two to three units in the upper jaw and one lower jaw unit. Each of these units can work independently of both adjacent bones on the same side of the head and of the units on the opposite side of the head. This gives the snake's skull flexibility unmatched by any other vertebrate and permits it to catch and swallow large prey. The lower jaw is composed of a long bone consisting of the fused articular, prearticular, and subangular bones and a somewhat shorter dentary bone. The halves of the lower jaws are attached by an elastic ligament, and attached posteriorly to the cranium by a loose double joint. The upper jaws are also loosely attached to the cranium. In addition, the body is quite distensible since the ribs are free of a sternum; consequently, snakes can swallow prey substantially larger than their usual body circumference. When swallowing large prey, a snake merely "walks" its mouth around the animal by first moving one-half of each jaw forward, then the other; it seems to literally crawl about its prey. As limb girdles are absent in most snakes, the remainder of their skeleton is essentially composed of at least 120 vertebrae and their accompanying ribs on the neck and trunk vertebrae. The number of caudal (tail) vertebrae depends on the length of the tail.

Because of its important contributions to breathing and locomotion, the muscular system is complex. Muscles link adjacent vertebrae to ribs, and more distant vertebrae to each other. They also link vertebrae and ribs to the ventral scutes. These various muscle attachments allow the body to be very flexible.

The internal organs are adapted to the snake's elongated body. The digestive tract is a long, expandable tube extending from the mouth to the anal vent and consists of an esophagus, stomach, small intestine, and large intestine or colon. A long liver and a pancreas discharge bile and digestive enzymes into the small intestine. The mouth usually has numerous teeth that serve to catch, hold, and ingest prey. The teeth also puncture the prey and allow the entrance of digestive enzymes into it. Palatine, labial, lingual, and sublingual salivary glands secrete saliva into the mouth cavity to cover the prey and make it easier

to pass along the esophagus to the stomach. Some enzymes injected into the prey may be venomous (see below). Just inside the anal vent is the cloaca, a shared receptacle into which the digestive, excretory, and reproductive systems empty.

Snakes rely on lungs for breathing. All snakes have a large right lung extending along the body cavity, and many also have a small left one. In many species a new lunglike structure has evolved from the wall of the trachea anterior to the heart. Both the normal and tracheal lungs are simple vascularized sacs with some alveoli and little internal division. No muscular diaphragm is present, as in mammals. Air is pumped in and out of the lungs by expansion and contraction of the ribs in a bellowslike fashion. To aid in breathing while ingesting prey, the epiglottis is protrusible and can be pushed under the food item during the swallowing process.

Most circulatory adaptations are related to the switch from breathing through gills to lung breathing. The heart has three chambers: two atria and a single ventricle (although the ventricle may be partially divided by an incomplete interventricular septum). A sinus venosus, incorporated into the wall of the right atrium, collects venous blood from the body via a postcaval vein. A full pulmonary system consisting of both pulmonary arteries and veins is present, and the systemic arch divides into right and left branches. The renal portal system, which drains blood from the posterior portion of the body, is reduced.

The paired kidneys are of the metanephric type, and some concentration of urine occurs. Within the kidneys, the renal tubules open into larger collecting tubules that eventually drain into a ureter, which, in turn, drains into the cloaca. No urinary bladder is present.

The reproductive system consists of paired ovaries or testes and their accompanying tubes. The saccular ovaries contain a lymph-filled internal cavity into which the eggs are expelled. The large-yolked (telolecithal) eggs leave the ovary and enter a glandular oviduct that provides a coating of albumen and an external leathery shell for each egg before the eggs empty into the cloaca. The lower end of the oviduct is expanded into a uterus in ovoviviparous and viviparous species (see below). Both the eggs and young, in those with "live birth," leave the female through the cloaca and anal vent. Males produce sperm in seminiferous tubules within their testes. Sperm drains from the testes via a sperm duct formed from the embryonic archinephric or Wolffian duct. The upper end of this tube consists of the epididymis, the middle section is the vas deferens, and the lower portion is expanded into a sperm-storing seminal vesicle before emptying into the cloaca. The male copulatory organ is termed the hemipenis. A pair lie in cavities in the base of the tail; when erected by turgidity and turned inside out, the hemipenis is projected from the cloacal vent. A retractor muscle is attached to the tip of the hemipenis, connecting with a series of caudal vertebrae. A deep groove, the sulcus spermaticus, which may be single or bifurcate, lies on the outer surface and carries sperm. The hemipenis is quite ornamental and may be adorned with spines, hooks, and calyxes, which serve to anchor it within the female's cloaca during copulation. Each taxon has its own type of hemipenis and ornamentation, and the organ is important in taxonomy.

The nervous system has several mammalian features. The center of brain activity shifts to the cerebrum, which is enlarged and contains a neopallium (the forerunner of the mammalian cerebral cortex) and a somewhat enlarged cerebellum. Twelve pairs of cranial nerves are present.

The ear is much reduced; the external ear opening, tympanum, and Eustachian tube are absent. Sound waves striking the side of the head are transmitted from the skin to muscle to bone, specifically through the jaw muscles to the quadrate bone, which is loosely attached to the underside of the cranium. The ear bone or columella lies beside the quadrate bone and transmits

minute vibrations from the quadrate bone to the sound-sensitive portions of the inner ear. This system is most effective for low frequency airborne sounds, and most snakes hear best in the 200–500 Hz range.

Except in a few burrowing forms, the eye is covered with a fixed transparent scale beneath which the eyeball moves; eyelids are missing, so snakes cannot close their eyes. The transparent eye scale is also shed when skin is periodically sloughed in one piece, leaving a new one beneath exposed. Accommodation is accomplished by changing the shape of the lens. In the predominately burrowing leptotyphlopids and typhlopids with poorly developed eyes, vision is probably restricted to the perception of light and dark. In the rest of the snakes, diurnal species usually have moderate-sized eyes with round pupils and predominately cone retinas. Nocturnal snakes have large eyes with vertically elliptical pupils and predominately rod retinas. Snakes apparently lack color vision.

The tongue is long, protractile, and forked; within limits the tongue forks can be moved independently. The tongue transfers chemical information and serves as an organ both of taste and of smell in conjunction with the fluid-filled Jacobson's or vomeronasal organ (a large, dorsal, olfactory structure opening directly into the mouth). When the tongue is retracted, its tips are wiped across the opening of the Jacobson's organ. The tongue is neither a stinger nor a heat sensor.

Taste buds are probably absent from the tongue but may be found along the middle of the roof of the mouth in some snakes.

The snake's integument is covered with dry, keratinous scales. Those on the snake's head may either be enlarged into plates or consist of only small scales. Dorsal body scales may either be smooth or have a longitudinal keel (carinate). They occur in rows along the body, which may be uniform in number or may vary in number at particular positions along the body. Usually there is a reduction in the number of rows from anterior to posterior; that is, 19 rows on the neck, 17–18 at midbody, and 14–15 near the tail. The numbers of scale rows at any point along the body may be distinctive and may be used as a taxonomic character. The number of scale rows does not change with growth. On the snake's belly are a series of enlarged, rectangular ventral plates arranged in a single row from the throat to anal vent; an enlarged flap, the anal plate (either single or divided), covering the cloacal opening; and one or two adjacent rows of small subcaudal scales posterior to the anal vent. Counts of the ventrals and subcaudals, and whether or not the anal plate is single or divided, are major taxonomic characters.

Another important character that can be used to determine relationships is the karyotype, or the number and physical appearance of the diploid chromosome pairs. Each chromosome has a small, unstaining, constricted region called a centromere, which may be located at different positions in different pairs of chromosomes. Its position is used to designate the chromosome as either metacentric, having the centromere located near the middle so the two arms are of equal or near equal length; acrocentric, having the centromere near one end of the chromosome so that the two arms are of unequal length (one long, one short); or telocentric, where the centromere is very near one end of the chromosome. Snakes possess sex chromosomes; in females the sex chromosomes are of unequal length (heteromorphic) and are termed ZW; in males the sex chromosomes are of equal or near equal length (homomorphic) and are termed ZZ. A nucleolus organizer region (NOR) is present on a pair of chromosomes.

Habitat

In North America, snakes can be found from the Atlantic coast west to the Pacific coast, from the Mexican border north to the southern Northwest Territories in Canada, and from below sea level to over 3,000 m elevation. Such a wide distribution has brought North American snakes into contact with many habitat types (deserts, dry grasslands, various woodlands, rivers, swamps, marshes, bogs, etc.), and they have evolved terrestrial, aquatic, and burrowing lifestyles in response. Habitat and lifestyle are discussed in the account of each species.

Activity Periods

Both the annual and daily activities of each snake are related in its account. Over most of the geographical area covered by this book, snakes are active only in the spring, summer, and fall and hibernate in the winter. Some living in hot, dry regions must even become inactive (estivate) or switch from diurnal to nocturnal activity during the summer. Most snakes are active when environmental temperatures are between 15 and 30°C. Because snakes are conformers with body temperatures generally matching that of their external surroundings (ectotherms), their body temperature varies, and they may also be termed poikilotherms. In the text, where possible, a discussion of the thermal ecology of each species is presented. In these discussions, the following abbreviations are used for the sake of brevity to denote various temperatures: environmental temperature (ET); air temperature (AT); surface or soil temperature (ST); body temperature (BT), cloacal temperature (CT), critical thermal maximum (CT_{max}), critical thermal minimum (CT_{min}), and incubation temperature (IT).

Movements

Snakes, like other vertebrates, usually are active in only a relatively small portion of the available habitat. This area is termed the home range or activity range, and all life behaviors are normally carried out within the home range. However, some do not have suitable overwintering habitat within their home range, and so must make a fall movement beyond the limit of their summer home range to a distant hibernaculum and return from it the next spring. Such one-way movements may be relatively short, 100–300 m, but sometimes they are of several kilometers.

Reproduction

All snakes have internal fertilization at the upper end of the oviduct, and direct development (no metamorphic stage occurs). The young either hatch out of shelled eggs laid by oviparous species after a suitable incubation period (IP) or are born alive in ovoviviparous and viviparous species after a gestation period (GP). In ovoviviparous snakes, the embryos (covered with a membranous amniotic sac) are retained and hatch within the female's reproductive tract, then pass out of her cloaca (parturition). No placental connection is formed between the embryo and the female, so no nourishment, other than the yolk within the original yolk sac, is provided. Viviparous snakes form a placenta or placenta-like membrane through which nourishment is provided by the female to the embryo. At full term, the young also undergo parturition.

In the text, when possible, the following reproductive parameters are provided for each species: size and age at maturity, gametic and hormonal cycles of both sexes, the mating season(s), courtship and mating behaviors, the season of egg laying (oviposition) of oviparous species, the season of birth (parturition) of ovoviviparous and viviparous species, and descriptions of eggs, hatchlings, or neonates. The relative clutch mass (RCM), the total clutch mass divided by the female postparturient mass (Barron 1997a; Seigel and Fitch 1984), is presented where known.

Diet

Snakes are carnivores that consume other animals. With so many different species adapted to various habitats, North American snakes take a wide variety of prey, and a prey list is presented for each species. Snakes capture their prey by grabbing them with their mouths and directly swallowing them; by grabbing them with their mouths, throwing several body loops around the prey, squeezing them to prevent their breathing (constriction), and then swallowing them when they have died; or by injecting venomous saliva into the prey, usually releasing them and later following their odor trail, and finally swallowing them when they are dead. Notes are presented on the feeding behavior of each species.

Predators and Defense

Those animals that prey on a snake are listed, and its means of defense are described.

Venoms

A venom is a highly toxic poison that one animal injects into another. The venom of snakes is produced in modified salivary glands (Duvernoy's glands or venom glands) located toward the rear of the upper jaw. These glands are ducted either to the base of a grooved tooth or into the hollow center of a special injecting fang (see the family accounts of Colubridae, Elapidae, and Viperidae for detailed descriptions). Each venomous species has unique venom composed of different components and different amounts of toxic and nontoxic compounds. The chemistry of such venoms is complicated, but overall, venoms are at least 90% protein (by dry weight), and most of the proteins are enzymes. About 25 different enzymes have been isolated from snake venoms. Ten of these occur in the venom of most snakes. Proteolytic enzymes (involved in the breakdown of tissue proteins), phospholipases (either mildly or highly toxic to muscles and nerves), and hyaluronidases (dissolve intercellular materials and speed the spread of venom through the prey's tissue) are the most common types. Other enzymes are collagenases (which break down connective tissues), ribonucleases, deoxyribonucleases, nucleotide amino acid oxidases, lactate dehydrogenases, and acidic or basic phosphatases (all of which disrupt normal cellular function) (for more complete discussions of venom chemistry see Ernst and Zug 1996; Russell 1983; Tu 1977). Venoms evolved first as a prey-capture device, and second as a defensive tool. Because North American snakes of the families Elapidae and Viperidae possess dangerous venoms, where applicable, the toxicity and symptoms in human envenomations are presented for each species in these families.

Populations

The population dynamics, including population sizes, sex ratio, juvenile to adult ratio, size and age classes, and survival status are given, as far as is known, for each species.

Conservation

Snakes are among our most persecuted wildlife, and their populations have been decreasing rapidly in North America. Many are killed or injured severely when discovered, and entire populations have been systematically eradicated over periods of time, especially those sharing communal hibernacula. Others have been removed from the breeding population to be sold in the pet trade. However, the most sinister cause of the decline of snakes is the habitat destruction that has resulted from the spread of North America's in-

creasing human population. You cannot have aquatic snakes without water or woodland snakes without trees. As humans move outward from our cities, they either bring with them new predators to attack snakes, especially domestic dogs and cats (Mitchell and Beck 1992), or create new habitats for old snake enemies such as raccoons, foxes, and coyotes. Also introduced into the environment are chemical pollutants, some of which are toxic to snakes and other reptiles. The modern increase in mechanized vehicular traffic has caused declines in many snake populations living adjacent to busy roads.

If snakes are to remain a part of our fauna we must initiate additional conservation measures. Unfortunately, we do not know enough about the life requirements of many of our snake species to formulate adequate conservation plans for many species. However, certain needs are obvious. The lands and waterways harboring important populations must be protected from undue human disturbance and pollution. The trend away from use of dangerous residual pesticides and other chemical pollutants must be continued. States must pass and enforce legislation controlling the capture of snakes in the wild, and the pet trade must be strictly monitored.

Most important, people must be educated as to the natural history, economic importance, and plight of our snakes. A fostering of awareness in people should make them more interested in protecting not only our snakes, but wildlife in general. The creation of a conservation mode toward snakes is a major purpose of this book.

Identification of the Snakes of the United States and Canada

The identification of a species of snake covered in this book is based on a series of dichotomous keys. Refer first to the following Key to the Families of Snakes in the United States and Canada. After comparing the snake to the characters expressed in the Key, the family to which it belongs should be evident. Next, go to the beginning of the family account in the text, where a second key to the genera of snakes belonging to that family is presented. Use this key to determine the proper genus for your snake and then go to the account of that genus in the text. (Each new genus is indicated by a shaded band.) There you will find a third key to identify the various species belonging to that genus (if the genus is monotypic, having only one species assigned to it, only the generic key is

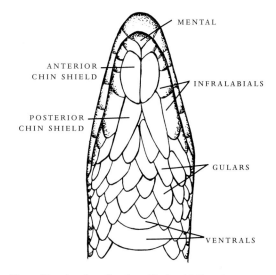

Ventral head scales of snakes. (Evelyn M. Ernst)

needed). Once the species of snake has been determined, its description (RECOGNITION) and color photograph should be compared with your animal to finalize the identification.

In the text three standard measurements are used: total body length (TBL), the distance between the

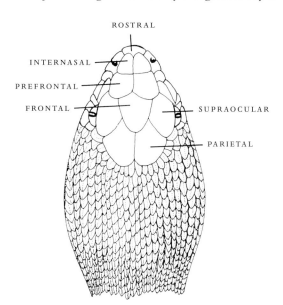

Dorsal head scales of snakes. (Evelyn M. Ernst)

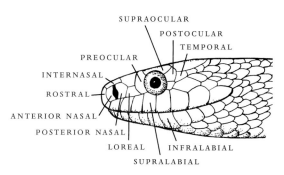

Lateral head scales of snakes. (Evelyn M. Ernst)

Counting snake scale rows. (Evelyn
M. Ernst)

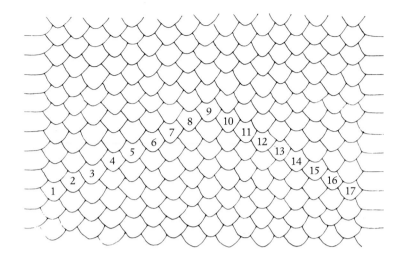

most anterior point of the snout and the posterior tip
of the tail; snout-vent length (SVL), the distance from
the most anterior tip of the snout to the posterior
border of the vent (because many snakes have lost a

portion of their tail for various reasons, this is a more
useful measurement than TBL); and tail length (TL),
the distance from the posterior border of the vent to
the posterior tip of the tail.

Key to the Families of Snakes of the United States and Canada

(adapted from Powell et al. 1998)

1a. Ventral scales transversely elongated 2
1b. Ventral scales not transversely elongated; if barely larger
than dorsal body scales, divided into two rows by a mid-
ventral sulcus 4
2a. Tail laterally compressed and oarlike . . . Elapidae (in part)
2b. Tail not laterally compressed; short, pointed, and tipped
with a spine 3
3a. Eighteen to 20 midbody scale rows . . . . . . Typhlopidae
3b. Fourteen midbody scale rows . . . . . . Leptotyphlopidae
4a. Facial pit present between the nostril and eye . . . Viperidae

4b. No facial pit between the nostril and eye 5
5a. Small scales on top of head behind eyes . . . . Boidae
5b. Large scales on top of head behind eyes 6
6a. Body unicolored or with pattern of stripes, crossbands,
or blotches; yellow bands never bordered by red; no
permanently erect fangs at the front of the maxillae
. . . . Colubridae
6b. Body with red, yellow, and red bands; yellow bands bor-
dered by red; permanently erect fangs present at the front
of the maxillae . . . . Elapidae (in part)

Leptotyphlopidae
Slender Blindsnakes

This family is composed of two genera and 87 species (McDiarmid et al. 1999) of small, slender, wormlike burrowing snakes distributed from the southwestern United States through Central America and South America to Argentina, over most of Africa, and in Arabia and Pakistan. Slender blindsnakes have blunt, solidly fused skulls with the premaxilla, maxilla, palatine, nasal, and prefrontal bones sutured tightly to the cranium, and the maxillae longitudinally oriented. The supratemporal bone is reduced or absent, allowing the quadrate bone to articulate directly with the cranium. The premaxilla, maxilla, and palatine bones are toothless, but four to five teeth are present on the reduced mandible. The hyoid is V-shaped. There is no visible neck. Vestiges of a pelvic girdle remain, including the ilium, ischium, pubis, and a rudimentary femur (which rarely shows as an external spur). The tracheal and left lungs, as well as the left oviduct, are absent. The head is covered with enlarged, platelike scales; the nasal and prefrontal scales are fused. The ocular scale is fused with one or more supralabials; the eyes are small, but visible through the ocular scale. The smooth body scales are uniform in size and shape. A spinelike scale adorns the tip of the tail. Reproduction is oviparous.

Only one genus and two species are present in North America.

Leptotyphlops Fitzinger 1843

Slender Blindsnakes

Key to the Species of *Leptotyphlops*

1a. Supraorbital scales present, rostral scale extends backward to the level of the anterior rim or center of the orbit . . . . *L. dulcis*

2a. Supraorbital scales absent, rostral scale usually does not extend rearward to the center of the orbit, and sometimes not to the anterior rim . . . . *L. humilis*

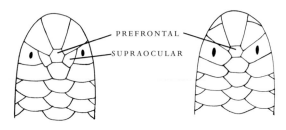

PREFRONTAL

SUPRAOCULAR

Head scales of *Leptotyphlops dulcis* (left) and *Leptotyphlops humilis* (right). (Evelyn M. Ernst)

Leptotyphlops dulcis (Baird and Girard 1853) | Plains Slender Blindsnake

RECOGNITION.   *L. dulcis* is a small (maximum TBL, 28.3 cm), cylindrical (body length/diameter, 50–54), grayish to pinkish or reddish brown snake (the pigment is in the seven most dorsal scale rows) with reduced eyes visible through large ocular scales. Countershading occurs, with the venter pinkish and lighter than the dorsum. The head is short, blunt, not wider than the neck, and has a countersunk lower jaw. The tail is short (approximately 5% of TBL), with a downcurved terminal spine. Body scales are smooth, pitless, uniform in size around the entire body, and in 14 anterior and midbody rows, 12 rows just anterior to the vent, and 10 rows around the tail. A series of 199–255 middorsal scales are present from the rostral scale to the tip of the tail. The anal plate is undivided, and 11–17 subcaudals lie beneath the tail. Head scalation is complex. Dorsal head scales from anterior to posterior, respectively, consist of 1 enlarged rostral, 1 prefrontal, 1 frontal, 1 interparietal, and 1 interoccipital scale. Laterally there are 2 nasals (1 upper, 1 lower), 1 large transluscent ocular covering the eye, 1 supraocular, 1 parietal (in contact with the posterior supralabial), 1 temporal, 1 occipital, 2–3 supralabials (1–2 anterior and 1 posterior, separated by the ocular scale), and 4–5 infralabials. No loreal scale is present. Usually three scales lie dorsally between the two enlarged oculars. The single hemipenis is smooth, not distally forked, and has a deeply grooved sulcus spermaticus. No teeth are present on the maxilla, and

teeth are present only on the anterior half of the lower jaw.

As no apparent sexual dimorphism exists, dissection of the anterior region of the tail is necessary to determine the sex of an individual.

GEOGRAPHIC VARIATION.   Four subspecies exist (Hahn 1979b; Smith et al. 1998); only two occur north of Mexico. *L. d. dulcis* (Baird and Girard 1853), the Texas slender blindsnake, is found from southwestern Oklahoma south through central and western Texas to San Luis Potosí, and northern Hidalgo and Veracruz, Mexico. It has only 1 large anterior supralabial, 206–255 (mean, 228) middorsal scales, and 12–17 (mean, 14.5) subcaudals (Han 1979b). *L. d. dissectus* (Cope 1896), the New Mexico slender blindsnake, ranges from the southern tier counties of Kansas south through central and western Oklahoma, western Texas, and southeastern Colorado to the Pecos and Rio Grande watersheds, the southwestern counties of New Mexico, and adjacent southeastern Arizona. It has the anterior supralabial subdivided into 2 smaller scales, 224–246 (mean, 238) middorsal scales, and 12–16 (mean, 13.9) subcaudals (Hahn 1979b). Intergradation occurs between the two subspecies in Oklahoma and northwestern Texas.

CONFUSING SPECIES.   The western slender blindsnake *(L. humilis)* lacks supraocular scales, the rostral

Plains slender blindsnake, *Leptothylops dulcis*; Cochise County, Arizona. (Photograph by Cecil Schwalbe)

scale barely extends beyond the anterior border of the eye (if at all), and there are 12–21 subcaudals. The Brahminy blindsnake *(Ramphotyphlops braminus)* is extralimital, has its eyes barely visible through the ocular scales, and has 18–20 midbody scale rows.

KARYOTYPE. Undescribed, but the mitochondrial RNA is discussed by Kumazawa et al. (1996).

FOSSIL RECORD. Pleistocene (Rancholabrean) vertebrae of *Leptotyphlops* sp. have been found in Arizona (Van Devender et al. 1991) and Texas (Parmley and Pfau 1997), but because the vertebrae of *L. dulcis* and *L. humilis* are indistinguishable, no specific designations have been made.

DISTRIBUTION. *L. dulcis* ranges from southern Kansas southwestward to New Mexico and southeastern Arizona, and southward to Hidalgo and Veracruz, Mexico.

HABITAT. *L. dulcis* lives in arid grasslands and desert fringes, usually with abundant surface rocks or logs for retreats and with some free water or moist soil available. Elevation ranges from sea level to about 2,100 m, and it can be found in a variety of plant habi-

Distribution of
Leptothyphlops dulcis.

tats: desert scrub with thornbush, yucca, and cacti; prairie grasslands; and oak-juniper woodlands. It is often found on rocky hillsides and on canyon bottoms (especially those with running water). Soils in these habitats range from sand to loam, and loose soils are preferred. The snake is often common in the suburbs of cities, where it takes advantage of well-watered lawns and flower beds, and compost piles. Gehlbach and Baldridge (1987) even found them living in debris at the bottom of eastern screech owl (*Otus asio*) nests, apparently having escaped predation by crawling into the litter, and enjoying the protection of the owls while feeding on larvae of insect parasites of the birds—a commensal relationship.

Clark (1967b) tested soil-type preferences of *L. dulcis* and found it preferred clay-loam soils over both sand and a mixture of sand and clay-loam, but when offered a mixture of sawdust and clay-loam, snakes chose it 50% of the time.

BEHAVIOR. Being mostly subterranean, *L. dulcis* is not often seen. In south-central Texas and New Mexico, it is active from March or early April to October (Degenhardt et al. 1996; Vermersch and Kuntz 1986). At higher elevations and latitudes it comes out later in the spring and retreats earlier in the fall; in Colorado, it seems active only from May to September (Hammerson 1986). Winter hibernacula are deep underground, and dry, hot summers may also cause some individuals to retreat underground and estivate.

L. dulcis is normally nocturnally surface active, leaving its hiding place about sunset and remaining out until at least 2230 hours, but most activity seems to occur at 2000–2100 hours. These snakes sometimes come to the surface in the early morning and on cool, overcast, or rainy days. Smith (1956) reported that in Kansas *L. dulcis* prefers ETs of 25–28°C and will only come to the surface after the AT is 16°C or higher. In three tests of ST preferences, *L. dulcis* chose temperatures of 15.9–27.5°C and averaged 19.4–22.2°C (Clark 1967b). Captives have been successfully kept at ATs of 25–30°C (Rossi and Rossi 1995). In the wild, thermoregulation is usually achieved by lying beneath a warm rock.

This snake probably does not move far from its burrow entrance. It is an extremely slow crawler, 1.2–1.5 m/minute, and may use the spiny tip of its tail to lever the body forward (Ortenburger, in Webb 1970). It is known to follow pheromone trails laid down by its conspecifics (Gehlbach et al. 1971), and this may explain why *L. dulcis* has been found in aggregations in both summer and winter. Cutaneous touch receptors on the rostral and anterior supralabial glands may aid navigation (Orejas-Miranda et al. 1977).

REPRODUCTION. Because *L. dulcis* carries out its breeding activities underground, few data have been reported. Females with TBLs of 19.3–22.5 cm have contained eggs (Force 1936a); and adults have been reported to be as short as 12.5 cm (Collins 1993), 13.2 cm (Wright and Wright 1957), and 15.8 cm (Taylor 1939c).

Males have spindle-shaped testes located at the front of the caudal third of the body, with four to six (two to seven) visible lobes (Fox 1965). The left testis usually has fewer lobes, but occasionally may have the same number or more than the right testis. When fully active, the lobes are 0.5–4.0 mm long and 0.5–2.0 mm wide. The seasonal testicular cycle has not been described for *L. dulcis*, but it is probably similar to that of *L. humilis*.

Female *L. dulcis* possess only a right oviduct, which has well-developed seminal receptacles at the base of its infundibulum, and a short vaginal pouch. The anterior third or more of the uterus contains single, well-spaced, possibly mucous-secreting, glands (Fox and Dessauer 1962). The full ovarian cycle has not been described, but Klauber (1940a) found large, well-developed eggs in early summer, indicating spring ovulation and late summer oviposition, and recently laid eggs have been found during late June and July.

The mating period lasts from late March and early April to June in Texas (Tennant 1984; Vermersch and Kuntz 1986). Males follow females' pheromone trails, and several may attempt to copulate with the same female at a time, forming a "ball" of blindsnakes. Mating usually occurs under cover of a rock or deep in a rock crevice. When mating, the male wraps his body around the female in a corkscrew fashion (Vermersch and Kuntz 1986).

Normal nesting sites are under rocks, within rotting logs, deep in rock crevices, in cavities in decaying plant litter, or as deep as 76 cm below the surface of loose, sandy soil (Tennant 1984). Nesting may be communal. On 10 July, Hibbard (1964) found such an ovipository in a series of cracks to 56 cm deep in a quarry wall in Kansas; it contained three females with their eggs, three more clutches of eggs, several other loose eggs, and old egg shells from nesting in previous years; all told, 42 eggs were present. Hibbard had also encountered four egg-bearing females in a similar setting in the bank of an arroyo on 5 July of the previous year. Although females may coil around their eggs, they do not incubate them; they do protect them from invertebrate predators.

Litters contain one to eight eggs, with an average of 4.75 for eight clutches. The long, narrow eggs have parchment shells, and are approximately 15.0 × 4.5 mm. Hatching takes place in late August or September. The minute, pinkish hatchlings are only 6.5–7.6 (mean, 6.8) cm long.

GROWTH AND LONGEVITY. No data are available.

DIET AND FEEDING HABITS. The natural diet consists mostly of termites and ants; Punzo (1974) found that adult termites made up 34.4% of the total diet, ants (all life stages) 29.8%, beetles (adults and larvae) 9.7%, and dipteran larvae 9.3%. *L. dulcis* will even attack and eat army ants (*Neivmyrmex* sp.) and fire ants (*Solenopsis* sp.) (Baldridge and Wivagg 1992; Watkins et al. 1967, 1969, 1972). Other reported prey are arachnids—harvestmen, sun scorpions (solpugids), and spiders; millipedes; and various insects—adult dermapterans, larval lepidopterans, larval neuropterans, and adult and nymphal orthopterans (Force 1936a; Punzo 1974; Reid and Lott 1963; Stebbins 1985; Tennant 1984; Vermersch and Kuntz 1986). Termites and ants are found by following their scent trails (Baldridge and Wivagg 1992; Gehlbach et al. 1971; Reid and Lott 1963; Watkins et al. 1967). *L. dulcis* has taste buds in the dermal folds around the paired openings of its vomeronasal (Jacobson's) organ in the roof of its nasal cavity, which may aid in "tasting" the scent trail (Kroll 1973). When prey is located, *L. dulcis* takes it into its mouth by "mandibular raking" (Kley and Brainerd 1999). The tooth-bearing bones of the lower jaw rotate synchronously in and out of the mouth to drag prey into the esophagus; this is accomplished by three unique hinges on the lower jaw that allow the various elements to move independently. *L. dulcis* can eat almost one ant larva per minute. Once the prey is ingested, the snake arches the anterior portion of its body and pushes downward, forcing the juices and soft internal organs of the insect into its mouth. The chitinous exoskeleton of adult ants and the potent-jawed heads of termites are not swallowed (Reid and Lott 1963). When attacked while feeding by a number of ants, the blindsnake forms a ball-like, writhing coil and smears cloacal gland fluids over its body (Gehlbach et al. 1968). This fluid is a glycoprotein with free fatty acids that repel the ants (Blum et al. 1971; Watkins et al. 1969).

PREDATION AND DEFENSE. *L. dulcis* is probably preyed on by numerous animals, but only a few observations have been reported. Renfro (in Tennant 1984) observed large centipedes eating a cold, lethargic *L. dulcis*, and snakes (*Hypsiglena torquata, Micrurus fulvius*), birds (*Geococcyx californianus, Otus asio*), and mammals—moles (*Scalopus aquaticus*), armadillos (*Dasypus novemcinctus*), skunks (*Mephitis* sp.), and domestic cats (*Felis catus*)—are known predators (Gehlbach and Baldridge 1987; Greene 1984; Milstead et al. 1950; Peterson 1950; Webb 1970).

If it cannot retreat down a hole when first disturbed, *L. dulcis* may tilt its individual scales, producing a silvery, startling, appearance (Conant and Collins 1998); writhe about and cover itself with anal gland secretions (see above); play dead; or begin semirigid crawling (Gehlbach 1970). It does not bite, but it may probe the fingers with its tail spine if held.

A few of these inoffensive snakes die on our highways each year, and some drown in swimming pools in the suburbs or are killed by domestic cats, but the greatest dangers to *L. dulcis* are habitat alteration and the use of pesticides. It is listed as threatened and is protected in Kansas.

POPULATIONS. The species is not uncommon across its range, but its subterranean, nocturnal behavior makes it appear so. It has a tendency to aggregate, so when found, several individuals are often detected at one time: 13 under one stone in Oklahoma (McCoy 1960), 11 under another stone in Kansas (Collins 1993), and the breeding aggregations found by Hibbard (1964), mentioned above.

REMARKS. The genus *Leptotyphlops* and the species *L. dulcis* have been reviewed by Hahn (1979a, 1979b).

Leptotyphlops humilis (Baird and Girard 1853) | Western Slender Blindsnake

RECOGNITION.   *L. humilis* in the United States are small (TBL to 38.9 cm), cylindrical (body length/diameter 55–63), purplish brown or pinkish snakes (the dark pigment is in the 5–9 dorsalmost scale rows), with their eyes reduced to mere spots beneath translucent ocular scales. The tail is short (approximately 5% as long as the TBL) with a downward-curved terminal spine. The head is blunt and not wider than the neck; the lower jaw is countersunk. Body scales are uniform in shape and size around the entire body (no ventral scutes are present), smooth and pitless, and occur in 14 anterior and midbody rows, 12–13 rows just anterior to the vent, and 10–12 rows around the tail. A series of 257–308 scales is present in a middorsal row from the rostral scale to the tail tip. The anal plate is undivided, and 12–21 subcaudals are present. Head scalation is complex. Dorsally, from anterior to posterior, lie an enlarged rostral scale, 1 prefrontal, 1 frontal, 1 interparietal, and 1 interoccipital scale. Laterally are 2 nasals (1 upper, 1 lower), 1 large translucent ocular scale covering the eye, 1 parietal (in contact with the posterior supralabial), 1 temporal, 1 occipital, 2 supralabials (1 anterior, 1 posterior, separated by the ocular scale), and 4 (3) infralabials. No supraocular or loreal scales are present. The hemipenis has not been described, but it is probably similar to that of *L. dulcis* in general features. Teeth are only found on the anterior half of the lower jaw.

No apparent sexual dimorphism exists; dissection of the anterior portion of the tail is necessary to determine the sex of an individual.

GEOGRAPHIC VARIATION.   Nine subspecies have been described (Hahn 1979c), but only four occur north of Mexico. *L. h. humilis* (Baird and Girard 1853), the southwestern slender blindsnake, ranges from southern California and southern Nevada east to central Arizona and south to northern Sonora and western Baja California. It has 12 scale rows encircling the tail, 15–21 (mean, 17.9) subcaudals, 7–9 pigmented dorsal scale rows, and more than 257 scales in the middorsal longitudinal row (257–283; mean, 272) (Hahn 1979c; Klauber 1940a). *L. h. cahuilae* Klauber 1931c, the desert slender blindsnake, occurs from southeastern California and southwestern Arizona to northern Sonora and eastern Baja California. It has 12 scale rows around the tail, 16–21 (mean, 17.4) subcaudals, 5 lightly pigmented dorsal scale rows, and more than 280 (280–305; mean, 295) scales in the middorsal longitudinal scale row (Hahn 1979c; Klauber 1940a). *L. h. segregus* Klauber 1939b, the Trans-Pecos slender blindsnake, ranges from southeastern Arizona and southern New Mexico to western Texas, Chihuahua, Coahuila, and northeastern Durango. This subspecies has 10 scale rows encircling the tail, 12–16 (mean, 14.0) subcaudals, 7 pigmented dorsal scale rows, and 1 middorsal longitudinal scale row containing more than 250 (261–275; mean, 271) scales (Hahn 1979c; Klauber 1940a). *L. h. utahensis* Tanner 1938, the Utah slender blindsnake, is found only in southwestern Utah and southeastern Nevada. This race is identified by the 12 rows of scales around its tail, 17–20 (mean, 18.0) subcaudals, 7–9 pigmented dorsal scale rows, and more than 280 (289–308; mean, 300) scales in the middorsal longitudinal scale row (Hahn 1979c; Klauber 1940a).

Intergradation occurs where the ranges of the respective subspecies meet (Hahn 1979c).

CONFUSING SPECIES.   The plains slender blindsnake *(Leptotyphlops dulcis)* has three scales situated between its ocular scales. The Brahminy blindsnake *(Ramphotyphlops braminus)* is extralimital, has eyes visible though the ocular scales, and has 18–20 midbody scale rows.

KARYOTYPE.   Undescribed.

FOSSIL RECORD.   Possibly, the Pleistocene (Rancholabrean) fossils reported by Van Devender et al. (1991) are of *L. humilis*.

DISTRIBUTION.   *L. humilis* ranges from southern California, southern Nevada, and southwestern Utah south and east to Baja California, Colima, southern Arizona, southern New Mexico, western Texas, Chihuahua, Coahuila, and northeastern Durango. It is also found on the islands of Santa Catalina, Carmen, Cerralvo, and Cedros.

Western slender blindsnake, *Leptothylops humilis*; Riverside County, California. (Photograph by Donald J. Fisher)

HABITAT. This small snake lives in habitats as diverse as grasslands, deserts, and mountain slopes, as long as loose soils (either sandy, loam, or occasionally gravelly and stony) are present, at elevations from below sea level in the Death Valley area of California to approximately 1,500 m in western Texas. Most records are from foothills or canyon bottoms with running water. Surface rocks, logs, or piles of plant debris are usually present, and the vegetation varies from grass to cacti, ocotillo, white sage, incense bush, greasewood, thornbush, chaparral, date palm, desert willow, and scrub oak.

Kay (1970) recorded the estimated chemical and physical characteristics of the soil and ground water at eight sites with elevations ranging from –78.5 m to 1,363.6 m where *L. humilis* was collected in Death Valley, California. The soils had salt contents of 0.25–3.80%, and pHs of less than 10 to 11.1. The pH of the soil water ranged from 6.8 to 8.5, and the percentage of total dissolved solids in the water was 0.03–2.80.

BEHAVIOR. *L. humilis* spends most of its time underground. It uses its blunt head, with its solidly compact cranium and large rostral scale, to force its way through loose soils, but it will also crawl into tunnels and burrows made by other animals.

Klauber (1940a) found *L. h. humilis* surface active in all months in Southern California, with most captures occurring in May through July and decidedly less activity occurring from October through March. *L. h. cahuilae* was surface active for a shorter annual period: April to December, with a peak in May. Annual activity in New Mexico is normally from April to September, but one individual has been collected in February (Degenhardt et al. 1996). Hibernation occurs at

ground depths varying from 15 cm (Wood 1945) to probably over 1 m, as long as the hibernaculum is beneath the frost zone. Summer estivation may occur at depths of 60 cm to 1.2 m (Grant, in Klauber 1940a).

Daily activity is almost exclusively nocturnal; although some *L. humilis* may come out at dusk and a few have been found on the surface in the morning hours, almost all daytime captures are of individuals hidden under rocks or some other object. Surface activity may be triggered by rains or cool, overcast skies. Klauber (1940a) found them active in Southern California from 1830 to 2129 hours, with most activity occurring from 1900 to 2029 hours. Brattstrom and Schwenkmeyer (1951) made 12 collecting trips in San Diego County, California, for *L. humilis* on moonlit nights and seven trips on dark nights; 28 snakes were found on moonlit nights, compared to only six caught on dark nights.

Distribution of *Leptotyphlops humilis.*

This species has been found active in California at ATs of 23–31°C, with optimum activity at 26–28°C (Klauber 1940a). Brattstrom and Schwenkmeyer (1951) found them active at ATs of 20–34°C and at relative humidities of approximately 20–52%. These snakes often crawl onto blacktop roads at night, presumably to warm themselves, and daytime thermoregulation is usually accomplished under a heated rock.

When crawling, *L. humilis* employs more of a caterpillar method than the ordinary lateral undulatory motion used by most snakes. On smooth surfaces it may use its tail spine to lever its body forward.

REPRODUCTION. The smallest female *L. humilis* containing eggs was 22.5 cm TBL, but Klauber (1940a) thought that no female under 24.5 cm was mature. Females have only a right functional oviduct, in which seminal receptacles are present at the base of the infundibulum (Fox and Dessauer 1962). The ovarian cycle has not been described, but females usually contain eggs in June (Banta 1953; Klauber 1940a), and females have been found attending eggs in August (Gates 1957). Perhaps they coil about the eggs to prevent them from drying out or to protect them from invertebrate predators; the females do not incubate the eggs as occurs in some pythons.

Male *L. humilis* have paired spindle-shaped testes at the front of the caudal third of the body. The testes resemble strings of closely abutting small lobes, with the largest in the center; two to seven (usually four to six) lobes are present per testis (Fox 1965). The left testis usually has fewer lobes, although occasionally the number of lobes in each testis is equal. Fully active testes have lobes that are 0.5–4.0 mm long by 0.5–2.0 mm wide. The diameter of the testis increases in the spring, but by July it is reduced, with a shrunk basement membrane. Spermatogenic activity is well along in March (Fox 1965). Lamina of the seminiferous tubules are packed with spermatids, but no mature sperm are present, and Sertoli cells and several layers of primary and secondary spermatocytes are evident along the lamina borders. All spermatogenic stages are well represented. By late April and May, spermatozoa begin to leave the seminiferous tubules and enter the epididymides and vas deferens, and the seminiferous tubules are of maximum diameter. Spermatogenesis continues through May and June, with the seminifer-

ous tubules becoming smaller in diameter until reaching their lowest size in July and August. Large quantities of sperm are present in the epididymides and vas deferens in July and August, but sperm production probably ceases in August. Courtship and copulatory dates and behavior have not been reported.

The IP is 30–60 days (Rossi and Rossi 1995), and clutches contain two (Klauber 1940a) to eight (Rossi and Rossi 1995) eggs; the average for 11 clutches was 4.6 eggs. Clutch size is positively correlated to female TBL, with larger females producing more eggs than smaller females. The eggs have parchmentlike shells, and are long and narrow: 6–15 (mean, 12.9) mm long by 2–5 (mean, 4.3) mm wide. Neonates have 7.5–12.9 (mean, 9.9) cm TBLs.

GROWTH AND LONGEVITY. No growth data are available. Rossi and Rossi (1995) maintained two *L. humilis* for nearly a year; wild individuals must survive several years.

DIET AND FEEDING HABITS. Small soft prey are preferred, particularly ants (all life stages) and termites (adults, nymphs). Ants and termites made up 54.2% of the total diet of the individuals examined by Punzo (1974). Additional reported prey are centipedes, millipedes, spiders, whip scorpions, and other insects (beetle grubs, dipteran larvae, lepidopteran caterpillars, and small orthopterans) (Brattstrom and Schwenkmeyer 1951; Perkins 1938; Punzo 1974). Perkins (1938) thought *L. humilis* perhaps also eats young slender salamanders (*Batrachoseps* sp.).

Captives will eat ant pupae, termites, and juvenile wax worms; a diet of 20 ant pupae or termites every one to two weeks seems sufficient (Rossi and Rossi 1995). The small snakes can consume one prey item every 10 seconds, and one individual ate at least 15 ant pupae at one feeding (Rossi and Rossi 1995). Although wild *L. humilis* have never been observed drinking, captives will drink if water is offered to them (Mosauer 1936).

PREDATORS AND DEFENSE. Being small and relatively slow, *L. humilis* is easy prey for many animals. Reported predators include scorpions (*Centruroides*), rainbow trout (*Onycorhynchus mykiss*), night snakes (*Hypsiglena torquata*), Sonoran coral snakes (*Micruroides euryxanthus),* curved-billed thrashers *(Toxostoma curvirostris),* and coyotes *(Canis latrans)* (Anderson 1956; Banta 1953; Klauber 1940a; Tennant 1984; Woodin 1953). Klauber (1940a) also reported that one was caught in the web of a black widow spider *(Latrodectus mactans),* and another was found crushed in a cow *(Bos taurus)* track. Some are killed each year while crossing highways (Klauber 1931a; Price and LaPointe 1990).

When detected, *L. humilis* tries to escape by crawling away, burrowing into loose soil, or entering a nearby burrow. If picked up, it may thrash about, release a malodorous musk, try to force its head and coils between the fingers, or coil around the fingers and jab them with its tail spine. When white light is shown on *L. humilis* at night it appears ghostly silver, and under an ultraviolet light it fluoresces, with the rostral scale appearing blue and the rest of the body pale green (Hulse 1971). Perhaps these color reflections startle or repel predators.

POPULATIONS. This species is not uncommon across its range. Because it is seldom seen, its presence and numbers are not often recognized. However, because it has a tendency toward aggregation, several are often found together at one time. Several dozen were uncovered beneath board planking about 1.2 m below the ground surface at a site in Death Valley, California (Turner and Wauer 1963). At a site in Imperial County, California, Slevin (1950) collected or observed 159 *L. humilis* in five days in a 449 × 12 m tract of land. Brattstrom and Schwenkmeyer (1951) recorded 69 *L. humilis* in two years while road-cruising in San Diego County, California. In contrast, Klauber (1940a) recorded 108 of these snakes while mostly road-cruising in San Diego County from 1923 to 1938, which accounted for only 0.83% of the 12,947 snakes of all species he found during that period.

L. humilis is considered a species of special concern in Nevada and Utah.

REMARKS. Few new data concerning *L. humilis* have been added since the 1970s, and ecological and behavioral studies are needed. The species has been reviewed by Hahn (1979c).

Typhlopidae
Blindsnakes

Six genera and 203 species (McDiarmid et al. 1999) of small, wormlike burrowing snakes belong to this mostly tropical family. Its natural range includes southern Europe, Africa, southern Asia, Australia, and tropical America, and species have been introduced to many oceanic islands and North America.

Typhlopids have solid skulls with a coronoid bone, and the prefrontal bone contacting the nasal bone; ectopterygoid, supratemporal, and circumorbital bones are absent. The maxilla lies transverse to the axis of the skull and is only loosely attached to the cranium. The maxilla has a few teeth, but the palatal bone and reduced mandible have none. The hyoid is Y-shaped. Vestiges of a pelvic girdle remain in the form of pubic, ischial, and iliac elements, with traces of pubic and ischial symphyses or a single elongated bone on each side. The left lung is usually absent, but a tracheal lung is present. The left oviduct is missing. The head is covered with enlarged plate-like scales; the nasal and prefrontal scales are fused. The small eyes are concealed beneath large ocular scales. No visible neck is present. The smooth body scales are uniform in size and shape; a spiny scale adorns the tip of the short tail. Reproduction is oviparous, but at least one species is ovoviviparous, and parthenogenesis occurs in another species.

One introduced species of long-tailed blindsnakes, *Ramphotyphlops braminus*, has become established in the United States.

Head scales of *Ramphotyphlops braminus*.
(Evelyn M. Ernst)

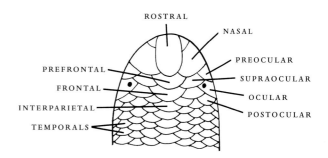

Ramphotyphlops braminus (Daudin 1803) | Brahminy Blindsnake

RECOGNITION. *R. braminus* consists of only females. It is small (TBL to 17.9 cm, but most are shorter than 12 cm), thin (body length/diameter = 30–55%), blunt-headed snake with a rounded snout, lateral nostrils, the lower jaw countersunk, barely visible eyes, and no visible neck. The tail is short (only 1.5–3.0% of TBL) and ends in a scaly spine. Dorsal body color is dark brown to black; the venter is tan to yellowish brown. A series of 249–348 rows (mean, 305) of smooth scales lies between the occiput and anal vent, and 8–15 (mean, 12) rows are present on the tail. Circling the body at the midpoint is a series of 18–20 scales. The head has a large rostral scale (25–33% as wide as the head) separated from the nostrils by an almost vertical suture. Other dorsal, midline scales behind the rostral are 1 prefrontal, 1 frontal, and 1 interparietal. Laterally are 2 nasals (1 small anterior [lower], and 1 larger posterior [upper]), 1 large preocular, 1 supraocular, 1 large ocular covering the eye, 1 postocular, 3+ temporals, 4 supralabials, and 4–6 infralabials. The suture below the nostril extends to the preocular scale, but not to the supralabials. Each maxilla has up to five teeth.

GEOGRAPHIC VARIATION. Wall (1921) recognized three varieties, but subspecific status of those introduced into the United States is unknown.

CONFUSING SPECIES. Slender blindsnakes *(Leptotyphlops)* have their eyes clearly visible through the ocular scales, and 12–13 midbody scale rows. The western slender blindsnake *(L. humilis)* also lacks supraocular scales. All other snakes in the United States have transverse ventral scutes.

KARYOTYPE. The karyotype is 3n = 42 chromosomes, arranged in 14 triplet sets (15 large macrochromosomes, 6 medium-length macrochromosomes, and 21 microchromosomes). One microchromosome has a secondary constriction, and one of the two smallest sets of microchromosomes has 2 subtelocentric and 1 submetacentric chromosomes. The 6 largest macrochromosomes are composed of 2 triplet sets: one consisting of 1 sub-metacentric and 2 metacentric chromosomes, and the other with 3 smaller submetacentric chromosomes (Ota et al. 1991; Wynn et al. 1987).

FOSSIL RECORD. Unknown.

DISTRIBUTION. Due to its accidental introduction in soil of potted plants and in soil used as ship ballast dumped on shores, *R. braminus* is the most widely distributed terrestrial reptile in the world. It now occurs in southern Asia from Arabia to Japan, the Malay Archipelago, the Philippines, Madagascar, southern Africa, Mexico, and on many islands in the Indian and Pacific Oceans, including all of the main Hawaiian Islands (McKeown 1996), and the Caribbean Sea. In the continental United States it is established in Florida from north-central Orange County and Highlands County northwest of Lake Okeechobee south to Dade and Monroe counties and the Upper Keys, and in Lee and Pinellas counties along the Gulf Coast (Ernst and Brown 2000). It has also been found in Louisiana (Thomas 1994) and Massachusetts (Jones et al. 1995; Wallach et al. 1991), but probably could not become established outside of buildings in Massachusetts because of its frozen winter soil.

HABITAT. This small burrower prefers loose, often shady soil (humus, loam, and sand) in mesic habitats, particularly that of flower beds. It is also commonly found in decaying logs and stumps and under rocks, moist leaves, or other plant debris on the ground; in

Brahminy blindsnake, *Ramphothylops braminus*; Myanmar. (Photograph by George R. Zug)

Distribution of *Ramphotyphlops braminus*.

Florida, it lives under human refuse in trash piles and dumps, and around plant nurseries. It apparently needs a moderately moist habitat to balance evaporative water loss through its skin.

At times it appears in unusual situations. Several writers have commented on its emergence through floor cracks in Asian homes, and Minton (1966) reported that some, particularly the young, have been found in the gutter in the most exclusive shopping district of Karachi, Pakistan, and on the second floor of a shop on the same street, a hospital ward, and the bathroom of a modern apartment. C. Ernst's former student, Dr. Christopher W. Brown, then a veterinarian in Dade County, Florida, sent Ernst two juveniles that had been brought to him by an excited woman who found them on the floor of her kitchen and thought her dog had passed them. Wall (1921) commented that *R. braminus* was certainly the snake that invaded the water supply in Calcutta, India, many individuals finding their way into the distribution pipes. Imagine the shock and consternation this would cause if it occurred today in the tourist and wealthy sections of southeastern Florida.

Daniel (1983) reported another potential problem with this small snake. In India it is believed to enter the ear of persons sleeping on the ground. There may be some truth to this, as captives the authors have had regularly entered crevices or holes to hide during the day.

BEHAVIOR. Almost nothing is known of the everyday behavior of *R. braminus*. It is almost entirely nocturnal, only occasionally coming to the surface at dusk or dawn. It may come to the surface during the day after rains; but it probably both overheats and desiccates in dry daytime air, so restricts its diel activity to the cooler, more humid night. Presumably, this snake is active all year in the tropics, but in more temperate areas, such as the United States, it may be less surface active in the cooler winter months and in the hot, dry summer months.

R. braminus is an active burrower that can disappear quickly into loose soil. The blunt head is pushed into the soil, and a serpentine, or sometimes thrashing, movement is used to progress through the soil. The tail spine may be used as an anchor while it forces the body into the soil (Tennant 1997). The rate of movement when crawling on the soil surface is slow, due to the lack of transverse ventral scutes to give it a grip.

REPRODUCTION. *R. braminus* seems to be an all female, triploid, oviparous species that produces eggs parthenogenetically without fertilization. Females with SVLs 9.1 cm or greater contain enlarged follicles (Kamosawa and Ota 1996). Ota et al. (1991) reported a female with a SVL of 9.46 cm that was mature, and Nussbaum (1980) found others 11.1 cm (TBL) or longer possessing enlarged, yolked follicles; so maturity probably occurs at a TBL of 9.5–10.0 cm.

Dissections by Nussbaum (1980) revealed that the ovarian eggs are arranged linearly and normally graded in size with the largest most anterior. He thought this arrangement meant that not all yolked eggs are laid simultaneously, so counts of enlarged follicles in preserved specimens are not good estimates of clutch size. In addition, he described a preserved female with three shelled oviductal eggs apparently ready to be laid, and a fourth yolked ovarian egg which was only half the size of those in the oviduct. Could this small snake lay more than one clutch a year? Ota et al. (1991) found no additional oviductal eggs or evidence of additional ovipositions after females from some temperate Japanese Islands had laid their initial clutch. Females from the Japanese Ryukyu Archipelago oviposit in June and July, and the young hatch in mid- to late August (Ota et al. (1991). However, Nussbaum (1980) found gravid females in the more tropical Seychelles Islands during July, August, October, and December; and Cagle (1946) reported a clutch was laid in the Mariana Islands on 21 April, and a small juvenile was collected on 9 May. Wall (1921) only found gravid females in the warm months, April–July, in Assam; and Pakistan females are gravid in December–January, and early May (Minton 1966). Multiple clutch production should be investigated in more tropical populations.

Clutches contain one to eight (mean, 3.7) eggs, and clutch size is directly correlated with female TBL and mass (Kamosawa and Ota 1996). Females invest much material into the production of young: the RCM is 0.31–0.99 (mean, 0.66), and when clutch mass is divided by female mass plus the clutch mass, the investment is 0.24–0.50 (mean, 0.39; Kamosawa and Ota 1996). The elongated, white eggs have a leathery shell, are 11.2–20.4 (mean, 15.4) × 3.0–5.1 (mean, 3.9) mm, and weigh 0.12–0.23 (mean, 0.18) g. The eggs contain well-developed embryos when laid (Ota et al. 1991); the IP is 38–56 (mean, 47) days, depending on IT. Hatchlings are 50–66 (mean, 58.6) mm long and resemble adults in body color.

GROWTH AND LONGEVITY.   Unknown.

DIET AND FEEDING HABITS.   Because of its small mouth, R. braminus is restricted to eating prey with narrow diameters. Ants (usually larvae and pupae, but occasionally adults) and termites (pupae and some adults) are the most important foods, but small beetles, the soft-bodied larvae of other insects, and possibly small earthworms are probably also consumed. Captives have eaten the eggs and larvae of ants and termites, small caterpillars, small crickets, and mosses and fungi (Sharma and Vazirani 1977), and Annandale (1907) observed a captive devour the excreta of caterpillars.

PREDATORS AND DEFENSE.   Attacks on R. braminus by snakes Bungarus coeruleus, Conopsis nasus, and Dinodon rufozonatus (Iraha and Kazazu 1995; Minton et al. 1997; Wall 1921) have been documented, and undoubtedly other snakes, birds, small mammals, and possibly even large invertebrates prey on it.

These small creatures are inoffensive when handled. They do not bite, but they may secrete musk and prick your fingers with the tips of their tails. When first discovered they try to escape, often frantically thrashing their bodies back and forth in a manner similar to the movements of nematodes. Lazell (1988) reported tail rattling in this species, but the authors have not observed this.

POPULATIONS.   In the tropics, it may be one of the most common snakes (Wall 1921), but populations seem smaller in Florida. Nevertheless, groups of up to six have been found under the same rock in Dade County, and the numbers of individuals in southern Florida will probably continue to increase if no natural catastrophe besets the population.

REMARKS.   It is generally believed that R. braminus is an all female, parthenogenetic species, but Wall (1921) and List (1958) reported finding males. Possibly these may have been wrongly sexed or misidentified as to species. Nussbaum (1980) believed that reports of males, in addition to taxonomic and distributional considerations, indicate that R. braminus, as now recognized, may be a complex of unisexual and bisexual species.

Boidae
Boas

The Boidae is composed of eight genera and 41 species (McDiarmid et al. 1999) of generalized oviparous, constricting snakes found from western North America and the Caribbean Islands south to north-central Argentina, fringing the Sahara Desert and in northeastern and east-central Africa and Madagascar, ranging from southwestern Europe through southern and eastern Arabia and the Middle East to Southwest Asia and India, and on some Pacific Islands and New Guinea. In the skull, the elongated, scalelike supratemporal bone extends beyond the occipital bones, and the premaxilla, septomaxilla, and vomer bones articulate with the cranium. The premaxillae are not sutured to the maxillae. The nasal bones contact the elongated prefrontals but are not sutured to them, allowing the entire nasal complex to articulate with the cranium. A large postorbital bone is present, but no supraorbital. The short quadrate is not enlarged laterally, and the long, laterally projecting, stapes is attached by cartilage to the quadrate. The lower jaws are loosely articulated, and a coronoid bone is present in the mandible. Numerous teeth are present on the maxillae and palatines, but the premaxillae are toothless. Vestiges of hind limbs and girdles are present, with external spurs, better developed in males, on each side of the anal vent. Hypapophyses project from the anterior vertebrae. The tail is short and blunt. Body scales are smooth. Infrared sensitive pits may exist between the labial scales. The family contains two subfamilies, and both are present in North America: the Erycinae, with the genus *Charina*, and the Boinae, with the genus *Boa*.

Key to the Genera of the Family *Boidae*

1a. Dorsal body pattern consists of transverse saddlelike blotches or bars; adults longer than 200 cm .... *Boa*

1b. Either no dorsal body pattern or a pattern of three longitudinal stripes; adults shorter than 120 cm ... *Charina*

Boa constrictor Linnaeus 1758 | Boa Constrictor

RECOGNITION. *B. constrictor* is the largest snake with a breeding population in the United States. Its record TBL is 4.2 m, but few wild individuals are longer than 3 m. The much quoted record length of 18.5 feet (564 cm) was based on a misidentified young anaconda *(Eunectes murinus)* (Joy 1992). The body is thick, and the blunt tail short (TL only 15–20% of SVL). The triangular head is distinct from the neck and has a blunt snout and vertically elliptical pupils. Body color varies from gray, or pink, to tan. A dorsal series of 15–30 dark brown or reddish brown saddle-like blotches or rectangular bars (each normally containing a light spot) is present. A corresponding series of dark, triangular-shaped blotches with light centers occurs on each side of the body. Tail markings are sometimes red, have black borders, and are separated by yellow pigment. The venter is cream, yellow, gray, or tan, with irregular-shaped black or dark brown spots. The head is gray or tan on top, with a narrow, dark medial stripe extending from just in back of the nostrils to the neck. Another dark stripe begins at the nostril, passes rearward through the orbit, and then passes obliquely downward to beyond the corner of the mouth. A small dark bar may be present below the eye, and the supralabials may have one or two small dark bars. Dorsal body scales are smooth and pitless and lie in 49–74 anterior rows, 58–75+ rows at midbody, and 34–49 rows near the vent. Beneath are 225–288 ventrals, a single row of 45–70 subcaudals, and an undivided anal plate. A spurlike remnant of the hind legs is present on each side of the vent. The dorsal surface of the head is covered with small scales, as is most of the lateral surface. Distinguishable on the side of the head are 2 nasals, an orbital ring consisting of 14–20 pre-, supra-, post-, and subocular scales, 17–25 supralabials, and 20–27 infralabials. A relatively small mental shield is present on the chin, followed by a series of small scales. The bilobed hemipenis has a single sulcus spermaticus that ends before the apex, a smooth base and a smooth apex, and flounces along the shaft. Maxillary teeth are aglyphous (ungrooved), long, and curved backward, and average 18–19 (15–24) in number.

Females are generally larger than males (Huang 1996), but males have better developed spurs adjacent to the vent.

GEOGRAPHIC VARIATION. Ten subspecies are recognized (McDiarmid et al. 1999), but which of these is (are) established in the United States has not been determined.

CONFUSING SPECIES. No other large snake in the United States has anal spurs. Other snakes with anal spurs are very small, thin, and lack ventral scutes *(Leptotyphlops* and *Ramphotyphlops);* are shorter and have an unpatterned body and enlarged dorsal head scales *(Charina bottae);* or are shorter, with three longitudinal body stripes and less than 50 midbody scale rows *(C. trivirgata).*

KARYOTYPE. The diploid chromosome compliment is 36: 16 macrochromosomes (6 metacentric, 2 submetacentric, and 8 acrocentric), and 20 microchromosomes (Becak et al. 1963; Singh et al. 1968). Sexual heteromorphy is not distinguished in this species, but Benirschke and Hsu (1971) tentatively designated the fourth pair of macrochromosomes in females as sex chromosomes (ZW?) after comparison to other species with this pair dimorphic in females.

FOSSIL RECORD. Unknown.

DISTRIBUTION. The natural range of *Boa constrictor* extends from Sonora and Tamaulipas in northern Mexico south through Central America to southern Brazil, Bolivia, Uruguay, and northern Argentina in South America, and approximately encompasses latitudes 30°N to 36°S (a winter AT of 10°C limits the range in the temperate zones). It also occurs on the West Indian islands of Dominica, St. Lucia, San Andrés, and Providencia and on other continental islands off the Atlantic and Pacific coasts of Mexico and Central and South America.

In the United States, a breeding population has been established in Dade County, Florida, by released

Boa constrictor, *Boa constrictor*. (Photograph by Carl H. Ernst)

or escaped snakes from the pet trade (Dalrymple 1994). The skeletons of an adult boa and two juveniles were removed from pinewoods on the Deering estate after a controlled burn in 1990, and several more observations of young-of-the-year have occurred since then.

HABITAT. *Boa constrictor* is a generalist as to habitat and became adapted to various habitats across its large range. In arid parts of Mexico it occurs in semi-deserts with thorn scrub; elsewhere it lives in wet and dry tropical forests and savannas. In parts of South America it inhabits high forests, and in agricultural areas it uses cultivated fields, especially those for sugar cane. It seems to thrive in disturbed settings. The total altitudinal range is sea level to about 1,500 m. It is a ground dweller where trees are scarce, but may be somewhat arboreal where trees are plentiful.

BEHAVIOR. In its tropical range, *Boa constrictor* is probably most active during the rainy season but has no extended period of inactivity during the year. Daily activity is usually crepuscular or nocturnal, but some boas prowl during the day (McGinnis and Moore 1969). Hardy and McDiarmid (1969) encountered these snakes most often at night between 1930 and 2400 hours in Sinaloa, Mexico. Mammal burrows, hollow logs and stumps, tree holes, and rock crevices are used as retreats. Living in warm habitats, the snake usually can maintain active BTs without basking, but some basking may occur in the early morning, especially at higher elevations. Active wild individuals have been found when ATs were 22–29°C (Brattstrom 1965; Myres and Eells 1968), and free moving wild and captive individuals have had BTs of 22–37°C (Brattstrom 1965; McGinnis and Moore 1969; Montgomery and Rand 1978; Myres and Eells 1968). A captive kept at 21–24°C never had its BT fall to ambient: it maintained its BT at 22–24°C for about the first three hours after feeding, then raised it to 31–36°C and maintained it there by basking under a heat source (Regal 1966).

Distribution of *Boa constrictor*.

B. constrictor sometimes aggregates, presumably to reduce heat loss. Lazell (1964) reported groups of 3–12 boas in the same hollow log or tree stump, and Myres and Eells (1968) found a large female and four smaller males outside the entrance of a small cavity in a rock ledge. BTs of four of the snakes were 30.4–31.0°C, and the fifth had a BT of 25.8°C. The appearance of the ground at the base of the ledge indicated that this was a regular basking site.

Water loss during the dry season or in dry habitats may be a problem but is countered behaviorally by remaining inactive during the day and foraging at night when ATs are cooler and the air more humid. Additionally, the skin of this species contains a relatively high quantity of water-proofing lipids (Burken et al. 1985). Close aggregations may also retard cutaneous water loss.

Long distance movements are probably seldom made, provided food and shelters are locally available. A radio-equipped individual moved a total of only 135 m in 12 days, spending much of its time underground in several armadillo burrows, seeking a new burrow every three to four days (Montgomery and Rand 1978). This snake is a good climber, particularly young individuals, and it readily climbs above ground into shrubs and small trees to a height of 12 m (Lazell 1964).

REPRODUCTION. Greene (1983) concluded that sexual maturity occurs at a TBL of 150–200 cm, but Scott (in Hardy and McDiarmid 1969) reported copulation by two approximately 120 cm individuals and birth of 17 young to another 120 cm female. Pope (1961) noted that a 119.4 cm female gave birth to four young. In addition, Foekema (1972) reported a 170 cm female was probably sexually mature, and Kauffeld (in Pope 1961) discovered that a wild female with a SVL of 142 cm was gravid. However, de Porben-Platón and Feuer (1975) reported an unsuccessful mating attempt by a 140 cm male. Females apparently mature in their fourth year (Foekema 1972). The gametic cycles have not been described, but these vary with latitude, as the species seems to have a very long breeding season.

Courtship/mating behaviors have been observed, either in captivity or in nature, in December–September, but most activity seems to take place in December–March. During courtship, the male approaches and crawls on top of the female. Next, he performs a series of strong contractions as he slides his body along her back towards her head. When his head is over that of the female, he may press his chin downward and rub the top of her head. He also rapidly strokes the female's sides and back with his cloacal spurs, especially in the region of her vent, often creating an audible scratching sound. Eventually, he manipulates his vent in contact with hers and inserts the hemipenis if she is receptive. Courtship may last several hours, and copulation usually lasts over an hour (Gadd 1983; Mole and Urich 1894). It is suspected that females store viable sperm.

The species is ovoviviparous. Only one litter is produced a year; it is not known if all females in a population reproduce annually. After a successful mating, the female may carry the developing young for 143–178 days, depending on ETs. Captives, kept constantly warm, may produce neonates in less time. Litters have been born from February to September, but the majority of births take place from March to July. Litters consist of 2–64 (mean, 23; n = 34 litters). Hatchlings are 37.3–63.5 (mean, 47.3) cm long and weigh about 145 g. Females may be slightly longer than males at birth (Hoge 1947).

GROWTH AND LONGEVITY. Growth data are scarce and are mostly based on captives reared under different feeding regimes. Growth of neonates may be rapid, but extremely variable, possibly accounting for the discrepancies in maturity lengths listed above. A captive kept by Emsley (1977) grew to 165 cm by its third birthday. Other length increases listed in Pope (1961) are 149.9 cm by a male in two years, 218.4 cm by a female in two years, and 109.2 cm by a male in 2.5 years. Another captive male gained 140.6 cm in approximately three years (de Porben-Platón and Feuer 1975). Growth slows in large individuals.

No natural longevity has been reported, but captives have had long lives: a female captured as an adult survived an additional 10 years, 1 months, and 15 days; a captive-born female lived 29 years, 11 months, and 9 days; and a male that was wild caught at an unknown age survived over 21 years in captivity (Snider and Bowler 1992).

DIET AND FEEDING HABITS. Captive *B. constrictor* may consume up to 159 g of food per week (Kirkwood and Gili 1994). A generalist predator, it eats a variety of animals in the wild, but small and medium-sized mammals, birds, and lizards are the most important prey. Reported prey are mammals—opossum *(Didelphis albiventris)*, bats *(Artebius jamaicensis, Brachphylla cavernarum, Desmodus rotundus)*, armadillos *(Chaetophractus)*, collared anteater *(Tamandua tetradactylus)*, murid mice and rats *(Mus musculus, Rattus norvegicus, R. rattus)*, cotton rats (Sigmodontinae), spiny rats *(Proechimys)*, squirrels *(Microsciurus, Sciurus)*, maras *(Dolichotis salinicola)*, agouti *(Dasyprocta noblei)*, cavies *(Microcavia australis)*, paca *(Agouti paca)*, viscachas *(Lagostomus maximus)*, Rothschild's prehensile-tailed porcupine *(Coendou rothschildi)*, hares and rabbits *(Lepus europaeus, Sylvilagus)*, pigs *(Sus scrofa)*, coatis *(Nasua narica)*, mongooses (Herpestidae), dogs and foxes *(Canis familiaris, Lycalopex gymnocerus)*, ocelots *(Leopardus pardalis)*, goats *(Capra hircus)*, and young deer (Cervidae); birds—rheas *(Rhea americana)*, tinamous (Tinamidae), domestic chickens *(Gallus gallus)*, turkeys *(Meleagris gallopavo)*, pekin ducks *(Anas platyrhynchus)*, cattle egrets *(Bubulcus ibis)*, doves (Columbidae), monk parakeets *(Myiopsitta monacha)*, antbirds (Formicariidae), blue-gray tanagers *(Thraupis episcopus)*, orange-billed sparrows *(Arremon aurantiirostris)*, and bright-rumped attilas *(Attila spadicus)*; lizards—racerunners *(Cnemidophorus)*, tegus *(Tupinambis)*, and ameivas *(Ameiva)*; frogs; and fish (Boback et al. 2000; Bogert and Oliver 1945; Emsley 1977; Greene 1983; Henderson et al. 1995; Janzen 1970; Mole and Urich 1894; Pope 1961; Sironi et al. 2000; Thomas 1974; Tolson and Henderson 1993). The colony of *B. constrictor* established in Florida possibly prey on domestic animals, opossum *(Didelphis virginianus)*, and raccoon *(Procyon lotor)* (Dalrymple 1994). Captives will eat house mice *(Mus musculus)*, brown rats *(Rattus norvegicus)*, golden hamsters *(Mesocricetus auratus)*, guinea pigs *(Cavia porcellus)*, house sparrows *(Passer domesticus)*, and rock doves *(Columba livia)* (C. Ernst, pers. obs.; Pope 1961).

Several hunting techniques are used. The snake may simply prowl until it comes upon an animal or the scent trail of a prey species, which it then follows until it finds the meal. It also uses an ambush method known as "sit-and-wait"—the snake selects a place near the prey's burrow or lies concealed beside a prey trail (Montgomery and Rand 1978). Juveniles may wave their multicolored tails at small prey to lure them into striking range (Radcliffe et al. 1980). Detection is via odor and is mediated by the vomeronasal system (Stone and Holtzman 1996).

Prey are seized in the mouth, quickly surrounded by body coils, and constricted. During constriction the snake's venter is turned anteriorly, and usually the right side of the body is used to apply pressure (Heinrich and Klaassen 1985). Warm prey is preferred over cold prey (Quesnel and Wehekind 1969), and the time required to consume prey is conversely related to the activity level of the prey (MacDonald 1973).

PREDATORS AND DEFENSE. Few reports of predation on *B. constrictor* are available, and all of these are of attacks by ophiophagous snakes: Beebe (1946) saw a mussurana *(Pseudoboa cloeli)* seize a young boa, Duellman (1963) found a boa fighting with a large indigo snake *(Drymarchon corais)* that was apparently trying to eat it, and Guyer and Laska (1996) observed a tropical racer *(Coluber mentovarius)* attempt to eat a juvenile boa. The greatest threats are from habitat destruction and overcollecting for the pet trade.

Although often mild-mannered, when disturbed some wild boa constrictors are aggressive. They hiss loudly, shake their tails, and release a pungent musk. Biting may occur, but often as a last resort. Most individuals become rather calm after being in captivity for some time, and those born in captivity usually grow up docile.

POPULATIONS. No study of the dynamics of a wild boa constrictor population has been reported. It may be common at some localities; Hardy and McDiarmid (1969) captured 150 boas during one summer in Sinaloa, Mexico.

REMARKS. The colony established in Dade County, Florida, should be studied to determine its dynamics and ecology. The taxonomy of *Boa constrictor* was reviewed by McDiarmid et al. (1999).

Charina Gray 1849

Rubber and Rosy Boas

Key to the Species of *Charina*

1a. Dorsal head surface covered with enlarged plates; three scales lie between the orbits, the middle one the largest; snout short with a large, broad rostral scalé; one to two loreal scales on each side; tail blunt; body color uniform, without stripes . . . . *C. bottae*

1b. Dorsal head surface covered with small scales; several small scales lie between the orbits; snout elongated, with the rostral scale longer than broad; three to eight loreal scales on each side; tail not blunt; body with longitudinal stripes . . . . *C. trivirgata*

Charina bottae (Blainville 1835) | Rubber Boa

RECOGNITION. *C. bottae* is a relatively short (TBL to 83.8 cm, but most individuals are smaller than 60 cm), stout-bodied snake with a short, bluntly rounded tail. Dorsal body color is usually uniform tan, brown, reddish brown, or olive green, but some dark flecking may be present along the sides. The brown to olive head is no broader than the neck and has large plate-like scales on its dorsal surface. The snout is broad and rather blunt, the lower jaw is countersunk, and the pupils are vertically elliptical. The supralabials are yellowish, and the chin and throat cream to yellow. The venter is yellow, with either dark flecking or a mottled pattern of orange, brown, and black. Dorsal body scales are small, smooth, and pitless and lie in 32–53 rows. The 182–231 ventrals are reduced in size, the 24–43 subcaudals occur in a single row, and the anal plate is undivided, with an external remnant (spur) of a hind limb on each side. Lateral head scales include 2 nasals, 1 (2) loreal(s), 1 preocular, 3–4 postoculars, 10 (9–11) supralabials, and 10 reduced infralabials. Temporal scales are the same size and shape as the body scales lying posterior to them, and the chin shields are small. The single hemipenis is distally clavate and transversely plicate, with a terminally forked sulcus spermaticus and a smooth basal segment (Stewart 1977). The maxillary teeth total 10–15.

Adult males are shorter and weigh less than females, with TLs averaging 13 (11.8–14.7) % of TBL, and well-developed, hooked, robust, spurs that are of uniform size; females are larger and weigh more than males, with TLs averaging 11.3 (9.5–12.9) % of TBL,

and spurs that are small, conical, often hidden, or even absent (Hoyer 1974; Hoyer and Stewart 2000a; Nussbaum and Hoyer 1974).

GEOGRAPHIC VARIATION. Two subspecies are recognized (the following descriptions are based on Cunningham 1966b; Erwin 1974; Rodriguez-Robles et al. 2001; and Stewart 1977). *C. b. bottae* (Blainville 1835), the northern rubber boa, occurs over the greater part of the range. It is large (TBL usually over 40 cm), with 39–53 dorsal scale rows, 188–231 ventrals, and 24–43 subcaudals; its frontal plate usually has a convex or angular posterior border, and its body color is brown to green. *C. b. umbratica* Klauber 1943b, the southern rubber boa, is only found in some mountain ranges in southern California. It is small (TBL less than 40 cm), with 32–42 dorsal scale rows, 182–217 ventrals, and 25–34 subcaudals; its frontal plate has a straight or only slightly convex posterior border, and it is light, usually tan, in body color. Formerly, a third taxon, *C. b. utahensis* Van Denburgh 1920, was recognized, but after examination of a large series of specimens, Nussbaum and Hoyer (1974) showed it not significantly different from *C. b. bottae*.

Rodriguez-Robles et al. (2001) studied mtDNA sequences to test the current phylogeographic interpretation of subspecific variation within *Charina bottae*. They identified two clades corresponding to the currently recognized subspecies—a northern *C. b. bottae* group, and a southern *C. b. umbratica* group—and thought that enough genetic and morphological data

Rubber boa, *Charina bottae*; California. (Photograph by Roger W. Barbour)

existed to recognize *C. b. umbricata* as a distinct species.

CONFUSING SPECIES. For the rosy boa *(Charina trivirgata)*, see the key to the species of *Charina* presented above.

KARYOTYPE. The karyotype consists of 36 diploid chromosomes with a total of 44 arms: 16 macrochromosomes (8 metacentric, 8 acrocentric) and 20 microchromosomes (Gorman and Gress 1970; Trinco and Smith 1971).

FOSSIL RECORD. The only known fossils are eight Pleistocene vertebrae from Shasta County, California (Bell and Mead 1996), and three vertebrae from a Holocene deposit in Washoe County, Nevada (Mead 1988; Mead and Bell 1994).

DISTRIBUTION. *C. bottae* ranges south from southern British Columbia and southwestern Alberta through Washington, Oregon, western Montana, and northwestern Wyoming to the Pacific Coast and Sier-

ras of California, central Nevada, and south-central Utah. Isolated populations also occur in south-central Montana and adjacent north-central Wyoming and in the mountain ranges of southern California.

HABITAT. Rubber boas are often found in uplands (to 3,050 m), where they live in habitats varying from scrub pine-oak woodlands and chaparral to coniferous forests, but they are also known from grasslands and desert fringes. Boulders, flat rocks, and logs and stumps for hiding places are a necessity, and the vegetation present is often scattered.

BEHAVIOR. *C. bottae* has a relatively long annual activity period that is basically determined by ET and therefore depends on both latitude and elevation. In the Willamette Valley of western Oregon, active individuals have been found from 30 January to early November, with peak surface activity in April–June (Hoyer 1974; Nussbaum et al. 1983). In British Columbia, they have been seen basking as early as 24 February (Grant 1969). Farther east at a higher elevation in Idaho, rubber boas are usually active April–

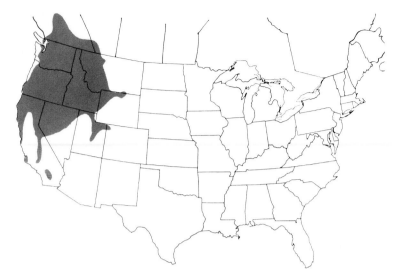

Distribution of *Charina bottae*.

October and sometimes into November during warm autumns (Dorcas, in Koch and Peterson 1995). *C. bottae* is probably active all year in southern California. Males emerge much earlier in the spring than do females (Hoyer 1974).

Hibernation sites include talus slopes, deep rock crevices, rodent burrows, and within logs. Hibernating *C. bottae* typically have BTs of 4–9°C; those placed in a refrigerator by Cunningham (1966b) could still right themselves at a BT as low as 3.1°C. A dormant period of cooling is needed to stimulate breeding after spring emergence (captives should be cooled to BTs of 10–13°C for three months; Spiess and Smith 1998).

These snakes seldom emerge before dusk and remain active through the night, although they are occasionally seen on the surface during cool, cloudy days, or shortly after sunrise. Surprisingly, nocturnal surface activity only occurs about once in every eight days (Dorcas and Peterson 1998). Days are normally spent hidden in rodent burrows, within the rotting wood of logs or stumps, beneath the bark of trees or stumps, or under flat rocks.

Occasionally the rubber boa basks, especially after feeding, on cool days, or early or late in its annual activity period. This is sometimes done while lying within rock crevices exposed to the sun (Stewart 1987). Active wild *C. bottae* have had 6.0–34.5°C BTs (Dorcas, in Koch and Peterson 1995; Dorcas and Peterson 1997). Thermal preference seems to be 27–28°C (Dorcas and Peterson 1997); the CT_{max} is 38°C. Nocturnal activity normally takes place at BTs

of 13–18°C (Cunningham 1966b), and crepuscular and daytime activity at 21–25°C (Dorcas and Peterson 1997, 1998). Those under cover have lower BTs than surface active individuals, with their BTs closely matching ST. Brattstrom (1965) found one under a log with a CT of 14°C (AT, 15.7°C; ST, 12.5°C), and another under a board with a CT of 18.2°C (AT, 18.5°C; ST, 16.5°C). Pregnant females try to maintain BTs near 31.5°C (Dorcas and Peterson 1998). Digestion and elimination are related to BT. In tests performed by Dorcas et al. (1997), rubber boas regurgitated all of their prey almost intact at ETs of 10 and 35°C. Gastric digestion rates rose steadily as BTs increased from 15 to 25°C, then leveled off or decreased slightly at 30°C. Passage rates were lowest at 15°C, about the same at 20 and 25°C, and highest at 30°C.

Home ranges of rubber boas are usually small. Dorcas (in Koch and Peterson 1995) found that many Idaho *C. bottae* never ventured farther than 100 m from their den site. Data from radio-equipped individuals indicate that this snake rarely moves from place to place during the day; almost all such behavior occurs at night (Dorcas and Peterson 1998).

Not all movements are made on the surface of the ground; it is a good climber, sometimes climbing to hide under the loose bark of a tree or raid a bird's nest. Stebbins (1954) has also observed it swimming in streams on several occasions.

REPRODUCTION. Stebbins (1985) reported the minimum adult length as 35.6 cm, and Wright and Wright

(1957) as 38.1 cm. More realistic are the TBLs of 45.0 cm for males and 54.5 cm for females reported by Nussbaum et al. (1983). Such TBLs are probably reached by wild rubber boas in three to five years (Hoyer and Storm 1991); Rossi and Rossi (1995) reported that well-fed captives may mature in two to three years.

The sexual cycles have not been formally studied, but pregnant females can be found throughout the summer months, indicating late spring ovulation, and parturition occurs in August–November in the wild. Hoyer (in Stewart 1987) believed that females normally reproduce once in every two to three years.

Courtship and mating occur in April–May (Hoyer and Stewart 2000a; Nussbaum et al. 1983), but captives have bred during February–May (Rossi and Rossi 1995; van der Pols 1988). Courtship is slow and deliberate. The male approaches the female and tongue-flicks over her body, and she opens her cloacal vent upon contact with the male. Both sexes have scent glands located within the cloaca at the base of the tail that release volatile secretions, possibly containing pheromones, onto the posterolateral margins of the cloaca (Oldak 1976). Further courtship behavior and the copulatory act have not been described. Males possibly use their enlarged spurs to hold or stimulate the female.

Captive litters have been delivered in June (van der Pols 1988); most wild neonates appear in August–September, but Hudson (1957) found a newborn on 25 November. When born, the neonates are enclosed in an amniotic membrane and have remnants of an umbilical cord. The GP is probably three to five months. Litters consist of 1 (Stewart 1987) to 10 (Spiess and Smith 1998) young and average 4 (27 litters). Mean RCM of 12 litters was 0.369 (0.288–0.436) (Hoyer and Stewart 2000a). Neonates are uniformly pinkish or tan with TBLs of 17.0–28.5 (mean, 20.7) cm, and weigh 3.9–8.0 (mean, 6.5) g.

GROWTH AND LONGEVITY. No growth data are available. *C. bottae* is long-lived if given proper care. One of unknown sex originally wild caught as an adult survived for 20 years and 5 months (Snider and Bowler 1992), and another was still living after over 17 years in captivity (Koch and Peterson 1995).

DIET AND FEEDING HABITS. *C. bottae* is a constrictor of small vertebrates. The prey is slowly stalked, sometimes with the snake's mouth held open (Stebbins 1954). When in range, the boa strikes quickly, seizes the prey behind the head, and immediately throws loops of its body around the animal's body. After the animal has stopped struggling, it is released from the snake's coils and swallowed head first. More than one small prey may be constricted at once, even as the snake is swallowing another (Nussbaum et al. 1983).

Rodríguez-Robles et al. (1999b) found that mammals (66%) were most commonly eaten, followed by lizards (17%), birds (7%), and squamate eggs (5%). Known prey of *C. bottae* are mammals—moles *(Scapanus latimanus),* shrews *(Sorex* sp.), voles *(Microtus californicus, M. longicaudus, M. montanus),* mice *(Peromyscus boylei, P. maniculatus, Perognathus* sp., *Zapus princeps),* pocket gophers *(Thomomys talpoides),* and young rabbits *(Sylvilagus* sp.); birds, both adults and nestlings *(Parus rufescens);* lizards *(Elgaria coerulea, Sceloporus occidentalis)* and their eggs; salamanders, both adults and eggs *(Ensatina eschscholtzii);* and snails *(Ariolimax)* (Bartholomew and Lleyson 1993; Fitch 1936; Linder 1963; Macey 1983; Nussbaum et al. 1983; Shaw and Campbell 1974; Rodriquez-Robles et al. 1999b; Stebbins 1954; Van Denburgh 1922; Wright and Wright 1957). Captives have eaten shrews *(Sorex* sp.), mice *(Mus musculus, Peromyscus* sp.), voles *(Microtus* sp.), lizards *(Elgaria multicarinata, Gerrhonotus* sp., *Sceloporus graciosus),* lizard eggs *(Sceloporus occidentalis),* snakes *(C. bottae, Thamnophis elegans),* snake eggs *(Diadophis punctatus),* birds *(Carpodacus mexicanus),* salamander eggs *(Ensatina eschscholtzii),* earthworms, and ground beef (Hoyer and Steward 2000b; Hudson 1957; Lewis 1946; Linder 1963; Stebbins 1954; van der Pols 1988). An age / size dietary shift occurs: smaller individuals 14.4–26.8 cm) eat squamate eggs and lizards; larger *C. bottae* eat lizards, birds, and mammals (Rodríguez-Robles et al. 1999b).

PREDATORS AND DEFENSE. Wild animals known to kill or possibly harm *C. bottae* are shrews *(Sorex* sp.), moles *(Neurotrichus gibbsii, Scapanus* sp.), voles *(Clethrionomys* sp., *Lagurus curtatus, Microtus* sp., *Phenacomys* sp.), mice *(Chaetodipus californicus, Onychomys* sp., *Peromyscus* sp., *Perognathus* sp., *Reithrodontomys megaloti, Zapus* sp.), rats *(Neotoma* sp.), kangaroo rats *(Dipodomys* sp.), squirrels *(Glaucomys sabrinus, Sciurus griseus, Spermophilus* sp., *Tamias* sp., *Tamiasciurus* sp.), badgers *(Taxidea taxus),* martins *(Martes* sp.), raccoon *(Procyon lotor),* ravens *(Corvus corax),* hawks *(Buteo jamaicensis),* owls, toads *(Bufo boreas),* lizards *(Elgaria multicarinata),* snakes *(Diadophis punctatus, Hypsiglena torquata, Lampropeltis getula, L. zonata, Masticophis lateralis),* carpenter ants *(Camponotus* sp.), and Jerusalem crickets *(Stenopelmatus* sp.) (Hoyer and Stewart 2000b; Koch and Peterson 1995; Larson in Koch and Peterson 1995; Van Heest and Hay 2000). Captives have been eaten by the Soloman Island boa *(Candoia carinata)* (Michaels 1985a, 1985b), and captive female *C. bottae* have eaten their newborn young (Hudson 1957). Some are killed on highways, and others drown in cisterns each year.

The rubber boa has several defense strategies. Because it is most active at night, its unicolored body blends in well with the soil background, and it will stop moving almost immediately when disturbed. If, however, it is near a rock crevice or the entrance to a rodent burrow, it may try to retreat into these. It seldom bites, but if further disturbed may loop its body into a ball with the head hidden beneath protective coils. Meanwhile, the short, blunt tail is exposed and waved as if it were a head. A pungent musk may be released from anal glands. A captive juvenile observed by Peabody et al. (1975) tried to prevent itself from being swallowed by a larger *C. bottae* by coiling about the larger snake's neck and pulling its head from the mouth of the larger snake. Similarly, Van Heest and Hay (2000) reported a rubber boa coiled around the neck of an attacking red-tailed hawk *(Buteo jamaicensis)* and strangled it. When this snake raids a mouse nest, it will fend off the female mouse as it eats the young by imitation strikes with its tail. The female mouse will often chew the snake's tail, thus most scars on the tails of rubber boas are probably from female mice, not predators (Nussbaum and Hoyer 1974).

POPULATIONS. In any given area, this snake may seem scarce, but this is likely due more to their secretive burrowing and nocturnal behavior than to actual low numbers. The only study of the population dynamics of *C. bottae* was by Hoyer (1974). The sex ratio at birth favors females, but females experience a greater postbirth mortality rate than males, and the adult sex ratio is closer to 1:1 (Hoyer and Stewart 2000a). In Hoyer's population in the Willamette Valley of Oregon, most males were 45.1–60.0 cm long, and most females were 55.1–75.0 cm. Of 338 different rubber boas caught, 296 (87.6%) were between 45.1 and 75.0 cm long, only 4 (1.1%) were longer than 75.1 cm, and only 38 (11.2%) were shorter than 45.1 cm. Twenty-two (6.5%) were juveniles, 28 (8.2%) were subadult, and 288 (85.2%) were adults. A second population studied by Hoyer and Stewart (2000a) in the San Bernardino Mountains of southern California was composed of 40 adult males, 32 adult females, and 13 immature individuals. *C. bottae* is considered a species of special concern in Nevada, and rare in Wyoming.

REMARKS. *C. bottae* is closely related to the rosy boa *(C. trivirgata)* (Kluge 1993). The species has been reviewed by Stewart (1977).

Charina trivirgata (Cope 1861b) | Rosy Boa

RECOGNITION. *C. trivirgata* is a short, stocky snake that grows to a maximum TBL of 111.8 cm (although most individuals are less than 90 cm long); the tail is short, tapered, and slightly prehensile. Body color is gray to light brown, with a dorsal and two lateral broad, reddish brown longitudinal stripes. The stripes may be complete, or interrupted to form a series of irregularly shaped blotches. The head is elongated, slightly broader than the neck, and covered dorsally with small scales. The eye has a vertically elliptical pupil. Chin, throat, and venter are cream to grayish white; the venter is usually spotted or mottled with gray. Dorsal body scales are smooth, pitless, and occur in 33–49 rows in populations north of Mexico. Be-

Rosy boa, *Charina trivirgata*; San Bernardino County, California. (Photograph by Donald J. Fisher)

neath are 216–245 ventrals, 38–52 subcaudals, and an undivided anal plate. On either side of the anal vent is an external remnant (spur) of a hind limb. Lateral head scales include 2 nasals, 3 (2–4) loreals, a ring of 7–11 ocular scales (including pre-, supra-, post-, and suboculars), several rows of 1–3 temporals, 13–15 (12–15) supralabials, and 14–16 (11–17) infralabials. No chin shields are present. The single hemipenis has a distally forked sulcus spermaticus, a smooth apex with pinnate lamina, and a smooth base. Each maxilla has 14–20 (mean, 17) teeth.

Adult males are shorter than females, with larger better-developed spurs and TLs averaging 14% of TBL; adult females are larger than males, with shorter less-developed spurs that barely break the skin surface and TLs averaging 13% of TBL.

GEOGRAPHIC VARIATION.   The number of subspecies is debatable; as many as six have been named, but only three occur north of Mexico. *C. t. trivirgata* (Cope 1861b), the Mexican rosy boa, ranges south from Maricopa and Pima counties, Arizona, to western Sonora and the southern half of Baja California. It has three dark brown longitudinal stripes with serrate borders on a gray to cream background, and a cream to white venter with only a few dark speckles. *C. t. gracia* (Klauber 1931a), the desert rosy boa, occurs in southeastern California, southwestern Arizona, and northeastern Baja California. It can be identified by its three rose-colored, reddish brown, or tan smooth-bordered, longitudinal stripes on a gray or tan

background; the lack, usually, of dark spotting between the longitudinal stripes; and the cream venter with dark flecks or mottling. *C. t. roseofusca* (Cope 1868), the coastal rosy boa, is found only along the Pacific Coast of southwestern California and northwestern Baja California. This snake has three pink, reddish brown, or dull brown irregularly bordered, longitudinal stripes on a bluish gray background; scattered dark-pigmented scales between the longitudinal stripes; and a gray to bluish gray venter with dark mottling.

Taxonomy of the races of *C. trivirgata* is in flux (Ottley et al. 1980; Spiteri 1988; Yingling 1982). Spiteri (1991) concluded that so much intergradation occurs between *C. t. roseofusca* and *C. t. gracia* in southern California that neither subspecies occurs in pure populations there. He considered *gracia* invalid (as did Yingling 1982) and relegated all California rosy boas to *C. t. myriolepis* (Cope 1868), a long unused name. This arrangement has not been universally accepted, so we have taken the conservative approach and continue to recognize three subspecies in the United States.

CONFUSING SPECIES.   The rubber boa *(C. bottae)* could be confused with some heavily pigmented rosy boas, but see the key to the species of *Charina* presented above.

KARYOTYPE.   The karyotype consists of 36 chromosomes with 44 arms: 16 macrochromosomes (8 acrocentric, 8 metacentric) and 20 microchromosomes (Gorman and Gress 1970).

FOSSIL RECORD.   Pleistocene (Rancholabrean) remains have been found in southern Arizona (Mead et al. 1984) and California (Van Devender and Mead 1978).

DISTRIBUTION.   The rosy boa ranges south from Hanaupah Canyon near Death Valley, California, to southern Baja California, southern Arizona, and western Sonora, Mexico.

HABITAT.   *C. trivirgata* lives in dry shrublands and the fringes of deserts; among scattered rocks and boulders, rock crevices, or talus slopes; usually on south-facing hillsides at elevations from sea level to

Distribution of *Charina trivirgata*.

over 2,000 m. It is rarely found anywhere without rock cover and seems to prefer habitats with some free water (possibly because of greater prey availability).

BEHAVIOR. Because of its secretive nature and nocturnal behavior, few life history data have been reported. It is most often found hiding under some object. The prime annual activity period in southwestern California extends from March to November, but rosy boas may be active in the winter months (Klauber 1924). Farther north and east and at its highest elevations, the annual activity period is shorter, probably lasting from April to October. It is chiefly nocturnal, but some may emerge early at dusk or during cool spring and fall days. On overcast or sometimes rainy days it may be active during the day, particularly in midmorning. Basking is not uncommon in the spring and at higher elevations. Klauber (1924) found it active on roads from 2010 to 2247 hours. Nocturnally active *C. trivirgata* caught by Klauber (1924) and Brattstrom (1965) had CTs of 23 and 25.2°C (AT, 33.2°C; ST, 32.4°C), respectively, and one collected in the sun by Brattstrom had a CT of 35.5°C (AT, 23.0°C; ST, 30.0°C). Captives have been successfully kept at daytime ETs of 26–34°C and night ETs of 15–24°C; gravid females are best kept at 24–29°C (Rossi and Rossi 1995).

Winter is usually spent underground, deep in a rock crevice or mammal burrow. A period of cooling is necessary to bring on breeding readiness in the spring. Breeders have successfully stimulated mating behavior by first cooling the snakes to BTs of 10–15°C for two to four months, and rosy boas show no ill effects when exposed to ETs as low as 3°C for short periods (Rossi and Rossi 1995).

Although no data on home range size have been reported, rosy boas probably make only short trips from their day retreats. They are slow crawlers, usually employing a rectilinear (caterpillar) form of locomotion, and average only 0.145 km/hour. Their maximum crawling speed is 0.361 km/hour (Mosauer 1935b). Climbing ability is good.

REPRODUCTION. Most reproductive data have come from captive breeding. Maturity is apparently attained at two to three years of age (Rossi and Rossi 1995). The smallest recorded breeding male had a TBL of 58 cm (Granger 1982), and the smallest breeding female was 60 cm TBL (Stebbins 1985). Almost nothing is known of its gametic cycles. A female captured on 29 June had embryos probably 67% developed (Taylor, in Wright and Wright 1957).

Courtship and/or copulation have been observed in captivity during the period 15 May to 20 July, but some matings in the wild probably occur before this. A courting male approaches a female and carefully examines her by flicking his tongue over most of her body; the female may concurrently tongue-flick the male. The male then slowly crawls on top of the female and stimulates her by erecting his spurs and stroking her posterior sides. If receptive, she twists the rear of her body to one side and slightly elevates her tail. Then the male quickly inserts his hemipenis into her cloaca (Granger 1982; Kurfess 1967; Norrie 1986).

Females are ovoviviparous; they retain the fertilized eggs for incubation within their bodies until they hatch, and then they give birth. The GP ranges from 103 to 143 days (Markx 1986; Rossi and Rossi 1995), and captive litters have been born from 29 September to 22 November. Litters contain 1–12 young (Rossi and Rossi 1995; Stebbins 1985) and average 4.9 (n = 15 litters). Neonates are 18.5–36.2 (mean, 29.9 cm; n = 36) cm long and weigh an average of 28.2 (23.0–31.2) g. They are colored and patterned like the adults.

GROWTH AND LONGEVITY. If young rosy boas are well fed, growth can be rapid. Available data on growth rates are based on captives raised under different conditions. Five neonates raised by Kurfess (1967) grew from an average of 35.2 cm to an average of 74.0 cm in nine months, and another 36.6 cm male grew to 45.7 cm in one year and added an additional 18.7 cm its second year. One, with a 77 cm TBL and a mass of 311 g when captured, grew to 91 cm and 405 g in six years (Mazzarella 1974), and an adult female 75 cm long and 250 g gained 150 g in 1.5 years (van der Pols 1986).

Two *C. trivirgata* of unknown sex (one a wild-caught juvenile *C. t. gracia*, the other a wild-caught adult *C. t. roseofusca*) survived in captivity 18 years and 8 months, and 18 years and 7 months, respectively (Snider and Bowler 1992).

DIET AND FEEDING HABITS. *C. trivirgata* slowly stalks its prey, seizes it in its mouth, wraps several body coils around it, and constricts it. Once the prey is dead, the snake releases it from the coils and swallows it head first. Two prey items can be constricted at a time, and the snake is capable of swallowing one prey while constricting a second (Shaw 1959).

It has been suggested that wild rosy boas eat mice, nestling birds, lizards, and snakes (Fowlie 1965; Stebbins 1985; Wright and Wright 1957; Shaw and Campbell 1974), but supporting data are lacking, and these generalizations are apparently based on captives. Atsatt (1913) and Shaw and Campbell (1974) reported that wild *C. trivirgata* eat deer mice *(Peromyscus maniculatus)*, and Klauber (1924) found one apparently watching a wood rat *(Neotoma* sp.) nest. Captives have taken mice *(Mus musculus, Peromyscus* sp.), small rats *(Rattus norvegicus),* nestling birds *(Passer domesticus),*

and a small sidewinder rattlesnake *(Crotalus cerastes)* (Klauber 1972; Kurfess 1967; Shaw 1959; Stebbins 1954; Van Denburgh 1922). A thorough study of the diet of wild *C. trivirgata* would be useful.

PREDATORS AND DEFENSE. No examples of natural predation have been reported. Some are killed, however, on roads each year, and many others are caught and sold into the pet trade.

Although newborns are nervous and may be quick to strike (van der Pols 1986), an adult rosy boa is not aggressive and seldom, if ever, bites, but when handled may release a pungent musk or wrap itself around the handler's arm. It may also form a tight ball with its coils and hide the head beneath the coils. It apparently does not display and wave its tail, as does *C. bottae.*

POPULATIONS. No thorough study of the population dynamics has been reported, and one is badly needed. Status of wild populations of the rosy boa is uncertain due to its secretive and nocturnal behavior. Many have been collected for the pet trade, and this continues to be a problem because breeding adults are favored. However, this species is relatively easy to breed in captivity, and it is hoped captive-born individuals will be able to satisfy the demand in the future.

Data from captive litters indicate that the neonate sex ratio may slightly favor females over males (Klauber 1933; Norrie 1986).

C. trivirgata is considered a species of special concern in Nevada.

REMARKS. *C. trivirgata* shares so many characters with the rubber boa *(C. bottae)* that Kluge (1993) relegated it to the genus *Charina. C. trivirgata* was reviewed by Yingling (1982).

Colubridae
Colubrid Snakes

This large family contains more living snakes than any other family, about 212 genera and about 1,650 species. It is found on all continents, except Antarctica, as well as on many islands. The United States and Canada have about 105 species in 42 genera. Most species are small to medium in length, but three native North American species: *Drymarchon corais* (indigo snake), *Elaphe obsoleta* (rat snake), and *Masticophis flagellum* (coachwhip) have grown to over 250 cm.

Colubrids are characterized by the lack of postfrontal, coronoid, and pelvic bones. The hyoid is Y-shaped with two superficially placed parallel arms. The horizontal, stationary, elongated maxilla articulates with the anterior frontal bone by a lateral process. Usually premaxillary teeth are absent, but teeth are present on the maxilla, palatine, pterygoid, and dentary. No anterior hollow fangs occur on the maxilla, but some posterior teeth on the maxilla may be enlarged with (opisthoglyphous) or without (aglyphous) grooves. The supralabial gland may produce a venomous secretion. The left lung is vestigial or absent, and the hemipenial surface morphology is variable. Oviparous, ovoviviparous, and viviparous species are included in the family.

The dorsal surface of the head usually has, anteriorly to posteriorly, the following enlarged scales: a rostral, an internasal, two prefrontals, a single large frontal, two supraoculars, and two or more elongated parietals in several rows. Laterally are one or two nasal scales, a loreal (absent in some), one or more preoculars, one or more postoculars, two or more temporals, and several supralabials. In a few genera *(Nerodia, Heterodon)*, some species have completed the ocular ring of scales around the eye by adding suboculars between the orbit and supralabials. On the lower jaw is a mental scale that is usually separated from the anterior of two pairs of chin shields by one or more of several pairs of infralabial scales. Normally on the back and sides of the body are overlapping keeled (ridged) or smooth scales. The lower body surface has a series of transversely expanded plates, the ventral scutes, extending from side to side. An anal plate is present that may be either single or divided, and beneath the tail is a double row of subcaudal scales (a few species have only one row).

The family Colubridae contains seven subfamilies, but only snakes belonging to three subfamilies occur north of Mexico.

1. Colubrinae (colubrine snakes). Snakes without hypapophyses, or with narrow, elongated hypapophyses on their posterior vertebrae. The hemipenis is usually spinose near the base and calyculate near the apex; neither capitation nor apical disk are present, and the single sulcus spermaticus is asymmetrical and extends only onto one lobe in those that are bilobed. A few have enlarged (sometimes opisthoglyphous) posterior maxillary teeth. Body scale row reduction is usually midlateral or vertebral. About 18 genera and about 650 species are

included worldwide. North American genera are *Arizona, Bogertophis, Cemophora, Chilomeniscus, Chionactis, Coluber, Drymarchon, Drymobius, Elaphe, Ficimia, Gyalopion, Lampropeltis, Liochlorophis, Masticophis, Opheodrys, Pituophis, Rhinocheilus, Salvadora, Senticolis, Sonora, Stilosoma, Tantilla,* and *Trimorphodon.*

2. Natricinae (water snakes). All body vertebrae have elongated, recurved hypapophyses. The symmetrical hemipenis has at least two basal hooks, lacks calyxes or an apical disk, but has a single or bifurcated, centripetal sulcus spermaticus. The maxillary teeth become gradually longer toward the rear; those most posterior may be greatly enlarged, usually aglyphous and separated from the anterior teeth by a diastema (gap). Body scale row reduction is usually midlateral or sublateral. There are about 38 genera and 200 species worldwide. Genera from the United States and Canada include *Clonophis, Nerodia, Regina, Seminatrix, Storeria, Thamnophis, Tropidoclonion,* and *Virginia.*

3. Xenodontinae (xenodontine snakes). The posterior body vertebrae either lack hypapophyses or are flat and broad. The spinose hemipenis normally has a capitate, calyculate apical region and a bifurcated, centrifugal (bilobed) sulcus spermaticus. Most species have two enlarged posterior (sometimes opisthoglyphous) maxillary teeth. Body scale row reduction is usually paravertebral. There are 92 genera and about 540 species worldwide. Genera occurring north of Mexico are *Carphophis, Coniophanes, Contia, Diadophis, Farancia, Heterodon, Hypsiglena, Leptodeira, Oxybelis,* and *Rhadinaea.*

Key to the Genera of Colubridae

(adapted from Ernst and Barbour 1989; Powell et al. 1998; Wright and Wright 1957)

1a. Anal plate divided 2
1b. Anal plate undivided (single) 25
2a Dorsal body scales smooth 3
2b. At least some dorsal body scales keeled 40
3a. Nineteen or more midbody dorsal scale rows 4
3b. Eighteen or fewer midbody dorsal scale rows 24
4a. Preocular scales present 5
4b. Preocular scales absent . . . . *Farancia* (in part)
5a. Pupil round 6
5b. Pupil vertically elliptical 34
6a. Nineteen midbody dorsal scale rows . . . . . . *Coniophanes*
6b. At least 25 midbody dorsal scale rows 7
7a. Either loreal or preocular scales absent 8
7b. Both loreal and preocular scales present 14
8a. Thirteen or fewer midbody dorsal scale rows 9
8b. Fourteen or more midbody dorsal scale rows 10
9a. One postocular scale, back uniformly brown . . . .
. . . . *Carphophis*
9b. Two postocular scales, back patterned with dark bands . .
. . . . *Chilomeniscus*
10a. Six supralabials, prefrontal scale touches the orbit . . . . .
. . . . *Virginia* (in part)
10b. Seven or more supralabials, prefrontal does not touch the orbit 11

11a. Fifteen or fewer midbody dorsal scale rows 12
11b. Seventeen or more midbody dorsal scale rows 13
12a. Snout rounded (not shovel-like), back unpatterned . . . . .
. . . . *Tantilla*
12b. Snout shovel-like, back with dark bands . . . .
. . . . *Chionactis* (in part)
13a. Rostral scale touches frontal scale, short thick tail . . . . .
. . . . *Ficimia*
13b. Rostral scale does not touch frontal scale, long slender tail
. . . . *Oxybelis*
14a. One preocular scale 15
14b. Two or more preocular scales 21
15a. Seventeen midbody dorsal body rows 16
15b. Sixteen or fewer midbody dorsal scale rows 18
16a. Rostral scale curved upward . . . . *Gyalopion* (in part)
16b. Rostral scale flat, not curved upward 17
17a. Normally 7 supralabials, dark stripe extends through orbit to corner of mouth . . . . *Rhadinaea*
17b. Normally 8 supralabials, no dark stripe extends through orbit to corner of mouth . . . . *Seminatrix*
18a. More than 65 subcaudals, anterior and posterior chin shields about equal in length . . . Liochlorophis (in part)
18b. Fewer than 65 subcaudals, anterior chin shields longer than posterior ones 19

19a. Light lateral stripe present on scale rows 4–5, ventral scales with dark anterior borders . . . . *Contia*

19b. No light lateral stripe present, ventral scales lack dark pigment or dark ventral pigment is extension of dorsal body bands 20

20a. Snout flat and shovel-like, nasal valves present . . . .
. . . . *Chionactis* (in part)

20b. Snout not shovel-like, nasal valves absent . . . . *Sonora*

21a. Rostral scale enlarged, and raised with free edges . . .
. . . . *Salvadora*

21b. Rostral scale not enlarged or raised with free edges . . . 22

22a. Two or more anterior temporal scales, lower preocular small and wedged into supralabial row 23

22b. One anterior temporal scale, lower preocular not entering supralabial row 24

23a. Fifteen dorsal body scale rows near the anal vent . . . *Coluber*

23b. Thirteen or fewer dorsal body scale rows near the anal vent . . . . *Masticophis*

24a. Light neck collar (may be interrupted), nasal plate divided
. . . . *Diadophis*

24b. No light neck collar, nasal plate single . . . .
. . . . *Liochlorophis* (in part)

25a. Dorsal body scales smooth 26

25b. At least some dorsal body scales keeled 36

26a. One row of subcaudals . . . . *Rhinocheilus*

26b. Two rows of subcaudals 27

27a. Pupil vertically elliptical 28

27b. Pupil round 29

28a. Snout shovel-like, subocular scales present . . . .
. . . . *Phyllorhynchus* (in part)

28b. Snout not shovel-like, subocular scales absent . . . .
. . . . *Trimorphodon* (in part)

29a. Supralabials touch parietal scales, no loreal scale . . . . . .
. . . . *Stilosoma*

29b. Supralabials do not touch parietal scales, loreal scale present 30

30a. No central dark pigment on ventral scutes 31

30b. Center of ventral scutes with dark marks 33

31a. Rostral scale upturned . . . . *Gyalopion* (in part)

31b. Rostral scale not upturned 32

32a. Body with red, black, and yellow bands, 7 or fewer supralabials, 8 infralabials . . . . *Cemophora*

32b. Body without red, black, and yellow bands, 8 or more supralabials, 12 or more infralabials . . . . *Arizona*

33a. Seventeen or fewer midbody dorsal scale rows . . . .
. . . . *Drymarchon*

33b. Eighteen or more midbody dorsal scale rows . . . .
. . . . *Lampropeltis*

34a. At least 2 loreals, 3–4 postoculars, at least 2 anterior temporal scales, at least 9 supralabials . . . . *Trimorphodon* (in part)

34b. On loreal scale, 2 postoculars, 1 anterior temporal, 7–8 supralabials 35

35a. Back with large dark blotches, no lateral spots . . . .
. . . . *Leptodeira*

35b. Back with small dark blotches, small lateral spots present
. . . . *Hypsiglena*

36a. Midbody dorsal scale rows total 27 or more, 4 prefrontals
. . . . *Pituophis*

36b. Midbody dorsal scale rows total 26 or less, 2 prefrontals
. . . . *Phyllorhynchus* (in part)

37a. Pupil vertically elliptical, suboculars present, rostral scale enlarged with free edges . . . . *Phyllorhynchus* (in part)

37b. Pupil round, no suboculars, rostral not enlarged with free edges 38

38a. Eight or more infralabials . . . . *Thamnophis*

38b. Seven or fewer infralabials 39

39a. Venter patterned with two rows of dark half-moon–shaped marks . . . . *Tropidoclonion*

39b. Venter unpatterned or with small scattered spots . . . . . .
. . . . *Virginia* (in part)

40a. Rostral scale upturned and medially keeled . . . *Heterodon*

40b. Rostral scale not upturned or medially keeled 41

41a. Loreal and preocular scales present 42

41b. Either loreal or preocular scales absent 50

42a. Seventeen or fewer midbody dorsal scale rows 43

42b. Nineteen or more midbody dorsal scale rows 45

43a. Sixty or fewer subcaudals . . . . *Seminatrix*

43b. Eighty or more subcaudals 44

44a. Seven or fewer supralabials, 7–8 infralabials, back green . .
. . . . *Opheodrys*

44b. Eight or more supralabials, 10–11 infralabials, back dark with a light spot on each scale . . . . *Drymobius*

45a. Dorsal scales strongly keeled, keel extends entire length of scale 46

45b. Dorsal scales weakly keeled, keel not extending entire length of scale 48

46a. Twenty-one or more midbody dorsal scale rows . . . *Nerodia*

46b. Nineteen or fewer midbody dorsal scale rows 47

47a. Seven or more supralabials, 2 preoculars . . . . *Regina*

47b. Six or fewer supralabials, 1 preocular . . . . *Clonophis*

48a. Suboculars present . . . . *Bogertophis*

48b. Suboculars absent 49

49a. Thirty or more midbody dorsal scale rows . . . *Senticolis*

49b. Twenty-nine or fewer midbody dorsal scale rows . . . *Elaphe*

50a. Nineteen or more midbody dorsal scale rows . . . .
. . . . *Farancia* (in part)

50b. Seventeen or fewer midbody dorsal scale rows 51

51a. Loreal present, prefrontal touches orbit . . . .
. . . . *Virginia* (in part)

51b. Loreal absent, prefrontal does not touch orbit . . . *Storeria*

Arizona elegans Kennicott, in Baird 1859 | Glossy Snake

RECOGNITION.   *A. elegans* is a pale (faded), rather slender species with a maximum TBL of 177.8 cm, but most individuals are under 100 cm. Dorsal body color ranges from tan, yellowish gray, or cream to pinkish. A series of 41–83 brown or gray, black-edged, dorsal blotches is present; another 12–27 dorsal blotches occur on the tail; and a series of smaller, sometimes obscured, blotches alternates laterally with the larger, darker, dorsal blotches. The head is the same color as the body, with a dark oblique stripe extending backward from the orbit to the corner of the mouth. Some supralabials or infralabials may bear dark bars. The lower jaw is countersunk, and the pupil is slightly vertically elliptical. The venter is usually immaculate white to cream or light brown. Dorsal body scales are smooth and shiny, with a single apical pit; they lie in 28–29 (25–27) anterior rows, 27–31 (25–35) midbody rows, and 19–20 (17–22) posterior rows. Ventral scutes total 183–241, along with 39–63 subcaudals and an undivided anal plate. Lateral head scales are 2 nasals (partially separated by the nostril), 1 (2) loreal(s), 1 (2) preocular(s), 2 (rarely 3) postoculars, 2 (1) + 3–4 (5–6) temporals, 8 (7–9) supralabials, and 12–13 (11–15) infralabials. The single hemipenis is swollen distally and tipped with flounces. The lower portion of its shaft has numerous small spines, with those approaching the middle of the shaft the largest. The distal portion of the shaft has small spines, and the transition from small spines to flounces is abrupt (Dixon and Fleet 1976). Each maxilla has 14–17 (mean, 15.2; n = 12) teeth.

Males are shorter than females and have 183–228 ventrals, 46–63 subcaudals, and TLs 13–17% of TBL; females have 192–241 ventrals, 39–54 subcaudals, and TLs 12–15% of TBL (see GEOGRAPHIC VARIATION for mean TLs of both sexes of the subspecies).

GEOGRAPHIC VARIATION.   Nine subspecies are considered valid (Dixon and Fleet 1976), but only seven occur north of Mexico. *A. e. elegans* Kennicott, in Baird 1859, the Kansas glossy snake, ranges from the sand hills of Nebraska, eastern Colorado, and western Kansas southwestward through western Oklahoma, western Texas, and eastern New Mexico to San Luis Potosí and Aquascalientes, Mexico. It is a dark form with 29–31 midbody scale rows, 39–69 (mean, 53) dorsal body blotches, 197–219 (mean, 206) ventrals in males and 208–227 (mean, 215) in females,

Mojave glossy snake, *Arizona elegans candida*; San Bernardino County, California. (Photograph by Donald J. Fisher)

51–62 (mean, 56) subcaudals in males and 49–53 (mean, 52) in females, and a long tail (mean, 15.6% of TBL in males and 14.9% of TBL in females). *A. e. arenicola* Dixon 1960, the Texas glossy snake, ranges from central to southern Texas. It is a brownish snake that has 29–35 midbody scale rows, 41–58 (mean, 49) dorsal body blotches, 207–225 (mean, 215) ventrals in males and 217–231 (mean, 225) in females, 54–58 (mean, 57) subcaudals in males and 49–52 (mean, 50) in females, and a long tail (mean, 15.4% of TBL in males and 13.8% of TBL in females). *A. e. candida* Klauber 1946a, the Mojave glossy snake, is found in the Mojave Desert of southeastern California and adjacent southwestern Nevada. Present on this pale snake are 26–29 (mean, 27) midbody scales rows, 53–75 (mean, 63) dorsal body blotches, 203–220 (mean, 214) ventrals in males and 220–232 (mean, 223) in females, 47–55 (mean, 50) subcaudals in males and 44–49 (mean, 46) in females, a short tail (mean, 13.9% of TBL in males and 12.5% of TBL in females), and a high frequency of paired preocular scales. *A. e. eburnata* Klauber 1946a, the desert glossy snake, is found from southwestern Utah, southern Nevada, and northwestern Arizona south through southeastern California to northeastern Baja California. This pale subspecies has 25–29 (mean, 27) midbody scale rows, 53–83 (mean, 69) dorsal body blotches, 208–238 (mean, 220) ventrals in males and 220–241 (mean, 231) in females, 47–59 (mean, 52) subcaudals in males and 43–54 (mean, 47) in females, and a short tail (mean, 13.7% of TBL in males and 12.6% of TBL in females). *A. e. noctivaga* Klauber 1946a, the Arizona glossy snake, is found from southeastern Nevada south through most of Arizona to Sinaloa, Mexico. This dark morph has 25–29 (mean, 27) midbody scale rows, 46–66 broad dorsal blotches (wider or equal to the light spaces between them), 204–214 (mean, 209) ventrals in males and 211–224 (mean, 220) in females, 46–52 (mean, 49) subcaudals in males and 43–48 (mean, 45) in females, and a short tail (mean, 13.7% of TBL in males and 12.7% of TBL in females). *A. e. occidentalis* Blanchard 1924a, the California glossy snake, ranges from the San Joaquin Valley south through the Central Valley of California to southwestern California and northwestern Baja California. This, the darkest subspecies, has 51–75 (mean, 63) dark brown body blotches on a darker than usual

ground color, dark spotted infralabials, some dark spotting along the sides of its ventrals, 26–29 (mean, 27) midbody scale rows, 207–223 (mean, 214) ventrals in males and 215–231 (mean, 223) in females, 47–54 (mean, 50) subcaudals in males and 43–50 (mean, 46) in females, and a short tail (mean, 13.6% of TBL in males and 12.5% of TBL in females). *A. e. philipi* Klauber 1946a, the Painted Desert glossy snake, ranges from southern Utah and northeastern Arizona south through west and central New Mexico and southeastern Arizona to Chihuahua, Mexico. It has 27 (rarely 25–29) midbody scale rows, 53–80 (mean, 64) dorsal body blotches, 183–202 (mean, 195) ventrals in males and 192–211 (mean, 204) in females, 50–60 (mean, 55) subcaudals in males and 45–53 (mean, 48) in females, and a long tail (mean, 16.4% of TBL in males and 14.8% of TBL in females). Zones of intergradation occur where the ranges of the various subspecies meet.

CONFUSING SPECIES. The species of *Elaphe* and *Pituophis* have keeled body scales, and the *Elaphe* have a divided anal plate. The night snake *(Hypsiglena torquata)* has a divided anal plate, distinct vertically elliptical pupils, and a flattened head. The western lyre snake *(Trimorphodon biscutatus)* has a dark lyre or V-shaped mark on the top of its head, distinct vertically elliptical pupils, and a single or divided anal plate. The western rattlesnake *(Crotalus viridis)* has a tail rattle, a heat-sensitive pit between its nostril and eye, and distinct vertically elliptical pupils.

KARYOTYPE. The karyotype is composed of 36 chromosomes with 50 arms: 16 macrochromosomes and 20 microchromosomes (Baker et al. 1972; Bury et al. 1970; Camper and Hanks 1995; Trinco and Smith 1971). Only macrochromosome pair six (by size) is acrocentric, and the rest of the macrochromosomes are biarmed (Bury et al. 1970; Camper and Hanks 1995). Females are heteromorphic ZW, males are homomorphic ZZ. The NOR is located on the first pair of microchromosomes (Camper and Hanks 1995).

FOSSIL RECORD. Pleistocene (Rancholabrean) fossils have been found in Arizona (Mead et al. 1984; Van Devender and Mead 1978; Van Devender, Mead, and Rea 1991; Van Devender et al. 1991), California

(LaDuke 1991), New Mexico (Van Devender and Worthington 1977), and Texas (Hill 1971; Holman 1963, 1964, 1966; Parmley 1988b, 1990a; Van Devender and Bradley 1994).

DISTRIBUTION. *A. elegans* occurs from central Texas, Nebraska and eastern Colorado, southern Utah, southern Nevada, and the San Joaquin Valley of California south to Taumaulipas, San Luis Potosí, Aquascalientes, Sinaloa, and Baja California in Mexico.

HABITAT. This snake lives in a variety of habitats with sandy or loamy soils, with or without rocks: deserts with thorn scrub, creosote-mesquite patches, chaparral, sagebrush, grasslands, and oak-hickory woodlands at elevations of from below sea level to approximately 2,200 m (most live at elevations of 900 m or less). Sullivan (1981b) found glossy snakes most numerous in an ecotone between a grassland and oak woodland/chaparral in the northwestern San Joaquin Valley of California.

BEHAVIOR. Seasonally, *A. elegans* is active from late February or early March to November in Southern California and Arizona; elsewhere, at higher elevations and latitudes, it is active from April or early May to September–November. Most surface activity occurs in May–July. It spends December–February hibernating underground in a mammal burrow or buried into the soil below the frost line, but it may still come to the surface to bask on warm, sunny, winter days (Cowles 1941b). A hibernating *A. elegans* in New Mexico was found 60 cm below the surface (Brown in Degenhardt et al. 1996), and Cowles (1941b) excavated California individuals on 20 February with a BT of 19.5°C.

Daily activity is crepuscular and nocturnal; only a few are active during the day, and then mostly in the spring and fall. Klauber (1946) found *A. elegans* surface active from 1800 to 0359 hours in southern California and at 1900–0359 hours in the Mojave Desert. Peak activity occurred at 2000–2100 hours. Its slightly vertically elliptical pupil is a nocturnal adaptation, as is its retina, which contains both cones and rods (Walls 1934).

Active *A. elegans* have had BTs of 13.5–32.0°C (Brattstrom 1965; Klauber 1946a; Stebbins 1954; Sullivan 1981a). The lowest BTs at which Cowles and Bogert (1944) found them above ground were 14–18°C; the snakes are only above ground for short periods at these BTs. At 19–20°C more snakes become active, and Cowles and Bogert thought this is probably the normal lower BT for voluntary surface activity. The mean CT_{max} is 41.8 (41.0–43.0) °C, and the lethal BT is 43–44°C (Cowles and Bogert 1944). Glossy snakes are accomplished burrowers that can disappear into loose soil within minutes, and during the day they remain buried beneath the surface just deep enough to escape the daytime heat.

REPRODUCTION. Females with SVLs of 50+ cm (Aldridge 1979b) and TBLs of 66 cm (Degenhardt et al. 1996) have contained viable eggs. Such lengths are probably reached in three to four years. The minimum length of mature males has not been reported.

Aldridge (1979a) studied the gametic cycle of male glossy snakes from New Mexico. During the spring (and probably also the winter), the epithelial lumen wall of the seminiferous tubules contains one to two layers of Sertoli cells and spermatogonia that are approximately equal in numbers. Recrudescence begins in late June, and the first spermatids are evident in mid-July. Spermatogenesis, with free mature sperm present, begins in July, but August–September is the peak period of sperm production (unfortunately Aldridge did not examine any males after 23 September), but probably mature sperm are stored in the epididymides or vas deferens over winter. Seminiferous tubule diameter is smallest in early spring and begins to increase as recrudescence advances. By mid-July the tubules have doubled their diameter. BTs of at least 24°C are necessary for completion of sperm production.

Aldridge (1979b) also studied the female gametic cycle in New Mexico. Yolk deposition occurs in two stages. Primary vitellogenesis occurs in ovarian follicles up to 4–6 mm in diameter; such follicles are present all year long. Follicles remain at this size until the second stage of vitellogenesis, which begins in April–May and continues to mid- or late June when ovulation occurs. Not all females reproduce annually; about 33% are not reproductively ready each year. Courtship and mating usually take place in April–June (the acts have not been described), and oviposition takes place during the period 31 May to 22 July.

Clutches contain 3 (Aldridge 1979b) to 23 or 24 (Cowles 1941b; Tennant 1985) eggs. The white eggs

Distribution of *Arizona elegans.*

have flexible, leathery shells and are 38.0–67.8 (mean, 57.5) × 16–18 (mean, 16.7) mm, and weigh 11.0–12.4 (mean, 11.6) g. IP averages 68–69 (57–90) days, depending on ET, and hatchlings appear from late August through September. Hatchlings average 24.8 (17.0–29.0) cm in TBL.

GROWTH AND LONGEVITY.   No data are available on growth rates of wild glossy snakes, but some captive data exist. A captive albino hatchling grew to a TBL of 29.4 cm in three months (Funk 1965b), and Ball (in Rossi and Rossi 1995) reported a growth rate of 17.1 cm/year for the first three years of life for both sexes of captive *A. e. elegans.* Snider and Bowler (1992) reported a captive longevity of 19 years, 1 month, and 8 days for a wild-caught adult male.

DIET AND FEEDING HABITS.   *A. elegans* is an active hunter that seeks its prey both on the surface and underground. Vision and olfaction are used to find prey, and once detected, it may be chased or, if close enough, seized immediately. Small animals are quickly swallowed, but larger ones are first constricted. If caught on the surface, the prey is constricted by wrapping body coils around it; however, when caught underground the prey is squeezed against the burrow wall and pressed hard enough to stop its breathing (C. Ernst, pers. obs.).

Wild glossy snakes eat many animals, but chiefly small mammals and lizards: mammals—pocket mice *(Chaetodipus formosus, C. hispidus, Perognathus inorna-*

tus), kangaroo rats *(Dipodomys merriami, D. ordii),* white-footed mice *(Peromyscus* sp.*),* and moles *(Scalopus aquaticus);* small birds; lizards *(Callisaurus draconoides, Cnemidophorus tigris, Coleonyx* sp.(?)*, Cophosaurus texanus, Dipsosaurus dorsalis, Holbrookia* sp.*, Phrynosoma coronatum, P. cornutum, P. hernandezi, Sceloporus magister, S. occidentalis, Uta stansburiana,* and *Xantusia vigilis);* small snakes *(Phyllorhynchus decurtatus);* and insects (Coleoptera, Orthoptera) (Brown 1997; Cunningham 1959; Klauber 1946; McKinney and Ballinger 1966; Marr 1944; Rodríquez-Robles et al. 1999a; Stebbins 1954; Tinkle 1967; Van Denburgh 1922; Wright and Wright 1957). In addition, captives have eaten mice *(Mus musculus),* gerbils *(Gerbillus* sp.*),* birds, and lizards *(Coleonyx variegatus, Uma* sp.*)* (Rossi and Rossi 1995; Stebbins 1954).

PREDATORS AND DEFENSE.   Probably many carnivorous mammals, raptorial birds, and ophiophagous snakes eat *A. elegans,* but published records are rare. Kirn (in Klauber 1946a) saw a Texas coral snake *(Micrurus fulvius tener)* try to swallow a small glossy snake; Ellis and Brunson (1993) reported an attack by a red-tailed hawk *(Buteo jamaicensis);* and Collins (1993) mentions snakes, mammals, and owls as predators. Many are killed on roads (Klauber 1946a; Price and LaPointe 1990; Rosen and Lowe 1994), and agriculture (Klauber 1946a) and habitat destruction take their tolls.

When first discovered, *A. elegans* will vibrate its tail and, if handled, spray musk. Some are rather gentle and seldom if ever bite, but the authors have had several very nasty glossy snakes in their laboratory that would strike and bite at the slightest provocation.

POPULATIONS. No study of the population dynamics of *A. elegans* has been published, but some ideas of its relative abundance at certain sites have been noted. Klauber (1946a) reported that *A. e. eburnata* comprised only 70 (8.5%) of the 827 snakes encountered along a road in San Diego County, California, and *A. e. candida* 95 (15.7%) of 605 snakes recorded in a section of the Mojave Desert. In southern Arizona, 15 (4.1%) of 368 snakes found in 1988–1991 on a stretch of road were *A. elegans* (Rosen and Lowe 1994); along a highway in New Mexico in 1975–1978, 24 (5.3%) of the 454 snakes encountered were this species (Price and LaPointe 1990); and Reynolds (1982) found only 26 (6.2% of 418 snakes) along a road in Chihuahua, Mexico, from 1975 through 1977.

Because its numbers are apparently low, the species is protected in Kansas and Utah.

REMARKS. In a morphological study of snakes belonging to the colubrid tribe Lampropeltini, Keogh (1996) found *Arizona* phylogenetically situated between *Lampropeltis* and *Pituophis*, but its mtDNA sequences are closer to *Bogertophis* (Rodriguez-Robles and Jesus-Escobar 1999). *A. elegans* has been reviewed by Dixon and Fleet (1976) and Klauber (1946a).

Bogertophis Dowling and Price 1988

Southwestern Rat Snakes

Key to the Species of *Bogertophis*

1a. No dark dorsal body pattern present, usually more than 81 subcaudals . . . . *B. rosaliae*

1b. Dark dorsal pattern of H-shaped blotches present, usually less than 81 subcaudals . . . . *B. subocularis*

Bogertophis rosaliae (Mocquard 1899) | Baja California Rat Snake

RECOGNITION. This unicolored rat snake is stout at midbody, has a short tail (to 19% of TBL), and grows to a maximum TBL of 151 cm (Hunsaker 1965). Adult head and body color varies from tan or yellow orange to olive brown, gray brown, or orange brown, with no pattern. Dark skin can be seen between the rather small body scales, accentuating their color. The venter is cream to yellowish gray or pinkish tan. The head is distinctly broader than the neck, and the eye is prominent, protruding, and has a yellow to bronze iris. Body scales are at least weakly keeled with two apical pits and lie in 29–33 anterior rows, 31–35 rows at midbody, and 20–23 rows near the tail. Ventrals total 276–288, subcaudals 78–94, and the anal plate is divided. Scales positioned on the side of the head are 2 nasals, 1 (2) loreal(s), 1 preocular, 2 (3) postoculars, 5 rows of temporals containing 3–6 scales each, 10–11 supralabials, and 13–14 (12–15) infralabials. Between the orbit and the supralabials is a series of usually 3 (2–6) suboculars (lorilabials). The hemipenis is small, only extending 8–10 subcaudals when inverted, and not bilobed, with a single sulcus

Baja California rat snake, *Bogertophis rosaliae*. (Photograph by R. D. Bartlett)

spermaticus, several rows of spinules near the head, and a naked base. Each maxilla has 17–21 ungrooved teeth of approximately the same length.

Males have slightly longer tails with 83–94 (mean, 90) subcaudals; females have 78–86 (mean, 83) subcaudals.

GEOGRAPHIC VARIATION. Unknown.

CONFUSING SPECIES. For the Trans-Pecos rat snake *(B. subocularis)*, see the key to the species of *Bogertophis*. North American rat snakes of the genera *Elaphe* and *Senticolis* have dorsal body patterns, much longer tails, and no subocular (lorilabial) scales. The glossy snake *(Arizona elegans)* has a dorsal body pattern, a slightly pointed rostral scale, no subocular scales, and body scales with only one apical pit. Bull snakes *(Pituophis)* have a dorsal body pattern, a dark stripe extending downward from the orbit onto the supralabials, and a single anal plate.

KARYOTYPE. The chromosome compliment is 2n = 38 (Mengden in Dowling and Price 1988).

Distribution of *Bogertophis rosaliae*.

FOSSIL RECORD. Unknown.

DISTRIBUTION. *B. rosaliae* is distributed from southern Imperial County, California, south through the Baja California peninsula in Mexico.

HABITAT. Although it is an arid or semidesert species, *B. rosaliae* seems to seek out microhabitats with some water and vegetation available, perhaps because of better prey availability. It is most often found in deep valleys or canyons with permanently flowing water or large springs, rocks, and brushy vegetation (palms, paloverde, ocotillo, elephant tree) at elevations from sea level to 1,780 m.

BEHAVIOR. *B. rosaliae* is probably better known from captivity in the pet trade than from observations by scientists in the wild. Annually it is active from 1 March to 27 October (Hunsaker 1965; Ottley and Jacobsen 1983). Most daily activity takes place between 2000 and 0100 hours, but it has been seen abroad in the morning in May and June and in the afternoon in March. It seems nocturnal or crepuscular and probably only occasionally ventures on the surface during the daylight hours (Ottley and Jacobsen 1983). Most days are probably spent in rodent burrows or rock crevices or beneath surface objects such as rocks, logs, and piles of plant debris. *B. rosaliae* is a good climber and readily ascends into low bushes or trees to forage or bask.

Captive males have engaged in fierce combat involving biting (Schulz 1996).

REPRODUCTION. Almost nothing has been reported concerning the breeding habits of this species. Individuals having greater than 50 cm TBL no longer have the juvenile body pattern (see below) (Staszko and Walls 1994); this length is probably reached in one to two years, but both the size and age seem low for the attainment of maturity. Schulz (1996) reported that captives mature in two to three years. A decomposing gravid female contained developing eggs on 30 May but was in too poor a condition to determine either clutch size or stage of development (Ottley and Jacobsen 1983); based on this, however, oviposition would have taken place in June. Tepedelen (in Price 1990b) observed captive copulations in late April after a 12 week hibernation. According to Schulz (1996) courtship behavior closely resembles that of *B. subocularis* (see species account), and the mating period in captivity may last three weeks. The GP is approximately 63 days (Brown 1997). Captive clutches have contained an average of 6–7 (4–11) eggs, with larger females laying more eggs per clutch (Brown 1997; Schulz 1996). IP has taken 80–90 days at ETs of 28–29°C.

Hatchlings are 30–35 cm long. A 39.5 cm individual that may have recently hatched was collected on 27 October, so hatching may occur in late summer or early fall (Ottley and Jacobsen 1983). Body coloration of hatchlings and juveniles seems faded or pale in comparison to that of adults, and young *B. rosaliae* have narrow (one scale row wide), cream to light yellow bands crossing their orange-yellow backs, but not their tails. These bands are short and stop four to six scale rows above the ventrals. Laterally, small, irregular, streaklike bands extend upward to sometimes coalesce with the dorsal crossbands (Ottley and Jacobsen 1983).

GROWTH AND LONGEVITY. Ottley and Jacobsen (1983) found a 47.4 cm juvenile they thought was almost one year old, so an individual longer that 50 cm may be in its second year. The yearling was caught on 1 June 1979 and was still alive on 16 February 1982 (an estimated age of 40.5 months).

DIET AND FEEDING HABITS. The species actively hunts for prey, and captives appear to use both olfaction and vision to find food. Once found, the snake seizes the animal in its mouth, coils itself around the prey, and constricts it. Swallowing, usually head first, occurs shortly after the death of the prey. Adult captives readily accept white mice *(Mus musculus)* and rats *(Rattus norvegicus),* and hatchlings will accept newborn mice. The wild diet is unknown, but probably consists of rodents and small birds (considering its arboreal foraging); Schulz (1996) thought wild *B. rosaliae* probably eat mice, bats, small birds, and lizards.

PREDATORS AND DEFENSE.   No data on predation exist. Although usually mild mannered, some recently wild-caught individuals will strike and bite, and release a strong musk.

POPULATIONS.   Too few individuals have been captured at any one site in the United States to calculate population dynamics.

REMARKS.   The name *rosaliae* does not refer to the snake's coloration; it instead refers to the type locality: Santa Rosalia, Baja California, Mexico.

Bogertophis is a member of the rat snake group of the colubrid tribe Lampropeltini, which also includes the North American genera *Arizona, Elaphe, Pituophis,* and *Senticolis.* The genus *Bogertophis* was established for this *rosaliae* and *B. subocularis* by Dowling and Price in 1988. The two species were formerly included in the genus *Elaphe,* but Dowling and Price found they differ in some morphological characters (dentition, vertebrae and skull structure, presence of subocular scales, and hemipenis structure), microdermatoglyphic structure of body scales, karyotype (40 chromosomes in *Bogertophis,* 36 in *Elaphe*), and electrophoretic albumin immunological distances. Consequently, Dowling and Price created the genus *Bogertophis* for them and, based on their immunological tests, suggested that *E. obsoleta* and *B. subocularis* last shared a common ancestor 13–14 million years ago. This arrangement has not been universally accepted. Schulz (1996) points out that the two *Bogertophis* differ less from another Mexican species, *E. flavirufa,* still included in *Elaphe,* than from the other four species of *Elaphe* occurring north of the Mexican border. *B. rosaliae* has been reviewed by Dowling (1957a), Dowling and Price (1988), and Price (1990b).

Bogertophis subocularis (Brown 1901) | Trans-Pecos Rat Snake

RECOGNITION.   This is a large snake (to 170 cm TBL, Tennant 1984; 176.6 cm, Conant and Collins 1998; 180 cm, Switak 1985) that is broadest at midbody and has a distinctly broader head than neck, H-shaped blotches on its back, a series of subocular (lorilabial) scales between the orbit and the supralabials, and large, very prominent, protruding eyes. The back and sides vary from grayish yellow to olive yellow or tan. Two dark longitudinal stripes are present on the neck, and 21–28 well-developed, dark brown to black, H-shaped blotches lie between the neck and tail. The tail usually has an additional 7–11 solid blotches. The long sides of the H-blotches are longitudinal, the shorter crossbar transverses the back. The crossbars of the posterior-most blotches are often broader than those more anterior, presenting a more rhomboid shape. Another series of dark blotches is present on the side, with a blotch directly below each H and another between the dorsal blotches. Small dark stipples may also occur along the sides. The head is grayish tan and unpatterned. Juveniles are patterned like the adults. The chin and throat are white, the rest of the venter grayish brown; the underside of the tail is often patterned with small irregularly shaped brown specks. The weakly keeled scales have two apical pits, and occur in 29–33 rows anteriorly, 31–36 rows at midbody, and 23–25 rows near the vent. Ventrals total 258–283, subcaudals 65–81, and the anal plate is divided. Pertinent lateral head scales include 1 nasal (divided by the nostril), 1 loreal, 1 large preocular, 2–3 postoculars, five rows of temporals each containing 3–5 scales, 10 (9) to 12 supralabials, 13–16 (17) infralabials, and between the orbit and the supralabials, 1–3 presuboculars and 2–3 suboculars. The hemipenis is

Trans-Pecos rat snake, *Bogertophis subocularis*; Brewster County, Texas. (Photograph by Carl H. Ernst)

small, only extending 9–10 subcaudals when inverted, lacks basal hooks or distal lobes, and has the proximal third covered with fine spinules (Dowling and Price 1988; Worthington 1980). Each maxilla has 19–21 ungrooved teeth of equal length.

Males have slightly longer TLs with 69–81 (mean, 76) subcaudals; females have 65–78 (mean, 70) subcaudals.

GEOGRAPHIC VARIATION. Two subspecies have been described, but only *Bogertophis subocularis subocularis* (Brown 1901), the Trans-Pecos rat snake (described above), is present in the United States. This subspecies is variable (Conant and Collins 1998). A "blond" morph that is lighter in ground color and has either no dorsal blotches or a reduced number of them occurs in the Lower Pecos River watershed of Brewster County, Texas. In the Franklin Mountains of extreme western Texas, the *B. subocularis* have a steel-gray ground color.

CONFUSING SPECIES. For the Baja California rat snake *(B. rosaliae),* see key to the species of *Bogertophis.* In addition, four other Texas snakes could be mistaken for *B. subocularis.* Adult Baird's rat snakes *(Elaphe bairdi)* have four faded longitudinal stripes and no dark dorsal blotches; juveniles have rounded or rectangular blotches instead of H-shaped marks. The Texas rat snake *(E. obsoleta lindheimeri)* lacks longitudinal stripes and has rectangular dark blotches. The Great Plains rat snake *(E. emoryi)* has longitudinal neck stripes that unite posteriorly instead of remaining separate, rounded or rectangular dark blotches, and a patterned head. The lyre snake *(Trimorphodon biscutatus)* has smooth scales and a vertically elliptical pupil and lacks H-shaped body blotches.

KARYOTYPE. *B. subocularis* has 40 diploid chromosomes: 18 macrochromosomes and 22 microchromosomes; the largest pair of chromosomes is submetacentric, with the only other distinctly biarmed

Distribution of *Bogertophis subocularis*.

elements being the subtelocentric Z and W chromosomes, which are the third largest pair in size (Baker et al. 1971, 1972). Other macrochromosomes are acrocentric or near acrocentric. According to Camper and Hanks (1995), however, there are 14 acrocentric and 6 biarmed macrochromosomes and only 20 microchromosomes, and the NOR is on the long arm of chromosome one.

FOSSIL RECORD. Trunk vertebrae of *B. subocularis* have been found in Pleistocene (Rancholabrean) deposits in New Mexico (Brattstrom 1964a) and Texas (Logan and Black 1979; Parmley 1990a; Van Devender and Bradley 1994).

DISTRIBUTION. The range of the Trans-Pecos rat snake lies basically in the Chihuahuan Desert, extending from the southwestern edge of the Edwards Plateau into northeastern Mexico. It has been reported from Doña Ana, Eddy, Lincoln, Otero, and Sierra counties in south-central New Mexico, and in Brewster, Crane, Crockett, Culberson, Edwards, El Paso, Hudspeth, Jeff Davis, Pecos, Presidio, Reeves, Terrell, Uvalde, and Val Verde counties in western Texas. In Mexico, records exist for Chihuahua, Coahuila, Durango, and Nuevo León.

The snake's range parallels that of its host-specific tick, *Aponomma elaphensis*. This is apparently due to

the snake's habit of avoiding the sun, which can kill the tick (Degenhardt and Degenhardt 1965). Most of the tick's reproductive and metamorphic life history takes place deep underground in the daily retreats of *B. subocularis* (Degenhardt 1986).

HABITAT. This snake lives in arid and semiarid, rocky (limestone, granite, basalt) habitats with sand, gravel, or alluvial soils at elevations of 450–1,600 m. Vegetation varies from grasses, yucca, creosote, saltbush, mesquite, and cacti in more arid habitats to persimmon, cedar, and shin oak in the uplands.

BEHAVIOR. Reports of active Trans-Pecos rat snakes range from February to September, with most for the rainy season in July–August, but this may reflect collecting bias. Schulz (1996) reported hibernation takes place from December to May. Although no hibernaculum has been found, *B. subocularis* apparently descends to below the frost line into rock crevices or mammal burrows.

B. subocularis is rarely active during the daylight hours, and then usually only at dusk. The main activity period is probably from shortly after sunset to midnight, with most foraging, and so forth, occurring between 2200 and 2300 hours (Cranston 1992), but individuals have been found crossing roads near dawn.

Sawyer and Baccus (1996) found that a variety of diurnal retreat sites is used; 13 snakes were found in holes or crevices, 6 were in abandoned rodent burrows, 5 in natural holes, 2 in crevices in rocks, and 1 each were in a bush and under a rock. None was in drainage areas prone to flooding, and 13 retreats were located in the shadow of woody shrubs or prairie grasses. Schulz (1996) found one approximately 1 m deep in a limestone crevice.

BTs of the inactive snakes found by Sawyer and Baccus (1996) averaged 3.5°C less than the ET and ranged from 24.4 to 32.8°C. In contrast, Schulz (1996) found an active individual on a windy, rainy July night at an AT of 17–18°C.

Three Trans-Pecos rat snakes radio-tracked by Sawyer and Baccus (1996) traveled long distances during successive series of movements: 1.14 km (16 days), 1.73 km (33 days), and 2.53 km (21 days), respectively. The longest displacement between retreats was 1.01

km. The snakes used two, four, and eight different retreats, respectively, while studied, and mean time
spent in a particular retreat was 4.27 days. A pre-
scribed home range may be occupied; Axtell (1959)
found the same snake crossing a road at the same
place and time on two consecutive nights, possibly indicating that a nearby retreat was continually used.
Not all movements are at ground level since *B. subocularis* is a good climber that ascends the rock faces of
cliffs and caves.

REPRODUCTION.   Almost all specific details of *B.
subocularis* reproduction have come from observations
on captives. Mature Trans-Pecos rat snakes are at least
85 cm in TBL, and captive born individuals have bred
at two to three years of age (Degenhardt et al. 1996).
The sexual cycles have not been described.

The major mating period in captive snakes occurs
between May and early August, with most copulations in late June, but some matings have occurred
earlier or later in the year (Cranston 1992; McIntyre
1977; Schulz 1996; Tryon 1976). While courting, the
male chases the female and bites her body, usually de-
livering quick bites but sometimes chewing her
(Tryon 1976). He may also bite to keep the female restrained during copulation, and the mating act may
take as long as eight hours.

Captives have usually produced clutches during
June to September, but Tryon (1976) reported a female oviposited on 6 April. Schulz (1996) reported a
GP of 34–39 days. Clutches average about 6 (3–14)
cream to white, nonadherent, flexible-shelled, 48–73
× 19–30 mm, 17.9–30.4 g eggs (Campbell 1972;
Cranston 1992; Degenhardt et al. 1996; Schulz 1996;
Tryon 1976). Probably only one clutch is laid a year.
The IP is temperature dependent and lasts 70–105
days. In the wild, hatching probably occurs from September to early December. Hatchlings are 28–40 cm
in TBL and weigh 13.8–18.7 g.

GROWTH AND LONGEVITY.   No data on wild
growth have been published. Tryon (1976) reported
that three captive hatchlings grew to 65.4, 69.9, and
72.0 cm TBL and weighed 64.1. 82.8, and 109.3 g, respectively, at the end of 12 months; and in 8 months,
two hatchlings raised by Campbell (1972) grew to 34
and 42 cm TBL.

Tennant (1984) reported captives have lived 24
years, and Snider and Bowler (1992) noted that an
adult male caught in the wild survived an additional
18 years, 9 months, and 23 days.

DIET AND FEEDING HABITS.   *B. subocularis* actively forages after dark. When prey is captured, it is
quickly constricted (sometimes several individuals at
a time). Wild snakes have eaten lizards *(Holbrookia,
Sceloporus, Uta)*, cliff swallows *(Petrochelidon)*, roadrunners *(Geococcyx)*, pocket mice *(Perognathus)*, cactus
mice *(Peromyscus)*, and kangaroo mice *(Dipodomys)*
(Cranston 1992; Dowling 1957a; Reynolds and Scott
1982; Switak 1985; Tennant 1984); and Axtell (1959)
found one near a pack rat *(Neotoma)* nest, so these rodents are probably also natural prey. Lizards make up
much of the food of juveniles (Conant and Collins
1998). Degenhardt et al. (1996) listed the following
prey of captives: rodents *(Dipodomys*; house mice,
Mus; Perognathus; Peromyscus; Neotoma; brown rats,
Rattus; and cotton rats, *Sigmodon)*, rabbits *(Oryctola-
gus?)*, bats *(Pipistrellus)*, and lizards *(Anolis, Coleonyx,
Cnemidophorus, Cophosaurus, Crotophytus, Lanius,
Urosaurus, Uta)*.

PREDATORS AND DEFENSE.   Camper and Dixon
(2000) found one in a *Masticophis taeniatus*, and vehicles kill them on roads. It is a rather docile snake, although some will bite when handled.

POPULATIONS.   Tennant (1985) reported the species
is widely distributed and sometimes locally common
in western Texas. It is popular in the pet trade, and
this poses a threat to wild populations.

REMARKS.   The Trans-Pecos rat snake belongs to
the *"rosaliae"* group of rat snakes (Dowling 1957a)
and is a morphological sister species to the Baja California rat snake *(B. rosaliae)* (Dowling 1957a; Keogh
1996). However, Rodriguez-Robles and Jesus-Escobar
(1999) reported that the mtDNA sequences of the two
presently recognized species of *Bogertophis* are different enough to not support monophyly in *Bogertophis*.
Schulz (1996) and Worthington (1980) have reviewed
B. subocularis.

Carphophis Gervais 1843

Worm Snakes

Key to the Species of *Carphophis*

1a. Light ventral pigmentation extends dorsally to body scale row one or two, dorsal coloration tan to dark or chestnut brown . . . . *C. amoenus*

1b. Light ventral pigmentation extends dorsally to body scale row three, dorsal coloration dark gray to gray violet . . . . *C. vermis*

Carphophis amoenus (Say 1825) | Eastern Worm Snake

RECOGNITION.   *C. amoenus* is small (TBL to 35.0 cm), cylindrical, and unpatterned, with a tan to dark or chestnut brown dorsum, a pinkish venter, a pointed head, and small black eyes. The pinkish ventral pigmentation extends dorsally onto body scale rows one to two. The tail is short and ends in a blunt, spinelike scale. Dorsal body scales are smooth, pitless, and opalescent and occur in 13 rows throughout (rarely to 15 rows near the tail). Beneath are 109–145 ventrals, 22–41 subcaudals, and a divided anal plate. Laterally on the head are 1 nasal, 1 loreal, 0 preoculars (rarely 1), 1 postocular, 1 + 2–3 (1) temporals, 5 (6) supralabials, and 6 (5–7) infralabials. Dorsally the internasals and prefrontals may be paired and free, or they may be fused into two large scales. No gulars occur between the posterior chin shields. The single hemipenis is 5–7 subcaudals long and has a forked sulcus spermaticus, a calyculate crown, numerous small spines along the shaft, and three large basal hooks. Each maxilla averages 10 (9–11) teeth.

Males are shorter than females and have 109–129 (mean, 123) ventrals, 31–41 (mean, 37) subcaudals, and TLs 17–21 (mean, 19) % of TBL; the larger females have 117–145 (mean, 133) ventrals, 22–34 (mean, 28–29) subcaudals, and TLs 11–16 (mean, 13–14) % of TBL. Adult males also have ridges on the body scales dorsal to the anal plate (Blanchard 1924b).

GEOGRAPHIC VARIATION.   Two subspecies are recognized. *C. a. amoenus* (Say 1825), the eastern worm snake, is found from Rhode Island, southwestern Massachusetts, and southeastern New York south

Eastern worm snake, *Carphophis amoenus*; Rowan County, Kentucky. (Photograph by Roger W. Barbour)

to South Carolina, northern Georgia, and central Alabama. It has separate internasals and prefrontal scales. *C. a. helenae* (Kennicott 1859a), the midwestern worm snake, occurs from southern Ohio west to southern Illinois, and south to the Gulf Coast of Mississippi, southeastern Louisiana, and eastern Arkansas. This subspecies has the internasal and prefrontal scales fused into one large platelike scale.

A large area of intergradation occurs between the two subspecies in Ohio, eastern Kentucky, and West Virginia (Barbour 1960; Pauley 1973; Smith 1948).

CONFUSING SPECIES. The western worm snake *(Carphophis vermis)* has the light ventral pigmentation extending onto the third body scale row, and a dark gray or gray-violet dorsum. The southeastern crowned snake *(Tantilla coronata)* has 15 midbody scale rows, a dark head, and a dark collar. The ringneck snake *(Diadophis punctatus)* has a light neck color and a yellow venter with or without black spots. Snakes of the genera *Storeria* and *Virginia* have keeled body scales.

KARYOTYPE. Undescribed.

FOSSIL RECORD. *C. amoenus* has an abundant Pleistocene record. Irvingtonian fossils are known from Maryland (Holman 1977b) and West Virginia (Holman and Grady 1989); Rancholabrean records are from Alabama (Holman et al. 1990), Florida (Auffenberg 1963; Gut and Ray 1963; Holman 1958b), Georgia (Holman 1967, 1985), Pennsylvania (Guilday et al. 1964, 1966; Richmond 1964), Tennessee (Van Dam 1978), Virginia (Holman 1986a), and West Virginia (Holman 1987c). The Florida sites are well south of the present range of the species. Also, the vertebrae identified only as *Carphophis?* sp. by Corgon (1976) are probably from this species.

DISTRIBUTION. *C. amoenus* ranges from southern New England, southeastern New York, eastern Pennsylvania, West Virginia, southern Ohio, southern Indiana, and southern Illinois south to South Carolina, northern Georgia, Alabama, southeastern Louisiana, and eastern Arkansas.

HABITAT. This snake is most common on the edges or in the ecotonal areas of open to thick woodlands, and the borders of wetlands. It may also be found in grasslands adjacent to woodlands. Moist soils that can support its earthworm prey, and abundant daytime retreats such as rocks, logs, or abundant leaf litter are required. Soil moisture must be such as to offset the evaporative water loss through the snake's skin.

BEHAVIOR. The annual activity period of the worm snake varies with latitude, and probably also elevation; BT and cutaneous moisture loss seem the controlling factors. Russell and Hanlin (1999) found it active in every month but February on the coastal plain of South Carolina. Farther north *C. amoenus* is active from March–April to October–November. Most seasonal activity takes place from April through June; few are surface active in the summer, but a second lesser period of activity occurs in the fall.

To escape overheating or desiccation, *C. amoenus* has adopted a fossorial lifestyle, and it usually spends the hot months underground or in a rotting log. Seven *C. amoenus* were found in a "ball" about 20 cm under the surface of the ground in late August in Kentucky (Barbour 1950). Winters are also spent in the same places. Neill (1948a) found that in Georgia they overwinter beneath rocks in small tunnels about 36–72 cm beneath the surface. Grizzell (1949) found one in Maryland about 72 cm deep in the soil in February at a temperature of 9.5°C, and in northern Virginia the authors have found them within rotting logs and stumps during the winter.

Most daily activity is probably nocturnal. Over the years the authors have found only two individuals surface active during the daylight hours on the coastal plain of northern Virginia; the rest were under cover. However, in the mountains of eastern Kentucky, Barbour et al. (1969) found no movements occurred between midnight and 0300 hours. Activity increased rapidly to a high of 55% between 1500 and 1800 hours, then declined toward midnight; 29% of the movements ceased between 0700 and 0900 hours and 58% between 2100 hours and midnight.

Russell and Hanlin (1999) reported that 63% of recaptures of pit-tagged South Carolina *C. amoenus* occurred within 30 m of the original capture site; mean distance moved was 63.8 (0–180) m in 3–238 days. Barbour et al. (1969) reported that the home ranges of 10 *C. amoenus* in Kentucky averaged only 253 m².

Distribution of *Carphophis amoenus.*

REPRODUCTION. The reproductive biology of *C. amoenus* is not as well known as that of *C. vermis.* Barbour (1960) found an 18.5 cm female *C. amoenus* in Kentucky that contained two eggs, and Wright and Wright (1957) thought a total length of 17.8 cm was adult size. Palmer and Braswell (1995) and Russell and Hanlin (1999) gave a minimum SVL of 17 cm for mature female worm snakes in the Carolinas. Clark (1970a) found that most males had developed ridges on the dorsal body scales near the vent by SVLs of at least 14.7 cm in *C. m. helenae* and 15.9 cm in *C. a. amoenus.*

The male gametic cycle has not been described, and little data exist regarding that of the female. Barbour (1960) found females with 5 mm follicles in February and March, 2.5–13.0 mm in April, 12–19 mm in May, and 13–22 mm in June. At the time of laying, the eggs averaged 24.2 mm in length.

Courtship and mating probably occur in the spring; the authors have most often found the sexes together between late April and June. Courtship and mating behaviors have not been described.

Developing eggs can be seen through the translucent venter of the female in late May and June. Oviposition takes place between early June and mid-July, 5 June to 15 July in northern Virginia. The authors have found clutches of eggs in depressions under rocks, in cavities in the rotting wood of logs and stumps, and in an old sawdust pile; and rodent burrows are probably also used for nesting. A female was nearby or with the eggs in 75% of the cases. Ninety-five clutches averaged 5.1 (1–12) eggs. The white, leathery eggs average 15.6 (10.6–25.0) mm when laid and are 8.1

(5.0–11.0) mm wide. The IP is unknown, but the authors have found newly hatched young from 30 July to 20 September in northern Virginia. Hatchlings are 7.5–13.8 (mean, 10.1) mm long and weigh about 0.5–0.8 g. They have much darker chocolate-brown dorsums and more pinkish venters than adults.

GROWTH AND LONGEVITY. No growth data exist, and the captive longevity record is short: only 1 year, 1 month, and 10 days for a wild-caught adult (Snider and Bowler 1992).

DIET AND FEEDING HABITS. *C. amoenus* is almost exclusively an earthworm predator (Barbour 1950, 1960; Brown 1979a; Bush 1959; Ernst et al. 1997; Hamilton and Pollack 1956; Minton 1972); however, Uhler et al. (1939) found dipteran larvae (Tabanidae) had been eaten, Wright and Wright (1957) listed slugs and snails among prey taken, and Clark (1970a) found a small salamander (*Eurycea* sp.) in the stomach of one.

PREDATORS AND DEFENSE. A variety of larger predatory vertebrates feed on *C. amoenus.* Those reported include snakes (*Agkistrodon contortrix, Coluber constrictor, Elaphe guttata, E. obsoleta, Lampropeltis getula, L. triangulum, Micrurus fulvius, Pituophis melanoleucus, Sistrurus miliarius*), birds (*Catharus guttatus, Turdus migratorius, Tyto alba*), mammals (*Didelphis virginiana, Felis catus*), and mudpuppies (*Necturus lewisi*) (Brown 1979a; Ernst et al. 1997; Hamilton and Pollack 1956; Holman 1958a; Klemens 1993; Palmer and Braswell 1995; Uhler et al. 1939). Other carnivorous mammals and predatory birds probably also take their share.

Occasionally accidents kill *C. amoenus*. Flooding of lowland forests and woodland fires are very destructive to worm snake populations. Some are run over by motorized vehicles, others die as a result of human habitat destruction, and insecticide poisoning occasionally kills *C. amoenus* (Ernst 1962).

C. amoenus is very shy and mild mannered. Of the hundreds the authors have handled, only one large individual has tried to bite. Usually they will twist and thrash, try to crawl between the fingers, probe the hand with their tail spine, and emit a strong-smelling musk.

POPULATIONS.   *C. amoenus* may occur in large numbers where the habitat is ideal. C. Ernst and his students collected 108 individuals from beneath rocks and debris in 100 m along a hillside overlooking the Kentucky River in one hour on an April afternoon. It is the most common snake in northern Virginia, and at one site there occurs in densities over 200/ha (Ernst et al. 1997). The 1.88:1.00 sex ratio of a population in South Carolina significantly favored males (64) over females (34), and hatchlings and juveniles made up only 18% of the individuals captured (Russell and Hanlin 1999). However, the sex ratio of those adults the authors have caught in northern Virginia is not significantly different from 1:1.

Due to human activities, *C. amoenus* is becoming rare in some areas. It is currently protected as threatened in Massachusetts and as a species of special concern in Rhode Island.

REMARKS.   Ecological studies are currently being conducted by C. Ernst and his students on a dense population in northern Virginia. The species has been reviewed by Barbour (1960) and Blanchard (1924b).

Carphophis vermis (Kennicott 1859a) | Western Worm Snake

RECOGNITION.   Although also small, *C. vermis* is longer (TBL to 39.1 cm) than its more eastern sister species, *C. amoenus*. It is cylindrical, with an unpatterned dark gray to gray violet dorsum, a pinkish venter, a pointed head, and small violet eyes. The pinkish ventral pigment extends upward to include the third lateral body scale row. The tail is short and ends in a blunt spinelike scale. Dorsal body scales usually occur in 13 rows and are smooth, pitless, and opalescent. On the underside are 120–150 ventrals, 21–41 subcaudals, and a divided anal plate. Each side of the head has 1 nasal, 1 loreal, no preocular, 1 (rarely 2) postocular(s), 1 + 1 (rarely 2) temporals, 5 supralabials, and 6 infralabials. Dorsally, the paired internasals and prefrontal scales are not fused, and on the chin no gulars occur between the posterior chin shields. The single hemipenis is similar to that of *C. amoenus*: it has a forked sulcus spermaticus, a calyculate crown, numerous small spines along the shaft, and three large basal spines and is five to seven subcaudals long. Each maxilla has 10–12 (mean, 11) teeth.

Males are shorter with 120–141 (mean, 131) ventrals, 21–41 (mean, 26) subcaudals, and TLs 17–23 (mean, 20) % of SVL; females are larger with 128–150 (mean, 140) ventrals, 21–31 (mean, 28) subcaudals, and TLs 12–17% (mean, 14) % of SVL (Clark 1970a). Males have ridges on the body scales dorsal to the anal vent (Blanchard 1924b).

GEOGRAPHIC VARIATION.   No subspecies are recognized.

CONFUSING SPECIES.   See the key to the species of *Carphophis* presented above to distinguish this species from *C. amoenus*. Snakes of the genera *Storeria* and *Virginia* have keeled scales, and the *Tantilla* have dark heads and often a dark neck collar. The ringneck snake *(Diadophis punctatus)* has a light neck collar and a yellow venter with or without black spots.

KARYOTYPE.   Undescribed.

FOSSIL RECORD.   Pleistocene (Rancholabrean) fossils of *C. vermis* are known from Arkansas (Dowling 1958b) and Missouri (Saunders 1977).

Western worm snake, *Carphophis vermis*; Douglas County, Kansas. (Photograph by Roger W. Barbour)

DISTRIBUTION. *C. vermis* ranges from southern Iowa and southeastern Nebraska south to northwestern Louisiana and northeastern Texas. Isolated populations also are found in west-central Illinois, southwestern Wisconsin, southeastern Arkansas, and northeastern Louisiana.

HABITAT. This species prefers moist, rocky woodlands and may follow riparian woodlands along streams flowing through prairies. Clark (1967b, 1970a) found that in Kansas it is most often associated with soil moisture levels of 21–30%, but occurs at levels of 11–80%. In Arkansas, *C. vermis* lives in soil moisture levels of 16–42% (Elick and Sealander 1972). It apparently requires a moderate level of soil moisture to offset evaporative water loss through the skin and to support its main earthworm prey. Those studied by Elick and Sealander (1972) lost 2.3–6.7 mg water/g body wt/hour through the skin and respiratory passages when subjected to desiccation. These small snakes soon disappear from recently cleared areas, apparently because of the increased heating and drying of the soil.

BEHAVIOR. Thanks to the efforts of Donald Clark and Henry Fitch the biology of *C. vermis* is much better known than that of its eastern cousin *C. amoenus*.

BT and cutaneous water loss are probably the controlling factors of habitat selection and activity patterns in this small snake. To escape overheating and desiccation, *C. vermis* has adopted a fossorial lifestyle, and it seems more so than *C. amoenus*. It has several morphological characters that facilitate burrowing in the soil: a narrow head, cylindrical body, small eyes, smooth scales, and a relatively short tail. To burrow, because they have no physical or behavioral traits that allow them to penetrate compact soil, western worm snakes first seek out the route of least resistance through the soil. The snout or entire head is pushed into an available crevice and rotated in a horizontal right-to-left then left-to-right manner, rotated vertically in an up-and-down fashion with the fulcrum at about eye level, or rolled from side to side along the longitudinal axis. These movements enlarge the original hole and allow the snake to enter the ground. This is done in a stepwise manner with the head and

Distribution of *Carphophis vermis*.

neck extended forward (in part by the movement of the body within the skin), where a grip is obtained, and then the remainder of the body is pulled forward (Clark 1970a).

In Kansas, the western worm snake is active from late March to November (Clark 1970a; Collins 1993), with most surface activity taking place from April to early June. In Missouri, it is active from March–October (Johnson 1987). Hot summer weather drives *C. vermis* underground, to the shelter of rotting logs or stumps, or under rocks, where it estivates until late August, when there is a second lesser peak in activity. Winter is spent underground in rodent burrows or in rotting logs or stumps, and Drda (1968) found some overwintering in a Missouri cave. Fitch (1956) found a dormant individual, with a BT of 3.5°C, beneath a rock on 29 March when light snow was falling and the AT and ST were −3°C and 3.5°C, respectively.

Most daily activity is probably nocturnal, although some individuals are active during the day, usually beneath leaf litter. This snake does not bask directly in sunlight, but instead thermoregulates by maintaining contact with the undersides of sun-warmed objects, such as rocks. Fitch (1956) recorded the BTs of 21 *C. vermis* in Kansas. Excluding one very low body temperature, these averaged 26.4 (19.0–31.7) °C. Henderson (1974) reported the preferred temperature range of Kansas *C. vermis* to be 24–30°C, with a preferred optimum temperature of 26–27°C. BTs of 42 Kansas *C. vermis* recorded by Clark (1970a) averaged 18.3 (9.9–23.8) °C; the corresponding STs averaged 17.5 (9.6–25.5) °C. In the laboratory, *C. vermis* chose an average ET of 23 (14.4–30.8) °C on a thermal gradient (Clark 1967b).

C. vermis has a rather small home range. Clark (1970a) calculated individual ranges of 0.016–0.173 ha, with adult males having the largest ranges and juveniles the smallest. Surface movements are only for relatively short distances. One female moved approximately 122 m in 19 days (Fitch 1958), and an adult crawled about 86 m (Clark 1970a).

REPRODUCTION. Most males are mature at a SVL of 21.6 cm (Clark 1970a). The smallest male with sperm found by Clark was 17.7 cm, and Blanchard (1924b) mentioned one that was mature at 19.0 cm. Males develop ridges on the posterior body scales

above the anal vent by SVLs of at least 17.0 cm. Such a length is reached in the second year of growth (Fitch 1999).

The male gametic cycle was described by Aldridge and Metter (1973). During the winter, Sertoli cells are prevalent in the luminal wall of the seminiferous tubules. During the spring, summer, and fall each meiotic stage becomes prevalent within the tubules, with sperm being the most common in the fall, having been formed from mid-July to mid-September. Mature sperm is stored in the vas deferens throughout the year.

All females are mature at 25.0 cm SVL or longer, and some may mature at 24.0 cm; such lengths are reached during the third year of growth (Clark 1970a; Fitch 1999).

The ovaries contain small follicles 1–2 mm in length throughout the year. After oviposition in June some of these begin to enlarge at a rate of about 0.3 mm/week, and by mid-September have grown to 7 mm. No additional growth occurs during the winter, but in April the follicles begin to yolk up and grow at a rate of about 1.5 mm/week to about 19 mm. Ovulation is in late May, and oviposition occurs about 37 days later (Aldridge and Metter 1973; Clark 1970a, 1970b). The number of eggs produced and the weight of the clutch increase with the age and size of the female (Clark 1970a, 1970b).

Courtship and mating occur in April–May and again in September–October (Clark 1970a). Apparently, females are capable of storing viable sperm over the winter. The courtship/mating behaviors have not been described.

Nesting occurs in late June and early July, almost always in the morning, and several hours may pass before all eggs in a clutch are laid (Clark 1970a). Typical nesting sites are depressions under rocks, inside rotting stumps and logs, old sawdust piles, and possibly ground squirrel burrows.

Apparently only one clutch is laid a year. Relative clutch masses determined for five Kansas clutches by Clark (1970b) were 32.0–36.3 (mean, 34.8) %. Clutches consist of 1–12 (mean, 4.5; n = 18) eggs. The elongated eggs are pale white or cream to translucent, thin-shelled, 14.0–40.6 (mean, 26.3) × 6.0–15.8 (mean, 9.3) mm, and weigh 0.9–1.1 (mean, 1.0) g. IP lasts 18–60 (mean, 43.5) days, depending on the ET. Hatching normally takes place from mid-August into September.

Hatchlings are more sharply two-toned than adults and have orange-red to bright pink venters. They have 7.5–12.4 (mean, 10.6) cm TBLs and weigh 0.7–1.1 (mean, 0.8) g.

GROWTH AND LONGEVITY. Females grow larger than males. The following SVLs for Kansas *C. vermis* are based on data presented by Clark (1970a, 1970b) and Fitch (1999): males—hatchlings, 11.2–12.4 cm; year 1, 10.7–17.9 cm; year 2, 17.3–21.5 cm; year 3, 20.6–23.5 cm; year 4, 23.0–24.7 cm; year 5, 24.2–25.3 cm; year 6, 25.4–26.3 cm, year 7, 26.5–27.4 cm, year 8, 27.5–28.0 cm; and year 9, 28.8 cm; females—hatchlings, 11.7–13.5 cm; year 1, 13.6–19.6 cm; year 2, 17.3–24.9 cm; year 3, 22.4–27.3 cm; year 4, 26.5–28.5 cm; year 5, 27.8–28.6 cm; year 6, 29.0–30.5 cm; year 7, 30.6–31.7 cm; year 8, 31.8–32.5 cm; and year 10, 33.4–33.8 cm.

Females achieve larger sizes by growing at a faster rate than males, but growth slows with age in both sexes. The growth rates for the first four years in Kansas were as follows: hatchlings—0.185 mm/day for males, 0.277 mm/day for females; first year—males 0.266 mm/day, females 0.296 mm/day; second year—males 0.172 mm/day, females 0.256 mm/day; third year—males 0.094 mm/day, females 0.113 mm/day; and fourth year—both sexes 0.054 mm/day (Clark 1970a).

Fitch (1999) had three wild females survive 10 years during his Kansas study.

DIET AND FEEDING HABITS. The small mouth and head of the *Carphophis* limit them to soft-bodied, narrow, elongated prey. Like *C. amoenus*, *C. vermis* subsists chiefly on earthworms (*Allolobophora caliginosa, A. trapezoides, Lumbricus* sp., and possibly *Eisenia* sp. and *Octolasium* sp.), but occasionally soft-bodied insects (beetle grubs, fly larvae) and small snakes (*Diadophis punctatus*) are eaten by wild *C. vermis* (Clark 1970a; Hurter 1911; Tennant 1985; Wright and Wright 1957). Earthworms are swallowed head first (Clark 1970a).

PREDATORS AND DEFENSE. Predatory snakes, such as the copperhead (*Agkistrodon contortrix*), common kingsnake (*Lampropeltis getula*), and milksnake (*L. triangulum*), are known predators, and moles

(*Scalopus aquaticus*), opossum (*Didelphis virginiana*), and an unidentified thrush have also been found with them in their stomachs, or have been seen attacking the snake (Anderson 1965; Clark 1970a; Collins 1993; Reynolds 1945; Sandidge 1955; Webb 1970). In addition, captives have been eaten by prairie kingsnakes (*Lampropeltis c. calligaster*), the least shrew (*Cryptotis parva*), and opossum (Clark 1970a). Probably any carnivorous vertebrate larger than *C. vermis* is a potential predator. Humans remain, however, the most destructive force, with their habitat destruction, motorized vehicles, and indiscriminate use of pesticides.

C. vermis is a gentle creature: very shy and mild mannered. It seldom, if ever, attempts to bite, but will, if handled, twist and thrash about, try to crawl between the fingers, probe with its pointed tail, and emit a rather pungent musk. Wright (1986) has reported that some captives have feigned death by suddenly going limp, and others have occasionally turned over and displayed their bright pinkish venters, perhaps to startle a potential predator.

POPULATIONS. *C. vermis* may exist in large numbers where the habitat is suitable. Based on capture-recapture records, Clark (1970a) found densities of 60–120 individuals/ha at his study site in Kansas, and Anderson (1965) reported that it was not unusual to see as many as 25 in a few hours of hunting in moist woodlands in Missouri; but elsewhere only a few may occur. Of 7,061 snakes collected by Fitch (1992) from 1980 through 1991 in Douglas, Jefferson, and Leavenworth counties in northeastern Kansas, only 16 were *C. vermis*. It is one of the rarer snakes in Texas, only occurring in a few northeastern counties (Tennant 1985), and it is protected as a species of special concern in Iowa and Louisiana.

The sex ratio of 926 individuals collected by Clark (1970a) did not differ significantly from 1:1. Of 913 individuals aged by Clark, 6.6% were hatchlings, 19.4% were first-year snakes, 18.2% were in their second year, 21.6% were three years old, 13.4% were four years old, and 20.9% were more than four years old.

REMARKS. Clark (1970a) proposed that it be elevated from subspecific, *C. a. vermis*, to specific status, *C. vermis*, because of the absence of fusion of the internasal and prefrontal scales, single posttemporal scale, ventral scale count, and extent of ventral coloration on the lateral scale rows. He concluded the Mississippi River formed an effective barrier to gene flow between *C. amoenus* and *C. vermis*. However, *C. vermis* occurs east of the Mississippi River in Illinois and Wisconsin, and *C. amoenus* is known from eastern Arkansas (Conant and Collins 1998), and the two species hybridize in northeastern Louisiana (Rossman 1973).

Cemophora coccinea (Blumenbach 1788) | Scarlet Snake

RECOGNITION. *C. coccinea* has a maximum TBL of 82.8 cm, but most individuals are shorter than 55 cm. The body supports a series of red, black-bordered, saddlelike bands (12–28 on the body; 1–10 on the tail) separated by yellow cream bands. The head is red, with a dark transverse bar between the eyes. The venter is immaculate white or cream. The head is barely broader than the neck, and the tail is short. The snout is rounded and projecting. Dorsal body scales are smooth with two apical pits; they lie in 19 (17–21) anterior rows, 19 (17–21) rows at midbody, and 19 (14–18) rows near the vent. Beneath are 149–195 ventrals, 31–50 subcaudals, and an undivided anal plate. Lateral head scales are 1 (sometimes divided into 2) nasal, 1 loreal, 1 (0–2) preocular, 2 (0–3) postoculars, 1 + 2 temporals, 6 (4–7) supralabials (the second and third contact the orbit if 6 supralabials are present, the third and fourth if there are 7 supralabials), and 7 (6–9) infralabials. The rostral scale is enlarged and projects beyond the lower jaw. The bilobed hemipenis has a forked sulcus spermaticus, has no adornments near the base of the shaft, is spinose distally on the shaft, and has calyxes on the apex. Each maxilla supports 9–10 teeth; the most posterior is elongate and bladelike (the posterior maxillary teeth are described in detail by Trauth (1993).

Males have 149–176 (mean, 162) ventrals, 34–50 (mean, 42) subcaudals, and TLs 11.5–18.0 (mean, 15.0) % of TBL; females have 155–195 (mean, 168) ventrals, 31–42 subcaudals, and TLs 11.1–16.3 (mean, 14) % of TBL.

GEOGRAPHIC VARIATION. Three subspecies have been described (Williams 1985). *C. c. coccinea* (Blumenbach 1788), the Florida scarlet snake, is restricted to peninsular Florida from Citrus, Lake, and Volusia counties southward. It has the first black band behind the eyes not in contact with the parietal scales (usually separated by at least two scale lengths), the 12–22 body bands closed laterally, fewer than 185 ventrals, and usually 7 supralabials. Duellman and Schwartz (1958) reported there is a definite reduction in the

Florida scarlet snake, *Cemophora coccinea coccinea*; Gainesville, Florida. (Photograph by Peter May)

Northern scarlet snake,
Cemophora coccinea copei;
Kentucky. (Photograph by
Roger W. Barbour)

number of red body blotches from north to south in peninsular Florida. *C. c. copei* Jan 1863, the northern scarlet snake, ranges from New Jersey, Delaware, and eastern Maryland south to peninsular Florida and west through Virginia and southern Tennessee to Oklahoma and eastern Texas. Isolated colonies also occur in West Virginia, Kentucky, southwestern Illinois, and central Missouri. It either has the first black band touching the parietal scales (it sometimes joins the black transverse bar) or separated from the parietals by no more than one scale length, the 13–28 (mean, 18.6) body bands closed laterally, fewer than 185 ventrals, and usually 6 supralabials. Intergradation with *C. c. coccinea* occurs in Levy, Alachua, and Marion counties, Florida (Williams and Wilson 1967). *C. c. lineri* Williams, Brown, and Wilson 1966, the Texas scarlet snake, is restricted to southern Texas. It has the first black band separated from the parietal scales by at least two scale lengths, the 14–17 body bands open laterally, 185 or more ventrals, and usually 7 supralabials.

CONFUSING SPECIES. The coral snake *(Micrurus fulvius)* has a black face, and its red and yellow bands are in contact. All other coral snake mimics have the dorsal body bands at least encroaching on the venter.

KARYOTYPE. Undescribed.

FOSSIL RECORD. *Cemophora* is known from the Pleistocene (Irvingtonian) of Citrus County, Florida

(Meylan 1982), and the Pleistocene (Rancholabrean) of Florida (Auffenberg 1963; Holman 1962a, 1976; Lynch 1965; Tihen 1962) and Virginia (Fay 1988; Guilday 1962; Holman 1986a).

DISTRIBUTION. *C. coccinea* ranges from the southern New Jersey and the Delmarva Peninsula south through peninsular Florida and west to Missouri, eastern Oklahoma, eastern Texas, and southern Texas.

HABITAT. Habitats of this snake lie between sea level and approximately 750 m. It is most often found in pine, hardwood, or mixed oak-pine woodlands with an understory of wiregrass. The soil is usually sandy or loamy, but sometimes rocky. There, it hides under leaf litter, rocks, logs, or in stumps. The authors have taken several from beneath old wooded ties along abandoned railways, especially in Florida.

It is semifossorial and burrows by thrusting its head right and left until the head and neck are concealed, then forcing its snout deeper into the soil and lifting the soil upward with the snout until it is completely covered with soil (Wilson 1951). Individuals have been found buried over 1.8 m deep (Tennant 1985).

BEHAVIOR. The annual activity period is typical for a snake within its distribution, and *Cemophora* is normally surface active between April May and September–November. Active snakes have been found in every month in North Carolina, with 87% of activity occurring in May–August (Palmer and Braswell 1995).

Distribution of *Cemophora coccinea*.

It is possible that the entire population in southern Florida may be active all year, although Enge and Sullivan (2000) recorded them in all months but January and March in 13 Florida counties, with peak activity in June (the peak season for availability of reptile eggs) and most activity in April–August. Nelson and Gibbons (1972) found no strong correlation between their activity and temperature in South Carolina, nor did rainfall seem to influence them. Hibernation is spent in underground burrows or in rotting logs or stumps.

Although a few may be found on the surface during the day, most activity is crepuscular or nocturnal (Neill 1957; Nelson and Gibbons 1972; Palmer and Braswell 1995; Palmer and Tregembo 1970). No temperature data are available.

Reynolds (1980), using a convex-polygon method, estimated the mean home range of four North Carolina males was 1,627 (930–2,790) m², and that of two females was 1,395 (930–1,860) m²; the mean activity radii for 11 males and six females that had moved were 30.5 (15.3–68.2) and 28.1 (15.3–36.1) m, respectively; and the mean distances moved between captures by males and females were 52.9 (20.3–136.4) and 54.0 (30.5–91.5) m, respectively. The overall mean distance between successive captures was 51.5 m (n = 34). In South Carolina, the minimal distances between successive captures were 1–600 m with no apparent relationship to snake size or time of year; four individuals traveled a minimum of 15 m/day (Nelson and Gibbons 1972).

Mara (1995b) observed a smaller captive male exhibit combat behavior toward an older male: he crawled up and down the larger male's back and along his sides and then began coiling and twisting with him head to tail rather than head to head.

REPRODUCTION. According to Conant and Collins (1998) both sexes are mature at a TBL of 36.7 cm, but Palmer and Braswell (1995) reported a gravid North Carolina female was only 32.9 cm long; such lengths would probably be reached in two to three years. The gametic cycles have not been described.

Mating apparently takes place in the spring (from March through June in Florida; Tennant 1997). Photographs in Mara (1994, 1995b) show the male's body looped over that of the female, his tail coiled around hers, and a hemipenis inserted into her anal vent. He is apparently also biting her back, possibly to restrain her or to maintain his position.

The nesting season extends from late May to late August, with most ovipositions occurring in July. This long nesting period prompted Fitch (1970) to suggest that *Cemophora* may lay more than one clutch per year. The nests are in underground burrows or under plant debris or rocks. The white, elongated eggs may be adherent, 12.0–44.8 (mean, 32.8; n = 46) mm long, 7–19 (mean, 11.5; n = 39) mm wide, and weigh 2.0–6.0 (mean, 3.0; n = 8) g. Most eggs hatch in September after an IP of 70–80 days, but neonates may rarely appear in October or early November, and Gibbons and Semlitsch (1991) reported a March hatching in South Carolina.

Clutches average five (n = 27) and contain two to nine eggs (Herman 1983; Palmer and Braswell 1995).

Hatchlings have 11.3–18.6 (mean, 14.7; n = 33) cm TBLs and weigh 2.1–5.9 (mean, 3.7; n = 17) g. Usually, hatchlings have no yellow pigment present between their red dorsal saddles, as these areas are whitish; a general darkening of pigmentation occurs with age (Neill 1950).

GROWTH AND LONGEVITY. Reynolds (1980) calculated the following rates of growth between captures for those North Carolina *Cemophora* that had increased in length: males (three)—1.0–1.5 (mean, 1.17) cm, 0.0159–0.0526 (mean, 0.037) cm/day; females (four)—1.0–3.0 (mean, 1.75) cm, 0.0254–0.0566 (mean, 0.041) cm/day. *C. coccinea* fed an artificial, enhanced diet gained 0.0015–0.12 (mean, 0.042) g/day (Brisbin and Bagshaw 1993). McIntyre (in Tennant 1997) kept a captive alive for over six years.

DIET AND FEEDING HABITS. *C. coccinea* apparently feeds predominately on reptile eggs, but it also consumes other prey. Recorded foods include lizard eggs *(Eumeces inexpectatus, Cnemidophorus sexlineatus),* snake eggs *(Cemophora coccinea, Diadophis punctatus, Elaphe guttata, Pituophis melanoleucus),* turtle eggs *(Graptemys* sp., *Pseudemys* sp., *Terrapene carolina, Trachemys scripta),* small lizards *(Anolis carolinensis, Eumeces inexpectatus, Scincella lateralis),* small snakes *(Diadophis punctatus, Tantilla coronata, Virginia* sp.), small frogs *(Acris* sp.), salamanders, young mice, insects, slugs, and possibly earthworms (Brodie and Allison 1958; Brown 1979a; Burger et al. 1992; Dickson 1948; Ditmars 1936; Hamilton and Pollack 1956; Minton and Bechtel 1958; Neill 1951; Palmer and Braswell 1995; Palmer and Tregembo 1970; Reynolds 1980; Williams and Wilson 1967).

Dickson (1948) reported that *Cemophora* enters large eggs to drink the contents; however, Minton and Bechtel (1958) proposed that the snake used its teeth to slit the eggshell, but did not enter the egg. Palmer and Tregembo (1970) observed several of these snakes feed on large eggs and never saw one enter an egg. Instead, the snake seized one end and began chewing. Its jaws extended forwards until the enlarged posterior maxillary teeth pierced the shell. The snake then looped part of its body over the egg and often wedged it against the cage wall; a combination of vigorous chewing and depressing the body then forced out the egg's contents. In contrast, the authors have seen a scarlet snake stick its head into a large egg through the slit made by its posterior teeth. Small eggs are swallowed whole (Brown 1979a, pers. obs.). Live prey, other than eggs, are apparently constricted. Willard (1977) reported that constricting *Cemophora* make irregular, somewhat overlapping coils with no consistent lateral surface against the prey.

PREDATORS AND DEFENSE. There are four known predators: *Cemophora* (devouring its own eggs), the coral snake *(Micrurus fulvius),* the southern toad *(Bufo terrestris),* and the loggerhead shrike *(Lanius ludovicianus)* (Brown 1979a; Guthrie 1932; Heinrich 1996; Palmer and Braswell 1995; Wright and Wright 1957). However, it is probable that an array of ophiophagous snakes, carnivorous mammals, and predatory birds eat the scarlet snake.

Cemophora is inoffensive and seldom, if ever, bites. If it cannot escape, it may try to conceal its head beneath its coils while elevating its tail, presumably to direct the predator away from the head. It may release musk or feces when handled.

POPULATIONS. *Cemophora* may be locally common, but because of its fossorial behavior gives the impression of being rare; of 230 snakes trapped in upland habitats in north-central Florida, only 10 (4.3%) were this species (Dodd and Franz 1995). During his study in North Carolina, Reynolds (1980) captured 130 snakes, 33 (25.4%) of which were *C. coccinea*. Population size estimates varied between 25 and 48 individuals using the Lincoln-Peterson method and between 29 and 33 individuals using the Schumacher-Eschmeyer method; density estimates using the two methods were 5–10/ha and 6–7/ha, respectively. The sex ratio was 2:1 in favor of males. Most individuals had 21–35 cm SVLs; only 16% had SVLs shorter than 21 cm, and approximately 4% were longer than 35 cm. The SVL structure of South Carolina *Cemophora* studied by Nelson and Gibbons (1972) was 11–51 cm, with most 21–40 cm.

The scarlet snake is considered threatened in Indiana and Texas and rare in Missouri.

REMARKS. Immunological studies by Dowling et al. (1996) indicate that *C. coccinea* is most closely related to the genera *Arizona, Bogertophis, Elaphe,* and *Lampropeltis,* but its morphology shows it is closest to *Stilosoma* (Keogh 1996). Previously, Williams and Wilson (1967) and Underwood (1967) had proposed *Lampropeltis triangulum* as its nearest relative, and Rodriguez-Robles and Jesus-Escobar (1999) presented mtDNA data that indicates *Cemophora* is a sister group to *Lampropeltis.* The extinct Miocene genus *Pseudocemophora* has characters in common with both *Cemophora* and *Lampropeltis* and may be ancestral to both (Auffenberg 1963). The genus *Cemophora* and *C. coccinea* were reviewed by Williams (1985) and Williams and Wilson (1967).

Chilomeniscus cinctus Cope 1861c | Banded Sand Snake

RECOGNITION.   This small (TBL to 28.5 cm) desert dweller is yellow, buff, or reddish orange with 14–49 narrow to broad, dark brown or black bands crossing the body and tail. Usually the bands on the tail completely encircle it, but the body bands may or may not cross the venter. The interspace between the bands may be colored entirely reddish orange, or the orange pigment may only form a saddlelike blotch. The venter is white to pale yellow; the chin and throat are white. A black head hood extends across the head to the supralabials below the orbit and first temporal on each side. The hood is usually concave anteriorly between the orbits, and it extends backward to a normally convex posterior border on the parietal scales.

Banded sand snake, *Chilomeniscus cinctus*; Baja California, Mexico. (Photograph by Brad R. Moon)

Distribution of *Chilomeniscus cinctus*.

The snout is yellow to orange. Body scales are generally smooth with apical pits (males may have keeled scales anterior to the vent), and occur in 13–15 anterior rows, 13(14) midbody rows, and 12–13 rows near the vent. The venter has 108–134 ventrals, 21–33 subcaudals, and a divided anal plate. The head is as broad as the neck, with a flattened snout, countersunk lower jaw, and round pupils. Lateral head scales consist of 2 (1) nasals, 0 (1) loreal, 1 preocular, 2 postoculars, 1 + 1–2 temporals, 7 (8) supralabials, and 8 (6–9) infralabials. The rostral scale is enlarged and separates the internasal scales. The hemipenis has numerous fringed calyxes (Wright and Wright 1957). Each maxilla has 11 teeth, with the most posterior weakly grooved.

Males have longer tails (13–15% of TBL), keeled scales just anterior to the anal vent, five to nine tail bands, 108–120 ventrals, and 25–33 subcaudals; females have shorter tails (9–13% of TBL), no or only weakly keeled scales just anterior to the anal vent, three to five tail bands, 111–134 ventrals, and 21–29 subcaudals.

GEOGRAPHIC VARIATION. Although much variation exists in ground color and the number and width of the body bands, *C. cinctus* is considered monotypic.

CONFUSING SPECIES. The western shovel-nosed snake *(Chionactis occipitalis)* has 15 midbody scale rows and a single anal plate, and its rostral scale does not separate the internasal scales. The Sonoran shovel-nosed snake *(Chionactis palarostris)* usually has 15 midbody scale rows and fewer than 21 dark body bands. The ground snake *(Sonora semiannulata)* lacks a countersunk lower jaw and has only few to no dark dorsal saddles that do not extend downward laterally to the ventrals. The Sonoran coral snake *(Micruroides euryxanthus)* has a bluntly rounded black snout.

KARYOTYPE. The karyotype is probably identical to that of its Baja California congener *C. stramineus*, which Bury et al. (1970) and Trinco and Smith (1972) reported as 2n = 36 chromosomes with 52 arms: 16 macrochromosomes and 20 microchromosomes, with macrochromosome pairs one and two approximately the same size and pair four subtelocentric.

FOSSIL RECORD. No fossils have been found.

DISTRIBUTION. The banded sand snake ranges from south-central and southwestern Arizona through southwestern Sonora, Mexico, and over most of Baja California and the islands of Magdalena and Tiburón.

HABITAT. *C. cinctus* lives in arid lands, often deserts, with loose sandy or sand-gravel soils, especially in riparian situations, and in arroyos and washes, from lowlands near sea level to rocky uplands over 900 m. Vegetation in these habitats varies from mesquite-creosote to paloverde-saguaro or thorn scrub. Surface rocks or other debris are necessary for shelters.

BEHAVIOR. As with most of our other small southwestern desert nocturnal colubrids, practically nothing is known about its ecology. It has been reported to be active annually from 8 April to 22 November (Gates 1957; Wright and Wright 1957), with most surface activity in May–July (Hensley 1950; Rosen and Lowe 1994). Daily activity seems almost entirely nocturnal, as it is seldom seen on the surface of the ground except at night.

It is a very efficient burrower in loose soils and is well adapted for burrowing. The head and neck are the same width (thus allowing a more powerful forward thrust of the flattened, somewhat wedge-shaped, snout), the nostrils are valved to keep out soil particles, the small eyes are angled somewhat dorsally, the lower jaw is countersunk, the body is thick and powerful with smooth and polished body scales to retard drag, the venter is flat with angular sides, and the tail is short (Mosauer 1936). It "swims" just beneath the surface of the sandy soil with a lateral undulatory motion and can progress some distance in this fashion before surfacing. When the snake is burrowing, the sand collapses behind it, forming looped, serpentine furrows that are usually found between bushes or other vegetation (Switak 1976, 1978).

REPRODUCTION. A limited amount of reproductive data is available. Wright and Wright (1957) listed the smallest adult TBL as 15.2 cm, but Stebbins (1985) gave 17.8 cm as the shortest adult length. The smallest reproductively active males and females examined by Goldberg (1995c) had SVLs of 15.1 cm and 17.3 cm, respectively. Therefore, SVL at maturity is probably about 16 cm. Goldberg (1995c) reported that males have regressed testes with the seminiferous tubules containing spermatogonia and Sertoli cells in July–September; the testes are in recrudescence with primary and secondary spermatocytes, and possibly some spermatids, in December–February; and sperm mature in March–June (a single January male was undergoing spermiogenesis). He found some females with inactive ovaries in every month; females only had active ovaries in June (yolk deposition, and 3–4 mm follicles) and July (two 6 mm oviductal eggs). A female taken on 27 July contained three 12 × 5 mm ova (Stebbins 1954). Not all females reproduce each year.

C. cinctus is oviparous and probably lays its eggs in July or August. Clutches contain two to three eggs. An egg analyzed by Vitt (1978) had ash and water contents of 6.9% and 39.3%, respectively, and a mean caloric value of 6.6 cal/mg (recalculated as 6.2 cal/mg by Congdon et al. 1982). RCM is 0.105 (Vitt 1978, Seigel and Fitch 1984). The 10–11 cm hatchlings resemble adults in body color and pattern. Gates (1957) found hatchlings in October, but most probably hatch in September.

GROWTH AND LONGEVITY. No growth data are available. A wild-caught C. cinctus survived four years at the Arizona-Sonora Desert Museum (Snider and Bowler 1992).

DIET AND FEEDING HABITS. C. cinctus is an active forager that takes both moving and stationary prey. It usually feeds on the ground surface but is capable of feeding underground. Wild individuals have eaten centipedes and insects (adult sand cockroaches, ant pupae) (Fowlie 1965; Stebbins 1954, 1985; Vorhies 1926; Wright and Wright 1957).

Vitt (1978) reported that the body of a C. cinctus contained 16.4% ash and 69.1% water and had a caloric value of 5.7 cal/mg (recalculated to be 4.9 cal/mg dry weight by Congdon et al. 1982), so its arthropod diet must supply this amount of energy.

PREDATORS AND DEFENSE. A Sonoran coral snake (Micruroides euryxanthus) was seen trying to eat a C. cinctus, and this small snake must be the prey of other ophiophagous snakes (Crotalus, Lampropeltis, Rhinocheilus, Salvadora), owls, and carnivorous mammals (Canis latrans, Conepatus, Mephitus, Vulpes). Motorized vehicles take a high toll of C. cinctus crossing roads at night (Rosen and Lowe 1994).

When discovered on the surface, it quickly burrows into the loose soil. If dug up and handled, it will thrash about, but seldom bites.

POPULATIONS. Despite being fairly common at some sites, population data are sparse. It made up only 7 (1.9%) of 368 snakes observed by Rosen and Lowe (1994) along an Arizona highway during a four-year study.

REMARKS. C. cinctus is in need of a thorough ecological and behavioral study. Banta and Leviton (1963) reviewed the genus Chilomeniscus.

Chionactis Cope 1861a

Shovel-nosed Snakes

Key to the Species of *Chionactis*

1a. Anterior border straight on a more extensive black head hood, usually less than 21 dark primary body bands, and usually fewer than 23 body bands or unmarked anterior band positions on the venter; snout blunt . . . . *C. palarostris*

1b. Anterior border concave on a less extensive black head hood, usually more than 21 dark primary body bands, and usually more than 23 body bands or unmarked anterior band positions on the venter, snout long . . . *C. occipitalis*

Chionactis occipitalis (Hallowell 1854) │ Western Shovel-nosed Snake

RECOGNITION. Ground color of this small (TBL to 43.2 cm) snake is white, cream, or yellow; 17–40 (usually more than 21) black or dark brown bands cross the back, and an additional 5–13 bands are present on the tail. These dark bands usually cross the venter. Also present, between the dark bands, may be smaller orange red, saddlelike bands that do not extend laterally to the ventrals (see GEOGRAPHIC VARIATION). The red, yellow, and black banded pattern is reminiscent of that of North American coral snakes (see CONFUSING SPECIES). A black hood with a concave anterior border and a convex to straight posterior border connects the orbits. The head is barely broader than the neck, the yellow snout is flattened and only slightly convex, and the lower jaw is countersunk. The pupils are round. Dorsal body scales are smooth, with an apical pit, and occur in 15 (16–17) anterior rows, 15 (14–16) rows at midbody, and 15 (13–14) rows near the tail. Beneath are 136–178 ventrals, 35–57 subcaudals, and a divided anal plate. Pertinent head scales include 1 nasal, 1 (0–2) loreal, 1 (2) preocular, 2 (1–3) postoculars, 1 (2) + 2 (1–3) temporals, 7 (6–8) supralabials, and 7 (6–8) infralabials; the rostral scale does not extend backward far enough to separate the internasal scales. The hemipenis has a single sulcus spermaticus and a distal section of fine, almost uniform calyxes. The tip forms two low mounds, but otherwise the hemipenis is not divided. Two large basal spines, one on each side of the sulcus, and about 30 smaller spines are present. Transition from spines to calyxes is abrupt.

Maxillary teeth total 11–12, with the three posterior teeth separated by a diastema.

Males have TLs 17.0–20.2% of TBL, 136–168 ventrals, and 35–57 subcaudals; females have TLs 15.5–18.4% of TBL, 153–178 ventrals, and 35–52 subcaudals.

GEOGRAPHIC VARIATION. Four subspecies exist in the United States. *C. o. occipitalis* (Hallowell 1854), the Mojave Desert shovel-nosed snake, occurs in the Mojave Desert in southern Nevada, west-central Arizona, and southeastern California. It is a yellow and brown snake that usually lacks orange red saddles between the brown body bands and normally has 45 or more dark body bands plus unmarked band positions on the venter. *C. o. annulata* (Baird 1859), the Colorado Desert shovel-nosed snake, ranges from southwestern Arizona and southeastern California south to Baja California and northern Sonora in Mexico. It is a yellow and black snake that also lacks orange red or brown saddles between the black body bands, or has only faint ones, and usually has fewer than 45 dark body bands plus unmarked band positions on the venter. *C. o. klauberi* (Stickel 1941), the Tucson shovel-nosed snake, occurs in southern Arizona in Maricopa, Pima, and Pinal counties. It has the black primary body bands separated by orange-red, orange-brown, brown, or black saddles, and usually fewer than 152 ventrals in males and fewer than 160 ventrals in females. *C. o. talpina* Klauber 1951, the Nevada shovel-nosed snake, lives in southwestern Nevada and the ad-

Mojave shovel-nosed snake, *Chionactis occipitalis occipitalis*; San Bernardino, California. (Photograph by Donald J. Fisher)

Tucson shovel-nosed snake, *Chionactis occipitalis klauberi*; Pine County, Arizona. (Photograph by Cecil Schwalbe)

jacent Death Valley region of eastern California. It has orange red, orange brown, brown, or black saddles separating the primary dark brown body bands, and usually more than 152 ventrals in males and more than 160 ventrals in females.

CONFUSING SPECIES. For characters distinguishing the Sonoran shovel-nosed snake *(C. palarostris)*, see the above key. The banded sand snake *(Chilomeniscus cinctus)* has the rostral scale separating the internasal scales, 19–49 dark body bands, and usually 13 scale rows at midbody. The ground snake *(Sonora semiannulata)* has no yellow bands, its snout is not yellow, flattened, or convex, and its lower jaw is not countersunk. North American coral snakes *(Micuroides, Micrurus)* have black snouts.

KARYOTYPE. The karyotype has 36 chromosomes (with a total of 52 arms), 16 macrochromosomes, and 20 microchromosomes (Bury et al. 1970; Trinco and Smith 1972). All macrochromosomes are biarmed, but pair six is distinctly subtelocentric.

FOSSIL RECORD. Pleistocene (Rancholabrean) fossils have been found in Arizona and California (Mead et al. 1982; Van Devender and Mead 1978).

DISTRIBUTION. *C. occipitalis* ranges from southwestern Nevada and the adjacent Death Valley region of California south to southwestern Arizona and southeastern California in the United States, and into northern Sonora and Baja California in Mexico.

Distribution of *Chionactis occipitalis*.

HABITAT. *C. occipitalis* is a resident of sandy deserts with only small rocks or stones and scant vegetation (grasses, cacti, creosote, mesquite). It is known from elevations below sea level in Death Valley, California, to about 1,400 m elsewhere.

BEHAVIOR. Across the range it has been found active from mid-March into November. In Nevada, activity has been recorded in May–September and November, with peak numbers of snakes being found in May–June and September (Elvin 1963). Southern California individuals are active from March through October, with peak activity in May–June, and a few surface active individuals after July (Klauber 1951). Elevation may play an important role in the annual period of activity, with individuals at higher elevations first becoming active later in the spring (May–June) (Elvin 1963).

The winter is spent underground (Cowles 1941b). An adult was found hibernating at a depth of approximately 60 cm. A juvenile overwintering 45 cm beneath the surface had a 18°C BT, approximately equal to the ST (Cowles 1941b). Another hibernating *C. occipitalis* had a BT of 19.5°C. By the end of March the snakes moved upward to 2.5–30.0 cm below the surface. Shaw (1953) found an adult in late January hibernating in a 25 cm straight burrow approximately 7.7 cm below the surface of a small sand dune. The

burrow was moist from recent winter rains and had an AT of 18.8°C.

Although mostly nocturnal, some individuals are surface active in the late afternoon (1700–1900 hours) or early morning (0700–1000 hours), but most activity occurs after 1900 hours, with the peak of daily activity taking place between 2000 and 2230 hours (Klauber 1951). Few individuals forage after midnight, and night surface activity usually ceases around 0230 hours (Cross 1970; Klauber 1951). Days are spent burrowed underground, in rodent burrows, or in scorpion holes. Emergence from the ground seems regulated by a circadian rhythm, and often there is a more or less synchronous emergence of several individuals in a short space and period of time (Norris and Kavanau 1966). This rhythm probably acts along with daily changes in ST near the surface, and the maximum duration of underground activity seems temperature dependent, being shorter at higher ETs.

C. occipitalis have been found surface active at ATs of 21.8–37.4°C; most observations occur at 24.0–29.2°C (Klauber 1951). BTs of voluntarily active individuals have ranged from 15.8 to 34.0°C (Brattstrom 1965; Cunningham 1966a), although most aboveground individuals probably have BTs of 26–28°C (Klauber 1951). Three found hiding under surface objects during the day had BTs of 20.4–31.2°C (Cunningham 1966a). Cowles and Bogert (1944) reported the CT_{max} is 37°C, with recovery occurring at 33°C. The highest voluntary BT of their captives was 31°C, and the minimum voluntary BT was 20°C.

Burrowing into loose soil is rapid and efficient. While digging into the soil, especially that of sand dunes, the head is bent downward and, along with the enlarged rostral scale that is at the lowest point of the advancing head, produces a soil-free cavity that is used for breathing. The countersunk lower jaw also aids in this process, and each nostril has a valve present that shuts off the cavity and prevents soil particles from entering while the snake digs with its snout (Stickel 1941). Entrance into the soil is accomplished with lateral undulatory movements of the body. Once under the soil, the small snake also uses this crawling motion to move laterally, and it is capable of both forward and backward movements.

Most night foraging is done on the surface, or just under the surface of the soil, when the snake makes short exploratory movements from one shrub-covered hillock to another. Most nocturnal underground movements are probably only for short distances; Mosauer (1932b, 1933, 1935a) doubted if this species travels more than 30 m/night, but some make longer journeys. Above ground movements are usually done at surface level, but Warren (1953) observed climbing behavior in this snake.

Male dominance combat occurs. Goode and Schuett (1994) observed that on 10 May after two captive males encountered each other snout to snout, the larger snake tried to press his chin on the nape of the smaller snake's neck and then slowly worked his way forward to its head. This caused the smaller attacked male to burrow into the sand bottom of their terrarium, and the larger aggressive male burrowed immediately on top of the smaller male. As both males submerged, their bodies were entwined. Once they were under the sand much writhing occurred, and occasionally portions of their bodies broke the surface. The entire combat encounter lasted about one minute. During subsequent combat sequences, on 16–19 May, the larger male was seen to bite his smaller rival, while the smaller male vibrated its tail. No further combat occurred after 19 May.

REPRODUCTION. Wright and Wright (1957) reported *C. occipitalis* as adult at 15.2–17.8 cm SVL. The smallest reproductively active California male examined by Goldberg (1997a) had a SVL of 19.4 cm; the shortest reproductive male from Arizona and Sonora, Mexico, examined by Goldberg and Rosen (1999) had a SVL of 20.1 cm. Klauber (1951) found a 28.9 cm gravid female, and Goldberg (1997a) and Goldberg and Rosen (1999) reported reproductive females with SVLs of 25.7 cm (California) and 26.5 cm (Arizona), respectively. Stebbins (1985) gave 25.4 cm as the minimum adult TBL; so the species probably matures when between 25 and 26 cm TBL.

California males have regressed testes with spermatogonia and Sertoli cells in the seminiferous tubules during June–November, undergo spermatogenesis with primary and secondary spermatocytes and occasional spermatids in March–April and September, and contain maturing sperm and spermatids in March–July (Goldberg 1997a). Fewer Arizona and Sonora males were examined by Goldberg and Rosen (1999), but one had regressed testes in August, two were undergoing recrudescence in May, and several were in spermiogenesis from April to July (approximating the months of above ground activity in Arizona).

Goldberg (1997a) found reproductively inactive females in March–September in California. Vitellogenesis had occurred in one female undergoing atresia in August; females with enlarged follicles were present in May–July, and they contained oviductal eggs May. In Arizona, a female contained enlarged follicles (> 10 mm) on 23 April, and another had oviductal eggs on 3 June (Goldberg and Rosen 1999). Cowles (1941b) found two 37.5 cm females contained 2 mm ova on 26 March: one contained six ova, the second female had six ova in one ovary and three in the other, and both contained abundant fat tissue.

Courtship and copulation have not been described, but Klauber (1951) found a male possibly trying to mate with a dead-on-the-road (DOR) female on 27 May.

The eggs are white and elongated (13–14 × 4.5–5.0 mm) with leathery shells. A typical clutch has two to four (two to six) eggs; with the six and nine ova found in two females by Cowles (1941b), possibly more than one clutch of eggs is laid each year. Nesting probably takes place in June or July, but no clutches have been found in the wild. The IP is unknown, but hatching probably occurs in August–September. Hatchlings are colored and patterned like the adults and are 12.1–12.4 cm long (Klauber 1951; Wright and Wright 1957).

GROWTH AND LONGEVITY. The growth rate is unknown. Klauber (1951) kept a *C. occipitalis* alive for over 42 months.

DIET AND FEEDING HABITS. Foraging occurs on the surface of the ground at night, but possibly the snake also feeds underground.

According to Glass (1972), *C. occipitalis* assumes a "vertical stance," with the anterior 25–33% of the body lifted off the ground in a sigmoid curve, when searching for or pursuing prey. The head is pointed downward, and the tongue rapidly flicked. However, the snake may also use a horizontal posture with the head only slightly raised, particularly when chasing scorpions. When caught, small prey may be simply seized in the mouth, worked about for ease of swallowing, and ingested. Large prey may be held to the ground with a body loop before being seized by the mouth. *C. occipitalis* seems immune to scorpion venom and may pursue these animals into their burrows. Scorpions are usually seized near the base of the tail stinger, and on two occasions witnessed by Norris and Kavanou (1966), the snake backed into the sand, dragging the scorpion behind its retreating snout, thus orienting it for ingestion. As the scorpion was swallowed, the jaw opposite that closest to the stinger was moved, the scorpion was slowly pulled down the throat as it was bent U-shaped, and the stinger and claws were swallowed last. However, Glass (1972) witnessed captives swallow scorpions head first on several occasions.

The natural diet is varied but consists of mostly arthropods: scorpions, centipedes, spiders, and insects—ants (pupae, adults), beetles (larvae, adults), cockroaches, and moths (pupae); but a lizard egg *(Uta)* was recovered from one, so it is possible that small lizards are also consumed (Cowles 1941b; Cunningham 1959; Klauber 1951; Norris and Kavanou 1966; Perkins 1938; Schwenkmeyer in Klauber 1951). Captives have eaten various insects, scorpions, centipedes, solpugids, and hatchling lizards *(Uta)* (Cunningham 1959; Glass 1972; Norris and Kavanou 1966; Regnery in Klauber 1951; Stebbins 1954).

PREDATORS AND DEFENSE. Klauber (1951) reported that one was killed by a domestic cat *(Felis catus)* and another was eaten by a coachwhip *(Masticophis flagellum piceus)*. He also assumed that this species is the natural prey of several types of snakes *(Arizona, Lampropeltis, Rhinocheilus, Salvadora)*, owls, and the coyote *(Canis latrans)*. The loggerhead shrike *(Lanius ludovicianus)* sometimes kills and impales it on ocotillo plants (Mahrdt and Banta 1996). Many are killed by automobiles (Rosen and Lowe 1994).

Being nocturnal and subterranean, *C. occipitalis* is seldom encountered without effort. Being negatively phototropic, it quickly burrows into the soil if disturbed by a light. A sidewinding locomotion may be used to escape across the surface of loose soil. It may form itself into a ball with head concealed beneath the coils (Mitchell 1978), but if cornered, it will put up a spirited defense: coiling and striking (usually with the mouth closed). When handled, some will bite, and almost all will spray musk and defecate.

POPULATIONS. *C. occipitalis* may be quite common in proper habitat. During a study of overwintering behavior of California desert reptiles, Cowles (1941b) found it to be the most abundant snake in the area studied, 41 (42.7%) of the total 96 reptiles collected. Klauber (1951) collected 397 in San Diego County, California, surpassed only by 523 spotted leaf-nosed snakes *(Phyllorhynchus decurtatus)*. In two hours, 12 *C. occipitalis* were collected by walking over about 0.33 ha of sand dunes at Palm Springs, California (Warren 1953). In contrast, only 5 (1.4%) *C. occipitalis* were included in 368 snakes seen in four years along an Arizona highway (Rosen and Lowe 1994). Obviously, the collecting method definitely makes a difference in determining the population density of this snake.

REMARKS. The species has been reviewed by Cross (1979), Klauber (1951), and Stickel (1941, 1943).

Chionactis saxatilis was described by Funk (1967) from individuals living in the Gila Mountains east of Yuma, Arizona. Unfortunately, only the holotype (Museum of Comparative Zoology, Harvard 77039) was deposited in a collection, and the other "paratypes" (including hatchlings) were subsequently lost by Funk. Cross (1979) examined and compared the holotype of *C. saxatilis* to populations of *C. occipitalis* of all compass directions from the Gila Mountains and found it did not differ significantly from the *C. occipitalis* in the region. Therefore, *C. saxatilis* is considered a synonym of *C. occipitalis*.

Chionactis palarostris (Klauber 1937) | Sonoran Shovel-nosed Snake

RECOGNITION. The maximum TBL is 40.6 cm. Body color is yellow, and a pattern of alternating black and orange red crossbands separated by yellow pigment occurs on the back. The black crossbands usually cross the ventrals, but the slightly broader, saddle-shaped orange red bands do not extend laterally to the ventrals. The black bands usually total less than 21 (13–22) on the body, and 4–5 on the tail. The snout is yellow, and an extensive black hood covers the top of the head to below and behind the orbits. Its forward border is straight, but the rear border is convex. Little or no orange pigment occurs on the head, but the nape is orange red separated from the black hood by a narrow yellow band. The venter is cream to yellow. The head is only slightly broader than the neck, the lower jaw is countersunk, and the pupils are round. The snout is shovel-shaped, flattened, and somewhat convex. Dorsal body scales are smooth with an apical pit and occur in 17 anterior and 15 midbody and posterior rows. The venter has 139–161 ventrals, 42–50 subcaudals, and a divided anal plate. Lateral head scales are 1 nasal, 1 loreal, 1 preocular, 2 postoculars, 1 + 2 temporals, 7 (6–8) supralabials, and 7 (6–8) infralabials. The hemipenis is similar to that of *C. occipitalis*. Each maxilla has eight to nine anterior teeth separated by a diastema from three enlarged, grooved, posterior teeth.

Males have TLs 18.5–20.8% of TBL, 139–150 ventrals, 42–50 subcaudals, and 13–16 dark body bands; females have TLs 16–17% of TBL, 155–161 ventrals, 42–43 subcaudals, and 18 or more dark body bands.

GEOGRAPHIC VARIATION. Two subspecies are recognized, but only the organ pipe shovel-nosed snake, *C. p. organica* Klauber 1951, occurs in the United States in extreme southern Arizona. It is described above.

CONFUSING SPECIES. See the above key for characters distinguishing the western shovel-nosed snake *(C. occipitalis)*. The banded sand snake *(Chilomeniscus cinctus)* has the rostral scale separating the internasals,

Sonoran shovel-nosed snake, *Chionactis palarostris*; Organ Pipe National Monument, Arizona. (Photograph by Cecil Schwalbe)

Distribution of *Chionactis palarostris*.

and 19–49 dark body bands. The ground snake *(Sonora semiannulata)* has no yellow bands, its snout is not flattened or convex, and its lower jaw is not countersunk. Coral snakes *(Micruroides, Micrurus)* have black snouts.

KARYOTYPE.   Unknown.

FOSSIL RECORD.   Van Devender et al. (1991) found Pleistocene (Rancholabrean) remains that they thought were probably those of *C. palarostris* at the Organ Pipe Cactus National Monument, Arizona.

DISTRIBUTION.   *C. palarostris* ranges in extreme southern Arizona along the Sonoyta-Ajo Road through the Organ Pipe Cactus National Monument to about 40 km north of the Mexican border, and in Mexico southward into northwestern Sonora.

HABITAT.   It prefers an upland desert habitat with sandy-gravelly soil and vegetation consisting of saguaro and other cacti, paloverde, creosote bush, and mesquite.

BEHAVIOR.   Little is known of the life history of this snake. It is annually active from March to early August, with most surface activity occurring in March–

June (Hensley 1950; Rosen and Lowe 1994). It is primarily nocturnal and spends the daylight hours in rodent or lizard burrows, beneath rocks, or within rock crevices, and these sites are probably also used as hibernacula.

REPRODUCTION.   Few reproductive data are known. The smallest reproductive male and female from Arizona and Sonora, Mexico, examined by Goldberg and Rosen (1999) had SVLs of 20.8 cm and 24.8 cm, respectively. One male had regressed testes with spermatogonia and Sertoli cells in its seminiferous tubules in April, and another was undergoing recrudescence with primary and secondary spermatocytes and some spermatids in May (Goldberg and Rosen 1999). Several males were in spermiogenesis in May–July, with mature sperm present in the epididymides. Four of seven females examined by Goldberg and Rosen (1999) in May and July had four to five enlarged follicles (> 6 mm) that would presumably have been ovulated. The only other available breeding data are of four eggs (mean length, 17.5 mm) found in a dead-on-the-road (DOR) female on 19 June (Hensley 1950).

GROWTH AND LONGEVITY.   Unknown.

DIET AND FEEDING HABITS.   Stebbins (1985) reported that *C. palarostris* eats invertebrates, but did not specify which kinds.

PREDATORS AND DEFENSE.   Unknown.

POPULATIONS.   In spite of the lack of data on the biology of *C. palarostris*, it is not particularly rare in Arizona: Rosen and Lowe (1994) found 46 individuals (32 DOR, 14 alive) during four years while slowly driving a road at night that mostly passed through the Organ Pipe Cactus National Monument. The species represented 12.5% of all snakes found and was only surpassed in numbers by *Crotalus atrox* and *Rhinocheilus lecontei*.

REMARKS.   So little is known about *C. palarostris* that a thorough study of its life history is needed.

Clonophis kirtlandii (Kennicott 1856) | Kirtland's Snake

RECOGNITION. This poorly known species is a small (TBL to 62.2 cm), moderately stout snake with a pink to red (rarely, white) venter, becoming yellow anteriorly, often with dark stippling, and bearing a row of black rounded spots on each side. The back and sides are gray brown to reddish brown with four alternating, longitudinal rows of 43–65 (mean, 56) black or dark brown, rounded blotches which may be lighter posteriorly, or indistinct in some individuals. The head is olive, brown, or black, and may contain some light mottling; the dark pigment extends ventrally onto the most posterior supralabial; other labials, chin, and throat are cream to yellow. In appearance, the head is barely wider than the neck and narrows gradually to the region of the nasals; the snout is broadly rounded. The eyes are small and the pupil round. Dorsal body scales are keeled and doubly pitted; they lie in 19 (17–21) scale rows anteriorly, 19 (17) at midbody, and 15–16 (14–17) posteriorly. Beneath are 121–137 ventrals, 44–69 subcaudals, and a divided anal plate. Lateral head scales are 2 nasals, 1 (0) loreal, 1 (2) preocular, 2 (1–3) postoculars, 1 + 2 (1) temporals, 6 (4–7) supralabials (fifth usually the largest, the third and fourth entering the eye), and 7 (6–9) infralabials (the last infralabial may have one to two small black spots). The hemipenis is weakly bilobed with smooth saccular tips and a simple sulcus spermaticus ending in the depression between the lobes. Most of the surface of the lobes is covered with small spines, but two at the base are large and hooked, and the apical surface is nude. There are 19–21 short, stout, weakly curved maxillary teeth; those that are most posterior are slightly enlarged.

Adult females have TBLs to 62.2 cm, TLs 19–24 (mean, 21) % of TBL, 123–137 (mean, 133) ventrals, and 44–61 (mean, 53) subcaudals; males grow to 33 cm, have TLs 23–28 (mean, 25) % of TBL, 121–135 (mean, 130) ventrals, and 56–69 (mean, 62) subcaudals.

Kirtland's snake, *Clonophis kirtlandii*; Indiana. (Photograph by James H. Harding)

Distribution of *Clonophis kirtlandii*.

GEOGRAPHIC VARIATION. No subspecies are recognized. Bavetz (1994) reported slight geographic variation in head scutellation and dorsal blotch number in Illinois *C. kirtlandii*.

CONFUSING SPECIES. The queen snake *(Regina septemvittata)* has a yellowish or cream-colored belly with four longitudinal dark stripes, and the red-bellied snake *(Storeria occipitomaculata)* has no dark spots at the sides of its belly.

KARYOTYPE. Undescribed.

FOSSIL RECORD. Not reported.

DISTRIBUTION. Kirtland's snake ranges from central western Pennsylvania westward through southern Ohio, Indiana, southern Michigan, north-central Kentucky, and central Illinois. The records of this species in Missouri and Wisconsin are old and based on single specimens; it is doubtful that viable populations exist in these states.

HABITAT. Although not as aquatic as many North American natricine species, *Clonophis* seems to require open damp habitats such as the edges of marshes, creeks, and canals, and wet pastures and fields, but it has been reported in wooded areas. Minton (1972) reported that in Indiana they are usually found in open grassy areas with few trees, clay soil that is quite dry in summer, some water (a sluggish creek, pond, or ditch), and earthworms. Some of the best known populations are from metropolitan areas, such as Toledo and Cincinnati (Conant 1951), Cook County, Illinois (Smith 1961), Indianapolis (Minton 1972), and Louisville (Barbour 1971). Minton (1972) captured one individual three times in a year at virtually the same spot, indicating these snakes have favorite refuges within their home ranges.

BEHAVIOR. Although they have been collected in all months of the year, *Clonophis* are most active in the spring, April and May, and fall, October (Conant 1938, 1943b; Minton 1972). In Toledo, Ohio, 43% of those caught were taken in April and 18% in May (Conant 1943b). Conant (1943b) found males more numerous in the spring, but the majority caught in July and August were females. Most *Clonophis* emerge from hibernation in late March or April and enter hibernation in late October or early November. Some, at least, spend the winter buried in the soil (Conant 1943b), although a laboratory investigation of fossorial behavior failed to demonstrate burrowing behavior by this species (Tucker 1994a). Many *C. kirtlandii* use crayfish burrows for hibernation, estivation, and daily cover.

Most activity is at night, especially during the summer; the days are spent under some sheltering debris, such as a log, piles of leaves, or rock, or in a crayfish burrow.

REPRODUCTION. The smallest mature male reported was 35 cm TBL (Wright and Wright 1957), and the smallest mature female was 36–37 cm TBL (Conant 1951; Conant and Collins 1998); such lengths would probably be reached in the second year of growth. Females 36–47 cm produced young in Ohio (Conant 1951), and a 41.5 cm female produced young in Illinois (Powell and Parmerlee 1991).

Courtship and mating occur in the spring. Mating pairs have been found on 1 May in Indiana (Minton 1972), and 10 and 14 May in Illinois (Smith 1961). Minton (1972) reported the snakes were tightly intertwined and remained together after being placed in the collecting bag.

Gestating females have been found in May, July, and August (Conant 1943b; Powell and Parmerlee 1991). Dates of parturition in this viviparous snake extend from 30 July (Minton 1972) to 24 September (Conant 1943b; Powell and Parmerlee 1991). Litters average 8 young (based on 40 litters), and may contain 4 (Conant 1943b) to 15 (Tucker 1976). A gravid Illinois *C. kirtlandii* collected on 16 May gave birth on 23–24 September (Powell and Parmerlee 1991). Litter size is positively correlated to female length. The only reported RCM is 0.305 (Tucker 1976). It is not known whether females produce more than one litter a year.

Tucker (1976) observed the birth of 7 of 15 young from a 48.5 cm female. The first five were born at approximately two-minute intervals. Three left their chorions within one minute of birth; two failed to break out of their chorions on their first attempt, but were successful on their second attempt after a 12 minute quiescent period. The births of the last two young were protracted, taking about five minutes each. All shed their skins within 24 hours. During parturition the female remained unconcealed and crawled slowly about the cage; as each fetus was slowly pushed toward the vent, a distinct bulge was visible at the posterior end of the female's body.

Powell and Parmerlee (1991) observed the birth of nine young (four males and five females) by a 41.5 cm female with a SVL of 33.5 cm and weighing 20.18 g after parturition. The first was born on the night of 23–24 September, the second at 1310 hours on 24 September, and the remaining seven between 1330 and 1445 hours on 25 September. Two of the young were stillborn, including the third, which Powell and Parmerlee suggested might explain the long delay in parturition, as that individual had broken through the fetal membranes prior to delivery and may have obstructed subsequent births.

Newborn young have 10.0–17.5 (mean, 14.3; n = 52) cm TBLs and weigh 1.01–1.40 (mean, 1.22; n = 16) g. The young are much darker than the adults and have indistinct dorsal blotches and deeper red venters.

GROWTH AND LONGEVITY.   Minton (1972) found that a wild *Clonophis* that measured 17.5 cm on 16 August had grown to 21.5 cm by 6 June of the following year. Another measured 19.5 cm when captured on 12 April, 25.0 cm when recaptured on 23 June, and 35.0 cm on 22 September of the same year.

DIET AND FEEDING HABITS.   In the wild, *Clonophis* are known to eat predominately earthworms and slugs, but also crayfish and, occasionally, minnows (Bavetz 1994; Conant 1943b; Minton 1972; Pope 1944); Thurow (1993) also reported an individual had eaten a water strider (*Gerris* sp.). In addition, chopped fish and the sympatric terrestrial leech, *Haemopsis terrestris,* have been eaten by captives (Conant 1943b; Minton 1972; Pope 1944; Tucker 1977).

Tucker (1994b) reported on the feeding behavior of four captive *C. kirtlandii* maintained in a simulation of their normal environment, including a series of earthworm burrows. On three occasions, snakes were observed to emerge from hiding places and assume a Z-shaped alert position, with the head up. When an earthworm was exposed in the vicinity of the snake, tongue flicking increased, and the snake searched for and attacked the earthworm. On five occasions, snakes that were initially seen in the Z-shaped alert position were later observed swallowing earthworms; on other occasions, snakes seen in the Z-shaped alert posture retreated to their refuges without attacking or feeding. On two occasions, *C. kirlandii* observed within earthworm burrows attacked and swallowed the earthworm occupying the burrow; on two other occasions, snakes were found swallowing earthworms inside burrows. However, snakes were not seen pursuing an earthworm into a burrow, and in no instance did the earthworms react to the presence of the snake until bitten.

PREDATORS AND DEFENSE.   An Indiana black kingsnake, *Lampropeltis g. nigra,* found in Indiana, had eaten a Clonophis (Minton 1972), and Brown (1987) reported predation by bullfrogs *(Rana catesbeiana)* in central Illinois. Harding (1997) thought that probably milk snakes *(Lampropeltis triangulum),* hawks and owls, shrews, weasels, skunks, raccoons, foxes, and domestic cats are also potential predators. When first discovered, *Clonophis* often flattens its body and becomes rigid. If further disturbed, it may thrash about or strike and spray musk.

POPULATIONS.   Kirtland's snake may be very common in some areas; Minton (1972) found 19 in two mild days following rain along a 0.6 km section of an Indianapolis street, but overall its populations are declining.

The sex ratios of the 264 *C. kirtlandii* examined by Conant (1943b) were 1:1 in 84 newborn young (42 of each sex) and 0.86:1 (84 males, 96 females) in the adults.

Clonophis kirtlandii is a typical snake of the Prairie Peninsula, where it has survived as a relict (Conant 1943b). With the increasing loss of natural prairie and the destruction of habitat due to the spread of our cities, this snake is in danger of extirpation over much of its range (Bavetz 1994; Edgren 2000). *C. kirtlandii* is now considered threatened in Illinois, Indiana, and Ohio and endangered in Pennsylvania, Michigan, and Kentucky.

REMARKS.   Rossman (1963a) studied the osteology of this species and recognized it as a separate genus. His studies also suggested a possible relationship to the genus *Storeria*; Varkey (1979) also found that *Clonophis* shared several cranial muscle characters with *Storeria*. However, Rossman et al. (1982) found *Clonophis* to be most similar to *Tropidoclonion* in relative size and placement of their internal organs. The genus and species were reviewed by Rossman and Powell (1985).

Coluber constrictor Linnaeus 1758 | Racer

RECOGNITION.   Adults are large (to 191.1 cm TBL) and almost uniformly shiny black to bluish (but see GEOGRAPHIC VARIATION and the description of hatchlings under REPRODUCTION). The gray to yellow adult venter is unmarked, and in adults the chin and throat may be white, gray, or tan. Dorsal body scales are smooth, pitted, and in 17 (16–19) anterior rows, 17 (15–19) midbody rows, and 15 (13–14) posterior rows. The venter has 151–193 ventrals, 66–120 subcaudals, and a divided anal plate. Lateral head scales are 2

Northern black racer, *Coluber constrictor constrictor*; Fayette County, Kentucky. (Photograph by Roger W. Barbour)

Buttermilk racer, *Coluber constrictor anthicus*; Louisiana. (Photograph by James H. Harding)

nasals, 1 (2) loreal, 2 (rarely 1 or 3) preoculars, 2 (rarely 1 or 3) postoculars, 2 + 2 + 2 temporals (rarely 1 or 3 scales may occur in any temporal row), 7–8 (6) supralabials, and 8–9 (7–11) infralabials. The cylindrical hemipenis is wide at its base, has an undivided sulcus spermaticus, and contains three large hooked spines on its smooth basal portion. Above these spines is a zone of small, recurved spines. Each maxilla has 13–19 (mean, 15) teeth.

Males have 160–193 (mean, 175) ventrals, 66–120 (mean, 95) subcaudals, and TLs 16–29 (mean, 26) % of TBL; females have 151–192 (mean, 179) ventrals, 70–106 (mean, 90) subcaudals, and TLs 19–29 (mean, 23) % of TBL.

GEOGRAPHIC VARIATION. Eleven subspecies are recognized; all range north of Mexico (Wilson 1978). *Coluber c. constrictor* Linnaeus 1758, the northern black racer, is found from southern Maine and central New York southwest to eastern Tennessee, northwestern Georgia, and northeastern Alabama. This large race (TBL to 191.1 cm) is shiny black dorsally, gray ventrally, has little white on the supralabials, and has a brown or dark amber iris; the hemipenile spine less than 2.5 times as large as the adjacent proximal spines. *C. c. anthicus* (Cope 1862), the buttermilk racer, is only found in southern Arkansas, northern Louisiana, and southeastern Texas. It is dark green, blue, or bluish black with numerous gray, white, yellowish, or tan spots or small blotches. The venter is white to gray white with few yellowish spots (TBL to 177.8 cm).

C. c. etheridgei Wilson 1970b, the tan racer, is restricted to a small range in southwestern Louisiana and adjacent Texas. It has a pale tan back with numerous pale spots, and a grayish white venter with some white spotting (TBL to 121.6 cm). *C. c. flaviventris* Say 1823, the eastern yellow-bellied racer, has an extensive range extending from extreme southern Saskatchewan, Canada, southeast through Montana, the western Dakotas, and most of Iowa to western Illinois, and south to the Gulf Coast of central and eastern Texas. Isolated populations are also found in central New Mexico and southwestern Louisiana. It is pale bluish gray, bluish green, or brownish dorsally and cream to lemon yellow ventrally, and usually has 7 supralabials, fewer than 99 subcaudals, and normally 14–16 maxillary teeth (TBL to 177.8 cm). *C. c. foxii* (Baird and Girard 1853), the blue racer, is found from southwestern Ontario, Michigan, Wisconsin, and southeastern Minnesota south to Ohio, Indiana, and Illinois. It has a pale bluish gray or bluish green back and a bluish gray venter, and the chin and throat are white (TBL to 182.9 cm). Some herpetologists regard it as merely a northwestern color morph of *C. c. constrictor*. *C. c. helvigularis* Auffenberg 1955b, the brown-chined racer, is only found in the lower Chipola and Apalachicola river valleys of the Florida Panhandle and adjacent Georgia. It is black dorsally and gray ventrally and has brown labials, chin, and throat, and its hemipenile spine is more than three times as long as the adjacent proximal spines (TBL to at least 150 cm). *C. c. latrunculus* Wilson 1970b, the black-masked racer,

Eastern yellow-bellied racer, *Coluber constrictor flaviventris*; Kimball County, Nebraska. (Photograph by Steve W. Gotte)

occurs in the Mississippi Valley from southwestern Tennessee south through western Mississippi and eastern Arkansas to that part of southeastern Louisiana west of the Mississippi River. It is has a dark gray back, bluish gray venter, and a black postocular stripe running through the orbit on each side of the head (TBL to at least 150 cm). *C. c. mormon* Baird and Girard 1852a, the western yellow-bellied racer, is found west of the Rocky Mountains from the interior dry belt of southern British Columbia south through western Washington, Oregon, Idaho, and western Montana to southern California, Nevada, Utah, and western Colorado. Scattered records (probably of intergrades) also exist for eastern Arizona, New Mexico, western Texas, and northeastern Mexico. It is green, olive, or greenish yellowish brown to reddish brown dorsally, with a yellow venter, and usually has eight supralabials and 13–14 maxillary teeth (TBL to 109.9 cm). Fitch et al. (1981) considered it a full species, but this interpretation has not been widely accepted. *C. c. oaxaca* (Jan 1863), the Mexican racer, is found from southern coastal Texas south through Mexico to northern Guatemala. It is small (TBL to 101.6 cm), green or olive or greenish gray dorsally, and yellow to yellow green ventrally, and usually has

eight supralabials, and 15–20 maxillary teeth. The young have dark crossbands on the neck and anterior body. *C. c. paludicola* Auffenberg and Babbitt 1953, the Everglades racer, is only found from Palm Beach, Hendry, and Lee counties south to the tip of Florida. It is bluish, greenish, or brownish gray dorsally and white to light bluish gray ventrally with some pale gray markings and has a red or reddish brown (rarely yellow) iris, usually 7 supralabials, and more than 99 subcaudals (TBL to 168.9 cm). The young are reddish with dorsal spots and reddish orange ventral spots. *C. c. priapus* Dunn and Wood 1939, the southern black racer, ranges from southern Illinois and southern Indiana and southeastern North Carolina south to south-central Florida, the Gulf Coast of the Florida Panhandle, Alabama, and Mississippi, and southeastern Louisiana, most of Arkansas, and extreme eastern Oklahoma and northeastern Texas. It has a black to dark gray back, a dark gray venter, almost completely dark supralabials, often a white chin and throat, and the enlarged hemipenile spine that is three times longer than the adjacent proximal spines (TBL to 165.1 cm).

CONFUSING SPECIES. Coachwhips (*Masticophis*) have 13 posterior scale rows. Rat snakes (*Elaphe obso-*

Distribution of *Coluber constrictor*.

leta), melanistic garter and ribbon snakes *(Tham-nophis)*, and rough green snakes *(Opheodrys aestivus)* have keeled body scales. Indigo snakes *(Drymarchon corais)* have red or orange pigment on the face, chin, and throat, and an undivided anal plate. Smooth green snakes *(Liochlorophis ventralis)* have a single nasal scale and one anterior temporal scale.

KARYOTYPE. The 36 chromosomes consist of 16 macrochromosomes (2 acrosome, 14 biarmed) and 20 microchromosomes (the NOR is located on the first pair); sex determination is ZZ/ZW (Baker et al. 1972; Bury et al. 1970; Camper and Hanks 1995).

FOSSIL RECORD. The racer has an extensive fossil record: Miocene (Clarendonian) of Kansas (Holman 1975); Miocene (Hemphillian) of Nebraska (Parmley and Holman 1995) and Texas (Parmley 1988b, 1988c); Pliocene (terminal Hemphillian) of Kansas and Oklahoma (Brattstrom 1967); Pliocene (Blancan) of Arizona (Brattstrom 1955b), Kansas (Brattstrom 1967), Nebraska (Holman and Schloeder 1991), and Texas (Holman and Schloeder 1991; Rogers 1976); Pleistocene (Irvingtonian) of Florida (Auffenberg 1963; Meylan 1982), Kansas (Holman 1972b, 1987a; Rogers 1982), Maryland (Holman 1977b), Nebraska (Holman 1995), Pennsylvania (Auffenberg 1955a), Texas (Holman and Winkler 1987; Slaughter 1966), and West Virginia (Holman 1982b; Holman and Grady 1989); and Pleistocene (Rancholabrean) of Alabama (Holman et al. 1990), Arkansas (Dowling 1958b), California

(LaDuke 1991), Florida (Auffenberg 1963; Brattstrom 1953b; Gut and Ray 1963; Holman 1958b, 1959a, 1996; Martin 1974; Meylan 1995), Georgia (Holman 1985), Illinois (Holman and Fay 1998), Kansas (Brattstrom 1967; Holman 1987a), Oklahoma (Brattstrom 1967; Smith and Cifelli 2000), Nevada (Brattstrom 1976; Mead and Bell 1994), New Mexico (Brattstrom 1964a), Ohio (Holman 1997), Pennsylvania (Guilday et al. 1964, 1966), Tennessee (Van Dam 1978), Texas (Hill 1971; Holman 1963, 1969a; Kasper and Parmley 1990; Parmley 1990b; Parmley and Pfau 1997), Virginia (Guilday 1962; Holman 1986a), and West Virginia (Holman 1982b; Holman and Grady 1987, 1989).

DISTRIBUTION. *C. constrictor* ranges from southern Maine, central New York, southwestern Ontario, Michigan, Wisconsin, southeastern Minnesota, southern Sasketchewan, and south-central British Columbia south to the Florida Keys and the Gulf Coast from the Florida Panhandle to the Rio Grande, and to New Mexico, Utah, Nevada, and southern California, southward through Mexico to northern Guatemala.

HABITAT. The racer lives in a variety of open to dry habitats: open hardwood and pine forests, brushy areas, sagebrush flats, scrub and prairie grasslands, meadows, old fields, and swamp and marsh borders at elevations of sea level to over 2,100 m. Retreats— mammal burrows, rock crevices, large rocks, rotting logs and stumps, piles of vegetation, and other prone debris—are required. Most habitats have available water, as dehydration is a problem. Bogert and Cowles (1947) reported that a *C. c. priapus* placed in a thermal drying chamber died after a 25% reduction of initial body weight through evaporative water loss.

BEHAVIOR. Over most of its range the racer emerges from hibernation from late March–May, and retreats for the winter from September–November, depending on both latitude and elevation. Most annual activity is in the spring, partly due to males searching for females; 59% of records in North Carolina are from April to June (Palmer and Braswell 1995). It is active in all months in southern Florida (Dalrymple et al. 1991), and in years with warm winters it may be active all year in Gulf Coast states. Even in the north, some individuals may bask on warm winter days.

Nevertheless, most hibernate in mammal burrows, caves, rock crevices, gravel banks, old stone walls, building foundations, cisterns and wells, or rotting logs and stumps. Site fidelity is high; only 7% of Utah racers used different hibernacula in successive years (Brown and Parker 1976). A hibernaculum also may be shared with other species of snakes, including copperheads *(Agkistrodon contortrix)* and various species of rattlesnakes *(Crotalus)*. At an Illinois hibernaculum excavated in February when the AT was 3°C and the frost line at 21 cm, the racers were dormant in a mammal burrow at depths of 91–106 cm, and both the AT and BT were 6.7°C (Schroder 1950). Hibernators in Utah had average CTs of 5°C (Parker and Brown 1974), and those in Michigan averaged 3.5 (3.3–3.7) °C (Rosen 1991). Such BTs are close to the species' CT$_{min}$. *Coluber* often shift positions to warmer areas of the den during the winter (Sexton and Hunt 1980), and their BTs are correlated with increasing ETs at greater hibernation depths. Spring emergence is gradual and usually involves several days of basking at the site before full activity is resumed (Cohen 1948a). Utah *Coluber* emerged when ATs were approximately 3–29°C; for most, the threshold AT is 11°C (Vetas 1951).

The racer is diurnal; its round pupil eye is well suited for daytime foraging, having a yellow lens and a retina composed of 100% cones (Wall 1934). Nights and dark or rainy days are spent under cover. Plummer and Congdon (1994) found it active on approxi-

mately 70% of the days during the annual activity period—40% of the time on the ground surface, 35% above ground in shrubs or trees, and 25% of the time underground.

Racers are often seen quickly crawling along with their heads raised above the ground (top speed—5.6 km/hour; Mosauer 1932c). Plummer and Congdon (1996) found them active from about 0900–1800 hours, with most surface activity occurring between 1200 and 1400 hours in South Carolina; in Virginia most activity is from 0900 to 1200 hours. In California, *C. constrictor* begins the day by protruding the head from its night retreat and exposing it to direct sunlight for 19–64 minutes; full emergence follows between 0912 and 1153 hours PDT. Ten to 30 minutes of basking usually follows, but ends when BT reaches 12°C above the emergence temperature (Hammerson 1987). The next 172–242 minutes are spent foraging, but the racer typically retreats beneath shelter during the hottest hours of the day. Peak BTs of 31.1–32.6°C are reached at about 1330 hours, and the snakes behaviorly thermoregulate around these BTs. Daily activity ends between 1555 and 1728 hours.

Coluber is often active at warmer ATs than other snakes. The authors have caught them prowling about with CTs over 32°C when other species of snakes had taken shelter. Clarke (1958) found active Kansas racers at ATs of 5–30°C; and Tucker (2000) reported that the average AT and ST when first-year *Coluber* were captured in Illinois were 28 (8–34) °C and 21 (3.0–30.8) °C, respectively. CT$_{max}$ of a Florida *C. c. priapus* was 43–45°C (Bogert and Cowles 1947). CTs of active racers are usually 25–38°C, but *Coluber* seem to prefer ATs of 22–33°C. Kitchell (1969) reported that racers on a thermal gradient chose temperatures of 22.4–37.4°C. In Michigan, moving racers had BTs of 27.2–36.8°C; those under cover on cool days had BTs of 21.0–23.4 (mean, 22.2) °C, and they emerged or retreated at BTs of 17.4–19.6 (mean, 17.7) °C (Rosen 1991b).

Racers are good climbers; the authors have seen them as high as 10 m in trees. They are fond of basking and can often be seen stretched out on the branches of some shrub or on a log; basking on the branches of low trees is very common on hammocks in the Florida Everglades. Basking racers in Michigan had BTs of 27.0–31.7 (mean, 29.2) °C (Rosen 1991b). *Coluber* is also a good swimmer and takes readily to water.

A rather large home range is used, but its extent depends on the habitat and sex. Fitch (1963a) reported Kansas males had average home ranges of about 10.5 ha, while females averaged 9.7 ha. Many individuals made movements of 600 m to 1 km, and some shifted their home ranges over time. Mean distance moved per day was 33.8 (0–454) m (males averaged 29.6 m; females, 41.4 m) (Fitch 1999; Fitch and Shirer 1971). The longest movement between captures was 1.2 km, after a lapse of four years (Fitch 1963a). Maryland racers moved 91 m to 1.8 km for one day and two years (Stickel and Cope 1947). Large adults in Michigan moved an average of 424 m between recaptures, yearlings 188 m, and small juveniles 62 m; males moved 40–470 (mean, 230) m, females 0–400 (mean, 134) m (Rosen 1991b). Mean movement on the home range in Utah was 31 m/day; females had a mean home range of 0.4 ha (that of nongravid females was 1.4 ha) (Brown and Parker 1976). South Carolina racers moved an average of 104 m/day during the summer within home ranges averaging 12.2 (5.3–20.5) ha (Plummer and Congdon 1994). In summer, some Virginia racers remain within 100 m of a specific retreat to which they apparently return each afternoon (C. Ernst, pers. obs.).

Many long trips are associated with migrations to/from distant hibernacula—Michigan *Coluber* may disperse up to 2.2 km from hibernacula (Rosen 1991b); olfaction seems to be the guiding sense (Brown and Parker 1976). Recoveries of Utah *Coluber* indicate they range about 250 m or more from a hibernaculum (Hirth et al. 1969), but at two other Utah hibernacula the maximum dispersal distances were 1.6 and 1.8 km, with a geometric mean for dispersal of 383 m (males dispersed a mean distance of 383 m, females 663 m) and a mean travel rate for females of 99 m/day (Brown and Parker 1976). Hibernacula may be 342 m from the summer home range in Kansas (Fitch 1999).

Males engage in combat behavior in the spring (McCauley 1945).

REPRODUCTION. Males mature in 11 months (Rosen 1991b) to two years (Fitch 1999) at TBLs of 50–68 cm (Stebbins 1985; Wright and Wright 1957) or SVLs of 46–50 cm (Fitch 1999; Rosen 1991b), but do not mate until at least their second spring. Females mature in two to three years (Fitch 1999; Rosen 1991b) at TBLs of 50–71 cm (Stebbins 1985; Wright and Wright 1957) or a SVL of 60 mm in Kansas (Fitch 1999). The various-sized subspecies possibly mature at different lengths.

Upon emergence from hibernation, the male seminiferous tubules are filled with Sertoli synctium but contain few germ cells. Spermatogonia proliferate in May and June, and by early July primary spermatocytes dominate. The first spermatozoa are present in early August, and by late October spermiogenesis is essentially over, and mature sperm have moved to the vas deferens and epididymides (Fitch 1963a). In females, vitellogenesis occurs in April–mid-June; follicles enlarge rapidly and are usually ovulated from late May through June. Callard and Leathem (1967) found a biphased pattern in ovarian weight; it was greater in March and June than in April or July. Female reproduction is annual, with a single clutch per year. Clutch size increases with the female's age and TBL (Fitch 1999); the longer subspecies generally produce larger clutches. RCMs range from 26.5 to 40.0 (Rosen 1991b; Seigel and Fitch 1984) and are strongly correlated to female length.

Courtship and mating occur from April through July, but Wright and Wright (1957) reported what may have been attempted mating in the fall in New York. Males use olfaction to find females (Lillywhite 1985), and several may simultaneously court the same female. When a female is found the male crawls alongside and examines her with his tongue. As he crawls onto her back, caudocephalic waves form along his body, and he aligns their two vents. The female raises her tail when receptive, and the male inserts a hemipenis, as the snakes entwine their bodies. The pair may remain still during copulation, or the female may become agitated and crawl around, dragging the attached male with her. After ejaculation, the male withdraws, and the female crawls quickly away (C. Ernst, pers. obs.).

The GP is 38–46 days (Velhagen and Savitzky 1998). Over most of the range, oviposition occurs from May or early June to early August, but Florida *Coluber* may nest as early as March or April (Gillingham 1976; Iverson 1978; Van Hyning 1931). The eggs are laid in nests dug in loose soil (particularly sand), placed in mammal burrows, rotting logs and stumps, old sawdust piles, compost heaps, and the mulch of flower beds; under large rocks or loose bark; or under human debris. Individual nesting is most common, but some nests may be communally shared year after year (Foley 1971; Swain and Smith 1978); communal nests also may be shared with other species (Nussbaum et al. 1983; Parker and Brown 1972; Porchuk and Brooks 1995).

Clutches contain 1 (Wright and Wright 1957) to 36 (Mitchell 1994) eggs and, for the entire species, average 13.6 eggs—some of the shorter subspecies usually lay less than 10 eggs per clutch, and some large subspecies commonly lay 20 or more eggs per clutch. The white, elliptical, nonadherent eggs have leathery, granular shells. One hundred and one eggs were 20.0–50.0 (mean, 33.7) mm long and 10.0–28.6 (mean, 19.1) mm wide; 45 eggs weighed 5.5–10.8 (mean, 7.1) g. Incubation takes 40–97 (mean, 64; n = 23) days and is temperature dependent.

Hatching occurs as early as June in Florida, but usually from late July–early November elsewhere. Hatchlings are 15.2–35.5 (mean, 24.3; n = 88) cm long and weigh 3.2–12.0 (mean, 5.6; n = 48) g; although the young of each subspecies differ somewhat, each has a dorsal row of 45–75 dark gray, brown, or reddish brown blotches on a lighter gray or brown ground color, and a series of small dark spots on the sides and venter. All traces of the blotches and spots gradually disappear as these patterns are replaced by the dark adult pigmentation, and they usually disappear completely when the snake reaches 70–80 cm TBL.

GROWTH AND LONGEVITY. Growth rates decline with age, but females grow faster and to greater lengths than males. Some subspecies grow faster and larger than others. Fitch (1999) reported the following SVLs by age and sex for Kansas *C. c. flaviventris*: year 1—males 23.8–58.8 cm, females 22.7–55.3 cm; year 2—males 52.5–69.0 cm, females 58.1–86.0 cm; year 3—males 53.8–87.2 cm, females 69.0–98.0 cm; year 4—males 67.6–88.0 cm, females 78.6–104.0 cm; year 5—males 71.5–90.0 cm, females 87.3–111.1 cm; year 6—males 77.0–90.2 cm, females 86.6–100.5 cm; year 7—males 81.3–90.0 cm, females 90.6–103.0 cm; year 8—males 84.5–90.2 cm, females 90.0–108.0 cm; year 9—males 90.0–91.2 cm, females 99.5–118.0

cm; and years 10+—males 92.6–111.0 cm, females 105.2–112.3 cm. SVLs of Michigan *C. c. foxii* measured by Rosen (1991b) were as follows: year 1—42.5–75.0 cm; years 1–2 and 2+—75.1–80.0 cm; they grew approximately 27.9 cm the first year, 23.7 cm between years 1 and 2, and 10.6 cm in their third year. Illinois first-year *C. c. foxii* had 19.2–37.4 cm SVLs and 3.0–17.0 g body masses (Tucker 2000). Mean SVLs of Utah *C. c. mormon* by age and sex were as follows: year 1—males 36.5cm, females 43.0 cm; year 2—males 48.6 cm, females 52.4 cm; year 3—males 52.0 cm, females 57.5 cm; year 4—males 54.1 cm, females 59.9 cm; year 5—males 56.4 cm, females 62.0 cm; year 6—males 57.3 cm, females 63.3 cm; and year 7—males 58.4 cm (Brown and Parker 1984).

No captive longevity data are available, but wild individuals 10 years or older are known (Fitch 1999; Harding 1997).

DIET AND FEEDING HABITS. Contrary to its specific name, *C. constrictor* does not constrict. Prey is detected by smell (Cooper et al. 2000) or sight (Nussbaum et al., 1983, reported it can detect crickets from 50 m away and is capable of seeing larger prey at greater distances). The racer crawls rapidly after prey and seizes it with its mouth. Small animals are swallowed alive, but larger prey may be held on the ground with the body and then chewed until dead before swallowing. Many of the insects and mammals commonly eaten are economically undesirable, so the racer should be regarded as beneficial to farmers.

The racer has a broad appetite, eating many different kinds of animals, apparently opportunistically as they become available: mammals—shrews (*Blarina brevidauda, B. hylophaga, Cryptotis parva, Sorex* sp.), bats (*Myotis evotis*), moles (*Scalopus aquaticus*), cottontails (*Sylvilagus floridanus*), squirrels (*Glaucomys volans, Tamias striatus*), lemmings and voles (*Clethrionomys gapperi, Microtus californicus, M. ochrogaster, M. pennsylvanicus, M. pinetorum, Synaptomys cooperi*), mice (*Mus musculus, Peromyscus leucopus, P. maniculatus, Ochrotomys nuttalli, Reithrodontomys flavescens, R. megalotis, R. montanus*), jumping mice (*Zapus hudsonius*), rats (*Neotoma floridana, Oryzomys palustris, Rattus norvegicus*), and small weasels (*Mustela* sp.); birds (and eggs) (*Agelaius phoeniceus, Cardinalis cardinalis, Pipilo erythrophthalmus, Progne subis, Sturnella magna, Turdus migratorius, Vireo griseus,* and *varius sparrows and warblers); reptiles—small turtles (and eggs) (Chrysemys picta, Malaclemys terrapin, Terrapene carolina),* lizards (and eggs) *(Anolis carolinensis, Cnemidophorus sexlineatus, Crotaphytus collaris, Eumeces egregius, E. fasciatus, E. inexpectatus, E. laticeps, E. obsoletus, E. skiltonianus, Gerrhonotus multicarinatus, Holbrookia maculata, Ophisaurus attenuatus, O. mimicus, O. ventralis, Phyrnosoma* sp., *Sceloporus graciosus, S. occidentalis, S. olivaceus, S. undulatus, Scincella lateralis),* and snakes (and skins) *(Agkistrodon contortrix, Carphophis amoenus, Coluber constrictor, Crotalus horridus, C. viridis, Diadophis punctatus, Elaphe obsoleta, Heterodon platirhinos, Lampropeltis getula, Liochlorophis vernalis, Masticophis flagellum, Nerodia sipedon, Opheodrys aestivus, Regina alleni, Rhadinaea flavilata, Sistrurus miliarius, Storeria dekayi, S. occipitomaculata, Tantilla coronata, Thamnophis radix, T. sauritus, T. sirtalis, Tropidoclonion lineatum, Virginia striatula, V. valeriae);* amphibians—salamanders *(Desmognathus fuscus)* and anurans *(Acris crepitans, Bufo terrestris, Gastrophryne carolinensis, Hyla chrysocelis, H. cinerea, H. femoralis, H. versicolor, Pseudacris brimleyi, P. crucifer, P. nigrita, Rana blairi, R. catesbeiana, R. clamitans, R. palustris, R. pipiens, R. sphenocephala, R. sylvatica);* fish eggs *(Ctenopharyngodon idella);* insects *(Coleoptera, Homoptera, Hymenoptera, Lepidoptera* [larvae], *Orthoptera);* and spiders (Anderson 1965; Blair 1960; Brown 1979a; Clark 1949; Cook and Aldridge 1984; Ernst et al. 1997; Fitch 1963a, 1999; Hamilton and Pollack 1956; Hammerson 1987; Hayes 1985a; Hoffman 1945; Iverson 1975; Klemens 1993; Klauber 1972; Klimstra 1959c; Marr 1944; Mattlin 1946; McCauley 1945; McIntosh and Gregory 1976; Mitchell 1994; Moler 1992; O'Brien 1998; Palmer and Braswell 1995; Plummer 1990b; Printiss 1994; Surface 1906; Tucker 2000; Uhler et al. 1939; Webb 1970; Wright and Bishop 1915). Young racers eat insects, small anurans, small lizards and snakes, and young mice; adults prey on larger prey—birds and their eggs and adult lizards, snakes, and mammals.

Several studies have commented on the percentage of occurrence of various prey in racer stomachs. In Virginia, Uhler et al. (1939) found the following prey by volume: snakes 26%, birds 18%, shrews 12%, caterpillars and moths 10%, frogs 9%, moles and lizards 6%, squirrels 5%, and other insects and arthropods 5%. Hamilton and Pollack (1956) recorded food percentages of occurrence in Georgia racers: lizards 65%, snakes 28%, amphibians 9%, mammals 3.5%, and insects 1.7%. In Illinois, Klimstra (1959c) noted the following percentages of occurrence: insects 48%, mammals 43.5%, birds 16.5%, amphibians 13%, and reptiles 12%. In Kansas, Fitch (1963a) found insects in 77% of racer stomachs, mammals in 15%, and snakes in 5%; and in North Carolina, Brown (1979a) found that reptiles, mammals, and insects made up 80% of prey items. The above indicates that the various subspecies have different prey preferences. Also, both Klimstra (1959b) and Fitch (1963a) observed seasonal shifts in prey preference and volume that apparently reflect the availability of various prey in different seasons.

PREDATORS AND DEFENSE. Racers have many natural enemies. Known predators are shrews *(Blarina hylophaga, Cryptotis parva),* opossum *(Didelphis virginianus),* mice *(Peromyscus leucopus, P. maniculatus, Reithrodontomys megalotis),* badger *(Taxidea taxus),* skunk *(Mephitis mephitis),* domestic cat *(Felis catus),* bobcat *(Lynx rufus),* eagles *(Aquila chrysaetos, Haliaeetus leucocephalus),* hawks *(Buteo albicaudatus, B. jamaicensis, B. lineatus, B. platypterus, B. regalis, B. swainsoni, Buteogallus anthracinus, Circus cyanus),* kestrels *(Falco sparverius),* owls *(Bubo virginianus, Tyto alba),* loggerhead shrikes *(Lanius ludovicianus),* roadrunners *(Geococcyx californianus),* crows *(Corvus brachyrhynchos),* snakes *(Agkistrodon contortrix, Coluber constrictor, Crotalus horridus, Elaphe obsoleta, Lampropeltus calligaster, L. getula),* glass lizards *(Ophisaurus attenuatus),* and ground beetles *(Calosoma* sp.) (Ernst and Barbour 1989; Fitch 1963a; Greene 1984; Hamilton and Pollack 1956; Jackson 1971; MacArtney and Weichel 1993; Mitchell and Beck 1992; Palmer and Braswell 1995; Ross 1989; Tyler 1991; Webb 1970). Owens (1949b) reported a captive tarantula ate hatchling racers; possibly wild spiders take some juveniles.

Adult racers have irascible tempers, and if prevented from fleeing (their most important defense), quickly coil, vibrate the tail, strike, and bite viciously. They may be very aggressive and even advance on one when thoroughly aroused. When handled and not able to bite, they will spray musk. If aggression does not drive off an enemy, some racers will play dead (Lynch 1978). The degree of defensive behavior is temperature dependent (Keogh and DeSerto 1994).

Racers normally remain nervous and high strung and make poor captives; many refuse to eat anything but their keeper's hands.

POPULATIONS. In areas with suitable habitat and abundant prey, racers are still abundant, but the density and number of individuals vary from site to site. At a northern Virginia wildlife refuge, *C. c. constrictor* occurs in a density of 1–3 adults/ha (Ernst et al. 1997), and elsewhere in the state it composes 4.5–10.4% of the total snake community (Mitchell 1994). During Fitch's (1992) studies at three Kansas sites, *C. c. flaviventris* had densities of 4.7–6.9 adults/ha. At a site in the Everglades, *C. c. paludicola* made up 11.6% (208) of the 1,782 snakes observed or collected by Dalrymple et al. (1991) from 1984 through 1986. In contrast, Clark (1949) recorded only 50 (2.4%) *C. c. anthicus* in a sample of 2,083 snakes from the uplands of Louisiana, and at a mixed pine-hardwood forest in eastern Texas, racers only made up 2.9% of the total snake

population (Ford et al. 1991). At hibernacula in Utah, *C. c. mormon* varied from 127 to 139 individuals (Parker and Brown 1973; Woodbury 1951), but only 23 occupied a hibernaculum in Saskatchewan (MacArtney and Weichel 1993). Unfortunately, populations of racers in many states have been drastically reduced by automobiles, pesticides, and widespread habitat destruction. The species is considered endangered in Maine, and *C. c. etheridgei* is listed as a species of special concern in Louisiana.

The sex ratio at hatching in Kansas favors males almost 2:1, but later in life females make up about 67% of the population (Fitch 1999). Annual survivorship of first-year *C. c. mormon* in Utah is only 15–20%, but adult survivorship is about 78% (Brown and Parker 1982).

REMARKS. *Masticophis* is the closest relative of North American *Coluber* (Dowling et al. 1996; Lopez and Maxson 1996). The genus *Coluber* and *C. constrictor* were reviewed by Wilson (1978, 1986).

Coniophanes imperialis (Baird 1859) | Regal Black-striped Snake

RECOGNITION. This small (to 50.8 cm TBL), slender, long-tailed, opisthoglyphous snake is mildly venomous. Its ground color is light brown, and three black, purplish gray, dull bluish gray, or dark brown longitudinal stripes are present on the body. The middorsal stripe is broad (one scale plus two half-scales); the two lateral stripes occur on the second half of the fourth dorsal scale row. The head is black with a pinkish to cream or white stripe extending from the snout through the dorsal orbit to the rear of the head. The venter is red to orange, the chin light brown. Body scales are smooth and pitless, with 19 rows at midbody. Ventral scutes total 118–143, subcaudals 67–94, and the anal plate is divided. Diagnostic lateral head scales are 2 nasals, 1 loreal, 1 preocular, 2 (3) postoculars, 1 + 2 temporals, 8 (7–9) supralabials, and 9 infralabials. The long, slender, deeply bifurcate hemipenis has a single sulcus spermaticus, lacks spines, and is calyculate but not capitate. Each maxilla has 10–15 teeth; the most posterior 1–2 teeth are enlarged and grooved. Sexual dimorphism has not been described.

GEOGRAPHIC VARIATION. Three subspecies are recognized, but only *Coniophanes imperialis imperialis* (Baird 1859), the regal black-striped snake, described above, reaches Texas.

Regal black-striped snake, *Coniophanes imperialis*. (Photograph by R. D. Bartlett)

Distribution of *Coniophanes imperialis*.

CONFUSING SPECIES. Other striped snakes within the range of *C. imperialis (Masticophis, Salvadora, Thamnophis)* have white, cream, yellow, or reddish stripes.

KARYOTYPE AND FOSSIL RECORD. Unknown.

DISTRIBUTION. The Texas range only includes Cameron, Hidalgo, and Willacy counties in the extreme south. In Mexico, this snake ranges south to Vera Cruz.

HABITAT. Areas with sandy soil and abundant surface hiding places (rocks, plant debris, logs) seem the natural habitat, but with suburban sprawl this snake is now found under trash and other materials lying on the ground about buildings or in vacant lots. It is also prone to foraging in the vegetation along canal banks and will take refuge in deep cracks when the soil dries out (Conant and Collins 1998). Moisture is a critical ingredient of the habitat. Beimler (in Conant 1955) reported that wild *C. imperialis* select moist conditions, ascending into piles of dead cactus when they are wet, but remaining beneath them when the rest of the pile is dry. Conant (1955) kept a captive in a pint jar. After each weekly cleaning the jar was left wet, and a damp crumpled paper towel was placed in the bottom with two other dry towels on top. The bottom towel re-

mained quite wet, the middle one damp, and that on top dry. When returned to the jar, the snake remained near the top of the towels, but retreated farther down during the week as the top two towels dried until it was at or near the bottom. Conant seldom saw the snake drink, although it was given water on numerous occasions.

BEHAVIOR. *C. imperialis* is secretive and seems rare, more so since much of its Texas habitat has been disturbed or destroyed. Brown (1937) found it active as early as March, and it probably is more active in the spring and fall than in summer. Most of the day is spent under some object or burrowed into loose sand; foraging usually occurs from late evening into the night, or early in the morning. It sometimes basks in the spring and fall.

REPRODUCTION. Few data are available on its reproductive habits. It is oviparous, usually laying clutches of 3–5 eggs in Texas (Brown 1937; Rossi and Rossi 1999b; Tennant 1984, 1985; Werler 1949), although Alvarez del Toro (1960) reported as many as 10 eggs per clutch in Mexico. The eggs are elongated (18.0–32.5 × 8–13 mm) with smooth, leathery, nonadhesive shells. Three eggs, laid by a female kept by Rossi and Rossi (1999b), averaged 1.3 g, and the total clutch mass was 4 g. Ovipositions have occurred from early May into late June (Rossi and Rossi 1999b; Tennant 1984); the number of clutches laid per year is unknown. The IP is 40–53 days (Rossi and Rossi 1999b; Tennant 1984). Hatchlings have TBLs of 14.0–16.5 cm.

GROWTH AND LONGEVITY. Unknown.

DIET AND FEEDING HABITS. Small anurans *(Bufo* sp., *Leptodactylus labialis, Syrrhophis cystignathoides)*, small lizards, and small snakes compose the natural diet (Brown 1937; Davis 1951; Tennant 1984, 1985); captives will accept small mice (Conant 1955), so possibly these are also eaten in the wild.

C. imperialis is an active hunter that seizes prey as soon as it is detected. The prey is usually worked to the back of the mouth where it is punctured by the enlarged, grooved teeth, allowing venom produced in serous Duvernoy's glands (Taub 1967) to enter the wounds and quickly immobilize the animal (Brown

1937). Swallowing is begun almost immediately after an animal is seized.

PREDATORS AND DEFENSE. No records of predation exist, but surely the species is eaten by large predatory snakes, birds, and mammals. When disturbed, *C. imperialis* turns the colorful underside of its tail upward and elevates, waves, and curls it to mimic a threatening head. Such behavior may divert a would-be predator's attention from the real head and upper body, which remain lowered during the tail display. Some individuals have incomplete tails that may have resulted from a predatory attack (Brown 1937). When handled, small individuals sometimes bite, but adults usually do not (Brown 1939).

POPULATIONS. Before 1945, *C. imperialis* was not uncommon, but conversion of its natural scrub habitat for agriculture has since destroyed many individuals and reduced its populations (Raun 1965; Tennant 1984). Where it still occurs, it seems rare, but this may be due to its secretive nature. Irwin (1995) recently observed several wild individuals in a short time period and considers it a "moderately common species in no immediate danger of being extirpated." Nevertheless, *C. imperialis* is listed as threatened and protected by the state of Texas.

REMARKS. Venom of *C. imperialis* may cause a strong reaction in humans (McKinistry 1978). Brown (1939) was accidentally bitten between fingers two and three of his left hand by a small snake, and experienced an itching, burning sensation at the site of the bite. Shortly, the two fingers became numb, swollen, and discolored red; they remained swollen for three days, although all pain had subsided. Later Brown allowed another, larger *C. imperialis* to bite him between fingers one and two of the same hand. The snake's rear fangs were only 2.5 mm long, but could be felt penetrating the skin. Although the snake attempted to chew, the fangs only pierced the skin once. Immediately, Brown experienced a sharp pain resembling a bee sting, and within an hour the pain had extended up the left arm to his elbow. The hand gradually became numb, swollen, and practically useless. The area at the bite site turned red, a small amount of amber liquid seeped from the fang punctures, and the hand perspired profusely. Five hours after the bite, the pain decreased and remained only in the swollen, discolored hand. All general pain was gone in 24 hours, but the wound was tender. After three days some swelling and lameness still existed. All symptoms, except some nervousness, disappeared in three weeks. The snakes that bit Brown were small to average size, so envenomation by a large individual could be serious.

Contia tenuis (Baird and Girard 1852b) | Sharp-tailed Snake

RECOGNITION. This small (TBL to 48.3 cm) northwestern snake has a short, tapered tail with a pointed terminal scale. The body is gray to reddish brown, and gray individuals usually have pink to red pigment on the top of the tail. Each dorsal scale is black bordered. A pale yellow to red stripe may occur on each side of the body; a series of black dots lies below the stripe, and below the stripe the body is darker than above it. The small head is dorsally flattened, rounded anteriorly, and distinct from the neck. The pupil is round. Dorsally, the head is olive brown to dark gray or black, and a dark mask begins on the side of the snout and passes rearward through the orbit to the neck. The rostral scale and supralabials often bear

white pigment. On the white venter, the anterior edge of each ventral scute is black, presenting a banded pattern. Dorsal body scales are smooth and pitless and occur in 15 rows along the length of the body. Beneath are 147–186 ventrals, 27–57 subcaudals, and a divided anal plate. Lateral head scales include 1–2 nasals (which may be whole, partially divided, or totally divided), 1 loreal, 1 (rarely 2) preocular(s), 2 (1) postoculars, 1 + 1–2 temporals, 7 (6) supralabials, and 7 infralabials. The anterior pair of chin shields is much larger than those that follow. The slightly bilobed hemipenis has a forked sulcus spermaticus, longitudinal rows of small spines (usually four to six per row) along the main shaft, larger spines at its base, small

Sharp-tailed snake, *Contia tenuis*; Kittitas County, Washington. (Photograph by William Leonard)

spines in the fork between the lobes, and four to five rows of calyxes near the tip of each short lobe. Each maxilla has 7–11 rather long teeth.

Few to no external characters separate the sexes, although in males the base of the tail may be swollen just behind the anal vent.

GEOGRAPHIC VARIATION. No subspecies are known, but considerable variation in the numbers of ventrals and subcaudals and in TL occur in Oregon (Hoyer et al. 2000); variation in the northernmost populations in Washington and British Columbia is practically unknown due to few recorded specimens (Nussbaum et al. 1983).

CONFUSING SPECIES. In its range, this snake can only be confused with melanistic ring-necked snakes (*Diadophis punctatus*), but these snakes have two to three preoculars and dark flecks on the venter.

KARYOTYPE. The diploid compliment is 36 chromosomes with 16 macrochromosomes and 20 microchromosomes (Bury et al. 1970; Trinco and Smith 1972). There is a distinct difference in size between macrochromosome pairs two and three.

FOSSIL RECORD. No fossils have been discovered.

DISTRIBUTION. *C. tenuis* ranges from the Gulf Islands and southeastern coast of Vancouver Island, British Columbia, and possibly also on the mainland from McGillary Lake near Chase in the southern interior of British Columbia (see Leonard and Ovaska 1998; Tanner 1967) south to San Luis Obispo and Tulare counties, California. North of northern California the snake occurs in isolated populations.

HABITAT. *C. tenuis* normally lives in moist habitats, sometimes with over 250 cm rain per year (Pimental 1958), and at elevations from near sea level to between 600 and 2,000 m (Leonard and Ovaska 1998). Oak-pine woodlands (especially the edges) and coniferous (*Sequoia*) forests seem preferred, especially if a stream flows through them and there are abundant logs and rocks on the ground surface, but it has also been found in grasslands, open meadows, pastures, scattered chaparral, and talus slopes, and even in vacant lots and back yards in city suburbs (Cook 1960). At the northern part of the range, relatively open, south-facing rocky slopes bordered by woods are important habitat features (Engelstoft and Ovaska 2000).

BEHAVIOR. Across its range, *C. tenuis* is usually active from February to December. However, sightings have occurred in every month in Oregon, with peaks in March–May and October–early November (Hoyer et al. 2000), and in central California it is most active from March to June, with a second peak in September and October, but in Washington and British Columbia it is also active over the warm months of July and August (Carl 1960). July and August in the south are spent within logs or under rocks. Cook (1960) found one Oregon *C. tenuis* underground, tightly coiled in a moist earthen cell, in August; the same summer he found another that was unearthed by a road grader. Winter individuals have been found under the moist

Distribution of *Contia tenuis.*

bark of oak trees and under pine logs (Banta and Morafka 1968), but most probably crawl into rotting logs, or possibly retreat underground into rodent burrows. Some *C. tenuis* hibernate underground at depths deeper than 20–30 cm (Engelstoft et al. 1999).

    C. tenuis is secretive, spending most of the day within logs, under the bark of trees, under rocks, or in rodent burrows. Surface activity is mostly nocturnal. Activity occurs at lower BTs than in most snakes, 10–17°C in the Willamette Valley (Nussbaum et al. 1983) and 11–16°C in February in California (Stebbins 1954). Brattstrom (1965) collected four *C. tenuis* near Corvallis, Oregon, on 7 June at 1000 hours, under rocks, that had BTs of 16.0–21.8 (mean, 19.5) °C when the AT was 16.3–18.5°C and the ST 16.7–18.0°C. He thought the snakes might have basked in semisun, near the rocks under which they were found, to raise their BTs above ET. High humidity is another important factor determining the snake's activity pattern, perhaps because its chief prey, slugs, are only active under such conditions, but probably also because of the dehydration problems faced by such a small-bodied animal.

    Dimensions of the home range have not been determined, but a female moved 44 m the first night it was followed, mostly under the ground surface, and spent five days within a log and an adjacent stump and three more days under a rock (Englestoft et al. 1999). Another moved 93 m between its farthest capture points. Carl (1960) reported that while climbing a slope the sharp terminal tail spine is brought forward and used as a fulcrum to help push the body up the in-

cline. *C. tenuis* will sometimes ascend trunks of trees or into shrubs as high as 2–3 m (Zweifel, in Cook 1960).

REPRODUCTION. Limited reproductive data are available. Stebbins (1985) gives 20 cm as the minimum adult size, but there has been no histological study to support this. The male sexual cycle is unknown; Storm (in Cook 1960) found some small ovarian follicles in Oregon females in June, August, and November, and preserved females in the University of California collection had 5 mm follicles in March, 10 mm follicles in April, 14 mm follicles in June, and 7 mm follicles in November (Cook 1960). Some females have oviductal eggs in June, and others have oviposited in June and July. Courtship and mating behaviors have not been observed, but the snake probably mates in the spring.

    Nesting has occurred from 10 June to 25 July. Brodie et al. (1969) found 43 eggs in natural rock outcrops in a small draw on an unshaded, grass-covered, southern Oregon slope. Most clutches were in outcrop cracks with little soil 15–30 cm below ground level, but one clutch was in a soil cavity within 7.5 cm of a nest of *Pituophis catenifer,* and another was in a bunch of grass roots 15 cm below the ground surface. Probably in more forested habitats, eggs are laid within or under rotting logs.

    Most clutches contain two to five (mean, 3.6; n = 8) eggs. Nussbaum et al. (1983) consider bunches of eight to nine eggs multiple deposits of two or more females. The elongated, white to cream eggs are 19.7–46.0 (mean, 28.7; n = 6) mm long and 6.4–7.2 (mean, 6.8; n = 6) mm wide and weigh about 0.8 g.

The shell is parchmentlike; Cook (1960) reported small rough longitudinal striations on the shell that were not present on eggs examined by Brodie et al. (1969).

The natural IP is unknown, but a full-term egg was found on 19 October, and a clutch hatched 23 October (Brodie et al. 1969; Stebbins 1954), so probably hatchlings emerge in September and October. They are reddish brown to gray brown dorsally with narrow dark stripes along the sides, have the adult ventral pattern, are 8.9–10.5 (mean, 10.3; n = 9) cm long, and weigh 0.4–0.6 g (n = 3).

GROWTH AND LONGEVITY. No data have been reported.

DIET AND FEEDING HABITS. Apparently, only small slugs and their eggs are eaten (Cook 1960; Darling 1947; Stebbins 1985; Zweifel 1954). Woodin (in Cook 1960) found slugs in 9 (13.4%) of 67 Contia stomachs he examined, and Darling (1947) found one to five slugs in 6 (26.1%) of 23 snakes. In both cases, slugs were the only prey found. The three species of small slugs usually present in its range belong to the introduced European genus Arion, but what the snake ate prior to its introduction 200–300 years ago is unknown (Cook 1960). Perhaps it consumed juveniles of the large banana slug (Ariolimax). Stebbins (1954) thought Contia probably also consumes earthworms, insects and other arthropods, and the salamanders (Batrachoseps, young Aneides) commonly found with it. Congdon et al. (1982) calculated the caloric values in milligrams (dry mass) for the body (5.005) and eggs (6.001) of C. tenuis, and their diet must support these material demands.

Its teeth seem modified for a slug diet. Except for the posterior pterygoid teeth, each tooth is longer than the depth of the bones bearing it (Stickel 1951). Such long recurved teeth seem specialized for grasping and holding slimy prey, allowing the snake to overcome a slug that, in a contracted state, may have a diameter greater than its head (Zweifel 1954).

PREDATORS AND DEFENSE. Predators of C. tenuis include the western toad (Bufo boreas), brook trout (Salvelinus fontinalis) (Hansen and Thomason 1991), and possibly ring-necked snake (Diadophis punctatus); birds also eat it (Ovaska and Engelstoft 1999; Shaw and Campbell 1974).

When first discovered, Contia may conceal its head beneath its body coils (Ovaska and Engelstoft 1999), remain rigid in a ball or pretzel-like coil, lie venter up, or flatten its mid- and lower body against the ground and elevate its anterior body into an S-shaped coil while facing and bluffing strikes (Leonard and Stebbins 1999). If handled, it will thrash about, release musk, and push the pointed terminal tail scale against the skin.

POPULATIONS. C. tenuis is locally common and lives in groups in suitable habitat—8–40 individuals have been found together at various sites and times (Cook 1960; Darling 1947; Engelstoft and Ovaska 2000; Leonard et al. 1996; Slevin, in Cook 1960). It comprised 89 (4.2%) of 2,138 snakes collected at five sites on the Gulf Islands from March through November 1997 (Engelstoft and Ovaska 2000).

REMARKS. The species was reviewed by Leonard and Ovaska (1998).

Diadophis punctatus (Linnaeus 1766) | Ring-necked Snake

RECOGNITION. This is a generally small (TBL to 85.7 cm, but most are smaller than 50 cm), olive, greenish gray, blue black, or black snake with a dark head and a cream, yellow or orange red neck band. The neck band is missing in some New Mexico populations, those from the Florida Keys, and occasionally in individuals from other parts of the range. The venter is yellow to orange or orange red and may be variously spotted or lack spots. Dorsal body scales are generally smooth (but see below) with an apical pit and occur in 13–17 anterior rows, 14–17 midbody rows, and 13–15 posterior rows. Beneath are 126–239 ventrals, 30–79 subcaudals, and a divided anal plate. On each side of the head are 2 nasals, 1 loreal, 2 (1–3,

Southern ring-necked snake, *Diadophis punctatus punctatus*; Collier County, Florida. (Photograph by Carl H. Ernst)

Northern ring-necked snake, *Diadophis punctatus edwardsii*; Jessamine County, Kentucky. (Photograph by Roger W. Barbour)

Northwestern ring-necked snake, *Diadophis punctatus occidentalis*; Washington. (Photograph by James H. Harding)

rarely 0) preoculars, 2 (1–4) postoculars, 1 (rarely 2) + 1 (rarely 2) + 2 temporals, 7–8 (6–9) supra- and infralabials. Body coloration, condition of the neck band, and scale counts are variable across the range (see GEOGRAPHIC VARIATION). The shallowly bilobed, single hemipenis has its head slightly basally constricted and has a distally forked sulcus spermaticus; the shaft is covered with spines. Each maxilla has 9–21 (mean, 13.2) teeth; the anterior teeth are slender and erect and are separated by a diastema from two larger, backward pointed, grooveless, posterior teeth.

Males have 126–225 ventrals, 37–79 subcaudals, and TLs 15–27 (mean, 21) % of TBL; females have 134–239 ventrals, 30–67 subcaudals, and TLs 10–25 (mean, 17) % of TBL. Some adult males have ridges on the body scales near the anal vent (Blanchard 1931, 1942).

GEOGRAPHIC VARIATION. All 12 subspecies occur in the United States and southeastern Canada; the above description is a composite of these. *D. p. punctatus* (Linnaeus 1766), the southern ring-necked snake, ranges from southeastern Virginia south through peninsular Florida and southwest to southeastern Alabama. It has an incomplete neck band, a medial row of large black ventral spots, usually 8 supralabials, normally 15 anterior scale rows, less than 175 ventrals, and fewer than 73 subcaudals (TBL to 48.2 cm). *D. p. acricus* Paulson 1966, the Key ring-necked snake, is known only from Big Pine Key, Florida. It has no neck ring, a medial row of black ventral half-moons, usually 8 supralabials, normally 15 anterior scale rows, less than 140 ventrals, and no more than 53 subcaudals (TBL to 28.9 cm). *D. p. amabilis* Baird and Girard 1853, the Pacific ring-necked snake, occurs from just north of San Francisco Bay south to Monterey on the California coast. It has a complete neck band, many small black ventral spots, ventral color extending to dorsal body scale rows 0.5–1.5, usually 7 supralabials, 15 anterior scale rows, fewer than 215 ventrals, and no more than 70 subcaudals (TBL to 53.2 cm). *D. p. arnyi* Kennicott 1859a, the prairie ring-necked snake, is found from southeastern Minnesota and southeastern South Dakota south to south-central Texas; although most of its range is west of the Mississippi River, it also occurs in southwestern Wisconsin and western Illinois. It has the neck band occasionally broken, scattered, black ventral spots, usually 7 supralabials, normally 17 anterior scale rows, up to 185 ventrals, and to about 52 subcaudals (TBL to 47.7 cm). *D. p. edwardsii* (Merrem 1820), the northern ring-necked snake, occurs from New Brunswick, Nova Scotia, southern Quebec, Ontario, Michigan, Wisconsin, and northeastern Minnesota south through western Virginia, western North Carolina, northern Georgia, and northeastern Alabama. It has a complete neck band, no dark ventral spots, usually 8 supralabials, normally 15 anterior scale rows, up to 170 ventrals, and fewer than 70 subcaudals (TBL to 70.6 cm). *D. p. modestus* Bocourt 1886, the San Bernardino ring-necked snake, inhabits southern coastal California. It has a complete neck band, prominent black ventral spots, ventral color only reaching the first row of dorsal body scales, usually 7 supralabials, 17 anterior body scale rows, fewer than 220 ventrals, and up to 75 subcaudals (TBL to 61 cm). *D. p. occidentalis* Blanchard 1923c, the northwestern ring-necked snake, ranges from southern Washington to northwestern coastal California, with isolated populations in south-central and southeastern Washington, northeastern Oregon, and western and south-central Idaho. It has a complete neck band, only a few dark ventral spots, a ventral collar extending onto 1.5–2.0 body scale rows, usually 7 supralabials, 15 anterior scale rows, fewer than 215 ventrals, and up to 70 subcaudals (TBL to 60 cm). *D. p. pulchellus* Baird and Girard 1853, the coral-bellied ring-necked snake, is found in the Central Valley of California. It has a complete neck band, no or only a few dark ventral spots, body scale rows one and two not flecked with black, 7 supralabials, 15 anterior scale rows, fewer than 210 ventrals, and up to 70 subcaudals (TBL to 47.5 cm). *D. p. regalis* Baird and Girard 1853, the regal ring-necked snake, is found in southeastern Idaho, central Utah, western Utah, eastern Nevada, north-central Arizona, western New Mexico, and the Rio Grande Valley of Texas south into Mexico. It has the neck band usually absent, irregular black ventral spots, the ventral pigment orange or red near the tail and extending onto body scale rows one and two, normally 7 supralabials, usually 17 anterior scale rows, fewer than 235 ventrals, and up to 68 subcaudals (TBL to 85.7 cm). *D. p. similis* Blanchard 1923c, the San Diego ring-necked snake, is only found in southwestern San Diego County, California, and northern Baja California. The neck band is complete, and it has the

Distribution of *Diadophis punctatus*.

venter usually dark spotted, the ventral color only reaching the first body scale row, 7 (8) supralabials, 15 anterior scale rows, up to 215 ventrals, and less than 70 subcaudals (TBL to 52.4 cm). *D. p. stictogenys* Cope 1861a, the Mississippi ring-necked snake, ranges from southern Illinois south in the Mississippi Valley to western Alabama and eastern Texas. It has a narrow (often interrupted) neck band, irregular clumps of dark spots clustered along the median of the venter, usually 7 supralabials, 15 anterior scale rows, fewer than 145 ventrals, and up to 52 subcaudals (TBL to 45.7 cm). *D. p. vandenburghi* Blanchard 1923c, the Monterey ring-necked snake, is found along the Monterey coast of California. Its neck band is complete, the few ventral dark spots are small, the ventral color extends onto body scale rows 1.5–2.0, and there are 7 (8) supralabials, 17 anterior scale rows, usually no more than 210 ventrals, and up to at least 75 subcaudals (TBL to 57.8 cm) present. Broad zones of intergradation occur where the ranges of the subspecies meet.

CONFUSING SPECIES. The brown and red-bellied snakes *(Storeria)* have keeled body scales, and lack ventral spots. Black-headed snakes *(Tantilla)* have white or tan neck bands and lack ventral spots and loreal scales. The sharp-tailed snake *(Contia tenuis)* lacks a neck band, has narrow black crossbars on a grayish venter, and has a terminal tail spine. Earth snakes *(Virginia)* have an unmarked venter and usually only five to six supralabials.

KARYOTYPE. Present are 16 macrochromosomes and 20 microchromosomes (Bury et al. 1970).

FOSSIL RECORD. Pleistocene fossils have been found in Irvingtonian deposits in a Maryland cave (Holman 1977b) and at Rancholabrean sites in Alabama (Holman et al. 1990), California (Brattstrom 1953c; Gilmore 1938; LaDuke 1991; Tihen 1962), Florida (Auffenberg 1963; Gut and Ray 1963; Holman 1959a), Georgia (Holman 1967), Kansas (Holman 1986a, 1987b; Preston 1979), Missouri (Saunders 1977), New Mexico (Van Devender and Worthington 1977), Pennsylvania (Guilday et al. 1964), Tennessee (Van Dam 1978), Texas (Hill 1971; Parmley 1990a; Parmley and Pfau 1997); Virginia (Guilday 1962; Holman 1986a), and West Virginia (Holman and Grady 1987).

DISTRIBUTION. *D. punctatus* ranges from New Brunswick and Nova Scotia west to Lake Superior and from southern Washington south to the Florida Keys and the Gulf Coast from the Florida Panhandle to Texas, New Mexico, Arizona, and southern California. Isolated populations occur in the Great Basin from southeastern Washington to northwestern Arizona, and in southeastern California. It also is found in northern Baja California and ranges south to San Luis Potosí in eastern Mexico.

HABITAT. In the east this snake lives in woodlands and is rarely found more than a few meters from the woods. In the Midwestern prairie regions, however, it has become an ecotonal species, living in both riparian woods and in shrubs between these woods and the prairie grasslands. In the southwest it may be found in low elevation chaparral, or at elevations from 980 m to over 2,000 m in piñon-juniper-ponderosa pine woods; and in the Northwest it is often found in oak-pine woods in rocky canyons. It is secretive and requires rocks, logs, stumps, loose bark on fallen trees, cow-pats, or human debris under which to hide. Also, these habitats are usually moist (either at the surface or beneath), at least in the spring and fall, and *Diadophis* seems to require moist soil to balance evaporative water loss from its body (Myers 1965; Clark 1967), for it becomes subterranean and estivates over hot, dry periods. Occasionally, it even enters moist caves.

Diadophis is quite social, and in proper habitat, aggregations are often found under rocks or within rotting logs; the authors have found as many as 10 at one time in such places.

BEHAVIOR. This snake may be active in every month in Florida (Myers 1965; Dalrymple et al. 1991) and some other southern states, especially during years with mild winters, but farther north it is active from late March or April to October or early November. Klauber (1928) recorded most individuals from February to July. In the mountains, *D. punctatus* may not become active until May and often retreats for the winter in September. Overall, it is most active in the spring, with a second lesser active period in September and October. The authors have found it extremely abundant during March and April in Florida. From mid-July through August it is seldom seen, although Palmer and Braswell (1995) reported 59% of North Carolina records are from June through August. Degenhardt et al. (1996) and Fitch (1975) reported average annual activity periods of 208 and 213 days for New Mexico and Kansas, respectively.

Some populations make spring and fall migrations from and to hibernacula (Blanchard et al. 1979), which include animal burrows, cisterns and wells, stone walls, brush piles, rotting logs and stumps, sawdust piles, gravel banks, rock outcrops, and buildings. Often several individuals use the same hibernaculum. Winter temperatures in Kansas hibernacula 30–80 cm beneath the surface are usually 0–10°C (Fitch 1975).

Most daily activity is nocturnal, but if weather conditions are right, some daylight activity may occur, especially during the breeding season. The authors have seen ring-necked snakes occasionally bask, but they most often thermoregulate through contact with sun-warmed objects. Their CT_{min} is about 0°C, and the CT_{max} is approximately 41.0°C. BTs of 21 Virginia *D. punctatus* found in April and July under exposed rocks in the mountains were 18.6–31.0 (mean, 24.1) °C (Mitchell 1994). Fitch (1975) recorded BTs of 11.7–34.4°C for 129 Kansas *D. p. arnyi* found beneath surface objects. In 109, the BT exceeded AT. For 37 snakes found in the open, BT averaged 26.6 (18.2–33.3) °C, an average of 3.7°C above AT. One basking had a BT of 30.3°C when the AT was 16.3°C. Most found on the surface had BTs of 25–27 or 29–31°C. Clarke (1958) collected *D. p. arnyi* when ATs were 2–32 (median, 22) °C. BTs of six *D. p. modestus* averaged 19.2 (18.2–20.4) °C (Brattstrom 1965). Both digestion and water loss increase with rising ET (Buikema and Armitage 1969; Henderson 1970).

Fitch (1975) found that nearly 25% of movements made by Kansas *D. punctatus* were less than 10 m, 33% were 10–70 m, 22% were 70–140 m, and the rest longer trips up to 1.7 km. The movements up to 70 m were probably movements within the home range. Home ranges were often elongated, with maximum axes of about 140 m, and seemed progressively altered through time. The snakes habitually returned to particular spots within the home range, even after long intervals of time.

D. punctatus has some climbing ability; the authors have found them 1–2 m above the ground hidden beneath loose bark on dead trees.

REPRODUCTION. Maturity may occur in both sexes at 17.8–18.0 cm TBL (Myers 1965; Wright and Wright 1957), and individuals over 22 cm TBL are certainly mature (C. Ernst, pers. obs.). Degenhardt et al. (1996) thought New Mexico *D. punctatus* become mature in 13–14 months, but Fitch (1975) reported it takes two to three years for this snake to mature in Kansas.

Males larger than 20 cm produce sperm (Myers 1965). The testes are smallest in the winter and spring. Spermatogenesis begins in the spring, and sperm production is greatest during the summer. Mature sperm are released from the testes in late summer and fall to be stored in the vas deferens until the next spring mating. In Kansas, Fitch (1975) found active sperm in 98% of males in April, 95% in May, 91% in September, and 93% in October.

Florida females in their first fall have 1.0 mm ovarian follicles, and the follicles grow to 1.5–2.0 mm by the first spring (Myers 1965). Once the female is mature, the follicles increase from 3 mm in April to nearly 24 mm oviductal eggs in July. From January to May, the female's reproductive tract is quiescent; from mid-August to June it is vitellogenic; and females are gravid from May to August (Perkins and Palmer 1996). Ovulation takes place in June in Kansas (Fitch 1975). The reproductive tract is divided into four distinct regions: infundibulum, uterine tube, uterus, and vagina (Perkins and Palmer 1996). The posterior portion of the tube contains temporary storage receptacles for the sperm from spring matings, and Fitch (1975) reported that sperm can survive for relatively long periods in these vascularized pouches (but probably survive only a few days in the cloaca). Cyclic changes related to shell formation occur in the oviduct. The uterus retains eggs throughout gestation and secretes the eggshell constituents. The endometrial glands of the uterus hypertrophy during vitellogenesis and become depleted of the secretory granules while the snake is gravid. The vagina has thick longitudinal and circular smooth muscle layers that help retain the eggs during gestation. It also has long furrows in its lining that also serve to store sperm over winter from fall matings. Female *D. punctatus* apparently reproduce annually.

Although females normally lay eggs, Peterson (1956) reported a case of ovoviparity in a Florida female that gave birth to six living young after apparently having retained the eggs within her oviducts. In newly laid eggs, the embryos are somewhat more advanced than those of other species of oviparous colubrids.

Pheromones released from the skin of female *Diadophis* attract males, and aggregate them for mating in the spring and fall (Dundee and Miller 1968; Noble and Clausen 1936). Actual observations of copulation in this species are rare: only on 4 and 7 May (Fitch 1975; Nussbaum et al. 1983); 15, 16, and 24 September (Fitch 1975; Payne, in Mitchell 1994; Wray, in Palmer and Braswell 1995); and possibly 4 October (Storm 1955); and Fitch (1975) found active sperm in about 6% of females in April, 20% in May, 16% in June, 8% in September, and 2.5% in October. While courting, the male rubs his closed mouth up and down the side of the females as he progresses forward beside her. When he encounters her neck ring he bites her there, aligns the lower part of his body against her, wraps his tail about her tail, and inserts his hemipenis (Fitch 1975; Nussbaum et al. 1983). The female's neck ring appears to serve as a releaser for male aggressive biting behavior.

Nesting occurs from 29 May to 1 September, with most ovipositions taking place in June–July. A rare Florida nesting occurred on 22 September with hatching on 16 October (Iverson 1978). Typical nest sites are under rocks, fallen bark, vegetation mounds, or sawdust piles, behind the loose bark on trees, in rotting logs and stumps, or in the walls of animal burrows. Preferred sites may be used by several females at the same time: Blanchard (1942) found 48 and 55 eggs in two communal nests, and Gilhen (1970) found 47 in another. Clutches are normally composed of 1–10 (mean, 4.8; n = 172) eggs, but Gehlbach (1965) found 18 eggs in a *D. p. regalis*. Females apparently reproduce each year, and probably lay more than one clutch per year. Larger females normally produce larger clutches (Barbour 1950). During dry years smaller clutches are produced (Seigel and Fitch 1985). RCM varies from 0.279 to 0.720 (Clark et al. 1997; Seigel and Fitch 1984; Vitt 1975) and may increase with the age and size of the female (Clark et al. 1997). The elongated eggs are white with rough, but thin, leathery shells, are 16.0–44.0 (mean, 25.0) × 5.5–13.0 (mean, 8.0) mm (n = 108) in size, and weigh 0.56–3.4 (mean, 1.45; n = 14) g. The eggs increase in size and weight as water is absorbed during incubation. IP is temperature dependent and averages 51.7 (28–75, n = 23) days. Most clutches in a given geographic area hatch within 10–20 days. Hatching, depending on location, may take place from mid-July to late September (but see above).

Hatchlings have 7.6–18.8 (mean, 12.4; n = 120) TBLs and weigh 0.55–2.90 (mean, 0.94; n = 26) g. Mean hatching mass is highly correlated with mean egg mass, but is not significantly related to female size or clutch size (Clark et al. 1997). The larger subspecies usually produce the largest hatchlings.

GROWTH AND LONGEVITY. Blanchard et al. (1979) reported the following estimated lengths for Michigan *D. punctatus*: females—first year, to 20 cm (60% increase in length); second year, to 24.5 cm (23% increase); third year, to 29.0 cm (18% increase); fourth year, to 34.0 cm (17% increase); and fifth year, to 39.0 cm (15% increase); males—first year, to 21.9 cm (68% increase); second year, to 26.0 cm (24% increase); third year, to 28.0 cm (8% increase); and fourth year, to 31.0 cm (11% increase). Fitch (1975) found similar growth rates in Kansas.

The record longevity in captivity is 6 years and 2 months (Snider and Bowler 1992), but both Fitch (1975) and Blanchard et al. (1979) had wild individuals live more than 10 years during their studies.

DIET AND FEEDING HABITS. *D. punctatus* preys on a variety of small animals: amphibians—salamanders (adults + eggs) *(Aneides aeneus, Batrachoseps attenuatus, Desmognathus fuscus, D. welteri, Eurycea bislineata, E. cirrigera, E. longicauda, E. quadridigitata, Plethodon cinereus, P. cylindraceus, P. glutinosus* [plus other western *Plethodon*], *Taricha torosa)* and frogs *(Eleutherodactylus planirostris, Gastrophryne carolinensis, Pseudacris regilla, Rana pipiens, R. sphenocephala);* reptiles—snakes *(Diadophis punctatus, Liochlorophis vernalis, Phyllorhynchus browni, Pituophis catenifer, Storeria occipitomaculata, Tantilla wilcoxi, Thamnophis hammondii, T. ordinoides)* and lizards *(Anniella pulchra, Eumeces skiltonianus, Ophisaurus attenuatus, Scincella lateralis);* insects (ants, beetle grubs, moth larvae); slugs; and earthworms (Barbour 1950; Bell and Bowden 1995; Blanchard 1942; Brown 1979a; Bush 1959; Darling 1947; Ernst 1962; Ernst et al. 1997; Fitch 1975; Goodman and Tate 1997; Hamilton and Pollack 1956; Kats et al. 1998; Klemens 1993; Mitchell 1994; Myers 1965; Palmer and Braswell 1995; Stebbins 1954; Tennant 1997; Uhler et al. 1939; Van Denburgh and Sleven 1913). In addition, captives have eaten hylid frogs *(Acris gryllus, Pseudacris feriarum),* snakes *(Contia tenuis, Sonora semiannulata, Virginia* sp.), and lizards *(Urosaurus ornatus)* (Anton 1994; Blanchard 1942; Cunningham 1959; Gehlbach 1974; Stebbins 1954). Whereas other researchers inevitably mention earthworms as prey, Uhler et al. (1939) reported that food items by volume from Virginia *D. punctatus* consisted of 80% salamanders, 15% ants, and 5% miscellaneous insects and arthropods. Fitch (1975) thought the average individual feeds about once every eight days, and that half of that period is required to digest and assimilate the meal. Digestion increases with a rise in BT, and Henderson (1970) found that when *Diadophis* was maintained at 35°C, the first defecation after feeding occurred in 7 hours; but when *Diadophis* was maintained at 24–33°C, defecation occurred only after 15–30 hours.

Prey is probably located by scent (Lancaster and Wise 1996). Differences in feeding behavior occur between the southwestern reptile-eating populations (Gehlbach 1974) and those from more northern prairie and eastern worm-eating populations (Fitch 1975; Henderson 1970; Myers 1965). Earthworms are usually grabbed in the mouth and held there as the snake works to one end of the worm and then begins swallowing. Salamanders and lizards are also treated in this way, but may also be held tight and chewed until they stop struggling, then swallowed head first. This snake is mildly venomous, with the enlarged posterior teeth used to introduce toxic saliva into prey. The saliva is produced in a Duvernoy's gland with mixed serous and mucous cells (Taub 1967) and is 100% protein (Hill and Mackessy 1997). Typically a snake will produce 5–20 (mean, 10) μl (two samples pooled totaled 2.88 mg dry yield) (Hill and Mackessy 1997). Lizards usually become paralyzed in a few minutes; a *Urosaurus ornatus* bitten by a *D. p. regalis* stopped breathing 71 minutes later (Anton 1994; see also PREDATORS AND DEFENSE). Myers (1965) and Shaw and Campbell (1974) reported bites of humans (perhaps from large *D. punctatus)* produce a burning sensation, but Henderson (1970) was bitten several times without experiencing discomfort.

Cunningham (1959) and Mitchell (1994) stated that vertebrate prey is killed by constriction, but although this may be done by some of the larger western subspecies, it is difficult to believe that the smaller eastern races practice constriction. The authors have seen them pin struggling prey to the substrate with a body loop to hold it still while commencing swallowing, but this is hardly true constriction.

PREDATORS AND DEFENSE. Several vertebrate animals prey on *D. punctatus*: snakes *(Agkistrodon contortrix, Coluber constrictor, Crotalus horridus, Lampropeltis getula, L. triangulum, Masticophis flagellum, Sistrurus miliarius, Micrurus fulvius),* lizards *(Crotaphytus collaris),* hawks *(Buteo jamaicensis, B. platypterus),* owls *(Bubo vir-*

ginianus, Otus asio), shrikes *(Lanius ludovicianus),* foxes *(Urocyon cinereoargenteus, Vulpes* sp.), domestic cats *(Felis catus),* raccoons *(Procyon lotor),* skunks *(Mephitis mephitis),* opossum *(Didelphis virginiana),* shrews *(Blarina brevicauda),* bullfrogs *(Rana catesbeiana),* toads *(Bufo americanus),* and brown trout *(Salmo trutta)* (Anderson 1965; Baird 2000; Blanchard 1942; Brown 1979a; Ernst 1962; Ernst et al. 1997; Fitch 1975; Greene 1984; Hamilton and Pollack 1955, 1956; Harding 1997; Klemens 1993; McCauley 1945; Minton 1972; Mitchell 1994; Mitchell and Beck 1992; Myers 1965; Palmer and Braswell 1995; Tyler 1991). In addition, Barber (in Myers 1965) reported an attack by a carabid beetle larva. Small *D. punctatus* have been found in the webs of *Theridion* spiders (Groves 1978; Klemens 1993), and the authors have seen a black widow spider *(Latrodectus mactans)* feeding on one in Virginia.

D. punctatus has several defensive behaviors. When first handled, it tries to escape by vigorously squirming or crawling between the fingers and releasing a strong musk, and *D. p. amabilis* and *D. p. regalis* may salivate copiously (Blanchard 1942). A *D. p. punctatus* attacked by a captive *Rhinocheilus lecontei* remained motionless and allowed itself to be almost entirely swallowed before turning its head 90° and biting the floor of the predator's mouth. The *Diadophis* held on for over 16 hours, during which the *Rhinocheilus* died, and the ring-necked snake emerged and crawled away at the 17th hour (Rossi and Rossi 1994). Occasionally one may pretend to be dead (Gehlbach 1970), and some may tuck their heads beneath body coils while rolling the tail into a tight coil and displaying its bright underside in a flash display (Davis 1948; Smith 1975). Whether this latter behavior is to startle a predator or to direct its attack toward the less crucial tail is unknown.

POPULATIONS. In good habitat, *D. punctatus* may be very common. It represented 6.7% of the 1,782 snakes captured over three years at Long Pine Key, Florida (Dalrymple et al. 1991). In three northeastern Kansas counties the ring-necked snake made up 59.2% of the 7,062 snakes captured by Fitch (1992) in 1981–1991, and it made up 30.3% of the 33,117 snakes in 44 samples from well-distributed localities over

Kansas (Fitch 1993). Blanchard et al. (1979) and Fitch (1975) have conducted long-term ecological studies of *D. punctatus* in Michigan and Kansas. At the Michigan study site, the population size was estimated to be 77–150 snakes, and because many of the marked individuals were never recaptured, it was thought that at any time a large proportion of the snakes was transient (Blanchard et al. 1979). At two Kansas sites, Fitch (1975, 1982) estimated the populations contained 2,700–7,000 and 4,400–10,400 snakes, for densities of 719–1,808 and 775–1,800 snakes/ha.

The juvenile to adult ratio in Michigan was 1:8, which may indicate how secretive the young are rather than a great juvenile mortality rate; in fact, both Blanchard et al. (1979) and Fitch (1975) thought the mortality rather constant throughout life, a 21–29% loss in each age or size class. In Kansas, the sex ratio varied drastically with the season, but was skewed toward males. Myers (1965) found a 1:1 adult sex ratio in Florida, but in juveniles the ratio favored males. Females were predominant in a Nova Scotia population (Gilhen 1970).

Many populations of this snake have been lost or drastically reduced as a result of habitat destruction. Today the species is protected in Idaho and Nevada, and *D. p. acricus* is protected in Florida.

REMARKS. Collins (1991), based on presumed morphological differences and allopatry, suggested *D. p. amabilis* be elevated to full species rank and include *modestus, occidentalis, pulchellus, similis,* and *vanderburghi* as subspecies. An antiserum prepared against the serum albumin of the eastern subspecies *arnyi, edwardsii, punctatus,* and *stictogenys* and the western subspecies *amabilis* and *occidentalis* indicated high levels of variation across the geographic range of *D. punctatus* (Pinou et al. 1995). A primary division, dating from approximately the Miocene, separated eastern *edwardsii* and *punctatus* from the Midwestern and western *amabilis, arnyi, modestus, occidentalis, pulchellus, similis, stictogenys,* and *vandenburghi.* However, Gehlbach (1974) reported a captive mating between a Texas *arnyi* and a western *regalis* that resulted in six fertile eggs. Additional research is needed to determine the exact status of the currently recognized subspecies.

Drymarchon corais (Boie 1827) | Indigo Snake

RECOGNITION. *D. corais* is the largest colubrid north of Mexico. Its record TBL is 263 cm, but most adults are 100–180 cm long. This species is shiny, bluish black, stout-bodied, with reddish, brownish orange, or cream pigment on the chin, throat, and sides of the head. The venter is olive gray to blue gray. Body scales are smooth with two apical pits; they occur in 17 (rarely 18–19) anterior rows, 17 rows at midbody, and 14–15 (rarely 13 or 16) rows near the vent. On the underside are 182–196 ventrals, 55–70 subcaudals, and a single anal plate. Each side of the head has 1 nasal, 1 loreal, 1 preocular, 2 postoculars, 2 + 2 (1–3) temporals, 8 (7–9) supralabials, and 8 (7–10) infralabials. The third supralabial from the rear may be small and not touch the postocular or temporal scales. The bilobed hemipenis is naked at the base, has a medial band of small spines, and has numerous fringed calyxes distally. Each maxilla has 17–18 aglyphous teeth.

No sexual dimorphism exists in the numbers of ventrals or subcaudals. A low, inconspicuous keel, requiring very close inspection to detect, is located near the anterior edge of the dorsal body scales on some males, but not on females; the keels start to appear at about 25–33% of the TBL behind the head to near the vent. Presence of the keels is clearly related to male length and maturity, as the frequency increases with size over 140 cm and is apparently associated with reproductive status (Layne and Steiner 1984). Mount (1975) reported that females from Alabama have more prominent reddish or cream-colored pigment about the chin, throat, and cheeks than do males; but Moulis (1976) found the opposite true in Georgia males.

GEOGRAPHIC VARIATION. Eight subspecies are recognized (McCranie 1980c), but only two are found in the United States. *Drymarchon corais couperi* (Holbrook 1842), the eastern indigo snake, occurs from southern Georgia south through peninsular Florida to the Keys, and westward through the Florida Panhandle and extreme southern Alabama to Mobile Bay. It is uniformly blue black dorsally, except for reddish, brownish orange, or cream pigment on the sides of the head, chin, and throat, and has a uniformly colored venter; lacks prominent dark lines extending downward from the orbit; has the third supralabial from the rear small and prevented from contacting the postocular or temporal scales by the two larger adjacent supralabials meeting above it; and usually 15 posterior body scale rows. *D. c. erebennus* (Cope 1861b), the Texas indigo snake, is found from southern Texas southward to northern Veracruz, San Louis Potosí,

Eastern indigo snake, *Drymarchon corais couperi*; Florida. (Photograph by James H. Harding)

Texas indigo snake, *Drymarchon corais erebennus*; Texas.
(Photograph by R. D. Bartlett)

and Hidalgo, Mexico. It has a brownish anterior dorsum with remnants of a spotted or banded pattern, and an unpatterned blue black posterior dorsum; a venter that is paler anteriorly and dark posteriorly; dark lines extending downward from the orbit; the third supralabial from the rear in contact with either a postocular or a temporal scale, or both; and usually 14 posterior body scale rows.

CONFUSING SPECIES. The racer *(Coluber constrictor)* and the coachwhips *(Masticophis)* have an elongated preocular scale that extends downward to partially separate two supralabials, and a divided anal plate.

KARYOTYPE. The diploid chromosomes total 36: 20 macrochromosomes (12 metacentric and submetacentric, 2 acrocentric) and 14 microchromosomes. Fe-

males are heteromorphic ZW (Z metacentric, W acrocentric); males are ZZ (Becak et al. 1973).

FOSSIL RECORD. A Pleistocene (Rancholabrean) fossil from Denton County, Texas, was reported by Harrington (1953), but the type specimen has been lost, so its identity cannot be confirmed (Holman 1981). Other Rancholabrean fossils are from Alabama (Dobie et al. 1996) and Florida (Auffenberg 1963; Brattstrom 1953b; Gilmore 1938; Gut and Ray 1963; Holman 1959a, 1959b, 1978, 1996; Meylan 1982, 1995; Weigel 1962). Holocene remains have been found in Yucatan, Mexico (Langebartel 1953).

DISTRIBUTION. The indigo snake has a disjunct range. Its distribution east of the Mississippi River is described above under *D. c. couperi*; west of the Mis-

Distribution of *Drymarchon corais*.

sissippi River it ranges from southern Texas southward along the Atlantic versant of Mexico and southward from Sonora, Mexico, on the Pacific versant to southern Brazil and northern Argentina east of the Andes and to northwestern Peru west of the Andes. It is also found on Trinidad and Tobago and several other islands off the coasts of Latin America (see McCranie 1980c).

HABITAT. Over much of its range in the eastern United States, *D. corais* prefers high dry habitats adjacent to water (pine barrens, oak forest, palmetto flats), but in southern Florida it can be found along canals, streams, or wet fields, and possibly into mangrove thickets. In Georgia, most sightings are in dwarf oak forest (longleaf pine–turkey oak) or planted slash pine–dwarf oak woodlands (Diemer and Speake 1983). Its North American habitats are generally under 1,000 m elevation.

The best habitat is one with relatively high humidity to offset the moisture lost by *D. corais* though its body surfaces. Bogert and Cowles (1947) studied moisture loss in a small (368.5 g) *D. corais* by placing it in a thermal chamber and allowing its body temperature to rise to 37.5°C within two hours. When they removed the snake after 9.5 hours, it was abnormally sluggish and died within seven hours. It had lost moisture to the extent of 46.2 g (12.5% of its initial body weight) at a mean rate of nearly 5 g (1.3%) per hour. A larger (1,247.4 g) indigo snake was placed in the chamber for more than five hours before it died, after losing 211 g (16.9%) of its body water. These studies indicate a rapid desiccation rate and may explain why *D. corais* spends so much time underground in humid animal burrows.

BEHAVIOR. Considering its size, relatively little is known of its life history. Most of our knowledge on feeding and reproduction is based on captives. It is possible we may never be able to learn much of its natural behavior because *Drymarchon* is threatened or endangered over most of its range in the United States. It would be a great loss if this magnificent creature should become extinct.

Indigo snakes are active in every month over most of their United States range, but they are definitely more active during the spring. Moulis (1976) reported them most active in Georgia in April, which he thought was the mating period. Estivation may occur during the summer, followed by a second period of slightly lesser activity from late summer into fall. In Georgia they may hibernate for a short time in winter; Moulis (1976) observed only one snake (in January) from October to March, and none during June and July in Georgia.

Daily activity is diurnal. Unfortunately, the thermal ecology of *Drymarchon* has been inadequately studied. Some data do exist, however, through the efforts of Bogert and Cowles (1947), who placed a 114.5 cm *D. corais* in direct sunlight; after 10 minutes, at a BT of 42.2°C, its movements became uncoordinated. The snake was removed from the sunlight, and it recovered. Apparently the snake's BT approached its CT_{max}.

During the warmer months Florida indigo snakes range widely, with individuals using home ranges of 50–100 ha or more (Moler 1992). During the winter they usually remain close to some deep retreat and normally have home ranges of less than 10 ha. When gopher tortoises (*Gopherus polyphemus*) are present, their burrows are used as winter retreats and as estivation sites in summer, and Lawler (1977) reported that in areas of southern Florida where tortoises do not dig burrows, indigo snakes use crab holes instead. Indigo snakes are good climbers, and they may raid birds' nests in trees.

Males are territorial, at least during the breeding season. When two adult males meet, combat may occur in which the two snakes raise their heads, necks, and anterior portions of the trunk and push against each other (Neill and Allen 1959).

REPRODUCTION. Females mature at about three years of age (Beardsley and Barten 1983) at a TBL of 152 cm (Conant and Collins 1998); the size and age of maturity in male *D. corais* are unknown. No details of the gametic cycles of either sex have been reported.

Courtship and mating have occurred in captivity from 30 October to 11 March, but according to Moulis (1976) wild *D. corais* mate in April in Georgia. Courtship has been described in detail by Gillingham and Chambers (1980). First, the male approaches the female and touches his snout to her body, then places his head on her back. Sometimes he must pursue her or move along with her to maintain his chin on her back. He then mounts her back. This is followed by a rhythmic sliding, twisting, and turning movement with local dorsoventral trunk movements; a strong nudging of his snout against the female's body that pushes her along; pinning her anterior body to the substrate with a U-shaped curve of his neck (usually when she crawls forward); and sliding his neck under hers, passing to the opposite side of her body, lifting her upwards, and curling his neck rearward to cradle her anterior body on his back (at times the female will respond with a neck curl in the opposite direction). The male follows these behaviors with a tail-search copulatory attempt that ends, as the female opens her vent, in insertion of a hemipenis, and he may perform some caudocephalic waves during this phase. Copulation is completed over two hours later when the male withdraws his hemipenis. Gillingham and Chambers (1980) and Beardsley and Barten (1983) did not observe biting by either sex during mating; but captive females have often received slashlike wounds that appear to be bite marks while mating, and Tinkle (1951) and Waide and Thomas (1984) reported aggressive biting during courtship.

About five to six weeks after mating, females pass a postcopulatory "plug" (O'Conner 1991). These masses are tan and consist of two separate oblong lobes that taper downward and join at the base. The larger of the lobes is approximately 3.4 × 1.5 cm, and the smaller lobe 3.0 × 1.5 cm. These "plugs" do not seem to prevent or interfere with subsequent copulation.

Female *D. corais* are capable of storing viable sperm for a considerable period. A female purchased from a dealer and housed alone laid a clutch of five eggs, one of which contained an embryo, after four years and four months (Carson 1945).

The GP is approximately 140 (126–176) days (O'Conner 1991), and captive ovipositions typically occur in May. Natural nests are unknown, but it is suspected that the eggs are laid in the underground burrows of pocket gophers *(Geomys pinetis)* or gopher tortoises. Clutches average 9.2 eggs (23 clutches), with a range of 4 (Wright and Wright 1957) to 14 (Whitecar 1973). Younger (shorter) females lay fewer eggs, and larger females also probably lay larger eggs. The eggs are elongate, with cream-colored leathery shells bearing calcified patches. They measure 50.8–100.0 (mean, 65.4; n = 21) × 27.0–44.8 (mean, 36.5; n = 21) mm and weigh 26–50 (mean, 43.7; n = 13) g. Hatching takes place in August and September after an IP of 70–115

(mean, 86.2; n = 25) days, depending on the IT. Hatching success varies from 7–100 (mean, 61.9; n = 8) %. Hatchlings have TBLs of 34.0–69.8 (mean, 54.9; n = 26) cm and weigh 26.0–50.0 (mean, 43.7; n = 13) g. Hatchlings differ from adults in having faint cross-bands or light anterior speckling.

GROWTH AND LONGEVITY.   Growth data on wild indigo snakes are unavailable. Two hatched in 1973 and raised in captivity grew to a TBL of almost 122 cm in about three years (Moulis 1976). One of these grew from 40.6 cm to 104 cm in its first year. Two other hatchlings grew 19.1 cm and 16.2 cm, respectively, in one year.

Snider and Bowler (1992) reported a captive longevity of 25 years and 11 months.

DIET AND FEEDING HABITS.   *D. corais* is a generalist feeder that will probably eat any vertebrate animal smaller than itself that it can overpower. It forages both at ground level and in shrubs and trees and uses both odor and sight to find food. Prey is not constricted, but instead is pinned down by the bulk of the body and often swallowed alive. Snakes, including venomous species, are seized by the head and chewed vigorously until immobilized (Keegan 1944; Moulis 1976). *D. corais* crawls along the side of the snake until reaching its head, then quickly seizes the head, often in such a way as to prevent the prey snake's jaws from opening. After the head is almost chewed to a pulp, the snake is quickly swallowed head first. Moulis (1976) reported that when pit vipers bite attacking indigo snakes, reactions to the venom do occur, but *Drymarchon* usually survives.

Wild *D. corais* prefer reptilian prey and feed on a variety of snakes (including venomous species) *(Crotalus adamanteus, C. horridus, Heterodon simus, Masticophis bilineatus, M. flagellum, Micrurus fulvius, Sistrurus miliarius),* lizards *(Cnemidophorus costatus, C. sexlineatus, Ctenosaura pectinata),* small turtles *(Gopherus polyphemus),* and turtle eggs; other prey recorded include mammals (cotton rats, *Sigmodon* sp.), nestling birds (green-cheeked Amazon parrots, *Amazona viridigenalis,* and scrub jays, *Aphelocoma coerulescens),* anurans *(Bufo* sp., *Phrynohyas venulosa),* fish, beetles, and slugs *(Philomycus)* (Babis 1949; Belson 2000; Carr 1940; Enkerlin-Hoeflich et al. 1993; Hardy and McDiarmid

1969; Leary and Razafindratsita 1998; Mount 1975; Mumme 1987; Neill and Allen 1956; Rossi and Lewis 1994; Tennant 1997; Wehekind 1955). Captives have eaten snakes *(Agkistrodon contortrix, Coluber constrictor, Crotalus adamanteus, C. atrox, C. horridus, Elaphe guttata, E. obsoleta, Farancia abacura, Lampropeltis getula, L. triangulum, Nerodia erythrogaster, N. fasciata, Opheodrys aestivus, Regina rigida, Sistrurus miliarius, Storeria dekayi, Thamnophis sauritus, T. sirtalis, Virginia striatula)*, lizards *(Cnemidophorus sexlineatus, Eumeces fasciatus, E. inexpectatus, E. laticeps, Ophisaurus attenuatus, O. ventralis, Sceloporus undulatus)*, anurans *(Acris crepitans, A. gryllus, Bufo terrestris, Rana utricularia* tadpoles, *Scaphiopus holbrooki)*, mammals *(Felis catus, Mus musculus, Rattus norvegicus, Sciurus carolinensis)*, and birds *(Gallus domesticus* chicks) (Beardsley and Barten 1983; Carson 1945; Groves 1960; Klauber 1972; LeBuff 1953; Moulis 1976; Rossi 1992; C. Ernst, pers. obs.).

PREDATORS AND DEFENSE. Data regarding natural predation are lacking. Young *D. corais* are probably preyed on by ophiophagous snakes *(Lampropeltis, Micrurus*, and possibly larger members of its own species), raptors, owls, and carnivorous mammals, but large indigo snakes have few natural enemies. Neill (in Moulis 1976) saw an alligator *(Alligator mississippiensis)* eat an adult, but humans are their worst enemies, with their automobiles, commercial collecting, habitat destruction, and indiscriminate killing of snakes. A major problem is the gassing of gopher tortoise burrows by pouring gasoline into the burrow. This is known to kill indigo and other snakes, as well as other vertebrates, that may have retreated there (Speake and Mount 1973).

When first disturbed *Drymarchon* often flattens its neck and makes threatening gestures, and if handled, it releases a potent musk. It also may shake its tail; in some tropical subspecies, the tail and posterior part of the body are deep yellow while the rest of the body is black, and when approached the snake may raise the tail in the air and wave it about (Neill 1960). The indigo snake seldom bites if handled, but when it does, the wounds may be severe.

POPULATIONS. No study of the dynamics of an indigo snake population has been published. Even though the indigo snake has both federal and state protection, it is disappearing from most of its range in the United States (see DISTRIBUTION above). In Texas, the encroachment of agriculture on its habitat has restricted it to smaller and smaller tracts. In spite of this, *D. corais* can still be locally common there: Irwin (1995) trapped five and saw another basking during an 82 day period in the lower Rio Grande Valley. The story is much the same in the East, where habitat destruction has cut up the living area of *D. corais* into smaller and smaller units, and both the gassing of gopher tortoise burrows and the collection of individuals for the pet trade have decimated local populations (Moler 1992; Tennant 1997). Currently, *Drymarchon corais* is federally listed as threatened throughout its range in this country, and it is also protected as threatened or endangered in all states in which it occurs. Unfortunately, even with this protection, the future of this species looks bleak if its habitat is not preserved.

REMARKS. *D. corais* is one of the most iridescent species of snakes. It has a pattern of undulating lines on the surface of the skin, formed by the junction of rows of cells that act as a two-dimensional optical diffraction grating to produce this iridescence (Monroe and Monroe 1968). In addition, the dermal melanocytes have fine, dendritelike processes that extend through the basement membrane into the first layer of the epidermis (Baden et al. 1966). *D. corais* has been reviewed by McCranie (1980c).

Drymobius margaritiferus (Schlegel 1837) | Central American Speckled Racer

RECOGNITION. This moderately large, slender snake has a greenish body (to 133.9 cm TBL), a long tail, and a brownish head with large black eyes. Each body scale has a black border; scales on the neck and upper body are bluish green, those at midbody are more yellow, and the posterior scales are greenish.

Central American speckled racer, *Drymobius margaritiferus*; Puerto Lempira, Honduras. (Photograph by John H. Tashjian, San Diego Zoo)

The center of each dorsal scale is yellow to orange. The supralabials, chin, throat, and underside of the neck are yellow; the remaining ventral scales are cream to white with dark borders. A distinct black stripe extends backward from the eye to the corner of the mouth. Each dorsal scale has two apical pits, and the scales are weakly keeled, except for the first 3–4 rows. Anterior and midbody scales occur in 17 rows, those near the tail in 15 rows. Ventrals total 137–168 scales; subcaudals 85–138 scales. The anal plate is divided. Lateral head scales present are a nasal partly divided by the nostril, 1 loreal, 1 preocular, 2 postoculars, 2 + 1–3 temporals, 8–10 (usually 9) supralabials, and 9–12 (usually 10) infralabials. The single, slightly bilobate, hemipenis is subcylindrical, with a single, straight sulcus spermaticus. It has 12–13 longitudinal rows of small basal and moderate-sized midbody spines, which gradually become smaller distally and are replaced with 20 or more rows of papillate calyxes. The apex lacks both spines and calyxes. Each maxilla bears 22–34 ungrooved, recurved teeth, which become slightly larger to the rear of the jaw. The sexes are similar.

GEOGRAPHIC VARIATION. Several subspecies are recognized, but only one reaches the United States—*Drymobius margaritiferus margaritiferus* (Schlegel 1837), the Central American speckled racer (described above).

CONFUSING SPECIES. The green snakes *(Liochlorophis vernalis)* and *(Opheodrys aestivus)* have no black-bordered body scales or subcaudals, no dark head stripe, one plus two temporals, and usually only six to seven supralabials; *Liochlorophis* also has smooth body scales. The racer *(Coluber constrictor)* and whipsnakes *(Masticophis)* have a lower preocular scale that extends downward to partially separate the two supralabials below it, and smooth body scales.

KARYOTYPE. Diploid chromosomes total 36, with 16 macrochromosomes (8 metacentric, 2 submetacentric, 6 subtelocentric) and 20 microchromosomes (Guitiérrez et al. 1985). The fourth pair of macrochromosomes may be sex determining (ZZ, ZW).

FOSSIL RECORD. Early post-Pleistocene vertebrae have been recovered from a cave in Yucatán (Langebartel 1953).

DISTRIBUTION. *D. margaritiferus* reaches its northernmost distribution in the Rio Grande watershed of extreme southern Texas, where it has been found in Cameron and Hidalgo counties (a questionable record also exists for Kleburg County; Dixon 1987). From Texas and southern Sonora, Mexico, the snake ranges south at lower elevations along both the Atlantic and Pacific versants of Mexico through Central America (including the Corn Islands of Nicaragua) to the Caribbean coast of Colombia (Wilson 1975b). An isolated record also exists in Coahuila, Mexico (Conant and Collins 1998).

HABITAT. *D. margaritiferus* normally lives near waterways that serve as the habitat of its amphibian prey. It is often found in dense, somewhat humid, vegetation in areas with much debris on the ground surface. In Mexico, it has been found in the ecotonal zones be-

Distribution of *Drymobius margaritiferus*.

tween pastures and forests, and in Central America to elevations of at least 1,500 m in both pine-oak assemblages and cloud forests.

BEHAVIOR. Almost nothing has been reported of the behavior and ecology of this snake, and most data are from the tropics. Like the North American racers and whipsnakes, *D. margaritiferus* is active. Temperature permitting, it is probably diurnally active all year, especially in southern Mexico and Central America. It is usually seen prowling through underbrush in search of prey, and occasionally climbs into low bushes.

REPRODUCTION. Age and length at maturity are unknown, but females as small as 63.9 cm TBL have laid fertile eggs. A pair was found copulating on 30 March in Sinaloa by Hardy and McDiarmid (1969).

Some females have contained eggs without developed shells from early June to August (Hardy and McDiarmid 1969), and very small ova in July (Landy et al. 1966), but others have oviposited or contained fully developed eggs from 19 February to August (Solórzano and Cerdas 1987; Werler 1951; Wright and Wright 1957). The eggs are white and elongated with nonadherant, smooth shells. Data on 17 eggs taken from the literature gives the following average dimensions: length, 37.3 (32–48) mm; width, 13.8 (12.0–15.8) mm; and mass, 5.65 (3.4–7.2) g. Clutches average 5 (2–8) eggs; it is not known if more than one clutch is pro-

duced a year. Length of the IP depends on the IT—reported IPs have averaged 59 (48–68) days (Solórzano and Cerdas 1987; Tennant 1984; Wright and Wright 1957).

Young *D. margaritiferus* are not as brightly colored as adults, and those of some subspecies have small dark bars crossing the back and a dark vertebral stripe. Hatchlings have average 21.4 (12.3–27.7) cm TBLs and 4.85 (4.3–5.4) g masses.

GROWTH AND LONGEVITY. No growth data have been reported. A wild-caught adult female lived 4 years, 4 months, and 17 days at the Philadelphia Zoo (Snider and Bowler 1994).

DIET AND FEEDING HABITS. *D. margaritiferus* is an active forager that hunts in damp places, mostly for anurans. Possibly the snake's saliva is toxic to its prey (Neill and Allen 1959).

Seib (1984) reported that the diet of 36 wild individuals he examined consisted of 90% anurans. Natural prey reported for the species are as follows: frogs and toads (*Bufo, Eleutherodactylus, Ptychohyla, Rana, Smilisca, Syrrophus*), lizards (*Ameiva, Anolis, Cnemidophorus*), reptile eggs, and cricetid rodents (Duellman 1961, 1963; Seib 1984). Captives have eaten frogs, lizards, small white mice, and chicks (Mehrtens 1987; Trutnau 1986).

PREDATORS AND DEFENSE. No data on predation have been published. This snake first tries to escape when found, but will bite if handled. Neill and Allen (1959) thought that its saliva may contain an anticoagulant because bites bleed excessively even though they are only small lacerations.

POPULATIONS. Unfortunately, no specific data exist on the dynamics of wild populations. The species is more plentiful in Mexico and the tropics than in Texas; in fact, it is one of the rarer reptiles in that state. Because of its limited range in the state and the destruction of its habitat, *D. margaritiferus* is considered endangered and is protected in Texas.

The male to female ratios of two clutches of hatchlings were 4:1 and 1:1, respectively (Solórzano and Cerdas 1987).

REMARKS. The genus and species were last reviewed by Wilson (1975a, 1975b).

Elaphe Fitzinger, in Wagler 1833

Rat Snakes

Key to the Species of *Elaphe*

1a. Neck stripes cross the parietals to unite on the frontal scales forming a V-shaped dark mark on the head 2

1b. Neck stripes absent from neck, not forming a V-shaped dark mark on the head 3

2a. Distinct orangish red, black-bordered dorsal blotches, found mostly east of Mississippi River . . . . *E. guttata*

2b. Often indistinct gray, tan, or brownish dorsal blotches with dark, but not black borders, found west of Mississippi River . . . . *E. emoryi*

3a. More than 220 ventrals 4

3b. Less than 220 ventrals . . . . *E. vulpina*

4a. Dorsal body pattern consists of four longitudinal stripes, range Texas into Mexico . . . . *E. bairdi*

4b. Dorsal pattern usually consists of blotches; if of longitudinal stripes, east of Mississippi River . . . . *E. obsoleta*

Elaphe bairdi (Yarrow, in Cope 1880) | Baird's Rat Snake

RECOGNITION. *Elaphe bairdi* is a large (to 157.5 cm TBL), stout, usually striped rat snake of the southwestern United States and northeastern Mexico. Its ground color is grayish brown, but the borders of the anterior scales are yellow to orangish yellow, and those of the posterior scales are deeper orange, giving the snake an overall somewhat iridescent orangish red appearance. Four somewhat faded brown longitudinal stripes are present on most adults, with the two most central darkest; however, some large individuals may lack stripes, and juveniles have 44–61 brown crossbands or pairs of small blotches on the back. Juveniles have spots on the top of the tail and an alternating row of small spots along the side of the body (see also Dial 1965). Juveniles may also have a stripe extending from the eye to the posterior corner of the mouth and/or a transverse bar between the eyes. The weakly keeled body scales are pitted, and occur in 25–27 rows anteriorly, 27–29 rows medially, and 19–21 rows near the tail. The chin, throat, and venter are cream with some grayish brown lateral spots and grayish speckles along the middle; the un-

Baird's rat snake, *Elaphe bairdi*; Alpine, Texas. (Photograph by John II. Tashjian, Dallas Zoo)

derside of the tail is often pinkish along the midline. Ventrals total 234–264, subcaudals 81–105, and the anal plate is divided. Lateral head scales include 2 nasals, 1 loreal, 1 preocular, 2 (3) postoculars, 2 + 4 + 5 temporals, 8–9 (10) supralabials, and 13–14 (12–16) infralabials. The single hemipenis is narrower at the base, swollen distally, and has a single, straight sulcus spermaticus. The basal half is naked, the proximal portion of the second half has a complete fringe of large spines, and the part distal to this is covered with small calyxes. Each maxilla has 16–18 ungrooved teeth of equal length.

Males normally have more than 250 ventrals and 92 subcaudals; females normally have less than 250 ventrals and 92 subcaudals; but some overlap occurs.

GEOGRAPHIC VARIATION. No subspecies have been described, but some differences exist in scale counts between the eastern and western populations (Lawson and Lieb 1990). The Mexican populations differ in body and head coloration from those in Texas (Schulz and Philippen 1991).

CONFUSING SPECIES. Other species of *Elaphe* can be identified by using the key presented above. The Trans-Pecos rat snake *(Bogertophis subocularis)* has prominent bulging eyes, a distinctive pattern of dark H-shaped crossbars on its back, and a row of small scales (suboculars) lying between the orbit and the subralabials.

KARYOTYPE. Like other North American *Elaphe*, *E. bairdi* has 36 chromosomes: 16 macrochromosomes (2 acrocentric, 14 biarmed), 20 microchromosomes. The NOR is on the first pair of microchromosomes (Camper and Hanks 1995).

FOSSIL RECORD. No fossils have been discovered.

DISTRIBUTION. Baird's rat snake has been reported from Kimble, Kerr, Bandera, and Medina counties in central Texas to Jeff Davis and Brewster counties in western Texas, and the Mexican states of Coahuila, Nuevo Léon, and Tamaulipas.

HABITAT. In Texas, this species is mostly a resident of semiarid upland (300–3,000 m) rocky habitats, such as forests, wooded canyons, riparian situations, and

Distribution of *Elaphe bairdi*.

boulder-and debris-covered hillsides. It sometimes enters outbuildings, presumably in search of rodents, and is a good climber.

BEHAVIOR. *E. bairdi* is nocturnal and secretive, and most of its natural history is unknown. It seldom leaves its daytime retreat before dusk, and forages, weather permitting, long into the night. Activity is more crepuscular during the spring and fall, and some may even venture out in the daylight in these seasons, but movements are almost entirely nocturnal in the hotter summer months. Most *E. bairdi* captured are taken on roads at night. It apparently hibernates from late October or early November to late February or March, and can be stimulated to activity by rains, particularly during July and August. At such times it probably drinks from puddles, but it is apparently also capable of swallowing rain droplets that roll down its head and suprlabials (Somma 1989).

Captive males have been observed engaging in combat behavior (Brecke et al. 1976). Male recognition is by taste/odor as a male touches his tongue to another's back. One male then longitudinally aligns his body along and across the second male's back, with its head anterior to the bottom male, and raises the anterior third of its body above the ground. The male beneath similarly responds but at a lower height, and both snakes crawl slowly forward. The top snake then laterally bends its body into loops across the dorsal anterior trunk of the lower male and tries to pin the bottom male's head to the ground. The bottom male retracts its head and usually tries to escape, causing a repeat of the behavioral sequence. The dorsal male may occasionally bite the other snake if it tries to crawl away.

REPRODUCTION. The reproductive cycles of both sexes have not been described. TBL at attainment of maturity is also unknown, but captive 93, 128, and 133 cm males and 91 and 117 cm females have engaged in courtship activity and copulation (Brecke et al. 1976; Dathe and Dedekind 1985).

The natural mating period is from April to June (Schulz 1996; Tennant 1984, 1985), and captives have been known to copulate in March and May (Brecke et al. 1976; Dathe and Dedekind 1985). The male initiates courtship with a series of body jerks when he touches a female. She responds with a midbody twitch and slowly crawls away, and he slowly follows. He then attempts to mount her by crawling forward along the middle of her back, and performs a series of close body coils and jerks as he lies across the center of her dorsum. She continues to move forward, and he pursues, repeating these behaviors. Finally, coitus is achieved when the male coils over the female, twists his tail beneath hers to bring their vents together, and inserts his hemipenis (Brecke et al. 1976).

According to Tennant (1984, 1985), the eggs are laid in midsummer; a GP of 43–44 days occurred between captive copulations and ovipositions observed by Brecke et al. (1976) and Dathe and Dedekind (1985). Typical clutches average about 6.0 (4–15) white, leathery-shelled, elongated eggs averaging about 58 (51–72) mm in length, 23 (19–26) mm in width, and 18 (15–22) g in weight. Possibly females are capable of laying two clutches a year in the southern part of the range (Brecke et al. 1976; Schulz 1996). Captive clutches incubated at 25–30°C have hatched in 60–83 days during June, July, and September (Brecke et al. 1976; Dathe and Dedekind 1985; Schulz 1996). Probably most natural nests would yield young in late August and September. Hatchlings are patterned as described in RECOGNITION, are 27.9–39.2 cm long, and have body masses of 10.1–18.2 g.

GROWTH AND LONGEVITY. Nothing has been reported concerning growth of *E. bairdi*, but a male caught in the wild survived 14 years, 5 months, and 3 days at the Fort Worth Zoo (Snider and Bowler 1992).

DIET AND FEEDING HABITS. *E. bairdi* actively searches for its prey, and when the prey is found seizes the animal in its mouth, wraps its coils around the prey's body, and constricts it. Foraging is nocturnal, presumably in response to the activity periods of arid-habitat rodents.

Unfortunately, little specific data have been published on the prey. Olson (1967) found a large adult coiled in a recess among nests of the cliff swallow (*Petrochelidon pyrrhonota*) that contained five adult swallows. Tennant (1984, 1985) and Vermersch and Kuntz (1986) listed rodents and other small mammals, bats, birds (eggs, nestlings, adults), and lizards as prey. The latter are probably eaten more frequently by juveniles. To take bats, the snake would have to enter the crevices or caves that serve as the flying mammals' day retreats, and climb rock walls to reach hanging bats. Captives do well on a diet of white mice, rats, or hamsters.

PREDATORS AND DEFENSE. Nothing has been reported of the predation on *E. bairdi,* but those crawling on roads at night are often killed by vehicles. Pet trade collecting is also a problem, as many individuals fail to adjust to captivity or receive poor care.

This is a relatively calm snake that does not always respond to human disturbance. However, some vibrate their tails; flatten the posterior portion of their heads; hiss, strike, and bite; or even spray musk or defecate.

POPULATIONS. No survey has been done to determine the number of *E. bairdi* composing the Texas populations. Tennant (1985) thought the species was spottily dispersed throughout the central Texas hill country and Trans-Pecos, but nowhere abundant. Such an impression may be due more to the snake's secretive behavior than to actual fact.

REMARKS. Keogh (1996) conducted a cladistic study of 17 morphological characters and found *Elaphe bairdi* most closely related to *E. guttata*, but also closely related to *E. obsoleta* and *E. vulpina* through common ancestry. It has often been considered a subspecies of *E. obsoleta*, based on supposed intergradation with *E. o. lindheimeri* in western Texas, but Lawson and Lieb (1990), Parmley (1986), and Olson (1977) have shown that interbreeding is rare, and probably

the result of hybridization between species, not intergradation between subspecies. Gene data from an electrophoretic survey upholds speciation and indicates that *E. bairdi* has undergone genetic differentiation in isolation from an *E. obsoleta* precursor (Keogh 1996).

Elaphe emoryi (Baird and Girard 1853) | Great Plains Rat Snake

RECOGNITION. *E. emoryi* is a light gray snake (TBL to 153 cm) with 25–59 dark gray, brown, or olive brown blotches with narrow black borders on the body, and another 9–28 blotches on the tail. Individuals from north in the range often have narrow blotches resembling crossbands. On the head are a black-bordered, spear-shaped mark extending forward between the eyes from the neck; a dark, black-bordered stripe running diagonally backward from the orbit to the corner of the mouth, a dark transverse bar in front of the eyes, and dark bars on the supralabials. Dark head and body marks may fade with age. The white venter has large, square black marks, and the underside of the tail usually has dark stripes. The pitted body scales are weakly keeled dorsally and often smooth along the sides; they occur in 25 (23–27) anterior rows, 27 (25–29) midbody rows, and 19 (18–21) rows near the anal vent. Beneath are 197–245 ventrals, 50–86 subcaudals, and a divided anal plate. Each side of the head has 2 nasals, 1 loreal, 1 (rarely 2) preocular(s), 2 (rarely 3) postoculars, 2 (1–4) + 3 (2–5) + 3–4 (2–5) temporals, 8 (7–9) supralabials, and 11–12 (14) infralabials. The fringed hemipenis has a single sulcus spermaticus and numerous calyxes. Each maxilla has 13–14 equal-sized teeth.

Males have 197–232 (mean, 211) ventrals and 57–86 (mean, 72) subcaudals; females have 201–245 (mean, 219) ventrals and 50–77 (mean, 66) subcaudals.

GEOGRAPHIC VARIATION. Two subspecies are known. *Elaphe emoryi emoryi* (Baird and Girard 1853), the northern Great Plains rat snake, has more than 45 dorsal body blotches and 18 tail blotches, fewer than 213 ventrals and fewer than 72 subcaudals in males, and fewer than 220 ventrals and 70 or more subcaudals in females, and subcaudal stripes are usually present. It ranges from western Illinois west to Colorado

and Utah, and south to northwestern Arkansas and western Louisiana through the northern two-thirds of Texas to eastern New Mexico. An isolated population is present in western Colorado and adjacent eastern Utah. *E. e. meahllmorum* Smith, Chizar, Staley, and Tepedelen 1994, the southern Great Plains rat snake, has 44 or fewer body blotches, fewer than 18 tail blotches, 214 or more ventrals and 73 or more subcaudals in males, 220 or more ventrals and fewer than 72 subcaudals in females, and usually no subcaudal stripes. It is found from southern Texas and southern New Mexico south to central Mexico. The two subspecies intergrade in a roughly 150 km wide zone from east of San Antonio to the El Paso region (Vaughan et al. 1996).

CONFUSING SPECIES. Other species of *Elaphe* can be identified with the key presented above. The Trans-Pecos rat snake (*Bogertophis subocularis*) has subocular scales and H-shaped dorsal blotches. The green rat snake (*Senticolis triaspis*) is greenish, lacks the spear-shaped head mark, and has a plain whitish venter. Bullsnakes (*Pituophis*) and water snakes (*Nerodia*) have strongly keeled body scales, and kingsnakes and milk snakes (*Lampropeltis*) and the glossy snake (*Arizona elegans*) have smooth body scales and undivided anal plates. The copperhead (*Agkistrodon contortrix*) has no dorsal head mark, a hole between the nostril and eye, and vertically elliptical pupils.

KARYOTYPE. Present are 16 macrochromosomes (12 submetacentric, 2 acrocentric, 2 telocentric) and 20 microchromosomes; sex determination is ZZ/ZW (Baker et al. 1971, 1972). The NOR is located on the first pair of microchromosomes (Camper and Hanks 1995).

FOSSIL RECORD. Fossil *E. emoryi* have dated from the Pliocene (Hemphillian and Blancan) of Nebraska

Great Plains rat snake, *Elaphe emoryi*; Texas. (Photograph by R. D. Bartlett)

(Parmley and Holman 1995; Rogers 1984) and Texas (Rogers 1976; Holman and Schloeder 1991); the Pleistocene (Irvingtonian) of Arkansas (Dowling 1958b) and Texas (Holman and Winkler 1987); the Pleistocene (Rancholabrean) of Nebraska (Holman 1995), New Mexico (Holman 1970), and Texas (Gehlbach and Holman 1974; Hill 1971; Kasper and Parmley 1990; Parmley 1986, 1988a, 1990a); and the late Holocene of Texas (Parmley 1990b).

DISTRIBUTION. *E. emoryi* ranges from western Illinois, central Iowa, southern Nebraska, and southeastern Colorado south to western Louisiana, Texas, and eastern New Mexico, and to central Mexico. Isolated populations are present in southwestern Colorado and adjacent Utah and in northeastern Utah.

HABITAT. *E. emoryi* lives in a variety of habitats with cover and permanent water—prairie grasslands, farm fields and pastures, riparian zones, thorn scrub, open woodlands, wooded rocky arroyos and canyons, caves, rock crevices, edges of deserts, and farm buildings—to elevations near 1,900 m.

BEHAVIOR. Surface activity takes place from March or April to October. Apparently all populations in the United States hibernate, at least for short periods, in winter. Typical hibernacula are rodent burrows, hollow logs, old stumps, rock crevices, caves, and the foundations of old buildings. These are often shared with other snakes—Webb (1970) reported that six *E. emoryi* were found hibernating with 27 *Coluber constrictor* in the foundation of an Oklahoma house.

Distribution of *Elaphe emoryi*.

Daily surface activity is usually nocturnal, but some individuals also may be found basking during the day. Schulz (1996) frequently observed them from shortly after sunset to approximately an hour after sunset. Clarke (1958) found them active at ATs of 18–29°C in Kansas. *E. emoryi* seems rather sedentary; the distance moved by Kansas individuals between captures in 34 instances averaged 109.6 m (Fitch 1999). The snakes showed a strong fidelity to specific sites—in 32 instances successive captures were beneath the same shelter after intervals of two days to 12 months, and if these captures are included, the average distance moved between captures was only 56.5 m. Although this snake does not climb as often as some other *Elaphe*, it has good climbing ability (Anderson 1965; Brumwell 1951).

REPRODUCTION. According to Stebbins (1985) individuals of both sexes with a TBL of 60 cm are adult; Johnson (1987) reported the shortest adult TBL as 61 cm. Some *E. emoryi* may grow to this length in 18 months, but probably most individuals mature in two to three years. Few data are available on the sex cycles. Iverson (1975) found three Nebraska females with enlarged follicles on 13 May; presumably ovulation occurs in May. Fitch (1999) found gravid females in Kansas throughout May and early June.

The natural breeding period extends from late March through May (Fitch 1999), but captives have mated in late February after artificial hibernation. Gillingham (1979) presented a composite description of courtship behavior in all North American species of *Elaphe*, except *E. bairdi*, that included three phases: tactile-chase, tactile-alignment, and intromission and coitus. Unfortunately, the specific courtship sequence of *E. emoryi* was lost in the generalization.

The average GP is 41 (30–49; n = 4) days, and nesting occurs from late May through July. Typical nest sites are mammal burrows and rotting logs and stumps. Possibly more than one female may lay her eggs at the same site; Fitch (1999) found aggregations of gravid females in Kansas. Twenty-four clutches reported in the literature contained 3 (Stebbins 1985) to 27 (Dundee and Rossman 1989) eggs, and averaged 10. Clark (1953) found that two clutches of 4 and 5 eggs weighed 31.6% and 33.4%, respectively, of female body mass; and Seigel and Fitch (1984) reported a RCM of 0.332 for a clutch.

The eggs have smooth shells and are white and adherent; 38 were 27–61 (mean, 47.2) mm long and 15–31 (mean, 24.1) mm wide and had masses of 12.0–25.5 (mean, 19.2) g. They hatch in August and September after an IP of 51–77 (mean, 57; n = 8) days, depending on IT. Hatchlings are 24.1–39.7 (mean, 35.5; n = 17) cm long and weigh 8.0–19.5 (mean, 14.5; n = 13) g.

GROWTH AND LONGEVITY. Limited growth data have been reported. Hatchlings (average TBL, 24.2 cm) fed a mouse per week grew to an average 73.6 cm TBL by November of the following year (Perkins 1943). The largest Kansas *E. emoryi* measured by Fitch (1999) grew from 131 cm SVL and 445 g in 1986 to 134 cm SVL and 530 g in 1991. Adult growth in his population was very small—only 1.1% in length and 5.1% in body mass; he attributed this to a deteriorating habitat and food supply. Three males he thought to be in their second year had SVLs of 70.8–79.2 cm. A wild-caught adult of undetermined sex survived 21 years, 1 month, and 15 days at the Topeka Zoo (Snider and Bowler 1992).

DIET AND FEEDING HABITS. Mammals are the preferred prey. Young opossums *(Didelphis virginianus),* shrews *(Cryptotis parva),* bats *(Myotis velifer, Plecotus rafinesquii, Tadarida brasiliensis),* young cottontails *(Sylvilagus floridanus),* rodents *(Microtus ochrogaster, Peromyscus maniculatus, Sigmodon hispidus, Rattus norvegicus),* young birds and birds eggs *(Bartramia longicauda, Ictalurus bullocki),* lizards *(Eumeces fasciatus, E. obsoletus, Sceloporus jarrovi, S. olivaceus),* small snakes *(Diadophis punctatus),* frogs, and insects have been eaten by wild *E. emoryi*; and captives have consumed house mice *(Mus musculus),* young brown rats *(Rattus norvegicus),* white-footed mice *(Peromyscus sp.),* house sparrows *(Passer domesticus),* garter snakes *(Thamnophis sirtalis),* and skinks *(Eumeces sp.)* (Anderson 1965; Cavitt 2000b; Clark 1949; Fitch 1982, 1999; Fouquette and Lindsay 1955; Gloyd 1928; Herreid 1961; Hibbard 1934; Marr 1944; McCoy 1975; McCrystal 1982; Ramírez-Baitista et al. 2000a; Tennant 1985; Twente 1955; Vermersch and Kuntz 1986; Wright and Wright 1957). Most prey are actively sought and probably are detected by both smell and sight, but ambush behavior may be practiced in rodent colonies or bat caves. Large animals are constricted, but smaller ones may be swallowed directly.

PREDATORS AND DEFENSE. *E. emoryi* is preyed on by hawks *(Buteo albicaudatus, B. jamaicensis)*, owls, carnivorous mammals, and larger snakes (Collins and Collins 1993; Ross 1989), and a captive coachwhip *(Masticophis flagellum)* ate one (Boyer and Heinze 1934). Grassland fires are a danger (Cavitt 2000a), and automobiles and habit destruction have reduced populations. When disturbed this snake will vibrate its tail and strike, and if handled it will void musk (C. Ernst, pers. obs.). Because their coloration and blotched pattern are similar, Burt and Hoyle (1934) thought *E. emoryi* might mimic the venomous massasauga *(Sistrurus catenatus)*.

POPULATIONS. This snake is secretive and remains hidden most of the time, resulting in few reports of its relative numbers, and these are probably underestimates. *E. emoryi* made up less than 1% (22) of 33,117 snakes collected by Fitch (1993) in 44 samples from scattered localities in Kansas, and only 100 (1.4%) of the 7,062 snakes collected by him in three counties in northeastern Kansas during 43 years (Fitch 1992). In 10 years, 31 individuals were captured a total of 109 times at a 4 ha Kansas farm by Fitch (1999); most of the snakes were found beneath cover boards placed around a collection of old buildings. However, Heinrich and Kaufman (1985) found this snake common on the Konza Prairie, Kansas, where 11 were killed during a controlled one-day fire, and Cavitt (2000a) reported 48 (8.7%) *E. emoryi* of a total of 550 snakes collected from 1994 through 1996 at the same site. The species also seems rare in arid habitats; Reynolds (1982) recorded only 7 (1.7%) in a three-year collection of 418 snakes on a road in Chihuahua, Mexico. The species is protected in Illinois and Utah.

REMARKS. The species was reviewed by Schulz (1996), Smith et al. (1994), and Vaughan et al. (1996).

Elaphe guttata (Linnaeus 1766) | Corn Snake

RECOGNITION. The corn snake (TBL to 182.9 cm) is gray with 15–50 black-bordered orange or red dorsal blotches and spots, black bars on the supralabials, and large black square blotches on a white venter. Nine to 18 dorsal blotches are present on the tail. A prominent black-bordered, spear-shaped mark extends forward from the neck between the eyes, and another black-bordered stripe extends diagonally backward on each side from the eye past the corner of the mouth onto the neck. Dark stripes are usually present on the venter of the tail. The keeled, pitted dorsal body scales occur in 25 (23–27) anterior rows, 27 (23–29) midbody rows, and 19 (20–23) rows near the anus. Beneath are 201–245 ventrals, 47–84 subcaudals, and a divided anal plate. Lateral head scales are 2 nasals, 1 loreal, 1 (rarely 2) preocular(s), 2 postoculars, 2 (3) + 3 (2, 4) temporals, 8 (6–9) supralabials, and 11–12 (10–15) infralabials. The fringed hemipenis has a single sulcus spermaticus and numerous calyxes. About 9–12 smooth, equal-sized teeth occur on each maxilla.

Males have 201–238 (mean, 221) ventrals, 54–84 (mean, 66) subcaudals, and tails that are thick at the base; females have 208–245 (mean, 228) ventrals, 47–81 (mean, 62) subcaudals, and tails that are not thickened at the base.

GEOGRAPHIC VARIATION. No subspecies are currently recognized. Formerly the reddish corn snakes of the Lower Florida Keys were designated *E. g. rosacea* (Cope 1888), but Christman (1980), Duellman and Schwartz (1958), and Mitchell (1977a) showed these snakes represent the southern end of a cline in the number of ventrals, subcaudals, and dorsal body blotches. So the taxon was synonymized with *E. guttata*.

CONFUSING SPECIES. Other species of *Elaphe* can be distinguished by using the key presented above. Milk snakes and kingsnakes *(Lampropeltis)* have smooth body scales, undivided anal plates, and no dark stripes beneath the tail. Bullsnakes and pine snakes *(Pituophis)* have a well-developed rostral scale and undivided anal plates. Copperheads *(Agkistrodon contortrix)* lack a dark mark on the head, have a hole between the nostril and eye, and have vertically elliptical pupils.

Corn snake, *Elaphe guttata*; Kentucky. (Photograph by Roger W. Barbour)

KARYOTYPE. Undescribed—the karyotype ascribed to *E. guttata* by Baker et al. (1971, 1972) and Camper and Hanks (1995) was from *E. emoryi*.

FOSSIL RECORD. All known fossils of *E. guttata* are from the Pleistocene: Irvingtonian—Florida (Meylan 1982); and Rancholabrean—Alabama (Holman et al. 1990), Florida (Auffenberg 1963; Gut and Ray 1963; Holman 1962a, 1978; Martin 1974), Georgia (Holman 1995), Oklahoma (Parmley and Lacy 1997), Pennsylvania (Guilday et al. 1964), Tennessee (Holman 1995), Texas (Parmley 1990a), and Virginia (Guilday 1962; Holman 1986a).

DISTRIBUTION. *E. guttata* ranges east of the Mississippi River from southern New Jersey to the Florida Keys and Tennessee, Mississippi, and southeastern Louisiana at elevations from sea level to over 400 m. Isolated populations occur in Kentucky, southern Arkansas, northwestern Louisiana, and southeastern Texas.

HABITAT. Corn snakes are most often found in pine barrens, brushy fields, open hardwood forests, caves, and mangrove thickets, or around trash dumps and abandoned buildings.

BEHAVIOR. Over most of the range corn snakes are active from April to November, with most surface ac-

tivity occurring in April–June, but in the southern states individuals may be found in all months, and in southern Florida it is doubtful that the population ever undergoes weather-related inactivity. Farther north, these snakes hibernate during the winter in rodent burrows, old stumps, hollow logs, caves, rock crevices, and old stone walls and building foundations.

Daily activity is mostly nocturnal, but some individuals may occasionally be found in the morning or late afternoon, and daytime activity increases during the cooler months. The authors once caught one in Florida in the early afternoon of a very hot August day. Although most activity is terrestrial, *E. guttata* is an accomplished climber and a good swimmer. Unfortunately, nothing has been reported on the thermal ecology of wild corn snakes.

Males often perform dominance combat dances (especially when a new male is introduced into their cage). This usually starts with a series of short, jerky, spasmodic, forward movements and can end with the dominant, usually larger, male pinning the head or body of the other male to the ground. Shaw (1951) has observed such behavior in relation to both sexual and feeding activity.

REPRODUCTION. Females mature at a SVL of 53–68 cm (Bechtel and Bechtel 1958; Ford and Seigel 1994b; Mitchell 1994); such lengths are attained in 9–32 months (Bechtel and Bechtel 1958; Ford and

Distribution of *Elaphe guttata*.

Seigel 1994b; Golder 1981; Witwer and Bauer 1995). Although the length has not been reported, males become sexually mature when about 18 months old (Bechtel and Bechtel 1958). Little is known of the sexual cycles of *E. guttata*. A Virginia female contained four large unshelled yolk masses on 15 June (Hoffman 2000), and the authors have found females with oviductal eggs in late May and June.

The mating period extends from March into early June depending on latitude, with most reported wild courtship or copulation records occurring in May. Ashton and Ashton (1981) reported winter mating in Florida. Ford and Cobb (1992) had corn snakes mate 29 days after emergence from forced hibernation. During courtship, the male pursues the female, crawls onto her, and undulates his body along her back, sending caudocephalic waves along his body toward the female's head. He then moves forward along her back, entwines his tail about her tail, and inserts his hemipenis into her vent. After intromission, the male aligns his body along the female's back, and both snakes occasionally elevate and lower their bodies from slightly anterior to the vent tailward (for a comprehensive description of courtship behavior in eastern *Elaphe,* see Gillingham 1979). Copulations may last up to 25 minutes (C. Ernst, pers. obs.).

The GP is 29–68 (mean, 44.5; n = 10) days. The eggs are laid in June and the first half of July over most of the range, and during May in Florida (Iverson 1978); they are laid in mammal burrows, sawdust piles, and rotting logs and stumps.

The white, elongated eggs are partially adherent with tough leathery shells. Measurements of 60 eggs were 28.5–61.0 (mean, 35.8) × 13–32 (mean, 19.7) mm, and 2.0–12.5 (mean, 7.0) g. RCM varies from 0.320 to 0.793 (mean, 0.538) (Seigel and Fitch 1984; Seigel and Ford 1991). The number of eggs laid per clutch and egg width are correlated with female length, and when adjusted for female length, increasing clutch size is negatively correlated with egg length (Ford and Seigel 1989a). Clutches contain 3–40 eggs, with an average of 13.6 (n = 105 clutches) eggs. Well-fed females produce larger clutches with larger clutch masses (Seigel and Ford 1991). More than one clutch may be laid in a season (Golder 1981; Tryon 1984); a captive laid 54 eggs over a 57 day period (van der Eerden 1985).

IP is 36–102 (mean, 62.4; n = 26 clutches) days, and hatching occurs in August and September, with most young emerging in August. Hatchlings are more red than adults, have 15.0–37.5 (mean, 29.7; n = 49) cm TBLs, and weigh 5.4–9.3 (mean, 7.3; n = 12) g.

GROWTH AND LONGEVITY. The amount of growth in corn snakes depends on their food intake; those consuming more food (and energy) grow faster (Barnard et al. 1979; Ford and Seigel 1994b). Actual growth data, however, are sparse, and are confined to individuals raised in captivity under different feeding regimes. Neonates at the University of Florida averaging 32.5 mm (7.5 g) at hatching grew to 57.7 mm (45.1 g) in six months and were 89.2 mm (164.3 g) after a year; the relationship between the weight and length of these snakes was demonstrated by the regression equation $y = 0.000134x^{3.14}$ (Barnard et al.

1979). In eight months, hatchlings at the Baltimore Zoo grew to 39.3 mm (12 g) (Groves 1957).

An unsexed *E. guttata*, originally caught as an adult, lived another 21 years and 9 months at the Philadelphia Zoo (Snider and Bowler 1992).

DIET AND FEEDING HABITS. *E. guttata* seem to prefer warm-blooded prey, such as mammals and birds and their eggs, but will also eat lizards, snakes, small frogs, and some insects. Hamilton and Pollack (1956) reported that mammals made up 59% by occurrence and 45% by volume of the diet. Reported natural prey are mammals—rodents *(Microtus pennsylvanicus, M. pinetorum, Mus musculus, Peromyscus gossypinus* [?], *P. leucopus, Oryzomys palustris, Sigmodon hispidus)*, moles *(Condylura cristata)*, and shrews *(Cryptotis parva)*; birds and their eggs *(Colinus virginianus, Passer domesticus, Toxostoma rufum)*; reptiles—lizards *(Anolis carolinensis, A. sagrei, Cnemidophorus sexlineatus, Eumeces fasciatus, Sceloporus undulatus, Scincella lateralis)* and snakes *(Carphophis amoenus)*; frogs *(Hyla chrysocelis)*; and insects (cave crickets and moth larvae) (Brode 1958; Brown 1979a; Ditmars 1936; C. Ernst, pers. obs.; Hamilton and Pollack 1956; Holman 1958a; Love 1978; McCauley 1945; Palmer and Braswell 1995; Uhler et al. 1939). In addition, our captives have eaten the common kingsnake *(Lampropeltis getula)*, bats *(Eptesicus fuscus, Pipistrellus subflavus)*, shrews *(Blarina brevicauda, Sorex longirostris)*, deer mice *(Peromyscus maniculatus)*, and young rats *(Rattus norvegicus)*. *E. guttata* has also eaten members of its own species in captivity (Hillis 1974; Ippoliti 1980; Polis and Myers 1985). Corn snakes have an assimilation efficiency of 88.9% when eating *Mus musculus* (Smith 1976).

Several orientational cues are used to find prey. The snake responds positively to the body heat of rodents (Austin and Gregory 1998). Odors of other snakes are also detected (Weldon et al. 1990), and corn snakes increase the rate of tongue flicking after both striking and swallowing (Cooper et al. 1989), so odors probably play a role in prey capture. Movement and proximity of prey appear to be more important than color conspicuousness in visual selection of food items (Smith and Watson 1972).

Small animals may be swallowed alive, but most prey are constricted (usually with the right side of the body; Heinrich and Klaassen 1985). Constriction is not always within the coils, as captives often squeeze prey against the floor or walls of the cage with their bodies—perhaps they also do this in rodent burrows.

PREDATORS AND DEFENSE. Known predators include snakes *(Drymarchon corais, Lampropeltis getula, Masticophis flagellum, Micrurus fulvius)*, lizards *(Gekko gekko)*, hawks *(Buteo sp.)*, foxes *(Urocyon cinereoargenteus, Vulpes vulpes)*, cats *(Felis catus, Lynx rufus)*, skunks *(Mephitis mephitis, Spilogale putorius)*, and opossums *(Didelphis virginianus)* (C. Ernst, pers. obs.; Greene 1984; Linzey and Clifford 1981; Love 2000; Neill 1961a; Tennant 1997). Captive corn snakes have been eaten by other corn snakes (see above), and a scarlet snake *(Cemophora coccinea)* devoured a corn snake egg (Minton and Bechtel 1958).

Wild *E. guttata* can be worthy opponents. They vibrate the tail and strike with amazing speed. C. Ernst once had the embarrassing problem of trying to board a train in Florida with a corn snake he had just caught in the parking lot firmly biting his pant leg. This snake reacts negatively to the odors of potentially harmful snakes, such as the common kingsnake *(Lampropeltis getula)* (Weldon et al. 1990).

POPULATIONS. Very limited data on population are available; a good study of population dynamics of this species would be useful. At a site in the Florida Everglades, *E. guttata* made up only 4.6% (83) of 1,782 snakes caught or observed by Dalrymple et al. (1991). Humans kill corn snakes when they mistake them for venomous copperheads *(Agkistrodon contortrix)*, and automobiles, habitat destruction, and collecting for the pet trade have thinned some populations. *E. guttata* is now considered a species of special concern in Florida, and it is given legal protection in Illinois, Kentucky, and New Jersey.

REMARKS. *E. guttata* is most closely related to *E. obsoleta* (Keogh 1996). Several mutant skin colors exist, whose heredity has been well documented (Bechtel and Bechtel 1978, 1989; McEachern 1991). The species was reviewed by Shulz (1996).

Elaphe obsoleta (Say, in James 1823) | Rat Snake

RECOGNITION. One of the largest snakes in North America, it has a record TBL of 256.5 cm. Color and body pattern are quite variable (see GEOGRAPHIC VARIATION), making a composite description difficult. The sides of the body are straight, not rounded, as in some other black snakes, presenting a cross-sectional profile like that of a loaf of bread. Body color varies from gray to olive gray, black, yellow, or orange, and the back may have a pattern of 24–42 dark blotches or dark longitudinal stripes. Some races become more melanistic with age but still retain some light pigment between the body scales. The head is anteriorly truncated, not rounded, and is wider behind the eyes near the corner of the mouth. Always present is a dark stripe extending from the eye to the corner of the mouth, and a dark transverse bar may occur between the eyes. The supralabials may contain dark bars. The venter of the tail lacks stripes, the dark marks on the ventral scales are small and often indistinct, and the chin and throat lack dark pigment. Body scales are pitted, weakly keeled, and in 25 (23–29) anterior rows, 25 or 27 (23–29) midbody rows, and 17 or 19 (18–21)

Black rat snake, *Elaphe obsoleta obsoleta*; Estill County, Kentucky. (Photograph by Roger W. Barbour)

Everglades rat snake, *Elaphe obsoleta rossalleni*; Collier County, Florida. (Photograph by Roger W. Barbour)

Gray rat snake, *Elaphe obsoleta spiloides*; Northern Alabama. (Photograph by Christopher W. Brown, DVM)

rows near the vent. Beneath are 218–258 ventrals, 46–102 subcaudals, and an anal plate that is usually divided or semidivided. Lateral head scales are 2 nasals, 1 (rarely 0, 2) loreal, 1 (rarely 2) preocular(s), 2 (rarely 1, 3) postoculars, 2 + 3–4 temporals, 8 (7–9) supralabials, and 11 (9–14) infralabials. The single hemipenis is slightly bilobed with a single sulcus spermaticus extending up one lobe, a naked base, spiny middle, and some calyxes at the base of the lobes. Each maxilla has 12–15 ungrooved teeth of equal length.

Males have 218–243 (mean, 232) ventrals, 63–102 (mean, 84) subcaudals, and TLs that are 15–21 (mean, 19) % of TBL; females have 224–258 ventrals (mean, 238), 46–92 (mean, 77) subcaudals, and TLs that are 14–20 (mean, 17) % of TBL.

GEOGRAPHIC VARIATION. Five subspecies are currently recognized. *Elaphe o. obsoleta* (Say, in James 1823), the black rat snake, is found from western New England and eastern and central New York west to southeastern Minnesota, southern Iowa, southeastern Nebraska, eastern Kansas, and eastern Oklahoma,

and south to central Georgia, northern Alabama, northern Louisiana, and northeastern Texas; isolated populations occur in southern Ontario. Adults are black with some indications of blotches and light pigment (white, yellow, orange, or red) on the skin between the body scales, and a white to yellow venter with faded gray or brown blotches or a black checkerboard pattern. *E. o. lindheimeri* (Baird and Girard 1853) the Texas rat snake, ranges from south-central Kansas south through west-central Oklahoma, eastern Texas, and central and southern Louisiana. It is gray or yellowish with a pattern of auburn brown or bluish black blotches, and often a black head. *E. o. quadrivittata* (Holbrook 1836), the yellow rat snake, occurs along the Atlantic Coastal Plain from southeastern North Carolina south through all but southern peninsular Florida. It is yellow to gray or greenish yellow with four dark longitudinal stripes and a black tongue. *E. o. rossalleni* Neill 1949b, the Everglades rat snake, is restricted to southern Florida and the Keys. It is bright orange, orangish yellow, or orangish brown with four faint gray longitudinal stripes and a red tongue. *E. o. spiloides* (Duméril, Bibron, and Duméril 1854), the gray rat snake, ranges from southwestern Indiana and southern Illinois south in the Mississippi Valley to Mississippi, central and southern Alabama, western Georgia, and northwestern Florida. It is gray or light brown with brown or dark gray blotches. Zones of intergradation occur where the ranges of these subspecies meet, and significant genetic variation occurs between populations from Ontario and Maryland, whereas less DNA variation is evident between Ontario populations, and populations 15–50 km apart in Ontario have only moderate genetic distinction (Prior et al. 1996). [Note: Based on phylogenetic analysis of two mitochondrial gene sequences, Burbrink (2001) recently published a revision of *Elaphe obsoleta* in which he proposed four molecular clades to be recognized as full species: (1) an eastern clade, *E. alleghaniensis* (Holbrook 1836); (2) a central clade, *E. spiloides* (Duméril, Bibron, and Duméril 1854); (3) a western clade, *E. obsoleta* (Say, in James 1823); and (4) *E. bairdi* (Yarrow, in Cope 1880). The reader is referred to that paper for details.]

Several other color or pattern morphs are known, and at times have been, but are no longer, recognized as taxa; for descriptions and discussions of these, see Christman (1980), Dowling (1952), Duellman and Schwartz (1958), or Schulz (1996). Bechtel and Bechtel (1985) reported on the genetics of color mutations popular in the pet trade, particularly the distinctively colored Lower Florida Keys morph.

Juveniles of all subspecies and adults of the western races are blotched. Christman (1980) theorized the blotched pattern is ancestral, and that *E. o. lindheimeri* most closely matches it. He also proposed that geographic variation led in Florida to development of the striped pattern of *E. o. quadrivittata* and *E. o rossalleni*, and in eastern North America to the virtually unpatterned adult *E. o. obsoleta*. Populations from extreme southern Florida have probably diverged less from the ancestral pattern, and still retain the dark pigmentation and blotches. More recent geographic variation on the Florida peninsula has led to the reduction in dark ground pigment along the coasts and in the Everglades. Development of the striped phenotype on peninsular Florida was probably expedited by a reduction in gene flow while parts of Florida were isolated during periods of higher seas. Popula-

tions in the Gulf Hammock region represent intergrades from subsequent contact between mainland blotched and peninsular striped morphs. That all combinations of striped and blotched phenotypes can be found in the Gulf Hammock area today suggests a pattern of recombinants such as would be observed when isolated populations come secondarily into contact.

CONFUSING SPECIES. The genera *Coluber, Masticophis, Drymarchon,* and *Lampropeltis* have smooth dorsal body scales, a single anal plate, or both, and *Coluber* and *Masticophis* also have a preocular that pushes downward between two supralabials. Garter and ribbon snakes *(Thamnophis)* have undivided anal plates. Fox snakes *(Elaphe vulpina)* have 216 or fewer ventral scutes (this is very important to remember when comparing juveniles). *Pituophis* species have four prefrontal scales; *E. obsoleta* has only two. Hog-nosed snakes *(Heterodon)* have an elongated, often upturned, rostrum, and water snakes *(Nerodia)* have strongly keeled body scales and brown bars on their supralabials.

KARYOTYPE. The diploid chromosome complement is 36: 16 macrochromosomes (12 submetacentric, 2 acrocentric, 2 subtelocentric) and 20 microchromosomes (Baker et al. 1971, 1972; Camper and Hanks 1995; Chang et al. 1971). Sex determination is ZZ(male)/ZW(female). The NOR is situated on the first microchromosome pair (Camper and Hanks 1995).

FOSSIL RECORD. Fossils of *E. obsoleta* are known from the Pliocene (Hemphilian) of Kansas (Brattstrom 1967; Holman 1979a) and Nebraska (Parmley and Holman 1995) and the Pliocene (Blancan) of Kansas (Brattstrom 1967; Holman 1979a; Holman and Schloeder 1991; Peters 1953; Rogers 1976) and Texas (Holman 1979a; Holman and Schloeder 1991; Rogers 1976). Pleistocene records are from the Irvingtonian of Florida (Meylan 1982, 1995), Kansas (Brattstrom 1967), and possibly Nebraska (Holman 1995), and the Rancholabrean of Alabama (Holman et al. 1990), Florida (Auffenberg 1963; Brattstrom 1953b, 1954b; Holman 1962a; Holman and Clausen 1984; Gut and Ray 1963; Young and Laerm 1993), Georgia (Holman 1995), Kansas (Brattstrom 1967; Holman 1995; Pres-

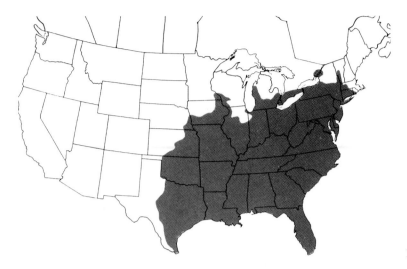

Distribution of *Elaphe obsoleta*.

ton 1979), Oklahoma (Smith and Cifelli 2000), Pennsylvania (Guilday et al. 1964), Tennessee (Holman 1995), Texas (Kasper and Parmley 1990), and Virginia (Guilday 1962; Holman 1986a, 1995; Holman and McDonald 1986).

DISTRIBUTION. The rat snake ranges from southwestern New England and southeastern Ontario west to southeastern Minnesota and eastern and southern Iowa south to the Florida Keys, and the Gulf Coast, and in Mexico possibly to Coahuila, Nuevo León, and Tamaulipas.

HABITAT. *E. obsoleta* lives in a variety of wooded or scrub habitats—deciduous hardwood forests, scrub pine and mixed palmetto-pine woods, edges of swamps and marshes, bayous, mangrove thickets, and old fields. It is often common about abandoned or partially demolished buildings where rodents are abundant, and can be found in bat caves. Weatherhead and Charland (1985) found that Ontario rat snakes prefer fields or the ecotone between fields and deciduous forests during the bird breeding season, and McAllister (1995) reported that at another Ontario site they are found in marshes during the bird nesting season.

BEHAVIOR. This snake may be active in all months in southern Florida and in other southern states, basking on warm winter days, but it usually hibernates for an extended period during the winter. In the southern portion of the range it normally emerges in late February or March and remains active well into November, but farther north the annual activity period is shortened to from late March, April, or early May to October or early November. Ontario *E. obsoleta* begin to emerge from hibernation in mid-April, but some snakes do not emerge until about 1 June, an emergence period of approximately 40 days (Blouin-Demers et al. 2000). Larger individuals emerge before smaller ones. Maximum AT cannot explain all the variance in emergence dates. In North Carolina, *E. obsoleta* usually has a bimodal surface activity cycle with spring and fall peaks, but most sightings occur in May–July (Palmer and Braswell 1995). The annual activity period of the northernmost Ontario populations may be shortened to only four to five months, with at least seven months of hibernation (Weatherhead 1989).

Winters are spent in south-facing rock crevices or slides, rock quarries, caves, hollow logs or trees, old stumps, mammal burrows, stone walls, foundations of old buildings, spring houses, cisterns and wells, or under large rocks (for characteristics of Ontario hibernacula, see Prior and Weatherhead 1996). When in cisterns or wells, *E. obsoleta* may hibernate at least partially underwater (Owens 1949a). Those using caves may shift position several times during the winter, apparently seeking a more favorable ET (Sexton and Hunt 1980). If hibernation conditions are not entirely suitable or disease develops during the winter, the snakes may be weakened and die shortly after spring emergence (Prior and Shilton 1996). Often the hibernaculum is communal with other species of snakes (Minton 1972; Seibert 1965). Fitch (1999) found no fidelity by Kansas rat snakes for a particular hibernaculum, but the authors have recorded this in Virginia.

Most daily activity is diurnal, but some crepuscular or nocturnal foraging may occur in the summer. Landreth (1972) found that rat snakes become very active at 10°C, and can survive ETs of 0°C for two hours. ATs of 15–30°C seem to be preferred by active individuals, although Clarke (1958) found Kansas rat snakes active at 12–34°C. Fitch (1956) reported that BTs of 53 Kansas *E. obsoleta* found in the open were 18.2–38.0 (mean, 28.0) °C, with 73% between 24 and 31°C. Active Virginia *E. obsoleta* had BTs of 25.0–30.6 (mean, 27.6) °C; those hiding under cover had BTs of 15.0–18.9 (mean, 17.5) °C (Mitchell 1994). Metabolic heat production by *E. obsoleta* is associated with light-dark cycles—minimum heat is produced at midday when ATs are high and also at night (possibly related to inactivity) (Kroll et al. 1973). The snake's physiological activities increase with rising temperatures; the heart beat is 11 per minute at 18°C, but 83 per minute at 30°C (Jacob and McDonald 1975).

The movements by individual *E. obsoleta* have been studied in several localities. Home ranges of Tennessee rat snakes varied from 0.4 to 13.4 ha, with males averaging 6.3 ha and females 3.3 ha (Mullin et al. 2000). Fitch (1963b, 1999) reported that in Kansas the average distance moved from a hibernaculum was 384–403 m for males and 362 m for females; the range of distances traveled was 30.5–966.0 m. Most movements (93%) during the activity period were shorter than 500 m, and 81% were shorter than 300 m (Fitch 1999). Fitch (1999) considered movements longer than 500 m to be shifts beyond the limits of the home range, and those from 300–500 m may represent unusually large ranges or ranges of elongate shape. Excluding movements longer than 500 m, mean distance for 120 movements within supposed home ranges was 177 m, and was the same for movements by either sex. If the home ranges were circular in shape, a mean area would be 9.84 ha. Based on his observations, Fitch thought the home ranges to be fairly stable in size over periods of years. The average distance moved per day by snakes equipped with radio transmitters was 44.7 (0–260) m (Fitch and Shirer 1971). In Maryland, Stickel and Cope (1947) recorded movements of 40–536 m between captures (3–730 days).

Stickel et al. (1980) found that established home ranges were kept for many years, perhaps for life, and found no evidence of shifts or major changes in range among 38 male and 28 female *E. obsoleta*. Individual snakes traveled 0–1,333 m, and the diameter of their Maryland home ranges averaged at least 600 m for males and at least 500 m for females. At another Maryland site, convex polygon home ranges averaged 9.5 ha (Durner and Gates 1993). Males used more of the home range earlier in the spring (possibly while searching for mates) and traveled more during the late spring and early summer; in contrast, females used shelters more often than males. In Ontario, Weatherhead and Hoysack (1989) calculated individual home ranges from radiotelemetric records as convex polygons (areas of water within the polygons were subtracted): for eight males the average home range was 3.90 ha, and for six females 1.22 ha. Males had longer ranges that extended an average of 421 m; ranges of females averaged 179 m in length. Some individual movements were over 1 km; males traveled a mean distance of 69.3 m per move, whereas females moved only an average of 43.9 m. Two hibernacula were used, which averaged 247 m from the home range.

E. obsoleta is an excellent climber (Jackson 1978) and is often seen in trees; in fact, one looking for these animals should always search above ground as well as on the ground, as they often stretch out and bask on a limb or are seen with part of their body protruding from a tree hole. They also forage up to 15 m high in trees for bird nests and squirrels; this may pose a problem where nest boxes are used for bird or squirrel propagation. Females seem to climb higher than males (Durner and Gates 1993), and these snakes frequently return to the same tree (Stickel et al. 1980). Rat snakes are also good swimmers, and the authors have often seen them in the water or in trees surrounded by water.

Male rat snakes participate in dominance combat dances, probably in competition for mates, during which one male tries to pin the other male's head or body to the ground (Mitchell 1981; Rigley 1971; Stickel et al. 1980). Gillingham (1980) has analyzed this combat behavior and described the seven motor patterns involved—touch mount, dorsal pin, hover, push-bridge, avoid, head raise, and no response—and the reader is referred to his paper.

REPRODUCTION. Females in Kansas generally first reproduce in their fourth year when at least 82.5 cm in SVL; males probably mature a year earlier than females with a SVL greater than 80.0 cm. Details of the sexual cycles have not been reported; however, Callard and Leathem (1967) found that ovarian weights were comparable in May and July, but that oviduct weight was significantly greater in July. The authors have found shelled eggs in females' oviducts in late May and June in Kentucky, Pennsylvania, and Virginia, so ovulation probably occurs in May and early June.

The mating period extends from mid-April to early June, or possibly as late as early July, with most copulatory activity occurring in late April and May. Fitch (1963b, 1999) found sperm in a Kansas female's cloaca in mid-October, so fall mating may also occur. Courtship and mating are more successful if the snakes have hibernated first. During the mating act, the male crawls along the female's back and bites her neck to hold her still. He then positions himself along her side and performs caudocephalic undulations and vibrates his tail. The tail is then moved under that of the female, the vents brought together, and the hemipenis inserted (Johnson 1950; Kennedy 1978; Mansueti 1946). Mating may take place above ground in trees (Padgett 1987).

After a GP of 37–51 days females oviposit in late May, June, and July (rarely August). Those in southern populations nest earlier than those in populations farther north. Nest sites include hollow logs or stumps, tree holes, piles of manure, rotting vegetation and sawdust, and beneath rocks or debris; several females may lay at the same site (Clark and Pendleton 1995; Lynch 1966b). Usually only one clutch is laid a year, but Cohen (1978) reported that a female laid two clutches of 13 and 10 eggs, respectively, 59 days apart. Only about 33% of the females reproduce in any given year (Fitch 1999). Clutches contain 4 to 44 (mean, 15; n = 41) eggs (Fitch 1970). The white, leathery-shelled, elongated eggs are nonadherent; 85 eggs measured 25.0 71.0 (mean, 46.4))(14.0 39.5 (mean, 25.3) mm, and 18 eggs weighed 11.4–17.6 (mean, 14.7) g. RCMs range from 0.334 to 0.338 (Mullen 1999; Seigel and Fitch 1984).

Hatching usually takes place after an IP of 42–84 (mean, 62.4; n = 18) days from late July to early No-

vember, but is concentrated in August and September. Hatching success in our laboratory has ranged from 50 to 100 (mean, 88; n = 21) %. Hatchlings are blotched and resemble adults in ground color, except those of E. o. obsoleta, which are gray in contrast to the black adults. Fifty-seven hatchlings had 17.7–50.1 (mean, 38.6) cm TBLs, and weighed 7.7–18.3 (mean, 11.2) g.

GROWTH AND LONGEVITY. Growth is rapid in juveniles, but slows once maturity is reached. Males grow faster and achieve greater lengths than females. Stickel et al. (1980) reported that growth in Maryland male rat snakes slows conspicuously near 134 cm at about six to eight years; growth in females slows near 125 cm at an estimated age of 6.6 years. Rat snakes in Kansas follow the same general growth pattern—yearlings have 31.6–55.4 SVLs, 3-years-olds are 76.3–87.7 cm, 5-year-olds are 95.8–103.9 cm, 10-year-olds are 118.0–126.3 cm, and 14-year-olds have 132.1–143.2 cm SVLs (Fitch 1999).

E. obsoleta has a potentially long life span. Fitch (1999) captured and released a male in 1950 at a probable age of 13 years, and recaptured it again in 1958 at an estimated age of 21 years. Snider and Bowler (1992) listed captives that survived 22 years, 11 months, and 30 days and 21 years, 9 months, and 2 days; and Liner (1990) reported a captive survived 22 years, 6 months, and 12 days.

DIET AND FEEDING HABITS. The rat snake prefers to eat mammals and birds. Surface (1906) found that mammals made up 47% and birds and their eggs 32% of food items in Pennsylvania, and Barbour (1950) recorded 47% mammals and 53% birds in Kentucky. Clark (1949) found 78 mammals and 17 birds in 100 E. obsoleta from Louisiana. In Kansas, Fitch (1963b) recorded 66% mammals and 23% birds (most in June), and in 1999 reported 76% of the food biomass was mammal (32% the vole Microtus ochrogaster) and 22% bird. Brown (1979a) recorded 59% mammalian and 37% bird foods in North Carolina. Uhler et al. (1939) examined the stomachs of 85 rat snakes from Virginia and found the major food items by volume were mice 32%, birds 31%, chipmunks and squirrels 15%, cottontails 9%, and shrews 4%.

Prey recorded from E. obsoleta are mammals—bats

(Eptesicus fuscus, Myotis grisescens, M. sodalis, Pipistrellus subflavus, Tadarida braziliensis), shrews *(Blarina brevicauda, Cryptotis parva)*, moles *(Condylura cristata)*, opossum *(Didelphis virginiana)*, rabbits *(Sylvilagus floridanus)*, squirrels *(Glaucomys volans, Sciurus carolinensis, S. niger, Tamias striatus, Tamiasciurus hudsonicus)*, voles *(Microtus ochrogaster, M. pennsylvanicus, M. pinetorum)*, mice *(Mus musculus, Peromyscus leucopus, P. maniculatus, Reithrodontomys humulis, R. megalotis, Zapus hudsonius)*, rats *(Neotoma floridana, Oryzomys palustris, Rattus norvegicus, Sigmodon hispidus)*, and weasels *(Mustella sp.)*; birds and their eggs—waterfowl *(Aix sponsa, Branta canadensis, Dendrocygna autumnalis, Lophodytes cucullatus)*, fowl *(Colinus virginianus, Gallus gallus, Numida meleagris, Phasianus colchicus)*, raptors *(Falco sparverius, Rostrhamus sociabilis)*, owls *(Bubo virginianus, Tyta alba)*, doves and pigeons *(Columba livia, Columbina passerina, Zenaida macroura)*, cuckoos *(Coccyzus americanus)*, hummingbirds *(Archilochus colubris)*, kingfishers *(Ceryle alcyon)*, woodpeckers *(Colaptes auratus, Melanerpes carolinus, M. erythrocephalus, Picoides borealis, P. pubescens, Sphyrapicus varius)*, phoebes *(Sayornis phoebe)*, swifts *(Chaetura pelagica)*, swallows *(Hirundo rustica, Progne subis, Riparia riparia, Stelgidopteryx ruficollis)*, crows and jays *(Corvus brachyrhynchos, Cyanocitta cristata)*, titmice *(Parus bicolor)*, wrens *(Thryothorus ludovicianus, Troglodytes aedon)*, nuthatches *(Sitta pusilla)*, mimic thrushes *(Dumetella carolinensis, Mimus polyglottos, Toxostoma rufum)*, thrushes *(Hylocichla mustelina, Sialia sialis, Turdus migratorius)*, vireos *(Vireo belli)*, wood warblers *(Icteria virens, Mniotilta varia, Seiurus noveboracensis)*, blackbirds *(Agelaius phoeniceus, Molothrus ater, Quiscalis guiscula, Sturnella magna)*, starlings *(Sturnus vulgaris)*, weaver finches *(Passer domesticus)*, and finches and sparrows *(Cardinalis cardinalis, Melospiza melodia, Spizella passerina, Zonotrichia atricapilla)*; reptiles—turtle eggs *(Terrapene carolina)*, lizards *(Anolis carolinensis, Cnemidophorus sexlineatus, Eumeces fasciatus, Hemidactylus turcicus, Sceloporus olivaceus, S. undulatus, Scincella lateralis)*, and snakes *(Elaphe obsoleta, Heterodon platirhinos, Storeria dekayi, Thamnophis sirtalis)*; frogs *(Acris sp., Hyla chrysocelis, H. squirella, Rana blairi, R. sphenocephala)*; snails; and insects (beetles, moth caterpillars) (Aldrich and Endicott 1984; Allen and Neill 1950a; Anderson 1965; Barbour 1950; Barr and Norton 1965; Bell 1957; Bennetts and Caton 1988;

Blair 1960; Blem 1979; Brown 1979a; Campbell 1970; Carr 1940; Carter 1992; Cary et al. 1981; Cink 1977, 1990, 1991; Collins 1980; Conant 1951; Cox 1986; Easterla 1967; C. Ernst, pers. obs.; Ernst and Barbour 1989; Ernst et al. 1997; Fendley 1980; Fitch 1963b, 1999; Fowler 1947; Haggerty 1981; Hamilton and Pollack 1956; Harris 1999; Hensley and Smith 1986; Hopkins 1981; Hudson 1947, 1954; Huheey 1970; Hurter 1911; Jackson 1970, 1974, 1978; Jackson and Dakin 1982; Liner 1997; Means and Goertz 1983; Minton 1972; Mirarchi and Hitchcock 1982; Mitchell et al. 1996; Neal et al. 1993; Nealen and Breitwisch 1997; Palmer and Braswell 1995; Plummer 1977; Reams et al. 2000a; Ridlehuber and Silvy 1981; Silver 1928; Stewart 1981; Stickel et al. 1980; Surface 1906; Uhler et al. 1939; Withgott and Amlaner 1996; Wright and Wright 1957). There are also several records of unique feeding episodes—a smooth, oval stone and a china egg that had served as nest eggs in poultry houses (Holt 1919), a golf ball (Jacobson et al. 1980), and autophagy (trying to swallow oneself) (Mitchell et al. 1982; Morris 1984). Juveniles prey on frogs and small mammals.

Large prey are seized in the mouth and quickly constricted in the snake's coils; several prey may be constricted simultaneously. Small and helpless animals are swallowed alive. Eggs are swallowed whole and then broken in the esophagus by contracting the anterior portion of the body into S-shaped curves and pushing the eggs against the hypapophyses of the cervical vertebrae (Mullin 1996). Immediately after the shell is broken, the portion of the body posterior to the egg is laterally flexed into a U-shaped bend. The shells may be either disgorged or, more often, swallowed.

From our experience, most food is found either by sight or smell. Arboreal prey is discovered by sight (Mullin and Cooper 1998), and the snakes are more successful in habitats with low levels of complexity (Mullen and Cooper 2000). If the prey escapes once it is struck, the snake will follow its olfactory trail (Withgott 1996). A hatchling may use its tail to lure small frogs or lizards (Tiebout 1997). Capture success is lower in more complex habitats (Mullin and Gutzke 1999).

PREDATORS AND DEFENSE. Large adult rat snakes have few enemies other than humans, with their automobiles and habitat destruction, but juveniles and small adults are known prey of other reptiles—snakes *(Agkistrodon contortrix, Coluber constrictor, Drymarchon corais, Lampropeltis getula, Masticophis flagellum, Micrurus fulvius)* and alligators *(Alligator mississippiensis);* birds—roadrunners *(Geococcyx californianus),* hawks *(Buteo jamaicensis, B. lineatus, B. platypteros),* and great horned owls *(Bubo virginianus);* mammals—shrews *(Blarina* sp.), raccoons *(Procyon lotor),* weasels *(Mustella* sp.), dogs and coyotes *(Canis familiaris, C. latrans),* cats *(Felis catus),* and swine *(Sus scrofa)* (Ernst and Barbour 1989; Ernst et al. 1997; Fitch 1963b; Greene 1984; Harding 1997; Meshaka et al. 1988; Mitchell 1994; Mitchell and Beck 1992; Parmley 1982; Platt and Rousell 1963; Vandermast 1999). In addition, wood ibis, large egrets and herons, otters, foxes, and bobcats probably take a few individuals.

This snake either "freezes" in place when approached or tries to crawl away. When prevented from fleeing it may vibrate its tail, coil, and strike, and if handled it may deliver a strong musk (which is more malodorous in females; Kissner et al. 2000). It may wrap itself around the neck, feet, or body and constrict an animal attacking it (Meshaka et al. 1988; Vandermast 1999).

POPULATIONS. Rat snakes may be locally common in the right habitat if rodents are abundant, and they are often one of the more common snakes in most communities (Fitch 1993). Ford et al. (1991) reported *E. obsoleta* made up 7.2% (22) of 305 snakes collected in an eastern Texas mixed pine-hardwood forest, and it made up 7.6% (136) of 1,762 snakes observed or collected from 1984 through 1986 at Long Pine Key, Florida (Dalrymple et al. 1991). In the Hill Parishes of Louisiana, *E. obsoleta* totaled 4.8% (100) of a sample of 2,083 snakes (Clark 1949). The species made up 3.1% (218) of over 7,000 snakes captured from 1981 through 1991 in three northeastern Kansas counties

(Fitch 1992) and 1.9% (633) of 33,117 snakes collected in 44 samples from the entire state (Fitch 1993). At a site in northeastern Kansas, the mean density of rat snakes was estimated to be 0.9/ha (Fitch 1963b), and at the Patuxent Wildlife Research Center, Maryland, the density was 1/0.23 ha (Stickel et al. 1980).

Most individuals captured during a 21 year period in Maryland were 110–160 cm long (Stickel et al. 1980). The sex ratio from hatchings in the laboratory was four males to every female in Kansas, but for older wild rat snakes it was only 0.90:1.00 (Fitch 1961); in Maryland the sex ratio was 1:1 in laboratory hatchings, but in wild 90–130 cm size classes females predominated (Stickel et al. 1980). These figures suggest a higher mortality rate for males.

Populations of *E. obsoleta* have been reduced in Massachusetts, Michigan, and Mississippi, and these states protect it.

REMARKS. In the Appalachian Mountains, the name "pilot black snake" is often applied to *E. obsoleta,* because it is believed to lead the venomous snakes *Agkistrodon contortrix* and *Crotalus horridus* away from danger, thus acting as their "pilot." In central Kentucky and adjacent Indiana, it is thought to milk cows and is called "cowsucker." Neither tale is true.

Although it may occasionally enter poultry houses and eat eggs and fledglings, *E. obsoleta* is of positive economic importance. It is a highly efficient rodent catcher and consumes many destructive mice and rats about farms each year. Some farmers recognize its value, and when C. Ernst was at the University of Kentucky several local farmers came to him each year for excess rat snakes that they then released in their barns and corn cribs.

E. obsoleta is most closely related to *E. guttata* (Keogh 1996), and captive hybridization between them has been reported (Bröer 1978). The species was reviewed by Schulz (1996).

Elaphe vulpina (Baird and Girard 1853) | Fox Snake

RECOGNITION. *E. vulpina* (TBL to 179.1 cm) is the least known of North American rat snakes. It is yellowish brown with a dorsal series of large dark brown or black rectangular-shaped blotches, and a longitudinal series of smaller dark blotches on each side. The dorsal surface of the head is plain yellow to reddish

Eastern fox snake, *Elaphe vulpina gloydi*; Iron County, Michigan. (Photograph by James H. Harding)

brown; a dark stripe runs diagonally backward from the orbit to the corner of the mouth. The cream to yellow venter has numerous black spots. Dorsal body scales are keeled, have two apical pits, and lie in 25 (23–27) anterior rows, 23 (25–27) rows at midbody, and 21 (19) posterior rows. Ventrals total 190–218, subcaudals 45–71; the anal plate is divided. On each side of the head are 2 nasals, 1 loreal, 1 (rarely 2) preocular(s), 2 (rarely 3) postoculars, 2–3 + 3–4 temporals, 8 (7–9) supralabials, and 11 (9–13) infralabials. The fringed hemipenis has numerous calyces and an undivided sulcus spermaticus. Each maxilla has 16–17 teeth.

Males have 190–212 (mean, 200) ventrals, 51–71 (mean, 64) subcaudals, and a TL 13–19 (mean, 16) % of TBL; females have 198–218 (mean, 206) ventrals, 45–60 (mean, 56) subcaudals, and a TL 12–17 (mean, 14) % of TBL.

GEOGRAPHIC VARIATION. Two subspecies are recognized. *Elaphe v. vulpina* (Baird and Girard 1853), the western fox snake, has 32–52 (mean, 41) dorsal body blotches, and the dorsal surface of the head is brown. It occurs from the northern panhandle of Michigan and northwestern Indiana west through southern Minnesota and Iowa to extreme southeastern South Dakota and eastern Nebraska, and south to western Illinois and extreme northeastern Missouri. *E. v. gloydi* Conant 1940, the eastern fox snake, has fewer (28–43; mean, 35), larger, dorsal body blotches, and an orangish red head. It is found around lakes Huron and Erie in southern Ontario, eastern Michigan, and north-central Ohio. The ranges of the two taxa are now separated (possibly by human disturbance of the prairie corridor passing through northern Indiana), causing some herpetologists to consider them full species, but until reproductive isolation is proven they should remain subspecies.

CONFUSING SPECIES. Other rat snakes can be distinguished by the above key. Milk snakes and kingsnakes (*Lampropeltis*) have smooth body scales and single anal plates. Gopher and pine snakes (*Pituophis*) have a single anal plate, a pointed snout, and strongly keeled body scales.

KARYOTYPE. The karyotype is 14 biarmed macrochromosomes, 2 acrocentric macrochromosomes,

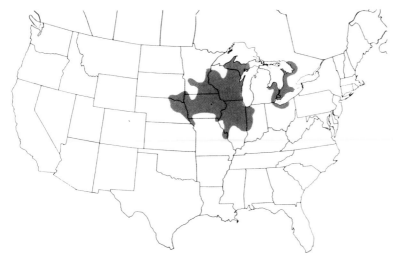

Distribution of *Elaphe vulpina*.

and 20 microchromosomes; the NOR is on the first pair of microchromosomes (Camper and Hanks 1995).

FOSSIL RECORD. Fox snake fossils date from the Pliocene (Hemphillian) of Nebraska (Holman 1982a); the Pliocene (Blancan) of Idaho, Kansas, Nebraska, Texas, and Washington (Eshelman 1975; Holman 1968b, 1972a, 1982a; Parmley and Walker 1998; Rogers 1976, 1984); the Pleistocene (Irvingtonian) of Nebraska, Maryland, Oklahoma, Pennsylvania, and South Dakota (Holman 1977a, 1977b, 1982b, 1986b); and the Pleistocene (Rancholabrean) of Alabama, Georgia, Michigan, Missouri, Ohio, Oklahoma, and West Virginia (Dowling 1958; Holman 1965b, 1974, 1979b, 1985, 1986b, 1997; Holman et al. 1990; Hood and Hawksley 1975; Parmalee et al. 1969).

DISTRIBUTION. *E. vulpina* is found around lakes Huron and Erie in southern Ontario, eastern Michigan, and north-central Ohio, and from the Upper Peninsula of Michigan and northwestern Indiana west to southeastern South Dakota and eastern Nebraska, and south to western Illinois and northeastern Missouri.

HABITAT. Over most its western range, *E. vulpina* lives in open grasslands, scrub brush, hedgerows, farm fields, and the edges of open woods, but in its eastern range it is found in (or along) marshes, vegetated sand dunes, beaches, farm fields, pastures, and open woodlots.

BEHAVIOR. Fox snakes are usually active from mid- or late April to October, but a few are occasionally surface active during the winter in Illinois (Brown and Brown 1995; Smith 1961); peak activity occurs in May and early June. The winter is spent underground in a rock crevice, animal burrow, or building foundation, and it is possible that those living in marshes use muskrat or beaver lodges and burrows as hibernacula. Several may aggregate at suitable overwintering sites; Smith (1961) found 16 and Vogt (1981) 166 (68 underwater) hibernating in old wells, and Zaremba (1978) found a group hibernating in a concrete cistern where 6 of the snakes were submerged under 90 cm of water. Murphy (1997) has also seen *E. vulpina* hibernating underwater through a layer of ice.

Daily activity is predominately diurnal, but fox snakes may prowl at night during warm rains. They are usually found prowling along rodent runways or marsh borders, especially during the morning (0600–1100 hours) and evening (1600–2000 hours), or basking at the base of shrubs. Little is known of this snake's thermal requirements. Dill (1972) reported no differences between the overall anterior and posterior BTs of an *E. vulpina* implanted with thermal transmitters, but during the diurnal warming period the anterior temperature was significantly lower ($p < 0.05$) than the posterior temperature.

Most activity is at ground level, but this snake sometimes climbs into shrubs, tree snags, and trees to heights of at least 2 m (Smith 1961), and Brown and Brown (1975) observed one exploring a bird's nest on a barn rafter about 10 m above the floor. The only movement data available is that of a 101 cm Illinois male crawling 39.6 m across ice in February when the AT was 9.4°C (Brown and Brown 1995).

Male *E. vulpina* may engage in combat behavior similar to that of other species of *Elaphe* (Barten 1992; Harding 1997).

REPRODUCTION. Conant and Collins (1998) considered 91 cm TBL *E. vulpina* adult; this length is probably reached in the third year of growth. Limited data on the sex cycles have been reported; Iverson (1975) found seven enlarged ovarian follicles in an 82 cm SVL female on 11 May, and another had shelled oviductal eggs on 4 July.

Harding (1997) reported that Michigan fox snakes mate in April and May, but literature records range from 25 May (captives; Hingley 1988) to 18 July (captives; Simonson 1951), with most observations clustered in June. The following description of courtship and mating is condensed from Gillingham (1974). Once the female is discovered, the male examines her with his tongue; she usually moves away, and he chases her. The female stops when receptive. The male then crawls alongside of her, examines her with his tongue, gently nudges her at midbody, and begins forward jerking motions with his entire body. The female immediately responds with similar jerks, and the male presses his head on her back and moves forward. When the male has progressed to between the female's head and midbody, he twitches his tail from side to side, pulls the posterior portion of his body forward into several S-shaped curves, and when these curves contact the female, lifts them 5–8 cm and places them on her back until he has completely mounted her. Next, he rubs his body against her back as she continues jerky motions, and positions his head just behind her head. Intromission follows, and the male bites the female's neck with his mouth, holding her thus during the rest of the copulation (which may take up to 40 minutes).

The eggs are laid after a GP of 30–34 days. Oviposition normally takes place in July, but has occurred from late June to early August. Nest sites include loose soil, hollow logs, rotting stumps, sawdust piles, under logs, and possibly mammal burrows, and several females may lay at the same place (Patch 1919).

Clutches contain 7–29 eggs (Wright and Wright 1957), with a mean of 14.4 eggs for 35 reported clutches. Seigel and Fitch (1984) reported a RCM of 0.319. The adherent eggs are white with leathery shells, 29.0–61.0 (mean, 46.2; n = 29) mm long and 14.5–30.0 (mean, 24.1; n = 24) mm wide. Most hatch in August, but hatching can occur until early October; IP is 35–75 (mean, 52.6; n = 10) days, depending on the IT. Hatchlings have dark markings on the dorsal surface of their heads, and 23.0–35.6 (mean, 29.4; n = 23) mm TBLs; seven weighed by Matlin (1948) averaged 11.7 (11.0–13.5) g.

GROWTH AND LONGEVITY. No growth data are available. A female *E. v. gloydi* caught as an adult lived another 7 years, 5 months, and 18 days at the Los Angeles Zoo (Snider and Bowler 1992).

DIET AND FEEDING HABITS. Mammals seem the most important prey of adults, but other animals are also eaten: mammals—young cottontails (*Sylvilagus floridanus*), pocket gophers (*Geomys bursarius*), chipmunks (*Tamias striatus*), ground squirrels (*Spermophilus tridecemlineatus*), mice (*Mus musculus, Peromyscus leucopus, P. maniculatus*), voles (*Microtus ochrogaster, M. pennsylvanicus*), and rats (*Rattus norvegicus*); birds—eggs (various ducks; pheasants, *Phasianus colchicus*) and nestlings (*Dendroica petechia*); and possibly various frogs. Juveniles eat small frogs, small lizards (*Eumeces fasciata*), insects, and earthworms (Aldrich and Endicott 1984; C. Ernst, pers. obs.; Harding 1997; Johnson 1987; Minton 1972; Vogt 1981; Wheeler 1984; Wilson 1985; Wright and Wright 1957). Anderson (1965) reported that captives ate mice (*Mus musculus, Peromyscus leucopus*), house sparrows (*Passer domesticus*), and pigeon (*Columba livia*) eggs; and Markezich (1962) had a captive eat a smooth green snake (*Liochlorophis vernalis*).

Fox snakes grab prey in their mouths and quickly constrict them. Most are detected by actively searching, but some *E. vulpina* may lie in ambush beside rodent runways.

PREDATORS AND DEFENSE. Reported predators of *E. vulpina* are prairie deer mice (*Peromyscus maniculatus*), on its eggs, bald eagles (*Haliaeetus leucocephalus*), and hawks (*Accipiter gentiles, Buteo jamaicensis*) (Evans and Roecker 1951; Pierce and Ross 1989; Ross 1989; Watermolen 1992); and probably carnivorous mammals, other birds of prey, and ophiophagus snakes also prey on them; but humans, with their automobiles and habitat destruction, are the worst enemy.

Adult fox snakes seldom bite if disturbed—instead they vigorously shake their tails and, if handled, spray musk; the young are more aggressive, and they strike and bite. The unmarked yellow or orangish red head of adults and the habit of vibrating the tail has led to many *E. vulpina* being mistaken for venomous pit vipers.

POPULATIONS. Few population numbers are available—Tucker (1995a) reported that *E. vulpina* made up only 6 (5.3%; 2 males, 4 females) of 113 snakes collected on an Illinois road in 21 October days; however, their numbers may be high at hibernacula (Vogt 1981). The species has declined over much of its range, particularly in the eastern portion; today it is considered endangered in Missouri, threatened in Michigan, and a species of special concern in Ohio, and it is protected in Ontario.

REMARKS. *E. vulpina* is most closely related to *E. obsoleta* and *E. guttata* (Keogh 1996). The species was reviewed by Powell (1990) and Schulz (1996).

Farancia Gray 1832

Mud and Rainbow Snakes

Key to the Species of *Farancia*

1a. One internasal scale . . . . *F. abacura* 1b. Two internasal scales . . . . *F. erytrogramma*

Farancia abacura (Holbrook 1836) | Mud Snake

RECOGNITION. *F. abacura* is a thick-bodied (TBL to 207 cm) black and red snake with a terminal tail spine. The back is bluish gray to black, often with a metallic sheen; the dark pigment on the sides is interrupted by a series of salmon pink to red bars; and alternating reddish and black transverse bars cross the venter. The labials, chin, and throat are yellowish with a black spot on each scale. The wedge-shaped head is almost as wide as the neck. Dorsal body scales are smooth and pitless (some near the anal vent may be weakly keeled), and occur in 19 (18–21) rows with no reduction along the body. On the venter are 167–200 ventrals, 31–55 subcaudals, and normally, a divided anal plate. Each side of the head has 1 nasal, 1 loreal, 0 preocular, 2 postoculars, 1 (2–3) + 2 (1–3) temporals, 7 (6–8) supralabials, and 8–9 (7–10) infralabials. A single internasal scale is present. The bifurcate hemipenis has a single sulcus spermaticus, dentate calyxes, and numerous spines. Maxillary teeth of 10 *F. abacura* the authors examined averaged 13.2 (11–16) teeth, with the posterior-most enlarged.

Males have 167–195 (mean, 176) ventrals, 31–55 (mean, 45) subcaudals, and TLs which are 12–19 (mean, 16) % of TBL; females have 185–208 (mean, 192) ventrals, 31–43 (mean, 35) subcaudals, and TLs 7–17 (mean, 11) % of TBL.

GEOGRAPHIC VARIATION. Two subspecies are recognized. *F. a. abacura* (Holbrook 1836), the eastern mud snake, ranges from southeastern Virginia south through peninsular Florida, and west to the Florida Panhandle and central Alabama. It has 53 or more tri-

Western mud snake, *Farancia abacura reinwardtii*; Hickman County, Kentucky. (Photograph by Roger W. Barbour)

angular-shaped red bars along its sides, the distal red bars on its tail frequently uniting medially, and three to four median scale rows separating the red bars on the neck. *F. a. reinwardtii* (Schlegel 1837), the western mud snake, is found from central Alabama west to eastern Texas and southeastern Oklahoma, and north along the Mississippi Valley to southern Illinois and southwestern Indiana. It has 52 or fewer rounded red bars along its sides, the distal red bars unite only at the tail tip, and eight to nine median scale rows separate the red bars on the neck. The two subspecies intergrade in the western panhandle of Florida, eastern and central Alabama, and west-central Georgia.

CONFUSING SPECIES. Rainbow snakes *(F. erytrogramma)* have two internasal scales, and three longitudinal red stripes on their bodies. Water snakes *(Nerodia, Regina)* have keeled dorsal body scales, and the black swamp snake *(Seminatrix pygaea)* does not have red bars crossing its venter.

KARYOTYPE. The 36 chromosomes are composed of 16 macrochromosomes (2 acrocentric, 14 biarmed) and 20 microchromosomes; the NOR is on the first pair of microchromosomes (Camper and Hanks 1995).

FOSSIL RECORD. Vertebrae of *F. abacura* and *F. erytrogramma* are almost impossible to distinguish (Auffenberg 1963), so fossils have usually been attributed only to the genus. Pleistocene remains have been found in Irvingtonian deposits in Citrus County, Florida (tentatively identified as *F. abacura*; Meylan 1982), and Rancholabrean fossils are known from several counties in central and northern Florida (Auffenberg 1963; Brattstrom 1953b; Gilmore 1938; Gut and Ray 1963; Hay 1917; Holman 1959b, 1978; Meylan 1995; Weigel 1962).

DISTRIBUTION. *F. abacura* ranges from southeastern Virginia south to the tip of Florida, west to eastern Texas and southeastern Oklahoma, and north

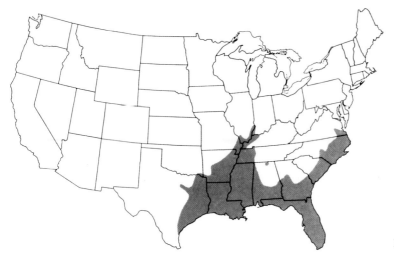

Distribution of *Farancia abacura*.

along the Mississippi Valley to southwestern Indiana and southern Illinois.

HABITAT. *F. abacura* lives in shallow, mud-bottomed, often tanic, slow-flowing waterways such as cypress swamps, marshes, bogs, creeks, and sloughs. It is common in the Everglades of Florida. Tolerant of brackish water, it may enter bays and tidal creeks.

BEHAVIOR. In the north it must hibernate in winter, but in the southern parts of its range, it may be at least sporadically active in every month: the authors have collected foraging individuals in February and early March in southern Florida. In South Carolina most activity occurs from March through May (Gibbons and Semlitsch 1991), in North Carolina from May through July (Palmer and Braswell 1995), and in Virginia from late May to early August (Mitchell 1994). Georgia mud snakes leave the water in late fall and burrow deeply in the pulpy wood of decaying pine stumps on hills or banks overlooking the water (Neill 1948a). Date of return to the water varies from year to year; Semlitsch (1988) reported that hatchlings enter South Carolina bodies of water from February through July and again in September–October and December, but most appear in April–May (60%) and September–October (16%). A captive kept by Meade (1935) stopped feeding in October and attempted to dig into the soil whenever possible. He allowed the snake to hibernate under dirt in a wooden box placed in a hole in the ground on 4 November. A pan of water was provided from which the snake occasionally drank, and when it emerged on 6 March, it had lost only about 3 g of weight. Scudder (1972) found a 24 cm juvenile in a mole cricket burrow in Florida, so possibly the young escape extremes of temperature in small animal burrows. The species is subject to desiccation, and will migrate from ponds that are drying (Seigel et al. 1995b).

F. abacura is chiefly nocturnal, especially in the summer and particularly during showers, hiding in burrows or aquatic plants during the day. In the spring there is some diurnal activity, at least in Florida, where the authors have collected several during the morning. Palmer and Braswell (1995) reported active individuals at ATs of 4.4°C during a dry day in January, 18.3°C on a rainy January night, and 18.0°C on a December evening.

REPRODUCTION. Wright and Wright (1957) reported females mature at TBLs of 85.2–92.0 cm, and males at 60.0–72.5 cm. These lengths are usually attained in 2.5 years (Robinette and Traugh 1992).

The sexual cycles have been studied by Robinette and Trauth (1992). Females have four size classes of ovarian follicles: (1) follicles with a diameter less than 1 mm, (2) those with diameters 1.5–6.5 mm undergoing primary vitellogenesis, (3) follicles 12–21 mm in diameter undergoing secondary vitellogenesis from mid-May to mid-July, and (4) oviductal eggs in a female in early September. Older, larger females complete secondary vitellogenesis earlier in the year than younger, shorter females. Male seminiferous tubules contain Scrtoli cells and spermatogonia in April, and the vas deferens are packed with mature sperm. Testicular recrudescence begins in May, when primary spermatocytes dominate in the seminiferous tubules, and some secondary spermatocytes are present by the end of the month. In June secondary spermatocytes predominate, and the vas deferens no longer contains many mature sperm. Spermatids appear in the testes in July, and mature sperm are present in both the seminiferous tubules and vas deferens in August. Testicular regression is completed in the fall, and mature sperm are stored over the winter in the vas deferens.

Matings have been observed in the water and on land from 24 April to 11 July (Meade 1937; Palmer and Braswell 1995). Meade (1937) observed captives copulate for most of the day; the female lay in a loose coil, while the male remained in a fairly straight line at right angles to the posterior part of her body. Courtship behaviors have not been described.

The nesting season begins in April–March in Florida, but elsewhere occurs from July to early September. Females construct a nest burrow and tend the eggs after oviposition, usually lying in a loose coil about them (Meade 1940; Reimer 1957). Rotting vegetation of American alligator *(Alligator mississippiensis)* nests is a favorite oviposition site (Hall and Meier 1993). The GP is about 56 days (Meade 1937). Reported clutches contain 4 (Kennedy 1959) to 104 (Van Hyning 1931) eggs, and average 27 (55 clutches); however, the 104 egg record may be based on several females ovipositing communally. If this is true, the upper limit of eggs in a clutch is 56 (Cook 1954), and the average is 25.6 eggs for 54 clutches reported in the literature. The white, elliptical eggs have smooth shells, and may be adherent. Measurements of 59 eggs reported in the literature were 22.7–47.6 (mean, 34.6) × 13.3–29.0 (mean, 20.8) mm, and 63 reported eggs weighed 7.9–11.0 (mean, 6.3) g. Auth (1992) reported the mass of a clutch was 36.8% of the female mass. IP lasts 37–80 (mean, 60) days, depending on the ET, and hatchlings normally appear in August–October. The young have 15.2–27.0 (mean, 22.0; n = 82) cm TBLs and weigh 2.5–8.0 (mean, 6.3; n = 25) g when hatched. They are occasionally found in large numbers among the roots of water hyacinths (Carr 1940).

GROWTH AND LONGEVITY. Goldstein (1941) reported that a hatchling grew 13.9 cm between hatching on 6 October and the next spring when it died. Snider and Bowler (1992) reported that a wild-caught adult female *F. a. reinwardtii* survived 18 years and 10 days at the Philadelphia Zoo.

DIET AND FEEDING HABITS. Urodeles *(Ambystoma talpoideum, Amphiuma means, A. pholeter, Pseudobranchus striatus, Siren lacertina)* are the natural prey of adult mud snakes, although various adult frogs, tadpoles, and occasionally fish are also eaten (Carr 1940; Clark 1949; Gibbons and Semlitsch 1991; Guidry 1953; Palmer and Braswell 1995; Van Hyning 1932). Young *F. abacura* probably eat small salamanders, small frogs, and tadpoles. Mud snakes have enlarged teeth at the rear of their upper jaws that probably give them a firmer grip on large slippery amphiumas and sirens. Taub (1967) found a Duvernoy's gland with numerous mucous cells in one *F. abacura,* but none in another, so it is not known if mud snakes use toxic saliva to subdue prey.

PREDATORS AND DEFENSE. Palmer and Braswell (1995) reported an American alligator *(Alligator mississippiensis)* and a cottonmouth *(Agkistrodon piscivorus)* had eaten *F. abacura,* and probably other ophiophagous snakes, carnivorous mammals, large wading birds, and birds of prey also prey on mud snakes, especially the young.

When disturbed, *F. abacura* often will tuck its head beneath its coils and curl the tail to display its red and black venter, and sometimes it will even roll over onto its back to display its red and black belly, feigning death as it does so (Davis 1948; Doody et al. 1996). Such flashes of color may act as warning displays mimicking venomous coral snakes *(Micrurus fulvius).* When handled, newly caught mud snakes do not bite; they sometimes jab the hand with their tail spines, but do not penetrate the skin.

POPULATIONS. *F. abacura* may occur in large numbers at some lowland sites—Hellman and Telford

(1956) collected 478 young mud snakes on a 2.7 km stretch of road fill in Alachua County, Florida, following torrential rains. At upland sites it is less numerous; the species constituted only 53 (2.5%) of the 2,083 snakes from the Hill Parishes of Louisiana recorded by Clark (1949).

REMARKS. A folk tale relates that the tail spine of snakes of the genus *Farancia* is a venomous stinger. This is entirely false. The genus *Farancia* and the species *F. abacura* were reviewed by Mitchell (1982a) and McDaniel and Karges (1983), respectively.

Farancia erytrogramma (Palisot de Beauvois, in Sonnini and Latreille 1801) | Rainbow Snake

RECOGNITION. *F. erytrogramma* is one of our most attractive snakes (TBL to 173.3 cm). It is iridescent black to violet or violet blue with three reddish longitudinal stripes and, often, red borders on its large head scales. The supralabials, infralabials, chin, and throat are lemon yellow; the centers of each supralabial, mental scale, chin shield, and anterior infralabial are usually violet. The venter is red to reddish yellow, with two anterior rows of black spots on the sides and a shorter medial row of black spots. The wedge-shaped head is about as wide as the neck; the tail ends in a spinelike scale. The mostly smooth (some near the anal vent may be weakly keeled), pitless, dorsal body scales usually occur in 19 (17–18) anterior rows, 19 midbody rows, and 17 or 19 (16–19) rows near the anal vent. Beneath are 155–182 ventrals, 34–50 subcaudals, and a divided anal plate (single in about 10% of individuals). Lateral head scales consist of 1 nasal, 1 loreal, 0 preocular (or rarely a very small one above the loreal), 2 (0–1) postoculars, 1–2 + 1–2 temporals, 7 (6–9) supralabials, and 7–8 (6–10) infralabials. The hemipenis is bifurcate with a single sulcus spermaticus, and numerous spines and some slightly serrate calyxes on each lobe. Two *F. erytrogramma* the authors examined had 14 and 15 maxillary teeth, respectively, with the posterior-most enlarged.

Males have 155–164 (mean, 159) ventrals, 44–50 (mean, 47) subcaudals, and TLs that are 16–20 (mean, 17.5) % of TBL; females have 170–182 (mean, 173) ventrals, 34–42 (mean, 38) subcaudals, and TLs that are only 10–16 (mean, 13) % of TBL.

GEOGRAPHIC VARIATION. Two subspecies are recognized. *F. e. erytrogramma* (Palisot de Beauvois, in Sonnini and Latreille 1801), the northern rainbow snake, ranges from southern Maryland south along the Atlantic Coast, to Lake and Pinellas counties, Florida, and west through the Gulf coastal states to southeastern Louisiana. It has red to pink ventrals with black spots restricted to lateral rows and a short medial row, black-spotted subcaudals with red pigment restricted to the borders of the spots, no black pigment on the first row of dorsal body scales, scale row two less than 25% black, scale row three 75% black, and no black encroachment on the red lateral stripes. *F. e. seminola* Neill 1964, the South Florida rainbow snake, has only been found at Fisheating Creek, Glades County, Florida, about 250 km south of the nearest populations of the northern rainbow snake. Its throat and anterior ventrals are heavily pigmented with black, the black subcaudal spots have only narrow red borders, the first two dorsal body scale rows are less than 50% black, scale row three is 100% black, and black pigment encroaches on the red lateral stripes. It is known only from the holotype; intensive collecting since 1964 has not revealed additional specimens.

CONFUSING SPECIES. The mud snake (*F. abacura*) has only one internasal scale, and a plain black back. The black swamp snake (*Seminatrix pygaea*) also has a plain black back.

KARYOTYPE. Undescribed.

FOSSIL RECORD. See account of *F. abacura*.

DISTRIBUTION. The species is found from southern Maryland southward to central Florida (Lake and Pinellas counties), with an isolated colony at Fisheating Creek, Glades County, and westward along the Gulf Coast to southeastern Louisiana.

Northern rainbow snake, *Farancia erytrogramma erytrogramma*; Hyde County, North Carolina. (Photograph by Roger W. Barbour)

HABITAT. This secretive snake prefers coastal plain waterways (rivers, streams, canals, lakes, swamps, and tidal and freshwater marshes) surrounded by sandy soil. Neill (1964) reported that Florida *F. erytrogramma* usually live in dens in the roots of bald cypress trees growing in about 60 cm of water. Man-made struc-

tures are also used for retreats—docks, log or stone piles; the authors once took several from the pilings of a boat ramp in North Carolina.

BEHAVIOR. In Florida, North Carolina, and Virginia, rainbow snakes are active in every month, with

Distribution of *Farancia erytrogramma*.

low activity from October–November to March and the greatest amount of activity in April–June. The increasing activity in March–May probably represents mating and foraging after partial inactivity in winter, and greater activity in June may be due to increased movements by gravid females. Higher winter water temperatures in Florida may allow this snake to be active for more extensive periods, but farther north thermoregulatory basking or hibernation may be necessary. *F. erytrogramma* caught in South Carolina during March and early April by Gibbons et al. (1977) were associated with warm periods (night ATs over 10°C) following two or more days of cooler weather, and captures were often made on the day prior to or following rainfall. However, they believed temperature was the more important cue. Neill (1964) thought October activity may represent increased foraging to build up body fat for winter.

Florida and Georgia *F. erytrogramma* probably spend the winter in the summer habitat, where the water temperature in headsprings does not vary from 22.2–23.4°C; but north of Georgia, adults usually abandon the water with the advent of cold weather and overwinter on higher ground, where Neill (1964) found them hibernating beneath a rotting pine stump, and in a rotting, beetle-infested log. As a result of drift-fence sampling in South Carolina, Gibbons et al. (1977) suggested that hatchling rainbow snakes overwinter in the soil near the nest, and move overland to an aquatic area during next March–April. If the aquatic site is "suitable," *F. erytrogramma* will remain there; but if it is, or becomes, undesirable, it emigrates overland to another aquatic site during a warm spell, and may remain terrestrial in a fossorial state for extended periods of time. Adults will also migrate from drying bodies of water during droughts (Seigel et al. 1995b). Such behaviors seem adaptations to aquatic habitats of the southeastern coastal plain, where water levels vary from year to year.

Most activity is nocturnal, but daytime foraging is not unknown. *F. erytrogramma* normally remain hidden during the day beneath the soil, under logs, or in old stumps. Those that live underwater among the cypress roots slowly stretch upward shortly after dusk until their eyes and nostrils are above water while their tails remain coiled among the roots (Neill 1964).

They do not emerge completely until 2100–2130 hours, and they then forage along the bottom of the waterway until about 2330 hours, when they begin to return to their retreats. Carr (1940) saw what he believed to be a rainbow snake on the bottom of a Florida spring over 4 m deep.

REPRODUCTION. Conant and Collins (1998) reported the minimum TBL at maturity for both sexes was 68.8 cm, but Mitchell (1994) reported that the shortest mature males and females had TBLs of 87.4 and 88.6 cm, respectively, and Gibbons et al. (1977) gave the shortest mature TBL for South Carolina females as 89.0 cm. The age at maturity is unknown, and no data exist on either male or female sexual cycles.

The period and behaviors of courtship/mating have not been reported. The nesting period extends from 30 June to 14 August, with most nests dug in July. According to Neill (1964), nests are dug in sandy soil to depths of 20–25 cm, and a nest measured by Richmond (1945) was 10 cm deep, 20 cm long, and 15 cm wide. N. Fry (in Wright and Wright 1957) reported that a female may excavate a burrow in sandy soil up to 30 cm or more wide. The female possibly remains with the eggs.

After an IP of about 75–80 days, the eggs hatch in September or early October. Clutches may contain 10 (Tennant 1997; Williamson and Roble 1999) to 52 (Mount 1975; Neill 1964) eggs (mean, 32.3; n = 21). The elongated, white eggs have leathery shells, are 25.8–40.0 (mean, 32.4; n = 25) mm long and 14.7–29.0 (mean, 20.8; n = 25) mm wide, and weigh 6.5–8.8 (mean, 7.7; n = 11) g. Hatchlings have 14.3–28.0 (mean, 22.1; n = 31) cm TBLs and weigh 3.6–8.7 (mean, 5.7; n = 10) g. Hatchlings use their caruncle (egg tooth) to slit open the eggshell, and after emergence may remain in the nest several weeks.

GROWTH AND LONGEVITY. Richmond (1954a) suggested that juveniles of both sexes grow about 2.4 cm during their first five months, and Rothman (1961) had a captive grow 9 cm in nine months. No longevity data are available.

DIET AND FEEDING HABITS. Natural and captive prey include freshwater eels *(Anguilla rostrata),* mole salamanders *(Ambystoma talpoidium),* amphiumas *(Amphiuma means),* greater sirens *(Siren lacertina),* other salamanders *(Desmognathus fuscus, Eurycea bislineata, Plethodon cinereus),* ranid frogs *(Rana heckscheri, R. pipiens, R. sphenocephala),* fish, and earthworms (Ashton and Ashton 1981; Dundee and Rossman 1989; Gibbons and Semlitsch 1991; Neill 1964; Palmer and Braswell 1995; Richmond 1945; Wright and Wright 1957). In the wild, adults feed primarily on freshwater eels, and juveniles eat tadpoles and earthworms.

It is not known whether or not *F. erytrogramma* uses venom to overcome its prey, but it has enlarged posterior maxillary teeth and a mixed serous-mucous Duvernoy's gland (Taub 1967).

PREDATORS AND DEFENSE. Reported predators are bullfrogs *(Rana catesbeiana),* indigo snakes *(Drymarchon corais),* common kingsnakes *(Lampropeltis getula),* hawks, and otters *(Lontra canadensis);* raccoons *(Procyon lotor)* and striped skunks *(Mephitis mephitis)* raid nests and eat the eggs and hatchlings (de Rageot 1992; C. Ernst, pers. obs.; Metrolis 1971; Neill 1964; Palmer and Braswell 1995; Richmond 1945).

When first discovered, this snake often remains perfectly calm and still, or it might try to slowly crawl away. In the authors' experience, rainbow snakes never bite when handled, but will press the pointed tips of their tails into their captor's hand, and some will expel musk.

POPULATIONS. Because of its secretive nature, *F. erytrogramma* gives a false impression of being rare. In fact, they can occur in rather dense populations—Richmond (1945) plowed up 20 in a 4.1 ha Virginia field, and Mount (1975) collected 8 within 30 m at an Alabama site. Unfortunately, Habitat destruction and collecting for the pet trade have decimated some populations. It is considered endangered in Mississippi and a species of special concern in Louisiana; the status of the subspecies *F. e. seminola* is undetermined.

REMARKS. Rainbow snakes usually do poorly in captivity, refusing food and eventually starving to death. The authors urge this be taken into consideration when these snakes are caught. The species was reviewed by Mitchell (1982b).

Ficimia streckeri Taylor 1931 | Taumaulipian Hook-nosed Snake

RECOGNITION. The maximum TBL of this small snake is 48.3 cm. Its ground color varies from tan or brown to gray or grayish olive, and its back is crossed by 33–60 narrow (1–2 scales wide), brown, dark gray or olive blotches or rows of small dark spots. The brownish to gray head lacks a dorsal pattern, but has an oblique dark spot extending backward from the rear bottom of the orbit, and a few small dark specks may occur along the upper sides of the supralabials. The narrow tip of the snout is upturned, concave, wide at its base, and hooklike. The venter is pale brown, lavender, or whitish. Body scales are smooth with a single apical pit, and lie in 17 (occasionally 18 or 19) rows at midbody. Beneath are 126–160 ventrals, 28–41 subcaudals, and a divided anal plate. The head

is not, or is only barely, broader than the neck. Diagnostic lateral head scales include 2 nasals (subdivided below the naris), 0 loreals, 1 preocular, 1–2 postoculars, 1 + 2 temporals, 7 supralabials, and 7–8 infralabials. The rostral scale is in wide contact with the frontal scale. The single hemipenis has one sulcus spermaticus, the base naked except for one enlarged spine on each side of the sulcus, very small spines near the base of the enlarged spine merging from spinulate calyxes on the distal half of the organ, and some larger spines positioned between the enlarged basal spines and calyxes, and the apex is nude (Hardy 1976a). Each maxilla has 13–14 aglyphous teeth.

The sexes are difficult to distinguish, but females are slightly longer and have greater numbers of ven-

Taumaulipian hook-nosed snake, *Ficimia streckeri*. (Photograph by R. D. Bartlett)

trals; males have longer tails and more subcaudals (Hardy 1976a).

GEOGRAPHIC VARIATION. No subspecies are recognized. *F. streckeri* has often been considered merely a northern subspecies of the Mexican snake *F. olivacea*, but Taylor (1949) found no evidence of intergradation between the two. The dark suborbital spot of *F. streckeri* distinguishes it from *F. olivacea* (Brown and Brown 1967); but some *olivacea* also have such a spot, although it is better developed in *streckeri* (Hardy 1975b). Differences in hemipenile structure, the number of maxillary teeth (14–17; 9 below the suborbital process in *olivacea*), and the absence of dorsal bands in adult *olivacea* indicate *streckeri* and *olivacea* are separate species.

CONFUSING SPECIES. The western hog-nosed snake *(Heterodon nasicus)* has keeled body scales. The Chihuahuan hook-nosed snake *(Gyalopion canum)* has

fewer body bands (25–48), a head patterned with dark bands, and a rostral scale that does not touch the frontal scale. The thornscrub hook-nosed snake *(G. quadrangulare)* has an extensive dorsal head blotch, broader dorsal bands, and an undivided anal plate.

KARYOTYPE. Undescribed.

FOSSIL RECORD. Pleistocene or Holocene vertebrae of *F. streckeri* were recovered from Howell's Ridge Cave, Grant County, Texas, by Van Devender and Worthington (1977).

DISTRIBUTION. *F. streckeri* ranges from the lower Rio Grande Valley in southern Texas (Brooks, Duval, Jim Hogg, Starr, Webb, and Zapata counties) southward to Hidalgo, Veracruz, and Puebla, Mexico.

HABITAT. The natural habitat is an area of grayish, gravelly or alluvial soil with brush composed of *Opun-*

Distribution of *Ficimia streckeri*.

tia cactus, mesquite, acacia, and paloverde. In such places the snake occurs most frequently in the more moist parts, especially around streams, stock ponds, irrigation ditches, and the borders of agricultural fields. Where the habitat has been incorporated into towns and suburbs, *F. streckeri* is sometimes found on freshly watered lawns.

BEHAVIOR. Due to its secretive, fossorial existence, few life history data have been recorded. In Texas, *F. streckeri* is most surface active during May and June, but is seldom seen during the heat of July and August or in the fall. Apparently it estivates over most of this period. It is not known if *F. streckeri* hibernates during the winter. It is seldom seen above ground during the daylight hours, preferring to remain buried in the ground or under some object. Most captures or observations have been after dark, so the snake seems nocturnal. It burrows by using its broad upturned snout to push into the soil.

REPRODUCTION. Reproductive data on this small snake are woefully lacking. Both sexes apparently mature at 25 cm TBL, and females are probably oviparous (Wright and Wright 1957). Although no supporting data have been published, its Latin American congener *F. publia* is definitely an egg layer (Greer 1966).

GROWTH AND LONGEVITY. Unknown.

DIET AND FEEDING HABITS. Foraging usually takes place after sunset. Spiders, centipedes, and possibly other small invertebrates are the usual foods, with spiders the favorite prey (Conant and Collins 1998; Mulaik and Mulaik 1943; Tennant 1984; Wright and Wright 1957). A longtime captive kept by Tennant (1984) ate a variety of spiders, but often had trouble capturing them. Another of his captives would not eat either spiders or centipedes, but survived for four months on cave crickets. In contrast, Mulaik and Mulaik (1943) reported that captives do not feed on termites or other insects.

The slightly elongated rear teeth have a series of very small, anterior corrugations that possibly channel the snake's saliva into its prey (Tennant 1984).

PREDATORS AND DEFENSE. The only recorded predator of *F. streckeri* was a coral snake (*Micrurus* sp.) (Martin 1958). Surely other ophiophagous snakes, as well as predatory birds and mammals, eat it, and humans kill many with their vehicles and habitat destruction.

When handled, *F. streckeri* tries to push its head between the fingers, reminiscent of its burrowing behavior. When threatened on the ground, it sometimes slowly waves its elevated head and forebody, resembling a viper. Disturbed snakes may throw their bodies into contortions while everting and contracting the cloaca through the vent, producing a strange, loud popping sound.

POPULATIONS. No population study has been undertaken, but large numbers of *F. streckeri* are commonly encountered at night on roads in undeveloped areas during late spring (Tennant 1984).

REMARKS. The genus *Ficimia* is most closely related to the genera *Gyalopion* and *Pseudoficimia* (Hardy 1975c). Its center of origin was probably the tropical lowlands southwest of the Mexican Plateau; ancestors of *F. streckeri* migrated to southern Texas, where they differentiated into that species (Hardy 1975c). Hardy (1976a, 1990) published reviews of *F. streckeri* and the genus *Ficimia*.

Gyalopion Cope 1861a

Hook-nosed Snakes

Key to the Species of *Gyalopion*

1a. Single anal plate; broad, black dorsal saddles . . . .
. . . . *G. quadrangulare*

2a. Divided anal plate; narrow, brown dorsal crossbands . . .
. . . . *G. canum*

Gyalopion canum Cope 1861a │ Chihuahuan Hook-nosed Snake

RECOGNITION. This small (to 38.4 cm TBL) south-western snake has an upturned snout and smooth scales. Its body color varies from gray brown or cinnamon brown to yellowish brown; 25–52 darker brown, dark-bordered, transverse bands cross the body, and another 8–15 cross the tail. Several broad, dark brown bars are also present on the head, including one that crosses the snout between the orbits and another that extends from the bottom of the orbit to the supralabials. The venter is cream or white with a salmon pink center. Dorsal body scales are smooth with a single apical pit, and lie in 20 anterior rows, and 17 rows at midbody and near the tail. Beneath are 122–146 ventrals, 25–37 subcaudals 25–37, and a divided anal plate. The head is only a little broader than the neck; laterally it has 2 nasals (subdivided below the

naris), 0 (rarely 1) loreal, 1 preocular, 2 postoculars, 1 + 2 temporals, 7 (6) supralabials, and 7 (8) infralabials. The narrow tip of the snout is turned upward, and the rostral scale is flat or concave at its broad base and extends backward to touch the preoculars. The single, slightly bulbous hemipenis extends 7–13 subcaudals when inverted and has a single sulcus spermaticus, an almost naked base with two to three large spines, spinulate calyxes on the distal half, and a nude (or practically so) apex. Females also have a small, less developed, hemipenis. The 12–15 maxillary teeth increase in length toward the rear; those most posterior are grooved.

Sex is difficult to distinguish. Females have slightly longer bodies than males, but males have slightly longer tails. Most scale counts overlap.

Chihuahuan hook-nosed snake, *Gyalopion canum*; Cochise County, Arizona. (Photograph by Cecil Schwalbe)

GEOGRAPHIC VARIATION. No subspecies have been described.

CONFUSING SPECIES. To distinguish the thornscrub hook-nosed snake *(Gyalopion quadrangulare),* see the key above. The Taumaulipian hook-nosed snake *(Ficimia streckeri)* lacks dark head bands, has a shorter rostral that only extends backward to the frontal scale, and has narrower body bands. The western hog-nosed snake *(Heterodon nasicus)* has keeled body scales and a ridge extending the length of its rostral scale.

KARYOTYPE. Not described.

FOSSIL RECORD. Pleistocene (Rancholabrean) remains have been found in northern Arizona (Mead et al. 1984), New Mexico (Van Devender and Worthington 1977), and Texas (Parmley 1990a).

DISTRIBUTION. *G. canum* ranges from western Texas and southern New Mexico to southeastern Arizona, and south in Mexico to Zacatecas and San Luis Potosí.

HABITAT. In the United States, *G. canum* inhabits semideserts and other arid terrains vegetated by short grasses, agave, blackbush, creosote bush, and mesquite. The soil is often loose, accommodating its burrowing habitat, but may not contain much sand or gravel. It occurs in highlands to at least the piñon-juniper zone, and has been found at elevations over 2,000 m in Texas. In New Mexico, most are found in grass-covered foothills at intermediate elevations, but small numbers live above in woodlands and below in deserts (Degenhardt et al. 1996).

BEHAVIOR. *G. canum* is an inveterate burrower that spends most of its life underground (which explains why its life history is poorly known). Using its upturned snout and stocky muscular body, it levers aside the soil particles until it is completely buried. Sometimes it will merely crawl beneath a rock or other object on the surface for shelter. It is a slow crawler, and when found on the surface, usually cannot move quickly enough to escape.

Most daily activity is nocturnal. A few begin to emerge at dusk, and as darkness deepens more come

Distribution of *Gyalopion canum.*

to the surface. Some have been found on the surface during the day, but such records are relatively rare. Cool rains seem to stimulate surface activity, and some of the day records occurred after such events. Annually, most have been collected from April to September, but it has also been captured in March (McCoy 1961b) and early November (Degenhardt et al. 1996). The annual activity period is possibly longer, since *G. canum* has been found active at rather cold temperatures, especially during or after rains. Its underground lifestyle is adaptive for water conservation, especially in desert habitats during the summer. No data are available on the snake's winter habits; but Degenhardt et al. (1996) thought that its range in New Mexico is probably restricted from farther northward extension because its rather shallow soil retreats are inadequate protection against severe winter temperatures.

REPRODUCTION. Wright and Wright (1957) reported that 16.8–30.2 cm males and 20.5–32.5 cm females are mature. Courtship and mating behaviors and the gametic cycles are undescribed.

G. canum is oviparous, laying one to four eggs in June or July (Degenhardt et al. 1996; Hardy 1975a). The white, leathery-shelled eggs are 23–29 mm in length and weigh 1.9–2.3 g (Degenhardt et al. 1996; Hardy 1975a).

GROWTH AND LONGEVITY.   Unreported.

DIET AND FEEDING BEHAVIOR.   Natural prey are
spiders, scorpions, and centipedes (Conant and
Collins 1998; Licht and Gehlbach 1961; Tennant 1984;
Webb 1960). Some captives have taken spiders, small
snakes, lizard eggs, rat legs, rat meat, and beef, but
others have refused spiders, millipedes, small frogs,
snakes, and newborn mice (Kauffeld 1948; Tanzer, in
Degenhardt et al. 1996; Wright and Wright 1957). One
captive spent over 14 hours eating a larger, dead ring-
necked snake *(Diadophis punctatus),* but died three
days later, apparently from the effects of consuming
too large a meal (the *Diadophis* was only about 33%
digested) (Vaeth 1980).

Prey is seized and worked to the rear of the mouth,
where the large grooved teeth take hold. Saliva then
flows down the tooth grooves into the wounds, help-
ing to immobilize the prey. No reports of the toxicity
of the saliva are available.

PREDATORS AND DEFENSE.   Spotted skunks *(Spilogale)* and larger snakes, such as *Crotalus lepidus* and
Micrurus fulvius, are reported predators (Milstead et al.
1950; Tennant 1984); other large snakes, birds of prey,
and carnivorous mammals probably also eat them. A
G. canum and a *Diadophis punctatus* were found gripping each other by the jaws: the larger *Diadophis* was
probably trying to eat the smaller *Gyalopion* (Degenhardt et al. 1996). Motorized vehicles are also a serious threat.

When touched or handled, *G. canum* displays the
peculiar defensive behavior referred to as "anal popping." It turns its anal vent towards the direction of
the encounter and everts the cloacal lining through
the vent, causing a bubbling or popping sound and
often the expulsion of feces. At the same time it twists
and contorts its body. The initial pops are of high amplitude (70–73 dB) and broad frequency range
(359–15,178 Hz), but in subsequent pops the amplitude drops off and the frequency range narrows; no
temporal pattern or harmonics are noticeable (Young
et al. 1999). The release of air is controlled mostly by
the cloacal sphincter muscle, but other extrinsic
muscles may also be involved.

G. canum strike with closed mouths and apparently
never bite. It is possible that its probable toxic saliva
(McKinistry 1978) could potentially deter smaller animals from harming it.

POPULATIONS.   An ecological study that includes
an assessment of population dynamics would be very
helpful, as no such data exist. This snake is common
in the Trans-Pecos and northern Stockton Plateau of
Texas (Tennant 1984), but Price and LaPointe (1990)
only found one during a four-year study of snakes on
a road in New Mexico.

REMARKS.   Systematics of the genus *Gyalopion* are
discussed by Hardy (1975a, 1975c, 1976b); it is closely
related to *Ficimia* and *Pseudoficimia,* and the three genera probably had a common ancestor, possibly during
the Oligocene in southern Mexico. Hardy (1975c)
thought that *G. canum* evolved in the Pliocene or Pleistocene at higher elevations in the Chihuahuan Desert
and later spread northward into its present range.

Gyalopion quadrangulare (Günther 1893) | Thornscrub Hook-nosed Snake

RECOGNITION.   This small hook-nosed species has
a maximum TBL of 35.4 cm. Its body is cream, white,
grayish white, or pink with 16–41 black, rectangular-
shaped dorsal blotches, and another 3–10 dark
blotches on the tail. All blotches extend downward on
the sides to varying degrees, sometimes to the ventrals (see GEOGRAPHIC VARIATION), and occasionally the
dorsal scales lying between the blotches are dark-
bordered. An orange red stripe, which is interrupted
by the black body blotches, is present along each side
of the body. A black head cap begins just anterior to
the orbits, passes between them, and then narrows
behind the orbits before joining the first rectangular
black blotch on the neck (how far it extends rearward
varies). The venter is cream to greenish yellow and is
usually unpatterned (some Mexican individuals have
black ventral pigment). The head is only a little broader
than the neck. Dorsal body scales are smooth with an

Thornscrub hook-nosed snake, *Gyalopion quadrangulare*; Mazetlen. (Photograph by Cecil Schwalbe)

apical pit, and lie in 17 (15–18) anterior rows, 17 (16) midbody rows, and 17 (15–18) posterior rows. Beneath are 116–140 ventrals, 20–32 subcaudals, and an undivided anal plate. Lateral head scales consist of 2 nasals (subdivided below the naris), 0 (1) loreal, 1 preocular, 2 (3) postoculars, 1 + 2–3 temporals, 6 (5–8) supralabials, and 6 (5–8) infralabials. The narrow tip of the snout is only slightly upturned; the rostral scale is flat or concave at its broad base, and extends posteriorly to meet the preoculars. The single, slightly bulbous hemipenis extends 6–12 subcaudals when inverted. It has a single sulcus spermaticus, a shaft with a naked base and 2–3 large basal spines, followed by a spinose region, spinulate calyxes on the distal half, and a nude apex. Unlike female *G. canum*, female *G. quadrangulare* lack a hemipenis (but retain hemipenile muscles). Each maxilla bears 13–15 teeth that increase in length from front to rear with no diastema; those most posterior are always grooved, but grooves may be present on all maxillary teeth.

Males have a slightly longer TL (11.7–16.0% of TBL) than that of females (10–14% of TBL). The numbers of ventral scutes, subcaudals, and body and tail blotches show no sexual dimorphism.

GEOGRAPHIC VARIATION. No subspecies are recognized. However, north-south clinal variation occurs (especially in Mexico) in TL as a percentage of TBL, presence or absence of loreal scales, number of scale rows on the neck and near the anal vent, presence or absence of lateral interblotches between the rectangular blotches, lateral extension of the dorsal rectangular blotches (closer to the ventrals in the north), and the amount of dark pigment on the sides of the venter (Hardy and McDiarmid 1969).

CONFUSING SPECIES. The Chihuahuan hook-nosed snake *(G. canum)* can be distinguished using the key presented above. The Mexican hook-nosed snake *(Ficimia streckeri)* lacks dark head bands and has a shorter rostral scute that extends rearward only to the frontal scale, narrower body bands, and a divided anal plate. The western hog-nosed snake *(Heterodon nasicus)* has keeled body scales and a ridge extending the length of its rostral scale. The long-nosed snake *(Rhinocheilus lecontei)* lacks an upturned snout, has more than 20 body scale rows, and most of its subcaudals are in a single row.

Distribution of *Gyalopion quadrangulare*.

KARYOTYPE.   Not reported.

FOSSIL RECORD.   Pleistocene (Rancholabrean) remains are known from Texas (Van Devender and Bradley 1994).

DISTRIBUTION.   *G. quadrangulare* ranges from near Nogales and Patagonia, Santa Cruz County, in extreme southern Arizona, south through Sonora and Sinaloa to Nayarit in Mexico.

HABITAT.   In Arizona, this snake lives in grass- and mesquite-covered, rolling foothills at elevations of 1,000–1,341 m.

BEHAVIOR.   It was not found in the United States until 1959 (Woodin 1962), and even today records of this snake only extend its range a relatively short distance north of Mexico. No concentrated effort has been made to gain data on its life history, and what information is available is mostly anecdotal or based on faunal or other accounts of Mexican populations.

Active *G. quadrangulare* have been found in June and July and in October and November. Most are dis-covered on roads at night, but two Arizona records are at 1600 and 1605 hours (Funk 1964d; Woodin 1962). In Sinaloa, *G. quadrangulare* are never collected at ATs below 27°C, and most are active at night ATs of 28–29°C (Hardy and McDiarmid 1969). One was found there floating on a stick in a water-filled irrigation ditch after a morning rain. Days are probably spent under rocks or buried in loose sand.

REPRODUCTION.   Greer (1966) found two gravid Sinaloan females in July. One contained six eggs on 12 July; the anterior-most oviductal egg was 8.0 × 4.5 mm, and the rest had an average size of 12.5 × 5.0 mm. The other contained three eggs ready for oviposition on 4 July; the eggs averaged 22.3 × 6.8 mm and were white with flexible, opaque shells. Newly hatched young are colored and patterned like adults, but their red areas may be a darker.

GROWTH AND LONGEVITY.   Unreported.

DIET AND FEEDING HABITS.   The wild diet consists mostly of spiders, but centipedes and small scorpions are probably also eaten (Bogert and Oliver 1945; Stebbins 1985; Woodin 1962).

PREDATORS AND DEFENSE.   No reports of predation are available, although some are killed on roads at night. This species is not known to use the cloacal popping defense regularly performed by *G. canum*.

POPULATIONS.   *G. quadrangulare* seems scarce in Arizona, but no concentrated effort to study its population has been made.

REMARKS.   The species has been reviewed by Hardy (1975a, 1976b). The spelling *quadrangulare* is used in place of *quadrangularis* following Frost and Collins (1988).

Hardy (1975c) thought *G. quadrangulare* evolved separately from *G. canum* in the coastal lowlands of western Mexico during the Pliocene or Pleistocene.

Heterodon Latreille, in Sonnini and Latreille 1801

Hog-nosed Snakes

Key to the Species of *Heterodon*

1a. Rostral scale straight or only slightly upturned, prefrontal scales touch, underside of tail lighter than venter . . . . *H. platirhinos*

1b. Rostral scale abruptly upturned, prefrontals separated by small scales, underside of tail colored same as venter . . . 2

2a. Two rows of dark spots on side of body, venter black with small white or yellow patches, rostral scale as broad as space between eyes . . . . *H. nasicus*

2b. One row of dark spots on side of body, venter light with faint brownish pigment posteriorly, rostral scale narrower than space between eyes . . . . *H. simus*

Heterodon nasicus Baird and Girard 1852a │ Western Hog-nosed Snake

RECOGNITION. *H. nasicus* is stout-bodied (maximum TBL, 154 cm; but most individuals are smaller than 80 cm), with a sharply upturned rostrum, which is dorsally concave and medially keeled. The body is buffy gray, brown, or olive, with a series of 23–52 dark brown dorsal blotches, two longitudinal rows of smaller dark brown blotches on each side, and 8–19 dark tail bands. A dark transverse bar lying between the eyes extends downward behind each eye to the corner of the mouth, and a middorsal and two elongated lateral blotches extend forward from the neck to the parietal scales. The venter is mostly black with yellow or whitish blotches. Dorsal body scales are keeled and pitted, and occur in 23 (21–26) anterior rows, 21–23 (19–26) midbody rows, and 19 (16–23) posterior rows. Beneath are 125–156 ventrals, 26–50

subcaudals, and a divided anal plate. Each side of the head has 2 nasals, 2 (0–4) loreals, an ocular ring of 7–13 scales below the supraocular scale, 4 (2–5) + 5 (3–7) temporals, 8 (7) supralabials, and 10–11 (9–13) infralabials. Behind the rostrum are 2–28 small accessory (azygous) scales between the internasal and prefrontal scales. The bilobed hemipenis has a bifurcated sulcus spermaticus, a spiny base, and distal calyces. Each maxilla has 9–10 teeth; a diastema separates the longer posterior tooth from the smaller teeth anterior to it, and the maxillae can rotate to elevate the enlarged posterior tooth.

The smaller males (TBL to 67 cm) have 125–147 (mean, 132) ventrals, 34–50 (mean, 42) subcaudals, 23–52 (mean, 34) dorsal body blotches, 11–15 (mean, 13) tail bands, and TLs of 12–19 (mean, 16.5) % of

Mexican hog-nosed snake,
Heterodon nasicus kennerlyi;
Cochise County, Arizona.
(Photograph by Carl H. Ernst)

TBL; the larger females (TBL to 154 cm) have 126–156 (mean, 142) ventrals, 26–49 (mean, 34) subcaudals, 30–50 (mean, 39) dorsal body blotches, 8–19 (mean, 11) tail bands, and TLs of 9–13 (mean, 12) % of TBL.

GEOGRAPHIC VARIATION. Two subspecies are recognized. *H. n. nasicus* Baird and Girard 1852a, the plains hog-nosed snake, has 9–28 accessory scales between the internasals and prefrontals on the snout behind the rostrum. It ranges from western Minnesota, southwestern Manitoba, southern Alberta, and southeastern Saskatchewan south to central and eastern Texas and eastern New Mexico, and also occurs in isolated populations in southeastern Minnesota, northwestern Iowa and eastern Nebraska, the prairies of western Illinois, northwestern and southeastern Missouri, central Wyoming, and northwestern Colorado. The taxon *H. n. gloydi* Edgren 1952, the dusky hognosed snake, has been synonymized with *H. n. nasicus*; see Platt (1969) and Walley and Eckerman (1999) for details. *H. n. kennerlyi* Kennicott 1860a, the Mexican hog-nosed snake, has only two to six small accessory scales between the internasal and prefrontal scales on the snout behind the rostrum. It is found in southwestern New Mexico and the Rio Grande Valley of Texas south and east in Mexico to Tamaulipas, San Luis Potosí, and eastern Aguascalientes.

CONFUSING SPECIES. Other species of hog-nosed snakes can be distinguished by the above key. The pygmy rattlesnake *(Sistrurus miliarius)* has a rattle, a

hole between the nostril and eye, and vertically elliptical pupils. The hook-nosed snake *(Gyalopion canum)* has a small upturned rostral scale that lacks a medial ridge, smooth body scales that normally lie in 17 rows at midbody, and a whitish venter. Leaf-nosed snakes *(Phyllorhynchus)* and patch-nosed snakes *(Salvadora)* have the tip of the rostrum turned back between the internasal scales.

KARYOTYPE. The karyotype is 2n = 36 chromosomes: 16 macrochromosomes and 20 microchromosomes (no chromosomes are acrocenteric), with sex determination ZZ in males and ZW in females (Baker et al. 1972). The NOR is located on the first pair of microchromosomes (Camper and Hanks 1995).

FOSSIL RECORD. The fossil record of *Heterodon* suggests that two lines of evolution occurred within the genus by the late Miocene (Barstovian). The Barstovian Midwestern species *Paleoheterodon tiheni* gave rise to the late Pliocene (Blancan) species *H. plionasicus* and to *H. nasicus* in the early Pleistocene (Blancan), and from *H. nasicus* evolved *H. simus*, possibly in the Pleistocene (Irvingtonian) of Florida. *H. platirhinos* apparently evolved in a different line, replacing the Pliocene (Hemphillian) species *H. brevis* in Florida (Meylan 1982).

Fossil *H. nasicus* are known from the Pleistocene Blancan of Kansas (Brattstrom 1967); Irvingtonian (?) of Florida (Meylan 1982), Kansas (Holman 1972b),

Distribution of *Heterodon nasicus*.

Oklahoma (Holman 1986b), and Texas (Holman 1965a); and Rancholabrean of Kansas (Brattstrom 1967), New Mexico (Van Devender and Worthington 1977), Oklahoma (Brattstrom 1967), and Texas (Hill 1971; Holman 1963, 1964). Other fossil remains identified only to the genus *Heterodon* that may be of *H. nasicus* are from the Rancholabrean of Arkansas (Dowling 1958b) and Irvingtonian and Rancholabrean of Texas (Kasper and Parmley 1990; Parmley 1988a, 1988b, 1990b).

DISTRIBUTION. *H. nasicus* ranges from western Minnesota, southwestern Manitoba, southern Alberta and southeastern Saskatchewan south to eastern and central Texas and New Mexico, and to Zacatecas, Aguascalientes, and San Luis Potosí in Mexico. Isolated populations also are found in northwestern Iowa, western Illinois, northwestern and southeastern Missouri, and central Wyoming.

HABITAT. It is a prairie or savannah species, preferring grasslands with well drained sandy or gravelly soil into which it burrows (see *H. platirhinos* for details) or from which it digs out prey, but it also occurs in suburbs, cultivated fields, pastures, floodplains, canyon bottoms, scrub brush, creosote deserts, and montane woodlands. It has been found at elevations from near sea level to over 2,400 m.

BEHAVIOR. The annual activity period is longer in the south than in the northern portions of the range, and at lower elevations versus higher elevations. In the south, it is probably active from late March–early April to October–November, but farther north or at higher elevations it may not surface until mid-April–May and may retreat underground in early October. In Alberta, *H. nasicus* has been seen as early as 10 May and as late as 20 September, an annual activity period of only 133 days (Pendlebury 1976), and is most active May–July, when daytime temperatures are highest (Russell and Bauer 1993). In contrast, Kansas *H. nasicus* are active from 24 April to 31 October, 190 days, and most active May–early August (Platt 1969). Hibernation probably takes place within the home range, underground below the frost line, in individual burrows the snake digs itself or in mammal burrows (Degenhardt et al. 1996; Smith 1961).

Daily activity is diurnal, mostly in the morning or late afternoon into evening. Platt (1969) occasionally saw them at dusk, but never found any active after dark, and Pendlebury (1976) caught 10 of 13 individuals in Alberta during the day. The night is spent in a temporary burrow the snake constructs in loose soil with its upturned snout, which is more upturned and larger than that of other species of *Heterodon* and forms a better shovel (Edgren 1955; Platt 1969). *H. nasicus* seldom takes shelter beneath rocks or logs.

Platt (1969) made no attempt to correlate surface activity with rainfall, but did conclude that surface activity was related to periods of rising ATs and that the greatest amount of activity occurred when the mean maximum AT was at least 2.2°C higher than the immediately preceding period. Maximum and minimum ATs on the day of capture in Alberta were 18.9–28.3 and 0.0–14.4°C, respectively (Pendlebury 1976). Platt (1969) reported CTs of active Kansas snakes were 21.4–36.2°C (STs, 17.6–36.0°C), with the usual activity range 27.0–35.0°C. One sluggish individual in a trap had a CT of 13.7°C, but others were able to make avoidance movements at 4.0°C and were able to right themselves at 5.6°C.

The mean distances between points of capture of *H. nasicus* at two Kansas sites were 79 and 207 m for males and 93 and 255 m for females (Platt 1969). A movement of 408 m in 17 days and one of 378 m in 79 days were made by males during the spring and autumn breeding seasons. Males that moved 777 m in 32 days and 602 m in 219 days may have shifted their home ranges. The longest trip was by a female who crawled about 1.6 km between 9 August and 12 June of the next year.

REPRODUCTION. Females attain maturity in 2–3 years; males in 1–2 years. Females mature at a TBL of 38–43 cm and males at a TBL of 38–40 cm (Conant and Collins 1998; Stebbins 1985; Wright and Wright 1957). Platt (1969) found Kansas females mature at 35.0 cm SVL and males at about 30 cm SVL.

In the spring, immature females contain 1–3 mm follicles. In late summer, preceding maturity, some of these enlarge to 3–5 mm. Approximately 50% of the enlarged follicles add yolk, grow rapidly, and mature the following spring. Mature females contain enlarged ova in late May–June, and oviductal eggs in mid-

June–July. In addition to enlarged follicles or oviductal eggs, a second compliment of smaller follicles is normally present, which represents ova to be matured the next year (C. Ernst, pers. obs.; Marr 1944; Pendlebury 1976; Platt 1969). Although females appear to have an annual gametic cycle, the production of litters seems to be on a biennial cycle that allows females to replenish lost energy stores. RCM is 0.224–0.735 (Iverson 1995; Seigel and Fitch 1984).

Most males initiate spermatogenesis when nine months old in their first spring, and they mature at 1.0–1.5 years. Spermatogonia and some primary spermatocytes are present in the testes during May. Spermatogenic activity reaches its peak in July–early August: primary spermatocytes and early spermatids are common in early July; by late July, spermatids of all stages and some mature sperm are present; by September sperm have passed into the vas deferens (Platt 1969).

Most mating occurs in late March–May (Guidry 1953; Platt 1969), but courtship/mating has also been observed to a lesser extent from August into the fall. Because this snake does not hibernate communally, males may wander widely and seek out more sedentary females in the first few weeks after emergence from hibernation (Platt 1969). Odor trails possibly lead them to mates. The courtship/mating behaviors have not been described. Females can store sperm over winter from fall matings.

The nesting period extends from early June to late July; most eggs are laid in July. Nests are excavated to 10 cm in sandy or other loose soil; at times the eggs are laid one after another in a tunnel instead of in a cluster in a depression (Platt 1969). Clutches contain 2 (Sabath and Worthington 1959) to 23–24 (Marr 1944; Wright and Wright 1957) (mean, 10.5; n = 40) eggs. They are nonadherrant, elliptical, and white or cream colored, and have smooth leathery shells; they are 20–42 (mean, 30.5; n = 37) mm long and 12.7–25.0 (mean, 18.0; n = 37) mm wide, and weigh 4.3–6.8 (mean, 5.9; n = 17) g. IP depends on IT and is 50–64 (mean, 56.9, n = 7) days. Hatching normally occurs from mid-August to mid-September. Hatchlings are brighter colored than adults, have 14.0–20.0 (mean, 17.5; n = 21) cm TBLs, and weigh 3.9–4.6 (mean, 4.2; n = 3) g.

GROWTH AND LONGEVITY. Females grow faster and larger. Platt (1969) reported the following probable growth rates for male *H. nasicus* in Kansas: 9 months of age, 17.9–25.5 cm SVL (2.06 cm/month increase); 21 months, 28.2–32.6 cm SVL (1.86 cm/month growth); 33 months, 33.0–35.6 cm SVL (0.63 cm/month); and 45 months, 36.0–37.7 cm SVL (0.48 cm/month growth). Similarly, females at 9 months old had 20.6–29.6 SVL (2.93 cm/month growth); at 21 months, 31.2–39.8 cm SVL (2.29 cm/month), at 33 months, 41.8–45.1 cm SVL (1.66 cm/month), and at 45 months, 47.1–49.0 cm SVL (0.77 cm/month growth). Of three recaptured Illinois *H. nasicus*, two grew 7.2 cm and gained 27–37 g (80–129%) in two years, and one gained 10 cm and 68 g (82%) in three years (Kolbe 1999). The longevity record for the species is of a *H. n. nasicus*, caught as an adult, which was still alive after 19 years, 10 months, and 28 days at the Oklahoma City Zoo (Snider and Bowler 1992).

DIET AND FEEDING HABITS. *H. nasicus* uses odor and sight to detect prey. When it is found, the snake crawls quickly toward it and seizes the animal in its wide-open mouth, often while attempting to hold it under a coil of its body. Buried prey is dug out with the upturned snout.

H. nasicus is not as dependent on amphibian prey as the other two species of *Heterodon*. Platt (1969) calculated that amphibians were taken 13–57% of the time, reptiles 17–48%, mammals 5–33%, and birds 1–14%; but, at an Illinois site, less than 7% of *H. nasicus* ate lizards, and only two individuals were observed feeding on turtle eggs (Kolbe 1999). Natural prey are amphibians—toads *(Bufo cognatus, B. punctatus, B. woodhousei),* spadefoots *(Scaphiopus bombifrons, S. hammondi),* frogs *(Rana catesbeiana* tadpoles, *R. pipiens),* and salamanders *(Ambystoma tigrinum);* reptiles—lizards *(Cnemidophorus sexlineatus, Crotophytus collaris, Eumeces septentrionalis, E. multivirgatus* eggs, *Holbrookia maculata, Phrynosoma* sp., *Sceloporus undulatus, Uta stansburiana),* snakes *(Coluber constrictor, Thamnophis radix,* and unidentified snake eggs), and turtles *(Chelydra serpentina* [eggs], *Chrysemys picta* [eggs], *Emydoidea blandingii* [eggs], *Kinosternon flavescens* [eggs and young], *Terrapene ornata* [eggs]);* birds—grasshopper sparrow *(Ammodramus savannarum),* western meadowlark *(Sturnella neglecta),* and eggs of ground-nesting birds (possibly quail, *Colinus virginianus;* or ring-necked pheasant, *Phasianus colchicus);* mammals—mice and voles *(Microtus ochrogaster, Peromyscus leucopus, Perognathus flavus, Reithrodontomys megalotus);* and insects (possibly ingested with other prey)—ants (Hymenoptera), beetles (Coleoptera), and grasshoppers (Orthoptera) (Breckenridge 1944; Diener 1957a; Gehlbach 1956; Gehlbach and Collette 1959; Kolbe 1999; Kolbe et al. 1999; Marr 1944; Murphy and Dloogatch 1980; Pendlebury 1976; Platt 1969; Stebbins 1954; Tennant 1985; Woodin 1953). Additional species eaten by captives are frogs *(Acris crepitans, Pseudacris crucifer, P. triseriata, Rana sylvatica),* salamanders *(Ambystoma opacum),* birds *(Passer domesticus, Turdus migratorius),* and mammals *(Blarina* sp., *Mus musculus, Rattus norvegicus* [young]) (Munro 1949b; Swenson 1950). *H. nasicus* has even practiced cannibalism on both its young and its eggs in captivity (Hammack 1991; Iverson 1975; Mitchell and Groves 1993).

Heterodon are well adapted for eating toads. Their large mouths, mobile maxillae, and elongated posterior maxillary teeth are ideal for holding and deflating struggling, inflated toads (Kroll 1976). The saliva of *H. nasicus* is toxic to prey (Kroll 1976; McKinistry 1978; Weaver 1965). The snake's enlarged rear maxillary teeth are used as fangs, and several cranial adaptations contribute to subduing prey, including rotation of the maxillae to elevate the posterior teeth into a stabbing position for the injection of the venom (Kapus 1964; Kroll 1976). The venom is produced with both serous and mucous elements in a Duvernoy's gland (Taub 1967) that is connected to the enlarged teeth by a duct. Hill and Mackessy (1997) reported venom yields of 10–28 µl that contained 55.8–84.0% protein. Painful human envenomations have occurred (Bragg 1960; Morris 1985); symptoms include discoloration and swelling of the bitten site and slight continuous bleeding from the wounds. Care should be taken when these snakes are handled.

Resistance to the powerful digitaloid and epinephrine-containing skin secretions of toads is inherent (Huheey 1958). The adrenal glands are enlarged, even at hatching (Spaur and Smith 1971), and Smith and White (1955) thought this is an adaptation for consuming toads, as the extent of toad-eating seems directly correlated to adrenal size in xenodontine snakes.

PREDATORS AND DEFENSE. Hawks *(Buteo regalis, B. swainsoni),* crows *(Corvus brachyrhynchos),* and coyote *(Canis latrans)* have attacked *H. nasicus* (Blair and Schitoskey 1982; Platt 1969); Greene and Oliver (1965) saw a massasauga *(Sistrurus catenatus)* eat a road-killed individual; and cannibalism on both the young and eggs has occurred.

H. nasicus has a sterotyped defensive display. If it cannot escape, it spreads its neck, hisses loudly, and occasionally strikes with its mouth closed. If this fails to drive away the disturber, it then contorts its body, writhes about, vomits up food, and finally rolls over onto its back and plays dead with tongue extended and blood seeping from the mouth.

POPULATIONS. Platt (1969) calculated the sizes of two Kansas populations as 57 and 121 snakes, with densities of 2.8 and 6.0/ha, respectively. At one site, individuals over two years old composed 88% of the population (first-year juveniles, 12%; second-year snakes, 30%; third-year individuals, 26%; and fourth-year and older snakes, 32%). The SVL structure of this population was as follows: < 36.0 cm, 21%; 36.0–39.9 cm, 19%; 40.0–43.9 cm, 26%; and > 48.9 cm, 21%. He thought the primary sex ratio was probably 1:1. In an Illinois population of 73 *H. nasicus,* 36 (mostly juveniles) had 15–30 cm SVLs, and 19 (mostly adult females) had 40–50 cm SVLs; estimated population size was 205, and the sex ratio was not significantly different from 1:1 (Kolbe 1999).

Over much of its range, *H. nasicus* has decreased in numbers. It is now protected in Arkansas, Illinois, Iowa, Minnesota, and Montana, is less common in Texas (Tennant 1985), and is rare in Missouri.

REMARKS. The genus *Heterodon* has been reviewed by Platt (1983), and *H. nasicus* by Walley and Eckerman (1999).

Heterodon platirhinos Latreille, in Sonnini and Latreille 1801 | Eastern Hog-nosed Snake

RECOGNITION. *H. platirhinos* is a thick-bodied snake (maximum TBL, 115.6 cm) with an unkeeled, only slightly upturned rostrum, and the underside of its tail lighter than the rest of the venter. It is gray, pinkish brown, yellow, olive, or black, with a 17–31 transverse dorsal blotches and 6–14 tail bands separating rows of dark spots on the sides and back, but some individuals are monocolored olive black. The black individuals are slate gray as juveniles, but darken with age and take on a satin appearance similar to that of the black racer *(Coluber constrictor)*. In North Carolina, the incidence of melanism decreases from the coastal plain toward the piedmont and mountains (Palmer and Braswell 1995). A dark V-shaped mark, with the apex on the parietal scales, occurs behind the eyes, and a transverse dark bar lies between the eyes and extends downward behind them to the corner of the mouth. The venter is mottled with gray or black. Dorsal body scales are keeled and pitted, and lie in 23–25 (21–27) anterior rows, 25 (21–27) midbody rows, and 19 (15–21) posterior rows. Ventrals total 112–154, subcaudals 30–64, and the anal plate is divided. Lateral head scalation consists of 2 nasals, 1 (2–4) loreal, an orbital ring of 8–13 scales below the supraocular scale, 3–4 + 4–5 (3) temporals, 8 (7–9) supralabials, and 10–11 (9–14) infralabials. Dorsally, behind the rostral scale, the internasals and prefrontals may either meet or be separated by 1–2 small azygous scales. The hemipenis is similar to that described for *H. nasicus*. Each maxilla has 11–13 teeth, with the anterior shorter teeth separated from the longer, most posterior tooth by a diastema.

Eastern hog-nosed snake, *Heterodon platirhinos*; Johnson County, North Carolina. (Photograph by William Leonard)

Eastern hog-nosed snake, *Heterodon platirhinos*; Columbia County, Georgia. (Photograph by Carl H. Ernst)

Males have 112–148 (mean, 126) ventrals, 30–62 (mean, 51) subcaudals, and TLs that are 14–24 (mean, 20) % of TBL; females have 126–154 (mean, 138) ventrals, 34–64 (mean, 39) subcaudals, and TLs that are only 12–20 (mean, 16) % of TBL.

GEOGRAPHIC VARIATION.   No subspecies are recognized (Blem 1981a).

CONFUSING SPECIES.   Use the above key to differentiate other *Heterodon*. Pygmy rattlesnakes *(Sistrurus miliarius)* have a rattle, facial pit, and vertically elliptical pupils. Hook-nosed snakes *(Gyalopion; Ficimia)* have small upturned rostral scales and smooth body scales that lie in fewer than 17 midbody rows. Patch-nosed snakes *(Salvadora)* are longitudinally striped and have smooth scales.

KARYOTYPE.   The karyotype has 36 chromosomes and is similar to that of *H. nasicus* (Baker et al. 1972).

FOSSIL RECORD.   *H. platirhinos* has an extensive fossil record, dating from the Miocene (Hemphillian) of Nebraska (Parmley and Holman 1995). Other known fossils are from the Pliocene (Blancan) of Kansas (Eshelman 1975; Holman 1979b) and Nebraska (Brattstrom 1967); the Pleistocene (Blancan) of West Virginia (Holman 1982b); the Pleistocene (Irvingtonian) of Florida (Auffenberg 1963), Kansas (Brattstrom 1967; Holman 1971), Maryland (Holman 1977b), Oklahoma (Holman 1986b), and West Virginia (Holman and Grady 1989); and the Pleistocene (Rancholabrean) of Florida (Auffenberg 1963; Gut and Ray 1963;

Holman 1958b, 1996; Martin 1974), Georgia (Holman 1967), Kansas (Brattstrom 1967), Missouri (Holman 1965b; Parmalee et al. 1969), Tennessee (Van Dam 1978), Texas (Hill 1971; Holman 1965c), and Virginia (Holman 1986a).

DISTRIBUTION.   *H. platirhinos* ranges from eastern Massachusetts, southern New Hampshire, and southwestern Ontario, west to Minnesota and southeastern South Dakota, and south through peninsular Florida, and along the Gulf Coast to central Texas.

HABITAT.   The habitat varies from wooded hillsides to grassy and cultivated fields; relatively dry areas with sandy, or sandy-loam soils are essential. The authors have most often encountered them at the edges of cultivated fields or open woodlands, on dirt roads passing through woods, or on sandy barrier beaches in tidal areas (where they occasionally enter seawater; Rodgers 1985). Although the authors have discovered many under logs in woodlands, most have been found in the open. In the south they may hide in pocket gopher *(Geomys pinetis)* mounds (Funderberg and Lee 1968).

BEHAVIOR.   This snake begins hibernation late, but emerges early in the spring. Records of active individual exist for each month of the year. In Florida and possibly along the Gulf Coast it may be active sporadically during December–February, especially in warm winters, but individuals in most southern populations first become active in March. Emergence time is later for more northern populations, April–May, de-

Distribution of *Heterodon platirhinos*.

pending on latitude and elevation. The prime activity period is April–November; in North Carolina, 53% of the records are from April–June, and 30% are from September and October (Palmer and Braswell 1995). The most northern populations may retreat underground in late September–October. The winter is usually spent in a mammal burrow or in a burrow in the soil excavated by the snake, but occasionally it overwinters within logs or stumps, under rocks or trash piles, or even above running springs of water. Arndt (1980) observed one bury itself to a depth of 58 cm in sandy soil to hibernate, and later recorded the BT of this snake as 9.2°C (ST, 8.5°C). *H. platirhinos* is usually active in the summer, but if needed, the same types of retreats are probably used for summer estivation. The authors have found it strictly diurnal. Most activity is in the morning (Platt 1969; Scott 1986; Plummer and Mills 2000), but a lesser activity period occurs in late afternoon or at dusk, especially during the anuran breeding season (Carr 1940; C. Ernst, pers. obs.; Plummer and Mills 2000). The normal voluntary BT range is about 22–34°C (Jones 1976; Mitchell 1994; Platt 1969); *H. platirhinos* chose ETs of 22.4–37.4°C when placed in a thermal gradient (Kitchell 1969). On Assateague Island, Virginia, these snakes are most active at 32–35°C STs (Scott 1986). Tucker (2000) found Illinois yearlings at ATs of 12–32°C and STs of 14–31°C, and Kansas *H. platirhinos* could still crawl slowly, spread their necks, and hiss at a BT of 5.6°C (Platt 1969).

Both sexes of *H. platirhinos* wander extensively dur-

ing the day, and usually burrow into the soil for the night wherever they happen to be when darkness approaches. A radio-equipped male appeared to trail a similarly equipped female, especially during the breeding season (Plummer and Mills 1996); he traveled about 1,500 m from his hibernaculum between 10 April and 9 June. From 10 April to 20 May, the female only moved 600 m, but the next year she moved 1,200 m in less than a month. Individuals recaptured by Platt (1969) at two Kansas sites had moved mean distances of 208 and 290 m, respectively; the longest movements were 783 and 858 m by males during the breeding season. Distances between captures of *H. platirhinos* in Virginia average 390 (40–760) m (Scott 1986). Stickel and Cope (1947) reported one snake was recaptured only 30 m from its original capture point 5.5 months later. Average daily movements in South Carolina were 119 m, and the average home range covered 50.2 ha (Plummer and Mills 2000). Not all movement is at ground level, as these snakes occasionally climb into low shrubs and stretch out on the branches to bask.

When not foraging or searching for a mate, *H. platirhinos* usually burrows into loose soil. This is accomplished by bending the head downward to apply the broad dorsal surface of the pointed rostrum to the soil, then moving the head laterally back and forth while pushing the snout into the soil. The flattened dorsal surface of the head may be used to bring soil to the surface, and the head is usually rotated slightly to the side on which the thrust is made (Davis 1946).

REPRODUCTION. Male *H. platirhinos* with SVLs of 40 cm and TBLs of 51 cm, and females with SVLs of 45 cm and TBLs of 51 cm are mature (Conant and Collins 1998; Wright and Wright 1957). In Kansas, females mature at SVLs of at least 55 cm and about 21 months of age (Platt 1969). The smallest mature female found by Platt had a 50 cm SVL. Males from Kentucky and Virginia are probably mature at SVLs of 45–50 cm and ages of 1.5–2.0 years (C. Ernst, pers. obs.).

Only generalities are known about the female gametic cycle: they contain yolked eggs and weigh the most in April–May, have oviductal eggs in late June–July, and probably reproduce annually. The male spermatogenic cycle is similar to that of *N. nasicus* (Platt 1969).

Most breeding occurs in the spring; the earliest date of copulation in nature is 28 March (Guidry 1953), but the primary spring breeding season is mid-April–May. A second breeding period may occur in September–October (Plummer and Mills 1996; Vogt 1981).

Since *H. platirhinos* usually hibernate individually, males must find receptive females in the spring after emergence. This may involve long-distance trailing, probably by following the female's pheromone trail (Plummer and Mills 1996). Once a female is found, the male crawls beside her, touches her side with his rostrum and tongue, and slowly crawls toward her head. When level with her neck, he coils his tail over hers, pushes a loop beneath her tail, and tries to insert a hemipenis into her vent with undulating pulsations. These pulsations soon become caudocephalic waves that progress anteriorly along his body. During this, the female may move slowly forward or remain still (Nichols 1982). Its spines and calyxes help anchor the base of the hemipenis to the female's cloacal wall in such a way that the distal portion of the organ remains in position despite movement by the snakes (Edgren 1953). Sometimes the female will crawl away dragging the attached male behind (C. Ernst, pers. obs.). Copulation may last several hours.

The nesting season is from early May through August, with most oviposition occurring in June–July. Captives have produced two clutches during a breeding season (Lardie 1976; Wenzel 1990). Most nests are depressions in loose soil or under rocks (Edgren 1955), but C. Ernst found clutches laid in sawdust piles, and probably some eggs are deposited in mammal burrows.

Clutches contain 4–61 (mean, 22.8; n = 70) eggs (Cagle 1942; Edgren 1955). Clutch size is positively related to female SVL. The cream to white, elliptical eggs are 20.0–43.1 (mean, 29.7) × 12.5–24.0 (mean, 20.1) mm (n = 63) and weigh 3.9–11.7 (mean, 8.3; n = 16) g. An RCM calculated by Seigel and Fitch (1984) was 0.439. IP is 39–65 (mean, 56) days, and depends on IT. Most eggs hatch in August–September, but Clark (1949) reported a natural nest in Louisiana hatched 4–12 July, and Tucker (2000) found Illinois hatchlings on 21 October.

Hatchlings are more vividly colored and marked than adults and have TBLs of 12.7–29.4 (mean, 23.6; n = 36) cm.

GROWTH AND LONGEVITY. The growth rate is rapid in juveniles, but slows after maturity; females grow faster and larger than males. Platt (1969) estimated the following probable growth rates for Kansas *H. platirhinos*: males—26.9–38.3 cm SVL (4.3 cm/month) at 9 months of age, 45.4–52.1 cm (3.4 cm/month) at 21 months, 54.0–55.3 cm (1.1 cm/month) at 33 months, and 58.0–59.7 cm (0.8 cm/month) at 45 months; females—24.0–38.5 cm SVL (4.3 cm/month) at 9 months of age, 55.5–56.7 cm (4.5 cm/month) at 21 months, 63.0 cm (1.2 cm/month) at 33 months, and 68.5 cm (0.96 cm/month) at 45 months. His largest female grew from 68.5 cm to 74.8 cm SVL in less than a year, a growth rate of 1.0 cm per active month. Illinois yearlings have 14.6–24.2 cm SVLs and weigh 10.6–30.9 g (Tucker 2000).

The record survivorship for the species is 7 years, 8 months, and 15 days (Snider and Bowler 1992).

DIET AND FEEDING HABITS. In Virginia, the majority of prey taken by volume are toads (40%), frogs (30%), salamanders (11%), and small mammals (19%) (Uhler et al. 1939), and amphibians are present in 58% and insects in 35% of the stomachs in Kansas (Platt 1969). Although most food items are amphibians, wild *H. platirhinos* have taken a variety of prey: amphibians—salamanders (*Ambystoma maculatum, A. opacum, A. texanum, A. tigrinum, Eurycea cirrigera, Notophthalmus viridescens, Plethodon* sp.), toads (*Bufo americanus, B. cognatus, B. terretris, B. woodhousei*), spadefoots (*Scaphiopus holbrookii*), treefrogs (*Hyla versicolor*), and true frogs (*Rana catesbeiana, R. clamitans,*

Eastern hog-nosed snake (death feigning), *Heterodon platirhinos*; Fairfax County, Virginia. (Photograph by Carl H. Ernst)

R. pipiens, R. sphenocephala); reptiles—small turtles *(Kinosternon subrubrum)*, lizards *(Cnemidophorus sexlineatus, Scincella lateralis)*, lizard eggs *(Ophisaurus [?] sp.)*, and small snakes *(Agkistrodon contortrix, Thamnophis sauritus)*; birds; mammals—shrews *(Blarina brevicauda)*, chipmunks *(Tamias striatus)*, mice *(Peromyscus sp.)*, and voles *(Microtus sp.)*; fish; and invertebrates—earthworms, snails, millipedes, centipedes, isopods, spiders, and insects (beetles, grasshoppers, lepidopteran larvae) (Carr 1940; Dundee and Rossman 1989; Ernst et al. 1997; Ernst and Laemmerzahl 1989; Fouquette and Lindsey 1955; Gibbons and Semlitsch 1991; Greenhall 1936; Hamilton and Pollack 1956; Mills and Yeomans 1993; Minton 1972; Palmer and Braswell 1995; Platt 1969; Surface 1906; Trauth 1982b; Tucker 2000; Uhler et al. 1939; Wright and Wright 1957). Captives seldom accept any food but amphibians; however, some can be induced to eat mice *(Mus musculus)* that have first been rubbed with a toad's skin.

PREDATORS AND DEFENSE. Documented predators of *H. platirhinos* are tarantulas *(Eurypelma californica)*, snakes *(Agkistrodon piscivorus, Coluber constrictor, Elaphe obsoleta, Lampropeltis getula, Masticophis flagel-*

lum), crows (Corvus brachyrhynchos), red-tailed hawks *(Buteo jamaicensis),* and barred owls *(Strix varia)* (Brittle and Brittle 2000; Edgren 1955; Hamilton and Pollack 1955, 1956; Hudson 1947; Klimstra 1959a; Over 1923; Owens 1949b; Platt 1969; Wright and Bishop 1915). However, humans cause the most damage with their habitat destruction, poisoning with pesticides or pollutants, vehicles, and outright killing of the snake.

Like other *Heterodon*, this snake has a stereotyped bluffing and death-feigning display (Platt 1969; Sexton 1979); even newborns resort to such behaviors (Raun 1962). Young et al. (1999) discuss the mechanics of head triangulation during the threat display. If bitten, the saliva of *H. platirhinos* can cause a burning pain, swelling, discoloration, and bleeding from the puncture wounds (Grogan 1974; McAlister 1963; Minton 1986).

POPULATIONS. *H. platirhinos* is locally common over most of its range (Scott, 1986, collected 66 on Assateague Island, Virginia), but in samples of snakes from large areas it tends to be less common than some other species. Clark (1949) only caught 86 (4.1%) in a sample of 2,083 snakes from the northern parishes of Louisiana, and Fitch (1993) reported it made up only 7 of 33,117 snakes collected throughout Kansas. Population sizes at Platt's (1969) two Kansas study sites were 10 and 42, for densities of 0.5 and 2.1/ha, respectively. At one site, snakes younger than two years made up 69% of the population (hatchlings 28%, first-year young 41%), two-year-olds 19%, and snakes three years and older 12%. The size structure of this population was as follows: < 56.0 cm SVL, 61%; 56.0–60.9 cm, 23%; 61.0–72.4 cm, 12%; and 72.5+ cm, 4%.

The sex ratio at hatching is 1:1, and this ratio usually carries through to adulthood (Platt 1969), but Platt (1969) caught 87 males and 38 females (2.29:1.00) at one of his study sites, and Scott (1986) collected 38 males and 28 females (1.36:1.00) on Assateague Island.

H. platirhinos is protected in Connecticut, Minnesota, South Dakota, and West Virginia.

REMARKS. The species was reviewed by Blem (1981a).

Heterodon simus (Linnaeus 1766) | Southern Hog-nosed Snake

RECOGNITION. *H. simus* (maximum TBL is 61 cm, but most adults are 45–55 cm long) is a light brown, blotched snake with a sharply upturned, keeled snout. It is gray brown to tan with 20–35 large, dark brown blotches outlined anteriorly and posteriorly with black; a similar row of alternating smaller dark spots on each side; and 6–11 dark brown tail bands. Also present are a dark brown or black stripe on each side of the neck, and a dark transverse bar on the snout in front of the eyes. The white, cream, yellowish or pinkish brown venter has faint brownish pigment posteriorly, 112–134 ventrals, 28–55 subcaudals, and a divided (rarely single) anal plate. Dorsal body scales are keeled and pitted, and occur in 25 (23–27) anterior rows, 25 (23 or 27) midbody rows, and 21 (19–20) posterior rows. On each side of the head are 2 nasals (occasionally the posterior nasal may be divided into a larger dorsal scale and a smaller ventral scale), 1 loreal, an ocular ring of 9–12 scales beneath the supraocular, 3–4 + 4–5 temporals, 8 (6–9) supralabials, and 10–11 (8–12) infralabials. The top of the head has 3–13 small accessory scales separating the internasal and prefrontal scales behind the rostrum. The hemipenis is divided into two distal lobes with papilla-like calyxes; the shaft has small proximal spines and longer medial spines, and a single, bifurcated sulcus spermaticus. Each maxilla has 6–11 anterior teeth separated by a diastema from two enlarged, grooveless, posterior teeth; the maxilla can rotate to erect the posterior teeth.

Males are shorter (usually < 50 cm TBL) with 112–122 (mean, 115) ventrals, 37–55 (mean, 45) sub-caudals, 20–27 (mean, 23) dorsal body blotches, 8–11 (mean, 9) tail bands, and TLs 18–23 (mean, 20–21) % of TBL; females are longer (usually > 50 cm TBL) with 123–134 (mean, 127) ventrals, 28–35 (mean, 32) subcaudals, 21–28 (mean, 25) dorsal body blotches, 6–8 (mean, 6.5) tail bands, and TLs 12–15 (mean, 13) % of TBL.

GEOGRAPHIC VARIATION. *H. simus* is monotypic.

CONFUSING SPECIES. Use the above key to identify other *Heterodon*. Pygmy rattlesnakes *(Sistrurus miliarius)* have a tail rattle, a hole between the nostril and eye, and vertically elliptical pupils.

KARYOTYPE. Undescribed.

FOSSIL RECORD. Several Pleistocene fossils have been discovered in Florida: Irvingtonian (?) at Medford Cave and Reddick in Marion County (Auffenberg 1963; Gut and Ray 1963), and Rancholabrean at Haille in Alachua County (Auffenberg 1963), Devil's Den Sinkhole in Levy County (Holman 1978), and Williston in Levy County (Holman 1959a, 1996).

DISTRIBUTION. *H. simus* ranges from Wake and Edgecombe counties in southeastern North Carolina south to St. Lucie, Okeechobee, Polk, and Pinellas counties in peninsular Florida, and west to the Pearl River separating southern Mississippi from southeastern Louisiana.

Southern hog-nosed snake, *Heterodon simus*; Aiken County, South Carolina. (Photograph by Carl H. Ernst)

Distribution of *Heterodon simus*.

HABITAT. This hog-nosed snake is found in generally xeric habitats with sandy or well-drained sandy-loam soils, such as sand hills, coastal sand dunes, wiregrass patches, abandoned old fields, cultivated fields, nursery groves, dry river floodplains, open longleaf and loblolly pine–turkey oak woodlands, and other scrub oak woods.

BEHAVIOR. *H. simus* is active in every month in Florida, but is most often seen there in May–June (C. Ernst, pers. obs.). Near Aiken, South Carolina, active individuals have been recorded from January through October and in December, with most collected between April and October (Gibbons and Semlitsch 1991); in North Carolina it has been found from late March to early November, with 35% of records from May through June and 47% from September through October (Palmer and Braswell 1995). It spends much time underground, and it is sometimes turned up during the plowing of fields. The winter is probably spent buried in the soil or within mammal burrows, but no observations on hibernation have been reported.

Activity is mostly diurnal, with some early morning or early evening behavior, especially in the summer. No natural thermal data are available, but Rossi and Rossi (1991) reported that all captive matings occurred when the AT was higher than 23°C.

REPRODUCTION. Both sexes are mature at 36 cm TBL (Conant and Collins 1998). The only data reported concerning the gametic cycles are oviductal eggs found by Palmer and Braswell (1995) in North Carolina females on 20 May and 13–14 June.

It breeds from mid-April through August (Rossi and Rossi 1991; Tennant 1997). A courting male may chase a female at a speed much faster than for normal crawling. If the female is receptive, she raises her tail over her dorsum and begins to back up. The male then crawls beside her, moves anteriorly along her side, and rubs her neck with his rostral scale. While continuously nudging the female with his rostrum, he moves his tail beneath her tail, inserts his hemipenis into her vent, and begins a series of caudocephalic waves. Copulation may last three to five hours (Rossi and Rossi 1991; Griswold, in Tennant 1997). Neill (1951) found a captive simultaneously mating with two males; one had inserted his right hemipenis, the other its left. During the copulation, a third male crawled over the three snakes with his tail upraised and made a few ineffectual attempts to participate before moving away. The female crawled away, dragging the two connected males with her, leaving a trail of blood that Neill thought resulted from the males lacerating each other with their hemipenile spines. Neill (1951) also reported an interspecific mating between a large captive female *H. simus* and a smaller male *H. platirhinos*. Afterwards the female's cloaca was swollen and bloody, and she died three days later, possibly from injuries sustained during the abnormal mating. Edgren (1952) and Tregembo (in Palmer and Braswell 1995) also reported captive matings between a large female *H. simus* and a male *H. platirhinos*, but such events between these two species in nature are rare.

Clutches are normally laid in July, but an October oviposition in captivity is known (Price and Carr 1943). Clutches contain 6–14 eggs (Palmer and Braswell 1995) and average 9.6 eggs (n = 17). The white, elongated eggs are 22.0–37.0 (mean, 29.8) × 11.0–19.3 (mean, 17.3) mm (n = 26) and weigh about 2.1–2.5 g. Saul (1968) reported that a possible hybrid *H. platirhinos* × *H. simus* laid 18 infertile eggs; however, judging by the large size of this clutch, the snake was probably a *platirhinos*.

The IP is 56–60 (mean, 57.5) days; most hatching occurs in September, but emergence may continue to late October (Jensen 1996). Neonates resemble adults, but their body color and pattern are more pronounced, and some are distinctly orange dorsally. Hatchling TBLs are 13.4–18.0 (mean, 14.4; n = 25) cm.

GROWTH AND LONGEVITY. No growth data are available. One of unknown sex, originally caught in the wild as a juvenile, was still alive after 3 years and 28 days (Snider and Bowler 1992).

DIET AND FEEDING HABITS. *H. simus* feeds predominately on anurans *(Bufo quercicus, B. terrestris, Hyla gratiosa, Pseudacris ornata, Scaphiopus holbrookii),* but small lizards *(Cnemidophorus sexlineatus, Sceloporus undulatus, Scincella lateralis)* and small mammals are sometimes taken (Ashton and Ashton 1981; Beane et al. 1998; Carr 1940; Deckert 1918; Gibbons and Semlitsch 1991; Goin 1947; Martof et al. 1980; Palmer and Braswell 1995; Tennant 1997; Van Duyn 1937; Weaver 1965; Wright and Wright 1957). Captives will eat newborn house mice *(Mus musculus)* rubbed with a toad, as well as anurans (Palmer and Braswell 1995; Rossi and Rossi 1991).

The upturned rostral scale is used to dig out buried anurans; Goin (1947) watched one use this scale as a "shovel" to excavate a *Scaphiopus holbrookii* that was 11.5 cm underground. Inflated toads and spadefoots apparently are deflated by puncturing them with the enlarged posterior maxillary teeth (Ashton and Ashton 1981), but the snake may simply be injecting toxic saliva into the anuran. The saliva is produced in Duvernoy's glands with some mucous cells intermingled with serous cells (Kapus 1964; Taub 1967), but its toxicity has not been tested, and it may only be toxic to anurans and lizards.

PREDATORS AND DEFENSE. The only record of predation on *H. simus* the authors have found is by a common kingsnake *(Lampropeltis getula)* in North Carolina (Palmer and Braswell 1995); however, larger ophiophagous snakes, predatory birds, and carnivorous mammals must eat some. This small snake is sometimes killed while crossing roads.

It displays the same stereotypic pattern of bluffing and death-feigning that occurs in the other two *Heterodon* (Myers and Arata 1961; Van Duyn 1957), but seldom bites humans. Its blotched pattern and tan to gray body color perhaps mimic the gray morph of the venomous pygmy rattlesnake *(Sistrurus miliarius),* and this may award it some protection.

POPULATIONS. *H. simus* is seldom seen, and appears uncommon to rare over much of its range. It is locally common in Florida (Tennant 1997), but its numbers have declined so much that it is now protected in Alabama and Mississippi.

REMARKS. *H. simus* has been reviewed by Meylan (1985).

Hypsiglena torquata (Günther 1860) | Night Snake

RECOGNITION. This is a small (to 64.2 cm TBL), slender, pale snake with vertically elliptical pupils. Body color is from gray or pale brown to brown, with a darker gray or brown, elongated blotch on the side of the neck, another extending backward and downward from the eye (these two blotches may fuse to form one long blotch), a dark blotch on the nape 9–13 scales long and tapered to the rear (which also may fuse with the lateral neck blotch), a series of 50–70 dark gray or brown, irregularly shaped blotches on the back, and smaller dark spots on the sides. Supralabials are white, and sometimes spotted with small brownish olive marks. Body scales are smooth, usually with a single apical pit but sometimes with two, and lie in 19–21 rows anteriorly and at midbody, and 15 rows near the anal vent. The venter is immaculate

Night snake, *Hypsiglena torquata*; Owyhee County, Idaho. (Photograph by William Leonard)

white to cream. Ventrals total 161–204 and subcaudals 38–66; the anal plate is divided. Lateral head scales present are a single nasal partially divided by the nostril, 1 loreal, 2 preoculars (the smaller lower one is partially inserted between two supralabials), 2 postoculars, 1–2 temporals, 8 supralabials, and 10 (11) infralabials. The hemipenis has a single head, and apical calyxes with only small inferior marginal spines. Each maxilla has 7–10 recurved teeth of approximately the same size in front of a diastema, and two large, ungrooved, fanglike teeth in the rear.

Mature females have greater SVLs and body masses than mature males (Diller and Wallace 1986; Fitch 1981), but males have longer tails (20–21% of TBL, females 17%; Klauber 1943). Females usually have over 170 (170–204) ventrals and fewer than 49 (38–52) subcaudals; males usually have less than 170 (161–193) ventrals and normally more than 49 (42–66) subcaudals.

GEOGRAPHIC VARIATION. Six subspecies are recognized in North America, and several others occur in Mexico and Central America. The desert night snake, *Hypsiglena torquata deserticola* Tanner 1944, is found from British Columbia, eastern Washington, eastern Oregon and adjacent Idaho south through western Utah, Nevada, and southeastern California to eastern Baja California and northwestern Sonora. It is dark gray with three dark spots on the nape, with the middle one enlarged posteriorly to cover the nape and contact the parietal scales. The Texas night snake, *H. t. jani* (Dugès 1865), occurs from south-central Kansas and southeastern Colorado south through western Oklahoma and western Texas and New Mexico into Mexico. It is grayish to light brown with three dark spots on the nape, with the lateral two elongated toward the rear. The San Diego night snake, *H. t. klauberi* Tanner 1944, occurs in southwestern California and western Baja California. It is yellowish to grayish brown with three dark spots on the nape. The Mesa Verde night snake, *H. t. loreala* Tanner 1944, is found in eastern Utah, western Colorado, northern Arizona, and possibly northwestern New Mexico. It is grayish brown with three dark blotches on the nape and two large loreal scales (all other North American subspecies have only one large loreal scale; if a second is present, it is small). The California night snake, *H. t. nuchalata* Tanner 1943, occurs in north and central California, exclusive of the Central Valley. This is

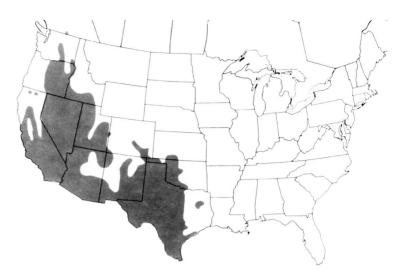

Distribution of *Hypsiglena torquata*.

the most aberrant of the subspecies, with a dark gray ground color, a dark band on the nape, seven supralabials (all other North American subspecies have at least eight supralabials), and 17–19 midbody scale rows (all other North American subspecies normally have 21 or more midbody scale rows). The spotted night snake, *H. t. ochrorhynchus* Cope 1861a, has only small dark blotches on the nape and small dorsal body blotches. It ranges from southern Utah south through western New Mexico, Arizona, and extreme southern Nevada into northern Mexico.

Geographic variation in the night snake is confusing, as most diagnostic characters greatly overlap. Dixon and Dean (1986) thought the westernmost populations probably represent two species, one based on the Mexican *H. torquata* and the other on the northern *H. ochrorhynchus*, but other snake systematists disagree. Dixon and Dean also proposed that *Hypsiglena* from the central and eastern populations represent a single taxon, *H. t. jani*.

CONFUSING SPECIES. The western lyre snake, *Trimorphodon biscutatus*, also has vertically elliptical pupils, but it has a V- or lyre-shaped mark on its head. Other similar snakes have rounded pupils. The glossy snake, *Arizona elegans*, has an undivided anal plate and at least 29 midbody scale rows. The gopher snake, *Pituophis catenifer*, has keeled body scales.

KARYOTYPE. The karyotype consists of 36 chromosomes: 16 macrochromosomes (2 acrocentric, 14 biarmed) and 20 microchromosomes (Camper and Hanks 1995). The NOR is located on a pair of microchromosomes (Camper and Hanks 1995).

FOSSIL RECORD. Pleistocene (Rancholabrean) remains of the night snake have been found in Arizona, California, Nevada, New Mexico, Texas, and Sonora, Mexico (Brattstrom 1976; LaDuke 1991; Mead and Bell 1994; Mead et al. 1982, 1984; Parmley 1990a; Van Devender and Bradley 1994; Van Devender and Mead 1978; Van Devender et al. 1977; Van Devender and Worthington 1977).

DISTRIBUTION. In the east, *H. torquata* ranges from south-central Kansas and southeastern Colorado south through western Oklahoma, western Texas, and New Mexico. Western subspecies are found from southern British Columbia, central Washington, eastern Oregon and western Idaho south through the Great Basin, the southern three-quarters of California and Arizona. The species range continues through Mexico to Costa Rica.

HABITAT. The night snake's habitat is usually arid (although it is occasionally found in moist riparian zones), with loose (often sandy) soil and abundant surface hiding places such as flat rocks, logs, or piles of plant debris. These sites may be in deserts, grasslands, mesquite savanna, chaparral, sagebrush flats, thorn scrub, thorn forest, or upland oak-juniper woodlands to an elevation to at least 2,200 m. It often uses rodent burrows or cracks in rock outcrops as retreats.

BEHAVIOR. Because of its almost totally nocturnal existence, much is unknown of the life history of *H. torquata*. The annual activity period lasts from late March to October in western Texas (Minton 1959; Tennant 1985), from April to October in New Mexico (Degenhardt et al. 1996; Price and LaPointe 1990), from May to October in Colorado (Hammerson 1986), and May to September with a quiescent period in August in Idaho (Diller and Wallace 1986). The greatest amount of activity seems to occur in May and June, and in the southern portion of the range the snake is probably active during warm periods from November to March. The coldest days of winter and those of the hottest, driest summer months are spent underground in mammal burrows or rock crevices. One emerged on 2 February from a rabbit burrow where it had apparently been hibernating. The ground had been covered by snow the night before, and the snake emerged only after an attempt was made to smoke out the rabbit (Koster 1940). Night snakes may also hibernate in tunnels dug in the ground by the desert tortoise *(Gopherus agassizii)* (Trutnau 1986).

In the spring to fall, daylight hours are usually spent in hiding. The snakes emerge in late evening and forage after dark, returning to their diurnal retreats close to dawn. Most specimens have been collected during night road cruising, but Milstead et al. (1950) and Minton (1959) have found them about in the morning. The night snake's elliptical pupil and colorless lens concentrate dim light on its pure rod retina (Stovall 1976; Walls 1934) and are ideal for a nocturnal forager.

H. torquata is an accomplished burrower that can easily disappear into soft sand.

Summer rains may stir night snakes to more activity; Dundee (1950) collected eight when the ground was still moist several days after rains.

Woodin (1953) found a night snake coiled on top of a rock in late afternoon on 13 August at an elevation over 1,800 m in Arizona. Possibly it was basking to warm itself for later foraging. Brattstrom (1965) took the BTs of three active night snakes: 30.2 (AT, 34.0°C; ST under tin covering, 36.5°C), 31.2 (AT, 30.0°C; ST,

30.0°C; road ST, 30.0°C), and 27.0°C. An individual found under a boulder by Cunningham (1966a), the date not given, that had a BT of only 5.4°C could only make slow lateral body movements.

REPRODUCTION. Sizes and ages of the two sexes at the attainment of maturity and their respective sexual cycles have not been entirely discovered, but some data exist. In Idaho, mature males contain spermatozoa in the distal portion of the vas deferens from late April to September, but their testes are only enlarged in midsummer, suggesting spermatogenesis occurs then (Diller and Wallace 1986). The sexual segments of the male kidney tubules are enlarged in the spring and early summer and slowly shrink through late summer and fall. The smallest five Idaho males with spermatozoa examined by Diller and Wallace (1986) were 28.6–28.8 cm SVL, but three of these captured in late April lacked development of the sexual segment of the kidney and probably would not have matured for several months. Based on these data, male *H. torquata* from the northern portion of the range probably mature during their first full summer of growth.

H. torquata is oviparous, and Arizona females with a SVL of 30.7–42.5 cm (Clark and Lieb 1973) and Idaho females with a SVL of 38.5–52.3 cm (Diller and Wallace 1986) have oviposited. This suggests that those from more northern portions of the range mature at a greater length. Females have contained enlarged, yolked ovarian follicles of 12.0–24.0 mm in diameter from 10 April to 5 June, and ovulation probably occurs at about 28 mm (Clark and Lieb 1973; Diller and Wallace 1986). Shelled oviductal eggs have been found on 18 May in Arizona (Clark and Lieb 1973) and 12 June in Kansas (Hibbard 1937). Smaller ovarian follicles with diameters of 11.2–14.9 mm have been found on 23 June in Arizona (Clark and Lieb 1973), and some with diameters of 8.4–8.9 mm have been found on 19 June and 10 July in Idaho (Diller and Wallace 1986), indicating that females in the southern portion of the range may be capable of laying two clutches a year, but those farther north are restricted to one clutch per year. Data on the presence of enlarged ovarian follicles and oviductal eggs suggest a south-north cline in the timing of the annual female reproductive cycle, and Clark and Lieb (1973) further thought the timing to be influenced by local rainfall patterns.

Oviposition dates in the literature have ranged from 25 April (Werler 1951) to 1 September (Vitt 1975), but females seem most capable of egg laying in June and July. Clutches average about 4.2 (2–9) eggs. The eggs are white with smooth to granular, flexible shells, are 29.2 (15.0–44.3) mm long and 10.3 (9–12) mm wide, and weigh 2.62 (1.8–4.3) g. The RCM is approximately 0.447 (Seigel and Fitch 1984). Development at ITs of 20–33°C takes 54–59 days (Diller and Wallace 1986; Tanner and Ottley 1981; Werler 1951).

In nature, most hatchlings probably emerge in August or September. They have average TBLs of 15.8 (10.2–19.5) cm and weigh about 1.25 (0.7–2.3) g. The body is light gray with olive brown dorsal blotches, the head is gray with olive speckles, and the venter is plain white.

GROWTH AND LONGEVITY. No growth data are available. An unsexed adult originally wild caught survived 9 years and 3 months at the Lincoln Park Zoo, Chicago (Snider and Bowler 1992), and three captives from Arizona and New Mexico lived for 92, 98, and 106 months (Brown, in Degenhardt et al. 1996).

DIET AND FEEDING HABITS. *H. torquata* forages at dusk and after dark, probing under rocks for reptiles and their eggs, and amphibians. Prey is seized immediately and worked to the rear of the mouth. There, the enlarged maxillary teeth pierce the animal, allowing toxic saliva, or venom, to enter the wound and immobilize the prey. Its chewing behavior is similar to that of a lyre snake *(Trimorphodon)* injecting venom (Cowles 1941a). Lizards have died in 45–120 minutes after the initial bite (Cowles 1941a; Goodman 1953). The venom is produced in a serous Duvernoy's gland (Taub 1967). Once it is injected into the animal, massive discoloring edema at and around the wound and death by paralysis occur. Apparently the venom contains a neurotoxic element, coupled with a hemorrhagic component that causes edema (Goodman 1953). The venom is composed of approximately 49.8 (21.7–100.0) % protein; the average venom yield extracted from eight *H. torquata* by Hill and Mackessy

(1997) was 12 (5–30) µl, and the average dry yield was 0.53 (0.28–1.05) mg. Vest (1988) had previously reported an average dry venom yield of 0.40 mg. Fortunately *H. torquata* does not readily bite when handled, so the effects of its venom on humans are unknown.

The diet of wild *H. torquata* consists primarily of adult lizards and their eggs *(Anniella, Cnemidophorus, Coleonyx, Cophosaurus, Crotaphytus, Dipsosaurus, Elgaria, Gambelia, Gerrhonotus, Holbrookia, Podarcis, Sceloporus, Uta, Xantusia),* amphisbaenians *(Bipes),* small snakes *(Crotalus, Leptotyphlops, Sonora, Tantilla, Thamnophis),* anurans *(Bufo, Hyla, Pseudacris, Scaphiopus, Spea),* and salamanders *(Ambystoma, Batrachoseps)* (Barry 1933; Cowles 1941a; Degenhardt et al. 1996; Dundee 1950; Glaser 1955; Goodman 1953; Jameson and Jameson 1956; Kassay 1957; Kauffeld 1943a; Lacey et al. 1996; Minton 1959; Rodríguez-Robles et al. 1999d; Stebbins 1954; Tennant 1985; Tinkle 1967). Earthworms and miscellaneous insects—beetle larvae (Coleoptera), cicadas (Homoptera), and grasshoppers (Orthoptera)—are occasionally consumed, and Glaser (1955) found a 6.6 × 5.3 × 4.9 mm piece of granite in a 34.2 cm night snake.

Prey is normally taken alive, but Kauffeld (1943a) observed a night snake eating a road-killed spadefoot toad *(Scaphiopus couchii),* so carrion is occasionally ingested. Lizards are typically swallowed head first, but anurans are swallowed rump first. Prey mass increases with snake mass, and prey mass to snake mass ratios determined by Rodríguez-Robles et al. (1999d) ranged from 0.03 to at least 0.50. Although included in the above list of prey, abundant lizards of the genera *Cnemidophorus, Coleonyx,* and *Xantusia* are infrequently eaten, suggesting that they chemosensorily avoid night snakes (Rodríguez-Robles et al. (1999d).

Captives have lived on anurans *(Hyla, Rana, Scaphiopus)* and lizards *(Sceloporus, Uta),* and Degenhardt et al. (1996) reported a case of captive cannibalism. They also related that a captive night snake went into violent contortions after biting an eastern narrow-mouthed frog *(Gastrophryne carolinensis).*

PREDATORS AND DEFENSE. Few predators are known: cats *(Felis catus),* hawks *(Buteo jamaicensis),* owls *(Asio otus),* and snakes *(Crotalus willardi, Micruroides euryxanthus)* (Diller and Wallace 1986; Gates

1957; Minton 1959; Ross 1989; Vorhies 1948). Motorized vehicles kill many snakes crossing roads.

The snake's first instinct when uncovered is to find a place of concealment; it will crawl away or burrow into loose soil if possible. Some form a tight, ball-like coil with the head in the center (Price 1987), or rigidly snap the body (Stuart 1988). A few, however, will flatten the head and neck and strike viciously (Dundee 1950; Fitch 1949).

POPULATIONS.   Tennant (1985) thought the spotted night snake common in Texas, but seldom seen because of its nocturnal activity pattern. In Idaho, it was the third most frequently captured snake in a drift fence study; only the gopher snake *(Pituophis catenifer)* and striped whipsnake *(Masticophis taeniatus)* were caught more frequently (Diller and Wallace 1996). However, *H. torquata* only made up 4.4% of the

snakes seen on a New Mexico highway during four years (Price and LaPointe 1990), and in Kansas it only made up 0.15% of the snakes recorded by Fitch (1993). The male to female ratio of 77 Idaho *H. torquata* captured by Diller and Wallace (1996) was 2.5:1.

H. torquata is listed as threatened and protected in the state of Kansas.

REMARKS.   Rodríguez-Robles et al. (1999d) proposed that the genus *Hypsiglena* arose within a Neotropical snake clade of predominantly nocturnal anuran predators, and that its occurrence in arid western North America correlates with two derived feeding traits: at least occasional ambushing of diurnal lizards and the use of lizard eggs as food.

Reviews of the species have been published by Dixon and Dean (1986), Tanner (1944, 1985), and Taylor (1939b).

Lampropeltis Fitzinger 1843

Kingsnakes and Milksnakes

Key to the Species of *Lampropeltis*

1a. Dorsal ground color black; unpatterned, or patterned with white or yellow speckles, chainlike bands, or longitudinal stripes (only in the western United States) . . . . .
. . . . *L. getula*

1b. Dorsal ground color red, brown, or tan 2

2a. Dorsal color tan to dark brown with small reddish blotches . . . . *L. calligaster*

2b. Dorsal color red or reddish brown 3

3a. Dorsal pattern consists of saddlelike blotches 4

3b. Dorsal pattern consists of red, black, and yellow or white crossbands 5

4a. A light Y- or V-shaped mark on the head, more than 20 dorsal, saddlelike, reddish body blotches . . . .
. . . . *L. triangulum* (in part)

4b. No light Y- or V-shaped mark on the gray head, less than 15 dorsal, saddlelike, orangish body blotches . . . *L. alterna*

5a. Body and tail with more than 40 yellow or white crossbands, snout white (sometimes with black flecks) . . . . . .
. . . . *L. pyromelana*

5b. Body and tail with more than 40 yellow or white crossbands, snout entirely black or heavily speckled with black
. . . . 6

6a. More than 31 yellow or white crossbands on body and tail, bands not broader on lower sides, usually 23 midbody scale rows . . . . *L. zonata*

6b. Fewer than 31 yellow or white crossbands on body and tail, bands broader on lower sides, usually 21 midbody scale rows . . . . *L. triangulum* (in part)

Lampropeltis alterna (Brown 1902) | Gray-banded Kingsnake

RECOGNITION.   This is a very attractive, colorful snake much favored in the pet trade. Its body (TBL to

147.1 cm) is blue gray, olive gray, or dark gray with 9–39 red or orange dorsal crossbands (9–18 in the

Gray-banded kingsnake, *Lampropeltis alterna*; Brewster County, Texas. (Photograph by Carl H. Ernst)

broad-banded *blairi* morph, 15–39 in the more nar-row-banded *alterna* morph), and 3–11 crossbands on the tail. The bright crossbands have black borders, which in turn have narrow white borders. Some individuals lack, or nearly lack, the red or orange dorsal crossbands, having only white-bordered black bands instead, and still others are melanistic. The head is gray with a dark, sometimes broken, stripe extending obliquely downward and backward from the eye to the corner of the mouth. Other head marks vary from none to black mottling on the snout and top, or black spots forming a V-shaped blotch behind the eyes. The white venter has many dark brown or black blotches, some fused. The large eyes are somewhat protrusive and have grayish white to silvery gray irises and round pupils. Dorsal body scales are smooth with two, some-times indistinct, apical pits, and occur in 23 (20–25) anterior rows, 25 (23–27) rows at midbody, and 19–20 (18–21) rows near the tail. The venter has 194–232 ventrals, 55–69 subcaudals, and an undivided anal plate. Lateral head scalation consists of 2 nasals almost completely separated by the nostril, 1 loreal, 1 preocular, 2–3 postoculars, 2 (3) + 2–4 (5) temporals, 7–8 supralabials, and 9–12 infralabials. The slightly bilobed, subcylindrical hemipenis has a single sulcus spermaticus; the distal portion of the shaft has heavily spinulated calyxes grading into long (0.6–0.8 mm), oval spines that decrease in size and grade into a basal area of longitudinal ridges. These ridges are naked proximally, but are spinululated distally. Each maxilla has 13–14 teeth with no diastema; the last two are slightly enlarged, but ungrooved.

Males are larger, with 212–229 ventrals and 58–69 subcaudals; the shorter females have 194–217 ventrals and 58–69 subcaudals.

GEOGRAPHIC VARIATION. Although considerable variation occurs in body color and pattern, as noted above, this variation seems to occur across the species range, and no subspecies are currently recognized (Garstka 1982; Gehlbach and McCoy 1965; Tanzer 1970). However, Miller (1979) has shown that variation occurs in both body scale row counts and the numbers of ventrals and subcaudals within populations from the Texas counties inhabited by *L. alterna*. A thorough study of variation in this species would be helpful.

CONFUSING SPECIES. Other *Lampropeltis* can be distinguished by using the key presented above. The coral snake *(Micrurus fulvius)* has alternating red, yellow, and black body bands, in that order, that extend across the ventrals, a black face, and black eyes. The long-nosed snake *(Rhinocheilus lecontei)* has many black speckles along its sides, a raised rostral scale on a pinkish red snout, black eyes, and a single row of subcaudals. The western lyre snake *(Trimorphodon biscutatus)* has vertically elliptical pupils and a divided anal plate. The rock rattlesnake *(Crotalus lepidus)* has a tail rattle, keeled scales, vertically elliptical pupils, and a loreal pit.

KARYOTYPE. The karyotype consists of 36 chromosomes: 16 macrochromosomes and 20 microchromosomes (Baker et al. 1972).

FOSSIL RECORD. Pleistocene (Rancholabrean) to Holocene remains of *L. alterna* have been found in Texas (Parmley 1990a, 1990b; Van Devender and Bradley 1994; Van Devender, in Miller 1979).

DISTRIBUTION. *L. alterna* ranges from southeastern New Mexico (Eddy and Otero counties) east to Edwards County, Texas, and south through Coahuila and eastern Chihuahua to extreme western Nuevo León, Zacatecas, and eastern Durango in Mexico.

HABITAT. The species is found in dry habitats of the Chihuahuan Desert and Edwards Plateau of western Texas among the broken limestone and igneous areas with thin gravelly soils vegetated with various desert plants (acacia, desert willow, creosote bush, mesquite, ocotillo, opuntia cacti, sotol) at elevations of 450–2,257 m.

BEHAVIOR. This snake is very secretive, spending most of its life deep in rock crevices from which it emerges at twilight or night to forage on the surface. Most activity occurs between the hours of 2100 and 2400. Only a few have been found surface active during the day, and these were in the early morning or late afternoon (Miller 1979). Rainstorms sometimes bring them to the surface in fair numbers, perhaps in pursuit of lizards.

L. alterna are active from mid-April to mid-October in western Texas, but most are seen from mid-May to late June. When ATs heat up in July and August, surface activity declines, and some individuals probably even estivate (Miller 1979). Nocturnal surface foraging increases again in September as ATs again fall. November to April or May is spent in hibernation. Probably most hibernate deep in rock crevices or mammal burrows; one was found dormant above ground in January, under a pile of rocks (Miller 1979). Based on captive breeding, a period of cold dormancy must precede successful mating.

Males engage in dominance combat bouts (Murphy et al. 1978). Initially nose-to-nose contact is made, and then the males raise their heads and anterior bodies and hover about 4 cm above the ground. Then one crawls alongside the other, and with tongue rapidly flicking, moves anteriorly along the other male's body. Once anteriorly aligned, both snakes bite their opponent's neck, body, and tail, possibly to maintain alignment posture, and jerk their bodies forward with heads still held off the ground. Next, body bridges or bows are formed by pressing the head and neck upon the ground and raising a loop of the body 10–37 cm above the horizontal surface at a 45° angle. The vertical body loops are maintained and kept aligned by moving forward, but no head alignment occurs. Violent body jerks are used by the less dominant male to resist alignment of the opponent's loop. The dominant male then presses the body loop of his opponent to the ground as each snake tries to maintain his head and anterior trunk upright to counteract the force the other is exerting. Body loops are used to press down the head and anterior trunk of the less dominant male as the snakes crawl slowly forward. When finally pinned, the subservient male pulls his head free, but is turned onto its back. Captive males sometimes engage in homosexual activity, even to the point of intromission (Tryon and Murphy 1982).

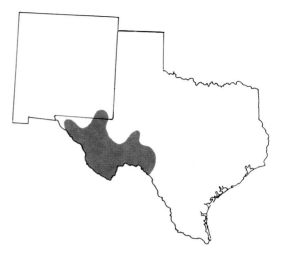

Distribution of *Lampropeltis alterna*.

REPRODUCTION. Considerable information on the reproductive biology of *L. alterna* has been obtained from captive breeding programs; unfortunately, similar data are nonexistent for the wild. Captive females as small as 79.9 cm TBL and males as small as 84.0 cm TBL have successfully mated. Female maturity is reached as early as the second spring, and almost all can produce eggs after their third spring.

Courtship and mating have not been observed in nature, but have occurred in captivity from March to July and in late September (Greatwood 1978; Hilken and Schlepper 1998; Murphy et al. 1978; Tryon and Murphy 1982). Mating lasts 4–15 minutes, and males sometimes mate two to three times with the same female or copulate with several females during a 24 hour period. Males even court females anteriorly while posteriorly in coitus with another female. First the male establishes the female's sex with tongue flicks, presumably identifying her pheromones, then performs a series of body jerks when contact is made (Murphy et al. 1978). She also jerks her body, and usually crawls away with the male following and attempting crawl alongside her. She twitches her tail from side to side while he continues tongue flicking and sometimes bites her. When aligned, he uses his tail to search for the female's anal vent, while gaping his vent, until intromission is accomplished. He does not wrap his tail around that of the female, but keeps it to her side.

Females are gravid in May, and eggs have been laid in captivity from mid-May to late August, but most eggs are deposited in June or July. The GP averages 39.6 (38–41) days (Tryon and Murphy 1982). More than one clutch can be laid a year (Greatwood 1978; Tryon and Murphy 1982). Clutches average 7.5 (3–13) eggs, which are white with leathery, adherent shells, are 37.1 (26.4–49.2) mm long and 21.0 (12–26) mm wide, and weigh 11.4 (9.1–13.3) g. The IP is 57–76 days, depending on the IT, and most young hatch in August–September. Hatchlings resemble adults in color and pattern, average 25.6 (19.0–32.3) cm TBL, and weigh an average of 8.8 (6.3–10.8) g.

GROWTH AND LONGEVITY. Some captive growth has been documented. *L. alterna* grows rapidly if fed properly. A female kept by Assetto (1978) grew from 45 to 91.5 cm between July 1974 and 1977, and Tryon and Murphy (1982) reported hatchlings grew from 22.5–27.9 to 60–78 cm and increased their weight from 6.5–10.5 to 86.3–190.0 g in approximately 19 months. A captive male grew 5.1 cm in 162 days (Axtell 1951).

A wild-caught female survived 19 years and 7 months in captivity (Salmon et al. 1997).

DIET AND FEEDING HABITS. Lizards and their eggs make up the bulk of the food of wild *L. alterna* (*Cnemidophorus, Cophosaurus, Eumeces, Sceloporus*), but pocket mice (*Perognathus*) and canyon frogs (*Hyla arenicolor*) are also eaten (Degenhardt et al. 1996; Gehlbach and Baker 1962; Mecham and Milstead 1949; Miller 1979; Tennant 1984). No records exist of wild *L. alterna* having consumed another snake, but cannibalism sometimes occurs in captivity (Miller 1979). Captives have taken other lizards (*Anolis, Crotaphytus,*

Urosaurus, Uta) and mice *(Mus, Peromyscus)* (Asseto 1978; Wright and Wright 1957; C. Ernst, pers. obs.).

Foraging is nocturnal, and probably occurs mostly in rock crevices and rodent burrows, since this species is a poor constrictor more prone to pin its prey against some object than to wrap around it. In captivity, the authors have observed that it has a difficult time subduing living prey in a spacious enclosure and often tries to swallow it alive.

PREDATORS AND DEFENSE. Tryon and Guese (1984) reported attacks by ringtail cats *(Bassariscus astutus)* on individuals in Texas, and Miller (1979) considered raccoons *(Procyon lotor),* badgers *(Taxidea taxus),* skunks *(Mephitis),* weasels *(Mustela),* foxes *(Vulpes),* coyotes *(Canis latrans),* peccaries *(Pecari),* and the great horned owl *(Bubo virginianus)* as potential predators. Many *L. alterna* die on Texas highways each year, and others are collected only to eventually die through neglect in the pet trade.

L. alterna is rather docile and seldom attempts to bite, but there are exceptions. It is more likely to thrash about and release musk and feces on its handler. In nature, its banded pattern may be mistaken for that of the venomous coral snake, giving it protection from some would-be predators. Tryon and Guese (1984) reported that a wild adult female played dead when apparently attacked by a ringtail cat *(Bassariscus)* and that a captive hatchling also played dead.

POPULATIONS. Since most individuals have been taken at scattered locations, little has been determined about this species' population dynamics. Its nocturnal behavior and a habitat with abundant rock crevices make it difficult to detect in numbers. Most wild individuals are seen along roads at night. Undoubtedly many more are in subterranean retreats, and the population size in suitable rocky habitats is considerably greater than one might imagine. In addition, although the sex ratio of hatchlings is essentially 1:1 (Miller 1979; Tryon and Murphy 1982), few females are captured. Of 85 *L. alterna* collected by Miller (1979) in Val Verde County, Texas, 70 were males, and only 2 of the 15 females were gravid. Females, especially when gravid, merely remain underground for longer periods than do males. Juveniles are also scarce; only about 4% of wild *L. alterna* caught by Miller (1979) were juveniles. Do juveniles suffer a higher mortality rate, or do they also remain mostly underground, possibly to avoid desiccation?

REMARKS. *L. alterna* was formerly considered a subspecies of *L. mexicana* (Gehlbach 1967), but Garstka (1982) elevated it to a full species. Recently, however, Hilken and Schlepper (1998) questioned this elevation after crossbreeding the two "species" in captivity. *L. alterna* has been reviewed by Gehlbach and Baker (1962).

Although the pet trade has taken, and still does take, individuals from the wild, thus depleting populations of breeding stock, captive breeding programs are now numerous and should be able to supply the pet trade with enough individuals in the future to reduce wild collecting.

Lampropeltis calligaster (Harlan 1827) | Yellow-bellied Kingsnake

RECOGNITION. *L. calligaster* (TBL to 142.2 cm) is shiny gray to brown with a dorsal pattern of 40–79 brown to red, dark-bordered blotches, and a cream to yellow venter with square to mottled brown blotches. Two alternating rows of dark spots (which may be fused) are present on each side of the body. Some individuals may be very dark with an obscured dorsal pattern, and occasionally an individual may be striped. The head has three dark marks—a stripe extending backward and downward from the eye to the corner of the mouth, a second stripe extending downward from the eye onto the supralabials, and a horizontal bar that crosses the face immediately anterior to the eyes. Dorsal body scales are smooth with two apical pits, and lie in 25 (19–23) anterior rows, 23–27 (21–22) midbody rows, and 20 (17–21) posterior rows. On the underside are 170–219 ventrals, 31–59 subcaudals, and a single anal plate. Lateral head scales include 2 nasals (partially separated by the nostril), 1 (0–2) loreal, 1 preocular, 2 (1–3) postoculars, 2 (1–3) + 3 (2–4) temporals, 7 (6–8) supralabials, and 8–9 (6–11) infralabials. The unequally bilobed hemipenis has a smooth base, a single sulcus spermaticus extending to the tip of the shortest lobe, calyxes on each lobe (usually larger on the longer lobe), and a few fringes and short spines. Each maxilla usually has 12–15 teeth.

Males have TLs that average 13.8 (10.1–15.0) % of TBL, 37–59 (mean, 48) subcaudals, and 170–215 (mean, 200) ventrals; females have TLs averaging 12.2 (8.9–14.5) % of TBL, 31–52 (mean, 42) subcaudals, and 186–219 (mean, 204) ventrals.

GEOGRAPHIC VARIATION. Three subspecies have been described. *Lampropeltis c. calligaster* (Harlan 1827), the prairie kingsnake, is found from western Indiana and western Kentucky west to southern Iowa and southeastern Nebraska south to the Gulf Coast of western Louisiana and eastern Texas. It has about 60 brown dorsal blotches with concave anterior and posterior borders, a yellow venter with square brown blotches, 25–27 midbody scale rows, and 9–10 (occasionally 8) infralabials. *L. c. rhombomaculata* (Holbrook 1840), the mole kingsnake, ranges from the western shore of the Chesapeake Bay in Maryland and Virginia west to central Tennessee and south to South Carolina, central Georgia, and the Gulf Coast from Mobile Bay west through Mississippi to eastern Louisiana. Scattered isolated populations also are known from the panhandle and peninsula of Florida.

Mole kingsnake, *Lampropeltis calligaster rhombomaculata*; Fairfax County, Virginia. (Photograph by Christopher W. Brown, DVM)

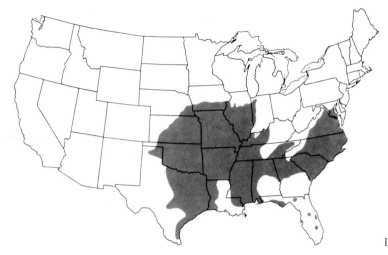

Distribution of *Lampropeltis calligaster*.

It has about 55 (no more than 71) reddish, well-separated, dorsal blotches with straight or convex anterior and posterior borders, a white to cream venter with square, rounded, or mottled brown blotches, 21–23 midbody scale rows, and 8 (occasionally 6–9) infralabials. *L. c. occiptolineata* Price 1987, the South Florida mole kingsnake, is found only on the central peninsula of Florida. It has over 75 small, juvenile-like, dorsal blotches, a white to cream venter with square, rounded, or mottled brown blotches, no more than 21 midbody scale rows, and a complexity network of dark lines on the back of the head not found in the other two subspecies.

CONFUSING SPECIES. Other *Lampropeltis* can be differentiated by the key presented above. Rat snakes (*Elaphe*) have keeled body scales and divided anal plates. The glossy snake (*Arizona elegans*) is somewhat faded in appearance, and its white venter lacks a dark pattern.

KARYOTYPE. The normal chromosome complement is 36: 2 acrocentric and 14 biarmed macrochromosomes and 20 microchromosomes (Baker et al. 1972; Camper and Hanks 1995). The fourth pair of microchromosomes is submetacenteric and heteromorphic ZW in females and homomorphic ZZ in males (Baker et al. 1972). A NOR is located on the first pair of microchromosomes (Camper and Hanks 1995).

FOSSIL RECORD. Pleistocene fossils date from the Blancan of Kansas (Holman 1979b) and the Ran-cholabrean of Arkansas (Dowling 1958), Florida (Holman 1996), Kansas (Brattstrom 1967), Oklahoma (Smith and Cifelli 2000), Pennsylvania (Guilday et al. 1966), and Texas (Hill 1971; Holman 1966). The Pennsylvania record is well north of the species' present range.

DISTRIBUTION. *L. calligaster* ranges from Maryland, central Kentucky, western Indiana, southern Iowa and southeastern Nebraska southward to South Carolina, central Georgia, the Gulf Coast of southwestern Alabama and Mississippi, and southeastern Louisiana, western Louisiana, and eastern Texas. Isolated populations are also present on the peninsula and panhandle of Florida.

HABITAT. This snake lives in a variety of open or semiopen habitats, including prairie grasslands, savannas, meadows, old fields, the borders of marshes, the edges of cultivated fields and pastures, thickets, open woodlands, and even trash-strewn urban lots.

BEHAVIOR. Relatively little is known of the biology of this snake; it is so secretive that it is seldom seen.

In Florida and along the Gulf Coast, *L. calligaster* may be active most of the year, especially if the winter is mild. Farther north it is forced to hibernate in winter, and the annual activity period becomes shorter with increased latitude. In Mississippi it is surface active from March to October (Cook 1945), and in North Carolina from February through December, with 48% of sightings occurring in April–June and

29% in August–September (Palmer and Braswell 1995); but Kansas and Virginia *L. calligaster* are only active from April to October or November (Clarke 1958; Mitchell 1994). Overwintering biology of *L. calligaster* is practically unknown. Smith (1961) reported that they occasionally use road embankments as winter retreats in Illinois, and individuals in Kansas used a rock ledge as a hibernaculum (Fitch 1978). Rodent burrows are also probably used as hibernacula.

During the spring and fall *L. calligaster* can be found prowling during the early morning hours, but with the onset of warm weather it shifts its daily activity to twilight and night, becoming primarily nocturnal. The days are usually spent underground in animal burrows or rock crevices, in hollow logs or stumps, or under surface objects.

The thermal requirements of this species are poorly known. Illinois first-year young were found at ATs of 19–26°C and STs of 14–21°C (Tucker 2000). Clarke (1958) found it active in Kansas at ATs of 6–31°C, and the only BTs reported are 30.4–33.0°C (Fitch 1956). Reaction times become faster with increasing temperatures (Keogh and DeSerto 1994).

Movement data are also limited. In Kansas, an adult male and an adult female were radio equipped by Fitch (1978). The male made successive daily movements of 4.5–18.5 (mean, 11.2) m; the female's daily movements were 0–29 m, and averaged 11.2 m for the 11 days it had moved (it did not move on 9 days). An additional 25 *L. calligaster* were recaptured by Fitch after intervals of 9 days to 46 months, but none was recaptured more than five times. For 35 distances between successive capture points, these snakes moved 18.3–764 (mean, 232) m. After exclusion of an exceptionally long 764 m record, the remaining 23 records of males formed a graduated series of 18–482 (mean, 265) m. Females moved 52–348 (mean, 169) m. This suggests males have larger home ranges; if these movements are taken as representing radii of circular home ranges, the home range size averaged 22 ha for males and 9 ha for females. During 50 years (1947–1997), Fitch (1999) only recorded 74 movements. The snakes were recaptured after intervals of three days to three years, and the five longest distances traveled between captures were 408–950 (average, 606.6) m, and in each instance the snake was believed to have shifted its home range to a new area. The

other 69 records formed a graded series up to 370 m; 33 males averaged 150 m, and 36 females averaged 123.8 m. Because the movements of both sexes were rather evenly distributed up to 350 m, Fitch (1999) thought the home ranges may have had about that diameter and encompassed 9.86 ha. However, some individuals are rather sedentary; Fitch (1999) found one female in the same place five times within a month. In another study, another individual moved 183 m in six weeks (Stickel and Cope 1947).

A dominance system occurs in male *L. calligaster*, especially during the mating season, consisting of behaviors similar to those found in other *Lampropeltis* (Collins 1993; Moehn 1967).

REPRODUCTION. Females mature at a SVL of about 70 cm—Fitch (1978) reported it as 65.1 cm in Kansas, with most females shorter than 70 cm lacking the prominent thickening of the cloacal wall normally associated with sexual maturity; and Mitchell (1994) gave 67.2 cm SVL as the smallest mature length of females in Virginia. Similarly, males longer than 70 cm SVL usually contain sperm—Mitchell (1994) reported a mature Virginia male with a SVL of 66.5 cm, and in Kansas the smallest mature male examined by Fitch (1999) was 62.9 cm. Females and males probably reached these lengths in two to three years.

Almost nothing has been reported concerning the gametic cycle of either sex. Females have enlarged follicles in late April and early May, contain oviductal eggs in late May and June, and are postovipositional by late July or early August (C. Ernst, pers. obs.; Fitch 1999). Males contain mature sperm in their vas deferens in September–October (C. Ernst, pers. obs.). Not all females breed each year (Fitch 1999).

The breeding season begins soon after *L. calligaster* emerge from hibernation and lasts from early April to early June. When they first meet, both sexes tongue flick and body jerk, position their bodies alongside each other, and then the female may rub her cloacal vent along the male's cloacal and tail regions (Tryon and Carl 1980). Females may also spasmodically jerk the anterior portion of their bodies. While copulating the male lies either to the side or on top of the female, places his head on her neck, and intermittently waves and pulsates his tail. He may bite her body and neck (Krysko et al. 2000). The female may hold her tail vertically during mating. Matings usually last over an hour. Tryon (1984) reported that a captive female mated twice during one year and subsequently laid two clutches of eggs.

Oviposition may take place as early as 16 May or as late as 25 July after a GP of 32–62 days (Krysko et al. 2000; Palmer and Braswell 1995). Most nesting occurs in July. Typical nest sites include rodent burrows, sawdust piles, or the loose soil of recently ploughed fields. Normally, it takes a female two to seven minutes to extrude an egg (Clark 1954). Clutches contain 3 (Brown 1992) to 21 eggs (Carpenter 1985) (mean, 10; n = 71). The elongated eggs are white and adherent, are 23.3–57.0 (mean, 37.7) mm long and 13.6–28.0 (mean, 19.2) mm wide, and weigh 3.5–12.4 (mean, 6.3) g. Generally, clutch size increases with female body length; the shorter subspecies, *L. c. rhombomaculata* and *L. c. occipitolineata*, produce fewer eggs per clutch, and their eggs are smaller. Reported RCMs have been 0.375–0.380 (Seigel and Fitch 1984; Tryon and Carl 1980). The IP is temperature dependent and averages 66.8 (44–110) days. Hatching occurs from July through October.

Hatchlings are more brightly patterned than adults, are 17.2–30.6 (mean, 23.2) mm long, and weigh 2.7–12.2 (mean, 6.5) g.

GROWTH AND LONGEVITY. Fitch (1999) believed one-year-old *L. c. calligaster* have 26.4–49.6 cm SVLs, approximately twice the length of hatchlings (these snakes probably grew over 4 cm per active month; Fitch 1978). Other SVLs listed by age include 2 years, 50.0–69.5 cm; 3 years, 70.0–82.0 cm; 4 years, 78.0–89.2 cm; 5 years, 83.3–94.5 cm; 6 years, 85.5–100.0 cm; 7 years, 99.1–104.2 cm; 8 years, 94.0–111.4 cm; and 10 years, 105.0–107.0 cm (Fitch 1999). Males generally grow faster and larger than females; on average females are 92.7% of male SVL and 81.9% of male mass. Illinois first-year young had 26.2–38.0 SVLs and 8.2–25.9 g masses (Tucker 2000).

A male *L. c. calligaster*, originally wild caught as an adult, survived 23 years, 8 months, and 23 days at the Oklahoma City Zoo (Snider and Bowler 1992).

DIET AND FEEDING HABITS. The authors' experience with *L. calligaster* indicates that it is an active hunter of small rodents and lizards. It often pursues rodents into their burrows, and seeks out lizards in their hiding places behind bark or in crevices. Other observers, however, have reported that it may ambush prey (Seigel and Fitch 1984).

Prey is seized in the mouth, body coils are wrapped around it, and the animal is constricted. Constriction can be either by the right or the left side of the snake (Heinrich and Klaassen 1985). The authors have seen captives constrict mice by squeezing them against a wall of their cage, a method probably used when constricting rodents in their underground burrows.

Wild and captive prairie kingsnakes have eaten a variety of prey: mammals—shrews (*Blarina brevicauda, B. carolinensis, B. hylophaga, Cryptotis parva, Sorex* sp.), moles (*Scalopus aquaticus),* young rabbits (*Sylvilagus floridanus),* pocket gophers (*Geomys* sp.), chipmunks (*Tamias striatus),* ground squirrels (*Spermophilus* sp.), voles (*Microtus ochrogaster, M. pennsylvanicus, M. pinetorum, Synaptomys cooperi),* mice (*Mus musculus, Peromyscus leucopus, P. maniculatus),* and rats (*Neotoma* sp., *Rattus norvegicus, Sigmodon hispidus);* lizards (*Cnemidophorus sexlineatus, Eumeces fasciatus, E. obsoletus, Ophisaurus attenuatus, O. ventralis, Sceloporus undulatus);* snakes (*Carphophis amoenus, Coluber constrictor, Crotalus horridus, Diadophis punctatus, Lampropeltis triangulum, Opheodrys aestivus, Storeria dekayi, S. occipitomaculata, Virginia striatula);* anurans (*Acris crepitans, Bufo* sp., *Hyla versicolor, Pseudacris crucifer, P. triseriata, Rana clamitans, R. pipiens);* bird eggs and young (*Colinus virginianus, Passer domesticus, Spizella passerina);* and insects—Coleoptera (Carabidae, Scarabeidae), Homoptera, Hymenoptera, Lepidoptera, and Orthroptera (Gryllidae, Locustidae) (Boyer and Heinze 1934; Brown 1979a; C. Ernst, pers. obs.; Fitch 1978, 1999; Gloyd 1928; Guidry 1953; Hamilton and Pollack 1956; Kern 1956; Klimstra 1959b; Lockwood 1954; Palmer and Braswell 1995; Schmidt 1919; Trauth 1983; Tucker 2000; Vermersch and Kuntz 1986; Webb 1970).

Klimstra (1959b) studied the diet of Illinois *L. calligaster* and most frequently found mammals as the prey (79.8% of stomachs examined), followed by a combination of frogs, bird eggs, and insects (15.3%). Surprisingly, lizards and snakes were only found in 8% of the stomachs. Fitch (1999) also found mammals the most important prey in Kansas, with snakes, lizards, and bird eggs of relatively minor importance. In terms of biomass, he calculated that mammals made up 81%, lizards 9%, snake eggs 5%, and bird eggs 5%. Adults eat larger prey (mammals and reptiles); young snakes prey on small shrews, small mice and voles, amphibians, small snakes, lizards, and insects.

That a small timber rattlesnake *(Crotalus horridus)* was eaten is not surprising, since the blood serum of *L. calligaster* has pit-viper-venom–neutralizing properties (Weinstein et al. 1992).

PREDATORS AND DEFENSE. Known predators of *L. calligaster* are common kingsnakes *(Lampropeltis getula)*, hawks *(Buteo albicaudatus, B. jamaicensis, B. platypterus)*, opossums *(Didelphis virginianus)*, ground squirrels *(Spermophilus* sp.), raccoons *(Procyon lotor)*, badgers *(Taxidea taxus)*, skunks *(Mephitis mephitis)*, and red fox *(Vulpes vulpes)* (Black 1983b; Brown 1979a; Linsey and Clifford 1981; Knable 1970; Minton 1972; Palmer and Braswell 1995; Ross 1989; Viets 1993). Humans also kill many prairie kingsnakes either directly or with their automobiles and habitat destruction.

Although most *L. calligaster* remain quietly coiled or try to flee when disturbed, some may be quite vicious—flattening, jerking and twitching their heads, shaking their tails, striking and biting, and spraying musk and cloacal contents. Defensive behavior is temperature dependent—the colder the snake, the slower it reacts (Keogh and DeSerto 1994).

POPULATIONS. Fitch (1978) trapped *L. calligaster* in Kansas, catching 10 in a continuous block of approximately 32 ha of grassland and 13 others on four separate grassland areas of about 32 ha combined. This suggests a minimum density of one snake / 2.6 ha or 0.38 individuals / ha. After 50 years of study and many captures later at a 9.46 ha site, Fitch (1999) estimated a range of maximum annual densities of *L. calligaster* over the years of 2.47–8.06 / ha. This probably means 9–38 prairie kingsnakes used the site in any given year, for a density of 1–4 / ha. In a three-county area in northeastern Kansas *L. calligaster* made up only 76 (1.1%) of 7,062 snakes caught by Fitch (1992), and of 33,117 snakes from over the entire state, it only accounted for 0.68%; however, 216 were caught at one site (Fitch 1993). C. Ernst found six neonates in an approximately 10 m^2 in a coastal plain open woodland in northern Virginia. Because of its secretive and nocturnal habits, these figures probably do not represent typical densities of this snake.

Limited data on sex ratios exist. Mount (1975) reported a ratio of 19 males to only 6 females (3.16: 1.00), perhaps because males are more active than females. Tryon and Carl (1980) reported a hatchling sex ratio of 11 males to 6 females (1.83:1.00) from a clutch of 17 eggs, and Ernst et al. (1985) recorded a male to female ratio of 4:5 (0.80:1.00) for nine hatchlings.

L. calligaster is a species of special concern in Louisiana and is considered rare in Florida.

REMARKS. Using morphological characters, Keogh (1996) reported that *L. calligaster* is most closely related to *L. getula,* but immunological tests by Dowling and Maxson (1990) showed it to be closely related to *L. mexicana.* This species was last reviewed by Blaney (1979b).

Lampropeltis getula (Linnaeus 1766) | Common Kingsnake

RECOGNITION. *L. getula* (TBL to 208.3 cm) is glossy black to brown with 15–97 white or yellow rows of spots or bands crossing its back. Size and patterns of the light spots or bands vary considerably (see GEOGRAPHIC VARIATION), but dark bars are always present on the lips. The venter is usually patterned with a mixture of cream or yellow and black. Dorsal body scales are smooth and doubly pitted, and occur in 21–23 (17–25) anterior rows, 21–23 (19–25) midbody rows, and 17–19 (20–21) posterior rows. The venter has 197–255 ventrals, 30–63 subcaudals, and a single anal plate. Pertinent lateral head scales are 2 nasals, 1 (rarely 0) loreal, 1 (2, rarely 0) preocular, 2 (1–3) postoculars, 2 (1–3) + 3 (2–4) temporals, 7 (6–8) supra-

Eastern kingsnake, *Lampropeltis getula getula*; Fairfax County, Virginia. (Photograph by Carl H. Ernst)

California kingsnake (banded phase), *Lampropeltis getula californiae*; Riverside County, California. (Photograph by Carl H. Ernst)

labials, and 9–10 (7–11) infralabials. The bilobed or clavate hemipenis has a single sulcus spermaticus extending toward the longer lobe, calyxes near the nude tips, small spines on the lower half of the shaft, and a base partially naked or with short spines. Each maxilla has 12–20 teeth.

Males have 197–255 ventrals, 40–63 subcaudals, and TLs 11–15 (mean, 13.5) % of TBL; females have 199–250 ventrals, 30–57 ventrals, and TLs 9–13 (mean, 12) % of TBL.

GEOGRAPHIC VARIATION. Although quite variable, electrophoretic analyses of blood proteins indicate *L. getula* is a single species (Dessauer and Pough 1975). Eight subspecies are recognized. *L. g. getula* (Linnaeus 1766), the eastern kingsnake, ranges from southern New Jersey to southern Florida and southeastern Alabama east of the Appalachian Mountains. It is black with a chainlike dorsal pattern of 15–44 nar-

row white to yellow crossbands, and usually no more than 21 dorsal scale rows. *L. g. californiae* (Blainville 1835), the California kingsnake, occurs from Douglas County in southwestern Oregon south to northern Baja California and east through southern Nevada, southern Utah, and western Arizona. It is dark brown or black, has more than 23 dorsal scale rows, and has two pattern morphs: (1) a chainlike pattern of 21–44 light crossbands with or without brown pigment on the white crossbands and (2) a middorsal longitudinal light stripe and, in some individuals, lateral longitudinal stripes on scale rows 1–3 or 1–6. *L. g. floridana* Blanchard 1919, the Florida kingsnake, resides in peninsular Florida from Pinellas and Hillsborough counties south to Monroe and Dade counties, with disjunct populations in Nassau, Duval, and Baker counties of northeastern Florida and in the panhandle from Jefferson to Gulf counties. It is cream to pale yellow with each dorsal scale brown at the tip, has

Speckled kingsnake, *Lampropeltis getula holbrooki*; Tuscaloosa County, Alabama. (Photograph by Carl H. Ernst)

22–66 faint light crossbands (especially on the neck), and has more than 23 dorsal scale rows. *L. g. holbrooki* Stejneger 1903, the speckled kingsnake, occurs from southwestern Illinois and Iowa south to Mobile Bay, Alabama, western Louisiana and eastern Texas. It normally has no more than 21 dorsal scale rows and is dark brown or black, and each dorsal scale has a white or yellow spot, producing a salt-and-pepper pattern. *L. g. nigra* (Yarrow 1882), the black kingsnake, is found generally west of the Appalachian Mountains and east of the Mississippi River from West Virginia and southern Ohio west to southwestern Indiana and adjacent southeastern Illinois and south to northwestern Georgia, central Alabama, and northeastern Mississippi. It is black with the chainlike pattern absent, incomplete, or reduced to a series of 21–70 small white or yellow spots, and normally has no more than 21 dorsal scale rows. *L. g. nigrita* Zweifel and Norris 1955, the black desert kingsnake, ranges south from Santa Cruz County, Arizona, through Sonora to northern Sinaloa, Mexico. It has more than 23 dorsal scale rows, is dark brown or gray black, is normally without faint crossbands or stripes, and has a black venter with a light anal plate. *L. g. splendida* (Baird and Girard 1853), the desert kingsnake, is found from central Texas to southeastern Arizona, and south to San Louis Potosi and Zacatecas, Mexico. It is brown or black above with a series of 42–97 narrow light crossbands, and has 5–10 rows of light-spotted scales on the sides of the body; the venter is black with large white or yellow spots along the sides; and it has more than 23 dorsal scale rows. *L. g. sticticeps* Barbour and Engels 1942, the Outer Banks kingsnake, is known only from the coastal barrier islands of North Carolina from Nags Head to Cape Lookout. It is brown with small white spots on the dark areas between about 25 chainlike crossbands, and has no more than 21 dorsal scale rows.

The validity of *L. g. sticticeps* was questioned by Blaney (1979a) and recently by Palmer and Braswell (1995), but was upheld by Lazell and Musick (1981) and Ernst and Barbour (1989). The confusion occurs from intergradation with *L. g. getula* about Cape Hatteras, but kingsnakes from the more southern barrier islands are quite distinct and easily separated from *L. g. getula*.

CONFUSING SPECIES. Other *Lampropeltis* can be distinguished with the key presented above. Rat snakes *(Elaphe)* and gopher and pine snakes *(Pituophis)* have keeled body scales, and the *Elaphe* have a divided anal plate. Racers *(Coluber)* and whipsnakes *(Masticophis)* lack dark bars on their supralabials and have an elongated preocular scale that invades the supralabial series and a divided anal plate.

Outer Banks kingsnake, *Lampropeltis getula sticticeps*; Carteret County, North Carolina. (Photograph by Carl H. Ernst)

KARYOTYPE. It has 36 chromosomes (16 macro-chromosomes, 20 microchromosomes); sex determination is ZZ (male), ZW (female) (Baker et al. 1972; Bury et al. 1970). The NOR is located on the first pair of microchromosomes (Camper and Hanks 1995).

FOSSIL RECORD. *L. getula* possibly dates from the Miocene (Hemphillian) of Nebraska (Parmley and Holman 1995), but most fossils are from the Pleistocene: Blancan—Kansas (Brattstrom 1967); Irvingtonian—Florida (Meylan 1982, 1995), Oklahoma (Holman 1986b), and Texas (Holman 1969b); and Rancholabrean—Alabama (Holman et al. 1990), Arizona (Mead et al. 1984; Van Devender et al. 1977, 1991), California (Brattstrom 1953b, 1953c, 1958a; Hudson and Brattstrom 1977; LaDuke 1991; Van Devender and Mead 1978), Florida (Auffenberg 1963; Brattstrom 1953b; Gut and Ray 1963; Holman 1959b, 1978; Weigel 1962), Georgia (Holman 1967), Kansas (Brattstrom 1967), Nevada (Brattstrom 1954a, 1976), New Mexico (Brattstrom 1964a; Van Devender and Worthington 1977), Oklahoma (Smith and Cifelli 2000), Tennessee (Van Dam 1978), Texas (Gehlbach and Holman 1974; Hill 1971; Holman 1964; Holman and Winkler 1987; Kasper and Parmley 1990; Parmley 1988b, 1990a), and Virginia (Holman 1986a).

DISTRIBUTION. *L. getula* is one of the few snakes that range coast to coast in the United States. Its northern limits are New Jersey, Delaware, and Maryland (there is an old record from southeastern Pennsylvania) to southern Illinois in the East, southern Iowa and Nebraska in the central states, and southwestern Oregon, northern California, and central Nevada in the West. It ranges southward through peninsular Florida, and west along the Gulf Coast, through Texas, southern New Mexico, and most of Arizona to southern California and northern Baja California, and south in Mexico to San Louis Potosi and Zacatecas.

HABITAT. The habitat varies with the subspecies, but most eastern populations are found in dry pine or deciduous woods. Those living in Florida and along the Gulf Coast sometimes enter marshes and live along swamp borders, and some Florida populations and *L. g. sticticeps* may enter brackish water. In the Midwest, prairies and farmlands are inhabited, and in the West it is found in deserts, chaparral, piñon-juniper woodlands, and river bottoms. Elevations range from sea level to about 2,000 m.

BEHAVIOR. *L. getula* is normally annually active from late March or April to October or early Novem-

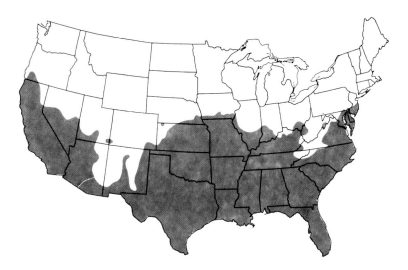

Distribution of *Lampropeltis getula*.

ber, but it may be active in all months in peninsular Florida, along the Gulf Coast, and elsewhere in years with warm winters. Most surface activity in the East occurs in April–June with a second period in September and October, but in western deserts *L. getula* is most active from July through September. Over most of the range it hibernates individually in winter, and may also estivate in the summer. Hibernacula include caves, rock crevices, clay and gravel banks, mammal burrows, tortoise *(Gopherus agassizii, G. polyphemus)* burrows, hollow logs and stumps, old sawdust mounds, and the foundations of abandoned buildings. Daily activity is diurnal in the winter, spring, and fall, but during the summer it shifts to crepuscular and nocturnal. Those active during the day in the West are usually associated with water (Degenhardt et al. 1996). Nonactive daily hours are spent under or in some shelter. Brattstrom (1965) reported the CT_{min} and CT_{max} of *L. getula* are –2 and 42°C, respectively, and that the minimum and maximum voluntary BTs are 15.1 and 31.4°C. In Kansas, *L. getula* are active at ATs of 13–31.5°C (Clarke 1958), and Sullivan (1981a) found them active in California at road STs of 22–34°C (BTs, 17–33°C). Brattstrom's active kingsnakes had an average BT of 28.1 (18.0–31.4) °C. BTs of active Georgia *L. getula* were 23.0–33.5 (mean, 28.7) °C (Bothner 1973). BT is highly correlated with ST (Sullivan 1981).

Few data exist concerning movements by *L. getula*. Stickel and Cope (1947) recaptured one 1.8 years later that had moved more than 100 m, and Fitch (1949) re-ported movements of 46–561 m in four days to about a month. *L. getula* apparently follows scent trails left by conspecifics (Burger 1991a). It is not restricted to land or to ground level. The authors have seen one swimming in a Florida swamp, and on another occasion found one in a tree hole 2 m above ground (it is known to raid bird nests).

Males sometimes engage in dominance combat behavior (Carpenter and Gillingham 1977; Krysko et al. 1998)—see Carpenter and Gillingham (1977) for a detailed analysis of the combat sequence.

REPRODUCTION. Maturity is achieved at two to four years of age (Zweifel 1980). Stebbins (1985) gives a minimum TBL of 51 cm for mature males and females, and Wright and Wright (1957) reported 55 cm, but most *L. getula* probably mature at greater lengths. The gametic cycles have not been described.

The principal breeding period extends from mid-March in Florida (Knepton 1951), and April elsewhere, to June, and captives have mated in January and February. Males apparently find females by following their scent (pheromone?) trails. When a female is located, the male examines her with his tongue, crawls alongside of her and then onto her back, and performs caudocephalic waves while he searches with his tail for her vent. He holds her still by biting her neck. When the female's vent is located, the male slides his tail, aligns their vents, and inserts one hemipenis (the opposite hemipenis may be used in subsequent matings; Zweifel 1997). Once intromission is accomplished, the male continues rhythmic undulations of his body and pumps with his cloacal region. The female usually remains passive during the male's behaviors (Lewke 1979; Secor 1987). Copulation often lasts over an hour. A female may mate with more than one male during the breeding season and may produce a clutch with offspring from several males (Zweifel and Dessauer 1983). Females may also produce more than one clutch per season as a result of more than one mating (Tryon 1984). The GP is about 60 (37–73) days (Zweifel 1980).

Nesting occurs as early as May in Florida (Iverson 1978; Knepton 1951), but over the geographic range most eggs are laid in June–July. Typical nest sites are rotting logs and stumps, sawdust mounds, mammal burrows, and rock crevices. Clutches contain 1–29 eggs (mean, 10.5; n = 89); clutch size is probably directly related to female body size. The eggs are adherent and white, are 27.8–69.0 (mean, 37.9; n = 65) mm long and 13–30 (mean, 22.1; n = 58) mm wide, and weigh 8.3–25.9 (mean, 11.2; n = 28) g. Seigel and Fitch (1984) reported RCMs of 0.325, 0.402, and 0.413.

The IP is about 59 (39–83) days, depending on the IT; eggs incubated at 22°C do not hatch (Burger 1990). Hatching occurs as early as mid-July in Florida, but elsewhere from late July through mid-October, with most hatchings occurring in August–September. Hatchlings resemble the adults in color and pattern, and have TBLs of 20.2–36.1 (mean, 27.1; n = 64) cm and masses of 4.4–7.0 (mean, 5.8; n = 12) g when they emerge. Hatchlings from eggs incubated at 28°C have longer SVLs and better escape and strike development than those incubated at 32°C (Burger 1990).

GROWTH AND LONGEVITY. Limited growth data are available. Fitch (1949) reported the following length and weight gains between captures for California *L. getula*: 13 months, 0 cm, 2 g; 24 months, 1.9 cm, 124 g; 72+ months, 13.0 cm, 99 g; 74+ months, 23.3 cm, 220 g; and 75 months, 18.2 cm, 366 g. Captive hatchlings may double their length in a year.

The longevity record for the species is 40 years and 11 months by a *L. g. californiae* (Dibble 2000).

DIET AND FEEDING HABITS. A captive may consume 25.9–39.1 g/week of food (Kirkwood and Gili 1994). *L. getula* preys on a great variety of animals, but seems to prefer reptiles and their eggs: reptiles—snakes (*Agkistrodon contortrix, A. piscivorus, Carphophis amoenus, Clonophis kirtlandii, Coluber constrictor, Crotalus atrox, C. cerastes, C. horridus, C. mitchellii, C. viridis, Diadophis punctatus, Elaphe obsoleta, Farancia erytrogramma, Heterodon platirhinus, H. simus, Lampropeltis calligaster, L. getula, Masticophis flagellum, Micrurus fulvius, Nerodia erythrogaster, N. fasciata, N. rhombifer, Opheodrys aestivus, Pituophis catenifer, Regina alleni, R. grahamii, Rhinocheilus lecontei, Sistrurus miliarius, Storeria dekayi, S. occipitomaculata, Tantilla sp., Thamnophis sirtalis, Virginia valeriae*), lizards (*Anolis carolinensis, Cnemidophorus sexlineatus, C. tigrus, Eumeces fasciatus, E. gilberti, Ophisaurus attenuatus, O. ventralis, Sceloporus graciosus, S. occidentalis, S. undulatus, Scincella lateralis*), and turtles (*Chelydra serpentina, Graptemys flavimaculata, Kinosternon subrubrum, Pseudemys concinna, Sternotherus odoratus, Trachemys scripta*); amphibians—frogs (*Rana* sp.) and urodeles (*Notophthalmus viridescens, Siren lacertina*); mammals (*Microtus ochrogaster, M. pennsylvanicus, M. pinetorum, Mus musculus, Peromyscus leucopus, P. maniculatus, Rattus norvegicus, Sigmodon hispidus, Thomomys* sp.); birds and their eggs (*Agelaius phoeniceus, Cardinalis cardinalis, Colinus virginianus, Gallus gallus, Mimus polyglottis, Molothrus ater, Spiza americana*); and sphinx moth larvae (Brauman and Fiorillo 1995; Brown 1979a; Byrd and Jenkins 1996; Cavitt 2000b; Clark 1949; Cunningham 1959; Dundee and Rossman 1989; C. Ernst, pers. obs.; Facemire and Fretwell 1980; Forks 1979; Gates 1957; Godley 1982; Hamilton and Pollack 1956; Jaksic and Greene 1984; Knight and Loraine 1986; LaDuc et al. 1996; Lewke 1982; Megonigal 1985; Minton 1972; Mitchell 1994; Plummer 1990b; Plummer and Congdon 1992; Posey 1973; Stebbins 1954; Wilson and Friddle 1946; Wright 1988). Lizards may constitute up to 46% of the diet (Hamilton and Pollack 1956). Turtles nests are searched for and then dug up by pushing the head sideways into the soil.

Prey is located primarily by smell, and the odors of colubrid and crotalid snakes are distinguished (Brock and Myers 1979; Weldon and Schell 1984; Williams and Brisbin 1978). Vision also plays a role in prey detection (C. Ernst, pers. obs.), but thermal cues seem of little importance (Austin and Gregory 1998). *L. getula* is a constrictor, and large prey are immobilized in its coils (with the left side usually toward the prey;

Heinrich and Klaassen 1985). Snakes are often grabbed by the head and chewed and twisted before constriction. Small animals may be swallowed immediately. Venomous crotalid snakes can be attacked because of venom-neutralizing factors in the kingsnake's blood serum (Weinstein et al. 1992).

PREDATORS AND DEFENSE. *L. getula* is known to cannibalize smaller members of its own species (Mitchell 1986). Other natural predators are bullfrogs *(Rana catesbeiana),* racers *(Coluber constrictor),* golden eagles *(Aquila chrysaetos),* red-tailed hawks *(Buteo jamaicensis),* great horned owls *(Bubo virginianus),* and coyotes *(Canis latrans)* (Fitch 1949; Klauber 1972; Palmer and Braswell 1995; Ross 1989).

When cornered, *L. getula* puts up a spirited fight—vibrating its tail; hissing, striking, and biting viciously; and spraying a pungent musk (the musk may serve as a warning substance to other kingsnakes; Brisbin 1968).

POPULATIONS. No detailed population study has been reported, but some data on the relative abundance of *L. getula* are available—it may be locally common, or scarce. It made up 14.4% (301) of 1,083 snakes collected by Clark (1949) in the Hill Parishes of Louisiana. However, in a Kansas tall grass prairie, *L. getula* only made up 38 (6.9%) of 550 snakes trapped by Cavitt (2000a); at another Kansas site only 2 (0.03%) were included in a sample of 7,062 snakes (Fitch 1992), and the species only made up only 2.25% of 33,117 snakes collected statewide by Fitch (1993). In five years in central California, Fitch (1949) only collected 43 *L. getula;* and at Laguna Dam, Imperial County, California, Slevin (1950) recorded only 4 (1.8%) in a total of 219 snakes. During road surveys in southern Arizona, New Mexico, and northeastern Chihuahua, Mexico, the species only made up 2.7–10.6% of the snakes seen (Price and LaPointe 1990; Reynolds 1982; Rosen and Lowe 1994), and at two sites in the Everglades of Florida, only 10 (3.5%) of the 2,809 snakes recorded (Dalrymple et al. 1991).

The secretive nature of *L. getula* contributes to some degree to its apparent low numbers, but populations have been reduced by habitat destruction, the use of pesticides, vehicles, and collection for the pet trade. Today, the subspecies *L. g. californiae* and *L. g. sticticeps* are protected in Oregon and Utah and North Carolina, respectively, and the species is considered endangered in Iowa and rare in Florida.

REMARKS. Keogh's (1996) morphological studies indicate *L. getula* is most closely related to *L. calligaster.* The species was last reviewed by Blaney (1977).

Lampropeltis pyromelana (Cope 1867) | Sonoran Mountain Kingsnake

RECOGNITION. *L. pyromelana* is strikingly attractive, with red, black, and white (or yellow) bands forming 37–61 triads along its body (TBL to 108.8 cm, but most individuals are less than 90 cm long). The red bands vary in width and completeness, are bordered on each side by black bands that narrow toward the venter, and either completely separate the black bands or are merely wedge-shaped marks on the sides that allow the black bands to unite dorsally. Red and white (or yellow) bands are never in contact. The snout is white or cream-colored, with or without red pigment. The infralabials, chin, and anterior throat are white or cream colored. A black hood extends from in front of the orbits backward onto the parietals, and downward on the sides to the supralabials below the orbits. The venter is white to yellow with dark spots; the red and black body bands do not often reach the venter. Dorsal body scales are smooth with two apical pits, and lie in 23 (21–25) anterior rows, 23 (25) midbody rows, and 17–19 (21) posterior rows. Beneath are 213–238 ventrals, 59–79 subcaudals, and a single anal plate. Lateral head scales are 1 nasal, 1 loreal, 1 preocular, 2 (3) postoculars, 2 (3) + 3 (4) + 4 (5) temporals, 7 (8) supralabials, and 9–10 (8–12) infralabials. The posterior chin shields are shorter and narrower than the anterior ones. The small, slender hemipenis has few calyces, short fringes, and slightly larger, slender spines above the fringes (that begin to decrease rapidly in size about halfway along the shaft, and finally disappear entirely, or remain over most of

Arizona mountain kingsnake, *Lampropeltis pyromelana pyromelana*; Santa Cruz County, Arizona. (Photograph by Brad R. Moon)

the basal portion of the shaft as minute, more or less imbedded, spinules). Each maxilla has 13–20 teeth.

Males have 217–238 ventrals, 66–79 subcaudals, and TLs 15.0–18.2% of TBL; females have 213–230 ventrals, 59–69 subcaudals, and TLs 14.3–17.6% of TBL.

GEOGRAPHIC VARIATION. Four subspecies have been described (Tanner 1983), but only three occur north of Mexico. *Lampropeltis p. pyromelana* (Cope 1867), the Arizona mountain kingsnake, is found in central and eastern Arizona, adjacent southwestern New Mexico, and Chihuahua, Mexico. It has 10 infralabials, 50% or fewer of the light bands complete across the venter, and 43 or more light dorsal bands. *Lampropeltis p. infralabialis* Tanner 1953, the Utah mountain kingsnake, is found in scattered populations in eastern Nevada, Utah, and north-central Arizona. It normally has only 9 infralabials, 50% or more of the light bands complete across the venter, and 42 or more light dorsal bands. *Lampropeltis p. woodini* Tanner 1953, the Huachuca mountain kingsnake, is only found in southern Arizona and adjacent Sonora, Mexico. It has 10 infralabials, fewer than 50% of the light bands completely crossing the venter, and 40 or fewer light dorsal bands.

CONFUSING SPECIES. See the above key to differentiate other *Lampropeltis*. The Sonoran coral snake *(Micruroides euryxanthus)* has a black snout, and red bands contacting the white (or yellow) bands. Long-nosed snakes *(Rhinocheilus lecontei)* have only a single row of subcaudals, black bars on the supralabials, and a more wedge-shaped snout.

KARYOTYPE. Undescribed.

FOSSIL RECORD. Pleistocene (Rancholabrean) fossils are from Arizona (Mead and Bell 1994; Mead et al. 1984), Nevada (Banta 1966; Brattstrom 1954a; Mead and Bell 1994; Mead et al. 1982), and New Mexico (Van Devender and Worthington 1977).

DISTRIBUTION. *L. pyromelana* is found in disjunct populations in eastern Nevada; central Utah; northern, central, and southern Arizona; and southwestern New Mexico. In Mexico it occurs in Chihuahua and Sonora.

HABITAT. This snake, as its common name implies, is a highland species; Wright and Wright (1957) reported it from as low as 838 m in New Mexico, but few are found below 1,500 m, and it has been observed as high as 2,724 m (Lowe 1967). Its habitats vary with elevation, being chaparral and piñon-juniper woodlands at lower elevations, and coniferous forest at the highest elevations. Often it is found in mesic canyons and valleys with permanent streams, or near highland springs. Surface rocks or logs and dense clumps of vegetation are usually present for shelter.

BEHAVIOR. *L. pyromelana* is active from April through October in New Mexico (Degenhardt et al. 1996), and active individuals have been taken from May through October in Arizona (Wright and Wright 1957) and Utah (Tanner and Cox 1981; Wright and Wright 1957). Most surface activity takes place from mid-May through July. No data are available on its overwintering habits, and probably some from lower elevations estivate during the hot summer.

Most activity records are from the daytime, particularly in the morning from 0800 to 1100 hours, but it has been collected in the afternoon, at dusk, and at night until 2115 hours. It is often surface active on overcast days or during or just after daytime showers. Temperature data are sparse; Stebbins (1954) reported a BT of 26°C (AT, 23°C), and one was basking at an AT of about 27°C (Fowlie 1965).

Distribution of *Lampropeltis pyromelana*.

Most activity is at ground level, but *L. pyromelana* has good climbing ability and sometimes ascends into bushes and low trees, perhaps while pursuing lizards or searching for bird nests.

REPRODUCTION. Most reproductive data have come from captives. Wright and Wright (1957) reported the minimum length of a mature male *L. pyromelana* as 42.4 cm, and that of a female as 51.9 cm; Stebbins (1985) gave the minimum adult TBL as 45.7 cm. The smallest male undergoing spermiogenesis examined by Goldberg (1997b) had a SVL of 44.3 cm. The age of maturity is unknown.

Males have regressed testes in May–July and October, have recrudesced testes in May–August, and undergo spermiogenesis in August and September (Goldberg 1997b). Sperm is apparently stored over the winter, as the vas deferens of May males with regressed testes contain sperm, as do those of males from August through October. Females (May, July–October) examined by Goldberg (1997b) were not reproductive, but one from June contained three enlarged (7–9 mm) follicles.

Matings in nature have been observed on 5 May in Arizona (Painter, in Degenhardt et al. 1996) and on 12 June in Nevada (Linsdale 1940). Copulations by captive *L. pyromelana* have taken place between 25 March and 1 June (Assetto 1982; Martin 1976a). These dates

indicate that mating in the wild occurs in the spring following hibernation.

Males are aggressive toward each other during the mating period. Aggression is shown by chasing, biting, constricting, and pressing the opponent against the ground or objects (Martin 1976a), and captive mating has been stimulated by placing a foreign male in the cage with a previously introduced male and female (Martin 1976a). The first male will attack the second male, and after the second male is removed, the original male usually promptly mates with the female.

Assetto (1982) and Martin (1976a) observed that in captivity courtship behavior might not occur. The male simply crawls alongside the female and begins to copulate with her; and Assetto (1982) reported that this male inserted only his left hemipenis. The matings lasted as long as 15 minutes. After several matings, the female rejected the male's advances. Assetto's female quickly crawled away when the male approached, and thrashed from side to side when he made contact with her. She also pressed her tail against the cage floor, effectively shutting her vent to him.

Oviposition occurs 32–59 days after copulation (Mattison, in Rossi and Rossi 1995), and egg-laying dates have range from late April through early July in captivity. One female laid her eggs in a shallow depression, possibly made by her (Assetto 1982). No data are available on natural nesting or nest sites.

Clutches contain one to nine eggs (Rossi and Rossi 1995) and average four to five eggs. The adherent, white eggs have smooth leathery shells, are 30.0–71.0 (mean, 48.1) mm long and 10.0–19.0 (mean, 16.7) mm wide, and weigh 4.9–5.9 (mean, 5.5) g. No evidence exists to show that clutch size becomes larger with an increase in female body length. The RCMs of two clutches were 0.387 (Martin 1976a; Seigel and Fitch 1984) and 0.174 (Assetto 1982). Zweifel (1980) reported a 70% fertility rate for 40 eggs laid in captivity.

After an IP of 57–81 (mean, 67) days, the eggs hatch from late July through late September, depending on the date of oviposition and IT. Hatchlings are colored and patterned like adults, are 20.3–29.4 (mean, 24.4) cm long, and weigh 4.3–10.3 (mean, 8.3) g.

GROWTH AND LONGEVITY. No growth data have been reported. A male *L. p. pyromelana* of unknown origin survived 22 years, 5 months, and 10 days at the

Pittsburgh Zoo, and a *L. p. woodini* of unknown sex that was wild caught when juvenile lived 19 years and 4 days in a private collection (Snider and Bowler 1992).

DIET AND FEEDING HABITATS. The foraging strategies of *L. pyromelana* have not been described, but when caught, small, weak prey are eaten at once; larger prey, such as adult lizards or mice, are constricted before being swallowed. Wild *L. pyromelana* have been found with lizards *(Sceloporus jarrovi, S. graciosus)* and mice *(Peromyscus)* in their stomachs (Gehlbach 1956; Stebbins 1954; Woodin 1953). Fowlie (1965) suspected that *L. pyromelana* preys on rats *(Neotoma?)*, and this kingsnake, like others, probably also eats small snakes and nestling birds in the wild. Captives have consumed lizards *(Sceloporus, Urosaurus)*, birds, the multimammate mouse *(Mastomys natalensis)*, and the house mouse *(Mus musculus)* (Assetto 1982; Even 1995; Martin 1976a; Rossi and Rossi 1995; Tanner and Cox 1981).

PREDATORS AND DEFENSE. The one published report of predation on the Sonoran mountain kingsnake is that of a spotted owl *(Strix occidentalis)* eating it. Dorsal body scales are smooth with two apical pits, and lie in 19–21 (17–23) anterior rows, 19 (17–23) midbody rows, and 17–19 (15–16) posterior rows. The venter has 135–244 ventrals, 21–78 subcaudals, and an undivided anal plate. Pertinent lateral head scales include 2 nasals (partially separated by the nostril), 1 (0–2) loreal, 1 (0–2) preocular(s), 2 (1–3) postoculars, 1–2 + 2 (3–4) temporals, 7 (6–9) supralabials, and 8–9 (7–11) infralabials. The bilobed hemipenis has a single sulcus spermaticus extending onto the left lobe. Its shaft is proximally naked, has spines beginning at the middle that gradually merge distally with papillate calyxes, and a naked apex (Williams 1988). The everted hemipenis is 5–11 (mean, 6.5) subcaudals long. Maxillary teeth total 11–15, with the two most posterior the largest.

one in Arizona (Duncan 1992). In addition, Ronald I. Crombie (pers. comm.) witnessed a Cooper's hawk *(Accipiter cooperii)* pick up a dead *L. pyromelana* from a road and fly away with it.

Captives are usually mild mannered (particularly those hatched in captivity), but wild individuals may bite when handled. Woodin (1953) observed that while exploring one's hands and arms, captives occasionally deliberately open their mouths and chew for several seconds.

The red, black, and white (or yellow) color pattern of *L. pyromelana* mimics that of the North American coral snakes *(Micruroides, Micrurus)*; this may explain the lack of observed predation on this species.

POPULATIONS. No data exist concerning population dynamics. Some populations have been adversely affected by habitat destruction and collecting for the pet trade. The subspecies *L. p. infralabialis* is protected in Utah.

REMARKS. *L. pyromelana* was reviewed by Tanner (1953, 1983).

Lampropeltis triangulum (Bonnaterre 1789) | Milksnake

RECOGNITION. *L. triangulum* is extremely variable (see GEOGRAPHIC VARIATION), and the description presented here relates only to those milksnakes living north of Mexico. For descriptions or photographs of all races of *L. triangulum*, see Markel (1990) and Williams (1988, 1994).

This is a small to medium-sized snake (TBL to 132.1 cm) varying in body color from grayish brown, olive brown, pinkish brown, and reddish brown to red, with a series of white or yellow and black bands on the body (yellow/white bands never contact red bands). The slightly pointed head has a variable dorsal color ranging from red to mostly black, or has a light V- or Y-shaped mark near the back. The supralabials may be patterned with black bars. The venter is white, cream, or yellow and has either rectangular black blotches, or dorsal light and dark bands crossing

Males have TLs 11–16 (mean, 14.5) % of TBL,

Eastern milksnake, *Lampropeltis triangulum triangulum*; Madison County, Kentucky. (Photograph by Roger W. Barbour)

28–78 (mean, 47) subcaudals, and 135–236 (mean, 199) ventrals; females have TLs 10–14 (mean, 13.4) % of TBL, 21–60 (mean, 39) subcaudals, and 161–244 (mean, 201) ventrals.

GEOGRAPHIC VARIATION. Twenty-five subspecies are recognized, but only nine occur in the United States and Canada. *Lampropeltis t. triangulum* (Bonnaterre 1789), the eastern milksnake, ranges from southern Maine, Quebec, and Ontario west to Minnesota and northeastern Iowa, and south to North Carolina, eastern Tennessee, and Kentucky. It reaches a TBL of 132.1 cm, and has 24–54 grayish brown, olive brown, or reddish brown, black-bordered dorsal blotches, a V- or Y-shaped light mark on the nape, a white venter with a black checkerboard pattern, normally 2 + 3 temporals, and 21 midbody scale rows. *Lampropeltis t. amaura* Cope 1861a, the Louisiana milksnake, ranges from southeastern Louisiana and adjacent southwestern Mississippi west to southwestern Arkansas. It has a maximum TBL of 78.7 cm, a black

head with a lighter snout, a body with 13–25 alternating broad red and narrower black and white to cream-colored rings that extend onto the venter (the red and white scales are not black tipped), normally 2 + 2 (3) temporals, and 21 midbody scale rows. *Lampropeltis t. annulata* Kennicott 1860a, the Mexican milksnake, ranges from southern Texas south to

Louisiana milksnake, *Lampropeltis triangulum amaura*; Caddo Parish, Louisiana. (Photograph by Carl H. Ernst)

Mexican milksnake, *Lampropeltis triangulum annulata*;
South Texas. (Photograph by John H. Tashjian, Fort
Worth Zoo)

New Mexico milksnake, *Lampropeltis triangulum celaenops*.
(Photograph by Robert E. Lovich)

Tamaulipas, Mexico. This race grows to a maximum
TBL of 105.4 cm, and has a black head and snout and
14–26 broad red body bands; its red and white scales
are not black tipped, the venter is mostly black, and
the snake has 2 + 3 (2) temporals and usually 21 rows
of scales at midbody. *Lampropeltis t. celaenops* Stejneger
1903, the New Mexico milksnake, ranges from the Rio
Grande Valley of central and southern New Mexico
east into adjacent Texas, and south to Brewster
County in the Big Bend of Texas. The maximum TBL
is 83.9 cm; it has a black head and either an entirely
black or black and white mottled snout, 17–30 red
body bands or blotches (its red and white scales are
not black tipped), a light midventer, 2 + 3(2) temporals, and 21 midbody scale rows. *Lampropeltis t. elapsoides* (Holbrook 1838), the scarlet kingsnake, is found
from southeastern Virginia and southwestern Kentucky south to the Florida Keys and the Gulf Coast
from southeastern Louisiana to the Florida Panhandle. Its maximum length is 68.6 cm, and it has a red
head with a black line across the posterior portion of
the parietal scales, 12–22 red body bands, the red and
white (yellow) scales without black tips, dorsal body
bands crossing the venter, usually 1 + 2 temporals,
and 17 or 19 scale rows at midbody. *Lampropeltis t. gen-*

tilis (Baird and Girard 1853), the Central Plains milksnake, occurs from south-central and southwestern
Nebraska, eastern Colorado, south through the western half of Kansas and western Oklahoma to the panhandle of northwestern Texas. It reaches 91.4 cm
TBL, and has a black head with a black and white
mottled snout, 20–39 red body bands (some posterior
ones may be crossed with black pigment), a black midventer, 2 + 2 (3) temporals, and 21 midbody scale
rows. *Lampropeltis t. multistriata* Kennicott 1860a, the
pale milksnake, is found from central South Dakota
west to central Montana, and south to northwestern
Nebraska and northeastern and north-central
Wyoming. Its maximum size is 85 cm, and its head has
black pigment on the posterior borders of the frontals
and supralabials and the parietals, and a light snout
mottled with black (sometimes with orange flecks); it
has 22–32 red or orange body blotches, a midventer
that is pale or has a few scattered black marks, 2 + 3
(2) temporals, and normally 21 midbody scale rows.
Lampropeltis t. syspila (Cope 1888), the red milksnake,
ranges from southeastern South Dakota and adjacent
Iowa and Nebraska east to Illinois and southwestern
Indiana and south to eastern Oklahoma and Mississippi. This orangish red snake reaches 106.7 cm TBL,
and has a red head and snout (occasionally with black
flecks), often a dark chevron on the posterior border
of the prefrontals (the prefrontals may be almost en
tirely black in some individuals), 16–31 red body
blotches, a ventrolateral row of small, alternating
blotches on each side (usually involving the edge of
the ventrals), a venter with a black checkerboard pattern, 2 + 2 (3) temporals, and usually 21 midbody

Scarlet kingsnake, *Lampropeltis triangulum elapsoides*; Volusia County, Florida. (Photograph by Peter May)

Red milksnake, *Lampropeltis triangulum syspila*; Missouri. (Photograph by Carl H. Ernst)

scale rows. *Lampropeltis t. taylori* Tanner and Loomis 1957, the Utah milksnake, is only found in the Great Basin from south of Salt Lake City and Vernal, Utah, south to west-central Colorado, and the Colorado River watershed of Arizona. It grows to 71.9 cm TBL, and has a black head with either a black or a pale-colored snout, 23–34 red body bands, a black midventer, 2 + 3 (2) temporals, and usually 21 midbody scale rows.

Intergradation zones occur where the ranges of the subspecies meet. Intergrades between *L. t. triangulum* and *L. t. elapsoides* on the Atlantic Coastal Plain from southern New Jersey to southeastern Virginia were formerly assigned to the taxon *L. t. temporalis* (Cope 1893), known as the coastal plain milksnake, but this color morph is no longer considered valid (Williams 1988). Individuals resulting from such a cross are very attractive, having orangish red blotches alternating with narrow black-bordered cream bands, and a black-bordered complete band or separate blotch on the nape. Recently, Dongarra (1998) and Grogan and Forester (1998) have tried to revive subspecific status for the coastal plain milksnake. Regardless of its official taxonomic status, this morph is highly prized in the pet trade.

CONFUSING SPECIES. Other *Lampropeltis* can be identified by using the key presented above. Species similar to blotch-pattened *L. triangulum* are the corn snake *(Elaphe guttata)* and juvenile black rat snake *(E. obsoleta),* which have keeled body scales and a divided anal plate; water snakes *(Nerodia)* have keeled scales and divided anal plates; juvenile racers *(Coluber constrictor)* have an elongated preocular scale that invades the supralabial row and a divided anal plate; the copperhead *(Agkistrodon contortrix),* which has a reddish unmarked head, dumbbell-like dorsal blotches, vertically elliptical pupils, and a pit between the nostril and eye; and the long-nosed snake *(Rhinocheilis lecontei),* with its rectangular red and wide black saddlelike dorsal body blotches above black-speckled yellowish lower sides, a white venter, an elongated snout, and a single row of subcaudal scales. The red, black, and yellow (white) banded *L. triangulum* may be confused with the venomous coral snakes *(Micruroides euryxanthus, Micrurus fulvius),* which have yellow bands adjacent to red bands, and heads that at least anteriorly are totally black; the scarlet snake *(Cemophora coccinea),* which has an immaculate, cream-colored venter; and the ground snake *(Sonora semiannulata),* banded sand snake *(Chilomeniscus cinctus),* and the two shovel-nosed snakes *(Chionactis occipitalis, C. palarostris),* which all have 16 or fewer midbody scale rows and divided anal plates.

KARYOTYPE. Undescribed, but presumably the diploid chromosome number is 36, as in other *Lampropeltis.*

FOSSIL RECORD. Fossils of *L. triangulum* are known from the late Miocene (Hemphilian)—Nebraska (Parmley and Holman 1995); Pliocene (Blancan)—Nebraska (Holman and Schloeder 1991) and Texas (Rogers 1976); Pleistocene (Blancan)—Kansas (Brattstrom 1967), Nebraska (Rogers 1984), and West Virginia (Holman 1982b); Pleistocene (Irvington-

Coastal plain milksnake, *Lampropeltis triangulum triangulum* × *L. t. elapsoides*. (Photograph by Carl H. Ernst)

ian)—Kansas (Brattstrom 1967), Maryland (Holman 1977b), Oklahoma (Holman 1986b), Texas (Holman and Winkler 1987), and West Virginia (Holman and Grady 1989); and Pleistocene (Rancholabrean)—Alabama (Holman et al. 1990), Arkansas (Dowling 1958b), Florida (Auffenberg 1963; Brattstrom 1953b; Holman 1978; Martin 1974), Georgia (Holman 1967), Kansas (Brattstrom 1967), Missouri (Holman 1965b; Parmalee et al. 1969; Saunders 1977), Nevada (Mead et al. 1982), Pennsylvania (Guilday et al. 1964; Richmond 1964), Tennessee (Van Dam 1978), Texas (Hill 1971; Holman 1963, 1964, 1966; Kasper and Parmley 1990; Parmley 1988b, 1990a; Van Devender and Bradley 1994), Virginia (Guilday 1962; Holman 1986a), and West Virginia (Holman and Grady 1994). The late Miocene (Barstovian) fossil species *L. similis* is the immediate ancestor of *L. triangulum* (Parmley 1994).

DISTRIBUTION. *L. triangulum* is one of the most widely distributed of North American snakes, ranging from 48°N latitude in Canada to nearly 4°S latitude in Ecuador, a distance of almost 5,800 km. The greatest longitudinal range in the United States is almost 3,000 km.

HABITAT. With such a wide range in latitude and longitude north of Mexico, *L. triangulum* lives in a great variety of habitats ranging from sea level to over 2,700 m. In eastern North America it is found in both deciduous and pine forests, rocky hillsides, brushy fields, bog and marsh borders, river floodplains, in the debris around abandoned buildings, about farm sheds and barns where rodents are plentiful, and even in trash-strewn suburban lots. In the Midwest and West, it hides under high-tide driftwood on Gulf Coast beaches and lives in short and tall grass prairies, farmlands, rocky canyons, wooded stream valleys, pine and hardwood forests, semiarid thorn brush, and desert lowlands. In spite of occurring in riparian zones and the borders of wetlands, it is seldom found in wetlands proper, being a distinct upland species.

BEHAVIOR. The milksnake is secretive, seldom seen in the open, and most frequently found hiding under rocks, logs, or the bark of old stumps. Because of its secretive nature, less is known about its behavior than that of many other snakes.

In the southern portion of the range, it becomes active earlier in the year and enters hibernation later. Those from peninsular Florida may be active all year, especially during years with warm winters, but over most of the geographic range, it is active from late March–April to October–November. Most surface activity is in April–June, with a second peak in August–October. In the spring or fall, *L. triangulum* is often found in more upland situations than during the

Distribution of *Lampropeltis triangulum*.

summer, presumably moving to and from hibernacula. After spring emergence, these snakes remain basking near their hibernacula before dispersing to their summer feeding ranges. Hibernacula include the walls of old wells and cisterns, stone walls, gravel and dirt banks, crevices in rock outcroppings, and the crumbling foundations of old buildings; they are also found beneath the soil of cultivated fields and within and behind the loose bark of hollow logs and stumps.

It is primarily nocturnal, although it may be active during the daylight hours, especially in the spring or fall. The only ones the authors have found during the day have been under cover. Dyrkacz (1977) found most Illinois milksnakes were under cover either early in the morning (0700–0900 hours) or late in the afternoon (1800–2000 hours), but found only one active during midday at 1000 hours. Most roadkills occur at night. BTs of Kansas *L. triangulum* recorded by Fitch (1956) ranged from 22.3 to 31.7 (mean, 26.2) °C, and this is probably close to the normal active range of BTs. However, Henderson et al. (1980) recorded BTs of 13 to almost 30°C for Wisconsin milksnakes, Webb (1970) reported BTs of 18–21°C in Oklahoma (AT, 19.0–19.6°C; ST under rocks, 18.5–19.2°C), and Clarke (1958) found them active in Kansas at ATs of approximately 10–29°C. With the exception of basking immediately after emergence from hibernation, aerial basking is uncommon. Fitch and Fleet (1970) observed that while *L. triangulum* does not ordinarily bask in direct sunlight, it obtains heat through conduction from sun-warmed objects.

Fitch (1999) recorded 41 movements of marked *L. triangulum* in a span of 10 years at several sites in Kansas; the longest were 504, 457, and 337 m and were probably shifts in home range. Other movements, which Fitch believed were within the snakes' home ranges, were rather evenly distributed up to 300 m. Excluding the three long movements, the mean distance moved between captures was 118 m (males, 127 m; females, 106 m). Considering 300 m as the average home range diameter, the overall mean home range was 7.07 ha. In many instances individual snakes returned to the same shelters they had used before. A female used the same shelter on four different dates and was found at seven other places within 75 m over a six-year period; another female caught six times in three years had returned to the same place three times, and a male caught seven times in four years was found at the same spot four times. During another study in Kansas, six *L. triangulum* traveled 76–396 (mean, 254) m, and if 254 m represents the radius of the home range, the mean home range was about 20 ha (Fitch and Fleet 1970). Fitch and Fleet (1970) also reported that the same shelter is frequently used; a juvenile was at the same place three additional times (the last about nine months after the first capture), and another juvenile was found beneath the same shelter twice.

As with other *Lampropeltis*, male *L. triangulum* have an established dominance system in which social position is determined by a male combat dance (Shaw 1951).

REPRODUCTION. A fair amount of data exists concerning reproductive biology of captive milksnakes, but less has been reported for wild individuals.

The subspecies of *L. triangulum* are of different sizes and, consequently, attain maturity at different lengths. The smallest known mature females are as follows: *L. t. amaura*, 41.0 cm TBL (Conant and Collins 1998) and 42.5 cm TBL (Wright and Wright 1957); *L. t. annulata*, 61.0 cm TBL (Conant and Collins 1998); *L. t. celaenops*, 35.0 cm TBL (Stebbins 1985); *L. t. elapsoides*, 36.0 cm TBL (Conant and Collins 1998); *L. t. gentilis*, 35.0 cm TBL (Stebbins 1985), 41.0 cm TBL (Conant and Collins 1998), and 41.2 cm TBL (Wright and Wright 1957); *L. t. multistriata*, 35.0 cm TBL (Stebbins 1985); *L. t. syspila*, 41.2 cm TBL (Wright and Wright 1957) and 48.0 SVL (Fitch and Fleet 1970); *L. t. taylori*, 35.0 cm TBL (Stebbins 1985); and *L. t. triangulum*, 39.9 and 40.4 cm TBL (Wright and Wright 1957) and 61.0 cm TBL (Conant and Collins 1998). The smallest known mature males are *L. t. amaura*, 41.0 cm TBL (Conant and Collins 1998) and 41.3 cm TBL (Wright and Wright 1957); *L. t. annulata*, 61.0 cm TBL (Conant and Collins 1998); *L. t. celaenops*, 35.0 cm TBL (Stebbins 1985); *L. t. elapsoides*, 36.0 cm TBL (Conant and Collins 1998); *L. t. gentilis*, 35.5 cm TBL (Wright and Wright 1957) and 41.0 cm TBL (Conant and Collins 1998); *L. t. multistriata*, 35 cm TBL (Stebbins 1985); *L. t. syspila*, 35.5 cm TBL (Wright and Wright 1957); *L. t. taylori*, 35.0 cm TBL (Stebbins 1985); and *L. t. triangulum*, 39.7 cm TBL (Wright and Wright 1957) and 61 cm TBL (Conant and Collins 1998). These lengths are probably reached in two to five years of normal growth.

The gametic cycles have not been described. Fitch (1999) and Fitch and Fleet (1970) reported that in Kansas *L. t. syspila* vitellogenesis occurs mostly in late May and June, females contain enlarged oviductal eggs from the latter half of May until 17 June, and oviposition occurs from mid-June into early July.

In the wild, the breeding season extends from early April through May. Possibly some fall matings also occur; a male caught in mid October by Fitch (1999) vigorously courted a female when they were placed together in the same cage. In two captive matings of *L. t. triangulum* observed by C. Ernst, the males actively sought the female by following, with much tongue flicking, her scent trail. When she was found, he placed several loops of his body on her back, seized the nape of her neck with his mouth, and vigorously performed jerky body undulations. He twisted his tail around that of the female as he searched for her vent, and once it was found, inserted his hemipenis and straightened out his tail so that it lay beside that of the female. She usually raised her tail when insertion was accomplished and remained passive during courtship and copulation. Herman (1979) reported the male will rub his chin lightly along the female's neck during copulation, but C. Ernst did not observe this. The two copulations lasted 35 and 44 minutes, respectively, and the entire courtship/mating sequences from the time first observed lasted 53 and 68 minutes, respectively. The courtship/mating sequence of *L. t. sinaloae* is similar to that described above for *L. t. triangulum* (Gillingham et al. 1977).

The gestation period is about 30–40 days. Nesting in the wild normally extends from May to mid-July (9 May to 21 July), and begins and ends earlier in the South; but Groves and Assetto (1976) reported a female *L. t. elapsoides* from Florida oviposited on 8 October, and captives have laid eggs in March, April, August, and September (Tryon 1984; Tryon and Murphy 1982). The eggs are laid in rotting logs and stumps, behind the bark of trees, in piles of rotting vegetation, under rocks, in sawdust mounds, or in mammal burrows. Several females may oviposit at the same site (Henderson et al. 1980).

Clutch size for the species varies from 1 (Johnson 1987) to 24 (Wright and Wright 1957), and averages 7.6 eggs for 145 reported clutches. The number of eggs laid is in direct correlation with the female's body size, and the longer North American subspecies (*gentilis* and *triangulum*) often lay nine or more eggs per clutch, while the smaller subspecies (*amaura, celaenops, elapsoides, multistriata, syspila,* and *taylori*) normally produce clutches of up to nine eggs. Captives have laid more than one clutch per season (Tryon 1984).

The white eggs have parchmentlike, slightly granular shells, are 22.0–62.0 (mean, 38.2; n = 91) mm long and 6.0–22.0 (mean, 14.7; n = 91) mm wide, and weigh 2.6–13.8 (mean, 7.7; n = 15) g. Egg size is proportional to female length. Eight RCMs presented in the literature averaged 0.376 (0.171–0.468) (Fitch 1999; Seigel and Fitch 1984; Tryon 1984). When laid, the eggs adhere in groups of 6–20.

Incubation takes about 40–99 (mean, 56.8; n = 48) days, depending on the incubating temperature, with most hatching in 50–70 days. The natural hatching period lasts from late July to late September, with most young appearing in August and September. Surface (1906), however, reported that a Pennsylvania clutch hatched in November, and captive clutches have hatched in March, October, and November (Tryon 1984; Tryon and Murphy 1982). Dyrkacz (1977) reported that of 80 eggs from Illinois *L. t. triangulum*, 79 (99%) were fertile and 57 (72%) hatched.

Hatchlings of the banded, tricolored subspecies are colored and patterned like the adults, but those of *L. t. triangulum* often have deeper reddish brown blotches than the adults. Hatchlings are 12.7–26.7 (mean, 19.8; n = 131) cm TBL and weigh 2.8–12.3 (mean, 7.1; n = 16) g.

GROWTH AND LONGEVITY. Some growth data are available. The growth rate is fast in hatchlings and juveniles, but slows once maturity is attained, and is slowest in adults.

L. t. triangulum from Illinois grew from an average TBL of 23.8 cm at hatching to an average of 26.0 cm in 1 month (Dyrkacz 1977). The two smallest milksnakes from Indiana examined by Minton (1972) had TBLs of 20.9 cm and 23.2 cm and were probably 9–10 months old. Two Nebraska intergrade *L. t. gentilis* × *t. multistriata* had TBLs of 23.5 cm and 21.5 cm when they hatched on 12–13 August. The shortest grew to 24.0 cm by 8 December, when it died, and the larger grew to 25.5 cm by 30 May, when it died (Iverson 1975). Two yearling individuals collected by Iverson (1975) had 30.0 cm and 34.0 cm TBLs.

Two studies in Kansas have presented growth data for *L. t. syspila*. Fitch and Fleet (1970) found that first-year young had SVLs of 19.8–26.8 (mean, 23.7) cm; hatchlings had grown an average of 15% over their original length in about two months. Second-year young averaged 36.0 (29.6–39.7) cm SVL, and third-year juveniles were usually longer than 40.0 cm but shorter than 50.0 cm SVL. Fitch (1999), after 50 years of study, listed the following SVLs and weights by sex for *L. t. syspila*: males—1 year, 23.7 (19.8–27.3) cm, 4.6 (2.4–7.8) g; 2 years, 34.3 (26.1–39.7) cm, 12.8 (7.0–21.0) g; 3 years, 43.3 (38.3–47.4) cm, 21.8 (11.0–29.0) g; 4 years, 52.3 (48.0–55.0) cm, 39.4 (24.0–48.0) g; 5 years,

60.8 (56.3–62.4) cm, 62.6 (48.0–76.0) g; 6 years, 63.4 (62.4–64.5) cm, 74.0 (59.0–95.0) g; 7 years, 66.5 (6.8–67.3) cm, 77.0 (63.0–98.0) g; 8 years, 69.4 (69.0–72.0) cm, 117.2 (88.0–134.0) g; 9 years, 73.5 (73.0–74.0) cm, 116.4 (88.0–138.0) g; and 10 years or older, 76.6 (74.7–80.0) cm, 122.8 (110.0–143.0) g; females—1 year, 23.0 (19.9–26.8) cm, 4.4 (3.2–6.0) g; 2 years, 34.2 (28.0–38.0) cm, 12.2 (8.3–21.0) g; 3 years, 45.2 (41.3–47.8) cm, 27.0 (16.0–40.0) g; 4 years, 52.0 (48.4–55.3) cm, 43.3 (24.0–62.0) g; 5 years, 56.7 (56.8–58.8) cm, 56.6 (45.0–70.0) g; 6 years, 60.1 (59.2–61.5) cm, 65.8 (54.0–90.0) g; 7 years, 63.0 (61.8–64.0) cm, 75.2 (65.0–86.0) g; 8 years, 65.4 (65.0–66.2) cm, 74.5 (62.0–98.0) g; 9 years, 67.8 (67.0–69.2) cm, 89.4 (75.0–104.0) g; and 10 years or older, 75.4 (74.0–80.0) cm, 154.0 (130.0–172.0) g.

The milksnake is a hearty species that has a potentially long life span: a female *L. t. triangulum*, caught in the wild as an adult, lived an additional 21 years, 4 months, and 14 days at the Philadelphia Zoo; a wild-caught *L. t. amaura* lived 20 years and 7 months in the collection of George P. Meade; and a *L. t. annulata*, wild-caught as an adult, survived 20 years and 2 months in the collection of Dennis Harris (Snider and Bowler 1992). Fitch and Fleet (1970) thought the largest wild adults in their study were 6–10 years old, and the oldest individuals caught by Fitch (1999) were more than 10 years of age.

DIET AND FEEDING HABITS. The milksnake, especially individuals of the shorter subspecies, has a relatively small head and mouth, and its body is narrow. It is restricted to eating relatively slender prey, and a prey size dimorphism exists between the shortest and largest subspecies. *L. triangulum* is both an active hunter and an ambusher. Captives may consume 4.3–13.7 g of food per week, depending on their size (Kirkwood and Gili 1994). Prey is located by both olfaction and sight. The snake seizes the prey in its mouth and quickly wraps it in coils of the body, slowly squeezing it until the animal is suffocated. Some small foods, such as young mice or shrews and reptile and bird eggs, are swallowed without being constricted. The snake coils about its prey in such a way as to have its venter turned anteriorly, and places either the right or left side of its body (with no preference) against the animal (Heinrich and Klaassen 1985).

Animals eaten by *L. triangulum* include mammals—shrews *(Blarina brevicauda, B. hylophaga, Cryptotis parva)*, mice *(Mus musculus, Peromyscus leucopus, P. maniculatus, Zapus hudsonius)*, and voles *(Clethrionomys gapperi, Microtus ochrogaster, M. pennsylvanicus, M. pinetorum)*; birds—boobies *(Sula leucogaster, S. nebouxii)*, sooty tern *(Sterna fuscata)*, chipping sparrow *(Spizella passerina)*, phoebe *(Sayornis phoebe)*, and ovenbird *(Seiurus aurocapillus)*, and their eggs—sparrow (Emberizidae), brown-headed cowbird *(Molothrus ater)*, and American robin *(Turdus migritorius)*; reptiles—lizards *(Anolis carolinensis, Cnemidophorus angusticeps, C. costatus, C. sexlineatus, Ctenosaura pectinata, Eumeces fasciatus, E. inexpectatus, E. obsoletus, Sceloporus graciosus, S. occidentalis, S. undulatus, Scincella lateralis)*, snakes *(Agkistrodon contortrix, Carphophis amoenus, C. vermis, Crotalus sp., Diadophis punctatus, Lampropeltis triangulum, Leptotyphlops sp., Liochlorophis vernalis, Nerodia sipedon, Regina septemvittata, Storeria dekayi, S. occipitomaculata, Tantilla coronata, Thamnophis radix, T. sirtalis, Virginia striatula, V. valeriae)*, and reptile eggs *(Diadophis punctatus, Lampropeltis triangulum)*; amphibians—frogs and toads *(Bufo sp.)* and salamanders; fish—minnows (Cyprinidae) and killifish (Fundulidae); earthworms (Annelida); slugs (Mollusca); insects—beetles (Coleoptera), caterpillars (Leptidoptera), and roaches (Orthoptera) (Anderson 1965; Ashton and Smith 1999; Brown 1979b; Carr 1940; Collins 1993; C. Ernst, pers. obs.; Fitch 1999; Fitch and Fleet 1970; Guidry 1953; Hammerson 1986; Kamb 1978; Klemens 1993; Medsger 1922; Mitchell and Groves 1993; Palmer and Braswell 1995; Rodríguez and Drummond 2000; Skehan 1960; Surface 1906; Tennant 1985; Vermersch and Kuntz 1986; Uhler et al. 1939; Williams 1988). That *L. triangulum* eats venomous pit vipers is not surprising, as its blood serum has venom-neutralizing properties (Weinstein et al. 1992). Some prey are consumed as carrion; C. Ernst observed a *L. t. triangulum* eating a road-killed *Blarina brevicauda* in Pennsylvania.

Small mammals are the preferred prey. They made up 79% of the food volume and 60% of all items (59% were young). Birds made up 12.7% of food volume (19% frequency) and reptiles 8.1% of food volume (12.4% frequency) in milksnakes examined by Brown (1979b). Uhler et al. (1939) found mice made up 42% by volume, snakes 26%, song birds and their eggs

16%, insects 11%, and shrews 5% of the stomach contents of Virginia *L. triangulum* containing food. On Isla Isabel, Mexico, stomachs of *L. t. sinaloae* contained lizards and their eggs 75.6% of the time and avian nestlings 24.3% of the time, but mammals (black rats, *Rattus rattus*) were not eaten (Rodríguez and Drummond 2000).

PREDATORS AND DEFENSE. Reports of predation on wild milksnakes include the case of cannibalism mentioned above (Mitchell and Groves 1993); attacks by a bullfrog *(Rana catesbeiana)* (Hensley 1962), a brown thrasher *(Toxostoma rufum)* (Flanigan 1971), and hawks *(Buteo jamaicensis, B. nitidus)* (Gurrola-Hidalgo and Chavez C. 1996; Ross 1989); and an apparent attack by a black-footed feret *(Mustela nigripes)* (Holycross and Simonson 1998). However, predatory mammals (raccoons, coyotes, foxes, skunks, weasels, and opossums) and hawks and owls probably take only a few. Many die each year on our highways or through destruction of their habitats, and the tricolored subspecies are in demand in the pet trade.

When excited, wild milksnakes vibrate their tails, strike, retain hold, and chew. Some may spray musk and cloacal contents, and others may hide their heads beneath their coils. Tricolored individuals may be particularly pugnacious. However, once in captivity, most become more docile.

The geographic variation in color patterns of United States *L. triangulum* is correlated with the presence or absence of sympatric venomous coral snakes *(Micruroides euryxanthus, Micrurus fulvius)* with whom tricolored subspecies form a mimicry complex—present in the south where the banded, tricolored subspecies occur, absent in the north where coral snakes do not occur and milksnakes are blotched. In addition, the red bands appear gray at night, and the black and yellow bands break up the snake's elongated image when it forages nocturnally (Tennant 1985).

POPULATIONS. Milksnake populations vary in size according to the suitability of the habitat and the extent to which humans have disturbed them. It may be widespread and fairly common, but not often seen because of its nocturnal, subterranean habits. Or it may be only seasonally common, as *L. t. annulata* is in the scrub thickets of southern Texas. In Florida, where *L.*

t. elapsoides was formerly both widespread and common, it is now only locally abundant because of habitat destruction.

Several studies have reported data on specific populations of *L. triangulum*. Guidry (1953) collected 18 *L. t. amaura* in one afternoon in an area of approximately 1.6 km² in Texas. Fitch (1999) collected 138 *L. t. syspila* (81 adult males, 42 adult females, 15 hatchlings) in 50 years at his study site in northeastern Kansas, and estimated the average density was only 0.52 snakes/ha. During a three-year study of a tallgrass prairie reptile community in Kansas, only 26 *L. triangulum* were collected in a sample of 550 snakes of 10 species (Cavitt 2000a). However, Busby and Parmelee (1996) found milksnakes more common at the Fort Riley Military Reservation in the Flint Hills of Kansas, collecting 35 individuals in 1993. Of 33,117 snakes recorded by Fitch (1993) throughout Kansas, *L. triangulum* totaled only 198 (0.6%), and most of these were found in the glaciated region (124), Flint Hills (33), or high plains (26). Two Illinois quarries with an approximate area of 5,000 m², yielded 36 adults, two juveniles, and five hatchlings at the first, and 14 adults and two hatchlings at the second, giving population densities of 86 and 32 milksnakes, respectively (Dyrkacz 1977). *L. t. triangulum* made up only 49 (5.5%) of 885 snakes collected by Uhler et al. (1939) in the George Washington National Forest of Virginia.

Sex ratio data are scarce; Fitch's (1999) Kansas population had an adult male to adult female ratio of 81 to 42 (1.93:1.00), and a hatchling (15) to adult ratio of 0.12:1.00. Fitch and Fleet (1970) reported that a clutch of five hatchling *L. t. syspila* contained four males and a single female.

Because of decreasing numbers, *L. triangulum* is currently protected in Texas and Utah.

REMARKS. *L. triangulum* has been reviewed by Williams (1988, 1994). On the basis morphology, Keogh (1996) reported *L. triangulum* is most closely related to *L. pyromelana* and *L. zonata*, but an immunological study by Dowling and Maxson (1990) placed it closer to *L. getula*.

A folktale explains the common name "milk snake." Because it is often found around or in barns and farm outbuildings, where it undoubtedly seeks mice, the mistaken idea has arisen that it sucks milk from cows' udders. This is entirely false. The snake probably has little ability to suck fluids, and besides, what cow would stand still while having its teats grasped by a mouth full of so many sharp teeth!

Lampropeltis zonata (Lockington 1876 ex Blainville 1835) | California Mountain Kingsnake

RECOGNITION. This pretty snake (TBL to 122.5 cm, but most are shorter than 100 cm) is a coral snake mimic living in a range where no wild coral snake exists. Its body is patterned with black, white, and red crossbands occurring groups of three (triads). The red bands are always bordered by black bands, and they may be interrupted dorsally to form a wedge-shaped blotch on each side within a broad black band, or the red pigment may be reduced or totally absent. Much variation occurs in the numbers of body triads present, the completeness of the red bands, and the width of the black bands (see GEOGRAPHIC VARIATION). The red and black bands often extend onto the white venter, and posteriorly, the venter may be speckled with black marks. The head is black dorsally, but the chin

St. Helena mountain kingsnake, *Lampropeltis zonata zonata*; Katherine Creek, Washington. (Photograph by Robert E. Lovich)

Coast mountain kingsnake, *Lampropeltis zonata multifasciata*; Santa Cruz County, Arizona. (Photograph by Brad R. Moon)

San Bernardino Mountain kingsnake, *Lampropeltis zonata parvirubra*; San Bernardino County, California. (Photograph by Robert E. Lovich)

and throat are usually white. Dorsal body scales are smooth with two apical pits, lie in 23 rows anteriorly and 23 (21–25) rows at midbody, and are reduced to 21 (17–19) rows near the tail. The venter has 194–227 ventrals, 45–62 subcaudals, and an undivided anal plate. On the side of the head are 2 nasals, 1 (0) loreal, 1 (2) preocular(s), 2 (3) postoculars, 2 + 3 + 4 temporals, 7 (8) supralabials, and 9 (8–10) infralabials. The posterior pair of chin shields is equal to or slightly smaller than the anterior pair. The hemipenis has not been described. Each maxilla has 11–13 teeth, with numbers 2–5 the longest and the others shorter, except the posterior-most 2 teeth, which are enlarged and bladelike.

The sexes are difficult to distinguish superficially. Males have 45–62 subcaudals and TLs that average 18.2% of TBL; females have 46–56 subcaudals and TLs that average 17.5% of TBL.

GEOGRAPHIC VARIATION. Seven subspecies are recognized (Markel 1990; Zweifel 1975), but only five occur north of Mexico. *Lampropeltis z. zonata* (Lockington 1876 ex Blainville 1835), the St. Helena mountain kingsnake, occurs from Mendocino, Napa, and Sonoma counties in California north to Curry, Douglas, Jackson, and Josephine counties in southwestern Oregon. It also occurs in Klickitat, Skamania, and

Yakima counties in southern Washington. It has the posterior border of the first white band positioned behind the corner of the mouth; 24–30 (mean, 27) body triads, of which at least 60% are divided by red; and a dark snout. *Lampropeltis z. multicincta* (Yarrow 1882), the Sierra mountain kingsnake, ranges south in the Sierra Mountains from Shasta County to northern Kern and Tulare counties in California. It has the posterior border of the first white band situated behind the corner of the mouth; 23–48 (mean, 35) body triads, with usually less than 60% of these divided by red (red pigment may be absent); and a dark snout. *Lampropeltis z. multifasciata* (Bocourt 1886), the coast mountain kingsnake, is found from Santa Clara, Santa Cruz, and Monterey counties southward to Santa Barbara and Ventura counties in California, mostly along the coast. This race is separated from the two subspecies found farther south by the Santa Clara River. It has the posterior border of the first white band either in front or behind the corner of the mouth; it has 26–45 body triads, with 60% or more completely divided by red, making the black bands seem narrow; and red pigment may be present on the snout. *Lampropeltis z. parvirubra* Zweifel 1952, the San Bernardino Mountain kingsnake, is present in the San Bernardino, San Gabrial, and San Jacinto mountains of Los Angeles, Riverside, and San Bernardino counties in Southern California. It is distinguished by having the posterior border of the first white band in front of or on the last supralabial; 35–56 (mean, 41) body triads, with usually fewer than 60% divided by red; and a dark snout. *Lampropeltis z. pulchra* Zweifel 1952, the San Diego mountain kingsnake, only occurs in the Santa Ana and Santa Monica mountains, and Verdugo Hills of Los Angeles County, and in the mountains of San Diego County in Southern California. It has the posterior border of the first white band in front of or on the last supralabial; 26–39 (mean, 33) body triads, with usually 60% or more divided by red; and a dark snout. Intergradation is common among these subspecies. The southern Washington populations are possibly intergrades between *L. z. zonata* and *L. z. multicincta* (Markel 1990), and wherever the ranges of the subspecies meet, an intergradation zone has formed.

Rodríguez-Robles et al. (1999c), using mitochondrial DNA sequences from all seven subspecies, reported two clades corresponding to the southern and northern segments of the species distribution. The southern clade includes populations from southern California and northern Baja California. The northern clade is divided into two subclades: a coastal subclade consisting of populations from the central coast of California and the southern Sierra Nevada Mountains of eastern California, and a northeastern subclade mainly composed of populations north of San Francisco Bay and most of the Sierra Nevada Mountains. They suggested that the two major clades resulted from gene barriers formed by past island seaways in southwestern California and the embayment of central California. The northern clade has experienced instances of range contraction, isolation, differentiation, and finally, expansion and secondary contact. Their research also indicated that the two main color pattern characters used to define subspecies (the number of triads and how many are separated by red) are too variable to reliably differentiate subspecies, and that a serious reevaluation of geographic variation within *L. zonata* is necessary.

CONFUSING SPECIES. Other *Lampropeltis* can be identified by the key presented above. The long-nosed snake *(Rhinocheilus lecontei)* has a single row of subcaudals, black bars on its supralabials, a more wedge-shaped snout, and no dark bands extending onto the venter. The Sonoran coral snake *(Micruroides euryxanthus)* has its red bands bordered by white or cream-colored bands.

KARYOTYPE. Undescribed.

FOSSIL RECORD. Pleistocene (Rancholabrean) fossils of *L. zonata* have been found in Nevada (Mead 1988; Mead and Bell 1994). Brattstrom (1955b) thought the Pleistocene (Blancan) species *L. intermedius* from Arizona a possible ancestor of *L. zonata*.

DISTRIBUTION. *L. zonata* ranges from Klickitat, Skamania, and Yakima counties in southern Washington, and Curry, Douglas, Jackson, and Josephine counties in southwestern Oregon south in the coastal and interior mountains of California to northern Baja California. It is also present on South Todos Santos Island off Baja California and in numerous disjunct populations within its California range.

Distribution of *Lampropeltis zonata*.

HABITAT. With such an extended north-south range, *L. zonata* occurs in a variety of habitats, but it is most often associated with moist woodlands, usually coniferous forests, oak woodlands or chaparral. In such places it is commonly found in riparian zones with abundant rocks and rotting logs, or on the south-facing, rocky, slopes of stream canyons. It has been found from sea level to an elevation of 3,000 m (Goodman and Goodman 1976).

BEHAVIOR. Annually, this snake is active from late March through early November in California, but if the winter is mild Southern California individuals will come out to bask on warm, sunny days. Peak activity in San Diego County occurs in mid-April–mid-May, the period when most mating takes place (McGurty 1988). Winters are spent deep in rock crevices or within mammal burrows.

Most daily activity is diurnal in the spring and fall, but during the summer *L. zonata* is crepuscular or nocturnal to as late as 2200 hours. BT of a wild *L. zonata* taken by Brattstrom (1965) was 27.5°C (AT, 26.0°C; ST, 35.0°C); three other active snakes had BTs of 24.2–26.4°C, and one found under a rock was had a BT of 23.8°C (Cunningham 1966a). Another found under a rock by Cranston (1994) had a BT of 34°C. Cowles (in Brattstrom 1965) determined the CT_{max} of two snakes to be 42 and 43°C.

Limited movement data are available. Mosauer (1935b) reported the maximum crawling speed to be 0.32 m/second (1.16 km/hour) and indicated that normal prowling occurs at 0.08 m/second (0.28

km/hour). One displaced up to 0.4 km repeatedly returned (Wentz 1953). *L. zonata* is a good climber; Cunningham (1955) found one over 1.5 m above ground coiled in a decaying cavity of an oak tree.

REPRODUCTION. According to Wright and Wright (1957) males are mature at 50.7 cm TBL, and females at 54.7 cm TBL. The smallest male undergoing spermiogenesis examined by Goldberg (1995d) had a SVL of 45.4 cm, and the smallest female with enlarged follicles had a 52.2 cm SVL.

Goldberg (1995d) found males with regressed testes in March–July, and a regressed male had sperm in his epididymis in June. Other males were in recrudescence in June–August. Most spermiogenesis occurred in June–September, although a male had mature sperm in June; sperm are apparently stored over winter in the vas deferens for mating the following spring. Four females examined by him had 8–10 mm follicles in late May, 6–10 mm follicles in early June, and 9–11 mm follicles on 1 July. An April female was yolking eggs, but two other April females and single females in May, June, and July were not experiencing vitellogenesis. Ovulation occurs in May and early June. Only 58% of the females examined by Goldberg were reproductively active, indicating a biennial cycle.

The breeding period is from April through early June (McGurty 1988; Newton and Smith 1975), but copulation by captives has taken place as early as March (C. Ernst, pers. obs.). Wild males may find females by following their pheromone trails (Newton and Smith 1975), and captive males are certainly interested in places where females have coiled or crawled. Courtship behavior has not been described, but C. Ernst has found captives copulating and observed that the anterior portion of the male's body was looped partially over the female's back, while his tail was aligned with her tail, and one hemipenis was inserted into her vent. The observed matings lasted 15–60 minutes.

In nature, females oviposit in late May–July, and it is possible, although not proven, that some may lay more than one clutch a year. Clutches average about 7 eggs, with as few as 2 (Goldberg 1995d) or as many as 10 (C. Ernst, pers. obs.). No evidence exists to show that clutch size increases proportionately with increased female body size. The elongated eggs are white and adherent, and average 42.2 (40.0–45.0) mm in length, 17.2 (15.8–18.0) mm in width, and 6.6 (5.0–9.0) g in mass. In four clutches examined by McGurty (1988), the mean RCM was 0.379 (0.319–0.482), and the mean weight of individual eggs versus female body mass was 10.78 (9.36–11.96) %. Twenty-two (95.6%) of 23 eggs in the four clutches were fertile.

Developmental time is dependent on the IT; IPs average 62 (47–87; n = 15) days at ITs of 23–29°C. Hatchlings are as vividly colored as adults, are 20.0–27.2 (mean, 26.6) cm long, and weigh 5.7–7.7 (mean, 6.6) g.

GROWTH AND LONGEVITY. No growth data are available. An adult of unknown sex and origin lived 26 years, 4 months, and 1 day at the Pittsburgh Zoo (Snider and Bowler 1992).

DIET AND FEEDING HABITS. *L. zonata* is an active hunter that chases lizards once they are seen. It is also possible that some prey, particularly hidden lizards and their eggs, are discovered by olfaction. Bird nests are also raided, both on the ground and in low trees and bushes. The snake is aided in its search by the intensity of the attack response of the parent birds (Goodman and Goodman 1976). The colorful pattern of *L. zonata* seems to serve as a reinforcement signal to maintain the birds' attacks, as well as to provide directional signals to the snake.

Once caught, small or helpless prey are swallowed at once, but large, struggling prey must be constricted before ingestion.

Lizards and nestling birds are the most important

natural prey of *L. zonata;* adult lizards and their eggs *(Eumeces gilberti, E. skiltonianus, Sceloporus graciosus, S. occidentalis),* small snakes *(Crotalus viridis),* nestling birds *(Catharus ustulatus, Empidonax oberholseri, Pipilo chlorurus),* quail eggs, and occasionally small mammals are all eaten (Cranston 1994; Cunningham 1959; Fitch 1936; Klauber 1972; McGurty 1988; Newton and Smith 1975; Petrides 1941; Stebbins 1954, 1985; Wentz 1953). Fitch (1936) found fragments of a green beetle (Coleoptera) in an Oregon *L. zonata,* but either the insect was probably ingested accidentally or its remains were from the stomach of a lizard the snake had eaten. Captives have taken lizards *(Eumeces, Sceloporus, Uta),* a garter snake *(Thamnophis butleri),* and mice (Blanchard 1921; Bogert 1930; Fitch 1936; Kauffeld 1969; Rossi and Ross 1995).

PREDATORS AND DEFENSE. No acts of natural predation have been reported. This snake's bold, advertising pattern has been considered a mimic of venomous coral snakes *(Micruroides* and *Micrurus)* (Brattstrom 1955a; Hecht and Marien 1956) even though no coral snake occurs within its United States range. However, its bright red, black, and yellow triads may serve other purposes (see DIET AND FEEDING HABITS).

Flight is the first line of defense of this snake, and when given a chance it will crawl to cover. If prevented from doing so, it may coil and strike, and when handled, twist violently to escape, release musk and fecal matter, and bite viciously. Its teeth can cause rather deep lacerations.

POPULATIONS. No study of population dynamics has been undertaken. Some populations have been detrimentally affected by habitat destruction. The historic range of this species near Los Angeles has shrunk since the late Pleistocene to the point that it is now found only in relict pockets (Newton and Smith 1975). Collection for the pet trade has also helped destroy habitats and raped populations (McGurty 1988). Fortunately, the species breeds in captivity, and hopefully this will fulfill the demand for pets. The species is protected in Oregon, and California protects the subspecies *L. z. pulchra.*

REMARKS. *L. zonata* has been reviewed by Zweifel (1975).

Leptodeira septentrionalis (Kennicott, in Baird 1859) | Northern Cat-eyed Snake

RECOGNITION. The cat-eyed snake is one of four unusual snakes that reach their northernmost distribution in extreme southern Texas. Its rounded body has reached a TBL of 98.5 cm, but individuals are usually shorter than 60 cm. Ground color varies from cream or yellowish to light reddish brown. A series of 20–35 dark brown or black bands or saddles 5–9 scales wide cross the back, and another 8–19 cross the tail. The head is much broader than the neck, and appears swollen just behind the eyes. It is gray to brown with dark dorsal blotches on the parietal scales, and a dark postorbital stripe extending backward and slightly downward from the eye may be present. The eyes are yellow with vertically elliptical pupils. Chin, throat, and venter are yellowish to orange; the underside of the tail is pinkish orange. Ventral scutes have a dark posterior border and dark speckles. Body scales are smooth with two apical pits, and occur in 21–23 rows anteriorly, 19–23 rows at midbody, and 15–17 rows near the anal vent. Ventrals total 181–208 and subcaudals 60–94, and the anal plate is divided. Lateral head scalation consists of a single nasal, 1 loreal, 3 (1–2) preoculars, 2 (3) postoculars, 1 + 2 + 3 temporals, 8 supralabials, and 10 (9–12) infralabials. The single hemipenis has an unforked sulcus spermaticus, a spiny head, and one or more longitudinal rows of large spines opposite the sulcus. It extends only 7–9 subcaudals when inverted. Each maxilla has 13–18 long, sharp, recurved anterior teeth separated by a diastema from two enlarged, grooved, fanglike teeth.

Sexual dimorphism in body length is pronounced, with females (to 98.5 cm TBL) much larger than males (to 77.4 cm TBL) (Duellman 1958a; Fitch 1981). However, males have longer tails than females; the TL is about 28 (22.2–34.9) % of TBL for males and 24 (19.0–28.3) % of TBL for females (Clark 1967a; Duellman 1958a). Subcaudals in males average 78.7 (66–94), those of females only 70.5 (60–81); males average 13.1 tail blotches, females 11.6; and the minimum number of posterior dorsal scale rows is 15 in males and 17 in females (Duellman 1958a).

GEOGRAPHIC VARIATION. Four subspecies are recognized, but only *Leptodeira septentrionalis septentrionalis* (Kennicott, in Baird 1859), the northern cat-eyed snake, described above, reaches Texas.

CONFUSING SPECIES. The spotted night snake *(Hypsiglena torquata)*, western lyre snake *(Trimorphodon biscutatus)* and rattlesnakes *(Crotalus, Sistrurus)* also have elliptical pupils, but the latter have a rattle at the ends of their tails. *Trimorphodon* has an extra scale (lorilabial) between the loreal and supralabials and a V- or lyre-shaped mark on its head, and *Hypsiglena* has three prominent dark blotches on its nape.

KARYOTYPE. Not reported.

FOSSIL RECORD. Unknown.

DISTRIBUTION. *L. septentrionalis* is found at elevations to 2,440 m (Fouquette and Rossman 1963) from Frio, LaSalle, McMullen, Live Oak, and Bee counties in the Rio Grande Valley of southern Texas and in Nuevo León and Tamaulipas in northeastern Mexico (an isolated colony also is present in Coahuila) in the east, and in central Nayarit in the west, southward and eastward along both coasts of Mexico and Central America to Colombia and Peru in northwestern South America.

Northern cat-eyed snake, *Leptodira s. septentrionalis.* (Photograph by R. D. Bartlett)

Distribution of *Leptodeira septentrionalis*.

HABITAT. In southern Texas, this snake is most often found in dense vegetation along waterways flowing through the arid thorn-brush habitat.

BEHAVIOR. Almost nothing is known of its behavior and ecology. It is almost entirely nocturnal in Texas, although tropical individuals are sometimes active in the day, and it is semiarboreal and an accomplished climber, often ascending into low trees and bushes while hunting for prey. While moving from branch to branch, the body is compressed and used much like an I beam (Duellman 1958a).

REPRODUCTION. Wright and Wright (1957) suggested a minimum adult SVL of 38 cm, and Duellman (1958a) reported the smallest mature individuals are 30–35 cm long. It lays clutches averaging 8.4 (6–12) elongated eggs, which are 25.9 (21.1–34.5) mm long and 11.7 (10.8–12.3) mm wide, and weigh 2.6 (2.1–3.1) g. No Texas ovipositions have been reported, but captives and tropical subspecies lay their eggs in the spring from February to May (Duellman 1958a). The IP is 79–90 days (Petzold 1969; Tennant 1985). A hatchling found on 28 August in Belize had an umbilical scar and had probably hatched that month (Neill 1962). Hatchlings are about 21.8 (17.8–25.4) cm in TBL, 1.8–2.3 g, orangish tan, and more vividly marked than adults.

Females are capable of maintaining viable sperm for up to five years following a copulation (Haines 1940). The female of record was found in a shipment of bananas from Central America in March 1934 and was acquired by Haines in August of that year. She laid viable eggs in 1936, 1938, and 1939 without having been with a male while in captivity. That the female skipped oviposition in 1935 and 1937 perhaps indicates she had to rebuild her body reserves between ovipositions, as occurs in rattlesnakes (Keenlyne 1978; Martin 1988).

GROWTH AND LONGEVITY. Haines (1940) reported that the female discussed above grew from 75 to 96 cm while in captivity for 6 years. An adult female caught in the tropics survived 10 years, 11 months, and 26 days at the Baltimore Zoo (Snider and Bowler 1992), and Wright and Wright (1957) kept another cat-eyed snake for 10 years.

DIET AND FEEDING HABITS. Foraging is done at night, both on the ground and in bushes and trees. Prey is seized and worked to the back of the mouth, where it is punctured by the snake's enlarged, grooved fangs. The venom of the cat-eyed snake must be chewed into the wound, and it immobilizes, paralyzes, and kills small snakes and lizards within 10 minutes (Burchfield 1993). It is produced in a Duvernoy's gland that is at least partially serous (Taub 1967) and allows the snake to immobilize hard-to-swallow prey (Rodríquez-Robles 1994).

Wild *L. septentrionalis* eat all life stages of frogs and toads *(Agalychnis, Bufo, Engystomops, Hyla, Leptodactylus, Phrynohyas, Phyllomedusa, Scinax, Smilisca)* and lizards *(Ameiva, Anolis, Ctenosaura, Sceloporus, Sphaerodactylus)* (Burchfield 1993; Duellman 1958a, 1963; Russell et al. 1999a; Tennant 1984; Warkentin 1995), and captives have subsisted on frogs *(Acris, Pseudacris, Rana),* salamanders, small snakes *(Nerodia, Tantilla),* minnows (Cyprinidae), and mice *(Mus)* (Burchfield 1993; Tennant 1984; Wright and Wright 1957).

The cat-eyed snake is a formidable predator. During a study of responses to predation by tadpoles of the Costa Rican treefrog, *Agalychnis callidryas,* the snake destroyed many of the frog's arboreal egg clutches (Warkentin 1995). *Leptodeira septentrionalis* attacked 60% of monitored clutches before they hatched, and ate 48% of the monitored eggs at one pond in 1991. In 1992, the snake attacked 50.5% of the clutches and consumed 50% of the eggs at the same pond, and at a second pond the snake attacked 27% of the clutches and ate 15% of the eggs. The above data include repeated attacks, but on first attacks the snake consumed an average of 79% of a clutch.

PREDATORS AND DEFENSE.   The only report concerning predation is that of the rear-fanged middle American snake *Clelia clelia* attempting to eat a *L. septentrionalis* in Costa Rica (Russell et al. 1999b). *L. septentrionalis* is fast, and its slender body allows it either to quickly flee or to hide from predators; but it will bite if handled, and it is large enough to envenomate if it can bring its rear fangs into play. A human envenomation resulted in more bleeding than expected from the small bite wounds, and a slight temporary edema and inflammation occurred around the bite site (Tennant 1984). Ditmars (1939) warned against careless handling of this snake, as the venom may predispose the area around the bite to secondary bacterial infection.

POPULATIONS.   *L. septentrionalis* is rare in Texas, but it is quite common in more tropical habitats (Duellman 1963). Because of its rarity, the disappearance of suitable vegetation, and use of pesticides in southern Texas, *L. septentrionalis* is near extinction in Texas, and it has been declared endangered and given full protection under the law.

REMARKS.   The species and genus have been reviewed by Duellman (1958a) and Taylor (1939a).

Liochlorophis vernalis (Harlan 1827) | Smooth Green Snake

RECOGNITION.   *L. vernalis* is an unpatterned green snake with a white to cream venter, yellow supralabials, and smooth body scales. Maximum TBL is 79.7 cm, but most individuals are shorter than 50 cm. The smooth body scales have a single apical pit and occur in 15 midbody rows. Beneath are 106–154 ventrals, 59–102 subcaudals, and a divided anal plate. Lateral head scales consist of 1 nasal, 1 loreal, 1 (2) preocular(s), 2 postoculars, 1 + 2 (3) temporals, 7 (6–8) supralabials, and 7–8 (5–9) infralabials. The short hemipenis has numerous deep fringed calyxes and a nude apex. Each maxilla has 15–21 (mean, 18) teeth.

Males are shorter-bodied (seldom to 50 cm TBL) with 106–145 (mean, 125) ventrals, 65–102 (mean, 86) subcaudals, and TLs 29–37 (mean, 34) % of TBL; females are longer-bodied (to 79.7 cm) with 111–154 (mean, 131) ventrals, 59–90 (mean, 80) subcaudals, and TLs 25–34 (mean, 29) % of TBL.

GEOGRAPHIC VARIATION.   Three subspecies have been named (Grobman 1941, 1992a, 1992b), but none are currently recognized (Collins 1992).

CONFUSING SPECIES.   The rough green snake *(Opheodrys aestivus)* has keeled body scales that occur in 17 midbody rows. The green rat snake *(Senticollis triaspis)* has keeled body scales that occur in 25 or more midbody rows. Greenish whipsnakes *(Masticophis)* and racers *(Coluber constrictor)* have a narrow, vertically elongated preocular scale that penetrates the supralabial row.

KARYOTYPE.   Undescribed.

FOSSIL RECORD.   Pleistocene fossils are known from the Irvingtonian of Florida (Meylan 1982), Maryland (Holman 1977b), and Texas (Holman and Winkler 1987) and the Rancholabrean of Indiana (Holman and Richards 1981), Ohio (Holman 1997), Virginia (Holman 1986a), and West Virginia (Holman and Grady 1994).

DISTRIBUTION.   *L. vernalis* is found from Nova Scotia and Manitoba south to northwestern Virginia and eastern West Virginia and west to southeastern Saskatchewan, Montana, Wyoming, Utah, and New Mexico. Isolated populations also occur in southeastern Texas and Chihuahua, Mexico.

HABITAT.   This snake lives in a variety of mesic habitats—wet prairies, meadows, bog and marsh bor-

Smooth green snake, *Liochlorophis vernalis*; Clare County, Michigan. (Photograph by James H. Harding)

ders, and open woodlands—at elevations of about sea level up to 2,895 m.

BEHAVIOR.   Over most of its range, *L. vernalis* is active from mid-April to October, but in the north or at higher elevations it may be surface active only from late May to September. Hibernation is underground, often communal: it has been found overwintering in a gravel bank in Pennsylvania (Lachner 1942), and in mammal burrows and the horizontal spaces between granite slabs in New Mexico (Degenhardt et al. 1996; Stuart and Painter 1993); but ant mounds, where it has been found buried at depths greater than 15 cm, seem preferred (Carpenter 1953a; Criddle 1937; Lang 1969; Young 1973). In a Manitoba ant mound containing water at a depth of 145 cm, some *L. vernalis* were partly submerged with their heads pointed upward (Criddle 1937). The majority of large adults were at the lowest level of the mound, but most of the smaller snakes were nearer the surface; perhaps larger individuals enter first. *L. vernalis* shares its hibernacula with other reptiles, especially where suitable hibernacula are scarce.

Most surface activity is during the warmer parts of the day, although Vogt (1981) found *L. vernalis* cross-

Distribution of *Liochlorophis vernalis*.

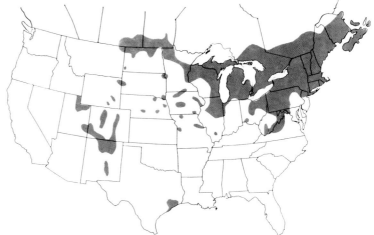

ing roads at night during warm summer and fall rains. Brattstrom (1965) recorded BTs of 18.0–31.2 (mean, 25.6) °C for active smooth green snakes, and Seibert and Hagen (1947) reported the species was most active when ATs were 21–30°C. The maximum metabolic heat *L. vernalis* is capable of producing is 3°C, and metabolic heat production is directly related to the snake's diurnal activity cycle, as its BT decreases at night (Kroll et al. 1973). After eating, the BT rapidly increases, then increases slightly and levels off; the maximum difference between the snake's BT and the AT during this period is +1.2°C (Kroll et al. 1973).

Although predominantly a ground dweller, *L. vernalis* occasionally will climb into low bushes and shrubs.

REPRODUCTION. Females mature at TBLs as short as 28 cm, and males 30 cm long may be mature (Wright and Wright 1957). Nothing is known of the gametic cycle of either sex.

The authors found a copulating pair in Pennsylvania on 15 April, and mating is known to occur in May (Collins 1993). August copulations have also been reported in southern Canada (Dymond and Fry 1932), so a second fall mating period may take place from which sperm possibly is stored over the winter.

Nestings have been observed from 9 June to 29 August, and females may lay two or more clutches a season (Blanchard 1932). Those from southern populations oviposit in June and July, but northern populations lay eggs from late July through August. Typical nest sites are piles of rotting vegetation, sawdust piles, rotting logs and stumps, and mammal burrows. Clutches contain 2 (Mitchell 1994) to 18 (Stebbins 1985) eggs, and average 6.9 (n = 40). Several females may share a nest site, and communal nests have contained up to 31 eggs. Gordon and Cook (1980) reported aggregation of gravid females near the time of laying. The whitish eggs are loosely adhered, thin-shelled, and elongate; measurements for 21 eggs were 19.0–38.0 (mean, 28.1) × 8.0–18.0 (mean, 11.6) mm.

The eggs are far advanced when laid, and possibly females aid egg development by incubating them internally while basking, an apparent adaptation for northern living. The young emerge from early August to early October, but most hatch in late August and early September after a short IP of 4–25 (mean, 14.8; n = 14) days. Hatchlings have gray to olive brown backs, and average 13.3 (8.3–16.7) cm in TBL.

GROWTH AND LONGEVITY. Growth data are lacking. The captive longevity record is 6 years, 1 month, and 9 days (Snider and Bowler 1992).

DIET AND FEEDING HABITS. *L. vernalis* feeds almost exclusively on arthropods—insects (ants, fly maggots, grasshoppers, crickets, beetle adults and grubs, and lepidopteran caterpillars), harvestmen, spiders, centipedes, millipedes, and crayfish; but earthworms, slugs, snails, and salmanders are other reported prey (Hammerson 1986; Surface 1906; Uhler et al. 1939; Wright and Wright 1957). Stomachs of Virginia *L. vernalis* examined by Uhler et al. (1939) contained by volume 36.8% caterpillars, 31.8% spiders, 20% grasshoppers, 10% ants, 1% slugs and snails, and 0.4% fly larvae. Prey is seized and either chewed or swallowed whole. Taub (1967) found *L. vernalis* has a purely serous Duvernoy's gland, but no evidence exists that its saliva is venomous.

PREDATORS AND DEFENSE. Neill (1948b) reported that a black widow spider (*Latrodectus mactans*) killed a *L. vernalis*, and ophiophagous snakes, domestic chickens (*Gallus domesticus*), hawks (*Buteo lineatus, B. platypterus*), and cats (*Felis catus*) (and probably other predatory mammals) all take their toll. Klemens (1993) reported predation by a "hawk."

Generally inoffensive, *L. vernalis* may void the contents of its cloaca and musk glands when handled, and Schlauch (1975) reported they may occasionally gape and pretend to strike, but do not bite. Cochran (1987) observed a captive *L. vernalis* perform rhythmic lateral head movements that may have been either defensive or an attempt to enhance binocular vision. The green body color is a natural camouflage when the snake is in vegetation.

POPULATIONS. Seibert (1950) estimated that a population of *L. vernalis* near Chicago totaled 237 with a density of approximately 185/ha. At a hibernaculum in Manitoba, it made up 148 (57.6%) of 257 hibernating snakes (Criddle 1937), and at another hibernaculum there, Grobman (1992a) found 84. However, the species is not always so plentiful: it constituted only 0.9% (8) of 885 snakes collected by Uhler et al. (1939) in the George Washington National Forest of western Virginia.

Of 32 *L. vernalis* collected in Manitoba by Gregory (1977a), 19 were males and 13 females (1.46:1.00), but Grobman (1992a) reported male to female ratios of 0.61:1.00 and 0.82:1.00, respectively, for two sites in Manitoba and Illinois.

L. vernalis is a useful species that eats some harmful insects, and is probably most numerous where insects abound. The common use of pesticides in such places has had a detrimental effect on its populations: two smooth green snakes died of insecticide poisoning after a section in northern Indiana was heavily sprayed (Minton 1972). This and other forms of habitat destruction have reduced populations of *L. vernalis* in many states to the point that it is now protected in Indiana, Missouri, Montana, North Carolina, and Wyoming, and of uncertain status in Idaho.

REMARKS. This species was formerly included in the genus *Opheodrys* with the rough green snake *(O. aestivus)*, but Oldham and Smith (1991) reviewed the species, and found nine distinct differences between the two green snakes, and erected the genus *Liochlorophis* for the *L. vernalis.*

Masticophis Baird and Girard 1853

Whipsnakes

Key to the Species of *Masticophis*

1a. Fifteen (or fewer) midbody scale rows 2
1b. Usually 17, but more than 15, midbody scale rows 3
2a. Dorsal head scales uniformly dark, paired light spots on the dorsal scales, or light borders on the middorsal scales . . . . *M. schotti*
2b. Dorsal head scales with light borders, no light spots or borders on the dorsal scutes . . . . *M. taeniatus*

3a. Lateral longitudinal stripe(s) absent . . . . *M. flagellum*
3b. Lateral longitudinal stripe(s) present 4
4a. Single lateral longitudinal stripe present, extending onto the tail . . . . *M. lateralis*
4b. Two or three lateral longitudinal stripes present, not extending onto the tail . . . . *M. bilineatus*

Masticophis bilineatus Jan 1863 | Sonoran Whipsnake

RECOGNITION. This large (TBL to 170 cm), slender, long-tailed (TL 40% of TBL) snake is greenish, bluish gray, or brownish gray. On each side are two to three white to cream longitudinal stripes separated by a continuous to dashed black line. These stripes normally fade out toward the tail; the widest occurs on scale rows 1–1.5, and the more dorsal narrow stripe is on scale rows 3.5–4.5. A pale spot is present at the anterior corner of dorsal body scales. The iris is yellowish. The supralabials are white to cream and are bordered dorsally by a black stripe extending backward from just below the eye to the corner of the mouth (no light temporal spot is present). The chin and throat are white to cream, often with small black spots. The venter is pale yellow; some dark spots may be present on the subcaudals. Dorsal body scales are smooth with only 1 (0–3) apical pit(s); they occur in 17 (19–20) anterior rows, 17 (15–18) rows at midbody, and 13 (10–14) rows near the tail. Ventrals total 182–216 and subcaudals 120–167; the anal plate is divided. The slightly bilobed hemipenis extends 5–14 subcaudals when inverted and is thick and rounded, with a single sulcus spermaticus, and calyxes and spines along the shaft. Each maxilla has 17–23 teeth.

The sexes are practically identical: males have 182–221 ventrals and 120–167 subcaudals; females have 183–216 ventrals and 121–165 subcaudals.

GEOGRAPHIC VARIATION. Presently, *M. bilineatus* is considered monotypic (Camper 1996a). The former subspecies *M. b. lineolatus* Hensley 1950 and *M. b. slevini* Lowe and Norris 1955 were synonymized with *M. bilineatus* by Camper and Dixon (1994), who found little variation across the geographic range of the species.

CONFUSING SPECIES. Other *Masticophis* can be distinguished by using the above key. The garter snakes *(Thamnophis)* have keeled body scales and an undivided anal plate. Patch-nosed snakes *(Salvadora)* have an enlarged rostral scale and black longitudinal stripes.

KARYOTYPE. Unreported.

FOSSIL RECORD. Unknown. Whipsnake vertebrae found within the range of this species have only been assigned to *Masticophis* sp. because of the similarity in the structure of vertebrae of all species in the genus (Holman 2000).

Sonoran whipsnake, *Masticophis bilineatus*; Santa Cruz County, Arizona. (Photograph by Brad R. Moon)

DISTRIBUTION. The entire United States range of *M. bilineatus* is west of the Continental Divide. It is found from central Arizona and Hidalgo County in extreme southwestern New Mexico, south in western Mexico to Jalisco and Colima, and in the islands of Tiburón and San Esteban in the Gulf of California.

HABITAT. This snake is most often found to elevations of about 2,300 m in semiarid highlands (Camper 1996a) with rocks and low, dense, woody vegetation (chaparral, oaks), or in rocky canyon bottoms with water and dense vegetation. In more lowland areas it occurs in deserts with Saguaro, paloverde and ocotillo, and grassland habitats.

BEHAVIOR. Life history data are sparse. *M. bilineatus* is active from March through October in New Mexico (Degenhardt et al. 1996), and while it is primarily diurnal, it has been observed foraging at night between 2200 and 2400 hours in Sinaloa, Mexico (Hardy and McDiarmid 1969). A retreat in a dirt road bank in Arizona was shared with the rattlesnake, *Crotalus atrox* (C. Ernst, pers. obs.).

M. *bilineatus* is an accomplished climber and is often seen above ground in low bushes or trees.

A thorough ecological study of *M. bilineatus* would yield much valuable data.

REPRODUCTION. Wright and Wright (1957) reported that 76 cm TBL individuals are mature. Little data concerning the female sexual cycle is available. Arizona females collected 10–15 April had large, yolked follicles, and clutches have been laid on 7 June and 12 July (Van Denburgh 1922; Vitt 1975). The three reported clutches had 6, 7, and 13 (average, 8.7) eggs, respectively (Stebbins 1985; Van Denburgh 1922; Vitt 1975). The elongated, white eggs are 37–54 (mean, 42) mm long and 18.0–19.2 (mean, 18.9) mm wide, and weigh about 12 g. The RCM of a clutch of 6 eggs was 0.439 (Vitt 1975). Hatchlings are colored and patterned like adults.

GROWTH AND LONGEVITY. No growth data have been reported. Like other whipsnakes, *M. bilineatus* is a poor captive; the record longevity in captivity is 2 years, 4 months, and 23 days (Snider and Bowler 1992), but wild individuals survive much longer.

Distribution of *Masticophis bilineatus*.

DIET AND FEEDING HABITS. *M. bilineatus* is an active forager during the day and night that hunts both at ground level and in bushes and small trees. Active prey is pursued, seized, and quickly swallowed head first. No constriction occurs, and although it has a purely serous Duvernoy's gland (Taub 1967), envenomation does not occur. The primary food of wild individuals is lizards. Camper and Dixon (2000) found 20 lizards in 18 *M. bilineatus*; lizards made up 91% of the prey taken, and mammals the remainder. Recorded prey include lizards *(Cnemidophorus, Cophosaurus, Eumeces* [?], *Sceloporus, Urosaurus, Uta),* mice *(Peromyscus),* young ground squirrels *(Ammospermophilus* or *Spermophilus),* young birds, and frogs (Bogert and Oliver 1945; Camper and Dixon 2000; Fowlie 1965; Gates 1957; Groschupf 1982; Lewis and Johnson 1956; Nickerson and Mays 1970; Stebbins 1954, 1985; Van Denburgh 1922; Woodin 1953).

PREDATORS AND DEFENSE. The only record of predation is by a black hawk *(Buteogallus anthracinus)* (Ross 1989). Some *M. bilineatus* are killed on our roads each year, and Hensley (1950) found several trapped in a steep-walled rock hole, some of which were already dead and others starved. These whipsnakes will try to escape if disturbed, but if handled, some will put up a spirited fight.

POPULATIONS.   *M. bilineatus* is locally common in some canyons and desert habitats. Hensley (1950) found 19 during three visits to the deep rock hole mentioned above.

REMARKS.   Albumin protein and mitochondrial DNA and RNA nucleotide sequencing studies by Lopez and Maxson (1995, 1996) show a Nearctic racer clade that includes the genera *Coluber* and *Masticophis*. Wilson (1973a) reviewed the genus *Masticophis*; Camper (1996a) and Camper and Dixon (1994) reviewed the species *M. bilineatus*.

Masticophis flagellum (Shaw 1802) | Coachwhip

RECOGNITION.   The coachwhip is a long (TBL to 259 cm, but most individuals are 100–150 cm) snake with the scales on its tail arranged in a pattern resembling a braided whip. Anterior body color varies from olive brown, dark brown, or black to yellow, pinkish, or reddish; body color fades gradually posteriorly until the tail is much lighter. The venter is pigmented like the dorsum, but the head is usually dark. Some lighter-colored individuals may retain the juvenile body pattern of dark, narrow crossbands, while others are melanistic and totally dark brown or black. Dorsal body scales are smooth with two apical pits, and occur in 19 (17, 21) anterior rows, 17 (15) midbody rows, and 13 (11–12) rows just in front vent. Beneath are 185–212 ventrals, 91–125 subcaudals, and a divided anal plate. Lateral head scales consist of 2 nasals (separated or partially separated by a nostril), 1 (2–3) loreal(s), 2 (1–4) preoculars, 2 (1–3) postoculars, 2–3 (1) + 3 (2) + 3 temporals, 8 (7–9) supralabials, and 10 (8–13) infralabials. The bilobed hemipenis has a

Eastern coachwhip, *Masticophis flagellum flagellum*; Kentucky. (Photograph by Roger W. Barbour)

Sonoran coachwhip, *Masticophis flagellum cingulum*; Santa Cruz County, Arizona. (Photograph by Brad R. Moon)

single, oblique sulcus spermaticus that extends onto the left lobe, a smooth apex, 40–60 spines in 4–6 rows, 2–3 large basal spines (one much larger than the other 1–2), and 9–13 rows of deep calyxes. It extends to the level of the 11th (6th–13th) subcaudal (Ortenburger 1928; Wilson 1970a). Each maxilla has 18–19 (16–21) teeth.

Males have 185–212 ventrals, 94–125 subcaudals, and TLs 22–28% of TBL; females have 186–208 ventrals, 91–123 subcaudals, and TLs 21–26% of TBL.

GEOGRAPHIC VARIATION. Seven subspecies are recognized based on body color and pattern (Wilson 1970a, 1973b); all occur in the United States. *M. f. flagellum* (Shaw 1802), the eastern coachwhip, is the only whipsnake east of the Mississippi River. It ranges from southeastern North Carolina west to eastern Nebraska, and south through peninsular Florida and to the Gulf Coast to eastern Texas. Its dorsal body color is dark brown to almost black anteriorly, but usually becomes lighter posteriorly. Occasionally some Florida or Georgia individuals have a tan dorsum on which narrow dark crossbands are visible. *M. f. cingulum* Lowe and Woodin 1954, the Sonoran coachwhip,

ranges from southern Arizona south to Sinaloa, Mexico. It is reddish brown above with widely separated narrow pink crossbands, which tend to be paired posteriorly. Occasionally individuals are totally reddish brown or black. *M. f. fulginosus* (Cope 1895), the Baja California coachwhip, can be found in extreme southwestern California from San Diego south through Baja California. This predominately Mexican snake has two color phases: (1) a light morph that is yellowish, tan, or gray with a zigzag pattern of black bands along the body and wider dark bands on the neck, and (2) a dark grayish brown morph with light lines on the sides, particularly near the front, and a variable amount of cream pigment on the venter. *M. f. lineatulus* Smith 1941b, the lined coachwhip, is found in southwestern New Mexico and adjacent southeastern Arizona south to Durango, Zacatecas, and western Nuevo León, Mexico. This is a tan to light gray snake, and each dorsal scale on the anterior portion of the body has a central longitudinal dark streak or a posterior dark spot. No marks are present on the neck, and the white loreal bar is missing. Juveniles have crossbands that are two to three scales long, and do not cross the venter. *M. f. piceus* (Cope 1892b), the red coachwhip, ranges from central Nevada and southern Utah south through southern California and most of Arizona to northern Sonora and adjacent northern Baja California, Mexico. Two color phases are present: (1) A red morph is pink to red with dark brown to black or dark-bordered reddish, sometimes united, crossbands on the neck, and a loreal with a white, black-bordered bar, and the juveniles are blotched or heavily spotted. (2) Black phase individuals are completely black dorsally and salmon pink to red posteroventrally; such snakes are found in scattered localities in the southern portion of the range. *M. f. ruddocki* Brattstrom and Warren 1953, the San Joaquin coachwhip, occurs from central California south to southern California. Dorsal body color is yellowish to olive with only faint or no crossbands on the neck, and the head is dark. *M. f. testaceus* (Say 1823), the western coachwhip, has a broad range extending from southwestern Nebraska and eastern Colorado south through western Kansas, western Oklahoma, eastern New Mexico, and central and western Texas to central Mexico. This subspecies is light yellow brown, tan, pinkish red, or dark brown, with or without short dark crossbands on the neck or long crossbands on the anterior portion of the body, and has a double row of dark spots on the cream-colored venter.

CONFUSING SPECIES.   To differentiate *M. flagellum* from the other species of *Masticophis* in the United States, use the key presented above. The racer *(Colu-* *ber constrictor)* has 15 body scale rows just anterior to the anal vent, and no reddish pigment on the sides of the tail. The green rat snake *(Senticolis triaspis)* has at least 25 midbody scale rows, and weakly keeled mid-dorsal scales. Melanistic garter and ribbon snakes *(Thamnophis)* have keeled body scales.

KARYOTYPE.   The karyotype consists of 36 chromosomes with 50 arms (16 macrochromosomes, 20 microchromosomes); sex determination is ZZ/ZW with the females heteromorphic (Baker et al. 1972; Bury et al. 1970; Trinco and Smith 1971).

FOSSIL RECORD.   The coachwhip's fossil record dates from the Peistocene (Rancholabrean) of Arkansas (Dowling 1958b), Florida (Auffenberg 1963; Gut and Ray 1963; Holman 1958b, 1959b; Martin 1974; Meylan 1982), California (Hudson and Brattstrom 1977), Nevada (Brattstrom 1954a, 1958b), New Mexico (Brattstrom 1964a), and Virginia (Guilday 1962). In addition, fossils found that have only been assigned to the genus *Masticophis* or to *Coluber-Masticophis* may be of this species.

DISTRIBUTION.   The coachwhip ranges from southeastern North Carolina westward to Nebraska, eastern Colorado, New Mexico, Arizona, southwestern Utah and Nevada, and mid- and southern California, and southward through peninsular Florida and eastern and central Mexico to Veracruz, Queretaro, Durango, and Sinaloa, and south through Baja California.

Distribution of *Masticophis flagellum*.

HABITAT. *M. flagellum* is a dry grassland, savannah, scrubland, or desert dweller; but it is also known from chaparral, mesquite-creosote brush, thornbush, pine and palmetto flatwoods, and pine-juniper and oak woodlands (scattered vegetation is helpful for both its foraging mode and its rapid escape behavior). Soils vary from loose sand to solid loam, and rocks do not need to be present. Elevation varies from near sea level to approximately 2,300 m.

BEHAVIOR. Seasonally, *M. flagellum* is first active in March, but more often in April–early May, depending on both elevation and latitude. Over most of the range, it remains surface active to September–November; but in Florida some are active in every month. It retreats underground, often into animal burrows, to escape the severe summer heat.

Little is known of its hibernating behavior. Neill (1948a) reported that in Georgia it overwinters in tunnels formed by the decay of pine roots on dry hillsides. In Kansas, coachwhips hibernate in deep rock crevices on hillsides or in small mammal burrows on the prairie (Collins 1993), and they may hibernate in western diamondback rattlesnake *(Crotalus atrox)* dens in Oklahoma (Ortenburger and Freeman 1930). Cowles (1941b) found one overwintering in the desert that had a CT of 17°C, and Secor and Nagy (1994) reported BTs of approximately 7–24°C.

Daily activity is strictly diurnal, and coachwhips are often seen foraging in the hottest summer hours. Jones and Whitford (1989) found them active from approximately 0800–1700 hours from spring to fall. However, many were inactive or in burrows at 0800 and from 1000 to 1600 hours in the spring, and at 0800 and 1600 in the summer and fall. Most basking occurs from 0800 to 1000 hours in all three seasons, but some individuals can be found basking at any daylight hour. Foraging occurs all day, but is most concentrated from 0900 to 1600 hours.

Its lowest voluntary BT is 21°C; but observations on caged individuals show that 24°C is more likely the normal lower voluntary BT for the species (Cowles and Bogert 1944). The maximum voluntary BT is 37°C, with normal activity occurring at 27–35°C, and the preferred highest BT is probably 33°C; 42.4–44.0°C BTs are lethal (Cowles and Bogert 1944). Field BTs of two western subspecies recorded by Brattstrom (1965) were 24–37 (mean, 31.6) °C, and Secor (1995) found that most active California *M. flagellum* have BTs of 30–35 (mean, 33.1) °C. Bogert and Cowles (1947) reported a field BT 32.6°C for a Florida *M. f. flagellum*.

California coachwhips studied by Hammerson (1977, 1989) emerge from their burrows with BTs of 16.3–25.2 (mean, 21.0) °C. Morning emergence is strongly correlated with deep burrow ATs, and the snakes typically leave their night retreat after direct sunlight enters the mouth of their burrow. Emergence STs in the direct sun average 33.4 (21.1–47.5) °C. Basking follows emergence, and lasts about 38.8 (4–122) minutes. Basking cause BTs to rise rapidly; basking ends and movement activity begins when the snake's BT reaches about 31.8 (28.0–35.2) °C. Daily surface activity ends in late afternoon when the coachwhips again retreat underground with BTs of 25.9–34.9 (mean, 30.4) °C (the warmest STs experienced by Hammerson's snakes were 25.6–50+ [mean, 36.6] °C). After entering its burrow, the snake's BT drops quickly to ET and continues to decline slowly until after emergence the following morning. Weather conditions that alter the amount of direct sunlight change the timing and duration of daily activity, and recently fed snakes are less active. Head temperatures were significantly elevated above those of the stomach prior to morning emergence and through the entire day (Hammerson 1977), as the head is first warmed in the sun before morning emergence. *M. flagellum* from San Bernardino County, California, are surface active for an average of 3.9 hours/day (Secor and Nagy 1994).

Bogert and Cowles (1947) found that two Florida *M. flagellum* were very resistant to desiccation. One that weighed 536 g when placed in a thermal chamber with an AT of 38°C for 46+ hours lost only 0.14% of its body weight per hour. The second 655 g snake lost only 11.3% of its initial body weight after 99.5 hours in the same chamber. As body water loss seems not to be a problem, this partially explains why this species can be active during the hottest period of the day.

When foraging or crawling across open country, the coachwhip does so with its head held vertically high above the ground, and it is capable of prowling at a rate of 0.48 km/hour and has a maximum speed of 6.01 km/hour (Mosauer 1935). The home range in California is 40.1–66.7 (mean, 53.4) ha, and individuals travel an average of 186 m, with average long distance moves of 241 m (Secor 1995). Activity is not restricted to ground level, as *M. flagellum* may climb into shrubs and low trees to bask or forage.

Dominance combat behavior between males occurs during the breeding season (Kennedy 1965b; Webb 1970).

REPRODUCTION.   Adults probably mature at a TBL of 70–90 cm (Stebbins 1985; Wright and Wright 1957), but no study of the sexual cycles and maturity of this snake has been reported. Mating occurs soon after emergence from hibernation; literature dates of observed copulations range from 18 April to 29 May, but the courtship and copulatory behaviors have not been described.

Nesting has been observed or fresh clutches have been found from 6 June to 30 July. The eggs are laid in loose soil at depths to 30 cm below the surface (Collins 1993), in rotting logs or decaying plant matter (Vermersch and Kuntz 1986), or in animal burrows. The mean number of eggs in 26 clutches reported in the literature is 10.7 (4–24). The eggs are white with nonadherent, granular-surfaced, leathery shells; they are 25.0–63.0 (mean, 40.0) mm long by 14.0–27.9 (mean, 22.0) mm wide. The IP averages of 64.4 (42–88) days.

Hatching takes place in late August–early September. Hatchlings are 20.5–41.0 (mean, 25.6; n = 20) cm long and are reddish brown to olive brown dorsally with a series of narrow to broad dark transverse bands beginning on the neck and continuing to varying distances along the body. A double row of reddish spots is present on the venter.

GROWTH AND LONGEVITY.   No growth data are available. Snider and Bowler (1992) reported that a male, originally wild-caught at an unknown age, survived 18 years, 1 month, and 29 days at the Philadelphia Zoo.

DIET AND FEEDING HABITS.   The coachwhip is an active forager, crawling about, often with its head and neck well off the ground, until a scent trail is discovered (Cooper et al. 1990; Secor 1995), or a small animal is flushed from its hiding place. It then chases rapidly after the prey, seizes it, and quickly swallows it. Being long and slender, *M. flagellum* can follow small animals into narrow crevices or burrows, and probably captures many lizards and small mammals underground. Active hunting is not restricted to ground level or subterranean burrows, as coachwhips often climb high into trees to raid birds' nests. It may also assume a "sit and wait" ambush behavior to capture swift lizard prey (Jones and Whitford 1989). It selects a site in total shade and remains inactive, with its head resting on top of vertically oriented body coils, until a lizard enters the area. The snake then responds by lifting its head above the coils and initiates pursuit of the lizard. This pursuit consists of extending the body outward toward the lizard, with the tail anchored onto some object. Such a hunting technique results in a greater rate of capture (80% versus 17%) than free-moving pursuit of fast prey. The energy demand for California coachwhips during the active season averages 24.1 g/kg body wt/day, and during an entire year a snake consumes about 212 kJ of usable prey flesh (Secor 1995).

Having such a wide distribution brings *M. flagellum* into contact with many small animals, so the list of natural prey is long: insects—lepidopteran larvae (Lepidoptera), grasshoppers (Orthoptera), and cicadas (Homoptera); amphibians—frog eggs and spadefoots *(Scaphiopus bombifrons);* reptiles—turtles (eggs, hatchling *Kinosternon subrubrum)*, lizards *(Callisaurus draconoides, Cnemidophorus sexlineatus, C. tigris, Cophosaurus texanum, Crotaphytus collaris, Dipsosaurus dorsalis, Eumeces egregius, E. laticeps, Holbrookia maculata, Phrynomoma cornutum, P. platyrhinos, Scincella lateralis, Sceloporus clarkii, S. olivaceus, S. undulatus, Urosaurus ornatus, Uta stansburiana)*, and snakes *(Arizona elegans, Coluber constrictor, Crotalus adamanteus* [in captivity], *C. atrox, C. cerastes, C. viridus, Diadophis punctatus, Heterodon* sp., *Masticophis flagellum, Opheodrys aestivus, Sonora semiannulata);* birds—adults, nestlings, and eggs *(Aphelocoma coerulescens, Chordeiles minor* [carrion], *Cyanocitta cristata, Molothrus ater, Passerculus sandwichensis, Pipilo aberti*, woodpecker); and mammals—bats, shrews *(Blarina* sp.), jackrabbits *(Lepus californicus)*, cottontails *(Sylvilagus floridana)*, cotton rats *(Sigmodon hispidus)*, wood rats *(Neotoma* sp.), mice *(Mus musculus, Perognathus hispidus, Pero-*

myscus leucopus), and ground squirrels *(Spermophilus mexicanus);* in addition, a captive ate a Great Plains rat snake *(Elaphe emoryi)* (Blair 1960; Boyer and Heinze 1934; Carpenter 1958; Clark 1949; Cliff 1954; Cunningham 1959; Finch 1981; Fouquette and Lindsay 1955; Gates 1957; Gehlbach 1956; Guidry 1953; Hamilton and Pollock 1956; Jones and Whitford 1989; Klauber 1972; Lohrer 1980; Marr 1944; McKinney and Ballinger 1966; Milstead et al. 1950; Minton 1959; Mueller and Whiting 1989; Ortenburger and Freeman 1930; Punzo 2000; Reams et al. 2000b; Secor 1994; Small et al. 1994; Stebbins 1954; Tabor and Germano 1997; Tennant 1985; Tyler 1977; Vermersch and Kuntz 1986; Webber 1980; Whiting et al. 1992; Woodin 1953). Of 30 stomachs examined by Clark (1949), 18 contained mammals and 12 had birds. Hamilton and Pollock (1956) reported the following percentages of occurrence and volume (in parentheses) for foods of 45 coachwhips: lizards, 68.9% (63.4%); mammals, 17.8% (14.7%); snakes, 8.9% (8.9%); insects, 8.9% (8.3%); birds, 2.2% (2.2%); and a turtle, 2.2% (2.2%).

PREDATORS AND DEFENSE. Natural enemies include various carnivorous mammals, raptors *(Aquila chrysaetos, Buteo albicaudatus, B. jamaicensis),* greater roadrunners *(Geococcyx californianus),* and other snakes *(Coluber constrictor, Masticophis flagellum)* (Fitch 1963a; Hammerson 1986; Parmley 1982; Ross 1989; Webb 1970). Accidents also claim the lives of coachwhips each year: many are killed while crossing roads (Price and LaPointe 1990; Rosen and Lowe 1994), others are killed in wild fires (Carr 1940; Simons 1989), and insecticides probably also adversely affect them (Herald 1949).

When first discovered in the open, *M. flagellum* quickly crawls away, and sometimes even climbs into trees or bushes to escape. If prevented from fleeing, it will turn, strike, and bite viciously, often aiming for the face. When handled, it thrashes about, bites (and often chews), and sprays musk and fecal matter. However, some play dead—cocking the head downward until the sclera are well exposed, opening the mouth, and partially extending the tongue (Gehlbach 1970; Smith 1975).

There is a folk tale that states that a large coachwhip will wrap its forebody around a human's leg and then lash its antagonist with its whiplike tail. This is entirely unfounded.

POPULATIONS. Unfortunately, no study of the population dynamics of this species has been reported. *M. flagellum* remains common in many undeveloped areas, where it can still be seen foraging during the day. It is one of the most common snakes in scrub woods in eastern Texas, accounting for 11.5% of snake captures (Ford et al. 1991), and it constituted 4.4% of the snakes found on Arizona State Road 85 by Rosen and Lowe (1994) in 1988–1991. Nevertheless, in disturbed habitats it is probably declining. It is currently protected in Alabama and Illinois.

REMARKS. *M. flagellum* was reviewed by Wilson (1970a, 1973b).

Masticophis lateralis (Hallowell 1853) | Striped Racer

RECOGNITION. This slender, long-tailed (29–30% of TBL) snake (TBL to 152.4 cm) is dark brown, dark gray, olive black, or black with a white to orange, black-bordered stripe extending down each side from just behind the posterior corner of the mouth to the anal vent or just beyond it. The labials are white to cream with some black speckles, and white spots may be present on other lateral head scales and the rostrum. The venter is white, cream, yellow, or orange; the underside of the tail is pink, and black speckles may be present on the anterior ventrals. Dorsal body scales are smooth, usually have apical pits, and occur in 17 rows both anteriorly and at midbody and in 13–14 rows near the tail. Present are 183–204 ventrals and 115–137 subcaudals; the anal plate is divided. Lateral head scales include 1 nasal, 1 loreal, 2 preoculars (the ventral most is small), 2 (2) postoculars, 2 + 2–3 + 2–4 temporals, 8 (7–9) supralabials, and 9 (8–10) infralabials. The bilobed hemipenis has a smooth tip, a single sulcus spermaticus, 3 large basal spines, 35–36

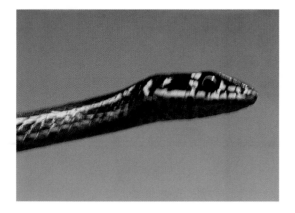

California striped racer, *Masticophis lateralis lateralis*; San Diego County, California. (Photograph by Robert E. Lovich)

Distribution of *Masticophis lateralis*.

smaller spines in 3–5 rows, and 10–11 rows of calyxes on the shaft. Each maxilla has 17–19 teeth, with the last 2–3 separated by a diastema.

Males average 194 ventrals and 129 subcaudals and have TLs about 30% of TBL; females average 196 ventrals and 121 subcaudals and have TLs about 29% of TBL.

GEOGRAPHIC VARIATION. Two subspecies have been described. The California striped racer, *M. l. lateralis* (Hallowell 1853), occurs from northern California south to central Baja California. It is dark brown, dark gray, or olive black with a white to pale yellow lateral stripe 0.25–1.0 scales wide, and anterior ventrals with dark spots. The Alameda striped racer, *M. l. euryxanthus* Riemer 1954, is found only in Alameda and Contra Costa counties, California. It is black with a yellow orange lateral stripe 1.5–2.0 scales wide, and no dark spots on the anterior ventrals.

CONFUSING SPECIES. To identify other *Masticophis*, refer to the key presented above. Garter and ribbon snakes *(Thamnophis)* have keeled body scales.

KARYOTYPE. Undescribed.

FOSSIL RECORD. Pleistocene (Rancholabrean) skeletal remains of *M. lateralis* are from the Rancho La Brea tar pits in California (LaDuke 1991).

DISTRIBUTION. This snake occurs from Trinity County in northern California southward west of the Sierra crest and desert and excluding most of the Central Valley of California to the vicinity of Socorro, Baja California Norte, and in Baja California Del Sur near San Ignacio.

HABITAT. The striped racer occurs from sea level to 2,100 m. In California, it is mostly found in foothill gullies, canyons, riparian zones along waterways, and rocky hillsides with grasses or extensive brush and chaparral. It ascends mountains to the scrub oak and pine belt, and in Baja California has even been found in desert habitats.

BEHAVIOR. Some active *M. lateralis* can be found in every month in southern California, but most California individuals hibernate from late October–early November to April–May, depending on latitude. Schwenkmeyer (1949) found one hibernating on 26 November in a cavity in loose packed soil and rocks about 30 cm below ground level on a steep shady side of a canyon in San Diego County. Annually most activity takes place in April–July; this snake does not estivate in the hot summer.

Daily activity is diurnal, usually between 0800 and 1800 hours, and follows closely the activity pattern of sympatric heliothermic lizards. Emergence is later on cloudy or foggy mornings, and prior to emergence the snake usually exposes only its head and neck for a period of time, with the head oriented to receive the direct rays of the sun. Following full emergence, the snakes usually bask with the body completely in full sunlight before beginning to forage. Basking normally ends when the deep BT has been raised about 13°C above the emergence BT; the amount of heating averages 0.45 (0.15–0.72) °C (Hammerson 1979). Those monitored by Hammerson (1979) had BTs of 17.1–27.6 (mean, 20.5) °C at morning emergence, 28.3–37.7 (mean, 33.4) °C while basking, and 27–35 (mean, 31.7) °C while retreating to their burrows at 1340–1820 hours. STs in full sunlight during the day were 17.7–50.0°C.

Like other *Masticophis*, the striped racer is an accomplished climber that has been seen as high as 3.5 m above ground in trees (Cunningham 1955).

Males become quite territorial and belligerent toward other males during the breeding season, often resorting to chasing and biting other males (Hammerson 1978).

REPRODUCTION. Stebbins (1985) gave 76 cm as the smallest adult TBL, and Goldberg (1975) found females with SVLs of 76.5–79.9 cm containing eggs.

Spermiogenesis begins in August and is completed in October in southern California; the sperm is stored in the vas deferens over winter. Upon emergence in March–April, the testes are regressed; the walls of the seminiferous tubules contain only spermatogonia and Sertoli cells, the lumina are partially or totally occluded by Sertoli syncytium, and the vas deferens is packed with mature sperm. The testes remain regressed through most of June. The spermatogonia begin to divide in late June, and primary and secondary spermatocytes are present in July (Goldberg 1975).

Yolking of eggs begins in mid-April in southern California, and enlarging follicles are found in May (Goldberg 1975). Oviductal eggs are present late May–July, and reported ovipositions have occurred from 27 May to 30 July, with most eggs laid in June and July. In view of this long nesting period, it is possible that more than one clutch is produced each year.

Mating occurs in April–May, either on the ground or up in shrubs (Hammerson 1978). Females engage in courtship for as long as 10 days after initial copulation, but whether or not multiple matings with different males occur is unknown. Males direct no courtship activity toward the same female the day

after copulation. Females remain passive prior to and during courtship. A courting male approaches a female, crawls onto her, and forms his body into a series of S-shaped loops along her back with his head facing toward her head. He then holds his head and neck several centimeters above those of the female, entwines his tail around her tail, and produces caudocephalic waves along his body. Simultaneously, he jerks his head from side to side, and rapidly tongue flicks. He does not rub his chin or head along the female's body, as is done by some other *Masticophis*. Insertion of a hemipenis occurs, and the tails unwind. The male does not undulate his body during copulation, but he may slowly thrust the rear portion of his body to insert the hemipenis deeper. Sometimes, the female may attempt to crawl off at this point, dragging the engaged male with her. Copulations observed by Hammerson (1978) lasted 15–130 minutes, but Perkins (1943) observed one that lasted 140 minutes.

Each clutch has 5–11 (mean, 7.5; n = 23) eggs. The elongated eggs are white and nonadherent, and average 42.8 (36–54) mm in length, 16.5 (12–20) mm in width, and 7.9 (7.5–8.2) g in mass. IP in the laboratory has lasted 60–94 (mean, 81) days. In the wild, hatchlings have been found in late October (Hammerson 1978); most eggs probably hatch from late August to October.

Hatchlings average 34.0 (33.8–34.3) mm in SVL and have the same coloration and two-striped pattern as adults; however, the contrast between light and dark pigment is more noticeable than in adults, and their lateral stripes may extend farther onto the tail (Ortenburger 1928).

GROWTH AND LONGEVITY. No growth data have been published. A male survived 4 years, 11 months, and 2 days at the Los Angeles Zoo (Snider and Bowler 1992). This species does poorly in captivity, often refusing to eat.

DIET AND FEEDING HABITS. Foraging is diurnal, both on the ground and in bushes and trees. When hunting at ground level, the snake glides forward with its head and neck held above the ground, and often stops and remains motionless with its head raised for some time as it visually searches. If a moving prey is detected, the snake crawls quickly after it, but if the prey is stationary, the snake may slowly approach it. All prey is seized in the mouth and quickly swallowed head first; no venom or constriction are applied.

Lizards *(Cnemidophorus, Eumeces, Gerrhonotus, Sceloporus, Uta)* are the primary prey (57% of the diet; Jaksic and Greene 1984), but small snakes *(Crotalus scutulatus, C. viridis),* voles *(Microtus),* birds *(Icterus galbula,* wrens), frogs, and insects are also consumed (Cornett 1982; Cunningham 1959; Fitch 1949; Hammerson 1978; Jaksic and Greene 1984; Klauber 1972; Ortenburger 1928; Stebbins 1954, 1985; Van Denburgh 1922; Walker 1946; Wright and Wright 1957).

PREDATORS AND DEFENSE. Fitch (1949) recorded 50 incidents of predation on *M. lateralis* by red-tailed hawks *(Buteo jamaicensis),* 7 by great horned owls *(Bubo virginianus),* and 7 by coyotes *(Canis latrans);* and a kestral *(Falco sparverius)* attacked a juvenile (Jennings 1997). Many are also killed on California highways each year.

The striped racer is a shy animal that usually flees along the ground or through bushes and trees when detected. When a burrow or some other subter-ranean retreat is nearby, the snake quickly crawls into it and disappears. If near water, it does not hesitate to dive in and swim to safety (Ortenburger 1928). Sometimes, it darts away, only to suddenly freeze in place farther along, or double back to its original position. When handled, *M. lateralis* often thrashes about, sprays musk, and may bite.

POPULATIONS. *M. lateralis* is probably one of the most common snakes in some parts of California. Juveniles are not often seen, and Fitch (1949) reported that 80–100 cm individuals were the most often recorded in the Sierra Nevada foothills of central California.

The subspecies *M. l. euryxanthus* is protected by California, and its chaparral habitat in Alameda, Contra Costa, San Jaquin, and Santa Clara counties is protected as critical habitat under the federal Endangered Species Act.

REMARKS. *M. lateralis* has been reviewed by Jennings (1983) and Riemer (1954).

Masticophis schotti Baird and Girard 1853 | Schott's Whipsnake

RECOGNITION. This snake was formerly considered a subspecies of the striped whipsnake *(M. taeniatus),* but was elevated to species status on the basis of a study of morphological and protein characters by Camper and Dixon (1994). It is a long, very thin snake (maximum TBL, 168 cm) with a bluish gray to greenish gray body with rusty red pigment on the sides of the neck and snout. Two white longitudinal stripes are present on each side of the body, one just above the ventral scutes, and the other on scale rows three to four. Midbody dorsal scales in rows seven to eight have light anterior borders. The venter is white anteriorly, but is speckled with bluish gray or is plain bluish gray behind this. The underside of the tail may be reddish. The smooth dorsal body scales have only one apical pit, and lie in 15 (13–14) anterior rows, 15 (13–14) rows at midbody, and 13 (9–14) posterior rows. The venter has 181–218 ventrals, 113–166 subcaudals, and a divided anal plate. Laterally on the head are 1 nasal, 1 (2–3) loreal(s), 2 (1–3) preoculars (the ventralmost is small), 2 (1–3) postoculars, 2 + 2 (1–3) + 2 (3) temporals, 8 (6–9) supralabials, and 9 (8–10) infralabials. The strongly bilobed hemipenis extends 6–13 subcaudals when inverted and has the single sulcus spermaticus extending to the tip of the longest lobe; the distal surface is smooth, but surrounded with deep, strongly fringed calyxes that change to spines about half-way along the shaft. Each maxilla has 15–23 teeth, with the last three longest teeth separated from the others by a diastema.

Males have longer SVLs than females, 181–212 ventrals, 120–166 subcaudals, and 9–12 preanal scale rows. Females have 181–218 ventrals, 113–162 subcaudals, and 11–14 preanal scale rows.

GEOGRAPHIC VARIATION. Two subspecies are recognized (Camper 1996b; Camper and Dixon 1994). Schott's whipsnake, *M. s. schotti* Baird and Girard 1853,

Schott's whipsnake, *Masticophis schotti schotti*; South Texas. (Photograph by John H. Tashjian, California Academy of Science)

Ruthven's whipsnake, *Masticophis schotti ruthveni*; South Texas. (Photograph by John H. Tashjian, California Academy of Science)

is found south of San Antonio in Texas, and ranges west into adjacent Mexico. It has paired pale cream spots on the border of the anterior dorsal scales, and always two prominent light dorsolateral stripes. Ruthven's whipsnake, *M. s. ruthveni* Ortenburger 1923, is found from the extreme southern Rio Grande Valley in Hidalgo and Starr counties, Texas, southward into Mexico. It has paired cream, yellow, or orange spots on the border of the anterior dorsal scales, zero to two narrow dorsolateral stripes, and a pinkish gray to green or almost black body.

CONFUSING SPECIES. Other species of *Masticophis* can be distinguished using the above key. Patch-nosed snakes *(Salvadora)* have a slightly projecting flap on each side of the rostral scale. Garter and ribbon snakes *(Thamnophis)* and the rough green snake *(Opheodrys aestivus)* have keeled body scales.

KARYOTYPE. The karyotype consists of 18 pairs of chromosomes, with 16 macrochromosomes (the sixth pair is acrocentric) and 20 microchromosomes. Females are ZW (the Z chromosome is submetacentric, and the W chromosome subtelocentric); males are ZZ (Baker et al. 1972).

FOSSIL RECORD. Unknown.

DISTRIBUTION. *M. schotti* ranges from Texas south of San Antonio on the Balcones Escarpment west to Coahuila and Nuevo León and south into Tamaulipas on the Gulf Coastal Plain and Guanajuato and Michoacán on the Mexican Plateau.

HABITAT. This snake lives in arid or semiarid brush (acacia, creosote, mesquite, ocotillo, opuntia cacti, thornbush), grassland, or desert habitats, but it can also be found in highlands to 2,000 m and along streams in riparian vegetation.

BEHAVIOR. The paucity of data on the life history of *M. schotti* is appalling, for it is not uncommon in proper habitat. It is more abundant than the sparsity of data regarding it would indicate; it has merely been

Distribution of *Masticophis schotti*.

neglected. It is active from late March through late September in Texas; no data are available on its over-wintering habits. This snake seems entirely diurnal, and may be found crawling along the surface of the ground at speeds up to 6 km/hour (Vermersch and Kuntz 1986). Occasionally it climbs into low bushes or trees to forage or bask.

REPRODUCTION. The TBL of the shortest adult *M. schotti* examined by Wright and Wright (1957) was 76.2 cm, but Conant and Collins (1998) reported a minimum adult TBL of 101.6 cm. Males mature in one to two years, and females in three years (Vermersch and Kuntz 1986). Courtship and mating apparently take place in the spring after the snakes emerge from hibernation.

All data available on eggs and hatchlings are based on clutches laid by captives. Oviposition dates range from 6 May to 14 June, and clutches average 7.5 (3–12) eggs (Gloyd and Conant 1934b; McCrystal and Dixon 1983). The white, ellipsoidal eggs have leathery, non-adherent, roughly granulated shells; mean length, width, and mass are 48.6 (36.5–80.2) mm, 22.4 (17.2–27.0) mm, and 15.3 (11.3–18.1) g, respectively. The RCM of a clutch was 0.430 (Gloyd and Conant 1934b). Eggs incubated by McCrystal and Dixon (1983) at 25–27°C hatched 80–81 days later, so in nature the young would probably hatch in August and early September. Hatchlings differ somewhat from adults; they have more white on the face and pink on the sides of the head and throat, and they are more brown (McCrystal and Dixon 1983).They average 39.3 (35.5–43.2) cm in TBL and 9.8 (9.3–10.6) g in mass.

GROWTH AND LONGEVITY. No data are available on either growth rates or survivorship.

DIET AND FEEDING HABITS. *M. schotti* is an active diurnal forager that cruises along with its head and forebody raised above the ground. Prey are apparently detected by sight: moving prey are attacked quickly, while those that remain still require a longer time to find and attack. Moving prey are chased and seized in the mouth. If the prey is small, it is swallowed immediately, but if it is large, the animal may be pinned on the ground with a body loop while the snake manipulates it to be swallowed head first.

M. schotti is a generalist feeder on a variety of small vertebrates. Camper and Dixon (2000) and Vermersch and Kuntz (1986) reported it eats lizards (*Cnemidophorus, Eumeces, Sceloporus, Scincella*, and family Polychridae), so lizards probably make up the bulk of its diet (78% in the study by Camper and Dixon). Wild *M. schotti* also eat small mammals (22%; Camper and Dixon 2000). Captives have consumed mice (*Mus musculus*), small rats (*Rattus norvegicus*), eggs and fledglings of house sparrows (*Passer domesticus*), garter snakes (*Thamnophis*), and ranid frogs (*Rana clamitans, R. pipiens*), and a large *M. schotti* even tried to eat a smaller one (Gloyd and Conant 1934b). Toads, however, are probably avoided, as parotoid gland poison from a marine toad (*Bufo marinus*) administered orally by Licht and Low (1968) caused cardiac stimulation and lethal cardiac arrest in a *M. schotti* within an hour.

PREDATORS AND DEFENSE. No reports of predation on *M. schotti* exist, but it must be the prey of many carnivorous mammals, hawks, and snake-eating serpents. Many are killed on Texas roads each year, and this and the destruction of its natural habitat are the greatest threats it faces.

M. schotti will first try to flee, and can quickly disappear among vegetation if given the chance. Its striped pattern helps conceal how fast the snake is moving until suddenly the tail crosses our path of vision and it is gone. Tennant (1984) has also commented as to its resemblance, when its body is held rigid, to the seasonally bare stems and branches of thorny vegetation. If prevented from escaping, *M. schotti* is a good fighter, viciously striking and biting, and if handled, thrashing and spraying musk and feces.

POPULATIONS. *M. schotti* is locally and seasonally abundant in the proper habitat. It was formerly quite common in Hidalgo and Starr counties, Texas, but is now rare because of destruction of its thornbush habitat (Tennant 1984).

REMARKS. *M. schotti* was reviewed by Camper (1996b) and Camper and Dixon (1994).

Masticophis taeniatus (Hallowell 1852) | Striped Whipsnake

RECOGNITION.   *M. taeniatus* is a large (TBL to 183.9 cm), slender, long-tailed (36–40% of TBL), variably colored and patterned snake (see GEOGRAPHIC VARIATION). Body color is reddish brown to dark brown, gray, or black, and it sometimes has a bluish or olive cast. Usually two cream or white longitudinal stripes are present along the sides of the body, but some individuals lack these, others have the dark sides further bisected to form up to four stripes, and still others merely have a series of white patches along their sides. Narrow patches of white pigment on the back may resemble light crossbands. The head is distinct from the neck, with large eyes, and white labials, chin, and throat. Some dorsal head scales may be light bordered. The venter is white, cream, or yellow; the underside of the tail is pink or red. Dorsal body scales are smooth with 2 (0–3) apical pits; there are 15 anterior rows, 15 (occasionally 12–14) midbody rows, and 9–13 rows near the vent. Ventrals total 183–236, subcaudals 105–178; the anal plate is divided. Each side of the head has 1 nasal, 1 (2) loreal(s), 2 (1–3) preoculars (the lowest is small), 2 (1–3) postoculars, 2–3 + 2–3 + 2–3 temporals, 8 (7–9) supralabials, and 9 (8–11) infralabials. The cylindrical, bilobed hemipenis extends 4–15 subcaudals when inverted; it has a single sulcus spermaticus, a naked apex, 9–10 continuous rows of calyxes with blunt spines at their edges around the shaft, 3–5 rows of small spines near the base (increasing in size toward the base), and three large basal spines. Each maxilla has 15–17 teeth; the three most posterior ones are longer and stouter than the rest, and are separated from the other teeth by a diastema.

Sexual dimorphism is not pronounced. Males have 183–236 ventrals, 117–175 subcaudals, and TLs 44.4% of TBL; females have 187–232 ventrals, 105–178 subcaudals, and TLs 44.1% of TBL.

GEOGRAPHIC VARIATION.   Two subspecies are recognized (Camper 1996c; Camper and Dixon 1994). The desert striped whipsnake, *M. t. taeniatus* (Hallowell 1852), ranges from south-central Washington and southern Idaho, eastern Utah, and western Colorado south through western Oregon, western California, Nevada, and central and southeastern Arizona to New Mexico. It is dark brown, dark gray, or black,

and it usually has the light longitudinal body stripe bisected by a black line to form two light stripes, additional black lines along the lower sides, no light crossbands on the back, and a yellowish venter grading to white anteriorly and pinkish posteriorly. The Central Texas whipsnake, *M. t. girardi* (Stejneger and Barbour 1917), occurs from central Texas west to Coahuila and south in Mexico to Guanajuato and Michoacán. It is reddish brown, dull purplish black, or shiny black, and its light longitudinal stripe may either extend the length of the body or be interrupted to form white blotches along the sides. Light crossbands are present on the back, the grayish venter has dark spots at the edge of the ventral scutes, and the underside of the tail is coral red. The dorsal pattern is quite variable across the range; a light pattern is found throughout the Chihuahuan Desert, a dark pattern commonly on the Edwards Plateau, and an intermediate pattern throughout the subspecies' range (see Camper 1996c

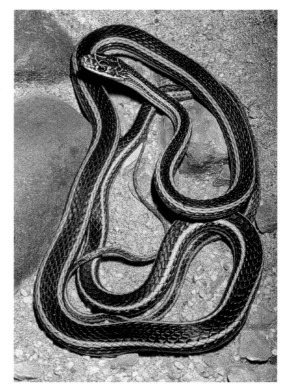

Striped whipsnake, *Masticophis taeniatus*; Yavapai County, Arizona. (Photograph by Brad R. Moon)

or Camper and Dixon 1994). To add to the confusion, there is a high incidence of melanism in *M. t. girardi* in the Cuatro Cienegas Basin of Coahuila, Mexico (Camper and Dixon 1990).

CONFUSING SPECIES. Other whipsnakes can be identified by the above key. Patch-nosed snakes *(Salvadora)* have black longitudinal body stripes, and a slightly projecting flap on each side of the rostral scale. Garter and ribbon snakes *(Thamnophis)* have keeled body scales and a light medial stripe. The racer *(Coluber constrictor)* is uniformly olive, dark gray, or brown dorsally and yellowish ventrally.

KARYOTYPE. The total chromosome compliment is 36, with 2 acrocentric and 14 biarmed macrochromosomes and 20 microchromosomes. The NOR is on the first pair of microchromosomes (Camper and Hanks 1995).

FOSSIL RECORD. Pleistocene (Rancholabrean) to early Holocene remains of *M. taeniatus* are known from Nevada (Brattstrom 1954a), and fossils of either *M. taeniatus* or *M. flagellum* have been found in New Mexico (Van Devender and Worthington 1977) and Texas (Hill 1971; Holman 1966, 1969a).

DISTRIBUTION. *M. taeniatus* ranges from south-central Washington south through the Great Basin to New Mexico and central Texas, and south to Hildalgo, Guanajuato and Michoacán, Mexico.

HABITAT. A variety of habitats are used, ranging from arid grasslands and sagebrush flats to piñon-juniper woodlands and pine-oak forests, but deserts are avoided. Over most of the range *M. taeniatus* is an upland snake, living in rock and brush covered foothills, mesas, valleys, brakes, and mountain canyons with elevations to 3,077 m (Stumpel 1995), but usually below 2,000 m.

BEHAVIOR. *M. taeniatus* is strictly diurnal and is most active in the morning and late afternoon. Annually, active individuals have been observed as early as late March or early April, with peak activity in May and June in Washington and Oregon (Storm and Leonard 1995), and from late March to early November in New Mexico (Degenhardt et al. 1996). They usually bask after emerging in the morning, sometimes above ground in shrubs. Active whipsnakes in northwestern Utah had mean CTs of 28.5 (20.0–36.5) °C in the spring, 28.8 (27.0–35.0) °C in the summer, and 27.5 (18.0–36.0) °C in the autumn (Hirth and King 1969). Hirth et al. (1969) reported BTs of 29–35°C for active *M. taeniatus* on their foraging grounds. In northern Utah, Parker and Brown (1980) found that those moving on clear days had the following mean seasonal CTs: spring, 32.8 (31.2–34.8) °C; summer, 32.76 (19.9–38.4) °C; and autumn, 32.64 (31.2–33.7) °C. Mean CTs taken on cloudy days were as follows: spring, 32.6 (25.6–37.6) °C; summer, 33.0 (25.8–37.2) °C; and autumn, 27.1 (21.0–33.5) °C. The preferred BT was 32–33°C. Mean ETs for these conditions and seasons

Distribution of *Masticophis taeniatus*.

were lower than the snakes' mean CTs, and *M. taeniatus* seems to achieve above ground temperature regulation by placing a portion of its coiled body (either more or less than 50%) in full sunlight.

The amount of body fat varies throughout the year, coinciding with the reproductive cycles and preparation for hibernation. Males have relatively constant body fat in spring–early summer, but the amount of fat increases considerably in July–September, then decreases from late September through early April (Parker and Brown 1980). Female fat body indexes are higher, and vary during the year; from October through April female fat content is relatively constant, but as eggs are yolked in the spring–early summer the amount of stored fat declines rapidly. After oviposition, fat is quickly deposited until hibernation begins in September–October.

The winter months are spent in hibernation, often in communal dens shared with other snake species (Parker 1976; Woodbury and Hansen 1950). Usually these sites are in deep, south-facing, rock crevices, but probably some *M. taeniatus* use mammal or desert tortoise burrows to hibernate. Striped whipsnakes entering northern Utah hibernacula begin to arrive in early September and continue to come for 35–48 days (Parker and Brown 1980). Arrivals are rather evenly spaced throughout this period, with no difference in the arrival dates of adult males and females, but most juveniles reach the hibernaculum later than adults. Maximum daily AT during the arrival period is generally over 15 °C, but occasionally is as low as 11 °C; the snakes seldom arrive on rainy days. Early arrival seems correlated to a particularly early spring emergence that year, and late arrivers are generally those who left the den late the previous spring. On average, Utah *M. taeniatus* remain surface active around the den for up to 37 days before disappearing below ground for good. Males normally spend fewer days (151–238) in hibernation than females (149–246). Juveniles stay underground 184–227 days. Hirth (1966a) found that adult females hibernate an average of 209 (162–245) days, and adult males 212 (190–233) days. Spring emergence occurs from late April through late May. BTs of subterranean *M. taeniatus* averaged 22.7 (19.0–27.9) °C in the fall and 29.0 (26.0–32.3) °C in the spring, while the ETs were 17.0–22.4°C in the fall and 16.6–25.6°C in the spring (Parker and Brown 1980).

Hibernating *M. taeniatus* usually lose body weight over the winter. During Hirth's (1966a) study, adult females lost an average of 9.4 (2.8–19.0) % of their body mass during hibernation, and adult males 9.4 (0.9–21.3) %. In a hibernation study by Parker and Brown (1980) males lost 0–19.3% of body mass, females 0–25.4%, and juveniles 1.15–21.4%.

Overwintering mortality at northern Utah hibernacula can be high. Nineteen (38.7%) of 49 *M. taeniatus* marked by Hirth (1966a) could not be found the next spring, and at the dens studied by Parker and Brown (1980) only 25.8 (0–75) % of juveniles overwintered successfully. However, mean adult survivorship during Parker and Brown's study was much higher: 97.0 (93.4–100) % for males, and 94.9 (87.5–100) % for females.

Most striped whipsnakes return to the same hibernaculum each year, but about 2% use other hibernacula in some years (Parker and Brown 1980). Hirth (1966b) displaced 20 *M. taeniatus* 50–274 m in all compass directions from a Utah hibernaculum; 14 were later recovered at the den site. The majority of the whipsnakes displaced 50 m returned in 1–2 days; but only one female returned after displacement of 100 m (in 39 days). A male Hirth had moved 274 m northeast of the hibernaculum in the fall was recovered at the den the following spring. Of 15 *M. taeniatus* displaced up to 300 m north, east, and south of a hibernaculum by Parker and Brown (1980), all but one returned to the den within 14 days, including a male temporarily blinded by painting over its eye spectacles. Displaced males outfitted with radio transmitters made counterclockwise movements using a north-south ridge as an orientation landmark while returning to the den (Parker and Brown 1980). Six snakes were displaced 0.85–16.8 km in light-tight boxes to different hibernacula by Parker and Brown (1980). Four displaced over 3 km remained at the new den sites, but two displaced 0.85 km came home, and another traveled to a strange den.

After spring emergence, males were seen more often than females and at a greater number of locations within 200 m of the hibernaculum; the mean distance moved by males was 54.4 (5–163) m, and females moved an average of 65.3 (18–170) m (Parker and Brown 1980). Males finally migrated away from the area around the hibernaculum in 19–51 days after emergence, and females left in 13–42 days. Mean daily distance moved by males from the den site was 272 (32–368) m; females averaged 267.2 (66–415) m. Males moved a mean maximum distance from the hibernaculum of 0.99 (0.37–1.69) km; females moved 1.45 (0.83–2.75) km. Gravid females with radio transmitters averaged more than one move per day, made trips of 7.0–339.5 m before oviposition, and made trips of 46.1–151.0 m after laying their eggs (Parker and Brown 1972, 1980). Hirth et al. (1969) found that some *M. taeniatus* moved 1.5–3.6 km from their hibernaculum, and most dispersed 150–220°S.

Male combat occurs in this species, particularly if one male invades the breeding territory of another male. Storm and Leonard (1995) observed a large male *M. taeniatus* grasp another large male by the neck; then the two snakes entwined and thrashed about, but the bitten snake received superficial wounds, which is inconsistent with normal ritualized male combat in snakes. Similar entwining and rolling behavior was noted in Utah by Bennion and Parker (1976) and Parker and Brown (1980).

M. taeniatus is quite arboreal, and may ascend into low bushes or trees to bask or forage; the usual climbing height is 0.6–1.0 m (Hirth et al. 1969).

REPRODUCTION. The minimum SVL of mature Utah males examined by Parker and Brown (1980) was 53 cm, and that of females was 74 cm; but Hirth (1966a) reported a minimum SVL for sexually mature Utah males of 62.5 cm, and of 58 cm for females with ovarian follicles with diameters of at least 4 mm. Maturation occurs in two to three years.

The sexual cycle of males from northern Utah begins in June when spermatogonia begin to divide and produce primary spermatocytes (Goldberg and Parker 1975). By July secondary spermatocytes and some spermatids are present in the tubules, and Sertoli cells are common. Spermatogenesis begins in late July, when spermatids begin to metamorphose, and continues through September, when mature sperm are present in the tubule lumens, the tubules are at their greatest diameter, and the testes are their largest. Regression begins in October as sperm pass into the vas deferens for storage over winter. The testes are regressed in the spring (April–May) following hibernation, with tubule diameters and epithelial thickness greatly reduced and spermatogonia and Sertoli cells present. Large numbers of sperm are present in the vas deferens and interstitial cells are at their greatest diameter throughout the spring–early summer, and mating occurs then.

Courtship and mating take place in the spring soon after emergence from hibernation. Males remain near the hibernaculum actively searching for females, and females probably mate with several different males or the same male several times. In northern Utah, mating activity occurred from 3 April to 23 May (Hirth et al. 1969; Parker and Brown 1980). Males probably find females by following their pheromone trails, although a female is pursued if seen. While searching for a mate, the male crawls for several minutes, stops, and then remains motionless for several minutes with his head about 10–12 cm above the ground, perhaps visually searching for a mate (Bennion and Parker 1976)—very similar to foraging behavior. He then crawls off and repeats the sequence somewhere else. Females usually lie motionless near or under cover and generally remain passive throughout the courtship. When the male detects a female, he approaches from the rear, crawls onto her back, and follows every curve along the length of her body until his head is about 20 cm in front of her head. He then turns to face her, and remains stationary for two to three minutes; then he makes a series of S-shaped loops around the female, with two to three individual loops per set. Following each loop series, he remains motionless for up to three minutes. Once 15–20 such loop sets are performed, the male places his head directly onto that of the female and begins to entwine his anterior body around her head and neck. She responds by lowering her head to the ground. He finally uncoils his body from her, slides posteriorly, coils the remainder of his body around her posterior two-thirds and tail, and begins to rub her back with his chin. The pair usually uncoil and coil about each other during this phase. They then uncoil and remain motionless beside each other. The male repeats the S-shaped loop phase several times after this, and finally places his tail beneath that of the female, undulates his body, and inserts a hemipenis into her cloaca. He also may attempt to pin her head to the ground at this point (Bennion and Parker 1976).

Reported ovipositions have occurred from 1 June

through 12 July, but most nesting occurs in June. Parker and Brown (1972) tracked two radio-equipped females, and found their nests were within abandoned rodent burrows situated on a gently sloping, south-facing, relatively open slope, where the clutches were laid in horizontal tunnels at depths of 36 and 41 cm from the surface.

The elongated, white, nonadherent eggs have leathery shells with rough granulated surfaces. They average 46.6 (33.0–65.4) mm in length and 15.2 (6.0–25.4) mm in width, and weigh about 9 g. Clutch size averages 6 (3–12) eggs; it is not known if more than one clutch is produced each year. RCM is about 0.410 (Parker and Brown 1980; Seigel and Fitch 1984). The IP in northern Utah is 44–58 days, but clutches from there incubated in the laboratory at 30°C took an average of 53.8 (50–58) days to hatch (Parker and Brown 1980), and Degenhardt et al. (1996) hatched eggs in the laboratory in 62–81 days. The young emerge from natural nests in August and September.

Hatchlings resemble adults in color and pattern, but are often more reddish, have a light crossband just behind the head, and have the most prominent light longitudinal stripe on scale rows three to four. Average TBL of hatchlings is 34.9 (25.4–43.2) cm, and mass averages 7.2 (4.4–9.2) g.

GROWTH AND LONGEVITY. Growth has only been studied in northern Utah populations. Heyrend and Call (1951) and Parker and Brown (1980) showed that the growth rate of smaller/younger individuals of both sexes is faster than that of larger/older adults, and that a steady decrease occurs in the growth rate as the snakes become longer. Those studied by Heyrend and Call (1951) had the following average TBLs: age one, 60.7 cm; age two, 78.9 cm; age three, 86.3 cm; age four, 87.3 cm; and age five, 85.8 cm. SVLs of *M. taeniatus* measured by Parker and Brown (1980) were slightly longer, averaging as follows: age one, approximately 67 cm; age two, 83 cm; age three, 87 cm; age four, 89 cm; and age five, 90 cm. In both studies females grew slower than males. While growth decreased with size/age, body mass increased as the snakes grew.

A captive lived 3 years, 11 months, and 26 days at Chicago's Brookfield Zoo (Snider and Bowler 1992).

These very nervous snakes do poorly in captivity, and although the maximum natural survival time is unknown, Parker and Brown (1980) estimated that few would survive 20 years in the wild.

DIET AND FEEDING HABITS. *M. taeniatus* is an active, diurnal forager that crawls through brush and grass with its head elevated as it looks for prey (Smith et al. 1999). It may pause for periods of time with its head raised, resembling a male searching for a female (see above), or even climb into bushes or low trees to raid bird nests. If the prey remains in place when sighted, the snake slowly crawls to it, but if the prey moves it is chased and caught. Small prey are quickly swallowed, usually head first, but if the prey is large, *M. taeniatus* may pin the prey to the ground with a coil while it changes position for easier swallowing. This snake has a Duvernoy's gland with some mucous cells mixed in with the serous cells (Taub 1967), but there is no evidence that it envenomates prey, nor does it constrict it.

A wide variety of animals are consumed: lizards (*Callisaurus, Cnemidophorus, Cophosaurus, Holbrookia, Phrynosoma, Sceloporus, Urosaurus, Uta,* Anguidae, and Crotaphytidae) and snakes *(Bogertophis subocularis, Crotalus atrox, C. scutulatus, C. viridis, Salvadora hexalepis, Sonora semiannulata, Thamnophis elegans)* are the main prey items, but bats *(Tadarida brasiliensis),* small rodents, nestling birds (possibly also eggs), spadefoots *(Scaphiopus* sp.), and insects (beetles and ants, probably secondarily ingested) are also ingested (Camper and Dixon 2000; Klauber 1972; Pack 1930; Punzo 2000; Storm and Leonard 1995; Tennant 1984; Vermersch and Kuntz 1986; Woodbury 1933, 1952). Lizards made up 88%, snakes 4%, mammals 5.5%, and insects 2.4% of the prey found in *M. taeniatus* by Camper and Dixon (2000). Juveniles eat the same foods as adults. Captives accept small mice *(Mus),* lizards *(Anolis, Cnemidophorus, Leptodactylus, Sceloporus, Urosaurus, Uta),* and snakes *(Thamnophis).* Live, moving prey are more readily accepted than stationary or dead prey (Smith et al. 1999).

PREDATORS AND DEFENSE. Predatory records are scarce. Hawks *(Buteo jamaicensis, B. regalis, B. swainsoni;* Pritchett and Alfonzo 1988; Ross 1989), and probably carnivorous mammals, other birds, and snakes, feed on it. Motorized vehicles are also a major concern.

This nervous snake will flee if given a chance, and it is very difficult to catch as it moves through brush where its striped pattern masks its rate of speed. If a rock crevice or rodent burrow is nearby, it quickly retreats underground. It may even ascend low bushes and trees and "jump" from one to another if pursued (Storm and Leonard 1995). However, some will freeze in place and remain motionless when discovered. If restrained, the snake thrashes about, sprays musk, and quickly bites.

POPULATIONS. In Texas, *M. taeniatus* is locally common in the west, but is uniformly common throughout the rest of its range in the state. It only seems scarce because it lives in brushlands, where it is difficult to detect.

In northern Utah hibernacula have provided useful population data. From 1939 through 1950 Woodbury and his associates (Heyrend and Call 1951; Julian 1951; Woodbury and Hansen 1950) researched a hibernaculum in the Tintic Mountains that yielded 1,056 *M. taeniatus*: 654 males and 402 females, for a sex ratio of 1.6:1.0. This same den was later studied by Hirth and King (1968), who calculated biomasses of 170 g for hatchlings/juveniles in 1964, but only 31 g in 1965 and 90 g in 1966. For the same years, the biomass assessments of adults were as follows: 1964, 2.96 kg for males and 5.19 kg for females; 1965, 3.92 kg for males and 5.26 kg for females; and 1966, 2.86 kg for males and 4.61 kg for females. The combined adult sex ratio for the three years was 0.65:1.00; the combined hatchling/juvenile to adult ratio was 0.07:1.00. The sex

ratio at this hibernaculum was 1.23:1.00 in 1970–72 and 1.00:1.00 in 1971–72 (Parker 1976). A steady decline in numbers of snakes using the den occurred from 1950 through 1972 (Parker and Brown 1973), partially caused by dynamiting of the den in the 1950s in an attempt to kill the rattlesnakes (*Crotalus viridis*) that also hibernated there.

A series of seven hibernacula on Tooele County, Utah, including the original Woodbury den, were studied from 1969 through 1972 by Parker (1976), who estimated the combined 1974 population of *M. taeniatus* to be 543 individuals, and estimated a summer density on the foraging grounds of 0.19 (0.15–0.22)/ha. Woodbury (in Hirth and King 1968) had projected the maximum summer density to be 39/ha. Summer biomass densities for this snake at three hibernacula were 17.7, 22.5, and 26 g/ha, respectively, and the adult sex ratio for the winter of 1973–74 was 1.64:1.00. Further calculations of population and biomass densities from data collected from 1969 through 1972 at these dens yielded the following ranges of numbers of individuals and biomass on the summer feeding grounds: 0.11–0.33 individuals/ha, and 14.3–39.9 g/ha (Parker and Brown 1980). The sex ratio of four clutches of eggs incubated by Parker and Brown (1980) was 1.60:1.00.

Annual survivorship for first-year *M. taeniatus* in northern Utah was low, but one- to five-year-olds had 80–100% survivorship, and adults exhibited an 80% annual survivorship rate (Parker and Brown 1980).

REMARKS. *M. taeniatus* was reviewed by Camper (1996c), Camper and Dixon (1994), and Parker (1982).

Nerodia Baird and Girard 1853

Water Snakes

Key to the Species of *Nerodia*

1a. Eye separated from supralabials by one or more small subocular scales 2
1b. No subocular scales present 3

2a. Venter cream colored and largely unmarked (some small brown lateral spots may be present near the tail); found east of Mobile Bay, Alabama .... *N. floridana*

2b. Venter dark with light markings; found west of Mobile Bay, Alabama . . . . *N. cyclopion*

3a. Dorsum patterned with four alternating rows of dark blotches (occasionally fused to form transverse bars); central Texas 4

3b. Dorsum not patterned as in 3a; not restricted to central Texas 5

4a. Venter patternless (or with only a few small, indistinct spots); Colorado / Concho watershed . . . *N. paucimaculata*

4b. Each side of venter marked with dark spots; Brazos watershed . . . . *N. harteri*

5a. Venter unmarked red or yellow, or with markings only along the outer edges of the ventrals . . . *N. erythrogaster*

5b. Venter heavily patterned with dark markings 6

6a. Parietal scales posteriorly divided into smaller scales, dorsal pattern consisting of 21–26 distinct blotches in adults, normally 11 or more infralabials . . . . *N. taxispilota*

6b. Parietal scales not posteriorly subdivided; adult dorsal pattern (if present) consists of more than 26 blotches; normally 10 infralabials 7

7a. Dorsum normally has 27 rhomboid-shaped dark blotches

connected at the corners; midbody scale rows usually 27 (25–31) . . . . *N. rhombifer*

7b. Dorsal markings neither rhomboidal nor connected at corners; midbody scale rows usually less than 25 (19–25) 8

8a. Dark stripe from eye to corner of mouth; dorsum usually with transverse light bands (rarely stripes) . . . *N. fasciata*

8b. No dark stripe from eye to corner of mouth; dorsum unpatterned or patterned with longitudinal stripes, dark spots, or dark transverse bands 9

9a. Venter black or dark brown to reddish brown with a median longitudinal row of light spots; dorsal pattern of light or dark longitudinal stripes, dark spots, or dark transverse bands . . . . *N. clarkii*

9b. Venter cream or yellow with a pattern of either reddish brown half-moon-shaped marks or reddish brown pigment along the transverse seams; dorsum with dark transverse bands on neck and anterior portion of body and alternating dark dorsal and lateral blotches on rest of body and tail (Lake Erie individuals may lack or have only a faint dorsal pattern) . . . . *N. sipedon*

Nerodia clarkii (Baird and Girard 1853) | Saltmarsh Snake

RECOGNITION. *N. clarkii* is gray, olive, or black to yellow or brick red, and may be unpatterned or have light or dark longitudinal stripes, dark dorsal spots, or transverse bands (see GEOGRAPHIC VARIATION). The supralabials have dark bars. The venter is yellow, brown, or reddish brown and is patterned with a single medial row of light spots or with a medial row flanked by two rows of small light spots. Dorsal body scales are keeled and doubly pitted, and occur in 21 anterior, 21–23 midbody, and 17 posterior rows. Beneath are 123–138 ventrals, 57–88 subcaudals, and a divided anal plate. On each side of the head are 2 nasals (partially divided by the nostril), 1 loreal, 1 preocular, 2 (3) postoculars, 1 + 2–3 temporals, 8 (7–9) supralabials, and 10 (9–11) infralabials. The hemipenis has few spines, but many spinules, and several enlarged basal hooks; the single sulcus spermaticus is not forked. Each maxilla has 18–20 teeth.

Males are shorter, with 125–131 ventrals, 76–88 subcaudals, and TLs 25.8–48.1 (mean, 30.0) % of TBL.

The larger females have 123–138 ventrals, 57–76 subcaudals, and TLs 22.5–26.4 (mean, 24.5) % of TBL.

GEOGRAPHIC VARIATION. Three subspecies are recognized. *N. c. clarkii* (Baird and Girard 1853), the Gulf saltmarsh snake, ranges along the Gulf Coast from Citrus County, Florida, west to southern Texas. It has two dark brown and two tan or yellow longitudinal stripes on each side, and a medial row of white or yellow spots on a brown to reddish brown venter (some individuals have an additional row of small light spots on each side). *N. c. compressicauda* Kennicott 1860a, the mangrove saltmarsh snake, can be found along the coast of Florida from Palm Beach County west to Hernando County, on the Florida Keys, and on the northern coast of Cuba. It is gray, olive, black, yellow, or brick red, and may either be unpatterned or have dark dorsal spots or transverse bands; the venter has a medial row of light spots that becomes indistinct or irregular posteriorly. It inter-

Mangrove saltmarsh snake, *Nerodia clarkii compressicauda*; Monroe County, Florida. (Photograph by Carl H. Ernst)

grades with *N. c. clarkii* along the Gulf coastal plain of Florida. *N. c. taeniata* (Cope 1895), the Atlantic saltmarsh snake, probably originally occurred along the Atlantic Coast of Florida from Volusia County south to Martin County, but today is restricted to the coast of Volusia County (Kochman and Christman 1992). It intergrades with *N. c. compressicauda* in Brevard and Indian River counties (Dunson 1979; Hebrard and Lee 1981). It has dark anterior lateral stripes, dark blotches posteriorly, and a medial row of light spots on the venter. Moler (1992) noted that there is a striking resemblance between *N. c. taeniata* and intergrades of *N. c. clarkii* and *N. c. compressicauda* from nearly the same latitude of the Florida Gulf Coast, and thought that *N. c. taeniata* may represent a Pleistocene relict population of intergrades with an ancestor that no longer occurs on the Atlantic Coast of Florida.

CONFUSING SPECIES. Crawfish snakes of the genus *Regina* have less than 20 midbody scale rows. Garter and ribbon snakes *(Thamnophis)* have an undivided anal plate and one light lateral stripe. The lined snake *(Tropidoclonion lineatum)* has two rows of dark half-moon marks extending down its venter, and an undivided anal plate. The cottonmouth *(Agkistrodon piscivorus)* has a hole between the nostril and eye, vertically elliptical pupils, light facial markings, and only a single row of subcaudals.

KARYOTYPE. Undescribed.

FOSSIL RECORD. No fossils have been assigned directly to *Nerodia clarkii*, but some of the Pleistocene remains from Hillsbourgh County, Florida, identified only to the genus *Nerodia* or tentatively assigned to *N. fasciata* by Meylan (1995) may be *N. clarkii*.

DISTRIBUTION. It ranges from Volusia County to Brevard and Indian River counties on the Atlantic coastal plain of Florida, and from Palm Beach County and the Florida Keys west along the Gulf coastal plain to the vicinity of Corpus Christi, Texas, and also occurs on the northern coast of Cuba.

HABITAT. *N. clarkii* is a saltmarsh resident that requires at least brackish waters, but may occasionally enter freshwater. It occupies shallow salt marshes, red mangrove swamps, and estuaries ranging in salinity from brackish to seawater. Nevertheless, it prefers to live in freshwater rather than seawater (Pettus 1958, 1963; Zug and Dunson 1979), and maintains water balance through utilization of rainwater (Miller 1985), preformed water from its prey, and water derived from oxidative metabolism. Its skin is impervious to sodium and saltwater influx, and Dunson (1980) thought the species to be in the process of evolving into a true marine species.

Dehydration is a problem. Dunson (1982) kept *N. c. compressicauda* in air (at 30°C) pumped at 300 ml/minute, and the snakes lost 21–55% of their mass per day.

Distribution of *Nerodia clarkii*.

BEHAVIOR. *N. clarkii* is active in every month, especially in southern Florida. More northern populations are probably inactive in the winter, especially during very cold years.

Our experience in Florida indicates that this snake is mostly nocturnal, and is infrequently found during the day. Days are spent under cover, often under rocks, logs, or other debris, but sometimes in crab (*Uca*) burrows or muskrat lodges; it seldom basks. Foraging begins at dusk, especially at low tide, and continues to near midnight. The authors have successfully maintained these snakes in the laboratory at a mean AT of 27 (25–28) °C, but wild individuals are probably forced to withstand ETs below or above this.

N. clarkii frequently moves about. Phillips (1939) recovered one about 0.47 km from where it had been originally captured a year earlier. No other movement data are available.

It is an excellent swimmer, usually moving near the surface, but it can dive and progress underwater for some distance, particularly when trying to escape. The authors have seen them dive to depths of nearly 2 m.

REPRODUCTION. Both sexes mature at a SVL of about 38 cm, and possibly as short as 36.7 cm (Wright and Wright 1957), probably in two to three years. Mitchell (in Wright and Wright 1957) found a female in January in Texas that contained 14 embryos (4 on one side and 10 on the other); 1 embryo was 15.3 cm long.

Depending on latitude, the mating season extends from January through the early spring. Swanson (1948) thought the mating season of *N. c. compressicauda* from the Florida Keys is 24 January–22 February. During courtship observed by him, the male approached a female, moved his snout anteriorly along her body until his head covered her head, and erratically jerked his body and head. When in contact with her body, this jerking had a rubbing function. He next tried to position his tail beneath her tail to accomplish intromission, and often had to thrust a U-shaped loop of tail beneath the posterior portion of the female's body to locate the cloacal vent.

This species is viviparous, and after a GP of at least 90–100 days most young are born in late July to late August, but an October parturition is know (Kochman and Christman 1992). Litters consist of 1 (Kochman and Christman 1992) to 24 (Wright and Wright 1957) young (mean, 11; n = 32), and the number of offspring per litter increases with female body length. Neonates are colored and patterned like the adults, are 14.0–26.7 (mean, 19.5; n = 19) cm long, and weigh 4.3–9.0 (mean, 6.0) g.

GROWTH AND LONGEVITY. No growth data are available. Because of their special environmental requirements, *N. clarkii* is not often kept in captivity, and longevity data have not been reported. The authors have had them survive over three years in their laboratory, but wild individuals live much longer than this.

DIET AND FEEDING HABITS. Saltmarsh snakes feed primarily on small fish (*Cyprinodon variegatus, Eu-*

cinostomus argenteus, Fundulus grandis, F. heteroclitus, F. seminolis, F. similis, Lucania parva, Poecilia latipinna, Tilapia sp., and Mugilidae), but also takes crabs (Uca sp.) and small frogs (Rana catesbeiana) and toads (Allen 1939b; Carr 1940; Miller and Mushinsky 1990; Neill 1965; Phillips 1939; Swanson 1948; Wright and Wright 1957). A captive ate a salamander (Ambystoma jeffersonianum) (Swanson 1948).

Foraging begins at dusk and continues until about midnight. Prey is located by both sight and odor. In Florida, most foraging is done amongst the prop roots in red mangrove (Rhizophora mangle) thickets where small fish often congregate. Here the snakes lie on the exposed prop roots and wait for a fish to swim beneath, then quickly seize it and swallow it alive. Capture success is best in areas where the prop root density is 30 m^2, but the snakes spend more time in a stationary search mode from perches at prop root densities of 0–15 m^2 (Mullin and Mushinsky 1995, 1997). Prey size depends on the gape limit of the individual snake's mouth, and gape size is positively correlated to the length of the snake (Mullin 1994). Large N. clarkii are more discriminating among prey sizes than are smaller individuals, and consequently, they ingest smaller prey relative to gape size (Miller and Mushinsky 1990).

PREDATORS AND DEFENSE.   No reports of predation exist, but N. clarkii are probably attacked by large carnivorous fish inhabiting red mangrove thickets, large wading birds, cottonmouths (Agkistrodon piscivorus), alligators (Alligator mississippiensis), and American crocodiles (Crocodylus acutus). Smaller individuals are most likely to fall victim to a predator, but larger snakes are not immune. Mushinsky and Miller (1993) reported that 42.8% of the male and 30.3% of the female N. c. compressicauda they examined had wounds apparently caused by a predator's attack. Generally, wound frequency increased with increased body size; however, most small individuals attacked were probably swallowed by the predator. Reddish morphs are generally more rare in populations of N. c. compressicauda, and Mullin (1994) thought their brightness attracts predators. In addition, some are killed on coastal roads each year.

The saltmarsh snake is docile for a Nerodia. When first discovered, it flattens its head and body and remains motionless, or it may attempt to flee, often down a nearby crab hole. When handled, few bite (usually only the larger females), but they may thrash about and release musk.

POPULATIONS.   Once very common along the coasts of Florida and Texas, N. clarkii is less so today. Large numbers of N. c. compressicauda and N. c. clarkii are still present in certain areas, but elsewhere are scarce: on Pahayokee in the Everglades, N. c. compressicauda totaled only 8 of 1,019 snakes collected in 1987/88 by Dalrymple et al. (1991). Of 42 adult N. c. compressicauda collected in Pinellas County by Mullin (1994), only 5 (11.9%) were the reddish morph, and the other 37 (88.1%) were green; 6 (14.3%) were males, and 36 (85.7%) were females. Pure N. c. taeniata have become rare, but specific sites in Brevard and Volusia counties may still support sufficient numbers of N. c. compressicauda × c. taeniata intergrades (Hebrard and Lee 1981).

Development of the narrow, fragile, coastal strip supporting N. clarkii has greatly decreased its viable habitat. Chemical pollution, and possibly the influx of raccoons (Procyon lotor) have also contributed to its decline. As its habitat shrinks, the possibility of genetic introgression by Nerodia fasciata, its close relative, also has increased, particularly in the populations of N. c. taeniata along the Atlantic Coast (Kochman and Christman 1992). Consequently, Florida has declared N. c. taeniata an endangered species and N. c. clarkii rare, and now protects both subspecies (Kochman and Christman 1992). N. c. taeniata is also considered threatened under the federal Endangered Species Act, and N. c. clarkii is now protected in Alabama.

REMARKS.   Conant (1963) tentatively included N. clarkii in N. fasciata pending additional research. Since then, molecular evidence for their separation has been presented by Lawson (1987) and Lawson et al. (1991), who while considering N. clarkii and N. fasciata sister species, recommended they both be elevated to full specific status.

Nerodia cyclopion (Duméril, Bibron, and Duméril 1854) | Mississippi Green Water Snake

RECOGNITION. *N. cyclopion* is heavy bodied (TBL to 129.5 cm), olive to brown, with subocular scales between the eye and supralabials, and heavy dark spotting on the posterior venter. Faint transverse bars cross the back, and grayish spots or half-moons are present on the cream to light yellow venter. Body scales are keeled, with two pits, and lie in 27 (25–29) anterior rows, 25 or 27 (23–29) midbody rows, and 21 (19–23) rows near the tail. Beneath are 133–148 ventrals, 57–78 subcaudals, and a divided anal plate. Laterally on the head are 2 nasals (partially divided by the nostril), 1 loreal, 1–2 preoculars, 1–2 suboculars, 2 postoculars, 1 + 2–3 temporals, 8 (7–9) supralabials, and 9–13 infralabials. The hemipenis has an unforked sulcus spermaticus, numerous spicules, a few spines, and enlarged basal hooks. Each maxilla has 20–21 teeth, with those most posterior elongated.

Males are shorter with TLs 23.9–26.4 (mean, 24.5) % of TBL, and 64–78 (mean, 70+) subcaudals; females are larger with TLs 19.9–24.9 (mean, 22.5) % of TBL, and 57–75 (mean, 64.5) subcaudals.

GEOGRAPHIC VARIATION. None reported.

CONFUSING SPECIES. Other water snakes of the genus *Nerodia* can be distinguished by the above key. The cottonmouth *(Agkistrodon piscivorus)* lacks subocular scales, has white facial marks, a hole between the nostril and eye, a single row of subcaudals, vertically elliptical pupils, and an undivided anal plate.

KARYOTYPE. The karyotype has 36 chromosomes (34 macrochromosomes, and 2 microchromosomes; pairs one, two, three, five, and six are submetacentric, and pair four is metacentric; Camper and Hanks 1995; Eberle 1972).

FOSSIL RECORD. Unknown.

DISTRIBUTION. This species ranges south in the Mississippi Valley from southern Illinois to the Gulf Coast, and east along the Gulf coastal plain to southwestern Alabama and the extreme western portion of the Florida Panhandle, and west to southeastern Texas.

HABITAT. *N. cyclopion* prefers quiet waters in wooded habitats: tree-lined swamps, shallow lakes, oxbows, marshes, bayous, ponds, rice fields, sluggish streams, canals, and sloughs. Along the Gulf Coast, it sometimes occurs in brackish water (Guidry 1953).

BEHAVIOR. In southern Louisiana, *N. cyclopion* may be active all year, but peak occurrence is in June–July (Mushinsky et al. 1980). Farther north it must undergo a period of winter inactivity, and is active from late March or April–October or November. In Illinois, it leaves the water in September–October to hibernate in adjacent bluffs, returning in the spring (Garton et al. 1970). Beaver and muskrat bank burrows and lodges, and earth or rock dams and rock crevices are also used as hibernacula.

Mississippi green water snake, *Nerodia cyclopion*; Madison County, Louisiana. (Photograph by Roger W. Barbour)

Distribution of *Nerodia cyclopion*.

It is most active during the day in the spring and fall, spending much time basking on emergent objects or along the bank. Low bushes may also be used as basking sites in the cold months (Mushinsky et al. 1980). Summer foraging usually occurs in the early morning, but may also occur at night; in the spring and fall much hunting is diurnal. In Louisiana, *N. cyclopion* seasonally adjusts its daily activity periods to maintain a fairly uniform BT—average CTs taken by Mushinsky et al. (1980) ranged from 26.1 to 28.9°C.

Little is known regarding its movements. Tinkle (1959) recaptured a "possibly gravid" female only 24 m from the spot where she was released 57 days earlier, and Trauth (1990) reported overland movements in Arkansas following an autumn flood.

REPRODUCTION. The smallest female known to be reproductive had a SVL of 63.7 cm, and the smallest known male producing sperm had a 54.6 cm SVL (Kofron 1979a); such SVLs are probably reached in years three to four.

Only limited data are available concerning the gametic cycles of Louisiana *N. cyclopion*. The largest ovarian follicle in the female mentioned above was 9.7 mm; follicles in 30 other April females were 10.3–39.7 mm, and during January–February, follicles were 10–20 mm; vitellogenesis began in late March, and by April–May follicles were 20–46 mm; ovulation occurred from late April through June; and embryos were present in late May–early June (Kofron 1979a).

Tinkle (1959) reported a Louisiana female was "certainly gravid" on 10 April. By 25 July, one female was postpartum, containing 11 corpora lutea; the young were born from mid-July through September. The GP was < 90 days, and the female gametic cycle appeared to be annual. Barbour (1971) thought the GP in Kentucky was about four months; possibly the cooler temperatures there retard development. Conway and Fleming (1960) reported the placental transmission of ions from mother to embryos.

The breeding period is usually in April. Meade (1934a) reported that his captives invariably mated out of water, but Kofron (1979a) observed wild *N. cyclopion* mate in water. Courtship apparently takes place in the water, and females probably exude pheromones to attract males. Several males may court one female. Tinkle and Liner (1955) saw nine swimming back and forth, occasionally nudging one another, in a Louisiana slough. The snakes were oblivious to Tinkle and Liner's presence, and were easily approached and captured. Unfortunately, Tinkle and Liner did not sex the snakes, but thought on the basis of body size that they were all males; however, females may have been involved. While courting, the male sways his head and anterior neck region forward and backward in a raised position and nudges the female with his head (Carpenter and Ferguson 1977). During mating the female stretches straight out with the male lying on her back with his body in sinuous curves (Meade 1934a). Copulation may last several hours. Kofron (1979a) found a mated pair swirling around in shallow water in a tidal pool. The female left the pool dragging the coupled male. She was killed, and the joined pair was placed in a cloth sack; 75 minutes later the male was still attached to the female (possibly the male could not disengage his spined hemipenis from the female's cloaca).

Litters contain 7–37 (mean, 17.2; n = 18) young (Kofron 1979a; Meade 1934a). Neonates have 18.7–30.5 (mean, 22.4; n = 14) cm TBLs, and are more vividly patterned than adults, with dark crossbands and spots.

GROWTH AND LONGEVITY. Growth slows with age; although females grow larger. At birth males have TBLs of 20.7–21.7 cm, and females 20.6–22.2 cm; at one year, males are 29.4–46.1 cm, females 39.9–48.3 cm; at two years, males are 34.0–61.8 cm, females 50.5–62.1 cm; at three years, males average 72.4 cm, females 72.3 cm; and by the end of the fourth year, females average 82.6 cm (Scudder-Davis and Burghardt 1996; Trauth 1990). Longevity has not been reported.

DIET AND FEEDING HABITS. *N. cyclopion* is predominately a fish eater, but will take some amphibians and crayfish. Mushinsky and Hebrard (1977a) reported that fish made up 98.4% and amphibians only 1.6% of the total volume of food, and 94% of the identifiable food remains from stomachs examined by Kofron (1978) were fish (crayfish, 3%; amphibians, 2%). Tennant (1985) examined 75 stomachs and found frogs in 10 (13.3%), fish in 4 (5.3%), and a single large salamander in another (1.3%). Garton et al. (1970) found sirens and sunfish in the stomachs that they examined, and Clark (1949) and Tinkle (1959) found these snakes had eaten only fish. Natural prey includes: fish (*Cyprinodon variegatus, Dorosoma cepedianum, Elassoma zonatum, Fundulus confluentus, F. pulvereus, Gambusia affinis, Heterandria formosa, Ictalurus furcatus, Lepomis* sp., *Mugil cephalus, Notemigonus crysoleucas, Poecilia latipinna*), amphiumas (*Amphiuma tridactylum*), sirens (*Siren intermedia*), unidentified adult and larval frogs, and crayfish (*Procambarus* sp.) (Clark 1949; Fontenot and Platt 1993; Garton et al. 1970; Kofron 1978; Mushinsky and Hebrard 1977a; Tennant 1985; Tinkle 1959). Although these snakes

eat fish throughout their lives, with maturity and increased body size they change portions of their diet to include more centrarchid fish (Mushinsky et al. 1982). Tennant (1985) thought juveniles feed mostly on insects, tadpoles, and minnows.

We have seen *N. cyclopion* actively pursue and capture small fishes, and believe this is their normal feeding behavior. Clark (1949) reported that two captives would climb about on the braces of their cage and hang over the water. When small fish were placed in the water, the snakes would drop into the water and rush frantically after them. As soon as one fish was swallowed, the chase resumed, and when the last fish had been eaten, the snakes returned to the cage braces. The two snakes would consume up to 12 approximately 50 mm fish at one feeding. Evans (1942) observed this snake swim with its mouth open while foraging, and other species of *Nerodia* are known to open-mouth forage (Gillingham and Rush 1974), but the authors have not observed such behavior. Both live and dead fish are eaten.

PREDATORS AND DEFENSE. *N. cyclopion* had the highest predatory wound frequency of five water snake species examined by Mushinsky and Miller (1993). The number with wounds increases with age/size, but small individuals attacked by a predator may be totally devoured and not be available for wound inspection. Adults are preyed on by American alligators (*Alligator mississippiensis*), cottonmouths (*Agkistrodon piscivorus*), and probably by large aquatic birds (anhingas, comorants, herons, egrets), loggerhead shrikes (*Lanius ludovicianus*), carnivorous mammals, and possibly large predatory fish. The young fall victim to all classes of vertebrates.

Humans cause the most damage to this snake, destroying many each year in the mistaken belief that they are venomous. In addition, much critical habitat is drained and destroyed, or poisoned by pesticides or other chemical pollutants. Studies have shown that *N. cyclopion* is vulnerable to both DDT and rotenone poisoning (Fontenot et al. 1994; Herald 1949). Although DDT is no longer used in mosquito control, some commercial fishermen still use rotenone. If a highway runs adjacent to a body of water, many will be run over by vehicles (Trauth 1990).

The several *N. cyclopion* the authors have handled had nasty dispositions, would bite at the least provocation, and frequently sprayed musk and feces. When warm they are very alert. Males are more aggressive than females.

POPULATIONS. Population size varies with locality, and the farther north, the smaller the population size. This snake occurs in large numbers in the extensive still waters of southern Louisiana; Viosca (in Dundee and Rossman 1989) once saw more than 80 of these snakes basking along a canal in New Orleans, and collected 119 of them on Delacroix Island in St. Bernard Parish. It is the second most abundant snake in the Atchafalaya Basin (Kofron 1978) and at a site in Ascension Parish (Mushinsky et al. 1980). Of 478 snakes collected at a southern Louisiana 3 km site, *N. cyclopion* was the most abundant (32.2% of captures), especially during the summer months (Mushinsky and Hebrard 1977b). In northern Louisiana, where the habitat often involves deeper, more flowing waters, its numbers are lower; Clark (1949) captured only 6 (0.3%) in a sample of 2,083 snakes. In northeastern Arkansas this snake only totaled 4 (0.8%) of 477 *Nerodia* collected by Hanebrink and Byrd (1986), but 72 (88.9%) of 81 snakes collected by Trauth (1990) after a flood at another site.

Size classes favor adults, and the sex ratio is not significantly different from 1:1.

Due in large part to the loss of cypress swamps along the Mississippi floodplain, *N. cyclopion* is disappearing from many sites in the northern portions of its range. In 1965, Anderson thought it rare and restricted to the southeastern most counties of Missouri, by 1987 Johnson reported it endangered, and today it is considered extirpated in that state. It is listed as endangered in Kentucky, threatened in Illinois, a species of special concern in Arkansas, and in need of management in Tennessee.

Nerodia erythrogaster (Forster 1771) | Plain-bellied Water Snake

RECOGNITION. *N. erythrogaster* (TBL to 163.6 cm) has a uniformly brown to olive gray back (or with faint cross bars); a yellow, orange, or red unpatterned venter; and dark bars on the supralabials. The keeled, doubly pitted body scales occur in 22–23 (19–25) anterior rows, 23–25 (20–27) midbody rows, and 17–19 (16–21) posterior rows. Beneath are 132–161 ventrals (with no apparent sexual dimorphism), 46–90 subcaudals, and a divided anal plate (undivided in about 10% of individuals). On each side of the head are 2 nasal scales (partially separated by the nostril), 1 loreal, 1 (2) preocular(s), 3 (1–4) postoculars, 1 + 3 (rarely 2) temporals, 8 (7–10) supralabials, and 10 (8–11) infralabials. The bilobed hemipenis (which extends to subcaudals seven to eight) has a subcylindrical shaft with spines and spinules that become smaller distally, nude patches at its base adjacent to the basal and accessory hooks, a single sulcus spermaticus ending at the junction of the two nude apical lobes, one large basal hook beside the sulcus that is followed distally by several small spines, and a more distal and smaller accessory hook on the opposite side of the sulcus. Each maxilla has 22–27 teeth.

Males are shorter and have 67–90 subcaudals, and TLs 23–30 (mean, 25) % of TBL; the larger, thicker bodied females have 46–79 subcaudals, and TLs 19–26 (mean, 21) % of TBL.

GEOGRAPHIC VARIATION. Six subspecies are recognized, but only four occur north of Mexico (McCranie 1990). *N. erythrogaster erythrogaster* (Forster 1771), the red-bellied water snake, ranges from the Delmarva Peninsula south to northern Florida, and west to southeastern Alabama. It has a plain red to orange red venter, a plain brown to brownish gray dorsum (occasional individuals have faint light crossbands), the lower sides greenish gray, and usually no parietal spots or postparietal streak on the head. *N. e. flavigaster* (Conant 1949), the yellow-bellied water snake, is found from southeastern Iowa south to eastern Texas, and southeast to north-central Georgia. It is gray or olive gray to black dorsally (some individu-

Red-bellied water snake, *Nerodia erythrogaster erythrogaster*; Hickman County, Kentucky. (Photograph by Roger W. Barbour)

Copper-bellied water snake, *Nerodia erythrogaster neglecta*; Indiana. (Photograph by James H. Harding)

als may have faint light crossbands) and yellow (sometimes orangish) ventrally (sometimes with faint gray markings at the base or sides of the ventral scutes), and occasionally has parietal spots or a postparietal streak. *N. e. neglecta* (Conant 1949), the copper-bellied water snake, occupies a disjunct northern range in south-central Michigan and adjacent Illinois and Indiana, and in southwestern Indiana, southern Illinois, southeastern Iowa, and western Kentucky and adjacent Tennessee. Isolated colonies also exist in west-central Ohio and south-central Indiana. Dorsally, it is gray to olive or brown with at least faint dark blotches, its venter is yellow to orange with some of the dorsal pigment invading along the sides, and it almost always has parietal spots and a postparietal streak. *N. e. transversa* (Hallowell 1852), the blotched water snake, occurs in the central plains from west-central Missouri and eastern and southern Kansas south to northwestern Missouri and southern Texas, the Rio Grande watershed in western Texas and southeastern New Mexico, and Coahuila, Mexico. An apparently isolated colony is present in the panhandle of Oklahoma. The dorsum varies in color from gray to brown or olive brown, and it is patterned with dark-bordered, light crossbands and dark, lateral blotches 1.5–2.0 scales wide (old adults may be uniformly dark); the venter is plain yellow or orangish (sometimes with dark pigment on the bases and outer edges of the ventrals); and parietal spots and a postparietal streak are usually present. Intergrade zones occur where the ranges of the various subspecies meet.

CONFUSING SPECIES. All other species of *Nerodia* have strongly patterned venters. Kirtland's snake *(Clonophis kirtlandii)* has two rows of dark ventral spots. The cottonmouth *(Agkistrodon piscivorous)* has white facial markings, a pitlike hole between the nostril and eye, vertically elliptical pupils, and a single row of subcaudals.

KARYOTYPE. Chromosomes total 36: 32 macrochromosomes and 4 microchromosomes (8 large submetacentrics, 6 medium-sized submetacentrics, 6 small subtelocentrics, and 14 small metacentrics); sex determination is ZZ/ZW (Z chromosomes are submetacentric, the W is subtelocentric) (Baker et al. 1972; Eberle 1972; Kilpatrick and Zimmerman 1973).

FOSSIL RECORD. Upper Pliocene (Blancan) and Pleistocene (Rancholabrean) fossils of *N. erythrogaster* are known from Texas (Hill 1971; Holman 1969a, 1979a; Kasper and Parmley 1990; Parmley 1988a, 1990a; Rodgers 1976); Pleistocene (Irvingtonian and Rancholabrean) fossils have been found in Florida (Auffenberg 1963; Meylan 1982); and Rancholabrean

remains have been found in Oklahoma (Smith and Cifelli 2000).

DISTRIBUTION. *N. erythrogaster* occupies a large geographic range extending from southern Delaware, south-central Michigan, and southeastern Iowa south to northern Florida, Texas, and southeastern New Mexico in the United States, and to eastern Durango and Zacatecas in Mexico.

HABITAT. This snake prefers slow moving waters—bayous, wet bottomland woods, marshes, lowland and cypress swamps, lakes, mill and cattle ponds, oxbows, rivers, streams, sloughs, and ditches. These bodies of water usually have soft (often mud) bottoms, abundant emergent vegetation, and brushy banks. Cool moist areas seem to be a requirement, and often the waters are quite tannic. This snake is sometimes found in moist woodlands some distance from water, especially during hot, humid weather (Clark 1949; Conant and Collins 1998). It occurs at elevations from sea level to 2,042 m (McCranie 1990).

BEHAVIOR. The start of the annual activity period for *N. erythrogaster* varies with latitude and seasonal temperatures. It may be sporadically active at the surface during the winter in the south (Guidry 1953; Kofron 1979a). Vermersch and Kuntz (1986) found them basking in January–February in south-central Texas when the AT and WT reached 21.5 and 18.0°C, respectively, but most individuals first emerge from hibernation in March–April. In North Carolina the an-

Distribution of *Nerodia erythrogaster*.

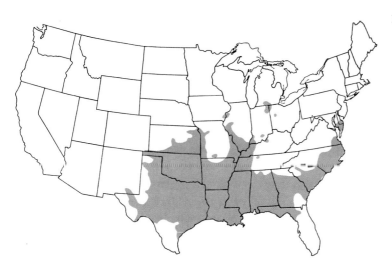

nual activity period extends from late February into November (Palmer and Braswell 1995), and in Kansas from March through October (Collins 1993). In both Louisiana and North Carolina the peak surface activity occurs in May–July, when 60% or more of captures or observations occur (Mushinsky et al. 1980; Palmer and Braswell 1995). Hibernation sites include animal burrows, rock piles, earth and rock dams, hollow logs or stumps, and beaver *(Castor canadensis)* and muskrat *(Ondatra zibethica)* lodges or bank burrows near or in water, and rocky, often elevated, upland sites may also be used by some populations. Kingsbury and Coppola (2000) found that radio-equipped *N. e. neglecta* from southern Indiana and western Kentucky, did not tend to make extensive migrations to dry upland hibernacula, but instead hibernated singly in or immediately adjacent to their wetlands during the winter. They usually selected lowland inactive crayfish burrows or rotting stumps in palustrine forest over adjacent uplands less than 20 m away. Only one hibernaculum was situated below flood level, and individual snakes tended to return to the same site in adjacent years.

N. erythrogaster is predominately nocturnal (Mushinsky et al. 1980), although Palmer and Braswell (1995) thought it equally active during the day and night in the summer. Daytimes from 0800 to 1700 hours are usually spent either in hiding or in basking (Diener 1957b). Basking may be on the bank, above ground on branches overhanging the water, on partially submerged logs, or possibly when the snake is submerged just below the surface in shallow water. Foraging begins with dusk, and may last until 0300 hours (Diener 1957b).

Mushinsky et al. (1980) found that BTs of active Louisiana *N. erythrogaster* ranged between 24 and 29°C, and that the yearly average CTs for 1976, 1977, and 1978 were 25.8, 25.7, and 28.0°C, respectively. Brattstrom (1965) recorded CTs of 29.0°C. Collins (1993) and Diener (1957b) reported these snakes active at ATs as low as 13°C in Kansas, and the species may enter water 41°C or higher in Mexican hot springs (Conant 1969).

Data on movements by *N. erythrogaster* are sparse. During a study at a large impoundment in Texas, it moved an average of 64.35 (12.8–179.0) m/day (Whiting et al. 1998).

REPRODUCTION. The smallest TBLs of mature female *N. erythrogaster* are 68.5 cm (Wright and Wright 1957), 73.4 cm (Kofron 1979a), and 76.0 cm (Conant and Collins 1998). Males mature at 72.4–76.9 cm TBLs (Conant and Collins 1998; Wright and Wright 1957). Such TBLs are probably attained during the third year of life.

The gametic cycles have not been thoroughly studied. Vitellogenesis begins in late April in Louisiana (Kofron 1979a). Before this follicles are 5–10 mm in diameter, but during late April–May they enlarged to over 35 mm. Ovulation occurs in late May–June. Oviducts of pregnant Kansas females contain developing ova in late June–July (Diener 1957b). The definitive shape of the embryo is not apparent until mid-July, and by late July the coil diameter of embryos averages 14 mm.

Courtship and mating normally occur from April to mid-June in the United States, but Conant (1969) reported possible sexual activity on 2 August in Mexico. During courtship, the male trails the female with much tongue flicking (apparently following her scent trail), eventually crawls alongside, and then loops his body back and forth along her back. He uses his head to press the female's head to the substratum, and tries to twist his tail beneath her tail to align their vents. If the female is receptive, she will raise her tail slightly to aid him. During copulation the two snakes may remain still, or intertwine (C. Ernst, pers. obs.). Females may store viable sperm for almost two years after mating (Conant 1965b). Gestation probably lasts approximately three to four months (Tennant 1985).

The young are usually born from August to October; however, an occasional litter is produced in late July. Kofron (1979a) found a juvenile of newborn length with the remnant of an umbilical cord on 10 April in Louisiana that he interpreted as evidence of spring parturition. Litters contain 2 (Conant 1969) to 37 young (Minton 1972) and average 17.8 (n = 75); litters of 10–20 are normal. Litter size increases with greater female body length. RCMs are 0.233–0.265 (Seigel and Fitch 1984; Thornton and Smith 1996a). Often a series of stillborn young or unfertilized eggs is also passed at the time of birth (Laposha et al. 1985), and Minton (1972) thought this indicates the female reproductive cycle is not particularly well adapted to a northern climate. Neonates have 18.1–30.6 (mean, 25.1; n = 103) cm TBLs; the mass is 3.5–10.9 (mean,

6.4; n = 66) g. The young are more strongly patterned, both dorsally and ventrally, than adults, having pronounced dorsal blotches and dark pigment on the venter.

GROWTH AND LONGEVITY.   Little growth data are available. Twenty neonates that averaged 26.3 (25.0–27.1) cm and 6.1 (5.5–6.4) g at birth on 5 September were fed chopped fish by Conant and Downs (1940). By 9 December they averaged 25.9 cm and 6.6 g; on 5 April, 30.7 cm and 10.9 g; on 13 June, 33.2 cm and 13.3 g; and on the following 2 May the three survivors averaged 42.0 cm and 26.7 g.

Snider and Bowler (1992) reported longevities of 14 years, 11 months, and 17 days for a female *N. e. transversa* originally wild caught when juvenile, and 8 years, 10 months, and 2 days for a *N. e. erythrogaster* that was wild caught when adult.

DIET AND FEEDING HABITS.   This snake feeds primarily on amphibians and fish. Recorded prey are fish—catfish *(Ictalurus* sp., *Noturus insignis, N. miurus),* suckers (Catostomidae), pickerel *(Esox* sp.), mosquitofish *(Gambusia affinis),* livebearers *(Poecilia latipinna),* killifish *(Fundulus* sp., *Heterandria formosa),* cyprinids *(Campostoma anomalum, Chrosomus erythrogaster, Nocomis biguttatus, Pimephales notatus),* darters *(Etheostoma spectabile),* sunfish *(Lepomis humilis),* pygmy sunfish *(Elassoma zonata),* and black bass *(Micropterus salmoides);* anurans (tadpoles and small adults)—ranid frogs *(Rana berlandieri, R. blairi, R. catesbeiana, R. pipiens, R. sphenocephala),* tree frogs *(Hyla chrysoscelis, H. cinerea),* and toads *(Bufo houstonensis, B. terrestris, B. valliceps, B. woodhousei);* salamanders and sirens *(Ambystoma* sp., *Amphiuma means, Siren intermedia);* crayfish *(Procambarus* sp.); and aquatic insects (Ashton and Ashton 1981; Byrd et al. 1988; Cagle 1942; Carpenter 1958; Clark 1949; Collins 1980; Diener 1957b; Ditmars 1931a; Dundee and Rossman 1989; Freed and Nietmann 1988; Guidry 1953; Hamilton and Pollack 1956; Hurter 1911; Kofron 1978; Liner 1954; Marvel 1972; Mushinsky and Hebrard 1977a; Mushinsky and Lotz 1980; Palmer and Braswell 1995; Penn 1950; Vermersch and Kuntz 1986; Webb 1970). Carrion may be ingested (Conant 1969). Diener (1957b) reported that anurans made up 91.8% and fish only 5.5% of the diet of 34 *N. erythrogaster,* and Mushinsky and Hebrard

(1977a) reported that at their Louisiana site 67.4% of the total food volume was frogs or tadpoles. Minton (1972) thought the preponderance of amphibians in the diet of this species at some localities may reflect the snake's choice of temporary waters where fish are uncommon.

Louisiana neonates did not respond preferentially at first to extracts of various fish, frogs, and toads during a food preference study conducted by Mushinsky and Lotz (1980). By two months of age, however, a significant response rate was established that persisted for several months regardless of dietary restrictions. The snakes then subsequently shifted their preference to frog extract when eight months old. Mushinsky and Lotz thought these shifts may reflect a maturational process.

Most *N. erythrogaster* that the authors have seen feeding in the wild or in their laboratory have actively sought and pursued prey; however, Gillingham and Rush (1974) observed *N. erythrogaster* with their tails anchored to rocks, their heads facing into the current, and their mouths gaping. Evans (1942) also reported open-mouthed foraging.

PREDATORS AND DEFENSE.   Known predators are the cottonmouth *(Agkistrodon piscivorus),* common kingsnake *(Lampropeltis getula),* snapping turtle *(Chelydra serpentina),* largemouth bass *(Micropterus salmoides),* and loggerhead shrike *(Lanius ludovicianus)* (Berna and Gibbons 1991; Diener 1957b; Hamilton and Pollack 1956; Palmer and Braswell 1995; Parmley and Mulford 1985; Tyler 1991). At least the young are probably also preyed on by other large fish, alligators, ophiophagous snakes, large aquatic birds, raptors, and various carnivorous mammals. Humans are the leading cause of decline in this species, through destroying their habitat, driving over them on roads, shooting them, and polluting their waterways.

A large *N. erythrogaster* is a nasty opponent. It thrashes about, bites hard, and sprays musk when not allowed to escape, and may even ooze blood from its gums (Smith et al. 1993). If given a chance, it will almost always try to crawl away, often diving into the nearest water and swimming away or hiding on the bottom. While capable of remaining submerged for over an hour (Baeyens et al. 1980), usual voluntary dives last about 26 minutes (Jacob and McDonald 1976).

POPULATIONS. *N. erythrogaster* is usually common in the proper habitat. Nineteen percent of the 477 *Nerodia* taken by Hanebrink and Byrd (1986) in northeastern Arkansas were this species; Fitch (1993) reported they made up 14.9% of the snakes at one site in Kansas; and the species made up 8.9% of 2,083 snakes collected by Clark (1949) in upstate Louisiana. However, in a mixed pine-hardwood forest in eastern Texas only five (1.6%) *N. erythrogaster* were included in a sample of 305 snakes (Ford et al. 1991). Population density also varies with habitat; Lacki et al. (1994) found densities of *N. e. neglecta* varied from 6.8 to 48.8 snakes/km in several different oxbows in southern Indiana.

Populations of *N. e. neglecta* have been severely reduced, and is now considered either endangered or threatened in the states in which it occurs. Some other populations of *N. erythrogaster* have also been severely depleted during the last 30 years, and are now also considered endangered or threatened (Iowa, Michigan, New Mexico, Ohio), or are given other forms of protection.

Although Keck (1994) reported a 0.81:1.00 male to female ratio in northeastern Texas, the adult sex ratio is probably 1:1 (Byrd et al. 1988). However, the sex ratio of neonates may favor either males or females (Palmer and Braswell 1995; Thornton and Smith 1996).

REMARKS. Studies of the various allozyme frequencies in several tissues indicate that *N. erythrogaster* is most closely related to *N. fasciata* and *N. clarkii* (Lawson 1987). Similarly, examination of mitochondrial DNA has showed a close kinship with *N. fasciata*, as well as with *N. harteri* and *N. paucimaculata* (*N. clarkii* was not studied) (Densmore et al. 1992). The species has been reviewed by McCranie (1990).

Nerodia fasciata (Linnaeus 1766) | Southern Water Snake

RECOGNITION. *N. fasciata* has a maximum TBL of 158.8 cm, although most individuals are 90–110 cm long. It varies from gray, tan, and brown to reddish brown, has a dorsal pattern of dark brown or red, and often has black-bordered, transverse bands of varying width; and a dark lateral spot may be present in the light area between the transverse bands (see GEO-GRAPHIC VARIATION). A dark stripe extends obliquely backward to the corner of the mouth, and dark bars are usually present on the supralabials. The yellow or cream-colored venter is marked with dark spots or transverse lines. Older individuals may become melanistic. Dorsal body scales are strongly keeled, have two apical pits, and occur in 23 (21–25) anterior

Banded water snake, *Nerodia fasciata fasciata*; Columbus County, North Carolina. (Photograph by Roger W. Barbour)

Florida water snake, *Nerodia fasciata pictiventris*; Dade County, Florida. (Photograph by Christopher W. Brown, DVM)

and midbody rows and 17 (16–19) posterior rows. The venter has 120–143 ventrals (with no sexual dimorphism), 50–89 subcaudals, and a divided anal plate. Each side of the head has 2 nasals (partially divided by the nostril), 1 loreal, 1 (2) preocular(s), 3 (1–4) postoculars, 1 + 3 (2) temporals, 8 (6–9) supralabials, and 10 (9–12) infralabials. The thermal environment during incubation may affect the development of meristic characters in embryos (Osgood 1978). The hemipenis has a single, unforked sulcus spermaticus, several enlarged basal hooks, and few spines, but many spicules, along the shaft. Eleven of 12 *N. fasciata* examined by the authors had 18–21 (mean, 19) teeth on each maxilla, but the larger 12th individual had 23 teeth.

Adult males are shorter, with TLs 22.6–29.8 (mean, 26.6) % of TBL, and 51–89 (mean, 78.3) subcaudals. Females are larger, with TLs 19.3–28.1 (mean, 23.8) % of TBL, and 50–86 (mean, 68.5) subcaudals.

GEOGRAPHIC VARIATION.   Three subspecies are recognized. *N. f. fasciata* (Linnaeus 1766), the banded water snake, ranges southward, mostly on the coastal plain, from Albemarle Sound, North Carolina, to northern Florida and west to southern Alabama. It has dark, often black-bordered, dorsal transverse bands, and dark rectangular-shaped spots along the sides of the venter. *N. f. confluens* (Blanchard 1923a), the broad-banded water snake, occurs from southern Illinois, adjacent Kentucky, and southeastern Missouri south in the Mississippi Valley to the Gulf Coast in Mississippi and Louisiana, and west through eastern and central Arkansas to southeastern Oklahoma and central Texas. It has the dark body bands so wide that only 11–17 are present (the other two subspecies have 19 or more bands), and large, rectangular, reddish brown spots on the sides of the venter. *N. f. pictiventris* (Cope 1895), the Florida water snake, is found from southeastern Georgia south through peninsular

Distribution of *Nerodia fasciata*.

Florida. It has dark brown or black, or sometimes reddish, transverse body bands, dark lateral spots between the bands, and wavy reddish brown transverse lines on the venter.

CONFUSING SPECIES. Other species of *Nerodia* may be distinguished from *N. fasciata* by the key presented above. Cottonmouths *(Agkistrodon piscivorus)* have vertically elliptical pupils, a hole between the nostril and the eye, and a single row of subcaudals.

KARYOTYPE. Eberle (1972) reported that this species has 36 chromosomes: 18 pairs of macrochromosomes and no microchromosomes, with pairs one through three, five, and six submetacentric and pair four metacentric. In contrast, Camper and Hanks (1995) reported the species has 34 biarmed macrochromosomes and 2 michrochromosomes. Sex determination is ZZ in males, and ZW in females; both the Z and W chromosomes are submetacentric (Kilpatrick and Zimmerman 1973).

FOSSIL RECORD. Meylan (1995) tentatively assigned Pleistocene (Irvingtonian) vertebrae from Hillsbourgh County, Florida, to *N. fasciata*, and Holman and Winkler (1987) found a Pleistocene (Irvingtonian) trunk vertebra of *N. fasciata* in Fyllan Cave, Travis County, Texas.

DISTRIBUTION. *N. fasciata* is found from Albermarle Sound, North Carolina, south on the Atlantic Coastal Plain through peninsular Florida, west along the Gulf Coastal Plain, and south from southern Illinois to central Texas.

HABITAT. *N. fasciata*, while it may spend some time in brackish water, is primarily a freshwater species found in the shallow parts of rivers, streams, lakes, swamps, marshes, ponds, sloughs, oxbows, and wet prairies. Usually some emergent or floating vegetation (water lilies, hyacinths, cattails) are present.

It prefers freshwater to seawater (Pettus 1958, 1963; Zug and Dunson 1979). Unfortunately, it will drink seawater, dying as a result; and because it drinks the water, it is restricted to freshwater. At 15% seawater, it has a slight preference for freshwater, but at 10% seawater it shows no preference for either fresh- or seawater (Zug and Dunson 1979). It has higher body water influx and efflux, and body sodium influx than other *Nerodia* (Dunson 1980). The skin is permeable, and when the snake is placed in seawater, it loses weight, but gains sodium (probably by drinking), and dies (Dunson 1978). When kept in air (at 30°C pumped at 300 ml/minute), it also loses weight (0.21–0.55% mass/day) (Dunson 1982).

BEHAVIOR. In southern Florida, *N. fasciata* is active in every month. More northern populations must hibernate during the winter and are active from February or March to November or December (C. Ernst, pers. obs.; Mushinsky and Hebrard 1977b; Tinkle 1959). In North Carolina they are encountered in all months but December; 83% of the records are from April–August, with April–May yielding most records

(Palmer and Braswell 1995). It has been found hibernating beneath logs or rocks in swampy areas in Georgia (Neill 1948a), and Kofron (1978) reported that during cold weather these snakes are found under debris that is always near water. Most, however, probably spend the winter underground in muskrat burrows or crayfish holes, or in muskrat or beaver lodges.

The authors' experience with this species over much of its eastern range indicates that it is primarily nocturnal. Most foraging and other movements are done from dusk into the night, and N. fasciata is often found crossing roads during this period. Daylight hours are spent under cover or in basking, especially in the morning, either on the banks or on branches overhanging the water. In contrast, Louisiana N. f. confluens are mostly diurnal in the summer, but become nocturnal in September, possibly in response to other water snake species becoming more diurnal at that time of the year (Mushinsky and Hebrard 1977b). Tinkle and Liner (1955) found them active at midday during the breeding season in Louisiana.

The BT of N. fasciata remains near the WT (Osgood 1970), but varies during the day depending on the amount of direct sunlight on the snake. When it leaves the water at about 1400 hours to bask, the snake's BT increases to 26–29°C. The general BT pattern of wild gravid females is one of warming in the morning when the sun appears, then maintaining the BT at about 26–31°C as long as possible into the afternoon (Osgood 1970). When the AT drops below the WT, the snakes slide back into the water, thus slowing the decline in BT. Minimum and maximum BTs recorded in the field for active individuals are 21.5 and 32.0°C, respectively. Tinkle (1959) found a Louisiana N. f. confluens torpid at an AT of 17°C.

N. fasciata is a good swimmer that uses exclusively lateral undulations (Jayne 1985); usually only the head and anterior neck are at the surface. It is capable of diving and remaining underwater for extended periods—voluntarily to < 24 minutes (Jacob and McDonald 1976).

Limited data have been published on movements by N. fasciata. Holman and Hill (1961) observed a mass unidirectional south-southwest movement in 107/108 N. f. pictiventris across a Florida road between 1945 and 2225 hours on 2 June 1961, and an additional 21/22 individuals crossing the road on 3 June between

2017 and 2110 hours. They thought these movements were related to a general drought in the area. Similar movements during a drought in South Carolina were noted by Seigel et al. (1995b). The South Carolina N. fasciata used discrete, nonrandom corridors when exiting drying water bodies.

N. fasciata uses both lateral undulatory movements and sidewinding (on loose sand) for crawling on the surface of the ground, and concertina and laterally undulatory locomotion when in tunnels (Jayne 1986). In tests run by Jayne (1986), it reached a maximum speed of 1.88 TBL/second (164.1 cm/second) while laterally undulating, and 0.05 TBL/second while using concertina crawling.

REPRODUCTION. The smallest sexually mature female and male N. fasciata had 45.0–57.9 and 52.0 cm SVLs, respectively (Palmer and Braswell 1995; Semlitsch and Gibbons 1982; Tinkle 1959). Such SVLs are usually reached in two to three years.

Data regarding the female gametic cycle of N. fasciata are sparse, and mostly biochemical. Kofron (1979a) found female N. f. confluens ovulate from early May to mid-June and give birth from July to September. Tinkle (1959) reported that a female dissected on 10 April had 11 preovulatory follicles larger than 12 mm, and another examined on 24 April contained 27 follicles larger than 16 mm. He found the first pregnant females on 1 May, and by 27 June embryos had scales and color patterns. Oviduct growth is related to ovarian activity and gestation. Callard and Leathem (1967) found that the alkaline phosphatase level decreases with increase in oviductal size from March through April, suggesting that the enzyme level does not change but instead is diluted by tissue growth. Also, the level of β-glucuronidase increases from May to July during the gestational period, perhaps due to estrogen production. Glycogen levels in the oviduct were high in March but decreased afterwards until June, when no further decrease occurred. Sodium concentration in the oviduct decreased significantly during pregnancy, but potassium concentration increased significantly between March and April and then remained at the higher level. Changes in the sodium/potassium ratio and other electrolytes reflect the tissue growth that occurs during the early reproductive phase, and changes in oviduct size and chemistry possibly reflect changes in ovarian steroid production. In addition, significant changes occur in the cytosolic and nuclear hepatic estrogen receptor levels during the vitellogenic stage of the female cycle (Riley and Callard 1988).

A male dissected on 6 June contained active sperm (Tinkle 1959). Once the sperm reaches the sperm duct, changes occur on its surface. Several proteins that are not present in the serum increase in the sperm duct during spermiogenesis (Esponda and Bedford 1987). Whereas testicular sperm do not bind antibody to duct secretions, those in the sperm duct do so over both head and tail, thus acquiring one or more of the duct's secretory components. These changes may be related to sperm survival or storage, as well as capacitation and the sperm binding to the ova.

The breeding season varies with locality and subspecies. In Florida, it might extend from autumn to early spring (Ashton and Ashton 1981). Meade (1934a) found *N. f. confluens* mating in April, and Anderson (1965) saw an attempted mating of two male *N. f. confluens* with the same female at Reelfoot Lake, Tennessee, on 16 April. Captives have mated as early as 7 and 16 February and 14 and 18 March (Sleijpen 1991), but over most of the natural range, the courtship/mating period probably extends from early April to mid-June. Males pursue females, and when the female is caught, the male crawls onto her back and crawls anteriorly by undulatory motion (Meade, 1934a, observed similar courtship posture) while undergoing some caudocephalic waves. Once the female's head is reached, the male pins it down, then attempts to position his tail beneath that of the female to bring their vents together. Copulation may last over an hour (C. Ernst, pers. obs.).

Tinkle (1959) and Tinkle and Liner (1955) observed aggregate swimming bouts in Louisiana *N. f. confluens* that may have been associated with mating. The snakes appeared to be males, and they swam back and forth across a pond, coming at frequent intervals to the shoreline with continual tongue flicking. At times one snake would approach another, hesitate briefly beside it, then move away in a diagonal direction and continue swimming. The snakes were unwary and easily approached, displaying curiosity at disturbances.

Developing embryos are nourished via a placenta. The GP averages about 79 days (48–109), depending on the ambient temperature. The embryos cannot tolerate temperatures beyond the 21–30°C range for the entire GP (Osgood 1970); but short periods at temperatures beyond this range probably can be tolerated, except during critical times of development.

Parturition usually occurs from late June into October, although most litters are born from mid-July to mid-September. Guidry (1953) reported a litter born on 20 October, and Iverson (1978) another on 23 November. There is a positive correlation between female length and the number of offspring produced per litter. Litters contain 6–83 (mean, 22.8; n = 84) young (Kofron and Dixon 1980; Palmer and Braswell 1995). The litter of 83, and another of 73, reported by Palmer and Braswell (1995) are exceptionally high. The other 82 litters contained 50 (Ashton and Ashton 1981; Tennant 1985) or fewer young, and averaged 21.4 young. An RCM of a litter was 0.201 (Seigel and Fitch 1984).

Neonates are more vividly colored and patterned than adults. Neonate TBL varies from 17.6 to 31.5 cm and averages 22.1 cm (n = 89); birth weight averages 5.1 (2.6.1–8.0) g.

GROWTH AND LONGEVITY. Information on growth of the southern water snake is based on captive-reared individuals, and only indicates possible trends or potentials. The growth rate depends on the feeding regime, and changes in the quantity of food available or the timing of feeding bouts affects females more than males (Scudder and Burghardt 1985). A reduction in growth efficiency occurs with age, and males and females experience similar reductions. Females allocate more of the ingested resources for increases in mass and SVL than do males, but males put more resources into TL than females (Scudder-Davis and Burghardt 1996). Both strategies are probably related to reproduction and the attainment of sexual maturity. At birth females averaged 18.4 (17.9–19.1) cm in SVL, 4.8 (4.5–5.4) cm in TL, and 3.6 (3.1–4.5) g in weight; neonate males averaged 18.0 (16.4–19.5) cm in SVL, 5.4 (4.7–6.0) cm in TL, and 3.7 (2.6–4.7) g in weight (Scudder-Davis and Burghardt 1996). By the first year the females had average SVLs of 40.9 (40.2–41.6) cm, TLs of 10.3 (10.2–10.4) cm, and average weights of 41.8 (38.9–47.0) g, and at the end of two years were 55.8 (55.1–56.8) cm in SVL and 13.8

(12.7–14.7) cm in TL, and weighed 107.3 (96.2–116.8) g. First-year males were 37.7 (35.3–40.0) cm in SVL and 10.8 (9.5–11.7) cm in TL, and weighed 38.6 (32.9–43.6) g; second-year males were 49.0 (46.6–51.0) cm in SVL, had 12.9 (11.1–15.0) cm TLs, and weighed 91.4 (82.6–101.3) g (Scudder-Davis and Burghardt 1996).

N. fasciata is not particularly long-lived in captivity; the authors have only had a male N. f. confluens, originally caught as an adult, survive 3 years and 3 months, and a female N. f. pictiventris, originally wild caught when adult, survived 3 years and 4 months.

DIET AND FEEDING HABITS. Most foraging is nocturnal, and prey is located both visually and by smell. N. fasciata prowl about while foraging, often exploring crevices and vegetation with their heads. Much tongue flicking occurs during foraging. Response to fish odors is innate, but responses to fish odors become more variable after six months of age, and stronger responses to the smell of frogs develop (Mushinsky and Lotz 1980). When food is located, it is quickly seized and swallowed.

This snake takes a great variety of prey, but mostly small fish and anurans. Both live animals and carrion are eaten; Brown (1979a) observed N. fasciata devouring dead frogs off a highway on a rainy June night in North Carolina. Clark (1949) found 60 fish, 85 frogs, and 5 birds in the stomachs of N. f. confluens from Louisiana. In two other Louisiana food studies, Mushinsky and Hebrard (1977a) found the following percentages of total food volume: 71.5% large fish, 13.6% frogs, 6.3% small fish, 4.9% tadpoles, 3.3% toads, and 0.3% crayfish; and Kofron (1978) recorded 10 frogs (including two tadpoles) from nine snakes, and 22 fish from another snake. In Georgia, Camp et al. (1980) found fish, frogs, toads, tadpoles, and sirens in stomachs of N. f. fasciata. Mushinsky et. al. (1982) reported that the major prey changes from fish to frogs as the snakes grow larger than 50 cm SVL. As the mouth gape increases in size the snakes are capable of seizing and swallowing larger prey.

Recorded natural prey are fish—American eels (Anguilla rostrata), pirate perch (Aphredoderus sayanus), suckers (Catostomidae), shad (Dorosoma sp.), banded pygmy sunfish (Elassoma zonatum), redfin pickerel (Esox americanus), killifishes (Fundulus sp.), mosquitofish (Gambusia affinis), least killifish (Heterandria formosa), white catfish (Ameiurus catus), sunfish (Lepomis macrochirus, L. punctatus), rainwater killifish (Lucania parva), black bass (Micropterus sp.), golden shiner (Notemigonus crysoleucas), livebearers (Poecilia sp.), and eastern mudminnow (Umbra pygmaea); anurans—cricket frogs (Acris sp.), southern toad (Bufo terrestris), spadefoots (Scaphiopus holbrookii), microhylids (Gastrophryne carolinensis), treefrogs (Hyla chrysoscelis, H. cinerea, H. femoralis, H.gratiosa H. squirella, H. versicolor), chorus frogs (Pseudacris crucifer, P. triseriata), and ranid frogs (tadpoles and small adults) (Rana capito, R. catesbeiana, R. clamitans, R. palustris, R. sphenocephala, R. virgatipes); salamanders (Desmognathus auriculatus); mudpuppies (Necturus beyeri, N. punctatus); newts (Notophthalmus viridescens); sirens (Siren lacertina); small turtles; small snakes; birds; earthworms; and crayfish (Aresco and Reed 1998; Ashton and Ashton 1981; Brown 1979a; Byrd et al. 1988; Camp et al. 1980; Carpenter 1958; Clark 1949; Collins 1980; Dundee and Rossman 1989; Ernst and Barbour 1989; Jensen 2000; Kennedy 1964; Kofron 1978; Mushinsky and Hebrard 1977a; Mushinsky et al. 1982; Palis 2000; Palmer and Braswell 1995; Tennant 1997; Wright and Wright 1957). Sleijpen (1991) reported a case of cannibalism in captivity.

PREDATORS AND DEFENSE. N. fasciata is preyed on by American alligators (Alligator mississippiensis), cottonmouths (Agkistrodon piscivorous), and common kingsnakes (Lampropeltis getula) (Palmer and Braswell 1995; C. Ernst, pers. obs.), and surely other ophiophagous snakes, large wading birds, hawks, owls, and carnivorous mammals take their toll. In addition, the young are probably eaten by large predatory fish. About 15% of the N. fasciata examined by Mushinsky and Miller (1993) had wounds from a previous predatory attack. Wound frequency increases with increasing body length, suggesting that predators may be less efficient as the snakes grow larger.

Humans also contribute to the destruction of this snake. Many are killed crossing highways adjacent to their water bodies, and draining of these habitats also causes much mortality. Pesticides may kill them, and Hopkins et al. (1999) have found elevated concentrations of arsenic, cadmium, and selenium in the tissues of N. fasciata taken from a site polluted by coal combustion wastes.

When disturbed, *N. fasciata* can put up a spirited defense. It coils, flattens its head and body, strikes, bites viciously, and sprays a pungent musk. A bite from a large individual may result in deep scratches. The species is not considered venomous, but Klynstra (1959) received a bite from a large female that resulted in a painful arm and swollen lymph nodes (perhaps from a secondary bacterial infection?).

POPULATIONS.   It may be very populous at some localities, but uncommon in others. Of 477 *Nerodia* collected in northeastern Arkansas by Hanebrink and Byrd (1986), 134 (28%) were *N. f. confluens*, and of the 2,083 snakes collected by Clark (1949) in northern Louisiana, 370 (17.8%) were *N. fasciata*. In two snake assemblages in the Florida Everglades, *N. f. pictiventris*

totaled only 13 (0.7%) of 1,782 snakes collected at an upland pinewoods site with intersecting wetlands, and 233 (22.9%) of 1,019 snakes collected in a vast seasonally flooded wetland with scattered dwarf cypress forest and marshland (Dalrymple et al. 1991). The species is considered endangered in Illinois and Kentucky.

In three reports on sex ratios, females were more numerous (Byrd et al. 1988; Keck 1994; Sabath and Worthington 1959), but the sample sizes were low and the male to female ratio did not differ significantly from 1:1.

REMARKS.   Molecular and mitochondrial DNA studies indicate *N. fasciata* is closest to *N. harteri, N. clarkii, N. sipedon,* and *N. erythrogaster,* in that order (Densmore et al. 1992; Lawson 1987).

Nerodia floridana (Goff 1936) | Florida Green Water Snake

RECOGNITION.   *N. floridana* is the largest North American water snake, with a record TBL of 188 cm. It is olive to brownish, or occasionally reddish brown, with up to 57 dark bars on each side that fade with age until absent in large individuals. The venter is plain white to cream except near the vent and beneath the tail, where spots or half-moon–shaped marks may be present. Dorsal body scales are keeled and doubly pitted, and occur in 27–29 anterior rows, 25–27 (28–31) midbody rows, and 21–23 posterior rows. The venter has 129–142 ventrals, 63–84 subcaudals, and a divided

anal plate. Lateral head scales are 1 nasal (sometimes divided into two by the nostril), 1 loreal, 1 (2) preocular(s), 1–3 postoculars, 1–2 suboculars (shared only with *N. cyclopion*), 1 + 2 (3) temporals, 7–8 supralabials, and 12–13 (11–14) infralabials. The hemipenis has not been described. Each maxilla has 20–21 teeth.

Males are shorter (to 100 cm TBL), and have 129–137 ventrals, 70–84 subcaudals, and TL 26–27 (25–30) % of TBL; females (to 188 cm TBL) have 131–142 ventrals, 63–79 subcaudals, and TL about 22 (20–24) % of TBL. The relative height of the first dor-

Florida green water snake, *Nerodia floridana*; Alachua County, Florida. (Photograph by Roger W. Barbour)

sal scale row (maximum vertical height of dorsal scale row one divided by maximum width of the vertebral row) is 1.8 (1.7–1.9) in males, and 2.3 (2.1–2.9) in females (Rossman 1995).

GEOGRAPHIC VARIATION. Subspeciation has not been noted, but possible variation between the isolated population in South Carolina and the major southern population should be examined. However, Thompson and Crother (1998) found no allozymatic divergence between the disjunct populations, and thought the apparent break in the range only artificial because this snake is largely nocturnal and rarely captured by hand.

CONFUSING SPECIES. The Mississippi green water snake *(N. cyclopion)* has a heavily spotted venter, and all other species of *Nerodia* lack subocular scales. Cottonmouths *(Agkistrodon piscivorus)* have light facial markings, loreal pits, vertically elliptical pupils, an undivided anal plate, and a single row of subcaudals.

KARYOTYPE. Presumably 36 diploid chromosomes in the same proportions and arrangements as those of *N. cyclopion.*

FOSSIL RECORD. Florida Pleistocene fossils are from an Irvingtonian site in Citrus County (Meylan 1982) and Rancholabrean deposits in Alachua, Columbia, and Manatee counties (Auffenberg 1963). In addition, other fossil Irvingtonian and Rancholabrean remains from Florida identified only to *Nerodia* sp. may possibly be from this species (Brattstrom 1953b; Meylan 1995). Hirschfeld (1968) reported post-Pleistocene remains of *N. floridana* from Dade County, Florida.

DISTRIBUTION. *N. floridana* has a split geographic range. Its main distribution is from southern Georgia south through peninsular Florida, and west through the Panhandle of Florida to Baldwin County, Alabama. A second isolated population occurs in southern and western South Carolina.

HABITAT. This snake is a resident of the littoral zone of quiet waters in lakes, ponds, swamps, sloughs, and drainage canals, but it will swim in open

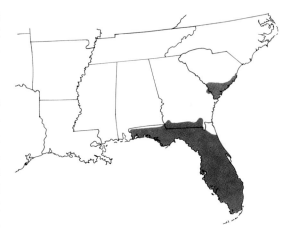

Distribution of *Nerodia floridana.*

water and occasionally enters brackish water. Most of its habitats contain abundant shoreline and/or aquatic vegetation: panic grass *(Panicum),* umbrella grass *(Fuirena),* cattails *(Typha),* water hyacinths *(Eichornia),* pickerel weed *(Pontederia),* and pond lily *(Nuphar).* Lodges of the round-tailed muskrat *(Neofiber alleni)* may be used as dens (Lee 1968a).

BEHAVIOR. Because this large snake is quite visible, it is surprising how little of its life history has been published. Active individuals have been seen in Florida in all months (Wright and Wright 1957), but even there it may be forced to become dormant during severe cold weather. Observations at Lake Conway, Orange County, Florida, seem to indicate nocturnal aquatic activity peaks in spring and fall, with lulls in June–July and winter, but *N. floridana* captured in aquatic traps in summer suggest it is active from spring to fall. Overwintering usually occurs in rodent burrows or lodges. It has been captured in every month except January and October in Aiken County, South Carolina (Gibbons and Semlitsch 1991). Most northern *N. floridana* hibernate during the winter.

Much of the day is spent basking on the bank or emergent vegetation; most foraging is crepuscular or nocturnal, and *N. floridana* is often encountered crossing roads and dikes at such times, especially on rainy nights. A radio-equipped adult female had a small home range along a mere 50 m stretch of shoreline, but other marked *N. floridana* at Lake Conway had a mean home range shoreline length of 202 (0–310) m

(Bancroft et al. 1983). One moved 140 m in two hours, and another 223 m in 1.67 hours. A good swimmer, *N. floridana* can dive and remain underwater for a relatively long time (Murdaugh and Jackson 1962).

The thermal ecology of wild individuals is unknown, but captives do well when kept at 23–27°C (Rossi 1992).

REPRODUCTION. Wright and Wright (1957) gave the minimum adult size as 50.8 cm TBL, and Franz (in Bancroft et al. 1983) found it to be about 70 cm SVL for females and 55 cm SVL for males. Males probably mature in one to two years, and females in two to three years. The gametic cycles have not been reported.

Mating occurs in February–June. Unfortunately the courtship and mating behaviors have not been described. During development, the embryos are associated with the female's uterine wall by a placenta. One ovary may be more active than the other, and some eggs may make intracoelomic migrations to the opposite oviduct (Betz 1963a). Parturition occurs from late June or July to September (Bancroft et al. 1983). Neonates are born approximately 2.5 minutes apart with the chorioallantoic membranes intact, and can usually free themselves from the membranes within 10 minutes (Betz 1963a). Once their heads are free of the membranes, they repeatedly open their mouths widely in an apparent attempt to clear their glottal openings of amniotic fluid, after which they immediately begin to breathe.

Litters contain 7–128 (mean, 47; n = 20) young. Litter size and neonate length and mass are positively correlated with female TBL (Betz 1963a). The mean RCM is 0.151 (0.110–0.199) (Betz 1963a); that of the litter of 128 young was 0.310 (Wray and Morrissey 1999). Each litter usually contains several stillborn young.

Neonates are lighter in color, and have better-developed dark lateral bars than adults. Their TBL is 17.0–28.0 (mean, 24.7; n = 229) cm, and their mass is 2.4–11.7 (mean, 7.6; n = 11) g.

GROWTH AND LONGEVITY. Lake Conway newborns average 32.5 (27.0–40.3) cm SVL by the end of September. Growth rates are rapid, at least from late March through September, and probably average about 32.5 and 15.0 cm in the first and second years, respectively (Bancroft et al. 1983). At Paynes Prairie, Alachua County, Florida, *N. floridana* average about 55 and 70 cm SVL at the end of their first and second years (Franz, in Bancroft et al. 1983). No longevity data are available.

DIET AND FEEDING HABITS. Fish and frogs are the preferred prey, but Ashton and Ashton (1981) reported that in the wild they also eat salamanders, tadpoles, small turtles, and invertebrates. Van Hyning (1932) examined 75 stomachs of *N. floridana* from Florida, and found 66% of the food bulk consisted of frogs, which were found in 10 stomachs. Fish were found in 4 stomachs (26% of the bulk), and 1 stomach contained a salamander (8% of the bulk). Stomachs of three *N. floridana* from Lake Conway contained fish, and one had a "purple fishing worm" (Bancroft et al. 1983). Five other individuals regurgitated fish (principally centrarchids and poeciliids), and another snake regurgitated a greater siren (*Siren lacertina*).

Taub (1967) reported that *N. floridana* has a purely serous Duvernoy's gland, but the secretions from this gland do not appear to be toxic to cold-blooded prey.

PREDATORS AND DEFENSE. Adults are eaten by alligators (*Alligator mississippiensis*) and cottonmouths (*Agkistrodon piscivorus*), and the young are preyed upon by a variety of large fish, snakes, alligators, predatory birds, and otters (*Lontra canadensis*). Captive female *N. floridana* sometimes eat their newborn young (Van Hyning 1931), but this is probably rare in nature.

The greatest losses, however, come from humans who destroy the habitat or kill the snakes outright (confusing them with venomous cottonmouths, *Agkistrodon piscivorus*). The indiscriminate use of insecticides and chemicals, such as rotenone, to catch fish could result in the deaths of many *N. floridana*. Herald (1949) reported that captives sprayed directly with DDT developed paralysis and died within four days, and that several wild *N. floridana* died after their pond was sprayed.

This snake has a vile temper, and if it cannot escape, it will bite and spray musk. Adults are large, and have long teeth that can inflict deep cuts. Generally speaking, it is rather obnoxious, which may, in part, explain why it has been so little studied.

POPULATIONS. It may occur in large numbers in suitable habitat. Carr (1940) counted 13 of them in a 100 m stretch of beach at Lake Okeechobee, and remarked that they are frequently found in groups of six or more basking on rafts of maiden-cane roots in Lake County. This species was the most abundant snake at Lake Conway during studies by Bancroft et al. (1983). About 120 resided in one pool, which supported a mean density of 0.26 N. floridana per meter of shoreline (snake biomass of 116.8 g/m). Most had 51–63 cm SVLs; few under 47 cm or over 95 cm were captured. The sex ratio at Lake Conway was 1.00:1.42, suggesting a bias toward females, but females were recaptured almost three times as often as males, and Bancroft et al. (1983) did not believe the sex ratio different from 1:1. However, Betz (1963a) recorded a sex ratio of 45 females to 34 males in a litter, so perhaps the normal sex ratio does favor females.

REMARKS. Formerly thought to be a Florida subspecies of N. cyclopion, N. floridana is now considered a separate species. Electrophoretic and molecular studies by Lawson (1987) and Pearson (1966) showed a low relationship between N. floridana and N. cyclopion, indicating that the two are separate species. Sanderson (1993) found significant differences in the numbers of ventrals, subcaudals, and dorsal scale rows between the two snakes, and discriminant function analysis of head-scale measurements was also helpful in separating them. Although hybrids have been reported from Alabama (Mount 1975), Sanderson (1993) found no evidence of recent gene exchange between the two species.

Our knowledge of the life history of this poorly known water snake would benefit from a thorough behavioral and ecological study.

Nerodia harteri (Trapido 1941) | Brazos River Water Snake

RECOGNITION. This slender snake is one of the smallest species of Nerodia; its maximum TBL is 90.2 cm, but most individuals are shorter than 60 cm. Body color is light brown, gray brown, or occasionally, olive brown. A pattern of two alternating rows of 44–69 dark spots is present on each side of the body, and the upper spots on the two sides may sometimes unite across the back to form saddles. The head is light brown, with dark brown bars on the supralabials and a small dark spot at the anterior corner of each parietal scale. The chin and throat are cream colored; the rest of the venter is pinkish brown to orangish brown with a row of dark spots on each side. Each dorsal body scale is keeled and has a pair of apical pits; they lie in 21 (22–28) anterior rows, 21 (19–23) midbody rows, and 16–17 (15–18) rows near the tail. On the underside are 143–151 ventrals, 67–88 subcaudals, and a divided anal plate. Laterally on the head are 2 nasals, 1 loreal, 1 (2) preocular(s), 2–3 postoculars, 1 + 2–3 temporals, 8 (9) supralabials, and 10 (9–11) infralabials. The posterior chin shields are separated by two rows of small scales. Each hemipenis is forked and has

an enlarged basal spine and a single sulcus spermaticus bordered by numerous smaller spines, which become shorter distally. Each maxilla has 20–21 teeth.

Males have 143–149 ventrals, 76–88 subcaudals, and TLs 26–27 (25–29) % of TBL; females have 146–151 ventrals, 67–79 subcaudals, and TLs only 23–24 (22–26) % of TBL.

GEOGRAPHIC VARIATION. No subspecies are recognized.

CONFUSING SPECIES. Other species of Nerodia can be identified by the above key. Kirtland's snake (Clonophis kirtlandii) occurs far to the north; it has 17 midbody scale rows and, normally, six supralabials and seven infralabials.

KARYOTYPE. The 36 chromosomes (34 macrochromosomes, 2 microchromosomes) have 68 arms (Baker et al. 1972); in contrast, Eberle (1972) reported that all 36 chromosomes were either submetacentric or metacentric macrochromosomes. Females are ZW and

Brazos River water snake, *Nerodia harteri*; Palo Pinto County, Texas. (Photograph by Norman J. Scott, Jr., U.S. Fish and Wildlife Service)

males ZZ, with the Z chromosome submetacentric and the W chromosome subtelocentric (Baker et al. 1972).

FOSSIL RECORD. None.

DISTRIBUTION. *N. harteri* is found only in the Brazos River drainage of north-central Texas in Bosque, Haskell, Hood, Johnson, Jones, Palo Pinto, Shackelford, Somervell, Throckmorton, and Young counties.

HABITAT. This snake is best associated with the rocky shorelines of swift-moving sections of rivers and streams with water depths seldom more than 30 cm. It has secondarily adapted to the shorelines of impoundments. Juveniles prefer shallow rocky waters for foraging and medium to large rocks on the banks for hiding (Scott et al. 1989).

BEHAVIOR. Few life history data are available. During its annual activity period of March–November, *N. harteri* is most active during the day, although some crepuscular foraging may occur (Tennant 1984; Wor-

ley 1970). It may bask in the morning and afternoon. Temperature data from wild individuals have not been reported, but captives have been successfully maintained at ETs of 18–35°C, with 27°C seemingly the best for them (Carl 1981; Rossi and Rossi 1995).

Distribution of *Nerodia harteri*.

Winters are spent underground in mammal burrows or crevices in the bank.

REPRODUCTION. Males probably reach maturity in one to two years at a SVL of 42–45 cm, and females in two to three years at a SVL of 45+ cm. The gametic cycles have not been described, but females probably ovulate in May or early June, and the neonates appear in late July–September after a gestation period of 2.5–4.0 months (Carl 1981). Carl (1981) observed mating in captivity during the second week of May.

Each litter has 4–24 (mean, 12.2) young (Carl 1981; Conant 1942; McCallion 1944). Litter size is directly correlated with female body length; larger females produce more young. A RCM reported by Seigel and Fitch (1984) was 0.164.

Neonates are patterned like the adults, only brighter; their TBL is 17.0–25.2 (mean, 21.2) cm, and they weigh 2.2–3.9 (mean, 2.9) g (Carl 1981; Conant 1942). SVL and TL are sexually dimorphic within litters, with females averaging longer SVLs and shorter TLs and males shorter SVLs and longer TLs (Carl 1981).

GROWTH AND LONGEVITY. No growth data are available. A female survived five years in captivity after being captured as an adult (Carl 1981).

DIET AND FEEDING HABITS. N. harteri probably begins to feed shortly after emerging from hibernation in the spring, and continues to hunt until the onset of cold weather in the fall. Feeding occurs, particularly by the juveniles, in shallow water.

Fish are probably the most important wild prey, but larval and adult anurans may also be taken. Captives have eaten fish—perch *(Perca flavescens),* smelt, killifish; frogs *(Rana clamitans, R. catesbeiana* tadpoles, *R.*

sylvatica); salamanders *(Desmognathus fuscus, Eurycea bislineata);* and small crayfish (McCallion 1944).

PREDATORS AND DEFENSE. Predators of *N. harteri,* especially of neonates and juveniles, are probably many, but reported examples of predation are almost nonexistent—a western cottonmouth *(Agkistrodon piscivorus leucostoma)* regurgitated one (Jay, in Tennant 1984).

Flight is the first defense, and a disturbed *N. harteri* immediately makes for the water, dives in, and swims rapidly away, usually downstream toward the opposite bank. If pursued, it dives to the bottom and either swims away underwater or hides among the rocks. It can remain submerged for up to 15 minutes (McIntyre; in Tennant 1984). If held, *N. harteri* will spray musk and sometimes defecate or bite.

POPULATIONS. Detailed studies of its distribution and habitat use from 1979 to 1987 by Scott et al. (1989) revealed that *N. harteri* is restricted to about 303 km of stream and two reservoirs in the upper Brazos River drainage. It is locally abundant in the proper habitat; 14 were observed in a 137 m stretch of riffles in Palo Pinto County (Tennant 1984). Nevertheless, it is considered a threatened species.

REMARKS. *N. harteri* is most closely related to *N. paucimaculata* (which was long considered a subspecies of *N. harteri;* see the account of that species for details), and secondarily to *N. fasciata* and *N. erythrogaster* (Densmore et al. 1992; Lawson 1987). The species was reviewed by Mecham (1983).

Since many of its important life history parameters are unknown, a good life history study of *N. harteri* would be beneficial.

Nerodia paucimaculata (Tinkle and Conant 1961) | Concho Water Snake

RECOGNITION. This is the smallest North American species of *Nerodia;* its maximum TBL is only 65.2 cm. Its body is reddish brown to olive brown, and a pattern of two alternating rows of 44–67 faded brown spots is present on each side, with the upper of these spots less developed. The head is brown to reddish

brown, with dark bars on the supralabials, and a small, dark spot at the anterior corner of each parietal scale. The chin and throat are cream colored; the remainder of the venter is cinnamon buff with the center orangish. Dark circular spots are absent from the venter, or are greatly reduced in size. Dorsal body scales

Concho water snake, *Nerodia paucimaculata*; Paint Rock, Texas. (Norman J. Scott, Jr., U.S. Fish and Wildlife Service)

are keeled and doubly pitted, and lie in 21 (22–23) anterior rows, 21 (19–23) midbody rows, and 16–17 (15–18) posterior rows. The venter has 139–151 ventrals, 64–83 subcaudals, and a divided anal plate. Lateral head scales consist of 2 nasals, 1 loreal, 1 (2) preocular(s), 3 postoculars, 1 + 2 temporals, 8 (9) supralabials, and 10 (9–11) infralabials. The posterior chin shields are separated by one row of small scales. The hemipenis has not been described. Each maxilla has 22 teeth.

Males have 139–149 ventrals, 77–83 subcaudals, and TLs 25–26 (24–28) % of TBL; females have 142–151 ventrals, 64–74 subcaudals, and TLs 23–24 (22–26) % of TBL.

GEOGRAPHIC VARIATION. None reported.

CONFUSING SPECIES. See the above key to identify other species of *Nerodia*. Kirtland's snake (*Clonophis kirtlandii*) ranges far north of Texas, has 17 midbody scale rows, and normally has six supralabials and seven infralabials.

KARYOTYPE. Undescribed, but probably similar to that of *N. harteri*.

FOSSIL RECORD. A post-Pleistocene trunk verte-

bra, possibly from *N. paucimaculata*, was found near the Colorado River in Coke County, Texas (Thornton and Smith 1995b).

DISTRIBUTION. *N. paucimaculata* is restricted to the Concho-Colorado River drainages of central Texas in Brown, Concho, Coke, Coleman, Lampasas, McCulloch, Mills, Runnels, San Saba, and Tom Green counties.

Distribution of *Nerodia paucimaculata*.

HABITAT. The prime habitat is a fast-moving section of riffles in a rocky stream with sandy banks, but some now inhabit the banks of lakes, ponds, and impoundments or abandoned oil rigs in aquatic settings. Sixty-two of these snakes observed by Rose (1989) were within 1 m of a riffle, and all but two of the remainder were found within 4 m of a riffle. Juveniles prefer habitats with medium to large, flat rocks for hiding (on unshaded banks), and rocky shallows for foraging (Scott et al. 1989).

BEHAVIOR. N. paucimaculata emerges from hibernation in March and remains active to mid-November (Greene et al. 1994; Rose 1989). Based on capture rates, juveniles are most active in May–July, and show little seasonality in their activity; adult males are most active in late April–early June; adult females are less active than either juveniles or males, with more being captured in May–June and late August–September; most pregnant females are caught in August (Whiting et al. 1996). Winter is spent underground in a burrow among or under rocks. Rose (1989) saw two N. paucimaculata in late March lying near an opening in the north bank of the Concho River; both snakes moved into the burrow, which was about 15 cm from the water surface. Daily retreat sites are usually within 3 m of water, but pregnant females may select sites up to 15 m from water (Whiting et al. 1997).

All those basking, as observed by Rose (1989), did so no more than 2 m above the water surface, and 78% were within 1 m of the water. Exposed roots, overhanging vegetation, and fallen trees were the most-used basking sites; rocks were not used.

It is more sedentary than other Nerodia sharing the same habitat, and usually only undertakes long movements (up to 0.8 km) after habitat loss (Whiting et al. 1998). Eight radio-equipped N. paucimaculata studied by Whiting et al. (1997, 1998) moved an average of only 30.9 (0–458.9) m/day. Males moved on 64% of the monitored days, and pregnant females on only 43% of the days (Whiting et al. 1997). The mean linear home (activity) range was 278 m for males, 219 m for pregnant females, and 210 m for juveniles. A single nonpregnant female had a home range of 271 m.

REPRODUCTION. All males with SVLs greater than 42 cm examined by Greene et al. (1999) contained sperm, and one 38 cm long male had sperm in its cloacal fluids. Of 154 females examined, the minimum SVL of one containing cloacal sperm was 46 cm (Greene et al. 1999). Such lengths are probably reached in one to three years, with males maturing at a shorter length and before females. The gametic cycles have not been described, but females probably ovulate in May or early June, and the young are born in late July–September (most births occur in August). The percentage of females pregnant in a given year varies from 79.5 to 88.8%; larger females are more likely to be fertilized than smaller ones (Greene et al. 1999).

Females found with sperm in their cloacal fluids indicate that mating occurs mostly in April and May, and secondarily in October; the only females found to have mated in the fall were maturing and too small to have mated the previous spring (Greene et al. 1999).

Litters average 13.2 (4–29) young (Greene et al. 1999; Rose 1989). The number of embryos produced increases by one for every 22 mm increase in female SVL; and RCMs average 0.460 (0.310–0.660; n = 27 litters) (Greene et al. 1999).

The body pattern of the young is similar to that of adults, only bolder. Neonates average 1.74 (1.41–1.95) cm in SVL and weigh an average of 3.8 (1.5–4.8) g (Greene et al. 1999). SVL and TL are sexually dimorphic within litters, with females averaging longer SVLs and shorter tails than males (Greene et al. 1999).

GROWTH AND LONGEVITY. No data are available.

DIET AND FEEDING HABITATS. N. paucimaculata feeds from mid-March to early November; pregnant females feed throughout the spring to mid-July, then resume feeding after giving birth (Greene et al. 1994). Neonates and juveniles take prey in proportion to apparent availability, but adults take most of the larger prey; a positive correlation exists between prey size and the snake's SVL.

Most feeding, particularly by juveniles, occurs in shallow water but some prey are taken in open water and from the surface; 69% of all adults, 93% of juveniles, and 100% of the young-of-the-year observed by Rose (1989) foraged in less than 0.2 m deep water. Adults usually forage in riffles, probing between rocks and into cavities under rocks, but juveniles may lie motionless on immovable objects, while completely or partially submerged, near schools of cyprinids, which are attacked when they swim within striking range (Greene et al. 1994).

Fish make up most of the diet, and cyprinids the greatest percentage (75% of the prey recorded by Greene et al. 1994). Recorded prey taken by wild *N. paucimaculata* include fish—Antherinidae *(Menidia beryllina)*, Centrarchidae *(Lepomis cyanellus, L. macrochirus, L. megalotis, Micropterus punctatus)*, Clupeidae *(Dorosoma cepedianum)*, Cyprinidae *(Cyprinella lutrensis, Cyprinus carpio, Nacomis* sp., *Pimephales promelas, P. vigilax)*, Cyprinodontidae *(Cyprinodon rubrofluviatilis, C. viriegatus)*, Ictaluridae *(Ictalurus melas, I. punctatus, Pylodictus olivaris)*, Percidae *(Etheostoma spectabile, Percina macrolepida)*, Poecilidae *(Gambusia affinis)*, and Sciaenidae *(Aplodinotus grunniens)*—and cricket frogs *(Acris crepitans)* (Greene et al. 1994; Rose 1989). Captives have eaten fish *(Carassius auratus, Cyprinella lutrensis, Hybognathus plicata, Ictalurus punctatus, Pimephales* sp.), frogs *(Acris crepitans,* tadpoles of *Rana blairi)*, and hellgrammites (Neuroptera) that had their jaws removed (Rose 1989).

PREDATORS AND DEFENSE. Teeth marks on two radio transmitters of predated *N. paucimaculata* were probably left by a coyote *(Canis latrans),* a raccoon *(Procyon lotor),* or a skunk *(Mephitis mephitis)* (Whiting et al. 1997).

This snake will flee directly to the water when disturbed. If restrained, it will spray musk, defecate, and sometimes bite.

POPULATIONS. Because its habitat has been depleted by past impoundment projects and its populations have declined, the Concho water snake is now considered endangered by the state of Texas and is also listed as threatened under the national Endangered Species Act.

N. paucimaculata occupies 396 stream-km in the Concho-Colorado river watershed, and approximately 25 km of lake (Scott et al. 1989). About 90–99% of the entire population of *N. paucimaculata* is concentrated in only 52% of its current range (Anon. 1986b; Tennant 1984). Even so, the species can be locally abundant in proper habitat: 114 were found along the Concho River in Coke County (Rose 1989); Greene et al. (1994) captured 192 individuals during food studies in 1987–1990; and Greene et al. (1999) recorded 27 pregnant females from 1988 through 1992 at Lake Ballinger, Lake Spence, and two other sites on the Colorado River. The adult sex ratio is essentially 1:1 (Rose (1989; Whiting et al. 1996). The sex ratio of 296 neonates and sexable stillborn embryos examined by Greene et al. (1999) also did not differ significantly from 1:1.

REMARKS. *N. paucimaculata* is most closely related to *N. harteri*, of which it was originally considered a subspecies (Tinkle and Conant 1961). Rose and Selcer (1989) found that the combined number of postoculars on each side equaled five scales in 96% of *N. paucimaculata*, but in only 29% of *N. harteri*; and more than five scales in 71% of *harteri*, but in only 4% of *paucimaculata*. The posterior scale row count was 16 in 85% of *harteri* and 57% of *paucimaculata*, but 17 in 39% of *paucimaculata* and only 15% of *harteri*. On the basis of these scale differences, and a few other minor ones, Rose and Selcer proposed that *N. paucimaculata* be considered a full species. However, they found no genetic differences between the two taxa during protein electrophoretic analyses of 10 isozymes, two plasma proteins, and hemoglobin; also, no polymorphic loci were found. Densmore et al. (1992) reported that the mitochondrial DNA of the two taxa differed by about 2.5%, and were distinguished by two unambiguous apomorphic characters and three homoplastic apomorphic characters. Based on these differences, the scale characters noted by Rose and Selcer, and the allopatry of the populations, Densmore et al. supported the contention that the two taxa are separate species. The species was reviewed by Mecham (1983).

Nerodia rhombifer (Hallowell 1852) | Diamondback Water Snake

RECOGNITION. *N. rhombifer* (maximum TBL 175.3 cm, but most individuals are under 110 cm) has a dorsal pattern of square to diamond-shaped, dark-bordered light brown or gray brown areas, with the dark borders connected in a chainlike pattern. The head is darker brown, with dark bars on the yellow supralabials. The venter is cream to yellow with a pattern of dark gray to black or brown half-moons. Dorsal body scales are keeled and doubly pitted, and lie in 25 (21–28) rows anteriorly, 27 (25–31) rows at midbody, and 21 (18–26) rows near the vent. On the venter are 132–152 ventrals (with no distinct sexual dimorphism), 56–88 subcaudals, and a divided anal plate. Each side of the head has 2 nasals (partially separated by the nostril), 1 loreal, 1 (rarely 2) preocular(s), 3 (2–5) postoculars, 1 + 2 (rarely 3) temporals, 8 (7–11) supralabials, and 11 (10–14) infralabials. The bilobed hemipenis extends caudally to the level of subcaudals six to eight, and its sulcus spermaticus terminates at the junction of two nude lobes; it has a subcylindrical main shaft that is nude at the base, but with two groups of accessory spines above (the proximal spines and spinules are replaced abruptly on the distal half by masses of very small papillose structures ending in minute spines), and a large basal hook, followed distally by another hook, and flanked by a cluster of enlarged spines. Each maxilla has 23–24 teeth.

The shorter males have conspicuous projecting tubercles on their chins, 68–88 (mean, 78.5) subcaudals, and TLs 22–27 (mean, 25) % of TBL; the longer females lack chin tubercles, and have 56–73 (mean, 65.5) subcaudals and TLs 19–24 (mean, 22) % of TBL.

GEOGRAPHIC VARIATION. Three subspecies are recognized (McAllister 1985), but only one, the northern diamondback water snake, *Nerodia r. rhombifer* (Hallowell 1852), described above, occurs north of Mexico.

CONFUSING SPECIES. Other water snakes of the genus *Nerodia* can be distinguished by using the above key. The cottonmouth (*Agkistrodon piscivorus*) lacks the diamond-like dorsal pattern, and has white facial markings, vertically elliptical pupils, a hole between the nostril and eye, and a single row of subcaudals.

KARYOTYPE. Chromosomes total 36. Eberle (1972) found 18 pairs of macrochromosomes (with pairs one, two, three, five, and six submetacenteric, and pair four metacentric), but Baker et al. (1972) reported 17 pairs of macrochromosomes and 1 pair of microchromosomes.

FOSSIL RECORD. Pleistocene (Rancholabrean) remains have been found in Oklahoma (Smith and Cifelli 2000).

DISTRIBUTION. *N. rhombifer* is found from southwestern Indiana, southwestern Illinois, and southeastern Iowa, west to eastern and southern Kansas, south to central Alabama and Mobile Bay, and west through most of Texas, to Chiapas, Tabasco, and Campeche, Mexico.

HABITAT. This snake is one of the more aquatic species of *Nerodia* (Keck 1998). It lives in a variety of bodies of water: lakes, oxbows, bayous, ponds (both natural and cattle), swamps, marshes, sloughs, ditches, and streams. The authors have even taken them from the bank of the Mississippi River. It is partial to waterways with vegetated banks, especially ones with overhanging trees, and is often found where stumps, driftwood, logs, or large rocks are present for hiding or basking places on the bank.

BEHAVIOR. In the deep South, *N. rhombifer* may be active most of the year, especially during those with warm winters, but to the north it must hibernate. It normally becomes active in February–mid-April, and remains active to September–November, depending on the latitude. Hibernation occurs in muskrat (*Ondatra zibethica*) or beaver (*Castor canadensis*) lodges or bank burrows, or possibly in the mud bottom of some waterway.

Most foraging and other activity is nocturnal, particularly during the summer, but occasionally they prowl during the day, especially in the spring and fall. Summer daytime activity consists of basking on banks, logs, branches overhanging the water, or partially submerged stumps or logs. Mushinsky et al. (1980) found it more arboreal in summer than in other seasons.

The thermal ecology of *N. rhombifer* is well defined. Brattstrom (1965) reported that the BTs of active in-

Diamondback water snake, *Nerodia rhombifer rhombifer*; Shelby County, Tennessee. (Photograph by Roger W. Barbour)

dividuals are 24.0–29.8°C, and average 26.8–28.5°C (Brattstrom 1965; Mushinsky et al. 1980). Daily body temperatures are usually close to ambient temperatures, and are higher during the day than at night (Lutterschmidt et al. 1996). In a laboratory study, Jacobson and Whitford (1970) determined the CT_{max} to be 40 and 41°C for *N. rhombifer* acclimated to 15 and 30°C, respectively. Tu and Hutchison (1995b) reported females and males had similar mean preferred BTs, 24.8 (19.6–29.2) and 24.9 (21.3–28.7) °C, respectively. Females carrying young have significantly higher pre-

ferred BTs than nonpregnant females (Tu and Hutchison 1994). BT is apparently not influenced by recent feeding or photoperiod (Tu and Hutchison 1995a, 1995c), but combinations of photoperiod and ET (such as short day and low temperature, or long day and higher temperature) influence the duration of daily activity (Tu and Hutchison 1995c).

Little has been reported concerning movements. One *N. rhombifer* moved 5.8 km in 12 days, but the average distance traveled is only 86.2 (2–321) m/day (Whiting et al. 1998).

Distribution of *Nerodia rhombifer*.

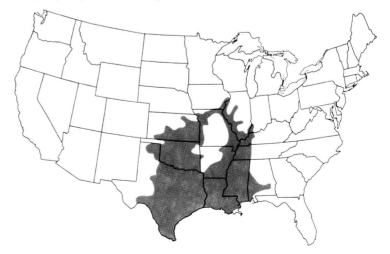

REPRODUCTION. Both sexes mature at an age of 2.5–3.0 years (Betz 1963b; Kofron 1979a). The shortest known male producing sperm (from Veracruz, Mexico) had a SVL of 47.5 cm (Aldridge et al. 1995), but most males probably do not mature until 68–80 cm long. Small mature females have SVLs of 65.5– 68.0 cm (Aldridge et al. 1995; Cagle 1937; Kofron 1979a).

In Veracruz, Mexico, spermatogenesis begins in September, spermatocytes progress to spermatids by October, with peak sperm production in November–early January (Aldridge et al. 1995). From October through early January most males have spermatozoa in the seminiferous tubules. From mid-January through July, the seminiferous tubules contain primarily spermatogonia and spermatocytes, but all sperm have usually passed out of the seminiferous tubules by February. Seminiferous tubule diameter is significantly lower from February through August.

Vitellogenesis is seasonal in Mexico, with some females yolking eggs throughout the year (Aldridge et al. 1995). In the United States, final vitellogenesis occurs in April; ovulation is in May–June in Mexico (Aldridge et al. 1995), but extends from early May through the third week of July in Louisiana (Kofron 1979a), and in Missouri from mid-May to mid-June (Betz 1963b). United States females are noticeably pregnant by late June, and the young are born in late July–early November, but usually in August–September (Gloyd 1928; Judd and Bray 1996; Kennedy 1964). A south-central Texas female contained fully developed fetuses in March, possibly from a fall mating (Vermersch and Kuntz 1986), and a captive that had mated in March gave birth on 15 June (Termeer 1987). Most females probably produce young annually (Aldridge et al. 1995; Betz 1963b, 1963c; Cagle 1937).

Recently ovulated eggs of *N. rhombifer* contain 41–48% water, 46–56% organic matter, and 3–5% inorganic salts; total protein is higher in the yolk than total lipid (Steward and Castillo 1984). Some placental transfer of certain mineral ions, particularly sodium and potassium, occurs.

Mating occurs in April and May soon after the emergence from hibernation (C. Ernst, pers. obs.; Meade 1934a). C. Ernst observed an early May mating in a shallow pool in a western Kentucky swamp. The snakes were entwined with the male on top. Contrary to popular belief (Collins 1993; Vermersch and Kuntz

1986), the male did not rub his chin tubercles on the female, but frequently touched her nape with his tongue.

Litters contain 8–62 (mean, 26.8; n = 56) young (Anderson 1965; Cagle 1937). A direct correlation exists between the number of young per litter and female body size, with larger females producing more offspring. Reported RCMs range from 28.9 to 37.0% (Plummer 1992; Seigel and Fitch 1984; Tucker and Camerer 1994). Neonates normally have 20.0–33.2 (mean, 25.8) cm TBLs and weigh 3.2–13.6 (mean, 9.0) g. Their body pattern is more pronounced than that of adults.

GROWTH AND LONGEVITY. No data exist on natural growth rates, but growth of a litter was monitored in the laboratory for two years by Scudder-Davis and Burghardt (1996). Growth efficiency (growth per unit of food consumed) decreased with age. Growth of both sexes decreased at approximately the same rate, but females allocated more ingested food resources for increases in mass and SVL, while males devoted more resources to increasing TL. Females had SVLs of 24.0–25.5 cm at birth, 35.0–40.4 cm at one year; and 48.0–56.9 cm at two years. Males were 23.4–25.3 cm SVL at birth, 33.8–37.5 cm at one year, and 46.7–51.5 cm at two years.

Snider and Bowler (1992) reported a longevity record of 4 years and 11 months.

DIET AND FEEDING HABITS. This species is decidedly piscivorous, but anurans also constitute a large part of the diet. Bowers (1966) reported that fish made up 50.0% and anurans 44.6% of the total volume of his sample, and Mushinsky and Hebrard (1977a) reported 95.2% of the total volume of prey in their study was fish. Natural prey are fish—American eel (*Anguilla rostrata*), shad (*Dorosoma cepedianum*), catfish (*Ameiurus melas, A. natalis, Bagre marinus, Ictalurus furcatus, I. punctatus, Pylodictos olivaris*), suckers (*Carpiodes carpio*), cyprinids (*Cyprinodon variegatus, Cyprinus carpio, Notemigonus crysoleucas, Notropis sp., Pimephales promelas*), mosquitofish (*Gambusia affinis*), livebearers (*Poecilia latipinna, P. mexicana*), killifish and topminnows (*Fundulus grandis, F. notatus, Lucania parva*), silversides (*Menidia audens*), sunfish (*Lepomis cyanellus, L. punctatus*), pygmy sunfish (*Elassoma zonatum*), crappies (*Pomoxis sp.*), black bass (*Micropterus punctatus, M. salmoides*), white bass (*Morone chrysops*), drums (*Aplodinotus grunniens*,

Cynoscion arenarius), gobies *(Dormitator maculatus, Gobionella shufeldti)*, and mullet *(Mugil cephalus, M. curema)*; anurans (tadpoles and small adults)—toads *(Bufo woodhousei)*, ranid frogs *(Rana blairi, R. catesbeiana, R. clamitans, R. sphenocephala)*, green treefrogs *(Hyla cinerea)*, and tropical frogs *(Leptodactylus melanonotus)*; small turtles *(Chelydra serpentina)*; snakes; birds; cotton rats *(Sigmodon hispidis)*; crayfish *(Procambarus* sp.); shrimp *(Palaemonetes* sp.); and insects—grasshoppers (Caelifera), dipterans (Chironomidae, Culicidae), beetles (Coleoptera), dragonflies (Odonata), and damselflies (Zygoptera) (Bowers 1966; Byrd et al. 1988; Cagle 1937; Carpenter 1958; Clark 1949; Hess and Klimstra 1975; Kofron 1978; Laughlin 1959; Manjarrez and Macias Garcia 1991; Mushinsky and Hebrard 1977a; Mushinsky et al. 1982; Plummer and Goy 1984; Sisk and McCoy 1963; Webb 1970). Most fish captured are rather slow swimmers, and some fish are taken as carrion.

Prey is located both by olfaction and sight. *N. rhombifer*'s prey-attack response is elicited by fish extracts (Czaplicki 1975), and Czaplicki and Porter (1974) found that the contrast of fish with their background is a major factor in prey selection, while size, activity, and proximity are of little or no importance. Kofron and Dixon (1980) observed that diamondback water snakes feeding in shallow water trap fish in their coils before seizing them with their mouths, and Byrd et al. (1988), Evans (1942), and Gillingham and Rush (1974) have described a peculiar open-mouthed feeding behavior. Snakes may lie facing into the current with their mouths open and their tails anchored to rocks, or they may swim with open mouths. Neonates are negatively buoyant and forage only at the surface of their aquatic habitat, capturing live fish mostly by the head (Savitsky and Burghardt 2000). Open-mouthed foraging is only rudimentarily developed in young snakes. With age they shift from hunting in patches of dense aquatic vegetation to more open water foraging, and spend more time foraging underwater and less time at the surface. They become more proficient in capturing and handling prey, and open-mouthed foraging develops slowly with time.

A gradual ontogenetic shift in the diet from small fish species to larger ones occurs as *N. rhombifer* grows larger and the gape of its mouth becomes greater. Individuals longer than 80 cm SVL feed entirely on large fish (Mushinsky et al. 1982; Plummer and Goy 1984).

PREDATORS AND DEFENSE. The young are preyed upon by large predatory fish, bullfrogs *(Rana catesbeiana)*, snapping turtles *(Chelydra serpentina)*, other ophiophagous snakes, shrikes *(Lanius ludovicianus)*, large wading birds, raptors, and carnivorous mammals. A captive was eaten by a cat-eyed snake *(Leptodeira septentrionalis)* (Burchfield 1993).

Humans cause the most damage to populations of *N. rhombifer*. Many are killed when they are mistaken for venomous snakes, and many others die on our roads. Habitat destruction has also taken a heavy toll. Fortunately, the indiscriminate use of insecticides has slowed, and this may save many individuals. Death of *N. rhombifer* from DDT and heptachlor poisoning has been documented (Boyd et al. 1963; Ferguson 1963).

Disturbed *N. rhombifer* drop or crawl quickly into the water, dive to the bottom, and swim rapidly away. They are capable of remaining underwater for over an hour (Baeyens et al. 1978). If handled, they bite viciously and spray musk.

POPULATIONS. *N. rhombifer* is often very common at some localities, but rare at others (it is considered threatened in Iowa). The species only constituted 6.3% of over 33,000 snakes recorded statewide in Kansas by Fitch (1993), but in the Cheyenne Bottoms *N. rhombifer* constituted 56.5% of the snakes recorded where 218 were collected in a little more than a month (Collins and Collins 1993). In the upstate parishes of Louisiana, it accounted for 12% of the 1,083 snakes recorded by Clark (1949). Diamondback water snakes made up 49.5% of 477 snakes examined in northeastern Arkansas by Hanebrink and Byrd (1986). Size classes of these populations favor individuals with SVLs larger than 70 cm (Clarke 1958). Litter sex ratios have ranged from 3:1 in a litter born in captivity (Conant 1969), to 0.27–0.69:1.00 in captive litters reported by Plummer (1992), to 0.82:1.00 for litters examined by Tucker and Camerer (1994). Keck (1994) found a 1:1 sex ratio in *N. rhombifer* captured in northeastern Texas.

REMARKS. Cliburn (1956) reported that *N. rhombifer* overlaps *N. taxispilota* in both the number of dorsal body scale rows and the dorsal color pattern, and he believed the two snakes represented subspecies of the single species *N. taxispilota*. However, Mount and

Schwaner (1970) found no evidence of intergradation. Analysis of allozyme frequency data from several tissues and mapping analysis of mitochondrial DNA indicate these two snakes are separate but closely related species (Densmore et al. 1992; Lawson 1987). *N. rhombifer* has been reviewed by McAllister (1985).

Nerodia sipedon (Linnaeus 1758) | Northern Water Snake

RECOGNITION. *N. sipedon* is medium sized (TBL to 150 cm), usually tan to gray, with wide brown or reddish brown dorsal blotches along its anterior third and dark brown rectangles alternating along back and sides posterior to this. Dark bars are present on the supralabials, but no dark stripe extends from the orbit to the corner of the mouth. The chin, throat, and venter are cream to yellow; a pattern of reddish half-moons is present on the venter. Neonates are more contrastingly marked than adults, which become darker with age until the dorsal and ventral patterns are obscured. Individuals lacking dorsal bands or ventral half-moons occur in some populations (Bulmer 1985). Dorsal body scales are strongly keeled with two apical pits, and occur in 21 (22–23) anterior rows, 23 (21–25) midbody rows, and 17 or 19 (16) posterior

Northern water snake, *Nerodia sipedon sipedon*; Fayette County, Kentucky. (Photograph by Roger W. Barbour)

Midland water snake, *Nerodia sipedon pleuralis*; Tuscaloosa County, Alabama. (Photograph by Steve W. Gotte)

Carolina water snake, *Nerodia sipedon williamengelsi*; Carteret County, North Carolina. (Photograph by Christopher W. Brown, DVM)

rows. The venter has 123–155 ventrals, 42–84 subcaudals, and a divided anal plate. Lateral head scales include 2 nasals (partially divided by the nostril), 1 (rarely 2) loreal(s), 1 (2) preocular(s), 3 (2) postoculars, 1 + 2–3 (4) temporals, 8 (7–9) supralabials, and 10 (9–12) infralabials. The hemipenis has a single sulcus spermaticus, numerous spinules but only a few spines, and several enlarged basal hooks. Each maxilla has 23–25 teeth.

Adult females are larger and heavier than adult males and have 42–77 (mean, 64) subcaudals and TLs 20.0–25.0 (mean, 22.0) % of TBL; males have 62–84 (mean, 75) subcaudals and TLs 23.5–29.0 (mean, 25.5) % of TBL.

GEOGRAPHIC VARIATION. Four subspecies are recognized. *N. s. sipedon* (Linnaeus 1758), the northern water snake, occurs from southern Quebec, Maine, and southern Ontario south to northern South Carolina, Georgia, and Alabama, and west to eastern Minnesota, Kansas, eastern Colorado, and northeastern Oklahoma. It has dark dorsal crossbands on the neck and forepart of the body, dark lateral blotches that are wider than the light spaces between them, and dark brown or reddish brown half-moons scattered on the venter that continue to the tip on the underside of the tail. *N. s. insularum* (Conant and Clay 1937), the Lake Erie water snake, is only found on islands in the Put-in-Bay Archipelago of Lake Erie. It is pale gray to olive, usually lacks a dorsal pattern, and has a cream venter. If a dorsal pattern is present, it is similar to that of *N. s. sipedon*, but usually faded (for discussions of the patterns and their possible evolution, and the size variation that occurs among the island populations, see Beatson 1976; Camin et al. 1954; Camin and Ehrlich 1958; Ehrlich and Camin 1960; King 1986, 1989, 1992, 1993b, 1993c; King and Lawson 1997; Pough 1976). *N. s. pleuralis* (Cope 1892b), the midland water snake, ranges from the southern portions of Indiana, Illinois, and Missouri west to eastern Oklahoma, and south to the Gulf Coast from Escambia County, Florida, west to eastern Louisiana. This race has the lateral dark blotches smaller than the light spaces between them, and the venter has a double row of half-moons. Some individuals have dark dorsal crossbands the entire length of the body and tail. *N. s. williamengelsi* (Conant and Lazell 1973), the Carolina water snake, occurs only on the Outer Banks of North Carolina and the adjacent mainland coasts of Pamlico and Core sounds. It is almost completely black dorsally, and those ventral half-moons posterior to the 50th ventral are solid black. Intergrade individuals are common in areas where the ranges of the subspecies meet.

CONFUSING SPECIES. Other *Nerodia* can be distinguished by using the key presented above. The cottonmouth (*Agkistrodon piscivorus*) has vertically elliptical pupils, a hole between its nostril and eye, and a single row of subcaudals under the tail. The queen snake (*Regina septemvittata*) has a yellow stripe on each side flanked by three narrow dark stripes, and four dark stripes on its venter.

KARYOTYPE. The karyotype consists of 36 macrochromosomes (30 submetacentrics and 6 subtelocentrics); sex determination is ZZ/ZW, and both Z and W chromosomes are submetacentric (Eberle 1972; Kilpatrick and Zimmerman 1973).

Prosser et al. (1999) described the characters of eight microsatellite DNA loci of *N. sipedon*, and found they showed heterozygosity of 29–91%. After examining local populations of the snakes, they concluded that microgeographic genetic structure exists, possibly due to limited dispersal.

FOSSIL RECORD. The fossil record of *N. sipedon* dates from the early Blancan of the Pliocene, and is quite geographically diverse: Pliocene (Blancan)—Nebraska (Holman and Schloeder 1991); Pleistocene (Blancan)—Kansas (Eshelman 1975; Holman 1972b; Rogers 1982), Nebraska (Holman 1972a), and West Virginia (Holman 1982b); Pleistocene (Irvingtonian)—Kansas (Brattstrom 1976; Holman 1971, 1972b), Maryland (Holman 1977b), South Dakota (Holman 1977a), and West Virginia (Holman and Grady 1989); and Pleistocene (Rancholabrean)—Alabama (Holman et al. 1990), Georgia (Holman 1967, 1985), Kansas (Brattstrom 1967; Holman 1986c, 1987b), Missouri (Holman 1974), Ohio (Holman 1997), Pennsylvania (Guilday et al. 1964), Tennessee (Van Dam 1978), Virginia (Holman 1986a; Holman and McDonald 1986),

and West Virginia (Holman and Grady 1994). The Irvingtonian record from South Dakota is extralimital and indicates that the species once had a more extensive range.

DISTRIBUTION. *N. sipedon* ranges from extreme southern Quebec, Maine, and southern Ontario, south to the Carolinas, central Georgia, and the Gulf Coast of the Florida Panhandle, west to eastern Minnesota, Iowa, Kansas, eastern Colorado, Oklahoma, central Arkansas, and Louisiana.

HABITAT. This aquatic snake can be found in any freshwater body within its range as long as there is abundant food and cover. It has been recorded from lakes, ponds, swamps, marshes, bogs, rivers, oxbows, streams, creeks, brooks, canals, and sloughs, with bottoms varying from rock or gravel to sand or mud. Abundant aquatic vegetation may or may not be present. *N. s. williamengelsi* lives in salt marshes and brackish water habitats closely associated with the plants *Spartina* and *Juncus* (Conant and Lazell 1973), and at some other sites *N. s. sipedon* also occasionally enters brackish water. However, *N. sipedon* requires freshwater. When compared with the estuarine *N. clarkii* and some marine species of snakes, it has a greater rate of water influx (Dunson 1980; Zug and Dunson 1979).

BEHAVIOR. The literature concerning *N. sipedon* is extensive, and much of its life history is well documented. In the North, it usually emerges from hiber-

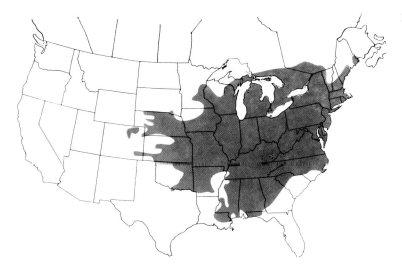

Distribution of *Nerodia sipedon*.

nation in March–April or as late as early May and remains active to October–November, with most activity in April–August. Southern *N. sipedon* may not be forced to hibernate for long durations, but instead may only seek shelter during cold periods and become sporadically active on warm winter days.

When forced to hibernate, those in the north use a variety of sites such as earthen and rock dams, stone causeways, flood walls, levees, beaver *(Castor canadensis)* and muskrat *(Ondatra zibethica)* bank burrows and lodges, meadow vole *(Microtus pennsylvanicus)* tunnels, ant mounds, crayfish burrows, the bases of sedge clumps, hollow logs and stumps, and deep cracks in upland rock ledges. Anderson (1965) found *N. sipedon* hibernating approximately 400 m from the water, and Breckenridge (1944) observed 35 *N. sipedon* moving in the fall toward hills overlooking their body of water; so a short overland migration may be needed to reach a hibernaculum. Several individuals may share the same hibernaculum (73 were found together under a stream bank in Missouri; Anderson 1965). The electrolyte composition and osmolality of the plasma is different during the winter than in the summer, presumably an adaptation for overwinter survival (Wasser 1990). Carpenter (1953a) reported a BT of 7°C for a hibernating individual in Michigan, and Brattstrom (1965) reported a questionable CT_{min} of –2°C. *N. sipedon* is diurnal during the cooler periods of the spring and fall, but becomes more nocturnal during the summer. In summer, the day is spent either hiding or basking; most foraging is done from twilight to midnight (Brown 1958; Diener 1957b). Although these snakes are nocturnal at most localities in the summer, Tiebout and Cary (1987) reported them equally active at all times of the day from May through July in southeastern Wisconsin; and in coldwater Appalachian trout streams in Pennsylvania they are decidedly diurnal during the entire annual activity period (Swanson 1952).

N. sipedon spends much time basking on the shore or while lying on branches overhanging the water (mean perch height, 11 cm; Tiebout and Cary 1987). At a site in Ontario, basking peaked at 0900 hours and then declined steadily until 1400 hours before increasing again (Robertson and Weatherhead 1992). BTs of baskers averaged 26.3°C, and none exceeded 33.0°C. Snakes basking at lower heights retreated to the water sooner than those perched higher (Weatherhead and Robertson 1992).

In Kansas, Clarke (1958) observed 36 *N. sipedon* at ATs of approximately 15–39°C, with 21 (58.3%) of the records falling between 26 and 34°C. BTs of active wild individuals are 16.0–30.0°C, and average about 26°C (Brattstrom 1965; Brown and Weatherhead 2000; Fitch 1956). When given a choice of ETs in a thermal gradient, this species normally selects 20.8–34.7 (mean, 28.0) °C, but chooses gradients of 22.2–31.6 (mean, 28.8) °C after feeding, and temperatures of 17.2–20.4 (mean, 18.7) °C while shedding (Kitchell 1969). Justy and Mallory (1985) subjected *N. sipedon* to another thermal gradient exam, and found that the ETs selected in the morning under light and dark regimes were not significantly different from those chosen in the afternoon under the same conditions. The snakes had mean BTs of 30.4°C in the light and 32.0°C in the dark during the morning, and 34.0°C in the light and 29.5°C in the dark in the afternoon. Lutterschmidt and Reinert (1990) found that *N. sipedon* chose a mean ET of 27.7°C before being fed or made to swallow a radio transmitter, and 36.0 and 36.4°C, respectively, afterwards. Northern water snakes that have just eaten usually seek a warmer ET, and their metabolic rate (as measured by oxygen consumption) increases following a meal, presumably to enhance digestion (Sievert and Andreadis 1999). However, Brown and Weatherhead (2000) found that feeding did not elicit a thermophilic response under laboratory conditions or when the snakes were fed experimentally in the field, suggesting that the benefits of increasing BT after eating do not outweigh the costs. In Ontario, Canada, the typical BT pattern is an increase in late morning to a plateau BT in the preferred range, followed by a decrease in the evening, with a night plateau similar to the water temperature (Brown and Weatherhead 2000). Preferred BT may be influenced by developmental temperature (Blouin-Demers et al. 2000).

After snakes enter cold water, the BT declines rapidly and then stabilizes at approximately 2°C above the WT (Weatherhead and Robertson 1992). The metabolic heat generated by the snake's activity probably prevents its BT from completely equilibrating with the WT, and may have a slight retarding effect on the cooling rate. Smaller individuals cool more rapidly than larger ones. *N. sipedon* acclimates rather quickly to changes in ET, but acclimation is a significant function of body mass, with small snakes acclimating more rapidly than large ones (Blem and Blem 1990a). Escape responses are correlated with neither WTs (17.8–27.4°C) nor ATs (16.0–29.1°C). Reproductive females thermoregulate more carefully during the GP than nonreproductive females, possibly to aid embryo development; males thermoregulate less than females of any condition (Brown and Wheatherhead 2000).

During most of their annual activity period, *N. sipedon* seldom moves far. Two adult males and two adult females equipped with radios in Kansas moved an average of 21 m/day; movements were both aquatic and terrestrial (Fitch 1999), and a juvenile was recaptured three times within a 4.6 m radius (Fitch 1956). A radio-equipped male was found 15 times in 23 days within a space of 9 m along the edge of the pond; and a pregnant female located 24 times in 35 days (with an 8 day interruption while she gave birth in the laboratory) made one shift of 21 m, two of 10.5 m, and one of 9 m, but otherwise stayed in the same place or moved no more than 4.5 m (Fitch and Shirer 1971). Another pregnant female made only short movements of 1.2–7.5 m in 4 days. At another site, Stickel and Cope (1947) recaptured an individual two years later only 116 m from its initial capture spot.

The rate of movement on land is temperature dependent; *N. sipedon* with masses of 7.1–149.2 g had mean maximum terrestrial velocities of 0.10 m/second at 10°C, 0.31 m/second at 20°C, and 0.43 m/second at 30°C (Finkler and Claussen 1999). The mean crawling speed of radio-equipped females in Wisconsin was 5.2 m/hour (Tiebout and Cary 1987).

N. sipedon marked in ponds at an Indiana fish hatchery tended to stay in one pond; 61% of recaptures in small ponds and 80% of recaptures in large ponds were in the same pond as the previous capture (Fraker 1970). If an adjacent pond was included, 81% of the snakes from small ponds were recaptured in either the original or the adjacent pond, and for large ponds the percentage rose to 98% (water snakes living in an adjacent stream were recaptured less often). The mean home range of Wisconsin *N. sipedon* was 5.4 ha, with a very concentrated core area averaging 7.7% of the entire range (Tiebout and Cary 1987).

This snake does make some long-distance movements, especially during migrations to and from hibernacula (Breckenridge 1944). Fitch (1999) reported that 8.2% of the *N. sipedon* in a Kansas pond were found in fields away from water; 6.0% were found along a small intermittent creek draining the pond, or its diversion ditch; 6.0% were found at far ponds and streams; 4.7% were on roads; and 2.8% were found in the fall and spring at upland limestone outcrops that served as hibernacula. The greatest straight-line distances recorded by Fitch (1999) were 1.15–1.73 km, and movements over 1 km were made by both sexes in almost all compass directions. Ten radio-equipped females followed by Tiebout and Cary (1987) used a hibernaculum 0.5 km from their summer home range, and some in Missouri hibernated 0.4 km from their summer range (Anderson 1965).

Fraker (1970) displaced some *N. sipedon* 0.12 and 0.31 km, both up- and downstream, to determine homing ability—about 20% of the snakes returned home. However, only larger snakes returned from 0.31 km, while shorter snakes could home from 0.12 km. Homing movements of 0.23–0.68 km were made in intervals of 11–51 days. Fraker thought odors may have aided the snakes' orientation, but Newcomer et al. (1974) have shown that *N. sipedon* is capable of sun compass orientation.

N. sipedon is a good swimmer that is often seen swimming with only its head above the surface. It is capable of foraging underwater and can remain submerged for over 65 minutes (Ferguson and Thornton 1984). Adults can sustain maximum activity at 25°C for about 42 minutes because of their increased blood oxygen capacity and decreased blood oxygen affinity, but neonates become exhausted in 5 minutes (Pough 1978).

REPRODUCTION.   Female *N. sipedon* usually mature in two to three years; males mature in 21–24 months (Bauman and Metter 1977; Feaver 1976; Pope 1944). Most females are mature at SVLs of 50–65 cm, but Feaver (1976) reported one from Michigan was mature at 47.5 cm. Males mature at a slightly smaller SVLs, 37–45 cm (Feaver 1976; King 1986; Mitchell 1994).

The female gametic cycle is well documented. Follicular growth is minimal throughout the year except for a short four- to six-week spring period during which yolking and rapid growth take place prior to ovulation in late May–June (Callard et al. 1991). Follicle mass increases from about 0.2 g to almost 4 g between mid-May and late June, and females are pregnant by June (Bauman and Metter 1977; King 1986). Aldridge (1982) found that the number of previtellogenic follicles is approximately three times greater than the number of vitellogenic follicles or embryos present in a pregnant female. Follicles smaller than 5 mm do not appear to have a seasonal growth pattern, but larger follicles undergo marked seasonal changes. Those bigger than 5 mm are absent during gestation, begin to appear after parturition, and reach a maximum size of 9 mm by hibernation. When vitellogenesis occurs in the spring, all follicles larger than 5 mm become yolked and are either ovulated or become atretic. Testosterone and estradiol are the dominant follicular phase plasma steroids, when vitellogenin is also present; progesterone is present at high levels throughout the pregnancy (Callard et al. 1991).

The GP is 9–12 weeks (Bauman and Metter 1977; Callard et al. 1991), during which the embryos are nourished through a placenta (Conway and Fleming 1960). The uterine region of the female's oviduct begins to grow coincident with spring follicle yolking, and continues to increase in size through the gestation period to late pregnancy, when the embryonic mass is greatest (Koob and Callard 1982). Both estradiol and progesterone receptors are present in the oviduct, and the progesterone receptors are apparently controlled by the estradiol (Callard et al. 1991). Langlois (1924) reported that in Michigan the embryos increase in length from about 75 to 180 mm between 10 July and 21 August. Occasionally, extrauterine embryos occur (Neill 1948c).

Males produce sperm after the breeding season and store it over winter for use the next spring (Bauman and Metter 1977; Weil and Aldridge 1981). Upon emergence from hibernation, the male's seminiferous tubules are filled with Sertoli cells and some sperm and germinal elements that were not released the preceding fall (Bauman and Metter 1977). In mid-April, spermatogonia increase in number, and many cells transform into primary spermatocytes and migrate to the center of the tubules. By early May primary spermatocytes are dominant, but some secondary spermatocytes are also present. The first spermatids appear in early June, and mature sperm are present by mid-July. The rate of spermatogenesis increases with increased ETs (Weil and Aldridge 1979). As the sperm mature, they move out from testes and are stored in the vasa deferentia. The testes contain both sperm and spermatids until early October, when Sertoli cells again fill the lumina of the seminiferous tubules. Seminiferous tubule diameter increases from a minimum at the time of spring emergence to a maximum during July–August, the peak of spermatogenesis, then shrinks during September and October as sperm leave the testes until it is once again at minimum size in December (Bauman and Metter 1977). Correspondingly, seasonal plasma testosterone levels are highest in the spring at the time of mating, decrease in July, and increase again in late summer and fall during maximum spermiogenesis (Weil and Aldridge 1981). Young males experience elevated testosterone levels early in life; King et al. (2000) found testosterone levels uniformly low during the first 30 days after birth, but significantly increased by 250–267 days of age. Increased amounts of follicle stimulating hormone (FSH) cause great increases in testis mass, seminiferous tubule diameter, and epithelial thickness; increased levels of luteinizing hormone (LH) induce lipid accumulation, enlargement of the mitochondria in the Leydig cells, and consequent male hormone production (Krohmer 1986).

The breeding season extends from mid-April to mid-June, although most mating occurs in May–June. It is possible that a second, less intense mating season occurs in the fall; Anderson (1965) observed an apparent attempt at mating on 26 September in Missouri. Courtship and mating usually take place during the day, but night matings do occur (C. Ernst, pers. obs.). Most courtship and copulation take place on land, or sometimes above ground in bushes (Casper 1993), but the authors have seen *N. sipedon* mating in shallow water.

Males actively search for females, possibly by following pheromone trails (Scudder et al. 1980), and when a female is found, the male examines her closely with tongue flicks. The male then aligns himself beside the female and rubs his body against hers. He subsequently places his head on her back, begins to rub her dorsum with his chin, and as he moves his body forward, jerks it spasmodically. Next, he coils around the female and explores for her vent with his tail. When the vent is found, the male inserts his hemipenis (Brophy 1998; C. Ernst, pers. obs.; Mushinsky 1979; Perry 1920). The entire courtship-mating sequence may take two to three hours.

Birth usually occurs in late August–September, but wild litters have been delivered from 8 August (Brown 1992) to 17 October (Palmer and Braswell 1995). Litters contain 6 (Minton 1972) to 99 (Slevin 1951) young; the average is 27.2 young (n = 132). Most litters are composed of 20–40 young. Females in northern populations have larger litters than those from the south (Fitch 1985a). Also, litter size tends to increase with increased female body size (Barron 1997a; Bauman and Metter 1977; King 1986). Barron (1997a) reported relative clutch masses of 0.35 and 0.38 for litters from Indiana, and Koob and Callard (1982) found that females carry an average total conceptus weight equal to 20% of maternal weight, though they might accommodate as much as 43% of body weight.

More than one male may father a particular litter; Barry et al. (1992), through protein electrophoretic analysis, found that the young in 12 of 14 Ontario litters from naturally mated females had more than one father. Since males cannot force copulations, multiple matings are the result of female choice. Also, Skalka and Vozenilek (1986) reported an apparent case of parthenogenesis by a female N. sipedon kept alone for 40 months.

The average TBL and mass of 76 neonates the authors examined were 21.8 (15.8–30.1) cm and 4.1 (1.5–4.8) g, respectively.

GROWTH AND LONGEVITY. Early growth of neonates is rapid, but the rate of growth slows with age. Raney and Roecker (1947) found that New York N. sipedon collected in their first fall and early the next spring had 20–25 cm TBLs, while those one year old were 35–40 cm long. These lengths represented an annual growth rate for juveniles of slightly greater than 50%. In Missouri, one-year-old males averaged 43 cm SVL, as compared with 19 cm when born (Bauman and Metter 1975).

In Kansas, first-year young averaged 18.7 cm SVL in September, 19.7 cm in October, 20.0 cm the next April, 22.8 cm in May, 23.1 cm in June, 28.9 cm in July, and one-year-olds in August–October averaged 31.3

cm (Fitch 1999). Masses of these snakes increased from an average of 3.83 g in the September after birth to 18.7 g in August–October of the next year. King (1986) studied seasonal growth of yearling N. sipedon on islands in Lake Erie. Growth rates estimated from mean cohort SVL sampled at 20 day intervals beginning 4 May were 0.002, 0.034, 0.083, 0.128, 0.256, and 0.066 cm/day; the most rapid growth occurred between late July and mid-August. The growth rate over the entire sampling period was 0.092 cm/day. From this, the annual growth rate of these young snakes was estimated to be 0.033 cm/day, two to three times that of older juveniles and adults. Juvenile and adult males grew an average of 0.012 (maximum 0.053) cm/day; juvenile and adult females grew an average rate of 0.014 (maximum 0.058) cm/day. Females grew much longer (59–144 cm SVL) than males (43–125 cm SVL). Brown and Weatherhead (1999b) reported sexual growth dimorphism in Ontario N. sipedon.

Snider and Bowler (1992) reported the maximum known longevity of N. sipedon is 9 years, 7 months, and 24 days.

DIET AND FEEDING HABITS. Fish are the favorite prey. In studies listing food incidence or volume, fish made up 50–96% of the food volume and 56–90% by frequency of occurrence, and amphibians 4–52% by volume and 17% by frequency. While N. sipedon does take some game and pan fish, most fish species eaten are rough fish, and many are taken as carrion. Because of its preference for a diet of fish, N. sipedon can create a serious problem when present at a fish hatchery (Baumen and Metter 1975). It is primarily a fish eater, but other prey are also taken. Reported wild prey include fish—lampreys (Ichthyomyzon castaneus, Lampetra appendix, Petromyzon marinus), freshwater eels (Anguilla rostrata), herrings and shads (Alosa pseudoharengus, Dorosoma cepedianum), trout (Oncorhynchus mykiss, Salmo trutta, Salvelinus fontinalis), mudminnows (Umbra limi), pickerel (Esox americanus), minnows, daces and chubs (Campostoma anomalum, Carassius auratus, Cyprinella lutrensis, C. spiloptera, Cyprinus carpio, Margariscus margarita, Nocomis biguttatus, N. leptocephalus, Notemigonus chrysoleucas, Notropis heterodon, N. heterolepis, N. hudsonius, N. rubellus, Phoxinus eos, P. erythrogaster, Pimephales notatus, Rhinichthys atratulus,

R. cataractae, Semotilus atromaculatus), suckers *(Catostomus commersoni, Erimyzon* sp., *Hypentelium nigricans, Moxostoma* sp.), catfish *(Ameiurus melas, A. nebulosus, Ictalurus punctatus, Noturus flavus),* trout-perch *(Percopsis omiscomaycus),* burbets *(Lota lota),* topminnows and killifish *(Fundulus notatus),* livebearers *(Gambusia affinis),* sculpins *(Cottus bairdi, C. cognatus),* gobies *(Neogobius melanostomus),* temperate basses *(Morone mississippiensis, M. saxatilis),* black bass, crappies and sunfish *(Lepomis cyanellus, L. macrochirus,L. punctatus, Micropterus dolomieu, M. punctulatus, M. salmoides, Pomoxis annularis),* and darters and perch *(Etheostoma blennioides, E. caeruleum, E. flabellare, E. nigrum, Perca flavescens, Percina caprodes);* amphibians—salamanders *(Ambystoma texanum, Desmognathus fuscus, D. monticola, Eurycea bislineata, Gyrinophilus porphyriticus, Necturus maculosus, Notophthalmus viridescens, Plethodon glutinosus, Pseudotriton montanus, P. ruber, Siren* sp.), toads *(Bufo americanus, B. woodhousei, B. terrestris),* spadefoots *(Scaphiopus holbrooki),* hylids *(Acris crepitans, Hyla chrysoscelis, Pseudacris crucifer, P. triseriata),* and ranid frogs *(Rana blairi, R. catesbeiana, R. clamitans, R. palustris, R. pipiens, R. sphenocephala, R. sylvatica);* snakes *(Nerodia sipedon);* mammals—shrews *(Sorex* sp.) and voles *(Microtus pennsylvanicus);* crayfish *(Cambarus* sp.); millipedes; spiders; insects (beetles, dipteran larvae, dragonfly nymphs, grasshoppers, lepidopteran larvae, stonefly nymphs); snails *(Lymnea);* and annelids—earthworms and leeches (Anderson 1965; Barbour 1950; Bauman and Metter 1975; Brown 1958, 1979a; Bush 1959; Camp et al. 1980; Collins 1980; Conant 1951; Diener 1957a; C. Ernst, pers. obs.; Fitch 1999; Hamilton 1951a; Iverson 1975; Kats 1986; King 1993a; King et al. 1999; Klemens 1993; Krevosky and Graham 1987; Lagler and Salyer 1947; Langlois 1964; Laughlin 1959; McCauley 1945; Minton 1972; Palmer and Braswell 1995; Raney and Roecker 1947; Surface 1906; Uhler et al. 1939; Webb 1970; Zelnick 1966). A positive correlation occurs between body length of *N. sipedon* and size of prey (King 1993); as expected, as the snake grows it eats larger prey. Conant and Bailey (1936) reported that captives have eaten fence lizards *(Sceloporus undulatus),* and the authors have fed captives small mice *(Mus musculus)* first rubbed with a fish.

Most foraging occurs from 1800 to 2400 hours, but easily captured prey may be eaten during the daytime. *N. sipedon* is an active hunter. The authors have often seen adults crawling about in shallow water exploring and probing with their snouts every little crevice or place where prey could be hidden; both olfaction and vision are used to find food (juveniles use a mixed strategy of active hunting and remaining stationary; Balent and Andreadis 1998). They may also swim after fish with their mouths wide open. When the prey is seized, it is usually worked about in the mouth until it can be swallowed (typically head first for fish and frogs). Large prey, especially if caught in deep water, are brought to more shallow water or onto the bank before being swallowed. If the snake has had previous experience in capturing cryptic prey, a specific search image may be adopted, whereby prey that are similar in color to the background are more readily captured than are more conspicuous prey (Porter and Czaplicki 1977). Laboratory tests have shown that food preferences are innate (Dix 1968), but geographic variation in food preferences exists, probably due to differential prey availability between sites.

Prey is detected by either sight (Czaplicki and Porter 1974; Drummond 1979, 1983, 1985) or odor (Burghardt 1968; Gove and Burghardt 1975). When both are integrated, the capture success is enhanced (Drummond 1979). Juveniles may be imprinted early with the odors of their main prey species, and this feeding experience may result in chemical food preferences later in life (Dunbar 1979). Also, Qureal-Regil and King (1998) have shown that juvenile *N. sipedon* fed large fish increased in body size and jaw length more than did individuals offered small fish, apparently to accommodate the swallowing of larger prey.

N. sipedon is not considered venomous. A study of the enzymes in its saliva showed the saliva contained only 16.5% protein and had little proteolytic or hemolytic ability. It did contain 7.4 units of cholinesterase, a neurotoxic factor, but this was not like that of elapid snakes (Hegeman 1961). The saliva is produced in a Duvernoy's gland with some mucous cells intermingled with serous cells (Taub 1967).

PREDATORS AND DEFENSE. *N. sipedon* has many natural enemies; the young are particularly vulnerable to predation. Known and suspected predators are fish *(Esox* sp., *Ictalurus punctatus, Micropterus* sp.); amphibians *(Rana catesbeiana);* reptiles—turtles *(Chelydra serpentina),* alligators *(Alligator mississippiensis),* and snakes (*Agkistrodon piscivorus, Coluber constrictor, Lampropeltis getula, Nerodia* sp.); birds—rails (*Rallus longirostris*), bitterns (*Botaurus lentiginosus*), egrets (*Egretta* sp.), herons (*Ardea herodias*), vultures (*Cathartes, Coragyps*), hawks (*Buteo jamaicensis, B. lineatus, Circus cyaneus*), and gulls (*Larus argentatus*); mammals—raccoons (*Procyon lotor*), otters (*Lontra canadensis*), mink (*Mustela vison*), and skunks (*Mephitis mephitis*); and possibly crabs (Black 1983a; Conant and Lazell 1973; C. Ernst, pers. obs.; Ernst et al. 1997; Fitch 1999; King 1986; Ross 1989; Webb 1970). Human predation is also a major problem.

The first defensive response is to escape; *N. sipedon* immediately dives into the water when alarmed, or crawls away if not near water. Defensive behavior and escape velocity are correlated with BT—the colder the snake, the slower it reacts (Weatherhead and Robertson 1992). *N. sipedon* has a vile temper, and it will flatten its head and body, strike, bite viciously (often retaining its hold and chewing), and spray a pungent musk if not allowed to escape.

POPULATIONS. *N. sipedon* may occur in large colonies where other water snakes are rare: over 6,000 were killed at a Missouri fish hatchery in a year. King (1986) caught 1,371 during his study of *N. s. insularum* in Lake Erie, Conant (1951) reported the capture of 395 (less than 50 juvenile) *N. s. insularum* in one day on an island in Lake Erie, and King (1986) estimated the average adult density of this subspecies to be 90.5 (22–381) per kilometer of island shore. In Kansas, Fitch (1999) caught 336 at one site, and Beatson (1976) captured 197 in 6.4 km at another Kansas site and estimated this number to be only 75–90% of the entire population (the density was 4–41 juveniles and adults/km of stream). At two Ontario marshes, estimated population sizes were 101.4 (85.5–117.4) and 83.6 (24.5–128.4), and the calculated densities at these two sites were 25.4 and 33.4 snakes/ha (Brown and Weatherhead 1999b). However, where there is com-

petition with other species of *Nerodia*, the numbers of *N. sipedon* are often reduced. Hanebrink and Byrd (1986) collected 477 individuals of five species of *Nerodia* in northeastern Arkansas; of these, only 12 (2.5%) were *N. sipedon*. Similarly, it totaled only 45 (6.9%) of 7,062 snakes caught from 1980 through 1991 by Fitch (1992) in northeastern Kansas.

The sex ratio seems to favor females, but probably is not significantly different from 1:1. Weatherhead et al. (1998) recorded 821 males and 883 females (0.92:1.00) from 88 litters of *N. sipedon*; Slevin (1951) reported a litter sex ratio for 99 *N. sipedon* of 0.75:1.00 (42 males, 56 females; one individual was not sexed); and Fitch (1999) caught 108 males and 153 females (0.70:1.00). However, Bleakney (1958b) reported a nearly 1:1 ratio for a litter of 32 from Ontario that had 16 males, 14 females, and two malformed young that were not sexed; and Brown and Weatherhead (1999b) found essentially a 1:1 ratio at two Ontario marshes. In contrast, King (1986) captured 728 male and 643 female *N. s. insularum*, a 1.13:1.00 sex ratio, and at Chaffey's Lock in eastern Ontario, Robertson and Weatherhead (1992) caught 76 males and 46 females (1.65:1.00).

The size and age classes of only a few populations have been reported. At two marshes in Ontario, most individuals were in the 45–65 cm SVL range (Brown and Weatherhead 1999b), and in Kansas most had 30.0–59.2 cm SVLs (Fitch 1999). Brown and Weatherhead (1999b) estimated that less than 2% of the population survived over nine years at the Ontario sites, with most mortality occurring in the first three years; those with 45–55 cm SVLs experienced the highest survivorship.

N. s. insularum is considered threatened in Ohio.

REMARKS. Multiple-method analyses of allozyme frequency data by Lawson (1987) indicate that *N. sipedon* is most closely related to *N. harteri* (including *N. paucimaculata*).

Nerodia taxispilota (Holbrook 1838) | Brown Water Snake

RECOGNITION. *N. taxispilota* is a large (TBL to 176.6 cm), thick-bodied, brown water snake with a dorsal pattern of three longitudinal rows of 22–29 (36) alternating, square, dark brown blotches. These blotches may be only slightly darker than the chocolate brown ground color, especially in older individuals. The head is plain brown with some dark bars on the supralabials; the chin and infralabials may be lighter in color. The venter is cream to tan with a pattern of dark spots or half-moons. Dorsal body scales are strongly keeled, have two apical pits, and lie in 29–31 (27–32) anterior rows, 29–31 (25–33) midbody rows, and 21–23 (20–25) rows near the tail. Beneath are 128–152 ventrals, 59–87 subcaudals, and a divided anal plate. Each side of the head has 2 nasals (partially divided by the nostril), 1 loreal, 1–2 (3) preoculars, 2–3 (1–4) postoculars, 2–3 (1) + 2–3 (4–5) temporals, 8–9 (7–11) supralabials, and 11–12 (9–13) infralabials. The parietals are shortened and subdivided posteriorly into several small scales. The hemipenis is greatly expanded apically, with a straight sulcus spermaticus and a very extensive nude apical area. Each maxilla has an average of 21 teeth.

Males have 130–152 (mean, 138) ventrals, 70–87 (mean, 80) subcaudals, and TLs 25–28 (mean, 27) % of TBL; females have 128–137 (mean, 134) ventrals, 59–79 (mean, 70) subcaudals, and TLs 19–26 (mean, 24) % of TBL. Females grow significantly larger and heavier than males; males seldom grow as long as 90 cm, but females may grow to 176 cm (Semlitsch and Gibbons 1982). Males also seldom have more than 31 midbody scale rows (females often have 32+ rows), and males may have knobby body scales near the vent.

GEOGRAPHIC VARIATION. Not determined.

CONFUSING SPECIES. Other water snakes of genus *Nerodia* can be distinguished by using the above key. The cottonmouth (*Agkistrodon piscivorus*) lacks dark body blotches, and has white facial markings, a hole between the nostril and eye, vertically elliptical pupils, and a single row of subcaudal scales.

KARYOTYPE. Each body cell has 36 chromosomes (34 macrochromosomes, 2 microchromosomes); macrochromosome pairs one, two, three, five, and six are submetacentric, and pair four is metacentric (Eberle 1972).

FOSSIL RECORD. Pleistocene (Rancholabrean) fossils have been found in Florida (Auffenberg 1963; Weigel 1962).

DISTRIBUTION. This snake ranges from southeastern Virginia south along the Atlantic coastal plain to southern Florida, and westward along the Gulf coastal plain to Mobile Bay. It also occurs on the piedmont of North Carolina, South Carolina, and Georgia.

HABITAT. Its habitat is open, quiet rivers, lakes, and cypress swamps, but although often abundant along such shores, it is rarely found in small creeks or weedy

Brown water snake, *Nerodia taxispilota*; Hyde County, North Carolina. (Photograph by Carl H. Ernst)

Distribution of *Nerodia taxispilota*.

sloughs. Near the mouths of rivers it may occur in brackish tidal areas; the authors have caught it in such places in Virginia and North Carolina. Partially submerged trees and stumps are often present, and it may also use man-made structures such as duck blinds, buoys, jetties, and old piers as basking and hiding places.

BEHAVIOR. *N. taxispilota* is probably active in all months in Florida, especially during years with warm winters, but more northern populations are forced to hibernate. The earliest record for surface activity in North Carolina is 12 February, and the latest 31 December; most activity there takes place in April–June (Palmer and Braswell 1995). In Virginia, the species is active from early April through early November, but some individuals may be active in all months (Mitchell 1994). Neill (1948a) thought it overwintered in cavities or burrows near the edge of the water in Georgia, since a rise in water level brought them out in numbers regardless of AT. The authors have also seen this along the James River in Virginia where an old pier was used as a hibernaculum.

This snake is primarily diurnal during the spring and fall, but is more nocturnally active in the summer. It exhibits circadian rhythms of nocturnal activity when exposed to ETs of at least 29°C, but at 27°C or less such rhythms disappear (Luckeydoo and Blem 1993). Most daylight activity is either foraging or basking. *N. taxispilota* is a good climber, and often ascends onto bushes and the limbs of short trees overhanging the water while basking, although it may also lie on

the bank or on partially submerged objects to bask. Larger adults bask on higher perches than juveniles and smaller adults (Mills et al. 1995). Osgood (1970) recorded the stomach temperatures of four (three pregnant females and a male) unrestrained *N. taxispilota* in an outdoor cage. Generally, the gravid females left the water and basked in the morning when the sun appeared, and maintained their BT at 26–31°C as long as possible into the late afternoon. When the AT finally fell to below that of the water, the females reentered the water and slowed the drop in their BTs. They were active during this period, and this was probably when most long movements would have occurred. The extremes in BT were 21 and 36°C for pregnant females, and 20 and 37°C for the male. Blem and Blem (1990a) reported that the mean preferred BTs of *N. taxispilota* in the field and laboratory were 24.8 and 28.2°C, respectively. At warm BTs, this snake consumes more food, although it does not grow faster (Semlitsch 1979). Interestingly, the metabolic rate of *N. taxispilota* is highest during its nocturnal phase (Blem and Killeen 1993).

In a study of movements in South Carolina, Mills et al. (1995) found that 70% of the recaptured individuals had moved less than 250 m from the previous capture site, but six moved more than 500 m, and three traveled over 1 km (1.05, 1.30, and 1.65 km). The snakes moved an average of 270 m (13 m/day) during the study, with time between recaptures ranging from 1 to 649 days. Ten of the 11 individuals that moved more than 10 m/day between captures did so from 12

August to 15 October, indicating a possible seasonal movement pattern. Only individuals larger than 80 cm SVL crossed the Savannah River.

REPRODUCTION. The minimum SVL of mature female *N. taxispilota* is 71.0–72.5 cm (White et al. 1982; Wright and Wright 1957); such a length is reached in three to four years of growth. The smallest mature males have 50.3–56.0 cm SVLs (Herrington 1989; Mitchell and Zug 1984; White et al. 1982); males probably mature in two to three years.

Spermatogenesis begins in April and terminates in November in Virginia (Mitchell and Zug 1984). Recrudescence reaches its peak in midsummer, and spermiogenesis occurs principally from September through November. The seminiferous tubules increase in diameter with spermatogenic activity, and sperm that passes from the testis are stored in the epididymides. Testes are small during April–June, reach their maximum size in August, then decrease in size from September through November as sperm leave (Herrington 1989; White et al. 1982).

Vitellogenesis occurs from April through early June in Virginia females (White et al. 1982), and the normal female lipid cycle reflects this (Blem and Blem 1990b). Follicles may reach 20 mm in length before ovulation in late May–late June (Herrington 1989; White et al. 1982). Most females reproduce annually (Herrington 1989; Semlitsch and Gibbons 1978; White et al. 1982).

Parturition normally takes place on land from late August into the fall, but births may occur as early as June in Florida (Tennant 1997) or as late as 1 November in Georgia (Wright and Wright 1957). The number of young produced per litter is positively correlated with female body size (Herrington 1989; Semlitsch and Gibbons 1978). The absolute amount of body tissue partitioned into reproduction increases with female body size, but the proportion does not (Semlitsch and Gibbons 1978). Most resources are devoted to the developing eggs during the summer, and the total lipid content of the eggs increases. At the same time, between May and July, a decline of slightly over 2% in female body fat occurs.

Breeding takes place from late February through early May in Florida, and again in mid- to late summer (Ashton and Ashton 1981; Tennant 1997), but in more northern populations April–May is the breeding period. Mating may take place in the water, on land, or above ground while the snakes are suspended from branches. More than one male may simultaneously court a female (Herrington 1989), and the successful male temporarily seals the female's cloaca with a gelatinous, semirigid plug at the end of the mating act (Devine 1975; Herrington 1989).

Litters contain 11–63 young (Palmer and Braswell 1995) and average 28 (n = 44). Thirty-nine neonates had an average TBL of 27.3 (17.4–36.0) cm and an average mass of 10.9 (7.4–14.0) g. Newborns are lighter brown in ground color, making the pattern of dorsal spots more vivid.

GROWTH AND LONGEVITY. Herrington (1989) released 83 marked neonates (mean SVL, 23.3 cm) back into the wild to study their growth patterns. Little growth occurred before hibernation, and the following spring the small snakes emerged with SVLs of 23–26 cm. One neonate marked on 14 September had grown only 0.4 cm when captured the following 16 March. Growth rates of first-year young (SVLs, 23–33 cm) averaged 9.6 (3.8–13.6) cm. At the beginning of their second full season, juveniles were 39–53 cm long, and in their third season they had a modal SVL of 62 cm. Growth occurred at a rate of 4–19 cm/season. Females grew much faster, but experienced a reduction in the rate of growth once maturity was reached. No data on longevity are available.

DIET AND FEEDING HABITS. Wild *N. taxispilota* feed almost exclusively on fish: catfish (*Ameiurus brunneus, A. catus, A. natalis, Ictalurus punctatus, Noturus gyrinus, N. insignis, N. leptacanthus*), cyprinids (*Cyprinella analostana, C. venusta, Notropis texanus*), darters (*Etheostoma swaini, Percina nigrofasciata*), sunfish (*Lepomis macrochirus*), bass (*Micropterus* sp., *Morone* sp.), gar (*Lepisosteus* sp.), and pickerel (*Esox* sp.) (Camp et al. 1980; Collins 1980; Hamilton and Pollack 1956; Mills and Hudson 1995; Palmer and Braswell 1995; Richmond 1944). Small adult frogs and their tadpoles (*Rana catesbeiana*) and toads (*Bufo* sp.) are also occasionally eaten (Camp et al. 1980; Palmer and Braswell 1995), but the small snakes and lizards mentioned by Allen (1939b) are probably seldom, if ever, consumed. Captives the authors have maintained refused everything but fish. Carrion, as well as fresh prey, is ingested (Tennant 1997).

The fish are actively chased and caught in the water, although they are sometimes brought to land before being swallowed, and the authors have seen *N. taxispilota* drop from a branch into the water to ambush fish swimming below. Similarly, Reams and Stevens (1999) observed this snake make open-mouthed attacks at passing sunfish *(Lepomis)* from a place of partial concealment in an algal mat.

PREDATORS AND DEFENSE. Natural predators include the American alligator *(Alligator mississippiensis),* cottonmouth *(Agkistrodon piscivorus),* snapping turtle *(Chelydra serpentina),* and cormorants *(Phalacrocorax auritus)* (Palmer and Braswell 1995; White et al. 1982; C. Ernst, pers. obs.), and surely large predatory fish, wading birds, carnivorous mammals, and ophiophagous snakes also eat them. However, humans are by far their worst enemy. Each year fishermen slaughter these snakes indiscriminately because they believe either that they are venomous or that they compete for pan or game fish. Draining and polluting of wetland habitats have also harmed *N. taxispilota* and other snakes.

When first caught *N. taxispilota* is a formidable opponent that can inflict deep lacerations when it bites. It also shares the obnoxious habit of spraying a pungent musk and fecal matter. When kept for a period in captivity, it will often calm down, but does not usually do well.

POPULATIONS. Although the brown water snake may occur in large numbers in its habitat, only scattered data are available regarding its population dynamics. In a South Carolina riverine population, the *N. taxispilota* ranged from 20–30 to 110–120 cm in SVL; with 50–90 cm adults and 30–40 cm juveniles comprising the bulk of the population (Mills et al. 1995). The snakes occurred in a density of 43 snakes/km of river habitat.

Some data concerning sex ratios have been reported. White et al. (1982) found a sex ratio over a three-year collecting period in Virginia of 1.2:1. They recorded a 1:1 sex ratio in the spring and summer, but a 2.5:1 male to female ratio in the fall. If only mature individuals were considered, the proportion of males to females increased from 1.4:1 in the spring to 1.9:1 in the fall. Herrington (1989) counted 33 males and 26 females in a sample of 59 brown water snakes with SVLs greater than 38 cm collected in Georgia (1.27:1). In South Carolina, Mills et al. (1995) found a sex ratio of 1.07:1, but Franklin (1944) recorded a sex ratio of 0.73:1 in three Florida litters, and Duellman and Schwartz (1958) reported another Florida litter sex ratio of 1.28:1.

REMARKS. Multiple analyses of tissue allozyme frequencies and study of mitochondrial DNA have shown that *N. taxispilota* is most closely related to *N. rhombifer* (Densmore et al. 1992; Lawson 1987). The species was reviewed by McCranie (1983).

Opheodrys aestivus (Linnaeus 1766) | Rough Green Snake

RECOGNITION. *O. aestivus* grows to a maximum of 115.9 cm, but most individuals are shorter than 75 cm. The dorsal body is unpatterned green; the venter is white, cream, yellow, or greenish yellow and unmarked, and the supralabials and lower portion of the head are light yellow. The keeled dorsal body scales lie in 17 (15–19) rows anteriorly and at midbody, and in 15 (13–17) rows near the vent. On the venter are 139–171 ventrals, 105–161 subcaudals, and a divided anal plate. Lateral head scales include 1 nasal, 1 loreal, 1 (rarely 2) preocular(s), 2 (1–3) postoculars, 1 (2–3) + 2 (3) temporals, 7 (6–8) supralabials, and 8 (7–10) infralabials. The long posterior chin shields are widely separated for half their length. The hemipenis bears numerous fringed calyxes. Each maxilla has 20–25 teeth.

Males have 149–168 (mean, 152) ventrals, 110–161 (mean, 135) subcaudals, and TLs 34–43 (mean, 39.5) % of TBL; females have 139–171 (mean, 155) ventrals, 105–149 (mean, 129) subcaudals, and TLs 32–42 (mean, 36) % of TBL.

Rough green snake, *Opheodrys aestivus*; Rowan County, Kentucky. (Photograph by Roger W. Barbour)

GEOGRAPHIC VARIATION. *O. aestivus* is currently considered monotypic (Walley and Plummer 2000); however, Grobman (1984) considers the species to have four subspecies—*O. a. aestivus, O. a. carinatus, O. a. conanti,* and *O. a. majalis*—based on scale count variations (for discussions regarding geographic variation, see Collins 1992; Grobman 1992b; Plummer 1987; Walley and Plummer 2000).

CONFUSING SPECIES. The smooth green snake (*Liochlorophis vernalis*) has smooth dorsal body scales, which usually lie in 15 rows at midbody. The two green water snakes (*Nerodia cyclopion, N. floridana*) are stocky, with dark bars on the supralabials, a patterned venter, and nine or more infralabials; and the crayfish snakes (*Regina*) usually have 19 midbody dorsal scale rows, and either have lateral body stripes or ventral markings. The green rat snake (*Senticolis triaspis*) has 25 or more dorsal body scale rows, and the brown vine snake (*Oxybelis aeneus*) has smooth dorsal body scales and a dark eye stripe.

KARYOTYPE. Undescribed.

FOSSIL RECORD. Late Pleistocene (Rancholabrean) remains have been found in Alabama (Holman et al. 1990), Florida (Auffenberg 1963; Gut and Ray 1963; Holman 1962a, 1976; Lynch 1965; Tihen 1962), Georgia (Fay 1988; Holman 1995), Pennsylvania (Guilday et al. 1964; Lynch 1966a), Texas (Holman 1962b, 1963, 1966, 1969b, 1980; Lynch 1966a; Parmley 1988c,

1990a; Patton 1963; Preston 1979), and Virginia (Fay 1988; Holman 1986a).

DISTRIBUTION. *O. aestivus* ranges from southern New Jersey south through peninsular Florida, and west to eastern Kansas, central Texas, and to Tampico, Mexico. Isolated colonies occur in northeastern Missouri and Coahuila, Mexico.

HABITAT. *Opheodrys* is most frequently found in or near moist habitats, particularly along waterways in woodlands, along marsh or lake borders, or in moist meadows, but it also occurs along the fringes of woodlands. It is quite arboreal, and trees or large shrubs are usually present.

BEHAVIOR. Over most of the range, *O. aestivus* is active from March–April to October–November, but occasionally, in the South and in southern Florida, it may be active in every month. It has been observed in every month in North Carolina, with 73% of the records occurring in May, July, and September–October (Palmer and Braswell 1995). This latter pattern is followed in Illinois, where the snake is most active in April–July, and again in September–October (Morris 1982). However, some northern populations do not emerge from hibernation until May. The winter is spent in a rotting stump or log, in an ant hill, or buried in the soil to depths of 20 cm or more.

Opheodrys seems strictly diurnal. In Arkansas, it is active most of the day, first emerging shortly after

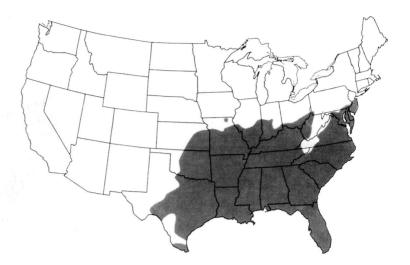

Distribution of *Opheodrys aestivus*.

daybreak and retreating 30–60 minutes before sundown; nights are usually spent on some arboreal perch (Plummer 1981b). In Arkansas, *O. aestivus* is diurnally active at BTs of 17.9–36.8 (mean, 29.3) °C (Plummer 1993). BTs of females were higher than those of males, especially in June. Although arboreal basking has been reported in other populations, the Arkansas snakes avoided basking, and their BTs usually correlated with cooler shaded ETs. However, recently fed laboratory individuals may have higher mean CTs (Touzeau and Sievert 1993).

Home ranges are rather restricted, especially within a season (Plummer 1981b). In an Arkansas population, most movement was at the vegetation line parallel to the shoreline of a lake. Mean length of the home range in 1979 was 62 m; males had home ranges averaging 56 (15–102) m, females, 68 (21–247) m (by 1992, more recaptures increased the average home range length to 67 m; Plummer 1997b). The greatest horizontal distance moved in one day was 60 m, and for 75 *Opheodrys* captured at least twice in each of two seasons, the interseasonal shifts in location of the home range averaged 45 (0.5–420) m. As the time of oviposition neared, gravid females descended from their arboreal habitats and moved terrestrially away from the shoreline an average of 32.7 m; after oviposition they returned immediately to their normal activity ranges (Plummer 1990a). Gravid and nongravid females from this population with BTs of 26.6–28.8°C tested by Plummer (1997a) achieved crawling speeds

of 2.15–3.78 (mean, 3.11) and 2.73–5.13 (mean, 4.15) cm/second, respectively. As its primary habitat usually involves a water body, *O. aestivus* sometimes enters the water, where it is a good swimmer (Richmond 1952).

O. aestivus is also a good climber, and at night most often sleeps above ground in shrubs and trees. In Arkansas, day and night perches are usually not over 3 m high (75% night, 71% day), 1 cm in diameter or less (99% night, 83% day), located distally on a branch (87% night, 63% day), and at an angle of less than a 60° (92% night, 88% day). Also, 88% of night perches and 86% of day perches are within 3 m of water (Plummer 1981b). It has been seen at heights over 10 m in trees: McComb and Noble (1981) found one in a tree hole 10.6 m above ground. Such a retreat would give protection from both predators and desiccation. Arboreal perching among transpiring leaves may retard moisture loss: Dove et al. (1982) reported mean rates of cutaneous water loss of 0.18 and 0.39 mg/cm^2/hour for adults and hatchlings, respectively, and Baeyens and Roundtree (1983) recorded a water loss rate of 0.21 mg/cm^2/hour for adults. The snake is less arboreal during the spring and fall, possibly because of the reduced number of leaves.

REPRODUCTION. Females become sexually mature at SVLs of 30–40 cm (Mitchell 1994; Plummer 1984; Tinkle 1960). Such lengths are achieved in approximately two years. Follicles 1–5 mm long are present throughout the annual activity period. Those 1–3 mm proliferate in postpartum females in July–August and increase to a maximum of 5 mm by October. Sets of 1–3 mm and 3–5 mm follicles are present in September and February, indicating little yolking occurs over the winter. Vitellogenesis resumes in the spring and yolk is rapidly added. The follicles enlarge to 15–25 mm in May, and oviductal eggs are present from late May through July. The amount of body fat is greatest in early spring and late fall, and least in June following secondary vitellogenesis; stored body fat may be reduced up to 70% during spring yolking of follicles. Illinois females have equal numbers of secondary vitellogenic follicles in the two ovaries or oviducts, but in Arkansas the right ovary averages 3.6 enlarged follicles while the left ovary only has an average of 2.6. About 60% of Arkansas females experience extrauterine transfer of ova (Morris 1982; Plummer 1983, 1984).

Males mature at about 12 months of age at SVLs of 24.5–30.0 cm (Aldridge et al. 1990; Mitchell 1994). The testes become progressively longer, wider, and more cylindrical as the male grows, eventually reaching 22 mm long and 4 mm wide; the right testis may be slightly longer than the left (Tinkle 1960). During the first spermatogenic season, the testes produce enough sperm for mating the following spring, when the male is 20–21 months old (Aldridge et al. 1990). Thereafter, spermatogenesis begins in June and reaches a peak in July–August. Sperm is passed to the vas deferens in the fall for storage until the next spring mating season. Levels of serum testosterone cycle the opposite of the spermatogenic cycle, being highest in early spring and late summer and fall (which may permit early spring mating). Body fat also decreases from April through June, corresponding to the mating period and probably reflecting the energy used in finding and courting a mate (Aldridge et al. 1990).

As noted above, mating occurs chiefly in the spring; although Morris and Vail (1991), Richmond (1956), and Cooper (in Palmer and Braswell 1995) reported fall matings in Illinois, Virginia, and North Carolina, and males in Illinois are very active in September, possibly reflecting an autumn increase in sexual activity (Morris 1982). The normal breeding season extends from late March to June, depending on latitude; most mature Arkansas females contain sperm in the spring, but not at other times of the year (Plummer 1984). A male visually locates a female; rapidly approaches her, while laterally jerking his head and waving and laterally undulating his tail; makes body contact; tongue flicks her body; and aligns his body along her back, while generally moving toward her head and touching his chin to her back (Morris and Vail 1991; Goldsmith 1988). Following alignment, he searches for the female's vent with his tail, and once it is found inserts his hemipenis. Copulation may last over 35 minutes, and can occur in bushes and trees as well as on the ground.

The eggs are principally laid in June and July, but ovipositions have occurred in both August and September. Conant (1951) and Holfert (1996) reported females may lay two clutches per year, and possibly nestings in late July–September involve second clutches.

Natural nest sites include rotting logs and stumps, cavities in moss and beneath flat rocks, spaces behind loose bark, and tree holes—narrow (about the width of an egg), vertical slits resulting from rotting (Plummer 1989, 1990a). Most *Opheodrys* probably nest individually, but communal nesting has been reported (Palmer and Braswell 1976). The same nest site may be used in succeeding years (Plummer 1989, 1990a). Females prefer to nest in moister substrates of –200 to –300 kPa rather than substrates of –600 to –2000 kPa, but they can nest on a wide range of substrate moisture levels without adverse effects on eggs or hatchlings (Plummer and Snell 1988). Moisture levels in tree holes are more variable and dry (mean, –1025 kPa) than in other nests (mean, –760 kPa) (Plummer 1990a). Eggs incubated in dryer situations produce smaller hatchlings; larger hatchlings from more moist nest sites have greater survivorship. ATs during incubation in Arkansas tree holes were 25–34.5°C (Plummer 1990a).

Clutches (n = 117) average 5.9 eggs and contain 1–14 (Fitch 1985a; Minton 1972). Egg and clutch size are both positively correlated to female size. Mean RCM is 0.372, and may vary from year to year depending on resources and environmental conditions (Seigel and Fitch 1984). The white, adherent eggs are 17.3–39.3 (mean, 25.1) mm long and 9.9–17.0 (mean, 10.8) mm wide, and have thin leathery shells. About

89% of the eggs are fertile, and 90% of these hatch (Plummer 1984). The eggs are laid about 35 days (30–39, n = 7; C. Ernst, pers. obs.) after copulation. The IP is temperature dependent, and may last 30–90 (mean, 51; n = 28) days. Most eggs hatch in August–September, but have occurred from 16 June to 20 October. Hatchlings have 11.4–24.5 (mean, 20.2; n = 81) cm TBLs and weigh 1.1–2.4 (mean, 1.55; n = 24) g.

GROWTH AND LONGEVITY.   Female *O. aestivus* grow faster and achieve a larger body size than males (Plummer 1997b). Growth is a decreasing linear function of SVL, and body mass is closely correlated with SVL (Plummer 1987). In Illinois, hatchlings had a maximum growth rate of 2.6 cm, while the greatest growth in the first season following hatching was 14.1 cm. During the second season, growth slowed to a maximum of 6.7 cm (Morris 1982).

A wild-caught juvenile of unknown sex was still living after 6 years, 8 months, and 21 days in captivity at the Los Angeles Zoo (Snider and Bowler 1992).

DIET AND FEEDING HABITS.   *Opheodrys* has been reported to eat chiefly insects, but millipedes, isopods, spiders, land snails *(Polygyra),* and rarely even small tree frogs (Hylidae) have been taken by wild individuals (Brown 1979a; Bush 1959; Clark 1949; Dundee and Rossman 1989; Goldsmith 1986; Guidry 1953; Hamilton and Pollack 1956; McCauley 1945; Minton 1972; Palmer and Braswell 1995; Plummer 1981b, 1991; Tennant 1985; Uhler et al. 1939; Van Hyning 1932; Wright and Wright 1957). Insects consumed by wild *Opheodrys* include beetles (Coleoptera); damselflies and mayflies (Ephemeroptera); moth and butterfly larvae (Lepidoptera); dragonflies (Odonata); and crickets, grasshoppers, katydids, wood roaches, preying mantids, and walking sticks (Orthoptera).

Foraging is usually above ground in bushes or trees, and involves searching leaves and small branches as the snake slowly moves distally on a limb (Plummer 1981b). Sometimes they will stalk insects with almost imperceptible gliding movements until the prey is seized with a quick strike (Minton 1972). Apparently vision is the sole sense used to detect moving prey; motionless insects may be overlooked (Goldsmith 1986). Once the insect is seen, the snake initially approaches it rapidly and sporadically, but the final

approach is slow and deliberate. Tongue flicking and lateral head movements are not used during the approach. When the insect is within strike distance (mean, 1.64 cm; Goldsmith 1986), the snake quickly seizes it. Insects are usually swallowed head first.

PREDATORS AND DEFENSE.   Several animals have been observed preying on *O. aestivus:* snakes *(Coluber constrictor, Lampropeltis calligaster, L. getula, Masticophis flagellum, Micrurus fulvius),* birds *(Buteo* sp., *Cyanocitta, cristata, Elanoides forficatus, Melanerpes carolinus),* domestic cats *(Felis catus),* alligator gar *(Atractosteus spatula),* and spiders *(Nephila clavipes)* (Brown 1979a; Clark 1949; Greene 1984; Gritis 1993; Guthrie 1932; Hammerson 1988; Klemens 1993; Mitchell 1994; Mitchell and Beck 1992; Mueller and Whiting 1989; Nugent et al. 1989; Palmer and Braswell 1995; Plummer 1990b, 1991; Reams et al. 2000b; Tomkins 1965; Zippel and Kirkland 1998); and probably opossums, raccoons, skunks, weasels, foxes, and coyotes also prey on the adults, and squirrels may eat eggs deposited in tree holes. In addition, mowers, hay-cutting equipment, motorized vehicles, and probably, lumbering and insecticides take their toll each year.

Opheodrys normally "freezes" when first discovered, and its body color blends in so well with green vegetation, that it is very difficult to distinguish. If touched, it will try to flee, but if further disturbed, the snake may gape its mouth, displaying a dark lining. It is inoffensive and rarely bites if held, but will void musk and fecal matter or wrap itself around some object.

POPULATIONS.   Because of its arboreal habits and blending coloration, this snake is usually overlooked, thus giving the false appearance of being uncommon or rare, when it may be quite common. It made up only about 0.1% of the snakes recorded in Kansas by Fitch (1993) and northern Louisiana by Clark (1949), 0.2% of the Virginia snakes examined by Uhler et al. (1939), and only 3.6% of the snakes found by Ford et al. (1991) in eastern Texas. In contrast, Goodman (in Anderson 1965) collected as many as 10 a night where day hunting only yielded one or two snakes, and Plummer (1997b) made over 2,700 captures (density, about 800/ha) hunting at night in Arkansas during a seven-year study of the species. The sex ratio is about 1:1 throughout life (Morris 1982; Plummer 1997b;

Tinkle 1960). Tinkle (1960) and Plummer (1997b) reported that juveniles composed 38 and 39%, respectively, of their populations. Adult survivorship in Plummer's population was relatively low: hatchlings, 15–19%; first-year young, 21.5%; adult males, 28%; and adult females, 41%.

O. aestivus is protected in Pennsylvania as a threatened species, and in Ohio as a species of special concern.

REMARKS. The species was reviewed by Walley and Plummer (2000).

Oxybelis aeneus (Wagler 1824) | Brown Vine Snake

RECOGNITION. No other snake in North America looks like *O. aeneus*. Its common name is quite appropriate, as it is a long (TBL to 152.4 cm), extremely thin snake with a long tail (TL 40–41% of TBL) and a narrow, elongated, pointed head. The SVL to head length ratio is approximately 41%. Body color is gray to grayish brown with some yellowish brown coloration anteriorly. The immaculate venter is gray to white, with the chin and throat often cream to yellow. The head is broader than the neck, with small eyes, cream-colored labials, and a dark brown stripe extending from the snout through the eye. Dorsal body scales are smooth or only weakly keeled dorsally, with or without apical pits, and lie in 17 (16) anterior rows, 17 (15–16) rows at midbody, and 13–14 rows near the vent. On the underside are 173–205 ventrals, 158–203

subcaudals, and a divided anal plate. Lateral head scales include 2 nasals, 0 loreal, 1 preocular, 1–2 postoculars, 2 (1–3) + 2 (1–4) temporals, 8–9 supralabials, and 9 (8–11) infralabials. The hemipenis has a single sulcus spermaticus situated laterally that may fork near the tip; has no enlarged basal spines, but instead has relatively small hooks or recurved, clawlike spines in about 10 (2–12) rows that merge with the calyxes and become smaller and less strongly denticulate toward the distal end; and has small scattered granular bodies in the flesh of the apex (Bogert and Oliver 1945; Keiser 1974). Normally, it extends 6–8 (4–10) subcaudals when inverted. Each maxilla has about 20 (18–21) long, curved teeth, with the most posterior two deeply grooved.

Little to no external sexual dimorphism exists; males have 173–205 ventrals and 169–188 subcaudals,

Brown vine snake, *Oxybelis aeneus*; Guairacoba, Sonora, Mexico. (Photograph by John W. Tashjian, San Diego Zoo)

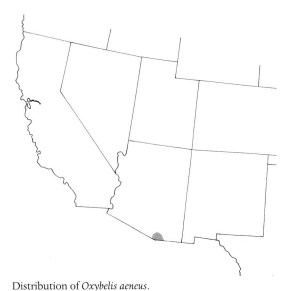

Distribution of *Oxybelis aeneus.*

and females have 173–204 ventrals and 158–203 subcaudals. However, differences do occur in the structure of the hemapophyses of the caudal vertebrae, with those of females open ventrally and those of males closed (Keiser 1970).

GEOGRAPHIC VARIATION.   No subspecies are currently recognized (Keiser 1974, 1982).

CONFUSING SPECIES.   No other snake north of Mexico has a head shaped like that of *O. aeneus.*

KARYOTYPE AND FOSSIL RECORD.   Unknown.

DISTRIBUTION.   In the United States, *O. aeneus* only occurs a few kilometers north of the Mexican border in Pima and Santa Cruz counties, Arizona (Van Devender et al. 1994). The species ranges from southern Arizona through western Mexico and from Neuvo León in eastern Mexico south through Central America to Bolivia and southern Brazil. Its northern distribution is apparently limited by winter freezing above 1,650 m elevation and by summer aridity below 1,160 m (Van Devender et al. 1994).

HABITAT.   In southern Arizona, *O. aeneus* occurs on dry, brushy hillsides, in brush-filled canyons, and along riparian stream bottoms, primarily with wild grape, or sycamore, oak, and walnut trees, to elevations of about 1,200 m. The restricted area it occupies in Arizona has relatively mild winters and relatively high annual precipitation that falls mainly as summer monsoon rains (Van Devender et al. 1994).

BEHAVIOR.   *O. aeneus* is uncommon in Arizona, and little has been recorded concerning its behavior and ecology there. Most life history data are from tropical populations.

It has been seen from 1 May to 11 October in the Pajarito Mountains (Stebbins 1954). How and where it spends the winter months is generally unknown. Van Devender et al. (1994) reported that Arizona *O. aeneus* does not have a fixed inactivity period in winter tied to the annual day-length cycle. It has been found on four occasions in total darkness within a cave in the Santa Rita Mountains; possibly such subterranean retreats are sought in winter. Henderson (1974b) collected it from 6 October to 6 July in the vicinity of Belize City, Belize. The rainy months there were October–January and June–July; May was the driest month.

The snake is diurnal, with most activity in Arizona taking place in the morning or late afternoon, although it has been captured at 0125 hours in Veracruz, Mexico (CT, 34.8°C; AT, 34.6°C; Kennedy 1965a). It retreats to higher, possibly safer, perches after sunset and sleeps there until soon after daybreak, when it climbs to a lower arboreal level to forage or bask (Henderson 1974b). It is less prone to overheating when in vegetation than when crawling across the hot earth. Perch height of individuals collected during the day in Belize was 1.5 (0.5–2.0) m, and mean night perch height was 2.9 (1.1–5.0) m (Henderson 1974b). In captivity, free-ranging *O. aeneus* in a greenhouse assumed a loosely coiled, head-down sleeping position at the distal end of a branch at the top (2.3 m) of a bush at 1645 hours (< 1 footcandle of light) and remained there until 0810 hours (200 footcandles of light), when it began to slowly descend through the branches to 0835 hours and 0.65 m lower, where it assumed a typical ambush posture (Henderson and Nickerson 1977).

REPRODUCTION.   Data concerning reproduction of *O. aeneus* are mostly anecdotal. The minimum size of mature males is unknown; the smallest male undergoing spermiogenesis examined by Goldberg (1998a) had a SVL of 60.5 cm. Males from Arizona and Mexico had regressed testes with the seminiferous tubules containing spermatogonia and Sertoli cells in July and August (Goldberg 1998a). During recrudescence in October and November, spermatogenesis occurred, and primary and secondary spermatocytes and some spermatids were present. Spermiogenesis followed in February and April–July, with spermatids and mature sperm present in the testes, and sperm in the epididymides and vas deferens.

The smallest female from the Yucatan Peninsula of Mexico with enlarging ovarian follicles or oviductal eggs had a SVL of 65.0 cm (Censky and McCoy 1988). The smallest reproductively active Arizona or Mexican female reported by Goldberg (1998a) had a 77.3 cm SVL, but Keiser (in Goldberg 1998a) found a 59 cm SVL female with fully formed eggs. Females probably mature at about two years of age. According to Censky and McCoy (1988), reproductive activity of females on the Yucatan Peninsula spans a 12–13 week period beginning in March and ending in June or July. Vitellogenesis begins in March, and the ovarian follicles grow rapidly during the spring. Most spring follicles are 3.1–10.0 mm in diameter, and 10 mm follicles or larger are present in May. Ovulation occurs between June and August at a minimum diameter of 29.9 mm. Presence of oviductal eggs in July and of females with stretched oviducts as late as September indicate a laying season of about 2.5 months, and possibly oviposition of more than one clutch, during the height of the Yucatan rainy season. Females are reproductively quiescent after oviposition for a period extending from July–September to the end of the following dry season. Goldberg (1998a) found some females from Arizona and Mexico reproductively inactive in January–May and July–September. Vitellogenesis occurred there in June and August, and females had enlarged follicles in July and August and oviductal eggs in July. Sexton and Heatwole (1965) found a Panamanian nest containing four eggs in a depression in leaf litter on 1 July, and Scott (in Hardy and McDiarmid 1969) found females with oviductal eggs in mid-August. Courtship and mating behaviors have not been described.

The adherent, elongated eggs are white with some brown stains, and average 41.5 (30.0–62.0) mm in length and 15.0 (14.6–15.2) mm in width. Clutches contain three to eight (mean, four) eggs. Hatchlings have been found from 13 July to 5 October. Their TBL is about 37.4 cm (Sexton and Heatwole 1965).

GROWTH AND LONGEVITY. The smallest Yucatan hatchling had a SVL of 29.0 cm; juveniles there reach 45 cm SVL by the end of their first year, and females grow to 65 cm in two years (Censky and McCoy 1988). In Belize, recaptured adult females grew as much as 61, 45, and 26 mm in approximately two, six, and one months; and adult males grew 88, 62, and 51 mm in approximately 1.5, 3, and 7.5 months, respectively (Henderson 1974b). Belize males averaged a 12.2 mm/month increase in length, and females grew an average of 7.3 mm/month, but some individuals of each sex failed to grow for as long as nine months (Henderson 1974b). Belize females tended to be longer (maximum SVL 97.5 cm) than males (maximum SVL 92.1 cm).

A female survived 11 years, 10 months, and 9 days at the Houston Zoo (Snider and Bowler 1992).

DIET AND FEEDING HABITS. *O. aeneus* is a diurnal feeder, predominantly on lizards, and captures prey both at ground level and above ground in bushes and trees. Four hunting techniques are employed. The snake may actively seek or trail prey while crawling along the surface of the ground with head elevated (Zweifel and Norris 1955); apparently both vision and odor detection are used at this time. The prey may also be actively pursued above ground along the limbs of bushes and trees. Pursuit may be rapid, or the snake may "sneak up" on its prey by slowly, almost imperceptibly, advancing on a branch toward the animal until within strike range. It may also ambush prey by lying still along a branch or slowly swaying back and forth from a branch imitating wind-blown vegetation (Fleishman 1985). It possibly lures small animals to within reach of its mouth by rigidly extending its tongue from its mouth and holding it motionless in front of the head (Kennedy 1965a; Keiser 1975). Prey are usually seized just behind the head, and during a strike the snake usually rotates the anterior portion of its body 90° (Henderson and Binder 1980). Once seized, the prey is worked to the rear of the mouth and impaled by the enlarged teeth. Toxic saliva from the serous Duvernoy's gland (Taub 1967) flows down the grooves in the rear fangs and enters the wound. The venom is very effective on lizards. The prey is held and the venom chewed in until the prey is immobilized; then it is swallowed headfirst.

A variety of small animals are eaten: lizards *(Anolis, Basiliscus, Cnemidophorus, Ctenosaura, Holbrookia, Iguana, Sceloporus, Urosaurus, Uta)* are the most common prey, but leptodactylid frogs, fish, small birds, small rodents, and insects are also consumed (Groschupf and Lower 1988; Hardy and McDiarmid 1969; Henderson 1982; Henderson and Binder 1980; Stebbins 1954; Stuart 1954; Van Devender et al. 1994; Wehekind 1955).

PREDATORS AND DEFENSE. Although its animal enemies are probably numerous, particularly when it is small, nothing has been reported about predation. Defensively, *O. aeneus* relies first on the concealment its long, thin, grayish brown body provides when resting among the leaves on a branch. It truly resembles a thin vine. Normally when danger is detected it remains motionless, often with tongue rigidly extended. If further disturbed the brown vine snake will form an S-shaped coil of its anterior body and gape its mouth to show the dark blue lining. It may also vibrate the tail. A strike may or may not follow, as the snake is a good bluffer.

Bites of humans by *O. aeneus* have been few (McKinstry 1978; Minton 1990) and have resulted from the human handling the snake. While the venom is highly toxic to lizards, it causes mild symptoms in humans. When the snake is allowed to chew in its venom, itching, swelling, blistering, and numbness may occur at the bite site, and fluid draining from the blister and rubbed into a fresh cut can produce another blister (Crimmins 1937). There is a heavy concentration of melanin on the sides of the snake's head that marks the position of the Duvernoy's gland (Pough et al. 1978).

POPULATIONS. Although now rather uncommon in Arizona (it is a candidate species for protection), *O. aeneus* may occur in dense populations in the tropics. Dunn (1949) reported that over 1,600 individuals had been caught in Panama from 1933 through 1945; the species was the most common snake, comprising 11.3–13.5% of all snake species recorded at the various collection sites. At Guirocoba, Sonora, Mexico, it was the third most abundant snake during a study by Zweifel and Norris (1955).

REMARKS. In Sonora, Mexico, *O. aeneus* was the species associated with the milk-snake myth. Natives believed it would suck milk from a cow, leaving the udder hard and dry (Zweifel and Norris 1955). The species was reviewed by Keiser (1974, 1982).

Phyllorhynchus Stejneger 1890

Leaf-nosed Snakes

Key to the Species of *Phyllorhynchus*

1a. Fewer than 17 dark, often saddle-shaped, body bands before the tail; 2–4 bands on the tail; lateral spots usually absent . . . . *P. browni*

1b. More than 18 dark, irregular-shaped, body bands before the tail; 2–15 bands on the tail; irregular-shaped lateral spots present . . . . *P. decurtatus*

Phyllorhynchus browni Stejneger 1890 | Saddled Leaf-nosed Snake

RECOGNITION. *P. browni* (TBL to 51 cm) has a blunt snout and a large, triangular-shaped, rostral scale with its free edges raised above the adjacent scales and curved upward and back over the snout. The pale body is pinkish cream with fewer than 17 (12–16) large, black-bordered, brown saddlelike bands on the back that extend laterally but do not reach the ventrals; 2–3 more bands are present on the tail. Some body bands may have light centers, and the light spaces between them may be mottled with brown. A dark band crosses the orbits, and the parietal scales may be either immaculate or contain a dark blotch. The pupil is vertically elliptical. Dorsal body scales are smooth and lie in 21 (19–20) anterior rows, 19 midbody rows, and 17 rows near the tail. The immaculate white venter has 154–187 ventrals, 18–40 subcaudals, and an undivided anal plate. Lateral head scales are 2 nasals, 2–3 (1–4), 0 loreals, 2 (3) preoculars, 2 (3) postoculars, 2–3 suboculars, 2 (3–4) + 3 (4) temporals, 6–7 (5–9) supralabials, and 8–9 (7–11) infralabials. Only one pair of chin shields is present. The single hemipenis has a sulcus spermaticus that forks near the tip, and a naked base; the midportion of the shaft has spinules that grade into calyxes on the head. Each maxilla has 10–12 teeth; three posterior teeth follow a diastema.

Males have 154–174 ventrals, 30–40 subcaudals, and TLs approximately 13% of TBL; females have 168–187 ventrals, 18–33 subcaudals, and TLs 7–8% of TBL.

GEOGRAPHIC VARIATION. Two subspecies occur in the United States. The Pima leaf-nosed snake, *P. b. browni* Stejneger 1890, is found in southern Arizona in Maricopa, Pinal, and Pima Counties. It is has the dark dorsal bands much wider than the light areas between them, no dark pigment on the parietal scales, and 166 or fewer ventrals in males, 168 or more ventrals in females. The Maricopa leaf-nosed snake, *P. b. lucidus* Klauber 1940c, occurs north of the range of *P. b. browni* in Maricopa and Pinal Counties, Arizona. It has the dorsal bands only slightly broader than the light interspaces, 168 or more ventrals in males, 180 or more ventrals in females, and dark pigment on the parietal scales.

CONFUSING SPECIES. See the key for characters separating *P. browni* from *P. decurtatus*. Patch-nosed

Pima leaf-nosed snake, *Phyllorhynchus browni browni*; Organ Pipe National Monument, Arizona. (Photograph by Donald J. Fisher)

snakes *(Salvadora)* are longitudinally striped, not banded, and have the internasal scales only partially separated by the rostral scale. The rostral scale of the western hog-nosed snake *(Heterodon nasicus)* projects forward, not upward, and has a medial keel, and its anal plate is divided.

KARYOTYPE.   Unknown.

FOSSIL RECORD.   Skeletal remains from the Pleistocene (Rancholabrean) of Arizona identified only to the genus *Phyllorhynchus* may be from *P. browni* (Holman 1995, 2000).

DISTRIBUTION.   *P. browni* ranges from Pinal, Maricopa, Pima, and southeastern Yuma Counties in Arizona southwestward into Mexico to Sinaloa.

Distribution of *Phyllorhynchus browni*.

HABITAT.   It lives in open sandy to gravelly, rock-strewn deserts with paloverde, mesquite, saltbush, and Saguaro and other cacti.

BEHAVIOR.   Although apparently common at some localities in Arizona, almost nothing is known of the biology of this small, secretive snake. It is most active from May to early August (Rosen and Lowe 1994); the majority of collection dates are in June–July, particularly after rainstorms. Nothing is known of its over-wintering habits. Daily activity is nocturnal, lasting approximately from 2000 to 2400 hours (Kauffeld 1943a; Klauber 1940c), although it has been found as late as 0400 hours after a rain shower (Shannon and Humphrey 1959), and most individuals are found as they cross roads. Daylight hours are spent under cover beneath rocks or other shelters, in rodent burrows, or burrowed into the soil. ATs at the time of capture of active individuals reported by Kauffeld (1943a), Klauber (1940c), and Shannon and Humphrey (1959) were 23–33°C. A female collected on a road with a ST of 31°C (AT, 29.2°C) had a BT of 31.2°C (Shannon and Humphrey 1959).

REPRODUCTION.   Reproductive data are sparse. Goldberg (1996) studied the reproductive cycles in Arizona. Males had regressed testes from June through August, when the seminiferous tubules contained only spermatogonia and Sertoli cells. No males were found in recrudescence (when spermatogenic cells proliferate and spermatogonial divisions are common, and primary and secondary spermatocytes and spermatids present). Those in spermiogenesis were found from April through September, when both metamorphosing spermatids and mature sperm were present. In June 96% of the 45 males collected were undergoing spermiogenesis, and 71% had sperm present in their epididymides. The minimum SVL for a spermiogenic male was 22.9 cm. June–July females were depositing yolk in their follicles, and some had both enlarged (4–9 mm) follicles and oviductal eggs 5–6 mm in diameter. Only 34% of the females were reproductively active. The smallest female with oviductal eggs had a SVL of 29.3 cm.

P. browni is oviparous, laying two to five eggs per clutch (Stebbins 1985). A female collected on 6 August contained five 16×7 mm ova that appeared about to be oviposited (Stebbins 1954).

GROWTH AND LONGEVITY.   Unreported.

DIET AND FEEDING HABITS.   The enlarged rostral scale may be used to dig up lizard eggs. Lizards and their eggs seem to be the main foods of adults (Klauber 1940c; Stebbins 1985), but juveniles may eat insect larvae (Fowlie 1965).

PREDATORS AND DEFENSE. Records of natural predators are nonexistent, but many *P. browni* are killed by vehicles while crossing roads (Rosen and Lowe 1994).

When molested, *P. browni* flattens its throat into a dewlap and hisses loudly. Some will bite if handled.

POPULATIONS. *P. browni* totaled 14 (3.8%) of 368 snakes recorded along Arizona State Route 84 in 1988–1991 by Rosen and Lowe (1994). The sex ratio is approximately 1:1.

REMARKS. So little is known of the life history and ecological requirements of this snake that a thorough study would be very helpful. The genus *Phyllorhynchus* was reviewed by McDiarmid and McCleary (1993).

Phyllorhynchus decurtatus (Cope 1869) | Spotted Leaf-nosed Snake

RECOGNITION. *P. decurtatus* (TBL to 51 cm) is pale gray, cream, pink, or tan with 18–60 brown body blotches, and another 2–15 tail blotches. The blotches are variable in size and shape, but none reach the venter. A dark brown band crosses the head between the orbits and continues diagonally to the posterior corners of the mouth; other head markings consist of variable dark spots. The rostral scute often contains a white or gray patch. Dorsal body scales are smooth with a single apical pit and lie in 21 anterior rows, 19 midbody rows, and 17 (16) posterior rows. The im-maculate white venter has 151–196 ventrals, 20–42 subcaudals, and an undivided anal plate. The head is slightly broader than the neck, with a blunt snout and vertically elliptical pupils. The large rostral scale is raised and extends backward to completely separate the internasal scales. Lateral head scales are 2 nasals, 2 (1–4) loreals, 2–3 (1–4) preoculars, 2 (3) postoculars, 2–3 suboculars, 2–3 + 3–4 temporals, 6–7 (5) supra-labials, and 9 (8–10) infralabials. The hemipenis is slightly bifurcate, with a single sulcus spermaticus that divides near the tip, a band of enlarged spines on

Desert leaf-nosed snake, *Phyllorhynchus decoratus perkinsi*; San Bernardino County, California. (Photograph by Donald J. Fisher)

either side of the sulcus (the proximal spines are large, but spine length decreases distally). Each maxilla has six to nine anterior teeth separated from three to four posterior teeth by a diastema.

Males are larger (to 51.0 cm), with TLs 14–15% of TBL, 151–187 ventrals, and 29–42 subcaudals; females are shorter (to 48.6 cm), with TLs 8–10% of TBL, 165–196 ventrals, and 20–34 subcaudals.

GEOGRAPHIC VARIATION. Five subspecies are recognized (McCleary and McDiarmid 1993), but only two occur in the United States. The cloudy leaf-nosed snake, *P. d. nubilus* Klauber 1940c, is found in south-central Arizona and northern Sonora, Mexico. It has 42–60 body blotches and 7–15 tail blotches, 157–162 ventrals in males and 171–176 ventrals in females, and 30–33 subcaudals in males and 20–24 subcaudals in females. (Doubts exist as to the validity of this taxon; McCleary and McDiarmid 1993). The desert leaf-nosed snake, *P. d. perkinsi* Klauber 1935a, ranges from south-central California and southern Nevada south through western Arizona and southeastern California to northwestern Sonora and northeastern Baja California. It has 24–48 body blotches and 2–9 tail blotches, 164–183 ventrals in males and 173–196 ventrals in females, and 32–42 subcaudals in males and 24–34 subcaudals in females. Intergradation between these subspecies occurs in central Arizona.

CONFUSING SPECIES. See the above key for characters distinguishing *P. decurtatus* and *P. browni*. The patch-nosed snakes *(Salvadora)* are striped, not blotched, and have round pupils and a divided anal plate. The western hog-nosed snake *(Heterodon nasicus)* has its rostral scute pointed forward with the point free, keeled body scales, the anal plate divided, and round pupils.

KARYOTYPE. The karyotype consists of 36 chromosomes with 50 arms: 16 macrochromosomes and 20 microchromosomes (Baker et al. 1972; Bury et al. 1970; Trinco and Smith 1972). The sixth largest pair is acrocentric; all other macrochromosomes are biarmed.

FOSSIL RECORD. Fossils are from the Pleistocene (Rancholabrean) of Arizona (Mead et al. 1984; Van Devender and Mead 1978).

Distribution of *Phyllorhynchus decurtatus*.

DISTRIBUTION. This snake ranges from south-central California and southern Nevada south through southeastern California and south-central and southwestern Arizona to near the southern tip of Baja California and to Matzatlán, Sinaloa, Mexico. Its distribution in the United States closely follows the range of the creosote bush (Stebbins 1985).

HABITAT. *P. decurtatus* is a resident of open, sandy to sand-gravel deserts with elevations of near sea level to above 800 m. Typical vegetation includes creosote and catclaw bush and various cacti.

BEHAVIOR. This snake is almost exclusively nocturnal. Brattstrom (1953a) found a few active as early as 1800–1900 hours and others as late as 0400–0500 hours; but most surface activity takes place between 1930 and 2400 hours, with a peak period at 2100–2400 hours. Few are active after midnight. During the day, it hides under rocks or other surface debris, or takes shelter in rodent burrows. It is capable of digging into loose soil with its enlarged rostral scale, but is not as good a burrower as either *Chilomeniscus cinctus* or the species of *Chionactis*.

At low elevations in the southern part of the range, active individuals have been found in every month, particularly in Mexico, but there is little surface activity in November–February in the United States.

Spring emergence begins in March–April in southern California (Brattstrom 1953a; Klauber 1940c) and as late as May in Arizona (Rosen and Lowe 1994). No emergence dates are available for the northern portions of the range, but spring emergence there is probably delayed to late April or May. Peak activity is in April–July in southern California (Brattstrom 1953a; Klauber 1940c), and in June–July in Arizona (Rosen and Lowe 1994). After July, the number of surface active *P. decurtatus* declines rapidly. The winter is spent underground. Cowles (1941b) found *P. decurtatus* hibernating as deep as 76 cm in a small sand dune where the ST at 101 cm was 19.5°C. Probably animal burrows are also used as winter retreats.

P. decurtatus displays acute discomfort when its BT rises to 36.5°C, and its CT_{max} is 38°C. A BT of 39.3°C is lethal, but if the snake is heated to 38°C and then allowed to cool, recovery takes place at 31°C (Cowles and Bogert 1944). Its minimum voluntary BT is 24°C. Klauber (1940c) found active individuals on roads at ATs of 29–34°C, and he (1935a) recorded a BT of 31°C for one snake. Based on published temperature data, *P. decurtatus* is probably most active at ATs of 28–30°C.

REPRODUCTION. According to Stebbins (1985) and Wright and Wright (1957), both sexes are adult at 30 cm TBL. The smallest spermiogenic male examined by Goldberg (1996) had a SVL of 24.4 cm, and the smallest female containing oviductal eggs had a 24.8 cm SVL.

The male sexual cycle is similar to that of *P. browni* (Goldberg 1996). Testes are regressed in May, June, and August, and spermiogenic males are present in April–July. Eighty-nine percent of June males were maturing sperm, and sperm was present in the epididymides of 100% of the males Goldberg examined. June females had enlarged follicles (4–9 mm); those in July had 4–6 mm oviductal eggs. No vitellogenesis was observed. Only 36% of the females examined by Goldberg were reproductively active. Eggs have been previously found in females in April, May, and August (Brattstrom 1953a).

Courtship and copulatory behaviors have not been described. Most nesting probably takes place in June–July, and the fact that a female contained eggs in August may indicate that more than one clutch is laid a year. Clutches contain two to four (mean, 3.6),

35–37 × 8–10 mm eggs (Brattstrom 1953a). Duration of the IP unknown, but the young probably hatch during late August to late September. Hatchlings resemble adults in color and pattern, and are about 16–18 cm long (Trutnau 1986).

GROWTH AND LONGEVITY. Unknown.

DIET AND FEEDING HABITS. Nothing is known of the hunting behavior of this snake, besides its being a nocturnal forager. Its diet consists of lizards *(Callisaurus, Coleonyx)* and their eggs (Brattstrom 1953a; Klauber 1940c; Thule and Greene, in McCleary and McDiarmid 1993). Perkins (1938) reported the species eats insect larvae, but this has not been substantiated. Adult lizards are probably captured as they sleep, and exposure to skin secretions from *P. decurtatus* will elicit a defensive attack, tail displays, and flight by western banded geckos *(Coleonyx variegatus)* (Dial et al. 1989).

PREDATORS AND DEFENSE. Records of predation on *P. decurtatus* only show snakes *(Arizona, Crotalus, Micruroides)* (Klauber 1935a, 1972; Lowe et al. 1986), but owls and carnivorous mammals probably also eat them. Motorized vehicles kill many spotted leaf-nosed snakes on southwestern roads each year (Klauber 1940c; Rosen and Lowe 1994).

When discovered, *P. decurtatus* usually tries to flee. When escape is prevented, it will puff out its throat vertically and hiss, and if handled, it tries to bury its head between the fingers and releases musk. Biting is rare.

POPULATIONS. This species is one of the most abundant snakes in the southwestern deserts. Gates (1957) collected about 100 *P. decurtatus* in two years in the vicinity of Wickenburg, Arizona, and Rosen and Lowe (1994) recorded 18 (4.9%) in a total sample of 368 snakes in four years along an Arizona highway. Klauber (1940c) reported that 110 (39.4%) of the 279 live snakes encountered on the roads of San Diego County, California, were *P. decurtatus*. Brattstrom (1953a) collected 487 in 30 years in San Diego County. Most of his records were of 13.1–41.0 cm snakes, and the sex ratio was 1.57:1.00.

REMARKS. *P. decurtatus* has been reviewed by McCleary and McDiarmid (1993).

Pituophis Holbrook 1842

Bullsnakes, Gopher Snakes, and Pine Snakes

Key to the Species of *Pituophis*

1a. A dark stripe extends obliquely downward from the orbit to the corner of the mouth; usually over 50 (32–106) dorsal body blotches; usually over 15 (6–36) tail blotches . . . . *P. catenifer* (in part)

1b. No dark stripe extends from the orbit to the corner of the mouth; fewer than 45 (25–42) dorsal body blotches; fewer than 14 (6–13) tail blotches 2

2a. Body either black (melanistic) or, if light, with 31 or fewer dark dorsal body blotches . . . . *P. melanoleucus*

2b. Body not black (melanistic); body light, usually with 32 or more dark dorsal body blotches . . . *P. catenifer* (in part)

Pituophis catenifer (Blainville 1835) | Gopher Snake

RECOGNITION. The somewhat slender gopher snake is a large (TBL to 274.3 cm) cream, yellow, tan, or gray species with 32–106 black, brown, or reddish brown dorsal blotches; a series of lateral dark blotches; 6–36 dark tail bands; four prefrontal scales; and a rounded snout with an enlarged rostral scale on its narrow head. A dark bar usually extends downward from the eye to the corner of the supralabials, a second extends obliquely downward from the eye to the posterior corner of the mouth, and the supralabials bear dark bars. Body color, patterns, and markings vary considerably (see GEOGRAPHIC VARIATION). The venter is white, cream, or yellow, and often has dark marks. Body scales are keeled with two apical pits; dorsal scale rows counts are as follows: anterior, 27–29 (25–33); midbody, 31 or 33 (27–37); and posterior, 23 (21–27). On the venter are 207–260 ventrals, 48–84 subcaudals, and a single anal plate. Lateral head scales consist of 2 nasals (partially divided by the nostril), 1 (rarely 0 or 2) loreal(s), 1–2 (rarely 3) preoculars, 3–4 (1–6) postoculars, 1 + 2–3 + 3–5 temporals, 8–9 (rarely 7 or 10) supralabials, and 12–13 (10–15) infralabials. Present also are 0–1 (rarely 2) azygous scale(s), 4 prefrontals, and a rostral scale that is as broad as long, or longer than broad. The hemipenis is subcylindrical and slightly bilobed with a single sulcus spermaticus, and the basal and distal ends are spinose. Spines at the base are generally small, those on the middle of the shaft larger and recurved, and those at the distal terminus small. Each maxilla has 16–17 teeth.

Pacific gopher snake, *Pituophis catenifer catenifer*. (Photograph by John H. Tashjian)

Sonoran gopher snake, *Pituophis catenifer affinis*. (Photograph by Carl H. Ernst)

San Diego gopher snake, *Pituophis catenifer annectens*; Riverside County, California. (Photograph by Donald J. Fisher)

Males have 209–253 (mean, 229) ventrals, 48–84 (mean, 69) subcaudals, and TLs 10.4–18.8 (mean, 14.3) % of TBL; females have 207–260 (mean, 236) ventrals, 48–82 (mean, 60) subcaudals, and TLs 10.1–16.6 (mean, 12.0) % of TBL.

GEOGRAPHIC VARIATION. Seven subspecies occur north of Mexico. *P. c. catenifer* (Blainville 1835), the Pacific gopher snake, ranges from northwestern Washington south along the Pacific Coast to approximately Los Angeles. It has a dark postorbital bar; 47–90 brown or black, separated, dorsal blotches (reduced to dark streaks anteriorly); 14–31 black tail bands; gray pigment on the side of the tail; 33 (29–35) midbody scale rows; and the rostral scale as broad as it is long. *P. c. affinis* Hallowell 1852, the Sonoran gopher snake, is found from south-central Utah, central New Mexico, and extreme western Texas west through Arizona to southeastern California, and south in Mexico to Baja California and northern Mexico. It has a dark postorbital bar; 34–63 brown to reddish brown, saddle-shaped, dorsal blotches; 9–21 dark tail bands; no lateral gray pigment; 31 or 33 (27–35) midbody scale rows; and the rostral scale slightly longer than it is broad. *P. c. annectens* Baird and Girard 1853, the San Diego gopher snake, occurs along the Pacific coast from approximately Los Angeles south to northwestern Baja California. It has a pale or absent postorbital bar; 57–106 black or brown, rounded, dorsal body blotches (those anterior are usually connected, and also in contact with the lateral blotches; 16–33 dark

tail bands, no gray lateral pigment, 29–37 (mean, 33) midbody scale rows; and the rostral scale as broad as it is long. *P. c. deserticola* Stejneger 1893, the Great Basin gopher snake, ranges south in the Great Basin from south-central British Columbia to western California, Nevada, Utah, western Colorado, northern Arizona, and northwestern New Mexico. It has a dark postorbital bar only in the north; is grayish, cream, or yellowish rather than tan to brownish, with 43–71 square, connected, dorsal body blotches (black anteriorly, brown posteriorly); has lateral blotches that connect to form a dark band; 12–22 black tail bands; dark keels on the anterior light scales; 27–35 (mean, 31) midbody scale rows; and the rostral scale as broad as it is long. *P. c. pumilus* Klauber 1946b, the Santa Cruz gopher snake, is isolated on that island. It has a dark postorbital bar; 64–82 dark dorsal blotches (those anterior contact the lateral blotches); 17–28 dark tail bands; black streaks on the dorsal scales in the anterior light spaces; 27–29 midbody scale rows; and the rostral scale as broad as it is long. *P. c. ruthveni* Stull 1929, the Louisiana pine snake, is found in only a small range from west-central Louisiana into adjacent eastern Texas. It rarely has a postorbital bar; is white or tan; has 28–42 dorsal blotches (those anterior dark brown and connected, those near the tail often reddish brown and separated); 6–13 brown or reddish brown tail bands; 31 (27–33) midbody scale rows; and the rostral scale high, keeled, and as broad as it is long. Principal component and discriminant-function analyses performed by Reichling (1995) indicate that *ruthveni* has diverged from the eastern species *P. melanoleucus* and is more closely related to *P. c. sayi*, suggesting an independent evolutionary pathway. In addition, no evidence exists of intergradation with the nearest eastern populations of *P. m. lodingi*. In accordance, it is treated here as a subspecies of the western species *P. catenifer*. *P. c. sayi* (Schlegel 1837), the bullsnake, ranges from southeastern Alberta and southwestern Saskatchewan south, west of the Mississippi River, into Mexico, with populations east of the Mississippi in Wisconsin, northwestern Illinois, northeastern Illinois and adjacent northwestern Indiana, and southwestern Indiana. It has a dark postorbital bar; 33–66 (usually 41 or more) black, brown, or reddish brown, unconnected, dorsal blotches; 9–19 black tail bands; the bases of the interblotch scales dark; 29, 31, or 33 (27–32) midbody scale rows; and the rostral scale high, keeled, and about twice as long as it is broad.

Rodríguez-Robles and Jesus-Escobar (2000) studied the mtDNA sequences of the various taxa of *Pituophis*. Their interpretations of the relationships within the taxa of the United States are essentially like the one presented here, except that they elevated *P. c. ruthveni* to full species status.

CONFUSING SPECIES. Rat snakes *(Elaphe)* and milk- and kingsnakes *(Lampropeltis)* have only two prefrontal scales, and *Elaphe* has a divided anal plate. Glossy snakes *(Arizona elegans)* have smooth scales and an unmarked venter. Whipsnakes *(Masticophis)* and juvenile racers *(Coluber)* have smooth scales and a divided anal plate. The lyre snake *(Trimorphodon biscutatus)* has vertically elliptical pupils, and light-centered dorsal blotches. The western rattlesnake *(Crotalus viridis)* has a tail rattle, vertically elliptical pupils, and a pit between the nostril and eye.

KARYOTYPE. The karyotype consists of 16 macrochromosomes and 20 microchromosomes (Baker et al. 1972; Bury et al. 1970; Trinco and Smith 1971); the sex chromosomes are ZW / ZZ, and a cloned ZFY gene (a supposed testis determining factor in mammals) is expressed in embryos of both sexes (Bull et al. 1988).

FOSSIL RECORD. *P. catenifer* has an extensive fossil record that parallels its current distribution (originally reported as *P. melanoleucus*, but here assigned by geo-

Louisiana pine snake, *Pituophis catenifer ruthveni*. (Photograph by R. D. Bartlett)

graphic location): Miocene (Hemphillian) of Nebraska (Parmley and Holman 1995); Pliocene (Blancan) of Idaho (Sankey 1996), Kansas (Brattstrom 1967; Eshleman 1975; Holman 1972b; Wilson 1968), Nebraska (Holman and Schloeder 1991), and Texas (Holman and Schloeder 1991; Rogers 1976); Pleistocene? of Illinois (Gilmore 1938); Pleistocene (Irvingtonian) of Arkansas (Dowling 1958b), Colorado (Holman 1995; Rogers et al. 1985), Kansas (Holman 1972b, 1986c), and Oklahoma (Holman 1986b); and Pleistocene (Rancholabrean) of Arizona (Mead et al. 1982, 1984; Van Devender et al. 1977; Van Devender and Mead 1978), California (Brattstrom 1953c; Hudson and Brattstrom 1977; LaDuke 1991), Kansas (Brattstrom 1967; Holman 1987a; Preston 1979), Missouri (Holman 1965b; Parmalee et al. 1969), Nevada (Brattstrom 1954a, 1954b, 1976; Mead 1985; Mead and Bell 1994; Mead et al. 1982, 1989), New Mexico (Brattstrom 1964a; Van Devender et al. 1976; Van Devender and Bradley 1994; Van Devender and Worthington 1977), Oklahoma (Brattstrom 1967; Preston 1979), Texas (Hill 1971; Mecham 1959; Mead and Bell 1994; Parmley 1986b, 1988b, 1990a; Preston 1979), and Utah (Mead and Bell 1994; Mead et al. 1989).

DISTRIBUTION. *P. catenifer* ranges from northwestern Illinois and Wisconsin west to southwestern Saskatchewan, southeastern Alberta, and south-central British Columbia, and south to Louisiana, Texas, New Mexico, Arizona, and southern California in the United States, and to southern Sinaloa, Veracruz, and Baja California in Mexico. Isolated populations also occur in northeastern Illinois and adjacent northwestern Indiana, southwestern Indiana, and on Santa Cruz Island, California.

Bullsnake, *Pituophis catenifer sayi*; Kiowa County, Colorado. (Photograph by Carl H. Ernst)

HABITAT.   With such an extensive range, the gopher snake lives in a variety of habitats at elevations from sea level to approximately 2,800 m: rocky canyons, dry prairie grasslands, open brushland, sand hills, the edges of open deciduous woods, coniferous forests, deserts, agricultural tracts (particularly around abandoned buildings), and the edges of marshes. It is not uncommon in suburbs and along coastal sand dunes.

Necessary are deep, usually loose but sometimes hardpan or rocky, sand, loam, or gravelly soils, an abundant supply of rodents, and at some sites, animal burrows for shelter.

BEHAVIOR.   Over most of its range, *P. catenifer* is active from April or May to September or October, but occasionally also from March to November in warm

Distribution of *Pituophis catenifer*.

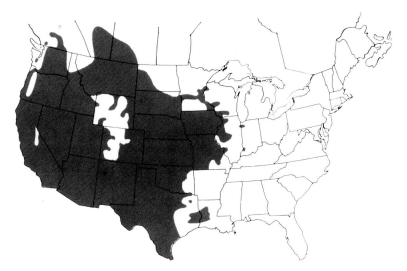

years. In southern Louisiana it may be active in every month. Most observations occur in May and June. The snake becomes less active as the summer gets hotter and dryer from late June onward, and probably uses underground shelters to escape the more intense daytime heat.

As many as 180–250 days may be spent in hibernation each year (Parker and Brown 1980), usually deep in mammal burrows or rock crevices. Schroder (1950) excavated an Indiana hibernaculum situated on the north rim of a large dune riddled with abandoned mammal burrows. The hibernaculum contained two chambers 91 and 107 cm deep, respectively, and the AT in the chambers was below 9°C (Landreth, 1972, reported the species first starts to awake from cold narcosis at 8°C). The average CT of *P. catenifer* entering a Utah den in autumn was 24.4°C compared with an average of 27.9°C for those on the surface near the den in the spring (Parker and Brown 1980). Fitch (1958) reported that a female caught in three successive Octobers near the same rock ledge apparently returned there each year to hibernate (although Parker and Brown, 1980, reported much interhibernacula movement). *P. catenifer* often shares its hibernaculum with other species of snakes, including rattlesnakes (*Crotalus*).

P. catenifer is diurnal in the spring and fall, but more crepuscular or nocturnal during hot, dry periods in summer. It basks in the morning after emergence, often only exposing its head, to raise its BT. This can cause regional heterothermy, with the head becoming warmer than the unexposed body (Ashton 1998). Brattstrom (1965) reported the threshold BT for normal locomotion of juveniles in laboratory tests was about 18°C. He also reported a thermal activity range of 16.4–34.6°C, a CT_{min} of 3.0°C, and a CT_{max} of 40.5°C. The BTs of 12 active Kansas *P. catenifer* averaged 28.2 (23.4–37.6) °C and 3.8°C above ET; only one snake had a BT below AT (Fitch 1999). Moving Utah *P. catenifer* had BTs of 21.5–34.7°C on clear days and 18.6–32.5°C during cloudy days (Parker and Brown 1980), and active Idaho gopher snakes had mean CTs of 28.6°C (Diller and Wallace 1996). Collins (1993) stated *P. catenifer* is active at ATs above 16°C in Kansas. Clarke (1958) recorded ATs of 13–37°C for other active Kansas individuals, but Parks (1973) found one crawling along a Kansas road in February at an AT of only 4°C. Sullivan (1981a) observed active California individuals at road STs of approximately 18–38°C.

This species is an accomplished burrower, and may simply dig itself into the ground to escape uncomfortable temperatures. Its pointed snout and enlarged rostral scale are quite effective for tunneling in loose soil. The digging sequence is stereotyped: spading actions by the snout are followed by scooping a load of soil in a head/neck flexure, moving backward, and dumping the soil away from the burrow (Carpenter 1982). Such behavior is important for digging retreats or nests and for excavating rodents (especially pocket gophers). A burrowing *P. catenifer* can possibly move up to 3,400 cm³ soil/hour (Carpenter 1982). Skulls of the two species of *Pituophis* differ in structure, particularly in the nasal/premaxilla articulation (Knight 1986), possibly indicating a difference in excavating ability or behavior.

Burrowing may help the snake avoid excessive evaporative water loss during dry weather. Prange and Schmidt-Nielson (1969) found the skin to be relatively impermeable, but water is lost during hibernation, and the snake emerges in spring up to 16% lighter than when it entered in the fall (Parker and Brown 1980).

Hibernacula may be some distance from the annual feeding grounds, and *P. catenifer* may make rather long spring and fall migrations between them; Moriarty and Linck (1997) reported movements up to 1–4 km, and the 2.4 km trip reported by Imler (1945) may have been between the feeding range and the hibernaculum. Parker and Brown (1980) reported an average seasonal migration of 508 (maximum, 875) m for Utah gopher snakes, and Fitch's (1999) Kansas individuals averaged 434 (21–1,390) m. Females may make additional migrations to nesting sites (Parker and Brown 1980). Displaced individuals show homing ability (Parker and Brown 1980). The orientation and navigational cues used to home or migrate are not known.

Movements on the feeding grounds are usually shorter, averaging 81.6 (6–270) m in Utah (Parker and Brown 1980) and 354 (54–1,140) m in Kansas (Fitch 1999). The average distance crawled per day by radio-equipped snakes in Kansas was 142 m (Fitch and Shirer 1971). Home ranges were 1.5–12.8 ha in Minnesota (Moriarty and Linck 1997), 1.15 (1.1–1.2) ha for males and 2.09 (0.9–3.3) ha for females in Utah (Parker and Brown 1980), and probably about 12.9 ha in Kansas (Fitch 1999).

P. catenifer is an accomplished climber that may ascend into low bushes or even trees (Bullock 1981).

Males of the various subspecies are known to engage in dominance combat bouts, particularly during the breeding season (Rundquist 1997; Shaw 1951).

REPRODUCTION. Male *P. catenifer* mature in one to two years at a TBL of 90–96 cm (Conant and Collins 1998; Diller and Wallace 1996; Parker and Brown 1980). Testes are regressed when males emerge from hibernation in April and May, but enlarge in June as recrudescence begins, reach their largest size in July, begin to shrink in August through the fall, and further regress during the winter (Goldberg and Parker 1975; Parker and Brown 1980). Spermiogenesis occurs in late summer and early autumn, after which the sperm enters the epididymides and vas deferens and is stored over winter until the spring breeding season. Some mature sperm may be found in the vas deferens during the entire annual activity period (April–October).

Female *P. catenifer* mature in three to five years at 90–95 cm TBL (Conant and Collins 1998; Parker and Brown 1980; Stebbins 1985). The female gametic cycle has been less studied than that of the male. Dissected Utah females had ovaries weighing 0.8–1.3 g in July and August, 1.1–2.5 g in September–October, 1.3–3.0 g in April, and 4.8–4.9 g in May (Parker and Brown 1980). One had the ovaries partially enveloped by the oviducts and was close to ovulation in May, and another female ovulated between 8 and 25 June. Parturient females with visible corpora lutea were present in early and mid-July. Ovulation occurs between 1 and 20 June in Idaho (Diller and Wallace 1996). Gestation takes about 49 days.

All reported natural matings have occurred in spring or early summer (21 April–25 June), with most concentrated in May; captive matings have occurred as early as February at the San Diego Zoo (Stebbins 1954). Most breeding activity takes place in the vicinity of the hibernaculum before the snakes disperse, and males probably identify females by odor (Fitch 1936; Parker and Brown 1980; Smith and Iverson 1993). During courtship the male crawls beside and over the female until he eventually rests loosely almost over her entire body. While doing this, the male performs ventrally directed caudocephalic waves with the posterior of his body. He may or may not bite the female's body at this time, but just prior to coitus the male may seize the her head or neck with his mouth. The female usually remains passive except for elevating and waving her tail and turning it sideways to better bring the snakes' anal vents together. The male curls his tail beneath hers until their vents are aligned and then inserts one hemipenis. Both snakes may wave their tails about and pulsate during the copulation (Gloyd 1947; Reichling 1988; Stebbins 1954). Copulation may last over an hour (Stebbins 1954).

Oviposition occurs principally in June and July, but has taken place from 4 May through 1 September. Females appear to have an annual breeding cycle: Diller and Wallace (1996) reported that 97% are reproductive each year in Idaho. Although not proven, the possibility exists, because of the extended nesting and hatching periods, that occasionally more than one clutch is laid each year. Nest sites include animal burrows, areas beneath rocks or logs, and excavations dug in loose soil by the female. Communal nesting occurs.

Ninety-four literature clutches contained 2–24 eggs (Stebbins 1985), with an average of 11.1 eggs per clutch. The white eggs are elliptical with a rough, leathery shell and often adherent, are 40–130 (mean, 61; n = 43) mm long and 19.0–43.0 (mean, 30.6; n = 43) mm wide, and have masses of 33.0–81.0 (mean, 62.7; n = 14) g. Reported RCMs have ranged from 0.189 to 0.47, and averaged 0.38 (Diller and Wallace 1996; Seigel and Fitch 1984).

Development takes 50–125 (mean, 67; n = 49) days, depending on the IT (Treadwell, 1962, describes embryological development). Clutches have hatched from 30 June to 7 November, but most hatched in late August and September. Hatchlings have 20.0–55.5 (mean, 37.5; n = 116) cm TBLs and weigh 5–30 (mean, 19; n = 60) g. They are dull in color at first, but brighten after their first shedding.

GROWTH AND LONGEVITY. Relative growth varies from year to year, probably due to weather factors or prey availability, and *P. catenifer* grows more slowly with age. First-year Kansas *P. c. sayi* grow at a mean rate of 5.6 cm/30 days, a mean relative growth rate of 9.4%; second-year snakes grow 2.7 cm/30 days (3.1%); third-year snakes grow 1.2 cm/30 days (1.2%); those over three years of age grow 0.6cm/30 days (0.5%); and some Kansas snakes grow to 110 cm SVL in four years (Platt 1984). An adolescent length of 90–130 cm SVL is typically attained in the fifth year (Fitch 1999). Based on recaptures of marked Kansas snakes, Fitch (1999) tentatively assigned the following SVLs to age classes: second year, 90.0–105.5 cm; third year, 108.2–118.0 cm; fifth year, 126.0–133.5 cm; seventh year, 140.7–144.7 cm; and ninth year, 160.0–162.4 cm. Imler (1945) reported that young *P. c. sayi* in Nebraska grow about 38 cm their first year and 17.8–20.0 cm the second year. Young California *P. c. catenifer* can grow more than 10 cm during late spring following their first hibernation, and a two-year-old grows to more than 80 cm SVL, but after this the growth rate slows (Fitch 1949). Male Utah *P. c. deserticola* grow an average per year of approximately 14.3 cm (a mean 24.2% increase) in years one and two, 7.8 cm (9.3%) in years three and four, and 2.0 cm (2.0%) in years five and six; similarly, females grow an average of 10.0 cm/year (15.6%) in years one and two, 6.0 cm/year (11.2%) in years three and four, and 3.5 cm (3.9%) in years five and six (Parker and Brown 1980).

Several *P. catenifer* had rather long lives in captivity: a wild-caught male *P. c. deserticola* lived for 33 years and 10 months; a wild-caught *P. c. sayi* (sex unknown) survived 22 years, 5 months, and 1 day; and a captive-bred *P. c. annectans* lived 20 years, 5 months, and 18 days (Snider and Bowler 1992).

DIET AND FEEDING HABITS. *P. catenifer* is an active forager, and prey is found by either olfaction (Chiszar et al. 1980; Dyrkacz and Corn 1974; Smith and Iverson 1993) or sight, and as a mammal predator it prefers warm prey over cold (Chiszar et al. 1989). It hunts along the surface of the ground, in subterranean mammal burrows, and in trees (Eichholz and Koenig 1992). Small prey may be merely pinned to the ground or against the wall of a burrow, but larger more dangerous animals are more often constricted. The type of prey, regardless of size, affects prey-handling behavior, and animals are handled three ways: (1) pinion—the prey is pinned to the ground by the snake's unlooped body as its head is grasped in the snake's mouth (used more often for adult mice, less

often for helpless young of larger prey), (2) pinion plus nonoverlapping loop—as above, but with the snake's body in a partial loop over that of the prey (pinioning is aimed more at holding the prey than at incapacitating it), and (3) fully encircling coils—typical constriction (used more for incapacitating larger prey) (de Queiroz 1984). Small prey are rarely ingested alive; large prey are only ingested when dead. The snake does not always win these battles, and some prey, especially larger ones, may escape. Large prey may also wound or kill a *P. catenifer* (Haywood and Harris 1972). Its appetite is voracious; one was found with 35 mice in its stomach (Van Denburgh 1922).

Mammals are the primary prey, but birds and other small vertebrates are also eaten: mammals—moles *(Scalopus aquaticus)*, gophers *(Geomys bursarius, Thomomys* sp.), voles *(Microtus longicaudus, M. montanus, M. ochrogaster, M. pennsylvanicus)*, mice *(Mus musculus, Onychomys leucogaster, Peromyscus boylii, P. leucopus, P. maniculatus, P. truei, Perognathus parvus)*, rats *(Neotoma albigula, Rattus norvegicus, Sigmodon hispidus)*, kangaroo rats *(Dipodomys merriami, D. ordi, D. spectabilis)*, ground squirrels *(Amnospermophilus leucurus, A. nelsoni, Cynomys* sp., *Spermophilus beecheyi, S. lateralis, S. townsendii, S. tridecemlineatus, Tamias* sp.), tree squirrels *(Sciurus nayaritensis)*, and rabbits and hares *(Lepus californicus, Sylvilagus floridanus, S. nuttalli)*; birds—curlew *(Numenius americanus)*, ducks *(Anas acuta, A. platyrhynchus)*, domestic chicken *(Gallus gallus)*, quail *(Colinus virginianus)*, owls *(Micrathene whitneyi)*, doves and pigeons *(Columba livia, Zenaida macroura)*, swallows *(Stelgidopteryx serripennis)*, woodpeckers *(Colaptes auratus, Melanerpes formicivorus)*, tyrant flycatchers *(Tyrannus* sp.), passerines *(Icterus galbula, Junco oreganus, Parus atricapillus, Serinus canaria, Sialia currucoides, Spiza americana, Sturnella neglecta, Troglodytes aedon, Turdus migratorius)*, and weaver finches *(Passer domesticus)*; reptiles—turtle eggs, lizards *(Cnemidophorus sexlineatus, Sceloporus occidentalis, Uta stansburiana)*, and snakes *(Crotalus viridis, P. catenifer, Thamnophis elegans)*; frogs; and insects (Orthoptera) (Blair 1985; Boal et al. 1997; Burt and Hoyle 1935; Cunningham 1959; Diller and Johnson 1988; Diller and Wallace 1988, 1996; Eichholz and Koenig 1992; Engeman and Delutes 1994; C. Ernst, pers. obs.; Fitch 1936, 1999; Hammerson 1986; Howitz 1986; Hurter 1911; Jaksic and Greene 1984; Jennings et al. 1996; Kingery and Kingery 1995;

Klauber 1972; Kneeland et al. 1995; Marr 1944, 1985; McKinney and Ballinger 1966; Nussbaum et al. 1983; Poran and Coss 1990; Randall et al. 1995; Redmond and Jenni 1986; Rodríguez-Robles 1998; Stull 1940; Van Denburgh 1922; Vogt 1981; Webb 1970; Wellstead 1981; Wright and Wright 1957; Zaworski 1990).

PREDATORS AND DEFENSE. Over the extensive range of *P. catenifer*, it comes into contact with a variety of potential predators, but few predatory data have been published. Known natural predators are raccoons *(Procyon lotor)*, badgers *(Taxidea taxus)*, coyotes *(Canis latrans)*, great horned owls *(Bubo virginianus)*, kestrels *(Falco sparverius)*, hawks *(Buteo albicaudatus, B. jamaicensis, B. regalis, B. swainsonii, Buteogallus anthracinus)*, golden eagles *(Aquila chrysaetos)*, ringnecked snakes *(Diadophis punctatus)*, and kingsnakes *(Lampropeltis getula)* (Blair and Schitosky 1982; Eckle and Grubb 1986; Giles 1940; Fitch 1949; Jennings 1997; Koch and Peterson 1995; Parker and Brown 1980; Ross 1989; Van Denburgh 1922; Young and Vandeventer 1988). A woodrat *(Neotoma* sp.) attacked a *P. catenifer* in captivity (Grater, in Klauber 1972). Humans kill many each year with their habitat destruction, automobiles, mowers, and pesticides, and gopher snakes are taken from wild populations each year for the pet trade.

When disturbed, *P. catenifer* throws itself into a coil, flattens its head into a triangle, puffs its body, rapidly vibrates its tail, and strikes repeatedly, while uttering a series of sounds that are audible for some distance. Although the behavior is largely bluff, some large individuals will inflict serious bites. The degree of defensive behavior is temperature dependent (Keogh and DeSerto 1994).

Two types of defensive sounds are made: hisses and bellows (Young et al. 1995). Hisses are characterized by lack of frequency and amplitude modulation, but bellows have a brief initial period of high-amplitude, broad-frequency sound followed by a longer period of lower-amplitude, constant-frequency sound. Both contain distinct harmonic elements; the modulation and harmonic nature of the sounds seems unique for snakes. The larynx has an epiglottal keel, a dorsal extension of the cricoid cartilage that, in contrast to previous suggestions (Martin and Huey 1971; Saiff 1975), plays only a small role in increasing the amplitude of the bellows. Within the larynx, a flexible, horizontal, shelflike laryngeal septum divides the anterior portion of the larynx and contributes to the harmonic elements of the sounds. The hisses and bellows overlap the 150–600 Hz optimum hearing range of snakes, and possibly are involved in intraspecific acoustic communication (Young 1997). Do such airborne sounds transmit a warning message to other *P. catenifer*? Probably not, as snakes respond more to vibrations conducted via solid objects to the lower jaw and anterior venter.

Western North American races of *P. catenifer* share aspects of coloration, pattern, and defensive behavior with the common sympatric rattlesnake, *Crotalus viridis*, and some populations are good mimics of that venomous snake (Sweet 1985).

POPULATIONS. *P. catenifer* can be common in an area, but because it remains underground much of the time, its population size is underestimated. Reported percentages of occurrence in some populations include the following: 14.8% of 454 snakes encountered on highway 85, Doña Ana County, New Mexico, 1975–1978 (Price and LaPointe 1990); 7.8% of 33,117 snakes recorded from throughout Kansas (Fitch 1993); 7.6% of 418 snakes observed on highways in Chihuahua, Mexico, 1975–1977 (Reynolds 1982); 4.7% of the 550 snakes captured in a Kansas tall grass prairie (Cavitt 2000a); and 2.1% of 1,730 snakes recorded at a Utah hibernaculum in 10 years (Woodbury 1951). Parker and Brown (1980) reported a density and biomass of 0.32/ha and 30.4 g/ha in Utah.

Sex ratios of both adults and hatchlings may be significantly different from 1:1; Gutzke et al. (1985) recorded adult and hatchling ratios of 0.67 in Nebraska. They attributed this to females typically dispersing shorter distances from hibernacula than do males, and thus being more likely to compete for local resources with other females more genetically similar to themselves than are males to compete with genetically similar males (clutches with sex ratios skewed toward males would have intersibling competition). Adult male to female ratios may vary seasonally due to differential activity patterns of the two sexes: Nebraska males are more active during the spring mating period than are females, probably because they are searching for mates; the sex ratio is about even in late May–June when females are searching for nest sites;

and females remain more active than males through August (Iverson 1990). Adult male to female ratios of 3.12:1.00 and 0.87:1.00 were recorded at two hibernacula in Utah (Parker and Brown 1980), and hatchling male to female ratios of 1.90:1.00, 1.60:1.00, and 1.00:1.00 have been found in Kansas (Fitch 1999), Utah (Parker and Brown 1980), and Nebraska (Iverson 1990), respectively.

P. c. ruthveni is considered endangered in Texas.

REMARKS. The genus *Pituophis* is often considered monotypic, containing only *P. melanoleucus* with 15 subspecies (Sweet and Parker 1990), but Ballinger et al. (1979) and Knight (1986) have presented evidence that it involves two species: the western *catenifer* and the eastern *melanoleucus*. It is most closely related to the genera *Arizona, Lampropeltis,* and *Rhinocheilus* (Dowling et al. 1996; Keogh 1996). Sweet and Parker (1990) reviewed the species.

Pituophis melanoleucus (Daudin 1803) | Pine Snake

RECOGNITION. The heavy-bodied pine snake (TBL to 228.6 cm) is white to cream, grayish tan, pink, or black, with a series of 19–39 (mean, 26) brown, reddish brown, dark gray, or black dorsal, saddlelike, blotches (darker anteriorly, lighter posteriorly), 2–3 rows of lateral spots, and 5–10 (mean, 7) dark tail blotches. Dark or pinkish mottling or flecking is usually present in the light spaces between the body blotches. The small head and nape are light colored with numerous dark mottlings, the supralabials have dark bars, and a dark vertical bar extends from the orbit to the supralabials, but no dark postorbital bar is present. Body scales are weakly keeled (smooth on the first 4–5 rows) with two apical pits; dorsal body

scales lie in 27 or 29 (25–31) rows anteriorly, 27, 29, or 31 (27–35) rows at midbody, and 19 or 21 (19–23) rows near the tail. The normally plain venter (some dark mottling may be present) is white, cream, tan, or grayish, with 203–249 ventrals, 29–67 subcaudals, and an undivided anal plate. A high, elongated (twice as long as broad) rostral scale, no (rarely 1–2) azygos scales, and 4 (2–6) prefrontals are present dorsally on the head; laterally are 2 nasals, 1 (rarely 0) loreal, 1 (2) preocular(s), 3 (2–4) postoculars, 1 + 3–4 + 4–6 temporals, 8 (6–9) supralabials, and 12–14 (11–15) infralabials. The subcylindrical, slightly bilobed hemipenis (9–11 subcaudals long when inverted) has a single sulcus spermaticus extending to the end of the larger

Northern pine snake, *Pituophis melanoleucus melanoleucus.* (Photograph by Christopher W. Brown, DVM)

Black pine snake, *Pituophis melanoleucus lodingi*; Alabama. (Photograph by Carl H. Ernst)

lobe. The basal half of the shaft has scattered spinules, the midportion larger spines, and the distal region many small spines grading into papillate calyxes near the crotch of the lobes (Cliburn 1975; Sweet and Parker 1990). Each maxilla has 14–18 teeth.

Males have 203–249 (mean, 214) ventrals, 44–67 (mean, 60) subcaudals, and TLs 12–16 (mean, 14.5) % of TBL; females have 212–235 (mean, 221) ventrals, 29–67 (mean, 52) subcaudals, and TLs 11–15 (mean, 12.8) % of TBL.

GEOGRAPHIC VARIATION. Three subspecies are recognized. *P. m. melanoleucus* (Daudin 1803), the northern pine snake, is found from the pine barrens of southern New Jersey, the coastal plains of North Carolina and South Carolina, and the mountains of western Virginia and eastern West Virginia west to southern Kentucky, Tennessee, and Alabama. It is white to pinkish cream with black anterior body blotches and brown posterior ones, and a heavily mottled nape. *P. m. lodingi* Blanchard 1924c, the black pine snake, occurs from southwestern Alabama to extreme southeastern Louisiana. Adults are nearly or totally black or dark brown with reddish labials and snout; juveniles may have dark blotches, but become melanistic with age. *P. m. mugitus* Barbour 1921, the

Florida pine snake, occurs from southwestern South Carolina west to Mobile Bay, and south in Florida to Lee and Dade counties. It is pale tan or grayish with gray, brown, or rusty brown, faded or indistinct body blotches, and a pale nape.

Integradation between *melanoleucus* and *mugitus* occurs over a broad area in South Carolina and along the Georgia fall line, and some intergradation between *mugitus* and *lodingi* occurs in the Florida panhandle.

CONFUSING SPECIES. Rat snakes *(Elaphe)* and kingsnakes *(Lampropeltis)* have only two prefrontal scales, and *Elaphe* has a divided anal plate. Coachwhips *(Masticophis),* racers *(Coluber),* and indigo snakes *(Drymarchon)* have smooth body scales.

KARYOTYPE. Past descriptions of the karyotype of *P. melanoleucus* were based on *P. catenifer* (see above), but the karyotype of this species is probably similar.

FOSSIL RECORD. Fossil remains of the pine snake have been found in Florida Pleistocene deposits: Irvingtonian (Holman 1991; Meylan 1982) and Rancholabrean (Auffenberg 1963; Brattstrom 1953b; Gut and Ray 1963; Holman 1959a, 1996).

DISTRIBUTION. *P. melanoleucus* occurs from southern New Jersey south along the Atlantic coastal plain to southern Florida (but only in scattered colonies in southern Florida) and west along the Gulf coastal plain to southeastern Mississippi and extreme southeastern Louisiana. It is also present in scattered populations in the mountains of western Virginia and eastern West Virginia, across southern Kentucky, in eastern and central Tennessee and northern Georgia, and in western Tennessee.

HABITAT. Habitats usually have well-drained sandy or loamy soils and dense vegetation. Habitats occupied include pine barrens, mixed scrub pine and oak woods, dry rocky mountain ridges, sand hills, and old fields. Disturbed habitats are used as much as 90% of the time in New Jersey (Burger and Zappalorti 1988a, 1989; Zappalorti and Burger 1985). In New Jersey over 50% of the observations by Burger and Zappalorti (1989) were near blueberry or pitch pine, although males were near blueberry twice as often as females, and males were associated with logs and bark extensively, while females were more frequently found under oak leaves.

BEHAVIOR. *P. melanoleucus* is highly fossorial, and in Florida may spend up to 85% of the time underground (Franz, in Tennant 1997), often using mammal burrows as retreats (Lee 1968a). Surface activity is usually diurnal, but occasionally crepuscular. The average activity pattern in New Jersey, where pine snake CTs were approximately 7–34°C and were highly correlated with ST, was 41% inactive, 36% basking, 20% moving, and 3% nesting (Burger and Zappalorti 1988a).

The pine snake must hibernate during the winter, and sometimes estivate in the summer. Possibly *P. m. mugitus* is active throughout the year in Florida, but normally it is only found from March to October, with peak occurrence in May–July and in October (Franz 1992). Palmer and Braswell (1995) reported an annual activity period of 5 March to 4 November in North Carolina, with 69% of records occurring in April–June, and in New Jersey it can be found on the surface from April into October (Zappalorti et al. 1983).

The home ranges of Florida *P. m. mugitus* average about slightly over 50 ha; two radio-tracked females had home ranges of 11 and 12 ha, respectively, while those of three radio-equipped males were approximately 23–92 ha (Franz 1992).

Occasionally an individual may be active in the winter (McDowell 1951), but winter is usually spent underground in excavated burrows (see *P. catenifer* for burrowing behavior), mammal burrows, or possibly rock crevices in the mountains. There the soil is warmer than at nearby areas. Both hibernacula and summer dens are usually dug by the snakes. Hibernacula are often also used as summer dens, but some dens are strictly for summer use (Burger et al. 1988). Both burrows are normally situated beside old fallen logs, the entrance tunnels following decaying roots into the soil. Hibernacula usually have significantly more plant cover within 5 m and much leaf cover over two entrances, and they are closer to trees than are summer dens, which have only one entrance (Burger et al. 1988). Hibernacula average 624 cm of tunnels and eight side chambers; summer dens average less than one side chamber and 122 cm of tunnels. Except for hatchlings, *P. melanoleucus* found hibernating in New Jersey were in individual chambers off the main tunnel at depths of 50–111 (mean, 79) cm. Mean temperature of the hibernacula was lower (7–11°C; mean, 8.8°C) than the CTs of the hibernating snakes (8–14°C; mean, 9.8°C) (Burger et al. 1988). Male *P. melanoleucus* will engage in dominance combat bouts during the breeding season (for details, see Shaw 1951).

REPRODUCTION. According to Conant and Collins (1998), both sexes are mature at a TBL of 122 cm; Wright and Wright (1957) reported minimum TBLs for mature males and females of 101 cm and 125 cm, respectively. Both sexes of *P. m. mugitus* mature at a SVL of 91 cm (Franz 1992). Such lengths may be reached in three years. The gametic cycles of *P. melanoleucus* have

Distribution of *Pituophis melanoleucus*.

not been described, but are probably similar to those of *P. catenifer*. Females appear to have an annual breeding cycle (Fitch 1970; Zappalorti et al. 1983).

Over most of the range the mating season extends through April and May, but possibly some mating occurs during the winter in Florida (Ashton and Ashton 1981). Neonate pine snakes recognize the odor of their species (Burger 1989b; Burger et al. 1991), so adult males probably recognize that of reproductive females and trail them during courtship (Reichling 1982). When the female is found, the male crawls over her, rubs the female's head with his chin, grasps her head or neck in his mouth (chewing them if she tries to escape), aligns his body along her side, undergoes caudocephalic waves, seeks her cloacal vent, and inserts one hemipenis (Hammock 1984; Merli 1992; Reichling 1982). Copulation may last from 25 minutes to over an hour.

GP averages 35 (28–39) days, and during late May through July the eggs are laid at the end of long subterranean tunnel-like burrows excavated in loose soil to depths of 25–30 cm (Burger and Zappalorti 1991), or are deposited beneath large rocks or logs, or possibly in small mammal burrows. Burger and Zappalorti (1986) studied nest site selection in New Jersey. All nests were in large clearings with less than 10% tree cover in pitch pine–scrub oak uplands and were in soft sand in open, unvegetated sections of the clearings. Sixteen females nested alone, eight nested communally in double clutches, three laid in one nest, and four oviposited in another nest. Few differences occurred between solitary and communal nests, except that more solitary nests were in sedge rather than grass in areas with greater tree cover and close to roads. The nests were 90–304 (mean, 187.6) cm long with chambers about 14 cm wide; the eggs were about 15 cm beneath the surface. While digging the nest, the female pushes her face and neck into the soil and pulls out loose soil with loops of the neck and body (Burger and Zappalorti 1991; Merli 1992). She flexes her coils and contracts her body inside the burrow, compressing the soil to widen the entrance and strengthen the walls. Once she is completely concealed beneath the ground the female widens the terminal end of the tunnel into a nest chamber and lays her eggs. The same nest burrow may be used for several years (Burger and Zappalorti 1992).

The eggs are elliptical with a rough leathery shell and often adherent, are 45.0–117.5 (mean, 63.5; n = 67) mm long and 25.4–45.7 (mean, 35.2; n = 67) mm wide, and weigh 20.3–74.4 (mean, 39.8; n = 16) g. Eggs increase in width and mass during incubation, and the variation above is due to eggs being measured and weighed at various times during incubation. Clutches may contain 3–24 eggs (Wright and Wright 1957) and average 8.7 eggs (n = 111). Since females often nest communally, perhaps the 24 eggs represent more than one clutch: New Jersey clutches averaged 8–9 (3–14) eggs (Zappalorti et al. 1983). RCM averages 0.325 (0.250–0.391) (Conant and Downs 1940; Seigel and Fitch 1984).

IP is 51–100 (mean, 68.8; n = 26) days, with 70–75 days most common. The young hatch from August to October, with TBLs of 33.0–55.5 (mean, 45.8; n = 70) cm and masses of 23.2–60.0 (mean, 42.6; n = 31) g. They are dull in color at first, but brighten after their first molt. Those of *P. m. lodingi* have a distinct blotched pattern on a dark brown ground color over about 75% of the posterior body; the anterior 25% of the body is uniform black (Reichling 1982).

IT produces long-term effects in young pine snakes (Burger 1989a, 1991a, 1998a, 1998b; Burger and Zappalorti 1988b; Burger et al. 1987). Lower ITs (21–23°C) produce shorter, larger-headed hatchlings with more abnormalities and higher mortality that shed late (Burger et al. 1987). Hatchlings incubated at 26 and 28°C performed better in behavioral tests than those incubated at low temperatures (21 and 23°C) or high temperatures (30 and 32°C) (Burger 1989a). Low ITs also affected hatchling emergence time and postnest survival—hatchlings remained in nests longer, and after emergence, they moved slower, took longer to find shade or search for cover and hibernacula, had a hard time capturing prey, and were more vulnerable to predation and overheating (Burger 1991a, 1998a). Hatchlings from intermediate incubation regimes fulfilled all of these behaviors more quickly and more successfully. Males suffer increased embryonic mortality at lower ITs; this affects the primary sex ratio of the surviving hatchlings, and later population dynamics (Burger and Zappalorti 1988b).

GROWTH AND LONGEVITY. No data on natural growth rates are available. A captive-born female survived 20 years, 9 months, and 2 days at the San Diego Zoo (Snider and Bowler 1992).

DIET AND FEEDING HABITS. *P. melanoleucus* is an active forager, and prey are chiefly found by olfaction (Burger 1991b), but sight may also play a role in detection. Prey may be hunted both on the surface or in underground tunnels. Surface prey are seized and then constricted in the snake's coils, but if they are caught within a burrow, prey are usually constricted against a wall.

Small mammals are the pine snake's main food, but other animals consumed include moles (*Parascalops breweri* [?], *Scalopus aquaticus* [?]), rabbits (*Sylvilagus floridanus*), voles (*Microtus pennsylvanicus*), mice (*Peromyscus leucopus, P. maniculatus*), rats (*Sigmodon hispidus*), squirrels (*Tamiasciurus hudsonicus*), pocket gophers (*Geomys pinetis*), quail eggs (*Colinus virginianus*), lizards (*Cnemidophorus sexlineatus*), and snakes and their eggs (*Carphophis amoenus*) (Ashton and Ashton 1981; Bloomer 1976; Brown 1979a; Carr 1940; C. Ernst, pers. obs.; Franz 1992; Hamilton and Pollack 1956; Linzey 1979; Linzey and Clifford 1981; Palmer and Braswell 1995; Wright and Wright 1957). Captives will eat domestic mice and rats (*Mus musculus, Rattus norvegicus*) and birds and their eggs (*Gallus gallus, Meleagris gallopavo, Passer domesticus*) (Cliburn 1962; C. Ernst, pers. obs.). Linzey and Clifford (1981) reported that when a large egg is eaten, it is swallowed for a short distance, and then the snake's strong neck muscles break the shell. The liquid contents are swallowed; the shell may either be swallowed or disgorged.

PREDATORS AND DEFENSE. Not much has been documented about natural predation of *P. melanoleucus*. Juveniles and adults are attacked by shrews (*Blarina brevicauda*), raccoons (*Procyon lotor*), skunks (*Mephitis mephitis*), red foxes (*Vulpes vulpes*), dogs (*Canis familiaris*), and cats (*Felis catus*), and the eggs are eaten by scarlet snakes (*Cemophora coccinea*) (Burger et al. 1992; C. Ernst et al., pers. obs.). Predation may be high when the snakes are underground in hibernacula (Burger et al. 1992). Automobile traffic, human poaching, on both adults and eggs, and habitat destruction and fires are also major causes of population declines.

If allowed to escape, *P. melanoleucus* will do so as its first defense, but the pine snake is also quite a fighter. When cornered it emits loud hisses and strikes. Dogs attacking it are often severely bitten on the nose (Carr 1940). Predatory behavior of hatchlings is affected by both ET (22–23, 27–28, or 32–33°C) and prey type (Burger 1998a, 1998b). Hatchlings respond more protectively (withdraw into tunnels) than defensively (strike), respond with less intensity to a vibration than to a predator sighting, and require longer to respond to a face model without eyes than to all other predatory types. It is more adaptive for small snakes to return to the burrow than to attack a much larger predator. Hatchlings incubated at medium temperatures (27–28°C) take less time to emerge from the burrow when undisturbed and have stronger protective responses than those incubated at other temperatures. Hatchlings also avoid scent trails made by potential predators (Burger 1989b).

POPULATIONS. *P. melanoleucus* seems to be uncommon over most of its range (*P. m. lodingi* is protected in Alabama and Mississippi; *P. m. melanoleucus* is considered a species of special concern in North Carolina and threatened in Kentucky, New Jersey, and Tennessee; and *P. m. mugitus* is protected in Alabama and South Carolina and is listed as a species of special concern in Florida). This impression of rarity may be due to its spending much time underground; however, much of its habitat has been destroyed or disturbed, and the snake is in decline over most of its range. It is seldom seen anymore in Florida due to habitat destruction, road mortality, and overcollection (Franz 1992). Only two (0.9%) of 230 snakes collected in upland habitats in Putnam County were this species (Dodd and Franz 1995). The pine snake is still fairly common in proper habitat in New Jersey (see papers by Burger and Zappalorti). The hatching sex ratio generally favors males, but adult females greatly outnumber adult males (Burger and Zappalorti 1988b). The overall sex ratio of the New Jersey pine snakes studied by Burger and Zappalorti (1988b) was 0.39:1.00.

REMARKS. The species has been reviewed by Sweet and Parker (1990).

Regina Baird and Girard 1853

Crayfish Snakes

Key to the Species of *Regina*

1a. Dorsal body scales smooth, one internasal scale present, no dark pigment on venter . . . . *R. alleni*

1b. Dorsal body scales keeled, two internasal scales present, venter with dark stripes or no dark pigment 2

2a. A single dark median stripe on venter or no dark pigment present . . . . *R. grahamii*

2b. Two dark longitudinal stripes or rows of half-moons on the venter 3

3a. Venter with two longitudinal rows of half-moons, lower dorsal scale rows smooth . . . . *R. rigida*

3b. Venter with two longitudinal stripes not divided into half-moons, lower dorsal scale rows keeled . . *R. septemvittata*

Regina alleni (Garman 1874) | Striped Crayfish Snake

RECOGNITION. *R. alleni* is a shiny, brown snake (TBL to 70.5 cm, but most adults are 50–60 cm) with dark dorsal stripes, and a broad yellowish stripe along its lower sides. Dorsal body scales are smooth (occasionally weakly keeled), usually lack pits, and occur in 19 anterior and midbody rows and 17 or 19 posterior rows. The immaculate pink to yellow or orange venter (occasionally a medial row of dark spots is present) has 110–133 ventrals, 53–69 subcaudals, and a divided anal plate. On each side of the short head are 2 nasals (partially divided by the nostril), 1 loreal, 1 preocular, 3–4 postoculars, 1 + 2 temporals, 8 (7–9) supralabials, and 11 (9–10) infralabials. The nasal scales meet be-hind the rostral scale and are followed by a single internasal scale. The single or slightly bilobed hemipenis has two enlarged basal hooks, many rows of small spines, and a single, undivided sulcus spermaticus. Rossman (1963a) reported a total of 26–29 stout maxillary teeth with chisel-like tips; Wright and Wright (1957) reported 16–18 teeth on each maxilla, and Auffenberg (1950) reported 12–15.

Adult females are larger (often longer than 60 cm), and have 120–133 ventrals and 53–61 subcaudals. The smaller males (normally shorter than 60 cm) have 110–127 ventrals and 59–69 subcaudals. Males also have a reduction of body-scale rows to 17 near the tail

Striped crayfish snake, *Regina alleni*; Florida. (Photograph by Roger W. Barbour)

(females have 19 posterior rows), and weakly keeled dorsal body scales near the vent (Blanchard 1931).

GEOGRAPHIC VARIATION. No subspecies are recognized. Auffenberg (1950) referred southern Florida *R. alleni* to the race *lineapiatus*, characterized by having ventral spots, but Duellman and Schwartz (1958) showed that these snakes are the terminal population of a continuous north-south cline showing increased ventral spotting toward the south.

CONFUSING SPECIES. Other species of crayfish snakes can be distinguished by using the key presented above. Garter and ribbon snakes *(Thamnophis)* have keeled body scales and an undivided anal plate.

KARYOTYPE. The karyotype consists of 36 macrochromosomes (Eberle 1972; Kilpatrick and Zimmerman 1973).

Distribution of *Regina alleni*.

FOSSIL RECORD. Pleistocene (Irvingtonian) vertebrae of *R. alleni* have been found in Hillsborough County, Florida (Meylan 1995), and Pleistocene (Rancholabrean) remains are known from elsewhere in Florida (Auffenberg 1963; Hirschfeld 1968; Tihen 1962).

DISTRIBUTION. *R. alleni* is found from southern Georgia southward through peninsular Florida.

HABITAT. *R. alleni* is highly aquatic, and prefers slow-moving or standing bodies of water with soft bottoms—swamps, marshes, bogs, lakes, ponds, sluggish streams, and sloughs—where it can be found hiding within the aquatic vegetation, especially in mats of water hyacinths *(Eichhornia crassipes)*, but also among panic grass *(Panicum hemitomon)*, cattail *(Typha* sp.), pickerel weed *(Pontederia lanceolata)*, and lake rush *(Fuirena scirpoides)*. The authors have also found it curled up in a mat of green filamentous algae, and Carr (1940) related that it may form a well-defined tunnel in tightly packed vegetation that connects to another tunnel in a mud bank. Near the coast, it sometimes enters brackish, tidal waters (Neill 1958).

BEHAVIOR. Relatively little has been reported regarding the life history of this secretive snake. *R. al-*

leni is probably active all year in southern Florida, but farther north, where colder winters occur, it may hibernate, or at least retreat for short periods. Sphagnum bogs are favorite overwintering sites (Carr 1940).

Most daily activity is diurnal, but in the warmest months most forging is nocturnal (Godley 1980). Feeding during the day when WTs are highest probably maximizes the snake's pursuit and capture success, and higher BTs may help the digestion of hard-bodied prey. Godley (1980) found individuals with food in their stomachs at mean WTs of 15.5–27.4°C, and Brattstrom (1965) reported its CT_{max} is 41.6°C. *R. alleni* can sometimes bask on floating mats of plants or along the bank. Terrestrial activity is often restricted to basking, but after warm rains it may crawl about on land. Since its prey are aquatic, it does not forage on land.

REPRODUCTION. Both sexes become sexually mature at a TBL of approximately 35 cm in two to three years. Conant and Collins (1998) reported the minimum size of both sexes to be 33.0 cm, and Wright and Wright (1957) reported 35.6 cm; Duellman and Schwartz (1958) had 37.2 cm and 41.5 cm females give birth to young. Nothing is known of the gametic cycle of either sex.

Based on the appearance of neonates from late June to September, mating probably occurs in the spring. The courtship and mating acts have not been described.

R. alleni might be viviparous, as living young are produced, but the placental arrangement has not been described. Size of litters ranges from 4 to 12 (Duellman and Schwartz 1958; Neill 1951) and averages 9.6 young (n = 12 litters). Larger females produce larger litters. Apparently more ova are fertilized than are born: Telford (1952) found 15 embryos, about 50 mm long, in a 50.8 cm female, and Tschambers (1950) reported that a 65.4 cm female contained 34 embryos, 19 mm long (confirmed by Neill 1951).

Neonates are 13.6–18.0 (mean, 16.7; n = 10) cm long and are more boldly marked than adults.

GROWTH AND LONGEVITY. Unknown.

DIET AND FEEDING HABITS. The nasal and frontal bones are reduced in the skull, producing a rhinokinetic snout adapted to feeding on hard-shelled prey (Dwyer and Kaiser 1997). Juvenile *R. alleni* with 12–20 cm SVLs feed primarily on dragonfly nymphs, but may shift seasonally to abundant palaemonid shrimp and astacid crayfish. At SVLs between 20 and 30 cm a major dietary shift occurs, and crayfish slowly replace insects and shrimp as the primary prey (Godley 1980). In most seasons juveniles consume more, but smaller, prey than adults; however, since they feed on insects that are higher in protein and lower in ash content than the primary crayfish prey of adults, their energetic intake per gram body mass is generally higher. Reported prey of all age classes are crayfish (*Procambarus alleni, P. fallax*), glass shrimp (*Palaemonetes paludosus*), dragonfly nymphs (Odonata; Coenagrionidae, Libellulidae—*Miathyria, Pachlongipennis*), damselfly nymphs (*Argia sedula*), and lesser sirens (*Pseudobranchus striatus*) (Carr 1940; Franz 1977; Godley 1980; Penn 1950; Tennant 1997; Van Hyning 1932), and it is possible that small toad and hylid tadpoles are also eaten. Van Hyning (1932) reported that crayfish made up 73% of the bulk of foods, lesser sirens 14%, and frogs 13% in nine *R. alleni* stomachs.

Franz (1977) observed that the foraging behavior of captive *R. alleni* consisted of crawling and probing about the bottom in exploratory patterns. Once a crayfish was detected, it was bitten, and the snake wrapped its body around the crayfish to hold it tight. The crayfish was not constricted, but only held while being swallowed. Crayfish were swallowed tail first, and ingestion took four to five minutes.

PREDATORS AND DEFENSE. Few observations on predation of *R. alleni* have been published. Adult crayfish and largemouth bass (*Micropterus salmoides*) prey on the newborn young and juveniles; greater sirens (*Siren lacertina*), cottonmouths (*Agkistrodon piscivorus*), common kingsnakes (*Lampropeltis getula*), racers (*Coluber constrictor*), great blue herons (*Ardea herodias*), great egrets (*Casmerodius albus*), red-shouldered hawks (*Buteo lineatus*), raccoons (*Procyon lotor*), and river otters (*Lontra canadensis*) feed on adults, and alligators (*Alligator mississippiensis*) probably also prey on *R. alleni* (Bancroft et al. 1983; Godley 1982; Godwin 1992; O'Brien 1998; Szelistowski and Meylan 1996). Godley (1982) used tail loss as an indication of the rate of predation on *R. alleni*, and found that 10.2% of the snakes had tail damage.

R. alleni is inoffensive and seldom bites, but does discharge musk and fecal matter. Godley (1982) observed an unusual gape and sway behavior when the snake is handled. If grasped firmly in the middle, it may rigidly arch its back, open its mouths nearly 180° (exposing the white interior), and sway its head and neck laterally. Usually the mouth is closed after a few lateral oscillations of the head. Godley thought this behavior to be a flash display used to startle predators or to mimic the more noxious water snakes (*Nerodia*) or venomous cottonmouths (*Agkistrodon piscivorus*) that do bite. He also observed *R. alleni* occasionally coiling into a ball, concealing the head beneath a coil, and laterally flattening its body. O'Brien (1998) saw one wrap the lower third of its body around vegetation to prevent being swallowed by a racer (*Coluber constrictor*).

POPULATIONS. Habitat destruction in Florida has caused declines in some populations, and many are killed on the roads each year; however, *R. alleni* is still locally common over much of the state. Bancroft et al. (1983) and Godley (1980) recorded a density of

1,287 snakes/ha of water hyacinth habitat in a Florida slough. The calculated biomass of this population was 30.79 kg/ha. Density of the population varied seasonally, being low in summer, increased in fall and winter, and decreased in spring. In contrast, at two Everglades sites only seven *R. alleni* were included in a total sample of 2,801 snakes (Dalrymple et al. 1991).

REMARKS. *R. alleni* was reviewed by Rossman (1963a; 1985).

Regina grahamii Baird and Girard 1853 | Graham's Crayfish Snake

RECOGNITION. *R. grahamii* is a slender, olive brown to dark brown, striped snake (to 119.4 cm TBL) with a yellow to buff-colored venter. On each side of the body is a broad, cream to yellow, longitudinal stripe on scale rows one to three. A dark-bordered, light brown, vertebral stripe is also present, and a narrow, wavy black line separates the dorsal body scales from the ventrals. A medial row of black spots may be present on the venter. The chin and throat are cream to yellow. Dorsal body scales are keeled (the first row may be smooth) and pitted, and occur in 19–21 anterior rows, 19 midbody rows, and 17 posterior rows. The venter has 155–178 ventrals, 51–67 subcaudals, and a divided anal plate. Each side of the head has 2 nasals (partially separated by the nostril), 1 loreal, 2 preoculars, 2–3 postoculars, 1 + 2 (1–3) temporals, 7 (8) supralabials, and 9–10 (8–11) infralabials. The single hemipenis may be slightly bilobed, with a single, undivided sulcus spermaticus, two enlarged basal spines, and many rows of small spines on the shaft. Each maxilla has 25–28 teeth, with the posterior-most slightly enlarged.

Adult females are larger than adult males; in a northwestern Missouri population, females averaged 59.2 cm SVL and 116.4 g in mass, while males averaged only 54.3 cm SVL and 64.9 g (Seigel 1992). Females have 155–178 (mean, 170) ventrals, 51–64 (mean, 57) subcaudals, and TLs 16–20 (mean, 18) % of TBL; males have 162–175 (mean, 167) ventrals, 60–67 (mean, 64) subcaudals, and TLs 17.5–20.5 (mean, 19.0) % of TBL.

GEOGRAPHIC VARIATION. No subspecies are recognized, but variation in body color and size occurs across the range.

CONFUSING SPECIES. Other species of crayfish snakes can be distinguished by using the above key.

Garter and ribbon snakes *(Thamnophis)* have an undivided anal plate and an unpatterned venter. The lined snake *(Tropidoclonion lineatum)* has an undivided anal plate and two longitudinal rows of dark half-moons on its venter. The Mississippi green water snake *(Nerodia cyclopion)* has several subocular scales, dark marks on its venter, and over 25 midbody scale rows. Other *Nerodia* have at least 23 midbody scale rows, lack a narrow dark line separating the dark dorsal body color from the lighter ventral pigment, and usually have dark spots or half-moons on the venter.

KARYOTYPE. The karyotype consists of 36 macrochromosomes (Eberle 1972; Kilpatrick and Zimmerman 1973). The autosomal chromosomes are 8 large submetacentrics, 6 medium-sized submetacentrics, 10 small submetacentrics, and 10 small to medium subtelocentrics (Kilpatrick and Zimmerman 1973). Sex determination is ZZ/ZW; the Z chromosomes are large submetacentrics, and the W chromosome is a medium-sized subtelocentric (Kilpatrick and Zimmerman 1973).

Graham's crayfish snake, *Regina grahamii*; Missouri. (Photograph by Peter May)

Distribution of *Regina grahamii.*

FOSSIL RECORD. Pliocene (Blancan) fossils have been found in Nebraska (Rogers 1984); Pleistocene fossils are from the Irvingtonian of Nebraska (Holman 1995) and the Rancholabrean of Kansas (Holman 1987b; Preston 1979; Tihen 1962), Oklahoma, and Texas (Parmley and Pfau 1997).

DISTRIBUTION. *R. grahamii* is found from Illinois, Iowa, and southeastern Nebraska southward west of the Mississippi River to the Gulf Coast of Louisiana and eastern Texas. It is absent over most of the Ozark-Ouachita highlands, but does occur east of the Mississippi River in northwestern Mississippi and probably also western Tennessee.

HABITAT. This snake is usually found about sluggish waterways, such as slow-flowing streams, bayous, swamps, marshes, lakes, ponds, sloughs, rice fields, and roadside ditches. Normally the bottom is soft, and abundant aquatic or emergent vegetation (often cattails), rocks, logs, or debris, and abundant crayfish burrows in which to hide and hibernate are present. As long as its principal crayfish prey is present, *R. grahamii* may be found nearby.

BEHAVIOR. The annual activity cycle varies with latitude. The snake can be found above ground in February–November in the southern portions of its range (C. Ernst, pers. obs.). Cleveland (1986) collected one on 15 February in Kansas, but most individuals are active there in April–October (Collins 1993). The species is active in Missouri from late March or April to November (Johnson 1987; Seigel 1992), but 70% of the *R. grahamii* collected in northwestern Missouri by Seigel (1992) were taken in April, May, and October, and only 14.6% in July–September. In Illinois they may be active to late November (Wright and Wright 1957). Winters are spent underground in crayfish burrows.

In the spring and fall it is more active during the daylight hours, but as the average daily temperature rises in summer, some forage at night. Seigel (1992) found only 8 (6.4%) of 125 *R. grahamii* active after sunset; the snakes were exclusively diurnal in April and in August–November. Most activity is concentrated between 1200 and 2000 hours. Summer days are often spent basking along the banks or in bushes overhanging the water.

Mushinsky et al. (1980) reported that most BTs of the 27 Louisiana *R. grahamii* they caught fell between 22 and 27°C; the average BT of males was 26.1°C, that of females 25.7°C. From 1976 through 1978, the average yearly BTs were 26.2, 25.8, and 28.4°C, respectively. The snakes' BTs were closely correlated with both AT and WT. Clarke (1958) found active *R. grahamii* only at ATs of 27.0–31.5°C. Nonactive periods are spent under rocks, logs, and leaf litter; in crayfish burrows; or in burrows they construct themselves in moist, soft soil or in the soft bottom of a waterway. Burrows in bank soil usually end in a chamber below the water level into which the snake can withdraw its entire body (Kofron and Dixon 1980). Breathing is accomplished by extending only the nostrils and eyes above the water for short periods. The maximum period of submergence observed by Kofron and Dixon (1980) was 46 minutes.

Not much has been reported concerning the movements of *R. grahamii*. Hall (1969) recaptured 3 of 14 marked individuals. One was recaptured after three days in its original pond, and two others were recaptured eight to nine weeks later in ponds adjacent to those of their initial capture. None of these snakes had moved more than 100 m.

REPRODUCTION. Female *R. grahamii* bearing embryos have had SVLs as short as 42.2 cm (Hall 1969) and 48.5 cm (Seigel 1992). Such lengths are attained in the third growing season, but females probably do not breed during their third year (Hall 1969). The smaller males are reproductively mature at SVLs of 32.0–40.0 cm and one year of age (Hall 1969).

In Louisiana, ovulation occurs during the period of late April through the third week of June. *R. grahamii* is viviparous, and in Kansas, females have 2 mm embryos in early June, 55–68 mm embryos in the second half of June, and 136–182 mm embryos in late July (Hall 1969). Females do more than just retain the eggs. Those with enlarged ovarian eggs also have thickened and folded oviducts (Hall 1969). The eggs lack a shell at all developmental stages, and when the eggs are in the oviduct the thin chorionic membrane is in intimate contact with the oviduct wall. The dry weight of developing embryos increases during June and July, indicating placental transmission (Hall 1969).

Sperm are present in the male testes in April–October (Hall 1969).

Mating occurs in the water during April and May, and several males may court the same female (Anderson 1965). Males push and prod the female's body with their heads and stroke her neck with their tongues (C.Ernst, pers. obs.). The pair entwine during copulation (Vermersch and Kuntz 1986).

Parturition occurs from late July to early September. Litters consist of 3 (Thornton and Smith 1995a) to 39 (Hall 1969) young; the average number of young in 36 litters reported in the literature was 14.9. A positive correlation exists between the number of young per litter and female body length (Hall 1969). Neonates have 15.3–29.1 cm TBLs and weigh 3.0–5.9 (mean, 4.3) g.

GROWTH AND LONGEVITY. Hall (1969) reported that males may grow to a SVL of 42 cm in one year, but that much variation is size occurs. Females attain a SVL of approximately 40 cm in the first year, and have SVLs of 50–55 cm by the end of the second year. No longevity data are available.

DIET AND FEEDING HABITS. Like other species of *Regina*, *R. grahamii* is primarily a crayfish eater, although other prey types are occasionally taken, perhaps when crayfish populations are low. Strecker (1927) reported that in a small lagoon where crayfish were abundant it fed almost entirely on them, but in a stream where crayfish were less plentiful the snake fed on other prey. Recorded prey are crayfish (*Orconectes nais, O. palmeri, Procambarus clarkii, P. vioscai*), minnows (Cyprinidae), catfish (Ictaluridae), cricket frogs (*Acris* sp.), chorus frogs (*Pseudacris triseriata*), salamanders, shrimp, prawn, and snails (Anderson 1965; Clark 1949; Godley et al. 1984; Hall 1969; Kofron 1978; Laughlin 1959; Liner 1954; Mushinsky and Hebrard 1977a; Seigel 1992; Strecker 1926, 1927; Vermersch and Kuntz 1986; Young 1977).

More than one prey item may be taken at a time, and prey may be ingested either head or tail first (Godley et al. 1984; Seigel 1992). Although adults eat larger crayfish than juveniles, the minimum prey size does not change during growth of the snake (Godley et al. 1984). Seigel (1992) found the frequency of feeding highest in juveniles smaller than 40 cm SVL.

During foraging, *R. grahamii* prowls about searching for crayfish, and when they are found, quickly seizes and devours them. Crayfish that have recently molted are more easily digested and are taken in relatively high percentages, especially in the spring. Since crayfish in this stage are almost always in hiding, this supports observations of active foraging rather than an ambush prey-capture strategy. Burghardt (1968) studied the chemical preference of neonates and found they responded only to crayfish extracts, and most strongly to extracts from newly molted crayfish.

PREDATORS AND DEFENSE. Forty-four percent of the *R. grahamii* examined by Mushinsky and Miller (1993) had wounds from predator attacks. Alligators (*Alligator mississippiensis*); ophiophagous snakes, such as cottonmouths (*Agkistrodon piscivorus*) and common kingsnakes *(Lampropeltis getula)*; large wading birds; raptors; shrikes; and various predatory mammals are natural predators. Their diurnal basking habit exposes these snakes to high rates of attempted predation, but humans, with their motorized vehicles and habitat destruction, are the principal enemy.

R. grahamii is shy and retiring in disposition and seldom bites when handled. Instead, it tries to crawl out of the grasp; if this does not work, it sprays musk, urine, and fecal matter . When first discovered, these alert snakes almost always try to escape into the water and swim away.

POPULATIONS. *R. grahamii* is often locally common, especially where crayfish are plentiful. They made up 21% of the snakes collected at Cheyenne Bottoms, Kansas (Fitch 1993), and Seigel (1992) captured 134 of these snakes in less than five years at another site in northwestern Missouri. Overall, however, it often occurs in smaller numbers than other species. Clark (1949) recorded only 21 (1%) *R. grahamii* in a sample of over 2,000 snakes from the uplands of Louisiana, and Fitch (1993) reported it made up only 2.7% of over 33,000 snakes in Kansas. Loss of crayfish populations because of pollution and acid rain in other parts of the species' range has reduced its numbers drastically.

Hall (1969) found the sex ratio did not differ significantly from 1:1 in the Kansas population he studied, and also found a 1:1 ratio in 87 unborn young. Similarly, in Louisiana, Mushinsky et al. (1980) reported a 1:1 adult sex ratio. Of 134 *R. grahamii* sexed by Seigel (1992) at his northeastern Missouri site, 63 were adult males, and 46 were adult females; this too is not significantly different from 1:1. Seigel (1992) also collected 25 juveniles, for a juvenile to adult ratio of 0.23:1.00.

The status of *R. grahamii* across its range should be determined, as it is probable that in the future it will need legal protection in some states. It is considered a species of special concern in Arkansas.

REMARKS. Molecular studies by Lawson (1987) indicate that *R. grahamii* is most closely related to *R. septemvittata*.

Regina rigida (Say 1825) | Glossy Crayfish Snake

RECOGNITION. *R. rigida* is a shiny brown to olive brown snake (TBL to 79.7 cm) with two faint brown or blue to black longitudinal stripes on its dorsum, and a light green to yellow venter with two longitudinal rows of black half-moons or triangular spots. Its labials and chin are yellow. The keeled (except dorsal row 1), pitted, dorsal body scales occur in 19 (18–21) anterior and midbody rows and 17 (15–19) posterior

Glossy crayfish snake, *Regina rigida rigida*; Volusia County, Florida. (Photograph by Peter May)

rows. The venter has 124–144 ventrals, 50–71 subcaudals, and a divided anal plate. On each side of the head are 2 nasals (partially divided by the nostril, 1 loreal, 2 (1–3) preoculars, 2 (3) postoculars, 1 + 2 (3) temporals, 7 (8) supralabials, and 10 (9–11) infralabials. The single or slightly bilobed hemipenis has two enlarged basal hooks, many rows of small spines (the spine adjacent to the hook is slightly smaller than the hook), and an undivided sulcus spermaticus. Each maxilla has 20–24 curved, chisel-like teeth.

Males are smaller and thinner than females, and have 124–139 ventrals, 55–71 subcaudals, and TLs 20.0–23.5 (mean, 22.7) % of TBL; females have longer, thicker bodies, 132–144 ventrals, 50–64 subcaudals, and TLs 18.0–21.7 (mean, 19.9) % of TBL.

GEOGRAPHIC VARIATION. Three subspecies are recognized (Huheey 1959). *R. r. rigida* (Say 1825), the eastern glossy crayfish snake, occurs along the Atlantic Coast from southeastern Virginia south to central peninsular Florida. It has two preoculars on each side, dark pigment along the edges of the lateral throat scales, and no more than 62 subcaudals in males and 54 or less in females. *R. r. deltae* (Huheey 1959), the delta glossy crayfish snake, occurs only in the Mississippi River delta in Louisiana and adjacent Mississippi. It has only one preocular scale on each side, no dark pigment on the lateral throat scales, at least 58 subcaudals in males, and no more than 58 subcaudals in females. *R. r. sinicola* (Huheey 1959), the Gulf glossy crayfish snake, ranges from west-central Georgia and the Florida panhandle west to southeastern Oklahoma and eastern Texas. It also has two preoculars on each side, but lacks dark pigment along the edges of the lateral throat scales and has at least 63 subcaudals in males and 55 or more in females. Intergrades have been reported between *rigida* and *sinicola* from south-central Georgia to Apalachee Bay, Florida, and between *deltae* and *sinicola* in south-central Louisiana (Huheey 1959).

CONFUSING SPECIES. Other *Regina* can be distinguished with the key presented above. Garter and ribbon snakes *(Thamnophis)* and the lined snake *(Tropidoclonion lineatum)* have light dorsal stripes and single anal plates. Some saltmarsh snakes *(Nerodia clarkii)* have two dark stripes and two tan or yellowish stripes on each side of the body.

KARYOTYPE. The karyotype consists of 36 macrochromosomes (Eberle 1972; Kilpatrick and Zimmerman 1973).

FOSSIL RECORD. Unknown.

DISTRIBUTION. *R. rigida* ranges from New Kent County in southeastern Virginia south to Hernando and Volusia counties, Florida, and west to southeastern Oklahoma and eastern Texas.

HABITAT. This species is a resident of lowland, slow-flowing waterways, such as swamps, marshes,

Distribution of *Regina rigida*.

sphagnum bogs, lakes, ponds, sloughs, and small streams. It enters brackish tidal waters at the mouth of the St. Johns River in Florida (Neill 1958).

BEHAVIOR.   Relatively little is known of its life history, due mostly to its secretive, subterranean habits. It is seldom seen on land except after rains. Wright and Wright (1957) gave the annual activity period as 5 March to 28 October. In Florida, South Carolina, and Texas it is active in March–November (Gibbons and Semlitsch 1991; Tennant 1985, 1997), but it is probably active in all months in peninsular Florida and the Gulf states, especially during years with warm winters. Most captures in North Carolina occur during July–September (Palmer and Braswell 1995).

It is usually active at night. During the day it hides under logs, stones, or plant debris at the water's edge, tunnels into sphagnum, or possibly retreats into crayfish burrows. Occasionally individuals bask on the bank or on branches overhanging the water.

REPRODUCTION.   A variety of minimum mature lengths have been reported for females. Conant and Collins (1998) presented the mature TBL of both sexes as 36.0 cm, Moulis and Williamson (1996) reported possible courtship involving a 45.2 cm female, and Palmer and Braswell (1995) noted that a 47.0 cm female had embryos. Wright and Wright (1957) thought the minimum TBL was 47.3 cm, and the smallest mature female examined by Kofron (1979a) was 51.5 cm long. Wright and Wright (1957) give a minimum mature TBL of 35.0 cm for males, and Moulis and Williamson (1996) observed a 37.8 cm male engaged in possible courtship behavior. Such TBLs are probably reached by two to three years of age.

Like other *Regina*, *R. rigida* is viviparous. In Louisiana, females have follicles with diameters to about 6 mm in January and February (Kofron 1979a). Vitellogenesis begins in late March, when follicles may be as large as 12 mm. By May, some Louisiana females have follicles with diameters of 20 mm, and ovulation probably occurs in May and early June.

Courtship and mating behaviors are poorly known. Mating may take place in April–May in Florida (Ashton and Ashton 1981), and in Louisiana the female gametic cycle indicates spring mating (Kofron 1979a). Possible courtship behavior was observed on 2 March

in southeastern Georgia (Moulis and Williamson 1996), during which a male bit a female midway along her body, but no copulation occurred.

Litters contain 6–14 young (Huheey 1959); the average number of young for 10 litters reported in the literature was 10. Neonates usually appear in August–September. They resemble adults in coloration and pattern, but have more pinkish venters. Neonate TBL is 16.5–22.8 (mean, 18.9; n = 17) cm. A positive correlation exists between litter size and female TBL.

GROWTH AND LONGEVITY.   No growth data are available, and longevity is unknown.

DIET AND FEEDING HABITS.   Adults feed predominantly on both soft- and hard-shelled crayfish (usually of the genus *Procambarus*), but other prey are occasionally taken: small fish, two-toed amphiumas *(Amphiuma means),* cricket frogs *(Acris* sp.), eastern narrow-mouthed toads *(Gastrophryne carolinensis),* and southern leopard frogs *(Rana sphenocephala)* (Ashton and Ashton 1981; Brown 1978; Clark 1949; Hamilton and Pollack 1956; Huheey 1959; Huheey and Palmer 1962; Kofron 1978; Myer 1987; Palmer and Braswell 1995; Strecker 1926; Tennant 1997). Young *R. rigida* feed on dragonfly nymphs (Odonata) and aquatic beetles (Coleoptera) (Brown 1978; Ashton and Ashton 1981).

The skull and teeth of *R. rigida* are designed to crush hard-shelled prey (Dwyer and Kaiser 1997; Rossman 1963a). When eating a hard-shelled crayfish, the snake pursues and seizes the crayfish on the abdomen while simultaneously wrapping its body around the carapace (Franz 1976, 1977), and Myer (1987) has observed constriction by one or more coils at the junction of the carapace and abdomen of the crayfish. After constriction, the snake aligns its mouth with the crayfish's uropods and telson and ingests it. The behavior is different when attacking a soft-shelled crayfish. Such prey is approached and bitten in the same way, and a single coil is used to pin (but not constrict) it. Ingestion is normally tail first (Myer 1987).

PREDATORS AND DEFENSE.   Only three predators, the two-toed amphiuma *(Amphiuma means),* bullfrog *(Rana catesbeiana),* and common kingsnake *(Lampropeltis getula),* have been documented (Enge 1998; Hensley 1962; Viosca 1926), but probably other aquatic feeding predators, such as alligators *(Alligator mississippiensis)*, cottonmouths *(Agkistrodon piscivorus)*, large water snakes *(Nerodia)*, turtles, wading birds, raptors, and various carnivorous mammals also eat *R. rigida*.

This shy, secretive snake is seldom seen, as it remains hidden most of the time, especially during the day. When it is approached, it invariably dives into the water and hides under bottom debris, but if trapped on land it will flatten its head and spray musk. It may also bite, but the authors have not observed this.

POPULATIONS. In some parts of Florida, this species is common, if one is willing to search diligently for it. However, over most of its range it seems uncommon; Clark (1949) collected only 18 (0.8%) in a sample of 2,083 snakes from the Hill Parishes of Louisiana, and Ford et al. (1991) reported only three (1%) *R. rigida* in a total sample of 305 snakes collected in Smith County, Texas. Whether or not this is simply due to its secretive habits is unknown.

R. rigida is considered a species of special concern in Arkansas and Oklahoma.

REMARKS. So little is known of this snake's life history that a good behavioral and ecological study is needed.

Regina septemvittata (Say 1825) | Queen Snake

RECOGNITION. *R. septemvittata* is a slender, brownish to olive snake (TBL to 92.2 cm) with a yellow stripe on each side flanking three narrow, dark dorsal stripes, and four brown stripes on its yellow venter. The labials, chin, and throat are cream to yellow. The keeled, pitted, dorsal body scales occur in 19 anterior and midbody rows, but are reduced to 17 rows posteriorly. The venter has 118–159 ventrals, 47–89 subcaudals, and a divided anal plate. Lateral head scales include either 1 or 2 nasals (if only a single nasal, the nostril is located centrally; if 2 nasals are present, the nostril partially separates the scales), 1 loreal, 2 (1) preoculars, 2 (1–3) postoculars, 1 + 2–3 + 2–4 temporals, 7 (6–8) supralabials, and 9–10 (8–11) infralabials. The hemipenis is single (occasionally weakly bilobed), with a single, undivided sulcus spermaticus, one enlarged basal hook, and many rows of small spines on the shaft. The pointed maxillary teeth are short and stout, and normally 23–27 are present on each maxilla.

Females are longer and stouter than males and have 118–157 (mean, 138) ventrals, 47–87 (mean, 66) subcaudals, and TLs 19–30 (mean, 23–24) % of TBL; males are shorter and slimmer, with 127–159 (mean, 141) ventrals, 65–89 (mean, 74) subcaudals, and TLs 22–34 (mean, 26–27) % of TBL.

GEOGRAPHIC VARIATION. No subspecies are recognized.

CONFUSING SPECIES. Other species of *Regina* can be distinguished by using the key presented above. Garter and ribbon snakes *(Thamnophis)* have a single anal plate, no pattern on their venters, and a light middorsal stripe. The lined snake *(Tropidoclonion lineatum)* has a single anal plate, two ventral rows of dark half-moons, and a light middorsal stripe. Most water snakes *(Nerodia)* sympatric with the queen snake have patterned backs, and dark bars on the supralabials. *Nerodia floridana* has a dark speckled dorsum. The Gulf saltmarsh snake *(Nerodia clarkii clarkii)* has a dark venter with one to three longitudinal rows of yellow spots.

KARYOTYPE. The 34 autosomal macrochromosomes consist of 8 large submetacentrics, 6 medium-

Queen snake, *Regina septemvittata*; Madison County, Kentucky. (Photograph by Roger W. Barbour)

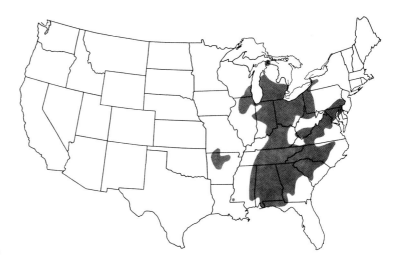

Distribution of *Regina septemvittata*.

sized submetacentrics, 10 small metacentrics, and 10 small to medium-sized subtelocentric chromosomes; males have 2 large metacentric Z chromosomes, and females have a Z chromosome and a medium-sized W chromosome (Eberle 1972; Kilpatrick and Zimmerman 1973).

FOSSIL RECORD. Pleistocene (Rancholabrean) vertebrae of *R. septemvittata* have been found in northwestern Ohio (Holman 1997), Pennsylvania (Guilday et al. 1964; Lynch 1966a), and Virginia (Fay 1988; Holman 1986a).

DISTRIBUTION. The main range of this snake is from southeastern Pennsylvania, western New York, and southwestern Ontario west to southeastern Wisconsin and adjacent northeastern Illinois, and south to northern Georgia, Alabama, and eastern Mississippi. Isolated populations also occur in the southwestern corner of Mississippi and in the Ozark Mountains of northern Arkansas and southern Missouri. Conant (1960) discussed the distribution and possible zoogeography of the two major populations.

HABITAT. *R. septemvittata* lives in clean, unpolluted brooks, streams, rivers, or marshes in open areas or woodlands. Crayfish must be present, and the bottoms and banks of the waterways are often rocky. Stokes and Dunson (1982) found that it has the most permeable skin of any snake, and this probably restricts it to at least the near vicinity of water.

BEHAVIOR. Seasonally, *R. septemvittata* may be active in all months in the southernmost portions of its range, but farther north and at higher elevations it is forced to hibernate during the winter. The length of the annual activity period varies with latitude. In North Carolina it has exhibited surface activity from late March to late October; in Virginia from late February to early October (Mitchell 1994); in Kentucky from early April to mid-November (Branson and Baker 1974); and in southeastern Pennsylvania from early April to early November (C. Ernst, pers. obs.), although Reinert (1975) found one active on 5 December. In Ohio it is active in March–October (Wood 1949), and in Wisconsin it can be seen in May–September (Vogt 1981). In North Carolina, most sightings occur in May–August (Palmer and Braswell 1995).

Overwintering is often communal, and queen snakes may aggregate at a hibernaculum prior to settling in for the winter (Wood 1949; C. Ernst, pers. obs.). On warm, sunny, late fall days, several individuals may be seen basking around such sites. The authors have found them hibernating in muskrat *(Ondatra zibethica)* bank burrows, and crayfish burrows are probably used. Earth and stone dams are also used as hibernacula. Vogt (1981) thought those in Wisconsin probably hibernate under rocks in or near spring-fed streams.

Although Wood (1949) stated *R. septemvittata* is active at all hours and Branson and Baker (1974) and Mount (1975) thought them predominately nocturnal, the authors have found them chiefly diurnal in southeastern Pennsylvania, Virginia, and Kentucky. Most foraging occurs in the morning, followed by a period of basking in branches overhanging the water or along the bank. On very hot days, queen snakes retreat under stones, logs, or other debris on the shore, and other favorite retreats are muskrat burrows and earth and stone dams. Often several may be found basking in close proximity, particularly in the spring and fall, or hiding in the same retreat.

Branson and Baker (1974) recorded the CTs of 116 Kentucky queen snakes that were partially or completely submerged in water, and found their temperatures were 0.2–6.2°C above the WT. The highest recorded BT was 30.4°C, the lowest 12.2°C, and the mean CT for all individuals was 25.6°C. The adult CT_{max} varied from 43.4 to 44.5°C, and that of juveniles varied between 39.5 and 41.5°C. Most activities are influenced by the ET, and both crawling and swimming velocities increase with increasing temperature (Finkler and Claussen 1999).

Home ranges are relatively small. Of 13 recaptures by Branson and Baker (1974), the straightline distances from point of release to point of recapture were 3–137 (mean, 22.6) m. Most of the activity by a population of 205 individuals in southeastern Pennsylvania centered around a stone dam used as both a summer and winter retreat. The greatest distance any of the snakes was found away from the dam was 55 m (a male), and 80% of 75 recaptures were within 25 m. No significant difference was found by C. Ernst (unpubl. data) between the distances moved by adults of either sex, and most juveniles occupied home ranges extending no more than 10 m from the dam. The maximum aquatic and terrestrial velocities of *R. septemvittata* recorded by Finkler and Claussen (1999) were 0.71 m/second and 0.39 m/second, respectively.

The queen snake apparently possesses the ability to use the sun for Y-axis orientation toward a particular shoreline (Newcomer et al. 1974).

REPRODUCTION. The smallest recorded females with embryos or enlarged follicles are 34.4 cm TBL (Branson and Baker 1974), 37.5 cm TBL (Wood and Duellman 1950), and 31.8 cm SVL (Mitchell 1994). Conant and Collins (1998) reported the mature length for both sexes as 38 cm TBL, and Mitchell (1994) reported a male producing sperm at 30.5 cm SVL. Fe-

males probably mature in their second year, but do not reproduce until their third year of life; males seem to mature in their second year.

The female gametic cycle has been insufficiently described. Branson and Baker (1974) found 7–49 immature eggs in 35 Kentucky specimens. Fifteen other females contained only immature follicles; most of these were captured in June–July. One containing seven ova was captured on 13 August. Only two females captured during June contained both immature follicles and mature ova; four females captured in August contained both immature follicles and embryos. Fourteen females taken 12–13 August contained immature follicles and had given birth. The presence of immature follicles in females that had produced young probably indicates that such follicles would mature and produce the next year's litter. *R. septemvittata* is viviparous, and the chorionic membrane surrounding the embryo lies in intimate contact with the wall of the female's oviduct during development. Both the chorionic membrane and the oviduct wall become richly supplied with a fine network of blood vessels (Branson and Baker 1974).

The male gametic cycle is also poorly known. Spermatogenesis begins in late spring and peaks during the summer. Spermiation begins in mid-July, and the sperm are subsequently stored in the vas deferens (Minesky and Aldridge 1982; Trauth 1991a).

The main breeding period is probably the spring, although Branson and Baker (1974) thought some individuals may mate in the fall. Minton (1972) found a copulating pair in Indiana on 28 May, Ford (1982b) reported spring courtship activity by recently captured males, and Ashton and Ashton (1981) thought mating occurred in the spring in Florida, possibly as late as June. According to Ford (1982b), the male begins courtship by approaching and examining the female with numerous tongue flicks. He then mounts her back, crawls forward to longitudinally align their bodies, and bounces up and down on her by oscillating the first 6–20 cm of his neck. Each bobbing lasts about 0.05 seconds, and the bounces occur at two speeds. The slower rate of 60–70/minute involves higher up and down movements, while during the faster rate of 91–115/minute the male does not lose contact with the female's back. Following the bouncing behavior, the male tries to initiate insertion of his hemipenis into the female's cloaca; when this is achieved he performs caudocephalic waves.

Reported births have occurred from 6 July to 1 October, but most take place from mid-August to mid-September. Litters contain 4–39 young (Fitch 1985a). The average number of young in 81 reported litters was 11. Limited data indicate that litter size increases with female TBL. RCMs range between 0.278 (Fontenot and Platt 1996) and 0.315 (Seigel and Fitch 1984). Fifty-three neonates from southeastern Pennsylvania measured by the authors had 16.6–23.1 (mean, 20.5) cm TBLs and weighed 2.7–3.1 (mean, 2.9) g.

GROWTH AND LONGEVITY. Raney and Roecker (1947) and Branson and Baker (1974) reported average increases of 75–79% in TBL for yearling queen snakes. Wood and Duellman (1950) reported a 50% increase in TBL during the second year and diminishing rates of growth in subsequent years. Branson and Baker (1974) noted a growth rate of 44.8% during the second year.

Queen snakes are difficult to maintain in captivity, as most refuse to eat. Nevertheless, a male—originally caught when adult—survived 19 years, 3 months, and 17 days at the Racine Zoo in Wisconsin (Snider and Bowler 1992).

DIET AND FEEDING BEHAVIOR. The authors' experience with queen snakes strongly suggests that they eat almost nothing but crayfish, and these observations agree with those of other researchers. Crayfish the primary prey, but only those that have recently molted and are still in a soft-shelled stage are eaten. Of 44 stomachs containing prey examined by Raney and Roecker (1947), crayfish made up 99.2% of the total volume of food items, and in 110 stomachs containing food examined by Branson and Baker (1974) 98.6% of the food consisted of crayfish. However, frogs, fish, and some aquatic invertebrates are occasionally taken. Reported prey include crayfish *(Orconectes juvenalis, O. obscurus);* anurans—toads *(Bufo* sp.), cricket frogs *(Acris* sp.), and tadpoles of true ranid frogs *(Rana* sp.); newts *(Notophthalmus* sp.); fish—catfish (Ictaluridae), fantail darters *(Etheostoma flabellare),* and mudminnows *(Umbra lima);* dragonfly nymphs (Odonata); and snails *(Physa* sp.) (Adler and Tilley 1960; Ashton and Ashton 1981; Branson and Baker

1974; Brown 1979a; Godley et al. 1984; Judd 1955; Palmer and Braswell 1995; Penn 1950; Raney and Roecker 1947; Surface 1906; Wood 1949; Wright and Wright 1957). McCauley (1945) found the head of an ant in a queen snake's stomach, but thought it probably was the stomach contents of a frog or fish the snake had eaten. Carrion may be taken: the authors have seen a wild queen snake swallow a partially decomposed soft-shelled crayfish *(Procambarus* sp.).

The authors have observed *R. septemvittata* forage among rocks in a small Pennsylvania stream, and on several occasions they disturbed crayfish from their hiding places, seized them by the tail, and proceeded to swallow them tail first. All the crayfish were small and appeared to have just molted. Odor probably plays an important role in finding prey. Pinder (1996) noted that much tongue flicking is done while foraging underwater; and Burghardt (1968) tested the response of newborn *R. septemvittata* to water extracts of several small animals, but the newborns only responded to extracts of crayfish, especially those that had recently molted.

PREDATORS AND DEFENSE. Few reports of predation on *R. septemvittata* exist. Minton (1972) saw a fish seize and subsequently release a small Indiana queen snake, and he had a report of another taken from the stomach of a great blue heron *(Ardea herodias).* Branson and Baker (1974) observed juveniles being attacked by crayfish in Kentucky, but few queen snakes show wounds caused by crayfish. Branson and Baker also found young *R. septemvittata* in the gut of a hellbender *(Cryptobranchus alleganiensis).* Palmer and Braswell (1995) reported predation by a racer *(Coluber constrictor),* and large water snakes *(Nerodia)* and cottonmouths *(Agkistrodon piscivorus)* probably also occasionally eat them. C. Ernst has seen a red-shouldered hawk *(Buteo lineatus)* feeding on a dead queen snake, and alligators *(Alligator mississippiensis),* raccoons *(Procyon lotor),* and otters *(Lontra canadensis)* may take a few. During hibernation, dormant queen snakes may be attacked by crayfish and mice (Branson and Baker 1974; Wood 1949).

The first defense of the queen snake, and in fact all snakes if given a chance, is to flee to a place of safety. This may be accomplished by diving into the water and swimming away (flight speed and distance are greatly influenced by temperature; Layne and Ford 1984) or by crawling under a rock or log or down a crevice or crayfish burrow. At any given time of day, most *R. septemvittata* are hiding under objects; Branson and Baker (1974) reported that almost 96% of the queen snakes they collected during their Kentucky study were found beneath rocks. When caught and handled, *R. septemvittata* may bite, though rarely, but will more often squirm violently and expel musk and feces.

POPULATIONS. Queen snakes may be very common at suitable sites with crayfish and hiding places. Branson and Baker (1974) found densities of 35/192 m and 62/237 m at two sites in a Kentucky stream, and Wood (1949) reported collecting 125 individuals within 92 m in a stream in Ohio. An old rock dam in southeastern Pennsylvania was home for 205 of these snakes (C. Ernst, per. obs.).

Of 229 queen snakes examined by Branson and Baker (1974) during their study in Kentucky, 113 were males and 116 females, a 1:1 sex ratio. Similarly, the sex ratio of 128 young born in captivity during their study was 65 males to 63 females. In the Pennsylvania population studied by C. Ernst, 115 individuals were males and 90 were females, essentially a 1:1 male to female ratio. The juvenile to adult ratio in the Pennsylvania population was 65 to 140, or 0.48:1.00.

Humans cause much damage to natural populations of *R. septemvittata*. Fontenot et al. (1996) found one contaminated with PCBs in South Carolina, and drainage and damming of their waterways as well as automobile traffic have killed many. At one site in southeastern Pennsylvania, about 100 queen snakes were shot while they basked by local teenage boys. Unfortunately, water pollution and acid rain have combined to reduce crayfish populations in many parts of its eastern range, and this, along with habitat drainage, has consequently eliminated *R. septemvittata* from many areas where it was once common. It is now considered endangered in Wisconsin and a species of special concern in Arkansas.

Rhadinaea flavilata (Cope 1871) | Pine Woods Snake

RECOGNITION. *R. flavilata* is a short (TBL to 40.3 cm), slender, yellowish brown to reddish brown snake with a white to yellow unmarked venter. Its sides are often lighter than the middorsum, and a diffused vertebral stripe may be present. A dark brown stripe extends rearward from the nose through the orbit and diagonally downward to the corner of the mouth. The chin and labials are white to yellow with dark flecks. The tail ends in a spinelike scale. Body scales are smooth and pitless, and lie in 18 (17–19) anterior rows and 17 midbody and posterior rows. On the underside are 112–141 ventrals, 59–83 pairs of subcaudals, and a divided anal plate. Lateral head scales consist of 2 nasals (the nostril is in the anterior-most), 1 (rarely 0) small loreal, 1 preocular, 2 (3) postoculars (the lower is small), 1 (rarely 2) + 2 (3) temporals, 7 (6–8) supralabials, and 9 (7–10) infralabials. The hemipenis extends to the ninth subcaudal, and has a bifurcate head, a single sulcus spermaticus that forks distally, a smooth base, a spiny middle with the largest spines on the surface opposite the sulcus, and distal heads with calyxes (papilla-like apically, spiny basally). Each maxilla has 13–15 teeth, with the posterior-most separated from those in front by a diastema and enlarged .

Females are longer-bodied with 126–141 (mean, 133) ventrals, 59–74 (mean, 67) subcaudals, and TLs that are 29–32 (mean, 29) % of TBL; males are shorter-bodied with 112–135 (mean, 128) ventrals, 69–83 (mean, 75) subcaudals, and TLs that are 26–36 (mean, 32) % of TBL. Males possess weakly keeled body scales near the anal vent.

GEOGRAPHIC VARIATION. No subspecies are recognized (Walley 1999), but clinal variation occurs in the number of dark flecks on the labials (greatest north, least south), occurrence of the vertebral stripe (greatest north, least south), and number of ventrals (decreasing slightly from south to north) (Myers 1967). Also, the number of supra- and infralabials varies more in peninsular Florida than elsewhere.

Pine woods snake, *Rhadinaea flavilata*; St. Johns County, Florida. (Photograph by James H. Harding)

CONFUSING SPECIES. No other small, basically unpatterned snake within its range has a dark stripe running through the eye.

KARYOTYPE. Undescribed.

FOSSIL RECORD. Known Pleistocene fossils are from Rancholabrean and Irvingtonian deposits in Citrus and Levy counties, Florida (Auffenberg 1963; Gut and Ray 1963; Holman 1958b, 1959a, 1996; Meylan 1982), and Rancholabrean deposits in Tennessee (Klippel and Parmalee 1982).

DISTRIBUTION. *R. flavilata* ranges from Dare and Beaufort counties, North Carolina, south on the Atlantic Coastal Plain through peninsular Florida to Palm Beach, Glades, and Sarasota counties, and westward along the Gulf Coastal Plain to Jefferson and Walton counties, Florida, and from Baldwin County, Alabama west to probably the Mississippi River in southeastern Louisiana. A population exists on the piedmont of northwestern South Carolina near Aiken (Whiteman et al. 1995), but most localities are less than 30 m elevation or 120 km from the coast.

Myers (1967, 1974) thought that *R. flavilata* or an ancestor migrated to the southeastern United States by a coastal route from the west, as all other members of the genus occur in Mexico and Central America.

HABITAT. This snake is usually found in coastal plain slash pine or longleaf pine woods characterized by poorly drained soils, and dependent on periodic fires to preserve the successionsal stage. A few have been taken in Florida hardwood hammocks adjacent to pine flatwoods, and some occur in dry woods or marshes on coastal islands off North Carolina and Florida. Within these habitats, *R. flavilata* spends most

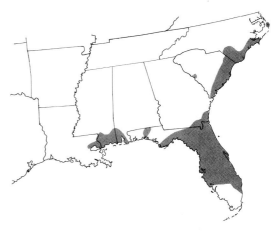

Distribution of *Rhadinaea flavilata*.

of its time under or within logs, under leaves or other surface debris, buried in sandy soil, or under the loose bark of pine trees.

BEHAVIOR. R. flavilata has been collected in every month, but most records are from April and May (57% in North Carolina; Palmer and Braswell 1995). When forced to hibernate, it enters rotting logs or stumps, or animal burrows, or digs below the frost line in sandy soil. During dry summer weather it retreats into crayfish burrows. It is probably predominately nocturnal, but its daily activity pattern has not been identified.

REPRODUCTION. Males with a TBL of 21.5–25.9 cm are mature (Conant and Collins 1998; Wright and Wright 1957), and females are mature at a TBL of 20.7–26.0 cm (Myers 1967; Palmer and Braswell 1995; Telford 1952; Wright and Wright 1957).

The male gametic cycle is unknown, and that of the female is poorly known. Myers (1967) reported that Florida females had 4 mm ovarian follicles in February, but by late April the follicles had grown to 12–15 × 4 mm, and from late April to late May females contained oviductal eggs. Funderberg (1958) found a gravid female on 11 May that laid four 13 × 5 mm eggs on 4 June. A 4 July female had 14–16 × 4–5 mm follicles (Myers 1967).

Breeding probably occurs in the spring, possibly as early as mid-February in Mississippi (Brode and Allison 1958). Palmer and Braswell (1995) found a male and a female entwined, but not copulating, on 17 April. The courtship/mating behaviors have not been described.

The eggs are laid from 31 May to 19 August, and possibly some females produce two clutches during this period (Palmer and Braswell 1995). Clutches contain 1–4 (mean, 2.5; n = 27) eggs. The elongated non- or slightly adherent eggs are white or cream with a leathery, granular shell; 44 eggs measured 18.0–36.4 (mean, 27.7) × 4.0–9.4 (mean, 7.3) mm. Hatchlings appear during mid-August to mid-October and have 12.5 16.7 (mean, 14.2; n – 15) cm TBLs.

GROWTH AND LONGEVITY. No growth data are available. The captive longevity record is 3 years and 4 days for a wild-caught adult of unknown sex (Snider and Bowler 1992).

DIET AND FEEDING HABITS. Few reports exist concerning the natural prey of R. flavilata exist, but captives have eaten a variety of animals. Natural and captive prey species include salamanders (Desmognathus fuscus, Eurycea quadridigitata, Plethodon glutinosus), toads (Bufo quercicus, B. terrestris), spadefoots (Scaphiopus holbrookii), treefrogs (Acris crepitans, A. gryllus, Hyla femoralis, H. squirella, Pseudacris crucifer, P. ocularis), leptodactylids (Eleutherodactylus planirostris), microhylids (Gastrophryne carolinensis), bullfrogs (Rana catesbeiana), lizards (Anolis carolinensis, Eumeces egregius, E. inexpectatus, Ophisauris ventralis, Scincella lateralis), snakes (Diadophis punctatus), newborn mice (Mus musculus), and earthworms (Allen 1939a; Brode and Allison 1958; Funderburg 1958; Malnate 1939; Myers 1967; Neill 1954; Palmer and Braswell 1995). It is doubtful that it eats insects.

Small frogs may be caught and swallowed immediately, but usually R. flavilata seizes an animal along the body, moves it to the rear of the mouth, embeds its elongated maxillary teeth, and chews it. The snake then lies quietly until the prey is immobilized by its venomous saliva before swallowing it (Malnate 1939; Neill 1954; Willard 1967). A ground skink (Scincella lateralis) died within 15 minutes of being bitten by a R. flavilata (Myers 1967). Normally an animal is seldom held for less than 45 minutes; usually a frog will be kept for 70–80 minutes; and a large active frog or lizard may be retained up to two to three hours (Neill 1954). The toxic saliva is produced in a combined serous-mucous Duvernoy's gland (Taub 1967); it is mild and of no danger to humans.

PREDATORS AND DEFENSE. The only reports of predation on R. flavilata are by snakes (Coluber constrictor, Lampropeltis getula, L. triangulum) (Palmer and Braswell 1995; Tennant 1997), but other ophiophagous snakes, birds of prey, and carnivorous mammals must take some. Humans probably kill many by clear cutting pine tree stands.

When found in logs or stumps, it may try to escape farther into the wood, but usually lies quietly in place, if picked up, it attempts to crawl through the fingers and expels a rather pungent musk. Seldom, if ever, does it bite.

POPULATIONS. Over its range, R. flavilata seems uncommon, but this is due to its secretive nature. The only reports of population numbers are those from Marion County, Florida, where Allen (1939a) caught 21 in a day, and a farmer later collected 80 in about 30 days; and from near Aiken, South Carolina, where 10 (7 males, 1 female, and 2 juveniles) were captured in approximately seven years (Whiteman et al. 1995). The sex ratio of a combined sample from Alachua and Marion counties, Florida, examined by Myers (1967) was 25 males and 43 females (0.58:1.00), but the combined ratio for specimens examined by him from all states was 93 males to 92 females, or 1:1.

REMARKS. The species has been reviewed by Myers (1974) and Walley (1999).

Rhinocheilus lecontei Baird and Girard 1853 | Long-nosed Snake

RECOGNITION. This attractive black, red, and yellow colubrid has a maximum recorded TBL of 104.1 cm. Its slim body is typically speckled with small black marks on the cream to yellow, pink, or red spaces lying along the sides between the 13–51 black dorsal blotches, but the dorsal red spaces between the dark blotches usually lack black speckles. The black blotches are also speckled, with yellow or white marks. Normally, the tail has about a dozen (3–18) black dorsal blotches. The pointed head is mostly black with a pink to red or orange, protruding or even upturned, snout, and countersunk mouth. The rostral scale is prominent. Some light speckles are present on the black portion of the head, and alternating black and yellow bars are present on the labials. The pupil is round. The venter is white to cream or yellow, with some dark spots, especially along the sides. The body scales are smooth with 0–2 apical pits, and lie in 23–25 rows near the head and at midbody and 19–20 rows near the tail. On the underside of the body are 181–218 ventrals, a mostly single row of 41–61 subcaudals (an unusual condition for a colubrid), and an undivided anal plate. Lateral head scales consists of 2 nasals divided by the nostril, 1 loreal, 1–2 preoculars, 2 postoculars, 2 + 3 temporals, 8 (7–10) supralabials, and 9 (8–11) infralabials. The rounded hemipenis is barely bilobed with a single sulcus spermaticus that crosses to the right lobe. Many tiny spines are present on the lower portion of the shaft, and large, recurved spines occur on the distal portion of the shaft that gradually change to calyxes near the bilobed section. Each maxilla has 11–12 teeth.

Males have 190–218 ventrals, 48–61 subcaudals, and TLs 16–17% of TBL. Females have 181–213 ventrals, 41–54 subcaudals, and TLs 15% of TBL. Adult males, on the average, have greater TBLs than females.

GEOGRAPHIC VARIATION. Four subspecies are currently recognized (Grismer 1990), but only two occur north of Mexico. *Rhinocheilus l. lecontei* Baird and Girard 1853, the western long-nosed snake, ranges south from southwestern Idaho, western California, northern Nevada, and western Utah through western and southern Arizona and extreme southwestern New Mexico to Baja California and Sonora, Mexico. It has a blunt snout that is not very upturned,

Western long-nosed snake, *Rhinocheilus lecontei lecontei*; California. (Photograph by Robert E. Lovich)

Texas long-nosed snake, *Rhinocheilus lecontei tessellatus*; Maverick County, Texas. (Photograph by Roger W. Barbour)

a rostral scale only slightly raised above the adjacent scales, 15–51 black body bands on a white to cream or yellowish background, scales in the light pigmented areas with or without red centers, and some individuals with black pigment on the venter. *R. l. tessellatus* (Garman 1884), the Texas long-nosed snake, ranges from southwestern Kansas and southeastern Colorado south through the western two-thirds of Texas and most of New Mexico to San Luis Potosí in Mexico. It has a more pointed, upturned snout, the rostral scale distinctly raised above the adjacent scales, 17–37 black body bands on a cream or yellow background, red pigment and black-centered scales in the light portion, and no black pigment on the venter.

Minton (1959) thought the *R. l. tessellatus* in the Big Bend region of western Texas differed from those from central Texas in having paler red areas between the black blotches, the rostral scale less sharply upturned, and the tip of the snout tan rather than reddish.

CONFUSING SPECIES. Other red and yellow or red, yellow, and black colubrid snakes, such as kingsnakes and milksnakes *(Lampropeltis)* and the scarlet snake *(Cemophora coccinea),* have two rows of subcaudals. The North American coral snake *(Micurus fulvius)* and the Sonoran coral snake *(Micuroides euryxanthus)* have the entire anterior portion of the head black; alternating body bands of red, yellow, cream, or white, and black (with the red bands bordered by yellow, cream, or white bands); and no loreal scales.

KARYOTYPE. The long-nosed snake carries a diploid compliment of 36 chromosomes: 16 macro-

chromosomes (pair six, by size, acrocentric; the rest biarmed) and 20 microchromosomes (Bury et al. 1970; Trinco and Smith 1972).

FOSSIL RECORD. The fossil record of *R. lecontei* is extensive, dating from the Upper Pliocene Blancan of New Mexico (Lucas et al. 1995) and Texas (Rogers 1976), and the Lower Pleistocene Blancan of Kansas (Brattstrom 1967), Irvingtonian of Texas (Holman 1969b), and Rancholabrean of Arizona (Mead et al. 1984; Van Devender and Mead 1978; Van Devender, Mead, and Rea 1991; Van Devender, Phillips, and Mead 1977; Van Devender, Rea, and Hall 1991), California (LaDuke 1991; Van Devender and Mead 1978), New Mexico (Van Devender and Worthington 1977), and Texas (Gehlbach and Holman 1974; Hill 1971; Van Devender and Bradley 1994).

DISTRIBUTION. The long-nosed snake is found from southwestern Kansas and adjacent Nebraska and western Utah, Nevada, and north-central California southward through western Texas, eastern and southern New Mexico, western and southern Arizona, and southern California to the Mexican states of Tamaulipas, San Luis Potosí, Zacatecas, Durango, Nayarit, and Baja California del Norte.

HABITAT. Its usual habitats are lowland desert, dry prairie, or scrubland (mesquite, acacia, opuntia cacti, thornbush) with sandy soil and rodent burrows or surface rocks, logs, and plant debris for diurnal retreats at elevations to slightly over 1,200 m.

BEHAVIOR. *R. lecontei* is relatively abundant across its range in the United States, and as a result more of its life history is known than for many other southwestern snakes.

Active individuals have been found in all months in the United States (Klauber 1941; Wright and Wright 1957), but in California it is most active from April through July (Klauber 1941). East of the 100th meridian it usually surfaces from winter dormancy in April and disappears in late September or October. In New Mexico, *Rhinocheilus* has been found active as early as 26 March and as late as 24 October (Degenhardt et al. 1996). Most observations have occurred in

Distribution of *Rhinocheilus lecontei*.

April, May, and June when the snake may be occasionally diurnally active in the morning or late afternoon, or more often crepuscular; but once the hot days of summer begin in July it is strictly crepuscular and nocturnal. Klauber (1941) found it active from 1900 to 1129 hours in California, but observed most between 2000 and 2100 hours.

Rhinocheilus is more cold than heat tolerant, and nocturnal individuals have been found foraging at temperatures as low as 15°C (Shaw and Campbell 1974), and Woodin (1953) collected one on a "very cold night during a rain." In California Klauber (1941) found them most active in early evening at ATs of 16.5–30.5°C (total range in AT for active snakes, 16.5–34.0°C), and in Sinaloa, Mexico, Hardy and McDiarmid (1969) observed them most often on nights with ATs of 26.4–28.2°C. Sullivan (1981a) found California *R. lecontei* active between 1800 and 2300 hours at CTs of 18.0–27.0°C, and Cunningham (1966) found another active with a cloacal temperature of 21°C. These temperature records seem to indicate that this snake is most active at a relatively narrow range of cool night temperatures, probably 21–27°C.

Its restriction to cooler ETs may be related to moisture loss in its arid environment, and its retreat into mammal burrows or under surface shelters during the day may also be related to preservation of body water. As with many other southwestern snakes, rains often bring *R. lecontei* to the surface, and it is often be found on roads after rainstorms.

According to Walls (1934), this snake has an intermediate stage retina containing both rods for nocturnal vision and cones for day use, and its round pupil is more of a diurnal adaptation.

The only reports of winter dormancy are of those upturned during plowing on 13 and 14 December in California (Klauber 1941), but surely this snake also uses rock crevices and mammal burrows to retreat below the soil frost depth in winter. One was seen using its enlarged rostral scale to push its way into loose soil during the warmer months (Fouquette and Lindsay 1955), so it also escapes from summer's drying heat by retreating underground.

Like many other colubrid, elapid, and viperid snakes, male long-nosed snakes engage in combat bouts. The two males wrap completely around each other from head to tail, and may crawl a considerable distance while so entwined (Osborne 1984).

REPRODUCTION. Sufficient data exist on the eggs of this species, but the reproductive cycles of both sexes are unknown. Wright and Wright (1957) listed 49.8 cm and 53.6 cm as the minimum sizes for mature males and females, respectively, and Klauber (1941) found eggs in 61.2 and 61.5 cm California females.

Mating probably occurs after emergence from winter dormancy in April or May, but neither courtship nor mating has been described. Perhaps these take place underground.

Most ovipositions have occurred in June and July

(Degenhardt et al. 1996; Klauber 1941; Kronen 1980; Lardie 1965; Stebbins 1985; Tennant 1984; Vitt 1975; Wright and Wright 1957), but one Arizona female laid her eggs on 15–16 August (Woodin 1953), so possibly more than one clutch can be laid during a reproductive season. Reported clutches average 6.5 eggs and have contained 3–11 eggs (Stebbins 1985; Vitt 1975). The elongated eggs have white, parchmentlike shells and are 38.5 (25–53) × 15.5 (13–16) mm in size. The only reported average egg mass was 6.8 g, and a RCM was 0.374 (Vitt 1975).

Clutches are apparently laid underground, as no data on natural nests exist. Reported IPs have ranged from 42 to 90 days, and average 71.8 days; IT undoubtedly determines the length of the IP. In the wild most eggs probably hatch in August or September. Hatchlings have an average TBL of 21.6 cm, but some may be as short as 16.6 cm, or as long as 24.4 cm. Hatchlings are paler than adults and lack the extensive adult dark flecking.

GROWTH AND LONGEVITY.   No growth data are available. A male originally captured as an adult survived 18 years, 10 months, and 22 days at the Staten Island Zoo (Snider and Bowler 1992).

DIET AND FEEDING BEHAVIOR.   *Rhinocheilus* is an active forager that seeks out its prey, usually at night, by examining rodent burrows and brush, and crawling beneath rocks, logs, and other surface shelters. Based on captive behavior the authors have observed, prey scent trails may be followed. Two adult males kept at different times in a large terrarium readily followed scent trails left by dead mice *(Mus musculus, Peromyscus leucopus)* the authors had dragged across the terrarium floor and then hidden. The mice were always found and quickly swallowed head first. Live mice were usually first discovered by sight, chased, grabbed in the mouth, positioned, and ingested head first. Use of venom was not apparent, but several times, the snakes squeezed the mice against the side of the terrarium and constricted them much in the way practiced by pine snakes *(Pituophis melanoleucus)* and mole kingsnakes *(Lampropeltis calligaster rhombomaculata)*. All three species forage underground in mammal burrows where little room is available for completely wrapping around prey.

Lizards *(Cnemidophorus, Eumeces, Holbrookia, Sceloporus, Uta)* seem to be the most important prey of smaller long-nosed snakes, perhaps because of the limitation of their rather small mouth gape (Rodríguez-Robles et al. 1999a), but rodents *(Dipodomys, Perognathus)* are taken by large individuals, and smaller snakes, reptile eggs, birds, grasshoppers (Orthoptera), and centipedes are also eaten (Collins 1993; Degenhardt et al. 1996; Fitch 1949; Fouquette and Lindsay 1955; Klauber 1941; McKinney and Ballinger 1966; Minton 1959; Rodríguez-Robles et al. 1999a; Stebbins 1954, 1985; Tennant 1984; Tinkle 1967; Wright and Wright 1957). Rodríguez-Robles and Greene (in Rodríguez-Robles et al. 1999a) found lizards that make up 66.4% and small mammals 26.1% of the diet of *R. lecontei*. In addition to the mice listed above *(Mus, Peromyscus)*, the authors' captives readily took five-lined skinks *(Eumeces fasciatus)* and fence lizards *(Sceloporus undulatus)*, and other captives are reported to have eaten geckos *(Coleonyx)*, side-blotched lizards *(Uta)*, and shovel-nosed snakes *(Chionactis)* (Klauber 1941).

PREDATORS AND DEFENSE.   Animals that prey on *R. lecontei* include large centipedes *(Scolopendra)*, large snakes *(Lampropeltis)*, owls *(Bubo)*, hawks *(Buteo)*, armadillos *(Dasypus)*, skunks *(Mephitis)*, foxes *(Vulpes)*, and coyotes *(Canis latrans)* (Easterla 1975b; Fitch 1949; Tennant 1984). Motorized vehicles are also a major mortality factor (Price and LaPointe 1990; Rosen and Lowe 1994).

Rhinocheilus has a nervous disposition, but even though it will fling and twist its body about and discharge musk if handled, it seldom bites. However, individual differences in temperament do exist, and some are more aggressive than others. Juveniles seem to strike and bite more fiercely than adults. Female *R. lecontei* have also been observed to discharge blood from their nose and feces and blood from the anal vent (Lardie 1961; McCoy and Gehlbach 1967; Smith et al. 1993). A wild snake will first try to flee from a potential predator. If it cannot escape, it may assume a defensive posture that emphasizes its red and black blotches, perhaps mimicking venomous coral snakes, and vibrate its tail; or it may hide the head beneath the body while holding its body coils rigid and somewhat raised and displaying the venter (Gorzula 1973).

Tests on its blood serum have revealed that *R. lecon-*

tei may have a slight immunity to pit viper venoms (Weinstein et al. 1992).

POPULATIONS.   Tennant (1984) thought this snake sparsely distributed and uncommon in central and western Texas. Price and LaPointe (1990) only found 12 (2.6%) *R. lecontei* among 454 individuals of 18 species of snakes they recorded along a New Mexico highway during a four-year study, and in Arizona Rosen and Lowe (1994) collected 47 (12.8%) in a sample of 368 snakes of 20 species in a similar four-year study. *Rhinocheilus* only had a calculated density of 0.5 km in a transect study in California (Sullivan 1981b), and Fitch (1993) found it made up only 5.47% of the snakes captured at one grassland site in Kansas. Unfortunately, statements and figures such as these give a false impression of low population size for this species. It is much more populous in some areas than others, and its nocturnal habits keep it from the attention of most persons.

According to Klauber (1941), about 63% of the specimens in collections are males, and 37% females, but he did not think this represents the true sex ratio of wild *R. lecontei*.

R. lecontei is listed as threatened in Kansas and as a species of special concern in Idaho.

REMARKS.   Keogh (1996) found *Rhinocheilus* to be most closely related to the genera *Cemophora, Lampropeltis,* and *Stilosoma* during a cladistic study of morphological characters of the snake tribe Lampropeltini, supporting the results of previous protein electrophoretic studies by Dessauer et al. (1987) and Dowling et al. (1983). However, a more recent study of mtDNA sequences by Rodríguez-Robles and Jesus-Escobar (1999) indicates that *Rhinocheilus* is a sister taxon to the lampropeltines. *R. lecontei* has been reviewed by Grismer (1990), Medica (1975), and Shannon and Humphrey (1963).

Salvadora Baird and Girard 1853

Patch-nosed Snakes

Key to the Species of *Salvadora*

1a.   Posterior chin shields touch or are only separated by one scale, dorsolateral stripe includes rows two and three, normally 8 supralabials . . . . *S. grahamiae*

1b.   Posterior chin shields do not touch and are separated by 2–3 scales, dorsolateral stripe includes scale row four (possibly just anteriorly), normally 9–10 supralabials 2

2a.   Two to 4 loreal scales present, 1 or no supralabials enter the orbit . . . . *S. hexalepis*

2b.   One loreal scale present, 2 supralabials enter the orbit . . . . *S. deserticola*

Salvadora deserticola Schmidt 1940 | Big Bend Patch-nosed Snake

RECOGNITION.   *S. deserticola* (TBL to 114.3 cm, but most are 60–90 cm) is the first of three snakes with a large, raised rostral scale. A pair of dorsolateral, dark brown or black stripes extend posteriorly from the eye along the length of the body. Between these stripes is a broad area of pale tan to orangish brown. The body is gray to olive gray or light brown, and the middorsal area is usually brighter than the sides below the dorsolateral stripes, where each body scale has some anterior orange brown pigment. Another narrower, dark longitudinal stripe, involving the fourth scale row (and sometimes also the third) anteriorly and the

Big Bend patch-nosed snake, *Salvadora deserticola*; Cochise County, Arizona. (Photograph by Roger W. Barbour)

third row near the tail, is also present along the body. The head lacks a dorsal pattern, and the venter is pinkish orange. Body scales are smooth with very small apical pits and occur in 18–20 anterior rows, 17 midbody rows, and 13–15 posterior rows. Present are 170–205 ventrals, 66–103 subcaudals, and a divided anal plate. Each side of the head has 2 nasals (partially divided by the nostril), 1–2 loreals, 2 (1–3) preoculars, 2 postoculars, 2 + 2–3 temporals, 9 supralabials, and 10–12 (rarely 9) infralabials. The posterior chin shields are partially separated by 2–3 scales. The single hemipenis is not capped or bifurcate, and has a single sulcus spermaticus, apical calyxes, and long basal spines. Each maxilla has seven to nine teeth preceding a slight diastema, which is followed by two to three larger teeth.

The shorter males have 76–103 subcaudals; females are longer, and have 66–82 subcaudals.

GEOGRAPHIC VARIATION. Mexican populations of *S. deserticola* have higher ventral counts, but no subspecies have been described.

CONFUSING SPECIES. To distinguish *S. deserticola* from other species of *Salvadora*, use the key presented above. The striped garter and ribbon snakes *(Thamnophis)* and lined snake *(Tropidoclonian)* have white, yellow, orange, or red stripes, keeled scales, and an undivided anal plate.

KARYOTYPE. Unreported.

FOSSIL RECORD. Fossil remains from the middle (Barstovian) and late (Hemphilian) Miocene of South Dakota and Nebraska, respectively (Green and Holman 1977; Holman 1979a; Parmley and Holman 1995), and the Pleistocene (Rancholabrean) of Arizona, New Mexico, Texas, and Sonora, Mexico, have been assigned to the genus *Salvadora*, but not to particular species (Holman 1970, 1995; Johnson 1974, 1987; Mead et al. 1984; Van Devender and Bradley 1994; Van Devender et al. 1985; Van Devender and Worthington 1977).

DISTRIBUTION. *S. deserticola* ranges from southeastern Arizona and adjacent southwestern New Mexico south through the Big Bend region of Texas and central Chihuahua in the east, and through eastern Sonora and western Sinaloa in the west; an isolated population is present in southern Chihuahua. In Texas it is known only from Brewster, Culberson, El Paso, Hudspeth, Jeff Davis, and Presidio counties (Dixon 1987).

HABITAT. As its specific name indicates, *S. deserticola* prefers the arid habitats of desert flats, arroyos, foothills, and mesas, with loose sandy or gravelly soils, and various dry-adapted plants such as grasses, cacti, ocotillo, mesquite, creosote bush, blackbush, and catclaw, at elevations between 1,000 and 1,600 m. Often large rocks, logs, piles of dead plant debris, and abundant rodent burrows are present that provide retreats and/or foraging sites.

BEHAVIOR. Little has been reported on the life history of *S. deserticola*. In New Mexico it is active from April into November (Degenhardt et al. 1996), and in western Texas from March through at least September (Minton 1959; Tennant 1984). No data exist on hibernation, but Degenhardt et al. (1996) reported that it practices "temperature-determined winter dormancy," and so may become surface active on warm days. Winter retreats are probably the same mammal burrows or rock crevices used to estivate in summer. During the spring and fall it is most active during the morning hours, and often basks before foraging. Basking may be performed either aerially or by burrowing beneath loose sand (Degenhardt et al. 1996). During the hotter periods of July to early September daily activity becomes crepuscular.

S. deserticola has a rather low CT_{min} (6.6–8.0°C; mean, 7°C; Jacobson and Whitford 1971), which allows it to be active when other competing species are dormant. This also assures that a minimum of morn-ing basking will raise the BT to within the activity range. Its CT_{max} of 48.8°C (Jacobson and Whitford 1971) is high, but by behavioral means the snake seems to avoid warm conditions that will raise its BT to near this upper limit. It probably keeps its BT below 39°C, and escapes a higher BT by withdrawing underground. In laboratory studies, Jacobson and Whitford (1971) determined that the species has a mean preferred BT of 33 (30.2–34.5) °C.

REPRODUCTION. During a study of the reproductive cycles of both sexes contained in a mixed sample of *S. deserticola* and *S. hexalepis* from Arizona, Goldberg (1995a) found that the smallest male producing sperm had a SVL of 46.8 cm and that the smallest female with oviductal eggs was 58.5 cm SVL. Conant and Collins (1998) reported the minimum TBL for adults is 61 cm, and Wright and Wright (1957) gave minimum adult TBLs of 68.4 cm for males and 70.9 cm for females.

Males have regressed testes with spermatogonia and Sertoli cells in the seminiferous tubules in February–April (Goldberg 1995a). Recrudescence, during which a renewal of sperm production takes place, occurs in April–June, and males undergoing spermiogenesis, with maturing spermatids and mature sperm can be found in May and July–October. Testes contain sperm in July–October, although two males examined by Goldberg had initiated sperm production in May, indicating that some males produce sperm as early as late spring. Spring mating is probably the rule.

Although females may contain 5–9 mm follicles in May–June, and oviductal eggs in June, vitellogenesis

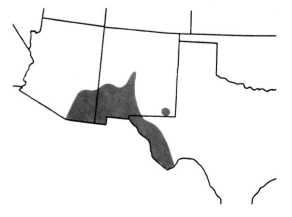

Distribution of *Salvadora deserticola*.

does not seem to occur in April and early May. It is possible that not all females reproduce each year (Goldberg 1995a).

Oviposition has occurred as early as 5 June, and probably most clutches are laid in June–July. However, August nesting has been reported, and Fitch (1970) thought more than one clutch may be laid per year because of such a long egg-laying period. Clutches have 3–10 (mean, 6) elliptical eggs. The white eggs have adherent, parchmentlike shells and average 33.5 (27–40) × 10.5 (9–12) mm in size. A clutch from *S. hexalepis* incubated in the laboratory took 85 days to develop (Stebbins 1954), and probably eggs from *S. deserticola* need a similar IP. In the wild, most hatching probably occurs in August or early September. Hatchlings resemble adults in color and pattern and have 21–28 (mean, 24.9) cm TBLs.

GROWTH AND LONGEVITY.   Unreported.

DIET AND FEEDING BEHAVIOR.   Few dietary data exist. Degenhardt et al. (1996) related that a large captive ate lizards *(Anolis, Cnemidophorus, Sceloporus)* and a pocket mouse *(Perognathus),* and Tennant (1984) noted that this snake eats lizards, small snakes, reptile eggs, and small mammals, but gave no specifics. Painter (in Degenhardt et al. 1996) reported lizards and grasshoppers as prey of wild individuals in New Mexico.

S. deserticola is an active forager, prowling through vegetation and exploring rodent burrows and beneath rocks, logs, and other surface debris. When prey is detected, it is seized, chewed, then swallowed head first. Most foraging occurs in the morning or in the evening during the hottest months.

PREDATORS AND DEFENSE.   Minton (1959) found the remains of a *S. deserticola* in the nest of a red-tailed hawk *(Buteo jamaicensis),* and probably a multitude of larger snakes, predatory birds, and carnivorous mammals prey on it.

The only *S. deserticola* the authors have experienced was particularly vile natured and would strike at the slightest provocation. When handled, it also sprayed musk and feces. Wild individuals probably first try to flee from predators, but if they can not escape, they coil, vibrate their tails, strike, and put up a vigorous defense.

Apparently, females cover the eggs with a pheromone scent at the time they are laid, which prevents egg predation by other *S. deserticola* (Shaw and Campbell 1974).

POPULATIONS.   No data are available regarding population dynamics. It seems rare throughout west Texas (Tennant 1984).

REMARKS.   So little is known of the biology of this species that any good field study would yield valuable data.

Salvadora grahamiae Baird and Girard 1853 | Mountain Patch-nosed Snake

RECOGNITION.   *S. grahamiae* (maximum TBL 119.4 cm, but most are 60–100 cm) is grayish to greenish gray or light brown with two broad, dark olive brown to black longitudinal stripes extending from at least the orbit, but usually from in front of the eye, backward along the length of the body. The portion of the back between the two dark stripes is slightly brighter yellow, pale orange, or gray than the sides below the stripes. Some also have a narrow dark, lateral stripe extending along the third scale row. The top of the head is unmarked; the pupils are round; and the large, raised, curved rostral scale is posteriorly notched and has a free, slightly projecting flap on each side. The unmarked venter is white, cream, or slightly pink. Dorsal body scales are smooth (except a few near the anal vent in adults that may bear faint keels) with small apical pits and occur in 19 anterior rows, 17–19 midbody rows, and 13–14 rows near the anal vent. The venter has 178–201 ventrals, 85–112 subcaudals, and a divided anal plate. Each side of the head has 2 nasals (partially divided by the nostril), 1–2 loreals, 2–3 preoculars, 2–3 postoculars, 2 + 2–3 tem-

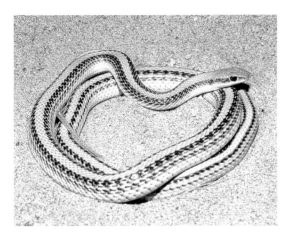

Mountain patch-nosed snake, *Salvadora grahamiae grahamiae*. (Photograph by R. D. Bartlett)

porals, 8 (9) supralabials, and 9 (8–10) infralabials. The two posterior chin shields are separated by a single scale (a few individuals may have contact between these two chin shields). The single hemipenis is not capped or bifurcate, and it has a single sulcus spermaticus, apical calyxes, and long basal spines. Each maxilla has eight to nine teeth anterior to a slight diastema, and three teeth behind it.

Males have 178–192 ventrals and 85–110 subcaudals; females have 188–201 ventrals and 91–112 subcaudals. Females are slightly longer and bulkier than males.

GEOGRAPHIC VARIATION. Two subspecies have been described. *S. g. grahamiae* Baird and Girard 1853, the mountain patch-nosed snake, occurs in Arizona, New Mexico, western Texas, east and central Chihuahua, and northeastern Sonora. It lacks, or only has a faint lateral stripe on scale row three. *S. g. lineata* Schmidt 1940, the Texas patch-nosed snake, ranges from central and southern Texas southward through Coahuila, Nuevo León, Tamaulipas, and San Luis Potosí to Hildago in Mexico. It has a very prominent, narrow, dark lateral stripe on scale row three.

CONFUSING SPECIES. Other species of *Salvadora* can be identified by the key presented above. Garter and ribbon snakes *(Thamnophis)* and the lined snake *(Tropidoclonian)* are also striped, but the stripes are either white, cream, yellow, or orange, not dark brown

or black, and they have keeled body scales and an undivided anal plate.

KARYOTYPE. The 36 chromosomes are comprised of 16 macrochromosomes (2 acrocentric and 14 biarmed, with the NOR on the short arm of the second large pair) and 20 microchromosomes (Baker et al. 1972; Camper and Hanks 1995). Baker et al. (1972) could not determine if heteromorphic sex chromosomes are present.

FOSSIL RECORD. See account of *Salvadora deserticola*.

DISTRIBUTION. The geographic range of *S. grahamiae* extends from Arizona, New Mexico, and Texas south in Mexico to northeastern Sonora in the west and Hidalgo in the east, with isolated populations in central Chihuahua and along the Chihuahua-Durango border.

HABITAT. In the west, *S. g. grahamiae* occupies dry, rocky habitats in mountains, mesas, arroyos, or canyons with open thorn brush and oak-juniper or oak-elm woods or forests; elevations are usually over 1,200 m. In the east, *S. g. lineata* is found at lower elevations in desert flats, dry grasslands, thorn brush, and along the fringes of cultivated fields.

BEHAVIOR. Although it is not particularly rare in some areas, few data have been published on the behavior and ecology of this snake. Capture dates show its annual activity period to be long, and active individuals have been found in every month (Wright and Wright 1957). In Texas, the snake is above ground from February or March to December (Minton 1959; Tennant 1984; Vermersch and Kuntz 1986), and in New Mexico from March into December (Degenhardt et al. 1996). It is rather tolerant of low ETs and is active when most other snakes are dormant. Unfortunately, no data regarding either hibernation or estivation are available.

Patch-nosed snakes resemble racers and whipsnakes in behavior, being very active, rapid crawlers. Foraging is done at ground level, but individuals sometimes climb into low bushes. Daily activity is during the daylight hours, especially on sunny morn-

Distribution of *Salvadora grahamiae*.

ings. At such times, the snake emerges from its nocturnal retreat, basks until warm, and then forages among vegetation, rocks, or logs. More basking occurs on cool days than on hot ones.

REPRODUCTION. More data are available on its reproductive biology. The smallest Arizona male producing sperm had a 48.3 cm SVL, and an Arizona female with a SVL of 56.8 cm contained eight oviductal eggs (Goldberg 1995a). The testes of a March and three May males were regressed, and sperm production occurred in others during August–October. Apparently the sperm is stored over winter in the vas deferens for use in spring matings (Goldberg 1995a).

April courtship and mating by *S. g. lineata* were observed at the Gladys Porter Zoo by Burchfield et al. (1982). When a male was placed into the cage of a female, she became excited and crawled rapidly away from him. This stimulated rapid breathing and much tongue flicking in the male. He then chased the female, but did not at first try to align himself beside her. He did, however, stop several times and twitch his tail from side to side. After four to five minutes of such behavior, the male moved forward along the female's back; when his head was parallel with and 2–3 cm above the female's head, he crawled an additional 9–12 cm forward, looped his neck to the right, turned his head to the left, and seized the female by the head. A series of undulations of his body at the level of the anal vent allowed his tail to search for her cloacal opening. After two to three minutes, the female elevated her tail, and the male aligned their tails and inserted his hemipenis. A slow lateral twitching of the entwined tails followed. Contractions in the male precloacal area occurred every 10–15 seconds, and the copulation lasted 45 minutes. A second mating following similar courtship behavior lasted 30 minutes.

Ovipositions have been observed from 1 April to 3 July, and clutches contain 3–10 (mean, 7) eggs. The elliptical eggs are white with leathery shells, and some in each clutch are adherent. Eggs are 24.1–40.0 (mean, 31.3) mm long and 13.0–15.9 (mean, 14.7) mm wide, and weigh 3.4–4.2 (mean, 3.8) g. The IP lasts 90–132 (mean, 107) days (unfortunately, ITs are not available). Most reported hatchings have taken place from 1 to 28 August, but one clutch hatched on 10–12 October (Degenhardt et al. 1996). Hatching success averages 55.8 (0–100) %. Hatchlings are similar to adults in color and pattern, are 21.6–29.0 (mean, 25.3) cm long, and weigh 1.8–3.2 (mean, 2.5) g.

GROWTH AND LONGEVITY. No data have been reported regarding either growth or life expectancy of the species.

DIET AND FEEDING BEHAVIOR. *S. grahamiae* is an active forager that apparently uses vision and odor to find its food. Behavior in captivity has shown that it can follow a scent trail left by lizards and small snakes and that the snake also detects buried reptile eggs by their odor (Blair 1960). Reptile eggs and other small, buried prey are excavated with the enlarged rostral scale. Larger prey detected visually on the surface are chased, seized, and swallowed. Taub (1967) found its Duvernoy's gland either to be purely serous or to have some mucous cells intermingled with the serous cells; since it also has enlarged rear maxillary teeth, Vermersch and Kuntz (1986) suspected *S. grahamiae* produces toxic saliva capable of immobilizing prey, but this has not been proven.

The chief prey are "cold-blooded": lizards *(Cnemidophorus, Sceloporus),* small snakes *(Sonora semiannulata),* and small frogs, for example; but small mammals and even birds may occasionally be taken (Blair 1960; Fowlie 1965; Minton 1959; Ramírez-Bautista et al. 2000b; Stebbins 1985; Tennant 1984; Vermersch and Kuntz 1986; Wright and Wright 1957). *S. grahamiae* is also an important predator on reptile eggs, and may excavate and destroy up to 75% of the eggs of the Texas spiny lizard *(Sceloporus olivaceus)* in one season (Blair 1960). Toads and their eggs are probably avoided since a *S. g. lineata* died in less than four hours after being fed eggs of a Gulf Coast toad *(Bufo valliceps),* and the toxic parotoid gland secretions of a ma-

rine toad *(Bufo marinus)* killed another in less than 2.5 hours (Licht 1968; Licht and Low 1968).

PREDATORS AND DEFENSE.   No information on predation has been reported, but surely this snake is eaten by a variety of larger ophiophagous snakes, birds, and mammals. Many are killed on roads each year.

If it cannot escape, *S. grahamiae* can put up a spirited fight: it coils, vibrates its tail, and strikes. If given an opportunity to crawl into brush, it can be very difficult to extract, and when crawling through grass or other vegetation, its striped pattern deceives the onlooker as to how fast it is moving.

POPULATIONS.   *S. grahamiae* is widely distributed and is not uncommon in the right habitat. Vermersch (in Vermersch and Kuntz 1986) found 35 under debris at a site in south San Antonio.

REMARKS.   A thorough study of the life history of this species would contribute valuable data. The taxonomy of *S. grahamiae* has not been reviewed since Schmidt (1940).

Salvadora hexalepis (Cope 1866) | Western Patch-nosed Snake

RECOGNITION.   Like the first two species of patch-nosed snakes, *S. hexalepis* (TBL to 116.8 cm) has a raised rostral scale and dark longitudinal stripes on its yellow or beige body. It differs from the other two *Salvadora* by having the dark dorsolateral stripes subdivided into two stripes, a narrow one on dorsal scale row three or four, and a broader one on rows six and seven. The medial, pale area between the dark stripes is normally only three scales wide (sometimes only two), and it may be obscured by faint crossbands. The venter is white with no dark markings, and in some individuals it is yellow or orangish toward the tail. The top of the head is unmarked; the pupils are round; and the large, raised and curved rostral scale has a free, slightly projecting, flap on each side. Dorsal body scales are smooth (except a few near the vent that may bear keels in adults) with indistinct apical

pits, and occur in 17–19 anterior rows, 15–17 midbody rows, and 13 rows near the tail. Beneath are 187–215 ventrals, 73–99 subcaudals, and a divided anal plate. Laterally on the head are 2 nasals (partially divided by the nostril), 2–4 (1) loreals, 1–2 preoculars, 2 (3) postoculars, 2–3 + 2–3 temporals, 9 (8–10) supralabials, and 10–11 (8–12) infralabials. Subocular scales may also be present. The two posterior chin shields are usually separated by two to three scales. The hemipenis is essentially like that described for *S. deserticola* and *S. grahamiae*. Occurring from anterior to posterior on the maxilla are 9–17 teeth, a diastema, and 3 larger teeth.

The larger males have 187–202 ventrals, and they may have noticeably keeled dorsal body scales near the anal vent; the shorter females have 200–215 ventrals and smooth or only faintly keeled dorsal body scales.

Desert patch-nosed snake,
Salvadora hexalepis hexalepis.
(Photograph by R. D. Bartlett)

GEOGRAPHIC VARIATION. Three subspecies are recognized in the United States, and a fourth occurs in Mexico. The desert patch-nosed snake, *S. h. hexalepis* (Cope 1866), is found from the lower Mojave Desert in southeastern California south to northwestern Sonora and northeastern Baja California. It has more than one loreal, only one supralabial reaching the orbit, the dorsal surface of the head gray, and the medial light area between the dorsolateral stripes three scales wide. The Mojave patch-nosed snake, *S. h. mojavensis* Bogert 1945, occurs from northwestern Nevada and Lassen County, California, south to southern Utah, northern and western Arizona, and the upper Mojave Desert of eastern California. It has one to two loreal scales, no supralabials entering the orbit (prevented from doing so by the presence of subocular scales), the dorsal surface of the head the same color as the back, and the area between the dorsolateral stripes three scales wide. The coast patch-nosed snake, *S. h. virgultea* (Bogert 1935), ranges from southwestern California to northwestern Baja California. Its has two to four loreals, usually only one supralabial entering the orbit, the dorsal surface of the head brown, and the area between the dorsolateral stripes only one to two scales wide.

CONFUSING SPECIES. See the above key to distinguish *S. deserticola* and *S. grahamiae*. Garter and ribbon snakes *(Thamnophis)* and lined snakes *(Tropidoclonian)* are striped, but the stripes are either white, cream, yellow, or orange, not dark brown or black, and they have keeled scales and an undivided anal plate.

KARYOTYPE. Undescribed.

FOSSIL RECORD. See account of *Salvadora deserticola.*

DISTRIBUTION. The species is distributed from northwestern Nevada and adjacent Lassen County, California, south to southern Utah, northern and western Arizona, and southern California in the United States, and in northwestern Sonora and throughout Baja California in Mexico.

HABITAT. It lives in flat deserts, rocky washes, arroyos, and canyons with sandy or sand-gravel soils and vegetation consisting of saltbush *(Atriplex)*, sagebrush, chaparral, creosote, Joshua tree, and various cacti at elevations of 240–2,100 m.

BEHAVIOR. Reported annual activity dates for *S. hexalepis* fall between February and December (Gates 1957; Wright and Wright 1957). In southern California, most surface activity is in May–June (Stebbins 1954; Wright and Wright 1957), but in Arizona most sightings are in April–June (Rosen and Lowe 1994; Vitt and Ohmart 1978). Observations on hibernating individuals have not been reported, but the winter is probably spent underground in rodent burrows, in rock crevices, or simply buried in the sand. These same sites are used as retreats in the summer (Grismer et al. 1994).

Most daily activity takes place in the morning, late afternoon, or early evening, with the majority of basking and foraging occurring before noon. Basking

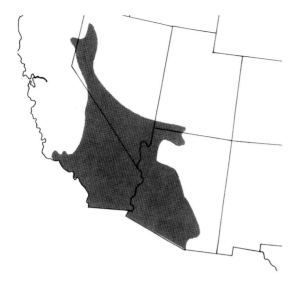

Distribution of *Salvadora hexalepis*.

individuals stretch out or coil their bodies to take advantage of the morning sun. Data collected during laboratory tests on a combined sample of *S. hexalepis* and *S. deserticola* by Jacobson and Whitford (1971) revealed a mean preferred BT of 33°C, with a range of observed BTs of 30.2–34.5°C. The mean CT_{min} is 7.0 (6.5–8.0) °C, and when AT drops below 20°C, the snake burrows into the soil. The mean CT_{max} is 43.8 (42.5–45.0) °C. At BTs of 33–37°C, it becomes hyperactive, and at BTs above 39°C it burrows. Burrowing is accomplished by thrusting the head into a hole scraped by the enlarged rostral scale, bending the neck S-shaped, and withdrawing and pushing back the loose soil with the neck loop (Pack 1930). Brattstrom (1965) found that a *S. hexalepis* crawling slowly in the shadow of a parked car had a BT of 37.5°C when the AT was 33°C, and the STs of the soil and desert road were 40°C.

S. hexalepis is capable of crawling at a maximum speed of 0.64 m/second (2.31 km/hour), but normal prowling speed is 0.10 m/second (0.36 km/hour) (Mosauer 1935b). Although foraging is done at ground level, *S. hexalepis* does occasionally climb into low trees and shrubs.

REPRODUCTION. Wright and Wright (1957) reported the minimum adult TBL of *S. hexalepis* as 50.8 cm, and Stebbins (1985) reported it to be 55 cm. The smallest male undergoing spermiogenesis and the smallest female with oviductal eggs examined by Goldberg (1995a) had SVLs of 46.8 cm and 58.4 cm, respectively.

The testicular and ovarian cycles were studied by Goldberg (1995a). The male testes are regressed over the winter when sperm are stored in the vas deferens. Recrudescence occurs in April–June. Spermiogenesis occurs in some males as early as May, but the primary period for sperm production is July–October. During regression, the seminiferous tubules contain spermatogonia and Sertoli cells. During recrudescence, spermatogonia begin to divide, producing primary and secondary spermatocytes and spermatids. Spermiogenesis is characterized by metamorphosing spermatids and mature sperm. Females have 7–9 mm follicles in early May, and oviductal eggs by early June. Mating occurs in April–June (Stebbins 1985). Nothing is known of the courtship and copulatory behavior or of the nest site conditions favored by this snake.

Clutches contain 3–10 (mean, 5.8) eggs, and clutch size is positively correlated to female body size. The elongated white eggs have parchmentlike shells and are 16–40 (mean, 26.2) × 9–12 (mean, 10.5) mm. Eggs are composed of 10.7% ash and 61.4% water, and contain 6.4 calories/mg of egg mass (Vitt 1978). Hatching probably takes place from late August to late October, depending on latitude; Gates (1957) reported hatching dates of 21 September to 23 October in southern Arizona. The only IP reported is 85 days for a clutch kept at "room temperature" (Perkins 1952). Hatchlings are probably about 25 cm in TBL.

GROWTH AND LONGEVITY. Wright and Wright (1957) thought 30.0–34.8 cm juveniles to be 5.0–7.5 cm beyond hatching size. A wild-caught adult male survived 14 years, 3 months, and 20 days at the San Diego Zoo (Snider and Bowler 1992).

DIET AND FEEDING HABITS. *S. hexalepis* is an active, diurnal forager that searches for its prey among rocks and vegetation. Probably both vision and olfaction are used to find prey, and when the animal is detected the snake quickly pursues it, sometimes with its head held off the ground while crawling. The prey is seized, worked into position, then swallowed, usually head first. No venom or constriction is used to subdue prey.

Lizards *(Cnemidophorus, Coleonyx)* are the usual prey, but small snakes, reptile eggs, and small rodents *(Dipodomys)* are also taken (Brown 1997; Cunningham 1959; Perkins 1938; Stebbins 1954). In addition, captives have eaten *Callisaurus* lizards (Gates 1957).

Vitt (1978) reported that the mean amount of calories per milligram of body weight for *S. hexalepis* is 5.5, and the body is composed of 21.8% ash and 74.1% water, which must be maintained by its diet.

PREDATORS AND DEFENSE. No reports of predation on this species have been published, but larger ophiophagous snakes, hawks, and carnivorous mammals probably eat them. Motorized vehicles may take a heavy toll where it is populous (Rosen and Lowe 1994).

Defensively, *S. hexalepis* uses two strategies. It may flee when disturbed. It is capable of crawling fast, and its striped pattern helps to conceal how rapidly it is moving. However, it may also lie motionless when detected, perhaps relying on its light color and pattern to conceal it. When handled the snake may bite and spray musk.

POPULATIONS. *S. hexalepis* is often common in proper habitat; Rosen and Lowe (1994) reported it constituted 7.3% of all the snakes they observed along a road in Arizona during a four-year study. Elsewhere it may be rare or declining; it is protected as a species of special concern in Utah.

REMARKS. For a snake that is common in some areas, relatively little has been reported concerning its life history. A thorough ecological and behavioral study would be helpful.

Seminatrix pygaea (Cope 1871) | Black Swamp Snake

RECOGNITION. *S. pygaea* (TBL to 55.5 cm, but most are shorter than 40.0 cm) has an unpatterned, shiny, black dorsum, and a red venter with black bars or triangular blotches at the anterior border of each ventral scute. Dorsal body scales on the lowest lateral rows have a pale streak resembling a keel. Buff to greenish yellow pigment is often present on the labials, and the chin may be brownish. Dorsal body scales are smooth and pitless, and lie in 17 (19) anterior rows, 17 rows at midbody, and 15 (14, 17) rows near the vent. The venter has 112–141 ventrals, 35–56 subcaudals, and a divided anal plate. Lateral head scales include 1 nasal, 1 loreal, 1 (2) preocular(s), 2 (1–3) postoculars, 1 + 2 temporals, 8 (6–10) supralabials, and 9 (7–11) infralabials. The spiny, unforked hemipenis has a single sulcus spermaticus with inconspicuous lips, two lateral basal hooks, and indistinct groups of enlarged spines near the base of the shaft. Each maxilla has 19–21 teeth; those most posterior are slightly longer.

The smaller males have 40–56 (mean, 50) subcaudals and TLs 18–25 (mean, 21) % of TBL; the longer, heavier females have 35–49 (mean, 40) subcaudals, and TLs 15–20 (mean, 17) % of TBL.

GEOGRAPHIC VARIATION. Three subspecies are recognized. *Seminatrix p. pygaea* (Cope 1871), the North Florida swamp snake, ranges from the Savannah River south to Pasco, Lake, and Orange counties, Florida, and west to Santa Rosa County, Florida, and Covington and Escambia counties, Alabama. Its red

Carolina swamp snake, *Seminatrix pygaea paludis*; Brunswick County, North Carolina. (Photograph by Roger W. Barbour)

venter is immaculate or has a pair of long, narrow, curved black bars at the anterior border of each of its 118–128 ventrals. *S. p. cyclas* Dowling 1950, the South Florida swamp snake, occurs in southern peninsular Florida. It has a short triangular-shaped black blotch at the anterior border of each of its 118 or fewer ventrals. *S. p. paludis* Dowling 1950, the Carolina swamp snake, is found from Albemarle Sound, North Carolina south along the Atlantic Coastal Plain to the Savannah River in South Carolina. It has a pair of heavy black bars at the anterior border of each of its 127 or more ventrals.

CONFUSING SPECIES. The red-bellied snake *(Storeria occipitomaculata)* and the various *Nerodia* have keeled dorsal body scales. The mud snake *(Farancia abacura)* has a terminal tail spine, and red pigment on its labials.

KARYOTYPE AND FOSSIL RECORD. Unreported.

DISTRIBUTION. *S. pygaea* ranges from Albermarle Sound in northeastern North Carolina south along the Atlantic Coastal Plain through peninsular Florida, and west through the panhandle of Florida to adjacent southern Alabama.

HABITAT. This highly aquatic snake inhabits many types of bodies of water with abundant aquatic vegetation: cyprus swamps, marshes, lakes, ponds, slow-flowing streams and rivers, sloughs, and canals. It is tolerant of brackish water and has been found in salt marshes in South Carolina, Georgia, and Florida (Neill 1958), and the authors have taken it from North Carolina tidal waters. It frequently burrows within mats of aquatic vegetation *(Eichhornia, Nuphar, Pontederia, Sagittaria),* and the best collection method is to rake out mats of floating vegetation, particularly water hyacinths *(Eichhornia crassipes).* When on land, it seldom ventures far from water, and is most often found beneath logs or plant debris.

BEHAVIOR. *S. pygaea* is probably active all year in southern Florida, but in northern Florida, Dodd (1993) found active individuals in all months but November and captured 49% of the snakes in the spring. North of Florida *S. pygaea* hibernates and is normally

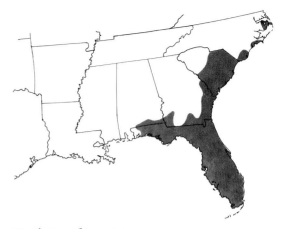

Distribution of *Seminatrix pygaea.*

active from late March–April to late October–early November. Near Aiken, South Carolina, where the snake is rarely trapped if the minimum WT is below 16°C, it is active from March through December (Gibbons and Semlitsch 1991). Males are usually active first in the spring, with females most active in May–June. Most activity takes place in shallow water along the shoreline.

During extended periods of cold weather, *S. pygaea* may leave the water and seek shelter under debris on the bank (Dowling 1950), and in winter it itself buries as deep as 60 cm (Carr 1940) in mud, sphagnum, or plant debris. It occasionally occupies mole cricket burrows (Scudder 1972) and round-tailed muskrat *(Neofiber)* lodges (Smith and Franz 1994).

Seminatrix is very secretive and mostly nocturnal, although the authors have found a few on land in the early morning and on roads during daytime rains. Warm rainy nights also stimulate this snake to move overland. Dodd (1993) observed movements on 52 days without rainfall during the previous 24 hours, and on 26 days when rain had fallen in the previous 24 hours (but only on four of those days did rainfall exceed 15 mm). Overcast conditions occurred on only 16 (34%) of 47 spring days when he captured active *S. pygaea.* The snakes moved both at high ATs (12–31°C; mean, 23.5°C), and low ATs (2–25°C; mean, 18.5°C). Overall, however, temperature and rainfall did not have much influence on terrestrial activity. *S. pygaea* seldom basks.

Severe drought may cause this snake to move to another body of water (Seigel et al. 1995b), and often it is juveniles who make such overland journeys, as adults burrow into the mud bottom of the drying body of water. However, both Dodd (1993) and Seigel et al. (1995b) thought that drought had little direct effect on overland migration and that emigration is more a response to prey decline. Movement orientation is directed to and from the nearest large body of water (Dodd 1993).

REPRODUCTION. Definitive data are lacking for both sexes as to age and size at attainment of maturity, but the female reproductive cycle has been studied (Dowling 1950; Sever and Ryan 1999; Sever et al. 1999, 2000; Seigel et al. 1995a). The oviduct contains four distinct regions, from anterior to posterior: an anterior infundibulum, a posterior infundibulum (containing sperm storage tubules), a uterus, and a vagina. Throughout, the oviduct the lining is composed of simple epithelial, cuboidal, or columnar tissue with invaginations forming both simple and compound tubular glands except in the anterior infundibulum and posterior vagina. The tubular glands are not areolar, and their linings are mere continuations of the oviduct lining with no additional specializations. The tissues lining the anterior infundibulum and vagina are irregular, and vary from squamous to columnar. Their cells are either ciliated or secretory. The secretory product of the infundibulum consists of lipids, while that of the vagina contains mostly glycoproteins (both products are also found in the other two regions of the oviduct). Glands in the uterus are simple tubes. Secretions produced in the sperm storage cells contain mucoproteins, and the lining contains many drops of lipids.

Rapid follicular vitellogenesis and growth occurs in the spring, ovulation usually takes place in June, and most young are born in August. Dowling (1950) examined the ovaries of females from Alachua County, Florida, and found 1–4 mm follicles throughout the year in females longer than 18 cm. Females shorter than 18 cm were probably immature, although a 15 cm female contained visible follicles. The largest female with undeveloped follicles was 35.5 cm, and the smallest with enlarged follicles was 24 cm. Females collected in the spring showed some follicular growth: April, 5 mm; May, nearly 10 mm, but without visible embryos; and June, 12–16 mm, with embryos. A fe-

male taken in July had seven well-formed young that would probably have been born in early August.

Courtship/mating behaviors have not been described, but females have contained sperm in their oviducts on 14 May and 9 June (Sever and Ryan 1999). So this ovoviviparous snake probably mates in the spring or early summer, although Ashton and Ashton (1981) reported possible fall mating. The sperm form tangled masses in the oviductal lumen and glands in the region of the sperm storage tubules. A carrier matrix composed of sloughed epithelial cells, a glycoprotein colloid, lipids, membranous structures, and possibly phagocytes surrounds the migrating sperm in the posterior uterus (Sever et al. 1999, 2000).

The 2–15 (mean, 7.9; n = 22 litters) young (Dowling 1950; Seigel et al. 1995a) are born from late July to mid-October, most frequently in August. Most females reproduce annually (Seigel et al. 1995a), and although litter size varies from year to year depending on resource availability, it is correlated to female SVL (Seigel et al. 1995a). Neonates have 13.5–16.5 (mean, 14.2; n = 15) cm TBLs and weigh 1.0–1.3 (mean, 1.2; n = 8) g.

GROWTH AND LONGEVITY. The only character to vary with age, other than body length, is the relationship of TL to TBL. The probable TL at any size can be obtained by the regression equations $0.287 \times$ TBL $- 0.588$ for males, and $0.204 \times$ TBL $+ 2.979$ for females (Dowling 1950). Longevity has not been reported, but the authors maintained captives for almost two years.

DIET AND FEEDING HABITS. Most foraging is probably aquatic and nocturnal, although the authors' captives have shown they can swallow food when out of the water. Prey is usually ingested head first. Animals eaten by wild and captive *S. pygaea* include worms (earthworms, leeches, oligochaetes), small fish (*Carassius auratus, Gambusia affinis, Lepomis* sp., *Poecilia latipinna*), anurans (*Acris gryllus, Bufo* sp., *Rana sphenocephala*), salamanders (*Ambystoma talpoideum, Desmognathus fuscus, Plethodon cinereus*), dwarf sirens (*Pseudobranchus striatus*), and small arthropods (Brown 1979a; Dowling 1950; C. Ernst, pers. obs.; Gibbons and Semlitsch 1991; Mills et al. 2000; Palmer and Braswell 1995; Rossman 1956; Tennant 1997).

PREDATORS AND DEFENSE. Large fish *(Micropterus salmoides)*, ophiophagous snakes *(Lampropeltis getula, Micrurus fulvius)*, bald eagles *(Haliaeetus leucocephalus)*, great blue herons *(Ardea herodius)*, armadillos *(Dasypus novemcinctus)*, and crayfish *(Procambarus* sp.) are known predators (Aycrigg et al. 1996; Dowling 1950; Godley 1982; Greene 1984; Kean and Tuberville 1995; Ross 1989).

Flight is this snake's best defense; it rarely bites, but may expel musk if handled.

POPULATIONS. *S. pygaea,* although secretive, is still common in specific localities, but its population dynamics have been little studied. The sex ratio of 225 captured near Aiken, South Carolina, was 1:1 (Gib-

bons and Semlitsch 1991). At a site in Putnam County, Florida, Dodd (1993) recorded 123 black swamp snakes from 1985 through 1990. Most had 10–25 cm SVLs, and 89% were juveniles shorter than 24 cm. For those that could be accurately sexed, the male-female ratio was 0.79:1.00 (not significantly different from 1:1). In South Carolina, the overall sex ratio for captive litters was 1.30:1.00 (Seigel et al. 1995a).

REMARKS. Biochemical tests have shown *S. pygaea* is most closely related to the natricines *Nerodia, Regina, Storeria, Thamnophis,* and *Tropidoclonion* (Dessauer 1967; Dowling et al. 1996; Schwaner and Dessauer 1982). The species has been reviewed by Dorcas et al. (1998) and Dowling (1950).

Senticolis triaspis (Cope 1866) | Green Rat Snake

RECOGNITION. As an adult, this slender greenish snake (maximum TBL 160 cm) has no body pattern and varies from greenish gray to green or olive. Hatchlings and juveniles are yellowish or tan with a dorsal pattern of narrow, brown, dumbbell-shaped blotches that, including those on the tail, may total over 100. Some blotches may be connected in a wavy or zigzag line or a chainlike pattern. Juveniles also have a dark brown or black head stripe, normally with a large light central area, transversely crossing the prefrontals and extending obliquely backward on each side through the orbit to the corner of the mouth. Adults usually lack this stripe. The lower portion of the supralabials, and the infralabials, chin, and throat are white to cream; the rest of the venter is yellowish. The head is distinct from the neck, and the pupils are round. Dorsal body scales are keeled with apical pits, and occur in 29 (27–33) anterior rows, 33 (30–39) midbody rows, and 21 (19–25) posterior rows. Beneath are 241–282 ventrals, 85–126 subcaudals, and a divided anal plate. On each side of the head are 2 nasals, 1 loreal, 1 (0–2) preocular(s), 2 (1–3) postoculars, 3 + 4 (5) temporals, 8 (7–9) supralabials, and 9–12 infralabials. When inverted, the subcylindrical hemipenis is 17–19 subcaudals long. It has a single sulcus spermaticus and is smooth on the proximal 20% of the shaft, followed

by two large, slightly recurved, hooklike spines; three to four rows of smaller spines distal to the large ones; and 19–24 oblique rows of papillate calyxes decreasing in size toward the tip, but continuous to the tip of the organ. Each maxilla has 19–24 (usually 21–22) recurved teeth, with the shortest teeth toward the rear.

The shorter males have 241–264 ventrals, 95–126 subcaudals, and TLs 30–35% of SVL; females have longer bodies, 256–282 ventrals, 85–110 subcaudals, and TLs 23–26% of SVL.

GEOGRAPHIC VARIATION. Three subspecies have been described (Dowling 1960; Price 1991), but only one, the northern green rat snake, *S. t. intermedia* (Boettger 1883), described above, is present north of the Mexico. It ranges from southeastern Arizona and southwestern New Mexico south through Mexico to Guatemala, but the range does not include the central plateau or the Yucatan Peninsula.

CONFUSING SPECIES. The corn snake *(Elaphe guttata)* may be confused with juvenile *S. triaspis,* but it has body blotches throughout its life, a pointed, dark mark between its eyes formed by the uniting of two dark longitudinal neck blotches, 25–31 midbody scale rows, and square, black blotches on the venter. The

Green rat snake, *Senticolis triaspis intermedia*; Chiricahua Mountains, Arizona. (Photograph by John H. Tashjian, Arizona-Sonora Desert Museum)

smooth green snake *(Liochlorophis vernalis)* has smooth body scales in approximately 15 rows at midbody, and usually only seven subralabials. Whipsnakes *(Masticophis)* and the racer *(Coluber constrictor)* have a prefrontal scale that invades the supralabial row, and smooth body scales. The lyre snake *(Trimorphodon biscutatus)* has vertical pupils, a distinct or indistinct lyre- or V-shaped head mark, and brown spots on the venter, and some have a single anal plate.

KARYOTYPE AND FOSSIL RECORD.   Unknown.

DISTRIBUTION.   *Senticolis* ranges from southeastern Arizona (Cochise, Pima, and Santa Cruz counties), southwestern New Mexico (Hidalgo County), and Tamaulipas southward through Mexico and Central America to Costa Rica.

HABITAT.   In the United States, it is a resident of rocky hillsides and the riparian zones of streams in up-

lands with elevations to about 2,000 m. Vegetation at these sites varies from wild grape, chaparral, and thornbush to pine, oak, sycamore, walnut, cottonwood, and willow.

BEHAVIOR.   Almost nothing is known of the everyday behavior of *S. triaspis*. It has been collected or observed from April through early November in the United States and northern Mexico. Cranston (1989a) found it most active in the afternoon and evening between 1700 and 2030 hours, but it has also been collected as early as 1645 hours and as late as 2100 hours, and from 0300 until 1030 hours. The preferred BT is 25°C, and this snake becomes torpid at a BT of 10–13°C (Cranston 1989a). Nothing is known of the overwintering habits in Arizona or New Mexico, but it probably hibernates for at least short periods each winter. In captivity, it can be induced to hibernate at a BT of 15°C (Cranston 1989a), and a cooling period seems necessary for successful reproduction.

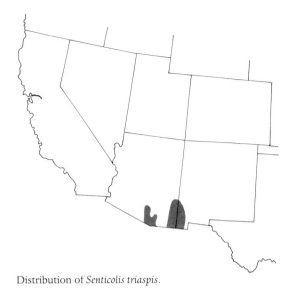

Distribution of *Senticolis triaspis*.

This species is good climber that spends much time in shrubs and low trees.

REPRODUCTION. Female *S. t. triaspis* from the Yucatan Peninsula of Mexico are mature at a SVL of 62.5 cm when about two years of age (Censky and McCoy 1988); size and age of maturity in both sexes of *S. t. intermedia* from the United States are unknown.

Censky and McCoy (1988) found that mature females from Yucatan contained five size classes of ovarian follicles: class I, < 1.0 mm diameter; class II, 1.1–3.0 mm; class III, 3.1–8.0 mm; class IV, 8.1–33.5 mm; and class V, 33.6+ mm in diameter. Oviductal eggs were larger than 35.0 mm. No seasonal reproductive pattern is evident, and at least in the tropics, this snake reproduces throughout the year. Yucatan females with follicles 30 mm or larger were found in March and November, a female had oviductal eggs in September, and females with stretched oviducts indicating recent oviposition were taken in November and February (Censky and McCoy 1988). Dowling (1960) reported that another Yucatan female had oviductal eggs in October. Captives of the tropical subspecies *S. t. mutablis* mate irregularly throughout the year and produce two clutches per year (Schulz 1992b, 1996).

Arizona *S. t. intermedia* apparently mate only in the spring, as courtship and mating activity in captives have been observed from 16 March to 1 May (Cranston 1989a, 1989b), and produce only one clutch per year in June or July (Cranston 1989b; Rossi and Rossi 1995; Schulz 1996). When courting the male crawls over the female's back with a forward jerking motion (Schulz 1992b).

Cranston (1989b) reported the GP as 68–84 days. Clutches contain two to nine (mean, 4.6) eggs (Censky and McCoy 1988; Cranston 1989a, 1989b; Dowling 1960; Rossi and Rossi 1995; Schulz 1992b, 1996). Clutch size does not seem related to female body length. The elongated, white, adherent eggs are usually 35.0–42.0 (mean, 37.6) mm long, but Rossi and Rossi (1995) reported a clutch of four eggs that averaged 76.3 mm in length and 29.5 mm in width. Cranston (1989b) reported a fertility rate of only 29%, but other breeders have recorded 100% fertility (Barry, in Rossi and Rossi 1995); the fertility rate of wild clutches is probably closer to 100%. RCM is 0.25–0.30.

Hatching occurs after an IP of 25–100 (average, 53) days, depending on the IT. Schulz (1996) reported an apparent case of sperm storage in a female *S. t. mutabilis* that had last mated on 5 March, and produced a clutch of five eggs on 6 June, which hatched on 29–30 August. On 9 October she laid a second clutch of four eggs, seven months after mating. Sperm storage could be an adaptation to assure fertilization in snakes that have the sexes separated for much of the year.

Hatchlings are described under RECOGNITION. They have 28.0–40.0 (mean, 34.7) cm TBLs and weigh 9.3–22.5 (mean, 17.5) g.

GROWTH AND LONGEVITY. Schulz (1992b) reported a 40 cm captive grew to 75 cm from 1989 to January 1991. No data on growth of wild individuals are available.

A *S. t. intermedia,* hatched in captivity, survived 19 years, 9 months, and 22 days in a private collection (Snider and Bowler 1992).

DIET AND FEEDING HABITS. Little has been reported regarding foraging behavior of wild green rat snakes, but they are probably active hunters, both on the ground and in shrubs and trees. It is a constrictor. Adults feed mostly on warm-blooded prey (mammals and birds), but juveniles prey mostly on lizards and possibly small mice (Schulz 1996). Reported wild prey includes woodrats *(Neotoma),* mice *(Mus, Peromyscus),* bats *(Glossophaga soricina),* birds, and lizards (Cranston 1989a; Duellman 1958b; Fowlie 1965; Mankins et al.

1965; Schulz 1996; Stebbins 1954). Captives will eat mice and birds (Rossi and Rossi 1995).

PREDATORS AND DEFENSE.   No data on predation are available. Wild green rat snakes are very nervous and will strike and bite when threatened.

POPULATIONS.   No data on dynamics of wild populations have been reported. The green rat snake is considered endangered in New Mexico.

REMARKS.   *Senticolis* belongs to the colubrid tribe Lampropeltini (Rodriquez-Robles and Jesus-Escobar

1999). *S. triaspis* is distinguished from its sister American rat snake genera *Bogertophis* and *Elaphe* by its unique hemipenis (see RECOGNITION); large numbers of dorsal scale rows and ventral scutes; and pointed, anteriorly projecting, almost as long as high, prefrontal bone (Dowling 1958a; Dowling and Fries 1987). On these bases, Dowling and Fries (1987) created the genus *Senticolis* and removed it from *Elaphe*, but this new designation has not been universally accepted (see Schulz 1996). The species has been reviewed by Dowling (1960), Dowling and Fries (1987), and Schulz (1996).

Sonora semiannulata Baird and Girard 1853 | Ground Snake

RECOGNITION.   Body color of this small snake (TBL to 38.4 cm, but most individuals are 18–32 cm) varies from gray to greenish or bluish gray, tan, brown, pink, or even orange. Individuals may also have either dark or light heads. Furthermore, the dark body pattern is extremely variable. Most have a series of light or dark brown, black, or orange bands crossing the back and sides, but not the venter; however, the number of bands (12–37), width of individual bands (narrow or broad), and shape of bands (straight-sided or saddle-shaped) is not constant within populations. Some ground snakes have the bands reduced to a single dark collar on the nape, others are plain with no dark marks, and still others (in the lower Colorado River watershed) lack dark marks but do have a bold pink, red, or orange vertebral stripe. Patterned snakes have dark pigment anteriorly on each dorsal scale, particularly along the sides. The venter is whitish to cream and lacks dark pigmentation, but the underside of the tail may be more vividly colored and have dark crossbands. Dorsal body scales are smooth, shiny, and pitless, and lie in 13–16 (mean, 14) anterior rows, 14–16 (mean, 15) rows at midbody, and 13–15 (mean, 14) rows near the vent. Present are 126–186 ventrals, 31–61 subcaudals, and a divided anal plate. The head is only slightly broader than the neck; the snout and black pupil are round. Lateral head scales include 1 nasal, 1 loreal, 1 preocular, 2 postoculars, 1 + 2 (1) temporals, 7 (rarely

6) supralabials, and 7 (6–8) infralabials. The hemipenis is shallowly divided with a single sulcus spermaticus; the crotch between the lobes is naked; a large spine is near the base to the side of the sulcus; several rows of slightly smaller spines are above this, followed by calyxes. One or two diastemata are present on each maxilla: about 11 teeth lie anterior to the first; 3 long, laterally grooved teeth lie posterior to the second; and 3–13 teeth are present between the two diastemata.

Males have 126–168 ventrals, 37–61 subcaudals, and TLs usually more than 19% of TBL; females have 136–186 ventrals, 31–54 subcaudals, and TLs usually less than 19% of TBL in females.

GEOGRAPHIC VARIATION.   *S. semiannulata* is one of the most variable snakes in North America. As many as seven subspecies have been described based on the many differences in body color and pattern described above, but now it is considered only a quite variable species without recognizable subspecies (Frost 1983; Frost and Van Devender 1979).

CONFUSING SPECIES.   Within the ground snake's range, the only other banded snakes are the coral snake *(Micrurus fulvius)* and the long-nosed snake *(Rhinocheilus lecontei),* in which the bands are red, yellow, and black. Ring-necked snakes *(Diadophis)* have a light neck ring instead of a dark collar, and most

Ground snake, *Sonora semiannulata*; Owyhee County, Idaho. (Photograph by William Leonard)

Ground snake, *Sonora semiannulata*; Santa Cruz County, Arizona. (Photograph by Brad R. Moon)

have some dark spots on the venter. Most confusion occurs between the unpatterned *Sonora* and other small, plain snakes: the species of *Tantilla* lack a loreal scale and have the second supralabial touching or almost touching the prefrontal scale; earth snakes *(Virginia)* and brown snakes *(Storeria)* have keeled scales; and blind snakes *(Leptotyphlops)* have the ventral scales the same size and shape as the dorsal scales.

KARYOTYPE. Undescribed.

FOSSIL RECORD. A possible fossil *Sonora* was reported from the late Pliocene (Blancan) of Kansas (Brattstrom 1967), and Pleistocene (Rancholabrean) or Rancholabrean/Holocene fossils of *S. semiannulata*

are known from Arizona (Mead and Bell 1994; Mead et al. 1984; Van Devender and Mead 1978; Van Devender et al. 1977, 1991), Kansas (Preston 1979), Nevada (Mead and Bell 1994), New Mexico (Van Devender and Worthington 1977), and western Texas (Van Devender and Bradley 1994).

DISTRIBUTION. The ground snake can be found from southern Kansas and southwestern Missouri in the east and western Nevada and adjacent eastern California in the west, south through central Oklahoma, central and western Texas, southern New Mexico, and western and southern Arizona. Isolated populations are also found in north-central Kansas, southeastern Colorado, northeastern and central Utah,

Distribution of *Sonora semiannulata*.

southwestern Idaho and adjacent Oregon, and north-western Nevada. In Mexico, the snake occurs in Baja California, Chihuahua, Coahuila, Durango, Nuevo León, Sonora, and Tamaulipas.

HABITAT. *Sonora* lives in dry habitats, at elevations usually below 2,000 m, such as grasslands, desert sand flats, rocky hillsides, scrub brush, riparian bottom-lands with willows, and oak-juniper stands. Loose soil, which may be clay or sand, with or without gravel or rocks present, is required for burrowing (wet soils are avoided), and surface rocks, logs, brush piles, or trash provide necessary foraging and hiding places.

BEHAVIOR. Few studies of *S. semiannulata* have been conducted, so most knowledge of its behavior and ecology is anecdotal. It has a relatively long an-nual activity period, and active individuals have been found in every month. Duration of the annual activity period varies with latitude. In the warmer, more southern portions of the range, the snake generally emerges in late February or March and remains active to October or early November. A few individuals may be active during the period December–February, and many estivate over the hot, dry periods of July–August (Kassing 1961). Farther north, activity starts later, usually in April in Missouri and Kansas (Collins 1993; Johnson 1987), and ends earlier (September in Kansas; Collins 1993). Hibernating *Sonora* found in Oklahoma were 60 cm underground; frozen ground depth at the site is usually 43 cm (Kassing 1961).

Most active ground snakes are found at dusk or during the night, seemingly indicating a preference for nocturnal foraging, but reports of diurnal activity also exist. Daytime activity is probably more common dur-ing the cooler spring and fall than in the summer, and daylight hours are usually spent under some surface shelter or in rock crevices or cracks in the soil. In con-trast to many other southwestern nocturnal snakes, *S. semiannulata* has a round pupil instead of an ellip-tically vertical one.

Precipitation is also a major stimulus for surface ac-tivity, and many *Sonora* have been found immediately after rains. Like other small snakes, body water loss is a limiting factor to diurnal activity on hot, dry days. Monthly records kept by Kassing (1961) of capture dates of Oklahoma *Sonora* indicate most activity oc-curs during the wettest months (April–June).

Degenhardt et al. (1996) thought thermoregulation normally occurs while the snake is concealed beneath warm rocks, but they have also observed some indi-viduals basking on the surface near retreat entrances. Ground snakes are equipped with numerous, scattered touch corpuscles on their head scales that may aid in finding a suitable microhabitat for burrowing, subter-ranean activity, or foraging in the dark (Jackson 1977).

Males may engage in combat behavior, particularly if a female is nearby; Kroll (1971) observed two cap-tive males fight, apparently over a female one had been courting. The larger, courting male released the female and bit the intruding smaller male twice. The males then intertwined their bodies, beginning at the tails and proceeding toward the head, and rolled over several times. This behavioral sequence was repeated several times over the next few days, but the individual combat bouts only lasted 1–10 minutes.

REPRODUCTION.   According to Kassing (1961), both sexes become sexually mature at a TBL of 23–24 cm when probably 1.0–1.5 years old, but Wright and Wright (1957) reported males matured at 29.6 cm and females at 30.5 cm. The gonads begin to enlarge when TBL exceeds 19 cm, during or following the first spring after hatching, and females probably first oviposit when at least 24 cm during their second spring (Kassing 1961).

Most breeding behavior occurs in April–June, but Kroll (1971) observed captives copulating in March, and Anderson (1965) and Kassing (1961) reported September matings. Apparently, *S. semiannulata* do not lay down pheromone trails by which the sexes can find each other (Gehlbach et al. 1971). Courtship consists of the male rubbing his chin along the female's back (possibly he is attracted to pheromones released from her dorsal skin glands), sending caudocephalic waves along his body, biting her nape, entwining his body around her to restrain her, and inserting his hemipenis into her cloaca (Kassing 1961; Kroll 1971). Copulation may last over an hour.

Nesting has been reported from 3 June to 25 August; perhaps more than one clutch is laid per reproductive year. The three- to six-egg (mean, 3.6) clutches are probably deposited under rocks or in rock crevices. The white eggs have smooth, leathery shells, are 13–28 (mean, 22.1) × 5–9 (mean, 7.8) mm in size, and weigh 0.9–1.3 (mean, 1.07) g. The typical RCM is approximately 0.226 (Seigel and Fitch 1984). Reported IPs have averaged 56.2 (49–70) days, and at this duration most young would hatch from late July through August, but Staedeli (1964) reported that the California clutch laid on 25 August hatched 20 October.

Hatchlings are patterned like adults and have 70–127 (mean, 97) mm TBLs.

GROWTH AND LONGEVITY.   No growth data are available. An adult, wild-caught male survived five years and six months in the authors' care.

DIET AND FEEDING BEHAVIOR.   Foraging seems to be nocturnal, but no direct observations of the behavior in the wild have been reported. The captive male noted above would trail prey placed in its cage with much tongue flicking, and when it was found, he seized it immediately, worked it to the rear of his mouth, and held it there for a short period before moving the prey around to swallow it, usually, head first.

The natural diet of ground snakes consists primarily of arthropods: spiders, both adults and egg masses—black widow (*Latrodectus mactans*) and wolf spiders (Lycosidae); windscorpions (Solifugae); scorpions (*Centruroides*); centipedes *(Lithobius, Scolopendra);* and insects—beetles (Coleoptera, adults and grubs), ants (Hymenoptera, adults and eggs), moths (Lepidoptera, adults and larvae), antlions (Neuroptera), and crickets and grasshoppers (Orthoptera) (Carpenter 1958; Degenhardt et al. 1996; Kassing 1961; Wright and Wright 1957). Degenhardt (in Degenhardt et al. 1996) found a ground snake attempting to swallow a road-killed Texas banded gecko (*Coleonyx brevis*), and Stebbins (1954) reported earless lizards (*Holbrookia*) and racerunners (*Cnemidophorus*) were prey, but ingestion of vertebrate prey is probably rare. The captive the authors kept fed primarily on crickets and mealworms (*Tenebrio*), but accepted earthworms on several occasions, and once ate a small dead five-lined skink (*Eumeces fasciatus);* it refused cricket frogs (*Pseudacris*) and baby mice (*Mus*).

The slightly enlarged rear maxillary teeth are grooved, so *Sonora* may use venomous saliva to immobilize prey. This has not been substantiated, and many of the crickets swallowed by the authors' captive were alive when ingested in spite of having been chewed by the snake's back teeth.

PREDATORS AND DEFENSE.   *S. semiannulata* probably has a multitude of vertebrate predators, but little has been reported. It is the food of larger snakes *(Crotalus cerastes, Hypsiglena torquata, Lampropeltis sp., Masticophis flagellum, M. taeniatus, Micruroides euryxanthus, Micrurus fulvius, Salvadora grahamiae);* lizards *(Crotaphytus collaris);* birds; and mammals—armadillos (*Dasypus*), skunks (*Mephitis, Spilogale*), and peccaries (*Pecari*) (Baird 2000; Camper and Dixon 2000; Cliff 1954; Collins 1993; Funk 1965a; Rodríguez-Robles et al. 1999d; Ruick 1948; Tennant 1984; Vitt and Hulse 1973; Webb 1970). Storm (1947) reported that a ringnecked snake (*Diadophis punctatus*) ate a *Sonora* in captivity, and Veer et al. (1997) reported the ingestion of one by a captive *Micruroides euryxanthus*.

The ground snake is mild tempered and seldom, if ever, bites when handled. Instead, it resorts to other defensive behaviors. Although relatively slow, it will attempt to flee or enter a hiding place when first detected. If prevented from doing so, it may spray musk or play dead (by contorting its body, opening its mouth, extending the tongue, and rolling over onto its back) (Gehlbach 1970; Hillis 1977). One even formed a complete loop with its body by gripping itself with its jaws about 5 cm behind the head in an unsuccessful attempt to prevent being swallowed by a *Micruroides euryxanthus*—although the *Sonora* was bitten and chewed several times by the coral snake, it was still struggling while being ingested (Veer et al. 1997). Tennant (1984) reported *Sonora* will also hide their heads and wave their tails about to divert a predator's attention.

Accidents sometimes claim the lives of ground snakes. In dry habitats, wild fires have killed them (Simons 1989), and Woodin (1953) reported that one was apparently killed by eating poisoned grasshoppers.

POPULATIONS. *S. semiannulata* can be locally common in the right habitat. Slevin (1950) reported that 56 ground snakes were caught during mammal trapping in Imperial County, California. He visited the site (a small spit of land of approximately 457 × 12 m, it contained a grove of cottonwoods on one end, and the rest was covered with mesquite trees and bordered by a heavy growth of willows and arrowweed) and in two days collected 53 more individuals. In contrast, Fitch (1993) found the species to represent only 2.75% of the snakes recorded at nine Kansas sites, and *Sonora* represented only 1.3% of the records during a four-year study of snakes found on a road in New Mexico (Price and LaPointe 1990).

Sonora is protected in Oregon, and also considered a species of special concern in Arkansas.

REMARKS. *S. semiannulata* was reviewed by Frost (1983).

Stilosoma extenuatum Brown 1890 | Short-tailed Snake

RECOGNITION. This extremely slender, cylindrical snake (to 65.5 cm TBL) has a TL of only 7–12% of its TBL. The body color is gray to silver gray with 50–80 dark brown or black lateral and dorsal blotches, and many have areas of yellow, orange, or red pigment separating the dorsal blotches. The tail has 8–16 similar blotches. The short, somewhat pointed head has a dark triangular or Y-shaped mark with a yellow orange center on the crown and a black postocular stripe; a distinct neck is lacking, and many black speckles dot the chin. The eyes are small, with a round pupil. The venter is gray to brown with white spots and flecks, and many of the dark lateral blotches extend onto the ventral surface, some reaching almost to the midline. The body scales are smooth and pitless, and are arranged in 19 anterior and midbody rows and 17 posterior rows. On the underside are 223–277 ventrals, 33–48 subcaudals, and an undivided anal plate. Laterally on the head are a single nasal scute with a central nostril, 0 loreals, 1 (0) preocular(s), 2 postoculars, 0 + 1 + 1 temporals (the anterior

separated from the postoculars by the parietal scale), usually 6 supralabials, and 5–8 infralabials. The rostral scale is prominent, and the internasals and prefrontals may fuse. The short (length 7–8 subcaudals) hemipenis is slightly clavate with a simple dextrally centrifugal sulcus spermaticus. The proximal portion of the shaft is naked, while the distal portion has spinules that rapidly graduate into about six rows of short spines, and the apex has one to two rows of large, irregular calyxes. Each maxilla has 10–11 short, stout, recurved and subequal teeth.

Females have 256–277 ventrals and 33–45 subcaudals; males 223–261 ventrals and 38–48 subcaudals. Females also have significantly longer TLs (9.5–14.1% of TBL) than males (8.8–12.1% of TBL).

GEOGRAPHIC VARIATION. No subspecies are recognized; see Highton (1956, 1976) and Woolfenden (1962) for discussions of discordant variation in the known geographically variable characters of this species.

Short-tailed snake, *Stilosoma extenuatum*; Marion County, Florida. (Photograph by Roger W. Barbour)

CONFUSING SPECIES. No other Florida snake has such a short tail. The mole kingsnake (*Lampropeltis calligaster*) has a brownish body and lacks an orangish vertebral stripe. The corn snake *(Elaphe guttata)* has an orangish body color, a spearpoint-like mark on its crown, a checkered belly, and a divided anal plate.

KARYOTYPE. The diploid number of chromosomes is 36 (Keogh 1996).

FOSSIL RECORD. A mid-Pliocene (Hemphillian) fossil from Alachua County, Florida, named *Stilosoma vetustum* by Auffenberg (1963), may be of this species, and another Pleistocene (Rancholabrean) vertebra from Alachua County seems to be *S. extenuatum*. Meylan (1982) has found vertebrae of *S. extenuatum* in early Pleistocene (Irvingtonian) deposits from Citrus County, Florida.

DISTRIBUTION. The species occurs from north and central peninsular Florida west of the St. Johns River from Suwannee and Columbia Counties southward to Highlands County.

HABITAT. This is a fossorial, xeric-adapted, upland snake occurring most frequently in the fine or sandy soils of longleaf pine–turkey oak woods or occasionally in xeric oak hammocks. Campbell and Christman (1982) reported that short-tailed snakes are more abundant in early successional stages in pine scrub than in the advanced stages with a full pine canopy, dense evergreen shrub layer, and matted ground cover. *Tantilla relicta*, believed to be the short-tailed snake's principal food, is also plentiful in such habitats.

BEHAVIOR. The habits of this secretive snake are poorly known, and few specimens reside in museum collections. Apparently it spends most of its life burrowed beneath sandy soil. Woolfenden (1962) reported that they enter the sand by pressing the nose against it and moving the head up and down. Once buried they use lateral undulations of the body to move through the sand.

Distribution of *Stilosoma extenuatum*.

Specimens have been taken between 25 January (Carr 1934) and 19 November (Highton 1956). It is seldom seen above ground except in spring (April) and fall (October); however, *Stilosoma* is probably active all year, weather permitting. Ashton and Ashton (1981) reported they are sometimes found in late fall under objects or leaf litter. On a daily basis, most activity is nocturnal.

REPRODUCTION. *Stilosoma* is apparently oviparous (Wright and Wright 1957), but the eggs have not been described. Most likely they are laid in underground burrows. Juvenile museum specimens resemble adults in pattern and coloration.

GROWTH AND LONGEVITY. A female *Stilosoma* captured in Gainesville, Florida, on 4 April (TBL 21.5 cm, SVL 19 cm) had an umbilical scar, suggesting the snake had hatched that spring or the previous fall; she grew 2.3 cm during five months in captivity (Rossi and Rossi 1993).

DIET AND FEEDING HABITS. *Stilosoma* is predominantly a snake eater, and *Tantilla relicta* may be its principal natural prey (Mushinsky 1984). Ditmars (1939) reported his captives ate brown snakes *(Storeria dekayi)* but refused small lizards and newborn mice, and in feeding trials conducted by Mushinsky (1984) over a seven-month period, a *Stilosoma* ingested only *Tantilla relicta*, avoiding five species of lizards and three other Florida snake species. In contrast, Allen and Neill (1953) reported it eats lizards as well as snakes, and Ashton and Ashton (1981) stated captives will occasionally devour ground skinks *(Scincella lateralis)*. A juvenile captured by Rossi and Rossi (1993) refused to voluntarily consume live or dead skinks placed in its cage, but did swallow a *S. lateralis* tail when the tail was placed in its mouth. This same juvenile consumed newborn *Storeria dekayi, S. occipitomaculata, Tropidoclonion lineatum, Virginia striatula* (and a juvenile), and a hatchling *Diadophis punctatus* during five months in captivity. The prey ranged in size from 7.0 to 10.15 cm in TBL; 17 of the snakes were offered alive, and 3 were prekilled (frozen and thawed). The only living snake refused by the captive was a 14 cm *D. punctatus*. The largest snake consumed by the captive was a 12.5 cm *Virginia striatula* with a head size and midbody circumference similar to that of the *Stilosoma;* the *V. striatula* was regurgitated, and the *Stilosoma* died the following day.

Rossi and Rossi (1993) concluded that the serpentine motion and size of the prey were the most important factors in producing a feeding response, although olfactory cues seemed to play a role in the recognition of prekilled food items. Larger snakes were seized posteriorly and constricted, and smaller snakes were seized near the head and swallowed without constriction. Constriction appeared to be used primarily as a means of restraining prey, as all prey were swallowed alive, even after prolonged struggles.

The constricting ability of *Stilosoma* is limited and may take considerable time (over two hours), and the prey may escape, particularly when the *Stilosoma* releases its bite to search for the head (Mushinsky 1984; Rossi and Rossi 1993). Mushinsky (1984) observed that *Stilosoma* used the anterior third of its body to wrap three coils around a *Tantilla*, then stretched the *Tantilla* between the coils and its more anterior bite. It then worked its mouth anteriorly as the *Tantilla* was pulled posteriorly by the coils. This is very similar to the boid pattern of constriction described by Greene and Burghardt (1978). Swallowing is a rapid side-to-side motion similar to that of *Lampropeltis,* and the bite appears powerful, visibly compressing the prey (Rossi and Rossi 1993).

PREDATORS AND DEFENSE. Short-tailed snakes have been found in the stomachs of coral snakes *(Micrurus fulvius)*. *Stilosoma* are very nervous when first caught, thrashing around, vibrating their tails, and striking with a short, sneezelike hiss.

POPULATIONS. No data reported. *Stilosoma* is threatened due to habitat destruction for citrus production and building sites, and clear cutting and other timber management programs.

REMARKS. Morphological and immunological studies show that the short-tailed snake is a member of the Lampropeltini tribe and is most closely related to *Lampropeltis*, with the point of divergence between *Stilosoma* and *Lampropeltis* occurring in the mid-Pliocene (Dowling and Maxson 1990). (See FOSSIL RECORD.) This species was reviewed by Dowling and Maxson (1990) and Highton (1956, 1976).

Storeria Baird and Girard 1853

Brown and Red-bellied Snakes

Key to the Species of *Storeria*

1a. One preocular scale on each side, 15 or 17 midbody scale rows, nape with or without pale blotches .... *S. dekayi*

1b. Two preocular scales on each side, 15 midbody scale rows, nape with pale blotches .... *S. occipitomaculata*

Storeria dekayi (Holbrook 1839) | DeKay's Brown Snake

RECOGNITION.   *S. dekayi* is a small (TBL to 52.7 cm, but most individuals are 20.0–40.0 cm) grayish brown to dark brown snake with a cream to pink venter and a variable pattern of two parallel rows of dark brown or black spots on the dorsum. The dark dorsal spots may be joined by narrow transverse bars, and most individuals have the middorsum lighter than the sides. Normally either a dark temporal stripe or dark blotches on the supralabials, or both, are present. The venter may have one to two longitudinal rows of small dark spots along the sides. The pitless, keeled scales usually occur in 15 or 17 dorsal rows along the length of the body. The venter has 112–149 ventrals, 36–73 subcaudals, and a divided anal plate. Laterally on the head are 2 nasals, 0 loreal, 1 (rarely 2) preocular(s), 2 (1–3) postoculars, 1 + 2 (1–5) temporals, 7 (6–8) supralabials, and 7 (5–9) infralabials. The rather spinose, single hemipenis is not greatly expanded, has a straight sulcus spermaticus, and may be shallowly forked (in *S. d. victa*). Each maxilla has 15 (14) teeth, with the posterior-most shorter than those anterior to them.

Males have 112–147 (mean, 126) ventrals, 43–73 (mean, 61) subcaudals, and a TL 18–32 (mean, 25) % of TBL; females have 119–149 (mean, 134) ventrals, 36–64 (mean, 56) subcaudals, and a TL 16–23 (mean, 21) % of TBL. Females have longer bodies and heads (King 1997; King et al. 1999).

GEOGRAPHIC VARIATION.   Eight subspecies are recognized (Christman 1982), but only five are found north of Mexico. *S. d. dekayi* (Holbrook 1839), the northern brown snake, occurs from southern Maine and southern Quebec and Ontario south to South Carolina. It has a dark diagonal or vertical bar on the first temporal scale, the two longitudinal rows of dark

Northern brown snake (gravid), *Storeria dekayi dekayi*; Fairfax County, Virginia. (Photograph by Carl H. Ernst)

Texas brown snake, *Storeria dekayi texana*; Douglas County, Kansas. (Photograph by Peter May)

spots on the dorsum not connected by a transverse bar, and the total of its ventrals and subcaudals fewer than 175. *S. d. limnetes* Anderson 1961, the marsh brown snake, ranges from central Minnesota and Wisconsin south, west of the Mississippi River, through eastern Iowa and southeastern Nebraska, western Missouri, eastern Kansas, and eastern Oklahoma to southern Mexico, and eastward along the Gulf Coast to Mobile Bay and Pensacola, Florida. A disjunct population is present in northwestern Texas. It has a dark horizontal bar on the first temporal scale, but lacks pigment on the supralabials. *S. d. texana* Trapido 1944, the Texas brown snake, ranges from Minnesota and Wisconsin southwestward to Texas and northeastern Mexico. It has no pigment on the first temporal scale, a large dark occipital blotch, and dark pigment on the supralabials below the orbit. *S. d. victa* Hay 1892, the Florida brown snake, is found from southeastern Georgia south through peninsular Florida, except along the Suwannee River Valley. It has a broad light neck collar, dark pigment on the supralabials below the eye, two rows of small dark spots on

each side of the venter, and 15 midbody scale rows (all other subspecies have 17 rows). *S. d. wrightorum* Trapido 1944, the Midland brown snake, ranges from southern Wisconsin south to the western Carolinas and the Gulf Coast. A wide zone of intergradation with *S. d. dekayi* occurs from southern Canada through Michigan, Ohio, and the western Appalachians to the Carolinas; and a second zone of intergradation between *texana* and *wrightorum* extends along the eastern edge of the former's range from Wisconsin south in the Mississippi Valley (Christman 1982; Conant and Collins 1998).

The taxonomic status of *S. d. victa* is debatable. It is the only race of *S. dekayi* that consistently has only 15 dorsal body scale rows instead of 17 (Christman, 1980, thought 15 rows primitive and 17 rows derived). In addition, adults retain a juvenile collar, the ventral pattern is different, and the hemipenis is slightly bilobed (another condition not found in the other races). Christman (1980) suggested that *S. d. victa* is indigenous to Florida and descended from the same ancestor as *S. d. wrightorum*, but with less differentiation,

Florida brown snake, *Storeria dekayi victa*; Alachua County, Florida. (Photograph by Roger W. Barbour)

and that no evidence suggests that *victa* and *wrightorum* are the same biological species. However, because the two taxa are allopatric, the consistent morphological and behavioral differences between them indicate that they are evolving independently (Christman 1980, 1982). The relationship between the two subspecies needs further clarification.

KARYOTYPE. The diploid chromosome complement consists of 36 macrochromosomes; sex determination is ZZ/ZW (Baker et al. 1972; Hardy 1971; Hubble 1971).

FOSSIL RECORD. Only Pleistocene fossils are known: Irvingtonian of Florida (Holman 1959a, 1996) and Rancholabrean of Florida (Auffenberg 1963; Gut

and Ray 1963; Holman 1962a), Georgia (Holman 1967), Kansas (Holman 1984, 1986c, 1987b; Preston 1979), Pennsylvania (Fay 1988; Guilday et al. 1964; Lynch 1966a), Tennessee (Klippel and Parmalee 1982), Texas (Holman 1962b; Preston 1979), and Virginia (Fay 1988; Guilday 1962; Holman 1986a).

DISTRIBUTION. *S. dekayi* is found from southern Maine, Quebec, and Ontario west to Wisconsin, Minnesota, and the eastern Dakotas, and south through Florida, to the Gulf of Mexico, and to Veracruz and Oaxaca, Mexico. In addition, a tropical subspecies ranges from Chiapas, Mexico, to Honduras.

HABITAT. *S. dekayi* can be found in nearly all terrestrial and marshland habitats within its range, and

Distribution of *Storeria dekayi*.

is particularly common along the edges of woods. It may occur in dense colonies and frequently inhabits urban areas. As long as there is an abundance of materials under which this snake can hide and a ready supply of earthworms, it flourishes.

BEHAVIOR. The annual activity period varies with latitude. In the Everglades of south Florida, Dalrymple et al. (1991) collected active *S. dekayi* from April to December and in February, so it is probably active every month in Florida. Farther north it normally must hibernate at least for short periods during the winter, but some will even emerge during warm days in winter: the authors have collected active individuals during December and January warm periods in northern Virginia, and Conant (1951), Mitchell (1994), and Palmer and Braswell (1995) collected them in every month in Ohio, Virginia, and North Carolina, respectively. *S. dekayi* becomes active soon after the ground begins to thaw in late March to April or May, and can often be found basking then. Over most of the range it will remain active to October or November. Most surface activity is in the spring: Palmer and Braswell (1995) and Fitch (1999) made 53 and 62%, respectively, of their captures from March through June. A second less intense activity period occurs in September and October when these snakes migrate to and aggregate at hibernacula (C. Ernst, pers. obs.; Vogt 1981). It is probably also as active in the summer, but then becomes crepuscular or nocturnal.

When the weather is severely cold, these small snakes must seek shelter beneath the frost line and hibernate. Hibernacula include stone walls, ant hills, old wells, building foundations, rock crevices, logs and stumps, rodent burrows, sawdust piles, and compost heaps, and they usually face south-southeast. There is high hibernaculum fidelity, with the same individuals returning year after year (C. Ernst, pers. obs.), and often several will hibernate together: Clausen (1936a) found over 200 in four hibernacula on Long Island. These hibernation aggregations may also include other snake species. In the north hibernation mortality from freezing may be high (Bailey 1948). BTs of 75 *S. dekayi* hibernating in an old stone wall in Pennsylvania were 3.0–7.0 (mean, 4.2) °C (C. Ernst, unpubl. data).

During the early spring and fall most activity is diurnal, especially in late morning, but during the summer activity shifts to dusk or nighttime (usually before 2400 hours; C. Ernst, pers. obs.). Clarke (1958) recorded Kansas *S. dekayi* at 2–27°C. Active *S. dekayi* collected by C. Ernst during late April to mid-July in Pennsylvania had BTs of 18.9–29.5 (mean, 25.3; n = 422) °C. BTs of active wild *S. dekayi* recorded by Fitch (1999) and Brattstrom (1965) ranged from 20.4 to 27.0°C.

Although the home ranges of most *S. dekayi* are probably small (less than 60 m; Freedman and Catling 1979), some individuals may travel rather long distances. A 31 cm male crawled 374 m in 30 days and a 39 cm female moved 226 m (Freedman and Catling 1979). Noble and Clausen (1936) found some of their marked snakes moved about 1.2 km. At two Pennsylvania sites, the average home range diameter was 47 (28–64, n = 41) m for males and 39 (22–54, n = 63) m for females (C. Ernst, unpubl.). The greatest distances moved were 670 m by a 30.5 cm male, 555 m by a 31.8 cm male, and 604 m by a 38.1 cm female, although most individuals (73% of males, 90% of females) were not found over 40 m from the last capture point.

REPRODUCTION. Female *S. dekayi* are mature at a minimum SVL of 17.0–17.5 cm (Kofron 1979b; Mitchell 1994); some males contain mature sperm at 15–16 cm SVL (Fitch 1999; King 1997; Mitchell 1994). It normally takes two to three years of growth to reach these lengths.

Female *S. dekayi* are viviparous, and apparently reproduce annually. In Louisiana vitellogenesis proceeds rapidly during the spring: in late winter or early spring the follicles have 3.1–6.0 mm diameters, but by April they have grown to 6.1–12.0 mm (Kofron 1979b). Ovulation usually occurs in late March or April in Louisiana, but Kofron found evidence of a July ovulation in one female (ovulation occurs in May in northern populations; C. Ernst, pers. obs.). Kofron also discovered that transcoelomic migration of ova to the opposite oviduct had occurred in 7 (41%) of 17 females containing young. Iverson (1978) reported that female *S. d. victa* contained enlarged follicles in March, enlarged ovarian eggs or embryos in May, and nearly full-term young in June, and parturition occurred in July or August. He also found some females with partial to nearly full-term embryos as late as 21

September (Do Florida *S. dekayi* produce more than one litter per year?).

Clausen (1936b) reported courtship and mating as early as February and March on Long Island, New York, but most observed matings have occurred from late March (Clausen 1936b) through May (pers. obs.), with April being the primary mating month. The breeding season is later in northern populations. Ashton and Ashton (1981) reported that these snakes may mate from early spring through early summer in Florida. Trapido (1940) found that a Canadian female collected in late August and sent to him in early October contained abundant sperm in her oviducts on 6 December, suggesting an August mating. Female *S. dekayi* can store viable sperm over winter for spring fertilization (Fox 1956).

Male *S. dekayi* follow pheromone trails to find the reproductive females. C. Ernst took a Pennsylvania female in April and rubbed her cloaca on a linoleum floor, leaving an intricate twisting pathway. When three males were individually released at the beginning of the trail, each rapidly tongue flicked and twitched its tail, then quickly followed the trail through all of its turns. Noble (1937) published the most detailed description of the courtship and mating behaviors of this snake. Courtship is stimulated by an increase in ET, imitating that which the snakes experience when leaving the hibernaculum in spring, and the rising morning ATs of spring. All of Noble's matings occurred in the morning. When a female is found, the male approaches from the side and identifies her by examination of her cloacal vent (apparently pheromones also play a role in distinguishing the sexes). Next he tongue flicks and rubs his chin along the female's back while moving forward along her back. She usually crawls away at this time, with the male following. He again approaches from the side, aligns his body parallel to hers, and moves his chin along her back until reaching her occipital region. Several males may court a single female, with one pushing the other(s) off the female's back. As soon as the male has his chin positioned about 1 cm behind her occipit, he attempts to encircle the female with the posterior portion of his body. As the two snakes' vents are brought into line, the male begins to writhe and produce a series of caudocephalic waves that pro-

ceed anteriorly along his body as he tries to keep his chin and head in position on her neck. The male lifts the female's cloacal region 2–3 cm above the ground and inserts a hemipenis into the female's vent. Now the female may crawl away, dragging the attached male with her. The male starts forward thrusts with his tail: two to three rapid thrusts followed by a short pause. Copulation may continue for at least 30 minutes (C. Ernst, pers. obs.).

GP averages 74 (14–113) days (Clausen 1936b; King 1997; Kofron 1979b; Velhagen and Savitsky 1998). Clark (1949) found Louisiana females near parturition from mid-July to mid-August. Births have occurred as early as 20 March in Florida, but the main period of birth ranges from early June to late September, with most young appearing in July and August. However, Ashton and Ashton (1981), Iverson (1978), and Meshaka (1994) reported that some young may be born in the spring in Florida. During parturition the female elevates her tail and then muscular contractions, visible along her body, expel the neonates out the cloacal vent. The young are born at about one-minute intervals (Morris 1974a, 1974b) and are surrounded by a transparent membrane that is soon ruptured. The RCM averages 0.38 (0.36–0.48) (Meshaka 1994; Seigel and Fitch 1984). After birth the young have a tendency to aggregate (Burghardt 1983).

Litters range from 3 (Wright and Wright 1957) to 41 (Morris 1974b) young; the average number of neonates in 169 litters reported in the literature was 13. They are dark brown, with an occipital collar, have SVLs of 6.9–11.7 (mean, 9.7; n = 109) cm, and weigh 0.20–0.50 (mean, 0.26; n = 109) g. A tradeoff exists between litter size and neonate size (King 1993d). Part of this is mediated through the timing of parturition, suggesting that transfer of nourishing materials across the placenta contributes to embryonic development, which alone is not sufficient to explain noncorrelation of litter size and neonate size. Female size and condition at ovulation exert indirect influence on both litter size and neonate size, so that larger females and those in better condition produce more, but smaller, young. Larger females also produce offspring in poorer condition. In addition, the amount of reproductive mass (that lost by the female at parturition in addition to the total offspring mass) is directly correlated with litter size, suggesting it represents a per-offspring allocation of resources by the female.

GROWTH AND LONGEVITY. Growth data are skimpy. Fitch (1999) recorded growth during September and October for wild Kansas neonates of 0.33–0.86 mm/day; first-year young had 8.4–13.9 cm SVLs, two-year males 14.8–19.8 cm SVLs, and two-year females 15.4–20.2 cm SVLs. Minton (1972) reported that Indiana young entering hibernation for the first time are 14.0–22.5 cm, and by the fall of their second year they grow to 28.0–30.5 cm and are probably mature. A 20.5 cm male he captured on 9 October grew to 29 cm by 28 March, and to 32 cm by 9 September of the next year. Captive young fed earthworms and slugs by Harwood (1945) grew from 10.5–14.8 cm (mean mass, 1.04 g) on 9 September, to 10.7–15.1 cm (mean mass, 1.12 g) by 1 October, and to 10.8–15.4 cm (mean mass, 1.16 g) by 31 October. Morris (1974a) kept a neonate born on 31 July. It shed on 30 September and assumed a light brown color, with most of its black markings fading to dark brown, the light neck collar becoming brownish, and the venter changing to pinkish brown. By 29 March, it had grown 9.3–13.7 cm and had lost its light neck collar completely. A wild-caught adult of unknown sex survived an additional 7 years and 13 days in captivity (Snider and Bowler 1992).

DIET AND FEEDING HABITS. Earthworms and slugs are the most common prey, but other animals are also taken occasionally: snails; insects—springtails (Collembola) and larvae of true bugs (Hemiptera, Miridae); isopods; mites; spiders; small fish; and amphibians—eggs, tadpoles (Bufo americanus), and cricket frogs (Acris sp.) (Brown 1979a; Catling and Freedman 1980b; Cebula and Redmer 1988; Clark 1949; Fitch 1999; Hamilton and Pollock 1956; Hurter 1911; Johnson 1987; Judd 1954; Langlois 1964; McCauley 1945; Minton 1972; Morris 1974b; Strecker 1930; Surface 1906; Tennant 1997; Wright and Bishop 1915; Wright and Wright 1957). An individual examined by Hamilton and Pollack (1956) contained over 30 springtails (Collembola). Captives have also eaten minnows (Cyprinidae) (Meier, in Rossman and Myer 1990), newly transformed Bufo americanus (Boyer and Heinze 1934), and their own young (C. Ernst, pers. obs.).

Most foraging is done in the early evening or at night, and individuals have fed as late as 30 October in Indiana (Minton 1972). The snakes actively search for their prey and are highly dependent on olfaction for locating them (Burghardt 1971; C. Ernst, pers. obs.). The authors have seen them capture earthworms many times. When the worm is located, the snake crawls rapidly to it, seizes it along the body, and then begins to work its jaws toward the closest end. Once the snake reaches the end, the worm is quickly swallowed. When preying upon a snail, S. dekayi approaches it, seizes the snail's soft body, pushes the snail along the substrate until it can wedge it against an immovable object, applies torsion to the soft body, extracts the snail from its shell, and swallows the soft body (Rossman and Myer 1990).

PREDATORS AND DEFENSE. Many animals have been reported to attack S. dekayi: mammals—shrews (Blarina, Sorex), opossums (Didelphis virginiana), raccoons (Procyon lotor), domestic cats (Felis catus), skunks (Mephitis mephitis), and weasels (Mustella sp.); birds—Virginia rails (Rallus limicola), robins (Turdus migratorius), shrikes (Lanius ludovicianus), brown thrashers (Toxostoma rufum), and hawks (Buteo lineatus); snakes (Agkistrodon piscivorus, Coluber constrictor, Lampropeltis calligaster, L. triangulum, Micrurus fulvius, Thamnophis sirtalis); toads (Bufo sp.); and spiders (Lactrodectes mactans) (Clark 1949; Contreras and Treviño 1987; Donahue 1995; Ernst and Barbour 1989; Ernst et al. 1997; Greene 1984; Hamilton and Pollack 1956; Klimstra 1959a, 1959b; Linzey and Clifford 1981; Mitchell and Beck 1992; Neill 1948b; Tyler 1991; Vogt 1981; Wauer 1999).

This species is inoffensive. When handled they rarely attempt to bite (the authors have had only one strike at them), but instead thrash about and spray musk and feces. Liner (1977) reported a case of death feigning (letisimulation); when touched the snake writhed, became contorted, and rolled onto its back and presented a dead, desiccated appearance. Similarly, one Hayes (1987) captured became flaccid and would not respond even when turned on its back. Two other S. dekayi captured by Hayes (1987) hid their heads under their body coils.

POPULATIONS. Local populations of S. dekayi in eastern woodlands can be large and dense. At one abandoned shantytown site in southeastern Pennsylvania, 603 individuals were found in slightly over 2 ha, a density of about 300/ha (C. Ernst, in Ernst and Barbour 1989). Freedman and Catling (1978) used four methods to estimate the population size at an abandoned quarry in southwestern Ontario, and found it ranged from 471 to 610 (mean, 545), with a density close to 70/ha. However, this species' contribution to total snake numbers in other habitats may be low: Louisiana hill parishes, 0.78% (Clark 1949); Kansas prairie grasslands, 0.18–3.6% (Cavitt 2000a; Clarke 1958; Fitch 1999); eastern Texas mixed pine-hardwood woodlands, 4.3% (Ford et al. 1991); and the Florida

Everglades, 5.8% (Dalrymple et al. 1991). Reported sex ratios for both newborn litters and adults favor females: neonates, from 0.64:1.00 to 1.00:1.00 (Brown 1992; Clausen 1936b; Sabath and Worthington 1959); adults, 0.36:1.00 (Ontario; Freedman and Catling 1978), 0.67:1.00 (Illinois; Tucker et al. 1995b), and 0.90:1.00 (Pennsylvania; C. Ernst, in Ernst and Barbour 1989). Some juvenile to adult ratios are 0.08 (Kansas; Fitch 1999) and 0.43 (Pennsylvania; C. Ernst, unpubl.).

REMARKS. The lower Florida Keys population of *S. d. victa* is threatened. *S. dekayi* was reviewed by Christman (1982).

Storeria occipitomaculata (Storer 1839) | Red-bellied Snake

RECOGNITION. The red-bellied snake is a small (TBL to 40.6 cm, but most individuals are 21–27 cm), light to dark brown, olive black, or grayish snake with a red, orangish, yellow, or tan venter, and three small, separate light blotches on the nape. A narrow vertebral stripe or indications of other dark dorsal longitudinal stripes may be present. The light nape blotches may fuse to form a complete ring or any of the three may be missing. A light spot is usually present on the fifth supralabial scale. The pitless, keeled body scales lie in 15 (16–17) anterior rows, 15 (13–17) midbody rows, and 15 (13–14) posterior rows. Beneath are 107–136 ventrals, 34–63 subcaudals, and a divided anal plate. Lateral head scales include 2 nasals, 0 loreals, 2 (rarely 1) preoculars, 2 (1–3) postoculars, 1 + 2 (1–3) temporals, 6 (5–8) supralabials, and 7 (5–8) infralabials. The short, single hemipenis has a medial sulcus spermaticus extending around the rear to the side and then straight to the tip, a flattened distal end, five lateral spines that are larger near the base, but no enlarged basal spines. Each maxilla has 14–15 teeth of equal length.

Males have 107–134 (mean, 120) ventrals, 42–63 (mean, 50) subcaudals, and TLs 20–27 (mean, 24.5)% of TBL; females have 111–136 (mean, 124) ventrals, 34–56 (mean, 43) subcuadals, and TLs 17–24 (mean, 21.5)% of TBL.

The distinct light (gray) and dark (brown) color morphs are found in varying proportions in eastern populations with no color intergradation between them. Because the morphs are members of a common gene pool, three possibilities for dorsal color polymorphism are suggested: (1) it is a selectively neutral trait, and color proportions vary due to drift; (2) there is balancing selection for the alleles involved in the color polymorphism; or (3) there is balancing selection for one or more genes that are linked to the genes controlling dorsal coloration (Grudzien and Owens 1991). More data are needed on the proportions of morphs over the geographic range to determine which possibility is in play.

GEOGRAPHIC VARIATION. Three subspecies are recognized (Rossman and Erwin 1980; Ernst 2002). *S. o. occipitomaculata* (Storer 1839), the northern red-bellied snake, ranges from Nova Scotia westward to southeastern Saskatchewan and south to South Carolina, northern Georgia, northeastern Alabama, Tennessee, central Arkansas, and eastern Oklahoma. It has a pinkish to red venter, the light neck marks usually separated from the venter, and less than 49 subcaudals in males and 42 in females. *S. o. obscura* Trapido 1944, the Florida red-bellied snake, ranges from northern Florida and southern Georgia west

Northern red-bellied snake, *Storeria occipitomaculata occipitomaculata*; Clare County, Michigan. (Photograph by James H. Harding)

along the Gulf Coast to southern Arkansas and eastern Texas. It intergrades with *S. o. occipitomaculata* in the eastern Carolinas, northern Georgia, eastern Alabama, northern Mississippi, and southeastern Oklahoma. It has a yellow, orange, or tan venter, the lateral neck blotches extending to the venter, and more than 53 subcaudals in males and 45 or more subcaudals in females. *S. o. pahasapae* Smith 1963, the Black Hills red-bellied snake, is found in the Black Hills of extreme western South Dakota and eastern Wyoming, and intergrades with *S. o. occipitomaculata* in southern Canada, North Dakota, eastern South Dakota, Minnesota (Ernst 1974), and northwestern Iowa. It has small neck blotches with the lateral ones either faint or lacking, no more than 54 subcaudals in males and 47 or fewer in females, often fusion of the oculars to present a two to one pattern (normally no fusion in *S. o. occipitomaculata*), and a maximum of 117 ventrals in males and 124 in females.

CONFUSING SPECIES. For *S. dekayi*, see the above key. Earth snakes *(Virginia)* have cream-colored venters. Kirtland's snake *(Clonophis kirtlandii)* has two longitudinal rows of black spots on its venter. Worm snakes *(Carphophis)* and black swamp snakes *(Seminatrix)* have smooth body scales.

KARYOTYPE. The karyotype consists of 34 macrochromosomes and 2 microchromosomes; sex determination is ZZ/ZW (Hardy 1971; Hubble 1971).

FOSSIL RECORD. Few fossils attributable to *S. occipitomaculata* have been found—the Pleistocene (Rancholabrean) of Pennsylvania (Fay 1988; Guilday et al. 1964; Lynch 1966a) and Virginia (Guilday 1962; Holman 1986a).

DISTRIBUTION. The red-bellied snake is found from Nova Scotia west to southeastern Saskatchewan, and south to central Florida and the Gulf Coast to eastern Texas. Relict populations also occur in the Black Hills of South Dakota and adjacent Wyoming.

HABITAT. This snake occurs predominately in moist woodlands (both pine and mixed) where it usually hides under rocks or logs, or within rotting logs. However, it is by no means restricted to woods and may also occasionally be found in open fields or bogs,

Florida red-bellied snake, *Storeria occipitomaculata obscura*; Volusia County, Florida. (Photograph by Peter May)

or along the borders of marshes or swamps. North-central populations often occur in more xeric habitats.

BEHAVIOR. It is probably active in every month from Florida to the Carolinas; in Missouri, Kansas, and Virginia the annual activity period is from March to October, or possibly early November; but farther north in Minnesota, northern New England, and southern Canada, the snake is not usually active until May, and often begins to hibernate as early as September. In North Carolina, 58% of the annual activity occurs in May–July (Palmer and Braswell 1995); in Connecticut there are two peaks of activity, 32% in May–June and 27% in September–October (Klemens 1993); and in Quebec, Canada, most activity occurs during the second week of August (Bider 1968).

Migration to hibernacula begins in September (Vogt 1981), and the winter is spent below the frost line in soil or gravel, ant mounds, rock crevices, or mammal burrows, but sawdust piles, rotting logs, and loose bark may also be used as hibernacula. Hibernation may be solitary, or as many as 101 (Criddle 1937) of these small snakes may use the same hibernaculum, which may also be shared with other reptiles.

The authors have found these snakes active during the late morning or afternoon in the spring and fall, but during the summer activity is predominately crepuscular or nocturnal, particularly between 2000 and 2400 hours. In Quebec, Bider (1968) observed *S. occipitomaculata* active during 2200–2400 hours in June, 2200–2300 hours in July, and at 1000–1100 hours and 1300–1400 hours in August. Semlitsch and Moran

Distribution of *Storeria occipitomaculata*.

(1984) found that when AT increased and a nearby body of water began to dry in South Carolina, activity increased. The sexes may have different thermoregulatory behavior, with females attaining higher BTs than males at the same ET, and this is related to the thermal gradient of the sexes' thermal retreats (Amaral 1994). Females seem to select warmer ETs to help incubate the broods they carry. BTs of two active individuals caught by Brattstrom (1965) were 24.3 and 28.2°C, respectively, and he proposed their CT_{max} was 37.8°C.

S. occipitomaculata may move considerable distances in a short time. Blanchard (1937a) recaptured a female that had moved about 400 m in 24 hours, but another was found after seven days only 30 m from the site of its first capture. Semlitsch and Moran (1984) thought home ranges in South Carolina were relatively small.

Red-bellied snakes will climb: Minton (1972) found one about 10 cm above ground in a tangle of weed stems, and Smith (1961) saw one climbing in low shrubs.

REPRODUCTION. Both sexes probably mature at the end of their first full year of growth, but probably do not mate until the following spring or summer when two years old (Blanchard 1937a; Semlitsch and Moran 1984). Dissections of South Carolina red-bellied snakes by Semlitsch and Moran (1984) revealed those of 9.4–11.0 cm SVL were immature. The shortest female with enlarged follicles was 12.6 cm, and the smallest male with enlarged testes was 11.8 cm long. In Virginia, the smallest mature male and female had SVLs of 13.7 cm and 15.1 cm, respectively (Mitchell 1994).

In South Carolina, females apparently reproduce annually, as all females larger than 12.6 cm SVL contained enlarged vitellogenic follicles (Semlitsch and Moran 1984). Follicles were largest in May (5.5 mm), and two females examined in July were parturient. South Carolina females contained an average of 9 (2–15) enlarged follicles. The number of follicles increased significantly with female size.

The vas deferens of all males dissected in the fall by Trapido (1940) contained mature sperm. He also found active sperm in the oviducts of females in October. The sperm may remain viable for at least four months in females (Fox 1956) and may be stored over winter in both male and female reproductive tracts.

Mating may occur during the spring, summer, or fall: the authors have seen them copulate on 29 May in Minnesota, Gregory (1977a) found a copulatory plug in a Manitoba female on 22 August, and Trapido (1940) reported a 6 September mating. In the mating the authors observed, the male was coiled around the female with his tail beneath hers and his hemipenis inserted into her vent.

S. occipitomaculata is ovoviviparous. Estimated gestation period for neonates incubated at 24–25°C is 59–77 (mean, 70) days (Velhagen and Savitsky 1998). Births have occurred from as early as May and June in Florida to as late as early September in Michigan, but over the range parturition usually occurs in July or August. Prior to giving birth, females aggregate at suitable sites (Gordon and Cook 1980; Gregory 1975). The young are born singly and are enclosed in a thin membrane that soon ruptures. Many are stillborn, and as much as 30 minutes may elapse between births (Nelson 1969). Several days may be needed to pass the entire litter (Cohen 1948b; Nelson 1969). Studies by Brodie and Dulcey (1989) have shown that large females produce litters with greater masses, and both litter size and mean neonate mass are positively correlated with litter mass.

Only one litter is produced a year, and litters contain 1 (Blanchard 1937a) to 23 (Tennant 1985) young, and average 8.2 young (n = 105). Most contain 4–9 young, so 23 neonates from one brood seems excessive for such a small snake, but other litters of 18–21 have been reported (Fitch 1970; Klemens 1993; Mount 1975; Nelson 1969; Wright and Wright 1957). Litters in the northern part of the range usually contain fewer young (mean, 7) than those from southern females (mean, 9). Neonates are similar to adults in color and pattern (although the ventral pattern may be brighter), have 6.1–10.9 (mean, 8.2) cm TBLs, and weigh 0.03–1.90 (mean, 0.084) g (Brodie and Dulcey 1989). RCMs average 0.60 (0.58–0.62) (Brodie and Dulcey 1989).

GROWTH AND LONGEVITY. South Carolina neonates grew from about 6.1 cm to about 9.0 cm in SVL by their first winter, and reached 11.0 cm by the following summer (Semlitsch and Moran 1984). In Michigan, red-bellied snakes grew to 17.0–21.0 cm TBL in one year (Blanchard 1937a).

A wild-caught adult female kept by the late Sherman A. Minton lived four years and seven months in captivity (Snider and Bowler 1992).

DIET AND FEEDING HABITS.   The feeding behavior of *S. occipitomaculata* has not been described. Its limited diet is predominately composed of slugs, but also includes earthworms and occasionally soft-bodied beetle larvae, isopods, and snails (Barbour 1950; Brown 1979a, 1979b; Hamilton and Pollack 1956; Johnson 1987; Klemens 1993; Minton 1972). Linzey and Clifford (1981) reported that it may occasionally eat "tiny frogs," and Ashton and Ashton (1981) thought salamanders are sometimes eaten.

PREDATORS AND DEFENSE.   This small snake is prey of many other animals: largemouth bass *(Micropterus salmoides),* snakes *(Coluber constrictor, Lampropeltis calligaster, L. getula, L. triangulum, Micrurus fulvius),* chickens *(Gallus gallus),* crows *(Corvus brachyrhynchos),* falcons and hawks *(Buteo jamaicensis, B. lineatus, B. platypterus, Falco sparverius),* and ground squirrels *(Spermophilus tridecemlineatus, Tamias striatus)* (Barrett and Villarroul 1994; C. Ernst, pers. obs.; Greene 1984; Hamilton and Pollack 1956; Herriot 1940; Klemens 1993; Knapik and Hodgson 1986; Medsger 1922; Minton 1972; Palmer and Braswell 1995; Ross 1989; Vogt 1981; Wilson and Friddle 1946; Wistrand 1972). There are also records of *S. occipitomaculata* being devoured in captivity by various animals: a spider (Swanson 1952), a fence lizard *(Sceloporus undulatus;* Busack 1960), a gray treefrog *(Hyla versicolor;* Puckette 1962), and a marbled salamander *(Ambystoma opacum;* Linzey and Clifford 1981). Habitat destruction and road mower deaths take a heavy toll.

When disturbed, red-bellied snakes flatten the head and body and expel musk and fecal matter. If handled, the upper lips are curled to expose the maxillary teeth, resulting in a startling "grin," and the side of the head may be pushed against the captor so that the teeth snag the skin (Amaral 1999; E. Ernst, pers. obs.). Other defensive displays have also been reported.

Some may go into convulsions, roll onto their back, gape open the mouth, and become motionless and contorted (Jordon 1970); merely become motionless (Watermolen 1991); or extend the body straight out and become rigid (Vogt 1981).

POPULATIONS.   *S. occipitomaculata* is considered uncommon to rare in most states; however, it is very secretive and, during most of the year, nocturnal, and it is probably locally more common than records show. The authors have collected 6 in 15 minutes at one Pennsylvania site, and 12 in 30 minutes at another site in Minnesota, and all were under cover; and Lang (1969) captured and marked over 1,500 *S. occipitomaculata* on a 24 ha grassy section in the woods near Itasca State Park, Minnesota. Nevertheless, most populations appear small. In eastern Texas, this snake made up only 6 (2%) of 305 snakes recorded from three habitats by Ford et al. (1991). In South Carolina, Semlitsch and Moran (1984) found relatively small populations at three study sites: 113 over four years at one site, 39 over two years at a second site, and 24 over four years at the third site. Only 3–13% of individuals marked at these sites in 1980–81 were recaptured during the rest of the study. Similarly, Blanchard (1937a) recaptured only 2 of 157 marked snakes during his study in Michigan.

In Michigan, Blanchard (1937a) caught 16 male and 9 female juveniles in 12 years. He also recorded the sex of 61 neonates, 28 males and 33 females, for a combined juvenile sex ratio of 44 males to 42 females. During this same period he collected 39 adult males and 71 adult females, a 0.55:1.00 ratio. Either males are more secretive and more greatly dispersed or they experience greater mortality. The sex ratio of 81 adults from South Carolina was no different from 1:1 (44 males, 37 females) (Semlitsch and Moran 1984).

Storeria occipitomaculata is considered threatened in Kansas and South Dakota and is rare and imperiled in Wyoming.

REMARKS.   The species was reviewed by Ernst (2002).

Tantilla Baird and Girard 1853

Black-headed Snakes

Key to the Species of *Tantilla*

Adapted from Ernst and Barbour (1989) and Wilson (1999)

1a. One postocular scale 2

1b. Two postocular scales 3

2a. Dorsal surface of head only slightly darker than the body color . . . . *T. gracilis*

2b. Dorsal surface of head distinctly darker than the body color . . . . *T. atriceps*

3a. Entire head dark above and below to a point three to four scales posterior to the parietals . . . . *T. cucullata* (in part)

3b. Head pattern not as above 4

4a. No pale parietal (nuchal) band present 5

4b. Pale parietal (nuchal) band present 7

5a. Head cap convex or posteriorly pointed . . . . *T. nigriceps*

5b. Head cap with a straight posterior border 6

6a. Tail length 18–22% of total body length (males 20–22%, females 18–20%), 41–48 subcaudals in females, hemipenis with two basal hooks . . . . *T. oolitica* (in part)

6b. Tail length 19–30% of total body length (males 28–30%, females 18–29%), 46–60 subcaudals in females, hemipenis with one basal hook . . . . *T. relicta* (in part)

7a. Pale parietal (nuchal) band crosses posterior portion of parietal scales 8

7b. Pale parietal (nuchal) band borders the parietal scales, or is one to three scales posterior to the parietal scales . . 12

8a. Ventrals total 160 or more . . . . *T. wilcoxi* (in part)

8b. Ventrals total less that 160 9

9a. Dark parietal (nuchal) band no wider than 1.5 scales . . . . *T. wilcoxi* (in part)

9b. Dark parietal (nuchal) band usually two or more scales wide 10

10a. Light pigment present on supralabials, tail length 22% or less of the total body length 11

10b. No light pigment on supralabials, tail length usually 23% or more of the total body length . . . . *T. relicta* (in part)

11a. Prominent pale parietal (nuchal) band present, usually three or fewer scales wide at the dorsal midline, subcaudals total 42–47 . . . . *T. coronata*

11b. Usually no prominent pale parietal (nuchal) band present, but if so, broken middorsally and usually confined to scales posterior to the parietals; subcaudals total 46–60 . . . . *T. oolitica* (in part)

12a. Pale parietal (nuchal) band distinct, bordered behind by a dark band . . . . *T. cucullata* (in part)

12b. Pale parietal (nuchal) band distinct or not, not bordered posteriorly by dark pigment, or if so, the dark pigment is reduced to spots 13

13a. Black head cap does not extend laterally below the corner of the mouth . . . . *T. hobartsmithi*

13b. Black head cap extends laterally below the corner of the mouth 14

14a. Extensive light postocular spot present, extending onto lower 25–75% of the anterior temporal scale . . *T. yaquia*

14b. No white pigment on the anterior temporal scale . . . . *T. planiceps*

Tantilla atriceps (Günther 1895) | Mexican Black-headed Snake

RECOGNITION. This small (to 23.0 cm TBL), poorly known species is often confused with the southwestern black-tailed snake, *T. hobartsmithi*. Its body is tan to grayish brown; the head cap is dark brown to black, usually straight or only slightly convex posteriorly, and extends only one to two scales behind the parietal scales. Laterally, it does not normally pass below the posterior corner of the mouth. Usu-

ally the dark head pigment is only present as low as the dorsal edge of the supralabials; 33–100% of individuals have some light pigment on the anterior temporal scale, and 70–100% have mostly light seventh supralabials (Cole and Hardy 1981). A light white to cream collar, 0–1.5 scales wide, lies behind the posterior border of the dark head cap, and no dark band or dark spots occur along its posterior edge. The chin and throat are grayish white; behind these the ventral scales have a pink to reddish tinge. The smooth, pitless body scales occur in 15 rows throughout. Ventrals total 123–140, and subcaudals 45–66; the anal plate is divided. Lateral head scalation consists of a single nasal scale, which is partly divided by the nostril, 0 loreal, 1 preocular, 1 (rarely 2) postocular(s), 1 + 1 temporals, 7 supralabials, and 6 infralabials. The rostral scale is broader than long, and the mental scale is usually separated from the anterior chin shields by the first pair of infralabials meeting at the midline. When everted, the subcylindrical hemipenis lacks a distinct swollen head (is not capitate or club-shaped as in *T. hobartsmithi*); it extends 9–14 subcaudals when inverted. Two medium-sized to large spines are present at the base of the organ, but no spinules are proximal to these large spines. A minimum of two to three rows of 26–40 spines approximately encircle the midsection of the shaft. Each maxilla has 10–12 smaller, anterior, ungrooved teeth separated by a diastema from two larger grooved teeth at the rear of the bone.

Sexual dimorphism has not been recorded.

GEOGRAPHIC VARIATION. Unknown, but the two isolated populations in southern Texas and northern Tamaulipas should be investigated.

CONFUSING SPECIES. Besides differences in the hemipenis and maxillary tooth row, *T. atriceps* and *T. hobartsmithi* can be distinguished by the mental scale touching the anterior chin shields in the latter species, and the fewer ventrals and subcaudals in the former. Other North American *Tantilla* can be distinguished using the key presented above. Ring-necked snakes *(Diadophis)* have a distinct, broad, neck ring and, usually, spotted venters.

KARYOTYPE AND FOSSIL RECORD. Unknown.

DISTRIBUTION. In the United States, *T. atriceps* is only known from Duval, Kleburg, and McMullen counties in southern Texas, but its Mexican range includes parts of the states of Coahuila, Durango, Nuevo Léon, Zacatecas, San Luis Potosí, and Tamaulipas.

HABITAT. *T. atriceps* has been found in a variety of habitats, ranging from wooded mountain canyons to

Mexican black-headed snake, *Tantilla atriceps*; McMullen County, Texas. (Photograph by Christopher R. Harrison)

desert flats (Conant and Collins 1998). Surface debris that retains moisture beneath is critical.

BEHAVIOR. Unknown.

REPRODUCTION. Unknown.

GROWTH AND LONGEVITY. Unknown.

DIET AND FEEDING HABITS. Unknown.

PREDATORS AND DEFENSE. The only known predator is the screech owl *(Otus asio)* (Ross 1989).

Distribution of *Tantilla atriceps*.

POPULATIONS. No data available.

REMARKS. *T. atriceps* has for most of its known existence been confused with other species of *Tantilla*, especially *T. hobartsmithi*, to which most life history published under the name *atriceps* can be attributed. Conant and Collins (1998) stated that it feeds on cen- tipedes and insects, but their source is not stated. With so little known of the life requirements of *T. atriceps*, a thorough study is needed.

The species is closely related to *T. nigriceps:* they have almost identical hemipenes (Cole and Hardy 1981). The species was reviewed by Cole and Hardy (1981, 1983a).

Tantilla coronata Baird and Girard 1853 | Southeastern Crowned Snake

RECOGNITION. The unpatterned body (to 33 cm TBL) is tan to pinkish brown or dark brown dorsally, gradually blending laterally into the pinkish white to cream-colored venter. The pointed to slightly rounded head does not have a countersunk lower jaw. Head pattern consists of a dark brown or black crown fol- lowed by a light white to cream-colored band two (one to three) scales wide that separates the dark cap from a dark brown or black collar, usually three or fewer (two to six) scales wide at the midline. A pale postocular blotch is present on each side of the head. Body scales are smooth with no pits, and they occur in 15 rows with no reduction at any point along the body. Ventral scales total 123–147 and subcaudals 34–58, and the anal plate is divided. Lateral head sca- lation consists of 2 nasal scales, 0 loreal, 1 preocular, 2 postoculars, 1+1 temporals, usually 7 supralabials, and 5–6 infralabials. The mental scale may touch the anterior chin shields. The hemipenis bears two basal hooks, the larger adjacent to the basal third of the sul- cus spermaticus, and the smaller along the middle third of the organ. Each maxilla has 13–18 (usually 16) teeth separated by a diastema from an enlarged pos- terior fang.

Maximum SVL is 24.6 cm for females and 22.3 cm for males (Semlitsch et al. 1981). Males have 123–141 ventrals, 35–50 subcaudals, and TLs 20–21 (17–23) % of TBL; females have 133–147 ventrals, 34–58 sub- caudals, and TLs 18–19 (15–21) % of TBL.

GEOGRAPHIC VARIATION. Semlitsch et al. (1981) suggested some geographic variation in SVL may occur in *T. coronata*. Telford (1966) has shown that *T. c. wagneri* (Jan 1862) is really *T. relicta,* and there is insufficient variation from other *T. coronata* to recog- nize *T. c. mitrifer* Schwartz 1953.

CONFUSING SPECIES. *T. relicta* may lack a neck col- lar, but if one is present, there is also either a light blotch on the snout or a lack of light pigment on the supralabials. Dekay's brown snake *(Storeria dekayi)* and red-bellied snakes *(S. occipitomaculata)* have keeled scales. Ring-necked snakes *(Diadophis punctatus)* have a pattern of black spots on their brightly colored ven- ters, and earth snakes *(Virginia)* lack a neck collar.

KARYOTYPE. Cole and Hardy (1981) found the diploid chromosome number to be 36; 16 macro- chromosomes (pairs one, three, and four are meta- centric; pairs two, five, and seven are submetacentric; pair eight is subtelocentric; and pair six is telocentric) and 20 microchromosomes.

Southeastern crowned snake, *Tantilla coronata*; Kentucky. (Photograph by Roger W. Barbour)

Distribution of *Tantilla coronata*.

FOSSIL RECORD. Fossils from north-central Florida reported as *T. coronata* by Auffenberg (1963) may be *T. relicta*.

DISTRIBUTION. *T. coronata* ranges southward from southern Virginia and southern Indiana to southern Georgia, the panhandle of Florida, and the Gulf Coast of Alabama, Mississippi, and southeastern Louisiana. It is not found west of the Mississippi River. The first recorded occurrence of *T. coronata* on the coastal plain of Virginia was reported in August of 1985 at Blackwater Ecologic Preserve; this is only the fifth recorded occurrence of this species in Virginia (Anon. 1986).

HABITAT. *T. coronata* is a secretive burrower that may be found in a variety of habitats ranging from mesic Appalachian forests to the wet borders of marshes, swamps, and the banks of rivers. It has been taken at elevations to 610 m in the southern Appalachians, almost always under stones, under moist logs, or within rotting stumps. Semlitsch et al. (1981) studied the habitat preferences by comparing drift-fence (with pitfall traps) captures in pine stands to those from the mesic areas around two Carolina bays at the Savannah River site, South Carolina, and found that pine and mesic areas were not utilized differently. However, within these various habitats, drift fences in more xeric conditions were more productive. They concluded that a xeric microhabitat with sufficient rocks, logs, or rotting stumps that provide cover ap-

pears more important for utilization of an area than either the predominant vegetation or the macrohabitat.

BEHAVIOR. The authors caught an active *T. coronata* on 16 March 1969 at Osewitchee Springs, Wilcox County, Georgia. Other active *T. coronata* have been found as early as 27 March in South Carolina (Semlitsch et al. 1981) and 29 March in Indiana (Minton 1949), and as late in fall as 28 October in North Carolina (Brimley 1941–42) and 6 November in South Carolina (Semlitsch et al. 1981). Trapping in South Carolina showed that regular captures of *T. coronata* began in April after a rise in mean maximum and minimum ATs above 20 and 10°C, respectively, and that the snake was most active during July and August (Semlitsch et al. 1981). Rainfall did not seem to affect activity.

The colder months are presumably spent in hibernation, although there are only two records of this. Allen (1932) found several inactive winter specimens below the surface of the ground on the inside of pine stumps, and Huheey and Stupka (1967) reported five were found in the ground at depths of 5–30 cm between 18 February and 16 March at Gatlinburg, Tennessee.

Most activity seems to occur at night. During the day these snakes hide beneath objects or remain underground. Captives also display nocturnal tendencies.

REPRODUCTION. Telford (1966) reported that the smallest mature male in his sample from throughout the range had a SVL of 13.4 cm while the smallest female had a SVL of 15.3 cm. Semlitsch et al. (1981) thought hatchlings matured during their second year (approximately 12 months old) because a distinct distribution of subadults (12.1–15.1 cm SVL) did not appear in their spring, summer, or fall samples. However, they speculated that possibly juveniles are subterranean and do not travel extensively above ground until mature. In South Carolina, sexual maturity in females is attained in the spring of their third calendar year (about 21 months of age) at a SVL of about 15 cm (Aldridge and Semlitsch 1992a.)

Female *T. coronata* have a complete, functional, right oviduct, but the left is reduced and nonfunctional; both ovaries are present and normally developed (Clark 1970c). The left and right ovaries do not differ in the number of follicles produced or the rate of atresia, indicating that the loss of the left oviduct is not accompanied by changes in ovarian function (Aldridge and Semlitsch 1992a). Eggs from both ovaries must descend through the right oviduct; the left oviduct terminates just anterior to the cloaca (Tennant 1997).

In South Carolina *T. coronata*, vitellogenesis begins in the spring, ovulation occurs in June, and oviposition takes place in June to early July (Aldridge 1992). Spermatogenesis begins in May and peaks in July and August; spermiation begins in late June, with sperm being stored in the vas deferens (Aldridge and Semlitsch 1982).

In males the sexual segment of the kidney has a cycle opposite that of the testis, and mating occurs during the period of sexual segment hypertrophy, in early spring (May) and summer (July–September) (Aldridge and Semlitsch 1992b). The youngest males, about 12 months of age, examined by Aldridge and Semlitsch (1992b) begin spermatogenesis at the same time of year as adults, and the course of spermatogenesis is similar to that of adults. Although insufficient sperm appear to be produced to allow successful mating following the first spermatogenic cycle, enough sperm are produced during the second spermatogenic season to permit mating in the summer or following spring.

Both males and females store sperm. Aldridge (1992) described seasonal changes in the oviduct and the temporal patterns of sperm storage in 27 adult females from South Carolina. Temporal distribution of sperm in the oviduct revealed that mating occurs in the late summer (and fall) and/or the following spring. Sperm from late summer matings overwinter in the posterior oviduct. In the spring, coinciding with vitellogenesis, some sperm are transported into the seminal receptacles, although other sperm remain in the posterior oviduct up to ovulation. Following oviposition, sperm are absent from the posterior oviduct but remain in the seminal receptacles for up to 10 weeks. The amounts of sperm in the seminal receptacles decrease through the summer, and by late summer and fall, sperm are absent from the seminal receptacles.

The only observed matings in this species took place in April and early May; Georgia mated pairs were intertwined beneath a scrap of bark at the base of a rotting tree stump (Neill 1951). Aldridge and Semlitsch (1992a) examined 68 female *T. coronata*; the absence of visible embryos in oviductal eggs and the absence of oviductal eggs in the majority of late June and July females possessing corpora lutea indicated that eggs were not retained in the oviduct for extended periods.

Aldridge and Semlitsch (1992a) found that the number of vitellogenic follicles is correlated with female SVL, although the numbers of oviductal eggs or corpora lutea are not correlated. Difference in the expected clutch size between snakes with vitellogenic follicles and snakes with oviductal eggs or corpora lutea was attributed to atresia of vitellogenic follicles, which Aldridge and Semlitsch suggested may represent the primary mechanism of clutch adjustment. The coelomic fat mass of adult females significantly declines during egg production, while fat mass increases significantly following oviposition (although some females had low reserves in late summer). Due to the variation in the size of vitellogenic follicles used to estimate mean clutch size, the differences in clutch size could not be compared to yearly variation in fat mass.

In the southern part of the range eggs may be deposited during late May or early June (Minton 1972), but most nesting occurs in June and July. Neill and Boyles (1957) dissected a gravid Alabama female on 25 May that contained three shelled eggs, and Minton (1949a) reported an Indiana female appeared to contain two to three elongated eggs on 30 May. Semlitsch et al. (1981) collected four females, each with shelled eggs, on 11 June, 16 June, and 18 July in South Carolina.

In addition to shelled eggs, Neill and Boyles (1957) reported the presence of smaller, spherical eggs, and concluded *T. coronata* may mature 8–12 ova, but produce only three young per year; Aldridge and Semlitsch (1992a) thought these spherical structures were probably ovarian follicles. It is possible that the one and two shelled eggs found in gravid July females by Semlitsch et al. (1981) represented second smaller clutches.

The eggs are white with a leathery shell. Although usually elongated (21.3–23.7 × 5.0–5.6 mm; Neill and Boyles 1957), those found by Neill (1951) were more nearly oval. Neill (1951) described the only reported nest as a cup-shaped depression beneath two overlapping bark fragments in a small mass of wood pulp and rotting bark near the base of an old stump. The nest seemed in an ideal location; it was shielded from rain and drainage from the stump, was exposed to sunlight in the morning and evening, but was shaded at midday.

GROWTH AND LONGEVITY. The young resemble adults in coloration and head pattern. The smallest measured by Telford (1966) had a 7.8 cm SVL; the smallest male measured by Minton (1949a) was 7.6 mm, and the smallest female was 8.0 mm. Two juveniles collected by Semlitsch et al. (1981) on 7 September and 2 August had SVLs of 10.0 mm and 11.9 mm. Semlitsch et al. (1981) thought South Carolina *T. coronata* with a SVL of more than 23 cm might represent individuals three years or older. Maximum longevity is unknown.

DIET AND FEEDING HABITS. Prey eaten by wild and captive *T. coronata* include tenebrionid beetle larvae, earthworms, snails, centipedes, spiders, cutworms, wireworms, and termites and their larvae. Vertebrates such as ground skinks (*Scincella lateralis*) are also reportedly taken (Tennant 1997). Although this species has venom glands and a pair of enlarged grooved teeth at the rear of its upper jaw, the efficiency of its venom apparatus is questionable. It has been presumed that the venom is used to subdue invertebrate prey, but Minton (1949a) forcibly made a *T. coronata* bite an earthworm, with seemingly no effect on the worm.

PREDATORS AND DEFENSE. This species is known to be eaten by the snakes *Micrurus fulvius, Stilosoma extenuatum, Lampropeltis getulus,* and *Lampropeltis triangulum elapsoides* and by the lizard *Ophisaurus ventralis.* It is probably also preyed on by a variety of birds and carnivorous mammals.

POPULATIONS. *T. coronata,* although locally common, often appears rare due to its secretive nature. Being largely nocturnal and spending the daylight hours undercover, it is seldom encountered. Drift-fence sampling in South Carolina has shown that a good population occurs at the Savannah River Plant (Semlitsch et al. 1981), and Brode and Allison (1958) collected 10 individuals from stumps on less than 5 ha in Harrison County, Mississippi. Neill (1951) reported it was unusually common on certain wooded hillsides bordering a small stream on the northwestern outskirts of Augusta, Georgia.

Of 274 *T. coronata* collected by Semlitsch et al. (1981), only 2 were juveniles; however, it was thought that juveniles probably move less than adults and may remain underground until mature. Most of those caught had 16–25 cm SVLs and were sexually mature. The sex ratio, calculated from dissected snakes, was 2:1 (36 males, 18 females). This ratio may reflect differential mortality, but it is more likely an indication of sampling bias toward the more active males (Semlitsch et al. 1981).

REMARKS. *T. coronata* was reviewed by Telford (1966, 1982). It is considered threatened in the state of Indiana.

Tantilla cucullata Minton 1956 | Trans-Pecos Black-headed Snake

RECOGNITION. *Tantilla cucullata* is the largest species of the genus in the United States, reaching a TBL of 65.4 cm. Its slender, light brown to grayish brown body has dark pigment only on the head and nape. The somewhat depressed head is pointed to slightly rounded anteriorly, as broad as the neck, and lacking a countersunk lower jaw. Head pattern is variable, consisting of four different morphs: (1) a collarless morph that has both the lateral and dorsal sides of the head covered with dark brown or black pigment, (2) a light-collared morph with the collar interrupted by dark pigment at its dorsal midpoint, (3) a light-collared variant with the collar interrupted dorsally by a dark X with three black spots along the posterior border (these first three head patterns are found in the Chisos and Davis Mountains of Trans-Pecos, Texas, in Brewster, Jeff Davis, and Presidio counties), and (4) a variant with an uninterrupted light collar separating the dark pigment on the head from that on the nape, and a light spot on the supralabials posterior to the orbit (found in the Pecos and Devil's river drainages in Val Verde, Terrell, and Pecos counties, and also in Crockett County, Texas). Dark pigment terminates posteriorly 2–4.5 scales behind the parietal. The tip of the snout is usually light brown, and some light flecking may be present on the anterior chin shields and first infralabials. A light mark is often present behind and slightly below the orbit. Body scales are smooth without apical pits and lie in 15 rows throughout. The venter is white to cream with 160–181 ventrals, 63–83 subcaudals, and a divided anal plate. Lateral head scalation consists of a nasal scale (partially subdivided in some), 0 loreals, 1 preocular, 2 postoculars, 1 + 1 temporals, 7 supralabials, and 6 infralabials. The rostral scale is broader than long. On the chin, the mental may, or may not, touch the anterior chin shields. The hemipenis has not been described. Maxillary teeth total 15–18 (mean, 16), with the anterior teeth separated by a diastema from two enlarged, grooved posterior teeth.

The sexes are similar and difficult to distinguish by external characteristics: males have 164–180 (mean, 169) ventrals, 63–83 (mean, 77) subcaudals, and TLs averaging 25 (23–29) % of TBL; females have 160–181 (mean, 173) ventrals, 63–83 (mean, 71) subcaudals, and TLs averaging 23 (21–28) % of TBL. Females are also slightly larger.

GEOGRAPHIC VARIATION. No subspecies are currently recognized (see REMARKS).

CONFUSING SPECIES. Neck collars of other western North American *Tantilla* are very narrow or absent (see the above key). Western ring-necked snakes (*Diadophis punctatus*) have dark spotted venters.

KARYOTYPE. Undescribed.

FOSSIL RECORD. Van Devender and Bradley (1994) reported Pleistocene (Rancholabrean) remains from Maravillas Canyon Cave, Brewster County, Texas.

DISTRIBUTION. *T. cucullata* occurs only in western Texas, where it is restricted to disjunct populations in

Trans-Pecos black-headed snake, *Tantilla cucullata*. (Photograph by R. D. Bartlett)

Distribution of *Tantilla cucullata*.

the Chisos and Davis mountains, and in the watersheds of the Pecos and Devil's rivers.

HABITAT. The species is most often found on rocky slopes or broken to flat rocky terrain with reddish lava soils at elevations of 1,300–1,700 m. Typical vegetation in this habitat is a piñon-oak-juniper mix. It has also been taken, however, in rolling arid grasslands with acacia, yucca, and cholla.

BEHAVIOR. *T. cucullata* is a secretive, fossorial, nocturnal species. Most time is spent underground, hidden under some object, or deep in a crevice. Tennant (1984) reported that one was discovered deep in a canyon-wall crevice during dry weather and that another was found in a maze of earthen burrows. Lack of much surface activity may be a reflection of dehydration problems in its usually dry habitat, and would explain its seeming bursts of above ground activity following rains. In fact, most individuals have been collected after a wet period. Except for an individual that was collected on 28 March (Fouquette and Potter 1961) and another collected in mid-April (Tennant 1984), almost all recorded dates for the species have been between early June and mid-September, with most during the wet periods of July and August. It is usually found crawling at twilight or after dark, especially following a shower, but Treadwell and Hibbitts (1968) found one active at 0800 hours.

REPRODUCTION. *T. cucullata* is an egg layer. Probably only a single clutch of two to three white, elongated, parchment-shelled eggs is laid each year. A captive kept by Tennant (1984) laid a clutch on 13 June, and Hillis and Campbell (1982) removed a mature 45 × 8 mm egg from a female captured on 25 June. It weighed about 8.9% of the female's mass. Behler and King (1979) reported that one to two eggs are laid in July, possibly based on Easterla (1975a), who found a female on 16 July containing two incompletely developed eggs that he thought would have been laid in about two weeks. The largest of these was 27.5 × 10.0 mm. A female examined by Clark (1970c) had the left oviduct reduced to smaller than the right one.

DIET AND FEEDING HABITS. Wild *T. cucullata* probably prey on centipedes and other small invertebrates, but data are lacking. Tennant (1984) observed one in the vicinity of the Devil's River struggling to swallow a centipede (*Geophilomorpha*) almost as large as itself. Captives have eaten centipedes from their habitat, and also small snails removed from their shells (Degenhardt et al. 1976; Tennant 1984). Foods refused by captives include millipedes, scorpions, moths and their caterpillars, spiders, small frogs (*Syrrhophus*), and hatchling lizards (Degenhardt et al. 1976; Tennant 1984). Its sister Mexican taxon *T. rubra* has a serous Duvernoy's gland (Taub 1967) whose secretions aid in subduing prey, and this condition probably also exists in *T. cucullata*.

PREDATORS AND DEFENSE. Unknown.

POPULATIONS. Seemingly rare (less than 100 have been collected), the snake may be more abundant than it appears; its numbers may be masked by its secretive fossorial habits and the favorite collecting periods of herpetologists. It is listed, under the name *T. rubra*, as threatened in Texas.

REMARKS. *T. cucullata* is most closely related to the Mexican species *T. rubra* Cope 1876, of which it was long thought to be a subspecies. Dixon et al. (2000) elevated it to full species status and placed the taxon *T. r. diabola* Fouquette and Potter 1961 in its synonymy. It was reviewed by Wilson et al. (2000).

Tantilla gracilis Baird and Girard 1853 | Flat-headed Snake

RECOGNITION.   This small (to 24.9 cm TBL), slender snake has an unpatterned tan to gray brown or reddish brown body, a salmon pink venter, and a flat head only slightly darker brown than the body. Posteriorly, the head cap is dorsomedially concave. The pointed head has a countersunk lower jaw. Body scales are smooth and usually occur in 15 rows along the entire body (some variation may occur in the pre-anal scale rows); 106–138 ventral scales, 33–57 subcaudals, and a normally divided anal plate are present. Lateral head scalation includes 2 nasals, 0 loreals, 1 preocular, 1 (2) postocular(s), 1 + 1 temporals, 6 (5–8) supralabials, and 6 (5–7) infralabials. The hemipenis bears two basal hooks, a large one adjacent to the basal third of the sulcus spermaticus, and another of similar size on the opposite side of the organ. Several smaller spines are present along the middle section.

Each maxilla has 10–14 teeth anterior to the slightly enlarged, grooved posterior fang; in most cases a small diastema separates the fang from the other teeth. Scanning electron microscopy studies of the maxillary teeth of 14 *T. gracilis* revealed fangs of two basic types, curved and linear (Trauth 1991b). A groove, which extends along the entire labial surface of the fang between the mesial and distal surfaces, projects anteriolaterally on the curved fangs, and laterally on the straighter linear fangs. It is presumably formed by an expansion of dental ridges that characterize all maxillary teeth. Dental ridges are more conspicuous in maxillary teeth near the fangs, and contribute to the semblance of grooves most noticeable on teeth near the fangs. Anterior maxillary teeth may also exhibit dental ridges with serrations, or these ridges may appear smooth.

Females grow longer (to 24.9 cm TBL) than males (to 21.5 cm), but males have slightly longer TLs (21–27% of TBL) than females (17–22% of TBL). Females have 115–138 ventrals and 33–53 subcaudals; males have 106–132 ventrals and 40–57 subcaudals.

GEOGRAPHIC VARIATION.   No subspecies are currently recognized; Dowling (1957b) and Hardy and Cole (1968) have shown that recognition of *T. g. hallowelli* Cope 1861 is unsupportable.

CONFUSING SPECIES.   Other *Tantilla* can be identified by using the key presented above. Earth snakes *(Virginia)* and brown snakes *(Storeria)* have at least weakly keeled body scales. The ground snake *(Sonora semiannulata)* has a loreal scale and a cream to white venter.

KARYOTYPE AND FOSSIL RECORD.   Unknown.

DISTRIBUTION.   *T. gracilis* ranges from southwestern Illinois west to eastern Kansas, and south to central Louisiana, southern Texas, and northwestern Coahuila, Mexico. Isolated populations also occur in the panhandle of Texas and extreme eastern Texas.

HABITAT.   This secretive, semifossorial species lives under rocks, rotting logs, or other moist debris in oak-hickory or mixed deciduous-pine woodlands and on brushy slopes, often situated in limestone areas. Soil conditions may play an important role in its distribution. It is found in loose, moist soil in wooded areas, but may also occur in fairly tight rocky soils (Vermersch and Kuntz 1986). Two isolated colonies at the Fitch Natural History Reservation in northeastern Kansas were at xeric limestone hilltop outcrops with southern exposure; they were eliminated when invading trees and brush (through succession) shaded their habitat (Fitch 1999). On the Great Plains, this species may inhabit grasslands.

T. gracilis was thought to prefer loose sandy soils, but in an experimental study Clark (1967b) found that it had no soil preferences and did not seem to be an extensive burrower. Most deep burrowing probably occurs in the summer when surface soils become dry. Jackson and Reno (1975) reported that the free margins of the dorsal, lateral, and ventral body scales of *T. gracilis* are of uniform length and presumably aid in limited burrowing activity.

BEHAVIOR.   Most individuals have been found in the spring and fall. The earliest record is 8 March (Wright and Wright 1957), while some Oklahoma *T. gracilis* have been active in November (Force 1935). Their relative scarcity in summer may be due to warmer and less moist soil conditions, as many sum-

Flat-headed snake, *Tantilla gracilis*; Payne County, Oklahoma. (Photograph by Steve W. Gotte)

mer captures have been during or after rains. Where they spend the summer is unknown, but they may use small animal burrows and ant mounds. Hibernation occurs during the colder months, when these small snakes retreat underground or into animal burrows. Clark (1967b) recorded the BTs of 10 *T. gracilis* in the laboratory as 19.6–27.5 (mean, 23.8) °C.

Smith (1956) thought the species probably nocturnal, and Force (1935) reported that one of its favorite foods is the meadow maggot or leatherjacket, a nocturnal insect.

REPRODUCTION. Reproductive data are limited. Force (1935) considered female *T. gracilis* to begin maturing when 12.5 cm at 1–1.5 years of age; females 12.5–15.5 cm contained noticeably developed ova 1–2 mm in length, and those shorter than 12.5 cm had only microscopic ova. Females 18.5 cm (1.5–2.5 years old) or longer were definitely mature. Mature females have both ovaries and a functional right oviduct, but the left oviduct is reduced to a vestige (Clark 1970c).

Twelve Kansas *T. gracilis* averaged 1.75 (1–3) oviductal eggs, while 16 Arkansas females, including those with previtellogenic follicles, averaged 4.9 eggs, and a second group of seven snakes averaged 3.1 (Fitch 1999).

Force (1935) thought males mature at 17.4 cm (1.5–2.5 years old); in those 15.5–17.5 cm in length, there was a gradual change from a flabby, white, immature testis to a firm, elongate, yellowish, apparently mature testis. Males 18.5 cm long were definitely mature.

Oklahoma males contained well-developed 5–9 mm testes during May, and presumably this is the mating period (Force 1935); prior to May the testes were much smaller. In south-central Texas, mating begins in April (Vermersch and Kuntz 1986). Courtship and mating have not been described, but males may find mates by following female pheromone trails (Gehlbach et al. 1971).

Eggs are deposited in June and the first half of July; Force (1935) reported that captives always oviposited at night. Normally two to three (one to four) eggs are laid. The white to cream-colored eggs are typically elongate or irregularly shaped with smooth shells and a distinctly visible germinal disc. The eggs usually hatch in late August or early September, but Wright and Wright (1957) reported that one young *T. gracilis* emerged in July.

Distribution of *Tantilla gracilis*.

Measurements of eggs and offspring of northeastern Texas *T. gracilis* are comparable to those in Oklahoma, although the IP is shorter in Texas. Force (1935) reported a size range of 13–26 × 4–6.5 mm for Oklahoma *T. gracilis* eggs, an IP of 83–84 days, and a TBL of 77–96 mm for hatchlings. Cobb (1990) reported a size range of 14.3–23.1 × 5.1–7.2 (mean, 17.7 × 6.2) mm for 13 Texas *T. gracilis* eggs, an IP of 50–51 days, and a TBL of 89–104 mm for hatchlings. In contrast, two eggs laid by a captive from Louisiana measured 19 × 15 mm and 19 × 16 mm (Fisher 1973). The average mass for Texas *T. gracilis* eggs was 0.45 (0.30–0.70) g.

Anderson (1965) found two clutches, one of two eggs and another of three eggs, in barely moist sand between two layers of limestone, and Collins (1993) reported that eggs are laid in a nest beneath a rock. Cobb (1990) located two nest sites in northeastern Texas; the first (15 July), under a stone in soil 12 cm deep with a ST of 29°C, contained five eggs; the second (15 September), under a stone in soil 11 cm deep, contained six empty egg shells. Both clutches were in underground chambers of 4–6 cm in diameter, and further examination of the chamber areas suggested they were remnants of underground tunnels excavated by carpenter ants. Cobb interpreted the clutch sizes and nest sites as evidence of communal nesting by *T. gracilis*.

GROWTH AND LONGEVITY. Force (1935) reported the following size-age relationships by sex for Oklahoma *T. gracilis*: females 9.0–12.5 cm (yearling), 12.5–18.5 cm (1–1.5 years), and 18.5–23.0 cm (1.5–2.5 years); males 8.5–12.5 cm (yearling), 12.5–17.5 cm (1–1.5 years), and 17.5–20.5 cm (1.5–2.5 years). Longevity is unknown.

DIET AND FEEDING HABITS. *T. gracilis* feeds primarily on centipedes and soft-bodied insect larvae, such as cutworms, wireworms, and leatherjackets. Sowbugs, spiders, and slugs have also been reported as prey. Gehlbach et al. (1971) found that captive *T. gracilis* followed pheromone trails left by army ants and termites, and concluded that the snakes use olfaction to detect prey.

The slightly enlarged tooth on the rear of the maxilla contains shallow lateral grooves and is probably used to subdue soft-bodied prey. Small venom glands are present, but the effectiveness of their secretions is questionable. Anderson (1965) macerated the head tissues of several *T. gracilis* and rubbed these into cuts in the skin of humans and laboratory mice with no adverse results; however, the venom may be specialized for invertebrates. In any case, *T. gracilis,* which is normally inoffensive, does not present a danger to humans.

PREDATORS AND DEFENSE. Collins (1993) reported birds, small mammals, lizards, and snakes as predators, and Tennant (1984) listed moles, shrews, skunks, armadillos, and screech owls. More specific observations include predation by a leopard frog *(Rana pipiens)* (Burt and Hoyle 1935) and coral snakes *(Micrurus fulvius)* (Fisher 1973; Hurter 1911). When held, *T. gracilis* does not bite, but instead sprays musk and thrashes about.

POPULATIONS. Although it may be common in some areas, little is known of the population structure of this small snake. Of the 411 Oklahoma *T. gracilis* collected and dissected by Force (1935), 245 were males and 176 females, a 1.39:1 sex ratio. The sex ratio of 246 *T. gracilis* from the vicinity of Winfield, Cowley County, Kansas, was 139 males to 107 females, 1.30:1 (Hardy and Cole 1968).

In a longitudinal study of the relative abundance of snakes in Kansas, Fitch (1993) found that a group of small, secretive, or fossorial species (including *T. gracilis*) that prey on invertebrates attained much higher population densities in at least one sample site than larger snakes that prey on vertebrates. *T. gracilis* was represented by 83 individuals constituting 7.48% of snakes collected in Chase, Cowley, Morris, Pottawatomie, and Marion counties, and by 5 individuals constituting 4.95% of snakes collected in Allen, Anderson, Douglas, Johnson, and Linn counties.

REMARKS. In parts of its range, this species is abundant in flower beds, gardens, and compost heaps, and is often kept as a pet. Unfortunately, it has almost no resistance to temperature changes and often dies from only moments of overheating in a glass jar or metal can (Tennant 1984).

Tantilla hobartsmithi Taylor 1937 | Southwestern Black-headed Snake

RECOGNITION. This small, slender, poorly known species reaches 31.3 cm TBL. Body color is tan to light brown; the head cap is much darker than the body. The dark brown or black pigment on the head does not extend below the posterior corner of the mouth, and it projects only 0.5–3 scales behind the parietals to end in a straight or convex border. A white to cream collar 0.5–2 scales wide follows the dark head cap, but no dark pigment is posterior to this light band. The chin and throat are grayish, but the venter becomes orange red to the rear. The smooth, pitless body scales are in 15 rows throughout. Ventrals total 124–172, and subcaudals 47–74; the anal plate is divided. Lateral head scalation consists of a nasal that is partially divided by the nostril, 0 loreals, 1 preocular, 2 postoculars, 1+1 temporals, 7 supralabials, and 6 infralabials. The rostral scale is broader than long. The mental scale contacts the first chin shields, thus preventing the first infralabials from touching at the midline. On the maxilla, 10–14 teeth lie anterior to a pair of slightly enlarged, grooved, posterior teeth. A short diastema may be present between the smaller anterior teeth and the enlarged rear ones. When everted, the hemipenis is subcylindrical to club-shaped with a head. Two medium to large spines are present at the base, but no smaller spines occur proximal to the basal spines, and a minimum of one to three rows of 16–37 spines approximately circle the midsection (Cole and Hardy 1981, 1983b). The inverted hemipenis extends posteriorly 7–14 subcaudals.

Males have 124–162 ventrals and 48–74 subcaudals; females have 130–172 ventrals and 47–65 subcaudals. In the series of *T. hobartsmithi* measured by Cole and Hardy (1981), males had both longer bodies and longer tails than females, and the male TL was a greater proportion of TBL than that of the female.

GEOGRAPHIC VARIATION. No subspecies are currently recognized, but a thorough study of geographic variation would be worthwhile.

CONFUSING SPECIES. Other species of the genus can be identified with the key presented above. Ring-necked snakes *(Diadophis)* usually have spotted venters.

KARYOTYPE. According to Cole and Hardy (1981), the diploid chromosome number is 36, consisting of 16 macrochromosomes (4 metacentric, 6 submetacentric, 2 meta-submetacentric, 2 telocentric, 2 submeta-subtelocenteric) and 20 microchromosomes.

FOSSIL RECORD. Pleistocene (Rancholabrean) remains of *T. hobartsmithi* have been found at Picacho Peak, Arizona (Van Devender et al. 1991), and in packrat *(Neotoma)* middens in Maravillas Canyon Cave, Texas (Van Devender and Bradley 1994). Other fossils

Southwestern black-headed snake, *Tantilla hobartsmithi*; Santa Cruz County, Arizona. (Photograph by Brad R. Moon)

have not been absolutely identified as *T. hobartsmithi*, but Holocene or Pleistocene *Tantilla* vertebrae found in western Texas and southwestern New Mexico by Gehlbach and Holman (1974), Parmley (1990a, 1990b), Van Devender and Bradley (1994), and Van Devender and Worthington (1977) may be from this species.

DISTRIBUTION. The range is disjunct, with populations in the United States in western Texas and southern New Mexico, western Colorado, southern Utah, central and southern Arizona, and southwestern Nevada and southern California. In northern Mexico, *T. hobartsmithi* is known from the states of Coahuila, Chihuahua, and Sonora.

HABITAT. As expected with such a scattered distribution, *T. hobartsmithi* is found in a variety of habitats, many riparian, at elevations under 1,000 m: grasslands; open chaparral; brushy areas with sagebrush, greasewood, creosote, mesquite, and yucca vegetation; thorn scrub; piñon-juniper woodlands; and open coniferous forests.

BEHAVIOR. Secretive and typically nocturnal, this snake spends most of the time buried in loose soil or under surface litter (especially if moisture is retained under the object). In New Mexico, it is active from March to September (Degenhardt et al. 1996), but most literature records are from May to July, and especially June. However, these records probably reflect the biased activity patterns of the collectors, not of *T. hobartsmithi*, although Cole and Hardy (1981) found collection dates in all months of the year. One Arizona individual was found hibernating in gravel along a road bank on 24 December (Little 1940).

Many of the sightings of *T. hobartsmithi* have come from riparian zones, and perhaps it requires a somewhat moist habitat to prevent the loss of body water. The rocks under which it hides are often in the shade, and Degenhardt et al. (1996) reported that the ET of such habitats is 15–25°C, and usually lower than nearby arid or desert habitats. Whether by design or chance, it occasionally enters water and can swim (Murray 1939).

REPRODUCTION. Mature males are at least 21.4 cm TBL, and mature females 16.7 cm (Wright and Wright 1957). Only the right oviduct is functional (Clark 1970c). Brown (1997) presumed that a clutch of one to three eggs is laid sometime between June and August, but no definite information is available on breeding by this snake.

GROWTH AND LONGEVITY. Unknown.

DIET AND FEEDING HABITS. Being arthropod specialists, wild *T. hobartsmithi* eat beetle grubs, lepidopteran caterpillars, millipedes, and scorpions (Cole and Hardy 1981; Degenhardt et al. 1996; Lindner 1963; Milstead et al. 1950; Minton 1959). One regurgitated a 44 mm *Scolopendra* scorpion that was 22% of

Distribution of *Tantilla hobartsmithi*.

its SVL (Tanner 1954). Captives will eat mealworm *(Tenebrio)* larvae (Stebbins 1954).

POPULATIONS. Although seldom encountered due to their fossorial way of life, Tennant (1984) thought the species moderately abundant in the Chisos, Davis, and Guadalupe mountains of western Texas, and Hammerson and Benedict (1998) found two Utah adults about 30 cm apart under debris. The male-female ratio of the series of specimens examined by Cole and Hardy (1981) was essentially equal.

REMARKS. On morphological grounds, Cole and Hardy (1981) thought *T. hobartsmithi* most closely related to *T. gracilis.* The species was reviewed by Cole and Hardy (1983b).

Tantilla nigriceps Kennicott 1860a │ Plains Black-headed Snake

RECOGNITION. Another small *Tantilla*, this slender species reaches a record TBL of 39.0 cm (Perry and Hauer 1996). Its back and sides are yellowish to grayish brown. The head cap is dark brown or black with a convex to pointed posterior border two to five scales behind the parietals. The dark pigment does not extend downward to cover all of the supralabials, and the snout is dark, not lighter brown. No light collar or band follows the dark head cap. The head is rounded anteriorly and not broader than the neck. Body scales are smooth and pitless, and occur in 15 rows throughout. The venter is mostly white to cream, but the medial area is pink to coral red. Ventrals total 123–168, subcaudals 33–66; the anal plate is divided. Lateral head scalation includes a single nasal (partially divided by the nostril), 0 loreals, 1 preocular, 2 (1) postoculars, 1 + 1 temporals, 7 supralabials, and 6–7 infralabials. The rostral scale is broader than long. The first pair of infralabials meet at the midline, preventing the mental scale from contacting the anterior chin shields. The noncapitate, somewhat narrow, hemipenis has only one large, curved, spine at its base, a moderate-sized spine on the opposite side, and no basal spinules (Coles and Hardy 1981). At least three rows of 31–39 small to large, curved, evenly and densely distributed spines encircle the middle of the organ. Spinules are present between these spines. The lower calyxes of the apical section contain large spines, while the distal calyxes are more papillate. Usually each maxilla has 13 teeth.

Females have larger TBLs, SVLs, and TLs (Perry and Hauer 1996); males have 123–153 ventrals and 43–66 subcaudals, and females have 135–168 ventrals and 33–58 subcaudals.

GEOGRAPHIC VARIATION. No subspecies are currently recognized (Cole and Hardy 1981), but Perry and Hauer (1996) have reported that males from the west-central region of New Mexico are significantly longer than those from eastern New Mexico, and females from the west-central region were also larger than eastern females.

CONFUSING SPECIES. Other species of *Tantilla* can be distinguished by using the key presented above. The ground snake *(Sonora semiannulata)* has a loreal scale. Ring-necked snakes *(Diadophis)* have a distinct light collar and usually a spotted venter.

KARYOTYPE. Undescribed.

FOSSIL RECORD. Hill (1971) found Pleistocene (Rancholabrean) remains in a cave in Kendall County,

Plains black-headed snake, *Tantilla nigriceps*; Maverick County, Texas. (Photograph by Roger W. Barbour)

Texas, that he thought belonged either to this species or to *T. gracilis*, and Van Devender and Worthington (1977) and Parmley (1990a, 1990b) reported that small Holocene or Pleistocene vertebrae found in west Texas caves were either of *T. nigriceps* or *T. hobartsmithi*.

DISTRIBUTION. The species ranges in the United States from southwestern Nebraska and eastern Colorado southward to southern Texas in the east and southwestern New Mexico and southeastern Arizona in the West. It also occurs in an isolated population in eastern Wyoming. In Mexico, the species range includes parts of the states of Chihuahua, Coahuila, Nuevo León, Tamaulipas, and Durango.

HABITAT. *T. nigriceps* has been found in a variety of vegetation types ranging from plains and desert grasslands to scrub brush and woodlands. The soil is usually loose, or cracks are present in the rocks that serve as retreats. Surface hiding places (rocks, logs, etc.) are normally present, and one *T. nigriceps* has even been found hiding under cattle dung.

BEHAVIOR. Small snakes living in dry habitats face the major problem of water loss from their bodies, and *T. nigriceps* is no exception. To combat this, it has adopted a fossorial lifestyle in which it remains underground or beneath some surface shelter during the day. Its body is well adapted to a burrowing existence, with its compact skull, head no wider than the neck, slightly countersunk mouth, reduced eyes, and mid-body scales that have free margins with the greatest extension at the distal tip (Jackson and Reno 1975).

Foraging is done at night, particularly after rains, and the snake probably seeks out those surface shelters that have retained some moisture in the soil beneath them. It is often found on roads at night.

Arizona *T. nigriceps* are especially active when the surface soil is damp in the spring (March–April) after winter rains, and in July–August after summer rains (Lowe 1967). Degenhardt et al. (1996) and Price and LaPointe (1990) found the main annual period of activity in New Mexico extends from April to September, but a few are also active in both March and October. Wright and Wright (1957) list collection dates from March to December, and Brown (1951) found active individuals under cover in junkyards on warm sunny winter days. Some *T. nigriceps* estivate during the dry stretches of summer, and annual activity is probably strongly correlated with AT, ST, and rainfall (Price and LaPointe 1990). Two were found apparently hibernating 2.44 m deep in Kansas soil on 13 January (Tihen 1938).

REPRODUCTION. Nothing is known of the sexual cycles of this secretive species, but Wright and Wright (1957) stated that it is adult at a TBL of 17.5–40.0 cm. Only the right oviduct is present and functional (Clark 1970c). According to Degenhardt et al. (1996) courtship and mating probably take place in the spring, followed by egg laying in June or July, and hatching about two months later. Clutches average two eggs (one to three) (Degenhardt et al. 1996; Iver-

Distribution of *Tantilla nigriceps*.

son 1975; Stebbins 1985; Tennant 1984). The oval eggs have white, leathery shells, and are 22–25 × 7 mm (Degenhardt et al. 1996). Hatching dates in the literature are 25 July (Tennant 1984) and 26 August (Degenhardt et al. 1996). Hatchlings are 64–123 mm in TBL and grayish silver to tan with black head caps.

DIET AND FEEDING HABITS.   By the types of prey it consumes, *T. nigriceps* must do much of its feeding underground. It preys on earthworms, millipedes, centipedes, spiders, and insects (adults, larvae, pupae) (Degenhardt et al. 1996; Stebbins 1985; Tennant 1984; Wright and Wright 1957). Most of the prey items are small, to match the snake's short jaw gape.

The enlarged rear maxillary teeth are grooved, and the snake uses venom to subdue its prey. Brown (in Degenhardt et al. 1996) observed that a captive female fed well on large centipedes *(Scolopendra),* which it grabbed behind the head and retained for three to five minutes, then ate. Hill and Mackessy (1997) extracted 10–15 μl (0.05–0.10 mg dry yield) of venom from the Duvernoy's glands of two *T. nigriceps* that was 95.6% protein in composition. Duvernoy's gland secretions immobolized three scolopendromorph centipedes in six to eight minutes, whereas it took venom from the rock rattlesnake *(Crotalus lepidus)* more than an hour to do so (Rodríguez-Robles 1994).

PREDATORS AND DEFENSE.   The only record of predation is that of ants killing and eating a *T. nigriceps* in Chihuahua, Mexico (Tanner 1985), but probably snake-eating serpents, small mammals, and possibly, large invertebrates also prey on it.

It is possible that its venom could deter a small would-be predator, but its small mouth prevents it from giving a human a serious bite.

POPULATIONS.   Fitch (1993) found that *T. nigriceps* made up 1.17–8.90% of the total numbers of snakes he collected at four sites in Kansas. Tennant (1984) thought the species relatively uncommon in West Texas, but more abundant both in the Panhandle and in the thorn brush of the Rio Grande plain. In four years, Price and LaPointe (1990) collected 34 *T. nigriceps* (7.5% of all snakes) while road cruising along a 25 km stretch of road in central New Mexico, and Fouquette and Lindsay (1955) collected 12 (6 of each sex) in just over a month at one northwestern Texas site, so *T. nigriceps* can be fairly common at some localities.

REMARKS.   Because so little of the life histories are known of this species and other southwestern *Tantilla*, comprehensive research is needed to determine their specific ecological requirements and status.

Tantilla oolitica (Telford 1966) | Rim Rock Crowned Snake

RECOGNITION.   This extremely rare, small snake (to 29.2 cm TBL) is most closely related to *Tantilla coronata*. It is tan to light brown dorsally with a pinkish white to cream-colored venter, the nape and rounded head dark brown to black, and the snout tan. On the unpatterned body, the darker dorsal coloration extends ventrally to about the level of the third scale row, below which it gradually lightens to the pale ventral coloration. A light-colored, sometimes broken, neckband may occur on the postparietal and posterior temporal scales in some individuals, and a pale postocular blotch is usually present on each side of the head. Body scales are smooth and pitless, and the anal plate is divided. There are 15 scale rows along the entire body, 135–146 ventrals, and 41–63 subcaudals.

Lateral head scalation consists of 1 nasal, 0 loreals, 1 preocular, 2 postoculars, 2 temporals, 6–7 supralabials, and 5–6 infralabials. The mental scale may touch the chin shields. The hemipenis has two similar-sized basal hooks, one along the basal third of the sulcus spermaticus and another along the middle third of the organ. Each maxilla contains 13–16 teeth separated by a diastema from the enlarged posterior fang.

Several points of sexual dimorphism are evident. Females reach a greater length (24.6 cm SVL) than males (17.1 cm maximum SVL). Males TLs are 20.8–22.4% of TBL, and the TLs of females are 19.1–19.6% of TBL; males also have a greater number of subcaudals (51–63) than females (41–48).

Rim rock crowned snake, *Tantilla oolitica*; Monroe County, Florida. (Photograph by Barry Mansell)

GEOGRAPHIC VARIATION. Variation occurs in the extent of development of the pale neckband, which is lacking in mainland individuals but occurs in varying degrees on those from the Keys. Porras and Wilson (1979) also pointed out the *T. oolitica* from Grassy Key have a shorter relative TL (17.9–18.1 to 19.1–19.6%) and fewer subcaudals (41–44 to 45–48) than other known specimens; however, once again, the authors caution that few specimens have been collected. In fact, *T. oolitica* may be rarest of North American snakes.

CONFUSING SPECIES. The more northerly *T. relicta pamlica* is smaller (to 21.6 TBL), has only one basal hook on its hemipenis, a longer tail in females (over 20% of total body length), fewer ventrals (115–129), a broad light neckband, and some white flecks on its snout. *Storeria dekayi victa* is larger (to 48.3 cm TBL), has two pale neckbands, a dorsal pattern of two rows of faint dark spots, and keeled body scales.

KARYOTYPE AND FOSSIL RECORD. Unknown.

DISTRIBUTION. *T. oolitica* is known from Dade County, Key Largo, Upper Matecumbe Key, Grassy Key, and Vaca Key (Krysko and Decker 1996) in Monroe County, Florida. One has been reported from Key West.

HABITAT. Pine rock lands and tropical hardwood hammocks in shallow sandy soils over oolitic limestone formations were probably the ancestral habitat; there this small burrowing snake hid in stumps and under logs, rocks, and fallen palmetto leaves. In habitats disturbed by humans, it has been found under boards, logs, and trash in vacant lots and pastures. Porras and Wilson (1979) thought that eroded cavities in

Distribution of *Tantilla oolitica*.

the limestone substratum probably provide refugia. With the rapid urbanization of southeastern Florida, the natural habitat of *T. oolitica* is disappearing, and its future is in jeopardy. Populations occurring in natural areas must be located and their habitat preserved from future development, otherwise this small snake faces extinction.

BEHAVIOR. Almost nothing is known of the life history of this secretive, semifossorial snake. It has been taken in September, February, April, and June, and Porras and Wilson (1979) thought it likely *T. oolitica* emerges principally from its hiding places during and after rains, since two of the snakes they reported were collected after rains.

REPRODUCTION. Nothing is known about reproduction in *T. oolitica,* but it is probably similar to that of other crowned snakes.

GROWTH AND LONGEVITY. Unknown.

DIET AND FEEDING HABITS. The feeding habits are unknown, but it may eat centipedes, insects, and other small invertebrates.

PREDATORS AND DEFENSE. Porras and Wilson (1979) suggested that the scorpion *Centruroides gracilis,* which is abundant where the snake occurs, may be a natural predator.

POPULATIONS. *T. oolitica* is considered threatened.

REMARKS. *T. oolitica* shows greater variability in scale characters than *T. coronata* and *T. relicta,* and resembles *T. coronata* more than it does *T. relicta* in characters of scutellation, body proportions, size, and hemipenile morphology (Telford 1980a). *T. oolitica* was reviewed by Telford (1980a).

Tantilla planiceps (Blainville 1835) | Western Black-headed Snake

RECOGNITION. This small (to 38.6 cm TBL) snake has a beige to light brown or olive gray body; the whitish, unmarked venter is orange or reddish along the midline, and the brown to black dorsal surface of the head is markedly darker than the body. The labials and lower surface of the head and neck are grayish white. The head pattern consists of a dark head cap extending ventrolaterally 0.5–2.0 scales below the corner of the mouth and on the middorsal line two to three scales beyond the posterior end of the interparietal suture, followed by a light white to cream-colored neck collar 0.5–1.0 scale wide, often with several distinct brown spots along the posterior edge of the collar. The posterior edge of the dark head cap is usually convex or straight. The pointed head has a countersunk lower jaw. Body scales are smooth and pitless, and usually occur in 15 rows along the length of the body, although the number may vary from 13 to 18 rows immediately anterior to the divided anal plate. Lateral head scalation includes one nasal (usually divided only below the naris, although often divided both above and below the naris), no loreals, one preocular, two postoculars, one plus one temporals, seven supralabials (with three plus four entering the orbit), and six infralabials. The mental scale usually touches the anterior chin shields. The proximal half of the basal section of the noncapitate hemipenis is essentially naked, while the distal part of the basal section bears numerous spinules, and there is usually a

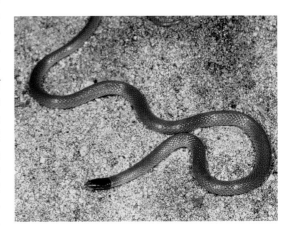

Western black-headed snake, *Tantilla planiceps*; Ventura County, California. (Photograph by Robert W. Hansen)

single, curved, small to large spine near the sulcus spermaticus at approximately the level of the proximal spinules. When inverted, the hemipenis extends 9–15 subcaudals. Each maxilla has 10–14 anterior teeth, usually separated by a diastema from two (rarely three) posterior, functional, grooved fangs.

Considerable sexual dimorphism and geographic variation exists in the number of ventrals and subcaudals. Ventrals range from 134 to 184 for males and from 148 to 197 for females; subcaudals present are 57–73 for males and 49–70 for females. A small degree of sexual dimorphism exists in TL; males have TLs that are 20.3–26.8% of TBL, and female TLs are 18.1–23.8% of TBL (Cole and Hardy 1981).

GEOGRAPHIC VARIATION.   No subspecies are currently recognized. Cole and Hardy (1981) have shown that *T. planiceps,* as recognized by Tanner (1966a), actually represented four distinct, monotypic species— *T. planiceps, T. yaquia, T. atriceps,* and *T. hobartsmithi*— based primarily on the anatomy of the male copulatory organs, with supporting evidence from features of head coloration, scutellation, and size. They considered *T. eiseni* and *T. planiceps transmontana* synonyms of *T. planiceps.* Stebbins (1985) reported that in individuals from the desert side of the mountains in southern California, the upper body surface is pale brown and the dark cap usually does not extend below the corner of the mouth. The white collar may be faint, but is rarely absent, and seldom has a dark border.

CONFUSING SPECIES.   The hemipenis of the southwestern black-headed snake *(T. hobartsmithi)* has an enlarged globular tip (capitate) and two enlarged spines at the base, the black head cap usually does not extend below the corner of the mouth, and no dark spots bordering the light neck collar are present. The ring-necked snake *(Diadophis punctatus)* has dark spots on a yellow or orange belly, and the underside of the tail is red.

KARYOTYPE AND FOSSIL RECORD.   Unknown.

DISTRIBUTION.   *T. planiceps* occurs in southern California from the vicinity of San Francisco Bay to the tip of Baja California, Mexico. Cole and Hardy

Distribution of *Tantilla planiceps.*

(1981) suggest that although some gaps in the range probably reflect inadequate collecting, others may indicate a relict distribution pattern.

HABITAT.   Little specific information is available on the habitats of this highly secretive and fossorial species. Stebbins (1954) reported that it occurs primarily in the Lower and Upper Sonoran life zones in arid and semiarid environments. Individuals have been collected in chaparral (Banta and Morafka 1968), grassland, an ecotone between grassland and oak woodland–chaparral (Sullivan 1981b), and desert (Klauber 1939a; Bostic 1971). In arid habitats *T. planiceps* occurs along rocky edges of washes, arroyos, and streams, and on rocky hillsides (Stebbins 1985).

BEHAVIOR.   *T. planiceps* is crepuscular to nocturnal, and appears to spend most of its time underground in crevices and animal burrows, but it may be found under rocks, logs, boards, and plant debris. Wright and Wright (1957) reported that *T. planiceps* (as *T. eiseni*) was frequently collected from road building areas, diggings, and excavations.

REPRODUCTION.   Clutches contain one to four eggs (Brown 1997; Stebbins 1985), laid between May and June. Other reproductive data are lacking.

GROWTH AND LONGEVITY.   Unknown.

DIET AND FEEDING HABITS. *T. planiceps* feeds mainly on insects (especially beetle larvae) and centipedes. A captive ate earthworms (Perkins 1938).

The species is rear-fanged, and possesses a Duvernoy's gland that produces the toxic saliva used to subdue its prey.

PREDATORS AND DEFENSE. The only reported incidence of predation on *T. planiceps* was by a loggerhead shrike *(Lanius ludovicianus)* in California (Ely 1997).

This inoffensive species usually does not bite, but while being captured may attempt to implant its sharp tail into the hand (Staedeli 1972). Whether this is a device for escape or a method of defense is unknown.

POPULATIONS. Population studies have not been reported, but as many as six *T. planiceps* have been found together under one rock (Brown 1997).

REMARKS. *T. planiceps* was reviewed by Cole and Hardy (1981, 1983c).

Tantilla relicta (Telford 1966) | Florida Crowned Snake

RECOGNITION. The unpatterned body of this small snake (to 24.1 cm TBL) is tan to reddish brown dorsally, gradually becoming lighter along the sides and blending with the pinkish white to cream-colored venter. The pointed to slightly rounded head has a pattern that varies from completely dark brown or black to having a prominent whitish to cream-colored neck band dividing the darker pigmented areas into a head cap and a neck collar; the dark neck collar is one to nine scales long (mean, 4.4; Telford 1980b). A pale postocular blotch is usually present on each side of the head, and it may connect with the neckband. The body scales are smooth with no pits, and occur in 15 rows with no reduction at any point along the body; the anal plate is divided. Laterally on the head are one nasal, no loreals, one preocular, two postoculars, two temporals, six to seven supralabials, and six infralabials. The mental scale may touch the anterior chin shields. The hemipenis bears a single basal hook along the proximal third of the organ. Each maxilla has 14–16 teeth (usually 15) separated by a diastema from the enlarged posterior fang.

Females are slightly longer than males (19.0–19.4 cm maximum SVL) and have more ventrals (119–142, compared with 115–135 in males) (Telford 1966). Males have TLs 28.7–29.7% of TBL, compared with 18.5–29.1% of TBL in females, and a greater number of subcaudals (44–67, compared with 40–60 in females) (Telford 1966).

Literature descriptions of *Tantilla coronata wagneri* (Jan 1862) from peninsular Florida by Blanchard (1938), Carr (1940), and Wright and Wright (1957) are based on *T. relicta*.

GEOGRAPHIC VARIATION. Three subspecies are recognized, based largely on head patterns, and appear to be ecologically separated by their habitat preferences (see HABITAT). *Tantilla r. relicta* Telford 1966, the peninsula crowned snake, occurs from Lake George, Marion County, southward along the central ridge of Florida to Highlands County and west to Tampa Bay, and has also been reported from the Florida west coast on Cedar Keys, Levy County, and in Sarasota and Charlotte counties. This subspecies intergrades with *T. r. neilli* in the vicinity of Lake George, Marion County, and around the former Suwannee Straits (Telford 1980b). *T. r. relicta* has a light neck band in most individuals (87%; Telford 1966), fol-

Peninsula crowned snake, *Tantilla relicta relicta*; Volusia County, Florida. (Photograph by Peter May)

lowed by a dark collar which is usually four (one to five) scales wide at the dorsal midline; a pointed head with a countersunk lower jaw; 117 to 134 ventrals; 40–59 subcaudals; and TLs 18–24% of TBL. *T. r. neilli* Telford 1966, the central Florida crowned snake, ranges in north-central peninsular Florida from Madison County southward to Hillsborough River and northern Polk County, and eastward to the St. Johns River. It lacks a light neckband, but has a narrowly rounded head on which the lower jaw is not countersunk, 123–142 ventrals, 46–67 subcaudals, and a relatively long tail, 19–29% of TBL. *T. r. pamlica* Telford 1966, the coastal dunes crowned snake, is found along the Florida east coast from Cape Canaveral southward to Palm Beach County. This race with a pointed head and countersunk lower jaw has a broad light neckband, and in over 60% of individuals, there is an absence of dark pigment on the parietal, supraocular, and temporal regions (Telford 1966); there is also extensive light pigment on the snout. The dark neck collar is usually three (two to five) scales wide at the dorsal midline. It has 115–129 ventrals, 45–51 subcaudals and TLs 20–24% of TBL. Christman (1980) reported that ventral and subcaudal counts tend to decrease clinally to the south in the various subspecies.

Telford (1980b) recommended that the southern population at Archbold Biological Station, Lake Placid, Highland County, be critically examined, since specimens from there have six supralabials, a condition rarely found in other *T. relicta* populations.

CONFUSING SPECIES. Other species of *Tantilla* can be identified by the key presented above. The brown snakes *(Storeria)* have keeled body scales, and the southern ring-necked snake *(Diadophis punctatus punctatus)* has a ventral pattern consisting of a central row of black half-moons.

KARYOTYPE. Undescribed.

FOSSIL RECORD. Auffenberg (1963) reported fossil *Tantilla* from middle or late Pleistocene deposits in north-central Florida that may be *T. relicta*.

DISTRIBUTION. It is restricted to peninsular Florida, where it ranges in the north from Madison County east to possibly Duval County and the St.

Distribution of *Tantilla relicta*.

Johns River, southward to Sarasota and Charlotte counties in the west and Highlands County in the center, and from Cape Canaveral to Palm Beach County in the east.

HABITAT. This species is a burrower, hiding beneath rocks, logs, or other prone objects. The three subspecies seem to prefer different habitats. *T. r. relicta* prefers scrub woodlands, while *T. r. neilli* is found in sand hills and xeric and mesic hammocks; where these subspecies are allopatric, *relicta* may occur in sand hills, suggesting it is prevented from living elsewhere by competing *neilli*. *T. r. pamlica* lives in isolated coastal dunes and scrub woodlands. In scrub habitats *T. relicta* is most often found in the early successional stages; thus it depends on periodic disturbance, such as fire or clear-cutting, to remove the matted understory or pine canopy (Campbell and Christman 1982). Mushinsky and Witz (1993) found that fire periodicity had no apparent influence on the local distribution of *T. relicta* in sandhill habitat in west-central Florida. Funderburg and Lee (1968) reported that *T. relicta* (as *T. coronata wagneri*) may take up permanent residence in the mounds of Florida pocket gophers *(Geomys)*. In 12 months Mushinsky (1984) collected 150 *T. relicta* in pitfall traps on approximately 20 ha of sandhill habitat. Greenberg et al. (1994) collected 29 *T. relicta* in pitfall traps and two individuals in single-ended funnel traps in sand pine scrub habitat over a period of 13 months.

Wilson and Porras (1983) reported that the habitat of *T. r. pamlica* in southeastern Florida has been reduced by increasing urban and agricultural development.

BEHAVIOR. Little is known of the life history of this small snake. Telford (1966) thought it a "submerged basker" since his captives lay beneath the surface of the sand with just the head above ground. Smith (1982) reported that *T. relicta* were completely fossorial, living under surface litter. Annually, *T. relicta* is active from late February to early December with peak activity occurring in late March and early April and again in late September and October (Smith 1982). In a 10 year study of *T. relicta* in west-central Florida, Mushinsky and Witz (1993) collected fewer individuals during the cooler months of the year than during the warmer months.

REPRODUCTION. All *Tantilla* are oviparous, but the eggs of *T. relicta* have not been described. Mushinsky and Witz (1993) observed eggs in the oviducts of 33 individuals in west-central Florida; two gravid females were captured in mid-March, 26 from late April to early June, and five in early August. The smallest female with visible eggs had a SVL of 15 cm. They suggested that the extended reproductive period may reflect considerable annual variation in the reproductive cycle, a poorly defined reproductive period, or production of more than one clutch per year. The smallest mature male examined by Telford (1966) had a SVL of 12 cm, while the smallest mature female had a SVL of 12.4 cm.

Ashton and Ashton (1981) suggested that the breeding habits of *T. relicta* are probably similar to those of the southeastern crowned snake.

Four west-central Florida hatchlings (with umbili-cal scars present) captured in May and June ranged from 8.8 to 9.5 cm SVL (Mushinsky and Witz 1993). Juveniles resemble the adults in pattern and coloration, but have large heads in proportion to body length; the smallest juvenile examined by Telford (1966) had a SVL of 7.7 cm.

GROWTH AND LONGEVITY. Unknown.

DIET AND FEEDING HABITS. Smith (1982) found that *T. relicta* specialized in feeding on tenebrionid larvae. In a study of 124 stomachs, he found that one species of tenebrionid beetle occurred in 85.5% of the stomachs containing food and made up 89.6% of the prey items. Centipedes and snails accounted for nearly all of the remainder of the diet. Mushinsky and Witz (1993) have suggested that this specialized diet probably reflects the small body size and burrowing habits of *T. relicta*.

PREDATORS AND DEFENSE. *T. relicta* is known to be eaten by other snakes *(Stilosoma extenuatum, Lampropeltis getula, Micrurus fulvius),* and probably various birds and mammals are also predators.

Telford (1966) suggested that the banded head pattern gives more protection from avian predators by breaking up the head outline, allowing *T. r. relicta* and *T. r. pamlica* to inhabit white sand areas, while the darker head of *T. r. neilli* would be at less disadvantage in areas of thick vegetation. This may account for some of the ecological separation noted between the three races.

REMARKS. Clark (1998) described a procedure for isolating DNA from the shed skin of *T. relicta* and other species. This species was reviewed by Telford (1980b).

Tantilla wilcoxi Stejneger 1902 | Chihuahuan Black-headed Snake

RECOGNITION. This small (to TBL of 35.5 cm) snake is pale or dark brown, gray, or olive green, and usually has dark spots on the sides. A distinct black or dark brown head cap extends posteriorly to near the tips of the parietals, then downward to or below the corner of the slightly countersunk mouth, including parts of the sixth and seventh labials. The dark head cap is bordered by a broad white collar, two scales wide, that crosses the tips of the parietals. The white collar is bordered posteriorly by a black band or spots 0.5–1.5 scales wide that may sometimes separate the white collar and join with the black head cap. The

Chihuahuan black-headed snake, *Tantilla wilcoxi*; Northern Mexico. (Photograph by Cecil Schwalbe)

pupil is small and round. The venter is dull white anteriorly, gradually changing from red to orange toward the posterior two-thirds of the body. The dorsal scales are smooth and occur in 15 rows along the length of the body. On the underside are 140–146 ventrals, 51–69 subcaudals, and a divided anal plate. Lateral head scalation consists of 2 nasals, 0 loreal, 1 preocular, 2 postoculars, 1 + 1 (+1) temporals, 6–7 supralabials, and 6–7 infralabials. The mental may be separated from the chin shields. The basal portion of the noncapitate hemipenis has many small spines; a large, thick, curved spine near the single sulcus spermaticus; and a second, somewhat smaller, spine on the opposite side. The midsection, which gradually merges with the apical region, is spinose, with numerous small to very large, densely distributed, curved spines arranged in at least five rows that encircle the organ (Cole and Hardy 1981). Each maxilla has 14 teeth (Smith 1941). The TL is 24–26% of the TBL (Conant 1965a; McDiarmid et al. 1976; Webb and Hensley 1959).

GEOGRAPHIC VARIATION. No subspecies are currently recognized (Cole and Hardy 1981).

CONFUSING SPECIES. *T. wilcoxi* can be distinguished from other species of *Tantilla* in its range by the broad white collar crossing the tips of the parietals.

KARYOTYPE. Unknown.

FOSSIL RECORD. Fossil remains of a Pleistocene (Rancholabrean) *Tantilla* from Rancho La Brea, California (LaDuke 1991), may be from this species.

DISTRIBUTION. The Chihuahuan black-headed snake is found in the Huachuca, Patagonia, and Santa Rita mountains of extreme southern Arizona southward into southwestern Chihuahua, northeastern Sinaloa, central Durango, Zacatecas, western San Luis Potosi, southeastern Coahuila, and southern Nuevo León in Mexico.

HABITAT. *T. wilcoxi* lives at elevations of 900–2,438 m on rocky slopes in desert grassland, and in pine-oak forests.

BEHAVIOR. Little has been reported about the behavior of this poorly known snake. It is nocturnal, and during the day is found under rocks, logs, and dead plants such as yucca, agave, and sotol, and may also be found in nearby dumps and trash piles adjacent to prime habitat (Lowe 1964; Fowlie 1965).

Distribution of *Tantilla wilcoxi*.

REPRODUCTION. Behler and King (1979) reported that *T. wilcoxi* lays one to three eggs in spring and summer. No other reproductive information has been published.

GROWTH AND LONGEVITY. Unreported.

DIET AND FEEDING HABITS. This small snake seems to feed primarily on spiders, but may also eat burrowing insect grubs and centipedes (Behler and King 1979; Fowlie 1965).

PREDATORS AND DEFENSE. Liner (1983) observed a *T. wilcoxi* being engulfed by a night snake, *Hypsiglena torquata,* in a collecting bag. Van Denburgh and Slevin (1913) commented on removing a specimen from the stomach of a *Diadophis punctatus* caught in Ramsey Canyon in the Huachuca Mountains.

POPULATIONS. Rare.

REMARKS. This species was reviewed by Liner (1983).

Tantilla yaquia Smith 1942 | Yaqui Black-headed Snake

RECOGNITION. The basic body color of this small snake (TBL to 32.5 cm) is brown, light brown, or brownish tan. In some individuals the dorsal scales have a speckled appearance, giving the impression of a faint stripe on each scale row; this is due to the posterior superimposition of each dorsal scale, which results in a greater concentration of pigment at each area of overlap. The tip of the snout may be lighter than the ground color. A distinct brown, brownish black, or black head cap extends onto the nape from two to four scales on the midline, and laterally 0.5–3.0 scales below the angle of the mouth. The posterior edge of the dark head cap is usually straight, and the head cap is bordered posteriorly by a narrow (1.0–1.5 scales) light or cream-colored nuchal collar, which may be bordered by several distinct brown to black spots. Most of supralabials one, four, five, and six, and the lower one-third to one-half of the anterior temporal, are white to cream-colored, contrasting sharply with the dark head cap. The venter is white anteriorly, gradually changing to pinkish orange beneath the tail. The body scales are smooth, without pits, and occur in 15 scale rows along the body. The anal plate is divided. Head scalation consists of a divided nasal, no loreals, 1 preocular, 2 postoculars, 1 + 1 temporals, 7 (6) supralabials, and 6 (7) infralabials. The mental scale is usually separated from the chin shields (McDiarmid 1968; Hardy and McDiarmid 1969). The hemipenis is subcylindrical to clavate when everted, semicapitate, with two very large basal spines and no spinules proximal to the basal spines; 37–58 spines arranged in two to four rows approximately encircle the spinose mid-

section, except at the sulcus spermaticus (Cole and Hardy 1981).

Males have 134–157 ventrals and 50–73 subcaudals, and the TL is 21.2–27.5% of the TBL. Females have 145–165 ventrals and 46–75 subcaudals, and the TL is 17.2–28.5% of the TBL. Females generally have more ventrals than males in the same population (McDiarmid 1968).

GEOGRAPHIC VARIATION. No subspecies are currently recognized. McDiarmid (1968) found evidence of clinal variation in several characteristics of *T. yaquia* based on a comparison of individuals from the northern, central, and southern portions of its range. Clinal

Yaqui black-headed snake, *Tantilla yaquia*; Santa Cruz County, Arizona. (Photograph by Brad R. Moon)

variation included a decrease in the number of ventrals plus subcaudals from north to south, shorter tails and a more extensive head cap in southern populations, the presence of one to nine dark spots posterior to the nuchal collar in the central and southern populations, and regional variation in the extent of white area posterior to the eye.

CONFUSING SPECIES. This species may be distinguished from other *Tantilla* occurring in its range by its light nuchal collar and the white to cream-colored spot on the side of the head.

KARYOTYPE AND FOSSIL RECORD. Unreported.

DISTRIBUTION. *T. yaquia* ranges south from southern Cochise and Santa Cruz counties in southeastern Arizona and Hidalgo County in New Mexico (Painter et al. 1992) into Mexico through eastern Sonora and extreme western Chihuahua, southern Sonora, and Sinaloa into the Rio Santiago Valley in Nayarit.

HABITAT. *T. yaquia* is found in evergreen and riparian woodland at elevations above 1,000 m, in deciduous short-tree forests along foothills and western slopes at elevations of 500–1,000 m, occasionally in drier thorn woodland, and in tropical semiarid and dry forests at elevations below 200 m.

BEHAVIOR. The limited information available on the life history and ecology of the Yaqui black-headed snake suggests that it is a nocturnal, secretive snake that spends most of its time beneath rocks and in crevices. McDiarmid (1968) reported that in the northern part of its range it has been found under rocks and surface litter in March, April, August, and September, especially following rains, when the soil is moist. *T. yaquia* have also been found in or near streams, and on paved roadways during summer nights (Degenhardt et al. 1996). Individuals have been collected in December, January, and February, and a few have been collected in July-September.

REPRODUCTION. Almost nothing has been recorded about the reproductive biology of the Yaqui black-headed snake. Stebbins (1985) suggested that it probably lays a clutch of one to four eggs in late

Distribution of *Tantilla yaquia*.

spring and summer. McDiarmid (1968) reported that two recently hatched individuals, a male and a female, measured 10.4 cm and 14.0 cm in TBL.

GROWTH AND LONGEVITY. Unreported.

DIET AND FEEDING. There is no documentation of the diet or feeding habits of *T. yaquia*, but it has been suggested that it probably feeds on small invertebrates such as millipedes, centipedes, larval and adult soft-bodied insects, and spiders (Degenhardt et al. 1996; Stebbins 1985).

PREDATORS AND DEFENSE. A specimen in the collection of the Museum of Vertebrate Zoology, University of California, was found in the stomach of the Tarahumara frog *(Rana tarahumarae)* (McDiarmid 1968). Degenhardt et al. (1996) reported that a small amount of musk and feces may be released from the vent when *T. yaquia* is captured.

POPULATIONS. No data are available on population dynamics.

REMARKS. *Tantilla yaquia* was reviewed by McDiarmid (1977). Additional studies are needed to understand the biology and ecology of this species, and to fill the gaps in its geographic range.

Thamnophis Fitzinger 1843

Garter and Ribbon Snakes

Key to the Species of *Thamnophis*

Modified from Ernst and Barbour (1989), Powell et al. (1998), and Rossman et al. (1996)

1a. Lateral light stripe occurs anteriorly on scale row four . . 2

1b. Lateral light stripe is absent or occurs anteriorly on scale rows two or three 8

2a. Head small, neck not distinct; lateral light stripe anteriorly involves scale row two 3

2b. Head normal, neck distinct, lateral light stripe anteriorly usually only involves scale rows three to four 4

3a. Usually 6 (rarely 7) supralabials; normally 17 midbody scale rows . . . . *T. brachystoma* (in part)

3b. Usually 7 (rarely 6) supralabials; normally 19 midbody scale rows . . . . *T. butleri*

4a. Tail long, usually more than 25% of TBL 5

4b. Tail not long, usually less than 25% of TBL 6

5a. Parietal spots bright, conspicuous, and often fused; dark pigment of sides usually not extending onto ventral scutes, but if so, covering less than 40% of each ventral . . . . *T. proximus*

5b. Parietal spots often absent, but if present, small, rarely bright or fused; dark pigment of sides always extending onto ventral scutes, and usually covering at least 40% of each ventral . . . . *T. sauritus*

6a. More than 19 midbody scale rows; dark bars present on supralabials 7

6b. No more than 19 midbody scale rows; no dark bars on supralabials . . . . *T. sirtalis* (in part)

7a. Eight to 9 supralabials; weak keels on dark dorsal scales . . . . *T. eques*

7b. Normally 7 supralabials; dark dorsal scales lack keels . . . . *T. radix*

8a. Light lateral stripe absent anteriorly, or only on scale row three; posterior set of supralabials light colored and bordered by dark bars . . . . *T marcianus*

8b. Light lateral stripe anteriorly involves scale row two; posterior supralabials not patterned as above 9

9a. Fewer than 19 midbody scale rows 10

9b. Nineteen or more midbody scale rows 11

10a. Usually 7 supralabials and 15 midbody scale rows . . . . *T. ordinoides*

10b. Usually 6 supralabials and 17 midbody scale rows . . . . *T. brachystoma* (in part)

11a. Seven supralabials . . . . *T. sirtalis* (in part)

11b. Eight or more supralabials 12

12a. Dark blotch present on side of neck; 19 or fewer anterior scale rows; two longitudinal rows of dark spots on each side . . . . *T. cyrtopsis*

12b. No dark blotch on side of neck; 19 or more anterior scale rows; no longitudinal rows of dark spots 13

13a. Prefrontal scale shorter than internasal scale . . . . *T. atratus* (in part)

13b. Prefrontal scale longer than internasal scale 14

14a. Usually only one supralabial contacts the orbit; no light lateral stripes; dorsum often conspicuously spotted . . . . *T. rufipunctatus*

14b. Usually two supralabials contact the orbit; light lateral stripe present; if present, dorsal spots not prominent 15

15a. Internasal scales broader than long, not tapered anteriorly; supralabials six and seven higher than broad . . . . *T. elegans*

15b. Internasal scales broader than long, tapered anteriorly; supralabials six and seven not higher than broad 16

16a. Fewer than 152 ventral scutes in males, and fewer than 144 in females . . . . *T. sirtalis* (in part)

16b. More than 152 ventral scutes in males, and more than 146 in females 17

17a. Large dark spots present below lateral stripe . . . . *T. sirtalis* (in part)

17b. If present below lateral stripe, dark spots not large 18

18a. No longitudinal stripes present, or only a faint, narrow vertebral stripe present; small dark nuchal blotches present . . . . *T. hammondii*

18b. One to three longitudinal stripes present; if present, dark nuchal blotches may be large 19

19a. Usually 11 infralabials present; the narrow vertebral stripe is occasionally faded posteriorly . . . . *T. couchii*

19b. Usually 10 or fewer infralabials; vertebral stripe varies . . 20

20a. At least 21 anterior scale rows; no more than 79 subcaudals in males, and 73 in females; the vertebral stripe dull and narrow . . . . *T. gigas*

20b. No more than 19 anterior scale rows; at least 85 subcaudals in males, and 76 in females; the vertebral stripe is often distinct and bright . . . . *T. atratus* (in part)

Thamnophis atratus (Kennicott 1860b) | Western Aquatic Garter Snake

RECOGNITION. This garter snake is a stout, short-bodied (TBL to 107 cm) species with an orange or yellow orange, one- to two-scale-wide, middorsal stripe, a pale yellow lateral stripe on scale rows two and three of each side, and a bright lemon yellow chin and throat. In western Santa Clara, Santa Cruz, San Mateo, and San Francisco counties, the lateral stripes may be obscured or absent, and the middorsal stripe yellow. Dorsal body color varies from black, dark brown, olive brown, and gray to bluish green with some salmon red or yellowish blotches on the sides between the medial and lateral stripes. The venter is bluish to olive. The supralabials bear black bars, and the iris is gray or black. Body scales are keeled without apical pits, and lie in 19 anterior rows, 19 (21) rows at midbody, and 15–17 rows near the tail. Beneath are 138–171 ventrals, 59–95 subcaudals, and an undivided anal plate. On each side of the head are a nasal scale, 1 loreal, 1 (2) preocular(s), 3 (2–4) postoculars, 1 + 2 + 3 (1–2) temporals, 8 (7) supralabials (the seventh is longer than the sixth), and 9–11 infralabials. The sixth and seventh supralabials are not greatly enlarged, the internasals are normally longer than wide, and the posterior pair of chin shields is longer than the anterior pair. The hemipenis has not been described. Each maxilla bears 21–28 teeth, with the most posterior enlarged.

Males have 145–171 ventrals, 65–95 subcaudals, and TLs 23–29% of TBL; females have 138–168 ventrals, 59–84 subcaudals, and TLs 22–27% of TBL. In addition, the relative height of the first dorsal scale row (maximum vertical height of dorsal scale row one divided by maximum width of the vertebral row) averages 2.6 (2.2–2.9) in females, but only 2.3 (2.1–2.6) in males (Rossman 1995).

GEOGRAPHIC VARIATION. Three subspecies are found in the United States (Boundy 1999). *Thamnophis atratus atratus* (Kennicott 1860b), the Santa Cruz garter snake, occurs along the Pacific Coast of California south of the San Francisco Bay from southern Solano County and the southern half of the San Francisco Peninsula southward to central Santa Barbara County. The distribution is interrupted by the Salinas Valley, in which the subspecies is absent. It is described above. *Thamnophis a. hydrophilus* Fitch 1936, the Oregon garter snake, is found north of the San Francisco Bay from the Gualala River on the Sonoma-Mendocino county line and on the eastern side of the Coast Ranges from Lake and Yolo counties, California, north to the Umpqua River Valley in Coos and Douglas counties, southwestern Oregon. It is pale gray with a dull, narrow middorsal stripe, often obscured or absent lateral stripes, dark checkerlike marks along the sides, and usually 10 infralabials. Overall, it is much darker than *T. a. atratus*. *Thamnophis a. zaxanthus* Boundy 1999, the broad-striped garter snake, occurs in the highlands of California from Napa and Solano counties south to Santa Barbara County. Body color is dark gray to black, with a broad (3.5 scales wide), intensive, yellow to orangish middorsal stripe, conspicuous greenish lateral stripes, no dark checkerlike marks on the sides, and usually 9 infralabials.

According to Boundy (1999) and Rossman and Stewart (1987), the taxon *T. a. aquaticus* Fox 1951 is based on intergrades between *T. a. atratus* and *T. a. hydrophilus*, and therefore not valid.

CONFUSING SPECIES. See the above key for characters distinguishing *T. atratus* from other garter snakes within its range.

KARYOTYPE AND FOSSIL RECORD. Unknown.

DISTRIBUTION. *Thamnophis atratus* ranges from Coos and Douglas counties in southwestern Oregon south to central Santa Barbara County, California.

HABITAT. The species is associated with a variety of bodies of water, ranging from permanent, swift-flowing streams with rocky bottoms and banks to sluggish streams with soft bottoms, rivers, ponds, and lakes, occurring in dense-canopy oak woodlands, grassy woodland ecotones, and chaparral at elevations from sea level to about 1,500 m. Occasionally it will move some distance from the water (especially *T. a. atratus*) into dense vegetation, and Fitch (1940) found a few in dry situations like chaparral-covered hillsides.

Oregon garter snake, *Thamnophis atratus hydrophilus*; Josephine County, Oregon. (Photograph by William Leonard)

BEHAVIOR. Data on the life history of *T. atratus* are lacking. It is a diurnal forager that occasionally is active at dusk. Wright and Wright (1957) reported it is annually active from 1 January to 2 December in central California, and from 15 April to 2 October in the northern portion of the range. It is most commonly encountered from April to July in both populations. Winter is probably spent underground in rodent burrows or in crevices within rock outcrops.

This snake is a confirmed basker, especially those in the northern populations where it is often seen lying on the bank or boulders beside its stream. The cool WT of these northern waterways probably makes it necessary for *T. atratus* to warm itself in the sun to maintain a BT that will allow both foraging and digestion. Based on temperature effects on male sperm production, Fox (1954) thought the normal BT range to be 20–35°C. His laboratory captives would voluntarily limit activity when their BTs reached 35°C.

T. a. hydrophilus seems more aquatic than *T. a. atratus*, but some southern populations are highly aquatic.

REPRODUCTION. Reproductive data are also sparse. Wright and Wright (1957) considered males with

SVLs of 30.8–33.0 cm, and females with a SVL of 35.5 cm or larger to be adults. Fox (1954) studied the male reproductive cycle, and found spermiogenesis to be prolonged. Early spermatids are present from early May to early October, late spermatids from late June to early October, and mature sperm from late June through late October. Fox thought that a greater sample size would have probably revealed mature

Distribution of *Thamnophis atratus*.

sperm in early June. Sperm production is more advanced in southern populations than in those from farther north. Interstitial cells are largest in spring. In females, yolk deposition and the final enlargement of follicles occur in the spring (Fox 1954).

Mating by wild *T. atratus* was observed from 16 March to 2 May, and a captive male courted a female on 31 August, four days after she had given birth (Fitch 1940). Courtship and copulatory behaviors have not been described.

All garter snakes are viviparous, giving birth to live young at some time in the summer. Litter size in *T. atratus* ranges from 4–30 (mean, 8–9) young (Brown 1997; Fox 1948a; Nussbaum et al. 1983; Rossman et al. 1996). Neonates are born from late August to mid-October (Burghardt 1969; Rossman et al. 1996); Fitch (1940) reported a 17 August parturition. They have 18.6–23.0 cm TBLs.

GROWTH AND LONGEVITY. Unknown.

DIET AND FEEDING HABITS. Foraging behavior by *T. atratus* depends on age (Lind and Welsh 1994). Neonates are usually found on the bank in the shallows, juveniles hunt in shallow riffles and edge waters, and adults forage in deeper, faster-flowing waters or on land. Adults are active foragers, and Boundy (in Rossman et al. 1996) observed several individuals foraging in a stream by anchoring their tails to submerged rocks and striking at passing minnows. Newborns use mainly a sit-and-wait, ambush method, lying along stream margins and allowing the prey to come to them; and juveniles use a combination of hunting and ambushing. Newborns and juveniles may employ tongue-luring behavior (Welsh and Lind 2000). Before tongue luring, young *T. atratus* approach the water slowly, crawling among the streamside rocks until they position themselves on rocks at the stream margin with their heads oriented toward the water and 1–2 cm from its surface. During this cautious positioning, the head may be swayed back and forth, possibly to gain a parallax view, which may help them locate juvenile fish *(Oncorhynchus mykiss, O. tshawytscha)* below the water surface. Short-duration tongue flicks often occur during positioning. Luring behavior begins only after the snake has taken an ambush position and a fish enters its field of vision. The

snake orients toward the fish and extends and holds the tongue rigid while quivering its tips at the water surface for varying lengths of time. When the fish investigates the tongue lure, the snake strikes and pulls it to shore.

Reported prey are fish—sculpins *(Cottus)*, trout and salmon *(Oncorhynchus mykiss, O. tshawytscha)*, minnows, and suckers; amphibians—ranid frogs *(Rana aurora, R. boylii, R. catesbeiana;* both adults and tadpoles), treefrogs *(Pseudacris regilla)*, toad tadpoles *(Bufo)*, and salamanders *(Aneides, Bratrachoceps, Dicamptodon, Ensatina, Triturus;* both adults and larvae); reptiles—lizards *(Gerrhonotus, Sceloporus)* and juvenile snakes *(Coluber constrictor mormon, Thamnophis atratus)*; birds *(Carduelis, Zonotrichia)*; mammals—mice *(Microtus)* and juvenile brush rabbits *(Sylvilagus bachmani)*; slugs; leeches; and earthworms (Brown 1997; Fitch 1936, 1940, 1941; Fox 1951; Lind and Welsh 1994; Nussbaum et al. 1983; Rossman et al. 1996; Welsh and Lind 2000; Wright and Wright 1957). Although consumed in the wild, rodents, slugs, and earthworms have been refused by captives (Burghardt 1969; Fox 1951).

Neonates and juveniles feed primarily on tadpoles and fish, in different microhabitats than adults (Lind and Welsh 1994; Welsh and Lind 2000). Juveniles have a higher success rate of prey capture (37%) than neonates (18%) (Lind and Welsh 1994). Adults are successful about 20% of the time.

Differences in food preferences occur between the two subspecies and probably reflect more terrestrial foraging by southern *T. a. atratus*, which consumes slugs (66% by incidence), mice (10%), lizards (10%), salamanders (5%), fish (5%), juvenile snakes (4%), birds (4%), fish eggs (4%), juvenile rabbits (2%), and earthworms (2%) (Fitch 1940, 1941). Northern *T. a. hydrophilus* depends more on aquatic prey: tadpoles (53.2% by incidence), sculpin (15.6%), unidentified fish (10.4%), trout (9.7%), aquatic salamanders (3.9%), ranid frogs (3.9%), fish eggs (2.0%), and minnows and suckers (2.0%) (Fitch 1936).

PREDATORS AND DEFENSE. The only references to predation on this species are of an adult *T. atratus* that cannibalized a juvenile of its own species (Fitch 1940), and of a western yellow-bellied racer *(Coluber constrictor mormon)* attempting to eat an adult *T. atratus* (Rossman, in Rossman et al. 1996).

T. atratus will first try to escape when disturbed; if near water, it will quickly dive in and swim away or hide under or among submerged rocks; if on land away from water, it will seek shelter among vegetation. When handled, one can expect to be bitten and musked.

POPULATIONS. The size structure of one population of *T. a. hydrophilus* from northern California is dominated by small snakes with SVLs of 15–35 cm (Kupferberg 1994); probably less than 30% of the individuals in this population are mature (Rossman et al. 1996). Unfortunately, no complete study of the dynamics of a population of *T. atratus* has been published, even though in the proper habitat, especially in northern California and Oregon, the species may be quite common.

REMARKS. *T. atratus* was originally thought to be a subspecies of *T. ordinoides* (Fitch 1940), later of *T. elegans* (Fox 1951), and still later of *T. couchii* (Lawson and Dessauer 1979; Rossman 1979). Finally, it was elevated to full species status by Rossman and Stewart (1987). It has been reviewed by Rossman et al. (1996).

Thamnophis brachystoma (Cope 1892a) | Short-headed Garter Snake

RECOGNITION. This small (TBL to 55.9 cm) garter snake is olive gray to light brown or black with a pale orange, yellow, or yellowish tan dorsal stripe, and a lateral buff-colored to yellow stripe on each side. The dorsal stripe may be indistinct. The lateral stripes are two scale rows wide, usually occurring anteriorly on rows two and three, but occasionally on the lower half of row four, and tend to be bordered by fine black lines. Normally, there is no longitudinal series of black spots between the dorsal and lateral stripes. The venter is olive gray to light gray or tan with some brighter pigment at the sides of the ventral scutes. The short head is as broad or only slightly broader than the indistinct neck. The snout is very short (relative snout length—snout length divided by frontal scale length—is 58.5%), and the eye is proportionately smaller than that of other garter snakes (relative eye size—eye diameter divided by frontal length—is 59.0%) (Rossman et al. 1996). Dorsally, it is olive gray to light brown with an orange or yellow parietal spot; dark seams separate the supralabials. Ventrally, the head is salmon pink, yellowish, or cream-colored. The body scales are keeled and pitless, and usually occur in 17 rows throughout (76% of 155 Pennsylvania snakes examined by Barton 1956), or 17-19-17 (11%), or 17-17-15 (8%). The anal plate is not divided. On the side of the head are a loreal, 1 (2) preocular(s), 2–3 postoculars, 2 temporals, 6 (7–9) supralabials, and 7–8 (9) infralabials. On the underside of the body are 131–146 ventrals and 51–75 subcaudals. The relatively stout hemipenis is not expanded distally (Rossman et al. 1996). Each maxilla has about 17 teeth; those in the rear are slightly enlarged.

Males have a more streamlined body than females

Short-headed garter snake, *Thamnophis brachystoma*; Forest County, Pennsylvania. (Photograph by Carl H. Ernst)

Distribution of *Thamnophis brachystoma*.

and longer TLs (Pisani and Bothner 1970). Males have 134–146 ventrals, 57–75 subcaudals, and TLs approximately 25% of TBL. Females have 131–146 ventrals, 51–64 subcaudals, and TLs only about 22% of TBL.

GEOGRAPHIC VARIATION. No subspecies are currently recognized.

CONFUSING SPECIES. Other species of garter and ribbon snakes occurring within the range of *T. brachystoma* can be distinguished from it by using the key presented above.

KARYOTYPE AND FOSSIL RECORD. Not reported.

DISTRIBUTION. The short-headed garter snake occurs mainly in the unglaciated portions of the upper Allegheny River drainage from southern Chautauqua, Cattaraugus, and Allegheny counties, New York, south to eastern Mercer, Venango, Clarian, and Jefferson counties, Pennsylvania, at elevations of 270 m to over 700 m (Bothner 1976; Price 1978). Colonies have also been established at Pittsburgh, Allegheny County, and in Butler, Clearfield, and Erie counties, Pennsylvania (Hulse and Hulse 1992; McCoy 1982), and an old, unverified record exists for Horsehead, Schemung County, New York, in the Susquehanna River drainage (Wright and Wright 1957). There is an introduced population in Youngstown, Mahoning County, Ohio (Novotny 1990). *T. brachystoma* is thought to have survived the Wisconsin glaciation in

essentially the same area it now occupies (Netting, in Conant 1950).

HABITAT. *T. brachystoma* is most often found under stones, logs, or boards in meadows or old fields or along marsh borders where the ground cover is predominantly low herbs. It is nearly always found in close proximity to water, and deep woodlands appear to be avoided. The introduced colonies in Allegheny, Butler, and Erie counties are all in urban settings.

BEHAVIOR. Like other garter snakes, *T. brachystoma* is predominately diurnal. Its annual activity cycle has not been reported. Klingener (1957) conducted a mark-recapture study of 14 *T. brachystoma* in Crawford County, Pennsylvania, and recovered 5 (35.7%) at the site of capture, a sheet of corrugated galvanized iron. He concluded the snakes were using the metal sheet as a home site or refuge, and Asplund (1963) reported it is very common to find 4–12 specimens of both sexes coiled together under one piece of cover.

Asplund (1963) took CTs from 128 *T. brachystoma*, most of which were under cover, and found the mean BT to be 30°C. The BTs of two active snakes were 31.8°C (late afternoon, 26 June) and 29.2°C (1430 hours, 16 July). Asplund thought the BTs of active individuals indicated an adaptation to a relatively cool climate and that thermal activity levels might have a great bearing on this snake's distribution.

Winter is apparently spent in an underground hibernaculum beneath the frost line. Such a site was excavated in Cattaraugus County, New York, during March 1962 by Bothner (1963). It was on a west-facing bluff with a 45° slope in loam soil having accumulations of shale and sandstone at an elevation of approximately 147 m. The opening was situated between two loose pieces of shale in a well-weathered outcropping. In three days, Bothner found 13 *T. brachystoma* (9 females, 4 males) buried at depths of 43–114 cm and soil temperatures of 2.8–3.3 °C. Most were situated alone, but two pairs of intertwined males and females were found, perhaps in preparation for mating. Bothner (in Pisani 1967) thought that the males emerge from hibernation before the females.

During the warmer months these snakes frequently bask.

REPRODUCTION. Males mature at about 28 cm TBL and females at approximately 33 cm TBL, both in their second year (Pisani and Bothner 1970); these are a small size and early age at maturity for garter snakes, especially from northern localities (Rossman et al. 1996).

The male sexual cycle is similar to that of *T. sirtalis*. Spermatogenic activity is clearly under way by the time of spring emergence in April, and mature sperm occur in the Sertoli cells by late July–early August, when the testes reach maximum size. Sperm pass into the lumen of the seminiferous tubules from mid-August through September, and then rapidly pass into the epididymides and vas deferens, where they apparently overwinter (Pisani and Bothner 1970).

In females, ovarian follicles 4–5 mm in diameter grow (add yolk) rapidly during the spring in preparation for ovulation. The area of a median cross section of a mature follicle increased from 4.5 mm² in early May to 38.5 mm² at ovulation (Pisani and Bothner 1970).

Mating begins in April just after emergence from hibernation, and the sperm is stored in seminal receptacles in the female's oviduct until ovulation. All of the mature females examined by Pisani and Bothner (1970) during April had motile sperm in their cloaca, but no sperm was found in females examined during the fall.

Pisani (1967) observed two pairs courting and mating on 17 April 1966 in Cattaraugus County, New York. A male *T. brachystoma* was observed pursuing a female over a distance of about 30 feet. During pursuit, the male's chin and labial regions were continually rubbed along the female's dorsum, and repeated attempts were made by the male to align his body with hers. When the female paused, the male attempted to insert his anal region beneath hers. As the pair passed other male *T. brachystoma* resting in the area, the males joined the chase, but stopped after about a meter.

The second pair was observed during mating. The male and female lay side by side, the female's head and part of the neck elevated above the leaves in which they were positioned. The head and part of the neck of the male lay along the female's back, his snout about one-fourth of the female's total length posterior to hers. Those regions of the male's body immediately anterior and posterior to his vent were draped in single loops over the female's back, the remainder of their tails being tightly entwined. The male made a rapid, spasmodic series of precoital courtship movements every 30 to 75 seconds, pressing his anal region tightly against the female's and lifting it up. After about 10 minutes, the male succeeded in inserting his left hemipenis into the female's cloaca; a series of caudocephalic waves was then initiated in the male, and continued for about 2 minutes. After a short pause, rhythmic waves were observed to progress cephalocaudally in the male, ending in a brief contraction of his anal region, presumably to expel sperm from his hemipenis. These waves continued at regular intervals of 10–20 seconds for the remainder of the time the two were in union. At this point their bodies were untwined, but still in close proximity. After about 20 minutes, the female waved her head and neck (which were still elevated) laterally several times, then lowered her head and crawled beneath some shaded leaves out of direct sunlight; the male was dragged after her. The pair remained in contact only at their anal regions, and the female's head was no longer elevated. An additional 10–15 minutes later, the female started to move into dense cover, the male still dragging behind; he made no attempt to crawl with her, but lay quietly, the cephalocaudal waves still in progress.

On 13 May at approximately 1130 hours, C. Ernst found a mating "ball" of 10 *T. brachystoma* (7 males, 3 females) under a flat rock in Forest County, Pennsylvania.

Pisani and Bothner (1970) concluded that female *T. brachystoma* probably have a biennial reproductive cycle, as 25% of the mature females examined between May and September showed no signs of ovulation that year (no enlargement of mature ovarian follicles, no embryos, no recent corpora lutea). They thought this possibly an adaptation to a habitat where short, cool summers are common.

Most young are born in August; Pisani and Bothner (1970) recorded parturition on days 2–9 and Swanson (1952) on days 5, 15–17, and 19–20; Ernst had litters born in his laboratory on 14 and 20 August (Ernst and Gotte 1986). However, Stewart (1961) reported a gravid female contained nine near-term young on 25 July, and Swanson (1952) reported the birth of a litter on 10 September. Swanson's litters averaged 8.6 (5–14) young, Ernst and Gotte's (1986) 6.5 (5–8), and Pisani and Bothner (1970) calculated the mean reproductive potential of their females as 7.2 young per litter, average: 2.4 (1–4) embryos in left oviduct, 4.8 (2–8) in right. The male to female ratio among Pisani and Bothner's prenatal and neonate *T. brachystoma* was 1.5:1. The largest females produced the greatest number of young in both Swanson's and Ernst and Gotte's samples.

The newborns resemble the adults in pattern, but are somewhat darker in ground color at first. The mean TBL of Ernst and Gotte's (1986) neonates was 13.3 (11.8–14.5) cm, while Swanson's (1952) were 12.5–15.8 cm long. Barton (1956) reported that in three litters produced in the laboratory and preserved at once, 12 males and 15 females each averaged 14.6 cm TBL. Pisani and Bothner (1970) reported average TBLs of 13.1 and 13.0 cm, respectively, for male and female neonate and immediately prenatal young.

GROWTH AND LONGEVITY. Barton (1956) studied the size of 194 *T. brachystoma* and concluded that neonates approximately double their length during the first year of life, reach mature size at the end of the second year, and then increase in length slowly throughout their remaining lives. Individuals have lived for more than three years in C. Ernst's laboratory.

DIET AND FEEDING HABITS. *T. brachystoma* seems to be strictly an earthworm eater, as no other animals have been found in its digestive tract (Asplund 1963;

Wozniak and Bothner 1966). Wozniak and Bothner (1966) found that 25% of the garter snakes they examined had earthworm remains, and Asplund (1963) reported that 55% of those he examined had eaten earthworms. Asplund found that an average earthworm meal totaled 4.75 (0.7–13.9) % of the snake's weight. Richmond (in Klingener 1957) suggested that *T. brachystoma* also feeds on isopods and slugs, and Asplund thought slugs or small salamanders might be eaten. Sweeny (1992) listed leeches as a possible food source for the short-headed garter snake. Captives readily eat earthworms; they seize them along the body, then work their mouths to one end of the earthworm and swallow it.

PREDATORS AND DEFENSE. Swanson (1952) felt that small mammals and possibly birds prey on *T. brachystoma*. Certainly, the automobile has killed many from colonies adjacent to roads. When approached they either remain quietly coiled or try to flee. When first handled they thrash about and spray musk, but never bite.

POPULATIONS. Asplund (1963) studied two Pennsylvania populations of *T. brachystoma* and found the colonies were large (555–1290 and 218–418 snakes, respectively), and that individuals moved freely in and out of each study area. Densities of colonies seem high, but due to its gregarious nature a false impression of abundance may be given. In areas where *T. sirtalis* is encroaching on *T. brachystoma,* the population density of *T. brachystoma* has suffered declines (Bothner 1976). *T. brachystoma* populations appear to be declining in New York due to habitat loss (Rossman et al. 1996).

Pisani and Bothner (1970) found a 1.4:1 adult male to female ratio, while Wozniak and Bothner (1966) reported a 0.6:1 ratio. Swanson (1952) found the sexes to be about equally represented in his study.

REMARKS. DeQueiroz and Lawson (1994) estimated the phylogenetic relationships of the garter snakes based on DNA sequence and allozyme variation. There is little doubt that *T. brachystoma* and Butler's garter snake, *T. butleri,* are closely related. Barton (1956) thought that before the Wisconsin glaciation *brachystoma* and *butleri* were members of a single species occupying a continuous geographical range, but the glacier's advance forced the main body of the species to retreat ahead of it to a point north of its terminal moraine, meanwhile leaving the segment of the population that has become *brachystoma* isolated in its high plateau locale. Due to pressures, competitive or climatic, *butleri* later migrated northward and has come to occupy primarily glaciated territory. Since *brachystoma* has remained virtually stationary during and since the Wisconsin glaciation, it likely is morphologically nearer the preglacial stock, whereas *butleri* has possibly evolved slightly more to fit the new demands of its glacier-modified habitat. The belief that *butleri* and *brachystoma* were once a single species is supported by the fact that most *butleri*-like *brachy-*

stoma are those from the southern and southwestern borders of the present range, the area presumably last in contact with *butleri*. Typical *butleri* characteristics (namely, 19 scale rows at midbody, seven supralabials, lateral stripes invading the fourth scale row) are possessed by more than twice as many individuals from this area than by those from the remainder of the range. While this finding must at present be regarded as tentative due to incomplete sampling, the fact that one-third of the southwestern *brachystoma* show one or more of these *butleri* characters is strongly suggestive, and the if two forms were in geographical contact, it is possible that this section would be regarded an area of intergradation.

This species was reviewed by Bothner (1976).

Thamnophis butleri (Cope 1889) | Butler's Garter Snake

RECOGNITION. This small stout-bodied snake (TBL to 73.7 cm) is olive brown to black with distinct yellow to orange longitudinal stripes. The lateral stripes occur on the second and third scale rows, and at least anteriorly, on the ventral half of row four; a double row of black spots may occur between the dorsal and lateral stripes. On the greenish yellow belly,

the sides of the ventral scutes are brownish, and there is usually a row of rounded black spots on each side; occasionally there is also irregular spotting medially. The olive to black head is small, and only broader than the neck. A small yellow spot often occurs on each parietal, and the supralabials may be tinged with orange or brown; the chin and throat are yellow. The

Butler's garter snake, *Thamnophis butleri*; Ingham County, Michigan. (Photograph by Carl H. Ernst)

body scales are keeled and pitless, and usually occur in 19 (occasionally 20–21) rows anteriorly and at mid-body, but only 17 rows near the anus. On the underside of the body are 129–154 ventrals and 49–72 subcaudals; the anal plate is not divided. Lateral head scalation consists of 2 nasals, 1 loreal, 1 preocular, 2–3 postoculars, 1 + 1 (2) temporals, 6–7 (rarely 8) supralabials, and 8–9 infralabials. The hemipenis has not been described. There are 19–23 teeth on each maxilla.

Males have 132–150 ventrals, 57–72 subcaudals, and longer tails (21.5–28.2% of TBL) than females (Rossman et al. 1996). Females have 129–151 ventrals, 49–64 subcaudals, and shorter tails (19.3–24.4% of TBL) than males (Rossman et al. 1996).

GEOGRAPHIC VARIATION. No subspecies are currently recognized.

CONFUSING SPECIES. Other species of garter and ribbon snakes occurring within the range of *T. butleri* can be distinguished from it by using the key presented above.

KARYOTYPE. Oguma and Makino (1932) reported that the diploid chromosome number of a male was 36.

FOSSIL RECORD. Not reported. *T. butleri* is considered a secondary invader of the post-Pleistocene Great Lakes region (Conant et al. 1945; Holman 1995; Smith and Minton 1957).

DISTRIBUTION. *T. butleri* ranges from central Ohio and central Indiana northward through eastern Michigan and the southern tip of Ontario. Isolated populations occur in southeastern Wisconsin and the Luther Marsh Conservatory Area in south-central Ontario (Coulson and Peluch 1984; Rossman et al. 1996).

HABITAT. Wet open areas, such as mesic prairies, pastures, fields in parks, marsh borders, the grassy sides of streams and canals, and vacant city lots are favored. Catling and Freedman (1980a) reported a large population of *T. butleri* in a seasonally dry upland area in Ontario, and suggested that although this snake is readily apparent in moist situations, it could still be very abundant, although inconspicuous, in sites that are dry in midsummer. *T. butleri* is one of the few reptiles to have benefited from urbanization, and large populations can often be found in cities (Minton 1968; Vogt 1981).

BEHAVIOR. The normal annual activity cycle extends from March to October or November. In Ohio, Conant (1951) collected *T. butleri* in every month except December, with a decided activity peak in April, when over 10 times as many were taken as in any other month, and a minor peak in October. Strathemann (1995) reported that *T. butleri* kept in outdoor enclosures throughout the year in Germany disappeared in late autumn for hibernation and reappeared in mid-March when the AT reached about 9°C.

Distribution of *Thamnophis butleri*.

Butler's garter snakes often are active during the morning hours, and the authors have also observed them foraging during the early evening; in the summer almost all activity is crepuscular. These snakes sometimes travel over broad areas while searching for food. Carpenter (1952a) reported an adult in Michigan moved a minimum distance of 121 m in two hours; the average distance moved during his study was 120 m for over 200 days between captures, and 115 m for less than 200 days. In over 200 days, females moved an average distance of 111 m, while males moved 125 m. For recaptures less than 200 days apart, females moved an average of 161 m, males 98 m. Carpenter never found *T. butleri* in the woods, and felt woodlands probably act as a natural barrier to their dispersal. The maximum distance between any two points of capture was 305 m and the maximum width 17 m, indicating a rather long, narrow home range. However, Carpenter found many individuals at distances of 30 m from the margin of the marsh and thought this distance was perhaps more indicative of the home range width.

In Ontario, Freedman and Catling (1979) found that 50% of their recaptures of *T. butleri* were at distances less than 50 m from the initial point of capture; however, a 31 cm male crawled 433 m and a 47 cm gravid female 517 m in 70 days. Minimum home ranges for three Ontario *T. butleri* were 50, 50, and 600 m², respectively. Freedman and Catling also noticed a tendency for *T. butleri* to avoid crossing roads.

In a laboratory study of five species of *Thamnophis* from across 25° of latitude, Doughty (1994) found that in general, *Thamnophis* species from high latitudes had lower CT_{min}, and this trend remained significant when interspecific differences in body mass were removed. *T. butleri* from Michigan had CT_{min} values of 4.2°C (unadjusted mean, neonates included) and 5.8°C (adjusted mean, without neonates). Doughty suggested that other morphological, behavioral, or physiological traits might explain some of the variation in CT_{min} across different habitats and latitudes.

Carpenter (1956) took the CT of 54 Butler's garter snakes and found them to average 26.1 (12.4–34.0) °C. Mean ETs measured at the same time were AT, 20.9 (7.0–29.0) °C; surface temperature, 24.2 (7.0–36.0) °C; and soil temperature (depth, 25 mm), 19.3 (7.0–32.0) °C. More than 70% of the CTs were between 20 and 30°C. During cold and hot weather, respectively, cloacal temperatures were higher and lower than immediate ETs. The CTs were most closely correlated with the surface temperature. *T. butleri* exhibited behavioral thermoregulation, basking in cool weather, seeking shelter in hot weather. In Michigan, they hibernated about 150 days, with emergence occurring from late March to late May (Carpenter 1952a, 1953a); ant mounds and meadow vole *(Microtus pennsylvanicus)* tunnels were used as hibernacula. In the ant mounds, *T. butleri* was found at depths of 35–68 cm.

Kamel and Gatten (1983) studied oxygen consumption and lactate accumulation during intense, short-term exercise at 25°C in Butler's garter snake. During a two-minute burst of activity, oxygen consumption rose 7.9-fold in *T. butleri*. The active metabolic rate, mass-specific aerobic scope, anaerobic scope, and total metabolic scope of *T. butleri* were found to be similar to those of other reptiles of its body size.

In a laboratory study of the effects of social and dietary experience on snake aggregation behavior, Lyman-Henley and Burghardt (1994) demonstrated that young *T. butleri* aggregate based on the characteristics of other individuals in a group, and that diet, familiarity, and perhaps relatedness are involved. (See DIET AND FEEDING HABITS.)

REPRODUCTION. The smallest gravid female *T. butleri* collected in Michigan by Carpenter (1952b) had a SVL of about 34.5 cm, which is within the size range reached by female *T. butleri* during their second spring. A male 32.1 cm in SVL was observed courting a larger female. This length is also within the range of those in their second spring (Carpenter 1952b). Smith (1946) noted that mature males develop tubercles on their mental scale, chin shields, and anterior labials.

During late March and April, breeding activities begin immediately after hibernation. The males actively seek females by following their pheromone trails (Ford 1982a). At times this leads several males to one female. Finneran (1949) observed four males closely intertwined about a female and a sixth smaller *T. butleri* of unknown sex, and later another male joined the aggregation.

During courtship, a male endeavors to achieve a dorsal position in relation to the female. He then rubs his chin along her back as he slowly crawls forward until reaching her neck. He also frequently touches her back with his tongue, probably smelling pheromones secreted through her skin. When his chin finally rests on her neck, several loops of his body lie across her back. Before the male's cloaca is pushed under the female, the region immediately anterior to the cloaca is thrown across the female's back, and his cloacal region is bent and forced under her body from the side opposite to that on which the most posterior portion of his body lies. The body and tail are then thrown into a series of rhythmic caudocephalic waves. These waves may occur at a frequency of less than one per second, and hemipenile insertion usually occurs within a few minutes after the beginning of these waves. After coitus is achieved, no further rhythmical tail thrusts occur (Noble 1937). Noble (1937) observed that in one mating, there occurred a rhythmical pulsation of the sides of the female's body immediately anterior to the cloaca (one beat approximately every three seconds), and he thought this due to the movements of the male's hemipenis. One copulation observed by Noble lasted 40 minutes.

The anterior cloaca of recently mated females contains a copulatory plug that blocks the oviductal openings (Devine 1977). The male apparently forms this plug after ejaculation. Devine (1977) interpreted this as a form of intrasexual competition in which the successfully copulating male makes the female temporarily unavailable to other males, and reduces the likelihood of multiple inseminations. Apparently, males recognize those females with plugs and treat them as if they were unavailable. In any given year, about 67% of the females become pregnant (Carpenter 1952a).

The 4–20 (typically 8–10), 125–185 mm young are usually born in August and early September. Data collected from clutches of 28 female Butler's garter snakes showed that the length and mass of newborn *T. butleri* are positively correlated with the length and mass of the female but negatively correlated with clutch size (Ford and Killebrew 1983). Ford and Killebrew (1983) reported that RCM (total offspring mass divided by female total mass) did not change with increase in female size; however, RCM per progeny decreased with female size, which would allow larger females to produce clutches of larger numbers with less

effect on neonate size. Seigel et al. (1986) reported a RCM of 0.362 for 25 females with an average SVL of 38.3 cm.

GROWTH AND LONGEVITY. Carpenter (1952b) studied growth in a marked population of *T. butleri* from Michigan. He estimated the annual growth period was the five months from May through September (153 days), and found a steady decrease in growth rate as the snake became larger. Females 20–24 cm in initial SVL grew 1.15 cm (7.0%) per month; those 30–34 cm, 1.24 cm (3.6%) per month; those 35–39 cm, 0.55 cm (1.5%) per month; and those 40–44 cm, 0.2 cm (0.5%) per month. Males 20–24 cm long grew 1.92 cm (8.9%) per month, those 25–29 cm, 2.93 cm (10.8%) per month; those 30–34 cm, 0.80 cm (2.5%) per month; and those 35–39 cm, 0.18 cm (0.5%) per month.

In a study of the effect of different diets on the growth of captive-born *T. butleri,* Lyman-Henley and Burghardt (1995) concluded that exclusive diets of fish or calcium-supplemented earthworms produced only minor differences in the growth rate of neonates.

Natural longevity is unknown. Strathemann (1995) reported maintaining *T. butleri* in outdoor enclosures in Germany for seven years.

DIET AND FEEDING HABITS. *T. butleri* is predominantly a worm eater (Ruthven 1908; Conant 1951; Carpenter 1952a; Catling and Freedman 1980b), and Catling and Freedman (1980b) reported *Lumbricus terrestris* and *Allolobophora chlorictica* were the earthworm species regurgitated most frequently, although other species of *Lumbricus,* as well as several species of *Aporrectodea,* were also regurgitated. Carpenter (1952a) reported that 83% of his food records were for earthworms and 10% for leeches, while Catling and Freedman (1980b) reported that 96% of the prey items regurgitated consisted of earthworms, and suggested that leeches were probably the principal constituent of the diet of *T. butleri* in Ontario prior to the introduction of Palearctic earthworms. Occasionally, small frogs are eaten (Carpenter 1952a; Ruthven 1908); Test (1958) reported a young *T. butleri* from Michigan regurgitated an adult spring peeper *(Hyla crucifer),* and a Canadian individual regurgitated a chorus frog *(Pseudacris triseriata)* (Catling and Freedman

1980b). Carpenter (1952a) reported that captive *T. butleri* ate a *Hyla crucifer,* a small *Bufo americanus,* a small *Rana pipiens,* and a *Plethodon cinereus,* but refused *Acris crepitans* and *Pseudacris nigrita.* Captives kept in Germany ate small fish and strips of trout fortified with vitamins and calcium from a long food needle, but did not catch fish from the pond in their outdoor enclosure (Strathemann 1995). Catling and Freedman (1980b) reported captive *T. butleri* capturing and eating fish placed in their water bowls; while they had no difficulty handling small fish, they had trouble subduing larger fish.

The eating of earthworms by *T. butleri* seems instinctive. Burghardt (1967, 1969) found that inexperienced young responded to extracts of fish, earthworms, slugs, and amphibians, but were most interested in earthworms and showed little interest in slug extract. *T. butleri* appears to be largely scent oriented, searching the surface of the ground or even "burrowing" to capture earthworms below ground, and frequently tongue flicking or nose pressing prey (Catling and Freedman 1980b). Responses to prey extracts by naive neonates may be mediated by the vomeronasal system, which appears to be functional at birth in the genus *Thamnophis* (Holtzman 1993; Holtzman and Halpern 1990). Since these behavioral responses are only partially dependent upon the presence of the tongue, the olfactory system may also be functional at birth. However, there is no direct evidence that a vomeronasal system stimulus is available to embryos or that embryos can detect it (Holtzman 1993).

Lyman-Henley and Burghardt (1995) reported *T. butleri* showed a striking prey-specific effect of experience upon prey preference. In a laboratory study, captive-born *T. butleri* tested at 10 days of age showed a strong preference for worm surface extracts prior to experience with prey, but barely discriminated fish extract from water. When retested at 157 and 159 days of age, snakes fed a diet of earthworms since birth exhibited no change in this preference. However, snakes fed a diet of mosquito fish *(Gambusia affinis)* since birth, while still showing a high response to earthworm cues, showed an even higher response to the familiar, though "unnatural" fish prey cues. When tested for preferences between sites marked with surface chemical cues of the prey items and sites marked with feces from conspecifics on the same or different diets, *T. butleri* showed an initial preference (at 11 days of age) for sites marked with feces of conspecifics fed earthworms. After experience with prey, *T. butleri* (at 136 days of age) showed changes in preference, dependant on the diet of the animals, between the initial and final feces choice test. Fish-fed *T. butleri* showed no significant change in preference, while worm-fed snakes showed a significant change from a bias toward worm-based feces to a preference for fish-based feces. Lyman-Henley and Burghardt (1995) concluded that the fact that some perceptual responses of *T. butleri* may be strikingly shaped by experience with atypical prey (fish) could reflect the retention of a plastic trait no longer under any prey-related natural selection.

PREDATORS AND DEFENSE. Since *T. butleri* is a small snake, its natural enemies are probably numerous. Vogt (1981) thought that birds, milksnakes (*Lampropeltis* sp.), and carnivorous mammals, including domestic cats *(Felis catus),* probably prey on it, and Carpenter (1952a) suggested crayfish may kill and devour them. Probably any carnivore larger than *T. butleri* will attack it on occasion.

When first encountered, *T. butleri* does not bite; instead it attempts to flee by vigorously throwing its body into a series of whipping, sideways motions. If handled it will expel musk from cloacal glands, and its tail may break off, but not as frequently as in *T. sirtalis* or *T. sauritus* (Willis et al. 1982). Gas chromatography–mass spectrometry analysis of scent gland secretions from five species of North American garter snakes, including eight *T. butleri,* revealed the same seven volatile compounds: trimethylamine, acetic acid, propanoic acid, 2-methylpropanoic acid, butanoic acid, 3-methylbutanoic acid, and 2-piperidone (Wood et al. 1995).

Defensive striking appears to be rare in *T. butleri.* Herzog and Burghardt (1986) and Herzog et al. (1989a, 1989b, 1992) conducted a series of experiments to investigate the development of antipredator responses in snakes. In two studies, newborn *T. butleri* (23 snakes from three litters and 71 snakes from seven litters, respectively) were confronted with a nonmoving and moving human hand. Few neonates struck at the threatening stimulus. Although males were more likely to strike than females and some individuals demonstrated significant habituation, there was no overall habituation of defensive strikes. Twenty-two individuals tested as juveniles (between the ages of 32 and 54 days) still showed no significant interactions, no differences in the number of strikes directed at moving and nonmoving stimuli, and no significant effects of litter or of order of stimulus presentation. Eight adult female *T. butleri* presented with the same stimuli were also very passive.

Ten *T. butleri* (from three litters) exposed to a series of five levels of escalating threat coiled and struck infrequently, but did perform numerous tail waves and reversals (Bowers et al. 1993).

POPULATIONS.   In his study in Michigan, Carpenter (1952a) found *T. butleri* made up only 13% of the three species of *Thamnophis* collected in three years, and 15% of those caught were neonates or less than one year old. His combined population estimate for the three years was only 121 individuals on the 48 acre site. In Ontario, Freedman and Catling (1978) estimated the population size for their 40 ha study area to be 900 (23/ha). Most individuals were over 30 cm

in total body length, and relatively few juveniles were caught. The male to female ratio in Ontario was not significantly different from 1:1.

T. butleri is considered threatened in Indiana, and a species of special concern in Wisconsin.

REMARKS.   That *T. butleri* is a separate species from *T. brachystoma* has been well documented (Smith 1945; Conant 1950; Barton 1956), and that both are closely related to *T. radix* is suspected (Ruthven 1908; Wright and Wright 1957). Rossman et al. (1996) stated that both morphological and biochemical evidence support the conclusion that *T. butleri* is a derivative of *T. radix,* and that it is probably ancestral to *T. brachystoma.* It is interesting that male *T. butleri* tested by Ford (1982a) apparently showed no preference for female pheromone trails of their species over those of *T. radix.*

Steehouder (1983) reported a captive female *T. butleri* produced three hybrid offspring after mating with a *T. sirtalis parietalis.* Catling and Freedman (1977) described melanistic *T. butleri* from a population in Ontario. The species was reviewed by Minton (1980).

Thamnophis couchii (Kennicott, in Baird 1859) | Sierra Garter Snake

RECOGNITION.   *T. couchii* is a large garter snake that has grown to 120 cm TBL (Brown 1997). It is olive brown, gray brown, dark brown, or black with a white to cream or yellow longitudinal stripe on scale rows two and three on each side. A cream to yellow middorsal stripe may be present on the neck, but is usually indistinct or absent on the body. Two alternating rows of square, dark olive to black spots are present between the lateral stripes and middle of the back. The dark spots and light stripes may be totally obscured in melanistic individuals. Two elongated black spots are present on the upper neck. The labials, chin, and cream-to-yellow venter may be mottled with black, particularly in the north and central portions of the range. Body scales are keeled and lack pits, and usually lie in 21 (22–23) anterior rows, 21 (19) midbody rows, and 17 posterior rows. On the underside are 161–187 ventrals, 68–98 subcaudals, and a single anal

plate. The snout is narrow and somewhat pointed. On the side of the head are 1 nasal (sometimes completely subdivided by the nostril), 1 loreal, 1 (2) preocular(s), 3 (2–4) postoculars, 1 + 2 + 2 temporals, 8 supralabials, and 11 (10) supralabials. The posterior pair of chin shields is usually longer than the anterior pair. The rather thick hemipenis is 13–17 subcaudals long when inverted, and is expanded distally with a single sulcus spermaticus. Each maxilla has 23–27 teeth, with the posterior-most 2–3 teeth elongated.

Males have 166–187 ventrals, 79–98 subcaudals, and TLs 22–27 (usually 25–27) % of TBL; females have 161–180 ventrals, 68–91 subcaudals, and TLs 20–25 (usually 22–24) % of TBL.

GEOGRAPHIC VARIATION.   *T. couchii* is monotypic.

CONFUSING SPECIES.   For characters distinguish-

Sierra garter snake, *Thamnophis couchii*; Tuolumne County, California. (Photograph by Brad R. Moon)

ing *T. couchii* from other garter snakes within its range, refer to the key above.

KARYOTYPE. Baker et al. (1972) reported that the karyotype consists of 36 chromosomes (34 macrochromosomes, 2 michrochromosomes) with 70 arms. No heteromorphy was found in the female sex chromosomes.

FOSSIL RECORD. The Pleistocene (Rancholabrean) remains at Rancho La Brea, California, assigned to the *T. couchii* group by LaDuke (1991) are probably not of this species.

DISTRIBUTION. The main range of *T. couchii* is found from the Pit and Sacramento rivers in north-central California south in the Sierra Nevada Mountains to the Tehachapi Mountains in south-central California. It also occurs in the Owens Valley of California, and along the Carson, Truckee, and Walker rivers in west-central Nevada.

HABITAT. The Sierra garter snake is one of the more aquatic species of *Thamnophis*, and is never found far from water. Typical habitats are the pools in rapidly flowing, rocky, mountain streams or rivers, seasonal creeks, meadow ponds, lakes, and reservoirs at elevations of 91–1,438 m. Riparian vegetation includes grasses, sedges, rushes, willows, cottonwoods, sycamores, oaks, fir, cedar, and chaparral.

BEHAVIOR. Unfortunately, relatively little has been reported of the life history of *T. couchii*. This is partly because in the past it has been variously included as a subspecies of either *T. elegans* or *T. ordinoides*, and some of its behavioral and reproductive data are masked under those names.

T. couchii living at low elevations are active from late March to early December (Fitch 1941; Wright and Wright 1957), but individuals living at high elevations emerge later in the spring and retreat early for the winter, and their entire active season may be as short

Distribution of *Thamnophis couchii*.

as 3.0–3.5 months (Hansen and Tremper, in Rossman et al. 1996). Nothing is known of its hibernation biology.

Daily activity is predominately diurnal. According to Rossman et al. (1996), this snake basks in the morning in protected areas, such as tall grass, then moves to the water to forage when warmed. At pond or stream sites it basks on the bank along the water's edge in the spring, but in summer *T. couchii* is more often found lying in shallow water or on mats of floating vegetation.

Fitch (1949) reported that all *T. couchii* that he marked left the several hundred meters of the creek within his study area, and that several recaptured snakes had made extensive trips. Only one marked male was recaptured, and it had moved 30 m in about 11 days. Six recaptured females had moved 1,661 m (12+ months), 1,482 m (8 months), 575 m (8+ months), 90 m (11+ months), 72 m (24+ months), and 30 m (1+ month), respectively.

REPRODUCTION. Few data are available on the breeding habits. Hanson and Tremper (in Rossman et al. 1996) suggested *T. couchii* may mature in 32–44 months. Wright and Wright (1957) listed the minimum lengths of adult males and females as 43 and 44 cm, respectively, and Brown (1997) gave the minimum adult size as 45.7 cm, so the species is probably mature when it reaches 50 cm.

Neither sex's gametic cycle has been described. Courtship and mating probably occur in the spring, but these acts have not been described. The young are born in late July to late September, with most neonates appearing in July and August. Litters average about 21 young, and have included 5–38 young (Brown 1997; Hansen and Tremper, in Rossman et al. 1996; Rossi and Rossi 1995). Litter size is probably positively correlated with female body size. Neonates resemble the adults and have 12–13 cm TBLs.

GROWTH AND LONGEVITY. The only available growth data were supplied by Fitch (1949), who measured and released 97 *T. couchii* and recaptured eight. Four of five recaptured females had grown 61.5–64.0 cm (24+ months), 79.0–79.5 cm (12+ months), 75.0–78.7 cm (11+ months), and 21.0–44.2 cm (8 months), respectively. Rossi and Rossi (1995) reported

that a *T. couchii* had been in their care for 2 years and 2 months and was still alive at the time of writing. Longevity in the wild is unknown, but is probably considerably longer than that reported for captives.

DIET AND FEEDING HABITS. *T. couchii* normally forages in shallow water, swimming slowly along at the surface or crawling along the bottom swaying its head back and forth as it searches between rocks and in clumps of vegetation or debris. It has a negative buoyancy that helps to keep it from being swept away by the current (Rossman et al. 1996). When prey are caught, especially large animals, they are dragged to shallow water before being swallowed.

Drummond (1983) studied foraging behavior of *T. couchii* in an artificial pool and recorded the following observations: (1) 68% of the snake's total search time was spent on aquatic foraging, (2) 28.2% of aquatic foraging time was spent in diving, (3) anterior diving occurred only 1.9% of the time, (4) aerial attacks only made up 4.3% of prey attacks, (5) crawling along the substrate made up 8% of foraging behavior (the body was held in an exaggerated sinuous posture and the elevated head was gently moved laterally back and forth), and (6) probing among rocks took up less than 1% of the foraging time. Of underwater attacks, 49% were during pursuit, 27% during substrate crawling, 6% during anterior diving, and only 3% while probing crevices. Rates of attack during overland searching totaled only 13% of the search time. In another set of tests, *T. couchii* depended more on olfaction than vision to find prey, although vision was not a minor behavior (Drummond 1985). To see underwater, *T. couchii* constricts its pupils to one-third their normal diameter, thereby increasing angular resolution by a factor of three (Schaeffel and de Queiroz 1990). The snake can compensate for refraction during air to water attacks on prey (Guillén and Drummond 1989).

Fish (and their eggs)—suckers (*Catostomus occidentalis*), trout, mosquitofish (*Gambusia affinis*)—and amphibians—larval salamanders (*Dicamptodon ensatus, Taricha* sp.), frog tadpoles (*Rana* sp.), treefrogs (*Pseudacris regilla*), toads and their tadpoles (*Bufo boreas*), and spadefoots (*Scaphiopus* sp.)—make up the bulk of the adult food; juveniles consume earthworms and leeches (Brown 1997; Cunningham 1959; Fitch 1940, 1941, 1949; Lind and Welsh 1990; Rossman et al. 1996). Fitch (1941) reported the percentages of prey in 44 stomachs as 62% tadpoles, 26% fish, 10% anurans, and 2% salamanders.

PREDATORS AND DEFENSE.   Fitch (1949) reported that a red-tailed hawk *(Buteo jamaicensis)* attacked a Sierra garter snake, and suspected that raccoons *(Procyon lotor)*, skunks *(Mephitis mephitis, Spilogale putorius)*, and the great blue heron *(Ardea herodias)* preyed on it.

The first line of defense for this species is to dive into the water and retreat to deep water or hide among rocks or submerged vegetation. If trapped, it has a vile temper and will bite viciously and spray musk.

POPULATIONS.   The only available data on populations are those provided by Fitch (1949). He collected 94 *T. couchii* in a few hundred meters at a site in California (36 males, 55 females, and 3 of undetermined sex) and found a male to female ratio for sexed individuals of 1.0:1.5. Male body lengths did not exceed 55 cm, but body lengths of females were to 90 cm.

Today, some populations of this species are declining, but most occurring in good habitat still contain large numbers of individuals of all size classes. If its habitats can be preserved, *T. couchii* is in no immediate danger.

REMARKS.   For much of its history *T. couchii* has been included as a subspecies of either *T. elegans* or *T. ordinoides*. Lawson and Dessauer (1979), on the basis of biochemical comparisons, and Rossman (1979), using morphological evidence, proposed that *T. couchii* was a separate species containing six subspecies (Fitch 1984). After further analyses, Rossman and Stewart (1987) demonstrated that this all-encompassing *T. couchii* was really a composite of four distinct species: *T. atratus, T. couchii, T. gigas*, and *T. hammondii*. They also concluded that some hybridization occurs between *T. couchii* and both *T. atratus* and *T. hammondii*. The monotypic *T. couchii* has been reviewed by Rossman et al. (1996).

Thamnophis cyrtopsis (Kennicott 1860a) | Black-necked Garter Snake

RECOGNITION.   This snake has a maximum TBL of 114.4 cm, but most are under 90 cm. Body color varies from olive gray to olive brown or dark brown. A distinct white, yellow, or orange dorsal stripe is present, which in United States populations completely divides a black neck collar into two large prominent blotches. White or yellow lateral stripes may be absent, but if present are on scale rows two and three. Between the dorsal and lateral stripes (or venter if the lateral stripes are absent) lie two alternating rows of large black spots or large black square-shaped blotches. The dark spots or squares may invade the upper border of the lateral stripe, causing it to appear wavy or scalloped. The head is either gray or black, and the supralabials are patterned with dark bars. The chin and throat are white to cream, and the rest of the venter is unpatterned greenish or bluish white to cream or tan. Body scales are keeled and pitted, and lie in 19 (21–23) anterior rows, 19 (rarely 21) midbody rows, and 17 rows near the tail. Beneath are 148–179 ventrals, 63–105 subcaudals, and a single anal plate. On the side of the

head lie 2 nasals, 1 loreal, 1 (2) preocular(s), 3 (1–4) postoculars, 1 + 2 + 3 temporals, 8 (7–10) supralabials, and 10 (9–11) infralabials. The everted hemipenis is stout and expanded distally with a single sulcus spermaticus. When inverted it is eight subcaudals long. Twenty-one to 29 teeth are present on the maxilla.

Males have 157–179 ventrals, 73–105 subcaudals, and TLs 23–27% of TBL; females have 148–177 ventrals, 63–95 subcaudals, and TLs 22.5–26.0% of TBL. Males average 3–4 more ventrals and 6–10 more subcaudals than females, and the male tail is usually 1–2% longer than that of the female.

GEOGRAPHIC VARIATION.   Three subspecies are currently recognized, but only two are present north of Mexico (Rossman et al. 1996). *T. c. cyrtopsis* (Kennicott 1860a), the western black-necked garter snake, is found in southeastern Utah, extreme southwestern and southeastern Colorado, Arizona, New Mexico, and western Texas. It also ranges south in Mexico through most of Sonora, the Sierra Madre Occiden-

Western black-necked garter snake, *Thamnophis cyrtopsis cyrtopsis*; Texas. (Photograph by James H. Harding)

Eastern black-necked snake, *Thamnophis cyrtopsis ocellatus*; Travis County, Texas. (Photograph by William Leonard)

tal, and the Mexican Plateau to northern Hildalgo. It has a gray head, few dark blotches on the sides, a pale dorsal stripe, small black, irregularly spaced spots along the lateral stripe, and 167–179 ventrals and 86–105 subcaudals in males and 163–177 ventrals and 75–95 subcaudals in females. *T. c. ocellatus* (Cope 1880), the eastern black-necked garter snake, ranges from central and western Texas to southern Chihuahua and northern Colima. It has a black head, large black square-shaped blotches on the sides, wavy lateral stripes, and 157–164 ventrals and 73–91 subcaudals in males and 148–165 ventrals and 63–76 subcaudals in females.

CONFUSING SPECIES. Other garter or ribbon snakes occurring within the range of *T. cyrtopsis* can be identified by using the key presented above. Whipsnakes (*Masticophis* sp.) with stripes have smooth body scales, a preocular that invades the supralabial line, no spots on the sides, and a divided anal plate. Patch-nosed snakes (*Salvadora* sp.) have smooth body scales, a large triangular-shaped rostral scale, no spots on the sides, dark stripes, and a divided anal plate. The lined snake *(Tropidoclonion lineatum)* has a narrow head not distinguishable from its neck, no spots on its sides, and two rows of spots or half-moons on the venter.

KARYOTYPE. The normal diploid complement of chromosomes is 36 (34 macrochromosomes, 2 microchromosomes) with 70 arms (Baker et al. 1972). Females do not have heteromorphic sex chromosomes.

Distribution of *Thamnophis cyrtopsis*.

FOSSIL RECORD. Pleistocene (Rancholabrean) fossils of *T. cyrtopsis* have been found in New Mexico, western Texas, and Sonora, Mexico (Van Devender and Bradley 1994; Van Devender et al. 1985; Van Devender and Worthington 1977).

DISTRIBUTION. *T. cyrtopsis* ranges from Utah, southwestern and southeastern Colorado, and central Texas southward and westward through Arizona, New Mexico, and Mexico to Guatemala.

HABITAT. This snake is mostly a highland species that lives along streams, pools, and springs on ravine and canyon bottoms, and on the rocky limestone hillsides above the waterways. Both permanent and intermittent streams are used as habitat, at elevations of 0–2,700 m. Over its broad range it has been found in such diverse habitats as deserts to upland oak woods and pine forests, and has been taken at stock ponds and in wetlands in urban settings. In the spring it is most often associated with flowing water, but in the summer, when less water is flowing, it occupies pools (Jones 1990).

BEHAVIOR. In the vicinity of Wickenburg, Arizona, *T. cyrtopsis* is active from 25 March to 1 October (Gates 1957). At other localities in the United States it probably emerges from hibernation in March or April and retreats for the winter in September or October, depending on the elevation and latitude (Degenhardt et al. 1996; Wright and Wright 1957). Nothing is known of its overwintering habits.

During the spring it is active in the morning, but in the hot weather of summer *T. cyrtopsis* shifts activity to early evening or night. Night retreats include exposed roots along stream banks, rodent burrows, crevices in stream banks or rocks, and piles of plant debris (Jones 1990). The CTs of 47 *T. cyrtopsis* at Wall Lake, New Mexico, averaged 26.7 (22.0–32.0) °C, while the AT and ST averaged 26.6 (16.0–35.0) and 27.3 (19.0–37.0) °C, respectively (Fleharty 1967). In Arizona, 14 black-necked garter snakes had a mean active-season BT of 27.5 (22.6–35.0) °C (Rosen 1991a). It is fond of basking in the early morning, usually on the bank, rocks, or floating mats of vegetation, and may have a particular basking site to which it returns each day (Mosauer 1932b). Fleharty (1967) found none basking when AT was 30°C or above, and few snakes were observed or captured at these ATs.

Black-necked garter snakes may move some distance overland away from their waterway; Jones (1990) found four Arizona adults in adjacent desert at least 0.5 km from the nearest water. However, most movements are probably within this species' aquatic habitat. At Wall Lake, New Mexico, the greatest distance traveled by a *T. cyrtopsis* was 233.5 m across the lake from the original capture point (Fleharty 1967). The greatest distance traveled in a day was only 10 m, although Fleharty observed one swimming across the lake, a distance of 45 m at that point.

REPRODUCTION. It probably takes two to three years for *T. cyrtopsis* to mature. The smallest known reproducing female was one 39.5 cm long from Texas that produced a litter (Sabath and Worthington 1959). Wright and Wright (1957) reported minimum lengths of mature females and males were 50.4 and 42.9 cm, respectively. Stebbins (1985) listed the size at maturity for both sexes as 40.6 cm, and Conant and Collins (1998) reported it was 41.0 cm. The smallest reproductive female and male examined by Goldberg (1998b) had SVLs of 41.2 and 33.8 cm, respectively.

Goldberg (1998b) studied the gametic cycles of both sexes of *T. cyrtopsis*. Males have regressed testes with seminiferous tubules containing spermatogonia and Sertoli cells from March through July. Recrudescence occurs from May to September, during which there is a renewal of spermatogenic cells characterized by meiotic divisions and the presence of primary and secondary spermatocytes and spermatids. Spermiogenic males are present from April through November. Sperm is present in the epididymides of spermiogenic males. The vas deferens contain sperm from March through November (the total duration of Goldberg's study), so sperm is probably stored there over the winter. Apparently, at least some males of this species can breed throughout the year.

The female gametic cycle is similar to that of other species of *Thamnophis*. Females enter hibernation with small, previtellogenic follicles that are yolked up during a secondary period of vitellogenesis in the spring prior to ovulation. Females may have follicles > 6 mm and contain developing embryos from March to June. About 61% of females produce litters each year, and females with inactive ovaries are present in the population throughout the year. Goldberg (1998b) noted a significant positive correlation exists between the number of enlarged follicles > 6 mm or embryos and female body size.

Courtship and mating apparently occur in the spring from March to May after the snakes emerge from hibernation; although Minton (1959) thought that some matings take place in the fall and winter. Courtship and mating behaviors are undescribed.

Neonates have been found from 29 June to 3 September, with most being born in July and August. A female took two hours to deliver six young (Meckel, in Tennant 1984). Litters contain 3–24 (mean, 9.9) young for 14 litters reported in the literature. Neonates are 14.5–28.1 (mean, 21.4) cm long. A litter

of eight young weighed by Vitt (1975) had an average mass of 3.31 g, and a RCM of 0.614.

GROWTH AND LONGEVITY. Published growth data are sparse and based on captives. One snake from a litter that averaged just over 20 cm per neonate at birth was a ravenous feeder, and grew to 56.5 cm in 11 months (Tennant 1984). A male *T. c. ocellatus* that was originally wild caught survived 10 years, 10 months, and 26 days at the Fort Worth Zoo; and an adult, wild-caught, *T. c. cyrtopsis* of undetermined sex survived 6 years, 3 months, and 29 days at the Brookfield Zoo (Snider and Bowler 1992).

DIET AND FEEDING HABITS. *T. cyrtopsis* either actively forages along the banks of streams for amphibians, or ambushes frogs while floating, semisubmerged, and camouflaged in algal mats on large pools (Jones 1990). When a snake fails to grasp a frog on its initial attack from ambush, it usually pursues its prey for at least a meter while swimming on the water's surface and diving only for short durations (< 10 seconds). It possibly cannot dive and forage on the bottom for longer periods because its specific gravity is less than one, and it naturally floats (Fleharty 1967). It is not known if this snake's saliva is toxic to prey, but it has a Duvernoy's gland with both mucous and serous cells, much like other colubrids that produce strong venom (Taub 1967). Natural food of the black-necked garter snake is made up mostly of amphibians: anurans (adults and tadpoles)—ranid frogs (*Rana berlandieri, R. blairi, R. catesbeiana, R. chiricahuensis* [?], *R. yavapaiensis*), toads (*Bufo mazatlanensis, B. punctatus, B. speciosus, B. woodhousei*), spadefoots (*Scaphiopus hammondii*), leptodactylid frogs (*Syrrhophus marnocki*), tree frogs (*Hyla arenicolor*), and narrow-mouthed frogs (*Gastrophryne olivacea*)—and salamanders (*Plethodon glutinosus* complex); other recorded prey include lizards (*Scincella lateralis*), an unidentified sparrow, small fish, crustaceans (*Triops*), and earthworms (Degenhardt et al. 1996; Fleharty 1967; Fouquette 1954; Milstead et al. 1950; Moeauer 1932b; Rossman et al. 1996; Stebbins 1954, 1985; Tennant 1984; Woodin 1953; Wright and Wright 1957; Zweifel and Norris 1955). Neonates and juveniles prey on earthworms, small fish, and small tadpoles; adults eat larger prey.

Fouquette (1954) reported that of the 40 Texas *T. cyrtopsis* he examined, 39 (97%) contained amphibians, and 1 (3%) had eaten a ground skink *(Scincella lateralis)*. Of the 39 snakes that had taken amphibians, 14 (36%) had eaten adult anurans, 24 (61%) had consumed tadpoles, 2 (5%) had eaten salamanders *(Plethodon glutinosus* complex), and 1 had eaten an unidentifiable amphibian. In two cases a snake had eaten both a young frog and a tadpole. Of the stomachs containing tadpoles, 13 (54%) had *Hyla arenicolor*, 8 (33%) had *Gastrophryne olivacea*, 2 (8%) had *Rana* sp. tadpoles, and 4 (17%) had unidentifiable tadpoles. Captives have eaten adult anurans *(Acris crepitans, Bufo punctatus, B. valliceps, Hyla cinerea, H. versicolor, Pseudacris clarkii, P. streckeri, Rana* sp.), tadpoles *(Pseudacris clarkii, P. streckeri, Scaphiopus holbrookii)*, fish *(Astyanax mexicanus, Gambusia affinis, Lepomis* sp.), scented mice *(Mus musculus)*, and raw horsemeat (Fouquette 1954; Rossi and Rossi 1995; Tennant 1984).

PREDATORS AND DEFENSE. Known predators of *T. cyrtopsis* are coral snakes *(Micrurus fulvius)*, Mexican gray-breasted jays *(Aphelocoma ultramarina)*, and hawks *(Buteo jamaicensis, Buteo gallus anthracinus)* (Contreras and Treviño 1987; Kennedy 1964; Ross 1989). In addition, fishermen are known to kill them (Fleharty 1967). The juveniles are probably eaten by predatory fish, bullfrogs *(Rana catesbeiana),* and wading birds; other snakes, owls, and carnivorous mammals most likely prey on the adult *T. cyrtopsis.*

When disturbed, the snake's first instinct is to flee. It will dive into the water if given a chance, and swim away on the surface or hide in crevices or rodent holes in the bank. If on land away from water, it will crawl under rocks, logs, or plant debris, down rodent burrows, or away into thick vegetation. When handled, some will bite, but almost all spray vile-smelling musk.

POPULATIONS. The black-necked garter snake can be common in the proper habitat (Tennant 1984); Woodin (1953) collected a dozen in a few minutes at the edge of an Arizona pond, and Minton (1959) reported that two to six of these snakes occupied every pool in certain canyons of the Big Bend National Park, Texas. Of 157 garter snakes captured at Wall Lake, New Mexico, by Fleharty (1967), 45 (29%) were *T. cyrtopsis* (37 females, 8 males).

REMARKS. A thorough study of the life history of *T. cyrtopsis* would expand our knowledge of the species. It has been reviewed by Milstead (1953), Rossman et al. (1996), and Webb (1980).

Thamnophis elegans (Baird and Girard 1853) | Western Terrestrial Garter Snake

RECOGNITION. This widely distributed western species reaches a maximum TBL of 109.2 cm, but most individuals are shorter than 80 cm. Body color varies from gray to gray brown, olive gray, dark olive, dark brown,or black. A well-developed white, cream, yellow, reddish yellow, or orange middorsal stripe is usually present (absent in some subspecies, see GEOGRAPHIC VARIATION), and on scale rows two and three of each side is a cream or reddish lateral stripe. Between the dorsal and lateral stripes are dark spots or red or white flecks. The dorsal surface of the head is red, brown, olive, or black. The supra- and infralabials are white to cream, and usually the supralabials have dark bars along the seams. Melanistic individuals occur about the Puget Sound in northwestern Washington, southwestern Washington, and eastern Oregon. The chin, throat, and venter are white, gray, cream, or tan, and a medial row of black or red flecks may be present on the venter. Body scales are keeled and pitted, and lie in 19 or 21 (17–23) anterior rows, 19 (17–21) rows at midbody, and 17 (15–16) rows near the tail. Present on the underside are 137–185 ventrals, 61–101 subcaudals, and a single anal plate. Lateral head scales are 2 nasals, 1 loreal, 1 (2) preocular(s), 3 (2–4) postoculars, 1 + 1–2 + 1–3 temporals, 8 (6–9) supralabials, and 10 (7–13) infralabials. The hemipenis has not been described. Each maxilla contains 14–27 teeth, with the 2–3 most posterior teeth bladelike and ridged (Wright et al. 1979). Variation in tooth counts occurs between populations (see Rossman et al. 1996).

Mountain garter snake, *Thamnophis elegans elegans*; Jackson County, Oregon. (Photograph by William Leonard)

Males have 148–185 ventrals, 71–101 subcaudals, and TLs about 26 (24–28) % of TBL; females have 137–177 ventrals, 61–91 subcaudals, and TLs only about 24 (18–26) % of TBL. As with other garter snakes, females usually attain a greater SVL than males. In females the mean relative height of the first dorsal scale row (maximum vertical height of dorsal scale row one divided by maximum width of the vertebral row) is 2.5 (2.3–2.8); that of males is only 2.3 (2.1 2.8) (Rossman 1995).

GEOGRAPHIC VARIATION. Rossman et al. (1996) recognize six subspecies, but only five occur north of Mexico. *T. e. elegans* (Baird and Girard 1853), the mountain garter snake, ranges from southwestern Oregon south to central California (exclusive of the coastal ranges), with an isolated population in the San Bernardino Mountains of southern California. Body color is dark olive, grayish brown, or black, with no red pigment between the well-defined dorsal (yellow or orange) and lateral (yellow) stripes. The venter is unmarked or has light gray speckles. There are 149–185 ventrals in males, 137–177 in females; and 76–101 subcaudals in males, 64–91 in females. *T. e. arizonae* Tanner and Lowe 1989, the Arizona garter snake, occurs in Apache and Navajo counties in eastern Arizona, and in Catron and McKinley counties in western New Mexico. Body color is light grayish brown or gray, with two alternating rows of black spots between the broad (to three scale rows wide) yellowish, orange, tan, or white dorsal stripe and the lateral stripes; the dorsal stripe is often indented (invaded by small mar-

ginal spots), and sometimes the lateral stripes are indistinct. The venter is plain or may have small dusky marks. There are 163–174 ventrals in males, 156–165 in females; and 80–92 subcaudals in males, 68–84 in females. *T. e. terrestris* Fox 1951, the coast garter snake, occurs in the Pacific coastal ranges from Curry County, Oregon, south to Ventura County, California. Body color is reddish brown, olive, or black, with orange, red, and dark flecks between the yellow to orange dorsal stripe and the yellowish lateral stripes (red pigment may invade the lateral stripes). The venter has dusky or reddish medial speckles. There are 148–178 ventrals in males, 137–178 in females; and 71–90 subcaudals in males, 61–88 in females. *T. e. vagrans* (Baird and Girard 1853), the wandering garter snake, ranges south from southwestern Saskatchewan, southern Alberta, and southern British Columbia to New Mexico, Arizona, and central Nevada (isolated populations also occur in northeastern Wyoming and west-central South Dakota). Body color is gray, grayish brown, or black, with small separated dark spots (sometimes enlarged or absent) and no red pigment between the dull yellow or tan, often indented, dorsal stripe and the sometimes indented lateral stripes. The venter has medial black flecks. Males have 155–184 ventrals, females 147–177; and 75–96 subcaudals occur in males, 65–90 in females. *T. e. vascotanneri* Tanner and Lowe 1989, the Upper Basin garter snake, is found in the Colorado and Green river watersheds of eastern Utah. Body color is gray or light grayish brown, with dark bars between the missing (most individuals) or interrupted light yellow dorsal stripe, and the often indented lateral stripes. The venter is gray with dark speckles at the edges of the ventral scutes. There are 164–180 ventrals in males, 158–170 in females; and 76–93 subcaudals in males, 64–85 in females.

CONFUSING SPECIES. Other *Thamnophis* occurring within the range of *T. elegans* can be distinguished from it by using the above key. Whipsnakes (*Masticophis*) have smooth scales, a preocular scale that invades the supralabial line, and a divided anal plate.

KARYOTYPE. *T. elegans* has 36 chromosomes (34 macrochromosomes, 2 microchromosomes) with 70 arms. No heteromorphic sex chromosomes are present in females.

Wandering garter snake, *Thamnophis elegans vagrans*; Pierce County, Washington. (Photograph by William Leonard)

FOSSIL RECORD. None.

DISTRIBUTION. The western terrestrial garter snake ranges from British Columbia, Alberta, and southwestern Saskatchewan south to California, Nevada, Arizona, and New Mexico. Scattered isolated populations occur in the San Bernardino Mountains of southern California, northwestern Wyoming, west-central South Dakota, British Columbia, Alberta, Saskatchewan, and northern Baja California.

HABITAT. With such an extensive range that includes great differences in elevation, latitude, and lon-gitude, the habitats in which *T. elegans* resides are quite variable. Usually it is found relatively close to water in riparian woodlands, or along the banks of ir-rigation ditches, ponds, marshes, and mountain lakes, but many populations occur in very dry habitats away from water in alpine meadows, cultivated pastures, and open grasslands. Regardless of where *T. elegans* lives, it is usually associated with some type of vege-tation (Fleharty 1967). *T. e. vagrans* seems to be more terrestrial than the other races.

T. elegans has been recorded from sea level to at least 3,992 m (Hammerson 1986). Hendricks (1996) observed a *T. e. vagrans* basking on a pocket gopher

Distribution of *Thamnophis elegans*.

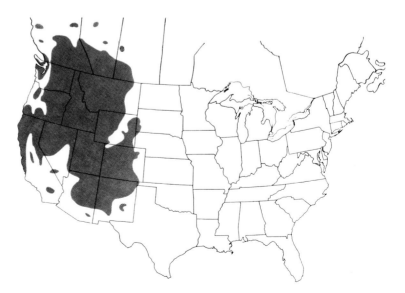

(*Thomomys talpoides*?) burrow 155 m above and 1.6 km from the treeline at an elevation of 3,182 m in the Shoshone National Forest, Park County, Wyoming.

BEHAVIOR. Next to *T. sirtalis*, *T. elegans* has been the most studied *Thamnophis*, and there is a good understanding of its biology even though some gaps exist in the data. Length of the annual activity period depends largely on latitude and elevation; generally those at lower elevations or more southerly latitudes emerge earlier in the spring and remain active longer into the fall than those of higher elevations and more northern latitudes. Spring emergence occurs between late March and mid-May, but primarily in April, and retreat for the winter occurs from mid-September to late October. Warm weather may bring the snakes out for the day in November or February, and Koch and Peterson (1995) reported them to be active during February in a hot springs area of Yellowstone National Park.

Hibernation takes place underground below the frost line in mammal burrows, rock crevices, or talus slopes, or beneath large rocks. Areas disturbed by humans are also used for hibernation—old wells, the base of bridge supports, road banks, and building foundations (Brown et al. 1974; Koch and Peterson 1995). The hibernaculum may be shared with other reptiles (*Eumeces multivirgatus, Charina bottae, Coluber constrictor, Crotalus viridis, Lampropeltis triangulum, Liochlorophis vernalis, Masticophis taeniatus, Pituophis catenifer, T. sirtalis*) (Brown et al. 1974; Degenhardt et al. 1996; Hammerson 1986; Storm and Leonard 1996; Wooodbury and Hansen 1950). CTs of hibernating Utah *T. elegans* taken by Brown et al. (1974) averaged 5°C, and closely approximated ambient ST. CTs were significantly, but inversely, related to increasing hibernation depth between 1.0 and 1.6 m. The snakes were found in groups of one to six individuals, and none was totally torpid. *T. elegans* is usually the last snake to enter the winter retreat and the earliest to emerge from hibernation. They first emerge on sunny days when conditions allow them to attain a BT of 15°C and bask near the entrance to the hibernaculum. Probably all leave the area of the hibernaculum within 30 days. Brattstrom (1965) recorded a BT of 14.2°C for a recently emerged *T. elegans*.

The hibernaculum may be 2–3 km from the sum-

mer foraging range, necessitating extensive migrations to and from it each year. While moving to or from the hibernaculum, newborn *T. elegans* apparently follow scent trails laid down by adults (Heller and Halpern 1981; Waye and Gregory 1993; Wood et al. 1995).

Most daily activity is diurnal, and *T. elegans* is particularly active on sunny days (Fleharty 1967), but some crepuscular and nocturnal activity occurs in the summer. Degenhardt et al. (1996) reported that the shift to more nocturnal activity may be related to food availability, as well as weather conditions. The normal mean CT of active *T. elegans* is 25.3–26.6°C (Brattstrom 1965; Fleharty 1967; Gregory 1984a, 1984b; Gregory and MacIntosh 1980). Surface activity takes place in a CT range of 14.2–37.0°C (Brattstrom 1965; Fleharty 1967; Peterson 1987; Scott et al. 1982), and Storm and Leonard (1995) reported a preferred BT of 30°C. In captivity, *T. elegans* has done particularly well in ATs of 27–35°C (Rossi and Rossi 1995). It emerges with low oral and cloacal temperatures, but rapidly reaches normal activity BT (approximately 26°C) and maintains this temperature with only a slight decline during the day (Gregory 1990). Oral temperatures are often much higher than CT while the snake warms up, but are only moderately higher once activity temperatures are reached. *T. elegans* often basks with only its head exposed to the sun, presumably to raise the brain temperature. As the year progresses to summer, the snake acclimates to higher seasonal temperatures, and the preferred BT rises accordingly (Scott and Pettus 1979).

BTs of active Colorado *T. e. vagrans* at an elevation of 2,600 m revealed that physical environments normally encountered by the snakes are surprisingly thermally harsh (Scott et al. 1982). The snakes only attain optimum BTs (26–32°C) for about 1.5–2.5 hours each day, and the CT_{max} is exceeded for at least three hours in bare-ground or rock microhabitats. Also, on cool or cloudy days in May or September, they can barely attain the minimum optimum BT in any microhabitat.

BT affects all normal behavioral and physiological activities, and both seasonal and daily variances can occur. Particularly correlated with BT are the speed and coordination of movement, the rate of tongue flicking, digestion, erythrocyte oxygen affinity, and metabolism (Fleharty 1967; Ingermann et al. 1991a, 1991b; Seidel and Lindeborg 1973; Stevenson et al.

1985). Oxygen consumption increases with higher BTs and size in *T. elegans*, but levels off at 28–38°C (presumably caused by the date of testing, acclimatization temperature, and geographical distribution of the snakes tested; Seidel and Lindeborg 1973).

Also affecting the female BT is the reproductive state. Pregnant females have higher BTs, and they behaviorally thermoregulate more precisely than nonpregnant females (Charland 1995). These differences persist throughout the pregnancy, but disappear following birth of the young. Pregnant females generally maintain higher BTs, apparently to help raise the metabolic rate of their developing embryos. This imposes an energy cost on females carrying young that is not found in nonpregnant females. Developmental temperature does not, however, affect the thermoregulatory temperature of the young after birth (Arnold et al. 1995).

Once *T. elegans* reaches its summer foraging range, it establishes a home (activity) range. In British Columbia, adults maintained home ranges of 10,000 to 100,000 m²; juveniles only used home ranges of about 1,000 m² (Farr, in Rossman et al. 1996). In New Mexico, Fleharty (1967) found that *T. elegans* probably used an entire lake surface area of 8.9 ha. However, the home range is determined by local environmental conditions and will vary from site to site. The longest known movement by a *T. elegans* was of a female who crawled 2 km from the hibernaculum to her summer home range in 7 days (Graves and Duvall 1990). Less extensive movements are made within the home range. The greatest distance moved in New Mexico was 357 m in 12 days, with 67 m covered in 1 day (Fleharty 1967). The speed, coordination, and duration of movements are affected by the BT and reproductive state of the individual (Charland and Gregory 1995). Whether or not the snake has recently eaten also plays an important role in movements, and those that have not fed recently can crawl faster during better coordinated, long trips (Garland and Arnold 1983).

REPRODUCTION. The reproductive biology of *T. elegans* has been well documented. Males mature at a SVL of 37–40 cm, females at a SVL of 42–46 cm (Farr, in Rossman et al. 1996; Hebard 1950; Riches 1967; White and Kolb 1974; Wright and Wright 1957). Normally, these lengths are attained during years two to

three (but see GROWTH AND LONGEVITY, below); well-fed captives kept active through their first winter have matured in as little as eight months (Riches 1967).

The male testes weigh least in December–February, increase in weight until reaching their maximum in July and early August, and then decline from mid-August through November (Fox 1982), although White and Kolb (1974) reported no change in length and width of the testes from 1 July to 19 September. The right (anterior) testis is usually longer than the left (posterior) testis. The average testis size index (length divided by width) obtained by White and Kolb (1974) was 2.3 (0.1–4.3). This index increases with greater SVL, that is, 0.4 (0.1–1.6) at 16.0–25.9 cm SVL, 1.0 (0.3–1.6) at 26.0–35.9 cm, 2.5 (1.0–4.3) at 36.0–45.9 cm, and 2.6 (1.8–3.9) at 46.0–55.0 cm. The volume of adult males 45–51 cm long averaged 163.3 mm³ for the left testis and 180.5 mm³ for the right one in January–March, and 766 mm³ and 841 mm³, respectively, in July and August (Fox 1952). Seminiferous tubule diameter follows a similar cycle: least in December–February, greatest in mid-June to mid-August (Fox 1952). Spermatogonia are present in the walls of the seminiferous tubules throughout the year, primary and secondary spermatocytes from March through November, spermatids from late April through November (low numbers are also present in December), and mature sperm from mid-June to early December (Fox 1952). The interstitial cells are smallest in late May and June, increase in size from June through October, then decline slightly from mid-October to December, increase again from January to early April, and finally decline from April through May (Fox 1952). Some slight timing differences may occur in the various populations (Fox 1954).

Data concerning the female cycle are fewer and mostly anecdotal. Of females collected from 1 July to 19 September in Sierra County, California, one had two enlarged (11–20 mm) ova, and another had degenerating embryos (White and Kolb 1974). Females have been found with large eggs from late May to early July, and others with near-term embryos in late June to early September (Wright and Wright 1957). Most young are probably born from July through September. Estrogen is the most important ovarian hormone regulating development of the uterus (Mead et al. 1981); it also influences the development of the subcaudal scale count in females, but not males (Osypka and Arnold 2000). Progesterone maintains conditions in the uterus during pregnancy: average progesterone concentrations of 1.1–2.0 ng/mg of corpora lutea and 1.8–2.8 ng/ml of plasma occur in the first trimester of pregnancy; progesterone concentrations are highest during the second trimester in the corpora lutea (2.6 ng/mg) and plasma (6.2 ng/ml); and the levels fall during the third trimester and are undetectable a week after parturition (Highfell and Mead 1975). At parturition, the serum progesterone level averages 1.0 ng/ml. Pregnancy is also associated with an increase in nucleoside triphosphate (NTP) concentration, and a simultaneous decrease in the oxygen affinity of the female's red blood cells. Increase in serum progesterone during pregnancy apparently causes the increase in red-cell NTP concentration (Ragsdale et al. 1993). The oxygen affinity of red cells from embryos is higher than that of their mother (Ingermann et al. 1991a).

Courtship and mating behavior begins almost immediately after emergence from hibernation, and has been observed from 16 and 21 March to 2 and 10 May (Ashton 1999; Fitch 1970; Riches 1967). Mating may also occur in September (Rossman et al. 1996), and Brown et al. (1974) found active sperm in females at a Utah hibernaculum in January. Female *Thamnophis* are capable of storing viable sperm for extended periods of time after mating (Fox 1956). The sperm is stored in seminal receptacles in modified alveolar glands at the base of the oviductal infundibulum that open into the lumen of the oviduct via branched, heavily ciliated ducts. Sperm from fall matings stored in these glands may be used to fertilize eggs ovulated the next spring.

Courtship and mating behaviors have not been described, but males apparently find their mates by following female pheromone trails, and several males may attempt to copulate with a female at the same time (Ashton 1999). Riches (1967) reported that a captive mating lasted 105 minutes. Young from this copulation were born 104 days later, and Rossi and Rossi (1995) reported GPs of 120–150 days for captive litters. Embryonic developmental stages have been described by Norman (1977), and Fox et al. (1961) have shown that low developmental temperatures may affect the scale patterns of neonates.

The bulk and weight of the litter carried by a female *T. elegans* causes changes in her behavior. She will bask more often, presumably to aid development of her offspring, but eats little or nothing, particularly late in the pregnancy, and becomes anorexic (Gregory et al. 1999). This causes an energy drain on the female, and she must be "fit and fat" before the pregnancy, with sufficient energy stores to carry her through. The bulk of the litter also retards her ability to escape predators by slowing her crawling speed and coordination. This—coupled with greater exposure during basking—results in a dangerous period for female *T. elegans*.

Schuett et al. (1997) have presented evidence that female *T. elegans* may produce offspring without fertilization by a male (facultative parthenogenesis). They reported four examples of females producing all male offspring with 87–100% of the DNA sequenced bands of their mothers, and without any male bands. The offspring had 22–52% fewer bands than their mothers. However, the females had been previously kept with other unsexed *T. elegans* presumed to also have been females, and because there is a possibility that some of the unsexed garter snakes may have been males, these records are in doubt.

Eight-eight litters recorded in the literature averaged 8.7 young, and ranged from 3 (Kasper and Kasper 1997) to 27 (Degenhardt et al. 1996). A literature review also revealed that the larger females produced the largest litters and largest young. However, feeding by the female during late pregnancy influences the postpartum mass of the mother but not the litter mass or size of the offspring (Gregory and Skebo 1998).

Newborn *T. elegans* are usually somewhat lighter in color than adults, with less bright dorsal and lateral stripes, and a distinct pattern of dark spots. Neonates have 16.7–27.6 (mean, 21.5; n = 27) cm TBLs and weigh 1.4–2.4 g.

Natural hybridization between *T. elegans* and both *T. ordinoides* and *T. sirtalis* has been reported (Norman 1978).

GROWTH AND LONGEVITY. Growth of this snake has seldom been reported, and then mostly for captive-reared individuals. Gregory and Prelypchan (1994) reported that first-year juveniles, maintained in exactly the same manner, had increased 13.4–17.4 cm in SVL and 12.5–17.1 g in body mass since birth. Males grew an average of 15.3 cm and increased their body masses by an average of 14.3 g; females increased an average of 14.2 cm and 13.9 g. Differences were pronounced between Gregory and Prelychan's six litters, apparently because of genetic influence. Three additional newborns measured by Kasper and Kasper (1997) grew from 10.3 to 10.6 cm SVL in about a month (without feeding), from 11.4 to 15.5 cm SVL in 11 days, and from 11.9 to 18.3 cm SVL, respectively; and an albino kept by Tanner (1966b) grew from 59.2 cm (43 g) to 69.4 cm (112.0 g) in five years.

Growth rate variation in *T. elegans* at Eagle Lake, Lassen County, California, was studied by Bronikowski and Arnold (1999) for 20 years in the wild and 6 years in the laboratory. Two ecotypes were revealed. Individuals living along the lake shore with continuous access to prey and water grew faster, matured at age three, and had higher fecundity, but low adult survival. In contrast, individuals from meadow populations with variable prey availability had slower growth rates, matured at age five to seven, experienced lower fecundity, but had high adult survival.

A female caught when 4–5 years old lived an additional 18 years in captivity (Schuett et al. 1997), and other *T. elegans* have survived over 12 years in captivity (Licht 1985; Slavens and Slavens 1991).

DIET AND FEEDING HABITS. *T. elegans* is in every sense a generalist feeder; wild individuals eat vertebrates of all classes and many types of invertebrates. The diet varies across the range, and between years, according to availability of prey species, and may even vary between local populations (Arnold 1981a, 1981b; Fitch, 1940, 1941; Gregory 1978, 1983, 1984a; Jennings et al. 1992; Kephart 1982; Kephart and Arnold 1982). High elevation populations may be entirely dependent on amphibian prey (Jennings et al. 1992), but coastal *T. elegans* forage on invertebrates in intertidal zones (Gregory 1978). Fitch (1940) reported that of 69 *T. e. vagrans* examined, 32 had eaten aquatic animals, and 37 had eaten prey that was mainly terrestrial. The latter prey was probably caught out of water, but mostly in riparian habitats.

Recently transformed anurans and tadpoles seem to be the most important and consistent prey. Amphibians totaled 51 (36.7%) of the 139 individual animals eaten (Fitch 1940). Of 100 individual animals eaten by *T. e. elegans*, 22 were aquatic and 78 terrestrial; 32 different amphibians were eaten (Fitch 1940), making up 31.7% of the diet (Fitch 1941). Slugs were the second most consumed prey. In New Mexico, where slugs are scarce, Gehlbach (1965) found frogs in 17 of 23 (73.9%) *T. e. vagrans* containing food, toads in 6 (26.1%), and a salamander in 1 (4.3%). Eating certain amphibians, however, may have its risks; *T. elegans* force-fed *Pseudacris regilla, Rana aurora,* and the skin of *Bufo boreas* showed no ill effects, but those fed the newt *Taricha granulosa* lost motor function. The effect was not fatal, as the snakes recovered within 24 hours (Macartney and Gregory 1981).

The following prey have been recorded from wild *T. elegans*: anurans (adults and tadpoles)—true frogs *(Rana aurora, R. blairi, R. boylii, R. mucosa, R. pretiosa, R. pipiens),* toads *(Bufo boreas, B. punctatus, B. woodhousei),* spadefoots *(Scaphiopus* sp.), and treefrogs *(Pseudacris regilla, P. triseriata);* salamanders *(Ambystoma tigrinum, Aneides hardii, Ensatina eschscholtzii, Hydromantes platycephalus, Plethodon neomexicanus);* lizards *(Eumeces skiltonianus, Phrynosoma douglassii, Sceloporus graciosus, S. occidentalis, S. undulatus, Uta stansburiana);* snakes *(Thamnophis elegans, T. radix);* small mammals—mice *(Microtus mexicanus, M. montanus, Perognathus flavus, Peromyscus leucopus),* chipmunks *(Tamias* sp.), brush rabbits *(Sylvilagus bachmani),* shrews *(Sorex emarginatus, S. vagrans),* and bats; birds (adults of small species, nestlings, fledglings, and broken egg contents)—junco *(Junco hyemalis),* Brewer's blackbird *(Euphagus cyanocephalus),* sparrows, cormorants *(Phalacrocorax* sp.), gulls *(Larus* sp.), crows *(Corvus* sp.), and quillemot *(Cepphus columba);* fish—sculpin *(Cottus* sp.), trout *(Oncorhynchus mykiss, Salmo trutta),* sunfish *(Lepomis* sp.), cyprinids *(Gila bicolor, Richardsonius balteatus, R. egregius, R. osculus),* mosquitofish *(Gambusia affinis),* lampreys *(Lampetra* sp.), suckers *(Catostomus tahoensis),* and fish entrails left by fishermen; leeches; earthworms; polychaetes; slugs; snails; crabs; insects (Coleoptera, Hymenoptera, Orthoptera); and spiders (Arnold and Wassersug 1978; Baker and Webb 1976; Bronikowski and Arnold 1999; Carpenter 1953b; Cunningham 1959; C. Ernst, pers. obs.; Finley et al. 1994; Fitch 1940, 1941; Fleharty 1967; Gregory 1978; Grismer 1994; Hebard 1951b; Koch and Panik 1993; Painter et al. 1999; Reaser and Dexter 1996; Tanner 1949; White and Kolb 1974).

Captives have consumed fish (*Gambusia affinis, Poecilia* sp., *Lepomis* sp.), frogs (adults and tadpoles—*Rana catesbeiana*), toads (*Bufo* sp.), salamanders *(Ambystoma tigrinum, Aneides* sp., *Batrachoseps* sp., *Plethodon jordani),* lizards *(Eumeces* sp., *Cnemidophorus* sp., *Gambelia* sp., *Sceloporus* sp., *Scincella lateralis, Uta stansburiana),* mice (*Microtus* sp., *Mus musculus, Peromyscus* sp.), leeches, earthworms, and slugs (Arnold 1981a, 1981b; Feder and Arnold 1982; Macartney and Gregory 1981; Rossi and Rossi 1995; Tanner 1949, 1966b).

Most foraging is diurnal, but some crepuscular and nocturnal hunting occurs in the summer or when frog choruses and tadpoles are prevalent. This species is an active hunter that forages on land, on the water surface, and underwater. It even climbs into low bushes or trees to examine bird nests (Storm and Leonard 1995). Prey is located both visually and by odor (Drummond 1985), and feeding behavior may vary between populations, depending on which prey is most available (Drummond and Burghardt 1983). Adults and juveniles in the same population may feed on different-sized prey requiring different hunting strategies. Pregnant females eat less food than nonpregnant females or males (Gregory et al. 1999).

When an animal is caught, it is quickly worked to the rear of the mouth where the enlarged maxillary teeth can hold it tight (C. Ernst, pers. obs.). Small prey are quickly swallowed, but larger, struggling prey may be held in the rear of the mouth for some time before becoming weakened or immobilized by the snake's saliva. The saliva is produced in Duvernoy's glands that contain a mixture of serous and mucous cells, and empty near the enlarged posterior maxillary teeth (Kardong and Luchtel 1986; Taub 1967). The average dry yield of saliva from one gland is 0.39 (0.10–0.46) mg, and the typical wet yield is 23 (10–45) μl (Hill and MacKessy 1997). The average percentage of protein in the saliva is 51.6 (32.7–84.6) %. The saliva is highly toxic to mice *(Mus musculus),* causing marked hemorrhaging in the lungs, diaphragm, mesentery, and stomach lining, and mild local hemorrhaging (Vest 1981b). The LD_{50} in *Mus musculus* is 13.85 mg/kg. In addition, Finley et al. (1994) and Jansen (1987) reported the venom caused proteolytic and myonecrotic effects in mice.

PREDATORS AND DEFENSE. Predators of this species are many, and include all vertebrate classes.

Large predatory fish introduced into the waterways of the West probably take some juveniles, as also does the introduced bullfrog *(Rana catesbeiana).* The snakes *Charina bottae, Masticophis taeniatus,* and *Pituophis catenifer,* and the red-tailed hawk *(Buteo jamaicensis)* have eaten it (Camper and Dixon 2000; Koch and Peterson 1995; Linder 1963; Stanford 1942; Zaworski 1990), and other ophiophagous snakes probably take their share. Small *T. elegans* may even be eaten by larger members of their own species (White and Kolb 1974). Koch and Peterson (1995) and Ross (1989) suspected herons, kestrels *(Falco sparverius),* ravens *(Corvus corax),* black-billed magpies *(Pica pica),* badgers *(Taxidea taxus),* raccoons *(Procyon lotor),* and even predaceous beetles (Coleoptera) of preying on *T. elegans,* and Turner (1955) saw a bear kill one. Each year many *T. elegans* fall victim to motorized vehicles and mowers, and many others have their habitat destroyed, or are killed outright by humans.

The first line of defense is to flee. The escape routes of *T. elegans* recorded by Fleharty (1967) in New Mexico included the following: diving underwater (7% of the snakes); going into the water on top of aquatic vegetation and stopping a short distance from shore but not diving (50%); under logs (23%); among grass and logs (2%); in vegetation without logs (14%); under logs and rocks (1%); and under rocks (3%). If not allowed to escape, *T. elegans* will spray musk and discharge feces. It may also attempt to bite, especially large individuals. Neonates can instinctively recognize the odor of *Lampropeltis getula* (Weldon 1982).

Because of the toxic nature of the Duvernoy's gland venom produced by *T. elegans,* this snake should be handled with care. An 11-year-old boy, whose hand was chewed for 10 minutes by a 79 cm *T. e. terrestris* (mistakenly at first identified as *T. couchii)* experienced swelling and discoloration of the hand and arm, and illness so severe he had to be hospitalized (McKinistry 1978), but he recovered within a few days. A second case of envenomation following a prolonged bite by a *T. e. vagrans* was reported (Vest 1981a).

POPULATIONS. *T. elegans* is a common snake over most of its range, and its populations may contain many individuals. It is the most populous and commonly seen snake in Yellowstone and Grand Teton

National Parks (Koch and Peterson 1995), and Farr (in Rossman et al. 1996) estimated that 5,520 individuals were present in 2,000 ha in British Columbia—a density of 2.8/ha. At another site in British Columbia, 134 (6.3%) captures of *T. elegans* were included in 2,138 captures of snakes by Engelstoft and Ovaska (2000).

Different habitats may support different numbers of *T. elegans*. Szaro et al. (1988) studied it for two years at two ungrazed riparian sites, and at a third grazed site in New Mexico. Mark-recapture estimates gave population sizes of 282 and 166 in the two years at the first riparian site, and 296 and 146 for the two years at the second riparian site. The times fixed-area plot method at these two sites gave estimates of 1.28 and 0.88 snakes/250 m² for the two years. In contrast, the grazed plot had mark-recapture estimates for the two years of 67 and 26 *T. elegans* and 0.28 and 0.11 snakes/250 m² by the times fixed-area plot method. At Wall Lake, New Mexico, *T. elegans* made up 29% of the individuals of three species of garter snakes (Fleharty 1967).

The sex ratio at Wall Lake was 1.00:3.37, but in Sierra County, California, it was 1.00:0.91 (White and Kolb 1974), and in British Columbia 1.00:1.34 (Waye 1999). Few snakes smaller than 30 cm SVL were present in the British Columbia population; the majority of males were 32.5–50.0 cm SVL, and most females were 40.0–70.0 cm SVL. The age class distribution of the British Columbia snakes ranged from neonates to 14 years; adult males and females two to seven years old made up the greatest portion of the population, with three- to four-year-old snakes most common.

T. e. vagrans is considered of special concern in Oklahoma.

REMARKS.   *T. elegans* has been reviewed by Fox (1951), Fitch (1940 1980a, 1983a), Rossman (1979), and Webb (1976).

Thamnophis eques (Reuss 1834) │ Mexican Garter Snake

RECOGNITION.   This stout-bodied garter snake has a maximum TBL of 112 cm and is best distinguished by the presence of a pair of black blotches behind the parietal scales; a light, crescent-shaped, pigmented area behind the corner of the mouth; black, wedge-shaped bars separating the supralabials; and light lateral body stripes on scale rows three and four. Body color varies from olive to dark brown or black, with

Mexican garter snake, *Thamnophis eques megalops*; Cochise County, Arizona. (Photograph by Cecil Schwalbe)

a yellow to orange middorsal stripe that is one to nine scales wide, a narrow pale yellow to greenish yellow longitudinal stripe on each side of the body, and checkered dark olive or black spots lying between the dorsal and lateral stripes. The top of the head is olive, and the pre- and postoculars are light colored. The venter is cream colored, and the labials and chin are cream to yellow. Body scales are keeled and occur in 21 (19) anterior rows, 19 (17–21) midbody rows, and 17 (15) posterior rows; the scale keels of black individuals may be brown or olive. Present are 143–176 ventrals, 59–95 subcaudals, and a single anal plate. Lateral head scales consist of 2 nasals, 1 loreal, 1 preocular, 3 (4) postoculars, 1 + 1–4 temporals, 8 (7–9) supralabials, and 10 (9–11) infralabials. The hemipenis has not been described. Each maxilla has 23–28 teeth, with the posterior teeth longer than those in front.

Males have 143–176 ventrals, 65–95 subcaudals, and TLs approximately 22–27 (usually 25–26) % of TBL; females generally have longer SVLs, 149–171 ventrals, 59–89 subcaudals, and TLs 20–25 (usually 22–24) % as long as the TBL.

GEOGRAPHIC VARIATION.   Three subspecies are currently recognized (Rossman et al. 1996), but only T. e. megalops (Kennicott 1860a), the Mexican garter snake, occurs in the United States. It is described above.

CONFUSING SPECIES.   To distinguish T. eques from the other garter snakes occurring within its North American range, refer to the above key. The striped whipsnakes (Masticophis) have smooth body scales in 15–17 midbody rows, and a divided anal plate.

KARYOTYPE AND FOSSIL RECORD.   Unknown.

DISTRIBUTION.   In the United States, T. eques is found only in Cochise, Graham, Maricopa, Pima, and Santa Cruz counties in southeastern Arizona, and Grant and Hidalgo counties in adjacent southwestern New Mexico. In Mexico, the species ranges in the highlands from Sonora and Chihuahua south to Oaxaca and Veracruz.

HABITAT.   In Arizona and New Mexico, the Mexican garter snake's habitat is now restricted to cattle

Distribution of *Thamnophis eques*.

tanks with abundant shoreline vegetation (knotgrass, spikegrass, bullrush, cattail, deergrass, willows, cottonwoods, mesquite) or valley cienégas (swamps) and their streams, at elevations to 2,590 m.

BEHAVIOR.   T. eques occupies the eastern water snake niche in the Southwest where species of Nerodia are absent. It is primarily diurnal, with a peak daily activity period in Mexico at 1000–1100 hours (Van Devender and Lowe 1977), but some crepuscular, and possibly even nocturnal, activity may occur. How early the snake emerges in the spring or how late in the fall it enters hibernation are not known, nor are its movement patterns. It is most active from June to August.

Arizona T. eques are active at BTs of 22.0–33.0 (mean, 27.3) °C, and their terrestrial BTs during stable periods at the middle of warm, clear days are 24.0–33.0 (mean, 28.0) °C (Rosen 1991a). They often bask, especially pregnant females.

REPRODUCTION.   Females are sexually mature at 53 cm TBL when two to three years old; males take two years to mature (Degenhardt et al. 1996). The female gametic cycle seems somewhat annually advanced from that of other garter snakes. Follicular enlargement occurs in the early fall, ovulation takes place during late March or the first half of April, and parturition normally takes place during June to early August (Degenhardt et al. 1996; Rossman et al. 1996). A late litter of 10 young was delivered on 28 September after an 11 month gestation period, and a female who mated on 7 April gave birth 118–119 days later on 3–4 August (Degenhardt et al. 1996). Rosen and Schwalbe (1988) found that only 50% of Arizona females produce litters each year, although they were not able to determine whether the breeding cycle was biennial. In Hidalgo, Mexico, Garcia and Drummond (1988) found 6 of 12 mature-sized females pregnant at one site, but only 1 of 9 and 3 of 16 carrying litters at two other sites. The male gametic cycle has not been described, and the only reported dates of mating are 29 October and 7 April in captivity (Degenhardt et al. 1996).

Litters average 14 (4–26) young with TBLs of 23.0–26.5 (mean, 24.5) cm (Degenhardt et al. 1996; Garcia and Drummond 1977; Ramirez-Bautista et al. 1995; Rosen and Schwalbe 1988; Rossi and Rossi 1995; Woodin 1950). Neonates have stocky bodies, and the same coloration and patterns as the adults.

GROWTH AND LONGEVITY. No study of the growth of *T. eques* has been reported. Rossi and Rossi (1995) reported a captive longevity of two years and three months; obviously wild individuals live longer than this.

DIET AND FEEDING HABITS. *T. eques* is an active forager, both along the bottom and at the surface of the water. It probably also takes amphibians along the shoreline, and since it is known to eat earthworms, lizards, and mice, also forages on land. Even so, most of its prey are associated with water. Reported prey species are fish—chubs *(Gila intermedia, G. robusta)* and goldfish *(Carassius auratus);* amphibians—salamander larvae *(Ambystoma tigrinum),* toads *(Bufo punctatus, B. woodhousei),* spadefoots *(Scaphiopus hammondii),* treefrogs *(Hyla arenicolor),* and ranid frogs *(Rana berlandieri, R. catesbeiana, R. chiricahuensis, R. yavapaiensis);* lizards *(Cnemidophorus, Sceloporus);* mice *(Microtus quasiater, Peromyscus maniculatus);* earthworms *(Eisenia);* leeches *(Erpobdella, Mooreobdella);* and slugs (Gastropoda) (Campbell 1934; Garcia and Drummond 1988; Rosen and Schwalbe 1988; Van Devender and Lowe 1977).

Garcia and Drummond (1988) identified the stomach contents of 126 Mexican *T. eques,* most containing a single prey species, and reported the following percentages of stomachs with each kind of prey: earthworms (41%), leeches (39%), fish (11%), frogs (5%), salamander larvae (3%), mice (1.5%), and slugs (0.8%). Vertebrates were eaten almost exclusively by larger individuals, while earthworms were the main food of juveniles; leeches were consumed by all size classes. Earthworms and leeches were taken most often in July and August. Captives have eaten small mice (Rossi and Rossi 1995).

PREDATORS AND DEFENSE. No direct observations of predation on *T. eques* have been reported; however, populations in Arizona have declined since the introduction of the bullfrog *(Rana catesbeiana),* and it is possible that the frog eats small *T. eques* (Schwalbe and Rosen 1988). Also, the snake in the talons of an eagle present on the Mexican coat of arms may be this species, as Cortez supposedly saw one seized by an eagle (Cope 1900).

T. eques is shy, and when on land usually hides in vegetation or beneath flat rocks or plant debris. It normally dives into the water if given a chance to escape, but if prevented from doing so will readily bite and spray its foul-smelling musk.

POPULATIONS. Populations of this species were probably, and still are at some sites, quite dense. Rosen and Schwalbe (1988) captured 95 individuals around an undisturbed 0.1 ha pond in Arizona, and Rossman et al. (1996) reported that other sites in Arizona also appear to have large populations in very small, restricted habitats. However, such sites are dominated by large, old snakes, suggesting a greater mortality of young snakes and little recruitment. Populations may also be large in Mexico; Garcia and Drummond (1988) captured 286 *T. eques* along 750 m of shoreline at a Hildalgo lake.

Unfortunately, populations of *T. eques* are declining in both Arizona and New Mexico. It has been listed as endangered by both those states, and is also listed as a Category 2 candidate species by the U.S. Fish and Wildlife Service.

REMARKS. *T. eques* is most closely related to *T. marcianus* and *T. sirtalis* (deQueiroz and Lawson 1994). It has been reviewed by Rossman et al. (1996).

Thamnophis gigas Fitch 1940 | Giant Garter Snake

RECOGNITION. *T. gigas* is the largest species of garter snake, growing to a maximum TBL of 162.6 cm. The body is olive to grayish brown, and two alternating rows of dark spots are present on each side. A pale yellow or olive gray middorsal stripe may be present, but it is often absent, and a pale yellow to gray lateral stripe is present on each side on scale rows two and three. The supralabials are cream colored, and are often separated by narrow, wedgelike black bars. The chin is cream colored, and the venter is olive gray. Body scales are keeled, and occur in 21 anterior rows, 21–23 rows at midbody, and 17 (18–19) rows near the tail. Ventrals total 150–170 and subcaudals 65–81; a single anal plate is present. Lateral head scales consist of 2 nasals, 1 loreal, 1 (2) preocular(s), 3 (2) postoculars, 1 + 1 + 1 temporals, 8 (7) supralabials, and 10 (9–11) infralabials. The hemipenis has not been described. Each maxilla has 23–27 teeth.

Males have 157–170 ventrals, 73–81 subcaudals, and TLs 23–26 (mean, 24) % of TBL; females have 150–164 ventrals, 63–73 subcaudals, and TLs 20–23 (mean, 21) % of TBL. The average relative height of the first dorsal scale row (maximum vertical height of dorsal scale row one divided by the maximum width of the vertebral row) is 2.9 (2.7–3.4) in females, but only 2.5 (2.3–2.8) in males (Rossman 1995).

GEOGRAPHIC VARIATION. No subspecies are recognized, but *T. gigas* in the Sacramento Valley have 162–168 ventrals in males and 156–164 in females, while those from the central San Joaquin Valley have 157–161 ventrals in males and 150–155 ventrals in females (Rossman et al. 1996).

CONFUSING SPECIES. For characters distinguishing *T. gigas* from other garter snakes in California, see the above key.

KARYOTYPE AND FOSSIL RECORD. Unknown.

DISTRIBUTION. The giant garter snake occurs only in the Central Valley of California from Butte County in the north to Kern County in the south. The range is divided into two populations, one living in the Sacramento Valley in the north and the other in the San Joaquin Valley in the south. Unfortunately, the snake has been extirpated south of northern Fresno County (Hansen and Brode 1980).

HABITAT. *T. gigas* is usually found along slow-flowing creeks, marshes, and sloughs with emergent vegetation (cattails, tules) and soft bottoms at elevations of 0–122 m. It is not found in large rivers.

BEHAVIOR. The giant garter snake is highly aquatic; it spends most of the day either in the water foraging or hiding or basking, either on the bank among emergent vegetation or on the branches of willow and saltbush overhanging the water. It may climb over a meter into brush to bask (Brode 1988), and often basks while stretched out and floating at the water surface. All daily activity is diurnal; nights are spent in rodent burrows, under logs or plant debris, or in brush piles on the bank. Its aquatic niche is similar to that of some eastern *Nerodia* water snakes.

T. gigas becomes active in mid- to late March and may remain active until October. Some estivate in rodent burrows or decaying piles of plant material, occasionally well away from the water, during the hot weather in July and August (Hansen and Tremper, in Rossman et al. 1996), and hibernation probably takes place in the same types of shelters.

REPRODUCTION. Males mature in three years, but it may take as long as five years for females to attain maturity (Rossman et al. 1996). Neither size at maturity nor the reproductive cycles of each sex have been reported.

Mating probably takes place in the spring after emergence from hibernation. The single litter of young is born in the summer. Hansen and Hansen (1990) reported data on 18 litters of *T. gigas* that were produced between 13 July and 1 September (9 in August, 8 in July, and 1 in September). Litter size ranged from 10 to 46 (mean, 23.1). Generally, the largest females produced the greatest number of neonates per litter: those with 90–100 cm TBLs averaged 18 (10–31) young per litter, females with 110–130 cm TBLs averaged 27 (16–46) young per litter. The litter of 46 young was produced by a 130 cm female. Neonates

Giant garter snake, *Thamnophis gigas*; Fresno County, California. (Photograph by Robert W. Hansen)

had SVLs of 15.2–23.2 cm; females over 110 cm TBL produced neonates averaging 21.3 cm SVL; females under 110 cm produced young averaging 19.8 cm SVL. Cunningham (1959) collected a female on 24 July that contained 24 eggs.

GROWTH AND LONGEVITY. Unknown.

DIET AND FEEDING HABITS. The giant garter snake forages by day, both in the water and along the bank. Prey is detected by sight or olfaction, chased, grabbed in the mouth, and swallowed. The reported diet includes fish *(Cyprinus carpio, Gambusia affinis, Gila crassicauda* [now extinct], *Orthodon microlepidotus)* and tadpoles and adults of ranid frogs *(Rana aurora, R. catesbeiana)* (Brode 1988; Cunningham 1959; Fitch 1941; Rossman et al. 1996).

PREDATORS AND DEFENSE. Other than that by humans, no predation has been reported, but introduced predatory fish possibly eat the juveniles.

T. gigas is an extremely alert snake and is very difficult to approach. Its main defense is to enter the water and swim away beneath the surface, often to a patch of submerged vegetation where it will hide for several minutes before again surfacing. Handling it usually brings a release of musk, and some individuals will bite.

POPULATIONS. Formerly common at some sites, especially Buena Vista Lake (Fitch 1941), *T. gigas* has been extirpated over much of its southern range in

the San Joaquin Valley (Brode 1988; Hansen and Brode 1980). The present population center is near Sacramento. Reduction in its numbers was caused primarily by human habitat alteration, especially the draining of the snake's original marsh habitat in the south. Today *T. gigas* is considered threatened by California and also by the U.S. Fish and Wildlife Service.

REMARKS. Originally described as a subspecies of *Thamnophis ordinoides* by Fitch (1940), and later considered a subspecies of *T. couchii* (Lawson and Dessauer 1979; Rossman 1979), *T. gigas* was elevated to full species rank by Rossman and Stewart (1987). The species has been reviewed by Rossman et al. (1996).

Distribution of *Thamnophis gigas*.

Thamnophis hammondii (Kennicott 1860a) | Two-striped Garter Snake

RECOGNITION. The two-striped garter snake (TBL to 106.8 cm) lacks a middorsal stripe, or only has remnants of one in the form of an elongated streak on the back of the neck. It is olive, brown, or brownish gray with a light lateral stripe on scale rows two and three of each side, and four rows of small black spots situated between the lateral stripes, but no red lateral spots. The head is grayish brown with grayish supralabials separated by black, wedgelike bars. The venter is yellow, orangish red, or pinkish, and either immaculate or with slight gray marks. The chin and throat are white to cream. Body scales are keeled and pitless, and occur in 21 (16–19) anterior rows, 21 (19) rows at midbody, and 17 (19) rows near the tail. Beneath are 149–178 ventrals, 61–96 subcaudals, and a single anal plate. Lateral head scales consist of 1 nasal, 1 loreal, 2 (1) preoculars, 3 (2–4) postoculars, 1 + 2 + 3 temporals, 8 (9) supralabials, and 10 (9–12) infralabials. The hemipenis has not been described. Each maxilla has 24–30 teeth, with the posterior-most enlarged.

Males have 155–178 ventrals, 66–96 subcaudals, and TLs 24–27 (mean, 24.9) % of TBL; females have 149–172 ventrals, 61–82 subcaudals, and TLs only 21–24 (mean, 22.9) % of TBL.

GEOGRAPHIC VARIATION. No subspecies are recognized.

CONFUSING SPECIES. Characteristics distinguishing *T. hammondii* from the other garter snakes living in California are covered in the above key.

KARYOTYPE. Undescribed.

FOSSIL RECORD. While no fossils have been directly assigned to this species, the Pleistocene (Rancholabrean) remains from Ranch LaBrea, California, identified as *T. couchii* species group by LaDuke (1991) may include *T. hammondii*.

DISTRIBUTION. *T. hammondii* ranges from Monterey County, California, southward along the Pacific Coast to northwestern Baja California. It also occurs in isolated populations in Baja California Sur, and on Catalina Island.

HABITAT. This snake is quite aquatic, and is normally found along permanent freshwater streams with rocky bottoms and much vegetation in riparian zones of willow, oak, pine, cedar, or even chaparral, at elevations from sea level to over 2,100 m.

BEHAVIOR. Unfortunately, some life history data concerning *T. hammondii* have been published under other garter snake species' names (see REMARKS), and what has been attributed directly to it is sparse. It is primarily diurnal, but may be occasionally active at night or at dusk or dawn during the hot summer periods. In California it is active in every month and is fond of basking, especially on cool mornings. It occasionally climbs into low bushes or trees. Mean BT of 14 *T. hammondii* taken by Cunningham (1966a) was 22.6 (18.6–31.8) °C; 5 of these were found swimming in water temperatures between 14.0 and 27.6°C, and those found under surface objects had BTs of 7.2–23.6°C.

REPRODUCTION. According to Wright and Wright (1957), males of the two-striped garter snake are mature at a SVL of 37.3 cm, and females mature at a SVL of 38.8 cm. No complete description of either the male or female reproductive cycle is available. On 28 May, Cunningham (1959) found a 46.1 cm TBL female that contained 6 eggs averaging 17 × 9 mm, and an-

Two-striped garter snake, *Thamnophis hammondii*; Southern California. (Photograph by Donald J. Fisher)

Distribution of *Thamnophis hammondii.*

other 64.9 cm female that contained 19 eggs. He and Rossi and Rossi (1995) observed copulations in the wild on 29 May and 3 April, respectively, so this species is a spring breeder. No description of the courtship and copulatory behaviors has been published. Litters are produced from July to late October and contain 3–36 (average 15–16) young. Neonates have 20–22 cm TBLs.

After mating, sperm is stored by female *Thamnophis* in special oviductal receptacles (Fox 1956). Apparently female *T. hammondii* can retain and support sperm for a considerable period of time after mating, as a female (79.5 cm SVL) who had not been with a male for 53 months gave birth to a small, dead, but fully formed, young (Stewart 1972).

GROWTH AND LONGEVITY.   No data on growth rates have been published. An adult *T. hammondii*, of unreported sex, previously captured in the wild, survived 7 years, 8 months, and 23 days at the Los Angeles Zoo (Snider and Bowler 1992).

DIET AND FEEDING HABITS.   Foraging is both diurnal and crepuscular, and is centered about the species' aquatic habitat. The diet consists of fish—

sticklebacks *(Gasterosteus aculeatus)* and trout; fish eggs; anurans, both adults and tadpoles *(Bufo boreas, Hyla arenicolor, Pseudacris regilla, Rana aurora);* and earthworms (Bell and Haglund 1978; Cunningham 1959; Fitch 1940, 1941; Grismer and McGuire 1993; Klauber 1931b; Van Denburgh 1897). Most prey are caught in the water or at the water's edge, but earthworms are probably taken on land. Captives will eat mice scented with fish (Rossi and Rossi 1995).

PREDATORS AND DEFENSE.   Aside from humans killing them (Brown 1997), the only report of predation on *T. hammondii* was that of two neonates regurgitated by a ring-necked snake *(Diadophis punctatus)* (Goodman and Tate 1997).

If given the opportunity, this snake will always choose to retreat into the water when disturbed. When prevented from doing so, some individuals will hide their heads beneath their body coils (Hayes and Baker 1986), and if handled they will bite and spray musk.

POPULATIONS.   Although once a fairly common animal along its waterways, no study of the population dynamics of *T. hammondii* has been published. Because of the deterioration and loss of its habitat, the species has declined in numbers to the point that it is considered threatened in California.

REMARKS.   *T. hammondii* is another garter snake with a confusing taxonomic history. Named originally as a full species by Kennicott (1860a), it was listed as a subspecies of *T. elegans* by Cooper (1870) and Ruthven (1908), and still later was relegated on the basis of morphological and biochemical information to a subspecies of *T. couchii* by Lawson and Dessauer (1979) and Rossman (1979). Rossman and Stewart (1987) studied meristic and mensural data and the color and patterns of members of the *T. couchii* complex, and they concluded that *T. hammondii* represented a separate species. So the status of the species has come full circle since it was first described in 1860. It was last reviewed by Rossman et al. (1996).

Thamnophis marcianus (Baird and Girard 1853) | Checkered Garter Snake

RECOGNITION. The record length for this pale species is 108.8 cm, but most individuals are less than 65 cm long. Body color varies from yellowish brown to light brown or olive, and a checkerboard-like pattern of black, squarish spots positioned on each side between the yellow or orange dorsal stripe and the venter distinguishes this snake. Each side also has a cream, white, or gray lateral stripe on scale rows two and three. Laterally at the back of the head is a cream or yellow crescent or triangular-shaped mark, which is followed by a large, dark, oblique blotch. Lateral head scales are white to cream with prominent black bars, and a black-bordered light spot is present on the parietal scales; chin, throat, and venter are cream, white, or gray. Body scales are keeled and pitted, and lie in 21 (19) anterior rows, 19 (21–23) rows at midbody, and 17 posterior rows. Beneath are 139–165 ventrals, 60–83 subcaudals, and a single anal plate. Lateral head scales consist of 2 nasals, 1 loreal, 1 preocular, 3 (4) postoculars, 1 + 2 + 2–3 temporals, 8 (7–9) supralabials, and 10 infralabials. The hemipenis has not been described. Each maxilla has 21–31 teeth.

Males are significantly smaller with shorter jaws than females (Seigel et al. 2000) and have 145–165 ventrals, 60–83 subcaudals, and TLs 22–26% of TBL. Females have 139–162 ventrals, 61–77 subcaudals, and TLs only 19–23% of TBL. The relative height of the first dorsal scale row (maximum vertical height of dorsal scale row one divided by the maximum width of the vertebral row) averages 2.4 in females, but only 2.2 in males (Rossman 1995).

GEOGRAPHIC VARIATION. Three subspecies are recognized, but only the nominate race, *T. m. marcianus* (Baird and Girard 1853), described above, occurs in the United States.

CONFUSING SPECIES. Other garter or ribbon snakes occurring within the range of *T. marcianus* can be identified by using the key presented above. The lined snake *(Tropidoclonion lineatum)* has a head barely wider than the neck, usually six supralabials, a divided anal plate, and a ventral pattern of dark spots. Whipsnakes *(Masticophis)* and patch-nosed snakes *(Sal-*

vadora) have smooth scales and a divided anal plate and lack dark lateral spots.

KARYOTYPE. The karyotype consists of 36 chromosomes (34 macrochromosomes and 2 microchromosomes) with 70 arms. The fifth chromosome pair is heteromorphic ZW in females, homomorphic ZZ in males (Baker et al. 1972).

FOSSIL RECORD. Garter snake bones, possibly of *T. marcianus*, have been recovered from Pleistocene (Blancan) and Pleistocene (Rancholabrean) deposits in Texas (Holman 1964, 1965a; Parmley 1988b, 1990a).

DISTRIBUTION. *T. marcianus* ranges from southwestern Kansas south and west through central and western Texas, New Mexico, and southern Arizona to southeastern California (where it seems to be expanding its range westward by following irrigation canals (Hollinsworth and Prosser 1997). In Mexico, it ranges from northeastern Baja California, Sonora, Chihuahua, and Coahuila south through Durango, Nuevo León, and Tamaulipas to northern Veracruz. It also occurs in isolated populations in central Veracruz, Tabasco, Chiapas, Campeche, Yucatan, and Quintana Roo, and on Cozumel Island, Mexico, and in Belize, Guatemala, Honduras, and Nicaragua.

HABITAT. The checkered garter snake is a low- to midelevation (to 2,200 m), dry grassland or desert species seldom found farther than 25 m from a waterway (stream, irrigation canal, marsh, spring, pond, cattle tank), and often in riparian woodlands. In southern Texas, it seems more terrestrial, and sometime occurs in open brush, around rocks in road embankments, backyards, and gardens (Ford, in Rossman et al. 1996).

BEHAVIOR. *T. marcianus* has a relatively long annual activity period: February to November or December in Texas and northern Mexico (Rossman et al. 1996; Vermersch and Kuntz 1986) and March–October in New Mexico and southeastern Arizona (Degenhardt et al. 1996; Rossman et al. 1996).

Checkered garter snake, *Thamnophis marcianus*; Santa Cruz County, Arizona. (Photograph by Brad R. Moon)

It is diurnal during the cooler portions of its annual activity period, but becomes crepuscular or nocturnal during the late spring and hot summer months. No data are available on natural overwintering habits, but Degenhardt et al. (1996) thought they probably hibernate either singly or in small groups. The CT_{min} determined in laboratory tests is 5.7°C, rather high for a garter snake (Doughty 1994). Holtzman et al. (1989) successfully artificially hibernated 27 individuals at ATs of 8–12°C for 104–112 days with only one mortality. Rossi and Rossi (1995) reported that daytime ATs of 27–35°C and nighttime ATs as low as 23°C are acceptable to active *T. marcianus*. These ATs match closely the mean active-season BT, 27.5 (22.6–35.0) °C, of Arizona *T. marcianus* (Rosen 1991a).

During the middle of warm clear days, the Arizona snakes had a mean BT of 29.4 (24.1–32.5) °C.

Home range size and the extent of movements by *T. marcianus* have not been reported. Speed of movement, however, has been studied, and is affected by both food load (the greater the mass of food eaten, the slower the crawling speed; Ford and Shuttlesworth 1986) and reproductive state (pregnant females are slower and have less endurance than nonpregnant females; Seigel et al. 1987).

Male *T. marcianus* do not exhibit male combat and territoriality, and are not affected by pheromones of other males of their species (Ford and Holland 1990).

REPRODUCTION. Both sexes probably mature in two to three years. Wright and Wright (1957) gave the minimum TBL of mature males and females as 32.5 and 32.2 cm, respectively, and Conant and Collins (1998) and Stebbins (1985) listed the minimum adult length as 45.7 cm. The smallest female with corpora lutea found by Ford and Karges (1987) had a 33 cm SVL, and Rossman et al. (1996) reported the minimum SVL of females at sexual maturity ranged from 34.5 cm in southern Texas to 51.5 cm in southern Arizona.

Ford and Karges (1987) studied the female gametic cycle and found females with 5–10 mm follicles or embryos in every month. Enlargement of follicles from < 5 mm to 5–10 mm occurs in both March and October. It is possible the enlarged follicles in fall females are previtellogenic, but the occurrence of 10–15 mm follicles in January and February indicates that

Distribution of *Thamnophis marcianus*.

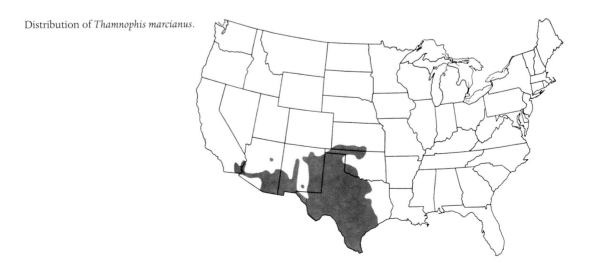

some females begin to yolk follicles in the fall, and that ovulation could occur in late February or March of the next year. Females with > 15 mm follicles, one pregnant and another with corpora lutea, were present in March; but the corpora lutea were small and probably from the previous year. Although some females had enlarged follicles in early spring, nearly half of the February females had not begun follicle enlargement. Ovulation is probably at its maximum in March and April. Birth occurs from mid-May to early October and is somewhat correlated to the local rainfall pattern. The right ovary is more productive than the left.

Some females probably produce two clutches in a year. Ford and Karges (1987) found several females with both corpora lutea and enlarged follicles or near-term embryos, but thought their evidence indicated an alteration of double-clutch years with single-clutch years. This is possibly due to the reduced physical condition of a female after giving birth twice in one year. In double-clutch years, ovulation in March or April and again in July would result in young in May or June and again in the fall. In a desert population in Arizona, parturition was in late May or June, and was possibly coordinated with the availablity of free water and prey (Seigel et al. 2000).

Most courtship and mating occur as early as March within 32 days following emergence from hibernation (Ford and Cobb 1992; Seigel et al. 2000). Vermersch and Kuntz (1986) reported copulation occurs through May and occasionally in the fall in south-central Texas. *T. marcianus* apparently is capable of storing viable sperm for several months, so a second clutch can be fertilized in the summer. Males find females by following their pheromone trails, and they frequently tongue flick while trailing (Ford and O'Bleness 1986; Perry-Richardson et al. 1990). Once the female is sighted, the male crawls slowly towards her. When the male contacts the female, she remains passive, performs a localized head-neck jerk, or tries to crawl away. If she flees, he chases her. After contact, he attempts to mount and maintain a chin press as he moves anteriorly along her back. Tail alignment is made initially and is maintained during courtship. The male searches with his tail for the female's vent, shaking his tail and pushing his body beneath her as he does this; caudocephalic waves may be performed at this time. Once their vents are aligned, the male inserts a hemipenis. Copulation lasts only about five to six minutes (Perry-Richardson et al. 1990). During coitus, the female may attempt to dislodge the male by crawling away or rotating axially while he attempts to remain on her back. Cloacal alignment before intromission is primarily accomplished by an alignment of tail tips, and stump-tailed *T. marcianus* may have difficulty performing this. However, stump-tailed females have successfully given birth, so it is not impossible to mate with a shortened tail.

Litter size varies from 3 (Ford and Karges 1987) to 35 (Lardie 1976d); the average number of young in 30 litters reported in the literature was 14.9. Mean RCM is 0.10–0.32 (Ford and Karges 1987; Seigel et al. 1986, 2000). Litter size is affected by the food and energy intake of the female; a typical female will produce a larger litter when well fed and nourished (Ford and Seigel 1989a; Seigel and Ford 1992). The average TBL of 42 neonates taken from the literature was 19.5 (12.3–27.9) cm. Neonates have body masses of 2.30–2.51 (1.64–3.99) g.

GROWTH AND LONGEVITY.   No data on growth are available. A wild-caught adult female survived 7 years, 6 months, and 26 days at the Los Angeles Zoo (Snider and Bowler 1992).

DIET AND FEEDING HABITS.   Wild *T. marcianus* hunt on land as well as along waterways, and consequently take a greater variety of prey than those *Thamnophis* that only feed in or along waterways. Nevertheless, amphibians seem to be the preferred prey. The natural diet consists of anurans (both small adults and tadpoles)—true frogs (*Rana berlandieri, R. blairi, R.catesbeiana*), tree frogs (*Pseudacris clarkii*), toads (*Bufo debilis, B. punctatus, B. speciosus, B. woodhousei*), spadefoots (*Scaphiopus couchii, S. holbrookii, Spea bombifrons, S. multiplicatus*), and microhylids (*Gastrophryne olivacea*); salamanders (*Ambystoma texanum*); snakes (*Tropidoclonion lineatum*); lizards (*Cophosaurus texanum, Holbrookia maculata*); small mice; fish; earthworms; slugs; and crayfish (Brown 1997; Degenhardt et al. 1996; Fouquette 1954; C. Ernst, pers. obs.; Lardie 1976c; Rossman et al. 1996; Stebbins 1954, 1985; Tennant 1984; Vermersch and Kuntz 1986; Woodward and Mitchell 1990; Wright and Wright 1957). Amphibian carrion is sometimes consumed (Rossman et al. 1996; Tennant 1984).

Captives have eaten bullfrog tadpoles *(Rana catesbeiana),* treefrogs *(Acris crepitans, Hyla cinerea, H. versicolor, Pseudacris clarkii, P. triseriatus),* toads *(Bufo speciosus, B. woodhousei),* spadefoots *(Scaphiopus couchii, S. holbrookii, Spea multiplicatus),* microhylids *(Gastrophryne olivacea),* lizards *(Gerrhonotus liocephalus),* fish *(Gambusia affinis, Lepomis* sp.), earthworms, and raw horse meat (Fouquette 1954; Kauffeld 1943a; Lutterschmidt and Rayburn 1993; Rossi and Rossi 1995; Stebbins 1954). Cannibalism has occurred in captivity (van het Meer 1996).

The checkered garter snake is an active forager that seeks its prey by both smell and sight. A potent proteinaceous chemoattractant from the common European frog *(Rana temporaria)* elicited an attack by *T. marcianus* in laboratory tests (Wattiaz et al. 1994); North American anurans probably also give off such attractants. Foraging shifts from daytime to early evening and night in the late spring and summer. Larger *T. marcianus* eat greater sized prey, while smaller individuals feed more on earthworms, slugs, and tadpoles. Captive males studied by Lutterschmidt and Rayburn (1993) ingested a weekly diet of bullfrog tadpoles *(Rana catesbeiana)* amounting to approximately 15–20% of their body mass. A study of the effects of surgery on food consumption by these snakes revealed the amount of food ingested during the week immediately following surgery was approximately five times the norm, and in week two it was twice the norm. By the fourth week after surgery, the ingestion rate returned to approximately normal.

PREDATORS AND DEFENSE. Natural predators of *T. marcianus* are many; they include bullfrogs *(Rana catesbeiana);* ophiophagous snakes *(Coluber constrictor, Lampropeltis* sp., *Masticophis* sp., *Micrurus fulvius);* hawks *(Buteo albicaudatus);* carnivorous mammals—skunks *(Mephitus* sp.), coyotes *(Canis latrans),* ar-

madillos *(Dasypus novemcinctus),* and pecaries *(Pecari tajacu);* and probably also owls (Ross 1989; Ruick 1948; Schwalbe and Rosen 1988; Tennant 1984). Individuals are also killed by vehicles on our roads, by mowing equipment, and by frightened humans who come upon them about their homes (C. Ernst, pers. obs.; Lardie 1976c).

When first disturbed most *T. marcianus* will try to flee, but some will occasionally assume a defensive posture in which the tightly coiled posterior third of their yellowish venter is displayed; this behavior is much like that of the ring-necked snake *(Diadophis punctatus)* (Tennant 1984). When held, it will bite and spray musk and feces.

POPULATIONS. No formal study of population dynamics has been published. It may be locally abundant (Tennant 1984) and may actually have increased its numbers in southwestern New Mexico, southeastern Arizona, and southern California due to construction of irrigation canals and cattle tanks (Degenhardt et al. 1996; Hollingsworth and Prosser 1997; Shaw and Campbell 1974). However, it is declining due to habitat destruction in other parts of its range (Stebbins 1985). Price and LaPointe (1990) reported that only 6 (1.3%) of 454 snakes found while road cruising in Doña Ana County, New Mexico, during 1975–1978 were this species, and only 30 (7.2%) of 418 snakes collected on a highway in Chihuahua, Mexico, between 1975 and 1977 were *T. marcianus* (Reynolds 1982).

The sex ratio of 101 checkered garter snakes collected in Arizona by Seigel (in Rossman et al. 1996) was 44 males to 57 females (0.77:1.00), and Seigel et al. (2000) reported an overall 0.67:1.00 male to female ratio, which varied seasonally, for an Arizona population. *T. marcianus* is considered threatened in Kansas.

REMARKS. *T. marcianus* has been reviewed by Mittleman (1949), Rossman (1971), and Rossman et al. (1996).

Thamnophis ordinoides (Baird and Girard 1852b) | Northwestern Garter Snake

RECOGNITION. The northwestern garter snake is of relatively moderate size (TBL to 96.5 cm, but most are much shorter) and is rather thick bodied. Its body color ranges from gray to olive, brown, or black, and some individuals have a greenish or bluish cast. A bluish, white, yellow, orange, or red middorsal stripe is usually present, but it may be only on the neck or be obscured or absent. The lateral stripes are white, cream, or yellow, but may also be obscure or absent. When present, they usually cover scale rows two and three. A series of dark, lateral spots normally lies between the dorsal and lateral stripes, but these may be obscured in black individuals. The top of the head is olive or brown, and black wedge-shaped bars may be present on the yellow supralabials. Two light spots are present on the parietals. The venter is cream, yellow, gray, or brown, often with red or black blotches. Body scales are keeled and pitless, and lie in 17 anterior rows, 17 (19) rows at midbody, and 15 (13) posterior rows. Beneath are 132–162 ventrals, 42–82 subcaudals, and an undivided anal plate. Lateral head scalation consists of 1 nasal (sometimes subdivided entirely by the nostril), 1 loreal, 1 (2) preocular(s), 3 (2–4) postoculars, 1 + 2 + 2 temporals, 7 (6–8) supralabials, and 8 (7–10) infralabials. The hemipenis has not been described. Each maxilla has 16–20 teeth, with the posterior-most longer than those preceding them.

Males have 137–162 ventrals, 56–80 subcaudals, and TLs 22–28 (normally 24–26; mean, 25.4) % of TBL; females have 132–158 ventrals, 42–72 subcaudals, and TLs only 21.0–23.5 (mean, 22.5) % of TBL. The average relative height of the first dorsal scale row (maximum height of dorsal scale row one divided by the maximum width of the vertebral row) is 2.6 (2.3–2.9) in females, but only 2.4 (2.2–2.5) in males (Rossman 1995).

GEOGRAPHIC VARIATION. No subspecies are recognized.

CONFUSING SPECIES. Other garter snakes overlapping the range of *T. ordinoides* can be identified using the key presented above.

KARYOTYPE AND FOSSIL RECORD. Unknown.

DISTRIBUTION. *T. ordinoides* ranges from southwestern British Columbia and Vancouver Island south, generally west of the Cascade Mountains, through western Washington and Oregon to Del Norte, Humbolt, and Siskiyou counties in northwestern California. It is also found on many islands in Puget Sound, and on Ozette Island off the coast of Washington.

HABITAT. *T. ordinoides* lives within the Pacific fog zone at elevations from sea level to 1,300–1,500 m. Its terrestrial habitats are relatively moist and consist of brushy meadows, swales, and grassy patches and sloped thickets in coniferous forests. Not usually found deep in the forest proper, this snake is most commonly found at the forest edge or in ecotones between forest and more open habitats. Although mainly terrestrial, *T. ordinoides* occasionally swims across waterways (Kirk 1983), in spite of the impression given by Fitch (1936, 1940) that it is reluctant to enter water.

BEHAVIOR. *T. ordinoides* emerges from hibernation in late March or early April, is most active between May and August, and returns to its winter retreat in rock crevice, talus slope, or rodent burrow from late October to early December. The snake may come to the surface and bask during warm winter days.

It is diurnal and most active on warm sunny days, remaining under cover on foggy or rainy days. When not foraging, basking, or searching for a mate, it hides under rocks, logs, or plant debris, or among vegetation or in rodent burrows. Pregnant females bask longer and more often than do males.

Stewart (1965) researched the thermal requirements of *T. ordinoides* in both the field and laboratory, and determined that its CT_{min} and CT_{max} were 4.2 and 38.9°C, respectively. His snakes had a preferred BT range of 24.4–30.4°C, with voluntary minimum and maximum BTs of 16.6 and 34.3°C, respectively; their mean BT was 27.4°C. Vitt (1974) recorded a mean BT of approximately 26°C for 27 high-latitude *T. ordinoides*, and Gregory (1984b) reported average BTs of 25°C for males and about 27°C for pregnant females. BTs of 9 *T. ordinoides* recorded by Brattstrom (1965) averaged 29.0 (12.6–31.5) °C.

Northwestern garter snake, *Thamnophis ordinoides*; Pacific County, Washington. (Photograph by William Leonard)

While foraging, searching for a mate, or moving to and from hibernacula, *T. ordinoides* may crawl long distances. It does not use sun compass orientation to set its direction, or follow pheromone trails produced by pregnant females (Lawson 1994). During displacement tests, some demonstrated homeward orientation, but others did not, and while the snake displayed solar-oriented behavior, it did not do so in the homeward direction. Movement speed is slower in pregnant females (Brodie 1989a).

REPRODUCTION. Some data exist on the breeding biology of this species, but much is still to be learned. Males mature in approximately one year at a TBL of 38–39 cm; females need two years to mature at a minimum TBL of 30–31 cm (Nussbaum et al. 1983; Wright and Wright 1957). The sexual cycles have not been researched, but ovulation occurs in late May or early June. Approximately 66–78% of adult females breed each year (Hebard 1951a; Stewart 1968). Mating occurs in late March or April after emergence from hibernation, and more females contain sperm in their reproductive tracts as the season progresses (Hebard 1951a; Stewart 1968). Some courtship and mating also occurs in late September and October when the snakes return to the hibernacula, but at a reduced rate. It is not known if females can store sperm from fall matings to fertilize eggs ovulated the next

Distribution of *Thamnophis ordinoides*.

spring. Courtship and mating have not been described.

The GP of this viviparous species is about nine weeks, and the young are born during June through August. During development egg yolk is the main source of organic nutrients, but embryos also receive a substantial allotment of inorganic materials via the placenta (Stewart et al. 1990).

The average number of young in 20 litters was 8–9, with a range of 3–20 (Brown 1997; Hebard 1951a; Nussbaum et al. 1983; Rossman et al. 1996; Stebbins 1985). Neonates are 14.9–19.1 cm in TBL and 11.8–14.9 cm in SVL, with males averaging longer than females (Stewart 1968). Litter size is positively correlated with female length (Stewart 1968), and RCMs average 31 (27–37) % of female body mass (Brodie 1989a).

GROWTH AND LONGEVITY. The only growth data available were provided by Stewart (1968) for Oregon *T. ordinoides*. He thought females two to three years old had SVLs of 36.0–38.5 cm; those three to four years old, 44.0–47.5 cm; and those four or more years old, 50.0–55.5 cm.

An adult, wild-caught, female survived 15 years, 11 months, and 6 days in captivity (Snider and Bowler 1992).

DIET AND FEEDING HABITS. In contrast with most other garter snakes in the Pacific states, *T. ordinoides* forages exclusively on land. It crawls slowly forward along a circuitous route with its head held close to the ground surface, tending to follow depressions below the general level of the ground surface (Fitch 1941). Pauses with lateral peering motions are occasionally made, but these seem guided by tactile stimuli and odor reception. Nooks and crannies, the undersides of logs, and areas between and under rocks are particularly investigated. In laboratory tests, *T. ordinoides* did not respond to fish odors (an unnatural prey), and its prey detection seemed about equally divided between sight and odor detection (Drummond 1983).

Slugs *(Ariolimax, Deroceras)* and earthworms make up the bulk of prey items, although small salamanders *(Aneides ferreus, Plethodon dunni, P. elongatus)* and frogs *(Rana aurora)* have also been found in its stomach (Fitch 1936, 1940, 1941; Gregory 1978, 1984a; Stewart

1968). Laboratory tests have shown that *T. ordinoides* responds with tongue flicks to the odors of other potential prey (Burghardt 1969; Carr and Gregory 1976), and some captives have accepted mice (Rossi and Rossi 1995), so possibly the list of acceptable prey species is longer. Fitch (1941) reported the frequency of predation to be 63% slugs (average length, 1.9 cm), 24% earthworms, 12% terrestrial salamanders, and 1% frogs. In two studies on Vancouver Island, Gregory (1978, 1984a) found slugs in 63 and 52 stomachs and earthworms in 67 and 49 stomachs, respectively. Unlike with other garter snakes, no apparent major shift of prey types occurs with size (Gregory 1984a). This snake suffered no apparent ill effects when force-fed *Rana aurora, Bufo boreas,* and *Pseudacris regilla,* but it lost motor function when force-fed entire *Taricha granulosa,* whose skin contains a potent neurotoxin (Brodie and Brodie 1990; MacCartney and Gregory 1981).

PREDATORS AND DEFENSE. Nussbaum et al. (1983) reported that a spotted owl *(Strix occidentalis)* killed and partially ate an adult *T. ordinoides*. Probably other predatory birds, mammals, and serpent-eating snakes also prey on them, and humans often kill them for no just cause. Others are killed by highway traffic each year.

T. ordinoides is shy and tries to flee to or hide in vegetation when disturbed. Its escape behavior is correlated with its color pattern (Brodie 1992, 1993a): snakes with well-developed stripes tend to crawl quickly and directly away from predators, as their stripes obscure their rate of movement. Spotted or plain individuals react differently, suddenly changing direction and then stopping abruptly and freezing in place, apparently depending on their pattern or body color to camouflage them. Brodie (1989b, 1992, 1993a) has shown that such correlations between behavior and pattern/color types have both genetic and developmental bases.

BT also affects its defensive behavior (Brodie and Russell 1999). BT has a substantial effect on sprint speed, distance crawled, and the number of reversals performed during flight and antipredator displays. *T. ordinoides* crawls more slowly for shorter distances and performs fewer reversals at 15°C than at either 22.5 or 30°C. Average sprint speed is less than 10 cm/second at 15.0°C, but about 13 cm/second at 22.5°C and 18 cm/second at 30.0°C. At 15.0°C the snakes move an average of only a little over 100 cm, at 22.5°C they move over 300 cm, and at 30.0°C the average distance moved is over 400 cm. They average less than 0.5 reversals at 15.0°C, about 1 reversal at 22.5°C, and about 1.3 reversals at 30.0°C. However, individual snakes show significant consistency in their behavior, which is not affected by temperature.

Although it is rather docile for a garter snake, do not be surprised if one bites and sprays musk when handled.

POPULATIONS. Presently, *T. ordinoides* is not in danger, and some populations are large. At a site in British Columbia, it made up 87% (1,865) of 2,138 captures of snakes (Engelstoft and Ovaska 2000). Fitch (1940) caught 80 in eight days at one site in Curry County, Oregon; Stewart (1968) caught 163 individuals at another four sites in the Willamette Valley of Oregon; and Gregory (1984a) recorded 654 captures at seven sites on Vancouver Island between 1974 and 1982. The sex ratio during Stewart's (1968) study was 83:80, or 1:1; the juvenile to adult ratio was 15:148 or 1.0:9.9, but the sex ratio among neonates was biased toward males 1.24:1.00.

REMARKS. Ruthven (1908) proposed that *T. ordinoides* formed a complex that included *T. atratus, T. couchii, T. elegans,* and *T. gigas.* Van Denburgh and Slevin (1918) added *T. hammondii* to the complex. Fox (1948a) presented morphological evidence that showed *T. ordinoides* is distinct from these other taxa, and this arrangement was confirmed biochemically by Lawson and Dessauer (1979), although they noted affinities with the *atratus* subspecies group of *T. couchii* (*atratus, aquaticus, gigas,* and *hydrophilus*). A study of mitochondrial DNA and allozyme variation by de Queiroz and Lawson (1994) confirmed this relationship (although *atratus, couchii, gigas,* and *hammondii* are now considered separate species; Rossman and Stewart 1987). Hybridization between *T. ordinoides* and *T. elegans vagrans* and *T. sirtalis fitchi* has been reported by Norman (1978).

T. ordinoides has been reviewed by Kirk (1979) and Rossman et al. (1996).

Thamnophis proximus (Say 1823) | Western Ribbon Snake

RECOGNITION. This is an elongated (to 126.8 cm TBL, usually 51–76 cm), black to dark brown or olive gray snake with a narrow orange vertebral stripe, a lateral yellow stripe on scale rows three and four, and a long narrow tail less than one-third the length of the body. A dark ventrolateral stripe is absent or narrow, and the labials and ventrals lack black markings. The large yellow parietal spots are fused, and the anterior portion of the face and chin are cinnamon brown or cream. A distinct neck separates the short head from the body. The eye is of moderate size, and the snout is long with a narrow tip. The body scales are keeled and pitless, and usually occur in 19 (rarely 21) rows anteriorly and at midbody, but only 17 rows near the tail. Present are 141–181 ventrals and 82–131 subcaudals; the anal plate is undivided. Differential head scales include 2 nasals (partially separated by the nostril), 1 lo-real, 1 preocular, 3 (2–4) postoculars, 1 + 2 temporals, usually 8 (7–9) supralabials (the fourth and fifth enter the orbit), and 10 (9–11) infralabials. The single hemipenis is short for the genus (usually extending only to subcaudals seven to eight when inverted), and it has a straight sulcus spermaticus that terminates at the apex (Rossman 1963b). It bears numerous rows of small spines on the distal half, the margins of the sulcus, and the extreme basal area; a pair of enlarged basal hooks occurs on each side of the sulcus; and the apical region lacks ornamentation. Each maxilla bears about 30 (27–34) teeth.

Males have 142–181 ventrals, 91–131 subcaudals, and TLs 26.0–33.3% of TBL; females have 141–177 ventrals, 82–124 subcaudals, and TLs 25.2–33.6% of TBL. The extent of sexual dimorphism in these characters varies depending on the population (Rossman

Western ribbon snake, *Thamnophis proximus proximus*; Madison County, Kentucky. (Photograph by Roger W. Barbour)

1963b; Rossman et al. 1996). The mean relative height of the first dorsal scale row is 1.6 in males and 1.7 in females (Rossman 1995).

See Rossman (1962, 1963b) and Gartside et al. (1977) for discussions of the validity of *T. proximus* as a distinct species from *T. sauritus*.

GEOGRAPHIC VARIATION. Six subspecies are recognized, but only four occur in the United States (Rossman 1970a). The subspecies are identified by their patterns; much overlap occurs in scutellation. *Thamnophis proximus proximus* (Say 1823), the western ribbon snake, ranges from Indiana, Illinois, and southern Wisconsin southwest to central Louisiana and eastern Texas. It has a black dorsum with a narrow orange vertebral stripe, and large, bright, connected parietal spots. *T. p. diabolicus* Rossman 1963b, the arid land ribbon snake, ranges from southeastern Colorado southward to Coahuila, Nuevo Leon, and west-central Tamaulipas, Mexico. It is olive gray to olive brown with an orange vertebral stripe, a brown ventrolateral stripe, and nondescript parietal spots. *T. p. orarius* Rossman 1963b, the Gulf Coast ribbon snake, occurs along the Gulf Coast from extreme southwestern Mississippi westward to southern Texas. It is olive brown with a broad gold vertebral stripe, and nondescript parietal spots. *T. p. rubrilinea-*

tus Rossman 1963b, the red-striped ribbon snake is confined to the Edwards Plateau of central Texas. It is olive brown to olive gray with a bright red vertebral stripe, a dark ventrolateral stripe in some individuals, and nondescript parietal spots.

CONFUSING SPECIES. The glossy crayfish snake (*Regina rigida rigida*) has a divided anal plate and black ventral markings. *T. sauritus* usually has only seven supralabials; if present, faint clearly separated parietal spots; and a tail at least one-third of the total body length. Other eastern *Thamnophis* with lateral stripes on scale rows three and four have tails usually less than one-fourth the total body length.

KARYOTYPE. The karyotype consists of 34 macrochromosomes and 2 microchromosomes; females are heteromorphic, ZW (Baker et al. 1972). Camper and Hanks (1995) reported that a pair of NORs is located terminally on the long arm of the first or second largest pair of chromosomes; one individual had an additional pair of microchromosomal NORs.

FOSSIL RECORD. Pleistocene remains of *T. proximus* have been found at Irvingtonian deposits in Kansas, Nebraska, and Texas, and in Rancholabrean deposits in Missouri, Oklahoma, Texas, and New

Red-striped ribbon snake,
Thamnophis proximus rubrilineatus;
Travis County, Texas. (Photo-
graph by William Leonard)

Mexico (Holman 1969b, 1981, 1987b, 1995; Kasper and Parmley 1990; Parmley and Pfau 1997; Smith and Cifelli 2000).

DISTRIBUTION. *T. proximus* ranges south from Indiana, Illinois, southern Wisconsin, and Iowa to southern Mississippi, Texas, and eastern New Mexico in the United States, and south through eastern Mexico to Costa Rica. Populations also occur in Guerrero and Oaxaca on the Pacific coast of Mexico.

HABITAT. Closely confined to the vicinity of permanent or semipermanent water, either standing

(marshes, ponds, lakes, sloughs) or running (brooks, creeks, rivers, swamps), where it is most frequently found in the bordering vegetation (grasses, cattails, shrubs). It sometimes enters wet woodlands or prairies, and individuals may climb into weeds or low bushes. Minton (1972) reported that all *T. proximus* he collected in Indiana were in drier, more open areas than its congener, *T. sauritus*.

BEHAVIOR. *T. proximus* is active from April through October over most of the range, but the annual activity period may either be shorter in the north or extend throughout the year in the extreme southern

Distribution of *Thamnophis proximus*.

portions of the range, if the winters are warm (Tinkle 1957). Clark (1974) reported that in Texas, trapping success during the spring and summer is correlated with rainfall, with fewer snakes captured during dry periods. A lack of precipitation may affect *T. proximus* either through desiccation or by reducing the availability of their amphibian foods.

A relationship between the phenology of vegetation and the density of *T. proximus* occurs in Louisiana (Tinkle 1957). Early in the year the snakes utilize open areas with maximum exposure to sunlight. When these areas become shaded due to the growth of vegetation, the snakes seek other open areas; however, when the daily temperatures increase in later months, they move back to the shaded sites to avoid the heat.

Even in the southern states, *T. proximus* may be forced to hibernate if WTs or ATs become too low. In Kentucky, they hibernate in rocky or gravelly banks near water, and in Illinois they have been found hibernating in rock crevices with copperheads and timber rattlesnakes (Ernst and Barbour 1989). Other hibernacula include springs, mammal burrows, anthills, rotten logs and stumps, and spaces behind the bark on trees and in pipes draining temporary ponds. Artificial hibernation studies conducted by Holtzman et al. (1989) resulted in a mortality rate of 13.8% for *T. proximus* neonates, compared to an estimated mortality rate of 45–85.5% for natural populations of colubrid snakes surviving their first hibernation.

On a daily basis this snake is mostly diurnal, being active in the morning and late afternoon hours, but if the nights are warm it may also prowl. It is very active during light summer rains.

Jacobson and Whitford (1970) found that *T. proximus* responded to acclimation by shifts in thermal tolerance, and suggested this might represent an important adaptation to seasonal variation in AT. The mean CT_{min} of *T. proximus* acclimated at 15°C was 4.2°C, while for those acclimated at 30°C it was 7.8°C; the mean CT_{max} of *T. proximus* acclimated at 15°C was 39°C, while for those acclimated at 30°C it was 42°C. At BTs above 25°C, *T. proximus* acclimated at 30°C had a significantly lower oxygen consumption than those acclimated at 15°C, and at BTs above 30°C, the heart rate for snakes acclimated at 15°C was significantly higher than that for those acclimated at 30°C,

suggesting that high BTs may act as a stress in low-temperature–acclimated snakes such as *T. proximus*.

Only limited data on movements are available. Clark (1974) found no significant differences in the mean distances between captures by sex or age. Omitting age distinctions, mean movement for males was 2.5 m/day, and for females, 1.1 m/day. Males moved up to 209 m between captures, and females 97 m. Immature females were much less prone to travel far than were adult females or males. An individual marked by Tinkle (1957) moved almost 100 m in about five months.

REPRODUCTION. The smallest sexually mature female examined by Tinkle (1957) was 48.5 cm in SVL, and he believed most females in the Louisiana population reached sexual maturity at about 50 cm SVL. However, Clark (1974) reported the smallest mature female in his Texas population was 51.5 cm and that none shorter was found pregnant. Females mature in their third year. Brood size averaged 13 in Tinkle's Louisiana population, but only 8.4 in Texas, although the average SVL of the females was similar (57.4 and 57.1 cm, respectively). Clark postulated that heavier mortality in the Louisiana population had resulted in selection favoring greater per season reproductive effort there. Seigel (in Shine and Seigel 1996) reported an average brood size of 10.2. Males mature in one to two years at SVLs of 36.8 cm or longer (Tinkle 1957; Clark 1974).

Tinkle (1957) studied the female reproductive cycle in a Louisiana population. From July through December, the maximum size of ovarian follicles was 5 mm, but most were smaller. Follicles probably remained at this size through January until ATs began to warm. In the spring the follicles increased in size until they became greater than 8 mm in April through June, and then were apparently ovulated. The right ovary, which was always longer and more anterior than the left, produced the majority of the eggs. Pregnant females were found as early as April and were present in the population through July.

Mating occurs during April and May over most of the range, but earlier farther south. In Kentucky it takes place almost immediately after emergence from hibernation. During this time the males actively pursue females, probably following pheromone trails (Ford 1978, 1981). Laboratory studies conducted by Graves et al. (1991) indicated that epidermal lipids are the source of chemical cues mediating attraction of *T. proximus* to shelters marked by other *T. proximus* and that these signals are detected by the vomeronasal system. The courtship and mating behaviors have not been described.

The birth period extends from late June to early October, but most young are born from July to early September. Females may produce two broods in a given year (Conant 1965b). Brood size ranges from 4 or 5 (Carpenter 1958; Powell 1982) to 36 (Bowers 1967), but most broods probably include only 10–15 young. Neonates are about 22.0 (13.3–29.8) cm in TBL and have a SVL of about 16.0 (15.0–21.4) cm and a mass of about 1.6–1.7 (1.6–2.0) g. Velhagen and Savitzky (1998) estimated a GP of 70–104 days based on neonate size (mass, TBL, SVL) and absolute growth rates of embryos. Neonates had relatively long tails (29% of TBL), and the absolute growth rate for SVL was 59% of the absolute growth rate for TBL, representing disproportionately rapid tail growth. Reported RCMs are 0.090 (unusually low), 0.185, 0.256, and 0.277 (Seigel et al. 1986; Thornton and Smith 1996b).

GROWTH AND LONGEVITY. Tinkle (1957) reported that a juvenile with a prominent yolk scar caught in December was 31.5 cm in SVL. Its growth represented at least a 50% increase in length since its birth earlier in the year. Clark (1974) presented growth curves for juveniles to 23 months.

Natural longevity is unknown, but a *T. proximus* at the Philadelphia Zoo lived three years, seven months, and one day (Snider and Bowler 1992).

DIET AND FEEDING HABITS. The diet is chiefly fishes and amphibians, with anurans being more often consumed than salamanders, but this may reflect a lesser availability of salamanders in the microhabitat of *T. proximus* rather than the snake's preference. Fouquette (1954) reported that 82% of its food consisted of amphibians. Clark (1974) found anurans or their tadpoles in 83% of the 24 stomachs he examined that contained food; salamanders and fish were found in only 4%, and 8% had eaten lizards (*Scincella laterale*). Reported prey species include 20 anurans (*Acris crepitans, A. gryllus, Bufo houstonensis, B. woodhousei, Gastrophryne carolinensis, G. olivacea* [larvae only], *Hyla crucifer, H. squirella, H. versicolor, Hypopachus variolosus, Leptodactylus labialis, Pseudacris clarki, P. streckeri, P. triseriata, Rana catesbeiana, R. clamitans, R. pipiens, R. sphenocephala, Scaphiopus bombifrons, Smilisca baudini*); two salamanders (*Ambystoma texanum, Plethodon cinereus*); and four fishes (*Cichlasoma cyanoguttatum, Gambusia affinis, Lepomis megalotis, Oncorhynchus mykiss*) (Clark 1949; Freed and Neitman 1988; Kennedy 1964; Rossman 1963b). Smith (1961) found a large *T. proximus* in Illinois that had eaten two smaller ribbon snakes, and Resetarits (1983) observed a *T. proximus* attempt to swallow the carrion of a road-killed toad *(Bufo)* in Missouri. In Mexico, *T. proximus* have been reported to eat *Leptodactylus melanonotus* and *Bufo valliceps* (Manjarrez and Marcias-Garcia 1992), *Hyla plicata*, tadpoles of toad, and possibly *Bufo bocourti* (Mutschmann 1999). Unlike most other species of *Thamnophis*, *T. proximus* apparently does not eat earthworms.

Responses to prey extracts by naive neonates may be mediated by the vomeronasal system, which appears to be functional at birth in the genus *Thamnophis* (Holtzman 1993; Holtzman and Halpern 1990). Since these behavioral responses are only partially dependent upon the presence of the tongue, the olfactory system may also be functional at birth. However, there is no direct evidence that a vomeronasal stimulus is available to embryos or that embryos can detect it (Holtzman 1993).

If the air is warm, *T. proximus* will forage as readily at night as during the day, and are often seen prowling among nocturnal choruses of hylid frogs (C. Ernst, pers. obs.). While hunting cricket frogs *(Acris)*, western ribbon snakes often make short thrusting probes with the forepart of their bodies into spots likely to hide prey (Wendelken 1978). These probes are made with closed mouths, and frequently this behavior involves a rapid sequence of three thrusts directed toward three different areas in a semicircle in front of the snake. When the frogs move, the snake rapidly crawls after them. If it misses, it assumes a motionless posture with its head raised. Wendelken (1978) believed this type of hunting behavior an adaptation to capturing such anurans as cricket frogs, which hide and then, when disturbed, hop away using erratic pathways. Fouquette (in Rossman 1963b) observed a *T. proximus* stalk a calling Mexican treefrog *(Smilisca baudini)*. When the frog's vocal sacs moved, the snake crawled closer, stopping each time the frog ceased calling.

PREDATORS AND DEFENSE. Large wading birds (such as herons), cranes, shrikes *(Lanius ludovicianus),* hawks *(Buteo albicaudatus),* raccoons, foxes, and large ophiophagous snakes (cottonmouths, king snakes, coral snakes) are the chief natural predators of *T. proximus.* Collins (1993) reported that large frogs and fish eat young individuals. Mulvany (1983) found a tarantula feeding on a juvenile western ribbon snake, and in Mexico, Manjarrez and Macias-Garcia (1992) watched an aquatic bug (Belostomatidae) attack and kill an adult female *T. proximus.*

T. proximus usually tries to escape when first discovered, and if near water will readily dive in, swim to the bottom, and hide under submerged objects. Occasionally one will hold its ground and give open-mouth threats, but they rarely bite, although they may expel musk.

POPULATIONS. Tinkle (1957) found *T. proximus* to be the most common snake at a Louisiana site (221 were encountered while eight other species of snakes only accounted for 199 individuals), but in the uplands of Louisiana, *T. proximus* only accounted for 37 (1.8%) of 2,083 snakes collected by Clark (1949). Population density peaks occurred in early spring after emergence from hibernation, during the summer because of the aggregation of gravid females and the presence of young snakes, and in winter because of the congregation around hibernating sites.

During his study of a Texas population, Clark (1974) found a decline in numbers from an estimated 104 (61/ha) in 1969 to 28 (16/ha) in 1971. The decline was correlated with an unusually dry winter that caused spring soil desiccation, resulting in no breed-

ing amphibians; Clark postulated that most died of desiccation while hibernating.

Thamnophis proximus accounted for only 5 (1.6%) of 305 snakes (representing 21 species) captured over a four-year period in a mixed pine-hardwood forest preserve in northeastern Texas (Ford et al. 1991). It represented less than 1% of 33,117 snakes (representing 34 species) collected during major field studies in Kansas (Fitch 1993) and 1 (0.9%) of 113 road-killed snakes (12 species) in Jersey and Madison counties, Illinois, during the month of October following summer flooding on the Mississippi River (Tucker 1995).

Carpenter (1958) gave the newborn male to female ratio of Oklahoma broods of *T. proximus* as 3:6, 5:7, 4:0, and 7:2 (plus one undetermined). In his Texas study, Clark (1974) reported a 143:114 (1.25:1) male to female ratio, but seasonally males were more abundant from March through June and females from August through October. He also found that immature females were recorded twice as often as mature females from March to June. Keck (1994) reported a 1:1 male to female ratio for *T. proximus* collected in funnel traps in northeast Texas, although the sampling size was quite small (six individuals) (Keck 1994).

Clark (1974) calculated a reproductive potential of 373 young for 1969 by assuming that breeding occurred each year, that there was a 1:1 sex ratio, and that there were 38 mature females that had average broods of 9.7 young. This increased the population 4.6 times.

Habitat disturbance (cultivation, draining, and filling of wet areas) is the major threat to the survival of *T. proximus.* The western ribbon snake is considered endangered in New Mexico and Wisconsin, threatened in Kentucky, and a species of special concern in Indiana.

REMARKS. A study on neonate size and embryonic growth rates in thamnophine snakes suggested that *T. proximus* is closely related to *T. sirtalis; T. sauritus* was not included in the study (Velhagen and Savitzky 1998).

The species was reviewed in Rossman (1970a).

Thamnophis radix (Baird and Girard 1853) | Plains Garter Snake

RECOGNITION. This relatively long garter snake (to 109.5 cm TBL, but typically 40–70 cm) has lateral light stripes on scale rows three and four, two rows of alternating black spots between the lateral and dorsal stripes, and black bars on the supralabials. Another row of black spots is located between the lateral stripe and the ventral scutes, and there may also be a row of dark spots along the sides of the venter. A pair of light spots is usually present on the parietals. Ground color is tan to dark brown, black, or greenish, the dorsal stripe yellow or orange, and some reddish pigment may be present along the sides of the body; some individuals are bright red brown (Redmer and Zaworski 1987). The pitless body scales are keeled, and occur in 19–21 rows anteriorly and at midbody but usually only 17 rows near the anus. On the underside are 135–175 ventrals, 54–88 subcaudals, and an undivided anal plate. Lateral head scales consists of 2 nasals (partially divided by the nostril), 1 loreal, 1 (2) preocular, 3 (1–2) postoculars, 1 + 2 + 2 temporals, 7 (6–8)

Plains garter snake, *Thamnophis radix*; Lyon County, Minnesota. (Photograph by Roger W. Barbour)

Plains garter snake, *Thamnophis radix*; Teton County, Montana. (Photograph by Carl H. Ernst)

supralabials, and 9 or 10 (8–11) infralabials. The eye occurs above supralabials four and five. The hemipenis contains an unbranched sulcus spermaticus, several large basal spines, small spines above these, but no spines or calyxes on the apex. Each maxilla has 20–27 recurved teeth; the posterior-most are enlarged.

Males have 183–175 ventrals, 64–88 subcaudals, and somewhat longer TLs (20.5–27.8% of TBL) than females; females have 135–174 ventrals, 54–74 subcaudals, and shorter TLs (17.6–27.5% of TBL) than males. The mean relative height of the first dorsal scale row is 2.2 in males and 2.5 in females (Rossman 1995). Smith (1946) reported the presence of tubercles on the chin shields of males.

GEOGRAPHIC VARIATION. No subspecies are currently recognized (Rossman et al. 1996). The number of ventral scales and dorsal scale rows once thought to differentiate the formerly recognized subspecies *T. r. radix* (Baird and Girard 1853) and *T. r. haydeni* (Kennicott 1860a) are now known to overlap; therefore males cannot be differentiated by these characteristics (Rossman et al. 1996).

CONFUSING SPECIES. Other *Thamnophis* can be distinguished from *T. radix* by using the above key.

KARYOTYPE. Each cell has 36 biarmed chromosomes (Baker et al. 1972). The females are heteromorphic ZW, with the Z chromosome submetacentric and the W chromosome acrocentric.

FOSSIL RECORD. Pliocene (Blancan) remains of *T. radix* have been found in Nebraska (Holman and Schloeder 1991; Rogers 1984). In addition, Pleistocene Irvingtonian fossils have been found in Kansas (Holman 1986c, 1995; Rogers 1982), Nebraska (Ford 1992; Holman 1995), and Oklahoma (Smith and Cifelli 2000); and Rancholabrean fossils are known from Kansas (Holman 1984, 1986c, 1987a, 1987b, 1995; Preston 1979) and Oklahoma (Holman 1986b, 1995; Preston 1979).

DISTRIBUTION. *T. radix* ranges from northwestern Indiana westward to the Rocky Mountains in Montana and Alberta, and from southern Alberta south to northwestern Missouri, northwestern Oklahoma, and northeastern New Mexico. Isolated populations also are present in west-central Ohio, southwestern Illinois, and adjacent east-central Missouri.

HABITAT. *T. radix* inhabits open areas such as prairies and meadows, with access to nearby water in marshes, ponds, brooks, or sloughs. In the western part of its range it may be found in swampy areas and along streams, sandy riverbeds, or other bodies of water. It was formerly common in the vacant lots of cities, but is now greatly reduced in numbers in such habitats due to building activities and widespread use of pesticides (Conant and Collins 1998).

We have observed that in Minnesota where it occurs sympatrically with *T. sirtalis,* the latter occupied more moist microhabitats, such as sloughs, ditches, or the banks of lakes, while *T. radix* was more commonly

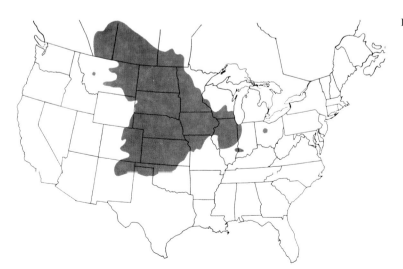

Distribution of *Thamnophis radix.*

found in open, less moist areas. Hart (1979) reported a similar partitioning of the habitat in Manitoba.

BEHAVIOR. The annual activity period extends from late March or early April to late October or mid-November, depending on locality and weather conditions. In Kansas, *T. radix* is active from March to November (Collins 1993), but farther north it is more restricted in annual activity; in Minnesota, the authors only found them active from late April through September.

The winter months are spent hibernating in some burrow, although *T. radix* may emerge occasionally to bask on exceptionally warm days. During a laboratory study of artificial hibernation, eight adult *T. radix* remained in hibernation for 119 days, 53 neonates hibernated for 87 days (mortality rate, 5.7%), and another 8 neonates hibernated for 150 days (Holtzman et al. 1989). Hibernacula are often the burrows of mammals such as pocket gophers, ground squirrels, or voles, but Criddle (1937) found them in anthills, and Dalrymple and Reichenbach (1981) and Reichenbach and Dalrymple (1986) thought they might hibernate in crayfish holes. Rock crevices, old wells, post holes, and holes under sidewalks may also be occupied during the winter (Pope 1944). Murphy (1997) observed *T. radix* hibernating underwater through a layer of ice.

Dalrymple and Reichenbach (1984) and Reichenbach and Dalrymple (1986) found *T. radix* active from 1100–1600 hours in the spring and fall, and from 0800–1700 hours in the summer, but less active between 1300 and 1400 hours. However, the authors have on several occasions found them in Minnesota feeding on *Pseudacris triseriata* after dark during that frog's breeding season. Diurnal activity usually consists of foraging or basking.

Activity seems to be controlled by AT. Seibert and Hagen (1947) reported that *T. radix* was most frequently observed when ATs were 21–29°C, and usually disappeared when the temperature fell below 7.2°C. Dalrymple and Reichenbach (1981) reported that the average field BT of 65 Ohio *T. radix* was 27.9°C. BTs ranged from 17 to 32°C during the months of March to September (Reichenbach and Dalrymple 1986). Hart (1979) found that *T. radix* in Manitoba had significantly higher oral and cloacal

temperatures than allopatric *T. sirtalis;* CTs depended most upon AT, but light intensity and ST were also important (*T. radix* occurred in a microhabitat of high AT but low ST). Heckrotte (1962, 1975) studied the effects of light and temperature in the laboratory on the circadian rhythm of *T. radix,* and found most activity occurred in the light period at a low constant temperature, but at a temperature of 31°C most activity shifted to the dark period; the snakes were either diurnal, crepuscular, or nocturnal, depending on the temperature. Reichenbach and Dalrymple (1986) reported that gravid *T. radix* and *T. sirtalis* spent an average of 2.8 hours/day at the surface compared with 1.4 hours/day for nongravid snakes. During the mating season, males spent approximately 4.8 hours/day at the surface compared with 2.8 hours/day for females; during the fall, both sexes spent about 2.8 hours/day at the surface. Seidel and Lindeborg (1973) reported an apparent lack of change or lag in the metabolic oxygen consumption rate at experimental temperatures between 18 and 34°C; they also reported that *T. radix* had its maximum metabolic rate at 38°C. Lueth (1941) determined the CT_{max} and CT_{min} for *T. radix* were 41 and 2°C. Doughty (1994) reported a CT_{min} of 4.6°C, while Bailey (1949) reported *T. radix* survived exposure to –2°C for one day.

During their study of population dynamics in Illinois, Seibert and Hagen (1947) observed that most individuals moved less than 2 m/day. One snake, recaptured four times, had moved 15 m in two weeks before the first recapture, and 6, 4.5, and 2.7 m in the following three weeks. When last seen in week five, it was only about 11 m from its original location, having traveled in a semicircular arc. No territorial behavior was observed during their study. Reichenbach and Dalrymple (1986) reported the distances moved between recaptures of Ohio *T. radix* and *T. sirtalis* were generally less than 76 m for intervals of several months to over a year.

The plains garter snake appears to have some homing ability. Thirteen of 32 marked *T. radix* released in distant habitats by Seibert and Hagen (1947) returned to the original area over a 70 day period; 8 wandered 1,208 m in one week. Lawson and Secoy (1991) examined the ability of adult *T. radix* to use solar cues as orientation guides during their fall return to a communal hibernaculum in southern Canada. Snakes were able to select a common compass direction at each of three test sites in the absence of landmark cues, suggesting that polarized light may be an orientation cue. Graves and Halpern (1988) found that *T. radix* neonates were attracted to skin extracts of postparturient female *T. radix,* and suggested the functional significance of such conspecific aggregation may relate to location of hibernacula, foraging areas, osmoregulation, or predation avoidance.

REPRODUCTION. Females apparently attain sexual maturity during years two to three (Seibert and Hagen 1947; Gregory 1977a). Male spermiogenesis occurs in late summer or early autumn, and the female ovarian cycle is essentially like that of other *Thamnophis* (Cieslak 1945). Mating usually takes place soon after the snakes emerge from hibernation in April or May, but Pope (1944) and Anderson (1965) also mentioned the possibility of autumn copulation. A female has been observed mating with several different males, and polygyny may also occur in the wild. Males apparently find females by following their sex pheromone trails (Kubie et al. 1978; Crews 1980; Ford and Low 1984; Ford and Schofield 1984). These pheromones are released from the dorsal skin, and shedding (ecdysis) enhances release (Kubie et al. 1978).

One or more males may simultaneously court a female. They crawl along her side poking her with their snouts while nonrhythmic contractions occur along the posterior portions of their bodies. They frequently touch her back with their tongues, and at last one male will successfully position himself to insert his hemipenis. Receptive females remain motionless and raise their tails. After the male releases his sperm, he may place a seminal plug in the female's cloaca that exerts an inhibitory effect on further courtship of that female (Ross and Crews 1977). Parthenogenesis was reported in *T. radix* by Murphy and Curry (2000a, 2000b).

The young are born from late June or July through September. Velhagen and Savitzky (1998) estimated a GP of 83–102 days based on neonate size and absolute growth rates. Litters may number 5–60 young, but most frequently number 10–20. Seigel and Fitch (1985) reported a minimum mean annual clutch size of nine for 32 females and a maximum mean annual clutch size of 11.87 for 15 females during a three-year study in western Missouri. Breckenridge (1944) noted

a litter of 92 young, but either this must be a mistake, or the litter came from an exceptionally large female. Possibly larger litters are produced in more northern populations; six Manitoba litters contained 14–54 (mean, 29.5) young (Gregory 1977a). Annual variations in litter size may also occur due to changes in environmental conditions (Fitch 1985a; Seigel and Fitch 1985). Neonates have 11.9–24.1 cm TBLs; the mass of 174 Illinois newborns was 0.93–2.48 (mean, 1.72) g (Arnold and Bennett 1988). Complete closure of the umbilical scar occurs in 72–110 hours, and the scar lies between the 124th and 150th ventrals in females and the 133rd and 156th in males (Smith 1947). Reported RCMs are 0.209 and 0.283 (Seigel et al. 1986).

GROWTH AND LONGEVITY. In Illinois, *T. radix* grew to lengths of about 45 cm their first year, or 15–20 cm over a period of 112 days or 16 weeks (20 May–9 September); the growth rate was approximately 1.1 cm/week (Seibert and Hagen 1947). Two-year-olds starting at 40–45 cm probably grew to 55–60 cm at a rate of 0.9 cm/week. Females grew at a faster rate (1.37 and 1.82 cm/week for the first two years, respectively). Gregory (1977a) found similar growth rates in Manitoba. Reichenbach and Dalrymple (1986) reported increases of 1.2 mm/day for immature *T. radix* from Ohio, and 0.17–1.4 mm/day after maturity was reached. Among neonates, *T. radix* females have larger heads and shorter tails than males; among adults, males have longer heads and a greater interocular distance, while females have wider heads and longer jaws (King et al. 1999).

Snider and Bowler (1992) reported a longevity of eight years, five months, and three days for a captive.

DIET AND FEEDING HABITS. The prey of *T. radix* includes small amphibians and their larvae—anurans *(Acris crepitans, Bufo americanus, B. cognatus, Hyla* sp., *Pseudacris triseriata, Rana blairi, R. pipiens)* and salamanders; fish *(Gambusia affinis, Phoxinus erythrogaster, Pimephales promelas);* birds *(Riparia riparia, Sturnella magna),* rodents; leeches; earthworms; and grasshoppers (Anderson 1965; Burt and Hoyle 1935; Cebula 1983; Degenhardt et al. 1996; C. Ernst, pers. obs.; Gray and Douglas 1989; Hjertass and Hjertass 1990; Matity et al. 1994). The foods eaten in the wild are very similar to those of *T. sirtalis.*

Halloy and Burghardt (1990) fed captive *T. radix* earthworms *(Lumbricus terrestris)* and mosquitofish *(Gambusia affinis);* captives have also been reported to eat goldfish *(Carassius auratus)* and smelt (Clupeidae). Fish and worm diets lead to different growth rates; Burghardt (1990) found that plains garter snakes fed on exclusive earthworm *(Lumbricus)* and fish *(Gambusia)* diets showed greater growth on the earthworm diet when the worms were supplemented with minerals rich in calcium and phosphorus, suggesting a trade-off between nutrition and prey availability. Dalrymple and Reichenbach (1984) estimated the ratio of prey biomass to *T. radix* biomass in Ohio to range from 40:1 to 91:1; a 1:4 predator-prey biomass ratio is sufficient for maintenance, growth, and reproduction (Reichenbach and Dalrymple 1986).

Prey trails are followed by olfaction until the animal is seen, then *T. radix* crawls rapidly after it and seizes it in its mouth (Chiszar et al. 1981; Czaplicki 1975; Kubie and Halpern 1979; Secoy 1979). In laboratory studies, Terrick et al. (1995) found that aversions to unpalatable prey are formed more readily if the prey is conspicuously colored, even though recognition of unpalatable prey depends on the prey's chemosensory characteristics rather than its coloration. A postbiting elevation in tongue-flicking rate coupled with apparent searching movements in newborn, ingestively naive garter snakes suggests a genetic basis for these chemosensory behaviors (Cooper 1992). Seven *T. radix* were trained in a two-choice apparatus to move into a compartment containing lemon-scented chips for a food reward, demonstrating *T. radix* are capable of learning a demonstrated response to an airborne odorant, presumably by use of one or more nasal chemical senses (Begun et al. 1988).

Yeager and Burghardt (1991) examined competition for food resources and its impact on aggregation behavior in the plains garter snake. Pairs of *T. radix* appeared to form dominance relationships, which suggests they may be able to discriminate between animals on the basis of their social relationships; such individual recognition appeared to persist over time.

PREDATORS AND DEFENSE. Hawks *(Buteo lineatus, B. swainsonii, Circus cyaneus)* and other birds of prey such as the kestrel *(Falco sparverius)* (Redmer 1988), predatory mammals *(Vulpes* sp., *Canis latrans, Mephi-*

tis mephitis, Mustela vison, Felis catus), possibly including *Didelphis virginiana* (Anton 2000a), and the milksnake *(Lampropeltis triangulum)* all prey on *T. radix;* but humans with their automobiles, mowers, and habitat destruction may kill more each year than all natural predators combined (Dalrymple and Reichenbach 1984). Seibert (1950) estimated a natural mortality rate of 20% for his Illinois population.

Plains garter snakes are milder tempered than *T. sirtalis,* but they will bite if handled. More commonly they secrete musk or defecate on their captor. Kissneras et al. (1998) found that females have significantly larger cloacal glands than males and speculated that the larger reserves of musk may be needed as a defense mechanism against predators when females are gravid.

Arnold and Bennett (1984) have described and tested the variation in antipredator displays in recently born *T. radix:* (1) Head-hide—The head is hidden under one or more loops of the body. (2) Head-expose—The head is motionless and flat on the substrate, not hidden under the body. (3) Closed-mouth attack—The snake strikes rapidly forward with the mouth closed. (4) Open-mouth attack—The snake strikes rapidly forward with the mouth open. The mouth is sometimes held open before or after the strike. Usually the snake does not actually bite. (5) Body-ball—The body is loosely rolled into a ball. The body is not dorsoventrally flattened. (6) Body-extend—The body lies flat and extended on the substrate. It may be linear or kinked, and there is no dorsoventral flattening. (7) Body-flat coil—The body is coiled with the tail on the outside and the head near the center of the coil. The body is dorsoventrally flattened by protraction of the ribs, giving the impression of a larger or stockier snake. (8) Tail-wave—The tail is elevated by dorsal flexure near the cloaca and moved sinuously from side to side. The movement ranges from a slow wave to a rapid wiggle, and may be accompanied by discharge of cloacal contents, which may be smeared over the body. (9) Tail-flat— The tail lies flat on the substrate. These behaviors were temperature dependent, with stronger responses when warm. The most frequently used behaviors were open-mouth attack from a coil, and body-extend with tail shake.

Herzog et al. (1992) reported that *T. radix* neonates showed low rates of striking and high rates of fleeing.

A study of 174 neonates suggests that minor variations in body and tail vertebral numbers may have a detectable impact on crawling performance and burst speed (Arnold and Bennett 1988).

Degenhardt et al. (1996) observed that New Mexico *T. radix* may take refuge in deep or muddy water, and may remain submerged for long periods of time.

POPULATIONS.   Of 383 snakes marked at an Illinois site, 298 (77.8%) were *T. radix* (Seibert and Hagen 1947). Estimation of the population size using the Lincoln Index was 1,152 (889/ha), and estimated population size by the Hayne method was 1,093 (845/ha) (Seibert 1950). Reichenbach and Dalrymple (1986) estimated that 222–531 *T. radix* occurred on their Ohio study tract, and calculated densities of 69, 52, and 123/ha during a three-year study; the estimated biomass was 3.5–8.6 kg/ha. Of 33,117 snakes from nine localities in Kansas, the overall relative abundance of *T. radix* was 4.11% (Fitch 1993).

Seibert and Hagen (1947) found a sex ratio of 75 males to 100 females in Illinois, but Reichenbach and Dalrymple (1986) reported a 1:1 sex ratio in Ohio.

Reichenbach and Dalrymple (1986) found that exploitative competition for food resources between *T. radix* and *T. sirtalis* in Ohio was unlikely to be a major factor in the population dynamics of either species. *T. radix* is endangered in Ohio due to habitat loss (Allen 1988). It is also considered a species of special concern in Arkansas.

REMARKS.   DeQueiroz and Lawson (1994) examined the phylogenetic relationships of the garter snakes based on DNA sequence and allozyme variation. Their data indicate *T. radix* is most closely related to *T. butleri* and *T. brachystoma*.

Thamnophis rufipunctatus (Cope, in Yarrow 1875) | Narrow-headed Garter Snake

RECOGNITION.   This poorly known garter snake (maximum TBL, 111.5 cm) is gray brown to brown or olive, with prominent reddish brown (black bordered), dark brown, or black spots along the length of the body. No dorsal or lateral stripes are present on the body, but faint ones may be present on the neck, and normally two dark, round nuchal spots are present. The head is olive gray to brown with lighter-colored, dark-barred labials, and no pale crescent behind the posterior corner of the mouth. The head is relatively long (5.2–5.6% of SVL; Rossman et al. 1996), and is laterally compressed with an elongated snout and the eyes positioned high, apparently adaptations for fish predation. The throat is cream colored, and the venter is grayish brown, usually with 2–4 (6) rows of large, dark, wedge-shaped marks on each side, or dark pigment extending across the anterior portion of each ventral scale. The pitless body scales are keeled, and lie in 21 (22–23) anterior rows, 21 (19) rows at midbody, and 17 (19) posterior rows. Surface ultrastructure of the body scales closely resembles that of the *Nerodia* water snakes (Chiasson and Lowe 1989). Ventrals range from 151 to 180, and 64–89 subcaudals are present; the anal plate is single. Laterally on the head are 2 nasals, 1 loreal, 2 (3) preoculars, 3 (2–4) postoculars, 1 + 2 + 3 temporals, 8 (7–10) supralabials, and 10 (9–11) infralabials. A postrostral scale is always present, and both pairs of chin shields are elongated. The hemipenis has not been described. Each maxilla has 24–29 teeth, with the most posterior longest.

Males have 155–180 ventrals, 71–89 subcaudals, and TLs 22–25% of TBL; females have 151–171 ventrals, 64–79 subcaudals, and TLs 21–23% of TBL.

GEOGRAPHIC VARIATION.   Three subspecies are recognized (Tanner 1990), but only *T. r. rufipunctatus* (Cope, in Yarrow 1875), the narrow-headed garter snake, described above, occurs in the United States.

CONFUSING SPECIES.   To separate *T. rufipunctatus* from other southwestern garter snakes, refer to the key presented above.

KARYOTYPE.   Each narrow-headed garter snake has a diploid chromosome total of 36, with 34 macrochromosomes, 2 michrochromosomes, and 70 chromosome arms (Baker et al. 1972).

Narrow-headed garter snake, *Thamnophis rufipunctatus*; New Mexico. (Photograph by James H. Harding)

Narrow-headed garter snake, *Thamnophis rufipunctatus*; Apache County, Arizona. (Photograph by Cecil Schwalbe)

FOSSIL RECORD. Unknown.

DISTRIBUTION. *T. rufipunctatus* has a split geographical distribution: the northern population ranges from north-central Arizona southeastward to the Gila and San Francisco watersheds of New Mexico; the southern population is found in Mexico from northern Chihuahua south to northern Durango.

HABITAT. This highly aquatic species lives at elevations of 700–2,400 m along the edge of riffles and in the pools of permanent and semipermanent, clear, rocky, streams flowing through open canopy stretches of riparian woodlands, and along the rocky shores of lakes.

Distribution of *Thamnophis rufipunctatus*.

BEHAVIOR. Little has been reported on the life history of the narrow-headed garter snake; studies by Fleharty (1967) in New Mexico and Rosen and Schwalbe (1988) in Arizona have provided the most information. The species seems primarily diurnal. A number of *T. rufipunctatus* were observed by Fleharty (1967) on cloudy days (75% cloud cover, 75% sunlight present), and it was even collected during rains and thunderstorms; however, the snake was most active on clear days. In Arizona it is active from late March to October (Rossman et al. 1996).

Most are found under rocks, but some individuals will bask on streamside rocks or in overhanging vegetation (Degenhardt et al. 1996). Rosen (1991a) found them active at BTs of 19.2–31.4 (mean, 25.0) °C; and in the middle of warm clear days, those out of the water had BTs of 26.7–31.4 (mean, 24.2) °C. Because it forages in rather cold streams, basking is probably necessary to bring the BT to the level required for proper physiological function.

T. rufipunctatus is very aquatic, and seldom strays far from its waterway. Two marked individuals recaptured by Fleharty (1967) had only moved a maximum distance of about 40 m between captures. Several were seen swimming well away from shore in the lake at his study site, and Fleharty thought they probably foraged throughout the entire 9 ha lake. All but two of the moving *T. rufipunctatus* observed by Rosen (1991a) were swimming.

REPRODUCTION. Females probably mature in their second year, while males take a little longer to become adults, probably 2.5–3.9 years (Degenhardt et al. 1996; Rosen and Schwalbe 1988; Rossi and Rossi 1995). The reproductive cycles have not been fully described, but Arizona females apparently ovulate in March (Rosen and Schwalbe 1988).

Courtship and mating occur in the spring, but the behaviors have not been described. A Mexican female collected 15 March gave birth to a litter in captivity on 17 July (Burkett, in Degenhardt et al. 1996), so unless she stored sperm from an earlier mating, the latest she could have mated was early March. Rossi and Rossi (1995) observed captives copulating in April. Females reproduce each year (Rosen and Schwalbe 1988).

Neonates appear in July or early August. The GP of the captive litter born on 17 July would have been at least 124 days. Litters contain 8–18 (mean, 12) young, which are patterned like the adults but have dull yellowish venters (Stebbins 1985). Their SVLs average 18.9 cm (14.7–25.4 cm), and their masses 2.4 (1.9–3.1) g. The maternal investment by a captive female into an unborn, nearly full term litter of 16 was 34–40 g, less than 15% of her body mass (Rossi and Rossi 1999a).

A comprehensive study of the reproductive parameters of the narrow-headed garter snake would provide valuable information.

GROWTH AND LONGEVITY. Growth rates for this snake have not been reported; and the maximum longevity is unknown. It has been kept for over two years in captivity (Rossi and Rossi 1995). Rosen and Schwalbe (1988) thought that wild individuals over two years of age had a 70% chance of surviving until the next year, and that some wild *T. rufipunctatus* probably live over 10 years.

DIET AND FEEDING HABITS. *T. rufipunctatus* is primarily a fish eater, and its narrow head, elongated snout, many teeth, and highly positioned eyes are adaptations for capturing such prey. Most foraging is probably aquatic, particularly in or at the edges of shallow riffles, but this snake probably also takes amphibians from the water's edge and on the bank. Reported prey are fish—suckers (*Catostomus clarki, C. insignis),* rainbow trout (*Oncorhynchus mykiss),* red shiners (*Cyprinella lutrensis),* speckled dace (*Rhinichthys osculus),* and green sunfish (*Lepomis cyanellus)*—and amphibians—larvae of the tiger salamander (*Ambystoma tigrinum),* and tadpoles and adult frogs and toads (Fleharty 1967; Hulse 1973; Rosen and Schwalbe 1988; Rossman et al. 1996; Stebbins 1954). Captives are picky eaters, but some have consumed fish-scented mice, and toads *(Bufo punctatus)* (Rossi and Rossi 1995; Woodin 1950).

PREDATORS AND DEFENSE. In Arizona, neonate mortality is about 93%, and *T. rufipunctatus* there have declined since predatory fish and bullfrogs *(Rana catesbeiana)* were introduced (Rosen and Schwalbe 1988). No direct observations of natural predation are available, but fishermen have killed *T. rufipunctatus* because they eat fish.

When disturbed, this snake usually dives to the bottom of the water and hides under or among the rocks (72% of observations), or if on the bank, it may crawl beneath the rocks or debris there (28%) (Fleharty 1967). It has a rather high body density (specific gravity approaching one), which helps it hug the bottom and stay submerged for considerable periods (Fleharty 1967). Most *T. rufipunctatus* have vile tempers, and if handled will attempt to bite and spray foul-smelling musk.

POPULATIONS. Formerly, it was not uncommon in its proper habitat, but there is no complete report on the population dynamics of this snake. It made up 18% of the 157 garter snakes collected at Wall Lake, New Mexico, by Fleharty (1967), but *T. rufipunctatus* was more secretive than the other two species present. Its sex ratio was skewed toward females three to one, and females had larger average body size than males. At a site in Coconino County, Arizona, Woodin (1950) captured 10 *T. rufipunctatus* and saw another about an hour later. The sex ratio of a captive litter of 16 was 1:1 (Rossi and Rossi 1999).

Unfortunately, since the above reports, the populations of *T. rufipunctatus* have declined to the point that it is now protected as a candidate species for listing in Arizona and endangered in New Mexico.

REMARKS. Because of its aquatic, fish-eating lifestyle, *T. rufipunctatus* shares several characters with the eastern water snake genus *Nerodia*, including the ultrastructure of the surface of its body scales (Chiasson and Lowe 1989). Lowe (1955) relegated the species to that genus because some individuals have a divided anal plate, and all have dorsally placed nostrils and an unstriped body pattern. However, Thompson (1957) retained *rufipunctatus* in *Thamnophis* on the basis that fewer than 10% have a divided anal plate, and the nostrils are no more dorsally situated than those of other semiaquatic species of *Thamnophis* that lack stripes as well as some species of *Nerodia* that are striped. A DNA sequencing and allozyme study by de Queiroz and Larson (1994) showed *T. rufipunctatus* is most closely related to the Mexican species *T. nigronuchalis*. The species was reviewed by Rossman et al. (1996), Tanner (1990), and Thompson (1957).

Thamnophis sauritus (Linnaeus 1766) | Common Ribbon Snake

RECOGNITION. The body of this slender, medium-sized (to 101.8 cm TBL) snake is uniformly tan, reddish brown, dark brown, or black with yellow, white, light blue, or bluish white lateral stripes on scale rows three and four. It has a golden yellow, yellow with a brown overlay, or tan-colored middorsal stripe that varies geographically and may be obscure or entirely absent. Two rows of black spots may be present between the lateral and the dorsal stripe. Below the lateral stripe is a dark (usually brown) ventrolateral stripe involving the first and second scale rows and extending onto about 40% or more of the area of each ventral scute. The venter is plain yellowish or light green. If present, spots on the short parietal scales are usually small, dull, and rarely fused. No dark bars are present on the labials. The head is very short for a garter snake: 39.9% of SVL. The eye is moderately

sized. The keeled, pitless body scales usually occur in 19 anterior rows, 19 rows at midbody, and 17 rows near the tail. On the underside of the body are 143–177 ventrals and 94–136 subcaudals, and an undivided anal plate. Lateral head scalation is similar to that of *T. proximus,* and consists of 1 loreal, 1 preocular, 3 (2–4) postoculars, 1 + 2 + 3 (4) temporals, 7 or 8 supralabials, and 10 (8–11) infralabials. The tail is long, up to 38.8% of TBL (Rossman et al. 1996). The hemipenis is short, extending only to the eighth subcaudal when inverted, and is virtually identical to that of *T. proximus* (Rossman 1963b). There are 27–34 teeth on each maxilla (Rossman et al. 1996).

Males have 145–177 ventrals and 98–136 subcaudals, females 143–169 ventrals and 94–131 subcaudals. Geographically proximate populations within a subspecies may have significantly different ventral or sub-

Eastern ribbon snake, *Thamnophis sauritus sauritus*; Fairfax County, Virginia. (Photograph by Carl H. Ernst)

Blue-striped ribbon snake, *Thamnophis sauritus nitae*; Levy County, Florida. (Photograph by Roger W. Barbour)

caudal counts (Rossman 1963). TLs overlap between the sexes, with ranges of 29.8–38.8% of TBL in males and 28.8–38.8% of TBL in females. The mean relative height of the first dorsal scale row is 1.2 in males and 1.5 in females (Rossman 1995).

GEOGRAPHIC VARIATION. Four subspecies are recognized (Rossman 1970b). *T. s. sauritus* (Linnaeus 1766), the eastern ribbon snake, ranges from southern New England west-southwestward through southern Ohio and Indiana to the Mississippi River and southward throughout the rest of the eastern United States except for southeastern Georgia and peninsular Florida. It has seven supralabials, a reddish brown to black back, and a golden yellow or yellowish orange middorsal stripe. The lateral stripes are slightly lighter yellow. *T. s. nitae* Rossman 1963b, the blue-striped ribbon snake, is restricted to northwestern peninsular Florida from the Withlacoochee River to Wakulla County. It has eight supralabials, a dark brown to black back, blue to bluish white lateral stripes, and an obscure middorsal stripe. *T. s. sackenii* (Kennicott 1859a), the peninsula ribbon snake, occurs in peninsular Florida and southeastern Georgia to the

Peninsula ribbon snake, *Thamnophis sauritus sackeni*; Collier County, Florida. (Photograph by Carl H. Ernst)

southern tip of South Carolina. It has eight supralabials, a tan to brown back, and a buff or tan-colored middorsal stripe that may be indistinct or lacking. The lateral stripes are light brown or bluish gray. Individuals from the lower Florida Keys have a well-developed yellow or orange middorsal stripe bordered by two narrow black stripes and only seven supralabials. *T. s. septentrionalis* Rossman 1963b, the northern ribbon snake, ranges from Nova Scotia and southern Maine westward to southern Ontario, Michigan, and Wisconsin. It has seven supralabials, a black or dark brown back, and a yellow middorsal stripe overlaid with brownish pigment. The lateral stripes are light yellow.

CONFUSING SPECIES. No other garter snakes are so thin or have such a long tail (up to 38.8% of TBL in both sexes).

KARYOTYPE. Undescribed, but presumably similar to that of *T. proximus*.

FOSSIL RECORD. Remains of *T. sauritus* have been found in Pleistocene Rancholabrean deposits in Ten-

Northern ribbon snake, *Thamnophis sauritus septentrionalis*; Michigan. (Photograph by James H. Harding)

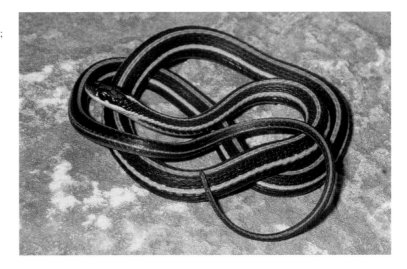

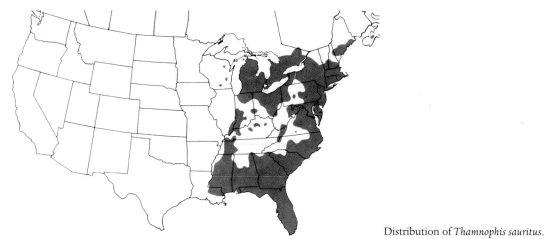

Distribution of *Thamnophis sauritus*.

nessee and Oklahoma, and in Pleistocene Irvingtonian deposits in Citrus County, Florida (Corgan and Breitburg 1996; Holman 1981, 1995; Smith and Cifelli 2000). Other possible *T. sauritus* fossils have been found in Pleistocene Rancholabrean deposits in Pennsylvania, Virginia, and Georgia, and a vertebra found in late Quaternary deposits in Saltville Valley, Virginia, may be *T. sauritus* or *T. sirtalis* (Holman 1995).

DISTRIBUTION. *T. sauritus* ranges from southern Maine and southern Ontario southward east of the Mississippi River to southeastern Louisiana and the Florida Keys. There are also isolated records of *T. sauritus* from Nova Scotia and northeastern Wisconsin; *T. s. sackenii* has been reported on New Providence Island in the Bahamas, probably transported there on plants imported from Florida (Buckner and Franz 1998a). The common ribbon snake is absent from large areas in Pennsylvania, West Virginia, Ohio, Indiana, Kentucky, Tennessee, Alabama, Georgia, North Carolina, and Virginia.

HABITAT. *T. sauritus* usually is found on the banks and within the vegetation bordering waterways. Bodies of water with either flowing (brooks, streams, rivers, swamps, marshes) or standing (bogs, wet meadows, sloughs, ponds, lakes) water are inhabited. It is not restricted to the ground, but frequently climbs into low vegetation, and has been observed foraging as high as 5.7 m above the ground (Bishop and Farrell 1994). It also uses animal burrows as retreats; the authors have seen it emerge from muskrat *(Ondatra*

zibethica) bank burrows, and Birkenholz (in Lee 1968a) has found them in the lodges of the round-tailed muskrat *(Neofiber alleni)* in Florida.

Minton (1972) reported that it seems to prefer a more moist habitat than does *T. proximus*.

BEHAVIOR. Common ribbon snakes are predominantly diurnal and are fond of basking (primarily on vegetation), but may also forage at night, at least during the frog-breeding season (Ernst et al. 1997; Rosen 1991a).

T. sauritus has a rather long annual activity cycle. In Florida and at other southern localities, it may be active year round, especially in years with warm winters, but in the north the snake may be forced to hibernate. Conant (1938) found them most active during the spring in Ohio, and Minton (1972) reported collecting them as early as late March and as late as 20 October in southern Indiana. *T. sauritus* was collected in every month but January and August in South Carolina (Gibbons and Semlitsch 1991), and Ernst et al. (1997) reported they were active from April to October in northern Virginia. This species requires a moist habitat, and during very hot and dry summers, it may estivate for short periods.

It has been found hibernating in ant mounds, vole tunnels, and crayfish burrows (Carpenter 1953a), and the authors suspect it also utilizes muskrat lodges and bank burrows. Hansknecht et al. (1999) observed five Virginia *T. sauritus* on and around a large fallen beech tree on an unseasonably warm day in January, and concluded that the snakes were overwintering in tunnels, probably created by mammals, within the root/soil base of the tree. Two of the snakes had CTs of 26.0 and 29.0°C; the AT was 22.0°C. BTs of seven hibernating Michigan *T. sauritus* were 5.4–5.8°C (Carpenter 1953a); these snakes were buried in an ant mound at depths to about 50 cm. In Michigan, Carpenter (1952a) found *T. sauritus* had a lower winterkill rate (for young) than did sympatric *T. sirtalis*.

Carpenter (1956) reported that the maximum and minimum CTs of 123 *T. sauritus* from Michigan were 34.0 and 12.6°C, respectively; the mean CT was 26.0°C. Rosen (1991a) found that the BT range of 135 surface-active *T. sauritus* collected near winter refugia in southern Michigan (from mid-September to mid-November and mid-February to mid-April) was 12.0–32.2°C, with a mean of 23.5°C for females and 25.0°C for males. Active-season (from mid-April to mid-September) BTs of 174 *T. sauritus* ranged from 19.0 to 33.4°C, with a mean of 27.5°C. The stable-phase (i.e., during the middle of warm clear days) mean BT for 34 of these Michigan *T. sauritus* was 30.0°C.

T. sauritus seems to remain within a relatively small home range near its waterway. Carpenter (1952a) reported that the maximum distance moved between captures in Michigan was 278 m, and the greatest width for any movement pattern was 49 m.

REPRODUCTION. Burt (1928) determined that female *T. sauritus sauritus* from Michigan were able to reproduce after attaining a TL of about 60 cm; Carpenter (1952a) reported females from southern Michigan attained maturity at two to three years of age at a SVL of 42 cm.

Gravid *T. sauritus* have been reported from June to October in southern Florida (Dalrymple et al. 1991). Rossman (1963b) gives the range of parturition dates as 2 July to 4 October. Young are born from July through September in northern Virginia (Ernst et al. 1997). There is some evidence to suggest that females in southern populations may produce two litters a year, but this has not been confirmed (Rossman 1963b; Rossman et al. 1996). Brood sizes range from 3 to 26, but 10–12 young are more common. Rossman et al. (1996) concluded that mean clutch size shows considerable geographic variation; southern populations appear to have larger clutch sizes and the longest neonates. Neonates have 14.1–23.9 cm TBLs.

GROWTH AND LONGEVITY. Carpenter (1952b) determined the annual growth period in southern Michigan to be the 153 days between 1 May and 30 September. He found that there was a consistent decrease in growth rate as *T. sauritus* became larger. Both sexes grew rapidly the first year, but the growth rates of males slowed more quickly. Carpenter found one female that had grown 26.8 cm in two years.

Natural longevity is unknown, but a captive-born male *T. s. septentrionalis* survived 10 years, 7 months, and 23 days at the Brookfield Zoo (Snider and Bowler 1992).

DIET AND FEEDING HABITS. Common ribbon snakes feed mostly on amphibians. Rossman (1963b) presented a table of prey listing 15 species of anurans of the genera *Bufo, Acris, Pseudacris, Hyla,* and *Rana;* three species of salamanders of the genera *Notophthalmus, Ambystoma,* and *Desmognathus;* and three fish (*Umbra, Gambusia, Heterandria*). Williamson and Moulis (1979) reported a captive feeding on slimy salamanders (*Plethodon glutinosus* complex). Brown (1979b) found that 21 snakes from Michigan contained only amphibians, of which 93% were anurans, and Carpenter (1952a) found 90% amphibian prey during his Michigan study. Apparently small *T. sauritus* feed on small frogs and toads and their tadpoles, but larger ribbon snakes are capable of swallowing medium-sized to full-grown ranid frogs. Love (1995) observed a *T. s. sackenii* feeding on a Cuban treefrog (*Osteopilus septentrionalis*) in Florida; it took 15 minutes for the snake to completely swallow the frog, which was eaten feet first.

Other animals taken include spiders (Hamilton and Pollack 1956), caterpillars, and other insects (Carpenter 1952a; Linzey and Clifford 1981; Surface 1906). Surface (1906) listed earthworms as food, but both Conant (1951) and Minton (1972) reported captives refused earthworms. Duellman (1948) reported a captive female ate her five young three days after their birth. Smith (1961) also reported a captive adult *T. sauritus* attacked a juvenile *T. sauritus*.

Most feeding is done in the morning or early evening, and the snakes actively prowl to find prey. Once discovered they rapidly crawl after it, seize it in their mouths and swallow it. Prey is detected both by olfaction and by vision.

Evans (1942) observed an unusual feeding behavior in *T. sauritus;* the snakes fed by swimming with their mouths open and then closing them upon contact with a fish. Bishop and Farrell (1994) observed a Florida female *T. sauritus* eating a *Hyla cinerea* in a red maple tree 5.72 m above the ground at an air temperature of 28–30°C in September.

PREDATORS AND DEFENSE.   Many wading birds and small predatory mammals eat this snake, as also do many other serpents. The young are particularly vulnerable, and may be preyed on by fishes, large crayfish, and turtles. Tail loss is frequently an indication of a predator attack, and Willis et al. (1982) found a greater frequency of tail loss in females than in males.

When first disturbed, *T. sauritus* usually tries to escape, and if near water, will not hesitate to dive in and swim rapidly away. Bowers et al. (1993) reported that it waves its tail and often reverses direction when fleeing. If handled, the common ribbon snake may thrash about and spray the captor with musk from anal glands.

Occasionally it will coil or flatten out, and may attempt to bite, but biting rarely occurs in these docile snakes.

POPULATIONS.   Carpenter (1952a) estimated the total population of *T. sauritus* on his 48 acre Michigan study plot was 508 (Hayne method) to 755 (Lincoln Index); 244–445 males, 264–310 females. When Carpenter adjusted this estimate for errors due to sampling techniques, the result was 477 *T. sauritus*.

Populations of *T. sauritus* are declining over much of its range because of habitat destruction. In addition, large numbers are killed on roadways (Rossman et al. 1996). *T. sauritus* is considered endangered in Illinois and Wisconsin, threatened in the Lower Keys of Florida, and a species of special concern in Connecticut, Kentucky, Maine, Rhode Island, and West Virginia.

REMARKS.   *T. sauritus* was reviewed by Rossman (1970b).

Thamnophis sirtalis (Linnaeus 1758) | Common Garter Snake

RECOGNITION.   *T. sirtalis* reaches a TBL of 137.2 cm; but most are shorter than 90 cm. Body coloration and patterns are variable (see GEOGRAPHIC VARIATION). The body may be greenish, gray, grayish brown, or black, and normally a vertebral and two lateral white, cream, yellow, gray, greenish, or blue stripes are present. The lateral stripes are always present and confined to body scale rows two and three, but the vertebral stripe may be absent. Two rows of black spots and red spots or blotches may occur between the vertebral and lateral stripe on each side. The head is distinct from the neck, and dorsally gray, olive, brown, black, or reddish. Most individuals have two small white or yellow spots on the parietal scales, and dark bars on the supralabials. The throat is light colored, and the venter gray, green, ivory, cream, or yellow with two rows of black (sometimes indistinct) spots partially hidden by the overlapping of the ventral scutes. Body scales are keeled and pitless, and occur in 19 (17–21) anterior rows, 19 (21) midbody rows, and 17 (15–19) posterior rows. The venter has 128–178 ventral scutes, 52–97 subcaudals, and an undivided anal plate. Lateral head scales are 2 nasals (partially di-

vided by the nostril), 1 loreal, 1 (2) preocular(s), 3 (2–4) postoculars, 1 + 2 (1–3) temporals, 7 (5–9) supralabials, and 10 (8–11) infralabials. The posterior pair of chin shields is usually longer than the anterior pair. The simple hemipenis has an unbranched sulcus spermaticus, five large spines at the base, and numerous very small, recurved spines in oblique rows on the shaft. Each maxilla has 16–26 teeth, with the posterior two enlarged.

Male SVL is only about 83% that of females, and male weight is only about 55% that of females (Fitch 1980b). Males have 133–178 (mean, 163) ventrals, 61–97 (mean, 85) subcaudals, TLs 18–30 (mean, 24) % of TBL, and those longer than 47 cm usually have knobs on the keels on the dorsal body scales near the vent (shorter males have only weakly developed knobs at best; Harrison 1933). Females have 128–174 ventrals (mean, 160), 52–93 subcaudals (mean, 76), and no knobs on the keels of their posterior body scales. The relative height of body scale row one (maximum vertical height of body scale row one divided by the maximum width of the vertebral row) is 2.4 in males but 2.6 in females (Rossman 1995).

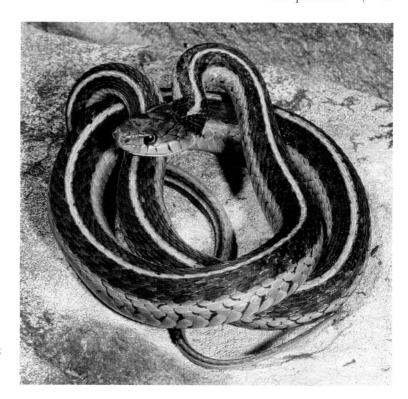

Eastern garter snake (striped phase), *Thamnophis sirtalis sirtalis*; Bell County, Kentucky. (Photograph by Roger W. Barbour)

Eastern garter snake (spotted phase), *Thamnophis sirtalis sirtalis*; Ingham County, Michigan. (Photograph by James H. Harding)

GEOGRAPHIC VARIATION. Eleven subspecies are recognized (Rossman et al. 1996). *T. s. sirtalis* (Linnaeus 1758), the eastern garter snake, has a dark gray, olive, or black head, a greenish, dark brown, or black dorsum, and three body patterns: (1) a prominent yellow vertebral and longitudinal yellow stripes; (2) no vertebral stripe, but yellowish lateral stripes with many dark spots between; and (3) no stripes, and the back and sides with many black spots. It ranges from Massachusetts and western New England west through Ontario, and south through peninsular Florida and the Gulf Coast from the Florida Panhandle west to eastern Louisiana. Isolated populations also occur in southwestern Louisiana and southeastern Texas. Some populations of *T. s. sirtalis* about western Lake Erie contain melanistic individuals, but the alleles are not in Hardy-Weinberg equilibrium (Lawson 1996). Inheritance of melanism has been thought due to homozygosity of a recessive allele, but occurrence of melanism does not match multifactor

Red-spotted garter snake, *Thamnophis sirtalis concinnus*; Clark County, Washington. (Photograph by William Leonard)

(two-gene) inheritance, and Zweifel (1998) thought that possibly cold temperature during a critical period of development may trigger its expression. Sattler and Guttman (1976) conducted an electrophoretic analysis of melanistic and normally colored individuals, but found no detectable genetic differences; Gibson and Falls (1988) thought the melanism may be related to thermoregulation. In Florida *T. s. sirtalis*, ventral and subcaudal counts are generally higher in the south (Christman 1980). *T. s. annectens* Brown 1950, the Texas garter snake, has a dark gray to black head, a black dorsum with yellow or white lateral flecks, longitudinal stripes that include a prominent orange vertebral stripe and yellow lateral stripes that invade scale row four (the only race of *T. sirtalis* with lateral stripes on row four, all others have the stripes on rows two and three). It occurs from southwestern Kansas southeast through central Oklahoma and the eastern Texas Panhandle to east-central Texas. *T. s. concinnus* (Hallowell 1852), the red-spotted garter snake, has a red head, a black dorsum with dark pigment extending onto the venter, a pale narrow vertebral stripe, and often obscure lateral stripes. This race is found from the Puget Sound south along the Pacific Coast to south of San Francisco Bay. *T. s. dorsalis* (Baird and Girard 1853), the New Mexico garter snake, has red pigment on the temporals of its dark head, the body olive gray to brownish olive with red flecks (usually confined to the skin between scales) alternating with rows of black spots on the sides, a black-bordered green to whitish yellow vertebral stripe, and yellow

lateral stripes. It is confined to a narrow north-south belt along the Rio Grande River from northern New Mexico to extreme western Texas, and isolated populations in northwestern Chihuahua, Mexico. *T. s. fitchi* Fox 1951, the Valley garter snake, has red pigment on the temporals of its dark head, a brown, gray, or black back, black pigment restricted to the tips of the ventrals, a broad yellow stripe with well-defined borders, and yellow lateral stripes. It ranges from the Pacific Coast of northwestern British Columbia south through central California to north of Los Angeles, and Idaho, western Wyoming, and northern Utah. *T. s. infernalis* (Blainville 1835), the California red-sided garter snake, has a red head, a dark gray body with some large black spots on the back, and red pigment on the sides (almost continuous in some individuals), a narrow greenish yellow to prominent yellow vertebral stripe, and yellowish lateral stripes. This race includes the formerly recognized *T. s. tetrataenia* (see Boundy and Rossman 1995). It is restricted to the San Francisco Bay area of California. *T. s. pallidulus* Allen 1899, the maritime garter snake, is a dark race with a gray black to brown head and body; the gray or tan vertebral stripe often absent or only present anteriorly; and gray to tan, often obscure, lateral stripes. It inhabits the maritime provinces of Canada, Maine, and northern Vermont and New Hampshire. *T. s. parietalis* (Say 1823), the red-sided garter snake, has a dark gray, olive, or black head with red pigment on the temporals, a dark gray, olive, or black body (the dark dorsal pigment may invade the venter), red or orange

Valley garter snake, *Thamnophis sirtalis fitchi*; Okanogan County, Washington. (Photograph by William Leonard)

lateral bars separated by black bars, a yellowish or greenish blue vertebral stripe, and yellow lateral stripes. It occurs over much of central North America from southern Manitoba west to eastern British Columbia, and south to central Texas, northeastern Colorado, eastern and north-central Wyoming, and Montana. A population isolated in southern Northwest Territory and northern Alberta is the northernmost in North America. Some *T. s. sirtalis* from Illinois and Wisconsin have reddish pigment along their sides similar to that found in *parietalis*, but no distinct populations of *parietalis* occur east of the Mississippi River. *T. s. pickeringii* (Baird and Girard 1853), the Puget Sound garter snake, has a dark gray or black head and body, a narrow yellow or bluish gray vertebral stripe, and yellow or bluish gray lateral stripes. It is confined to the area around the Puget Sound from southwestern British Columbia (including Vancouver Island) to northwestern Washington. *T. s. semifasciatus* (Cope 1892b), the Chicago garter snake, has a dark gray head and body, prominent broad black bars on its sides that interrupt the lateral stripes, a yellow vertebral stripe, and yellow lateral stripes. It is only found in southeastern Wisconsin, northeastern Illinois, and extreme northwestern Indiana in the vicinity of Chicago, Illinois. *T. s. similis* Rossman 1965, the blue-striped garter snake, has a dark gray or black head, a brownish body,

a narrow tan vertebral stripe, and bluish white lateral stripes. It is restricted to the Gulf Coast of Florida from Pinellis County north to Wakulla County.

CONFUSING SPECIES. Other garter and ribbon snakes can be distinguished by the above key. *Regina* and *Nerodia* have divided anal plates, and *Tropidoclonion* has a ventral pattern of dark half-moons. Striped *Masticophis* have smooth body scales and an elongated preocular that invades the supralabial row. Patch-nosed snakes *(Salvadora)* have an enlarged rostral scute, smooth body scales, and a divided anal plate.

KARYOTYPE. Its 36 chromosomes are composed of 34 biarmed macrochromosomes and 2 microchromosomes; the NOR is located on telocentric chromosome pair one or two (Baker et al. 1972; Camper and Hanks 1995).

FOSSIL RECORD. *T. sirtalis* has a widely distributed fossil record, possibly extending from the Miocene Hemphillian of Texas (Parmley 1988c); Pliocene Blancan records are from Nebraska (Holman and Schloeder 1991) and Texas (Holman 1979a); and known Pleistocene fossils are as follows: Blancan of Kansas (Rogers 1982); Irvingtonian of Kansas? (Holman 1972b) and South Dakota (Holman 1977a); and

Red-sided garter snake, *Thamnophis sirtalis parietalis*; Lyon County, Minnesota. (Photograph by Roger W. Barbour)

Rancholabrean of Alabama (Holman et al. 1990), Arkansas (Dowling 1958b), California (LaDuke 1991), Florida (Auffenberg 1963; Gut and Ray 1963; Holman 1959a, 1978, 1996), Georgia (Holman 1967), Missouri (Holman 1965b; Parmalee et al. 1969), Ohio (Holman 1997), Pennsylvania (Guilday et al. 1964, 1966; Rich-mond 1964), Tennessee (Van Dam 1978), Texas (Hill 1971; Kasper and Parmley 1990), and Virginia (Holman 1986a; Holman and McDonald 1986).

DISTRIBUTION. *T. sirtalis* ranges from the Atlantic Coast to the Pacific Coast and is found farther north

Puget Sound garter snake, *Thamnophis sirtalis pickeringii*; Pierce County, Washington. (Photograph by William Leonard)

Blue-striped garter snake, *Thamnophis sirtalis similis*; Marion County, Florida. (Photograph by Roger W. Barbour)

in Canada than any other species of snake. It occurs in Canada from Prince Edward Island, New Brunswick, Nova Scotia, and southern Quebec as far north as southern Hudson Bay, west through southern Canada from Ontario to British Columbia, and in northern Alberta and adjacent southernmost Northwest Territories. Isolated populations also occur along the Pacific Coast of northern British Columbia. In the United States the species ranges from Maine west to Puget Sound, Washington, and south to southern Florida, the Gulf Coast from the Florida panhandle to eastern Louisiana, southeastern and east-central Texas, eastern and western Wyoming, northern Utah,

southern Idaho, western Nevada, and the southern Pacific Coast of California to just north of San Diego. It is also found in the Rio Grande drainage of New Mexico, and isolated populations occur in southwestern Louisiana, central Texas, southeastern New Mexico and northwestern Chihuahua, Mexico. It has also been found in Abaco, Bahama Islands, apparently having arrived in a shipment of lumber from Florida (Buckner and Franz 1998b).

HABITAT. The common garter snake is found in a variety of habitats over its extensive geographic range at elevations of 0–2,540 m, but all have somewhat wet vegetation or free water: edges of deciduous woods and palmetto flats; banks of drainage ditches, sloughs, canals, streams, rivers, ponds, marshes, and swamps; meadows and pastures; old and cultivated fields; brushy fence rows; quarries and trash dumps; cemeteries; and vacant urban lots. The vegetation ranges from tall grasses to thick brush. On the prairies it is often found about swales, drainage canals, or streams. It has a strong affinity for freshwater, and seldom, if ever, enters brackish water (Duellman and Schwartz 1958; Neill 1958), but in Washington it has been observed feeding on intertidal fishes (Batts 1961).

BEHAVIOR. *T. sirtalis* is the most studied reptile in North America, being used in research on all aspects of biology; consequently, its life history is better known than that of any other North American snake.

Distribution of *Thamnophis sirtalis*.

T. sirtalis is more cold tolerant than many other snakes (Vincent and Secoy 1978), and it has a long annual activity period (March to late November or December over most of the range), but individuals are often surface active on warm winter days. Denman and Lapper (1964) reported Quebec *T. sirtalis* even work their way through frozen soil to emerge from hibernation in April, but most annual activity in Quebec occurs in the fall when *T. sirtalis* migrates back to hibernacula (Bider 1968). Hibernation may be prolonged in the north during severe winters, or of short duration in the south. In Florida and other Gulf Coast states, it may not occur during warm winters; Dalrymple et al. (1991) found active garter snakes in all months in the Everglades National Park.

Hibernacula include rock crevices, gravel banks, rock and earth dams, stone causeways, old wells and cisterns, ant mounds, crayfish burrows, beaver and muskrat bank burrows or lodges, and rotting logs and old stumps, and they are often shared communally by several *T. sirtalis* (Aleksiuk 1977a; Gregory 1974) or with other species of snakes. The best sites allow the snake's BT to remain slightly above freezing (Carpenter, 1953a, reported CTs of 3.4–7.0°C for hibernating Michigan *T. sirtalis*; MacArtney et al., 1989, recorded BTs of 2–7°C from hibernating individuals in British Columbia) and moist enough to prevent desiccation. However, this snake has a remarkable tolerance to very cold hibernation conditions (Costanzo 1986, 1989b; Joy and Crews 1987), and can even be frozen for varying periods of time (Churchill and Storey 1991, 1992; Costanzo and Claussen 1988; Storey 1990). Metabolic adjustments are made that aid survival: cryoprotectant synthesis does not occur, but the liver speeds up glycogenolysis, blood glucose increases dramatically during freezing, and a high free amino acid pool is present in the organs (Churchill and Storey 1991, 1992). Prolonged freezing, however, can result in death, and many *T. sirtalis* perish each winter (Bailey 1949; Churchill and Storey 1992). Some individuals may become completely submerged during hibernation, resulting in higher survival because of the resulting hydration effects and more constant thermal environment (Costanzo 1986, 1989b). The snakes make metabolic (metabolism may be reduced 5–20-fold), cardiovascular, and behavioral adjustments when submerged in cold water and become anoxic tolerant (Costanzo 1989a; Storey 1996). Cutaneous absorption of oxygen is sufficient to maintain enough aerobic metabolism for survival.

Hibernating *T. sirtalis* use up energy reserves during the winter (Crews et al. 1987) and are near starvation and somewhat desiccated when they emerge in the spring. Body lipids are low in the spring, increase during the summer after mating, and decrease during the fall and winter (Aleksiuk and Stewart 1971; Crews et al. 1987). Body water content has a reverse pattern, with the exceptions of a dehydration in the fall and a rehydration in the spring.

Spring, fall, and winter activity is mostly diurnal. On sunny days, *T. sirtalis* will emerge from its night retreat, bask in the early morning, and then forage before seeking the next night's retreat (C. Ernst, pers. obs.). Dalrymple and Reichenbach (1981) reported that in spring 88% of Ohio *T. sirtalis* are taken between 1300 and 1500 hours. However, some spring and summer crepuscular and nocturnal activity occurs when anurans are breeding (several times the authors have observed them feeding on anurans after dark), and in the summer most activity is either during the morning (0800–1000 hours) or early evening and at night (1800–2300 hours). In Quebec, this snake is most active at 2000–2100 hours in June, 2100–2300 hours in July, 1400–1500 hours in August, and 1300–1500 hours in October (Bider 1968).

The voluntary BT range is 9–35°C, the CT_{min} 2.7–3.6°C (Costanzo et al. 1990), and the CT_{max} 38–41°C for *T. sirtalis* (Brattstrom 1965). In a thermal gradient, *T. sirtalis* normally selected temperatures of 20–35°C, but after feeding chose 24–34°C, and while shedding, 16–26°C (Kitchell 1969). Stewart (1965) reported a similar normal range of BTs. At a Manitoba hibernaculum, active *T. s. parietalis* had spring BTs of 7.5–35.0°C at ATs of 8.0–23.8°C and STs of 9.5–45.5°C (Vincent 1975). Surface active *T. s. sirtalis* near a hibernaculum in southeastern Michigan had BTs of 16.8–32.0°C (female mean, 23.2°C; male mean, 26.3°C) (Rosen 1991a).

Most *T. sirtalis* are active at BTs of 18–30°C, and seek shelter when their BT falls below 17°C (Aleksiuk 1976b). It has a low BT when it first emerges in the morning but quickly reaches its normal activity BT and maintains it with only a slight decline during the day (oral temperatures are frequently higher than CTs during the warming phase; Gregory 1990). Carpenter (1956) found that about 50% of the CTs of active Michigan *T. sirtalis* fell between 25 and 30°C. Active *T. sirtalis* from Michigan examined by Rosen (1991a) had BTs of 20.4–34.4°C; Michigan *T. sirtalis* BTs during the stable period in the middle of warm clear days were 22.6–34.4°C, those from Georgia were 26.9–34.3°C, and individuals from Pennsylvania had BTs of 30.0–30.4°C. Moving snakes usually have BTs higher than the ET, those under cover about the same as ET, and those basking have CTs intermediate between moving snakes and those under cover (Gregory 1984a). Upon entering water, BT decreases rapidly; the BT of a swimming British Columbia snake that had just caught a fish was just over 14°C (Nelson and Gregory 2000). The ATs and STs at which Tucker (2000) collected first-year young in Illinois were 15–24 (mean, 21) °C and 11–23 (mean, 19) °C, respectively.

Gibson and Falls (1979a) found that BTs of wild *T. sirtalis* are cooler and more variable early and late in the day, and in the spring and fall. On sunny summer days, females average 1°C higher than males. On cloudy days, BTs are lower and more variable, and no difference exists between the BTs of the two sexes. Gibson and Falls thought females are better thermoregulators than males, and found (1979b) that melanistic *T. sirtalis* maintain a higher BT than striped morphs. Gibson and Falls (1979a) detected no indication that gravid females prefer elevated temperatures, as suggested by Fitch (1965); but Charland (1995) found that gravid females had mean higher BTs (30.5°C) and thermoregulated more precisely (mean, 1.6°C) than did nongravid females (mean BT, 29.6°C; mean precision, 6.0°C), and that these differences remained throughout gestation.

Diet may also influence thermal preference; recently fed *T. sirtalis*, and those about to shed, seek higher ETs (Gibson et al. 1989). Nelson and Gregory (2000) reported that in British Columbia the highest numbers of *T. sirtalis* at a fish hatchery were observed when maximum daily ATs exceeded 25°C, but at a nearby site where the snakes did not eat fish the numbers of garter snakes seen decreased in relation to maximum daily AT.

ETs may aid in differentiating the niches of sympatric *T. sirtalis* and *T. radix: sirtalis* apparently prefers lower ATs but higher STs than does *radix* (Hart 1979).

The average crawling speed is 1.4 (0.87–2.01) km/hour (Garland 1988), and speed increases with higher BT and greater body mass; but it increases with body length only to about 45 cm, as longer snakes crawl more slowly (Heckrotte 1967).

The extent of annual and daily movements is largely determined by local environmental conditions. If abundant prey and a suitable hibernaculum are present, little movement occurs, but long journeys are necessitated if the feeding range and the hibernaculum are widely separated. Some *T. sirtalis* travel long distances between summer feeding ranges and hibernacula. Yearlings and adults can distinguish the pheromones of conspecifics (Costanzo 1989b; Halpin 1990), and apparently follow their scent trails back to the hibernaculum in the fall. Gregory and Stewart (1975) recorded movements as long as 17.7 km in Manitoba, and Blanchard and Finster (1933) recovered individuals that had crawled about 2.4–3.2 km from the point of first capture. In Alberta, radio-equipped *T. sirtalis* emerged from a hibernaculum and moved along a constant bearing toward the closest freshwater marsh, approximately 3.75 km away (Larsen 1987). When they reached the marsh the snakes dispersed for the summer, but circled back during late summer, and eventually returned to the hibernaculum after a yearly round trip of over 15 km.

Most movements, however, are probably of shorter distances. Minton (1972) found marked *T. sirtalis* 457 m from their Indiana hibernaculum, and in Ontario Freedman and Catling (1979) recorded only short movements of 10–147 m for males and 10–153 m for females. Among 600 Kansas recaptures of *T. s. parietalis* over 50 years by Fitch (1999), movements less than 100 m were most common, relatively few movements were longer than 300 m, and 32 (5.4%) recaptures were at the place of previous capture (immature, 11.1%; adult females, 5.4%; adult males 2.4%). The average of the snake's circular home ranges varied from 0.21 ha for immatures to 0.72 ha for adult males, with an overall average of 0.54 ha for all individuals. Some snakes shifted their home ranges over time. The radio-equipped female with the most recaptures centered its activity on an old strip of sheet metal (which it was found beneath 21 times), and moved only 1.5–98 m from it (Fitch and Shirer 1971). Gravid females move less often and for shorter distances during the gestation period than nongravid females, but after parturition their movement behavior matches that of nonreproductive females (Charland and Gregory 1995). The longest trips made by Fitch's (1999) snakes were to and from the hibernaculum in the fall and spring, averaging 554 m: males 200–1,355 (mean, 747) m, and females 116–1,365 (mean, 480) m. Carpenter (1952a) recorded a maximum movement in Michigan of 300 m, with most less than 183 m. He thought the average home range was only about 0.8 ha. Illinois females moved an average of 1.05 m/day and males moved only 0.72 m/day (Seibert and Hagen 1947). When further differentiated according to age, first-year males moved 0.74 m/day; first-year females, 0.8 m/day; second-year males, 0.71 m/day; and second-year females, 1.58 m/day. The snakes averaged longer movements in May–July than in August–October. Odor detection is not needed for movement and orientation within the home range (Graves et al. 1993).

T. sirtalis is quite at home in water and can often be seen swimming along near the shoreline (Miller 1976). It is also a good climber. Lawson (1989, 1994) thought some individuals use sun compass orientation.

REPRODUCTION. Attainment of sexual maturity probably occurs at different SVLs in the variously sized subspecies. Male *T. sirtalis* mature in one to two years at a SVL of 36–39 cm (Rossman et al. 1996). The keels on the dorsal scutes in the anal region, an indication of maturity, are characteristically knobbed in males longer than 47.5 cm TBL, but absent or poorly developed in males shorter than this, and absent in females (Harrison 1933). When males emerge from hibernation, their vasa deferentia are packed with sperm in preparation for the spring matings, the androgen blood level is low, and the testes are small (Crews and Garstka 1982; Fox 1954; Krohmer et al. 1987). Plasma testosterone levels are highest in the spring and lowest in summer; testicular testosterone levels are higher in the spring than in the fall, but not significantly different in spring than in summer or in summer than in fall (Weil 1985). The androgen level starts to rise at about the time *T. sirtalis* disperse from hibernacula. During the summer the testes enlarge and spermatogenesis produces sperm for the next year's matings. Testes weigh the most in early summer, with a lesser peak in September. Testosterone is high in early spring, declines during the spring mating season, and peaks in late summer during gametogenesis (Moore et al. 2000). Corticosterone has a similar cycle, and does not seem to interact negatively with testosterone (Moore et al. 2000). The testosterone cycle delays the male's readiness to court until the next spring after emergence from hibernation (Crews 1991). Maximum spermatogenesis occurs in late summer. Manipulation of the photoperiod has no effect on the testicular cycle, as spermatogenesis is more controlled by a rise in the ET (Krohmer and Crews 1987, 1989a, 1989b).

Female *T. sirtalis* usually mature in two to three years at a SVL of 42–55 cm (Rossman et al. 1996). Little size increase occurs in the ovarian follicles over winter or in the early spring, and they generally lack yolk. Vitellogenesis begins in April or May, and the follicles grow dramatically (vitellogenic females emerge from hibernation with greater body masses than nonvitellogenic females; Whittier and Crews 1990); fertilization may occur from May to July. Florida females may contain enlarged follicles in late May, nearly full term embryos in early August, and full-term embryos in early October, and they give birth in mid-October to early November (Iverson 1978). Exposure to low ET and darkness during hibernation is required to start sexual receptivity and eventual vitellogenesis, but the relative importance of ET versus light is unknown (Bono-Gallo and Licht 1983). With few exceptions, females hibernating for at least 16 weeks will be sexually receptive, but only those that mate become vitellogenic. Mating causes the level of serum estrogen to rise, initiating vitellogenesis and enlargement of the follicles. The ovulated eggs are later fertilized by sperm the female has stored in her oviduct. After fertilization, the serum level of progesterone rises, but its production ceases after parturition. An excellent summary of the reproductive physiology of both sexes is presented by Crews and Garstka (1982).

As a result of their respective reproductive cycles, *T. sirtalis* mate at a time when the gonads are small and blood levels of sex steroid hormones are low (Crews et al. 1984). Male courtship is independent of both testicular hormones (Camazine et al. 1980; Crews 1983; Garstka et al. 1982) and ET (Shine et al. 2000). However, the pineal gland seems to play a role in mating readiness by controlling the diel cycle of melatonin (Medonca et al. 1996), and removal of the gland blocks male spring courtship behavior (Nelson et al. 1987).

Mating usually occurs in the spring from mid-March to mid-April after emergence from hibernation, but may also take place as late as mid-June (Fouquette 1954) and in the fall (Blanchard and Blanchard 1942; Fitch 1965; Medonca and Crews 1989). Cold exposure during hibernation followed by a rapid rise in BT triggers spring mating activity in males (Aleksiuk and Gregory 1974; Hawley and Aleksiuk 1975; Morris 1978; Vagvolgyi and Halpern 1983). Manitoba *T. s. parietalis* remain in the vicinity of the hibernaculum for about 1.5 months for intense mating activity, with males in excess of females (Gregory 1974).

During the mating period females release species-specific pheromones from their dorsal skin, which attract males (Crews and Garstka 1982; Ford 1978, 1982a; Ford and Schofield 1984). Males release pheromones that normally repulse other males, but some also release a pheromone that attracts other males. These "she-males" possess semichemical components intermediate to both sexes (Mason 1993), but mate with females significantly more than do normal males, demonstrating not only reproductive competency, but also a possible selective advantage over normal males (Mason and Crews 1985). Males follow pheromone scent trails to find females, but the ability to trail females changes during the year; males trail best in April–June, do not trail in late July, and show intermediate trailing ability in August–October (Ford 1981).

When the female is recognized by her scent, the male crawls alongside her, presses his chin against the female's back, and slowly moves anteriorly until his vent region lies parallel to that of the female. His vent is pressed against hers, and spasmodic ripples progress along his abdomen. The female's role is mainly passive, but insertion can only occur if she raises her tail to expose her gapping vent, and the male inserts his hemipenis almost immediately. Courtship may take from 5–10 minutes to over an hour; copulation typically takes about 15–20 minutes (Blanchard and Blanchard 1942; Fitch 1965; Gillingham and Dickinson 1980; List 1950; Noble 1937). Several males may simultaneously court a female, resulting in writhing "balls" of snakes (Rossman et al. 1996). Mating may occur at ground level or above ground in bushes (Gregory 1975b).

Immediately after mating, females become intolerant of other males' advances. This is partially because the male places a copulatory plug in the female's cloaca that blocks the oviductal openings for several days. The plug, apparently formed from kidney secretions, may prevent rival males from copulating with the female (Devine 1975, 1977; Ross and Crews 1977). In addition, males respond negatively to a pheromone released from residual male semen in the cloaca of a female that has recently copulated. Sexually active males do not court recently mated females, thus presenting a competitive advantage to the mated male. However, in spite of the plug, neonate DNA indicates that multiple matings with different males can occur (Gibson and Falls 1975; Schwartz et al. 1989).

Females may store sperm over winter from spring or fall matings, and such sperm may remain viable for a year (Fox 1956); females are known to have produced young after a spring when no mating occurred (Blanchard 1943; Rahn 1940). The sperm is stored in special grooves in the vaginal region of the oviduct, 3–6 cm anterior to the vent. The epithelial lining sloughs, associates with the sperm, and moves forward to special infundibular storage regions (Halpert et al. 1982). These carrier matrices not only facilitate the movement of sperm anteriorly, but also provide nourishment to the sperm. Stored sperm are evacuated from storage areas within six hours after a spring mating, but new sperm are not evident in the oviduct until a day after the mating.

T. sirtalis is viviparous, and nourishes its developing young through a placenta (Clark et al. 1955; Hoffman 1970a, 1970b). The RCM is typically 0.244–0.320 (Seigel and Fitch 1984; Seigel et al. 1986). Some females may breed bi- or triannually (Larsen et al. 1993), as only about 57 (10–100) % of females in a population produce young in a given year. Females possibly produce more than one litter a reproductive year, although this has not been proven. Gestation may take 80–90 or more days, and its duration is apparently dependent on the ET.

Litter size ranges from 1 (Kephart 1981) to 101 (Palmer and Braswell 1995) young, and averages 27 (n

= 325 clutches); large females produce more offspring than small females. The number of offspring produced by a female varies from year to year depending on environmental conditions (Seigel and Fitch 1985), and variances occur between populations (Gregory and Larsen 1993). The young are born from mid-June to early November, with most appearing in August and September. Prior to parturition pregnant females may aggregate in secluded places away from the hibernaculum (Gordon and Cook 1980; Gregory 1975a; Larsen et al. 1993; Reichenbach 1983). Neonates are brightly colored, with 12.0–27.8 (mean, 17.8; n = 255) cm TBLs and body masses of 0.6–4.2 (mean, 2.2; n = 61) g. The largest subspecies usually produce the largest offspring. After birth, neonates have a tendency to aggregate (Burghardt 1983), and it is not uncommon to find several under a shelter, possibly attracted by scent gland secretions.

GROWTH AND LONGEVITY. *T. sirtalis* grows throughout its life, although more slowly with age, during those periods of the year when prey are available and the ET is high enough for it to feed. Carpenter (1952b) considered the 153 day span from May through September as the growth period in Michigan. Farther north the feeding period may be shorter, and farther south it may be considerably longer, perhaps including every month in southern Florida. The more frequently the snake feeds, the faster it will grow (Myer and Kowell 1973), and as it grows larger, it becomes capable of taking bigger prey. In addition, individuals kept at a lower ET, or at the same ET but for shorter periods of time, grow more slowly than those with access to heat for longer periods of time (Arnold and Peterson 1989).

There is a constant decrease in growth rate as *T. sirtalis* becomes larger, particularly after maturity is reached, and much energy goes into reproductive effort at the expense of growth. During a 50 year study in Kansas, Fitch (1999) found the SVLs of male *T. s. parietalis* were as follows: year one, 13.6–41.0 cm; year two, 41.0–49.9 cm; year three, 50.0–55.9 cm; year four, 56.0–60.7 cm; year five, 60.8–63.9 cm; year six, 64.0–66.6 cm; and year seven, 66.7–68.3 cm. Females grew faster and consequently achieved greater SVLs: year one, 15.6–44.9 cm; year two, 45.0–60.0 cm; year three, 60.1–69.0 cm; year four, 69.1–76.5 cm; year five,

76.6–82.9 cm; year six, 83.0–87.5 cm; year seven, 87.6–90.9 cm; year eight, 91.0–94.0 cm; and year nine, 94.1–97.0 cm. The average gain per month of wild snakes by SVL class was as follows: 40–44.9 cm males, 14.1 cm; 45.0–49.9 cm males, 9.5 cm; 50.0–54.9 cm—males 7.0 cm, females 27.5 cm; 55.0–59.9 cm—males 4.6 cm, females 17.2 cm; 60.0–64.9 cm females, 10.9 cm; 65.0–69.9 cm females, 11.5 cm; and 70.0–90.0 cm females, 5.5 cm. Wild young 14.8–42.6 cm in SVL grew 0.1–0.2 cm/day (Fitch 1965). Carpenter (1952b) recorded comparable growth rates for wild Michigan *T. sirtalis*. In Illinois, Seibert and Hagen (1947) calculated that wild young *T. sirtalis* grew an additional 50–60% in length during year one; males grew 25–37% more and females 33–37% during year two; and females grew an additional 8–15% in year three.

Captive-born Kansas neonate males grew 18.9–24.4 cm from August through July of the next year; and year two males grew 2.5–2.7 cm from August to October (Fitch 1999). Similarly, captive-born neonate females grew 15.1–26.6 cm and 3.0–6.0 cm, respectively, over the same periods. A captive male and female fed exclusively fish grew 28.7 cm in 20 months and 48.0 cm in a little over two years, respectively (Riches 1962).

A wild-caught female of unknown age survived an additional 14 years in captivity (Snyder and Bowler 1992).

DIET AND FEEDING HABITS. Because of its long annual activity period, *T. sirtalis* may feed in every month in Florida, and from March or April through October in northern populations (C. Ernst, pers. obs.; Minton 1972). Both carrion and fresh prey are eaten, and feeding occurs both on land and in water. *T. sirtalis* may change prey according to annual or seasonal availability (Kephart and Arnold 1982). Also, the summer feeding range may be distant from the hibernaculum, requiring a long spring migration before feeding can begin (Gregory and Stewart 1975).

Juveniles eat worms, slugs, snails, insects, and salamanders, and seem more adept at catching transforming anurans than at catching adults. Adults are capable of eating full-grown frogs, toads, mice, and occasionally nestling birds. Amphibians may constitute up to 90% of adult prey of some populations (Pope 1944), but earthworms are eaten in large quantities (35–75%; Hamilton 1951b; Lagler and Salyer

1945) by most populations. Reichenbach and Dalrymple (1986) estimated that for wild *T. sirtalis*, a 1:4 predator-prey biomass ratio is sufficient for maintenance, growth, and reproduction.

Prey taken by this generalist feeder include fish *(Anoplarchus purpurescens, Carassius auratus, Catastomus* sp., *Gambusia affinis, Gobiosox meandricus, Notropis heterolepis, Noturus gyrinus, Oncorhynchus kisutch, O. mykiss, Rhinichthys atratulis, Salvelinus fontinalis, Schilbeodes mollis, Umbra lima, Xiphister atropurescens);* amphibians—adult and larval anurans *(Acris crepitans, A. gryllus, Bufo americanus, B. cognatus, B. quercicus, B. terrestris, B. valliceps, B. woodhousei, Gastrophryne olivacea, Hyla chrysocelis, H. cinerea, H. femoralis, H. versicolor, Osteopilus septentrionalis, Pseudacris crucifer, P. feriarum, P.nigrita, P. regilla, R. triseriata, Rana aurora, R. blairi, R. boylii, R. catesbeiana, R. clamitans, R. muscosa, R. palustris, R. pipiens, R. pretiosa, R. sphenocephala, R. sylvatica, Scaphiopus* sp., *Spea* sp.) and salamanders *(Ambystoma laterale, A. macultum, A. opacum, A. texanum, Desmognathus fuscus, Dicamptodon copei, D. ensatus, Ensatina eschscholtzii, Eurycea bislineata, Gyrinophilus porphyriticus, Necturus* sp., *Notophthalmus viridescens, Plethodon cinereus, P. cylindraceus, P. dunni, P. glutinosus, P. idahoensis, Pseudotriton* sp., *Taricha granulosa);* small snakes *(Agkistrodon contortrix, Diadophis punctatus, Nerodia sipedon, Storeria dekayi, T. sirtalis);* eggs and young birds *(Cardinalis cardinalis, Carduelis tristis, Dendroica petechis, Melospiza lincolni, Cistothorus platensis, Larus delawarensis, Passerella iliaca, Spizella pusilla, Sterna* sp., *Turdus migritorius, Vireo bellii);* mammals—shrews *(Blarina brecicauda, B. hylophaga, Cryptotis parva, Sorex cinereus),* chipmunks *(Tamias striatus),* mice *(Peromyscus leucopus, Reithrodontomys megalotis),* and voles *(Microtis ochrogaster, M. pennsylvanicus, Synaptomys cooperi);* and invertebrates—earthworms, leeches, slugs, snails, millipedes, isopods, spiders, crayfish, and various adult and larval insects (Coleoptera, Diptera, Lepidoptera, Orthoptera, Plecoptera) (Allen 1979; Barbour 1950; Batts 1961; Brown 1979a; Brumwell 1951; Carpenter 1951, 1953a; Catling and Freedman 1980b; Cavitt 2000a; Conant 1951; Davison and Bollinger 2000; Dundee and Rossman 1989; C. Ernst, pers. obs.; Ernst et al. 1997; Feldman and Wilkinson 2000a, 2000b; Fetterolf 1979; Fitch 1965; 1999; Fouquette 1954; Gregory 1978, 1983; Gregory and Nelson 1991; Hamilton 1951b; Hamilton

and Pollack 1956; Lagler and Salyer 1945; Lazell and Nisbet 1972; Loafman and Jones 1996; Martin 1979; McCauley 1945; Meshaka and Jansen 1997; Minton 1972; Palmer and Braswell 1995; Pope 1944; Poteet and Bell 1999; Sajdak and Sajdak 1999; Surface 1906; Uhler et al. 1939; Vogt 1981; Wilson and Wilson 1996; Wright and Wright 1957).

Laboratory tests of food preferences have shown innate intraspecific geographic variation: neonates from some populations preferred fish, while others were more interested in amphibians or worms (Burghardt 1970, 1975; Dix 1968; Kephart and Arnold 1982; MacArtney and Gregory 1981). This may be a means of avoiding intergeneric competition, as Fouquette (1954) reported that Texas *T. sirtalis* avoid competition with *T. proximus* by primarily eating worms and secondarily amphibians, while the latter species feeds mostly on amphibians.

The vomeronasal system mediates feeding behavior, and most food is probably found by following scent trails. Olfaction is critical to the onset of prey searching behavior (Burghardt 1990; Burghardt and Denny 1983; Burghardt and Pruitt 1975; Gillingham et al. 1990; Gove and Burghardt 1983; Halpern and Frumin 1979; Kubie and Halpern 1975, 1978), and chemical prey selection is influenced by initial diet, genetics, and sex (Lyman-Henly and Burghardt 1995). When prey is detected, vision supplements olfaction during the capture, and when both senses are used capture success is increased (Burghardt 1969; Drummond 1983, 1985). Visual cues alone are insufficient to elicit foraging behavior, but they are important in aquatic predation (Teather 1991). During foraging in water, open-mouth searching is common (Drummond 1983; Halloy and Burghardt 1990). All prey are seized in the mouth and swallowed as quickly as possible; fish are usually swallowed head first (Halloy and Burghardt 1990). Ontogenetic changes occur in the feeding anatomy (shape of head, length of snout, etc.) that seem to represent a shift from early emphasis on prey manipulation to a later emphasis upon prey capture (Young 1989).

Some evidence exists that the saliva of *T. sirtalis* has venomous properties. It is produced in a serous Duvernoy's gland (Taub 1967), and secretions from this gland may be lethal to mice (Rosenberg et al. 1985). When biting, the snake deeply embeds its rear maxillary teeth, piercing the skin of a restraining hand in a way that causes profuse bleeding. It is strongly possible that the saliva's enzymes may help to immobilize active prey, such as anurans or mice, and when the snake bites such prey it often chews before ingesting them.

PREDATORS AND DEFENSE. Many animals are known or suspected to prey on *T. sirtalis* (particularly juveniles): mammals—shrews *(Blarina brevicauda)*, chipmunks *(Tamias striatus)*, voles *(Microtus* sp.), raccoons *(Procyon lotor)*, badgers *(Taxidea taxus)*, skunks *(Mephitis mephitis)*, weasels *(Mustela frenata, M. vison)*, domestic dogs and coyotes *(Canis familiaris, C. latrans)*, and domestic cats *(Felis catus)*; birds—bald eagles *(Haliaeetus leucocephala)*, hawks *(Buteo albicaudatus, B. jamaicensis, B. lineatus, B. platypterus, B. swainsoni, Circus cyaneus)*, kestrels *(Falco sparverius)*, owls *(Bubo virginianus)*, herons *(Ardea herodias, Butorides striatus)*, American bittern *(Botaurus lentiginosus)*, Virginia rails *(Rallus linicola)*, goldeneye ducks *(Bucephala clangula)*, ring-necked pheasants *(Phasianus colchicus)*, ruffed grouse *(Bunasa umbellus)*, domestic chickens *(Gallus gallus)*, turkeys *(Meleagris gallopavo)*, crows *(Corvus brachyrhynchos)*, blue jays *(Cyanocitta cristata)*, loggerhead shrikes *(Lanius ludovicianus)*, and robins *(Turdus migratorius)*; reptiles—snakes *(Agkistrodon contortrix, Coluber constrictor, Lampropeltis getula, L. triangulum, Micrurus fulvius, Sistrurus catenatus, Thamnophis sirtalis* [neonates recognize the odors of some ophiophagous snakes; Weldon 1982]), collard lizards *(Crotaphytus collaris)*, and box turtles *(Terrapene carolina)*; amphibians—bullfrogs *(Rana catesbeiana)* and salamanders *(Ambystoma* sp.); predatory fish; large spiders; and crayfish (Aleksiuk 1977b; Barten 1982; Best and Pfaffenberger 1987; Breckenridge 1944; Carpenter 1952a; Conant 1951; Davis 1969; C. Ernst, pers. obs.; C. Ernst et al. 1997; S. Ernst 1945; Finneran 1948; Fitch 1965; Gutherie 1932; Lazell and Nisbet 1972; Littlefield 1971; McKeever 1958; Minton 1972; Netting 1969; Ortenburger 1928; Palmer and Braswell 1995; Parker and Brown 1980; Randall 1940; Ross 1989; Schueler 1975; Seigel 1986; Surface 1906; Vogt 1981; Voss 1991; Zorichak 1953). In addition, Aleksiuk (1977b) found hibernating *T. sirtalis* with portions of their heads chewed off, most likely by rodents, and Swanson (1952) found a small *T. sirtalis* with its head trapped by a trapdoor snail.

Despite the numerous predators listed above, humans are the biggest threat to *T. sirtalis*. Habitat destruction and the automobile kill many each year (Ashley and Robinson 1996; Krivda 1993), and the use of certain pesticides may poison others (Korschgen 1970).

Flight is the first defense, but if prevented from escaping *T. sirtalis* is spirited and puts up a good fight (blood levels of corticosterone increase when it is frightened; Moore et al. 2000). It flattens the head and body, sprays musk (several proteins and volatile components are involved—Weldon and Leto 1995; Wood et al. 1995; and the musk of females is more pungent—Kissner et al. 2000), strikes, bites, and chews; its saliva may be mildly venomous (see below). Some hide the head under a body coil (Stuart 1991) or play dead (Schueler 1975), and others break off their tails while escaping (Cooper and Alfieri 1993; Fitch 1999; Willis et al. 1982). The striped body pattern is also highly effective for concealing motion. Rapidity of defensive behavior is temperature related (Passek and Gillingham 1997; Schieffelin and de Queiroz 1991), and if the snake is too cold to crawl rapidly away, it will rely more on alternate defensive behaviors (Scribner and Weatherhead 1994). Antipredator behavior varies between populations and is apparently inherited (Garland 1988; Herzog and Schwartz 1990). *T. sirtalis* can instinctively recognize the odors of some potentially predaceous snakes (Weldon 1982).

Human envenomation has occurred; a 13-year-old boy was bitten by a large *T. s. sirtalis*, which chewed his index finger for about 10 minutes before releasing its grip (Hayes and Hayes 1985). The bitten hand swelled immediately, and the swelling increased over the next three hours. The next morning the victim's hand was bluish and cold, and his axillary and supratrochlear lymph nodes were swollen. The boy was admitted to a hospital, and responded to cortisone, antihistamine, and antibiotic treatments. Moderate edema and ecchymosis occurred at the bite site, and finger movements were somewhat impaired. As the swelling subsided, the lymphangitis took the form of linear discolorations along the full extent of the arm. The boy was released the next day. C. Ernst has developed a hyperallergic reaction to saliva of *T. sirtalis*; when bitten, a burning rash develops at the site. Severe reactions apparently occur only after a long-duration bite.

POPULATIONS. *T. sirtalis* may occur in very large numbers (500–600 to 10,000 individuals) at some Canadian hibernacula (Aleksiuk 1976a; Aleksiuk and Lavies 1975; Larsen and Gregory 1989). However, populations are smaller on the feeding range. Dalrymple et al. (1991) recorded 537 *T. sirtalis* (19.2%) in 2,801 total snake observations at two sites in southern Florida. Fitch (1992) collected 744 *T. sirtalis* (10.5% of 7,062 total snakes captured in 11 years) at three areas in northeastern Kansas, and Cavitt (2000a) collected 115 (20.9%) in a sample of 550 snakes at another site in Kansas; over the entire state, *T. sirtalis* averaged 6.50 (0.26–30.57) % of the total snake population at sites where it occurred (Fitch 1993). Some reported densities per hectare of suitable habitat for typical summer populations are 1.7 (Manitoba; Farr 1988), 4 (Ontario; Freedman and Cattling 1978), 5.4 (Illinois; Seibert 1950), 7.4–44.5 (Kansas; Fitch 1999), 18.7 (Illinois; Blaesing 1979), 24.8 (Michigan; Carpenter 1952a), 22.7–83.2 (Massachusetts; Seibert 1951), and 45–89 (Ohio; Reichenbach and Dalrymple 1986). Biomass estimates for the Ohio population studied by Reichenbach and Dalrymple (1986) ranged from 2.8 to 5.5 kg/ha. Typical male to female sex ratios of various populations are 0.60:1.00, adults (Kansas; Fitch 1965); 1.00:0.91, at birth (Michigan; Carpenter 1952a); 0.37:1.00 (Illinois; Tucker 1995a); 0.23–0.80:1.00, at birth (Minnesota; Dunlap and Lang 1990); and 1:1 (Alberta; Larsen and Gregory 1989). Most populations are composed primarily of subadults (50–60%), with adults over five years old comprising less than 10% (Fitch 1965). Survivorship varies between populations, about 29–43% for neonates, 51% for yearlings, 33% for two-year-olds, and 34–67% for adults (Rossman et al. 1996). Annual survivorship of large males in Alberta may be as high as 68–98% (Larsen and Gregory 1989).

Because of habitat loss and overcollecting in California, the subspecies *T. s. infernalis* is considered endangered.

REMARKS. Based on DNA sequence and allozyme variation, *T. sirtalis* is most closely related to the ribbon snakes *T. proximus* and *T. sauritus* (de Queiroz and Lawson 1994). *T. sirtalis* has been reviewed by Fitch (1980b) and Rossman et al. (1996).

Trimorphodon biscutatus (Duméril, Bibron, and Duméril 1854) | Western Lyre Snake

RECOGNITION. This mildly venomous, rear-fanged colubrid may grow to a TBL of 166.5 cm. It is gray to brown with 17–24 dark brown or black, light-bordered, saddle-shaped (broader in the middle, narrow at the sides) blotches crossing the back, and another 7–13 on the tail. The head is distinct from the neck, and whitish-gray with dark blotches on the dorsal surface forming a complete or incomplete V- or lyre-shaped pattern (best developed in western and Mexican subspecies). The pupil is vertically elliptical. The venter is white, cream, or gray, with a row of dark blotches on each side. Dorsal body scales are smooth and doubly pitted, and occur in 20–23 anterior and midbody rows and 15–18 posterior rows. Present are 222–244 ventrals, 58–86 subcaudals, and a divided anal plate. Lateral head scales consist of 2 nasals, 2–4 loreals, a small lorilabial situated between the loreals and supralabials, 3 (4) preoculars, 3–4 postoculars, 2–3 + 3–5 temporals, 9 (8–10) supralabials, and 11–13 infralabials. The long, single hemipenis is attenuated, with a single sulcus spermaticus running to the tip, and a naked base (or with tiny spinules). The rest of the organ is covered with large spines and spinules, with naked pouches and thick spinulate lips present near the tip. When inverted, the hemipenis extends posteriorly 14–25 subcaudals. The maxilla has 10–12 teeth, with the anterior 2–3 teeth longer than the rest, which gradually decrease posteriorly in size to a diastema followed by two large, anteriorly grooved, fanglike teeth.

The shorter males average 20 body blotches and 11 tail blotches, and have 222–230 (mean, 225) ventrals, 70–86 (mean, 79) subcaudals, and TLs averaging 16% of TBL; the larger females average 27 body blotches and 13 tail blotches, and have 222–244 (mean, 237) ventrals, 58–69 (mean, 62) subcaudals, and TLs averaging 14% of TBL.

Sonoran lyre snake, *Trimorphodon biscutatus lambda*; Pima County, Arizona. (Photograph by Brad R. Moon)

GEOGRAPHIC VARIATION. Six subspecies have been described (Gehlbach 1971; Scott and McDiarmid 1984b; Wilson and Meyer 1982), but only three occur north of Mexico. *T. b. lambda* Cope 1886, the Sonoran lyre snake, is found from southwestern Utah and southern Nevada south to southwestern New Mexico, Arizona, and southeastern California and Nayarit and central Baja California in Mexico. It is distinguished by having a well-developed lyre-shaped mark on its head, 34 or fewer dorsal blotches, a divided anal plate, and usually 24 midbody scale rows. *T. b. vandenburghi* Klauber 1924, the California lyre snake, is found in southern California and northwestern Baja California. It has a well-developed lyre-shaped mark on its head, 28–43 dorsal blotches, an anal plate that may be either single or divided, and 21–24 midbody scale rows. *T. b. vilkinsoni* Cope 1886, the Texas lyre snake, ranges from extreme western Texas and southern New Mexico south to Mexico. It lacks a distinct lyre-shaped mark on its head and instead has no mark or only small blotches, has faint, narrow bands crossing the back, and has, fewer, narrower, more widely spaced dorsal body blotches.

CONFUSING SPECIES. No other snakes with elliptically vertical pupils have a lorilabial scale (see RECOGNITION). In addition, the night snake (*Hypsiglena torquata*) has an unpatterned venter; the copperhead (*Agkistrodon contortrix*) has a heat-sensitive pit located between the nostril and eye, an unpatterned head, and an undivided anal plate; and the gray-banded kingsnake (*Lampropeltis alterna*) has a round pupil and an undivided anal plate.

KARYOTYPE. The karyotype is rather unique (Bury et al. 1970; Trinco and Smith 1972): the diploid compliment is 38 (18 macrochromosomes, 20 microchromosomes) with 46 chromosome arms. The 8 largest macrochromosomes are biarmed, while the other 10 are acrocentric.

FOSSIL RECORD. Pleistocene Rancholabrean remains have been found in Arizona and New Mexico (Mead and Bell 1994; Van Devender and Mead 1978; Van Devender and Worthington 1977).

DISTRIBUTION. The lyre snake ranges from southern California, Nevada, and southwestern Utah south-

Distribution of *Trimorphodon biscutatus*.

eastward to Trans-Pecos Texas, and south through mostly western Mexico to Costa Rica.

HABITAT. It is a resident of rocky, dry habitats, such as talus slopes, rock-strewn hillsides, and canyons with rock walls. It may occur in montane woodlands, grasslands, or even low-elevation desert scrub, but usually is found in rocky, upland situations at elevations of 1,000–3,000 m.

BEHAVIOR. *T. biscutatus* is another secretive, nocturnal snake of which little is known. Most have been collected on roads at night, but it is sometimes encountered prowling at dusk. Its large eye has a vertical slit pupil; clear, colorless lens; and conical visual cells that are ideal for night vision (Walls 1934). The daylight hours are spent deep in rock crevices, beneath rocks, or possibly, in rodent burrows.

Ordinarily, it is active above ground in March–October (Degenhardt et al. 1996; Rosen and Lowe 1994), although rare individuals have been found active in February, November, and December (Wright and Wright 1957). Hibernators have been found in deep, south-facing, rock crevices (Degenhardt et al. 1996; Repp 1998). The crevices are rather narrow and usually run perpendicular to the ground, with a hole at the base into which the snakes can retreat underground. More than one individual may use a crevice at the same time. Thermoregulation is achieved by moving up and down the crevice to find a proper ET, particularly as the sun shifts, and some may bask near the entrance of the crevice on warm winter days (Repp 1998).

Not all activity is at ground level. The snake is a very good climber that easily ascends bushes, trees, or cliff faces, and has been seen climbing rock crevices and trees to at least 4 m (Lowe et al. 1986).

REPRODUCTION. The size and age at which *T. biscutatus* attains sexual maturity are unclear. Goldberg (1995b) reported that a 44.8 cm SVL male contained sperm, and a 71.1 cm TBL female laid eggs (Tennant 1984). Wright and Wright (1957) reported the shortest adult TBL of both sexes is 55 cm.

Goldberg (1995b) found that spermiogenesis occurred in January–October, with peak sperm production in April–September. Recrudescent males were observed in May (33%), July (50%), and August (33%), and 23.5% of males examined from June through August had regressed testes. Spermatogenesis is interrupted by hibernation and is completed after spring emergence.

The female reproductive cycle is less understood. Some females examined in April and all those examined in May by Goldberg (1995b) were yolking eggs. Vitellogenesis was not observed in females examined from June through October and in March. In addition, Wright and Wright (1957) reported a September female contained no eggs and had inactive ovaries. Conversely, oviposition has occurred in December, January, March, and September in captives. Goldberg (1995b) thought this suggests that female lyre snakes do not necessarily produce clutches each year.

Captive courtship was observed in November by Werler (1951). The male vigorously chased the female, often stopping and, with his neck raised at a slight angle, moving his head from side to side in a slow waving motion though a horizontal arch of nearly 90°. The courtship lasted nearly three hours, but copulation was not observed; nevertheless, between 29 December and 7 January (57–66 days later), the female laid a clutch of 20 eggs. Many wild males have been found immediately after rains, which may indicate they were searching for mates. Perhaps female pheromone trails are enhanced at such times (Tennant 1985).

Clutches contain 6–20 (mean, 12) eggs. The white eggs are 21–45 (mean, 36.8) mm long and 9–25 (mean,

21.1) mm wide, and are of various shapes and sizes with nongranular, adherent shells. The only reported IPs are 77 and 79 days (Perkins 1952; Tennant 1985). The number of eggs per clutch increases with female length.

The only known date of natural hatching is 1 October (Cowles and Bogert 1935). Hatchlings are similar in color to adults, but the dark dorsal blotches are more contrasting and the dim head blotches may be joined by a dark peripheral line. Hatchling TBLs average 22.9 (20.5–26.4) cm.

GROWTH AND LONGEVITY. No growth data have been reported. A wild-caught juvenile male was still alive after 11 years, 10 months, and 30 days at the Fort Worth Zoo (Snider and Bowler 1992).

DIET AND FEEDING HABITS. Foraging is nocturnal, with *T. biscutatus* searching under rocks and other surface shelters, and particularly in rock crevices, for sleeping lizards. Possibly, vertical crevices possibly may be climbed to prey on roosting bats or nesting birds. Captives kept by Jones (1988) accepted prey between late March and late October, but refused food at other times, perhaps a biological clock phenomenon related to the natural period of hibernation.

As with other rear-fanged colubrids, suitable size prey is struck, retained, and then worked to the rear of the mouth, where the fangs can introduce the venomous saliva to immobilize the animal. The venom is produced in a purely serous Duvernoy's gland (Taub 1967). Three lyre snakes yielded 125–135 µl of venom (4.98–7.70 mg dry weight) that averaged 51.6 (32.7–84.6) % protein (Hill and Mackessy 1997). The grooved fangs are about 2 mm long and are attached to the posterior end of the maxilla at an angle of about 45° (Cowles and Bogert 1935).

Cowles and Bogert (1935) reported that a night lizard (*Xantusia*) seized and chewed by a lyre snake appeared lifeless in five minutes, and Duges (in McKinistry 1978) noted that a racerunner (*Cnemidophorus*) chewed by one died quickly. Rodents seem less affected by venom from *T. biscutatus*. A laboratory rat (*Rattus norvegicus*) and a house mouse (*Mus musculus*) chewed by a captive lyre snake exhibited swelling (edema) and purple discoloration at the bite site, more severe in the mouse than in the rat (Cowles and

Bogert 1935). Both rodents' symptoms diminished in five hours, although swelling was still present in the mouse after 1.5 days. Cowles and Bogert (1935) concluded that the lyre snake's venom is probably hemorrhagic rather than neurotoxic. The venom is probably also more specific for lizards.

Size of prey may also influence capture and ingestion time. During feeding by captives, *T. biscutatus* were unsuccessful in capturing mice (*Mus, Perognathus, Peromyscus*) on their initial strike seven times. Jones (1988) thought this a function of the size of the rodent prey, with laboratory mice (*Mus*) being larger than the two wild mice, but all of the rodents missed the first time were captured in a second attempt. Snakes took an average of 0.37 hours to capture and consume laboratory mice, but 0.53 hours to secure and eat the two wild mice. Lizards were secured on the first strike and swallowed in 0.27 hours.

Constriction of small mammals by lyre snakes has been reported by Murphy (1980) and Rodman (1939). Possibly the snakes involved were young, with venom delivery systems insufficient for controlling the rodents, or the prey might have been too large to be quickly immobilized by their venom. However, it is possible that the snakes' coiling around the mice to hold them in place while the venom took effect was mistaken for constriction. Were the mice actually suffocated? The question of whether or not *T. biscutatus* uses constriction as an alternate prey-catching strategy is still unanswered.

Wild lyre snakes have been observed to eat or attack lizards (*Cnemidophorus, Ctenosaura, Hemidactylus, Petrosaurus, Phyllodactylus, Sceloporus, Uta, Xantusia*), snakes, birds (*Crotophaga*), pocket mice (*Perognathus*), and bats (*Natalus, Tadarida*) (Degenhardt et al. 1996; Harris 1959; Klauber 1940b; Krutzch 1944; Reed 1997; Sánchez-Hernández and Ramírez-Bautista 1992; Scott and McDiarmid 1984b). Bats are ingested feet first and wings last (Sánchez-Hernández and Ramírez-Bautista 1992). Captives have consumed lizards (*Cnemidophorus, Coleonyx, Eumeces, Sceloporus, Urosaurus, Uta, Xantusia*), snakes (*Pituophis*), bats (*Tadarida*), mice (*Mus, Perognathus, Peromyscus, Sigmodon*), birds, and amphibians (Degenhardt et al. 1996; Dixon 1967; Klauber 1940b; Krutzch 1944; Rodman 1939; Scott and McDiarmid 1984b; Tennant 1984).

PREDATORS AND DEFENSE. Reports of predation on lyre snakes are nonexistent, but some are lost as roadkill each year (Rosen and Lowe 1994). Ramírez-Bautista and Uribe (1992) reported that a lyre snake died in 20 minutes after swallowing a large male Mexican spiny-tailed iguana *(Ctenosaura pectinata)*. Upon dissection, it was found that the lizard's spines had ruptured the snake's esophagus and stomach.

When first discovered, the lyre snake either will try to flee or will remain quietly in position. If further disturbed, it will coil, raise the anterior portion of its body, vibrate its tail, and usually as a last resort, open its mouth and strike. When it secures a hold, it will chew, probably trying to bring the enlarged rear teeth into play.

POPULATIONS. Tennant (1984, 1985) thought that because a number of lyre snakes are found each summer at widely separate localities across western Texas, the species is broadly, but sparsely, distributed throughout much of the northern Chihuahuan Desert. However, it can be locally common; Banicki and Webb (1982) reported they are not particularly rare in the El Paso area. Because of its seemingly rare occurrence, and because individuals have been collected for the pet trade, Texas declared *T. biscutatus* threatened in 1977 and has protected it ever since. It is also protected as a species of special concern in Utah.

REMARKS. Fortunately, human envenomation is rare, but minor symptoms do arise when it does occur: local inflammation, itching, swelling, and numbness (Brown 1997; Lowe et al. 1986). Envenomation is normally associated with careless handling of the snake.

The genus and species were reviewed by Scott and McDiarmid (1984a, 1984b).

Tropidoclonion lineatum (Hallowell 1857) | Lined Snake

RECOGNITION. This slender snake reaches a maximum TBL of 57.2 cm, but most individuals are shorter than 48 cm. The body is gray brown to olive brown with a grayish white to cream, yellow, or orange vertebral stripe, and a similarly colored lateral stripe on dorsal scale rows two and three on each side. The vertebral stripe is bordered on each side by a row of dark spots, and another row of dark spots lies dorsal to the lateral stripes. The small head is scarcely broader than the neck and body, and is gray to olive or brown with the scales behind the orbits heavily marked with black spots. The venter is pale green to yellowish green and has two rows of dark brown or black half-moon–shaped marks that begin as a single row on the throat, 132–156 ventrals, 24–47 subcaudals, and a single anal plate. Dorsal body scales are keeled and doubly pitted, and lie in 17 (14–16) anterior rows, 19 (16–18) midbody rows (formed by adding a fourth lateral row that is dropped posteriorly), and 15 or 17 (16) rows near the tail. Laterally, the head scales are 2 nasals, 1 loreal, 1 preocular, 2 postoculars, 1 + 1 temporals, 6 (5–7) supralabials, and 7 (5–6) infralabials. The mental scale may touch the anterior chin shields. The hemipenis is somewhat bilobed, with the lobes extending laterally into two elongated horns. The shaft has a single sulcus spermaticus that stops at the point between the lobes, four large basal spines, and several rows of spinules toward the distal end. Normally, 15 teeth occur on each maxilla, with the most posterior enlarged.

Males have 132–153 (mean, 141) ventrals, 32–47 (mean, 40) subcaudals, and TLs 13–23 (mean, 19) % of TBL; females have 135–156 (mean, 144) ventrals, 24–40 (mean, 33) subcaudals, and TLs 10–20 (mean, 14) % of TBL.

GEOGRAPHIC VARIATION. Currently, no subspecies are recognized (Collins 1990; Conant and Collins 1998), but this is controversial (Ramsey 1953; Smith and Chiszar 1994; Smith et al. 1996). The last study of geographic variation in *T. lineatum* was by Ramsey (1953), and a thorough reevaluation of the species is needed.

Lined snake, *Tropidoclonion linea-tum*; Kansas. (Photograph by James H. Harding)

CONFUSING SPECIES. The garter and ribbon snakes *(Thamnophis)* usually lack dark ventral spots, which if present, are never half-moon shaped. The crayfish snakes *(Regina)* have a divided anal plate.

KARYOTYPE. Undescribed.

FOSSIL RECORD. Pleistocene fossils are known from Irvingtonian deposits in Texas (Holman 1965a, 1969b, 1980; Holman and Winkler 1987; Parmley 1988a; Preston 1966), and Rancholabrean deposits in Kansas (Holman 1971, 1984; Preston 1979) and Texas (Johnson 1974, 1987).

DISTRIBUTION. The main range of *T. lineatum* extends from southeastern South Dakota south to the Gulf Coast of Texas, but it is also found in scattered populations in northern and central Illinois, southeastern Iowa, east-central Missouri, eastern Colorado, and New Mexico.

HABITAT. The lined snake was originally part of our midland prairie fauna, but it is now common in developed areas. It requires a relatively moist habitat, and often lives around springs, ponds, marsh borders, and the banks of brooks and streams. Presently, it is found in grasslands, oak woods with scattered trees, or even in suburbs, parks, gardens, cemeteries, and inner city lots and trash heaps. In such places, it hides under leaves, piles of vegetation, animal dung, rocks, logs, boards, or other debris, and even within cast-iron boxes

housing utility meters (McCoy 1961c). Its total elevational range is from near sea level to about 2,000 m.

BEHAVIOR. *T. lineatum* is active from late February or March to November or possibly early December in the south, but over most of its range the annual activity period extends from April to late September or October. No movement data are available.

Apparently, everywhere it spends some time dormant in the winter. Hibernation may occur singly or in groups, and most *T. lineatum* hibernate in burrows dug by themselves; however, these snakes may enter animal burrows, rock crevices, compost piles, or rotting logs and stumps, or they may simply crawl under rocks or other surface debris if it is available. Brumwell (1951) found Kansas *T. lineatum* hibernating 46 cm deep in the soil; and Hamilton (1947) found some buried 15–20 cm deep in Texas, all coiled with their heads inclined toward the center of the coils, and an aggregation of four was included. Whether or not BT controls the depth of winter sleep has been debated. Ramsey (1953) believed it does, but Hamilton (1947) presented conflicting evidence, and Gregory (1982) thought that hibernation may be controlled independently of BT. That some will emerge during warm spells in winter seems to point toward temperature control.

The lined snake is secretive and semifossorial. Days are spent under cover; foraging is crepuscular in the spring and fall, but nocturnal during the summer (Force 1931; Ramsey 1953). A few may be diurnally ac-

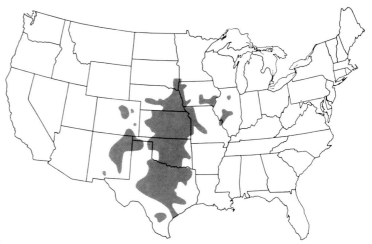

Distribution of *Tropidoclonion lineatum*.

tive, especially on cool days, and may even bask in the morning (Ramsey 1953). In Kansas, Clarke (1958) found *T. lineatum* active at ATs of approximately 17–27°C, and Fitch (1956) recorded BTs of 25.5–32.4 (mean, 30.5) °C from active individuals and thought the optimum BT to be 28°C and the preferred range to be 29–32°C. BTs of adult male and female Missouri *T. lineatum* did not differ significantly (nor did those of pregnant and nonpregnant females) and were 23–32 (mean, 28.8) and 22–34 (mean, 28.9) °C, respectively; however, BTs did differ significantly from both AT and ST, and the snakes apparently maintained an activity temperature range by using selected microhabitats (Krohmer 1989).

REPRODUCTION. Maturity occurs early in this small snake. Some males start spermatogenesis two months after birth at SVLs as short as 18.5–20.0 cm (Force 1936b; Krohmer and Aldridge 1985a), but most males mature in 8–12 months. Females mature in 19–24 months at SVLs as short as 22.1 cm (Krohmer and Aldridge 1985b). Mature *T. lineatum* possess knobs on the keels of the dorsal body scales near the vent, and Force (1936b) showed that about 50% of females larger than 19.5 cm had knobs, while none shorter than this size had them. She also found that 50% of 12.5–18.5 cm males had knobs, while 85% of those larger than 18.5 cm had them. Blanchard and Force (1930) reported that Oklahoma females were mature at TBLs of 24–35 cm, and that some bore young at 27.0–43.5 cm TBLs.

Testis mass is lowest in the early spring, but the testis reaches peak mass in late July (Krohmer and Aldridge 1985a). In early spring seminiferous tubule diameter is smallest and spermatogonia are prevalent. Tubule diameter increases during the summer and reaches maximum size by late July, corresponding to peak spermatogenesis. The most common cell types then are spermatids and spermatozoa. Spermiation begins in mid-July, with mating in late August or early September. Seminiferous tubule diameter and the rate of spermatogenesis decrease significantly by September. Sperm is stored over winter and in the early spring in the vas deferens. By mid-June, sperm is absent from the vas deferens, indicating the possibility of spring mating. Males born in August exhibit advanced spermatogenesis by September, with some spermiation in early October. Krohmer and Aldridge (1985a) considered this abortive, as all males began a new spermatogenic cycle in the spring.

In females, coelomic fat is significantly reduced by vitellogenesis prior to ovulation, but increases rapidly after parturition, and reaches maximum mass by mid-September (Krohmer and Aldridge 1985b). After parturition, follicular growth occurs slowly, and follicles reach a maximum length of 5 mm before hibernation. Vitellogenesis begins in the spring and the follicles enlarge accordingly. Ova are ovulated in June at an average length of 14 mm. Parturition occurs in August. The minimum SVL at which females initiate vitellogenesis is 21.4 cm, a length attained by July of their first year, indicating that females may produce a litter in their second active season. Mating occurs in late summer immediately after parturition; at this time sperm is abundant in the lower third of the oviduct (Krohmer and Aldridge 1985b). Sperm from fall matings remains viable in the female, and fertilization occurs at ovulation in late spring (Fox 1956).

Copulations have been observed in September and early October (Curtis 1949; Ramsey 1946), but courtship behavior has not been described. A pair observed by Ramsey (1946) mated for 6.5 hours; the male inserted only the left hemipenis, and the snakes laid calmly together during the entire period. The number of young per litter is significantly correlated to female SVL (Krohmer and Aldridge 1985b); a RCM of 0.426 was reported by Funk and Tucker (1978).

The GP lasts at least 10 months (Ramsey 1946), and the young are born in August and occasionally in early September. Litters contain 2–17 (mean, 7.6; n = 31) young. Neonates have 7.0–14.5 (mean, 11.1; n = 48) cm TBLs and weigh 0.38–1.2 (mean, 0.55; n = 33) g; their size is not correlated to female length. Neonates are grayish with poorly defined stripes, but well-defined ventral spots; body color darkens and stripes become more prominent with age.

GROWTH AND LONGEVITY. Blanchard and Force (1930) thought that the smallest young (mean TBL, 16.1 cm) collected in early May were those born the previous August and that they had grown about 5 cm in their first 3.5 active months. Both sexes grew at a rate of about 1.4 cm/month. Longevity has not been reported.

DIET AND FEEDING HABITS. T. lineatum is almost exclusively a worm eater, but rarely, sowbugs (Isoptera) and soft-bodied insects and insect larvae are eaten (Curtis 1949; Wright and Wright 1957), and a case of cannibalism by a female on her neonates was reported by Force (1931). The small size of the head and of mouth gape probably limit it to the above invertebrates.

Most hunting is done at night or after rains when earthworms are most often on the surface. Prey is primarily found by olfaction and taste, but sight may also play a role. Pregnant females usually feed only sparingly, if at all.

PREDATORS AND DEFENSE. Almost any larger carnivorous vertebrate is a potential predator of this snake. Known predators include snakes (Coluber constrictor, Micrurus fulvius, Tropidoclonion lineatum) and the loggerhead shrike (Lanius ludovicianus) (Fitch 1999; Force 1931; Greene 1984; Ramsey 1953; Tyler 1991).

Tropidoclonion seldom, if ever, bites, but if severely provoked it may flatten its head and body, coil, and strike. It almost always voids musk, and sometimes feces, when handled. Its striped pattern may confuse a predator in regard to the crawling speed of the snake.

POPULATIONS. T. lineatum gives the false impression of being rare, but this is because of its secretive and nocturnal behavior. No thorough study of its population dynamics has been conducted, and reported data are from Kansas and are fragmentary. Fitch (1992) recorded only two lined snakes in a sample of 7,062 snakes captured in 1980–1991 in northeastern Kansas, and only two were trapped (0.36% of 550 snakes) in 100 days at another Kansas site by Cavitt (2000a). Only 102 (0.31%) of 33,117 snakes collected statewide were this species (Fitch 1993). In contrast, Taggart (1992) collected 47 lined snakes in one day in Hodgeman County, and another 72 on another day in Ellis County.

T. lineatum is considered threatened in South Dakota.

REMARKS. Tropidoclonion is a member of the natricine complex of North American snakes (Dessauer 1967) and is most closely related to Thamnophis and Nerodia (Minton 1976).

Virginia Baird and Girard 1853

Earth Snakes

Key to the Species of *Virginia*

1a. Body scales keeled, one internasal scale, one preocular scale, normally five supralabials . . . .*V. striatula*

1b. Body scales smooth, two preocular scales, two internasal scales, normally six supralabials . . . .*V. valeriae*

Virginia striatula (Linnaeus 1766) | Rough Earth Snake

RECOGNITION.   *V. striatula* is a small (TBL 34.8 cm), gray brown to reddish brown snake with keeled dorsal body scales. The head is cone-shaped, much narrower at the pointed snout but increasingly broader toward the rear, making the neck difficult to distinguish. An obscure light band is sometimes present across the back of the head, especially in juveniles, and the labials are gray to cream. Dorsal body scales occur in 17 (15–16) anterior rows, 17 rows at midbody, and 16–17 (15–18) posterior rows. The unmarked cream to pink venter has 112–139 ventrals, 26–52 subcaudals, and normally, a divided anal plate. Lateral head scales consist of 2 nasals, 1 loreal, 0 preoculars, 1 (rarely 2–3) postocular(s), 1 + 2 (1) temporals, 5 (rarely 4 or 6) supralabials (the third and fourth con-tact the orbit), and 6 (5–7) infralabials. A single internasal scale is present. The subcylindrical hemipenis is five to seven subcaudals long and is asymmetrically bilobed, with the single sulcus spermaticus terminating distally between the lobes. The lower 50–75% of the shaft has laterally compressed, pointed, recurved spines set in fleshy lobes, and at the base are two large spines. Distally, smaller spines are present that become larger and less numerous toward the lobes. Each maxilla has 16–20 grooveless teeth.

Males have 112–132 (mean, 122) ventrals, 26–52 (mean, 43) subcaudals, and TLs 18–23 (mean, 19.5) % of TBL; females have 120–139 (mean, 135) ventrals, 29–45 (mean, 35) subcaudals, and TLs 14–20 (mean, 16) % of TBL.

Rough earth snake, *Virginia striatula*; Dallas, Texas. (Photograph by John H. Tashjian, Dallas Zoo)

GEOGRAPHIC VARIATION. No subspecies are recognized.

CONFUSING SPECIES. The smooth earth snake (*V. valeriae*) is recognized by the characters listed in the above key. The genera *Carphophis, Diadophis, Rhadinaea, Sonora,* and *Tantilla* have smooth body scales.

KARYOTYPE. The karyotype consists of 34 macrochromosomes and 2 microchromosomes; the NOR is on the long arm of telocentric chromosome one or two (Camper and Hanks 1995; Hardy 1971).

FOSSIL RECORD. Pleistocene (Rancholabrean) fossils are known from Georgia (Fay 1988; Holman 1995), Texas (Holman 1963), and Virginia (Guilday 1962); and fossils identified only to the generic level that may be from *V. striatula* were found in Pleistocene (Irvingtonian) deposits in Florida (Meylan 1982).

DISTRIBUTION. *V. striatula* ranges from southeastern Virginia south to northern Florida, west across Georgia, Alabama, and most of Mississippi to southeastern Louisiana, and from southern Missouri and extreme southeastern Kansas southward through western Arkansas, western Louisiana, eastern Oklahoma, and eastern Texas.

HABITAT. *V. striatula* is found in a variety of mostly open wooded or edge habitats: pinewoods, hardwood forests, wire-grass flatwoods, mesic hammocks, and swamp borders; beneath logs and stones; or behind the bark of dead trees or stumps. It also occurs in many cities and towns, where it hides beneath urban debris. During the July–August, it prefers thick shelters closely depressed to the ground (Clark 1964b).

BEHAVIOR. Few life history data are available. These snakes are active all year in the southern portions of the range, but farther north they first appear in late March or April and begin hibernation in late October or November. Cold weather forces them to hibernate during January–February over most of the range, and in the drier western portions, to estivate during June–August. Most surface activity is during the spring: 69% of captures in North Carolina occur during March–June (Palmer and Braswell 1995). Hibernation occurs underground or within logs, stumps, or possibly mammal burrows, and may be communal; Cook (1954) reported that clusters of 6–10 *V. striatula* of varying lengths have been plowed up in Mississippi in early spring.

On a daily basis, most activity is crepuscular or nocturnal, especially in summer; however, *V. striatula* is more active during the day in the spring and fall. Warm rains may bring them to the surface during the day, and movements are positively correlated with cumulative rainfall (Clark and Fleet 1976). *V. striatula* seeks moist hiding places and probably is easily desiccated.

In Texas, adults move greater distances than juveniles: mean distance moved by males was 0.24 m/day, and by females 0.13 m/day (Clark and Fleet 1976). Mean home ranges calculated with a circle-radius method were 81.7 m for males and 21.2 m for females, and by using a polygon method, 76.0 m and 100.1 m, respectively. *V. striatula* is capable of following odor trails left by conspecifics (Gehlbach et al. 1972).

REPRODUCTION. Males may mate their first spring at an age of seven to nine months. Clark and Fleet (1976) found a Texas male was mature at 11.8 cm SVL, and 96% of Texas males are mature at a SVL of 14.2 cm (Clark 1964b). Wright and Wright (1957) thought males mature at 18 cm TBL. Females become mature during their second fall, and probably first mate the next spring (Clark and Fleet 1976). Mitchell (1994) found a 17.8 cm SVL Virginia female mature, and Texas females with enlarged ovarian follicles have SVLs greater than 18.2 cm (Clark 1964b). Conant and Collins (1998) reported females mature at 18 cm TBL.

The female gametic cycle has not been fully described, but probably follows that of other colubrids, with yolking and enlargement of follicles during the spring, ovulation from mid-April to June, and oviductal eggs present from late May to July (Blem and Blem 1985; Clark 1964b). Females possibly store sperm from early spring matings until the eggs are ovulated. Male testes are at peak size from late August to October and are still enlarged the next April–June (Clark 1964b). A placental arrangement is formed, and the young are carried and nourished internally until birth by the female (Stewart 1989, 1990). Females probably

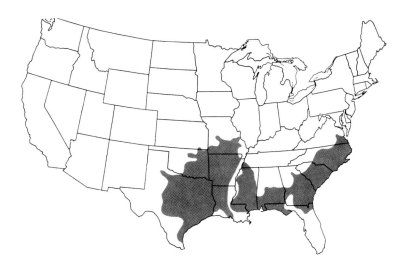

Distribution of *Virginia striatula*.

reproduce annually (Blem and Blem 1985). RCM of a litter was 0.428 (Ford et al. 1990).

Courtship and mating occur from late March to mid-June, but have not been described. Males possibly find females by following pheromone trails (Gehlbach et al. 1972).

After a GP of about 82 days, the young are born in July–October (most in July–August). Litters contain 2–13 (Wright and Wright 1957) (mean, 9.2; n = 106) young, and large females produce greater numbers of offspring per litter (Clark 1964b; Mitchell 1976). Neonates are 7.4–12.7 (mean, 9.4; n = 58) cm long and weigh 0.38–0.58 (mean, 0.44; n = 6) g. A distinct whitish transverse mark is present on the back of their heads.

GROWTH AND LONGEVITY. The only published growth data are that immature females grow rapidly in August–October, presumably because earthworms are more available then (Clark and Fleet 1976). A wild-caught adult female lived seven years, three months, and eight days at the North Carolina State Museum, Raleigh (Snider and Bowler 1992).

DIET AND FEEDING HABITS. Prey have been variously reported as insects, earthworms, isopods, snails, slugs, small anurans, and young lizards, but these accounts are probably exaggerated. Earthworms were the only stomach contents recorded by Brown (1979a), Clark (1964b), and Clark and Fleet (1976). Clark (1949) also found the remains of beetle larvae, and fed beetle larvae to captives. Vermersch and

Kuntz (1986) thought it consumes beetle larvae and ant and termite eggs and larvae, and Ashton and Ashton (1981) collected several *V. striatula* near pupae and larvae at the edge of ant colonies. Anderson (1965) reported a captive ate a snail.

V. striatula readily follows earthworm scent trails, so olfaction probably is the main means of detecting prey (Gehlbach et al. 1972). Earthworms are seized and swallowed; no venom appears to be used, although Taub (1967) reported the species has a purely serous Duvernoy's gland.

PREDATORS AND DEFENSE. Observed predators are the snakes *Coluber constrictor, Lampropeltis calligaster, L. triangulum elapsoides,* and *Micrurus fulvius* and domestic cats *(Felis catus)* (Greene 1984; Hurter 1911; Palmer and Braswell 1995; Vermersch and Kuntz 1986). When handled, *V. striatula* does not bite, but will writhe violently, spray musk, and void feces. Kirk (1969) observed one being swallowed tail first by a larger unidentified snake turn its head and clamp its jaws over the larger snake's glottis, causing it to eventually regurgitate the smaller snake. *V. striatula* may also pretend to be dead by becoming rigid, opening its mouth, and protruding its tongue (Thomas and Hendricks 1976).

POPULATIONS. Clark and Fleet (1976) estimated the size (including young of the year) for a Texas population ranged from 376 individuals (229/ha) in 1971 to 591 (348/ha) in 1969; the overall sex ratio was

281 males to 260 females, or about 1:1. Blem and Blem (1985) reported a sex ratio of 0.56:1.00 in Virginia. Vermersch and Kuntz (1986) calculated a density of 8.6/ha during a study in Brazos County, Texas, and stated that the density of *V. striatula* may be "many times this number" in some residential areas.

Habitat destruction and pesticide spraying (Ferguson 1963) have reduced populations of this snake in many areas.

REMARKS. As can be seen by the above narrative, little has been discovered about the biology of *V. striatula* in recent years, and a thorough life history study would be helpful.

The genus *Virginia* was reviewed by Rossman and Wallach (1991), and *V. striatula* was reviewed by Powell et al. (1994).

Virginia valeriae Baird and Girard 1853 | Smooth Earth Snake

RECOGNITION. This snake (TBL to 39.3 cm) is gray to greenish gray or reddish brown with a dorsal pattern of four longitudinal rows of small black dots, and some may have an inconspicuous light vertebral stripe. The head is cone-shaped with a pointed snout and light labial scales with some dark mottling, and

Eastern earth snake, *Virginia valeriae valeriae*; Rowan County, Kentucky. (Photograph by Roger W. Barbour)

Western earth snake, *Virginia valeriae elegans*; Hickman County, Kentucky. (Photograph by Roger W. Barbour)

Mountain earth snake, *Virginia valeriae pulchra*; Forest County, Pennsylvania. (Photograph by Carl H. Ernst)

is about as wide as the neck. Dorsal body scales are smooth to weakly keeled, lack apical pits, and occur in 15 (13–17) anterior rows, 17 (15–19) midbody rows, and 17 (13–15) rows near the tail. The unmarked, cream to light gray venter has 107–134 ventrals, 22–45 subcaudals, and a divided anal plate. Laterally on the head are 2 nasals, 1 long, horizontal loreal which contacts the orbit, 0 (very rarely 1) preoculars, 2 (1–3) postoculars, 1 + 2 (1–3) temporals, 6 (rarely 7) supralabials, and 6 (rarely 5 or 7) infralabials. Two internasals are present. The subcylindrical hemipenis is six subcaudals long and is asymmetrically bilobed, with a single sulcus spermaticus that terminates distally between the lobes; the proximal 50–67% of the shaft bears laterally compressed, sharply pointed recurved spines set in fleshy lobes. Two basal spines (the distal is shortest) are present, and the spines along the shaft become larger as they proceed toward the tip, reaching maximum size at about 20–25% of the distance along the shaft. Near the middle the spines become smaller, straight, and peglike, and lose the fleshy base, but they increase in length again and become fewer toward the apex. Each maxilla has 19–20 grooveless teeth.

Males have 107–126 (mean, 117) ventrals, 29–45 (mean, 36) subcaudals, and TLs 12–22 (mean, 19) % of TBL; females have 111–134 (mean, 123) ventrals, 22–36 (mean, 26) subcaudals, and TLs 11–24 (mean, 14) % of TBL.

GEOGRAPHIC VARIATION. Three subspecies are recognized (Powell et al. 1992). *V. v. valeriae* Baird and Girard 1853, the eastern earth snake, ranges from central New Jersey, Delaware, southeastern Pennsylvania, and western Maryland south to northern Florida, and west and north to Alabama, eastern Tennessee, eastern Kentucky, southern Ohio, and western West Virginia. It is gray to light brown with 15 midbody rows of mostly smooth scales and only faintly keeled dorsal scales near the anal vent. *V. v. elegans* Kennicott 1859a, the western earth snake, ranges from southwestern Indiana, southeastern and southwestern Illinois, and southern Iowa south to western Alabama, Mississippi, and southeastern Louisiana, and west to eastern Kansas, Oklahoma, and Texas. It is greenish gray to reddish brown with weakly keeled body scales in 17 rows at midbody. *V. v. pulchra* Richmond 1954b, the mountain earth snake, has a restricted range in the Appalachian Mountains from northwestern Pennsylvania south through extreme western Maryland and northeastern West Virginia to west-central Virginia. It is dark gray to a rich reddish brown with weakly keeled scales in 15 rows anteriorly, but 17 rows at midbody and posteriorly. Because *V. v. pulchra* is morphologically distinct and allopatric with no evidence of intergradation with the other two subspecies, Collins (1991) believes it may represent a separate species.

Distribution of *Virginia valeriae*.

CONFUSING SPECIES. *V. striatula* has five supra-labials, an internasal scale, a preocular, and distinctly keeled body scales. The ring-necked snake *(Diadophis punctatus)* has a distinct neck ring. Worm snakes *(Carphophis)* have 13 midbody scale rows, pink venters, and small rounded heads. The *Storeria* have strongly keeled body scales, and no loreal scale. Black-headed and crowned snakes *(Tantilla)* have dark-capped heads, one postocular, and entirely smooth body scales, and lack a loreal scale. The ground snake *(Sonora semiannulata)* has smooth body scales in 15 or fewer midbody rows, and a preocular scale.

KARYOTYPE. Hardy (1971) reported the presence of 36 chromosomes; sex determination is ZZ/ZW.

FOSSIL RECORD. Pleistocene (Rancholabrean) fossils are from Georgia (Fay 1988; Holman 1995), Pennsylvania (Gilmore 1938; Richmond 1964), and Virginia (Guilday 1962; Holman 1986a).

DISTRIBUTION. *V. valeriae* ranges from New Jersey, Delaware, Pennsylvania, and southern Ohio, west to southwestern Illinois and southern Iowa, and south to northern Florida and central Texas.

HABITAT. This is mostly an open, mesic, woodland (both hardwood and pine) and scrub resident that is also frequently found in fields near woods. The authors have collected it under leaf litter, rocks, and logs on both dry and moist soils, but more frequently under moist conditions, especially after rains. Occasionally it will occur in large numbers within suburbs, where it uses the debris of civilization for retreats.

BEHAVIOR. The annual activity cycle in Florida may be year long, but farther north, where *V. valeriae* is forced to hibernate, most surface activity is from April to October–November. Individuals have been found as early as February in North Carolina (Palmer and Braswell 1995) and Texas (Vermersch and Kuntz 1986), and as late as December in Texas (Tennant 1985; Vermersch and Kuntz 1986) and Virginia (Mitchell 1994). In North Carolina, the annual cycle appears to be bimodal, with 44% of captures occurring in April–May and 29% in September–October (Palmer and Braswell 1995). In winter, these snakes crawl deep into crevices on rocky hillsides (Collins 1993), burrow individually into the soil as deep as 76 cm (Grizzell 1949), enter rodent burrows, or crawl into rotting logs and stumps or compost piles, or under trash piles (Neill 1948a). One collected in Georgia in October by Hamilton and Pollack (1956) contained much visceral fat, possibly in preparation for hibernation.

Most daily activity is crepuscular or nocturnal, but occasional individuals may be found active during the day (Minton 1972), and heavy rains stimulate surface activity. Limited BT data are available; Fitch (1956) recorded 23.5 and 31.0°C BTs from two active snakes when the ATs were 21.7 and 24.2°C, respectively. Fitch also suggested *V. valeriae* is more cold resistant than *Diadophis punctatus*; two ring-necked snakes kept with a *V. valeriae* died when the water froze in the container in which all three were hiding, but the *Virginia* survived.

Little is known of the home range of *V. valeriae*. Stickel and Cope (1947) reported a marked individual moved only 6 m in four days.

REPRODUCTION.   This species probably matures in its second year at a TBL of about 18 cm (Conant and Collins 1998). Wright and Wright (1957) reported the minimum TBL of mature females was 18.3 cm, and that of mature males 19.0 cm. In Virginia, Mitchell (1994) and Blem and Blem (1985) found mature females with SVLs as short as 18.3 cm and 18.5 cm, respectively; the shortest mature male dissected by Mitchell had a SVL of 15.3 cm. The female and male sexual cycles are undescribed. The breeding period is March–April, and possibly into May, but the behaviors have not been reported.

V. valeriae is viviparous, and the young are born from 30 June to 30 September, with most appearing in August and September after a GP of about 88 (77–98) days. Sixty-two litters reported in the literature averaged 6.5 young, and contained 2 (Anderson 1965) to 14 (Groves 1961; Pisani 1971). However, Sinclair (1951) found a female with 18 ovarian eggs, and Martoff (1955) reported a female that gave birth to 4 young and then gave birth to 3 more 6 days later. RCMs of two litters were 0.500 (Pisani 1971) and 0.304 (Seigel and Fitch 1984). Neonates are darker colored than adults, have TBLs of 6.4–12.3 (mean, 9.6; n = 48) cm, and weigh 0.59–0.85 (mean, 0.69; n = 19) g.

GROWTH AND LONGEVITY.   No growth data have been reported. A wild-caught juvenile of unknown sex survived 6 years, 1 month, and 17 days in captivity (Snider and Bowler 1992).

DIET AND FEEDING HABITS.   Earthworms are the primary food, and in many diet studies were the only prey found (Blem and Blem 1985; Brown 1979a; Hamilton and Pollack 1956; Mitchell 1994; Palmer and

Braswell 1995). However, Cook (1954) recorded soft-bodied insects, insect larvae, and slugs as prey; and Anderson (1965) reported a captive ate cutworms (moth larvae, Noctuidae).

PREDATORS AND DEFENSE.   Known predators include snakes *(Coluber constrictor, Lampropeltis getula, Micrurus fulvius)* and domestic cats *(Felis catus)* (Greene 1984; Mitchell 1994; Palmer and Braswell 1995; Saenz et al. 1999; Yeatman 1983), but predatory birds and mammals probably also eat *V. valeriae*.

Its first reaction is to flee, and when handled, *V. valeriae* usually does not bite, but writhes about and releases musk and feces. A female *V. v. pulchra* collected in Pennsylvania by C. Ernst and his students played dead: it rolled onto its back, bent its neck so it could watch its handler, and when placed on its venter, quickly rolled over to again lie belly-up. An Ohio female pulled back its lips and exposed the inner surfaces and its teeth (Conant 1951), and Yeatman (1983) saw one form a loop knot with its body to prevent being swallowed by a *Coluber constrictor*.

POPULATIONS.   *V. valeriae* made up only 0.11% of 33,117 snakes collected statewide by Fitch (1993). Although seldom seen because of its nocturnal, secretive behavior, it may be locally abundant: Bothner and Moore (1964) collected 23 *V. v. pulchra* in one day in northwestern Pennsylvania. The species seems to have a 1:1 adult sex ratio. Richmond (1954b) reported an adult sample of 15 males and 14 females. However, snakes collected by Bothner and Moore (1964) included 5 adult males to 18 adult females, and 9 of the females were gravid and produced 61 young (25 males, 36 females). Sex ratios of other broods reported in the literature were 6:19 (Richmond 1954b), 3:1 (Cooper 1958), and 8:6 (Pisani 1971).

The species is listed as threatened in Iowa and Kansas, and the subspecies *V. v. pulchra* is protected in Maryland, Virginia, and West Virginia.

REMARKS.   *V. valeriae* was reviewed by Powell et al. (1992).

Elapidae
Elapid Snakes

The approximately 220 species of advanced snakes of the family Elapidae have extremely dangerous neurotoxic venom, and include the coral snakes, cobras, mambas, and sea snakes. The family is well represented in Australia, Southeast Asia, Africa, and South America; only three species live in the United States. Elapids are related to vipers and atractaspids, and probably evolved from colubrids. They differ by having one or more short, permanently erect, hollow (proteroglyphous) fangs near the front of the shortened maxillae that fit into a pocket on the outside of the mandibular gums (Bogert 1943). The venom duct is not attached directly to the fang, but enters a small cavity in the gum above the entrance lumen of the fang. Other shorter teeth may occur behind the fang on the maxillae, and also on the pterygoids, palatines, and dentaries. No teeth are present on the premaxillae. Postfrontal, coronoid, and pelvic bones are absent. The hyoid is Y- or U-shaped, with two superficially placed, parallel arms. The body vertebrae have short, recurved hypapophyses. Only the right lung is present. The spiny hemipenis has a bifurcate centripetal sulcus spermaticus. Dorsally, the head is covered with enlarged plates, but no loreal scale is present. Body scales are usually smooth, and the ventral scutes are well developed only in arboreal and fossorial species. The pupils are round. Reproduction is oviparous or ovoviviparous.

Four subfamilies exist, but only two occur in the United States: the terrestrial Micrurinae with two coral snakes (*Micruroides euryxanthus* and *Micrurus fulvius*) and the marine Hydrophiinae with one sea snake (*Pelamis platurus*).

Key to the Genera of *Elapidae*

1a. Tail oarlike, nostrils not valved, olive dorsally, yellow ventrally . . . . *Pelamis platurus*

1b. Tail not oarlike; nostrils not valved; body pattern of red, yellow (white), and black bands 2

2a. Most of head black, face black to level of angle of lower jaws; first broad body band behind the light collar red; usually one to two teeth on maxilla behind the fang . . . . *Micruroides euryxanthus*

2b. Only front of head black, face black to just behind eyes; first broad body band behind the light collar black; no teeth on maxilla behind the fang . . . . . . *Micrurus fulvius*

Micruroides euryxanthus (Kennicott 1860a) | Sonoran Coral Snake

RECOGNITION. This small (TBL to 66 cm) snake has 11–13 red, yellow (white), and black dorsal bands, its face is black anterior to the level of the angle of the lower jaws, and the first broad body band behind the light collar is red. The yellow nuchal band is four to eight scales wide; other yellow bands are usually three to five scales wide. Red and white (yellow) bands touch, but both the red and black bands are usually broader than the light bands, which may be restricted to only a few scale rows in width in some individuals. The banding extends onto the venter and follows a red-yellow-black-yellow-red pattern (the "tricolor monad" pattern of Savage and Slowinski 1990). The tail has one to two black bands separated by white or yellow. Black pigment usually does not occur in the red bands. The dorsal body scales are smooth and pitless, and lie in 17 anterior rows, 15 rows at midbody, and 15 rows just before the vent. Beneath are 205–245 ventrals, 19–32 subcaudals, and a divided anal plate. Lateral head scales include 2 nasals (the prenasal touches the first supralabial), 1 preocular (touching the postnasal), 2 postoculars, 1 + 2 temporals, 7 supralabials, and 6–7 infralabials. No loreal or subocular scales are present. The mental scale on the lower jaw is separated from the two small chin shields by a pair of infralabial scales. Behind these are several rows

Sonoran coral snake, *Micruroides euryxanthus*. (Photograph by Robert E. Lovich)

Sonoran coral snake, *Micruroides euryxanthus*; Cochise County, Arizona. (Photograph by Steve W. Gotte)

Distribution of *Micruroides euryxanthus*.

of gular scales before the ventrals. The hemipenis is about seven subcaudals long, bifurcate with a divided sulcus spermaticus, approaching a capitate condition with the spines expanded in the distal region, but gradually diminishing in size toward the apex, which bears a small papilla-like projection. A longitudinal naked fold begins at the base and extends almost parallel to the sulcus spermaticus. A few scattered small spinules may also be present up to the zone of larger spines. The fang on the maxilla is followed, after a diastema, by one or two solid teeth.

Males have 9–13 (mean, 11.4) black body bands, and average 222–223 (205–230) ventrals and 26–28 (23–32) subcaudals; females have 9–16 (mean, 12.6) black body bands, and average 231–233 (219–245) ventrals and 24 (19–27) subcaudals.

GEOGRAPHIC VARIATION. Three subspecies are recognized (Roze 1974), but only *M. e. euryxanthus* (Kennicott 1860a), the Arizona coral snake, lives in the United States. It ranges from central Arizona and southwestern New Mexico south to Chihuahua and Sonora, Mexico, and is described above.

CONFUSING SPECIES. For the coral snake, *Micrurus fulvius*, refer to the key above. Harmless red, black, and yellow (white) snakes within its range do not have body bands crossing the venter and usually have pale snouts, and normally the red bands touch the black bands. The shovel-nosed snakes (*Chionactis*) have white bands in contact with red saddlelike blotches, but their snout is not black, and the supralabials are normally light colored.

KARYOTYPE AND FOSSIL RECORD. Unreported.

DISTRIBUTION. *M. euryxanthus* ranges south from central Arizona and southwestern New Mexico into Mexico to Mazatlán and Sinaloa. It is also found on Isla Tiburón.

HABITAT. Living in arid habitats at elevations from sea level to 1,900 m with rocky or gravelly soils, *M. euryxanthus* is most often seen in arroyos or riparian zones, but also inhabits scrub and brushy areas (mesquite), grasslands, rocky hillsides, and even cultivated fields. It sometimes enters buildings, perhaps to escape the heat, and is also known to reside among the roots of termite-infested paloverde and creosote bushes. Its ecological distribution is closely tied to that of slender blindsnakes (*Leptotyphlops*), a major prey, and the coral snakes have been found within the channeled burrow systems of these small snakes (Lowe et al. 1986).

BEHAVIOR. In spite of increased research on snakes within its range in the past 50 years, many aspects of the life history of *M. euryxanthus* are unknown. Its secretive nature makes it difficult to research, and most data are anecdotal. An extensive ecological study is needed.

In Arizona, it is active from March to November and most frequently is seen after the monsoon rains in late June and early July (Lowe et al. 1986). Gates (1956) found one hibernating on 30 November more than a meter below the ground surface. In New Mexico, the annual activity period is April–September, with over 80% of sightings occurring in July–September (Degenhardt et al. 1996). Although sometimes abroad on overcast days after rains, it is mostly crepuscular or nocturnal in the summer. At night, the warm surfaces of roads are often sought out by this small snake, apparently to warm its self. Morning surface activity may be more common in March–May, and again in the fall; but because *M. euryxanthus* is a burrower, it is seldom seen above ground during the day, preferring to remain in some subterranean chamber beneath rocks or logs, or within old stumps. Unfortunately nothing has been reported on its thermal or humidity requirements.

REPRODUCTION. Stebbins (1985) gives 33.0 cm as the TBL of the smallest adult, and the shortest reproductive male and female dissected by Goldberg (1997c) had SVLs of 32.0 and 35.6 cm, respectively. Age at maturity is unknown.

Goldberg (1997c) studied the gametic cycles of both sexes. Males with regressed testes containing spermatogonia and Sertoli cells were found in June and August. No males were in recrudescence. Males undergoing spermiogenesis (metamorphosing spermatids) were present from April through November. Spermiogenic males had mature sperm in the epididymides and vas deferens, so males may be able to reproduce throughout the year. A female contained enlarging eggs on 31 May, and another contained oviductal eggs on 23 June; Funk (1964c) found a female with oviductal eggs on 20 July. Early vitellogenic females were found on 30 May and 13 July. Reproductively inactive females were present on 1 May and 1 June, suggesting that some females may not reproduce each year.

Courtship and mating behaviors have not been described. Mating probably takes place in the spring, but possibly also in the fall. Oviposition seems correlated with the summer rains of July and August (Lowe et al. 1986). The two to six eggs are laid underground, beneath rocks, or in rotting wood. A 41.6 cm female contained two eggs on 27 July that were 34.6 × 6.1 mm and 39.3 × 6.2 mm, respectively (Funk 1964c). Hatching occurs in September (Lowe et al. 1986; Shaw 1971), and the hatchlings have 19.0–20.3 cm TBLs.

GROWTH AND LONGEVITY. Nothing is known of the growth rate of this snake. Rossi and Rossi (1995) reported a captive longevity of over 10 years.

DIET AND FEEDING HABITS. The chief prey is the blindsnake (*Leptotyphlops humilis*) (Lowe et al. 1986; Vitt and Hulse 1973; Woodin 1953). Other wild prey include snakes (*Chilomeniscus cinctus, Chionactis occipitalis, Coluber constrictor, Diadophis punctatus, Gyalopion canum, G. quadrangulare, Phyllorhynchus browni, Sonora semiannulata, Tantilla* sp.) and lizards (*Cnemidophorus*

sp., *Elgaria kingi, Eumeces* sp., *Xantusia vigilis*) (Finnigan, in Rossi and Rossi 1995; Lowe et al. 1992; Roze 1996; Vitt and Hulse 1973). Fowlie (1965) reported that insect larvae are eaten, but there is no proof of this. Captives have eaten the snakes *Chionactis occipitalis, Diadophis punctatus, Hypsiglena torquata, Leptotyphlops dulcis, Rhinocheilus lecontei, Sonora semiannulata,* and *Tantilla planiceps* and the lizards *Anniella pulchra* and *Scincella lateralis* (Gates 1957; Lindner 1962a; Rossi and Rossi 1995; Veer et al. 1997; Vitt and Hulse 1973; Vorhies 1929; Woodin 1953). However, in feeding tests this snake rejected the snakes *Arizona elegans, Phyllorhynchus browni, P. decurtatus, Rhinocheilus lecontei,* and *Thamnophis cyrtopsis* and the lizards *Anniella pulchra, Cnemidophorus tigris, C. velox, Coleonyx variegatus, Sceloporus undulatus, Urosaurus ornatus, Uta stansburiana,* and *Xantusia vigilis* (Vitt and Hulse 1973). *Micruroides* seems to prefer smooth-scaled reptiles to those with keeled scales.

The venom delivery apparatus of *M. euryxanthus* is rather weak (see below), and reptilian prey are not always immediately incapacitated (Lindner 1962a; Lowe 1948b; Vitt and Hulse 1973; Vorhies 1929; Woodin 1953). From 7 to 40 minutes may elapse before the prey is weak enough to be swallowed (Lindner 1962a; Lowe 1948b; Vorhies 1929), and often the prey fights during this period (Veers et al. 1997).

Feeding behavior generally follows a consistent pattern. *M. euryxanthus* first responds to prey with increased tongue flicking, followed by approaching the prey with a series of jerky movements. When close, it touches the prey a number of times with its tongue, and then bites it. Usually, when bitten, the prey tries to crawl away; the coral snake then chews and moves its head toward the prey's head. In most cases envenomation does not take place (judging from the absence of puncture marks and the behavior of the prey after being bitten). *M. euryxanthus* continues to advance by biting until it reaches the anterior end of the prey's head and then begins swallowing. Swallowing is accomplished by a series of chewing motions separated by short rest periods. Once the prey is down, the coral snake seeks shelter where it can digest its food. A feeding on *Leptotyphlops humilis* observed by Vitt and Hulse (1973) took 22 minutes from start to finish. Large prey do not exhibit symptoms of envenomation by the time they are swallowed, but a few *L. humilis* do.

VENOM AND BITES. Eight *M. euryxanthus* 21.5–51.5 cm long that the authors examined had fangs 0.1–1.0 (mean, 0.6) mm long; Bogert reported that four *Micruroides* 40.1–45.6 cm long had fangs of 0.7–1.0 mm. Fang length is positively correlated with body length. The venom is neurotoxic; the maximum yield of dry venom is 6 mg, and the average yield is 0.12 mg (Roze 1996). Lowe (1948b) reported that within two minutes a bitten night lizard *(Xantusia)* showed slight paralysis of its hind limbs. In 3.5 minutes, the hindlimbs were completely paralyzed, and by 3.75 minutes the front legs were nearly completely paralyzed, and the lizard was experiencing involuntary lateral undulatory movements of its body. Death occurred 7.5 minutes after the initial bite.

Its small mouth and short fangs make it difficult for *M. euryxanthus* to penetrate the skin of a human. However, human envenomation has occurred. Russell (1967a) reported three cases, all of which occurred while the victim was handling the snake. Common symptoms included immediate, but not severe, pain at the site of the bite, with the pain persisting from 15 minutes to several hours. Nausea, weakness, and drowsiness occurred several hours later. Parethesia (abnormal sensations) also occurred, but was limited to the finger bitten in one case, and spread to the hand and wrist in the other two. Two victims experienced no symptoms within 7–24 hours of the bite, but symptoms persisted for four days in the third, the one bitten by the largest snake (55 cm). One of the victims was a physician who took detailed notes concerning the bite and its symptoms. He pulled the snake from his finger almost as soon as he was bitten. About 3 hours later there was parethesia involving the finger and hand, followed by progressive deterioration of handwriting ability over a period of about 6 hours, at the end of which his handwriting looked like that of a 5-year-old child. The doctor experienced headache, nausea, difficulty in focusing his eyes, and some slight drooping of the upper eyelids. He possibly also experienced some photophobia and increased lacrimation. Weakness and drowsiness occurred, and his memory was vague when he tried to remember the incident. There was no change in heart rate and no difficulty breathing. Roze (1996) reported the lethal human dose of dry venom to be 6–8 mg. This small snake has very potent venom and should be considered dangerous, especially to children.

PREDATORS AND DEFENSE. Few cases of predation have been recorded; however, due to its small size it probably is at least occasionally the victim of carnivorous mammals (skunks, badgers, foxes, coyotes, raccoons), kestrels, hawks, owls, roadrunners, and ophiophagous snakes *(Lampropeltis, Masticophis),* and possibly also tarantulas. It is cannibalized by its own species (Lowe et al. 1986), and some die on our highways each year (Rosen and Lowe 1994).

This species is rather shy and gentle if not severely disturbed. If startled, it may coil, tuck its head under its body, and elevate its tail, coil it so that the ventral surface faces toward the disturbance, and move it about. The moving, banded tail may draw predators away from the tucked-under head in a decoying behavior; Vitt and Hulse (1973) found that three (14%) of the snakes they studied had scars on the tail, possibly indicating a predatory attack there. *M. euryxanthus* will also discharge air and fecal matter from the cloaca, producing a rather consistent, moderately loud sound of low amplitude (50.0–53.5 dB), limited frequency range (422–5523 Hz), and distinct temporal patterning and harmonics (Bogert 1960; Young et al. 1999). Air is apparently drawn into the cloaca through the vent and then expelled through the vent; the popping is driven primarily by the m. sphinctor cloacae but may involve other extrinsic muscles. The sound lasts about 0.2 seconds and is repeated every 0.3–0.5 seconds. If neither of the above defensive behaviors wards off a predator, and the snake is touched or the predator comes very close, it will strike quickly and viciously in a side-sweeping motion, and if the mouth makes contact, it will bite and continue to chew for some time.

POPULATIONS. While *M. euryxanthus* seems rare, this is probably due more to its secretive habits than to actual scarcity. It may even prove to be common in some areas.

REMARKS. This is the northernmost of the coral snakes in western and tropical America. Due to this distribution and several characters considered primitive elapid features (such as additional solid teeth behind the fang on the maxilla), it has usually been thought to be close to the origins of coral snake evolution (Schmidt 1928; Bogert 1943). Immunological assessment of serum albumins by Cadle and Sarich (1981) shows that *M. euryxanthus* and *Micrurus fulvius* are close allies with other elapids instead of derivatives of South American colubrids, and that a late Oligocene–early Miocene separation between the New World and Old World elapid lineages may have occurred. Further studies based on allozymic and morphological characters show the two North American coral snakes not closely related even though they occur together at the northern extent of the range of American coral snakes (Slowinski 1995), with *Micruroides* more closely related to Asian kraits *(Bungarus)* and *M. fulvius* most closely related to several tropical species of *Micrurus*.

M. euryxanthus may participate in a mimicry complex with other coral snakes and red-, yellow-, and black-banded colubrids (see *Micrurus fulvius*). The species was reviewed by Roze (1974, 1996).

Micrurus fulvius (Linnaeus 1766) | North American Coral Snake

RECOGNITION. This black-snouted, red-, yellow-, and black-banded snake (TBL to 121.3 cm) has the red and yellow bands adjacent to each other, a banding pattern that is termed "tricolor monad" (Savage and Slowinski 1990). Black body bands total 13–25, those on the tail 3–7; 12–24 red bands cross the body. The bands continue onto the venter, and some black pigment may be present in the red bands. A bright yellow band crosses the occiput, separating the black neck band from the parietal scales. Body scales are smooth and pitless, and lie in 15 rows throughout. The venter has 180–237 ventrals, 26–59 subcaudals, and a divided (occasionally single) anal plate. Lateral head scales are 2 nasals, a preocular, 2 postoculars, 1 + 1 (2) temporals, 7 supralabials, and 7 infralabials; there are no loreal or subocular scales. On the lower jaw, the mental does not touch the chin shields. The posterior pair of chin shields is the largest. The bifurcate hemipenis has a forked sulcus spermaticus extending from its base to nearly the apex of each fork; each forks tapers gradually toward the apex and ends in a spinelike papilla. The organ is naked at the base, after which small spines and scattered spinules cover it up to the sulcus fork. Each lobe has large spines that shorten toward the apex. The lip of the sulcus is naked for its en-

Eastern coral snake, *Micrurus fulvius fulvius*; Georgia. (Photograph by Carl H. Ernst)

Texas coral snake, *Micrurus fulvius tenor*. (Photograph by R. D. Bartlett)

tire length, but is covered on both sides with small spines. A large longitudinal naked fold begins almost at the base of the organ and runs approximately parallel to the sulcus, ending shortly before the bifurcation where the large spines begin. The fang is the only tooth on the maxilla.

Males have 180–217 ventrals, 36–59 pairs of subcaudals, 11–17 (mean, 13.7) black body bands, 3–5 (usually 4) black tail bands, and TLs averaging 13.8% of TBL; females have 205–237 ventrals, 26–38 pairs of subcaudals, 12–19 (mean, 14.8) black body bands, 3–4 (mean, 3.2) black tail bands, and TLs averaging 9.3% of TBL. Males lack keels on the body scales anterior to and above the anal plate.

GEOGRAPHIC VARIATION. Five subspecies are recognized (Roze and Tilger 1983), but only two occur in the United States. *M. f. fulvius* (Linnaeus 1766), the eastern North American coral snake, occurs east of the Mississippi River from southeastern North Carolina southward through peninsular Florida, and westward to southeastern Louisiana. Its red body bands have either no black pigment or only small black spots or black tips on the scales (often the black pigment concentrates to form a pair of large dorsal spots), and the black neckband does not touch the parietal. *M. f. tener* (Baird and Girard 1853), the Texas coral snake, ranges from southwestern Arkansas and northern and central Louisiana southwestward through Texas to Coahuila, Nuevo Leon, and central Tamaulipas. Black pigment in its red bands is widely scattered, and the black neckband touches the parietal scales. Because of its apparent allopatry (Conant and Collins 1998; Roze and Tilger 1983), Collins (1991) has suggested that *M. f. tener* be designated a separate species, but this has not been widely accepted.

Coral snakes from southern Florida were formerly designated *M. f. barbouri* on the basis of a few specimens lacking black spots on their red bands (Schmidt 1928). Subsequently, Duellman and Schwartz (1958) reported that many southern Florida *M. fulvius* have black spotting on their red bands and that Schmidt's designation was invalid.

CONFUSING SPECIES. For the Sonoran coral snake *(Micruroides euryxanthus)*, see the above key. The scarlet snake *(Cemophora coccinea)* and several subspecies

of the milksnake *(Lampropeltis triangulum)* have a similar red, yellow, and black pattern, but their red and yellow bands are separated by black bands, and their snouts are red instead of black. Also, the scarlet snake has no bands crossing its venter. The long-nosed snake *(Rhinocheileus lecontei)* has reddish dorsal saddles instead of bands, a whitish venter with some dark speckles along the sides, and a single row of subcaudals.

KARYOTYPE. The karyotype consists of 32 chromosomes (16 macrochromosomes and 16 microchromosomes); the sixth pair is heteromorphic (ZW) in females and ZZ in males (Graham 1977).

FOSSIL RECORD. Pleistocene fossils have been found at an Irvingtonian site in Citrus County, Florida (Meylan 1982), and in Rancholabrean deposits in Alachua, Citrus, Indian River, Levy, and Marion counties, Florida (Auffenberg 1963; Gut and Ray 1963; Holman 1958b, 1959a, 1959b, 1996; Martin 1974; Weigel 1962), and Kendall and Travis counties, Texas (Hill 1971; Holman 1969a).

DISTRIBUTION. *M. fulvius* ranges from southeastern North Carolina southward, mostly on the coastal plain, through Florida, and west through central and southern Georgia, Alabama, and southern Mississippi to southeastern Louisiana. A gap occurs in south-central Louisiana, but the species is again found from central and northern Louisiana and southwestern Arkansas southwestward through southern Texas, and southward in Mexico, through eastern Coahuila, northeastern Nuevo León and Tamaulipas to San Luis Potosí, eastern Guanajuato, Querétaro, and Hidalgo.

HABITAT. As long as the habitat is dry, hiding places are available, and prey are present, *M. fulvius* will do well. In Florida, it seems to prefer woods or brushy areas (rosemary scrub), seasonally flooded pine flatwoods, and xerophytic and mesophytic oak-hardwood hammocks, but can also be found in a variety of other dry, open areas (Neill 1957; Jackson and Franz 1981; Tennant 1997). Occasionally it is seen along the edges of marshes, but wet habitats are generally avoided. Much time is spent buried in the sandy soil, leaf litter, logs, or stumps, and it may also hide in gopher tortoise burrows where the two reptiles are sympatric.

Distribution of *Micrurus fulvius*.

Farther west in western Louisiana and Texas, this species lives in dry semiopen habitats, such as mixed pine woods, oak-juniper brakes, thorn brush, and grasslands, with soils ranging from sand to clay or loam, and with rock crevices, flat rocks, logs, stumps, or thick plant litter where they can hide. Mammal burrows are also used for retreats.

BEHAVIOR.   Florida *M. fulvius* are probably active in every month, but least active during December–February. It has a distinct bimodal annual activity pattern, with more activity from March through May and August through November (Jackson and Franz 1981). North of Florida, it may be forced to hibernate during the winter. However, during years with warm spells in winter, it may be active then also; active North Carolina coral snakes have been found in all months but December (Palmer and Braswell 1995). In south-central Texas, adults are most active in March–May, but are observed throughout the summer and into the fall (Vermersch and Kuntz 1986).

Observations show that *M. fulvius* is most active during the day, and is most often seen on bright, sunny mornings, but occasionally it also prowls in the late afternoon or early evening. Neill (1957) reported that only one of 121 active *M. fulvius* was taken at night. Foraging is done in the early morning during April–August in Florida; it is surface active from 0700 to 0900 hours, remains under cover for much of the day, and resumes activity during the late afternoon, 1600–1730 hours (Jackson and Franz 1981). In March

and again in September–November, it appears in mid- or late morning (0900–1000 hours), and with the exception of a midafternoon quiescent period (1330–1600 hours), remains active most of the day. Vermersch and Kuntz (1986) reported that in south-central Texas its daily activities do not follow a strict schedule, but that most are found on cloudy days or in the early morning, early evening, or at night. In Mexico the species seems to be mostly crepuscular or nocturnal, but it is also active in the early morning on overcast days (Campbell and Lamar 1989). No temperature or movement data are available.

REPRODUCTION.   Females mature at a SVL of about 50–55 cm (Ford et al. 1990; Quinn 1979b; Jackson and Franz 1981). According to Roze (1996), *M. f. fulvius* matures in 11–16 months, and *M. f. tener* in 12–21 months. Ovary weights of Texas coral snakes increase in March–April, decline slightly in May, and then decline more rapidly in June; follicle lengths show the same pattern (Quinn 1979b). In Florida, vitellogenesis occurs in late winter and March–May, with follicles reaching preovulatory size by early June (Jackson and Franz 1981).

The smallest male *M. f. tener* undergoing spermiogenesis found by Quinn (1979b) was 40.2 cm SVL, and most with 45 cm SVLs or longer are mature (Jackson and Franz 1981). This size is reached in 11–21 months. In Texas, the testes undergo regression with spermatogonia and Sertoli cells in May through August, reaching a peak in June. Early recrudescence with spermatogonial divisions and primary spermatocytes occurs from June through October, and peaks in July. During August–September, males have late recrudescence with secondary spermatocytes and undifferentiated spermatids. Spermiogenesis producing mature sperm takes place in August–April. Seminiferous tubule diameter is greatest from November to March, and testes weigh the most in December–February. Sperm resides in the vas deferens from February through December, and in the epididymis from April through December (Quinn 1979b). The male sexual cycle is essentially the same in Florida (Jackson and Franz 1981).

Mating occurs in April–May, and possibly also in late August–early October. During courtship the male flicks his tongue several times over the female's midback, then raises his head and neck at about a 45° angle, tilts his head down to touch his nose to her back, and quickly and smoothly runs his nose along her back to about 5 cm behind her head (according to Quinn, 1979b, 60% of the time the male moves along the female's back from rear to front; when he moves from front to back he reverses himself when the area of the female's vent is reached). He usually does not tongue flick during this advance, but aligns his body over hers. His body anterior to the vent is positioned on the female's back, and immediately posterior to the vent his tail is elevated and wrapped under and around that of the female. She responds by slightly elevating her tail and gaping her cloaca; intromission soon follows (Quinn 1979b; Vaeth 1984; Zegel 1975).

The eggs are laid during May–July. Tryon and McCrystal (1982) reported a GP of 37 days. Clutches contain 1–13 (mean, 6.5; n = 19) eggs; 4–7 eggs are most common. The eggs are white, adherent, and very elongate—20.0–46.0 (mean, 32.5) × 6.0–14.1 (mean, 12.4) mm—and weigh 3–6 (mean, 4.5) g. Clutches are normally laid underground or beneath leaf litter; the authors found 4 eggs in a hollow depression beneath an old wooden tie on an abandoned railroad embankment in Collier County, Florida.

Neonates appear in August–September after an IP of about 45–92 (mean, 60.8) days, depending on the IT; they have 16.5–23.0 (mean, 19.1) cm TBLs.

GROWTH AND LONGEVITY. *M. fulvius* may double its size in less than two years, and by three years is nearly 60 cm SVL (Quinn 1979b; Jackson and Franz 1981). A female *M. f. tener*, of unknown age when captured, survived 18 years, 3 months, and 30 days at the Fort Worth Zoo (Snider and Bowler 1992).

DIET AND FEEDING HABITS. Wild *M. fulvius* prey almost exclusively on reptiles: amphisbaenids (*Rhineura floridana*), lizards (*Cnemidophorus gularis, Eumeces fasciatus, E. inexpectatus, E. tetragrammus, Ophisaurus attenuatus, O. ventralis, Neoseps reynoldsi, Sceloporus undulatus, Scincella lateralis*), and snakes (*Agkistrodon contortrix, Arizona elegans, Carphophis amoenus, Cemophora coccinea, Coluber constrictor, Diadophis punctatus, Elaphe guttata, E. obsoleta, Farancia abacura, Ficimia olivacea, Lampropeltis calligaster, L. getula, Leptotyphlops dulcis, Micrurus fulvius, Opheodrys aestivis, Salvadora grahamiae, Seminatrix pygaea, Sonora semiannulata, Stilosoma extenuatum, Storeria dekayi, S. occipitomaculata, Tantilla coronata, T. cucullata, T. gracilis, T. nigriceps, T. planiceps, T. relicta, Thamnophis cyrtopsis, T. marcianus, T. proximus, Tropidoclonion lineatum, Tropidodipsas sartori, Virginia striatula, V. valeriae*) (Chance 1970; Clark 1949; Curtis 1952; Greene 1984; Heinrich 1996; Hurter 1911; Jackson and Franz 1981; Kennedy 1964; Klauber 1946a; Loveridge 1938, 1944; Minton 1949b; Obrecht 1946; Palmer and Braswell 1995; Reams et al. 1999; Roze 1996; Ruick 1948; Schmidt 1932; Vermersch and Kuntz 1986). Anurans and rodents are rarely eaten (Greene 1984). Captives may consume 1.7–3.1 g of food per week (Kirkwood and Gili 1994).

Although these snakes may feed nearly year round in Florida, feeding activity is most intense in September–November, with a lesser peak in April–May (Jackson and Franz 1981). While foraging, *M. fulvius* usually crawls slowly and pokes or probes beneath leaf litter with its head in a stereotyped manner involving repeated forward and lateral head movements, accompanied by frequent tongue-flick clusters (Greene 1984). Both visual and chemical stimuli elicit attacks. Rapid prey movements seem to bring on a quicker attack by the coral snake and sometimes override aversive chemical cues. Approach is slow if the prey is stationary or moving slowly, but rapid if the prey is moving quickly away. Prey are usually seized with a quick forward movement of the anterior or entire body of the coral snake, but may occasionally be seized with a quick lateral jerk of the head and neck.

M. fulvius does not have an efficient strike, and Greene (1984) thought this might be due to poor vision since it has relatively small eyes. It typically holds a prey, sometimes chewing it, until the prey is immobilized by the venom.

The prey is not usually released before it is swallowed, and is almost always ingested head first. Preingestion maneuvers suggest that chemical and/or tactile cues, such as scale overlap, are used to recognize the head end of the prey (Greene 1976).

M. fulvius is opportunistic, taking whatever suitable prey crosses its path when it is hungry. However, the skinks *(Eumeces, Neoseps, Scincella)* and the smaller snakes it eats may not be cost-effective in the amount of energy gained compared with that needed to find, attack, and swallow them (Greene 1984).

VENOM AND BITES. The fangs are relatively short; those of individuals with TBLs of 27–88 cm that the authors measured were only 0.6–2.7 mm in length; adults (65–88 cm) had fangs 1.6–2.7 mm long. Bogert (1943) reported three 70.0–81.7 cm *M. fulvius* had 2.1–2.5 mm fangs.

Reported venom yields for *M. fulvius* vary. Roze (1996) reported the venom glands hold as much as 38 mg of dry venom and that the average yield is 10–12 mg; Fix and Minton (1976) also reported dry yields of 6–12 mg. Ernst and Zug (1996) reported the normal wet yield as only 3–5 mg. A positive correlation occurs, with larger snakes giving greater venom yields.

Venom of the North American coral snake attacks the nervous system, primarily the respiratory center, resulting in loss of muscle strength, difficulty in breathing, and in extreme cases, death. The main toxins in elapid venoms are post- and presynaptic neurotoxins and cardiotoxins, and in *M. fulvius* phospholipase A$_2$ with myonecrotic or cardiotoxin-like properties is an important toxic component (Brazil 1987; Roze 1996). Pain, sometimes severe, usually occurs at the bite site, and if the bite is on a limb, may slowly extend up that extremity. The LD$_{50}$ for a 16–20 g mouse ranges from 9 to 26 μg, and the lethal amount for a human is 4–7 mg (Bolaños et al. 1978; Minton and Minton 1969; Roze 1996).

M. fulvius can deliver serious, sometimes fatal, bites (Clark 1949; Neill 1957; Parrish and Kahn 1967; Stejneger 1898; Stimson and Engelhardt 1960; Werler and

Darling 1950). Fortunately, the percentage of human fatalities (about 20%) is not extremely high, especially if the bite is treated with antivenin (Neill 1957). Because *M. fulvius* has relatively short fangs, the chance of a human receiving a bite in the wild when not handling one is slim. Nevertheless, Carr (1940) has reported instances of large *M. fulvius* actually striking, but such behavior must be rare, and heavy shoes or boots and thick trousers should be sufficient protection for the hiker.

PREDATORS AND DEFENSE. Known predators of *M. fulvius* are hawks and kestrels *(Buteo jamaicensis, B. lineatus, Falco sparverius),* loggerhead shrikes *(Lanius ludoviscianus),* snakes *(Drymarchon corais, Lampropeltis getula, Micrurus fulvius),* bullfrogs *(Rana catesbeiana),* and domestic cats *(Felis catus)* (Belson 2000; Brugger 1989; Chance 1970; Clark 1949; Curtis 1952; Jackson and Franz 1981; Loveridge 1938, 1944; Minton 1949; Roze 1996). That it preys on smaller individuals of its own species is not surprising, as they are found in the same microhabitat, and *M. fulvius* is apparently immune to the venom of its own species (Peterson 1990). The imported fire ant *(Solenopsis invicta)* may prey upon the eggs and young of *M. fulvius*, and at least in Alabama, the population of coral snakes has declined since its introduction (Mount 1981).

Would-be predators of this snake do not always fare so well. Brugger (1989) observed an adult male red-tailed hawk die with a partially eaten, at least 80 cm, *M. fulvius* in its talons. The bird died of flaccid paralysis typical of the neurotoxic effects of elapid venoms and had 15 punctures (presumably by fangs) on its body.

When approached, *M. fulvius* will often flatten the posterior portion of the body, tuck its head under an anterior coil, ball up its tail and wave it about, thus drawing the predator's attention away from the head; Gehlbach (1972) demonstrated that this behavior will deter some potential mammalian predators. When pinned down, however, *M. fulvius* will strike and chew on the restraining implement. These strikes are usually sidewise, rapid, and often vicious, but not always entirely lateral. While photographing a wild *M. fulvius* at close range, C. Ernst narrowly escaped being bitten during a lateral and upward strike that just missed the hand holding the camera.

POPULATIONS. Being a secretive burrower, *M. ful-vius* is not readily observable (the species constituted only 22 of 1,782 snakes collected or observed at the Everglades National Park, Florida, from 1984 through 1986 by Dalrymple et al. [1991]), and can live in urban areas without being detected. This gives a false impression of rarity, when it is common. For instance, Beck (in Shaw 1971) reported that in a 39 month period 1,958 *M. fulvius* were turned in for bounties in Pinellas County, Florida. Tennant (1997) thought *M. fulvius* to be common in Florida and very common in Texas.

Roze (1996) reported the male to female ratio of hatchlings in two clutches was 2.33:1.00.

The most serious threats to populations of *M. ful-vius* are habitat destruction and motorized vehicles.

REMARKS. The question of whether or not coral snakes and other red-, yellow-, and black-banded snakes form a mimicry complex has long been debated. One view is that coral snake patterns are primarily aposematic (Gehlbach 1972; Hecht and Marien 1956; Mertens 1956b, 1957; Pough 1988), particularly since there is an absence of countershading with the continuation of the dorsal bands onto the venter. Also, the patterns may be cryptic, presenting a visual illusion of disruption as the snake crawls. Greene and Pyburn (1973) thought it perfectly feasible that coral snake patterns could be aposematic, cryptic, and mimic at the same time.

Grobman (1978) suggested that similar color patterns have arisen independently of natural selection in unrelated sympatric species occupying similar habitats (pseudomimicry), while Wickler (1968) suggested that the dangerously venomous coral snakes are the mimics of mildly venomous colubrid snakes, not the models for these species. In summaries of the debate, Greene and McDiarmid (1981) and Pough (1988) concluded that field observations and experimental evidence refute previous objections to the coral snake serving as the Batesian model in the mimicry hypothesis, and the coral snake's bright colors serve as a warning signal to predators. Smith (1975) showed that the naive young of some tropical reptile-eating birds instinctively avoid the red-yellow-black–banded pattern of coral snakes. Hallwachs and Janzen (in Pough 1988) reported that in Costa Rica scavengers (mostly birds) that quickly consume road-killed snakes of other species typically leave dead coral snakes alone. Similarly colored and patterned harmless snakes *(Cemophora coccinea, Lampropeltis triangulum, L. pyromelana)* or mildly venomous snakes would also gain protection by their resemblance to the coral snakes.

To learn whether the tricolor coral snake's banded pattern functions aposematically, Brodie (1993b) exposed plasticine replicas of snakes to free-ranging avian predators at La Selva Biological Station in Costa Rica. The number of attacks on unmarked brown replicas was greater than that on the coral snake replicas; this was true whether replicas were placed on natural or plain white backgrounds, suggesting that the coral snake's banded patterns function aposematically. In a separate experiment, replicas representing all six patterns of proposed coral snake mimics at the study site were attacked less often than unmarked brown replicas, although some of the banded patterns were attacked significantly more often than others. Brodie interpreted these results as direct evidence that the coral snake's banded patterns are avoided by free-ranging avian predators, supporting theoretical predictions that deadly models protect a wide range of imprecise mimics. Beckers et al. (1996) questioned whether predator behavior towards wooden or plasticine models is representative of behavior towards snakes. To investigate this question they tested the responses of temporarily caged, wild coatis *(Nasua narica),* captured in an undisturbed Costa Rican rainforest reserve, to two venomous brightly colored coral snake species, two non- or mildly venomous "mimic" species, one venomous cryptic species, and six non- or mildly venomous cryptic snake species. Responses ranged from avoidance to predation, but the coatis did not avoid any of the coral snakes or "mimics," and in one case a coral snake was even attacked. Beckers et al. (1996) concluded that results of studies using abstract snake models should not be unconditionally regarded as convincing evidence that supports the hypotheses of aposematic coloration and mimicry among coral snakes.

Past objections to the mimicry theory have been based largely on the supposition that once bitten by a coral snake a predator will die from the bite; however, the apparent poor vision and poorly developed venom delivery system of coral snakes precludes that every bite will be fatal. It has also been supposed that coral snakes are nocturnal and that their bright colors would be meaningless at night, but reports by Neill (1957), Jackson and Franz (1981), and Greene and McDiarmid (1981) have shown *Micrurus fulvius* to be largely diurnal.

Studies of concordant geographic pattern variation by Greene and McDiarmid (1981) strongly suggest that some colubrid species of *Atractus, Erythrolamprus, Lampropeltis,* and *Pliocerus* are involved in mimicry systems with local coral snakes. Savage and Slowinski (1992) presented a detailed classification of all coral snake color patterns and surveyed the taxonomic distribution of these patterns for mimics and the 56 species of highly venomous coral snakes. They favored the explanation that Batesian mimicry is involved (with the venomous coral snakes being the models and the other forms the mimics) and thought that as many as 115 species of harmless or mildly toxic species, representing nearly 18% of all American snakes, may be regarded as coral snake mimics. They concluded that a number of species in the genera *Elaphe, Farancia, Nerodia,* and *Thamnophis,* although they have red pigment, should not be included among the coral snake mimics.

Parent birds may respond to the sight of a nearby snake by actions that will reveal the location of their nest. If bright, ringed snake patterns elicit this behavior more than do cryptic patterns, then ringed snakes that eat eggs or nestling birds should have a hunting advantage over cryptic snakes. Smith and Mostrom (1985) examined this theory in field tests with American robins *(Turdus migratorius)* and a red-, yellow-, and black-ringed coral snake model. The model elicited no more response than did a plain brown snake model. So, based on current evidence, the most likely advantage of bright, ringed patterns to snakes is to confer protection against predators, either by camouflage or as warning coloration in mimicry systems.

Coral snakes appear to exhibit near infrared reflectance that renders the snake extremely visible against a leaf litter substrate (Krempels 1984), and this may advertise a warning to potential avian predators.

Micrurus fulvius has been reviewed by Roze (1996) and Roze and Tilger (1983).

Pelamis platurus (Linnaeus 1766) | Yellow-bellied Sea Snake

RECOGNITION. The maximum TBL is 114.3 cm, but most *P. platurus,* are shorter than 80 cm. It is the only snake in the United States with a broad, oarlike tail that is flattened from side to side. Other distinguishing characters are its sharply demarcated two-toned body coloration (dark back, yellow belly), and dorsally placed, valved nostrils. The dark dorsal body coloring is black, olive, olive brown, or brown, and the venter is yellow, cream, or pale brown. The most common pigment pattern in the eastern Pacific population is a tricolored black-yellow-brown (or olive-yellow-brown) pattern, followed by a bicolored black-yellow (or olive-yellow) pattern (Tu 1976). A rare unicolor yellow phase occurs in less than 1% of the population (Tu 1976), but in 3% of the snakes at Golfo de Dulce, Costa Rica (Kropach 1971b). Body pigmentation tends to be in the form of broad longitudinal stripes, but some individuals have undulating stripes, bars or spots. The laterally compressed tail has a variable pattern of dark and light reticulations or occasionally large spots. The nonoverlapping body scales are smooth and pitless, and lie in 39–47 anterior rows, 44–67 midbody rows, and 33–46 posterior rows. On the venter are 260–465 ventrals (with no apparent sexual dimorphism) that are divided by a midventral groove and are almost as small as the dorsal body scales, 39–66 subcaudals, and a divided anal plate. The head is angular, narrowing considerably in front of the eyes, except in entirely yellow individuals, where it is two toned, dark on top and light beneath. Dorsal head scales are enlarged, laterally the head scales consist of 1 (2) preocular(s), 1–2 suboculars, 2 (3) postoculars, 2–3 + 2–3 + 3–4 temporals, 8–10 (7–11) supralabials, and 10–13 infralabials. No loreal scale is present. On the chin, the mental scale is small and ungrooved, and separates the first infralabials on each side. Other chin

Yellow-bellied sea snake, *Pelamis platurus*; Playa de Coco, Costa Rica. (Photograph by John H. Tashjian, Dallas Zoo)

shields are relatively small. The short tongue is barely capable of protruding from the mouth. The narrow hemipenis is feebly bilobed, with the sulcus spermaticus forked near the tip, the lips of the sulcus prominent and fleshy (but not spiny), and small spines over most of its length, but papillate at the apex. Each maxilla has the anterior fang followed by a diastema separating it from 8–9 (5–10) solid posterior teeth.

The shorter adult males (mean SVL, 45.2 cm; Kropach 1975) have TLs 12–13 (mean, 12.1) % of TBL, and ventrals with longer tubercles; the longer females (mean SVL, 48.1 cm; Kropach 1975) have TLs 10–12 (mean, 11.4) % of TBL, and ventrals with

Distribution of *Pelamis platurus*.

shorter tubercles. Unfortunately, these characters are insufficient by themselves for sex identification.

GEOGRAPHICAL VARIATION.   Unknown.

CONFUSING SPECIES.   Only sea snakes have such a broadly flattened tail, and no other species of these snakes is established along the Pacific Coast of the Americas.

KARYOTYPE.   Thirty-eight chromosomes are present, with 20 macrochromosomes (pairs one and two are metacentric, pair three is subtelocentric, and pairs four through nine have the centromere in a terminal position) and 18 microchromosomes. Females are ZW, males ZZ (Gutiérrez and Bolaños 1980).

FOSSIL RECORD.   Unknown.

DISTRIBUTION.   *P. platurus* is the most widely distributed sea snake. Mostly restricted to tropical and subtropical warm oceans, it is found in the Indian and Pacific oceans from eastern Africa, Madagascar, Arabia, and India, throughout coastal southeastern Asia, Indonesia, Japan, Australia, New Zealand, and the Pacific islands to the western coast of the Americas from Ecuador and the Galapagos Islands north to Baja California and the Gulf of California. It is the only sea snake occurring off the Hawaiian Islands, and is particularly common during El Niño years (McKeown 1996). Waifs have also been collected at San Clemente, Orange County, California (Pickwell et al. 1983), and Los Angeles Bay (Shaw 1961), and seen in the San Diego area (Stebbins 1985). The California records also probably coincide with El Niño years.

HABITAT.   Being totally marine, *P. platurus* does not enter predominately freshwater bays or rivers. It is usually considered a pelagic species, but in the Pacific Ocean off Central America it is most often found within a few kilometers of the coast, and seems to prefer the more shallow inshore waters with WTs of 22–30°C. There it spends most of the time drifting at the surface (rough water will cause it to dive; Tu 1976), often in large numbers among the flotsam in surface slicks formed at the interface of two currents. Such habitats probably provide good foraging.

BEHAVIOR. *P. platurus* occur from early February through November in the Galapagos Islands (Reynolds and Pickwell 1984) and December–June off the Pacific Coast of Colombia (Alvarez-León and Hernández-Camacho 1998), but farther north in Panamanian and Costa Rican waters they are present year round, with greater numbers during the drier months. Seventy-nine percent of the 635 juvenile and adult *Pelamis* collected by Vallarino and Weldon (1996) off Panama were taken in July and September–December between 0700 and 1300 hours on days with similar tides and favorable weather conditions. Activity between 1930 and 2400 hours has been recorded at Bahia Honda, Panama, where Myers (1945) collected individuals 22–31 cm long, and probably juveniles. The snakes swam leisurely upwards towards the surface, raised their heads above the water and floated upward until nearly horizontal while breathing, and then slowly swam downwards toward the bottom; none seemed interested in feeding. Myers (1945) suspected *Pelamis* is a diurnal feeder that spends the night on the bottom, occasionally rising to the surface to breathe. This has been corroborated by Tu (1976), who collected 3,077 *Pelamis* (from 14 January to 3 February) between 0700 and 1300 hours, but none from 1500 to 1800 hours. Perhaps surface waters become too warm at that time, or the snake's fish prey are less active. Surfacing depends on the condition of the surface water; fewer snakes are seen during periods of rough water (Tu 1976; Rubinoff et al. 1986).

Pelamis may dive to 6.8 m in the dry season and to 15.1 m during the wet season (Rubinoff et al. 1986). Before diving deep (to 152 m; Pinney 1994), *Pelamis* overinflates its lung, possibly to as much as 20% of body volume (Graham et al. 1975; Priede 1990). The dive is accomplished in several phases: gradually descending at about 5 m/minute (it must swim vigorously to overcome the positive buoyancy of the lung), and later gradually ascending. Ascension may account for about 82% of the total underwater period of each dive, and reflects when the snakes, according to Boyle's Law, compensate for buoyancy lost because of the decline in lung volume. As the lung O_2 is used, the resulting CO_2 passes out through the skin rather than through the lung. An intracardiac blood shunt also exists that assures management of lung O_2 reserves in a manner that augments cutaneous breathing and es-

tablishes favorable transcutaneous diffusion gradients that help the removal of built-up blood N_2 (to avert the "bends") and the uptake of O_2 (Graham et al. 1987).

Subsurface swimming is slower than surface swimming; the snakes usually elevate the tail until the rear of the body is nearly vertical (the first descent phase) (Graham et al. 1987). Undulatory movements involve torsional and rolling motions of the body that, through changes in the curve of the tail keel and body, contribute thrust. A second descent phase involves a more bouncy descent, as the snake bobs at a rate of 1.7 m/minute until reaching a depth where there is no tendency to either sink or rise. The third descent phase is a gradual descent at about 0.11 m/minute, but during phase four the snake descends more rapidly, at about 3–4 m/minute (Graham et al. 1987; Priede 1990).

Pelamis can remain underwater for long periods; Rubinoff et al. (1986) reported a maximum voluntary submergence time of 213 minutes, but of 202 complete dive cycles observed, only 19 (9.4%) exceeded 90 minutes. A diving *Pelamis* avoids anaerobiosis by reducing its metabolic rate, increasing the rate of cutaneous O_2 uptake, or both. Its blood O_2 capacity (the average volume of O_2 that can be held as a percent of blood volume) is high (10.2%), but changes in accord with BT (Pough and Lillywhite 1984), increasing as BT rises from 10 to 20°C, but dropping if BT rises more. However, BT normally varies little during a 24 hour period.

Cutaneous breathing is one of the main physiological adaptations of *Pelamis*; it can remove O_2 from water at rates up to 33% of total standard O_2 uptake, and can diffuse CO_2 to the water at rates up to 94% of standard O_2 consumption (Graham 1974a). As much O_2 as 18 ml/g of body weight can be absorbed through the skin (Heatwole 1987).

Another serious problem is osmoregulation, balancing of the body's salt and water content with that of the ocean. The snake's kidney cannot excrete higher concentrations of Na^+ than are naturally found in its blood; its urine is always hypoosmotic to the blood plasma. Therefore, additional structures must supplement the kidneys to prevent excess Na^+ building up in the body fluids. No discrete salt removal gland has been found in *Pelamis* (Schmidt-Nielsen and

Fange 1958; Taub and Dunson 1976), but serial sections of the head confirm its presence (Burns and Pickwell 1972). Also, mucoid cell types are absent from the labial glands of *Pelamis*, so these may not help secrete Na$^+$. This snake may lack the above glands, but it does have a good posterior salt gland beneath its tongue (sublingual) that excretes a fluid with a higher NaCl content than seawater into the mouth for expulsion (Dunson 1971; Dunson et al. 1971). *Pelamis*'s skin is permeable to water but not to Na$^+$, so it exchanges little Na$^+$ with seawater (Dunson and Robinson 1976). Influx and efflux of Na$^+$ are balanced, but water is not, and there is a net loss of water amounting to about 0.4% body weight per day that occurs primarily through the skin. So, its major osmotic problem in seawater is water balance, not salt balance (Dunson and Robinson 1976; Dunson and Stokes 1983).

Pelamis latitudinal distribution in the eastern Pacific Ocean lies between the northern and southern 18°C surface isotherms, and its CT$_{max}$ and CT$_{min}$ are 36 and 11.7°C, respectively (Graham et al. 1971). With rapid cooling this snake will stop feeding at 16–18°C; but it has a high resistance to cold and can withstand 5°C for about an hour. In laboratory tests, it does not acclimate and cannot survive long in 17°C water (Graham et al. 1971). It generally avoids surface WTs cooler than 19°C (Rubinoff et al. 1986). BTs of individuals caught in Pacific surface waters have been 26.9–31.0°C (Dunson and Ehlert 1971; Hecht et al. 1974). Feeding is slowed at 26°C, and effectively stopped at 23°C (Hecht et al. 1974). Brattstrom (1965) gave the BT of *Pelamis* as 24.9°C (AT, 25°C). Pickwell et al. (1983) found one dying on a southern California beach after the WT had dropped to 16°C; *Pelamis* loses efficient motor control of its swimming and floating at this WT, but slowly acclimated individuals can survive for at least a week at 33–35°C (Hecht et al. 1974). The optimal BT range seems to be 28–32°C.

BT is mostly determined by the surrounding water, but Graham (1974b) reported that the snake's dark dorsal body surface absorbs solar radiation to consistently elevate BT slightly above WT when it is at the surface in a calm sea. However, there is no solid evidence that *Pelamis* moves up or down the water column to thermoregulate, and Graham's laboratory experiments indicate it neither seeks nor avoids heat when given thermal choices.

Surface swimming is by sideward undulations aided by the laterally compressed tail acting as a paddle. *Pelamis* can move rapidly through the water, but only does so during local movements (usually while foraging), and it is doubtful if this snake actively swims for long distances. Instead, long-distance dispersal is probably passive, as the snake is moved about while floating in ocean currents. Sometimes it may be blown or drift to the extremes of its range in the eastern Pacific, and this is most likely how it occasionally reaches southern California.

While a graceful swimmer, *Pelamis* is poorly adapted for crawling on land. Its laterally compressed tail is a hindrance, and the lack of elongated ventral scutes prevents gripping of the ground for crawling. When washed onto a beach, it is almost helpless, and soon dies of heat exhaustion. In addition, *Pelamis* may not be able to breathe normally when out of water (Minton 1966).

REPRODUCTION. The breeding biology of *P. platurus* needs serious study. Compared with that of the terrestrial and freshwater snakes of the United States, it is poorly known and based mostly on anecdotes.

Males are mature at TBLs of 50 cm or more, but females must grow to at least 60 cm (Kropach 1975). Panamanian females with TBLs of 60–74.2 cm have produced young (Vallarino and Weldon 1996). These TBLs are probably attained in two to three years. The gametic cycles have not been described.

Breeding populations apparently occur only where the mean monthly WTs are above 20°C (Dunson and Ehlert 1971). Kropach (1975) expected to find seasonal reproduction in the Gulf of Panama because of the ecological seasonality of the region, but instead found young of newborn TBLs in every month, so breeding along the Pacific Coast of the Americas may take place throughout the year.

Courtship behavior has not been detailed, but males and females have been seen intertwining their bodies while swimming (McKeown 1996). Possibly the paired secretory sacs situated at the base of the tail (Weldon et al. 1991) release pheromones to attract the opposite sex. All mating occurs in the water, possibly near the surface in the slicks. Vallarino and Weldon

(1996) collected a copulating pair off the coast of Panama at 1300 hours on 10 February. The male had the posterior 10–15 cm of his body wrapped in three coils around the female. The snakes remained attached for approximately 1.5 hours after capture, but frequently attempted to disengage and swim away from one another.

Pelamis is ovoviviparous, and the young are thought to be born at sea, but Minton (1966) found a 23 cm juvenile in a mangrove swamp, so possibly some females may enter such habitats at parturition.

Normally brood size is 1–8 (mean, 4.4; n = 9) young (Visser 1967), but possibly as many as 10 young may be produced at one time (Rose 1950). There is a slight correlation between the number of young produced and female body size (Vallarino and Weldon 1996). Clutch mass of these litters averaged 57.8 (12–79) g, and the mean RCM was 0.288 (0.120–0.345) of before-birth female mass and 0.422 (0.136–0.527) of after-birth female mass.

The GP is unknown, but Kropach (1975) observed gravid females in the laboratory, and thought it is at least five months and more likely over six months. The births reported by Vallarino and Weldon (1996) occurred during 10–23 September. Neonates are more brightly colored than adults, are 22.0–28.0 (mean, 25.1; n = 21) cm long, and weigh 6.0–14.3 (mean, 8.8; n = 20) g.

GROWTH AND LONGEVITY. Growth of young *Pelamis* is rapid, at least during year one. Individuals shorter than 30 cm are first-year juveniles; those 30–50 cm are mostly juveniles and subadults, but may include a few adult males; snakes 50–60 cm are adult males and subadult females; and individuals over 60 cm are adult males and females (Kropach 1975; Vallarino and Weldon 1996). When males reach 50 cm, their growth rate slows, while that of females is maintained (Kropach 1975). The record captive longevity belongs to an unsexed wild-caught *P. platurus* of unknown age that survived 3 years, 5 months, and 10 days at the Houston Zoo (Snider and Bowler 1992).

DIET AND FEEDING HABITS. Fish are the primary prey. In the eastern Pacific, fish from at least 19 families and 25 genera are eaten: *Abudefduf troschelli, Acan-thurus xanthopterus, Anchoviella* sp., *Auxis* sp., *Blenniolus brevipinnis, Caranx caballus, C. hippos, C. marginatus, Chaetodon humeralis, Chloroscombrus orqueta, Coryphaena hippurus, Diodon histrix, Engraulis* sp., *Fistularia corneta, Gillichthys mirabilis, Hypsoblennius* sp., *Kyphosus* sp., *Lobotes pacificus, Lutjanus* sp., *Melanorhinus cyanellus, Mugil cephalus, M. durema, Mulloidichthys rathbuni, Peprilus medius, Polydactylus approximans, Polynemus approximans, Pseudupeneus grandisquamis, Selar crumenophthalmus, Sphoeroides* sp., *Sphyraena* sp., *Thunnus* sp., and *Vomer declivifrons* (Klawe 1964; Kropach 1975). No preference for prey size has been found for any size class of *Pelamis*.

Foraging seems to occur only at the water surface during the day and is primarily associated with current slicks. Most snakes collected in slicks contain food, while those caught elsewhere usually do not (Kropach 1971a). *Pelamis* may slowly and deliberately stalk a fish before seizing it, but usually the snake employs a type of ambush behavior by floating motionless among the debris trapped in the slick. Small fish seek out such debris to feed or to hide from other fish predators, and may congregate among floating objects in large numbers. As a fish swims by, the snake strikes rapidly sideward with its head and seizes it. This is usually followed by the snake swimming backward with the prey. Occasionally small fish will congregate beneath a floating *Pelamis*, and it will swim slowly backward. The fish also reverse direction to remain beneath the snake, and as some come close to the snake's head, it strikes laterally and seizes one. Prey is immobilized quickly by the snake's venom, which is chewed into the bite wound, and is usually quickly swallowed head first to avoid impalement by the fish's fin spines.

Sensitivity to movement in the water and possibly olfaction seem to be more important in prey detection than vision; Heatwole (1987) reported that finely chopped fish dropped into an aquarium holding these snakes causes a "frenzy" in which any object encountered, even another snake, is bitten.

VENOM AND BITES. The venom delivery apparatus is poorly developed. More adaptive emphasis seems to have been placed on the development of numerous small teeth to hold fish than on well-developed fangs. The fang situated at the front of the maxilla is hardly larger than other teeth on this bone. Twenty-five 43.8–75.5 cm *Pelamis* the authors examined had 0.9–2.8 mm fangs, and a positive correlation between fang length and TBL was evident.

The venom gland is composed of several small compartments containing cuboidal, columnar, and mucoid cells, and accessory venom glands may be present, in the suborbital region, that circumscribe the main venom duct (Burns and Pickwell 1972).

The venom is postsynaptic-neurotoxic in action and is very deadly to fish, which usually die within 60 seconds of being bitten. Muscle paralysis eventually causes respiratory failure and subsequent death (Tu 1991). Tu et al. (1975) isolated a major toxin (*Pelamis* toxin a) from the venom that made up 4.5% of the venom, and two other toxins, b (0.95%) and c (1.6%). Liu et al. (1975) isolated and partially characterized a toxin (pelamitoxin a) that may be the same as *Pelamis* toxin b. The toxin discovered by Liu et al. (1975) was very similar to hydrophitoxin b from *Hydrophis* sea snakes and *schistosa* 5 toxin from the venom of *Enhydrina*. Venoms of these latter snakes are capable of killing humans.

Pelamis has dry venom yields of 1–4 mg (Ernst and Zug 1996); the average yield is up to 2.8 mg (Pickwell et al. 1972), and the longest snakes yield the most venom. The LD_{25} of *Pelamis* venom ranges from 3.7 mg for a human weighing 45 kg to 7.5 mg for one weighing 91 kg (Pickwell et al. 1972). The lethal dose for a human is probably about 3.5 mg (Priede 1990).

This sea snake, with its small mouth and fangs and relatively low venom yield, poses little hazard to most humans. Human envenomations that may have occurred have either been very mild, or very rare, for there are no records of symptoms or fatalities attributed to *Pelamis;* possible exceptions are Taylor's (1953) mention that the bite is mortal and cannot be treated, and Kinghorn's (1956) statement that one death had occurred in India many years ago. Kropach (1972) noted six *Pelamis* bites that resulted in no effects.

PREDATORS AND DEFENSE. Reports of predators of *Pelamis* are rare: fish—puffer (*Sphoeroides* sp.) and snappers *(Lutjanus aratus, L. argentiventris, L. guttata);* birds—magnificent frigatebird *(Fregata magnificens),*

lava gull *(Larus fuliginosus),* and brown pelican *(Pelecanus occidentalis);* mammals—leopard seal *(Hydrurga leptonyx)* and sea lion (?) *(Zalophus californicus?);* and octopi (Alvarez-León and Hernández-Camacho 1998; Bruggen 1961; Heatwole and Finnie 1980; Pickwell et al. 1983; Reynolds and Pickwell 1984; Weldon 1988; Wetmore 1965). Some of these records may represent carrion eating, rather than predation, because Rubinoff and Kropach (1970) showed potential predators from the eastern Pacific made no attempts to attack *Pelamis.*

This snake is mild mannered, and divers have swum among them without being attacked, but Minton (1966) reported that one tried to bite repeatedly when picked up with a forceps. The bright contrasting yellow belly may be a warning device to would-be predators (Caldwell and Rubinoff 1983), or the contrasting dark back and bright venter may act aposematically so that there is no selection of one particular pattern by a predator. Many *Pelamis* have wounds on their tails (Weldon and Vallarino 1988), so maybe the multicolored tail is used to direct predators away from more vital parts of the body. They also practice knotting and tight coiling of the body that may help retard predators (Pickwell 1971).

Some *P. platurus* fall victim to accidents each year. Individuals often have wounds caused by boat props, and those washed ashore during storms usually do not find their way back to the ocean: they die from overheating and desiccation.

POPULATIONS. *Pelamis* sometimes occur in large aggregations: Belcher (in Smith 1926) saw thousands swimming on top of the water in the Mindoro and Sulu seas; Tu (1976) collected 3,077 off the coast of Costa Rica in less than a month; Kropach (1971a) estimated thousands drifted in surface slicks off Panama; and Vallarino and Weldon (1996) collected 635 in the Gulf of Chiriquí, Panama, during a 19 month study. The sex ratio is usually about 1:1; Kropach (1975) reported 340 males out of a sample of 712 snakes. However, one sample of 73 *Pelamis* from the Philippines contained only 9 (12%) males (McCoy and Hahn 1979). Several size classes are usually present in *Pelamis* populations: 20–30 cm neonates and juveniles, 31–50 cm juveniles or young adults, and 51+

cm adults (McCoy and Hahn 1979; Vallarino and Weldon 1996).

REMARKS. Electrophoretic studies of serum and tissue enzymes, and gene sequencing studies of ribosomal RNA and mitochondrial DNA have shown *Pelamis* is most closely related to other hydrophine sea snakes of the genera *Aipysurus, Emydocephalus, Enhydrina, Hydrophis,* and *Thalassophina* (Cadle and Sarich 1981; Keough 1998; Mao et al. 1983; Murphy 1988).

Pelamis platurus was reviewed by Pickwell and Culotta (1980) and Smith (1926).

Viperidae
Viperid Snakes

The Viperidae consists of 32 genera and 223 species (McDiarmid et al. 1999) occurring in Asia, Europe, Africa, and the Americas. Postfrontal, coronoid, and pelvic bones are absent, as are premaxillary teeth. In the skull, the prefrontal bone does not contact the nasal bone, the ectopterygoid is elongated, and a scalelike supratemporal bone suspends the quadrate. The hyoid is either Y-shaped or U-shaped with two long superficially placed, parallel arms. Pupils are vertically elliptical. All body vertebrae contain elongated hypapophyses. Only a right lung is present. Body scales are keeled; head scales are essentially like those of colubrids, but some snakes have the dorsal surface covered with small scales instead of enlarged plates. Reproduction is either oviparous or ovoviviparous (ovoviviparous in North American species). The hemipenis is deeply bilobed or double, with proximal spines and distal calyxes, and a bifurcate or semicentrifugal sulcus spermaticus.

Vipers are venomous snakes with an advanced venom-injecting apparatus. Their maxillae have become shortened horizontally while becoming deep vertically and are capable of movement on the prefrontal and ectopterygoid bones. This allows the elongated hollow fangs on the maxillae to be rotated until they lie against the palate when the mouth is closed (solenoglyphous). During the strike the maxillae move, causing the fangs to rotate downward and forward into stabbing positions. Each maxilla contains no teeth but the fang. The secretions produced by the venom glands are predominantly hemotoxic, but several species contain neurotoxic components in their venom.

The family includes four subfamilies, but only one, Crotalinae, occurs in the Americas. Members of the Crotalinae are called pit vipers because of the small hole in their face, which opens between the eye and nostril (usually at the position of the loreal scale). The maxilla is hollowed out dorsally to accommodate the pit, and the membrane at the base of the hole is extremely sensitive to infrared radiation, especially that emitted from warm-blooded prey. Each pit is subdivided into an outer chamber and a smaller inner chamber by a cornified epidermal membrane about 0.025 mm thick. Virtually all the membrane surface is supplied with axons from the trigeminal cranial nerve (V), particularly its ophthalmic and maxillary branches, and thus a continual transmission of impulses occurs from the pit membrane to the brain. The membrane is highly sensitive to infrared wavelengths of 15,000–40,000 Angstroms, and any warm or cold object causes a temporary change in the rate of impulse transmission, creating a response to sudden temperature changes. So, the pit organ serves to recognize the presence of any object that is warmer or colder than its surroundings. Sensitivity varies with the infrared wavelength, but is generally greater to emissions in the range of 2–3 microns than to shorter or longer wavelengths. The snakes seem to be able to detect differences in temperature of as little as 0.2°C or less, and possibly as small a change as 0.003°C in 0.1 second may be detected (for more in depth discussions of pit organs, see Ernst 1992; Ernst and Zug 1996).

Vipers evolved from colubrid ancestors different from those that eventually gave rise to the elapids. Pit vipers are believed to have evolved from Old World vipers (Darlington 1957; Brattstrom 1964b), but how they reached the Americas is unknown. Seventeen species in three genera *(Agkistrodon, Crotalus, Sistrurus)* occur in the United States and Canada.

Key to the Genera of *Viperidae*

1a. No scaly rattle at tip of tail . . . . *Agkistrodon*
1b. Scaly rattle present at tip of tail 2
2a. Dorsal surface of head covered with nine enlarged plates
. . . . *Sistrurus*

2b. Dorsal surface of head covered with small scales, or less than nine enlarged plates . . . . *Crotalus*

Agkistrodon Palisot de Beauvois 1799

Copperheads and Cottonmouths

Key to the Species of *Agkistrodon*

1a. Head yellow brown to reddish brown; body pattern of brown dumbbell-shaped blotches on a pinkish or grayish to orange brown ground color; loreal present . . . . *A. contortrix*

1b. Head dark brown, black, or olive brown; body pattern of dark brown or black bars on olive or brown ground color, or no pattern present; loreal absent . . . . *A. piscivorus*

Agkistrodon contortrix (Linnaeus 1766) | Copperhead

RECOGNITION. *A. contortrix* has a maximum TBL of 134.6 cm, but most are shorter than 90 cm. It is pinkish to grayish brown with an orange to copper or rust red, unpatterned head; 10–21 (mean, 15) brown to reddish brown bands on the body, which are usually broader along the sides of the body and narrower across the dorsum (dumbbell-shaped or saddle-shaped); and small dark spots in the light spaces between the bands (see GEOGRAPHIC VARIATION for variation). The tail lacks a rattle and is yellow, brown, or green. The head is usually lighter below the eye than above it; no light stripes are present, but a dark postocular stripe often is present. The parietal scales usually have a pair of small dark spots. The pupil is verti-cally elliptical. The venter is cream, pink, or light brown, with dark lateral blotches. Dorsal body scales are keeled and pitted, and lie in 23 or 25 (24–29) anterior rows, 23 (21–27) midbody rows, and 19 or 21 (18–23) posterior rows. Beneath are 138–157 (mean, 148) ventrals, 37–63 (mean, 45.5) subcaudals, and an undivided anal plate. Pertinent lateral head scales include 2 nasals, 1 loreal, 2–3 preoculars, 2–3 suboculars, 3–4 postoculars, several rows of temporals, 8 (6–10) supralabials, and 10 (8–12) infralabials. The deeply bifurcate hemipenis has about 35 large spines on the basal one-third of each lobe (most are straight, but some are slightly hooked); small, irregularly arranged, flattened papillae with terminal spines on the distal

Southern copperhead, *Agkistrodon contortrix contortrix*; Columbus County, North Carolina. (Photograph by Carl H. Ernst)

Northern copperhead, *Agkistrodon controtrix mokasen*; Bell County, Kentucky. (Photograph by Roger W. Barbour)

two-thirds of each lobe; no spines between the lobes; and a forked sulcus spermaticus. The shortened maxilla contains only the elongated fang.

Males have TLs 10–19 (mean, 14.5) % of TBL and 38–63 (mean, 47) subcaudals; females have TLs 10–17 (mean, 13.7) % of TBL and 37–57 (mean, 44) subcaudals.

GEOGRAPHIC VARIATION. Five subspecies have been described (Gloyd and Conant 1990). *A. c. contortrix* (Linnaeus 1766), the southern copperhead, is pale gray to pinkish, with crossbands well marked and very narrow (often medially separated) across the back, dark lateral spots on the venter, and a pinkish or greenish yellow tail tip. It is found from southeastern Virginia southward along the coastal plain to Gadsden and Liberty counties, Florida, and west to eastern Texas and northward in the Mississippi Valley to southern Missouri and southwestern Illinois. *A. c. laticinctus* Gloyd and Conant 1934a, the broad-banded

copperhead, can be found from extreme south-central Kansas (Chautauqua and Cowley counties) southward through central Oklahoma and central Texas to Medina and Atascosa counties. Its deep reddish brown crossbands are not much narrower across the back than along the sides, the tip of the tail is greenish gray, and the cream venter has small reddish brown or black spots and larger irregularly shaped dark blotches. *A. c. mokasen* (Daudin 1803), the northern copperhead, is reddish brown, with a bright coppery head and dark, wide dorsal bands, round dark spots on the sides of the venter, and often a greenish tail tip. It ranges from Massachusetts and Connecticut southward on the piedmont and highlands to Georgia, Alabama, and northeastern Mississippi, and west through southern Pennsylvania and the Ohio Valley to Illinois. *A. c. pictigaster* Gloyd and Conant 1943, the Trans-Pecos copperhead, ranges in western Texas from Crockett and Val Verde counties westward through

Trans-Pecos copperhead, *Agkistrodon contortrix pictigaster*; Western Texas. (Photograph by Carl H. Ernst)

the Big Bend region and Davis Mountains to northern Coahuila and eastern Chihuahua, Mexico. Its dorsal pattern resembles that of *A. c. laticinctus,* but the venter has dark reddish brown to black mottles in sharp contrast to cream-colored areas extending onto the belly from the sides, and often the reddish brown mid-body crossbands contain a pair of dark, rounded, lateral spots. *A. c. phaeogaster* Gloyd 1969, the Osage copperhead, resembles *A. c. mokasen,* but is paler with more pronounced dark dorsal bands, no small dark spots between the dark bands, a yellowish green tail tip, and a gray venter with dark mottles. It is only found in northern and central Missouri, eastern Kansas, and the northeastern corner of Oklahoma. Broad bands of intergradation occur where the ranges of the various subspecies meet.

CONFUSING SPECIES. Cottonmouths *(A. piscivorus)* have a band through the eye and lack a loreal scale, and the rattlesnakes *(Crotalus, Sistrurus)* have a tail rattle. Colubrids of the genera *Elaphe, Lampropeltis, Nerodia,* and *Heterodon* lack facial pits, have rounded pupils, and may have patterned heads. The lyre snake *(Trimorphodon biscutatus)* has a patterned head.

KARYOTYPE. *A. contortrix* has 36 chromosomes: 16 macrochromosomes (4 metacentric, 8 submetacentric, 2 subtelocentric) and 20 microchromosomes. Sex determination is ZW (female) or ZZ (male), and the W is either acrocenteric or subtelocentric to telocentric (Baker et al. 1972; Zimmerman and Kilpatrick

1973; Cole, in Gloyd and Conant 1990). The NOR is on the long arm of telocentric pair four (Camper and Hanks 1995).

FOSSIL RECORD. Fossil *A. contortrix* date from the Miocene (Hemphillian) of Nebraska (Brattstrom 1954a, 1967; Holman 1979a, 2000); the upper Pliocene (terminal Hemphillian or Blancan) of Kansas, Nebraska, and Texas (Brattstrom 1967; Holman 1979b; Holman and Schloeder 1991; Rogers 1976, 1984); the Pleistocene (Blancan) of Kansas (Brattstrom 1967); the Pleistocene (Irvingtonian) of Kansas (Holman 1995; Rogers 1982) and West Virginia (Holman 1982b); and the Pleistocene (Rancholabrean) of Georgia (Holman 1967), Kansas (Brattstrom 1967; Preston 1979), Pennsylvania (Brattstrom 1954b; Guilday et al. 1964, 1966; Holman 1995), Texas (Hill 1971; Holman 1964, 1968a, 1969b, 1980, 1995; Johnson 1974; Parmley 1988b), Virginia (Guilday 1962; Holman 1986a), and West Virginia (Holman and Grady 1987). Also, a broken vertebra of Rancholabrean age identifiable to the genus *Agkistrodon* but not to species level has been found in Alabama (Holman et al. 1990).

DISTRIBUTION. *A. contortrix* occurs from western Massachusetts, Connecticut and southeastern New York west through the southern two-thirds of Pennsylvania to Illinois, Missouri, and eastern Kansas, and south to Georgia, the panhandle of Florida, Mississippi, Louisiana, eastern and central Texas, and the extreme portions of northern Coahuila and eastern Chi-

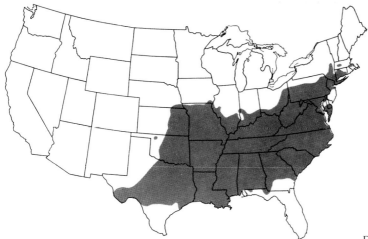

Distribution of *Agkistrodon contortrix*.

huahua, Mexico. Except in the northeastern part of its range, its distribution is mainly limited by the southern boundary of the Wisconsinan glacier.

HABITAT.   In the eastern United States, this snake inhabits relatively open oak-hickory woods with abundant brush piles, large logs, scattered rocks, and nearby rock crevices or slides. Along the southern coastal plains, it is found in wet woods and along swamp borders. In Texas and northern Mexico, it occurs near permanent or semipermanent waterways in dry woods, or even desert, with sandy soils and rocky outcrops and cliffs. Its entire elevational range is from near sea level to over 1,500 m. Gravid female *A. c. mokasen* prefer microhabitats that are clearly separated from those occupied by males and nonreproductive females (Reinert 1984b). Rocky, open, sparsely forested sites with warmer soil temperatures are used until the young are born. Such sites may be close to the hibernacula, or some distance away.

BEHAVIOR.   Annually, *A. contortrix* is active from April through October in the northern parts of its range, with most being seen from May through September, but farther south it may be active from March into December, or even emerge on warm days during January–February. Active copperheads have been found in February–December in North Carolina, where 62% of the records are from July–September (Palmer and Braswell 1995).

In the fall they become gregarious and may crawl some distance to communal hibernacula used each winter, and sometimes shared with other snakes. Weathered outcrops with crevices extending below the frost line are often used, as also are caves, gravel banks, old stone walls and building foundations, animal burrows, hollow logs and stumps, and sawdust piles. Drda (1968) observed several overwintering in a Missouri cave that were quite active most of the winter, as ATs there remained relatively constant and considerably above freezing. Juveniles moved deeper into the cave than adults. At Mason Neck National Wildlife Refuge, Fairfax County, Virginia, 15–25 adults share a hibernaculum under a broken concrete sidewalk each year with a few *Coluber constrictor* and *Elaphe obsoleta*. Formerly these snakes overwintered in the broken foundation of an abandoned house, but moved about 50 m to the sidewalk site after the building was torn down. Along the Atlantic Coastal Plain many copperheads hibernate singly, usually in hollow logs. In Virginia, it is usually the juveniles who hibernate singly, but the authors have found some adults also alone or in groups of two to three.

Although it is active during daylight in the spring and fall, this snake becomes crepuscular or nocturnal during the summer, and may be quite active in summer after an evening shower. Kansas copperheads are active at 7.5–32.0°C ATs (Clarke 1958), and Fitch (1956) determined their preferred BT is about 27°C, and their preferred BT activity range is probably 23–31°C. Brattstrom (1965) reported 17.5–34.5°C BTs, and Fitch (1960b) recorded BTs as low as 12.4°C for copperheads under rocks in the early spring. The CT_{min} and CT_{max} are 4–9 and 41°C, respectively. Most basking the authors have observed has been in either the spring or the fall. Fitch (1960b) found that gravid females basked more often and seemed to prefer warmer BTs. Sanders and Jacob (1981) found that those basking on clear winter days achieved BTs of at least 10°C, that summer BTs varied between snakes of different SVLs, and that the CT_{min} is negatively correlated with SVL.

Copperheads make three types of movements in Kansas (Fitch 1958, 1960b, 1999): movements within the home (or activity) range, abandonment of one home range and occupancy of a second, and migrations to and from hibernacula. Home ranges there vary between 3.4 ha for females and 9.8 ha for males; mean male home range area is 1.63 ha, and that for females is 1.85 ha. Short movements of up to 150 m are most common; the average distance of male movements is 70.3 m, and for females 77.5 m. Summer movements of 1.5–378 m are made within the home range, and snakes that shift home ranges move 442–762 m. Hibernacula may be 232–1,183 m from the summer home range. Males usually travel longer average distances to hibernacula (656 m) than do females (406 m).

Radio-equipped Kansas copperheads moved an average of 11 m/day (including days not moved). Mean distances moved for only those days when movement occurred were 18 m for a male, 12 m for a nongravid female, and 12 m for a gravid female (Fitch and Shirer 1971).

A marked copperhead in the Shenandoah National Park, Virginia, exhibited homing ability when it returned within two days to the place of original capture after having been displaced 0.8 km to a known den site (Martin, in Gloyd and Conant 1990).

The copperhead is a good climber that may ascend to 5 m in trees (C. Ernst, pers. obs.). It is also a good swimmer, and the authors have watched them swim across small creeks on several occasions.

Males engage in dominance combat bouts during the breeding season (Collins 1993; Fitch 1960b; Gloyd 1947; Mitchell 1981; Schuett 1986; Shaw 1948; Shively and Mitchell 1994). After meeting, the males make body contact and rise up facing each other to a height of 30–40% of their TBLs. After much tongue flicking,

they sway back and forth in unison with heads bent at a sharp angle, lean into each other, entwine, and try to push the opponent's head and neck to the ground (topping behavior). Eventually, one male (usually the smaller), is pinned to the ground, breaks off contact, and crawls away. Such bouts can last up to two hours. Female defense seems a stimulus. Schuett (1986) thought mate competition the major function of these encounters, but this is not certain, as combat occurs in captivity when no female is present, and at no particular elevated testosterone or corticosterone levels (Schuett et al. 1996).

REPRODUCTION. Some female copperheads are mature at 37.5–50.0 cm SVL and two to three years (Fitch 1960b; Ford et al. 1990; Mitchell 1994); males mature in two to three years at a minimum SVL of 47.5 cm (Mitchell 1994).

Females have several size groups of small (1–9 mm) ova in early spring, suggesting that they may mature at different times (Fitch 1960b). Vitellogenesis follows, and at the end of May the ova are ovulated. Female reproduction is normally biennial (Fitch 1960b; McDuffie 1961), but Vermersch and Kuntz (1986) reported that females from southern Texas produce young annually. Blood testosterone in adult males is lowest in April–May, increases in June, reaches its highest level in August, declines to early November, varies little during hibernation (November–January), increases quickly after spring emergence (February–March), and finally decreases in March–April (Schuett et al. 1997).

Two mating periods occur: April–May and September–October (Gloyd 1934; Schuett 1982). Female copperheads store viable sperm for long periods in special oviductal seminal receptacles (Allen 1955; Schuett 1992; Schuett and Gillingham 1986).

Males actively court females, who remain mostly passive. The male touches the female with his snout, places his head and neck on her back, rubs it with his chin, and crawls forward toward her head. She flattens her body, raises the tip of her tail, and moves the tail slowly back and forth or vibrates it. The male places his tail beside her tail and quivers it while looping it under her tail. He stops quivering his tail, but strokes her tail and vent region one to three times. If receptive, she gapes her vent, and intromission follows.

While copulating, both snakes normally remain motionless; although the female may raise her head 1–3 cm, and both snakes tongue flick. The female may crawl slowly forward pulling the male along, causing him to crawl backward to maintain his initial position. He may dismount until only contact at the vents is maintained. After ejaculation, the male retracts his hemipenis, withdraws, and crawls away (Schuett and Gillingham 1988). Head-raising behavior in courted females is similar to that of males during dominance behavior, and males may challenge females who head lift (Schuett and Duvall 1996).

The young are ovoviviparous; although Dolley (1939) reported the embryos are attached to the oviductal wall. After a GP of 83–150 (mean, 110) days, young are born in July–October, with September being the most important month. Females may aggregate near hibernacula about the time of parturition. Neonates are enclosed in a membranous, transparent sac at birth, and head-first emergence from it may take up to 15 minutes. Broods contain 1–21 (mean, 7; n = 192) young (Carpenter 1958; White 1979), but 4–8 are most common. Litter size is positively correlated to female SVL; larger females within each subspecies produce the greatest number of young. Brood size may vary from year to year, apparently due to different environmental conditions (Seigel and Fitch 1985). Neonate TBL is also positively correlated to female TBL. Mean RCM is 0.311 (0.273–0.419; n = 13) (Fitch 1960b; Ford et al. 1990; Seigel and Fitch 1984). Neonates have 16.0–30.0 (mean, 20.6; n = 158) cm TBLs, weigh 4.5–17.0 (mean, 10.6; n = 52) g, have yellow tails, and are patterned like adults, but paler.

GROWTH AND LONGEVITY. Kansas yearlings have SVLs of 30–40 cm; those two years old, 40–58 cm; three years old, 48–60 cm; four years old, 55–65 cm; five years old, 59–71 cm; seven years old, 65–76 cm; and nine years old, 68–80 cm (Fitch, 2000). Males grow faster than females (Fitch 1960b, 1999). In Indiana, yearlings are 30–43 cm, and two year olds are 53–59 cm (Minton 1972).

The longevity record for A. contortrix is 29 years, 10 months, and 6 days, and several others have survived over 20 years (Gloyd and Conant 1990; Snider and Bowler 1992).

DIET AND FEEDING HABITS. A. contortrix may consume over twice its body weight in prey each year (Schoener 1977). Carrion is consumed (Mitchell 1977b). Vertebrates are the usual prey, but it also eats invertebrates; prey include mammals—young opossum (Didelphis virginianus), moles (Condylura cristata, Parascalops breweri), shrews (Blarina brevicauda, B. carolinensis, B. hylophaga, Cryptotis parva, Sorex cinereus, S. longirostris), bats (Tadarida brasiliensis [?]), murid mice, rats, and voles (Clethrionomys gapperi, Microtus pennsylvanicus, M. pinetorum, M. ochrogaster, Mus musculus, Neotoma floridana, Peromyscus leucopus, P. maniculatus, Reithrodontomys humulis, R. megalotis, Sigmodon hispidus, Synaptomys cooperi), jumping mice (Napeozapus insignis, Zapus hudsonius), chipmunks (Tamias striatus), young squirrels (Sciurus carolinensis), and young cottontails (Sylvilagus floridanus); birds—mostly unidentified (Agelaius phoeniceus, Archilochus colubris, Cardinalis cardinalis, Carduelis tristis, Dendroica sp., Guiraca caerulea, Molothrus ater, Petrochelidon pyrrhonota, Pipilo erythrophthalmus [?], Seiurus sp., Sturnus vulgaris, Zonotrichia albicollis); reptiles—small turtles (Sternotherus odoratus, Terrapene ornata, T. carolina), lizards (Anolis carolinensis, Cnemidophorus sexlineatus, Crotaphytus collaris, Eumeces fasciatus, E. obsoletus, Ophisaurus attenuatus, Sceloporus undulatus, Scincella lateralis), and snakes (Carphophis amoenus, C. vermis, Coluber constrictor, Diadophis punctatus, Elaphe obsoleta, Lampropeltis triangulum, Nerodia rhombifera [in captivity], Rhinocheilus lecontei, Storeria dekayi, Tantilla coronata, Thamnophis proximus, T. sirtalis, Virginia striatula); amphibians—anurans (Acris gryllus, Gastrophryne olivacea, Pseudacris triseriata, Rana blairi, R. catesbeiana, R. clamitans, R. sphenocephala) and salamanders (Ambystoma opacum, Plethodon cinereus, P. cylindraceus, Pseudotriton ruber); insects (beetles, cicada, dragonfly, lepidopteran larvae, grasshoppers, locust, preying mantis); millipedes; and spiders (Anderson 1965; Barbour 1950; Barton 1949; Brown 1979a; Bush 1959; Carpenter 1958; Collins 1980; Ernst et al. 1997; Fitch 1960b, 1982, 1999; Garton and Dimmick 1969; Gloyd and Conant 1990; Greding 1964; Hamilton and Pollack 1955; Klauber 1972; Klemens 1993; Lagesse and Ford 1996; McCrystal and Green 1986; Mitchell 1994; Murphy 1964; Orth 1939; Palmer and Braswell 1995; Smith 1997; Surface 1906; Uhler et al. 1939; Walters et al. 1996).

The most frequently taken prey by Kansas copperheads are voles (*Microtus*, 24%), cicada (*Tibicen*, 15%), and white-footed mice (*Peromyscus*, 13%); *Microtus* and *Peromyscus* compose the greatest estimated biomass (1,051 g/ha) and so are the most readily available prey (Fitch 1982). In Tennessee, males feed mainly on voles (*Microtus*) and caterpillars; nongravid females eat white-footed mice (*Peromyscus*), voles (*Microtus*), and birds (unidentified); and gravid females take lizards (*Sceloporus*) and shrews (*Blarina, Cryptotis*) (Garton and Dimmick 1969).

Smaller individuals eat insects, salamanders, lizards, and small snakes, while adults prey more heavily on mammals. Gravid females usually fast, but when they do eat, they consume smaller volumes of food than either males or nongravid females (Garton and Dimmick 1969), and the prey they consume are those found in their restricted microhabitat.

Adults are mostly ambushers, although they sometimes actively forage. Juveniles actively stalk much of their prey, and neonates use their yellow tails to lure small frogs (Neill 1960). Large prey are bitten, released, and tracked later when the venom has taken effect; small prey and birds are often retained in the mouth until dead.

VENOM AND BITES. *Agkistrodon* have solenoglyphous fangs (Ernst 1964, 1965, 1982; Kardong 1979). A series of 214 copperheads 17–110 cm in TBL had 1.1–7.2 mm fangs; fang length increased linearly with increased length of both the body and head (Ernst 1965, 1982). Neonates have fully functional fangs and are capable of injecting venom (Boyer 1933). The fangs of all venomous snakes are shed and replaced periodically, an adaptation for replacing broken or loose fangs. A series of five to seven (in less than 3% of copperheads examined) replacement fangs occur in the gums behind and above the functional fang in alternating sockets on the maxilla (Ernst 1982). The replacement fangs lie close together, and those distal to the functional fang may be only 0.1–0.3 mm apart. In graduated lengths, they may range from a first reserve fang slightly longer than the functional fang (but never than 0.2 mm longer) to only a short spike about 0.2 mm long in the last of the series. The graduated reserve fang series shifts forward to occupy an alternate series of sockets on the maxilla. These sockets are divided by a wall of tissue that separates the developing fangs that will enter the outer socket from those that will enter the inner socket. The socket of the first reserve fang is also separated from that of the functional fang by a membrane. Beside the functional fang is a vacant socket into which the first reserve fang migrates just prior to loss of the functional fang. Even neonates have a replacement series. The fangs do not develop as a complete unit, but rather from the tip (represented by the most distal replacement fang) upward, and the hollow tube shape is in evidence from the earliest period of development in which shape can be ascertained. About 19% of the time, one or both fangs were in the process of replacement (Ernst 1982). Fitch (1960b) reported a 33 day fang shedding cycle.

The venom is highly hemolytic, and mice or rats dissected an hour or two after having been bitten show massive hemorrhaging. Copperheads contain 40–75 mg of venom (Ernst and Zug 1996). The LD_{50} of mice is 10.9 mg/kg (Ernst and Zug 1996); probably 100 mg or more are needed to kill an adult human (Minton and Minton 1969). Twenty-five to 75% of the contents of the venom glands may be discharged in one bite (Fitch 1960b), and juveniles are as toxic as their parents (Minton 1967). Copperhead venom exhibits moderately high levels of protease, low alkaline, phosphomonoesterase, and L-amino acid oxidase levels, high arginine esterhydrolase and hyluronidase activity, but no phosphodiesterase activity (Tan and Ponnudari 1990). Hemorrhaging is caused by a fibrinolytic enzyme. Venom of *A. c. laticinctus* contains a myotoxin that causes myelin sheath necrosis in mice (Johnson and Ownby 1993).

Symptoms of copperhead bites include pain and swelling, weakness, giddiness, breathing difficulty, hemorrhage, either an increased or a weakened pulse, occasionally shock and hypotension, nausea and vomiting, gangrene, ecchymosis, edema, unconsciousness or stupor, fever, sweating, headache, and intestinal discomfort (Hutchison 1929; Campbell and Lamar 1989). Copperhead bites are common, but death from a bite is almost nonexistent; the fatality rate has been estimated to be as low as 0.01–0.3% (Campbell and Lamar 1989; Minton 1969). Antivenin treatment should be sought at once: a 14-year-old boy died when treated too late with antivenin (Amaral 1927). Probably only the very young or old need worry about this snake. Case histories of bites are given by Boyer (1933), McCauley (1945), Fitch (1960b), and Diener (1961).

PREDATORS AND DEFENSE.   Bullfrogs *(Rana cates-beiana)*, alligators *(Alligator mississippiensis)*, ophiophagous snakes *(Coluber constrictor, Drymarchon corais, Lampropeltis calligaster* [?], *L. getula, L. triangulum, Micrurus fulvius, Thamnophis sirtalis)*, owls *(Bubo virginianus)*, hawks *(Buteo jamaicensis, B. platypterus)*, opossums *(Didelphis virginianus)*, moles *(Scalopus aquaticus)*, coyotes *(Canis familiaris)*, and domestic cats *(Felis catus)* are natural enemies (Clemens 1993; C. Ernst, pers. obs.; Fitch 1960b; Hurter 1911; Keegan 1944; Klauber 1972; Megonegal 1985; Mitchell 1994; Palmer and Brazwell 1995; Ross 1989). A young captive *A. contortrix* ate a dead litter mate (Mitchell 1977b), but it is not known if this species is naturally cannibalistic. Over much of the range, habitat destruction, insecticide poisoning, and the automobile have severely reduced populations.

Copperheads usually lie motionless when an intruder is first detected, and this behavior, along with their camouflaged pattern, makes them very dangerous. Many bites have resulted from persons unwittingly stepping on, sitting on, or touching unseen copperheads. If touched, they will strike, but if not touched, they remain quiet or try to crawl away. When handled, they try to bite and spray musk (contrary to the folktale, this musk has its own odor and does not smell like cucumbers). Recognition, by either the sight or smell, of an ophiophagous snake will cause a copperhead to body bridge.

POPULATIONS.   Copperheads can occur in large numbers, especially around hibernacula or sites with high prey density; Barbour (1962) captured seven adults in less than 15 minutes in a 3×6 m plot in Breathitt County, Kentucky, and the authors have caught 10 of these snakes in 15 minutes elsewhere in Kentucky. In a mixed pine-hardwood forest in Texas, copperheads made up 34.4% of the snakes captured (Ford et al. 1991).

Yearly densities, which included almost 3,000 individuals, at Fitch's (1999) Kansas study site varied from 3.9 to 34.6/ha. Biomass was estimated to be 0.80 kg/ha. The adult to juvenile ratio was about 4.26:1; smaller and younger size and age classes predominated, and snakes older than eight years represented only 5% of the population, while those no older than two years made up 55% (Fitch 1960b; Vial et al. 1977). The adult sex ratio was 1.22:1 (Fitch 1982). Vial et al. (1977) estimated a skewed sex ratio of 2.84:1 at birth, but calculated that males suffered higher mortality, and predicted a sex ratio of 1:1 by year eight. This is interesting, because sex ratios of litters are usually close to 1:1.

The copperhead is considered rare in Florida because of the limited panhandle distribution.

REMARKS.   Relationships of the American *Agkistrodon* to other genera of pit vipers, and between the three species within the genus, are muddled. American *Agkistrodon* share more slow-evolving proteins with the Asian genera *Hypnale* and *Trimeresurus* than with other American pit vipers (Dowling et al. 1996). However, data obtained from mitochondrial DNA indicate that the three American *Agkistrodon* are monophyletic (Knight et al. 1992) and are more closely related to American rattlesnakes *(Crotalus, Sistrurus)* than to Asian pit vipers (Kraus et al. 1996). Studies on venom by Jones (1976) and on scale surface contours by Chiasson et al. (1989) indicate *A. contortrix* has a greater affinity to neotropical *A. bilineatus* than to *A. piscivorus*, but mitochondrial studies by Knight et al. (1992) show *piscivorus* and *bilineatus* to be more closely related. In contrast, comparisons of skin kerotins by Campbell and Whitmore (1989) suggest *contortrix* is not closely related to *bilineatus* and that the three American *Agkistrodon* may not be monophyletic: *contortrix* and *piscivorus* seem closely related, while *bilineatus* is divergent. Recent mitochondrial DNA studies by Parkinson et al. (2000) suggest *contortrix* is ancestral to both *piscivorus* and *bilineatus*, that *piscivorus* is ancestral to *bilineatus*, and that *bilineatus* is a complex of two species.

Agkistrodon piscivorus (Bonnaterre 1790) | Cottonmouth

RECOGNITION. Adult cottonmouths are heavy-bodied, large (TBL to 189.2 cm), and olive, dark brown, or black. Juveniles are lighter olive or brown and become progressively darker with age until almost or totally black; the 20–27 (mean, 13) straight to slightly wavy dorsal body bands characteristic of juveniles fade with age until absent in old, large adults. The venter is tan to gray with numerous dark blotches. A light-bordered dark cheek stripe and dark rostral bars may be present. Dorsal body scales are keeled and doubly pitted, and occur in 25 or 27 (24–27) anterior rows, 25 (21–27) midbody rows, and 21 (17–23) posterior rows. On the underside are 125–145 ventrals, 30–56 subcaudals forming an undivided row (Burkett, 1966, reported that a female only had 17 subcaudals), and an undivided anal plate. Dorsal head scales consist of nine large plates, as in *A. contortrix*; laterally are 2 nasals, 0 loreals, 2–3 preoculars, 3 (2–4) postoculars, 2–4 suboculars, 3–5 temporals, 7–8 (6–9) supralabials, and 10–11 (8–12) infralabials. A heat sensitive pit is still situated between the nostril and eye. The bilobed hemipenis has a divided sulcus spermaticus, recurved spines near the base, and calyxes near the apex.

Males have 125–145 (mean, 136) ventrals, 30–54 (mean, 46) subcaudals, and TLs 12–24 (mean, 17) % of TBL; females have 128–144 (mean, 134) ventrals, 36–56 (mean, 43) subcaudals, and TLs 10–19 (mean, 15) % of TBL.

GEOGRAPHIC VARIATION. Three subspecies occur in the eastern United States. *Agkistrodon p. piscivorus* (Bonnaterre 1790), the eastern cottonmouth, lacks a pattern on its light snout, has dorsal bands that strongly contrast with the relatively lighter body color, and has 39–51 subcaudals in males and 40–50 in females. It is found along the Atlantic Coastal Plain from southeastern Virginia to east-central Alabama. *A. p. conanti* Gloyd 1969, the Florida cottonmouth, has two conspicuous dark vertical rostral bars, transverse body bands that are lost in the relatively dark body color, and 43–54 subcaudals in males and 41–49 in females. It is found from southern Georgia and Mobile Bay, Alabama, south through peninsular Florida. *A. p. leucostoma* (Troost 1836), the western cottonmouth, has no pattern on its dark brown to black snout, dorsal bands that are lost in the relatively dark body coloration, and 30–54 subcaudals in males and 36–56 in females (it is also the shortest subspecies; maximum TBL < 160 cm, while the other two may have TBLs > 180 cm). It ranges in the Mississippi Valley from southern Indiana, southwestern Illinois, southern Missouri, and southeastern Kansas, south to the Gulf Coast from Mobile Bay to central Texas. *Piscivorus* and *leucostoma* intergrade in Alabama and east-central Mississippi.

CONFUSING SPECIES. Use the above key to differentiate the copperhead *(A. contortrix)*. Rattlesnakes *(Crotalus, Sistrurus)* have a tail rattle. Water snakes

Eastern cottonmouth, *Agkistrodon piscivorus piscivorus*; Beaufort County, North Carolina. (Photograph by Carl H. Ernst)

Western cottonmouth, *Agkistrodon piscivorus leucostoma*; Hickman County, Kentucky. (Photograph by Roger W. Barbour)

(Nerodia) have no facial pits, divided anal plates, round pupils, and two rows of subcaudals. Also, when swimming, *A. piscivorus* inflates its lung, resulting in much of its body floating on the surface, while *Nerodia* elevate only the head and neck to the surface.

KARYOTYPE. The karyotype has 36 chromosomes: 16 macrochromosomes (4 metacentric, 8 submetacentric, 2 subtelocentric) and 20 microchromosomes. Sex determination in females is ZW (the W chromosome is submetacentric), in males, ZZ (Baker et al. 1972; Cole, in Gloyd and Conant 1990; Fischman et al. 1972; Zimmerman and Kilpatrick 1973). *A. piscivorus* also possesses a cloned ZFY gene (a supposed testis-determining factor in mammals) that was hybridized to the DNA of reptiles with sex chromosomes and is expressed in embryos of both sexes (Bull et al. 1988). A triploid *A. p. leucostoma* was described by Tiersch and Figiel (1991).

FOSSIL RECORD. Fossil *A. piscivorus* are known from the Pleistocene Rancholabrean of Florida (Auf-fenberg 1963; Brattstrom 1953b; Gilmore 1938; Holman 1958b, 1959a, 1978, 1995, 1996; Tihen 1962), Georgia (Holman 1967), and Texas (Hill 1971; Holman 1963, 1968a, 1980, 1995), and possible Pleistocene Irvingtonian remains have been found in Florida (Meylan 1995).

DISTRIBUTION. *A. piscivorus* ranges from southeastern Virginia south on the Atlantic Coastal Plain to the Florida Keys, and west along the Gulf Coastal Plain, and south through the Mississippi Valley from southern Indiana, southern Illinois, and Missouri to central Texas.

HABITAT. Cottonmouths occupy almost any type of aquatic habitat, from brackish coastal marshes to sand or mud-bottomed freshwater cypress swamps, bayous, ponds, lakes, rivers, streams, and drainage ditches within some southern cities. The authors have seen or collected them in such unlikely habitats as clear, gravelly, or rocky piedmont streams in Alabama, Arkansas, and Missouri. Occupied waterways usually

Distribution of *Agkistrodon piscivorus*.

have abundant mud or sand banks, logs, or brush piles for basking. They may be common in the rookeries of wading aquatic birds, such as ibis, anhingas, herons, and egrets (Wharton 1969), and may also occupy lodges of Florida round-tailed muskrats *(Neofiber alleni)* (Lee 1968a).

During droughts, most cottonmouths aggregate at remaining waterholes. Their skin has low water permeability, and they can apparently withstand much drying (Dunson and Freda 1985).

BEHAVIOR. With the advent of warm weather in March–April, cottonmouths emerge from their hibernacula and return to their water bodies. In late August–early September they begin a rather leisurely exodus from the water to upland hibernacula, and by October–November most have disappeared from their waterways. Exceptions occur, and individuals are occasionally active in winter. In southern Florida cottonmouths may bask in every month, but less so in December–February. Active cottonmouths have been found in every month in the Carolinas (Gibbons and Semlitch 1991; Palmer and Braswell 1995). Most activity in North Carolina is from May through October (Palmer and Braswell 1995), and in Virginia from April through September (Mitchell 1994). It is more tolerant of cold than most snakes, and is one of the last to enter hibernation (Neill 1947, 1948a). The winter is spent, often in groups, on shore at some upland site, such as a rock crevice on a hillside with a southern exposure, in hollow logs and stumps, under the roots of overturned trees, in palmetto patches, in piles of

leaves, or in crayfish, rodent, or gopher tortoise *(Gopherus polyphemus)* burrows. Wharton (1969) reported the CTs of cottonmouths in an underground Florida hibernaculum were 4.2–16.5°C and within a few degrees of the AT, and thought the STs kept the snake's CTs intermediate between the AT and the ST. The mean CT of hibernating Virginia cottonmouths was > 6°C (Blem 1997).

During the spring and fall, activity is mostly diurnal, but in summer it is predominately nocturnal; Virginia cottonmouths have a bipolar diel activity cycle, 0600–1000 hours and 1800–2100 hours (Blem and Blem 1995). The metabolic cycle seems to be circadian (Blem and Killeen 1993). During the day the snakes bask (especially in the morning), remain undercover, or lie quietly in ambush beside logs or other objects. CTs of active *A. piscivorus* average about 26 (21.0–35.0) °C (Bothner 1973; Brattstrom 1965; Wood 1954). It seldom climbs high out of the water, preferring instead to merely lie on the bank, although the authors have seen one climb about 1.6 m up a small tree in Florida.

When crawling, cottonmouths characteristically keep the head and neck elevated above the ground. Home ranges of *A. p. conanti* on Sea Horse Key, Florida, were 0.04–1.22 ha; males had slightly larger home ranges (mean, 0.17 ha) than females (mean, 0.14 ha). Some made long movements: a 132 cm male crawled 320 m in 27 months, and three females moved 380, 450, and 498 m, and another female left its home range to establish a new one on the other side of a mangrove inlet; but movements of 60–70 m between captures were most common (Wharton 1969). An *A. p. leucostoma* had a home range of approximately 0.16 ha (Tinkle 1959).

Like many other pit vipers, male cottonmouths participate in combat bouts in either shallow water or on land (Blem 1987; Burkett 1966; Carr and Carr 1942; Martin 1984; Perry 1978; Ramsey 1948). Apparently combat behavior only manifests itself in three-year-old or older males, and may be coincident with sexual maturity (Blem 1987).

REPRODUCTION. Male *A. p. piscivorus* with 60 cm SVLs, and male *A. p. leucostoma* with 52 cm SVLs are mature (C. Ernst, pers. obs.); minimum SVLs of mature female *A. p. piscivorus*, *A. p. conanti*, and *A. p. leucostoma* are, respectively, 61.9, 65.0, and 45.0 cm (Blem 1997; Burkett 1966; Wharton 1966). Such lengths are probably reached in two to three years.

The preliminary vitellogenesis begins in August–September, yolking ceases over winter, secondary vitellogenesis occurs in the spring, and the eggs are ovulated in May–June (Blem and Blem 1995; Kofron 1979a; Wharton 1966). Egg dry mass averages 4.7 g and is composed of about 24% nonpolar lipids, and decrease in dry mass remains relatively constant during early development but accelerates during the third trimester; a mean 57% of the original nonpolar lipids remain in neonates as parental investment, and at an ET of 30°C stored lipids could serve the neonate's metabolism for about 22 days (Fischer et al. 1994).

Female reproduction is either annual (Blem 1981b, 1982; Kofron 1979a) or biennial (Burkett 1966; Wharton 1966) and is probably determined by resource availability. More larger (older?) females than smaller females are likely to be gravid in a population. Total lipids decline in males and nongravid females during the first year of a biennium, but gradually increase during the second year; gravid females have their highest lipid levels prior to ovulation, after which both total lipids and fat body lipids decline through the GP until they are at their lowest point in the summer (Blem 1997; Scott et al. 1995).

In Alabama, testicular recrudescence occurs in April, spermiogenesis begins in June and peaks in July–August, spermatogenesis ceases in October, and sperm is stored over winter in the epididymides and vas deferens (Johnson et al. 1982).

Mating possibly occurs throughout the year in Florida (Wharton 1966), but elsewhere two breeding periods are evident, March–June and August–October. Females possibly store viable sperm for long periods. A complete description of the courtship and mating behaviors has not been published.

The GP is about 150 (120–170) days, during which the embryos probably receive some nourishment and oxygen from their mother. Most births occur in August–September, but births also occur in October. A positive correlation exists between the number and size of neonates and female length and mass (Blem 1981). Litters average 7.2 (1–20; n = 74) young, but 5–8 is probably most common. Females may congregate before giving birth, and remain with their broods to defend (?) them after birth (Heinrich and Studenroth 1996; Walters and Card 1996; Wharton 1966). When born, the neonates are enclosed in fetal membranes, from which they may take more than an hour to emerge (C. Ernst, pers. obs.).

Overall, neonates have 21.0–29.9 (mean, 26.2) cm TBLs and weigh 10.0–20.2 (mean, 16.9) g. Newborn *A. p. leucostoma* are about 21.0–29.9 (mean, 26) cm long; those of *A. p. piscivorus* are 22.2–29.3 (mean, 26.0) cm; and neonates of *A. p. conanti* have 28.5–35.0 (mean, 33.5) cm TBLs. The young are light brown with darker brown transverse bands and yellow tails.

Hybridization with *A. contortrix* has occurred in captivity (Mount and Cecil 1982).

GROWTH AND LONGEVITY. First-year Virginia *A. p. piscivorus* have mean SVLs of 35 cm, second-year juveniles average 60 cm, and third-year individuals are all > 60 cm (Blem and Blem 1995). Western Kentucky *A. p. leucostoma* have 26.0–29.8 cm TBLs at 7–8 months (having grown about 2.5 cm since birth) and 31.2–33.7 cm TBLs at 19–20 months (having grown about 4.5 cm), and those 31–32 months old average 42.5 cm (an increase of 9.5 cm) in TBL (Barbour 1956). The maximum known life span for *A. piscivorus* is 21 years, 4 months, and 10 days (Snider and Bowler 1992).

DIET AND FEEDING HABITS. The cottonmouth is an opportunist that eats a wide variety of foods, either live or as carrion, which are most available and easiest to catch at the time it is hungry.

Known prey are fish—bowfin (*Amia calva*), gizzard

shad *(Dorosoma cepedianium)*, mudminnows *(Umbra limi)*, eels *(Anguilla rostrata)*, catfish *(Bagre marinus, Ictalurus melas, I. natalis, I. punctatus)*, pickeral *(Esox americanus)*, live bearers *(Gambusia affinis, Heterandria formosa, Poecilia latipinna)*, cyprinids *(Cyprinodon variegatus, Notemigonus crysoleucas)*, killifish *(Fundulus dispar, Lucania sp.)*, pirate perch *(Aphedoderus sayanus)*, silversides *(Menedia sp.)*, bass and sunfish *(Acantharchus pomotis, Elassoma zonatum, Lepomis cyanellus, L. macrochirus, L. symmetricus, Micropterus dolomieui, Pomoxis nigromaculatus)*, sea bass *(Morone americanus)*, drum *(Aplodinotus grunniens, Cynoscion nebulosus)*, perch *(Perca flavescens)*, goby *(Gobionellus sp.)*, and mullet *(Mugil sp.)*; amphibians—salamanders *(Ambystoma opacum, A. talpoideum, Amphiuma means, Eurycea longicaudata, E. lucifugus, Notophthalmus viridescens, Pseudotriton montanus, Siren intermedia, S. lacertina)* and anurans *(Acris crepitans, A. gryllus, Bufo terrestris, Gastrophryne carolinensis, Hyla avivoca, H. cinerea, H. gratiosa, H. versicolor, Osteopilus septentrionalis, Rana catesbeiana, R. clamitans, R. palustris, R. sphenocephala, Scaphiopus hurteri)*; reptiles—juvenile alligators *(Alligator mississippiensis)*, turtles *(Chelydra serpentina, Kinosternon subrubrum, Pseudemys concinna, Sternotherus odoratus, Terrapene carolina, Trachemys scripta, Trionyx sp.)*, lizards *(Anolis carolinensis, Eumeces inexpectatus, E. laticeps, Ophisaurus ventralis, Scincella lateralis)*, and snakes *(Agkistrodon piscivorus, Coluber constrictor, Crotalus sp., Diadophis punctatus, Elaphe obsoleta, Farancia abacura, Heterodon platirhinos, Lampropeltis getula, Masticophis flagellum, Nerodia clarkii, N. cyclopion, N. erythrogaster, N. fasciata, N. rhombifer, N. sipedon, N. taxispilota, Opheodrys aestivus, Regina rigida, Sistrurus miliarius, Storeria dekayi, Thamnophis proximus, T. sauritus, T. sirtalis)*; birds, including eggs, nestlings and fledglings *(Aix sponsa, Ammodramus maritimus, Anhinga anhinga, Ardea alba, Cardinalis cardinalis, Corvus ossifragus, Egretta tricolor, Gallus gallus, Hylocichla mustelina, Pahalacrocorax auritus, Parus carolinensis, Pipilo erythrophthalmus, Plegadis falcinellus, Porzana carolina, Podilymbus podiceps, Zenaida macroura)*; mammals—moles *(Scalopus aquaticus)*, shrews *(Blarina carolinensis, Cryptotis parva, Sorex sp.)*, bats (species not named), squirrels *(Sciurus carolinensis)*, muskrats *(Neofiber alleni, Ondatra zibethicus)*, voles *(Microtus ochrogaster, M. pinetorum, M. pennsylvanicus)*, murid rats and mice *(Mus musculus, Oryzomys palustris, Peromyscus*

maniculatus, Rattus norvegicus, R. rattus, Sigmodon hispidus), pocket mice *(Perognathus sp.)*, and cottontail rabbits *(Sylvilagus aquaticus, S. floridanus, S. palustris)*; snails; conch; insects (beetles, cicadas, damselflies, grasshoppers, leptodopteran larvae); spiders; and crayfish (Allen and Swindell 1948; Barbour 1956; Berna and Gibbons 1991; Blem and Blem 1995; Burkett 1966; Carpenter 1958; Clark 1949; Collins and Carpenter 1970; Dundee and Rossman 1989; C. Ernst, pers. obs.; Gibbons and Semlitsch 1991; Gloyd and Conant 1990; Hamel 1996; Heinrich and Studenroth 1996; Hamilton and Pollack 1955, 1956; Keiser 1993; Klimstra 1959a; Kofron 1978; Laughlin 1959; Lutterschmidt et al. 1996; Mitchell 1994; Palmer and Braswell 1995; Palis 1993; Penn 1943; Platt and Rainwater 2000; Wharton 1969; Yerger 1953). Fish and amphibians are the most frequent prey; marine fish eaten are probably dropped by birds.

When foraging, *A. piscivorus* usually swims with its head elevated above the water, but occasionally explores pools with its head submerged (Bothner 1974). They often congregate under wading-bird rookeries and eat any young that fall from the nests (Wharton 1969). In contrast to the behavior of gravid females of other pit vipers, gravid *A. piscivorus* may continue to feed during gestation (Burkett 1966).

Odor, sight, and heat radiation (from birds and mammals) are used to detect prey. If in the water, when prey is identified, cottonmouths quickly swim to it, seize it, and retain it. On land, they ambush prey and/or actively pursue it. If the prey is large and struggles, it is usually held in the mouth until the venom immobilizes it. This is dangerous for the snake, which may be chewed by its prey. Striking and tasting animals triggers a chemosensory search pattern, causing it to trail released prey with much tongue flicking (Chiszar et al. 1986). Juveniles may use their yellow tails to lure frogs and other small prey (Wharton 1960).

VENOM AND BITES. Cottonmouths are large, sometimes aggressive, dangerous snakes. The solenoglyphous venom delivery system has adult fangs to 11 mm (Ernst 1964, 1965, 1982; Kardong 1974). Neonates have average fang lengths of 2.7 mm and fully developed venom glands (Ernst 1982). The fangs are shed periodically, and usually are replaced on one side at a time (Ernst 1982). The replacement process takes about five days to complete, and during this time venom may be ejected through either the old or the new fang, depending on the stage of development. The authors have found several cottonmouths with four functional fangs.

Adults may contain 80–170 mg of venom (Ernst and Zug 1996). The LD$_{50}$ of an adult mouse is 2.04 mg/kg (Ernst and Zug 1996), and the estimated lethal dose for a human is 100–150 mg (Minton and Minton 1969). Cottonmouth venom is very hemolytic, destroying red blood cells and exhibiting strong overall anticoagulant activity (although clotting at the bite site has occurred), and fatalities have been reported (Allen and Swindell 1948; Anderson 1965; Burkett 1966; Hutchison 1929). Symptoms of cottonmouth bites include swelling and pain at the site, weakness, giddiness, difficulty in breathing, hemorrhage, weakened pulse or heart failure, lowered blood pressure, nausea and vomiting, occasional paralysis, a drop in body temperature, unconsciousness or stupor, and nervousness (Burkett 1966; Essex 1932; Hutchison 1929). Nasty secondary bacterial infections, such as tetanus or gas gangrene, may also occur (sometimes resulting in amputation of a limb, toes, or fingers; Allen and Swindell 1948; Dart et al. 1992). Case histories of bites are given by Hulme (1952) and Burkett (1966).

PREDATORS AND DEFENSE. Known predators (mostly on juveniles) are predatory mammals *(Canis familiaris, Felis catus, Lontra canadensis, Lynx rufus, Procyon lotor)*; herons, egrets, cranes, and storks *(Ardea herodias, Cosmeroides albus, Egretta thula, Grus* sp., *Mycteria americana)*; owls *(Bubo virginianus)*; hawks *(Buteo* sp.); eagles *(Haliaeetus leucocephalus)*; alligators *(Alligator mississippiensis)*; snapping turtles *(Chelydra serpentina)*; snakes *(Agkistrodon piscivorus, Drymarchon corais, Lampropeltis getula)*; fish *(Ictalurus* sp., *Lepisosteus occeus, Micropterus salmoides)*; and ghost crabs *(Ocypode quadrata)* (Allen and Swindell 1948; Burkett 1966; Cross and Marshall 1998; Klauber 1972; Mitchell 1994; Penn 1943).

Individual cottonmouths vary in disposition from very timid to extremely aggressive, but all bite if handled. They can and will bite underwater. When first disturbed they either freeze in place or try to escape. When escape is not possible, they coil, flatten the body, vibrate the tail, and strike repeatedly. They may also gape the mouth to show the inner pinkish white lining. Schuett (in Gloyd and Conant 1990) has reported that gaping is probably innate, and that it is more frequently displayed by cool (BT, 10–18°C) snakes. Odors or sight of predator snakes results in body-bridging behavior (Carpenter and Gillingham 1975). If handled, cottonmouths thrash about violently, strike, and spray musk, and they may even bite themselves. Because they are common and some have violent tempers, cottonmouths should be approached with care.

POPULATIONS. *A. piscivorus* may be the most common reptile in certain habitats. At Murphy's Pond, Hickman County, Kentucky, they formerly occurred in densities of over 700/ha (Barbour 1956), and the authors have seen as many as 8 cottonmouths basking on a fallen cyprus tree in Florida. Viosca once collected 114 cottonmouths in one day on Delacroix Island, St. Bernard Parish, Louisiana (Dundee and Rossman 1989). Cottonmouths composed 8.6% of the snakes collected by Clark (1949) in the Louisiana uplands, 15.1% of the snakes captured by Ford et al. (1991) in eastern Texas, and 4.3% and 12.6%, respectively, at two sites in Florida's Everglades (Dalrymple et al. 1991).

Immature individuals made up 32.5% of those snakes examined by Burkett (1966) and about 45% of the Murphy's Pond population (Barbour 1956). Blem (1981b) reported a 1.80:1.00 male to female ratio in Virginia, but females made up 53% of adults and also of 48 embryos examined by Burkett (1966). Since the alligator has been protected, there has been a noticeable decrease in cottonmouth populations in certain areas of Florida, but the habitat has also dried and this may have played a role in the decline in its numbers (C. Ernst, pers. obs.). The cottonmouth is protected as threatened in Indiana.

REMARKS. *A. piscivorus* was reviewed by Gloyd and Conant (1990).

Crotalus Linnaeus 1758

Rattlesnakes

Key to the Species of *Crotalus*

1a. Supraocular scales raised or hornlike .... *C. cerastes*

1b. Supraocular scales not raised or hornlike 2

2a. Tail unicolored black or dark brown, or dark gray with very faint bands 3

2b. Tail not unicolored black or dark brown; tail bands usually distinct, but may be only confined to anterior portion of tail 4

3a. White scales occur within the dark dorsal blotches; usually six or fewer scales in the internasal-prefrontal region .... *C. molossus*

3b. No white scales within the dark dorsal blotches; usually more than seven scales in the internasal-prefrontal region .... *C. horridus*

4a. Tip of rostrum sharply raised; two pale stripes extend backward from the nostril and mental areas to corner of mouth .... *C. willardi*

4b. Tip of rostrum not sharply raised; no pale stripes on side of face, or two pale stripes extending diagonally backward from orbit to corner of mouth 5

5a. Upper preocular scale subdivided, either horizontally or vertically 6

5b. Upper preocular scale not subdivided 7

6a. No small scales separate the rostral scale from the prenasal .... *C. lepidus*

6b. A series of small scales separates rostral scale from the prenasal .... *C. mitchelli*

7a. Dorsal body pattern consists of dark crossbands, not blotches .... *C. tigris*

7b. Dorsal body pattern consists of dark blotches or spots, not crossbands 8

8a. Dorsal body pattern consists of a series of paired, small, circular or elliptical, dark spots .... *C. pricei*

8b. Dorsal body pattern consists of a series of large, square or diamond-shaped, dark blotches 9

9a. Dark tail bands decidedly narrower than light tail bands; normally only two rows of intersupraocular scales present .... *C. scutulatus*

9b. Dark tail bands wider than light tail bands; normally more than two rows of intersupraocular scales present 10

10a. Tail bands poorly developed or faded; usually more than two internasal scales .... *C. viridis*

10b. Tail bands well developed, not faded; usually only two internasal scales 11

11a. Light tail bands white or cream-colored ... *C. adamanteus*

11b. Light tail bands gray 12

12a. Pink, red, or reddish brown; usually no dark speckles in dorsal body blotches; anterior infralabials usually transversely divided .... *C. ruber*

12b. Gray or brown; dark speckles occur in dorsal body blotches; anterior infralabials not transversely divided .. .. *C. atrox*

Crotalus adamanteus Palisot de Beauvois 1799 | Eastern Diamondback Rattlesnake

RECOGNITION. *C. adamanteus* is the largest (maximum TBL, 251.5 cm; although most adults are 100–150 cm long) and bulkiest (maximum, 7+ kg; most adults weigh 2.0–2.3 kg) of any venomous snake in the United States. The body is brown with a dorsal pattern of 24–35 (mean, 31) dark, yellow-bordered, diamond-like (rhomboid), broader than long blotches, and the tail has 3–10 (mean, 6) brown and white bands. The face is adorned with a pair of dark, cream-to-yellow–bordered stripes, extending downward and backward from the eyes to the supralabials, and sev-

eral vertical light stripes on the rostrum. The venter is yellow to cream with some brownish mottling. Dorsal body scales are keeled and pitted, and lie in 29–30 (27–32) anterior rows, 27–29 (25–31) midbody rows, and 21 (19–23) rows near the tail. The venter has 159–187 ventrals, 20–33 subcaudals, and an undivided anal plate. Most dorsal head scales are small, but the higher-than-wide rostral, 2 internasals, 4 canthals (between the internasals and supraoculars), and 2 supraoculars are enlarged. Prefrontals are absent, but 6–7 intersupraoculars are present. Laterally are 2

Eastern diamondback rattle-snake, *Crotalus adamanteus*; Collier County, Florida. (Photograph by Roger W. Barbour)

nasals (the prenasal usually contacts the supralabial, but the postnasal is prevented from touching the upper preocular by loreal scales), 2 (1–3) loreals, 2 pre-oculars, 2 (3) postoculars, several suboculars and temporals, 14 (12–17) supralabials, and 17–18 (15–21) infralabials. The short, bifurcate hemipenis has a forked sulcus spermaticus, many recurved spines along the base, and spines in the crotch between the lobes. As in all North American viperids, only the enlarged, hollow fang occurs on the shortened, rotational maxilla.

Males have 159–176 (mean, 169) ventrals, 26–33 (mean, 30) subcaudals, and 5–10 (mean, 7) dark tail bands; females have 162–187 (mean, 176) ventrals, 20–28 subcaudals (mean, 24), and 3–7 (mean, 5) dark tail bands.

GEOGRAPHIC VARIATION. Individuals from the Florida Keys have higher ventral counts (Christman 1980), but no subspecies are recognized.

CONFUSING SPECIES. Other species of *Crotalus* in the United States can be identified by the key presented above.

KARYOTYPE. Undescribed.

FOSSIL RECORD. Pleistocene remains of *C. adamanteus* are known from several Irvingtonian and Rancholabrean sites in Florida (Auffenberg 1963; Brattstrom 1953b, 1954b; Gilmore 1938; Gut and Ray 1963; Hay 1917; Holman 1959a, 1959b, 1978, 1996; Holman and Clausen 1984; Meylan 1982, 1995; Tihen 1962; Weigel 1962) and at a Rancholabrean site in Augusta County, Virginia, far north of its present range (Guilday 1962). The fossil taxa *C. a. pleistofloridensis* Brattstrom 1953b and *C. giganteus* Brattstrom 1953b have been synonymized with *C. adamanteus* (Auffenberg 1963; Christman 1975).

DISTRIBUTION. *C. adamanteus* is limited to areas with mild winters and long growing seasons. It ranges from southeastern North Carolina south along the Atlantic coastal plain to the Florida Keys and west along the Gulf Coast to southeastern Mississippi and adjacent eastern Louisiana. The Louisiana population was thought possibly extinct (McCranie 1980a), but Dundee and Rossman (1989) cited recent records from Washington and Tangipahoa parishes. Overall, its original range has been shortened and fragmented by agriculture, forestry practices, urbanization, and plant succession after fire suppression (Martin and Means 2000).

HABITAT. Its presettlement habitat was probably open canopy, fire-climax pinewoods and savannas, including longleaf-pine–wiregrass sand hills, clay hills, and flatwoods (Martin and Means 2000). Today, it is best associated with dry, lowland palmetto or wiregrass flatwoods, pine or pine–turkey oak woodlands, but it also uses grass-sedge bogs, heaths, temperate hard-

Distribution of *Crotalus adamanteus*.

wood forests, tropical hardwood hammocks, sand-pine or scrub-oak habitats, and abandoned fields, especially if these are adjacent to pine-dominated habitats. Marshes and swamps are normally avoided, but occasionally it lives along their borders. Animal burrows (armadillo, gopher tortoise), hollow logs, or windfall mounds from uprooted trees must be present for the snake to use in winter or to avoid surface fires.

BEHAVIOR.   In North Carolina, *C. adamanteus* has been found in every month except December and January; 68% of observations are from June and August through October, and the latest record of activity is 13 November (Palmer and Brazwell 1995). Annually, it is probably active every month in Florida south of the 18°C isotherm; north of this line there are short periods of inactivity to avoid cold occur during the two to four months of winter (Clamp 1990). In the Florida Panhandle, one to four months of hibernation occur north of the 12°C January isotherm (Martin and Means 2000). Timmerman (1995) reported the snake is surface active 55% of the time during the winter in Putnam County, Florida. It must retreat underground and hibernate during the winter in the colder northern portions of its range. Typical hibernacula are the same retreats used during the summer to avoid excessive heat: mammal or gopher tortoise (*Gopherus*) burrows, hollow logs or stumps, or retreats among the roots of wind-felled trees or palmettos (Means 1985, 1986; Timmerman 1995). It does not live in uplands, and so does not usually have rock slides or

crevices as winter retreats, as do *C. horridus* or *Agkistrodon contortrix*. The Florida snakes studied by Timmerman (1995) always used more than one retreat during the winter.

C. adamanteus is decidedly diurnal; 60% percent (n = 449) of the 743 observations made by Timmerman (1995) were between 0600 and 1200 hours, and 32% more (n = 240) occurred between 1201 and 1800 hours. Only 7% (n = 54) of his observations occurred between 1801 and 0559 hours. Activities recorded for the 689 observations between 0600 and 1800 hours included the following: tightly coiled (49.7%, n = 346); under cover, not visible (33.4%, n = 230); loosely coiled, function unknown, but possibly thermoregulatory (10.7%, n = 74); and crawling (5.7%, n = 39). During 1801–0559 hours, the 54 observations included the following activities: tightly coiled (50.0%, n = 27); under cover, not visible (45.6%, n = 23); loosely coiled (5.5%, n = 3); and crawling (1.8%, n = 1). The snakes spent from one day to a week in the same tight coil. Except in winter, when they entered subterranean retreats, the rattlesnakes studied by Timmerman (1995) spent little to no time thermoregulating. The authors have found them actively foraging or traveling at ATs of 27–35°C; one recorded by Timmerman (1995) had a BT of 16°C at an AT of 19°C.

C. adamanteus establishes an initial home range and continues to use it for years. Daily underground retreats and hibernacula are the same and are included within the home range, so no seasonal migration occurs. Within the home range, the snake has favorite places to which it frequently returns; several underground retreats may be used over a period of time. Timmerman's (1995) snakes made their longest movements (+20 m/day, 2.9–45.5 m) in September–November, and their shortest movements (+10 m/day, 0–19.5 m) during December–February, when they were mostly underground. His males had mean home ranges of 84.3 ha, and females maintained mean home ranges of 46.5 ha; ranges of the sexes overlapped. Means (1985) reported mean home ranges in northwestern Florida of 200 ha for males and 80 ha for females.

Most activity is at ground level or subterranean, but this snake will rarely climb several meters into trees while pursuing prey (Klauber 1972). It is a good swimmer that regularly swims across streams and narrow bodies of freshwater, and also occasionally swims or rafts across saltwater to offshore islands.

A male social dominance system, determined during combat bouts, is present. When two males meet, particularly during the breeding season, the identity odor of each is determined by tongue flicking. The males then raise the anterior 30–40% of their bodies and face each other, as each tries to outstare the other. Bending their heads at a sharp angle to the ground, they entwine their anterior bodies and try to push each other off balance and to the ground. Such bouts may last for only a few minutes to almost two hours, and finally end when one male (usually the smaller) is pinned to the ground, unwraps itself from the victor, and crawls away (C. Ernst, pers. obs.).

REPRODUCTION. Wright and Wright (1957) and Conant and Collins (1998) reported minimum adult TBLs of 76 and 84 cm, respectively, which would probably be achieved in two to three years. However, Berish (1998) reported the SVL of the smallest mature female to be 109.3 cm, so the minimum mature TBL of females may be considerably longer than 76–84 cm. The reproductive cycles of both sexes have not been described, and it is not known if female C. adamanteus reproduce annually or biennially. It is suspected, however, that they can store viable sperm for relatively long periods after a successful mating (Klauber 1972).

In South Carolina, C. adamanteus has a spring breeding season, beginning in March (Kauffeld 1969), but Meek (in Klauber 1972) reported mid-September

matings, Ashton and Ashton (1981) believed that mating occurs in both fall and spring, and a 30 January copulation has occurred in captivity (Murphy and Shadduck 1978). During the captive mating, the snakes remained joined for about nine hours. Occasional pulsations near the cloaca of the male were seen, but the female remained passive. Females seek sheltered places to give birth from 16 July to 5 October (Klauber 1972), after a GP of possibly over 200 days. Such a long GP indicates a mating period in late winter or early spring, but a later spring breeding period is more likely. Most young are born in retreats such as gopher tortoise burrows or hollow logs, and the female may remain with her offspring for a short period until they shed and depart (Butler et al. 1995).

The number of young per litter ranges from 4 to 29 (mean, 12.7; n = 27). At the time of emergence from the fetal membranes the neonates have TBLs of 30.0–42.4 (mean, 36.8; n = 17) cm and weigh 32.0–48.5 (mean, 39.5; n = 9) g.

C. adamanteus has hybridized with C. horridus atricaudatus (Klauber 1972).

GROWTH AND LONGEVITY. The only record of natural growth was for a recaptured South Carolina C. adamanteus that grew from 60 cm TBL to 109 cm in about 26 months (Smith 1992). With proper resources growth may be rapid: a juvenile raised by Strimple (1992b) grew from 44.5 to 69.9 cm (64.5 to 284.5 g) in one year. The length of a midbody vertebra is directly proportional to the TBL of C. adamanteus ($y = 6.745 \times 0.674$), and the log body mass times log TBL can be calculated with the equation $y = 3.108x + 2.766$ (Christman 1975; Prange and Christman 1976).

A wild-caught juvenile survived 22 years, 9 months, and 3 days in captivity (Snider and Bowler 1992).

DIET AND FEEDING HABITS. Prey of C. adamanteus include small mammals—rabbits (Sylvilagus floridanus, S. palustris), squirrels (Sciurus carolinensis, S. niger), cotton rats (Sigmodon hispidus), woodrats (Neotoma floridana), and mice (Peromyscus gossypinus, P. maniculatus, Podomys floridanus)—and birds—king rail (Rallus elegans), young turkey (Meleagris gallopavo), bobwhite (Colinus virginianus), and towhee (Pipilo erythrophthalmus) (Carr 1940; C. Ernst, pers. obs.;

Klauber 1972; Martin and Means 2000; Timmerman 1995). The report by Rutledge (1936) of one raiding a pileated woodpecker *(Dryocopus pileatus)* nest is probably erroneous because this snake seldom climbs into trees. The young feed primarily on mice and rats, while adults seem to prefer rabbits, cotton rats, mice, squirrels, and birds. Carrion may be ingested (Funderberg 1968).

The eastern diamondback may actively seek out prey by following scent trails (Chiszar et al. 1986, 1991), but often it captures prey from ambush: it lies in wait for prey beside logs or among the roots of wind-felled trees. In addition to their odor, endothermic prey emit infrared heat waves that may be detected by the pit on the rattlesnake's face. Usually only one envenomating bite is delivered, and the wounded animal is released immediately after the strike and allowed to crawl away to die. Biting of the prey sets off a chemosensory search image for the tasted animal, and the snake slowly pursues its victim until it is found, then examines the prey with tongue flicks to determine if it is dead, and swallows it quickly, usually from the head end. Chemical searching may last for 2–62 minutes following a strike (Brock 1981).

VENOM AND BITES. *C. adamanteus* has a well-developed solenoglyphous venom delivery system (Klauber 1972), with fangs as long as 27 mm (Telford 1952). Its venom is strongly hemolytic, causing strong hemorrhagic, procoagulant, and anticoagulant reactions, but protease activity is low (Tan and Ponnudurai 1991). A myotoxin similar to those found in *C. durissus* and *C. viridis* is also present (Samejima et al. 1991). Total dry venom yield may be as high as 848 mg, but averages from about 492–666 mg/adult (Klauber 1972); minimum lethal doses for a 350 g pigeon and a 20 g mouse are 0.2–0.3 mg and 0.04 mg, respectively (Githens and George 1931; Githens and Wolf 1939). The minimum lethal dose for a rabbit is 0.25 mg/kg body weight (Boquet 1948). The human lethal dose has been estimated as 100 mg (Dowling 1975). Human deaths from severe untreated bites can occur in 6–30 hours, and the mortality rate may be 40% (Neill 1957). Venom toxicity varies regionally and between individual snakes, even from the same litter.

Symptoms in human bites include swelling, pain, weakness, giddiness, respiratory difficulty, hemor-

rhage, weak pulse or heart failure (or in some cases an increased pulse rate), enlarged glands, soreness, diarrhea (often bloody), collapse, shock, toxemia, and convulsion (Hutchison 1929; Kitchens and Van Mierop 1983). Necrosis at the site of the bite and occasionally involving much of the injured limb is common, and sensory disturbances, such as a sensation of yellow vision, may occur (Minton 1974). Bitten limbs often are at least partially crippled. Case histories of bites by *C. adamanteus* are in Klauber (1972).

PREDATORS AND DEFENSE. Young *C. adamanteus* have many potential enemies: hogs *(Sus scrofa)*, carnivorous mammals *(Procyon lotor, Ursus americanus, Mephitis mephitis, Lontra canadensis, Canis familiaris, C. latrans, Felis catus, Lynx rufus)*, raptors *(Bubo virginianus, Buteo jamaicensis, Caracara plancus)*, wood storks *(Mycteria americana)*, ophiophagous snakes *(Drymarchon corais, Coluber constrictor, Lampropeltis getula, Masticophis flagellum, Micrurus fulvius)* (it will bridge its body and inflate its body when coming in contact with *Drymarchon* and *Lampropeltis*; Weldon and Burghardt 1979), and ranid frogs *(Rana catesbeiana, R. heckscheri)* (C. Ernst, pers. obs.; Klauber 1972; Neill 1961b). Adults have little to fear except humans, who often kill one on sight, run over them with their automobiles, destroy their habitats, and collect them for the leather and meat industries (Berish 1998). White-tailed deer *(Odocoileus virginianus)* occasionally stamp *C. adamanteus* to death (Timmerman 1995), and some caught above ground are killed during grass fires (C. Ernst, pers. obs.).

Most will lie quietly coiled when first discovered, displaying a mild temperament for a rattlesnake. However, if provoked, it coils, shakes its tail—SVL-adjusted loudness to over 70 dB (Cook et al. 1994); frequency range, 1.5–18.6 kHz; dominant frequency, 7.1 kHz (Young and Brown 1993)—and raises the head and neck into a striking position; if further disturbed, it strikes. If picked up, it thrashes about and tries to bite. Overall, they are extremely dangerous and should be let alone.

POPULATIONS. It can be quite common in suitable habitats. This is especially true in the vicinity of Corkscrew Swamp Sanctuary, Collier County, Florida (C. Ernst, pers. obs.), and at Okeetee, South Carolina.

A series of 280 snakes caught in 74 days of actual hunting over a period of six years at Okeetee included 60 (21%) eastern diamondbacks (Kauffeld 1957). About 1,000 were killed each year on seven hunting preserves in the Thomasville-Tallahassee area of Florida, where a dollar bounty was offered for each snake (Stoddard 1942). The late Ross Allen reported that over a period of 28 years he had received 1,000–5,000 per year at his Florida snake exhibit, with a grand total of 50,000 (Klauber 1972). Timmerman (1995) reported a crude density estimate of approximately 0.2/ha at the Ordway Preserve, Putnam County, Florida. The sex ratio of *C. adamanteus* harvested in Florida is skewed toward males (Berish 1998).

Unfortunately, this magnificent creature is rapidly disappearing over much of its former range, and is now listed as endangered in North Carolina (Palmer and Braswell 1995).

REMARKS. Gloyd (1940) thought that *C. adamanteus* was a "climax form" derived from *C. atrox*, which he believed to be most close to the ancestral type for the *atrox* group of rattlesnakes. Studies by Meylan (1982) support this theory, but Christman (1980) noted there is no reason to believe it arose on the Mexican Plateau and then migrated to Florida. Both Florida and the southwestern United States seem to be refuges where rattlesnakes, like *adamanteus* and *atrox*, evolved more slowly, retaining ancestral characters. The species was reviewed by McCranie (1980a).

Crotalus atrox Baird and Girard 1853 | Western Diamondback Rattlesnake

RECOGNITION. *C. atrox* is the second largest venomous snake in North America, growing to a record TBL of 233.7 cm, but most individuals are shorter than 150 cm. It is brown to gray, with some individuals reddish, yellowish, or even melanistic (Pedro Almendariz lava field in Socorro and Sierra counties, New Mexico; Best and James 1984). The dorsum has 23–45 (mean, 36) dark, light-bordered, diamond- or hexagonal-shaped blotches, smaller dark blotches lie along the sides, and two to eight (usually four to six) alternating wide gray and black bands are present on the tail. Some individuals may lack the tail rattle (Holycross 2000a; Painter et al. 1999). Two light stripes extend downward and backward from in front and in back of the eye to the supralabials, the posterior one ends well in front of the corner of the mouth, and some dark pigment may be present on the top of the head. The venter is white, cream, or pink, with some fine dark mottling along the sides; the underside of the tail is often grayish. Dorsal body scales are keeled and pitted, and lie in 23–27 anterior rows, 25–27 (23–29) rows at midbody, and 22–23 rows near the tail. Beneath are 168–196 ventrals, 16–36 subcaudals, and an undivided anal plate. On the top of the head lie a higher-than-wide rostral scale followed by 2 small internasals and 11–32 additional scales. Between the 2 large supraoculars are 4–5 (3–8) inter-

supraocular scales. No prefrontals are present. Laterally are 2 nasals (the prenasal normally touches the supralabials, the postnasal usually contacts the upper preocular), 1 (2) loreal(s), 2 (3) preoculars, 3–4 (2–4) suboculars, 3 (2–6) postoculars, several temporals, 15–16 (12–18) supralabials, and 16–17 (14–21) infralabials. The bilobed hemipenis has a divided sulcus spermaticus, about 64 spines and 57 fringes, a soft apical projection on each lobe, and a few spines in the crotch between the lobes.

Males have 168–193 (mean, 182) ventrals, 19–32 (mean, 26) subcaudals, and five to six (three to eight) black tail bands; females have 173–196 (mean, 185) ventrals, 16–36 (mean, 20) subcaudals, and three to four (two to six) black tail bands. Adult males are larger than adult females.

GEOGRAPHIC VARIATION. Although some color, size, and rattle growth variation occurs between populations, no subspecies are recognized.

CONFUSING SPECIES. Other large rattlesnakes within its range can be identified by the key presented above.

KARYOTYPE. The karyotype consists of 36 chromosomes: 16 macrochromosomes (4 metacentric, 6

Western diamondback rattle-snake, *Crotalus atrox*; Clark County, Nevada. (Photograph by William Leonard)

submetacentric, and 4 subtelocentric) and 20 microchromosomes, with females ZW and males ZZ (the Z chromosome is either metacentric or submetacentric, and the W chromosome is either submetacentric or subtelocentric) (Baker et al. 1972; Zimmerman and Kilpatrick 1973). Porter (1994) has isolated two families of repetitive DNA sequences from *C. atrox*.

FOSSIL RECORD. Fossils are known from the Pliocene (Blancan) of Texas (Rogers 1976); the Pleistocene (Irvingtonian) of Texas (Holman and Winkler 1987); and the Pleistocene (Rancholabrean) of Arizona (Mead et al. 1984), California (Holman 1995), Nevada (Tihen 1962), New Mexico (Brattstrom 1954a, 1954b, 1958b; Holman 1970; Van Devender et al.

1976), Texas (Holman 1966, 1969b, 1995; Mecham 1959; Van Devender and Bradley 1994), and Sonora, Mexico (Van Devender et al. 1985).

DISTRIBUTION. *C. atrox* ranges from west-central Arkansas westward through eastern and southern Oklahoma, Texas (except the extreme east), central and southern New Mexico, Arizona, possibly extreme southern Nevada (Clark County; Emmerson 1982), and southeastern California (Riverside and Imperial counties), and southward in Mexico to Veracruz, Hidalgo, Queretaro, Sinaloa, and northeastern Baja California.

HABITAT. *C. atrox* lives in a variety of arid or seasonally dry habitats, from sea level to 2,135 m; these

Distribution of *Crotalus atrox*.

include deserts, grasslands, shrublands, scrub woods, or open coniferous forests, where the typical vegetation ranges from cacti and thornbushes to mesquite, paloverde, grasses, and even riparian oaks. It is often found among scattered rocks and boulders, or rock outcrops with crevices.

BEHAVIOR. The annual activity period of *C. atrox* is March or April to October or November, depending on latitude and elevation. It is principally active from June to September, with a decided peak in August. Rainfall is usually highest from July to September, allowing the snake to reach its greatest activity about a month later, possibly due to increases in rodent populations. In March–April, most hours are spent resting, but as summer continues periods of activity and alertness become longer than resting stages, especially during the wet months (15 July–15 October); in the fall (16 October–30 November) activity slows until the snake rests as much as it is active or alert; and normally in December–February the snake hibernates, and most time and energy are spent in resting underground (Beck 1995). If the weather warms, some *C. atrox* will bask at the mouth of their retreats around noon.

Hibernacula are most often rock crevices, small caves, or abandoned mines located on south-facing slopes, but sometimes wood piles, mammal burrows, desert tortoise burrows, or deep cracks in the soil are used. As many as 100–200 *C. atrox* may regularly congregate at a specific site to overwinter, and a hibernaculum may be used solely by *C. atrox* or be shared with other snake species.

C. atrox is more diurnally active during the spring and fall, foraging in the morning or early evening, with some basking in the morning (Landreth 1973). In the summer, it is more crepuscular and nocturnal, resting under some sheltering rock or shading vegetation during the day. Diel activity is determined by AT. Recorded BTs of active individuals range from 18 to 34°C, and average 27–30°C; snakes with BTs of 14°C were thought to be active only because of abnormal disturbance (Beck 1996; Brattstrom 1965; Cowles and Bogert 1944; Landreth 1973). The CT_{max} ranges from 39.0 to 46.5°C (Cowles and Bogert 1944; Mosauer and Lazier 1933).

Oklahoma *C. atrox* studied by Landreth (1973) made annual migrations of 0.7–3.5 km to and from winter dens. During such migrations, it does not wander randomly, but instead follows directed courses, possibly either using solar cues (sun compass [?]; Landreth 1973) or following scent trails (Weldon et al. 1990) to determine directional goals and pathways. In the spring, Landreth's males moved an average of 102.4 m/day, but only averaged 61.2 and 54.3 m in the summer and fall; females made average daily movements of 82.4 m in the spring, 46.1 m the summer, and 46.3 m in the fall. However, three different females made unexplained midsummer, overnight trips of 72.4–105.6 m. Average winter movements were short distances from the den (males, 3.5 m; females, 2.7 m). In southeastern Arizona, *C. atrox* maintained an average home range of 5.42 ha and traveled a mean distance of 12.9 km in 95 hours of surface activity (Beck 1995). During the annual activity period, the snakes moved an average of 50.8 m/day and 94.6 m per bout of activity. *C. atrox* climbs and swims well.

Males regularly participate in combat bouts or "dances," which have been well described by Armstrong and Murphy (1979), Lowe (1942, 1948a), and Repp (1998).

REPRODUCTION. The shortest TBL of a mature *C. atrox* has been reported variously as 76 cm (Conant and Collins 1998; Stebbins 1985), 76.2 cm (Wright and Wright 1957), and 80 cm (Simons 1986); but Klauber (1972) reported the shortest mature female SVL as 74.2 cm, and Tinkle (1962) as 80.0 cm. The heaviest immature female weighed by Tinkle (1962) was 450 g, while the lightest mature female weighed 320 g; most adults weighed more than 500 g. Fat makes up about 10.1% of body mass in mature females; mature males have fat 6.4% of body mass (Fitch and Pisani 1993). Maturity seems to take place in 30–36 months.

Females reproduce biennially (Fitch and Pisani 1993; Tinkle 1962). Vitellogenesis begins after emergence from hibernation in the previous nonreproductive year, and the follicles grow to a maximum length of 30 mm with considerable yolk deposition prior to the next hibernating period, but little follicular enlargement occurs over the winter. In the spring of the second (reproductive) year of the cycle, follicles continue to grow; by April most follicles are 30 × 10 mm. Ovulation and fertilization occur in early summer. No follicles enlarge when the female is gravid, and postpartum females have follicles no larger than 10 mm. Body fat slowly increases after parturition.

In Mexico, males are probably reproductively active during the entire summer. They begin spermiogenesis in July, and by August and September sperm production is in full swing (Jacob et al. 1987). Mass of testes does not vary significantly during the summer, but seminiferous tubule diameter is significantly greater in August. Mature sperm is stored over the winter for the next spring/summer mating (Jacob et al. 1987; Klauber 1972; Landreth 1973).

Some matings occur at the hibernaculum in spring, but most probably take place during the summer months. Spring copulations in the wild have occurred as early as 25 March (Bogert 1942) and as late as 14 May (Wright and Wright 1957), and in the summer as late as 29 August (Taylor 1935). Captives have courted and copulated in almost all months. Typically, a male locates and identifies a female by olfaction by rapid tongue flicking, then raises his forebody about 50–60 cm and jerks spasmodically. He crawls to her, closely examines her back and sides with his tongue, and increases the rate of spasmodic body jerking. He then rubs his chin sideways on the female's back at irregular intervals, and brings his entire body in contact with hers. At this point, she usually raises her tail and opens her cloacal vent, and the male places his vent next to her open vent and inserts a hemipenis. She may begin rhythmic body spasms at this time, but usually lies still, and he may pulsate his anterior tail region during the copulation. Copulation may last 15 minutes to four to five hours (one mating lasted eight hours; see Armstrong and Murphy 1979).

Births have been reported from late June to early October (Armstrong and Murphy 1979), but usually occur in August or September in nature (Price 1988). Females may remain with their neonates up to six days.

The number of young produced is positively correlated with female size (Fitch and Pisani 1993; Tinkle 1962). Litters average 11 young and normally contain 2–25 (n = 70) young. Klauber (1972) reported an unusual litter containing 46 young (26 alive, 20 dead;

most litters contain some stillborn individuals). Neonates average 28.5 (21.4–36.7, n = 41) cm in TBL.

Captive *C. atrox* have mated with other species of rattlesnakes (Klauber 1972), but hybridization is rare in natural populations.

GROWTH AND LONGEVITY. Growth rates vary between populations, with males equal to or larger than females throughout life (Beaupre et al. 1998; Fitch and Pisani 1993). Neonates of both sexes are similar in size, and the juvenile growth rate is uniform between the sexes; length divergence occurs after maturity. A 50.3 cm (62 g) wild female grew 38.1 mm (17 g) in 43 days between captures, and another wild female (77.4 cm, 258 g) grew 50.8 mm (8 g) in 59 days (Laughlin and Wilks 1962).

A wild-caught juvenile *C. atrox* survived 25 years, 10 months, and 27 days in captivity (Snider and Bowler 1992), and a 90 cm adult caught in 1964 was still alive in January 1991 (William W. Lamar, pers. com.).

DIET AND FEEDING HABITS. *C. atrox* finds prey either by infrared reception or olfaction. Two hunting strategies are used: active foraging and ambushing. When a fresh prey odor trail is discovered, it is followed with much tongue flicking (Chiszar et al. 1985; Gillingham and Clark 1981). When the warm-blooded prey is finally detected either visually or by infrared reception, the rate of tongue flicking slows. While ambushing, *C. atrox* lies quietly beside a frequently used rodent trail. When the prey comes within striking range, it is quickly bitten, then left to wander away and die, to be followed later by its odor. Once the body is discovered, the snake cautiously examines it with its tongue to make sure it is dead before it begins to ingest the prey head first. Envenomized prey seems to be preferred over fresh animals (Chiszar et al. 1999). Most of the annual energy budget is needed during May–September (Duvall and Beaupre 1998); yearly maintenance energy requirements can be satisfied in two to three large meals with a prey quantity equivalent to 93% of its body mass (Beck 1995).

Small mammals made up the largest part of the diet by weight (94.8%) and frequency of occurrence (86.7%) (birds were 7.6% by weight, 13.3% by frequency; lizards were 2.9% by weight, 11.1% by frequency) in 205 Texas *C. atrox* (78, 38.1% with food) examined by Beavers (1976). Particular mammals eaten were pocket mice *(Perognathus)* by 39% of the snakes, harvest mice *(Reithrodontomys)* by 9%, and white-footed mice *(Peromyscus)* by almost 7%. Similarly, in 43 *C. atrox* from Chihuahua, Mexico, Reynolds and Scott (1982) found that mammals were the predominant food (85.7% occurrence: pocket mice 26.5%; white-footed mice 16.3%; and ground squirrels, *Spermophilus*, 10.2%). (Reptiles made up 12.2% and birds 2.0%.) Prey were selected on the basis of size; animals either too large or too small were not eaten, nor were those that could seriously harm the snake. Known wild prey includes mammals—moles (unidentified), shrews *(Cryptotis parva),* murid mice, rats, and voles *(Baiomys taylori, Microtus mexicanus, M. ochrogaster, Mus musculus, Neotoma albigula, N. floridana, N. micropus, Peromyscus eremicus, P. maniculatus, Onychomys torridus, Rattus norvegicus, Reithrodontomys megalotis, Sigmodon hispidus),* pocket mice *(Perognathus flavescens, P. flavus, P. hispidus, P. intermedius, P. merriami, P. penicillatus),* kangaroo rats *(Dipodomys merriami, D. ordii, D. spectabilis),* pocket gophers *(Geomys bursarius, Pappogeomys castanops),* ground squirrels *(Spermophilus spilosoma, S. variegatus),* prairie dogs *(Cynomys ludovicianus),* fox squirrels *(Sciurus niger),* cottontails *(Sylvilagus audubonii, S. floridanus),* and jackrabbits *(Lepus californicus);* birds (including eggs and nestlings)—quail *(Colinus virginianus),* gulls *(Larus atricilla),* terns *(Sterna caspia),* black skimmers *(Rynchops niger),* burrowing owls *(Athene cunicularia),* doves *(Columbina sp.),* mockingbirds *(Mimus polyglottos),* towhees *(Pipilo erythrophthalmus),* horned larks *(Eremophila alpestris),* and sparrows *(Amphispiza bilineata, Melospiza melodia);* reptiles—lizards *(Cnemidophorus sp., Coleonyx brevis, Crotaphytus collaris, Eumeces brevilineatus, Holbrookia sp., Phrynosoma cornutum, Sceloporus magister, Uta stansburiana)* and snakes *(C. atrox);* amphibians—frogs and toads; and insects—lubber grasshoppers *(Brachystola),* beetles, and ants (Beavers 1976; Best and James 1984; Cottam et al. 1959; Fouquette and Lindsay 1955; Cates 1957; Hermann 1950; King 1975; Klauber 1972; Lowe et al. 1986; Marr 1944; McKinney and Ballinger 1966; Milstead et al. 1950; Minton 1959; Pisani and Stephenson 1991; Quinn 1985; Reynolds and Scott 1982; Smith and Hensley 1958; Tennant 1985; Tinkle

1967; Woodin 1953). The beetles and ants were found in a specimen that also contained mammal hairs and the remains of an iguanid lizard, and so may have been secondarily ingested with other prey (Klauber 1972).

Carrion is consumed when available (Gillingham and Baker 1981; Klauber 1972); perhaps this snake uses a scavenging feeding strategy. Being opportunistic, it probably eats what it can find, dead or alive, providing it is of the proper species and body size.

VENOM AND BITES. *C. atrox* has impressive fangs: 51 with 10–14 cm TBLs had fangs 9.6–12.9 mm long (Klauber 1939c).

This snake is extremely dangerous. Its venom is highly hemorrhagic; almost 53% of its enzymes are concerned with lytic breakdown of the circulatory system (three fibrinogenolytic proteases are present), but another 17% are neurotoxic in action, and 30% are digestive proteases (Tennant 1985). Intraspecific differences occur in concentrations of certain proteins; some individuals possess a neurotoxin analogous to the Mojave toxin of *C. scutulatus,* making them more dangerous than most. Hemorrhaging from the breakdown of vascular tissues occurs rapidly, and the venom also contains strong hemaglutinizing enzymes that clump red blood cells.

Venom yields are often very high. Adult *C. atrox* may yield a total of 175–600 mg of dry venom (Ernst and Zug 1996): the human lethal dose is approximately 60–100 mg. A 60 cm snake can yield about 0.10 ml of venom per bite (0.19 ml high yield), while one 150 cm long could inject 1.27 ml per bite (1.88 ml high yield) (Klauber 1972). One 165 cm long yielded a total of 1,145 mg of dried venom (3.9 ml liquid) (Klauber 1972).

Human envenomation by *C. atrox* is not uncommon and is often very serious. With or without antivenin treatment, death may occur, and this species is probably responsible for more human deaths than any other snake in the United States. Symptoms reported include intense burning pain, swelling, discoloration of tissues, edema, ecchymosis, hemorrhage, necrosis, hematemesis, hemolytic anemia, lowered blood pressure, lowered heart rate, increased heart rate, fever, sweating, numbness, weakness, stiffness, giddiness, nausea, vomiting, breathing difficulties, shock, and secondary gangrene infection (Dart et al. 1992; Hutchison 1929; Russell 1960).

PREDATORS AND DEFENSE.   Adults have few natural predators, but neonates and juveniles are probably eaten by a number of carnivorous animals. However, the only reports of predation are of a white-tailed hawk *(Buteo albicaudatus)*, a bobcat *(Lynx rufus)*, a bullfrog *(Rana catesbeiana)*, and snakes *(Drymarchon corais, Lampropeltis getula, Masticophis flagellum, M. taeniatus)* (Blair 1954; Clarkson and deVos 1986; Klauber 1972; Ross 1989; Shaw and Campbell 1974; Wilson 1954). In addition, Klauber (1972) reported a case of captive cannibalism of a juvenile by another juvenile *C. atrox*. Crimmins (1931) observed chickens *(Gallus gallus)* carrying small *C. atrox* in their bills, and after he killed one snake and chopped it up, the chickens and muscovy ducks *(Cairina moschata)* in the pen fought over the pieces. If one enters a pen through a chicken-wire fence and then feeds, it may become hopelessly stuck in the fence when it tries to leave (Campbell 1950).

Humans are still the major predator of this snake: the automobile, habitat destruction, and wanton killing (especially at dens) have severely decimated populations in some areas. One of the worst destructive actions by humans is in the form of the popular "rattlesnake roundups" in Oklahoma, Texas, and other southwestern states, where *C. atrox* is usually the snake most commonly captured.

A large, irate *C. atrox* is an awesome adversary. It will coil, raise its neck and head as high as 50 cm above its coils, continually rattle its tail—SVL-adjusted loudness is over 70 dB, the dominant frequency range is 5.14–6.60 kHz, and the total frequency range is 0.65–20.22 kHz (Cook et al. 1994; Fenton and Licht 1990; Young and Brown 1993)—strike (rarely venom is sprayed; Wheeler 1994), and sometimes even advance toward its "attacker" (presumably to get within better striking range). Some individuals will spray musk from anal scent glands (particularly if handled), and this secretion has been considered a possible deterrent to predators, but the truth of this is unknown.

POPULATIONS.   *C. atrox* is one of the most common snakes in the southwestern United States, and is surely the most common venomous snake over much of that area. In western Texas it may be found in dense populations, but not as dense as in the past. About 3,500 individuals were collected at Floresville, Wilson County, between 1 June and 1 September 1926 (Crimmins 1927), and a rancher killed 1,200 while clearing about 4,049 ha of cactus and brush in Shackelford County (0.3/ha) (Wood, in Klauber 1972). It is extremely abundant in Arizona: of 425 rattlesnakes collected by Klauber (1972), 218 (51.3%) were *C. atrox*, and Rosen and Lowe (1994) reported that 56 (15.2%) of 368 snakes observed on Rt. 85 in 1988–1991 were this species. In New Mexico, 209 (46%) of 454 snakes collected by Price and LaPointe (1990) while road cruising during 1975–1978 were *C. atrox*. Its numbers have increased as semidesert grasslands in Arizona and New Mexico have undergone succession with overgrazing to desert scrub (Mendelson and Jennings 1992). However, Vitt and Ohmart (1978) noted that due to its high trophic position, the species exists in relatively low densities in the lower Colorado River area. Fitch and Pisani (1993) thought that first-year young might make up as much as 40% of the spring population.

Fitch and Pisani (1993) examined 1,011 *C. atrox* collected in Oklahoma roundups and found the sex ratio was 1.4:1 in favor of males; but Boyer (1957) reported a sex ratio for 215 *C. atrox* from southwestern Oklahoma of 1:1.21 in favor of females. Probably the sex ratio does not differ significantly from 1:1.

REMARKS.   Based on morphology and scalation, *atrox* belongs in a complex with the *Crotalus* species *adamanteus*, *ruber*, and *tortugensis* (Brattstrom 1964b; Gloyd 1940; Klauber 1972). Data from electrophoretic studies of venom proteins by Foote and MacMahon (1977) have verified this arrangement, but have also shown a closer linkage to *viridis* than is shown by morphology.

Crotalus cerastes Hallowell 1854 | Sidewinder

RECOGNITION. *C. cerastes* has a maximun TBL of 82.4 cm, but most adults are 50–60 cm long. Its pale dorsum is pinkish, cream, tan, or gray with a series of 28–47 (mean, 36) darker tan, yellowish brown, orangish, or gray blotches, and three longitudinal rows of dark spots (often faded) on each side. The tail has two to seven dark bands, the last of which is usually darkest. A light-bordered dark stripe runs diagonally backward from the eye to the corner of the mouth, and dark spots or streaks may be present on the dorsal surface of the head behind the eyes. The white to cream venter may bear dark pigment. The keeled body scales occur in 21–23 (19–25) rows at midbody, and a strongly keeled, tuberculate spinal ridge is present. On the venter are 132–154 ventrals, 14–26 subcaudals, and an undivided anal plate. Dorsal head scales include a wider-than high-rostral, 2 moderate internasals, 12–34 scales before the 4–6 intersupraoculars, 0 prefrontals, and 2 supraoculars that are elevated into pointed, hornlike structures over the eyes. Laterally are 2 nasals (the prenasal touches the supralabials), 1 (2) loreal(s) (the loreal extends to the orbit splitting the preoculars), 2 preoculars, 2 postoculars, 2–3 suboculars, several temporals, 12–13 (10–15) supralabials, and 12–13 (10–17) infralabials. The bilobed hemipenis has a divided sulcus spermaticus, about 54 spines and 21 fringes on each of the short, thick lobes, and numerous spines between the lobes.

Males have 132–151 (mean, 142) ventrals, 17–26 (mean, 21) subcaudals, and three to seven (mean, five) dark tail bands; females have 135–154 (mean, 144) ventrals, 14–21 (mean, 17) subcaudals, and two to seven (mean, four) dark tail bands.

GEOGRAPHIC VARIATION. Three subspecies exist. *Crotalus cerastes cerastes* Hallowell 1854, the Mojave Desert sidewinder, is restricted to the Mojave Desert of California and adjacent Arizona, southern Nevada, and southwestern Utah. It has a brown proximal rattle-matrix lobe, usually fewer than 141 ventrals in males and fewer than 144 in females, 22 subcaudals in males and 17 or more in females, and 21 midbody dorsal scale rows. *C. c. cercobombus* Savage and Cliff 1953, the Sonoran Desert sidewinder, occurs from south-central Arizona southward to western Sonora and Isla Tiburon, Mexico. It has a black proximal rattle-matrix lobe, usually 141 or fewer ventrals in males and 145 or fewer in females, 20 subcaudals in males and 16 in females, and 21 midbody dorsal scale rows. *C. c. laterorepens* Klauber 1944, the Colorado Desert sidewinder, ranges in the Colorado Desert from southeastern California and southwestern Arizona south in Mexico to Baja California and the panhandle of Sonora. It has a black proximal rattle-matrix lobe, usually 142 or more ventrals in males and 146 or more in females, 21–22 subcaudals in males and 17 in fe-

Mojave Desert sidewinder,
Crotalus cerastes cerastes.
(Photograph by Donald J. Fisher)

Distribution of *Crotalus cerastes*.

males, and 23 midbody dorsal scale rows. Unfortunately, the above scale counts are not adequate characters for differentiating the subspecies (see table insert between pp. 124 and 125 in Klauber 1972), and in some individuals, tail color may also be a questionable.

CONFUSING SPECIES. No other snake in the southwestern United States has elevated hornlike projections over its eyes.

KARYOTYPE. The karyotype consists of 36 chromosomes: 16 macrochromosomes (4 metacentric, 6 submetacentric, and 4 subtelocentric; the Z sexual chromosome metacentric; and the W sexual chromosome subtelocentric) and 20 microchromosomes (Zimmerman and Kilpatrick 1973).

FOSSIL RECORD. Pleistocene vertebrae have been found in Rancholabrean deposits in Arizona (Van Devender et al. 1991; Van Devender and Mead 1978).

DISTRIBUTION. The sidewinder ranges from extreme southwestern Utah, southern Nevada, and southeastern California southward through southeastern Arizona to northwestern Sonora, eastern Baja California del Norte, and Isla Tiburon in Mexico.

HABITAT. Prime habitat is a desert with loose sand dunes in rather low-lying areas (from below sea level in Death Valley, California, to slightly over 1,800 m), but it is sometimes found in hardpan, rocky, or gravelly sites within deserts. Associated vegetation is creosote bush, mesquite, paloverde, burroweed, galleta grass, and various cacti.

BEHAVIOR. In California, spring emergence may occur as early as late February, but with increasing daylight and warmth, more and more individuals leave their hibernacula in March and April; fall disappearance occurs in October or November (Brown and Lillywhite 1992; Klauber 1972; Secor 1994). Most spring surface activity takes place in May and June; a fall activity peak occurs in late September or October.

Hibernation begins in October and all *C. cerastes* are underground by December (Brown and Lillywhite 1992; Secor 1994), although warm weather may bring a few to the surface to bask or crawl about. Winter is usually spent alone within a rodent burrow. Of 15 snakes monitored by Secor (1994), 14 hibernated in kangaroo rat burrows, and the other in a desert tortoise burrow. Cowles (1941b) speculated that this snake might hibernate at depths below 30 cm, and Brown and Lillywhite (1992) and Secor (1994) recorded hibernation depths of 20–70 cm. In rocky areas, crevices may be used as a hibernaculum, and during mild winters this snake may merely bury itself in the sand near the surface.

In the spring when STs are no higher than 35°C, *C. cerastes* will stay on the surface all day before seeking shelter at sunset. It avoids the summer daytime heat by entering animal burrows or by burying itself beneath the sand so that at most only the outer coil is uncovered. It enters a tight coil and then edges or nudges the sand outward from beneath the body or uses the head and neck to pull sand over its coils to form a saucer-shaped craterlike depression in which it lies with its back flush with the surrounding surface (Cowles and Bogert 1944; Cowles 1945; Secor 1994). Any appreciable drift of sand tends to submerge the snake either by surface movement of rolling grains or by the deposition of wind-blown material, and wind often blows away tracks leading to the spot. These roosts are usually in the shade of some bush.

The sidewinder is usually considered nocturnal; almost all summer activity takes place at night, but some diurnal movements occur in early spring and in the fall, particularly during the morning or late in the afternoon. Suitable daytime ATs for surface activity are 32–35 °C (Secor 1994). Nocturnal activity takes place from 1930 to 0500 hours, with the peak period occurring between 1000 and 0100 hours (Klauber 1944; Moore 1978). Sidewinders are nocturnal despite widely varying ET conditions (Moore 1978). The normal activity range in BTs is 6.3–40.8 °C, and STs are usually over 30 °C (Brown and Lillywhite 1992; Moore 1978; Secor 1994). Mean BT varies from month to month (November, 18.4 °C; August, 31.4 °C), but averages 25.8 °C. BTs of active sidewinders have ranged from 13.6 to 40.8 °C (Brattstrom 1965; Brown and Lillywhite 1992; Cunningham 1966a). Cowles and Bogert (1944) reported a voluntary minimum BT of 17.5 °C, an optimum BT of 31.5 °C, and the CT_{max} of 41.6 °C; and Brattstrom (1965) thought the CT_{min} was –2 °C. Basking sometimes occurs in the morning or late afternoon, probably following a meal (the region of the body containing the food bolus is usually exposed directly to the sun), and at night, *C. cerastes* near asphalt roads will crawl onto the highway to warm themselves by conduction of the residual heat remaining there.

Sidewinders may maintain rather large home ranges, probably due to the energy needs that result from widespread desert prey. In the eastern Mojave Desert, male *C. cerastes* have home ranges of 8.3–51.2 (mean, 18.2) ha, and females maintain home ranges of 3.7–21.3 (mean, 12.0) ha (Secor 1992, 1994). Secor (1992) found that in spring juveniles move an average of 100.2 m between captures, subadults 172.6 m, adult females 76.3 m, and adult males 122.5 m; movements for these same groups in the summer and fall are 163.7, 202.3, 73.0, and 99.1 m, and 140.8, 188.0, 78.5, and 237.5 m, respectively. One of his subadults moved 963 m between captures, and Brown and Lillywhite (1992) reported one made a night trip in October of 1.27 km. Such long-distance movements probably are not frequent: most of the sidewinders followed by Brown and Lillywhite moved less than 400 m/night.

Although *C. cerastes* is capable of performing all four typical methods of crawling by snakes (see Ernst and Zug 1996), its sandy habitat often dictates that it resort to the specialized method from which it derives its name. Sidewinding is essentially a series of lateral looping movements in which only vertical force is applied and usually no more than two parts of the body touch the sand at any one time. However, when the neck first makes contact, three points (neck, body, and tail) are in contact with the sand. The snake moves diagonally quickly forward, and separate J-shaped tracks (each paralleling the other and angling in the direction of movement) result, as it literally skips across loose sand. Its weight seems to shift from head to tail as it moves. Jayne (1986) observed that sidewinding is sometimes alternated with typical lateral undulatory crawling, even on loose sand, and reported maximum mean forward velocities of 0.75–1.7 TBLs per second. Mosauer (1935b) reported that this species could voluntarily sidewind at 0.14 m/second and, if harassed, could reach a speed of 0.91 m/second. Maximal burst speed observed by Secor et al. (1992) was 3.7 km/hour; adults were able to maintain a speed of 0.5 km/hour for 33–180 minutes. Typically, nighttime sidewinding is slow, 0.04–0.07 m/second (Secor 1994). When the snake moves through brush or plant debris, lateral undulation is used, while rectilinear crawling is typically used during courtship and the first 1–3 m of nighttime movement. Sidewinding seems ideally suited for movement in sandy deserts, but also allows some thermal regulation, as only two to three points of the body are in contact with the hot (or cold, at night) sand.

C. cerastes occasionally climbs into desert vegetation to heights of 10–30 cm. It is also a natural swimmer (Klauber 1972).

Male combat behavior has been recorded only once in *C. cerastes*, and took place in April with both males in breeding condition. The bout included a sequence of biting not known in other North American crotalids (Lowe and Norris 1950). While parrying in an upright position, the snakes suddenly bit each other in the neck approximately 50 mm posterior to the head. This behavior was repeated, but it is doubtful that either male ejected venom during the biting.

REPRODUCTION. The smallest TBLs of mature individuals of either sex are 42.0–43.4 cm (Klauber 1972; Stebbins 1985; Wright and Wright 1957). The age of maturity is not known.

Wild *C. cerastes* may mate in either the spring or fall. Spring copulations have occurred on 26 March–4 June; fall matings took place on 20 September, and 7,

18, and 22 October (Brown and Lillywhite 1992; Lowe 1942; Klauber 1972; Secor 1994; Stebbins 1954; Wright and Wright 1957). Possibly sperm from fall matings is stored by the female until ovulation the next spring. All observations of mating were in the morning, so courtship had begun the night before. The male nudges and performs jerky head movements along the female's body, then wraps his body around that of the female and inserts a hemipenis. After intromission, the male may hold his tail straight up, waving it slowly in a circle, but does not pulsate or pump. He may drag the female about while they are attached, as his body moves around and over her, while he still nudges her body with his head. This may be followed by a period of little movement before more tail waving and nudging occur, but not necessarily at the same time. A pronounced pulsating or pumping motion occurs in the female's cloacal region, possibly begun by her, continues at a rate of one per second for about 10 seconds, then a little faster or slower until stopped entirely. Eventually the two snakes pull apart and go their separate ways (Lowe 1942; Perkins, in Klauber 1972). Copulation may last over seven to eight hours.

The GP is 150+ days (Perkins, in Klauber 1972). Known birth dates range from 14 August to 28 November, but most occur in September or early October (Brown and Lillywhite 1992; Klauber 1972; Secor 1994; Wright and Wright 1957). Litters average 9.2 offspring (n = 57 litters) and may contain 1 (C. Ernst, pers. obs.) to 20 young (Langebartel and Smith 1954), but typically have 7–12. Mean TBL is 18.2 (16.1–20.5, n = 31) cm; they weigh about 6 g (n = 3). Larger females appear to produce more young per litter; RCM is approximately 0.40 (Secor 1994).

GROWTH AND LONGEVITY. The mean growth rate for 35 *C. cerastes* studied by Secor (1994) was 0.54 mm/day. The growth rate slows with increasing body length. Klauber (1972) noted that the Mojave Desert sidewinder *(C. c. cerastes)* is shorter than the Colorado Desert sidewinder *(C. c. laterorepens)*, which may be correlated with a shorter growing season. A *C. c. cerastes* born in captivity survived over 28 years (Goodman et al. 1997).

DIET AND FEEDING HABITS. Adult *C. cerastes* feed mostly on small rodents and lizards. Neonates and small juveniles rely almost exclusively on lizards, although possibly small snakes are also eaten. As the snakes grow they gradually take larger lizards and rodents. Funk (1965a) examined 226 sidewinders: 88 (51.5%) contained mammals (mostly *Dipodomys, Perognathus,* and *Peromyscus*), 73 (42.7%) contained lizards (mostly *Cnemidophorus* and *Uma*), 5 (2.9%) had eaten birds, and 5 (2.9%) contained small snakes. Reported prey of wild and captive *C. cerastes* are mammals—kangaroo rats *(Dipodomys deserti, D. merriami, D. platyrhinos),* pocket mice *(Perognathus baileyi, P. longimembris, P. penicillatus),* white-footed mice *(Peromyscus eremicus, P. maniculatus),* harvest mice *(Reithrodontomys megalotis),* house mice *(Mus musculus),* ground squirrels *(Ammospermophilus harrisii, A. leucurus, Spermophilus tereticaudus),* woodrats *(Neotoma albigula, N. lepida),* pocket gophers, *(Thomomys bottae),* and shrews *(Notiosorex crawfordi);* birds—sparrows *(Amphispiza bilineata, Chondestes grammacus, Passer domesticus),* wrens *(Campylorhynchus brunneicapillums),* and warblers *(Dendroica petechia);* reptiles—lizards *(Callisaurus draconoides, Cnemidophorus tigris, Coleonyx variegatus, Dipsosaurus dorsalis, Gambelia wizlizeni, Phrynosoma cornutum, P. mcalli, Uma inornata, U. notata, U. scoparia, Urosaurus ornatus, Uta stansburiana)* and snakes *(Arizona elegans, Chionactis occipitalis, Crotalus cerastes, Sonora semiannulata);* and a "caterpillar" (Brown and Lillywhite 1992; Cunningham 1959; Funk 1965a; Klauber 1972, Secor 1994; Van Denburgh 1922). The caterpillar was found in a juvenile that also contained a lizard *(Uma),* and Klauber (1972) thought that the lizard either had first eaten the caterpillar or had been captured while eating it. Carrion is consumed: Cunningham (1959) reported that a captive ate a mouse dead for at least two days, and Klauber (1972) found a sidewinder eating a DOR (dead-on-the-road) kangaroo rat *(Dipodomys).*

C. cerastes captures most prey from ambush, lying, partially concealed by sand, outside the entrances of rodent and lizard burrows; however, some active foraging does occur. Olfaction may play a minor role to visual or infrared prey detection; Chiszar and Radcliffe (1977) recorded no significant response by naive neonate sidewinders to prey odors. However, Secor (1994) observed that olfaction is more important in prey detection than vision or heat detection, as sidewinders usually tongue flick before striking and then use olfaction to trail wounded prey. Lizards are usually retained in the mouth when struck, but rodents are released after the strike.

VENOM AND BITES. *C. cerastes* has relatively long fangs for its size; 51.8–76.7 cm adults had fangs 5.0–8.1 mm long (Klauber 1939c).

The venom is only moderately toxic, and the amount injected per bite is low: 0.06 ml (0.018 g dried) for adults (Amaral 1928). Total yield is usually 20–45 mg of dried venom per adult, with a maximum yield of 63 mg (Ernst and Zug 1996; Klauber 1972). Only 0.10 mg/kg will kill a mouse (Ernst and Zug 1996); the human lethal dose is 40 mg (Dowling 1975). Sidewinder venom has hemorrhagic, anticoagulant, protease, and arginine ester hydrolase activities (MacKessy 1988; Tan and Ponnudarai 1991).

Human envenomation by a sidewinder is usually mild, but fatalities have resulted (Russell 1960). Symptoms include pain, swelling, an itching sensation, discoloration, weakness, dizziness, slight nausea (after administration of antivenin), paralysis, necrosis of the tissue at the bite site, an increase in BT, and tenderness at the site of the bite for several days after being bitten (Hutchison 1929; Lowell 1957; Minton 1956a; S. M. Secor, pers. comm.).

PREDATORS AND DEFENSE. *C. cerastes* has many predators, particularly of the young. The following are actual or potential predators: coyotes *(Canis latrans)*, kit foxes *(Vulpes macrotis)*, American kestrels *(Falco sparvarius)*, red-tailed hawks *(Buteo jamaicensis)*, great horned owls *(Bubo virginianus)*, roadrunners *(Geococcyx californianus)*, loggerhead shrikes *(Lanius ludovicianus)*, ravens *(Corvus corax)*, leopard lizards *(Gambelia wizlizeni)*, coachwhips *(Masticophis flagellum)*, kingsnakes *(Lampropeltis getula)*, rosy boas *(Charina trivirgata)*, and larger sidewinders *(C. cerastes)* (Brown and Lillywhite 1992; Funk 1965a; Klauber 1972; Ross 1989; Secor 1994). Many die at the hands of humans and their automobiles.

The sidewinder is a nervous snake, but often remains quietly coiled when first discovered. If prodded it will rattle and usually try to crawl away, but if further provoked, it will put up a spirited fight, coiling, rattling—SVL-adjusted loudness to about 70 dB; frequency range, 3.8–23.8 kHz; mean dominant frequency, 12.9 kHz (Cook et al. 1994; Fenton and Licht 1990; Young and Brown 1993)—jerking the head, alternately laterally compressing and inflating the body, and striking viciously. If confronted by a kingsnake, *C. cerastes* will flee, strike and bite, body bridge, hide its head under a coil, or inflate its body (Bogert 1941; Cowles 1938). It is also capable of changing its body melanism to somewhat match that of the substratum (Klauber 1931b; Neill 1951); although Neill (1951) thought this a thermal adjustment, it also may provide some protection from overhead avian predators.

POPULATIONS. *C. cerastes* may be locally common. It made up 4.3% of the snakes observed on Arizona Rt. 85 in 1988–1991 by Rosen and Lowe (1994); Fowlie (1965) found 47 on one moonlit night on a road between Yuma and Gila Bend, Arizona; and Armstrong and Murphy (1979) saw up to 30 per night while driving roads. Brown and Lillywhite (1992) marked 50 *C. cerastes* at their study site, and estimated the sidewinder's density at 0.29–0.71/ha. Secor (1994) marked 116 *C. cerastes* and thought the density closer to 1/ha at another site.

Of 116 *C. cerastes* sidewinders captured by Secor (1994), 59 were females and 57 males, a 1:1 sex ratio, and the ratio of immature to mature snakes was 0.33:1. The 50 individuals captured by Brown and Lillywhite (1992) included 25 males, 20 females (1.25:1), and five juveniles (0.11:1).

REMARKS. Brattstrom (1964b) thought *C. cerastes* most closely related to *C. mitchellii*, *C. tigris*, and *C. viridis* on morphological grounds, but Klauber (1972) grouped it with *C. durissus*, *C. molossus*, and *C. horridus*, and dorsal scale microdermatoglyphics place it with *C. mitchelli* and *C. pricei* (Stille 1987). Electrophoretic studies of venom proteins show it to be closely related to *C. pricei*, *C. willardi*, *C. lepidus*, *C. triseriatus*, and *Sistrurus ravus* (Foote and MacMahon 1977).

Cohen and Myres (1970) suggested that the snake's supraocular horns function as eyelids that protect the eyes while it moves through burrows entangled with such obstructions as creosote roots, rocks, and gravel, which could abrade the eye.

Crotalus horridus Linnaeus 1758 | Timber Rattlesnake

RECOGNITION. Adult *C. horridus* (TBL to 189.2 cm) have 15–34 (mean, 24) chevronlike or V-shaped body bands, a gray, dark brown, or black unpatterned tail, and numerous small scales on top of the head. Body color varies from yellow to gray or dark brown, and some individuals (especially in the Northeast) may be totally black. The light morph makes up 40–93% of eastern populations; dark morphs tend to predominate in montane, densely forested sites, particularly in the Northeast (Martin 1988). Those from the South have a red to reddish orange vertebral stripe, and juveniles have three to six tail bands. On each side of the head is a dark stripe that extends from the eye backward to beyond the corner of the mouth, and some individuals may have round occipital spots. The venter is pink, white, cream, or yellow with small, dark, stipples; on the venter are 154–183 ventrals, 13–31 subcaudals, and an undivided anal plate. Dorsal body scales are keeled and pitted, and form 25–27 (23–29) rows anteriorly, 23 or 25 (21–26) midbody rows, and 19 (17–21) posterior rows. Dorsal head scales include a higher-than-broad rostral, 2 internasals, 4 canthals (between the internasals and supraoculars), and 2 supraoculars; laterally are 2 nasals (separated from the preoculars by the loreal), 2 (1–3) loreals, 2 preoculars, 4 (2–6) postoculars, several suboculars and temporals, 13–15 (10–17) supralabials, and 14–16 (11–19) infralabials. The bifurcated hemipenis has a divided sulcus spermaticus, 70+ recurved spines, and 30+ fringes per lobe, but no spines in the crotch between the lobes.

Adult males are larger than females and have 154–179 (mean, 171) ventrals, 18–31 (mean, 26) subcaudals, and TLs 5–14 (mean, 8) % of TBL. Females have 154–183 (mean, 170) ventrals, 13–28 (mean, 21) subcaudals, and TLs 4–15 (mean, 6) % of TBL. Female *C. h. horridus* retain the dark postorbital stripe throughout life (the intensity may decrease), but it becomes obscured in mature males (Storment 1990).

GEOGRAPHIC VARIATION. Two subspecies are recognized (for a debate on their validity, see Brown and Ernst 1986; Pisani et al. 1973). *C. h. horridus* Lin-

Timber rattlesnake, *Crotalus horridus horridus*; Ohio. (Photograph by Roger W. Barbour)

Timber rattlesnake, *Crotalus horridus horridus)*; Warren County, New York. (Photograph by Carl H. Ernst)

naeus 1758, the timber rattlesnake, ranges from New Hampshire (formerly also southern Maine), Vermont, northeastern New York, and southeastern Ontario, west to southeastern Minnesota, and south to northern Georgia, northwestern Arkansas, and northeastern Texas. It is yellow to gray or black, lacks a distinct vertebral stripe, and has 23 (21–26) midbody scale rows and 15–34 dorsal body bands. *C. h. atricaudatus* Latreille, in Sonnini and Latreille 1801, the canebrake rattlesnake, occurs from southeastern Virginia along the Atlantic Coastal Plain to northern Florida, westward to central Texas, and northward in the Mississippi Valley to southern Illinois. It is pinkish brown or gray, with a distinct reddish orange vertebral stripe, 25 (21–25) midbody scale rows, and 21–29 dorsal body bands. Conant and Collins (1998) refer to color morphs instead of subspecies: a "yellow variation" and a "black variation" in the Northeast *(C. h. horridus),* a "southern variation" in the lowlands of the South *(C. h. atricaudatus),* and a "western variation" found west of the Mississippi River from the Ozarks northward *(C. h. horridus × h. atricaudatus* [?]).

CONFUSING SPECIES. Other *Crotalus* can be identified by the above key. Pygmy rattlesnakes and massasaugas *(Sistrurus)* have nine enlarged plates on top of the head.

KARYOTYPE. The 36 chromosomes consist of 16 macrochromosomes (4 metacentric, 6 submetacen-

Distribution of *Crotalus horridus.*

Canebrake rattlesnake, *Crotalus horridus atricaudatus*; Aiken County, South Carolina. (Photograph by Peter May)

tric, 4 subtelocentric) and 20 microchromosomes; sex determination is ZZ in males and ZW in females (Zimmerman and Kilpatrick 1973).

FOSSIL RECORD. Fossil *C. horridus* are known from the Pliocene (Blancan) of Nebraska (Rogers 1984); the Pleistocene (Irvingtonian) of Arkansas (Dowling 1958b), Maryland (Holman 1977b, 1980), Nebraska (Holman 1995), Pennsylvania (Holman 1995), Texas (Holman and Winkler 1987), and West Virginia (Holman 1982b; Holman and Grady 1989); and the Pleistocene (Rancholabrean) of Alabama (Holman et al. 1990), Georgia (Holman 1967), Indiana (Holman and Richards 1981; Richards 1990), Massachusetts (van Frank and Hecht 1954), Missouri (Holman 1965b, 1974; Parmalee et al. 1969), New York (Steadman and Craig 1993; Steadman et al. 1993), Pennsylvania (Guilday et al. 1964, 1966), Tennessee (Brattstrom 1954b; Holman 1995; Van Dam 1978), Virginia (Guilday 1962; Holman 1995), and West Virginia (Holman 1995; Holman and Grady 1987). In addition, a Nebraska Miocene (Hemphillian) fossil has been identified as close to *C. horridus* (Parmley and Holman 1995).

DISTRIBUTION. *C. horridus* formerly occurred in southern Maine and now ranges from south-central New Hampshire west through northeastern and southern New York to southeastern Minnesota, and south to northern Florida and eastern Texas. Scattered colonies formerly existed in Ontario, and still exist in eastern Massachusetts, North Carolina, and Ohio.

HABITAT. Elevation ranges from sea level to about 1,200 m. *C. h. horridus* inhabits upland woodlands, usually facing south, with nearby rock ledges or slides. *C. h. atricaudatus* lives in lowland thickets, pinewoods, and canebrakes, or along swamp borders. Gravid females occupy small, warmer home ranges with relatively open canopy and much leaf litter near the hibernaculum; their home ranges are more static and overlapping than are those of males and nongravid females (Reinert and Zappalorti 1988a). Males and nonreproductive females have larger, distant home ranges in the specific subspecies' habitats described above; canopy cover and vegetation are more extensive, and logs are often present (Peterson 1990; Reinert 1984a, 1984b; Reinert and Zappalorti 1988a).

C. h. horridus uses a gradient of habitats in Pennsylvania, from mature forests with numerous fallen logs to young forests with predominantly leaf litter cover (Reinert 1984b): dark morphs prefer the former, but yellow morphs are more frequently found in the latter. This habitat separation of the color morphs probably is primarily concerned with background matching for camouflage.

BEHAVIOR. Annual activity is usually from March–mid-April (occasionally early May) to October–November (occasionally early December); the farther south, the longer the annual activity period; the farther north, the shorter the time period above ground. In New York, this snake is annually active for 4.6 months and hibernates for 7.4 months (Brown 1993). Some temporary and sporadic emergence usually occurs in the spring before general emergence, and snakes leave the hibernacula over an extended 18 day to two-month period. In North Carolina, 88% of its records are from June through October (Palmer and Braswell 1995). The duration of dormancy usually depends on how warm the early spring or fall days are.

Formerly, *C. h. horridus* congregated in large groups of as many as 50–200 snakes at suitable hibernacula, usually in rock crevices or south-facing talus slopes; snakes from kilometers around would crawl over set pathways to reach these sites. Some heavily populated dens still exist in remote or protected areas, but many have been reduced or extirpated. Hibernaculum fidelity is high (Bushar et al. 1998); only 1 of 11 *C. h. hor-*

ridus translocated to a distant hibernaculum returned to that site the next fall (Reinert and Rupert 1999). *C. h. atricaudatus* hibernates individually or in much smaller groups in mammal burrows, old logs and stumps, or shallow rock crevices. In both subspecies, neonates and adults share the same hibernaculum. Apparently the neonates initially find the den by following adult odor trails (Brown and MacLean 1983; Reinert and Zappalorti 1988b). BTs of hibernating New York *C. horridus* were 4.3–15.7 (mean, 10.5) °C from September through May, mean rate of BT decline was 0.5°C per week through February, and the temperature stabilized at 4.3°C in March, then rose by 0.6°C per week in April–May (Brown 1982).

In the spring and fall *C. horridus* is primarily diurnal, but when the days become hot in summer it shifts to a more crepuscular or nocturnal mode. Cloudy, windless days with ATs of 20–25°C and a BT of about 25°C are preferred by *C. horridus*. Recorded BTs of active snakes are 5.5–33.3 (average, 27–30) °C (Brown et al. 1982; Oldfield and Keyler 1989; Reinert and Zappalorti 1988a; Wills and Beaupre 2000). Differences between BT and ET in Arkansas *C. horridus* during August were 1.0–4.5°C at 1900–0800 hours, and –2.0 to –8.0°C at 0900–1600 hours, but no significant difference occurred between 1700 and 1800 hours (Wills and Beaupre 2000).

Newborn young can follow the scent trail of their own species, and they use this ability to find a communal hibernaculum (Brown and MacLean 1983; Reinert and Zappalorti 1988b). Some may even travel with adults during these migrations (Reinert and Zappalorti 1988b). Radio-equipped New York adults moved an average of 504 m (females, 280 m; males, 1,400 m) and gained a mean 102 m in elevation from hibernaculum to summer feeding range (Brown 1987; Brown et al. 1982). The maximum single migratory movements were 7.2 km by a male, and 3.7 km by a nongravid female (W. S. Brown, pers. comm.). In contrast, gravid females move little distance from the hibernaculum; one only moved 39 m in 46 days (Brown et al. 1982). Mean migration distances in Virginia are 2.45 km for adult males, 2.16 km for nongravid females, 0.5 km for gravid females, and 1.73 km for juveniles (Martin 1990). Two females tracked by Brown et al. (1982) used the same migratory routes returning to the den in autumn as they had in leaving it the

previous spring. These snakes may remain at one spot for a period of time, then move a considerable distance, and then settle down again for some time (Galligan and Dunson 1982). Perhaps these erratic movements are stimulated by prey availability.

Males have home ranges of 65–207 ha, nongravid females 17–42 ha, but gravid females only 4–22 ha (Brown 1993; Reinert 1991; Reinert and Zappalorti 1988a). Both males and nongravid females continually shift their nonoverlapping home ranges, and normally move in a looping pattern during the active season that eventually returns them to their hibernaculum in the fall.

C. horridus will sometimes climb into bushes or small trees (Saenz et al. 1996). It is also a good swimmer, and often swims from the mainland to islands in northern lakes (W.S. Brown, pers. comm.).

Adult males, like other *Crotalus*, engage in combat dances during the breeding season (Anderson 1965; Collins 1993; Klauber 1972; Sutherland 1958).

REPRODUCTION. Usually 4–6 years (males) to 7–13 years (females) pass before *C. horridus* mature. SVLs of recently matured female *C. h. atricaudatus* are usually > 100 cm; and males are mature at SVLs 90–100 cm (Gibbons 1972). Female *C. h. horridus* are mature at SVLs of 67.7–90.0 cm (Brown 1991; Galligan and Dunson 1979; Keenlyne 1978; Martin 1988).

Females normally have either biennial or triennial reproductive cycles, with triennial most common, but some may take as long as six years before reproducing again (Brown 1991, 1993; Fitch 1985b; Galligan and Dunson, 1979; Gibbons 1972; Keenlyne 1978). Proportions of gravid females vary from year to year, and may be influenced by prey availability. If fat reserves are low, female reproduction may be delayed one or more years (Gibbons 1972). Proportions of gravid females each year vary throughout the range: 27–75% in New York, 18–51% in Virginia (Brown and Martin 1990), and up to 84% in Pennsylvania (Reinert 1991).

Follicular development and vitellogenesis occur from late July through October in the north (Brown 1991, 1995; Keenlyne 1978; Martin 1993). The eggs are ovulated the next May–June in the north, but South Carolina females may contain embryos in the spring (Gibbons 1972). Parturition occurs in August–October. Spermatogenesis begins in June and July, with maximum sperm production in late July–September, when seminiferous tubules have their greatest diameters. Sperm then passes into the epididymides and vasa deferentia for overwinter storage; tubular diameters are small in the spring (Aldridge and Brown 1995).

Some minor breeding activity may take place in the spring (Anderson 1965; Keenlyne 1978), but most mating occurs from mid-July through October, with the sperm being stored until ovulation the next spring (Brown 1987, 1991; Martin 1988, 1990; Sealy 1996). In northeastern New York, the mating season is concentrated in 72 days from 15 July through 23 August, and heterosexual grouping coincides with female vitellogenesis (Brown 1995). Males probably follow scent trails to find females (Brown and MacLean 1983). Once a female is found, the male rubs her neck with his chin, positions himself alongside the female, stimulates her with quick, rapid jerks of his head and body, and then curls his tail beneath hers until the vents touch and inserts his hemipenis; copulation may last several hours (C. Ernst, pers. obs.).

C. horridus is ovoviviparous, and parturition usually occurs between 15 August and 16 October. *C. h. atricaudatus* possibly give birth earlier; a captive produced a litter on 20 July (Kauffeld, in Klauber 1972). Birthing rookeries are sometimes located at the hibernaculum, but may be as far away as 0.5–1.0 km (Martin 1988; Reinert and Zappalorti 1988b).

Most broods consist of 6–10 (mean, 10.4; n = 88) young, but litters of 1–20 are known (Palmer and Braswell 1995). The female remains with the young for 7–10 days before all disperse (Martin 1988, 1990, 1996). Litter size is directly proportional to female SVL. Seigel and Fitch (1984) reported a RCM of 0.335. Neonates are believed to trail adults away from the birthing area and, later in the fall, to the hibernaculum (Reinert and Zappalorti 1988b).

Neonates are patterned like adults, but gray in hue, have 19.5–38.3 (mean, 32.5; n = 49) cm TBLs, and weigh 11.2–29.1 (mean, 22.5; n = 10) g. They have a buttonlike terminal tail scale that is exposed after the first shedding of the skin (normally in 7–10 days). They are dangerous even at this small size, having fangs 2.6–3.8 mm long (Stewart et al. 1960), and a ready supply of venom.

Schuett (1998) and Schuett et al. (1998) reported an apparent case of automictic parthenogenesis by a fe-

male *C. horridus*. She had been in captivity since birth and never with a male, but produced a litter of three triploid males (one live, two stillborn).

GROWTH AND LONGEVITY. Fitch (1985b, 1999) reported the following SVL to age correlations for Kansas *C. horridus*: fall of birth, 31.0–34.5 cm; first spring, 32.4–59.1 cm; year 1, 54.8–71.2 cm; year 2, 50.4–83.4 cm; year 3, 64.4–99.9 cm; year 4, 76.0–100.3 cm; year 5, 88.5–108.0 cm; year 6, 96.5–114.7 cm; year 7, 100.0–119.6 cm; year 8, 123.0–124.8 cm; year 9, 103.8–104.4 cm; and year 15, 127.0 cm. In Virginia, juveniles average 43.2 cm at one year, 58.4 cm at two years, and 70.6 cm at three years (Martin 1988). Shortly after birth in South Carolina, juveniles have 35–43 cm SVLs, and they grow to 50–60 cm by the next June; at two years they are 65–75 cm, and at three years 80–90 cm (Gibbons 1972). The growth rate depends on the frequency of feeding and the quality of the diet and can be accelerated with increased feeding; a captive grew from a TBL of 34.3 cm to 75.6 cm in only eight months (Schwab 1988). The longevity record for captives is 36 years, 7 months, and 27 days (Cavanaugh 1994); some wild *C. horridus* survive over 30 years (W.S. Brown, pers. comm.).

DIET AND FEEDING HABITS. *C. horridus* is a sit-and-wait ambusher at a place where small mammals will probably pass (Brown and Greenberg 1992; Reinert et al. 1984). Favored positions are coiled beside a fallen log with the head positioned perpendicular to the log's long axis and the chin resting on the side of the log, or lying beside a tree with the head elevated and held vertically against the trunk. Some prey may be actively sought, however, as evidenced by the abundant records of it climbing trees, presumably seeking birds or squirrels. Striking a prey starts a chemical search with much tongue flicking. Since white-footed mice and chipmunks are the preferred prey in the East (Brown 1987; Martin 1988), feeding must occur both day and night. Neill (1960) suggested the young may use their tails as a lure for small prey, but this has not been ascertained. *C. horridus* only eats 6–20 meals per year, and annually consumes 2.5 times its body weight (Brown 1987; Fitch 1982).

Most prey are taken alive, but carrion is eaten; warm-blooded prey are preferred. Mice composed 38%, squirrels and chipmunks 25%, rabbits 18%, shrews 5%, and birds (mostly songbirds) 13% of the prey taken by 141 Virginia *C. horridus* (Uhler et al. 1939). In Pennsylvania, mammals composed 94% of the diet (Surface 1906). Recorded prey are mammals—shrews *(Blarina brevicauda, Cryptotis parva, Sorex cinereus),* moles *(Scalopus aquaticus),* bats (not identified), murid rodents *(Clethrionomys gapperi, Microtus pennsylvanicus, M. pinetorum, M. ochrogaster, Mus musculus, Neotoma floridana, Oryzomys palustris, Peromyscus leucopus, P. maniculatus, P. nuttalli, Rattus norvegicus, Sigmodon hispidus, Synaptomys cooperi),* jumping mice *(Napaeozapus insignis, Zapus hudsonicus),* pocket gophers *(Geomys bursarius),* squirrels *(Glaucomys volans, Marmota monax* [young], *Sciurus carolinensis, S. niger, Tamiasciurus hudsonicus, Tamias striatus),* rabbits *(Sylvilagus floridanus),* raccoon (young) *(Procyon lotor),* and mustelids *(Mephitis mephitis, Mustela frenata);* birds (eggs, young, and adults)—galliforms *(Bonasa umbellus, Colinus virginianus, Gallus gallus, Melaegris gallopavo),* rails *(Rallus longirostris* [?]), woodpeckers *(Melanerpes carolinus),* and passeriforms *(Ammodramus savannarum, Bombycilla cedrorum, Coccyzus americanus, Dendroica caerulescens, Hylocichla mustelina, Pipilo erythrophthalmus, Seiurus aurocapillus, Setophaga rutilla, Spizella pusilla, Toxostoma rufum, Zonotrichia albicollis);* reptiles—lizards *(Eumeces* sp.) and snakes *(Coluber constrictor, Thamnophis sirtalis);* anurans *(Bufo* sp., *Rana* sp.); and insects (Bailey 1946; Barbour 1950; Brown 1979a; Brown and Greenberg 1992; Bush 1959; C. Ernst, pers. obs.; Fitch 1982, 1999; Grant 1970; Hamilton and Pollack 1955; Kennedy 1964; Klauber 1972; Minton 1972; Mitchell 1994; Myers 1956; Nicolletto 1985; Palmer and Braswell 1995; Smyth 1949; Surface 1906; Swanson 1952; Uhler et al. 1939). Barbour (1950) took a snail shell from a stomach, but thought it probably had been secondarily consumed in a chipmunk pouch.

The feeding behavior of females is strongly related to their reproductive condition (Keenlyne 1972; Reinert et al. 1984). Gravid females feed very little, if at all, while those with maturing follicles eat more often.

VENOM AND BITES. Adults have 8.7–10.4 mm fangs (Klauber 1939c), and replacement fangs for those lost or broken are already present at birth (Barton 1950).

The venom of *C. horridus* is strongly hemolytic. Human envenomation results in swelling, pain, weak-

ness, giddiness, breathing difficulty, myonecrosis, blood coagulation impairment, hemorrhage, weak pulse and lowered blood pressure, increased heart rate, heart failure, nausea, ecchymosis, paralysis, unconsciousness or stupor, shock, gastric disturbance, diarrhea, and heart pain, and death has resulted from bites (Barbour 1950; Brown 1987; Hutchison 1929; Guidry 1953; Kitchens et al. 1987; Klauber 1972; Parrish and Thompson 1958).

Typically *C. horridus* contains 75–210 mg of dried venom (Ernst and Zug 1996); the maximum known dry yield is 229 mg (Klauber 1972). Wet venom volumes are 0.23–0.71 ml/snake (Minton 1953). The LD_{50} for a typical mouse is 1.64 mg/kg (Ernst and Zug 1996), and the estimated lethal human dose is 75–100 mg (Minton and Minton 1969). Small basic peptide venom toxins may vary geographically in this snake (Straight et al. 1991).

PREDATORS AND DEFENSE. Known predators, particularly of juvenile *C. horridus* are hawks *(Buteo jamaicensis),* owls *(Bubo virginianus),* chickens and turkeys *(Gallus gallus; Meleagris gallopavo),* hogs *(Sus scrofa),* bobcats *(Lynx rufus),* dogs and foxes *(Canis familiaris, C. latrans, Vulpes* sp.), skunks *(Mephitis mephitis),* and snakes *(Agkistrodon piscivorus, Coluber constrictor, Drymarchon corais, Elaphe obsoleta, Lampropeltis getula)* (Klauber 1972; Klemens 1993; Mitchell 1994; J. B. Sealy, pers. comm.). Adults have few enemies except humans. Some may be trampled by deer *(Odocoileus virginianus)* (Minton 1972), but far more die on our highways, are blown apart by shotguns, or perish from destruction of their habitat. Collecting for the pet trade, bounty hunting (largely in the past), organized rattlesnake hunts (organized hunts may seriously damage the reproductive capacity of a population by removing a large proportion of the gravid females; Reinert 1990)—all at levels that are nonsustainable—are major threats to the timber rattlesnake throughout its range.

C. horridus is mild tempered for a rattlesnake, and will retreat if disturbed. Nevertheless, if prevented from escaping, it will form a loose coil, raise its head, strike (sometimes with mouth closed), and rattle—the SVL-adjusted loudness is 70 dB, the frequency, 1.47–20.63 kHz (Cook et al. 1994; Fenton and Licht 1990; Young and Brown 1993). It recognizes the odor and sight of ophidian predators *(Lampropeltis, Dry-marchon),* and responds by body bridging or striking (Gutzke et al. 1993).

POPULATIONS. Timber rattlesnakes vary in numbers according to the suitability of the habitat. In samples of 2,083 snakes from northern Louisiana and 7,062 snakes from three counties in northeastern Kansas, only 30 (1.4%) and 13 (0.18%), respectively, were *C. horridus* (Clark 1949; Fitch 1992). At one Kansas site, its density and biomass were only 0.3 snakes/ha and 0.16 kg/ha (Fitch 1982). In contrast, Harwig (1966) recorded 1,628 *C. horridus* in 10 years at various Pennsylvania sites. He found as many as 17 at one time at a 6 m rock, and as many as 40–80 neonates on one September day. From 1973 through 1987, Martin (1988, 1990) examined 509 sites in the Shenandoah National Park, Virginia, and collected 5,195 *C. horridus,* including 1,271 neonates. He estimated the total population to be 5,400–6,700 individuals. Individual dens there have populations of 10–205 snakes, and the population increases by an average of 63% with the birth of the young each fall (Martin 1988). A survey of Pennsylvania dens by Martin (1990) showed that 78 (25.6%) dens contained 0–15 snakes; 117 (37.5%), 15–30; 72 (23%), 30–60; and 37 (11.9%), 60–120. Only 8 dens (2.6%) had more than 120 rattlesnakes.

The adult sex ratio favors males: 1.79:1 and 1.84:1 from two Pennsylvania snake hunts (Galligan and Dunson 1979; Reinert 1991), 1.69:1 in Kansas (Fitch 1982), and 1:1 in Wisconsin (Oldfield and Keyler 1989). The sex ratio at birth is essentially 1:1 (Odum 1979). However, a Minnesota litter had a 2.5:1 ratio (Edgren 1948), two Pennsylvania litters combined had a 1.8:1 ratio (Galligan and Dunson 1979), and the juvenile to adult ratio in Kansas was 1:1.5 (Fitch 1982).

Survivorship of young-age classes may be low. Martin (1988, 1990) estimated that overwinter mortality rate was 50% for all age classes, and 61% for young of the year. The death rate was estimated at 40% for year 2, 25% for year 3, 17.5% for year 4, and 10% for years 5–14 for females and years 5–17 for males. Only about 17% of his total population was composed of snakes 15 years of age or older. Fitch (1985b) estimated the percentage survival through the fifth year in Kansas was about 17%. Adult females have a higher mortality rate than adult males.

C. horridus is a late-maturing species with a low lifetime reproductive rate and a long generation time (W.S. Brown, pers. comm.). Adult mortality is likely low, with a relatively low turnover making it susceptible to small amounts of exploitation. Given its demographic characteristics, there is a good case to be made for giving the timber rattlesnake total protection throughout its range. Some states have recognized its problems of fragmented distribution and small numbers of often isolated denning colonies by listing it as endangered (Connecticut, Massachusetts, New Hampshire, New Jersey, Ohio, Vermont, Virginia [*C. h. atricaudatus*]), threatened (Illinois, Indiana, New York, Texas), or a species of special concern (Minnesota, Pennsylvania, West Virginia, Wisconsin).

REMARKS. *C. horridus* is a member of the *C. durissus* subgroup, and in North America is biochemically and morphologically closest to *C. molossus* (Foote and MacMahon 1977; Gloyd 1940; Stille 1987). The species was reviewed by Collins and Knight (1980).

Crotalus lepidus (Kennicott 1861) | Rock Rattlesnake

RECOGNITION. *C. lepidus* (TBL to 83 cm) is gray, greenish, pink, or tan with a pattern of 13–31 narrow, dark brown or black, irregularly spaced dorsal bands and 2–3 (1–6) similar bands on the tail. The bands are often bordered by paler pigments (particularly those anterior), and small spots or irregular gray mottling may occur between the bands. A pinkish brown stripe runs backward from under the eye to the corner of the mouth. The venter is pink to light tan anteriorly, but more gray toward the tail. Dorsal body scales are keeled, and usually either in 23 or 25 (21–26) anterior rows, 23 (20–26) midbody rows, and 17–18 (14–20) rows near the tail. Beneath are 147–173 ventrals, 16–33 subcaudals, and an undivided anal plate. Dorsal head scalation consists of a rostral (usually wider than long), 2 internasals that touch medially, 5–15 scales in

Mottled rock rattlesnake, *Crotalus lepidus lepidus*. (Photograph by John H. Tashjian)

Banded rock rattlesnake, *Crotalus lepidus klauberi*. (Photograph by Barry Mansell)

the internasal-prefrontal area (a canthal is usually present on each side, but prefrontals are absent), 2 supraoculars, and 2 (1–4) intersupraoculars. Laterally are 2 nasals (the prenasal touches a supralabial, but the postnasal does not contact the upper preocular), 1 (2) loreal(s), 3 (0–7) prefoveals (a series of small scales anterior to the preoculars), 2 (3–4) preoculars, 2 (1–5) postoculars, 3 (2–5) suboculars, 12–13 (10–15) supralabials, and 11–12 (9–13) infralabials. The short, bifurcate hemipenis has a divided sulcus spermaticus, about 33 spines and 19 fringes per lobe, but no spines in the crotch between the lobes.

Males have 147–172 (mean, 160.6) ventrals, 20–33 (mean, 25) subcaudals, and TLs 6.9–10.4 (mean, 8.5) % of TBL; females have 149–173 (mean, 161.2) ventrals, 16–24 (mean, 20) subcaudals, and TLs 5.4–8.5 (mean, 7.0) % of TBL. Adult males are longer than adult females.

GEOGRAPHIC VARIATION. Four subspecies are recognized, but only two occur in the United States. *C. l. lepidus* (Kennicott 1861), the mottled rock rattlesnake, has a dark gray or brown stripe extending backward from the orbit to the corner of the mouth, no dark blotches on the nape of the neck, a mottled dorsal body pattern with the crossbands faded and only slightly distinct from the pale ground color, and a relatively dark venter. It is found from southwestern Texas (except the El Paso area) and southeastern New Mexico southward in Mexico to San Luis Potosí. *C. l. klauberi* Gloyd 1936, the banded rock rattlesnake, often lacks a dark stripe from the orbit to the corner of mouth, has two dark blotches on the nape of the neck, a darker ground color crossed by well-defined dark bands with little mottling between, and a light-colored venter. This subspecies is sexually dichromatic: males are greenish and females gray (Jacob and

Altenbach 1977). This difference may have evolved for background matching through natural selection influenced by predation pressure, and is a result of a sex-linked gene that either balances the percent of color morphs in the population or functions in sex recognition. It occurs from extreme western Texas, southwestern New Mexico and southeastern Arizona southwestward to northern Jalisco, Mexico. Much variation in body coloration and pattern occurs between populations. Ground color of *C. l. lepidus* is set at birth, and seems to be an adaptation to the dominant substrate color of its habitat (Campbell and Lamar 1989; Vincent 1982a, 1982b).

CONFUSING SPECIES. Other U.S. *Crotalus* are distinguished by the lack of a vertically divided upper preocular scale.

KARYOTYPE. Thirty-six chromosomes (16 macrochromosomes, 20 microchromosomes) are present, and the ZW sexual heteromorphism occurs on the female's fourth pair of macrochromosomes (Baker et al. 1972).

FOSSIL RECORD. A Pleistocene (Irvingtonian) vertebra from Arizona is assigned to *C. lepidus* (Brattstrom 1955b; Holman 2000), and another vertebra from the Pliocene (Blancan) of Arizona may be from *C. lepidus* (Brattstrom 1955b).

DISTRIBUTION. *C. lepidus* ranges from southwestern Texas, southern New Mexico and southeastern Arizona south in Mexico through Coahuila, western Nuevo León, Chihuahua, and northeastern Sonora to southwestern Tamaulipas, western San Luis Potosí, Aguascalientes, northern Jalisco, Zacatecas, and Southeastern Sinaloa, and may also be present in eastern Nayarit (Campbell and Lamar 1989).

HABITAT. In the United States, this snake lives in arid and semiarid areas at medium elevations (600–2,285 m). It is most often associated with steep rocky areas, particularly talus slopes, rock-strewn hillsides, rock outcrops with crevices, dry arroyos, and rocky canyons in brushlands (lechaguilla-creosote-cactus), piñon-oak-juniper woodlands, or open areas in pine forests, but is also found in mesquite grasslands, and deserts (only *C. l. lepidus*).

Distribution of *Crotalus lepidus*.

BEHAVIOR. The species is active throughout the year in Mexico if the temperature is warm, but few are seen before the rainy season (Armstrong and Murphy 1979). In the United States, it must hibernate during the winter, and is active from March to October in New Mexico (where 29% have been collected in August; Degenhardt et al. 1996). The winter is spent under rocks, in rock crevices, and within old logs or stumps.

Most activity is diurnal during the spring and fall, but shifts to crepuscular during the hotter periods of summer. *C. lepidus* is usually found in the open during the cool morning hours, and in the shade until 0930–1000 hours (Conant 1955). The hottest hours are spent under cover. Beaupre (1995a) found it surface active from 0700 to 1400 hours and at 1800–2200 hours. Night captures are rare, and mostly occur in August. Activity periods may differ between populations, depending on environmental conditions: Beaupre (1995a) found those living in a hot/dry habitat moved only 20–35 (mean, 33) % of the time, while those in a cooler/wetter habitat were found active 40–95 (mean, 62) % of the time. His snakes moved an average of 20.4 m/day. Temperature data are few, but living at relatively high altitudes, this snake may be adapted to cooler temperatures. Basking or otherwise active *C. lepidus* have been found at ATs of 24–35°C (Klauber 1972). BTs at Beaupre's (1995a) hot site averaged 29.9 (21.5–35.5) °C, as compared with 28.8

(17.4–38.0) °C at his cool site (snakes from the hot site showed 64% less surface activity in 1995). Average daily field respiration was significantly lower (only about 50%) at the hotter habitat than at the cooler habitat—2,019 J(day)$^{-1}$ compared with 4,872 J(day)$^{-1}$ (Beaupre 1996). The annual average energy budget for a 100 g adult was 113.3% of body mass per year (16.4 g of food per month) at the hot site, and 193% of body mass per year (32.7 g of food per month) at the cooler site. Oxygen consumption increased with rising ET (Beaupre 1993). It was lowest at both sites at 20°C (0700–1300 hours), and highest at 35°C in the afternoon (nongravid females had lower metabolic rates at 25°C than either gravid females or males). Snakes at the hotter site had a lower growth rate and achieved smaller adult body lengths (Beaupre 1995a), even though the resting metabolic rates of snakes from both populations were similar (Beaupre 1995b). Because Beaupre's (1996) two study sites differed in available water, water balance physiology was also different between snakes at the two sites. Usually snakes from both sites experienced negative water balance—the average water influx rate was 13.2 ml/kg/day^{-1} at the dry site and 9.3 ml/kg/day^{-1} at the moister site. Frey (1996) found a rock rattlesnake completely submerged in a pool of water (WT = 16°C; AT = 35°C), and thought it was either thermoregulating or possibly foraging for small fish.

C. lepidus does not often climb, but has been found as high as 61 cm behind the loose bark of a pine tree in complete shade (Rossi and Feldner 1993). It is, however, a good swimmer (Frey 1996; Klauber 1972).

Males may socially communicate through ritualized combat (Carpenter et al. 1976).

REPRODUCTION. Maturity is reached by both sexes at approximately three years of age; Stebbins (1985) gives a TBL of 38 cm for mature individuals of both sexes. SVLs of the smallest male undergoing spermiogenesis and the smallest female undergoing secondary vitellogenesis examined by Goldberg (2000a) were 35.2 and 34.0 cm, respectively.

Males examined by Goldberg (2000a) had regressed testes with spermatogonia and Sertoli cells in May, June, and October; spermiogenesis with maturing spermatids and mature sperm occurred from June to October. Mature sperm are stored over winter in the vas deferens.

Females examined by Goldberg (2000a) had inactive ovaries from July through October; vitellogenesis occurred from July through August, and again in October, enlarged follicles (> 6 mm) were present from April through October, and one female had six oviductal eggs in April. Beaupre (1995a) found gravid females on 17–18 May, and a female examined by Stebbins (1954) on 1 July contained 34 × 17 mm ova. Females probably have a biennial reproductive cycle, but Beaupre (1995a) reported that one produced litters in three consecutive years. Sanchez et al. (1999) and Seigel and Fitch (1984) reported RCMs of 0.353 and 0.414, respectively.

Courtship/mating activity occurs from late July to early October. The male directs head bobs (three to five every five seconds) on the female's back and tongue flicks at the same rate (Armstrong and Murphy 1979). It is possible that females store sperm.

The GP is long, 240–363 days (Swinford 1989; Tennant 1985), and the young are usually born in late June–August, but April and October births are known. Mexican females give birth earlier (Armstrong and Murphy 1979; Harris and Simmons 1972). Litters average four neonates (n = 49) and contain 1 (Harris and Simmons 1972) to 10 (Sanchez et al. 1999) young. Neonates have 16–24 (mean, 19.4; n = 26) cm TBLs and 3–7 (mean, 5; n = 10) g masses. They have yellowish tails.

GROWTH AND LONGEVITY. Growth data are scarce and are based on young raised in captivity. Kauffeld (1943b) reported that a male *C. l. klauberi,* 20 cm at birth, grew to 31.2 cm in 118 days. The male fed readily, as opposed to a female that had to be force-fed and grew only 3.2 cm during the same period. Woodin (1953) reported that two young *klauberi,* 20.5 and 21.0 cm when collected, grew to 21.4 and 21.8 cm, respectively, in 23 days. A *C. l. lepidus* kept by Falck (1940) grew from 40.7 to 47.6 cm in 409 days, and Strimple (1993a) had captive born *C. l. lepidus* grow an average of 17.8 cm (1.5 cm/month) and 37.2 g (4.2 g/month) their first year, and 9.2 cm (0.8 cm/month) and 50.7 g (3.1 g/month) the second year. One grew from 23.5 cm (13 g) to 52.1 cm (106.8 g) in two years, and to 63.9 cm (171.2 g) in three years. Longevity records for the species include 24.5 years (Russell 1983) and 23 years, 3 months, 24 days (Snider and Bowler 1992).

DIET AND FEEDING HABITS. *C. lepidus* seems to prefer cold-blooded prey (particularly lizards) to mammals. Wild prey include reptiles—lizards *(Cnemidophorus gularis, C. sacki [?], Cophosaurus texanus, Phrynosoma cornutum, Sceloporus clarki, S. jarrovii, S. merriami, S. poinsettii, Urosaurus ornatus)* and snakes *(Gyalopion canum)*; anurans *(Syrrhophus marnocki)*; rodents *(Dipodomys sp., Geomys bursarius, Perognathus sp., Peromyscus sp., Sigmodon sp.)*; and insects (caterpillars, grasshoppers) (Beaupre 1995a; Campbell 1934; Conant 1955; Klauber 1972; Marr 1944; Milstead et al. 1950; Stebbins 1954; Woodin 1953). In addition, captives have consumed lizards *(Anolis carolinensis, Eumeces laticeps, Sceloporus undulatus)*, snakes *(Crotalus lepidus, Virginia striatula)*, salamanders *(Ambystoma tigrinum)*, frogs *(Acris crepitans, Pseudacris triseriata, Rana pipiens, R. sylvatica)*, and rodents *(Microtus sp., Mus musculus, Peromyscus sp.)* (Axtell 1959; Campbell 1934; Falck 1940; Harris and Simmons 1977; Kauffeld 1943b; Milstead et al. 1950; Strimple 1993a; Williamson 1971; Woodin 1953).

Juvenile rock rattlesnakes have yellow tails, which they wave as a lure to attract lizards (Kauffeld 1943b; Neill 1960; Starrett and Holycross 2000). Adults may actively forage, but often ambush prey. They lie in an S-shaped coil with the head pointed upward along the side of a rock, or across the open surface of a boulder or a gap in vegetation (Beaupre 1995a). Lizards are struck on the body, held until comatose, and then quickly swallowed. Mice are struck, released, and later trailed. Chemoreception is used to find the dead rodents (Chiszar et al. 1986).

VENOM AND BITES. Five *C. l. klauberi* with 52.0–59.5 cm TBLs had 3.2–3.6 mm fangs (Klauber 1939c). Fresh adults may yield as much as 129 mg of dried venom (Klauber 1972).

The venom of this snake may be more specific for vertebrates than invertebrates: the venom took over an hour to kill a scolopendromorph centipede (Rodríguez-Robles 1994). The lethal intravenous venom dose for a typical mouse is 0.02–5.0 mg (Githens and Wolff 1939; Tu 1982), and the intraperitoneal dose is 0.90 mg (Githens and Wolff 1939); that for a typical pigeon is 0.01 mg (Githens and George 1931). Chemically, the venom contains 22 distinct protein bands (Forstner et al. 1997), and some populations contain a Mojave-like toxic protein that makes them more dangerous (Rael et al. 1992). Texas populations of *C. lepidus* have different venom chemical profiles. Those from the Rio Grande Valley, though geographically separated, are chemically homogeneous (supporting Vincent's [1982b] hypothesis of dispersal of the species along river canyons). These populations are also intermediate between the mountains and eastern plateau populations. Venom of rock rattlesnakes from populations in the Edwards and Stockton plateaus differs from that of rock rattlesnakes from the Rio Grande and western mountains. Venom toxicity across the Texas range of this species varies from 0.72 to 2.20 mg/kg of mouse, and the LD_{50} varies from 0.15 to 0.64 mg/kg (Forstner et al. 1997).

The venom is extremely hemorrhagic, and local necrosis often occurs, so *C. lepidus* should be treated with caution. The late A. H. Wright was bitten on the thumb by both fangs of a *C. lepidus*. The arm swelled considerably and his lymph glands were affected, but he fully recovered (Wright and Wright 1957). In another bite related by Klauber (1972), one fang pierced the middle finger. By the next day swelling had advanced to the forearm, and on the second day, to the shoulder. An intense and continual burning pain developed at the site of the puncture; it began on the day following the bite and became almost unbearable by the second day, but then lessened. Within a day or so after the bite, a large blood blister formed at the site of the puncture wound. The swelling remained for five weeks, with numbness and tingling sensations.

PREDATORS AND DEFENSE. Only two acts of possible predation on wild *C. lepidus* have been published. Tennant (1985) reported that one was eaten by a copperhead *(Agkistrodon contortrix)*, and another was seized by a collard lizard *(Crotaphytus collaris)* (Klauber 1972). Captives have cannibalized other members of their own species (Harris and Simmons 1977; Williamson 1971), so large individuals could also eat smaller ones in nature, and other ophiophagous snakes, birds of prey, and carnivorous mammals must eat at least the juveniles. Humans cause the most destruction, however, with their mining, grazing, road building, scientific and pet trade collecting, and recreational and urban development (Johnson and Mills 1982). Most of these involve habitat destruction, but with the exception of road building and grazing, are of local impact.

C. lepidus has a rather calm temperament. It will often remain quiet when first discovered, partially camouflaged by its body color matching the color of the substrate (Beaupre 1995a; Vincent 1982a). If given the chance, however, it will escape into a rock crevice or under some object. When it cannot escape, it will coil and strike, and attempt to bite if handled, rattling all the time. The frequency of rattling varies from 2.4 to 23.1 Hz (Young and Brown 1993), and the SVL-adjusted loudness is over 70 dB (Cook et al. 1994).

POPULATIONS. *C. lepidus* may be locally common, with large numbers occurring on some talus slopes, but most populations seem small. No more than 106 individuals were recorded at any of more than 40 Arizona localities sampled by Johnson and Mills (1982), and only six sites had more than seven rock rattlesnakes. In three years, Reynolds (1982) collected only three (0.72%) in a sample of 418 snakes captured along a Chihuahuan highway. It is considered endangered in New Mexico.

The only data on sex ratios are those of Beaupre (1995a), who recorded ratios of 1.33:1.00 and 1.92:1.00 at his two Texas study sites.

REMARKS. Electrophoretic studies of venom proteins by Foote and MacMahon (1977) and morphological similarities (Dorcas 1992; Gloyd 1940) indicate that *C. lepidus* is closely related to the Mexican rattlesnake, *C. triseriatus.*

Crotalus mitchellii (Cope 1861b) | Speckled Rattlesnake

RECOGNITION. *C. mitchellii* grows to a maximum TBL of 13.7 cm (most individuals < 10 cm). Its rostral scale is separated from the prenasal by at least one but usually several scales, and the preocular scale is subdivided. Ground color is variable, ranging from gray, cream, yellowish pink, tan, or brown to black (Pisgah lava flow, San Bernardino County, California); dorsal body scales are adorned with white and black specks. Usually a series of 23–46 (mean, 35) dark bands or blotches are present on the back, and 2–9 (mean, 4.5) on the tail. The head is marked dorsally with dark specks or spots. The venter is white, pink, cream, or yellowish brown with some grayish black blotches at the sides or borders of the ventrals. Body scales are keeled and pitted, and occur in 23 (25) anterior rows, 23 or 25 (21–27) midbody rows, and 23 (25) posterior rows. Beneath are 162–190 ventrals, 16–28 subcaudals, and a single anal plate. Dorsal head scalation includes a wider-than-high rostral, up to 50 scales in the internasal and prefrontal area (no prefrontal scales are present), 2 supraoculars, and 1–8 intersupraoculars; lateral scalation consists of 2 nasals (the prenasal may touch the first supralabial; the postnasal does not meet the

upper preocular), 2 (0–5) loreals, 2 (3) preoculars, 2 (3) postoculars, several suboculars, numerous temporals, 14 or 16 (12–19) supralabials, and 15–16 (12–19) infralabials. The bifurcate hemipenis has a divided sulcus spermaticus and 1–3 spines in the crotch; each lobe has 40–60 spines and 31 fringes.

Males have 162–187 (mean, 176) ventrals, 20–28 (mean, 24) subcaudals, 3–9 (mean, 5) dark tail rings, and TLs 6.7–8.0 (mean, 7) % of TBL; females have 163–190 (mean, 179) ventrals, 16–24 (mean, 20) subcaudals, 2–6 (mean, 4) dark tail rings, and TLs 5.0–6.8 (mean, 6) % of TBL.

GEOGRAPHIC VARIATION. Five subspecies are recognized, but only two range north of Mexico (McCrystal and McCord 1986). *C. m. pyrrhus* (Cope 1867), the southwestern speckled rattlesnake, occurs in southwestern Nevada and adjacent eastern California. It is white, gray, pink, or tan to orange red with dark crossbands often divided by light pigment, has small scales separating the rostral and prenasal scales, and has no pitting or furrowing on its smooth-edged supraocular scales. *C. m. stephensi* Klauber 1930, the

Southwestern speckled rattlesnake, *Crotalus mitchellii pyrrhus*. (Photograph by Barry Mansell)

Panamint rattlesnake, ranges from southwestern Utah through western Arizona to northwestern Sonora, Mexico, and through southern California and the northern half of Baja California. It is tan or gray with light brown blotches or crossbands bordered by light pigment, lacks small scales between the rostral and prenasals, and has supraoculars with pitted or furrowed outer edges.

CONFUSING SPECIES. Other *Crotalus* rattlesnakes can be distinguished by the key presented above.

KARYOTYPE. Its 36 chromosomes are made up of 16 macrochromosomes and 20 microchromosomes; sex determination is ZW for females and ZZ for males (Zimmerman and Kilpatrick 1973).

FOSSIL RECORD. Pleistocene (Rancholabrean) fossil vertebrae are from Gypsum Cave, Nevada (Brattstrom 1954a, 1954b); vertebrae from the Lower Grand Canyon, Arizona, may be from either *C. mitchellii* or *C. viridis* (Van Devender et al. 1977); and a Holocene fossil is from the Grand Canyon (Mead and Van Devender 1981).

DISTRIBUTION. *C. mitchellii* ranges from extreme southwestern Utah, southwestern Nevada, southeastern California, western and northwestern Sonora south through most of Baja California, Mexico. It also occurs on the islands of Angel de la Guarda, Carmen, Cerralvo, El Muerto, Espíritu Santo, Monserrate, Piojo, Salispuedes, San José, and Smith in the Gulf of California, and Santa Margarita off the Pacific Coast.

HABITAT. *C. mitchellii* is primarily a desert dweller (sometimes in areas with loose sand), and it usually occupies the hottest, driest, rocky microhabitats, such as canyons, foothills, buttes, and erosion gullies vegetated with thickets of chaparral, creosote bush, sagebrush, thorn scrub, and piñon-juniper woodlands at elevations of a few hundred to about 2,400 m.

BEHAVIOR. *C. mitchellii* is active from late February to December over its range, but April into early October seems to be the period of most activity. In the southwestern portion of the range, it is more active during the late summer rainy season (Armstrong and Murphy 1979). It initially becomes surface active in April, and the number of hours of daily activity increases in each successive month through September (Moore 1978). Activity is then reduced, and between

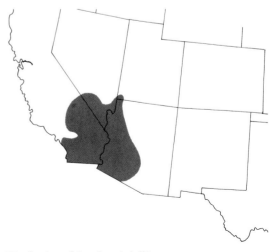

Distribution of *Crotalus mitchellii*

December and March most northern populations hibernate below the frost line in crevices or animal burrows, but caves or abandoned mines are also used. Although usually solitary during the activity period, *C. mitchellii* often congregate (20–180 individuals; Klauber 1972) at suitable hibernacula.

During most of its annual period (June to September) foraging is usually nocturnal, particularly between dusk and shortly after midnight (Klauber 1972; Moore 1978), but some diurnal activity occurs in the spring and fall. Since surface temperatures sometimes fall rapidly after sunset in the desert, *C. mitchellii* may be limited to only a few suitable hours of activity each night. Daytime ATs in its microhabitats are usually at least 32°C. BTs of active individuals have ranged from 18.8 to 39.3°C, but the overall preferred BT (April to December) seems to be about 31°C (Moore 1978). Brattstrom (1965), however, reported BTs of 26.3–31.8 (mean, 30.3) °C for active *C. mitchellii*. A copulating pair had a BT of 31.8°C (AT 31.8°C; ST 31.0°C) (Warren, in Brattstrom 1965). The CT_{min} is –2°C (Brattstrom 1965). Tightly coiled, inactive *C. mitchellii* may be able to conserve heat more effectively through circulatory adjustments than uncoiled snakes (Moore 1978). It may bask in the morning, particularly after feeding, but the hottest hours of the summer day are spent under cover beneath rocks or bushes, or in rock crevices, caves, or animal burrows.

C. mitchellii occasionally climbs as high as 90 cm into vegetation, and is also a natural swimmer (Klauber 1972). Competition or some other factor of habitat exclusion may occur between *C. mitchellii* and both *C. atrox* and *C. scutulatus*, as the other two rattlesnakes will only occupy the microhabitat of *C. mitchellii* when it is absent.

REPRODUCTION. Reproductive data for *C. mitchellii* are few. Both sexes are apparently mature at a TBL of 57 cm (Stebbins 1985); the shortest reported gravid female was 57.3 cm (Klauber 1972). Probably two to three years of growth are needed to reach this size. The gametic cycles of both sexes have not been described, but a female *C. m. pyrrhus* in San Bernardino County, California, contained small ova on 10 June (Cunningham 1959).

The natural breeding period is April–May, but captives have mated as early as January and as late as Oc-

tober; one captive pair mated four times between 8 January and 13 May in six years (Peterson 1983). Armstrong and Murphy (1979) observed a seven-hour (0800–1500 hours) captive copulation during which the right hemipenis was inserted, and a prominent bulge, extending 20 scale rows, developed anterior of the female's vent.

The GP is approximately 140 days, and parturition in nature usually occurs from July through September, but a rare litter may be produced in late June. Litters contain 1 (Armstrong and Murphy 1979) to 12 (Strimple 1992a) young, and average 6.4 (n = 22). Neonates are 20.3–30.5 (mean, 25.9; n = 12) cm in TBL, and weigh 17.5–26.6 (mean, 22.4; n = 12) g.

GROWTH AND LONGEVITY. Nothing has been published on the growth rate of this species. Snider and Bowler (1992) reported three *C. mitchellii* survived over 19 years; the record was 22 years and 16 days survival by a wild-caught adult.

DIET AND FEEDING HABITS. The speckled rattlesnake captures its food either by actively foraging or by lying in ambush. If a lizard is struck, the snake usually holds it until it dies and then swallows it immediately, but when a small mammal is bitten the snake normally releases it and later trails it until it is found dead or incapacitated, and then the snake swallows it (C. Ernst, pers. obs.).

Adults seem to prefer small mammals, either fresh or as carrion. Lizards are apparently the primary foods of juveniles, although some adults will also eat them. Natural prey include ground squirrels (*Ammospermophilus leucurus*, *Spermophilus* sp.), woodrats (*Neotoma* sp.), kangaroo rats (*Dipodomys agilis*), pocket mice (*Perognathus* sp.), white-footed mice (*Peromyscus crinitus*, *P. maniculatus*, *P. truei*), cotton rats (*Sigmodon* sp.), rabbits (*Sylvilagus auduboni*), lizards (*Callisaurus draconoides*, *Cnemidophorus maximus*, *C. tigris*, *Eumeces skiltonianus*, *Petrosaurus mearnsi*, *Sauromalus obesus*, *Sceloporus* sp., *Uta stansburiana*), goldfinch (*Carduelis* sp.), and insects (?) (Camp 1916; C. Ernst, pers. obs.; Klauber 1972). Klauber (1972) reported that of specimens containing food he examined, 18 had eaten mammals, 9 lizards, 1 a bird, and another both a mouse and a lizard. Most mammals taken are small, but Shaw (in Klauber 1972) found a large *C. mitchellii* that had taken a nearly grown cottontail rabbit

(S. auduboni). Although birds are often listed as prey, the only one yet identified has been the goldfinch (Batchelder, in Klauber 1972). Captive adults will eat *Mus musculus* and young *Rattus norvegicus* (C. Ernst, pers. obs.; Rossi and Rossi 1995), and Porter (1983) has related three instances of cannibalism by captive juveniles.

VENOM AND BITES.   Five *C. m. stephensi*, 74.6–88.5 cm in length, examined by Klauber (1939c) had fangs 5.6–7.1 mm long, but five *C. m. pyrrhus*, 82.6–111.4 cm long, had fangs 7.8–10.8 mm.

The venom contains Mojave toxin, which attacks the nervous system and is very potent, particularly for birds; the minimum lethal dose for a 350 g pigeon is only 0.002–0.04 mg dried venom, and for mice 0.05–0.12 mg (Klauber 1972). Lethality of dried venom is not even diminished with time; Russell et al. (1960) found it had not weakened after 26–27 years in storage. A typical adult may contain up to 227 mg of dried venom (Klauber 1972); however, on the average young individuals yield only about 0.06 mg (0.18 ml) of venom per bite, while adults may inject 0.1 mg (0.3 ml), and old snakes 0.16 mg (0.48 ml) (Amaral 1928).

Bites to humans may result in considerable swelling (edema), discoloration, and pain about the site of the area bite (Klauber 1972). When treated with antivenin, recovery is usually complete and uneventful.

PREDATORS AND DEFENSE.   Only four reports of predation exist: one was attacked by a kingsnake *(Lampropeltis getula)* (Klauber 1972); a late Holocene ringtail *(Bassariscus astutus)* had eaten one (Mead and Van Devender 1981); a gray fox *(Urocyon cinereoargenteus)* ate one (Zweifel, in Stebbins 1954); and notes accompanying a *C. m. pyrrhus* in the UCLA collection describe a bobcat *(Lynx rufus)* attack on it (Cunningham 1959).

Temperament varies between individual *C. mitchellii;* some lie quietly with only an occasional rattle when first discovered, but most seem very nervous, and if they cannot escape, they will coil, raise a loop of the body from the ground, inflate the trunk, and strike, while continuously rattling—the frequency is 1.9–20.0 kHz (Young and Brown 1993), SVL-adjusted loudness about 75 dB (Cook et al. 1994). The subspecies *stephensi* seems less excitable than *pyrrhus. C. mitchellii* reacts defensively to the odor of the California kingsnake *(Lampropeltis getula californiae)* (Bogert 1941).

POPULATIONS.   No data concerning populations of *C. mitchellii* have been published. The species is protected in Utah.

REMARKS.   Morphologically, *C. mitchellii* seems most closely related to *C. tigris* and *C. viridis* (Brattstrom 1964b; Gloyd 1940; Klauber 1972); however, electrophoretic studies of rattlesnake venoms by Foote and MacMahon (1977) indicate that it is closest to *C. pricei* and *C. cerastes*. It has been reviewed by McCrystal and McCord (1986).

Crotalus molossus Baird and Girard 1853 | Black-tailed Rattlesnake

RECOGNITION.   *C. molossus* grows to a maximum TBL of 133 cm, although most adults are smaller than 100 cm. It is olive gray, greenish yellow, yellow, or even reddish brown (dark individuals are usually from areas with dark substrates) with 20–41 dark brown or black, sometimes diamond-shaped, blotches or irregular crossbands, a black tail, and often a black snout. A dark band lies between the eyes, and a light-bordered, dark stripe extends diagonally backward from the eye to the corner of the mouth. The venter is white to cream anteriorly, but more greenish toward the tail. Dorsal body scales are keeled with apical pits, and occur in 25–27 (23–29) anterior rows, 27 (23–31) mid-body rows, and 21–23 (19–27) rows near the tail. Beneath are 166–201 ventrals, 16–30 subcaudals, and an undivided anal plate. Dorsal head scales include a slightly higher than wide rostral scute, 2 large internasals touching the rostral, 2 prefrontals, 2 large supraoculars, 2 pairs of canthals (the second pair lies between the supraoculars), and 2–5 intersupraoculars between the prefronatals. On the side of the face are 2 nasals (the prenasal rarely touches the supralabials, the postnasal rarely touches the upper preocular), 2–3 (1–9) loreals, 2–3 preoculars, several suboculars, 3–5 (6–7) postoculars, several temporals, 17–18 (13–20) supralabials, and 17–18 (14–21) infralabials. The short

Black-tailed rattlesnake, *Crotalus molossus molossus (yellow phase)*; Cochise County, Arizona. (Photograph by Steve W. Gotte)

Black-tailed rattlesnake, *Crotalus molossus molossus (gray phase)*; Western Texas. (Photograph by Carl H. Ernst)

bilobed hemipenis has a divided sulcus spermaticus, about 68 spines and 21 fringes per lobe, and no spines in the crotch between the lobes.

Males have 166–199 (mean, 187) ventrals, 22–30 (mean, 26) subcaudals, and TLs 5.8–8.6 (mean, 7) % of TBL; females have 177–201 (mean, 193) ventrals, 16–25 (mean, 22) subcaudals, and TLs 4.6–6.7 (mean, 5–6) % of TBL.

GEOGRAPHIC VARIATION. Three subspecies are recognized (Price 1980), but only the nominate race,

C. m. molossus Baird and Girard 1853, the northern black-tailed rattlesnake (described above), inhabits the United States. Individuals from the uplands of western Texas are generally darker than those from New Mexico and Arizona, which are more yellowish in color; and *C. molossus* living on dark-lava flows are melanistic, apparently adapted to matching the substrate color (Lewis 1949; Prieto and Jacobson 1968). Campbell and Lamar (1989) reported clinal variation in hemipenial morphology: individuals from the United States and adjacent Mexico have straight,

Distribution of *Crotalus molossus*.

thick, stubby lobes with more than 50 small spines at the base of each lobe; those from farther south in Mexico have slender lobes with fewer spines.

CONFUSING SPECIES. Other large rattlesnakes within its range can be differentiated by the key presented above.

KARYOTYPE. *C. molossus* has 36 chromosomes: 16 macrochromosomes (4 metacentric, 6 submetacentric, 4 subtelocentric) and 20 microchromosomes. Sex determination is ZZ/ZW (Baker et al. 1971, 1972; Zimmerman and Kilpatrick 1973). Baker et al. (1971, 1972) reported that the Z macrochromosome is submetacentric and the W macrochromosome is subtelocentric; but Zimmerman and Kilpatrick (1973) thought these chromosomes to be metacentric and submetacentric, respectively.

FOSSIL RECORD. No fossils have been reported.

DISTRIBUTION. *C. molossus* ranges from northern and western Arizona, the southern half of New Mexico, and west-central and central Texas south to the southern edge of the Mexican Plateau and Mesa del Sur, Oaxaca. It is also found on Tiburon and San Esteban islands in the Gulf of California.

HABITAT. The major habitats are upland pine-oak or boreal forests, where the snake is found in rocky sites: talus slopes, the sides of canyons, crevices in out-crops, caves, and abandoned mines. At lower elevations its habitat consists of mesquite grassland, chaparral, or even desert situations. The total range encompasses elevations of 300–3,750 m.

BEHAVIOR. *C. molossus* does not remain constantly torpid during the winter, as some bask on warm days in January–March (Greene 1990), but most surface activity occurs from April to October, and occasionally as late as November or December. It is more typically seen in the late summer or fall (Greene 1990; Reynolds 1982). Hibernation takes place below the frost line in animal burrows, rock crevices, caves, and possibly abandoned mines.

In eastern Arizona *C. molossus* is diurnal or crepuscular in the spring (C. Ernst, pers. obs.). Active Sonoran Desert *C. molossus* average 4,796 surface hours per year: 19.7 daylight hours during the summer (reduced to 12 hours in dry periods), 12.8 hours in the fall, but only 5–8 hours in the winter (Beck 1995). Most summer activity there occurs during 1600–2200 and 0800–1000 hours. The nights may be quite cold at higher elevations, restricting spring and fall activity to only the warmest days, but *C. molossus* is more crepuscular or nocturnal during the hotter summer months. It usually remains concealed during overcast days. Surface activity often occurs after summer rains, and probably it drinks water from puddles at such times: Greene (1990) observed one drinking water from the film seeping over a rock face.

The thermal ecology of *C. molossus* is poorly

known. One collected at twilight in May in eastern Arizona had a BT of 24°C (C. Ernst, pers. obs.). During the annual foraging period in the Sonoran Desert, the mean active BT is near 29.5 (21.8–29.5) °C, but in the winter, the mean BT of active individuals is only 14.5°C (Beck 1995). A *C. molossus* survived at 4°C for about 10 days (Bogert, in Klauber 1972), so the CT_{min} of this snake is lower than that temperature. The CT_{max} is unknown, but a *C. molossus* exposed for 10 minutes to bright summer sunlight died (Wright and Wright 1957). Those found in the morning are usually basking, apparently trying to warm after the chilling effects of night ATs, and nighttime basking on warm paved roads is not uncommon.

Sonoran Desert *C. molossus* have a mean home range of 3.5 ha (Beck 1995). They move an average of 88.7 m/day, with an average maximum movement of 103.6 m per bout of activity. Most traveling is done during the wet summer and fall months. In late summer, *C. molossus* moves from its summer foraging range to its hibernation site at a rocky slope, arroyo, or creosote flat. Total distance traveled during the year averages about 15 km.

C. molossus is an accomplished climber that sleeps and forages in bushes and trees to a height of about 3 m (Allen 1933; Campbell and Lamar 1989; Klauber 1972; Lowe et al. 1986). It also swims well when placed in water (Klauber 1972).

Male dominance combat may occur in late summer, sometimes when a female is nearby, during which each male attempts to pin his opponent's head to the ground, and the loser crawls away undamaged (Greene 1990).

REPRODUCTION. Little is known of the reproductive biology of this fairly common snake. The smallest reproductive male and female *C. m. molossus* examined by Goldberg (1999c) had 57.6 cm and 65.3 cm SVLs, respectively; the smallest mature female known to Klauber (1972) had a TBL 70.3 cm.

Goldberg (1999c) studied the gametic cycles of both sexes. Males have regressed testes with spermatogonia and Sertoli cells from March through June; spermatogonial division, with primary and secondary spermatocytes and a few spermatids, takes place during recrudescence in April–August; and spermiogenesis, with maturing spermatids and mature sperm,

occurs from May through September, with peak activity (83%) in July–September. Sperm is stored over winter for use in the next year's matings (Dancik, in Schuett 1992). Females with inactive ovaries are present in the population from April through October; those with enlarged follicles (> 12 mm), oviductal eggs, or embryos are found in April, June–July, and September–October. Females may contain oviductal eggs from late April to early June, and full-term young in mid-July. That some females have enlarged follicles, but no oviductal eggs, in July and September–October suggests at least a biennial cycle. A female collected on 5 July by Gates (1957) also had well-developed embryos.

The male apparently remains with the female after mating, perhaps guarding her from courtship by another male; a heterosexual pair of *C. m. molossus* radio tagged after being found in a woodrat nest traveled and basked together for several weeks, but by early fall they had moved apart and entered separate hibernacula in the same rocky bluff (Greene 1990). A possible mating attempt by a male *C. m. molossus* on a dead female occurred on 7 August (Wright and Wright 1957), a mating of wild *C. m. nigrescens* in Mexico was observed on 1 February, and in captivity this subspecies has mated on 2 March and 28 May (Armstrong and Murphy 1979). Copulation may last up to 105 minutes.

Thirty-one litters of *C. molossus* reported in the literature averaged 5.6 (3–16) young, but most litters contained less than 10 young. Parturition in wild *C. m. molossus* occurs from late July into September, but five Mexican *C. m. nigrescens* young were born in captivity on 9 June (Armstrong and Murphy 1979). Neonate *C. m. molossus* are 22.9–31.5 (mean, 27.2; n = 22) cm in TBL, weigh 11–28 g, and have dark tail bands. Savary (1999) reported an apparent case of a female defending five young in an opening at the base of a rock outcrop: she advanced rattling from the opening, then retreated and lay on top of the neonates.

A captive mating between a male *C. molossus* and a female *C. atrox* was reported by Davis (1936).

GROWTH AND LONGEVITY. Data on growth rates have not been reported. A female lived 20 years, 8 months, and 24 days at the Columbus (Ohio) Zoo (Snider and Bowler 1992).

DIET AND FEEDING HABITS. *C. molossus* probably captures its prey with a combination of ambush and active hunting. In the spring and fall most foraging is done in the morning or late afternoon, but crepuscular or nocturnal hunting is the summer norm. Prey is struck and later scent-trailed, found, and swallowed when dead (C. Ernst, pers. obs.). To fulfill its annual energy requirements, *C. molossus* needs to ingest prey quantity equal to 93% of its body mass; this requirement can be met in two to three large meals (Beck 1995).

Small mammals are the preferred prey, but birds and lizards are occasionally taken, and suitable carrion is probably also eaten. Prey recorded from *C. molossus* include mammals—rodents (*Dipodomys merriami, Neotoma albigula, Perognathus flavus, P. intermedius, Peromyscus eremicus, P. maniculatus, Sciurus* sp., *Tamias* sp.) and rabbits (*Sylvilagus* sp.); birds; reptiles—lizards *(Heloderma suspectum)* and snakes; anurans; and insects (Funk 1964a; Gehlbach 1956; Greene 1990; Klauber 1972; Lowe et al. 1986; Milstead et al. 1950; Minton 1959; Reynolds and Scott 1982; Vermersch and Kuntz 1986; Woodin 1953). In Arizona, typical prey are *Neotoma* and *Sylvilagus* (Greene 1990), but Chihuahuan *C. molossus* consume 33.3% *Perognathus*, 25.0% *Peromyscus*, 16.7% *Dipodomys*, 16.7% birds, and only 8.3% *Neotoma* (Reynolds and Scott 1982).

VENOM AND BITES. Adult *C. molossus* have fangs that are 9.6–13.5 mm long (Klauber 1939c). The average liquid venom yield is 0.60 ml (0.18 g dried) (Amaral 1928). The average dried venom yield per fresh adult is about 286 mg, and the maximum known dry yield is 540 mg (Klauber 1972). Minton (1959) reported the venom as of moderate toxicity: mouse LD_{50} is 17.4 mg/kg. Minimum lethal doses for 22–28 g mice are 0.06–14.0 mg/kg of dried venom (Githens and Wolff 1939; Macht 1937), and the minimum lethal dose for a 350 g pigeon is 0.40 mg of dried venom (Githens and George 1931). Phosphodiesterases are present, as also are two proteases that may cause hemorrhagic systems: N-benzoyl-L-arginine ethyl esterase and p-tosyl-L-arginine methyl esterase (Beasley et al. 1993; Stegall et al. 1994).

Although the venom is relatively mild, bites by this snake can be serious. The venom is strongly hemorrhagic and includes fibrinolytic and platelet-aggregating properties. A coagulant effect, although present, is much less marked. Human envenomation produces marked swelling and ecchymosis of the area bitten, thrombocytopenia, and in one case, hypofibrinogenemia (Hardy et al. 1982). Victims normally recover after treatment with antivenin, crystalloid solutions, fresh frozen plasma, and cryoprecipitates.

PREDATORS AND DEFENSE. A *C. molossus* was eaten (possibly as carrion) in captivity by a *C. atrox* (Klauber 1972). Natural enemies, particularly of the young, probably include ophiophagous snakes *(Lampropeltis, Pituophis),* hawks *(Buteo),* owls *(Asio, Bubo),* and carnivorous mammals *(Canis, Lynx, Mephitis, Tayassu).* Humans are the worst enemy, often killing this snake on sight, but also destroying many on the roads or through habitat destruction.

This is usually a mild-mannered snake that depends on its cryptic coloration and pattern to conceal it. It often remains calmly coiled, either quietly or with occasional rattling, or tries to crawl into some shelter. However, some will begin rattling when a human is still some distance away, and a few aggressively strike when first disturbed. Armstrong and Murphy (1979) observed that Mexican *C. m. nigrescens* may hold the mouth open with fangs folded for over five minutes when provoked. If confronted with either the sight or odor of snakes of the genera *Lampropeltis* or *Coluber, C. molossus* bridges a body coil (Weldon and Burghardt 1979). When it does rattle, the sound is rather loud (about 70 dB; Cook et al. 1994) with a dominant frequency range of 6.9–9.8 kHz, and total frequency range of 0.6–19.9 kHz (Young and Brown 1993).

POPULATIONS. No study of its population structure or dynamics has been published. Of 425 rattlesnakes collected in central Arizona, only 27 (6.4%) were of this species (Klauber 1972).

REMARKS. Gloyd (1940) thought *C. molossus* part of a complex with *C. horridus* and *C. durissus,* but actually closely related to the Mexican *C. basiliscus.* Electrophoretic studies of rattlesnake venom by Foote and MacMahon (1977) show it most closely related to *C. scutulatus, C. tigris,* and *C. horridus* (*C. basiliscus* was not tested). The species was reviewed by Price (1980).

Crotalus pricei Van Denburgh 1895 | Twin-spotted Rattlesnake

RECOGNITION. This small (TBL to 66 cm, but most are shorter than 55 cm), slender snake is gray to pale brown or occasionally reddish, with a dorsal pattern consisting of two longitudinal rows of 39–64 (usually about 50) dark brown or black spots, which may be united across the back or alternate, with those nearest the tail usually forming crossbands. Smaller dark spots may occur along the sides, and normally a dark stripe extends from below the eye backward along the cheek. The basal segment of the rattle is orange to red. The throat and venter are gray or light brown; the posterior-most ventrals contain much black mottling. Dorsal body scales are keeled (the lowest row is smooth) with two faint apical pits, and usually occur in 23 anterior rows, 21 (22–23) midbody rows, and about 17 rows near the anal vent. Beneath are 135–171 venters and 18–33 subcaudals, and the anal plate is undivided. The species is unique among crotalid rattlesnakes in having the first supralabial curving dorsally behind the postnasal scale to contact a small prefoveal scale lying between the postnasal and loreal scales. Dorsal head scales include a broader-than-long rostral, 2 internasals, 1 (2) canthal, 2 supraoculars, 2–3 intersupraoculars, and 4–11 scales in the internasal-prefrontal area (prefrontals are usually absent). Laterally are 2 nasals (the prenasal touches the supralabials, but the postnasal does not touch the upper preocular), 1 (2) loreal(s) (not touching any supralabial), 2–3 preoculars, 3–4 postoculars, several suboculars, numerous temporals, 9 (8–10) supralabials, and 9–10 (8–12) infralabials. The short, bifurcate hemipenis has a divided sulcus spermaticus, with about 52 spines and 22 fringes per lobe and many spines in the crotch (Klauber 1972). Only the fang is present on the maxilla.

Males have 135–164 (mean, 156) ventrals, 21–33 (mean, 25) subcaudals, and tails 6.6–11.0 (mean, 8.7) % of TBL; females have 143–171 (mean, 163) ventrals, 18–27 (mean, 22) subcaudals, and tails 5.2–8.6 (mean, 7.5) % of TBL.

GEOGRAPHIC VARIATION. Two subspecies have been described (McCranie 1980b), but only one, *C. p. pricei* Van Denburgh 1895, the twin-spotted rattlesnake (described above), occurs north of Mexico.

CONFUSING SPECIES. Other *Crotalus* can be identified by the key presented above.

KARYOTYPE AND FOSSIL RECORD. Not reported.

DISTRIBUTION. *C. pricei* is found from southeastern Arizona (the isolated Santa Rita, Huachuca, Pinaleno [Mt. Graham], Dos Cabezus, and Chiricahua mountains) south into Mexico, where its main range is from northeastern Sonora and western Chihuahua southward through western Durango to northern Nayarit. A second Mexican range occurs from southeastern Coahuila and southwestern Nuevo León to southern Tamaulipas. These ranges were probably continuous during the Pleistocene (Rancholabrean) glaciation, but later drying of the intervening lowlands caused restriction of the scrub pine-oak woodlands to high altitudes, and isolated the Arizona populations from each other and from those in Mexico.

HABITAT. In Arizona, this snake lives only at relatively high elevations, 1,900–3,200 m. There it occupies the rocky areas (particularly talus slopes) of canyons and ridges vegetated with scrub-brush, pine-oak, or coniferous woodlands. Water is probably obtained by drinking that trickling over rocks (Kauffeld 1943b).

BEHAVIOR. The annual cycle is poorly known. Armstrong and Murphy (1979) have collected *C. p. pricei* in Arizona on 17 March and in Mexico from May through September, sometimes under adverse weather conditions. It probably spends the colder months hibernating. Captives are most active in the late afternoon and at night (Kauffeld 1943b), but in nature the nights at higher elevations are usually cold, and although *C. pricei* may be nocturnally active on the warmest nights, most activity seems diurnal, particularly after 1100 hours. This is especially true immediately following precipitation, when this snake is commonly found basking, sometimes in pairs. Humid days also bring it out from its retreats under rocks and rock crevices.

C. pricei is adapted to rather low ETs. Active individuals have been found at ATs of 11°C (Armstrong

Twin-spotted rattlesnake, *Crotalus pricei pricei*. (Photograph by Cecil Schwalbe)

and Murphy 1979) to 27°C (Wright and Wright 1957), and BTs of five sent to Brattstrom (1965) averaged 21.1 (18.0–23.8) °C.

This snake swims with the same typical lateral undulations used in crawling, but does not elevate the tail rattle above the water (Klauber 1972). It climbs into shrubs to a height of at least 20 cm (Gumbart and Sullivan 1990).

REPRODUCTION. Very little is known of the breeding biology of *C. pricei*. According to Stebbins (1985), 30.5 cm *C. pricei* of both sexes are mature, and the smallest gravid female measured by Klauber (1972) was 30.1 cm. Goldberg (2000b) reported mature males with 32.2 cm and 33.3 cm SVLs, and mature females with 33 cm SVLs; these lengths are probably attained during the second year.

Goldberg (2000b) studied the gametic cycles of both sexes. No males had regressed (inactive) testes. Males were in recrudescence with primary and secondary spermatocytes and some spermatids from June through October. Spermiogenesis, with metamorphosing spermatids and mature sperm present, began in some males in June and lasted into October.

Apparently, sperm is stored over winter for spring matings. Three females examined on 7 May, 11 June, and 12 August, respectively, were not undergoing yolk deposition; two females had started yolk deposition by 6 July and 27 September and would probably have ovulated the next spring; another female that would

Distribution of *Crotalus pricei*.

probably have also ovulated the next spring had enlarged follicles (> 10 mm) on 23 January; and four females had ovulated by 18 May, 7 June, 29 June, and August and probably would have given birth later that year. The female reproductive cycle seems biennial.

No matings have been observed in the wild, but one in captivity occurred on 9 July (Armstrong and Murphy 1979). No description of courtship/mating behaviors has been published. Females possibly store viable sperm from matings for long periods (Lawler, in Schuett 1992).

C. pricei is ovoviviparous and bears live young in July or August. Litters contain three to nine young (Armstrong and Murphy 1979), and average 5.4 young (n = 11). Short females probably produce the smallest litters. Neonates are 12.7–20.3 (mean, 16.2; n = 13) cm long and weigh 2.4–6.4 (mean, 4.21; n = 13) g. A litter of seven had a RCM of 0.53 (Mahaney 1997).

GROWTH AND LONGEVITY. Five captive-born young grew an average of 9.8 cm and increased their mass an average of 11.5 g during their first 125 days (Kauffeld 1943b). The greatest increase (17 to 28 cm) was by the largest neonate. A captive-born male was still alive after 15 years, 8 months, and 9 days at Zoo Atlanta (Snider and Bowler 1992).

DIET AND FEEDING HABITS. Lizards seem the primary prey. Wild-caught adults had consumed *Sceloporus jarrovi* and *S. poinsetti* (Armstrong and Murphy 1979; Woodin 1953), and captives have readily taken *S. undulatus* and *Anolis carolinensis* (Kauffeld 1943b). Nestling birds may also be important prey: yellow-eyed juncos *(Junco phaeonotus)* (Gumbart and Sullivan 1990). Klauber (1972) found a mouse in a wild adult, and Wright and Wright (1957) listed both mice and a "shed skin" as foods of captives. Martin (1974) stated *C. pricei* eat invertebrates, but this is debatable.

Lizards are normally struck in the thorax and are usually held in the mouth following a strike, but mice are struck, released, and trailed with much tongue flicking (Cruz et al. 1987). *C. pricei* does not wave its tail to lure lizards, as do some other small pit vipers (Kauffeld 1943b). Digestion is rapid after a lizard meal, with defecation usually taking place on day two or three after feeding, and often again on day five (Kauffeld 1943b).

VENOM AND BITES. Adults 40.2–51.6 cm long that the authors measured had 2.0–3.3 mm fangs, and a 21.5 cm neonate had 1.0 mm fangs. Klauber (1972) reported that the body length to fang length and head length to fang length ratios were 155 and 7.5, respectively.

The venom is probably highly toxic, but yields are low; Klauber (1972) reported a dry yield of only 8 mg per adult, and Minton and Weinstein (1984) recorded a yield of only 4.1 mg per snake. The LD_{50} for mice is 0.95 mg/kg for intravenous and 11.39 mg/kg for subcutaneous injections, and the minimum lethal dose for a 350 g pigeon is 0.2 mg of dried venom (Klauber 1972). No protease activity is evident (Minton and Weinstein 1984).

Four human envenomations resulted in both local and systemic symptoms more serious than expected from such a small rattlesnake (Minton and Weinstein 1984), so one should not be careless around this species.

PREDATORS AND DEFENSE. Data on predation are lacking. Juveniles, at least, occasionally fall victim to birds of prey *(Bubo, Buteo)*, skunks *(Mephitis)*, badgers *(Taxidea)*, coyotes *(Canis)*, and kingsnakes *(Lampropeltis)*, and humans destroy many through habitat destruction, overcollection, and roadkills. Potential threats in Arizona include mining, grazing, overcollecting, logging, and recreational or other development (Johnson and Mills 1982).

C. pricei is shy, and quickly crawls to shelter if possible. Its rattle is soft and at times barely audible above accompanying insect noises; the total range of frequency is 4.9–24.1 Hz (Young and Brown 1993), and the SVL-adjusted loudness is about 70 dB (Cook et al. 1994). Although usually mild mannered, it will strike if provoked.

POPULATIONS. *C. pricei* is probably the most frequently encountered rattlesnake at higher elevations within its range (Armstrong and Murphy 1979). Several may occur in a small space of only a few square meters; Kauffeld (1943a) collected three within an hour in a small area of exposed boulders. Johnson and Mills (1982) found it at 21 sites during their survey. It was quite common in the Chiricahuas of southeastern Arizona, but somewhat less so in the four other mountains it occupies in that state (Klauber 1972);

now it is less common than before 1982 and has been given legal protection by Arizona.

REMARKS.   Electrophoretic studies of venom proteins by Foote and MacMahon (1977) indicate *C. pricei* is most closely related to *C. cerastes* and *C. willardi*; in contrast, a study of its dorsal scale microdermatoglyphics by Stille (1987) revealed its nearest relatives to be *C. mitchelli* and *C. cerastes*. The species was reviewed by McCranie (1980b).

Crotalus ruber Cope 1892a │ Red Diamond Rattlesnake

RECOGNITION.   *C. ruber* (TBL to 162.5 cm; a maximum length of 190.5 cm has been reported but not confirmed; Sibly 1951) is brick red, reddish gray, or pinkish brown with a series of 29–42 (mean, 35) light-bordered, diamond-shaped marks on its back, and two to seven conspicuous white or gray and black rings on its tail. Some individuals have the diamonds poorly outlined. Two diagonal light stripes are present on the side of the head. The unmarked venter is white to cream. Dorsal body scales are keeled with apical pits, and occur in 29 (25–30) anterior rows, 29 (25–32) midbody rows, and 27–29 (25–30) posterior rows. The ventrals total 179–206, subcaudals 15–29, and the anal plate is undivided. Dorsal head scalation consists of a rostral, 2 small internasals in contact with the rostral, several canthals (prefrontals are absent), 2 supraoculars, and 4–10 intersupraoculars; and lateral scalation includes 2 nasals (the prenasal touches the supralabials, the postnasal rarely contacts the upper preocular), 1–2 loreals, 1–2 preoculars, 2 postoculars, several suboculars, several temporals, 14–16 (12–19) supralabials, and 17–18 (13–21) infralabials (the first pair is unusually transversely divided). The long, bifurcate hemipenis has a divided sulcus spermaticus, about 62 spines and 50 fringes per lobe, and 1–3 spines in the crotch between the lobes.

Males have 179–203 (mean, 194) ventrals, 21–29 (mean, 26) subcaudals, and 3–7 (mean, 5) dark tail rings; females have 188–206 (mean, 197) ventrals, 15–26 (mean, 21) subcaudals, and 2–5 (mean, 4) dark tail rings.

GEOGRAPHIC VARIATION.   Three subspecies are recognized, but only the nominate race, *C. r. ruber* Cope 1892a, the red diamond rattlesnake, described above, occurs in the United States.

CONFUSING SPECIES.   Other species of *Crotalus* can be distinguished from *C. ruber* by the above key.

KARYOTYPE AND FOSSIL RECORD.   Unknown.

DISTRIBUTION.   *C. ruber* occurs from San Bernardino and Los Angeles counties, California, southward through Baja California, Mexico (except the northeastern corner), and also occurs on several islands in

Red diamond rattlesnake, *Crotalus ruber ruber*. (Photograph by Barry Mansell)

Distribution of *Crotalus ruber*.

the Gulf of California, and on Isla Cedros and Isla de Santa Margarita off the Pacific coast of Baja California.

HABITAT.   This species lives in rocky habitats with thick vegetation (desert scrub, thorn scrub, cacti, chaparral, and pine-oak woods) from near sea level to at least 1,500 m. It sometimes ventures into cultivated areas and grasslands. In California, it is most common in the western foothills of the Coast Ranges, but also lives in the dry, rocky inland valleys.

BEHAVIOR.   The earliest and latest recorded dates of surface activity for *C. ruber* are 20 February and 9 October (Wright and Wright 1957), but Klauber (1972), and Armstrong (in Armstrong and Murphy 1979) stated that they collected it in every month, although they did not provide dates. Most surface activity occurs from March to June, when the snake can be found abroad during the day or at dusk, especially on warm days following rains. It is almost entirely nocturnal during the hottest months and has been found active from 1840 to 0325 hours at ATs of 18–30°C (Klauber, in Wright and Wright 1957). The BT of an active snake recorded by Brattstrom (1965) was 24°C. Summer daily retreats include rock crevices, animal burrows, and brush piles. In the winter, cool temperatures bring on lethargy, and these snakes spend much time underground in rock crevices and animal burrows, where several may congregate. Klauber (1972) mentioned one such den

where 24 *C. ruber* were blasted out of a rock crevice during road construction.

This species is a good climber, and often ascends cacti, bushes, and small trees (Klauber 1972); Hollingsworth and Mellink (1996) saw one in Mexico climb to a height of 2 m in an elephant tree. It is also an accomplished swimmer that occasionally swims in reservoirs, and even in the Pacific Ocean (Klauber 1972).

Males may participate in dominance combat bouts, especially during the breeding season. Two males face each other with one lying on top of the other. Their heads and necks are raised and swayed from side to side while their tongues continually flick. One male rises above the other and bends his head toward the other snake until the heads touch. The head of the ventral male may only be raised 3–4 cm above his body, but he usually also elevates the anterior portion of his body 30–40 cm. The dorsal male rises at the same time to maintain a superior position, and then the snakes push their raised bodies and necks against each other. They may separate, then rejoin to repeat the process until one pushes the other to the ground and pins it there, after which the pinned male usually crawls away (Shaw 1948).

REPRODUCTION.   Wright and Wright (1957) gave 60 cm as the shortest adult TBL, and Stebbins (1985) reported the minimum adult TBL to be 75 cm; but the smallest gravid female examined by Klauber (1972) was 73.3 cm. The smallest male with sperm and the smallest female with enlarged follicles (> 6 mm) examined by Goldberg (1999b) had 63.7 cm and 66.2 cm SVLs, respectively. Attainment of such lengths probably takes one to two years.

Male testes are regressed with spermatogonia and Sertoli cells from February through May; are recrudescent with dividing spermatogonia, primary and secondary spermatocytes, and a few spermatids from April to August; and undergo spermiogenesis with metamorphosing spermatids and mature sperm in August (Goldberg 1999b). Spermiogenesis probably ends in September–October, and mature sperm is stored over the winter in the vas deferens. Females have enlarged (> 10 mm) ovarian follicles from March through June and in September, but some females have inactive ovaries in April–August (Goldberg 1999b). Ovulation occurs sometime between March and June. Female *C. ruber* typically begin vitellogenesis in one reproductive season and complete it the next spring, so their reproductive cycle is probably biennial: 47% of the females examined by Goldberg (1999b) were reproductive.

Courtship and mating in the wild have been seen from early March into May, and captives have mated at almost any time of the year, but most often from February to June. Copulations by captives witnessed by Perkins (in Klauber 1972) lasted from over 2 hours to almost 23 hours. The male nudges and tongue flicks the female's back and head, and may spastically jerk while courting. He may also slightly pulsate his tail while copulating (C. Ernst, pers. obs.). During a lengthy mating the male may change body positions several times, and the attached pair may move about, one crawling and dragging the other along with it.

The young are born in August and September, after a GP of 141–190 (mean, 165; n = 4) days. Litters contain 3–20 young (Klauber 1972), but average 8 (n = 40). Neonates are grayer than adults and have 28.0–35.0 (mean, 31) cm TBLs.

C. ruber is known to have hybridized with *C. viridis* both in the wild and in captivity (Armstrong and Murphy 1979; Klauber 1972).

GROWTH AND LONGEVITY. Klauber (1972) analyzed the growth patterns of 249 *C. ruber* from San Diego County, California. Neonates, averaging about 30 cm in TBL, appeared in September, and grew to 39 cm and had a button rattle by November. After emerging from hibernation in March, the snakes grew to nearly 50 cm and had two rattle segments by mid-April. By the end of April, most had three rattle segments, and some had grown to 60 cm (few were shorter than 45 cm). They were 45–65 cm long in May. The first four rattle segments appeared in June when the snakes were 46–70 cm. Those measured in July were 50–70 cm, and some had five rattle segments. By September, the yearlings averaged 67 mm. Two-year snakes probably averaged about 87 cm with seven to eight rattle segments and evident sexual dimorphism, and three-year males had TBLs of about 94 cm and females about 84 cm. By the next spring an additional 2.5 cm had been added to the length, and the tail had as many as 9–11 rattles. The male TBL exceeded that of the female by about 10%.

A wild-caught adult male survived an additional 19 years, 2 months, and 27 days in captivity (Snider and Bowler 1992).

DIET AND FEEDING HABITS. Prey taken by wild *C. ruber* include mammals—rabbits (*Sylvilagus auduboni, S. bachmani*), ground squirrels (*Amnospermophilus leucurus, Spermophilus beecheyi*), kangaroo rats (*Dipodomys*), wood rats (*Neotoma*), mice (*Mus musculus, Peromyscus*), voles (*Microtus*), and spotted skunks (*Spilogale putorius*); birds; and lizards (*Cnemidophorus tigris, Ctenosaura hemilopha*) (Hammerson 1981; Klauber 1972; Patten and Banta 1980; Tevis 1943). Of 57 snakes containing prey that were examined by Klauber (1972), 53 had eaten mammals, 3 lizards, and 1 a bird. Captives have consumed rodents (*Mus musculus, Microtus* sp.), lizards (*Anolis carolinensis, Eumeces fasciatus*), and a western rattlesnake (*Crotalus viridis*) (Cunningham 1959; C. Ernst, pers. obs.; Klauber 1972).

The normal method of prey capture is by ambush, but this snake will also actively follow scent trails (C. Ernst, pers. obs.). Young snakes feed on mice and lizards, adults on larger mammalian prey. Most prey are struck first, later followed by odor trailing, and then swallowed after they are dead, but carrion is also consumed (Cowles and Phelan 1958; Cunningham 1959; Patten 1981; Patten and Banta 1980).

VENOM AND BITES. *C. ruber* has relatively long fangs; those with 90–130 cm TBLs have 9.5–12.9 mm fangs (Klauber 1939c). The venom is usually injected during a bite, but Klauber (1972) received a spray of venom or saliva droplets from a strike by a snake with a previously injured jaw when he was beyond the snake's range, and he thought that the injury may have caused the juice, which was thrown onto him by the force of the strike, to accumulate on the snake's lower jaw.

C. ruber has high venom yields with lethal toxicities and hemorrhagic and enzyme activities similar to those of the *C. atrox* group (Glenn and Straight 1985) and is capable of killing a human (Shaw and Campbell 1974). The snake's total venom yield is 120–668 (mean, 364) mg; the lethal venom dose for a human is about 100 mg (Ernst and Zug 1996; Klauber 1972). The larger the snake, the greater the yield; adults typically secrete about 0.72 ml (0.24 g dried) of venom per strike, and an exceptional one may inject 1.65 ml (0.55 g dried; Amaral 1928). The venom causes local hemorrhaging by direct action on blood vessel walls. Two metalloproteinases (HT-1 and HT-2) are responsible for this (Takeya et al. 1990, 1993), and three proteolytic hemorrhagins degrade fibrinogen and cause myonecrosis (Mori et al. 1987). Human envenomation results in a slight increase in BT, pain, swelling, local discoloration, an initial increase followed by a lowering of blood pressure, bloody diarrhea, and a decrease in blood platelets (Clarke 1961; Klauber 1972; Lyons 1971).

PREDATORS AND DEFENSE. Kingsnakes *(Lampropeltis)* and other ophiophagous snakes, birds of prey *(Bubo, Buteo),* and carnivorous mammals *(Canis, Mephitis, Taxidea)* probably take juvenile and small adult *C. ruber,* but adults have few enemies other than humans. The automobile, rifle, and collection for the pet trade have taken their toll, but habitat destruction probably has caused the greatest loss.

C. ruber is mild mannered for such a large snake, and aggressive behavior seems rare. At times it will lie quietly without even rattling when closely approached; however, it can bite at the least expected moment, and if cornered or provoked can put up a spirited fight, coiling, raising up, and striking. It will perform a body bridge when introduced to the odor or sight of a *Lampropeltis* (Bogert 1941; Rubio 1998; Weldon and Burghardt 1979).

POPULATIONS. No quantitative population data have been published. Locally, *C. ruber* may be common, especially around a hibernaculum. Of over 12,000 snakes collected or observed from 1923 through 1938 in San Diego County by Klauber (1972), it made up 1.1–10.6% in any zone, but was most numerous in the inland valleys (10.6%), desert foothills (9.1%), and foothills (8.3%), and along the coast (6.6%). It made up 7.8% of all snakes collected.

REMARKS. Murphy et al. (1994) compared the genetic and morphological diversity of *Crotalus exsul* Garman 1884 from Isla da Cedros, Mexico, to *C. ruber* from mainland Baja California, southern California, and several islands in the Gulf of California; because of the closeness of the two snakes, they proposed that they both be included in the single species *C. exsul* by priority. However, the International Commission on Zoological Nomenclature (2000) gave the name *ruber* precedence for the species because it has been used extensively since 1892 for populations over the mainland and on the islands in the Gulf of California, while *exsul* has been used solely for the island populations off the southern Pacific coast of Baja California. Thus the authors use *"ruber"* for the species in this book.

C. ruber seems closely related to the other two diamondback rattlesnakes, *C. atrox* and *C. adamanteus,* and the Mexican *C. tortugensis* (Foote and MacMahon 1977; Gloyd 1940).

Crotalus scutulatus (Kennicott 1861) | Mojave Rattlesnake

RECOGNITION. Maximum TBL of *C. scutulatus* is 140 cm, but most adults are about 100 cm long. It is greenish gray, olive, yellowish green, or brown with 27–44 (mean, 37) dark gray or brown, light-bordered, diamond-shaped or oval to hexagonal, dorsal blotches. The light scales separating these blotches are usually unmarked with dark pigment. A dark, light-bordered stripe extends from the orbit downward to the corner of the mouth, and a pair of dark blotches is usually present on the occiput. Two to eight alternating light gray and dark bands cross the base of the tail, and the darker bands are much narrower than the light ones. The venter is white to cream with only slight pigment

encroachment along the sides, and some small dark spots under the tail. Dorsal body scales are keeled and pitted, and occur in 23 (21–25) anterior rows, 25 (21–29) midbody rows, and 21–23 (19–25) posterior rows. Beneath are 155–192 ventrals, 15–29 subcaudals, and an undivided anal plate. The rostral contacts 2 small internasals and is usually higher than wide. No prefrontals are present, but 6–21 scales lie between the internasals and the intersupraocular scales. Normally only 2 rows of intersupraoculars occur between the large supraocular scales, but sometimes 3 rows are present (those most posterior are smaller). Lateral head scales are as follows: 2 nasals (the prenasal touches

Mojave rattlesnake, *Crotalus scutulatus scutulatus*; Cochise County, Arizona. (Photograph by Carl H. Ernst)

the first supralabial; the postnasal rarely contacts the upper preocular), 1 (rarely 2) loreal(s), 2 preoculars, 2 (3) postoculars, several suboculars and temporals, 13–15 (12–18) supralabials, and 14–16 (12–18) infralabials. The bifurcate hemipenis has a divided sulcus spermaticus, each lobe has approximately 49 spines and 40 fringes, and 0–2 spines lie in the crotch.

Males have 155–190 (mean, 177) ventrals, 21–29 (mean, 25) subcaudals, and three to eight (mean, five) dark tail rings; females have 167–192 (mean, 181) ventrals, 15–25 (mean, 19) subcaudals, and two to six (mean, three to four) dark tail rings.

GEOGRAPHIC VARIATION. Two subspecies have been described, but only *C. s. scutulatus* (Kennicott 1861), the Mojave rattlesnake (described above), occurs north of Mexico. Within the United States, *C. s. scutulatus* has two distinct venom types, and also individuals with venom intergrade between the two types (venoms A and B, see VENOM AND BITES).

CONFUSING SPECIES. Other species of *Crotalus* that occur within the range of *C. scutulatus* can be identified by the key presented above.

KARYOTYPE. The Mojave rattlesnake has 36 diploid chromosomes: 16 macrochromosomes (including 4 metacentric, 6 submetacentric, and 4 subtelocentric) and 20 microchromosomes; females are ZW, males ZZ (the Z macrochromosome is metacentric; the W macrochromosome is submetacentric) (Baker et al. 1972; Zimmerman and Kilpatrick 1973).

FOSSIL RECORD. Pleistocene (Rancholabrean) fossils have been found in Distrito de Zumpango, Mexico (Brattstrom 1954b, 1955c), and in Deadman Cave, southern Arizona (Mead et al. 1984).

DISTRIBUTION. *C. scutulatus* ranges from southwestern Washington County, Utah; Lincoln and Clark counties, Nevada; and Kern, Los Angeles, and San Bernardino counties, California, southeast through Arizona and southward from Trans-Pecos, Texas, and southwestern Hildalgo and Otero counties, New Mexico, to the southern edge of the Mexican Plateau in Puebla and adjacent Veracruz.

HABITAT. The Mojave rattlesnake inhabits semiarid grasslands, open brush areas, or deserts at elevations

Distribution of *Crotalus scutulatus*.

from near sea level to about 2,500 m where the typical vegetation is clump grasses *(Sporobolus),* paloverde, mesquite, creosote, or cacti, and the soil is not particularly rocky.

BEHAVIOR. *C. scutulatus* is above ground from mid-March to November, but most activity probably takes place from late April or early May through September, with May and July–August the months of peak activity (particularly August; Degenhardt et al. 1996; Reynolds 1982). Much time is spent in animal burrows or under rocks. Such burrows help the snake in its thermoregulation by providing a cooler haunt during the hot, summer days, and a warmer retreat when the air is cool in the spring and fall. The snakes may hibernate in these if the burrows are deep enough, but if they are too shallow, the snakes must seek retreats below the frost line. One was found hibernating in a desert tortoise *(Gopherus agassizii)* burrow (Baxter and Stewart 1990), and another apparently estivating in an Arizona cave in June (Gates 1957). *C. scutulatus* apparently does not aggregate for hibernation, but instead spends the winter alone or in pairs (Lowe et al. 1986).

Although primarily nocturnal in the summer (1959–2337 hours; Klauber, in Stebbins 1954), *C. scutulatus* forages or basks (often on or along the side of a road) in early morning and may forage during the late afternoon in the spring and fall, and at higher elevations it is often abroad during the day even in sum-

mer. Klauber (1972) found them active at ATs of 17–27°C. Brattstrom (1965) recorded BTs of 22.2–34.0 (mean, 30.0) °C from wild *C. scutulatus,* and Pough (1966) reported a mean BT of 26.5 (21.9–29.8) °C. According to Brattstrom (1965), the species' CT_{max} is 42°C. Plummer (2000) observed an individual apparently become heat stressed while feeding on a dirt road at 1047 hours; it dragged its prey off the road to a shaded spot before it resumed swallowing.

No movement data are available. Boone (1937) reported a possible incident of climbing by this snake, relating that a "yellow Pacific rattlesnake" (thought to have been a Mojave rattlesnake by Klauber 1972) climbed 1.5 m into a mesquite tree. It is a good swimmer (Klauber 1972).

REPRODUCTION. According to Conant and Collins (1998) and Stebbins (1985), both sexes are adult at 61 cm TBL. The smallest reproductive females and males examined by Goldberg and Rosen (2000) had SVLs of 60.0–69.9 and 41.1–47.8 cm, respectively. Another female with a SVL of 54.3 cm was undergoing secondary vitellogenesis, but it is not known if these follicles would have completed development.

Goldberg and Rosen (2000) found females with inactive ovaries from May through September, some undergoing early yolk deposition in June and August–November, and others with enlarged follicles (> 12 mm) or embryos in March–April and June–July. Minton (1959) also found a gravid female in early July. Twenty-eight percent of the March–August females contained > 12 mm follicles or developing embryos, and would have probably produced young that year. Females probably reproduce biennially or triennially.

Males examined by Goldberg and Rosen (2000) had regressed testes in March–May and October, were undergoing recrudescence in March–July, or were undergoing spermiogenesis in June–September; mature sperm was present in the vas deferens throughout the annual activity season, so viable sperm apparently can be stored over winter. In Chihuahua, Mexico, male testicular activity peaks in August when the seminiferous tubule diameter is significantly greater than in other months. Testicular length does not vary significantly from month to month, but testicular mass does, peaking in September. Spermiogenesis occurs from July through August, and mature sperm are present in the accessory ducts throughout the summer (Jacob et al. 1987).

Mating takes place in April–May and possibly also in August–September. In August 1975, Jacob et al. (1987) found a heterosexual pair of *C. scutulatus* lying on a road. Soon a second male emerged onto the highway directly in line with the original pair and less than 2 m behind them; however, no copulation took place. The courtship/mating behaviors have not been described.

Birth occurs in July–September after a GP of about 170 days (Klauber 1972). Most newborn young have been found in mid-August. Litters contain 2 (Stebbins 1985) to 17 (Mellink 1990) young (mean, 8.2; n = 57). Neonates are 17.5–28.3 (mean, 25.1; n = 23) cm in TBL and 9.5–13.9 (mean, 11.3; n = 25) g in mass.

A natural hybrid *C. scutulatus* × *C. viridis* has been found in Hudspeth County, Texas (Murphy and Crabtree 1988), and captive hybridizations between *C. scutulatus* and *C. atrox*, *C. cerastes*, *C. durissus*, and *C. viridis* have also been reported (Cook 1955; Jacob 1977; Klauber 1972; Perkins 1951; Powell et al. 1990). Venom characteristics indicate that *C. scutulatus* and *C. viridis* regularly hybridize in New Mexico (Glenn and Straight 1990).

GROWTH AND LONGEVITY. No growth data are available. A wild-caught male survived 14 years and 5 days in captivity (Snider and Bowler 1992).

DIET AND FEEDING HABITS. Mammals are the main food of *C. scutulatus*. Known prey include mammals—kangaroo rats *(Dipodomys merriami, D. spectabilis)*, pocket mice *(Perognathus flavus, P. intermedius, P. longimembris, P. pencillatus)*, white-footed mice *(Peromyscus eremicus, P. maniculatus)*, ground squirrels *(Spermophilus spilosoma, S. tereticaudus)*, and hares and rabbits *(Lepus californicus, Sylvilagus audubonii)*; bird's eggs; reptiles—lizards *(Colenyx brevis, Cnemidophorus tigris, Holbrookia* sp., *Phrynosoma platyrhinos, Sceloporus* sp., *Uta stansburiana)* and snakes *(Phyllorhynchus decurtatus)*; amphibians—toads *(Bufo* sp.), spadefoots *(Scaphiopus* sp.), and frogs; centipedes; and insects (Boone 1937; Cromwell 1982; Jennings, in Brown 1997; Kauffeld 1943a; Klauber 1972; Lowe et al. 1986; Plummer 2000; Reynolds and Scott 1982; Turner, in Tennant 1984). Reynolds and Scott (1982) found mammals in 91.7% of the individuals

they examined: kangaroo rats occurred in 39.6% of the stomachs containing food items, pocket mice in 20.8%, white-footed mice in 16.5%, ground squirrels in 10.4%, jackrabbits in 4.2%, and cottontails in 2.1%. Klauber (1972) found mammal remains in 21 specimens and lizard remains in only 2 specimens. Captives have taken house mice *(Mus musculus)*, woodrats *(Neotoma albigula)*, lizards *(Anolis carolinensis, Eumeces* sp., *Holbrookia* sp., *Uta stansburiana)*, and a snake *(Crotalus cerastes)* (Brown and Lillywhite 1992; C. Ernst, pers. obs.; Klauber 1972; Strimple 1993b; Vorhies and Taylor 1940). Prey is selected on the basis of size; prey that are either too large or too small are rejected, and potential prey that could possibly harm the snake are not accepted (Reynolds and Scott 1982).

C. scutulatus either actively hunts or ambushes prey, using infrared detection, olfaction, and sight to find it. Bitten mammals are usually released immediately and allowed to wander off until dead from the venom. The snake then follows the animal's scent trail and swallows it.

VENOM AND BITES. *C. scutulatus* is probably our most dangerous rattlesnake, since its venom is highly neurotoxic. Its does not have particularly long fangs; seven individuals 81.2–108.5 cm long only had 6.7–8.8 mm fangs (Klauber 1939c). However, long fangs are not needed with such extremely virulent venom.

The venom affects the heart, skeletal muscles, and neuromuscular junctions. The lethal portion is an acidic protein, termed Mojave toxin, which blocks transmission of impulses from nerve to muscle and alters uptake and release of several neurotransmitters. Its amino acid sequence is very similar to that of related toxins from the venom of South American *C. durissus* and some populations of *C. viridis*. In addition, a virulent fibrinogenolytic hemorrhagic toxin is also present in some populations of *C. scutulatus*. Protein concentrations, presumably of these different toxins, vary between individual snakes (Johnson et al. 1968), so that in some cases smaller *C. scutulatus* may have more potent venom than larger individuals. However, larger snakes with less potent venom can be just as deadly because of their potential for injecting greater amounts of venom per bite. The seriousness of the envenomation is dependent upon both the quantity and quality of the venom injected.

Studies of the venom yield and venom toxicity of the Mojave rattlesnake indicate that the amount of venom injected in one bite is sufficient to cause the death of its natural prey as well as a human. The venom seems 10 times more toxic than that of most other North American crotalid snakes (Ernst and Zug 1996). The average dried venom yield is 77 (50–150) mg per fresh adult. The minimum lethal dose for a 350 g pigeon is 0.05 mg (Githens and George 1931), and the LD$_{50}$ for mice is 0.18 mg/kg (Ernst and Zug 1996). The estimated dry venom dosage needed to kill an adult human is relatively small, probably only 10–15 mg (Minton and Minton 1969).

Electrophoretic studies have revealed variation in the Mojave toxin from different populations in Big Bend, Texas, and southeastern Arizona, suggesting that several genetically diverse groups occur in the United States (Rael et al. 1984). Additional testing has shown that two distinct venom populations and a zone of intergradation occur in Arizona (Glenn and Straight 1989; Glenn et al. 1983; Huang et al. 1992). The venom of the Chihuahuan population (venom A) contains the neurotoxic Mojave toxin and is lacking in hemorrhagic and specific proteolytic activities. The Sonoran population (venom B) lacks Mojave toxin but produces hemorrhagic and proteolytic symptoms. Venoms of C. scutulatus from regions between the venom A and venom B populations in Arizona contain both the Mojave toxin of venom A and the proteolytic and hemorrhagic activities of venom B. Mouse interperitoneal LD$_{50}$ values of the A plus B venoms are 0.4–2.6 mg/kg, compared with 0.2–0.5 mg/kg for venom A individuals and 2.1–5.3 mg/kg for the venom B individuals. High-pressure liquid chromatography shows that A plus B venoms exhibit a combined protein profile of venoms A and B. These data indicate that an intergrade zone exists between the two venom types, which arcs around the western and southern regions of the venom B population. Within these regions, C. scutulatus can have three major venom types. Wilkinson et al. (1991) conducted starch gel electrophoretic studies of 55 enzymes from tissues of Mojave rattlesnakes within the venom intergrade zone and found high gene flow between venom A and B snakes, with low genetic divergence, indicating the two venom populations are conspecific.

Human envenomation by C. scutulatus is usually se-

vere, with high mortality occurring in untreated bites (Dart et al. 1992; Hardy 1983, 1986; Russell 1967b). In Arizona, most fatal cases are from bites by C. scutulatus and C. atrox. Contributing to this is the fact that the Mojave rattlesnake is often very common in some heavily populated areas. Symptoms of envenomation by the Mojave rattlesnake include local pain and swelling (edema), blood blisters, ecchymosis, necrosis, fragility of veins, cardiopulmonary arrest, elevated heart rate, lowered blood pressure, double vision, difficulty in speaking and swallowing water, decrease in blood platelets and fibrinogen levels, increase in fibrinolytic split products, shock, renal failure, drooping eyelids, depression, and diarrhea (Dart et al. 1992; Hardy 1983, 1986; Klauber 1972; Smith 1990). Rapid expansion of some Arizona cities where this snake is common has brought it into more frequent contact with humans, creating a potentially dangerous scenario, particularly regarding children and pets.

PREDATORS AND DEFENSE. *Masticophis lateralis* ate one (Klauber 1972), and the sight or odor of other ophiophagous snakes (*Drymarchon, Lampropeltis*) brings about body bridging and trunk inflation by C. scutulatus (Bogert 1941; Weldon and Burghardt 1979). However, humans are the worst enemy, slaughtering many each year, particularly on the highways.

Individual temperaments vary, and although some C. scutulatus are calm, in the authors' experience, others are extremely nervous, excitable, and aggressive. If not allowed to escape, it will coil, raise up, continuously rattle—the SVL-adjusted loudness is about 70 dB (Cook et al. 1994), and the dominant frequency and frequency range are 10.5 kHz and 3.3–20.3 kHz, respectively (Young and Brown 1993)—and strike viciously. Occasionally, this snake will even advance on the disturber (Bartholomew and Nohavec 1995), and sometimes will flatten the neck in a hoodlike display (Brown et al. 2000; Glenn and Lawler 1987) or even the head and trunk (Armstrong and Murphy 1979). Occasionally one will strike so violently that its entire body becomes momentarily airborne. It is also common for them to strike through collecting bags, so one must be very careful.

POPULATIONS. The Mojave rattlesnake appears to be at least locally common in some areas of Arizona.

Of 425 rattlesnakes collected in central Arizona, 147 (34.6%) were *C. scutulatus* (Klauber 1972); and of 368 snakes observed on Arizona Rt. 85 in 1988–1991, 18 (4.9%) were this species (Rosen and Lowe 1994). It was also the most observed snake found on Chihuahuan highways in 1975–1977, 104 of 418 (24.9%; Reynolds 1982). However, the numbers of *C. scutulatus* may be declining in some areas. Plant successional changes over 30 years caused a decline in *C. scutulatus* along two Arizona roads: in 1959–1961, 125 were found on Portal Road and U.S. 80 in Arizona, but in 1987, 1989 only 56 were observed (Mendelson and Jennings 1992).

REMARKS. On morphological grounds, Gloyd (1940) thought *C. scutulatus* close to the ancestral stock, and somewhat intermediate to the *atrox* and *viridis* groups of North American *Crotalus* evolution, but somewhat closer to *viridis*. In contrast, electrophoretic studies of venom proteins by Foote and MacMahon (1977) showed it closer to *horridus, molossus,* and *tigris*, but Glenn and Straight (1990) found that venom toxins of *viridis* from southwestern New Mexico more similar to the Mojave toxin of *scutulatus* than to similar toxins from *viridis concolor*, indicating hybridization between the two species in that region.

C. scutulatus was reviewed by Price (1982).

Crotalus tigris Kennicott, in Baird 1859a | Tiger Rattlesnake

RECOGNITION. *C. tigris* is a short rattlesnake, with a maximum TBL of 90 cm, a comparatively small head (body length at least 25 times longer than head length), and a proportionately large rattle. Body color is variable, ranging from gray or lavender to pink, yellowish brown, or orange. A series of 35–52 (mean, 43) faint, irregularly shaped gray, olive, or brown bands cross the back, and no other species of *Crotalus* has crossbands on the anterior portion of the body. The posterior-most bands are often the darkest. Four to 10 (mean, 7) indistinct bands are present on the tail. The venter is cream to greenish brown with gray, lavender, or brown spots on each scute. Head markings are poorly developed, but a dark cheek stripe is usually present. Dorsal body scales are keeled and pitted, and

occur in 23 (20–28) rows at midbody. On the underside are 156–183 ventrals, 16–27 subcaudals, and an undivided anal plate. Enlarged dorsal head scales include a wider-than-high rostral, 2 small internasals, 4 canthals, 2 supraoculars, and 3–8 intersupraoculars; prefrontals are absent. On each side of the head are 2 nasals (the prenasal usually touches the first supralabial, but the postnasal rarely contacts the upper preocular), 1–2 loreals, 2–3 preoculars, 1 (2) postocular(s), several suboculars and temporals, normally 12–14 (11–16) supralabials, and usually 13–15 (11–16) infralabials. The short, bifurcated hemipenis has a divided sulcus spermaticus, each lobe with about 64 spines and 40 fringes, and only 1–2 spines in the crotch.

Males have 156–172 (mean, 165) ventrals, 23–27

Tiger rattlesnake, *Crotalus tigris*. (Photograph by Barry Mansell)

(mean, 25) subcaudals, and 6–10 (mean, 8) dark tail bands; females have 164–183 (mean, 170) ventrals, 16–27 (mean, 20) subcaudals, and 4–7 (mean, 6) dark tail bands.

GEOGRAPHIC VARIATION. Although differences in ground color and patterns occur within populations, no subspecies are recognized.

CONFUSING SPECIES. Other species of *Crotalus* can be identified by using the key presented above.

KARYOTYPE AND FOSSIL RECORD. Unknown.

DISTRIBUTION. *C. tigris* is found in isolated populations from south-central Arizona southward through almost all of Sonora, Mexico. It also occurs on Isla Tiburon in the Gulf of California. Fowlie (1965) thought that the present isolated foothill distribution may have resulted from the displacement of the tiger rattlesnake in the intervening areas by *C. atrox* and *C. cerastes*.

HABITAT. It is found exclusively in local colonies living in rocky habitats (canyons, ravines, or hillsides in deserts) or in mesquite grasslands at elevations of near sea level to about 2,400 m. Typical plants in its microhabitat are creosote, various cacti (particularly saguaro and ocotillo), paloverde, and mesquite.

BEHAVIOR. *C. tigris* becomes active in late spring or early summer (it emerges after rains), and can be found into October or early November, when it becomes dormant over the winter in rock crevices or animal burrows.

It is chiefly nocturnal, beginning daily foraging at dusk and continuing into the night until its environment becomes too cold, but some individuals are occasionally found basking or foraging in the morning. Few data are available concerning its thermal requirements. Beck (1996) reported that the tiger rattlesnake prefers elevated ETs after feeding, and the BT of one that had fed was significantly higher than those of unfed rattlesnakes of other species (1200–1600 hours). This *C. tigris* moved 290 m to its hibernaculum during the nine days after it fed.

Activity is not restricted to the ground, and *C. tigris* has been found in bushes 60 cm above the desert floor

Distribution of *Crotalus tigris*.

(Klauber 1972; Stebbins 1954). In spite of being an inhabitant of the desert, the tiger rattlesnake swims readily with typical lateral undulations when placed in water (Klauber 1972).

REPRODUCTION. Little is known of the reproductive biology of this snake. Stebbins (1985) reported that the shortest TBL of mature males and females is 45 cm, a length probably reached in two to three years. The SVLs of the smallest male with sperm and smallest female with enlarged ovarian follicles examined by Goldberg (1999a) were 51.2 and 54.1 cm, respectively. The shortest TBL of a pregnant female examined by Klauber (1972) was 61.6 cm.

Spermiogenesis, with both metamorphosing spermatids and mature sperm, occurs in males during June–October, and sperm is present in the vas deferens in May–October, making males ripe for mating (Goldberg 1999a). However, recrudescence, with spermatogonial divisions, primary and secondary spermatocytes, and some spermatids, also occurs from May to August. Other males have regressed testes with spermatogenesis and Sertoli cells from October through July.

Females have enlarged follicles (> 6 mm) from August to November (Goldberg 1999a). Stebbins (1954) reported that two females taken in October contained "eggs" (presumably enlarged follicles). Vitellogenesis begins in the fall and is completed the next spring, when the eggs are ovulated. Females apparently have a biennial reproductive cycle.

Mating possibly takes place in both the spring and late summer to early fall, although most observations are from late summer or the fall. The young are born from late June through September, but most from late July to September, after a GP of about 150 days (Rossi and Rossi 1995). Litters contain 2–6 (mean, 4; n = 16) young. Neonates have 21.0–25.8 (mean, 22.8; n = 8) cm TBLs and 2–9 (mean, 6.8; n = 3) g masses.

GROWTH AND LONGEVITY. The growth rate is unknown. A wild-caught adult survived 15 years, 3 months, and 3 days at the Staten Island Zoo (Snider and Bowler 1992).

DIET AND FEEDING HABITS. Although it probably ambushes much of its prey, *C. tigris* may also actively forage, as evidenced by Armstrong and Murphy (1979) having taken one as it was investigating a woodrat nest. Prey recorded from wild individuals include small rodents (*Dipodomys* sp., *Neotoma* sp., *Perognathus hispidus, Peromyscus eremicus, Thomomys* sp.) and lizards (*Cnemidophorus* sp., *Sceloporus magister*) (Armstrong and Murphy 1979; Fowlie 1965; Lowe et al. 1986; Ortenburger and Ortenburger 1926; Stebbins 1954). Captives have taken rodents *(Mus musculus, Neotoma albigula, Perognathus intermedius)* and various lizards (Beck 1996; Kauffeld 1943a). Its small head may restrict the size of possible prey. Possibly young individuals rely heavily on lizards for food, while adults depend more on rodents.

VENOM AND BITES. *C. tigris* produces a potent whitish venom with neurotoxic elements (Klauber 1972), but because of its smaller head and shorter 4.0–4.6 mm fangs (Klauber 1939c), the adult venom yield is low: 6.4–11 mg dried venom per fresh adult (Klauber 1972; Minton and Weinstein 1984; Weinstein and Smith 1990) and 0.18 ml (Amaral 1928). The LD_{50} for mice is 0.070 mg/kg interperitoneal, 0.056 mg/kg intravenous, and 0.21 mg/kg subcutaneous; there seems to be low protease activity and no hemolytic activity (Minton and Weinstein 1984; Weinstein and Smith 1990). Weinstein and Smith (1990) isolated four toxins; one made up about 10% of the total venom protein and had an interperitoneal LD_{50} of 0.05 mg/kg in mice. This particular toxin showed complete immunoidentity with crotoxin and Mojave toxin, indicating the presence of isoforms of crotoxin and/or Mojave toxin exist in the venom. The several recorded human envenomations by tiger rattlesnakes produced little local reaction and no significant systemic symptoms.

PREDATORS AND DEFENSE. No records of natural predation exist, but habitat destruction, automobiles, and collection for the pet trade reduce populations.

C. tigris is behaviorally unpredictable, sometimes rattling when approached and at other times remaining silent. It is generally inoffensive, but will strike if greatly disturbed. Its rattling occurs at a frequency range of 0.7–19.0 Hz (Young and Brown 1993) and at a SVL-adjusted loudness of about 77 dB (Cook et al. 1994). When confronted with the odor of ophiophagous *Lampropeltis*, it reacts by bridging its body (Weldon and Burghardt 1979).

POPULATIONS. Only 6 (1.6%) of 368 snakes recorded along Arizona State Road 85 in Pima County between 1988 and 1991 were *C. tigris* (Rosen and Lowe 1994). Some local populations seem small, but nowhere has there been a concentrated study of its population dynamics.

REMARKS. Brattstrom (1964b) proposed that *C. viridis* was the probable ancestor of *C. tigris*; however, electrophoretic studies of venom proteins by Foote and MacMahon (1977) suggest that *C. tigris* is more closely related to *C. mitchellii, C. scutulatus*, and the tropical *C. durissus* than to the *C. viridis* group, and that it and *C. scutulatus* are closer to *C. molossus* and *C. horridus* than to either the *C. viridis* or *C. atrox* groups. *C. tigris* has long been thought to be closely related to *C. mitchellii* (Amaral 1929). Therefore, it was surprising that a recent study of dorsal scale microdermatoglyphic patterns shows it and *C. mitchellii* to be widely separated (Stille 1987). Perhaps scale sculpturing is a poor taxonomic character and more indicative of habitat use than of evolutionary relationships.

As can be seen from the lack of behavioral and ecological data above, such studies of *C. tigris* are needed.

Crotalus viridis (Rafinesque 1818) | Western Rattlesnake

RECOGNITION. *C. viridis* (TBL to 162.5 cm) is the most variable rattlesnake in North America, making a composite description difficult; so, after reading the following description, also examine GEOGRAPHIC VARIATION.

The body is black, gray, olive, greenish gray, greenish brown, brown, yellowish brown, tan, salmon, or reddish with 20–57 (mean, 41) brown or black, light-bordered dorsal botches, which often resemble crossbands near the tail. Two to 15 (mean, 7) faint dark bands are present on the tail. However, there is much ontogenetic variation: the pattern is usually vivid in juveniles, but fades with age, so the series of dorsal blotches may almost disappear in adults. Two light diagonal stripes occur on the side of the face; one extends backward from the anterior to the orbit to the supralabials, and the second from the rear of the orbit to in front of and above the corner of the mouth, from where it runs backward onto the neck. Narrow, light, transverse stripes may occur anterior to the eyes and over the supraocular scales. The venter is gray, cream, or white with no dark markings, and has 158–196 ventrals, 13–31 subcaudals, and an undivided anal plate. Dorsal body scales occur in 23–25 anterior

Prairie rattlesnake, *Crotalus viridus viridus*; Northeastern Wyoming. (Photograph by Roger W. Barbour)

Southern Pacific rattlesnake, *Crotalus viridis helleri*; San Diego County, California. (Photograph by Carl H. Ernst)

Great basin rattlesnake, *Crotalus viridis lutosus*. (Photograph by R. D. Bartlett)

rows, 23–27 (21–29) rows at midbody, and 19 (20–23) rows anterior to the tail. It is the only rattlesnake with more than 2 internasals touching the rostral, which is usually higher than wide. Behind the rostral, and touching it, are 3–4 (1–8) internasals, at least 8 scales before the 4–6 (1–9) intersupraoculars (prefrontals are absent). Lateral head scalation consists of 2 nasals (the prenasal touches the supralabials in some individuals; the postnasal seldom contacts the upper preocular), 1 (1–3) loreal(s), 2 preoculars, several suboculars, 2 (1–3) postoculars, 14–15 (10–19) supralabials, and 15–16 (11–20) infralabials. Each of the hemipenis lobes is adorned with about 40–92 spines and 26–37 fringes, but no spines lie in the crotch between the lobes; the sulcus spermaticus divides to extend up each lobe.

Males have 158–190 (mean, 175) ventrals, 18–31 (mean, 25) subcaudals, and 3–15 (mean, 8) dark tail bands; females have 164–196 (mean, 179) ventrals, 13–26 (mean, 19) subcaudals, and 2–11 (mean, 6) dark tail bands.

GEOGRAPHIC VARIATION. Nine subspecies are currently recognized, but one is confined to a Mexican island; the North American subspecies follow. *C. v. viridis* (Rafinesque 1818), the prairie rattlesnake, ranges generally east of the Rocky Mountains from Alberta, Saskatchewan, Montana, eastern Idaho, and North Dakota south barely to northeastern and southeastern Arizona, New Mexico, western Texas, northern Chihuahua, and northwestern Coahuila. It is greenish gray to brownish gray with oval to quadrangular-shaped, light bordered, dark blotches, and two loreals; TBL to 145 cm. *C. v. abyssus* Klauber 1930, the Grand Canyon rattlesnake, is found only on the floor of the Grand Canyon in Arizona. It is salmon to red with oval, rough-edged blotches that fade with age and two loreals; TBL to 98 cm. *C. v. cerberus* (Coues 1875), the Arizona black rattlesnake, ranges from Mohave and Yavapai counties southeast to Apache, Graham, and Pima counties, in Arizona, and adjacent Grant County, New Mexico. It is dark gray, olive, dark brown, or black with large, poorly defined dark blotches and two loreals; TBL to 100 cm. *C. v. concolor* Woodbury 1929, the midget faded rattlesnake, occurs in the Colorado and Green river watersheds in southwestern Wyoming, eastern Utah, and western Colorado. This small subspecies (TBL to 70 cm) is cream, yellowish brown, or tan with rectangular to oval only slightly darker (often faint or absent) body blotches and two loreals. *C. v. helleri* Meek 1906, the Southern Pacific rattlesnake, is found from southwestern San Luis Obispo and Kern counties,

Northern Pacific rattlesnake, *Crotalus viridis oreganus*; Klickitat County, Washington. (Photograph by Brad R. Moon)

California, south to northern Baja California; it also occurs on Santa Catalina and Coronado del Sur islands. It is colored like *C. v. oreganus*, and usually has only one loreal, but its dark blotches are angular or diamond-shaped; TBL to 135 cm. *C. v. lutosus* Klauber 1930, the Great Basin rattlesnake, ranges between the Rocky and Sierra Nevada mountains from southern Idaho, southwestern Oregon, and northwestern California south through western Utah and Nevada to northwestern Arizona. It is gray, yellowish brown, or tan with elliptical to oval brown or black blotches widely separated by lighter pigment, and two loreals; TBL to 135 cm. *C. v. nuntius* Klauber 1935b, the Hopi rattlesnake, lives in northeastern and north-central Arizona, and adjacent extreme northwestern New Mexico. It is pink, red, or reddish brown with irregularly oval to rectangular, narrowly light-bordered blotches, and two loreals; TBL to 70 cm. *C. v. oreganus* Holbrook 1840, the Northern Pacific rattlesnake, ranges west of the Rockies from British Columbia south to San Luis Obispo and Kern counties, California. It is dark gray, olive, yellowish brown, brown, or black, with hexagonal, oval, or almost circular dark blotches having well-defined light borders, and usually a single loreal scale; TBL to 162.5 cm. Intergrade zones occur where the various subspecies ranges meet.

Two clades exist within *C. viridis*, an eastern and southern clade consisting of only *nuntius* and *viridis*, and a second one composed of the rest of the subspecies (Pook et al. 2000). Venoms containing lethal toxins similar to Mojave toxin evolved within the western clade, which includes *concolor*; and small body size apparently evolved twice, once in each clade. Some island populations of *lutosus, helleri*, and *oreganus* have also evolved dwarfed populations (Ashton 2000).

CONFUSING SPECIES. Other North American *Crotalus* have facial stripes and body blotches, but only *C. viridis* has more than two internasals touching the rostral scale, and poorly defined tail bands. *Sistrurus catenatus* has nine large scales on the top of its head.

KARYOTYPE. The 36 chromosomes consist of 16 macrochromosomes (4 metacentric, 6 submetacentric, and 4 subtelocentric) and 20 microchromosomes (Baker et al. 1972; Zimmerman and Kilpatrick 1973). Males are ZZ, females ZW; the Z is metacentric or submetacentric, and the W subtelocentric or submetacentric. The isozyme patterns of a number of gene loci have been examined by Murphy and Crabtree (1985).

FOSSIL RECORD. *C. viridis* has an extensive fossil record: Miocene (Hemphillian) of Nebraska (Brattstrom 1967); Pliocene (Hemphillian) of Oklahoma (Brattstrom 1967; Parmley and Holman 1995); Pliocene (Blancan) of Kansas (Brattstrom 1967; Holman and Schloeder 1991; Peters 1953; Rogers 1976); Pleistocene (Irvingtonian) of Colorado (Holman 1995; Rogers et al. 1985) and Nebraska (Holman 1995); and Pleistocene (Rancholabrean) of California (Brattstrom 1953c, 1954b, 1958a; Gilmore 1938; Hud-

Distribution of *Crotalus viridis*.

son and Brattstrom 1977; LaDuke 1991; Miller 1942, 1971), Idaho (Lundelius et al. 1983; McDonald and Anderson 1975), Kansas (Brattstrom 1967; Holman 1971; Preston 1978), and Nevada (Brattstrom 1954b, 1958b; Holman 1979a, 1981; Mead and Bell 1994; Mead et al. 1982, 1989). There are also Rancholabrean vertebrae from Arizona that may be either from this species or *C. mitchellii* (Mead and Bell 1994; Van Devender et al. 1977), and an undesignated Pleistocene fossil from Iowa (Brattstrom 1954b; Gilmore 1938).

DISTRIBUTION. *C. viridis* is found from south-central British Columbia, southeastern Alberta, and southwestern Saskatchewan southeastward through the United States to extreme western Iowa, Nebraska, and Kansas, and south to northern Baja California and adjacent Sonora, and northern Chihuahua and north-western Coahuila in Mexico.

HABITAT. *C. viridis* is found in a variety of habitats at elevations near sea level to about 4,000 m, including deciduous and coniferous woods, scrub areas, prairie grasslands, shrub steppes, desert margins, and coastal and sand dunes; usually south-facing rocky outcroppings with deep crevices or prairie dog *(Cynomys)* towns are located within migratory distance. In Canada, the distribution coincides with the availability of suitable rock crevice hibernacula, and usually only involves river valleys.

BEHAVIOR. Typical hibernacula are prairie dog towns and other deep animal burrows, the walls of cisterns or wells, caves, and crevices in south-facing rock outcrops. Emergence from hibernation is generally earlier in the south (late February to early April) and later in the north (late March to mid-April or early May); no sexual differences exist in the dates of spring emergence (Fitch 1949; Graves and Duvall 1990). The earliest recorded appearances of active individuals are 11 February (North Dakota; Wheeler 1947) and 1 March (California; Fitch and Twining 1946). The normal annual activity period is probably April–September, but in New Mexico the snakes are active in March–December, with 40% of the observations in July–August (Degenhardt et al. 1996; Howell and Wood 1957); in Idaho, it is surface active in April–August (Diller and Wallace 1996); and in southern California active snakes are found in every month (Klauber 1972). The pivotal BT for both arousal and dormancy is 10°C (Jacob and Painter 1980), but a BT of 16°C may be necessary to bring them out of the den (Woodbury 1951), and increases in ST are probably more responsible for the emergence than is AT.

After spring emergence these snakes stay near the hibernaculum and bask for several days to weeks before migrating to their summer feeding range. The summer home range is occupied until September, when the return migration to the hibernaculum begins. From late September through November, the snakes remain near the den, frequently basking (possibly to help digest a last meal or to help the ovaries to mature), but they feed less often as the AT drops. Eventually the hibernaculum is entered for good, often in December, and although some may move about within it, most snakes lie there individually coiled or in bunches until the next spring (Duvall et al. 1985; Gannon and Secoy 1985; Ludlow 1981). Some hibernacula have been used for centuries, and theoretically the *C. viridis* now inhabiting them are descendents of the first to overwinter there. Den fidelity is strong (Duvall et al. 1985). The den may be shared with other reptiles, and once the rattlesnakes are torpid, homoiotherms may move into the den (foxes, badgers, even prey species such as packrats, prairie dogs, and burrowing owls).

The snakes probably seek the warmer portions of a hibernaculum and move deeper into the den as winter progresses (Marion and Sexton 1984; Sexton and Marion 1981). However, at a den in British Columbia, the spring thermal gradient was weak to nonexistent during most of the emergence period (MacArtney et al. 1989). BTs of hibernating *C. viridis* may drop to 2–7°C (Jacob and Painter 1980; MacArtney et al. 1989). Cooling of the BT during hibernation is probably necessary for proper reproduction the next year (Tryon 1985). BT drops more slowly when the snakes are lying in groups than when they are alone, but physical contact with several other snakes does not help raise the BT (Graves and Duvall 1987; White and Lasiewski 1971). The longer the snake is chilled, the longer the period of arousal once BT again rises.

Body mass is lost during hibernation, probably because of evaporative water loss and metabolic use of stored fat. Adults lose 4–9% and juveniles 20–50% of their body weight (Hirth 1966a; Klauber 1972; Parker and Brown 1974). This is an important factor influencing overwinter survivability of small snakes, particularly neonates (Charland, 1989, has reported a survivorship rate of only 55% for neonates in their first winter, but that survivorship seemed independent of both weight and condition at birth). Lying in bunches of several individuals with bodies in contact reduces water loss (White and Lasiewski 1971). If water is available, the snakes will drink; *C. viridis* must maintain an extracellular fluid volume of about 41.9% of their mass (Smits and Lillywhite 1985).

C. viridis forages in the morning and late afternoon or evening during the spring and fall, but in the summer it becomes crepuscular or nocturnal (but 75% to full moonlight retards activity; Clarke et al. 1996). When not foraging, it either remains under cover, coiled in the shade, or basking, depending on the AT. Populations occurring at both higher altitudes and higher latitudes seem to be more diurnally active in the summer. BTs recorded from wild, active *C. viridis* are 9.3–37.8°C (Cunningham 1966a), but most are active at 20–35°C BTs (Brattstrom 1965; Cunningham 1966a; Graves and Duvall 1993; Hirth and King 1969; Stebbins 1954; Vitt 1974). The CT_{min} and CT_{max} for *C. viridis* are probably 0°C (C. Ernst, pers. obs.) and 38–42°C (Brattstrom 1965). These snakes are capable of changing their body color in response to ETs, and become lighter, with melanophores maximally contracted, when at BTs of more than 34°C (Rahn 1942a). As BT drops to below 30°C, the melanophores disperse, and the snakes gradually assume normal color when their BT is about 23°C. Snakes chilled to about 8°C exhibit maximal darkening. These pigmental changes may aid in thermoregulation. Smaller snakes heat and cool faster than larger ones: two neonates had 16–18°C BTs, while adults had BTs above 21°C; in addition, mean BTs of adult females were 2.1 and 2.0°C higher than those of males in the spring and summer, respectively, and may be correlated with female viviparity (Hirth and King 1969).

Gravid females have 19–27°C voluntary BTs, and bask most commonly when ST is 15–25°C (Diller and Wallace 1996). Females regulate BT by shifting between warmer and cooler locations, with most periods of inactivity spent near a heat source (Gier et al. 1989). Most maintain a BT of 29–30°C. There is no significant difference in mean and range of BT between gravid and nongravid females before or after birth. Gravid females thermoregulate higher and with less variability before than after birth, and their BTs change significantly after parturition, dropping to 23.3–32.0 (mean, 28.5) °C (Gier et al. 1989). Both gravid and nongravid females have a triphasic diel BT pattern in the summer: BTs rise rapidly in the morning, remain stable in the afternoon, and decline slowly at night; during the afternoon stable period, mean BT of gravid (31.7°C) and nongravid females (30.7°C) are not significantly different, but those of gravid females are significantly less variable (Charland and Gregory 1990).

Scarcity of water is a problem in many of the xeric habitats of *C. viridis*. When it is available, as in puddles after rains, the snake often drinks to capacity, or it may coil and lick up the water that accumulates between its body coils (Aird and Aird 1990).

C. viridis may migrate long distances (11 km) to and from the hibernaculum in the spring and fall (Duvall 1986). These movements are not usually direct or nonstop, and may be related to prey availability (Duvall et al. 1985, 1990; King and Duvall 1990). Mean distances covered per movement recorded by King and Duvall (1990) were 237 m for males and 137 m for females. Males average 25.3 days between movements, females only 6.7 days (Duvall et al. 1990; King and Duvall 1990). Olfaction plays the major role in finding prey-rich areas, and odor trails are detected either by tongue flicking or, possibly, mouth gaping (Chiszar et al. 1990; Duvall et al. 1985, 1990; Graves and Duvall 1983). By traveling along paths of very high angular fixity or straightness, males, more than females, minimize the likelihood of covering the same area twice as they search for either food or mates, and prey odor detection brings about a slowing of male activity.

Once the summer feeding area is reached, a more or less permanent home range is established, and unless prey become scarce, it is maintained for the rest of the summer. Mean size of these ranges in California is 12.1 ha for males and 6.5 ha for females (Fitch 1949), but Stark (in MacArtney et al. 1989) found these home ranges to be only 2.4 ha for males and 1.8 ha for females (presumably in Alberta).

C. viridis has homing ability and can return to its hibernaculum if displaced varying distances at all four compass points from the den (Hirth 1966b). Conspecific odor detection is probably not the major orientation mechanism in homing to the den (King et al. 1983). Instead, the snakes use fixed-angle, sun-compass orientation in return to the hibernaculum (Duvall et al. 1985).

C. viridis will climb into bushes or trees as high as 7.6 m while foraging, or possibly basking (Cunningham 1955; Klauber 1972; Shaw 1966). One observed basking in South Dakota by C. Ernst had climbed almost 2 m up a slanting rock surface. It is also a good swimmer (Klauber 1972).

Male western rattlesnakes participate in combat dominance bouts during the mating season (Gloyd 1947; Hersek et al. 1992; Klauber 1972; Thorne 1977).

REPRODUCTION. Since there are considerable differences in size of the eight subspecies, the TBL at maturity is variable. In addition, males grow more rapidly than females and mature at a smaller size and earlier age (MacArtney et al. 1990). The shorter subspecies probably mature at TBLs of 40–50 cm, and the larger subspecies at 55–65 cm (Diller and Wallace 1984; DuVall et al. 1992; Glissmeyer 1951; Klauber 1972; MacArtney and Gregory 1988; MacArtney et al. 1990). Such lengths are usually attained in three to four years in males and four to seven years in females. The length at which maturity is reached may even vary between populations of the same subspecies (for details on the individual subspecies, see Ernst 1992). Because males mature earlier, their potential lifetime reproductive output is greater than that of females.

In males, Sertoli syncytia and spermatogonia are present in the seminiferous tubules during hibernation, and from mid-April through June the spermatogonia divide. Spermatids and spermatozoa are present from June through October. Spermatogenesis ceases in late August–November, but mature sperm are still present in the tubules. Peak sperm production occurs from mid-June through September, and spermiation apparently takes place between mid-June and mid-October. Sperm may be present in the vas deferens in every month (Aldridge 1979a, 1993; Diller and Wallace 1984). Seminiferous tubule diameter is smallest in the spring, is about twice the spring diameter in mid-July–September, and shrinks in October as sperm pass out of the tubules (Aldridge 1993). Temperature plays a major role in initiating spermatogenesis (Aldridge 1979a).

The female cycle seems biennial, with approximately 50–70% of the females breeding in any given year; but some females may reproduce annually, and others triennially (Diller and Wallace 1984; Fitch 1985a; King and Duvall 1990). A three-year cycle probably consists of two successive seasons of feeding and follicle development, with a peak of sexual receptivity and mating occurring in year two, associated with maximum follicle development, and a third season in which spring ovulation takes place, fertilization is accomplished with stored sperm, and there is a summer pregnancy and autumn birth of live young (King and Duvall 1990). Vitellogenesis occurs twice in the female ovary during the year. Primary vetellogenesis occurs in microscopic to 4–6 mm follicles (which are present throughout the year) in the summer after parturition, with follicles growing to 15–20 mm by hibernation. No yolking occurs during the winter. Secondary vitellogenesis occurs in the spring, and ovulation takes place in May or early June (Aldridge 1979b; Diller and Wallace 1984; Fitch 1949; Gannon and Secoy 1984; Glissmeyer 1951; MacArtney and Gregory 1988; Rahn 1942b). Reproductive females produce more body fat than females not reproducing that year (Diller and Wallace 1984).

Mating may occur in the spring in California (Fitch 1949; Fitch and Glading 1947; Klauber 1972), but spring matings are rare elsewhere (Holycross 1995). Most breeding activity occurs during mid-July to early September (Duvall et al. 1985; Graves and Duvall 1990; Hayes et al. 1992; King and Duvall 1990; MacArtney and Gregory 1988; Wright and Wright 1957). Males search for mates in the second half of the summer season, while females continue to forage for the duration of the season (King and Duvall 1990). Males must locate two goals in time and space (food and mates; females search only for food), and exhibit significantly greater spatial searching efficiency during spring foraging than do females, allowing them to concentrate foraging activities into the first half of the annual activity season, so the second half can be almost exclusively devoted to mate searching. The mating system is best described as a prolonged male mate-searching polygyny.

Males find and identify females by olfactory cues, which are enhanced by female ecdysis; females are usually courted within 48 hours after shedding (Chiszar et al. 1991; Klauber 1972; MacArtney and Gregory 1988; Scudder et al. 1988). Males perform straight-line, fixed-bearing searches for females; and males searching along a straight path find more females than those moving in less straight paths (Duvall and Schuett 1997). Once the female or her scent trail is found, he follows, and once she is reached, he maintains contact with her body and searches with his tail for her vent. During courtship and coitus, the female usually remains quietly coiled; only occasionally does she flee and the male chase her. After three to four tongue flicks, the male performs forward jerks or flexions of his body (the female may move her tail back and forth laterally in response to tactile movements

by the male). While this is occurring, he increases the rate of tongue flicking toward the female's dorsum, often making contact, and may rub her with his chin. This flexion cycle ceases when the male initiates tail-search behavior. While tail searching, the male generally withdraws his head and anterior trunk from the female and ceases both tongue flicking and flexing. Outstretched positions may be necessary for copulation, as a coiled female hinders courtship. A period of no movement by the male follows until flexions begin again and the entire courtship sequence is repeated (Duvall et al. 1985, 1992; Hayes 1986; Hayes et al. 1992).

Copulation may last several hours. As most mating occurs in the late summer, sexual encounters may normally occur at night. Mating activity in British Columbia coincided with the peak of male spermatogenic activity, and up to eight snakes took part (MacArtney and Gregory 1988). Because most matings occur in late summer when ovarian follicles are small, and ovulation does not occur until the next spring, the female must store viable sperm over winter in her oviducts.

Some gravid females may immigrate from their hibernaculum in the spring, but most remain relatively close and form maternity colonies either there or in secondary nearby dens. Little if any feeding may occur during the period of pregnancy, and the females must depend on the fat supply they have built up to carry them through the GP. After the birth of the young, the emaciated females apparently must double their weight before mating again, and those that cannot do so in a single summer must delay mating for another year or more (MacArtney and Gregory 1988; Charland and Gregory 1989). Basking becomes the prime activity. Females using maternity colonies give birth sooner than those that migrate away from the den, and their young may have a better chance to find suitable overwintering sites (Duvall 1986). The females often remain near until the neonates first shed their skins (Cunningham et al. 1996).

Parturition occurs during August–early October after a GP of 110–172 days (Diller and Wallace 1984; Fitch and Glading 1947). Litters average 9.8 young (n = 602), but may contain 1–25 young (Fitch 1949; Wright and Wright 1957). Litter size is generally proportional to female TBL, so the shorter subspecies usually produce less than 10 young per litter, while larger races may produce more than this (Klauber 1972). Younger females may produce smaller litters, averaging only about 6 young, while older (larger) females have 15–16 young. Neonates average 25.4 (11.2–30.8; n = 92) cm in TBL and weigh 13–16 (mean, 14.7; n = 14) g. Neonate size is correlated with female length, and females of the shorter subspecies may produce young less than 20 cm long. Some young may have yellowish or orange pigment on the tail, and occasionally one is born without a rattle (Holycross 2000).

Natural hybrids between *C. viridis* and both *C. ruber* and *C. scutulatus* are known (Armstrong and Murphy 1979; Klauber 1972; Glenn and Straight 1990; Murphy and Crabtree 1988).

GROWTH AND LONGEVITY. Individual growth is quite variable and is dependent on foraging success and weather conditions, making it difficult to present an overall growth rate. However, growth slows with age and length in both sexes. In Utah, 40 cm male *C. v. lutosus* grew an average of 20.7 cm (51%) between captures, while males 50 cm long grew only 7.5 cm (15%), those 70 cm long grew 3.8 cm (5%), and those 90 cm long increased only 1.6 cm (1%) (Heyrand and Call 1951). Females 40 cm long grew 13.4 cm (33%) between captures, those 50 cm long grew 7.1 cm (15%), those 70 cm long grew 2.7 cm (4%), and those about 79 cm long grew only 1.2 cm (1.5%). Young *C. v. helleri* grow from 27.5–28.0 cm to about 54 cm in one year, and by their second September males usually exceed 80 cm, but females are only about 72 cm (Klauber 1972). In British Columbia, male *C. v. oreganus* have mean SVLs of 28.5, 35.8, and 45.3 cm for years one, two, and three, respectively; females average SVLs of 28.2 and 35.2 cm during years one and two (MacArtney et al. 1990). Northern California *C. v. oreganus* only grow an average of 22 cm their first year (Fitch 1949). Saskatchewan *C. v. viridis* are 19.5–22.9 cm at birth, while those in their second summer are 35.0–59.5 cm long; average growth is 33.7 cm the first year, and 21.2 cm the second year (Gannon and Secoy 1984).

A *C. v. viridis*, estimated to have been two years old when captured, survived 27 years and 9 months in captivity (Bailey et al. 1989).

DIET AND FEEDING HABITS. *C. viridis* occurs within the ranges of numerous prey species, and it has one of the most variable diet lists of any rattlesnake in North America. Warm-blooded prey, especially mammals, are preferred by adults. In California, the ground squirrel (*Spermophilus beecheyi*) is the chief prey, followed by kangaroo rats (*Dipodomys*), cottontails (*Sylvilagus*), white-footed mice (*Peromyscus*), pocket mice (*Perognathus*), and pocket gophers (*Thomomys*); mammals predominate, but some birds, lizards (only about 9% of prey; Jaksic and Greene 1984), and spadefoot toads are also eaten (Fitch and Twining 1946). Juvenile ground squirrels (*Spermophilus*, 14% annually of the juvenile population) constitute 81% of prey in southwestern Idaho (Diller and Johnson 1988), and in northern Idaho voles (*Microtus*), deer mice (*Peromyscus*), and cottontail rabbits (*Sylvilagus*, 5–11% annually of the juvenile population) make up almost 92% of the biomass ingested and 80% of the total prey taken (Diller and Johnson 1988; Wallace and Diller 1990). Feeding usually takes place from mid-April to early October in most populations. In British Columbia, *C. viridis* feeds most often from June through August, and rodents make up 91%, shrews 5%, and birds 4% of the prey consumed (MacArtney 1989).

Newborn snakes and small juveniles prey on the smallest mammals, whereas adults eat larger prey of a greater diversity. Small reptiles make up the greatest food bulk for juveniles, and possibly are a major food source for the two smallest subspecies, *concolor* and *nuntius*. However, the only ontogenetic shift in prey found by Wallace and Diller (1990) was an increase in mammalian prey size with TBL; snakes less than a year old took shrews, but as they grew, more mice and voles were captured, and finally prey as large as cottontail rabbits were taken by adults. Yearlings have greater consumption rates (expressed as percent of body mass) than do older age classes (Diller and Johnson 1988). The production efficiency (proportion of prey mass consumed that is used for growth) is 28%.

In most populations, gravid females usually do not feed during gestation or after parturition, but Wallace and Diller (1990) reported that in northern Idaho reproductive females feed from the spring to early August, and again in the fall after the birth of the young. They thought feeding during the breeding year might explain how some females can reproduce in consecutive years.

C. viridis is either an active forager, or a sit-and-wait ambusher (Diller 1990). The first approach is used when prey are scattered, or often during migration to or from the den (Duvall et al. 1985). Ambushing is used more often (particularly by males) when colonies of rodents have been identified and the snake can lie near the openings of burrows or rodent runs. The snake is only capable of short bouts of maximal activity before exhaustion (Ruben 1983), so the latter strategy is more efficient from an energy standpoint.

Prey is found visually, by infrared detection (particularly for birds and mammals), or by olfaction. Movement of the prey seems to be the primary visual component that brings on a rise in the rate of tongue flicking, which provides additional olfactory information (Chiszar et al. 1981; Scudder and Chiszar 1977). The visual and infrared data are combined in biomodal neurons of the optic tectum that receive input from both the retina and the pit organ (Newman and Hartline 1981). This is extremely important during crepuscular or nocturnal hunting. However, the pit organ may not be the only means of detecting prey body heat: *C. viridis* anesthetized so that the trigeminal nerve could not mediate electrophysiological responses of the pit organs to thermal stimulation still exhibited behavioral responses to thermal cues (Chiszar et al. 1986). Either an auxiliary infrared-sensitive system (nociceptors) or the common temperature sense could be responsible. Intraoral thermal stimulation elicits response from the superficial maxillary branch of the trigeminal nerve (Dickman et al. 1987). Such responses to oral heat stimulation are independent of any responses associated with thermal stimulation of the pit organs. Histological preparations of tissues from the upper lip, palate, and fang sheath reveal dense ramifying neurons in the epidermal layers of the fang sheaths that are morphologically similar to the infrared sensitive neurons in pit organ membranes.

Visual and thermal cues are sufficient to bring on a strike response by the snake. It readily strikes when presented objects 1.5–4.5°C warmer than AT.

Olfaction also plays a major role in prey detection, as indicated by the spring migratory and habitat selection patterns (Duvall et al. 1990; Theodoratus and Chiszar 2000), and the modified behavior of *C. viridis* with vomeronasal organs sutured (Graves and Duvall 1985a). Such snakes have lower tongue-flick rates when presented with prey odor stimuli; unaltered *C. viridis* may mouth gape and actually shake their heads in two to three rapid horizontal jerks to help bring odors to the vomeronasal organ (Graves and Duvall 1983, 1985b). Possibly, prey chemical preferences must be learned. These are absent in neonates, but are present in adults (Chiszar and Radcliffe 1977). Food deprivation causes increases in tongue-flick rates in response to mouse odor (Chiszar et al. 1981), and often strikes are hurried and inaccurate (Hayes 1993).

When prey wanders into striking range, it is usually struck only once, after which it may walk freely off while the venom digests it. The strike is usually aimed at the forward portion of moving prey (Schmidt et al. 1993). Lizards and small rodents are usually held, but large rodents are released (Chiszar et al. 1986; Radliffe et al. 1980). The larger the snake, the more likely it is to hold, rather than quickly release, prey. Snakes possess a ready reserve of venom sufficient to envenomate up to four mice in close succession without loss of killing effectiveness; but when presented several mice in succession, the later mice are often struck repeatedly or held in the mouth rather than released (Kardong 1986a, 1986b), probably because venom reserves have been depleted (Hayes et al. 1992).

The head or chest is struck most often, and envenomation of these areas most quickly leads to death (possibly due to mechanical damage caused by the snake's fangs; Kardong 1996). Small prey may simply be swallowed alive without envenomation by adults. Retention of prey following a bite increases the severity of the envenomation, and a poor strike is usually rapidly followed by a second or third. The quantity of venom released in a strike is not related to prey size (Hayes 1992). Once prey has been struck and tasted, a chemical search image is created, resulting in an increase in the rate of tongue flicking (Chiszar et al. 1991; Haverly and Kardong 1996; Scudder et al. 1992). Prey trailing only occurs if the prey has been envenomated (Chiszar et al. 1988; Diller 1990; Furry et al. 1991; Golan et al. 1982; Lee et al. 1988, 1992). Once the odor trail of the bitten prey is located, the snake usually searches only about 15 minutes before returning to its hunting mode. Venom odors and odors from the head and nasal-oral tissues of the mouse are important cues for finally detecting the dead mouse, and for finding the mouse's head for easier swallowing (Duvall et al. 1980; Lavín-Murcio and Kardong 1995).

Recorded natural prey (fresh killed or carrion) are mammals—shrews (*Sorex* sp.), shrew moles *(Neurotrichus gibbsii)*, pikas *(Ochotona princeps)*, cottontail rabbits *(Sylvilagus audubonii, S. bachmani, S. nuttallii)*, juvenile jackrabbits (*Lepus* sp.), pocket gophers *(Geomys bursarius, Thomomys bottae)*, kangaroo rats *(Dipodomys heermanni, D. ordii, Microdipodops megacephalus, M. pallidus)*, pocket mice *(Chaetodipus californicus, Perognathus inornatus, P. parvus)*, chipmunks (*Eutamias* sp.), ground squirrels *(Ammospermophilus leucurus, Spermophilus beecheyi, S. townsendii, S. tridecemlineatus)*, juvenile prairie dogs *(Cynomys leucurus, C. ludovicianus)*, juvenile yellow-bellied marmots *(Marmota flaviventris)*, juvenile tree squirrels *(Sciurus niger, Tamiasciurus hudsonicus)*, juvenile muskrats *(Ondatra zibethica)*, voles *(Clethrionomys californicus, Microtus californicus, M. ochrogaster)*, various mice *(Mus musculus, Peromyscus boylii, P. maniculatus, P. truei, Reithrodontomys megalotis)*, woodrats *(Neotoma fuscipes, N. lepida)*, and brown rats *(Rattus norvegicus)*; birds (including eggs and nestlings)—juvenile pheasants *(Phasianus colchicus)*, quail *(Lophortyx californicus, Oreortyx pictus)*, domestic chickens *(Gallus gallus)*, turkeys *(Meleagris gallopavo)*, grouse *(Dendragapus obscurus)*, burrowing owls *(Athene cunicularia)*, woodpeckers *(Dryobates pubescens, Picoides* sp.)*, mourning doves *(Zenaida macroura)*, bushtit *(Psaltriparus minimus)*, horned larks *(Eremophila alpestris)*, and passeriforms *(Calamospiza melanocorys, Carpodacus mexicanus, Chondestes grammacus, Dendroica* sp.*, Euphagus cyanocephalus, Junco* sp.*, Melospiza melodia, Mimus polyglottos, Passerculus sandwichensis, Pipilo erythrophthalmus, Pooecetes gramineus, Sialia mexicana, Sternella neglecta, Sturnus vulgaris, Zonotrichia leucophrys)*; reptiles—lizards *(Cnemidophorus tesselatus, C. tigris, Eumeces gilberti, Gerrhonotus* sp.*, Holbrookia maculata, Phrynosoma douglassii, P. platyrhinos, Sceloporus graciosus, S. occidentalis, S. undulatus, Uta stansburiana)* and snakes *(Crotalus viridis)*; amphibians—spadefoots *(Scaphiopus bombifrons, S. hammondii, S. intermontanus)*, frogs (*Rana* sp.)*, and salamanders *(Aneides lugubris)*; fish—trout and salmon; and insects (mormon crickets, grasshoppers,

beetles, hymenopterans); and captives have also eaten snakes (*Crotalus viridis, Lampropeltis getula, Phyllorhynchus* sp.) (Banta 1974; Brown 1990; Bullock 1971; Chiszar et al. 1993; Cunningham 1959; Diller and Johnson 1988; Diller and Wallace 1996; Duvall 1986; Duvall et al. 1985; C. Ernst, pers. obs.; Fitch 1949; Fitch and Twining 1946; Gannon and Secoy 1984; Genter 1984; Graves 1991; Hamilton 1950; Hammerson 1986; Jaksic and Greene 1984; Klauber 1972; Lillywhite 1982; MacArtney 1989; Mahrdt and Banta 1997; McKinney and Ballinger 1966; Mosimann and Rabb 1952; Powers 1972; Stabler 1948; Stebbins 1954; Wallace and Diller 1990; Young and Miller 1980).

VENOM AND BITES. Fang length is positively correlated with body length in venomous snakes, so adults of the largest subspecies of *C. viridis* possess the longest fangs (5.3–9.6 mm), while adults of the smallest subspecies, *concolor* and *nuntius*, have the shortest fangs (3.8–5.2 mm) (Klauber 1939c). Strike kinematics are discussed by Kardong and Bels (1998).

The venom gland is composed of two discrete secretory regions, a small anterior accessory gland and a large posterior main gland, joined by a short duct (Mackessy 1991). The main gland has at least four distinct cell types: secretory cells (the dominant cell type), mitochondria-rich cells, horizontal (secretory stem) cells, and "dark" (myoepithelial) cells. The accessory gland contains at least six cell types, including mucosecretory cells and several types of mitochondria-rich cells. Release of venom into the lumen of the main gland is by exocytosis of granules and by release of intact membrane-bound vesicles.

Venom of *C. viridis* is predominately hemorrhagic (Tan and Ponnudurai 1991), but that of some subspecies also contains neurotoxic peptide elements (Griffin and Aird 1990; Russell 1983; Ziolkowaki et al. 1992). The overall toxicity is slightly higher than that of *C. atrox*, and this potency, coupled with the high irritability of many individuals, makes *C. viridis* very dangerous. Fortunately, human bites are relatively infrequent.

Chemistry of the venom is summarized by Aird et al. (1988), Li et al. (1993), Russell (1983), Soto et al. (1989), and Young et al. (1991). Two color shades of venom occur, white (colorless, with fewer lower molecular weight components, and less toxic) and yellow (Johnson et al. 1987). Juveniles have colorless venom, but qualitatively their venom is similar to the yellow venom of adults (Fiero et al. 1972).

Hemorrhagic, neurologic, and proteolytic activities may all result during the development of a single envenomation. Hemorrhagic activity occurs in less than 20 minutes, and its intensity varies between populations of *C. v. lutosus*. Venoms from snakes occupying northern ranges in Utah have high hemorrhagic ability, while venoms from snakes from southern Utah and northern Arizona have a lower hemorrhagic capability (Adame et al. 1990). Neurologic symptoms may be paralytic, but are not as severe as those produced from bites by *C. scutulatus*; although some New Mexican *C. v. viridis* contain the Mojave toxin usually associated with *C. scutulatus* (Glenn and Straight 1990). Venom from *C. v. concolor* has a similar amino acid sequence to Mojave toxin (Aird et al. 1990) and is 10–30 times more toxic than venom of other subspecies (Glenn and Straight 1977).

Potential venom yield increases with body length (Klauber 1972). Adults produce average dried venom yields of 35–250 mg (Ernst and Zug 1996). The average amount of dry venom secreted in a bite is 65–90 mg (Amaral 1928); the lethal dose for a human adult is 70–160 mg (Minton and Minton 1969).

Symptoms recorded during human envenomations include swelling; pain; tingling or numbness over the bitten area and over the tongue, mouth, and scalp; stiffness; weakness; giddiness; breathing difficulty; hemorrhage; lowered blood pressure; lowered blood flow; heart failure; nausea and vomiting; secondary gangrene infection; ecchymosis; paralysis; unconsciousness or stupor; nervousness; excitability; and possibly an increase in vascular permeability to protein and erythrocytes (Dart et al. 1992; Hutchison 1929; Russell 1960; Russell and Michaelis 1960; Schaeffer et al. 1973). Death has occurred from untreated and poorly treated bites (Hutchison 1929; Straight and Glen 1993; for case histories, see also Klauber 1972; Over 1928).

PREDATORS AND DEFENSE. Known predators of *C. viridis* are mammals—rodents *(Erethizon dorsatum, Marmota monax, Neotoma cinerea)*, mustelids *(Mephitis mephitis, Taxidea taxus)*, cats *(Felis catus, Lynx rufus)*,

canids *(Canis familiaris, C. latrans, Vulpes* sp., *Urocyon cinereoargenteus)*, and domestic hogs *(Sus scrofa)*; birds—eagles *(Aquila chrysaetos)*, hawks *(Accipiter cooperii, Buteo jamaicensis, B. swainsoni)*, owls *(Bubo virginianus)*, turkeys *(Meleagris gallopavo)*, roadrunners *(Geococcyx calfornianus)*, and jays *(Aphelocoma coerulescens)*; snakes *(Charina bottae* [captivity], *Coluber constrictor, Crotalus viridis* [captivity], *C. ruber* [captivity], *Lampropeltis getula, L. zonata, Masticophis flagellum, M. lateralis, M. taeniatus)*; trout *(Onycorynchus mykiss)*; and ants *(Formica* sp.) (Banta 1974; Bullock 1971; Cobb and Peterson 1999; Cunningham 1959; Duvall 1986; Duvall et al. 1985; Fitch 1949; Fitch and Glading 1947; Klauber 1972; Lillywhite 1982; MacArtney and Weichel 1993; Powers 1972; Tabor and Germano 1997; Toweill 1982; Woodbury 1952). Accidents involving other wild animals often prove fatal; deer, pronghorn, goats, horses, and cattle often trample *C. viridis* (Klauber 1972), and Metter (1963) found one with porcupine quills protruding from its head.

Humans cause this animal the most harm. They have killed it on sight, secondarily poisoned it, slaughtered it on our highways each year, and destroyed hibernacula. Formerly, large populations overwintered in specific dens, but many of these have been systematically eradicated with gas, bullets, and explosives (Brown and Parker 1982; Klauber 1972; Martin 1930), so that now *C. viridis* is in danger of totally disappearing from areas where it was once the most common snake.

Usually it will first rely on its cryptic coloration and pattern to escape detection (particularly pregnant females), especially when sufficient cover is present; when it realizes it has been discovered, it normally tries to crawl directly away from the threat, stretching out its body so that the head and upper third of the body are positioned, or cocked, for a potential bite while it backs away with the posterior two-thirds of its body. When this does not help, the snake may simply hide its head under the central (usually widest) coil of the body (the authors have only seen this once). If further disturbed, it forms a defensive coil with its head and the anterior portion of the body raised high, rotates its coils so that it always faces the intruder, and rattles continuously—SVL-adjusted loudness is about 75 dB; frequency varies from mean lows of 3.28–

3.34 kHz to mean highs of 10.40–10.62 kHz (Cook et al. 1994; Fenton and Licht 1990). If approached too closely, the snake will strike viciously (once one advanced toward C. Ernst each time it struck). An alarm pheromone may also be released from the cloacal glands that possibly warns other nearby *C. viridis* (Graves and Duvall 1988).

Potentially predatory snakes are recognized by sight or their odors, and *C. viridis* will strike, inflate its body, or body bridge when approached by these snakes (Gutzke et al. 1993; Weldon et al. 1992).

C. viridis serves as the model in several mimicry systems. Gopher snakes *(Pituophis catenifer)* share aspects of coloration, pattern, and defensive behavior with sympatric subspecies of *C. viridis* in what seems to be a case of Batesian mimicry (Kardong 1980; Sweet 1985), and the hiss of the burrowing owl *(Athene cunicularia)* and the sound of the snake's rattle are very similar (Rowe et al. 1986).

POPULATIONS. *C. viridis* may be common; generally the largest populations existing today occur in isolated areas. Of the snakes recorded from 1975 to 1980 at a northern Idaho site, 454 (45.9%) were *C. viridis* (Diller and Wallace 1996); Fitch (1949) reported a density of approximately 2.9/ha at his California site (males 1.3/ha, females 1.6/ha), and in parts of the Dakotas, Wyoming, and Montana it may be the most numerous snake species (C. Ernst, pers. obs.).

However, in many areas, populations have decreased or disappeared due to direct human predation at hibernacula. The population of a northwestern Utah den was studied from 1939 to the early 1970s by Brown and Parker (1982); Hirth and King (1968), Parker and Brown (1973, 1974), and Woodbury (1951). Woodbury (1951) and his students marked over 900 *C. viridis* in 1939–1950. Population size was estimated to be 769 snakes in 1940, but by 1950 it had dwindled to only 235, in the mid-1960s to only 53–58 (Hirth and King 1968), and by 1969–1973 the population had dropped to only 12–17 individuals (Parker and Brown 1974). Another Utah den contained only 69 adults in 1949 after an estimated 300 individuals had been killed there in 1937 (Woodbury and Hansen 1950). The population at a den in Saskatchewan was

estimated to be 149 (Gannon and Secoy 1984), and a den in Wyoming contained 42 adults (Duvall et al. 1985). *C. viridis* was also uncommon in other studies: of 454 snakes recorded during a four-year road-collecting study in New Mexico, only 6 (1.3%) were this species (Price and LaPointe 1990); and of 33,117 snakes collected statewide in Kansas, only 32 were *C. viridis* (Fitch 1993). MacArtney and Weichel (1993) estimated the total population of *C. viridis* in southern Saskatchewan was only 2,000–4,500 snakes.

Overwintering mortality is high, particularly among juveniles. Gannon and Secoy (1984) reported that the of the young-of-the-year proportion of the population decreased from 39% to only 12.7% from the fall of 1976 to the spring of 1977. Fitch (1985b) calculated a mortality rate of 60% in first-year young and 50% in each subsequent year for a population in Kansas. He thought few survive longer than eight years in the wild; however, most populations are composed predominantly of adults with SVLs greater that 50 cm. During Fitch's (1949) California study, individuals with 25–50 cm SVLs made up 34.2% of the population; adults longer than 70 cm constituted 52.9% of the snakes.

The sex ratio typically does not vary significantly from 1:1 (Fitch 1998), but the juvenile to adult ratio may vary from 1:1 or 1:2 (Diller and Wallace 1984; MacArtney 1985) to 2:1 (Fitch 1949).

Because its numbers have been severely depleted in some states, *C. viridis* is now considered endangered in Colorado *(C. v. concolor)* and Iowa, rare in Wyoming *(C. v. concolor),* and a controlled species in Utah.

REMARKS. Brattstrom (1964b) thought *C. viridis* morphologically close to the species *atrox, cerastes, mitchelli,* and *tigris,* but electrophoretic studies of venom proteins place it with *atrox* and *ruber* (Foote and MacMahon 1977). Venom proteins also show the subspecies *abyssus* is most closely related to the subspecies *lutosus* (Young et al. 1980).

C. viridis plays an important role in the culture of the Native American Hopi tribe. During the Hopi's snake dance, *C. v. nuntius* is carried in the mouths and hands of the participants (for a detailed description and discussion, see Klauber 1972).

Crotalus willardi Meek 1906 | Ridge-nosed Rattlesnake

RECOGNITION. This small (maximum TBL, 67 cm; but most are shorter than 55 cm) snake is gray, brown, or reddish brown with a series of 18–28 (mean, 23) white to cream-colored, dark-bordered crossbars, and only one to three anterior bands on the tail. Three longitudinal rows of small, indistinct dark spots occur along the sides. Individuals from Arizona have two white longitudinal stripes on the side of the face, one extending diagonally backward from the prenasal scale below the eye to the corner of the mouth, and a second extending backward along the supra- and infralabials. A median white, vertical stripe extends downward from the rostral and mental scales. Snakes from New Mexico lack the rostral-mental stripe, and have only faded longitudinal stripes on the side of the face. Dorsal body scales are keeled and pitted; they occur in 28–29 (25–31) anterior rows, 25 or 27 (23–31) midbody rows, and 19 (16–21) rows near the tail. The pink, cream, or tan venter is mottled with dark brown or black, and has 140–160 ventrals, 21–36 subcaudals, and an undivided anal plate. The rostral is higher than wide, anteriorly pointed, and slightly upturned. It combines with the recurved outer edges of the 2 internasals and 2/2 canthals to produce a distinctly raised snout. As many as 60 small scales (usually 20–40) occupy the intercanthal to parietal areas (no prefrontal scales are present). Also present are 6–9 intersupraoculars and 2 reduced supraoculars. Lateral scales consists of 2 nasals (the postnasal does not touch the upper preocular, but the prenasal contacts the supralabials), 2 (1–4) loreals, 2–3 preoculars, 3–4 (5) postoculars, 2–3 suboculars, several rows of temporals, 13–14 (10–17) supralabials, and 13–14 (12–16) infralabials. The bilobed hemipenis has a divided sulcus spermaticus, about 56 short heavy spines and 16 fringes on each lobe (reduction of the lobal spines to reticulations is sudden), and 1–2 spines in the crotch between the lobes. Each maxilla bears only the fang.

Males have 140–158 (mean, 151) ventrals, 23–36 (mean, 29) subcaudals, and TLs 9.1–11.5 (mean, 10.5) % of TBL; females have 144–160 (mean, 155) ventrals, 21–32 (mean, 24) subcaudals, and TLs only 7.9–9.8 (mean, 8.5) % of TBL.

GEOGRAPHIC VARIATION. In the United States and Mexico, populations of *C. willardi* are not continuously distributed, but instead occur in isolated pockets on separate mountain ranges, which has led to evolution of much variation. Five subspecies are recognized; only two occur in the United States. *C. w. willardi* Meek 1906, the Arizona ridge-nosed rattlesnake, ranges from the Huachuca, Patagonia, and Santa Rita Mountains in southeastern Arizona southward into the Sierra de los Ajos, Sierra Azul, and Sierra de Cananea of northern Sonora, Mexico. It has well-developed white stripes on the sides of the face and vertically on the rostral and mental scales, a brownish to reddish brown back, and little dark spot-

Arizona ridge-nosed rattlesnake, *Crotalus willardi willardi*; Arizona. (Photograph by Cecil Schwalbe)

ting on the head. *C. w. obscurus* Harris and Simmons 1976, the New Mexico ridge-nosed rattlesnake, lives only in the Animas and Peloncillo Mountains of New Mexico, and the Sierra de San Luis of extreme northeastern Sonora and western Chihuahua, Mexico. It lacks the vertical white stripe on the rostral and mental scales, and the lateral facial stripes are faded or absent. Its back may be either gray or brownish, and the head is heavily marked with dark spots.

The New Mexican population when first discovered was thought to represent the Mexican subspecies *C. w. silus* (Bogert and Degenhardt 1961), but reevaluation by Harris and Simmons (1976) showed it to be an undescribed form.

CONFUSING SPECIES. The raised rostrum and pattern of white facial stripes set this species apart from all other rattlesnakes in the United States. The western hog-nosed snake *(Heterodon nasicus)* also has an upturned snout, but lacks a loreal pit, elliptical pupils, and a tail rattle.

KARYOTYPE AND FOSSIL RECORD. Not reported.

DISTRIBUTION. The greatest portion of the geographical range of *C. willardi* is in Mexico, as it is known only from a few localities in south-central Arizona and extreme southwestern New Mexico. In Mexico, it occurs from north-central and northwestern Sonora and eastern Chihuahua southward through west-central Durango to southwestern Zacatecas.

HABITAT. It is a montane (elevation 1,475–2,800 m) pine-oak or scrub-oak forest species most often found in canyons along streams, near cool, shaded rock outcrops with crevices, in rock piles, or in old stumps or downed logs. Usually a thick mat of leaf litter or pine needles covers the ground.

BEHAVIOR. Data on the life history of *C. willardi* are few. The annual activity period in Arizona extends from April or early May to mid-November (Johnson 1983; Lowe et al. 1986). The colder months are spent under cover in rock crevices, talus slopes, or rotting stumps or logs; several have been found hibernating 40–46 cm deep in a talus slope (Degenhardt et al. 1996). It is most active during the day, particularly in

Distribution of *Crotalus willardi*.

the spring and fall, but some crepuscular or nocturnal foraging possibly occurs in the summer. Daily activity peaks on warm, humid mornings, and especially after rains, some will emerge late in the afternoon. Toward autumn, when daytime ATs fall, most activity shifts to the afternoon. Active *C. willardi* have been found when ATs varied from 20–26°C (Bogert and Degenhardt 1961; Degenhardt et al. 1996; Kauffeld 1943a) to 30–32°C (Brattstrom 1965; Wright and Wright 1957), but most foraging and basking takes place when ATs are 24–29°C (Armstrong and Murphy 1979; Degenhardt et al. 1996).

C. willardi sometimes ascends trees or bushes to heights of 42–61 cm (Kauffeld 1943a; Rossi and Feldner 1993).

REPRODUCTION. Stebbins (1985) reported the TBL at maturity to be 37 cm for each sex. Pregnant females with 45.2–48.1 cm TBLs have been found by Klauber (1949b, 1972) and Quinn (1977), and a 54.8 cm male has successfully mated (Tryon 1978). The male and female gametic cycles are undescribed. Pregnant females have been found from early May to early September (Delgodillo-Espinosa et al. 1999; Johnson 1983; Martin 1975b). Because females of other species of *Crotalus* have biennial cycles and Martin (1975c, 1976b) has reported an approximate 13 month GP in captivity, Tryon (1978) thought the female cycle to be at least biennial.

Courtship and mating activities by *C. willardi* have occurred in captivity on 29 January; 17–19 April; 16, 19, and 22 June; 15 and 28 July; in early August; and on 8–9 September (Armstrong and Murphy 1979; Martin 1975b, 1976b; Tryon 1978); and Lowe et al. (1986) observed mating in the wild in July. Copulation often follows soon after female ecdysis. Observed matings have lasted 11–24 hours (Armstrong and Murphy 1979; Tryon 1978), but these may have been even longer since entire sequences were not witnessed. When a male discovers a female, he immediately begins rapid, longitudinal chin rubbing and tongue flicks along the female's back and upper sides (Tryon 1978). If unreceptive, the female immediately slaps her tail rapidly from side to side and crawls away. This causes the male to intensify his activities. Once he assumes loose coils on and parallel to the female's body, she raises her tail slightly and stops moving. The male then loops his tail under hers and attempts to align their cloacal vents with several anterior-posterior strokes. If intromission is not accomplished, the male behavior sequence begins again. Once intromission is accomplished, most movement by both snakes ceases, but the male may periodically chin rub and tongue flick, and the female may rapidly bob her head. A captive male observed during courtship by Guese (in Armstrong and Murphy 1979) directed head bobbing and tongue flicking across a coiled, resting female's back, then moved his uplifted tail in both horizontal and vertical planes with an undulating motion. Another captive male twitched after discovering a female, and tongue flicked the entire dorsal surface of her body. He then rubbed along her back by holding his head at a 30° angle and sliding the area of the mental scale forward for 1 cm (Armstrong and Murphy 1979).

Litters contain two (Klauber 1949b) to nine (Martin 1976b) young, and average 5.8 (n = 11). There seems to be a positive correlation between the number of young produced and female length. Martin (1975c) and Delgodillo-Espinosa et al. (1999) reported RCMs of 0.358 and 0.402, respectively. Thirty-four neonates averaged 19.3 (165–22.2) cm TBLs and had 6.5 (4.3–8.5) g masses. Captive and wild birth dates range from 30 June to 10 September, with most records in August. Young *C. w. willardi* are brownish at birth and have either yellowish or gray-striped tails.

Young of *C. w. obscurus* are dark brown with distinctly blackish tails (Holycross 2000c; Martin 1976b).

An apparent natural hybridization between *C. willardi* and *C. lepidus* has occurred in the Peloncillo Mountains of New Mexico (Campbell et al. 1989).

GROWTH AND LONGEVITY.   The growth rate has not been reported. However, *C. willardi* may have a long life span; a captive female, wild-caught as a juvenile, lived for another 21 years, 3 months, and 24 days (Snider and Bowler 1992).

DIET AND FEEDING HABITS.   Wild *C. willardi* have eaten mice *(Peromyscus boylii, P. maniculatus);* lizards *(Gerrhonotus kingi, Sceloporus jarrovii);* birds—rufous-crowned sparrows *(Aimophila ruficeps)* and a small warbler; scorpions; and centipedes *(Scolopendra)* (Barker 1992; Klauber 1949b, 1972; Fowlie 1965; Greene 1994; Johnson 1983; Martin 1975b; Parker and Stotz 1977; Woodin 1953). In captivity, it has consumed white laboratory mice *(Mus musculus),* lizards *(Anolis carolinensis, Phrynosoma solare, Urosaurus ornatus),* snakes *(Hypsiglena torquata, Trimorphodon biscutatus),* and centipedes *(Scolopendra)* (Armstrong and Murphy 1979; Bogert and Degenhardt 1961; Johnson 1983; Kauffeld 1943b; Klauber 1972; Lowe et al. 1986; Manion 1968; Martin 1976b; Vorhies 1948). Juveniles are probably more dependent on lizards as prey than are adults.

C. willardi captures its prey either by striking it from ambush or by actively hunting for it. When bitten, rodents are usually released at once, and later trailed by olfactory cues; lizards are usually struck in the body region and retained until dead.

VENOM AND BITES.   Klauber (1939c) reported fang lengths of 5.3–6.0 mm for *C. willardi*.

The total volume of venom available for injection is small; Minton and Weinstein (1984) reported a venom yield of 3.1 mg, and Klauber (1972) could extract only a total of 3.7 mg of dried venom. The venom is also relatively weak; the minimum LD_{50} for a 20 g mouse is 0.24 mg (Githens and Wolf 1939), and for a 350 g pigeon it is only 0.1 mg (Githens and George 1931). The intravenous LD_{50} for 20–25 g mice is 1.61 mg/kg; a subcutaneous dose of 0.33 mg causes extensive subcutaneous hemorrhaging and is lethal (Minton and Weinstein 1984). The venom has a moderate amount of protease activity.

Russell (in Minton and Weinstein 1984) treated a human bite by *C. willardi* that showed only minimal local signs of envenomation.

PREDATORS AND DEFENSE. Natural predators of *C. willardi* are unknown, but probably include ophiophagous snakes, birds of prey, and carnivorous mammals.

This is a relatively secretive snake of mild disposition. Most lie still without rattling, or may try to crawl away, occasionally shaking their tails as they go. Seldom do they coil and strike at an intruder, but they do have the unpleasant habit of turning the head to bite the hand holding their neck, so one must be alert to avoid such an accident. Usually all rattling ceases once they are placed in a collecting bag or container.

POPULATIONS. At some Arizona sites, *C. willardi* may be the most common snake; Johnson (1983) has found as many as six in two hours in one canyon. It seems most common in the Huachuca Mountains, followed by the Santa Rita and Patagonia mountains, in that order (Johnson and Mills 1982). Klauber (1936) reported a sex ratio of 1.15 males for each female, and

Quinn (1977) noted a ratio of 1.5:1, but Tryon (1978) found twice as many females as males in litters.

The isolated populations of *C. willardi* could lead to extinction of some of the smaller isolated colonies if human interference or natural conditions become intolerable, and overcollection of *C. w. obscurus* has severely decimated the Animas population to the point that the species is now considered endangered in New Mexico. Fortunately, its microhabitat is not often visited by humans. The major populations in Arizona are on federally protected lands, and the snake is considered threatened there.

REMARKS. An electrophoretic study of venom proteins from *C. willardi* has shown that it is most closely related to the *Crotalus* species *cerastes, lepidus, pricei,* and *triseriatus,* and to the Mexican *Sistrurus ravus* (Foote and MacMahon 1977). Brattstrom (1964b) had previously proposed it close to *lepidus, pricei,* and *triseriatus* on morphological grounds. Greene (1994) proposed weighted "sister taxa" showing *C. w. willardi* separate from the other four subspecies, and *C. w. obscurus* and the Mexican *C. w. silus* closely related.

Because some day soon the populations of *C. willardi* may have to be managed to ensure its survival, it seems necessary that a thorough ecological study of both its U.S. subspecies be conducted.

Sistrurus Garman 1884

Massasaugas and Pigmy Rattlesnakes

Key to the Species of *Sistrurus*

1a. Prefrontal scale does not contact loreal scale; preocular scale contacts postnasal scale . . . . *S. catenatus*

1b. Prefrontal scale broadly contacts loreal scale; preocular scale does not contact postnasal scale . . . . . . *S. miliarius*

Sistrurus catenatus (Rafinesque 1818) | Massasauga

RECOGNITION. *S. catenatus* grows to a maximum TBL of 100.3 cm, but most individuals are shorter than 55 cm. It is gray to light brown with a dorsal se-

ries of 21–50 (mean, 40) dark brown to black blotches, three rows of small brown to black spots on each side of the body (occasional individuals are striped), and

Eastern massasauga, *Sistrurus catenatus catenatus*; Michigan. (Photograph by James H. Harding)

the tail with alternate dark and light bands. Individuals from loamy plains are usually grayish brown, while those from Arizona have a more reddish appearance. The black venter is mottled with yellow, cream, or white marks, or it may be nearly all black. A dark, light-bordered stripe runs backward from the eye, and another dark middorsal, light-bordered stripe extends posteriorly on the back of the head. Dorsal body scales are strongly keeled, and lie in 23 (24–27) anterior rows, 23 or 25 (21–27) midbody rows, and 17–19 posterior rows. Ventral scales total 129–160, subcaudals 19–36, and the anal plate is complete. Dorsally on the head are a higher-than-wide rostral scale, followed by 9 enlarged plates—2 internasals, 2 prefrontals, a large frontal, 2 supraoculars, and 2 parietals. Laterally are 2 nasals, a loreal, 2 preoculars (the upper touches the postnasal), 3–4 (2–5) postoculars, 1–2 suboculars, 11–12 (9–14) supralabials, and 11–13 (10–16) infralabials. The hemipenis is bifurcate with a divided sulcus spermaticus, about 33 recurved spines and 23 fringes per lobe, and some spines between the lobes.

Males have 129–155 (mean, 144) ventrals, 24–36 (mean, 32) subcaudals, 5–11 (mean, 8) dark tail bands, and TLs 9.0–12.5 (mean, 10.8) % of TBL; females have 132–160 (mean, 148) ventrals, 19–29 (mean, 27) subcaudals, 3–8 (mean, 6) dark tail bands, and TLs 7.5–9.5 (mean, 9) % of TBL.

GEOGRAPHIC VARIATION. Three subspecies are recognized (Minton 1983). *S. c. catenatus* (Rafinesque 1818), the eastern massasauga, is found from southern Ontario and central New York west to Iowa and eastern Missouri. It usually has 25 midbody scale rows, 129–157 ventrals, 24–33 subcaudals in males and 19–29 in females, 20–40 dorsal body blotches, the venter mostly dark gray or black, and 55–80 cm adult TBLs. *S. c. edwardsii* (Baird and Girard 1853), the desert massasauga, lives in southeastern Colorado, the Texas Panhandle, extreme southwestern Texas, eastern and southern New Mexico, and southeastern Arizona in the United States, and in the Cuatro Cienegas Basin of Coahuila and at Aramberri, Nuevo León, in Mexico. It averages 23 midbody scale rows and has 137–152 ventrals, 28–36 subcaudals in males and 24–29 in females, 27–41 dorsal body blotches, a whitish to cream-colored venter with only a few small dark spots, and a maximum TBL of 55 cm. *S. c. tergeminus* (Say 1823), the western massasauga, ranges from southwestern Iowa and northwestern Missouri southwest through extreme southeastern Nebraska, east and central Kansas, and western Oklahoma to western Texas, and south from Oklahoma through east-central Texas to the Gulf Coast. It usually has 24 midbody scale rows, 138–160 ventrals, 27–34 subcaudals in males and 21–28 in females, 28–50 dorsal body blotches, a whitish or cream-colored venter with dark lateral blotches, and 45–65 cm adult TBLs. Intergradation zones occur between *catenatus* and *tergeminus* in southwestern Iowa and adjacent Missouri, and between *tergeminus* and *edwardsii* from southwestern Colorado through extreme western Oklahoma and the central Panhandle of Texas.

CONFUSING SPECIES. The large rattlesnakes (*Crotalus*) have numerous small scales on the crown between the two supraocular scales. *S. miliarius* has its prefrontals in broad contact with the loreal scale. Hog-nosed snakes (*Heterodon*) lack the loreal pit, rattle, and elliptical pupil.

KARYOTYPE. The karyotype consists of 36 chromosomes: 16 macrochromosomes (4 metacentric, 6 submetacentric, 4 subtelocentric) and 20 microchromosomes; sex determination is ZZ in males and ZW in females (Zimmerman and Kilpatrick 1973).

FOSSIL RECORD. Pliocene (Blancan) fossil *S. catenatus* have been found in Kansas, Nebraska, and Texas (Brattstrom 1967; Holman and Schloeder 1991; Rogers 1976, 1984); Pleistocene fossils are known from the Irvingtonian of Nebraska and West Virginia (Holman 1982b, 1995) and the Rancholabrean of Kansas (Holman 1972b; Preston 1979).

DISTRIBUTION. This species ranges from southern Ontario, central New York, and northwestern Pennsylvania, west to eastern Iowa, and southwest to western Texas, southern New Mexico, and southeastern Arizona. Mexican populations occur in Coahuila and Nuevo León.

HABITAT. The massasauga occurs from sea level to about 2,100 m. Over most of the range it is found in

Distribution of *Sistrurus catenatus*.

moist habitats such as swamps, marshes, bogs, minerotrophic shrubby peatlands, wet meadows, seasonally moist grasslands, or wet woods, but in its dry range in Arizona, New Mexico, and parts of western Texas, it is restricted to habitats such as river bottoms, dry desert grasslands, short grass prairies, plains of mesquite, juniper, grass, yucca, creosote and cacti, and scrub oak woods. It is able to survive in such arid regions because it uses rodent burrows as daytime retreats and hibernacula; these burrows provide a humid microclimate that retards moisture loss.

Eastern massasaugas use low, poorly drained areas near the hibernaculum in the spring and fall, but in the summer gravid females use more dry habitats with low or sparse vegetation (Reinert and Kodrich 1982). In Missouri, they move from prairie habitats in spring to upland old fields and deciduous woods in summer, and then return to the prairies in the fall (Seigel 1986).

BEHAVIOR.   In the United States and Canada, S. catenatus is annually surface active from mid-March or April to October or early November; possibly Mexican populations are active all year, but less so in the summer and winter. Annual activity is bimodal with peaks in late April–June, and late September–October.

In the East, the winter is usually spent in crayfish burrows, old stumps or rotten logs within peat bogs and other wetlands, or moist, often coniferous, woodlands; but in the dry Southwest, where wetlands are seasonal and crayfish scarce or absent, hibernation takes place in rock crevices and rodent burrows. In northeastern Ohio, massasaugas are capable of maintaining CTs above ET for 45 minutes and can withstand freezing BTs for short periods without harm, but they usually hibernate in wet crayfish holes at depths below the frost line (Maple and Orr 1968).

Prior and Weatherhead (1994) recorded positive responses to disturbance at 15–31°C BTs from active Ontario massasaugas: to 15°C (2%), 16–20°C (25%), 21–25°C (31%), 25–30°C (45%), and 31+°C (71%). During the spring and fall, S. catenatus actively forages or basks (often on grass tussocks) during the day, but when daytime summer ATs reach 34°C it becomes more crepuscular or nocturnal (Tennant 1985). In northwestern Missouri, most spring activity is from 1200 to 1600 hours (55%), 1600 to 2000 hours (24%),

and 0800 to 1200 hours (17%); little activity (4%) occurs from 2000 to 2400 hours; summer activity is from 1600 to 2000 hours (42%), 1200 to 1600 hours (33%), and 2000 to 2400 hours (18%); and in the fall, most activity (70%) is at 1200–1600 hours (Seigel 1986). Pennsylvania S. catenatus are mainly summer active from 0900 to 1500 hours (Reinert 1978), but in Arizona, to avoid very warm summer day ATs, most S. catenatus are crepuscular or nocturnal (Lowe et al. 1986).

S. catenatus normally move some distance between the hibernaculum and the summer activity range, and often it is gravid females who migrate the greatest distance (King 1999). The snakes move freely during the annual activity period, but daily distances moved and home range areas are dependent on the amount of available habitat. Mean home range area and length in western Pennsylvania were 9,794 m² and 89 m, respectively, and the mean distance moved per day was 9.1 m, with no significant differences between the sexes; however, gravid females had significantly shorter home range lengths than nongravid females (Reinert and Kodrich 1982). In Illinois, the mean home range in a limited habitat was only 2.38 ha (Wilson and Mauger 1999); but in Wisconsin, mean home range for males was 161.5 ha, that of nongravid females was 6.7 ha, and that of gravid females was 2.8 ha (King 1999); and in New York these three classes had mean home ranges of 27.8 ha, 41.4 ha, and 2 ha, respectively (Johnson 2000). Ontario home ranges averaged 0.25 km² (Weatherhead and Prior 1992). Mean distances for snakes that had moved were 7–167 m/day, and 752–3,712 m/season, with gravid females traveling less distance than either nongravid females or males (Johnson 2000; Weatherhead and Prior 1992). Neonates have the shortest home ranges and move smaller distances per day and per season (King 1999). Massasaugas are good swimmers and readily enter water.

Males engage in dominance bouts; two males face each other with heads and the anterior portion of the bodies raised, venters pressed together, and necks intertwined, and each attempts to pin his opponent to the ground (Collins and Collins 1993).

REPRODUCTION.   The sexes are mature when TBLs are 40–54 cm (Stebbins 1985; Wright 1941); such lengths are reached at three to four years. The smallest mature male and female examined by Goldberg and Holycross (1999) had 28.0 and 32.9 cm SVLs, respectively.

First-summer Wisconsin females show no follicular growth; those in their second summer have follicles about 7 mm in diameter; 50% of third-summer females are gravid and 25% are postpartum (one collected 31 August had yellow follicles about 25 cm long); and only about 3% of fourth-summer females are not gravid or have not already given birth (Keenlyne 1978). Only 7% of third-summer or older Wisconsin females and only 3% of fourth-summer females or older are nonreproductive. This suggests an annual female reproductive cycle. However, Goldberg and Holycross (1999), Reinert (1981), and Seigel (1986) reported a biennial reproductive cycle in females from Arizona, Colorado, Pennsylvania, and Missouri, respectively. The annual percentage of reproductive females in Arizona and Colorado is only about 15%; in Pennsylvania, only 52–58%; and in Missouri, 33–71%. Significant size differences exist between females from Arizona, Colorado, and Pennsylvania and those from Wisconsin, those from Wisconsin being larger: perhaps SVL influences the breeding cycle.

Breeding may occur in the spring, and again in late summer or fall. During courtship, the male lies on the female's back with his tail coiled around her tail, and he frequently rubs her head and neck with his chin and writhes his body. He then massages the posterior portion of the female's tail with his tail loop by tightening it and stroking posteriorly until her rattle is touched, then reversing the stroke until he reaches the place of his original grip. This entire cycle is repeated several times. The chin-rubbing rate is relatively constant, and continues for the entire period of time between successive tail-stroke cycles (Chiszar et al. 1976). If mating occurs in late summer or early autumn and the young are not born until the next summer, the sperm is probably stored in the female's oviducts and not used until the next spring.

The GP is about 100 (71–115) days; the ovoviviparous young are born from late July to early October, but most births occur in August. From 1 to 10 minutes elapse between individual births, and the young rupture the fetal membrane within the first few minutes. Their first act after emergence from the membrane is to stretch their jaws as if yawning (Anderson 1965).

Litters average 8 young (n = 65), and vary from 2 (Stebbins 1954) to 20 (Anton 2000b; Vogt 1981). The smaller females from southwestern populations produce fewer young per litter, usually 5–6 (Goldberg and Holycross 1999), and Seigel (1986) found a significant positive relationship between female length and litter size in Missouri. Seigel and Fitch (1984) reported a RCM of 0.247. Neonates have 13.5–27.5 (mean, 21.2; n = 53) cm TBLs and weigh 3.4–13.3 (mean, 8.6; n = 18) g.

A natural hybrid *S. catenatus* × *Crotalus horridus* was reported by Bailey (1942).

GROWTH AND LONGEVITY. Yearlings from Illinois have 39–43 cm TBLs, an increase of about 65% from birth (Wright 1941), and Missouri yearlings have SVLs of 30–40 cm (Seigel 1986). Massasaugas with 50–54 cm SVLs are probably three to four years old (Wright 1941; Keenlyne 1978; Seigel 1986).

The longevity record is for a male who survived 20 years and 5 days at the Staten Island Zoo (Snider and Bowler 1992).

DIET AND FEEDING HABITS. Adults usually capture prey by ambush, but some active foraging is probably also important. Young *S. catenatus* tail lure by waving their tails back and forth over their heads to attract small frogs (Schuett et al. 1984). Warm-blooded prey are probably detected by the heat sensory facial pit, but sight and olfaction are also important feeding cues (Chiszar et al. 1976, 1979, 1981). Movement is the primary cue in eliciting exploratory behavior (Scudder and Chiszar 1977). Most prey are struck and then eaten only after they die, but anurans may be swallowed alive.

Reported natural prey are mammals—shrews *(Blarina brevicauda, Sorex cinereus),* voles *(Microtus ochrogaster, M. pennsylvanicus),* murid mice *(Mus musculus, Peromyscus leucopus, P. maniculatus, Reithrodontomys montanus),* jumping mice *(Zapus hudsonius),* and pocket mice *(Perognathus hispidus, P. merriami);* birds (eggs and nestlings)—quail *(Colinus virginianus),* sparrows *(Chondestes grammacus, Spizella pusilla),* and blackbirds *(Agelaius phoeniceus);* reptiles—lizards *(Cnemidophorus gularis, C. sexlineatus, Gambelia wislizenii, Holbrookia* sp., *Phrynosoma cornutum, Sceloporus olivaceus, Scincella lateralis, Uta stansburiana)* and snakes *(Heterodon nasicus, Liochlorophis vernalis, Storeria dekayi,*

Sonora semiannulata, Thamnophis sirtalis, Tropidoclonion lineatum); anurans *(Bufo* sp., *Pseudacris crucifer, Rana* sp.); fish; crayfish; centipedes *(Scolopendra);* and insects (Applegate 1995; Best 1978; Brush and Ferguson 1986; Degenhardt et al. 1996; Greene and Oliver 1965; Keenlyne and Beer 1973; Klauber 1972; Lardie 1976b; Mauger and Wilson 1999; McKinney and Ballinger 1966; Seigel 1986; Tennant 1985; Tinkle 1967; Vogt 1981; Webb 1970; Wright 1941; Wright and Wright 1957).

Nearly 95% of the prey of Wisconsin massasaugas were warm-blooded, and 85.7% of the entire diet consisted of voles; other prey were deer mice (4.4%), garter snakes (4.4%), jumping mice (2.2%), redwinged blackbirds (1.1%), shrews (1.1%), and an unidentified snake (1.1%); food items by sex and percentages of snakes containing prey were males, 83.6%, nongravid females, 55.6%, and gravid females, 10.4% (Keenlyne and Beer 1973). Two major categories of food were consumed by Missouri *S. catenatus*: small rodents and snakes (Seigel 1986). Fowlie (1965) reported that in Arizona *S. c. edwardsii* is primarily an amphibian predator; but Greene (1990), after examining museum specimens (mostly roadkills), concluded that they eat small lizards and pocket mice, and Lowe et al. (1986) reported that mice and lizards (especially whiptails and earless) are taken.

Ruthven (in Klauber 1972) thought snakes devoured were probably carrion; Greene and Oliver (1965) found a Texas massasauga attempting to swallow a recently road-killed snake, and Schwammer (1983) observed one eating carrion in Colorado.

VENOM AND BITES. Massasauga fangs are short; Klauber (1939c) reported lengths of 4.5–5.9 mm. The total dry venom yield for an adult massasauga is 15–45 mg, and the LD_{50} for a mouse is 2.9 mg/kg (Ernst and Zug 1996); however, the yield per bite is probably closer to 5–6 mg. The estimated human lethal dose is 30–40 mg (Minton and Minton 1969). Young only a few days old have venom toxic enough to cause bitten mice to die within several hours (Conant 1951).

The venom is largely hemolytic and causes much ecchymosis as capillary walls are destroyed, but neurotoxins may also be present (Tan and Ponnudurai 1991); other symptoms of bites include an initial burning sensation, pain, skin sensitivity, discoloration and swelling spreading from the bite site, swollen and painful lymph glands, bleeding from the puncture wounds, numbness at the bite site, a cold sweat, fever, faintness, nausea and loss of appetite, tremors, headache, and nervousness (Allen 1956; Atkinson and Netting 1927; Baldwin 1999; Dodge and Folk 1960; Hutchison 1929; Klauber 1972; LaPointe 1953; Menne 1959). Humans have died from massasauga bites (Lyon and Bishop 1936; Stebbins 1954; Menne 1959).

PREDATORS AND DEFENSE. Predation data concerning *S. catenatus* are scanty. Reported predators are fish (?), bullfrogs *(Rana catesbeiana),* turtles (?), racers *(Coluber constrictor),* loggerhead shrikes *(Lanius ludovicianus),* coyotes *(Canis latrans),* and weasels *(Mustela frenata, M. vison)* (Chapman and Casto 1972; Collins and Collins 1993; Johnson 1992; Minton 1972; Ross 1989); large hawks *(Buteo),* owls *(Bubo),* turkeys *(Meleagris),* large wading birds *(Ardea,* etc.), and carnivorous mammals *(Procyon, Mephitis, Taxidea, Canis, Felis, Lynx)* are also potential predators. However, humans (through habitat destruction and roadkills) probably eliminate more massasaugas each year than all natural predators combined.

This snake is usually rather sluggish and mild mannered, and only becomes aggressive if provoked. However, differences in disposition between individuals occur; a large female that the authors found in Missouri was very alert and irritable, rattling her tail and striking whenever approached. The SVL-adjusted loudness of rattling is about 70 dB, and the sound frequencies are 6.4–19.4 kHz, with a dominant frequency of 13.5 kHz (Cook et al. 1994; Fenton and Licht 1990; Young and Brown 1993). Massasaugas from disturbed populations adjust their behavior to become less visible (Parent and Weatherhead 2000).

POPULATIONS. Populations are normally rather small, but dense (Conant 1951; Fitch 1993; Kingsbury 1996; Mauger and Wilson 1999; Seigel 1986; Seigel et al. 1998). Recorded data on sex distributions in litters and natural populations show the male to female ratio to be essentially 1:1, and juveniles constitute about 30–40% of populations.

Populations crowded into small areas make *S. catenatus* more prone to extirpation (Conant 1951). In the past fairly dense populations of these snakes probably occurred at suitable sites. However, human and natural habitat destruction have eliminated most colonies (Kingsbury 1996; Menne 1959; Seigel et al. 1998). In the Southwest, loss of prairie grasslands to overgrazing has eliminated much of the snake's original habitat. As a result, *S. catenatus* is now considered threatened or endangered over most of its range. Suitable habitat must be preserved and populations protected, if it is to remain a viable species.

REMARKS. Molecular studies have shown the species of *Sistrurus* are most closely related to the larger rattlesnakes of the genus *Crotalus* (Dowling et al. 1996). *S. catenatus* was reviewed by Minton (1983).

Sistrurus miliarius (Linnaeus 1766) | Pigmy Rattlesnake

RECOGNITION. *S. miliarius* is small (maximum TBL 83.2 cm, but typically 40–55 cm) with nine enlarged scales on the dorsal surface of the head (see *S. catenatus*), a series of 22–45 (mean, 33) dark dorsal body blotches, one to three rows of dark spots on its sides, and a red to orange vertebral stripe. The body is normally gray or tan, but reddish orange to brick red individuals occur along the northeastern edge of the range, chiefly in Beaufort and Hyde counties, North Carolina. The venter is whitish to cream-colored with a moderate to heavy pattern of dark blotches. A black or reddish brown bar extends backward from the eye to beyond the corner of the mouth, and two dark longitudinal, often wavy, stripes are present on the back of the head. Dorsal body scales have keels, and occur in 23–25 anterior rows, 21–23 (19–25) midbody rows, and 17 (15–19) rows near the vent. The venter has 122–148 ventral scutes, 25–39 subcaudals, and an undivided anal plate. On the side of the head are 2 nasals, a loreal (lying between the postnasal and upper preocular), 2 preoculars, 3–4 (5–6) postoculars, 4–5 rows of temporals, 10–11 (8–13) supralabials, and 11–12

Carolina pigmy rattlesnake, *Sistrurus miliarius miliarius (gray phase)*. (Photograph by R. D. Bartlett)

Carolina pigmy rattlesnake, *Sistrurus miliarius miliarius (red phase)*; Hyde County, North Carolina. (Photograph by R. D. Bartlett)

(9–14) infralabials. The hemipenis is similar to that of *S. catenatus*.

Males are usually smaller, and have longer tails, which are thicker at the base (Bishop et al. 1996). They also have 122–148 (mean, 130) ventrals, 28–39 (mean, 34) subcaudals, 7–14 (mean, 11) dark tail bands, and TLs 10–15 (mean, 12.5) % of TBL; females have 123–148 (mean, 135) ventrals, 25–36 (mean, 30) subcaudals, 6–13 (mean, 9) dark tail bands, and TLs 9–12 (mean, 10.5) % of TBL.

GEOGRAPHIC VARIATION. Three subspecies have been described (Palmer 1978). *S. m. miliarius* (Linneaus 1766), the Carolina pigmy rattlesnake, is gray to reddish brown with a well-marked head pattern, one to two rows of lateral spots, usually 25 anterior and 23 midbody scale rows, and dark ventral spots at least two scutes wide. It ranges from Hyde County, North Carolina, southwestward to central Alabama. *S. m. barbouri* Gloyd 1935, the dusky pigmy rattlesnake, is dark gray with an obscured head pattern, three rows of lateral spots, usually 25 anterior and 23 midbody scale rows, and a heavily dark-spotted venter. Christman (1980) found that in Florida ventral and subcaudal counts decrease clinally toward the north, and that coastal populations have higher dorsal scale

Dusky pigmy rattlesnake, *Sistrurus miliarius barbouri*; Volusia County, Florida. (Photograph by Peter May)

Western pigmy rattlesnake, *Sistrurus miliarius streckeri*; Arkansas. (Photograph by Peter May)

row and blotch counts and larger, more rounded, dorsal blotches than inland populations. Its range is from extreme southwestern South Carolina south through peninsular Florida and west through southern Georgia, the Florida panhandle, and southern Alabama to southeastern Mississippi. *S. m. streckeri* Gloyd 1935, the western pigmy rattlesnake, is gray to tan with a well-marked head pattern, one to two rows of lateral spots, usually 23 anterior and 21 midbody scale rows, and diffuse ventral blotches about one scale wide. It occurs from "The Land Between the Lakes" in western Kentucky and Tennessee, southern Missouri, and eastern Oklahoma south to the Gulf Coast of Louisiana and central Texas.

CONFUSING SPECIES. Massasaugas *(S. catenatus)* can be differentiated by the key presented above, and larger rattlesnakes *(Crotalus)* have small scales between their supraoculars. Hog-noosed snakes *(Heterodon)* have upturned rostral scales and lack a rattle and facial pits.

KARYOTYPE. Karyotype is like that of *S. catenatus* (Zimmerman and Kilpatrick 1973).

FOSSIL RECORD. Pleistocene fossils have been found at Irvingtonian (Auffenberg 1963; Holman 1995; Meylan 1982, 1995) and Rancholabrean (Auffenberg 1963; Gut and Ray 1963; Holman 1959a, 1996; Martin 1974; Tihen 1962) sites in Florida.

DISTRIBUTION. *S. miliarius* ranges from Hyde County, North Carolina, south to the Florida Keys, and west to eastern Oklahoma and central Texas.

HABITAT. The pigmy rattlesnake lives in a variety of habitats at elevations of 0–500 m, but in the East none of these are very far from water; mixed turkey oak–longleaf pine forest, scrub pinewoods, sand hills, and wire-grass and palmetto flatwoods are all used. In the Everglades, it is seldom encountered in pinewoods or other dry habitats, but flooding may force it to higher ground such as canal banks and roads (Duellman and Schwartz 1958). It may use gopher tortoise *(Gopherus polyphemus)* and small mammal burrows as retreats. In the western, drier parts of its range, it is restricted to mesic grasslands.

Distribution of *Sistrurus miliarius*.

BEHAVIOR. In North Carolina, South Carolina, Georgia, and Florida, *S. miliarius* may remain active all year, but at lower numbers during the winter. In Florida, the highest incidence of surface activity occurs during periods of high water table. Over the entire range, most surface activity occurs in June–September, but in North Carolina, 82% of activity is in July–October (Palmer and Braswell 1995). Little is known of their overwintering behavior. Animal burrows, sawdust piles, and old logs are used as hibernacula (Klauber 1972; Neill 1948a; Palmer and Williamson 1971).

During the summer, *S. miliarius* is active from the late afternoon into the night, often basking in the morning. In the fall, winter, and early spring, activity is primarily in the afternoon, when it usually basks. Over 75% of individuals found are either coiled in an ambush mode or basking. May et al. (1996) reported it surface active in Florida at ATs of 14–32°C and CTs of 15–37°C (CT averaged 1.9°C above AT); microsites used averaged 0.4°C above surrounding STs. Clark (1949) found them basking in Louisiana at ATs as high as 38–45°C.

Florida pigmy rattlers have a bimodal seasonal movement pattern, peaking in March–April, moving least in December–February and July–August (May et al. 1996). Their home range is small. Those monitored by Hudnall (1979) moved a maximum distance from the first capture point of 9–242 m. One male averaged 179.6 m between recaptures, and two others only averaged 81.0–89.5 m between captures. Gravid females are rather sessile: one in Texas was never found more than 2 m from its original capture point in 34 days (Fleet and Kroll 1978). *S. miliarius* with pit tags and those without moved, respectively, an average of 98.9 and 92.5 m between captures, and 1.76 and 1.54 m/day (Jemison et al. 1995).

Although usually found on the ground, *S. miliarius* will climb into trees and bushes during flood events; Klauber (1972) found one 8 m high in a tree. The snake is also a good swimmer.

Males participate in dominance combat dances similar to those reported for other rattlesnakes (C. Ernst, pers. obs.; Lindsey 1979; Palmer and Williamson 1971). A pair will rise up, face each other, sometimes sway back and forth, lunge toward each other, entwine the posterior 40–50% of their bodies, and push with the raised anterior body until one of the two snakes is pinned firmly to the ground. The vanquished snake then crawls away unhurt. Such bouts last for a few minutes to over two hours and may be continuous or sporadic.

REPRODUCTION. Females with 33.2, 36.0, and 38.1 cm TBLs and masses of 50–150 g have reproduced (Clark 1949; May et al. 1997; Sabath and Worthington 1959), and Conant and Collins (1998) reported a minimum adult TBL of 38 cm for both sexes. Such lengths are probably reached in two to three years in nature, but one- to two-year-old captive females have produced young (Smetsers 1990). The male gametic cycle is undescribed, and data on the female cycle is sparse. Florida *S. m. barbouri* have had enlarged ovarian follicles on 7 January, partly developed embryos on 2 July, and nearly full term fetuses on 16 July, and they have given birth on 15 July, 2 August, and 4 October (Iverson 1978); and North Carolina *S. m. miliarius* have contained oviductal young on 27 May, 4 July, and 7, 8, 28, and 30 August (Palmer and Braswell 1995). Both annual and biennial reproduction occur in Florida females (Farrell et al. 1995).

Although no spring dates are available, mating probably occurs soon after emergence from hibernation. Several observations of mating in the wild exist for mid-August to early November (primarily September–October in Florida), and captives have mated in December and January. As most young are born from July through September, if spring matings do not occur, viable sperm must be stored over winter in the female's reproductive tract (Montgomery and Schuett 1989). When courting, a male waves his tail as he crawls after a female. When she is reached, he examines her with tongue flicks, crawls over her, and eventually inserts one hemipenis; copulation may last over six hours (Montgomery and Schuett 1989).

After a long 107–294 day GP (mean, 172; n = 7), the ovoviviparous young are born from late July through September, with August being the most important month; captive births have occurred in January and April to early June. At birth, the young are enclosed in a sheathlike membrane, and appear at intervals of 30–80 (mean, 46) minutes after a series of posteriorly progressing peristaltic contractions (Fleet and Kroll 1978). The young gape their jaws and appear to yawn after breaking through the fetal membranes.

Fifty-seven litters contained 2 (Farrell et al. 1995) to 32 (Carpenter 1960) young, and averaged 6.7. Northern *S. miliarius* produce smaller litters (Fitch 1985a). RCMs of seven litters averaged 0.327 (0.190–0.502) (Farrell et al. 1995; Ford et al. 1990; Seigel and Fitch 1984; Smetsers 1990). Both litter size and clutch mass are positively correlated with female body size (Bishop et al. 1996; Farrell et al. 1995). Neonates have 7.8–23.0 (mean, 15.5; n = 89) cm TBLs, weigh 0.8–6.2 g, and have cream, yellow, or orange tails.

An apparent defense of young by a captive female was witnessed by Verkerk (1987). When disturbed, the young hid behind the female's back while she rattled and tried to bite.

GROWTH AND LONGEVITY. In Florida, the mean annual growth rate of juvenile male *S. m. barbouri* is 3.5 cm, and that of juvenile females 2.6 cm; the growth rate is not significantly different between the sexes (Bishop et al. 1996). Florida juveniles grow about 10.5 cm and increase in weight about 75 g between birth and their third year. A male 23.5 cm in TBL when collected grew to 60.9 cm in two years in the authors' laboratory. Another male 65 cm long when captured in March 1981 grew to 80.3 cm by 1987; it was thought to be about 20 years old when it died in April 1993 (Snellings and Collins 1996). A female *S. m. streckeri* at the Houston Zoo lived 16 years, 1 month, and 4 days (Snider and Bowler 1992).

DIET AND FEEDING HABITS. Twelve of 16 Georgia *S. miliarius* examined by Hamilton and Pollack (1955) contained prey; reptiles were found in 50% of the stomachs, centipedes in 33%, and mammals in 17%. In Florida, the proportion of snakes with prey is highest in March, May, and June, lower in the summer, but increases again in September–October (May et al. 1996). Snakes make up less than 10% of the winter food, but 20–25% in late spring or fall (May et al. 1997).

Wild *S. miliarius* take a variety of small prey: small rodents *(Microtus pinetorum, Peromyscus maniculatus)*, nestling birds, small snakes *(Carphophis amoenus, Coluber constrictor, Diadophis punctatus, Nerodia sp., Sistrurus miliarius, Storeria dekayi, Thamnophis sauritus)*, lizards *(Anolis sp., Cnemidophorus sexlineatus, Eumeces inexpectatus, Scincella lateralis)*, anurans *(Acris sp., Bufo sp., Gastrophryne carolinensis, Hyla sp., Rana clamitans, R. sphenocephala)*, beetles, spiders, and centipedes *(Scolopendra)* (Chamberlain 1935; Clark 1949; C. Ernst, pers. obs.; Hamilton and Pollack 1955; Klauber 1972; Palmer and Braswell 1995; Palmer and Williamson 1971; Wright and Wright 1957). In addition, captives readily take house mice *(Mus musculus)*, lizards *(Eumeces fasciatus, Hemidactylus turcicus, Sceloporus undulatus)*, and crickets (C. Ernst, pers. obs.; Kennedy 1964; May et al. 1997; Montgomery and Schuett 1989; Verkerk 1987).

Most prey are ambushed, as the snake lies quietly along a prey trail by a grass clump or at the side of a log with its head oriented upwards. At such times, juveniles wave their yellowish tails to attract lizards and frogs (Jackson and Martin 1980; Neill 1960), but light levels must conceal the body while illuminating the bright tail (Rabatsky and Farrell 1996). Some prey, however, are actively sought. Many pigmy rattlesnakes the authors have found seemed to be searching for prey, and C. Ernst observed a Florida pigmy rattler stalk, strike, and swallow an *Anolis carolinensis*. Anurans may be more important in its diet than acknowledged; apparently Florida *S. miliarius* use frog odors when selecting hunting sites (Roth et al. 1999).

VENOM AND BITES. *S. miliarius* has short, 5.2–6.3 mm fangs (Klauber 1939c). Venom yield is also low, 12–35 mg (Ernst and Zug 1996), and a typical bite probably involves only about 20 mg. The LD_{50} for a mouse is 2.8 mg/kg (Ernst and Zug 1996). The lethal dose for an adult human has not been calculated, but is probably more than the total capacity of the snake. The venom seems rather virulent to mammals. Small mice bitten by the authors' adult *S. miliarius* have died in 30–90 seconds.

Human envenomation by the pigmy rattlesnake is not uncommon, particularly in Florida. The bite is more serious in children than adults, and small children may require several weeks of hospitalization when bitten. Case histories of human envenomation are given by Chamberlain (1935), Harris (1965), Klauber (1972), and Schmidt and Inger (1957). The venom contains no neurotoxic agents, but is strongly hemorrhagic (Scarborough et al. 1991; Tan and Ponnudarai 1991). Symptoms experienced have included swelling, pain, weakness, giddiness, respiratory difficulty, hemorrhage, nausea, ecchymosis, and the passage of bloody urine (Hutchison 1929).

PREDATORS AND DEFENSE. *S. miliarius* is preyed on by carnivorous mammals *(Canis familiaris, Didelphis virginianus, Felis catus, Mephitis mephitis),* hawks *(Buteo* sp.), and snakes *(Coluber constrictor, Drymarchon corais, Lampropeltis getula, Micrurus fulvius, Sistrurus miliarius)* (Allen and Neill 1950b; Klauber 1972; Printiss 1994). Most, though, are destroyed by habitat destruction and automobiles.

When disturbed, *S. miliarius* will either flee, flatten its body and strike sideways, or quickly coil (previously coiled individuals usually remain calm). But if further molested, the snake bobs its head and strikes with little warning. Its small rattle can barely be heard: the SVL-adjusted loudness is barely over 40 dB, and the frequency is 2.85–24.38 kHz (most common frequency, 9.95–14.3 kHz) (Cook et al. 1994; Young and Brown 1993). Those not coiled when first found are more active in their defense than those coiled. The pigmy rattlesnake recognizes the odor of *Lampropeltis getula,* and when introduced to this odor, it will hide its head, thrash about, or body bridge (Gutzke et al. 1993). The pattern and grayish coloration of this species helps camouflage it. This is especially true of *S. m. barbouri* in areas where pine trees have been partially burned and ashes are abundant.

POPULATIONS. In proper habitat, this snake can be quite numerous; the Florida population studied by May et al. (1996, 1997) had 400–500 within about 8 ha, a density of 50–62.5/ha; and Viosca (in Dundee and Rossman 1989) collected 103 on Delacrox Island, Louisiana, in 12 days when the snakes were forced onto levees by severe flooding. However, at other places it may be uncommon; Clark (1949) found only 11 in a sample of over 2,000 snakes from the upland parishes of Louisiana. It is considered threatened in Kentucky and Tennessee.

The sex ratio does not differ significantly from 1:1 (Bishop et al. 1996; Carpenter 1960; May et al. 1996).

REMARKS. Klauber (1972) thought *Sistrurus* ancestral to *Crotalus,* and believed it to have evolved in Mexico and later migrated north to the United States. Dorsal scale microdermoglyphics indicate *S. miliarius* is more closely related to *Crotalus pricei, C. cerastes,* and *C. mitchellii* than to other *Sistrurus* (Stille 1987). The species was reviewed by Palmer (1978).

Glossary

abyssus bottomless, referring to the Grand Canyon

abacura checkered, tessalated

acricus without a ring (neck band)

adamanteus diamond-like (pattern)

aeneus of bronze or copper

aestivus summer

affinis related by marriage

Agkistrodon hooked tooth

alleni named for Professor J. A. Allen

alterna alternating

amabilis lovely

amaura dark, dim

amoenus pleasing, charming

annectans, annectens to connect, referring to the dorsal body blotches *(Pituophis)* or adjacent subspecies *(Thamnophis)*

anthicus speckled with white

annulata bearing rings

arenicola sand-loving

Arizona dry zone

arizonae named for Arizona

arnyi named for Samuel Arny

atratus blackened

atricaudatus black-tailed

atriceps black head

atrox savage, fierce, cruel; referring to the nasty disposition of this snake

bairdi named for Spencer Fullerton Baird

barbouri named for Thomas Barbour

bilineatus two-lined

biscutatus two scales

Boa a water snake

Bogertophis Bogert's snake, named for Charles M. Bogert

bottae named for Paolo Emilio Botta, the nineteenth-century explorer who collected the original specimen

brachystoma short mouth

braminus belonging to Brahma

browni named for Herbert Brown

butleri named for the naturalist Amos W. Butler, who presented Cope with the type specimen

cahuilae for Lake Cahuila near the type locality

californiae named for California

calligaster beautiful belly

candida shining white, bright

canum whitish-gray, hoary

Carphophis dry twig snake

catenatus chainlike (pattern)

catenifer to carry

celaenops black or dark eyes

Cemophora muzzle-bearing

cerastes horned

cerberus black watchdog

cercobombus tail buzzer

Charina graceful

Chilomeniscus lip, crescent

Chionactis snow, white

cinctus belted, ringed

cingulum to circle, to go around

clarkii named for John H. Clark

Clonophis twiglike snake; violent, confused motion

coccinea scarlet, crimson

Coluber serpent, snake

compressicauda compressed, flattened tail

conanti named for the noted herpetologist Roger Conant

concinnus neat, well made; referring to the color pattern

concolor uniform coloration

confluens combined, joined; referring to the body pattern

Coniophanes dusky appearance

constrictor something that constricts

Contia named for John L. LeConte

contortrix twister

copei named for Edward Drinker Cope

corais raven, crow; referring to the black dorsal coloration

coronata crowned

couchii named for Lt. Couch of the U.S. Army

couperi named for J. Hamilton Couper

Crotalus rattle (tail)

cucullata hooded

cyclas garment ornate with a border around the bottom, referring to the ventral pattern

cyclopion round eye

cyrtopsis curved appearance, referring to the wavy lateral stripe in some individuals

dekayi named for James E. DeKay

deltae living in a delta, referring to the Mississippi Delta

decurtatus to shorten or cut off

deserticola desert-dwelling

diabolicus devilish, an allusion to the forked pattern of the parietal spots and to the aridity of the region inhabited by this race

Diadophis divided snake, referring to the neck band separating the head and body

dissectus divided, sectioned

dorsalis of the dorsum; referring to the vertebral stripe

Drymarchon wood ruler, probably referring to its large size

Drymobius forest dweller

dulcis sweet, soft

eburnata ivory

edwardsii named either for G. Edwards, or L. A. Edwards

Elaphe deerlike

elapsoides like *Elaps* (= *Micrurus*)

elegans elegant, neat

emoryi named for William H. Emory

eques horse

erebennus black

erythrogaster red belly

erytrogramma red-line character

etheridgei named for Richard Etheridge

euryxanthus broad yellow (bands or stripe)

extenuatum extended, elongated

Farancia a coined word, meaning unknown

fasciata banded

Ficimia a word without meaning, coined by Gray

fitchi named for Henry S. Fitch

flagellum whip, flail

flavigaster, flaviventris yellow belly

flavilata yellow, extensive

floridana named for Florida

foxii named for Rev. Charles C. Fox

fuliginosus sooty

fulvius reddish yellow, orange (bands)

gentilis of the same race or group

getula a proper name, Getulians, Morocco

gigas giant, mighty

girardi named for Charles Girard

gloydi named for Howard K. Gloyd

gracia gentile

gracilis slender, gentle

grahamiae, grahamii named for Col. James Duncan Graham

guttata spotted

Gyalopion hollow vessel

hammondii named for W. A. and J. F. Hammond

harteri named for Philip Harter who collected the type specimens

hellenae named for Helen Teunison

helleri named for Edmond Heller

helvigularis yellowish throat

Heterodon variable teeth

hexalepis six scales

hobartsmithi named for Hobart M. Smith

holbrooki named for John Edwards Holbrook

horridus horrid, dreadful

humilis small, ground-dwelling

hydrophilus water-loving

Hypsiglena high eye

imperialis imperial, kinglike

infernalis belonging to Hades

infralabialis of the lower labial scales

insularum of islands

intermedia intermediate, lying in between

jani named for Georg Jan

kennerlyi named for C. B. R. Kennerly, an army surgeon

kirtlandii names for Jared P. Kirtland, an early Ohio physician and naturalist

klauberi named for Laurence M. Klauber

lambda refers to the chevronlike head pattern

Lampropeltis shiny shield

lateralis lateral, on the side

laterorepens side-creeping

laticinctus broad band

latrunculus robber, freebooter; referring to the dark eye stripe

lecontei named for John L. LeConte

lepidus scaly, pretty, attractive

Leptodeira thin neck

Leptotyphlops slender and blind

leucostoma white mouth

limnetes marsh dweller

lindheimeri named for Ferdinand Lindheimer

lineata, lineatum, lineatus, lineatulus lined, marked with lines

lineri named for Ernest A. Liner

Liochlorophis smooth green snake

lodingi named for Henry P. Löding

loreala bearing loreal scales

lucidus lucid, bright

lutosus muddy

marcianus named for Capt. R. B. Marcy, one of the collectors of the first specimen

margaritiferus bearing pearls

Masticophis whipsnake

meahllmorum a name with no meaning derived from the names of 11 associates of Hobart M. Smith

megalops large eye

melanoleucus black and white

Micruroides like *Micrurus*

Micrurus small tail

miliarius milletlike (pattern)

mitchellii named for Dr. S. Weir Mitchell, a researcher of rattlesnake venom

modestus retiring, unpretentious

mojavensis of the Mojave Desert

mokasen moccasin

molossus after the Molossian wolfdog of antiquity

mormon named for the Mormon religious sect

mugitus bellowing, referring to the snake's loud hiss

multicincta many-girdled

multifasciata many-banded

multistriata many layers

nasicus nasal

neglecta neglected, not recognized

neilli named for Wilfred T. Neill

Nerodia wetlike

niger black

nigriceps black head

nigrita black

nitae named for Nita J. Rossman

noctivaga night wanderer

nubilus cloudy

nuchalata pertaining to the nape or neck

nuntius messenger

oaxaca named for the Mexican state of Oaxaca

obscura, obscurus dusky, obscure, faded, hidden

obsoleta obsolete, referring to the faded body pattern

occidentalis western

occipitalis back part of the head

occipitolineata lines on the back of the head

occipitomaculata spotted neck (occipit)

ocellatus having small eyes, referring to the dark spots on the first scale row that are arched over by the lateral stripe

orchrorhynchus brownish yellow snout

oolitica the Miami, Florida, oolite substratum

Opheodrys snake, oak

orarius of the (Gulf) coast

ordinoides similar to *ordinatus* (= *T. sirtalis*)

oreganus from Oregon

organica named for the Organ Pipe Cactus National Monument

Oxybelis sharp arrow

pahasapae Sioux Native American name for Black Hills

palarostris pale nose

pallidulus pale

pamlica the geological Pamlico Terrace, Florida

paludicola, paludis marsh dweller

parietalis of a wall; referring to the parietal scales

parvirubra little red

paucimaculata few spots

Pelamis fishlike

perkinsi named for Charles B. Perkins

phaeogaster dark belly

philipi named for Philip M. Klauber

Phyllorhynchus leaf nose

piceus pitch black

pickeringii named for Dr. Charles Pickering, the collector

pictigaster painted belly

pictiventris painted belly

piscivorus fish-eating

Pituophis pine snake

planiceps flat head

platirhinos flat or straight snout

platurus flat tail

pleuralis on the side, lateral

priapus named for Priapus, Roman god of male reproductive ability; referring to the large hemipenile spine

pricei named for W.W. Price, collector of the type specimen

proximus nearest or next

pulchellus beautiful, little

pulchra beautiful

pumilus dwarf

punctatus dotted, spotted

pygaea rump, buttocks

pyromelana flame-colored, black

pyrrhus flame-colored, orange, reddish

quadrangulare four angles or corners, referring to the dorsal blotches

quadrivittata four-striped

radix root

Ramphotyphlops beaked, blind

regalis royal, regal

Regina queen

reinwardtii named for C. G. C. Reinwardt

relicta a relic

Rhadinaea slender

Rhinocheilus nose lip

rhombifer bearing rhombs, referring to the diamond-like dorsal pattern

rhombomaculata spotted with rhomboid-shaped blotches

rigida rigid, stiff

rosaliae named for Santa Rosalis, Baja California, Mexico

roseofusca ruddy and dusky

rossalleni named for E. Ross Allen

ruber red

rubrilineatus bearing red lines

ruddocki named for Dr. John C. Ruddock, Medical Director for the Richfield Oil Corporation

rufipunctatus red-spotted

ruthveni named for Alexander G. Ruthven

rutiloris to be red and of the mouth

sackenii named for Baron Osten Sacken

Salvadora for the Linnean plant name

sauritus lizardlike

sayi named for Thomas P. Say

schotti named for Arthur Schott

scutulatus small shield, diamond-like pattern

segregus segregated, referring to its isolated geographical range

semiannulata half-ringed

semifasciatus half-banded

Seminatrix half *Natrix*

seminola the area of Florida inhabited by the Seminole Indians

Senticolis thorny penis

septemvittata seven-striped

septentrionalis northern

similis similar, like *Thamnophis sauritus nitae*

simus flat-nosed, snub-nosed

sinicola gulf inhabitant

sipedon a siren

sirtalis like a garter

Sistrurus rattle tail

Sonora named for Sonora, Mexico

spiloides spotted, stained

splendida splendid

stephensi named for Frank Stephens, a member of the collecting team

sticticeps dotted head

stictogenys narrow chin shield

Stilosoma pointed body

Storeria named for David H. Storer

streckeri named for John K. Strecker Jr.

striatula furrow or line

subocularis referring to the small scales positioned between the orbit and supralabials

syspila together, cap; referring to the snout pattern similar to that of other subspecies of *Lampropeltis triangulum*

taeniata, taeniatus thin-banded

talpina like a mole

Tantilla something small

taxispilota regularly patterned marks

taylori named for Edward H. Taylor

tener tender, delicate (appearance)

tenuis thin, narrow, slender

tergeminus triple, threefold (spotted pattern)

terrestris terrestrial, of the earth

tessellatus small cube of stone, referring to the dorsal pattern

testaceus covered with tiles (= scales)

texana belonging to Texas

Thamnophis bush snake

tigris tiger (pattern)

torquata bearing a neck chain

transversa to cross, referring to dorsal crossbands

triangulum triangle

triaspis three shields, referring to the three primary head scales

Trimorphodon three shapes, referring to the three tooth shapes on the maxilla

trivirgata three-striped

Tropidoclonion keeled twig

umbratica shade, seclusion

utahensis named for Utah

vagrans wandering

valeriae named for Valeria Blaney, collector of the holotype

vandenburghi named for John Van Denburgh

vascotanneri named for Vasco M. Tanner

vermis worm

vernalis spring

victa defeated, conquered

vilkinsoni named for Edward Wilkinson

virgultea little twig

Virginia named for the Commonwealth of Virginia

viridis green

vulpina either foxlike, or named for Rev. Charles Fox

wilcoxi named for Dr. Timothy E. Wilcox, M.D.

willardi named for Frank C. Willard, collector of the type specimen

williamengelsi named for William L. Engels

woodini named for William H. Woodin

wrightorum named for Albert Hazen and Anna Allen Wright

yaquia refers to the Yaqui Indians

zaxanthus intensely yellow

zonata banded

Bibliography

Adame, B. L., J. G. Soto, D. J. Secraw, J. C. Perez, J. L. Glenn, and R. C. Straight. 1990. Regional variation of biochemical characteristics and antigeneity in Great Basin rattlesnake *(Crotalus viridis lutosus)* venom. Comp. Biochem. Physiol. 97B:95–101.

Adler, K. K., and S. G. Tilley. 1960. A fish and a snail in the diet of *Natrix septemvittata* (Say). J. Ohio Herpetol. Soc. 2:28–29.

Aird, S. D., and M. E. Aird. 1990. Rain-collecting behavior in a Great Basin rattlesnake *(Crotalus viridis lutosus)*. Bull. Chicago Herpetol. Soc. 25:217.

Aird, S. D., W. G. Kruggel, and I. I. Kaiser. 1990. Amino acid sequence of the basic subunit of Mojave toxin from the venom of the Mojave rattlesnake *(Crotalus scutulatus)*. Toxicon 28:669–673.

———. 1991. Multiple myotoxin sequences from the venom of a single prairie rattlesnake *(Crotalus viridis viridus)*. Toxin 29:265–268.

Aird, S. D., C. S. Seebart, and I. I. Kaiser. 1988. Preliminary fractionation and characterization of the venom of the Great Basin rattlesnake *(Crotalus viridis lutosus)*. Herpetologica 44:71–85.

Aird, S. D., L. J. Thirkhill, C. S. Seebart, and I. I. Kaiser. 1989. Venoms and morphology of western diamondback/Mojave rattlesnake hybrids. J. Herpetol. 23:131–141.

Aldrich, J. W., and C. G. Endicott. 1984. Black rat snake predation on giant Canada goose eggs. Wildl. Soc. Bull. 12:263–264.

Aldridge, R. D. 1975. Environmental control of spermatogenesis in the rattlesnake, *Crotalus viridis*. Copeia 1975:493–496.

———. 1979a. Seasonal spermatogenesis in sympatric *Crotalus viridis* and *Arizona elegans* (Reptilia, Serpentes) in New Mexico. J. Herpetol. 13:187–192.

———. 1979b. Female reproductive cycles of the snakes *Arizona elegans* and *Crotalus viridis*. Herpetologica 35:256–261.

———. 1982. The ovarian cycle of the watersnake *Nerodia sipedon*, and effects of hypo-physectomy and gonadotropin administration. Herpetologica 38:71–79.

———. 1992. Oviductal anatomy and seasonal sperm storage in the southeastern crowned snake *(Tantilla coronata)*. Copeia 1992:1103–1106.

———. 1993. Male reproductive anatomy and seasonal occurrence of mating and combat behavior of the rattlesnake *Crotalus v. viridis*. J. Herpetol. 27:481–484.

Aldridge, R. D., and W. S. Brown. 1995. Male reproductive cycle, age at maturity, and cost of reproduction in the timber rattlesnake *(Crotalus horridus)*. J. Herpetol. 29:399–407.

Aldridge, R. D., W. P. Flanagan, and J. T. Swarthout. 1995. Reproductive biology of the water snake *Nerodia rhombifer* from Veracruz, Mexico, with comparisons of tropical and temperate snakes. Herpetologica 51:182–192.

Aldridge, R. D., J. J. Greenhaw, and M. V. Plummer. 1990. The male reproductive cycle of the rough green snake *(Opheodrys aestivus)*. Amphibia-Reptilia 11:165–172.

Aldridge, R. D., and D. E. Metter. 1973. The reproductive cycle of the western worm snake, *Carphophis vermis* in Missouri. Copeia 1973:472–477.

Aldridge, R. D., and R. D. Semlitsch. 1982. The reproductive cycle of the southeastern crowned snake *Tantilla coronata*. Progr. Ann. Jt. Meet. Soc. Stud. Amphib. Rept./Herpetol. League 1982:56.

———. 1992a. Female reproductive biology of the southeastern crowned snake *(Tantilla coronata)*. Amphibia-Reptilia 13:209–218.

———. 1992b. Male reproductive biology of the southeastern crowned snake *(Tantilla coronata)*. Amphibia-Reptilia 13:219–225.

Aleksiuk, M. 1976a. Reptilian hibernation: Evidence of adaptive strategies in *Thamnophis sirtalis parietalis*. Copeia 1976:170–178.

———. 1976b. Metabolic and behavioural adjustment to temperature change in the red-sided garter snake

(Thamnophis sirtalis parietalis): An integrated approach. J. Therm. Biol. 1:153–156.

———. 1977a. Cold-induced aggregative behavior in the red-sided garter snake *(Thamnophis sirtalis parietalis).* Herpetologica 33:98–101.

———. 1977b. Sources of mortality in concentrated garter snake populations. Can. Field-Nat. 91:70–72.

Aleksiuk, M., and P. T. Gregory. 1974. Regulation of seasonal mating behavior in *Thamnophis sirtalis parietalis.* Copeia 1974:681–689.

Aleksiuk, M., and B. Lavies. 1975. Manitoba's fantastic snake pits. Natl. Geogr. 148:714–723.

Aleksiuk, M., and K. W. Stewart. 1971. Seasonal changes in the body composition of the garter snake *Thamnophis sirtalis parietalis.* Ecology 52:485–490.

Allen, E. R. 1939a. Habits of *Rhadinaea flavilata.* Copeia 1939:175.

———. 1939b [1938]. Notes on Florida water snakes. Proc. Florida Acad. Sci. 3:101–104.

Allen, E. R., and W. T. Neill. 1950a. The life history of the Everglades rat snake, *Elaphe obsoleta rossalleni.* Herpetologica 6:109–112.

——— 1950b. The pigmy rattlesnake. Florida Wildl. 5(4): 10–11.

——— 1953. The short-tailed snake. Florida Wildl. 6(11): 8–9.

Allen, E. R., and D. Swindell. 1948. Cottonmouth moccasin in Florida. Herpetologica 4(suppl. 1): 1–16.

Allen, G. M. 1899. Notes on the amphibians and reptiles of Intervale, New Hampshire. Proc. Boston Soc. Nat. Hist. 29:63–75.

Allen, M. J. 1932. A survey of the amphibians and reptiles of Harrison County, Mississippi. Am. Mus. Novitates 542:1–20.

———. 1933. Report on a collection of amphibians and reptiles from Sonora, Mexico, with the description of a new lizard. Occ. Pap. Mus. Zool. Univ. Michigan 259:1–15.

Allen, T. A. 1979. Eastern garter snake predation on dark-eyed junco nests. Jack Pine Warbler 57:168–169.

Allen, W. B. 1955. Some notes on reptiles. Herpetologica 11:228.

———. 1956. The effects of a massasauga bite. Herpetologica 12:151.

———. 1988. State lists of endangered and threatened species of reptiles and amphibians and laws and regulations covering collecting of reptiles and amphibians in each state. Chicago, Illinois: Chicago Herpetological Society.

Alvarez-León, R., and J. I. Hernández-Camacho. 1998. Notas sobre la occurrencia de *Pelamis platurus* (Reptilia:

Serpentes: Hydrophiidae) en el Pacífico Colombiano. Caldasia 20:93–102.

Alvarez del Toro, M. 1960. Los reptiles de Chiapas. Tuxtla Gutierrez, Chiapas: Inst. Zool. Estudo.

Amaral, A. do. 1927. The anti-snake-bite campaign in Texas and in the subtropical United States. Bull. Antivenin Inst. Am. 1:77–85.

———. 1928. Studies on snake venoms. I. Amounts of venom secreted by Nearctic pit vipers. Bull. Antivenin Inst. Am. 1:103–104.

———. 1929. Studies of Nearctic ophidia. III. Notes on *Crotalus tigris* Kennicott, 1859. Bull. Antivenin Inst. Am. 2:82–85.

Amaral, J. P. do. 1994. Some ecological considerations on thermoregulation and prey capture behavior of the red-belly snake. Michigan Acad. 26:403.

Amaral, P. S. do. 1999. Lip-curling in redbelly snakes *(Storeria occipitomaculata):* Functional morphology and ecological significance. J. Zool. (London) 248:289–293.

Anderson, J. D. 1956. A blind snake preyed upon by a scorpion. Herpetologica 12:327.

Anderson, P. K. 1961. Variation in populations of brown snakes, genus *Storeria,* bordering the Gulf of Mexico. Am. Midl. Nat. 66:235–249.

———. 1965. The reptiles of Missouri. Columbia: Univiversity of Missouri Press.

Annandale, N. 1905–1907. Notes on the fauna of a desert tract in southern India. Part I. Batrachians and reptiles of the desert region of the North-west Frontier. Mem. Asiatic Soc. Bengal 1:183–202.

Anon. 1986a. Southeastern crowned snake. Virginia Conserv. News 17(1): 6.

———. 1986b. Concho water snake considered threatened. Herpetology 16(3):18–19.

Anton, T. G. 1994. Observation of predatory behavior in the regal ringneck snake *(Diadophis punctatus regalis)* under captive conditions. Bull. Chicago Herpetol. Soc. 29:95.

———. 2000a. *Thamnophis radix* (plains garter snake). Predation. Herpetol. Rev. 31:47.

———. 2000b. *Sistrurus catenatus* (massasauga). Litter size. Herpetol. Rev. 31:248.

Applegate, R. D. 1995. *Sistrurus catenatus catenatus* (eastern massasauga). Food habits. Herpetol. Rev. 26:206.

Aresco, M. J., and R. N. Reed. 1998. *Rana capito sevosa* (dusky gopher frog). Predation. Herpetol. Rev. 29:40.

Armstrong, B. L., and J. B. Murphy. 1979. The natural history of Mexican rattlesnakes. Univ. Kansas Mus. Nat. Hist. Spec. Publ. 5:1–88.

Arndt, R. G. 1980. A hibernating eastern hognose snake, *Heterodon platirhinos.* Herpetol. Rev. 11:30–32.

Arnold, S. J. 1981a. Behavioral variation in natural populations. I. Phenotypic, genetic and environmental correlations between chemoreceptive responses to prey in the garter snake, *Thamnophis elegans*. Evolution 35:489–509.

———. 1981b. Behavioral variation in natural populations. II. The inheritance of feeding response in crosses between geographic races of the garter snake, *Thamnophis elegans*. Evolution 35:510–515.

Arnold, S. J., and A. F. Bennett. 1984. Behavioural variation in natural populations. III. Antipredator displays in the garter snake *Thamnophis radix*. Anim. Behav. 32:1108–1118.

———. 1988. Behavioural variation in natural populations. V. Morphological correlates of locomotion in the garter snake *(Thamnophis radix)*. Biol. J. Linn. Soc. 34:175–190.

Arnold, S. J., and C. R. Peterson. 1989. A test for temperature effects on the ontogeny of shape in the garter snake *Thamnophis sirtalis*. Physiol. Zool. 62:1316–1333.

Arnold, S. J., C. R. Peterson, and J. Gladstone. 1995. Behavioural variation in natural populations. VII. Maternal body temperature does not affect juvenile thermoregulation in a garter snake. Anim. Behav. 50:623–633.

Arnold, S. J., and R. J. Wassersug. 1978. Differential predation on metamorphic anurans by garter snakes *(Thamnophis)*: Social behavior as a possible defense. Ecology 59:1014–1022.

Ashley, E. P., and J. T. Robinson. 1996. Road mortality of amphibians, reptiles, and other wildlife on the Long Point Causeway, Lake Erie, Ontario. Can. Field-Nat. 110:403–412.

Ashton, K. G. 1998. *Pituophis melanoleucus deserticola* (Great Basin gopher snake). Regional heterothermy. Herpetol. Rev. 29:170–171.

———. 1999. *Thamnophis elegans vagrans* (wandering garter snake). Mating. Herpetol. Rev. 30:104.

———. 2000. Notes on the island populations of the western rattlesnake, *Crotalus viridis*. Herpetol. Rev. 31:214–217.

Ashton, K. G., and H. M. Smith. 1999. *Lampropeltis triangulum blanchardi* (Blanchard's milk snake). Diet. Herpetol. Rev. 30:169.

Ashton, R. E., Jr., and P. S. Ashton. 1981. Handbook of reptiles and amphibians of Florida. Part 1. The snakes. Miami, Florida: Windward Publ.

Asplund, K. K. 1963. Ecological factors in the distribution of *Thamnophis brachystoma* (Cope). Herpetologica 19:128–132.

Assetto, R. 1978. Reproduction of the gray-banded kingsnake, *Lampropeltis mexicana alterna*. Herpetol. Rev. 9:56–57.

———. 1982. Captive reproduction in *Lampropeltis pyromelana*. Bull. Philadelphia Herpetol. Soc. 30:25.

Atkinson, D. A., and M. G. Netting. 1927. The distribution and habits of the massasauga. Bull. Antivenin Inst. Am. 1:40–44.

Atsatt, S. R. 1913. The reptiles of the San Jacinto area of Southern California. Univ. California Publ. Zool. 12:31–50.

Auffenberg, W. 1950. A new subspecies of the mud snake, *Liodytes alleni*. Herpetologica 6:13–16.

———. 1955a. On the status of the fossil snake *Coluber acuminatus*. Copeia 1955:65–67.

———. 1955b. A reconsideration of the racer, *Coluber constrictor*, in eastern United States. Tulane Stud. Zool. 2:89–155.

———. 1963. The fossil snakes of Florida. Tulane Stud. Zool. 10:131–216.

Auffenberg, W., and L. H. Babbitt. 1953. A new subspecies of *Coluber constrictor* from Florida. Copeia 1953:44–45.

Austin, J. D., and P. T. Gregory. 1998. Relative roles of thermal and chemical cues in the investigative behavior of prey in colubrid *(Elaphe guttata* and *Lampropeltis getulus)* and boid *(Python regius)* snakes. Herpetol. Nat. Hist. 6:47–50.

Auth, D. L. 1992. *Farancia abacura abacura* (eastern mud snake). Reproduction. Herpetol. Rev. 23:61.

Axtell, R.W. 1951. An additional specimen of *Lampropeltis blairi* from Texas. Copeia 1951:313.

———. 1959. Amphibians and reptiles of the Black Gap Wildlife Management Area, Brewster County, Texas. Southwest. Nat. 4:88–109.

Aycrigg, A. D., J. M. Farrell, and P. G. May. 1996. *Seminatrix pygaea pygaea* (black swamp snake). Predation. Herpetol. Rev. 27:84.

Babis, W. A. 1949. Notes on the food of the indigo snake. Copeia 1949:147.

Baden, H. P., G. Sazbo, and J. Cohen. 1966. Cutaneous melanocyte system of the indigo snake, *Drymarchon corais*. Nature (London) 211:1095.

Baeyens, D. A., C. T. McAllister, and L. F. Morgans. 1978. Some physiological and morphological adaptations for underwater survival in *Natrix rhombifera* and *Elaphe obsoleta*. Proc. Arkansas Acad. Sci. 32:18–21.

Baeyens, D. A., M. W. Patterson, and C. T. McAllister. 1980. A comparative physiological study of diving in three species of *Nerodia* and *Elaphe obsoleta*. J. Herpetol. 14:65–70.

Baeyens, D. A., and R. L. Rountree. 1983. A comparative study of evaporative water loss and epidermal permeability in an arboreal snake, *Opheodrys aestivus*, and a semi-aquatic snake, *Nerodia rhombifera*. Comp. Biochem. Physiol. 76A:301–304.

Bailey, J. R. 1939. A systematic revision of the snakes of the genus *Coniophanes*. Pap. Michigan Acad. Sci., Arts, Lett. 24(2): 1–48.

Bailey, J. W. 1946. The mammals of Virginia. Richmond, Virginia: Privately published.

Bailey, R. M. 1942. An intergeneric hybrid rattlesnake. Am. Nat. 76:376–385.

———. 1948. Winter mortality in the snake, *Storeria dekayi*. Copeia 1948:215.

———. 1949. Temperature toleration of garter snakes in hibernation. Ecology 30:238–242.

Bailey, V., M. R. Terman, and R. Wall. 1989. Noteworthy longevity in *Crotalus viridis viridis* (Rafinesque). Trans. Kansas Acad. Sci. 92:116–117.

Baird, S. F. 1859. Reptiles of the boundary. In: Report of the United States and Mexican Boundary Survey, U.S. 34th Congress 1st Session, Exec. Doc. 108, vol. 2, part 2, 1–35.

Baird, S. F., and C. Girard. 1852a. Characteristics of some new reptiles in the Museum of the Smithsonian Institution. Proc. Acad. Nat. Sci. Philadelphia 6:68–70.

———. 1852b. Descriptions of some species of reptiles collected by the U.S. Exploring Expedition under the command of Capt. Charles Wilkes, U.S.N. Proc. Acad. Nat. Sci. Philadelphia 6:174–177.

———. 1853. Catalogue of North American reptiles in the Museum of the Smithsonian Institution. Part 1. Serpents. Smithsonian Misc. Coll. 2(5): 1–172.

Baird, T. A. 2000. *Crotaphytus collaris* (eastern collard lizard). Predator-prey. Herpetol. Rev. 31:104.

Baker, R. H., and R. G. Webb. 1976. *Thamnophis elegans* captures *Sorex emarginatus*. Herpetol. Rev. 7:112.

Baker, R. J., J. J. Bull, and G. A. Mengden. 1971. Chromosomes of *Elaphe subocularis* (Reptilia: Serpentes), with the description of an in vivo technique for preparation of snake chromosomes. Experientia 27:1228–1229.

Baker, R. J., G. A. Mengden, and J. J. Bull. 1972. Karyotypic studies of thirty-eight species of North American snakes. Copeia 1972:257–265.

Baldridge, R. S., and D. E. Wivagg. 1992. Predation on imported fire ants by blind snakes. Texas J. Sci. 44:250–252.

Baldwin, A. S. 1999. Case report of an untreated human envenomation by the western massasauga rattlesnake *Sistrurus catenatus tergeminus*. Bull. Maryland Herpetol. Soc. 35:14–20.

Balent, K. L., and P. T. Andreadis. 1998. The mixed foraging strategy of juvenile northern water snakes. J. Herpetol. 32:575–579.

Ballinger, R. E., J. D. Lynch, and P. H. Cole. 1979. Distribution and natural history of amphibians and reptiles in western Nebraska with ecological notes on the herpetiles of Arapaho Prairie. Prairie Nat. 11:65–74.

Bancroft, G. T., J. S. Godley, D. T. Gross, N. N. Rojas, S. A. Sutphen, and R. W. McDiarmid. 1983. Large-scale operations management test of use of the white amur for control of problem aquatic plants. The herpetofauna of Lake Conway: Species accounts. Final Report. U.S. Army Corp. Eng., Aquatic Plant Contr. Res. Progr. Misc. Pap. A-83-5.

Banicki, L. H., and R. G. Webb. 1982. Morphological variation of the Texas lyre snake *(Trimorphodon biscutatus vilkinsoni)* from the Franklin Mountains, West Texas. Southwest. Nat. 27:321–324.

Banta, B. H. 1953. Some herpetological notes from southern Nevada. Herpetologica 9:75–76.

———. 1966. A check list of fossil amphibians and reptiles reported from the state of Nevada. Biol. Soc. Nevada Occ. Pap. 13:1–6.

———. 1974. A pre-Columbian record of cannibalism in the rattlesnake. Bull. Maryland Herpetol. Soc. 10:56.

Banta, B. H., and A. E. Leviton. 1963. Remarks on the colubrid genus *Chilomeniscus* (Serpentes: Colubridae). Proc. California Acad. Sci., ser. 4, 31:309–327.

Banta, B. H., and D. J. Morafka. 1968. An annotated check list of the recent amphibians and reptiles of the Pinnacles National Monument and Bear Valley, San Benito, and Monterey counties, California, with some ecological observations. Wasmann J. Biol. 26:161–183.

Barbour, R. W. 1950. The reptiles of Big Black Mountain, Harlan County, Kentucky. Copeia 1950:100–107.

———. 1956. A study of the cottonmouth, *Ancistrodon piscivorus leucostoma* in Kentucky. Trans. Kentucky Acad. Sci. 17:33–41.

———. 1960. A study of the worm snake, *Carphophis amoenus* Say, in Kentucky. Trans. Kentucky Acad. Sci. 21:10–16.

———. 1962. An aggregation of copperheads, *Agkistrodon contortrix*. Copeia 1962:640.

———. 1971. Amphibians and reptiles of Kentucky. Lexington: University Press of Kentucky.

Barbour, R. W., M. J. Harvey, and J. W. Hardin. 1969. Home range, movements, and activity of the eastern worm snakes, *Carphophis amoenus amoenus*. Ecology 50:470–476.

Barbour, T. 1921. The Florida pine snake. Proc. New England Zool. Club 7:117–118.

Barbour, T., and W. L. Engels. 1942. Two interesting new snakes. Proc. New England Zool. Club 20:101–104.

Barker, D. G. 1992. Variation, intraspecific relationships and biogeography of the ridgenose rattlesnake, *Crotalus willardi*, 89–105. In: J. A. Campbell, and E. D. Brodie, Jr. (eds.), Biology of the pitvipers. Tyler, Texas: Selva

Barnard, S. M, T. G. Hollinger, and T. A. Romaine. 1979.

Growth and food consumption in the corn snake, *Elaphe guttata guttata* (Serpentes: Colubridae) Copeia 1979:739–741.

Barr, T. C., Jr., and R. M. Norton. 1965. Predation on cave bats by the pilot black snake. J. Mammal. 46:672.

Barrett, G. C., and M. R. Villarroul. 1994. *Storeria occipitomaculata occipitomaculata* (northern red-bellied snake). Predation. Herpetol. Rev. 25:29–30.

Barron, J. N. 1997a. Condition-adjusted estimator of reproductive output in snakes. Copeia 1997:306–318.

———. 1997b. Calorimetric analysis of neonatal water snakes, *Nerodia sipedon*. J. Herpetol. 31:422–425.

Barry, F. E., P. J. Weatherhead, and D. P. Philipp. 1992. Multiple paternity in a wild population of northern water snakes. *Nerodia sipedon*. Behav. Ecol. Sociobiol. 30:193–199.

Barry, L. T. 1933. Snakes of Mesa Verde National Park. Mesa Verde Notes 4(2): 8–11.

Barten, S. L. 1982. Predation on a garter snake, *Thamnophis* sp. by a blue jay, *Cyanocitta cristata*. Bull. Chicago Herpetol. Soc. 17:99.

———. 1992. Combat behavior by two male western fox snakes, *Elaphe vulpina vulpina* (Baird and Girard), in Illinois. Bull. Chicago Herpetol. Soc. 27:232–233.

Bartholomew, B. D., and C. Lleyson. 1993. *Charina bottae* (rubber boa). Food. Herpetol. Rev. 24:105.

Bartholomew, B. D., and R. D. Nohavec. 1995. Saltation in snakes with a note on escape saltation in a *Crotalus scutulatus*. Great Basin Nat. 55:282–283.

Barton, A. J. 1949. Ophiophagy by a juvenile copperhead. Copeia 1949:232.

———. 1950. Replacement fangs in newborn timber rattlesnakes. Copeia 1950:235–236.

———. 1956. A statistical study of *Thamnophis brachystoma* (Cope) with comments on the kinship of *T. butleri* (Cope). Proc. Biol. Soc. Washington 69:71–82.

Batts, B. S. 1961. Intertidal fishes as food of the common garter snake. Copeia 1961:350–351.

Bauman, M. A., and D. E. Metter. 1975. Economics, feeding, and population structure of *Natrix s. sipedon* in a goldfish hatchery. Progr. Fish-Cult. 37:197–201.

———. 1977. Reproductive cycle of the northern watersnake, *Natrix s. sipedon* (Reptilia, Serpentes, Colubridae). J. Herpetol. 11:51–59.

Bavetz, M. 1994. Geographic variation, status, and distribution of Kirtland's snake (*Clonophis kirtlandii* Kennicott) in Illinois. Trans. Illinois St. Acad. Sci. 87:151–163.

Baxter, R. J., and G. R. Stewart. 1990 (1986). Excavation of winter burrows and relocation of desert tortoises (*Gopherus agassizii*) at the Luz Solar Generation Station Kramer Junction, California. Proc. Symp. Gopher Tortoise Council 1986:124–127.

Beane, J. C., T. J. Thorp, and D. A. Jackson. 1998. *Heterodon simus* (southern hognose snake). Diet. Herpetol. Rev. 29:44–45.

Beardsley, H., and S. Barten. 1983. A note on reproduction in a captive born indigo snake, *Drymarchon corais couperi*. Bull. Chicago Herpetol. Soc. 18:15–18.

Beasley, R. J., E. L. Ross, P. M. Nave, D. H. Sifford, and B. D. Johnson. 1993. Phosphodiesterase activities of selected crotalid venoms. SAAS Bull. Biochem. Biotech. 6:48–53.

Beatson, R. R. 1976. Environmental and genetical correlates of disruptive coloration in the water snake, *Natrix s. sipedon*. Evolution 30:241–252.

Beaupre, S. J. 1993. An ecological study of oxygen consumption in the mottled rock rattlesnake, *Crotalus lepidus lepidus*, and the black-tailed rattlesnake, *Crotalus molossus molossus*, from two populations. Physiol. Zool. 66:437–454.

———. 1995a. Comparative ecology of the mottled rock rattlesnake, *Crotalus lepidus*, in Big Bend National Park. Herpetologica 51:45–56.

———. 1995b. Effects of geographically variable thermal environment on bioenergetics of mottled rock rattlesnakes. Ecology 76:1655–1665.

———. 1996. Field metabolic rate, water flux, and energy budgets of mottled rock rattlesnakes, *Crotalus lepidus*, from two populations. Copeia 1996:319–329.

Beaupre, S. J., and D. J. Duvall. 1998. Integrative biology of rattlesnakes: Contributions to biology and evolution. Bioscience 48:531–538.

Beaupre, S. J., D. J. Duvall, and J. O'Leile. 1998. Ontogenetic variation in growth and sexual size dimorphism in a central Arizona population of the western diamondback rattlesnake *(Crotalus atrox)*. Copeia 1998:40–47.

Beavers, R. A. 1976. Food habits of the western diamondback rattlesnake, *Crotalus atrox*, in Texas. Southwest. Nat. 20:503–515.

Becak, M. L., W. Becak, F. L. Roberts, R. N. Shaffner, and E. P. Volpe. 1973. *Drymarchon corais corais* (Boie). In: K. Benerschke and T. C. Hsu (eds.), Chromosome atlas: Fish, amphibians, reptiles, birds, vol. 2. New York: Springer-Verlag.

Becak, W., and M. L. Becak. 1969. Cytotaxonomy and chromosomal evolution in Serpentes. Cytogenetics 8:247–262.

Becak, W., M. L. Becak, and H. R. S. Nazareth. 1962. Karyotypic studies of two species of South American snakes *(Boa constrictor amarali* and *Bothrops jararaca)*. Cytogenetics 1:303–313.

———. 1963. Chromosomes of snakes in short term cultures of leucocytes. Am. Nat. 97:253–256.

Bechtel, H. B., and E. Bechtel. 1958. Reproduction in captive corn snakes, *Elaphe guttata guttata*. Copeia 1958:148–149.

———. 1978. Heredity and pattern mutation in the corn snake, *Elaphe g. guttata*, demonstrated in captive breedings. Copeia 1978:719–721.

———. 1985. Genetics of color mutations in the snake, *Elaphe obsoleta*. J. Heredity 76:7–11

———. 1989. Color mutations in the corn snake *(Elaphe guttata guttata)*: Review and additional breeding data. J. Heredity 80:272–276.

Beck, D. D. 1995. Ecology and energetics of three sympatric rattlesnake species in the Sonoran Desert. J. Herpetol. 29:211–223.

———. 1996. Effects of feeding on body temperatures of rattlesnakes: A field experiment. Physiol. Zool. 69:1442–1455.

Beckers, G. J. L., A. A. M. Twan, and H. J. Strijbosch. 1996. Coral snake mimicry: Live snakes not avoided by a mammalian predator. Oecologia (Berlin) 106:461–463.

Beebe, W. 1946. Field notes on the snakes of Kartabo, British Guiana and Caripito. Zoologica (New York) 31:11–52.

Begun, D., J. L. Kubie, M. Plough-O'Keefe, and M. Halpern. 1988. Conditioned discrimination of airborne odorants by garter snakes *(Thamnophis radix* and *T. sirtalis sirtalis)*. J. Comp. Psychol. 102(1): 35–43.

Behler, J. L., and F. W. King. 1979. The Audubon Society field guide to North American reptiles and amphibians. New York: Alfred A. Knopf.

Bell, C. J., and J. K. Bowden. 1995. *Diadophis punctatus modestus* (San Bernardino ringneck snake). Diet. Herpetol. Rev. 26:38.

Bell, C. J., and J. I. Mead. 1996. *Charina* Gray, 1849 (Boidae: Erycinae) from the Pleistocene of California. Herpetol. Nat. Hist. 4:161–168.

Bell, E. D. 1957. The food habits of the pilot black snake *Elaphe o. obsoleta* with observations on a captive specimen. Mengel Nat. 2:19–22.

Bell, M. A., and T. R. Haglund. 1978. Selective predation of threespine sticklebacks *(Gasteroosteus aculeatus)* by garter snakes. Evolution 32:304–319.

Bellemin, J. M., and G. R. Stewart. 1977. Diagnostic characters and color convergence of the garter snakes *Thamnophis elegans terrestris* and *Thamnophis couchii aratus* along the Central California Coast. Bull. So. California Acad. Sci. 76:73–84.

Belson, M. S. 2000. *Drymarchon corais couperi* (eastern indigo snake) and *Micrurus fulvius fulvius* (eastern coral snake). Predator-prey. Herpetol. Rev. 31:105.

Benerschke, K. and T. C. Hsu, eds. 1971. Chromosome atlas: Fish, amphibians, reptiles, and birds, vol. 1. New York: Springer Verlag.

Bennetts, R. E., and E. L. Caton. 1988. An observed incident of rat snake predation on snail kite *(Rostrhamus sociabilis)* chicks in Florida. Florida Field Nat. 16:14–16.

Bennion, R. S., and W. S. Parker. 1976. Field observations on courtship and aggressive behavior in desert striped whipsnakes, *Masticophis t. taeniatus*. Herpetologica 32:30–35.

Benton, M. J. 1980a. Geographic variation in the garter snakes *(Thamnophis sirtalis)* of the north-central United States, a multivariate study. Zool. J. Linn. Soc. 68:307–323.

———. 1980b. Geographic variation and validity of subspecies names for the eastern garter snake, *Thamnophis sirtalis*. Bull. Chicago Herpetol. Soc. 15:57–69.

Berish, J. E. D. 1998. Characterization of rattlesnake harvest in Florida. J. Herpetol. 32:551–557.

Berna, H. J., and J. W. Gibbons. 1991. *Agkistrodon piscivorus piscivorus* (eastern cottonmouth). Diet. Herpetol. Rev. 22:130–131.

Best, I. B. 1978. Field sparrow reproductive success and nesting ecology. Auk 95:9–22.

Best, T. L., and H. C. James. 1984. Rattlesnakes (genus *Crotalus*) of the Pedro Armendariz Lava *Field, New Mexico.* Copeia *1984:213–215.*

Best, T. L., and G. S. Pfaffenberger. 1987. Age and sexual variation in the diet of collard lizards *(Crotaphytus collaris)*. Southwest. Nat. 32:415–426.

Betz, T. W. 1963a. Neonatal *Natrix cyclopion floridana.* Copeia 1963:575–576.

———. 1963b. The gross ovarian morphology of the diamond-backed water snake, *Natrix rhombifera*, during the reproductive cycle. Copeia 1963:692–697.

———. 1963c. The ovarian histology of the diamond-backed water snake, *Natrix rhombifera*, during the reproductive cycle. J. Morph. 133:245–260.

Bider, J. R. 1968. Animal activity in uncontrolled terrestrial communities as determined by a sand transect technique. Ecol. Monogr. 38:269–308.

Bishop, L. A., and T. M. Farrell. 1994. *Thamnophis sauritus sackenii* (peninsula ribbon snake) behavior. Herpetol. Rev. 25:127.

Bishop, L. A., T. M. Farrell, and P. G. May. 1996. Sexual dimorphism in a Florida population of the rattlesnake *Sistrurus miliarius*. Herpetologica 52:360–364.

Black, J. H. 1983a. Northern watersnakes eaten by a channel catfish. Bull. Oklahoma Herpetol. Soc. 8:5–56.

———. 1983b. Red-tailed hawk captures prairie kingsnake. Bull. Oklahoma Herpetol. Soc. 8:63–65.

Blaesing, M. E. 1979. Some aspects of the ecology of the

eastern garter snake, *Thamnophis sirtalis sirtalis* (Reptilia, Serpentes, Colubridae), in a semi-disturbed habitat in west-central Illinois. J. Herpetol. 13:177–181.

Blainville, M. H. D. de. 1835. Description de quelques espèces de reptiles de la Californie précédée de l'analyse d'un système général d'erpétologie et d'amphibiologie. Nouv. Ann. Mus. Hist. Nat. (Paris) 4:233–296.

Blair, C. L., and F. Schitoskey, Jr. 1982. Breeding biology and diet of the ferruginous hawk in South Dakota. Wilson Bull. 94:46–54.

Blair, M. 1985. Death from above. Kansas Wildl. 42(4): 10–11.

Blair, W. F. 1954. Mammals of the Mesquite Plains Biotic District in Texas and Oklahoma, and speciation in the central grasslands. Texas J. Sci. 6:235–264.

———. 1960. The rusty lizard. Austin: University of Texas Press.

Blanchard, F. C. 1943 [1942]. A test of fecundity of the garter snake *Thamnophis sirtalis sirtalis* (Linnaeus) in the year following the year of insemination. Pap. Michigan Acad. Sci., Arts, Lett. 28:313–316.

Blanchard, F. N. 1919. Two new snakes of the genus *Lampropeltis*. Occ. Pap. Mus. Zool. Univ. Michigan 70:1–12.

———. 1921. A revision of the king snakes: Genus *Lampropeltis*. U.S. Natl. Mus. Bull. 114:1–260.

———. 1923a. A new North American snake of the genus *Natrix*. Occ. Pap. Mus. Zool. Univ. Michigan 140:1–6.

———. 1923b. The snakes of the genus *Virginia*. Pap. Michigan Acad. Sci., Arts, Lett. 3:343–365.

———. 1923c. Comments on ring-neck snakes (genus *Diadophis*), with diagnoses of new forms. Occ. Pap. Mus. Zool. Univ. Michigan 142:1–9.

———. 1924a. A new snake of the genus *Arizona*. Occ. Pap. Mus. Zool. Univ. Michigan 150:1–5.

———. 1924b. The forms of *Carphophis*. Pap. Michigan Acad. Sci., Arts, Lett. 4:527–530.

———. 1924c. A name for the black *Pituophis* from Alabama. Pap. Michigan Acad. Sci., Arts, Lett. 4:531–532.

———. 1931. Secondary sex characters of certain snakes. Bull. Antivenin Inst. Am. 4:95–104.

———. 1932. Eggs and young of the smooth green snake, *Liopeltis vernalis* (Harlan). Pap. Michigan Acad. Sci., Arts, Lett. 17:493–508.

———. 1937a. Data on the natural history of the red-bellied snake, *Storeria occipitomaculata* (Storer), in northern Michigan. Copeia 1937:151–162.

———. 1937b [1936]. Eggs and natural nests of the eastern ringneck snake, *Diadophis punctatus edwardsii*. Pap. Michigan Acad. Sci., Arts, Lett. 22:521–532.

———. 1938. Snakes of the genus *Tantilla* in the United States. Zool. Ser. Field Mus. Nat. Hist. 20:369–376.

———. 1942. *The ring-neck snakes, genus* Diadophis. Bull. Chicago Acad. Sci. 7:1–144.

Blanchard, F. N., and F. C. Blanchard. 1942. Mating of the garter snake *Thamnophis sirtalis sirtalis* (Linnaeus). Pap. Michigan Acad. Sci., Arts, Lett. 27:215–234.

Blanchard, F. N., and E. B. Finster. 1933. A method of marking living snakes for future recognition, with a discussion of some problems and results. Ecology 14:334–347.

Blanchard, F. N., and E. R. Force. 1930. The age of attainment of sexual maturity in the lined snake, *Tropidoclonion lineatum* (Hallowell). Bull. Antivenin Inst. Am. 3:96–98.

Blanchard, F. N., M. R. Gilreath, and F. C. Blanchard. 1979. The eastern ringneck snake *(Diadophis punctatus edwardsii)* in northern Michigan. (Reptilia, Serpentes, Colubridae). J. Herpetol. 13:377–402.

Blaney, R. M. 1973. *Lampropeltis*. Cat. Am. Amphib. Rept. 150:1–2.

———. 1977. Systematics of the common kingsnake, *Lampropeltis getulis* (Linnaeus). Tulane Stud. Zool. Bot. 19:47–103.

———. 1979a. The status of the Outer Banks kingsnake, *Lampropeltis getulus sticticeps* (Reptilia: Serpentes: Colubridae). Brimleyana 1:125–128.

———. 1979b. *Lampropeltis calligaster*. Cat. Am. Amphib. Rept. 229:1–2.

Bleakney, J. S. 1958a. A zoogeographical study of the amphibians and reptiles of eastern Canada. Bull. Natl. Mus. Canada 155:1–119.

———. 1958b. Variation in a litter of northern water snakes from Ottawa, Ontario. Can. Field-Nat. 72:128–132.

———. 1959. *Thamnophis sirtalis sirtalis* (Linnaeus) in eastern Canada, redescription of *T. s. pallidula* Allen. Copeia 1959:52–56.

Blem, C. R. 1979. Predation of black rat snakes on a bank swallow colony. Wilson Bull. 91:135–137.

———. 1981a. Heterodon platyrhinos. Cat. Am. Amphib. Rept. 282:1–2.

———. 1981b. Reproduction of the eastern cottonmouth *Agkistrodon piscivorus piscivorus* (Serpentes: Viperidae) at the northern edge of its range. Brimleyana 5:117–128.

———. 1982. Biennial reproduction in snakes: An alternative hypothesis. Copeia 1982:961–963.

———. 1987. Development of combat rituals in captive cottonmouths. J. Herpetol. 21:64–65.

———. 1997. Lipid reserves of the eastern cottonmouth *(Agkistrodon piscivorus)* at the northern edge of its range. Copeia 1997:53–59.

Blem, C. R., and L. B. Blem 1985. Notes on *Virginia* (Reptilia: Colubridae) in Virginia. Brimleyana 11:87–95.

———. 1990b. Lipid reserves of the brown water snake *Nerodia taxispilota*. Comp. Biochem. Physiol. 97A:367–372.

———. 1995. The eastern cottonmouth *(Agkistrodon piscivorus)* at the northern edge of its range. J. Herpetol. 29:391–398.

Blem, C. R., and K. L. Blem. 1990a. Metabolic acclimation in three species of sympatric, semi-aquatic snakes. Comp. Biochem. Physiol. 97A:259–264.

Blem, C. R., and K. B. Killeen. 1993. Circadian metabolic cycles in eastern cottonmouths and brown water snakes. J. Herpetol. 27:341–344.

Bloomer, T. J. 1976. The northern pine snake *Pituophis melanoleucus melanoleucus* in New Jersey. HERP: Bull. New York Herpetol. Soc. 13:33–35.

Blouin-Demers, G., K. J. Kissner, and P. J. Weatherhead. 2000. Plasticity in preferred body temperature of young snakes in response to temperature during development. Copeia 2000:841–845.

Blouin-Demers, G., K. A. Prior, and P. J. Weatherhead. 2000. Patterns of variation in spring emergence by black rat snakes *(Elaphe obsoleta obsoleta)*. Herpetologica 56:175–188.

Blum, M. S., J. B. Byrd, J. R. Travis, J. F. Watkins II, and F. R. Gehlbach. 1971. Chemistry of the cloacal sac secretion of the blind snake, *Leptotyphlops dulcis*. Comp. Biochem. Physiol. 38B:103–107.

Blumenbach, J. F. 1788. Beytrag zur Naturgeschichte der Schlangen. Magazin f. d. Neuste Aug d. Physi u. Naturg. 5:1–13.

Boal, C. W., B. D. Bibles, and R. W. Mannan. 1997. Nest defense and mobbing behavior of elf owls. J. Raptor Res. 32:286–287.

Boback, S. M., E. Burroughs, C. Ugarte, and J. Watling. 2000. *Boa constrictor* (boa constrictor). Diet. Herpetol. Rev. 31:244–245.

Bocourt, M.-F. 1886. Etudes sur les reptiles et les batraciens. In: Duméril, Bocourt, and Mocquard, Recherches zoologiques pour servir à l'histoire et la faune de l'Amerique Central et du Mexique. Miss. Sci. Mexique et Am. Cent., Partie Troisième. Paris. Livr. 10:593–656.

Boettger, O. 1883. Herpetologische Mittheilungen. I. Kurze Notizen über Reptilien und Amphibien in der Heidelberger Universitäts Sammlung. Ber. Offenbacher Ver. Naturk. 22:147–152.

Bogert, C. M. 1930. An annotated list of the amphibians and reptiles of Los Angeles County, California. Bull. So. California Acad. Sci. 29:3–14.

———. 1935. *Salvadora grahamiae virgultea*, a new subspecies of the patch-nosed snake. Bull. So. California Acad. Sci. 34:88–94.

———. 1941. Sensory cues used by rattlesnakes in their recognition of ophidian enemies. Ann. New York Acad. Sci. 41:329–343.

———. 1942. Field note on the copulation of *Crotalus atrox* in California. Copeia 1942:262.

———. 1943. Dentitional phenomena in cobras and other elapids with notes on adaptive modifications of fangs. Bull. Am. Mus. Nat. Hist. 81:285–360.

———. 1945. Two additional races of the patch-nosed snake, *Salvadora hexalepis*. Am. Mus. Novitates 1285:1–14.

———. 1960. The influence of sound on the behavior of amphibians and reptiles, 137–320. In: W. E. Lanyon and W. N. Tavolga (eds.), Animal sounds and communication. Am. Inst. Biol. Sci. Publ.7:1–443.

Bogert, C. M., and R. B. Cowles. 1947. Results of the Archbold expeditions, no. 58. Moisture loss in relation to habitat selection in some Floridian reptiles. Am. Mus. Novitates 1358:1–34.

Bogert, C. M., and W. G. Degenhardt. 1961. An addition to the fauna of the United States, the Chihuahuan ridge-nosed rattlesnake in New Mexico. Am. Mus. Novitates 2064:1–15.

Bogert, C. M., and J. A. Oliver. 1945. A preliminary analysis of the herpetofauna of Sonora. Bull. Am. Mus. Nat. Hist. 83:297–426.

Boie, F. 1827. Bemerkungen über Merrem's Versuch eines Systems der Amphibien. Isis 20:508–566.

Bolaños, R., L. Cerdas, and J. W. Abalos. 1978. Venoms of coral snake *(Micrurus* ssp.): Report on a multivalent antivenin for the Americas. Bull. Pan Am. Health Org. 12:23–27.

Bono-Gallo, A., and P. Licht. 1983. Effects of temperature on sexual receptivity and ovarian recrudescence in the garter snake, *Thamnophis sirtalis parietalis*. Herpetologica 39:173–182.

Bonnaterre, J. P. 1789–1790. Encyclopédie méthodique. Tableau encyclopédique et méthodique des trois règnes de la nature. 2 vols. Paris: Panckoucke

Boone, A. R. 1937. Snake hunter catches snakes for fun. Pop. Sci. Monthly 131(4): 54–55.

Boquet, P. 1948. Venins de serpents et antivenins. Coll. Inst. Pasteur [Paris].

Bostic, D. L. 1971. Herpetofauna of the Pacific Coast of north central Baja California, Mexico, with a description of a new subspecies of *Phyllodactylus xanti*. Trans. San Diego Soc. Nat. Hist. 16(10): 237–264.

Bothner, R. C. 1963. A hibernaculum of the short-headed garter snake, *Thamnophis brachystoma* (Cope). Copeia 1963:572–573.

———. 1973. Temperatures of *Agkistrodon p. piscivorus* and *Lampropeltis g. getulus* in Georgia. HISS News-J. 1:24–25.

———. 1974. Some observations on the feeding habits of the cottonmouth in southeastern Georgia. J. Herpetol. 8:257–258.

———. 1976. *Thamnophis brachystoma*. Cat. Am. Amphib. Rept. 190:1–2.

Bothner, R. C., and T. R. Moore. 1964. A collection of *Haldea valeriae pulchra* from western Pennsylvania, with notes on some litters of their young. Copeia 1964:709–710.

Boundy, J. 1997. Snakes of Louisiana. Baton Rouge: Louisiana Department of Wildlife and Fisheries.

———. 1999. Systematics of the garter snake *Thamnophis atratus* at the southern end of its range. Proc. California Acad. Sci. 51:311–336.

Boundy, J., and D. A. Rossman. 1995. Allocation and status of the garter snake names *Coluber infernalis* Blainville, *Eutaenia sirtalis tetrataenia* Cope, and *Eutaenia imperialis* Coves and Yarrow. Copeia 1995:236–240.

Bowers, B. B., A. E. Bledsoe, and G. M. Burghardt. 1993. Responses to escalating predatory threat in garter and ribbon snakes. J. Comp. Psychol. 107:25–33.

Bowers, J. H. 1966. Food habits of the diamond-backed water snake, *Natrix rhombifera rhombifera*, in Bowie and Red River counties, Texas. Herpetologica 22:225–229.

———. 1967. A record litter of *Thamnophis sirtalis proximus* (Say). Southwest. Nat. 12:200.

Boyd, C. E., S. B. Vinson, and D. E. Ferguson. 1963. Possible DDT resistance in two species of frog. Copeia 1963:426–429.

Boyer, D. A. 1933. A case report on the potency of the bite of a young copperhead. Copeia 1933:97.

Boyer, D. A., and A. A. Heinze. 1934. An annotated list of the amphibians and reptiles of Jefferson County, Missouri. Trans. Acad. Sci. St. Louis 28:185–200.

Boyer, D. R. 1957. Sexual dimorphism in a population of the western diamond-backed rattlesnake. Herpetologica 13:213–217.

Bragg, A. N. 1960. Is *Heterodon* venomous? Herpetologica 16:121–123.

Branson, B. A., and E. C. Baker. 1974. An ecological study of the queen snake, *Regina septemvittata* (Say) in Kentucky. Tulane Stud. Zool. Bot. 18:153–171.

Brattstrom, B. H. 1953a. Notes on a population of leaf-nosed snakes *Phyllorhynchus decurtatus perkinsi*. Herpetologica 9:57–64.

———. 1953b. Records of Pleistocene reptiles and amphibians from Florida. Quart. J. Florida Acad. Sci. 16:243–248.

———. 1953c. Records of Pleistocene reptiles from California. Copeia 1953:174–179.

———. 1953d. The amphibians and reptiles from Rancho LaBrea. Trans. San Diego Soc. Nat. Hist. 11:365–392.

———. 1954a. Amphibians and reptiles from Gypsum Cave, Nevada. Bull. So. California Acad. Sci. 53:8–12.

———. 1954b. The fossil pit-vipers (Reptilia: Crotalidae) of North America. Trans. San Diego Soc. Nat. Hist. 12:31–46.

———. 1955a. The coral snake "mimic" problem and protective coloration. Evolution 9:217–219.

———. 1955b. Pliocene and Pleistocene amphibians and reptiles from southeastern Arizona. J. Paleontol. 29:150–154.

———. 1955c. Records of some Pliocene and Pleistocene reptiles and amphibians from Mexico. Bull. So. California Acad. Sci. 54:1–4.

———. 1958a. New records of Cenozoic amphibians and reptiles from California. Bull. So. California Acad. Sci. 57:5–12.

———. 1958b. Additions to the Pleistocene herpetofauna of Nevada. Herpetologica 14:36.

———. 1964a. Amphibians and reptiles from cave deposits in south-central New Mexico. Bull. So. California Acad. Sci. 63:93–103.

———. 1964b. Evolution of the pit vipers. Trans. San Diego Soc. Nat. Hist. 13:185–268.

———. 1965. Body temperatures of reptiles. Am. Midl. Nat. 73:376–422.

———. 1967. A succession of Pliocene and Pleistocene snake faunas from the High Plains of the United States. Copeia 1967:188–202.

———. 1976. A Pleistocene herpetofauna from Smith Creek Cave, Nevada. Bull. So. California Acad. Sci. 75:283–284.

Brattstrom, B. H., and R. C. Schwenkmeyer. 1951. Notes on the natural history of the worm snake, *Leptotyphlops humilis*. Herpetologica 7:193–196.

Brattstrom, B. H., and J. W. Warren. 1953. A new subspecies of racer, *Masticophis flagellum*, from the San Joaquin Valley of California. Herpetologica 9:177–179.

Brauman, R. J., and R. A. Fiorillo. 1995. *Lampropeltis getula holbrooki* (speckled kingsnake). Oophagy. Herpetol. Rev. 26:101–102.

Brazil, O. V. 1987. Coral snake venoms: Mode of action and pathophysiology of experimental envenomation. Rev. Inst. Med. Trop. Sao Paulo 29:119–126.

Brecke, B. J., J. B. Murphy, and W. Seifert. 1976. An inventory of reproduction and social behavior in captive Baird's ratsnakes, *Elaphe obsoleta bairdi* (Yarrow). Herpetologica 32:389–395.

Breckenridge, W. J. 1944. Reptiles and amphibians of Minnesota. Minneapolis: University of Minnesota Press.

Brimley, C. S. 1941–1942. The amphibians and reptiles of North Carolina: The snakes. Carolina Tips 4–5(19–26).

Brisbin, I. L., Jr. 1968. Evidence for the use of postanal musk as an alarm device in the kingsnake, *Lampropeltis getulus*. Herpetologica 24:169–170.

Brisbin, I. L., Jr., and C. Bagshaw. 1993. Survival weight changes, and shedding frequencies of captive scarlet snakes, *Cemophora coccinea*, maintained on an artificial diet. Herpetol. Rev. 24:27–29.

Brittle, D. L., and G. Brittle. 2000. *Heterodon platirhinos* (eastern hognose snake). Catesbeiana 20:82.

Brock, O. G. 1981. Predatory behavior of eastern diamondback rattlesnakes *(Crotalus adamanteus):* Field enclosure and Y-maze laboratory studies, emphasizing prey trailing behaviors. Diss. Abst. Int. B41:2510.

Brock, O. G., and S. N. Myers. 1979. Responses of ingestively naive *Lampropeltis getulus* (Reptilia, Serpentes, Colubridae) to prey extracts. J. Herpetol. 13:209–212.

Brode, J. M. 1988. Natural history of the giant garter snake *(Thamnophis couchii gigas),* 25–28. In: H. F. De Lisle, P. R. Brown, B. Kaufman, and B. M. McCurty (eds.), Proceedings of the Conference on California Herpetology, 1987. Southwestern Herpetological Society Special Publicaltion 4.

Brode, W. E. 1958. The occurrence of the pickerel frog, three salamanders, and two snakes in Mississippi caves. Copeia 1958:47–48.

Brode, W. E., and P. Allison. 1958. Burrowing snakes of the panhandle counties of Mississippi. Herpetologica 14:37–40.

Brodie, E. D., Jr., R. A. Nussbaum, and R. M. Storm. 1969. An egg-laying aggregation of five species of Oregon reptiles. Herpetologica 25:223–227.

Brodie, E. D., III. 1989a. Behavioral modification as a means of reducing the cost of reproduction. Am. Nat. 134:225–238.

———. 1989b. Genetic correlations between morphology and antipredator behaviour in natural populations of the garter snake *Thamnophis ordinoides*. Nature (London) 342:542–543.

———. 1992. Correlational selection for color pattern and antipredator behavior in the garter snake *Thamnophis ordinoides*. Evolution 46:1284–1298.

———. 1993a. Consistency of individual differences in anti-predator behaviour and colour pattern in the garter snake, *Thamnophis ordinoides*. Anim. Behav. 45:851–861.

———. 1993b. Differential avoidance of coral snake banded patterns by free-ranging avian predators in Costa Rica. Evolution 47:227–235.

Brodie, E. D., III, and E. D. Brodie, Jr. 1990. Tetrodotoxin resistance in garter snakes: An evolutionary response of predators to dangerous prey. Evolution 44:651–659.

Brodie, E. D., III, and P. K. Ducey. 1989. Allocation of reproductive investment in the redbelly snake *Storeria occipitomaculata*. Am. Nat. 122:51–58.

Brodie, E. D., III, and N. H. Russell. 1999. The consistency of individual differences in behaviour: Temperature effects on antipredator behaviour in garter snakes. Anim. Behav. 57:445–451.

Bröer, W. 1978. Bastarde bei zwei *Elaphe*-Arten (Reptilia: Serpentes: Colubridae). Salamandra 14:63–68.

Bronikowski, A. M., and S. J. Arnold. 1999. The evolutionary ecology of life history variation in the garter snake *Thamnophis elegans*. Ecology 80:2314–2325.

Brophy, T. R. 1998. *Nerodia sipedon sipedon* (northern water snake). Catesbeiana 18:45–46.

Brothers, D. R. 1992. An introduction to snakes of the Dismal Swamp Region of North Carolina and Virginia. Boise, Idaho: Edgewood Probes, Inc.

———. 1994. *Elaphe obsoleta* (rat snake). Reproduction. Herpetol. Rev. 25:124.

Brown, A. E. 1890. On a new genus of Colubridae from Florida. Proc. Acad. Nat. Sci. Philadelphia 42:199–200.

———. 1901. A new species of *Coluber* from western Texas. Proc. Acad. Nat. Sci. Philadelphia 53:492–495.

———. 1902 [1901]. A new species of *Ophibolus* from western Texas. Proc. Acad. Nat. Sci. Philadelphia 53:612–613.

Brown, B. C. 1937. Notes on *Coniophanes imperialis* (Baird). Copeia 1937:234.

———. 1939. The effect of *Coniophanes imperialis* poisoning in man. Copeia 1939:109.

———. 1950. An annotated checklist of the reptiles and amphibians of Texas. Waco, Texas: Baylor University Press.

———. 1951. The Texan hooded snake in the lower Rio Grande Valley of Texas. Herpetologica 7:175.

Brown, B. C., and L. M. Brown. 1967. Notable records of Tamaulipan snakes. Texas J. Sci. 19:323–326.

Brown, C. W., and C. H. Ernst. 1986. A study of variation in eastern timber rattlesnakes, *Crotalus horridus* Linnae (Serpentes: Viperidae). Brimleyana 12:57–74.

Brown, D. G. 1990. Observation of a prairie rattlesnake *(Crotalus viridis viridis)* consuming neonatal cottontail rabbits *(Sylvilagus nuttalli),* with defense of the young cottontails by adult conspecifics. Bull. Chicago Herpetol. Soc. 25:24–26.

Brown, E. E. 1958. Feeding habits of the northern water snake, *Natrix sipedon sipedon* Linnaeus. Zoologica (New York) 43:55–71.

———. 1978. A note on the food and young in *Natrix rigida*. Bull. Maryland Herpetol. Soc. 14:91–92.

———. 1979a. Some snake food records from the Carolinas. Brimleyana 1:113–124.

———. 1979b. Stray food records from New York and Michigan snakes. Am. Midl. Nat. 102:200–203.

———. 1992. Notes on amphibians and reptiles of the western piedmont of North Carolina. J. Elisha Mitchell Sci. Soc. 108:38–54.

Brown, G. P., and P. J. Weatherhead. 1996. Effects of reproduction on survival and growth of female northern water snakes, *Nerodia sipedon*. Can. J. Zool. 75:424–432.

———. 1999a. Growth and sexual size dimorphism in northern water snakes *(Nerodia sipedon)*. Copeia 1999:723–732.

———. 1999b. Demography and sexual size dimorphism in northern water snakes, *Nerodia sipedon*. Can. J. Zool. 78:1358–1366.

———. 2000. Thermal ecology and sexual size dimorphism in northern water snakes, *Nerodia sipedon*. Ecol. Monogr. 70:311–330.

Brown, J. F. W., W. M. Marden, and D. L. Hardy, Sr. 2000. *Crotalus scutulatus scutulatus* (Mojave rattlesnake). Defensive behavior. Herpetol. Rev. 31:45.

Brown, L. E. 1987. A newly discovered population of Kirtland's snake with comments on habitat and rarity in central Illinois. Bull. Chicago Herpetol. Soc. 22:32–33.

Brown, L. E., and J. R. Brown. 1975. Evidence of climbing ability by western fox snakes *(Elaphe vulpina vulpina)*. Bull. Maryland Herpetol. Soc. 11:179.

Brown, L. E., and K. A. Brown. 1995. Fox snake winter activity in central Illinois. Herpetol. Rev. 26:134–135.

Brown, P. R. 1997. A field guide to the snakes of California. Houston, Texas: Gulf Publishing Co.

Brown, T. W., and H. B. Lillywhite. 1992. Autecology of the Mojave Desert sidewinder, *Crotalus cerastes cerastes*, at Kelso Dunes, Mojave Desert, California, U.S.A., 279–308. In: J. A. Campbell and E. D. Brodie, Jr. (eds.), Biology of the pitvipers. Tyler, Texas: Selva.

Brown, W. S. 1982. Overwintering body temperatures of timber rattlesnakes *(Crotalus horridus)* in northeastern New York. J. Herpetol. 16:145–150.

———. 1987. Hidden life of the timber rattler. Natl. Geogr. 172:128–138.

———. 1991. Female reproductive ecology in a northern population of the timber rattlesnake, *Crotalus horridus*. Herpetologica 47:101–115.

———. 1992. Emergence, ingress, and seasonal captures at dens of northern timber rattlesnakes, *Crotalus horridus*, 251–258. In: J. A. Campbell and E. D. Brodie, Jr. (eds.), Biology of the pitvipers. Tyler, Texas: Selva.

———. 1993. Biology, status, and management of the timber rattlesnake *(Crotalus horridus)*: A guide for conservation. Soc. Stud. Amphib. Rept. Herpetol. Circ. 22:1–78.

———. 1995. Heterosexual groups and the mating season in a northern population of timber rattlesnakes, *Crotalus horridus*. Herpetol. Nat. Hist. 3:127–133.

Brown, W. S., and D. B. Greenberg. 1992. Vertical-tree ambush posture in *Crotalus horridus*. Herpetol. Rev. 23:67.

Brown, W. S., and F. M. MacLean. 1983. Conspecific scent-trailing by newborn timber rattlesnakes, *Crotalus horridus*. Herpetologica 39:430–436.

Brown, W. S., and W. H. Martin. 1990. Geographic variation in female reproductive ecology of the timber rattlesnake, *Crotalus horridus*. Catesbeiana 10:48.

Brown, W. S., and W. S. Parker. 1976. Movement ecology of *Coluber constrictor* near communal hibernacula. Copeia 1976:225–242.

———. 1982. Niche dimensions and resource partitioning in a Great Basin Desert snake community, 59–81. In: N. J. Scott, Jr. (ed.), Herpetological communities. U.S. Fish Wildl. Serv. Wildl. Res. Rep. 13.

———. 1984. Growth, reproduction, and demography of the racer, *Coluber constrictor mormon,* in northern Utah. Univ. Kansas Mus. Nat. Hist. Spec. Publ. 10:13–39.

Brown, W. S., W. S. Parker, and J. A. Elder. 1974. Thermal and spatial relationships of two species of colubrid snakes during hibernation. Herpetologica 30:32–338.

Brown, W. S., D. W. Pyle, K. R. Greene, and J. B. Friedlander. 1982. Movements and temperature relationships of timber rattlesnakes *(Crotalus horridus)* in northeastern New York. J. Herpetol. 16:151–161.

Bruggen, A. C. 1961. *Pelamis platurus,* an unusual item of food of *Octopus* spec. Banisteria 25:73–74.

Brugger, K. E. 1989. Red-tailed hawk dies with coral snake in talons. Copeia 1989:508–510.

Brumwell, M. J. 1951. An ecological survey of Fort Leavenworth Military Reservation. Am. Midl. Nat. 45:187–231.

Brush, S. W., and G. W. Ferguson. 1986. Predation of lark sparrow eggs by a massasauga rattlesnake. Southwest. Nat. 31:260–261.

Buckner, S. D., and R. Franz. 1998a. *Thamnophis sauritus sackenii* (peninsula ribbon snake). Herpetol. Rev. 29:55

———. 1998b. *Thamnophis sirtalis sirtalis* (eastern garter snake). Bahama Islands: Abaco. Herpetol. Rev. 29:55.

Buikema, A. L., Jr., and K. B. Armitage. 1969. The effect of temperature on metabolism of the prairie ringneck snake, *Diadophis punctatus arnyi* Kennicott. Herpetologica 25:194–206.

Bull, J. J., D. M. Hillis, and S. O'Steen. 1988. Mammalian ZFY sequences exist in reptiles regardless of sex-determining mechanism. Science (New York) 242:567–568.

Bullock, R. E. 1971. Cannibalism in captive rattlesnakes. Great Basin Nat. 31:49–50.

———. 1981. Tree climbing bullsnakes. Blue Jay 39:139–140.

Bulmer, W. 1985. Report on an unbanded population of *Nerodia sipedon* from Virginia. Virginia J. Sci. 36:106.

Burbrink, F. T. 2001. Systematics of the eastern ratsnake complex *(Elaphe obsoleta).* Herpetol. Monogr. 15:1–53.

Burchfield, P. M. 1993. An unusual dietary inclusion for the cat-eyed snake, *Leptodeira septentrionalis.* Bull. Chicago Herpetol. Soc. 28:266–267.

Burchfield, P. M., T. F. Beimler, and C. S. Doucette. 1982. An unusual precoital head-biting behavior in the Texas patchnosed snake, *Salvadora grahamiae lineata* (Reptilia: Serpentes: Colubridae). Copeia 1982:192–193.

Burger, J. 1989a. Incubation period has long-term effects on behaviour of young pine snakes *(Pituophis melanoleucus).* Behav. Ecol. Sociobiol. 24:201–207.

———. 1989b. Following of conspecific and avoidance of predator chemical cues by pine snakes *(Pituophis melanoleucus).* J. Chem. Ecol. 15:799–806.

———. 1990. Effects of incubation temperature on behavior of young black racers *(Coluber constrictor)* and kingsnakes *(Lampropeltis getulus).* J. Herpetol. 24:158–163.

———. 1991a. Effect of experience with pine *(Pituophis melanoleucus)* and king *(Lampropeltis getulus)* snake odors on Y-maze behavior of pine snake hatchlings. J. Chem. Ecol. 17:79–87.

———. 1991b. Effects of incubation temperature on behavior of hatchling pine snakes: Implications for reptilian distribution. Behav. Ecol. Sociobiol. 28:297–303.

———. 1991c. Response to prey cues by hatchling pine snakes *(Pituophis melanoleucus):* Effects of incubation temperature and experience. J. Chem. Ecol. 17:1069–1078.

———. 1992. Trace element levels in pine snake hatchlings: Tissue and temporal differences. Arch. Environ. Contam. Toxicol. 22:209–213.

———. 1998a. Effects of incubation temperature on hatchling pine snakes: Implications for survival. Behav. Ecol. Sociobiol. 43:11–18.

———. 1998b. Antipredator behaviour of hatchling snakes: Effects of incubation temperature and simulated predators. Anim. Behav. 56:547–553.

Burger, J., and R. T. Zappalorti. 1986. Nest site selection by pine snakes, *Pituophis melanoleucus,* in a New Jersey Pine Barrens. Copeia 1986:116–121.

———. 1988a. Habitat use in free-ranging pine snakes, *Pituophis melanoleucus,* in New Jersey pine barrens. Herpetologica 44:48–55.

———. 1988b. Effects of incubation temperature on sex ratios in pine snakes: Differential vulnerability of males and females. Am. Nat. 132:492–505.

———. 1989. Habitat use by pine snakes *(Pituophis melanoleucus)* in the New Jersey pine barrens: Individual and sexual variation. J. Herpetol. 23:68–73.

———. 1991. Nesting behavior of pine snakes *(Pituophis melanoleucus)* in the New Jersey pine barrens. J. Herpetol. 25:152–160.

———. 1992. Philopatry and nesting phenology of pine snakes *Pituophis melanoleucus* in the New Jersey pine barrens. Behav. Ecol. Sociobiol. 30:331–336.

Burger, J., W. Boarman, L. Kurzava, and M. Gochfeld. 1991. Effect of experience with pine *(Pituophis melanoleucus)* and king *(Lampropeltis getulus)* snake odors on Y-maze behavior of pine snake hatchlings. J. Chem. Ecol. 17:79–87.

Burger, J., R. T. Zappalorti, J. Dowdell, T. Georgiadis, J. Hill, and M. Gochfeld. 1992. Subterranean predation on pine snakes *(Pituophis melanoleucus).* J. Herpetol. 26:259–263.

Burger, J., R. T. Zappalorti, and M. Gochfeld. 1987. Developmental effects of incubation temperature on hatchling pine snakes *Pituophis melanoleucus.* Comp. Biochem. Physiol. 87A:727–732.

———. 1999–2000. Defensive behaviors of pine snakes *(Pituophis melanoleucus)* and black racers *(Coluber constrictor)* to disturbance during hibernation. Herpetol. Nat. Hist. 7:59–66.

Burger, J., R. T. Zappalorti, M. Gochfeld, W. I. Boarman, M. Caffrey, V. Doig, S. D. Garber, B. Lauro, M. Mikovsky, C. Safina, and J. Saliva. 1988. Hibernacula and summer den sites of pine snakes *(Pituophis melanoleucus)* in the New Jersey pine barrens. J. Herpetol. 22:425–433.

Burghardt, G. M. 1967. Chemical-cue preferences of inexperienced snakes: Comparative aspects. Science (New York) 157:718–721.

———. 1968. Chemical preference studies on newborn snakes of three sympatric species of *Natrix.* Copeia 1968:732–737.

———. 1969. Comparative prey-attack studies in newborn snakes of the genus *Thamnophis.* Behaviour 33:77–113.

———. 1970. Intraspecific geographical variation in chemical food cue preferences of newborn garter snakes *(Thamnophis sirtalis).* Behaviour 36:246–257.

———. 1971. Chemical-cue preferences of newborn snakes: Influence of prenatal maternal experience. Science (New York) 171:921–923.

———. 1975. Chemical prey preference polymorphism in newborn garter snakes *Thamnophis sirtalis.* Behaviour 52:202–225.

———. 1983. Aggregation and species discrimination in newborn snakes. Zeit. Tierpsychol. 61:89–101.

———. 1990. Chemically mediated predation in vertebrates: Diversity, ontogeny, and information, 475–499. In: D. W. MacDonald, D. Müller-Schwarze, and S. E. Natynczuk (eds.), Chemical signals in vertebrates 5. New York: Oxford University Press.

———. 1993. The comparative imperative: Genetics and ontogeny of chemoreceptive prey responses in natricine snakes. Brain Behav. Evol. 41:138–146.

Burghardt, G. M., and D. Denny. 1983. Effects of prey movement and prey odor on feeding in garter snakes. Zeit. Tierpsychol. 62:329–347.

Burghardt, G. M., and C. H. Pruitt. 1975. Role of the tongue and senses in feeding of naive and experienced garter snakes. Physiol. Behav. 14:185–194.

Burken, R. R., P. W. Wertz, and D. T. Downing. 1985. The effect of lipids on transepidermal water permeation in snakes. Comp. Biochem. Physiol. 81A:213–216.

Burkett, R. D. 1966. Natural history of the cottonmouth moccasin, Agkistrodon piscivorus (Reptilia). Univ. Kansas Publ. Mus. Nat. Hist. 17:435–491.

Burns, B., and G. V. Pickwell. 1972. Cephalic glands in sea turtles (Pelamis, Hydrophis, and Laticauda). Copeia 1972:547–559.

Burns, G., A. Ramos, and A. Muchlinski. 1996. Fever response in North American snakes. J. Herpetol. 30:133–139.

Burt, C. H., and W. L. Hoyle. 1935. Additional records of the reptiles of the central prairie region of the United States. Trans. Kansas Acad. Sci. 37:193–216.

Burt, M. D. 1928. The relation of size to maturity in the garter snakes, Thamnophis sirtalis sirtalis (L.) and T. sauritus sauritus (L.). Copeia 166:8–12.

Bury, R. B., F. Gress, and G. C. Gorman. 1970. Karyotypic survey of some colubrid snakes from western North America. Herpetologica 26:461–466.

Busack, S. D. 1960. Ophiophagy in Sceloporus. Herpetologica 16:44.

Busby, W. H., and J. R. Parmelee. 1996. Historical changes in a herpetofaunal assemblage in the Flint Hills of Kansas. Am. Midl. Nat. 135:81–91.

Busch, C., W. Lukas, H. M. Smith, D. Payne, and D. Chiszar. 1996. Strike-induced chemosensory searching (SICS) in northern Pacific rattlesnakes Crotalus viridis oreganus Holbrook, 1840, rescued from abusive husbandry conditions. Herpetozoa 9:99–104.

Bush, F. M. 1959. Foods of some Kentucky herptiles. Herpetologica 15:73–77.

Bushar, L. M., H. K. Reinert, and L. Gelbert. 1998. Genetic variation and gene flow within and between local populations of the timber rattlesnake, Crotalus horridus. Copeia 1998:411–422.

Butler, J. A., T. W. Hull, and R. Franz. 1995. Neonate aggregations and maternal attendance of young in the eastern diamondback rattlesnake, Crotalus adamanteus. Copeia 1995:196–198.

Byrd, J. G., and L. N. Jenkins. 1996. Lampropeltis getula niger (black kingsnake). Diet. Herpetol. Rev. 27:204.

Byrd, W., E. Hanebrink, and W. Meshaka. 1988. Food, feeding behavior, sex ratios, and measurements of three species of water snakes (Nerodia spp.) collected from northeastern Arkansas. Bull. Chicago Herpetol. Soc. 23:55–57.

Cadle, J. E. 1984. Molecular systematics of Neotropical xenodontine snakes. III. Overview of xenodontine phylogeny and the history of New World snakes. Copeia 1984:641–652.

———. 1988. Phylogenetic relationships among advanced snakes: A molecular approach. Univ. California Publ. Zool. 119:1–77.

Cadle, J. E., and V. M. Sarich. 1981. An immunological assessment of the phylogenetic position of New World coral snakes. J. Zool. (London) 195:157–167.

Cagle, F. R. 1937. Notes on Natrix rhombifera as observed at Reelfoot Lake. J. Tennessee Acad. Sci. 12:179–185.

———. 1942. Herpetological fauna of Jackson and Union counties, Illinois. Am. Midl. Nat. 28:164–200.

———. 1946. Typhlops braminus in the Marianas Islands. Copeia 1946:101.

Caldwell, G. S., and R. W. Rubinoff. 1983. Avoidance of venomous sea snakes by naive herons and egrets. Auk 100:195–198.

Callard, I. P., K. Etheridge, G. Giannoukos, T. Lamb, and L. Perez. 1991. The role of steroids in reproduction in female elasmobranchs and reptiles. J. Steroid Biochem. Molec. Biol. 40:571–575.

Callard, I. P., and J. H. Leathem. 1967. Some aspects of oviduct biochemistry in the snakes Natrix sipedon pictiventris, Coluber c. constrictor and Elaphe q. quadrivittata. Proc. Pennsylvania Acad. Sci. 40:59–62.

Camazine, B., W. Garstka, R. Tokarz, and D. Crews. 1980. Effects of castration and androgen replacement on male courtship behavior in the red-sided garter snake, Thamnophis sirtalis parietalis. Horm. Behav. 14:358–372.

Camin, J. H., and P. R. Ehrlich. 1958. Natural selection in water snakes (Natrix sipedon L.) on islands in Lake Erie. Evolution 12:504–511.

Camin, J. H., C. Tripplehorn, and H. Walter. 1954. Some indication of survival value in type "A" pattern of the island water snakes in Lake Erie. Chicago Acad. Sci. Nat. Hist. Misc. 13:1–3.

Camp, C. D., W. D. Sprewell, and V. N. Powders. 1980. Feeding habits of *Nerodia taxispilota* with comparative notes on the foods of sympatric congeners in Georgia. J. Herpetol. 14:301–304.

Camp, C. L. 1916. Notes on the local distribution and habitats of the amphibians and reptiles of southeastern California in the vicinity of the Turtle Mountains. Univ. California Publ. Zool. 12:503–544.

Campbell, B. 1934. Report on a collection of reptiles and amphibians made in Arizona during the summer of 1933. Occ. Pap. Mus. Zool. Univ. Michigan 289:1–10.

Campbell, H. W. 1950. Rattlesnakes tangled in wire. Herpetologica 6:44.

———. 1970. Prey selection in naive *Elaphe obsoleta* (Squamata: Serpentes)—a reappraisal. Psychon. Sci. 21:300–301.

Campbell, H. W., and S. P. Christman. 1982. The herpetological components of Florida sandhill and sand pine scrub associations, 163–171. In: N. J. Scott, Jr. (ed.). Herpetological communities. U.S. Fish Wildl. Serv. Wildl. Res. Rep. 13.

Campbell, J. A. 1972. Reproduction in captive Trans-Pecos ratsnakes, *Elaphe subocularis*. Herpetol. Rev. 4:129–130.

———. 1973. A captive hatching of *Micrurus fulvius tenere* (Serpentes, Elapidae). J. Herpetol. 7:312–315.

Campbell, J. A., and W. W. Lamar. 1989. The venomous reptiles of Latin America. Ithaca, New York: Comstock Publishing Associates, Cornell University Press.

Campbell, J. A., and D. H. Whitmore, Jr. 1989. A comparison of the skin keratin biochemistry in vipers with comments on its systematic value. Herpetologica 45:242–249.

Campbell, J. A., E. D. Brodie, Jr., D. G. Barker, and A. H. Potts. 1989. An apparent natural hybrid rattlesnake and *Crotalus willardi* (Viperidae) from the Peloncillo Mountains of southwestern New Mexico. Herpetologica 45:344–349.

Camper, J. D. 1996a. *Masticophis bilineatus*. Cat. Am. Amphib. Rept. 637:1–4.

———. 1996b. *Masticophis schotti*. Cat. Am. Amphib. Rept. 638:1–4.

———. 1996c. *Masticophis taeniatus*. Cat. Am. Amphib. Rept. 639:1–6.

Camper, J. D., and J. R. Dixon. 1990. High incidence of melanism in *Masticophis taeniatus girardi* (Reptilia: Colubridae), from the Cuatro Cienegas Basin of Coahuila, Mexico. Texas J. Sci. 42:202–204.

———. 1994. Geographic variation and systematics of the striped whipsnakes (*Masticophis taeniatus* complex: Reptilia: Serpentes: Colubridae). Ann. Carnegie Mus. 63:1–48.

———. 2000. Food habits of three species of striped whipsnakes, *Masticophis* (Serpentes: Colubridae). Texas J. Sci. 52:83–92.

Camper, J. D., and B. G. Hanks. 1995. Variation in the nucleolus organizer region among New World snakes. J. Herpetol. 29:468–471.

Carl, G. 1981. Reproduction in the captive Brazos water snake, *Nerodia harteri*. Texas J. Sci. 33:77–78.

Carl, G. C. 1960. The reptiles of British Columbia. British Columbia Prov. Mus. Handb. 3:1–65.

Carpenter, C. C. 1951. Young goldfinches eaten by garter snake. Wilson Bull. 63:117–118.

———. 1952a. Comparative ecology of the common garter snake (*Thamnophis s. sirtalis*), the ribbon snake (*Thamnophis s. sauritus*) and Butler's garter snake (*Thamnophis butler*) in mixed populations. Ecol. Monogr. 22:235–258.

———. 1952b. Growth and maturity of the three species of *Thamnophis* in Michigan. Copeia 1952:237–243.

———. 1953a. A study of hibernacula and hibernating associations of snakes and amphibians in Michigan. Ecology 34:74–80.

———. 1953b. An ecological survey of the herpetofauna of the Grand Teton-Jackson Hole area of Wyoming. Copeia 1953:170–174.

———. 1956. Body temperatures of three species of *Thamnophis*. Ecology 37:732–735.

———. 1958. Reproduction, young, eggs, and food of Oklahoma snakes. Herpetologica 14:113–115.

———. 1960. A large brood of western pigmy rattlesnakes. Herpetologica 16:142143.

———. 1982. The bullsnake as an excavator. J. Herpetol. 16:394–401.

———. 1985. *Lampropeltis calligaster calligaster* (prairie kingsnake). Reproduction. Herpetol. Rev. 16:81.

Carpenter, C. C., and G. W. Ferguson. 1977. Variation and evolution of stereotyped behavior in reptiles, 335–554. In: C. Gans and D. W. Tinkle (eds.), Biology of the Reptilia, vol. 7. London: Academic Press.

Carpenter, C. C., and J. C. Gillingham. 1975. Postural responses to kingsnakes by crotaline snakes. Herpetologica 31:293–302.

———. 1977. A combat ritual between two male speckled kingsnakes (*Lampropeltis getulus holbrooki*: Colubridae, Serpentes) with indications of dominance. Southwest. Nat. 22:517–524.

Carpenter, C. C., J. C. Gillingham, and J. B. Murphy. 1976. The combat ritual of the rock rattlesnake (*Crotalus lepidus*). Copeia 1976:764–780.

Carpenter, C. S. 1985. *Tantilla gracilis* (flat-headed snake). Albino. Herpetol. Rev. 16(3): 81.

Carr, A. F., Jr. 1934. Notes on the habits of the short-tailed snake. Copeia 1934:138–139.

———. 1940. A contribution to the herpetology of Florida. Univ. Florida Publ. Biol. Sci. Ser. 3: 1–118.

Carr, A. F., Jr., and M. H. Carr. 1942. Notes on the courtship of the cottonmouth moccasin. Proc. New England Zool. Club 20:1–6.

Carr, C. M., and P. T. Gregory. 1976. Can tongue flicks be used to measure niche sizes? Can. J. Zool. 54:1389–1394.

Carson, H. L. 1945. Delayed fertilization in a captive indigo snake with a note on feeding and shedding. Copeia 1945:222–225.

Carter, W. A. 1992. Black-and-white warbler nest failure in Pontotoc County, Oklahoma. Bull. Oklahoma Ornithol. Soc. 25(3): 22–23.

Cary, D. L., R. L. Clauson, and D. Grimes. 1981. An observation on snake predation on a bat. Trans. Kansas Acad. Sci. 84:223–224.

Casper, G. S. 1993. A note on reproductive activity in Wisconsin northern water snakes, Nerodia s. sipedon. Bull. Chicago Herpetol. Soc. 28:213.

Catling, P. M., and W. Freedman. 1977. Melanistic Butler's garter snakes (Thamnophis butleri) at Amherstburg, Ontario. Can. Field-Nat. 91:397–399.

———. 1980a. Variation in distribution and abundance of four sympatric species of snakes at Amherstburg, Ontario. Can. Field-Nat. 94:19–27.

———. 1980b. Food and feeding behavior of sympatric snakes at Amherstburg, Ontario. Can. Field-Nat. 94:28–33.

Cavanaugh, C. J. 1994. Crotalus horridus (timber rattlesnake). Longevity. Herpetol. Rev. 25:70.

Cavitt, J. F. 2000a. Fire and a tallgrass prairie reptile community: Effects of relative abundance and seasonal activity. J. Herpetol. 34:12–20.

———. 2000b. Tallgrass prairie snake assemblage. Food habits. Herpetol. Rev. 31:47–48.

Cebula, J. J. 1983. A note on the food choices of a plains garter snake. Bull. Chicago Herpetol. Soc. 18:46.

Cebula, J. J., and M. Redmer. 1988. Observations on the reproduction of Storeria dekayi in DuPage County, Illinois. Bull. Chicago Herpetol. Soc. 23:29.

Censky, E. J., and C. J. McCoy. 1988. Female reproductive cycles of five species of snakes (Reptilia: Colubridae) from the Yucatan Peninsula, Mexico. Biotropica 20:326–333.

Chamberlain, E. B. 1935. Notes on the pygmy rattlesnake Sistrurus miliarius Linnaeus, in South Carolina. Copeia 1935:146–147.

Chance, B. 1970. A note on the feeding habits of Micrurus fulvius fulvius. Bull. Maryland Herpetol. Soc. 6:56.

Chang, P., J. Balling, and R. Lister. 1971. Karyotype of the pilot black snake, Elaphe obsoleta obsoleta (Say). Mammal Chromosome Newsl. 12:9.

Chapman, B. R., and S. D. Casto. 1972. Additional vertebrate prey of the loggerhead shrike. Wilson Bull. 84:496–497.

Charland, M. B. 1989. Size and winter survivorship in neonatal western rattlesnakes (Crotalus viridis). Can. J. Zool. 67:1620–1625.

———. 1995. Thermal consequences of reptilian viviparity: Thermoregulation in gravid and nongravid garter snakes (Thamnophis). J. Herpetol. 29:383–390.

Charland, M. B., and P. T. Gregory. 1989. Feeding rate and weight gain in postpartum rattlesnakes: Do animals that eat more always grow more? Copeia 1989:211–214.

———. 1990. The influence of female reproductive status on thermoregulation in a viviparous snake, Crotalus viridis. Copeia 1990:1089–1098.

———. 1995. Movements and habitat use in gravid and nongravid female garter snakes (Colubridae: Thamnophis). J. Zool. (London) 236:543–561.

Chiasson, R. B., D. L. Bentley, and C. H. Lowe. 1989. Scale morphology in Agkistrodon and closely related crotaline genera. Herpetologica 45:430–438.

Chiasson, R. B., and C. H. Lowe. 1989. Ultrastructural scale patterns in Nerodia and Thamnophis. J. Herpetol. 23:109–118.

Chiszar, D., C. Andren, F. Nilson, B. O'Connell, J. S. Mestas, Jr., H. M. Smith, and C. W. Radcliffe. 1982. Strike-induced chemosensory searching in Old World vipers and New World pit vipers. Anim. Learn. Behav. 10:121–125.

Chiszar, D., C. Castro, J. B. Murphy, and H. M. Smith. 1989. Discrimination between thermally different rodent carcasses by bull snakes (Pituophis melanoleucus) and cobras (Naja pallida and Aspidelaps scutatus). Bull. Chicago Herpetol. Soc. 24:181–183.

Chiszar, D., D. Dickman, and J. Colton. 1986. Sensitivity to thermal stimulation in prairie rattlesnakes (Crotalus viridis) after bilateral anesthetization of the facial pits. Behav. Neurol. Biol. 45:143–149.

Chiszar, D., G. Hobika, and H. M. Smith. 1993. Prairie rattlesnakes (Crotalus viridis) respond to rodent blood with chemosensory searching. Brain Behav. Evol. 41:229–233.

Chiszar, D., G. Hobika, H. M. Smith, and J. Vidaurri. 1991. Envenomation and acquisition of chemical information by prairie rattlesnakes. Prairie Nat. 23:69–72.

Chiszar, D., T. Melcer, R. Lee, C. W. Radcliffe, and D. Duvall. 1990. Chemical cues used by prairie rattlesnakes (Crotalus viridis) to follow trails of rodent prey. J. Chem. Ecol. 16:79–86.

Chiszar, D., P. Nelson, and H. M. Smith. 1988. Analysis of the behavioral sequence emitted by rattlesnakes during feeding episodes. III. Strike-induced chemosensory searching and location of rodent carcasses. Bull. Maryland Herpetol. Soc. 24:99–108.

Chiszar, D., B. O'Connell, R. Greenlee, B. Demeter, T. Walsh, J. Chiszar, K. Moran, and H. M. Smith. 1985. Duration of strike-induced chemosensory searching in long-term captive rattlesnakes at National Zoo, Audubon Zoo, and the San Diego Zoo. Zoo Biol. 4:291–294.

Chiszar, D., and C. W. Radcliffe. 1977. Absence of prey-chemical preference in newborn rattlesnakes (Crotalus cerastes, C. enyo, and C. viridis). Behav. Biol. 21:146–150.

Chiszar, D., C. W. Radcliffe, R. Boyd, A. Radcliffe, H. Yun, H. M. Smith, T. Boyer, B. Atkins, and F. Feiler. 1986. Trailing behavior in cottonmouths (Agkistrodon piscivorus). J. Herpetol. 20:269–272.

Chiszar, D., C. W. Radcliffe, T. Byers, and R. Stoops. 1986. Prey capture behavior in nine species of venomous snakes. Psychol. Rec. 36:433–438.

Chiszar, D., C. W. Radcliffe, and F. Feiler. 1986. Trailing behavior in banded rock rattlesnakes (Crotalus lepidus klauberi) and prairie rattlesnakes (C. viridis viridis). J. Comp. Psychol. 100:368–371.

Chiszar, D., C. W. Radcliffe, R. Overstreet, T. Poole, and T. Byers. 1985. Duration of strike-induced chemosensory searching in cottonmouths (Agkistrodon piscivorus) and a test of the hypothesis that striking prey creates a specific search image. Can. J. Zool. 63:1057–1061.

Chiszar, D., C. W. Radcliffe, and K. Scudder. 1980. Use of the vomeronasal system during predatory episodes by bull snakes (Pituophis melanoleucus). Bull. Psychon. Soc. 15:35–36.

Chiszar, D., C. W. Radcliffe, H. M. Smith, and H. Baskinski. 1981. Effect of prolonged food deprivation on response to prey odors by rattlesnakes. Herpetologica 37:237–243.

Chiszar, D., C. W. Radcliffe, H. M. Smith, and P. Langer. 1991. Strike-induced chemosensory searching: Do rattlesnakes make one decision or two? Bull. Maryland Herpetol. Soc. 27:90–94.

Chiszar, D., K. Scudder, and L. Knight. 1976. Rate of tongue flicking by garter snakes (Thamnophis radix haydeni) and rattlesnakes (Crotalus v. viridis, Sistrurus catenatus tergeminus, and Sistrurus catenatus edwardsii) during prolonged exposure to food odors. Behav. Biol. 18:273–283.

Chiszar, D., K. Scudder, L. Knight, and H. M. Smith. 1978. Exploratory behavior in prairie rattlesnakes (Crotalus viridis) and water moccasins (Agkistrodon piscivorus). Psychol. Rec. 28:363–368.

Chiszar, D., K. Scudder, and H. M. Smith. 1979. Chemosensory investigation of fish mucus odor by rattlesnakes. Bull. Maryland Herpetol. Soc. 15:31–36.

Chiszar, D., K. Scudder, H. M. Smith, and C. W. Radcliffe. 1976. Observations of courtship behavior in the western massasauga (Sistrurus catenatus tergeminus). Herpetologica 32:337–338.

Chiszar, D., L. Simonsen, C. Radcliffe, and H. M. Smith. 1979. Rate of tongue flicking by cottonmouths (Agkistrodon piscivorus) during prolonged exposure to various odors, and strike induced chemosensory searching by the cantil (Agkistrodon bilineatus). Trans. Kansas Acad. Sci. 82:49–54.

Chiszar, D., H. M. Smith, C. M. Bogert, and J. Vidaurri. 1991. A chemical sense of self in timber and prairie rattlesnakes. Bull. Psychon. Sci. 29:153–154.

Chiszar, D., H. M. Smith, and R. Defusco. 1993. Crotalus viridis viridis (prairie rattlesnake). Diet. Herpetol. Rev. 24:106.

Chiszar, D., H. M. Smith, J. L. Glenn, and R. C. Straight. 1991. Strike-induced chemosensory searching in venomoid pit vipers at Hogle Zoo. Zoo Biol. 10:111–117.

Chiszar, D., S. W. Taylor, C. W. Radcliffe, H. M. Smith, and B. O'Connell. 1981. Effects of chemical and visual stimuli upon chemosensory searching by garter snakes and rattlesnakes. J. Herpetol. 15:415–423.

Chiszar, D., A. Walters, J. Urbaniak, H. M. Smith, and S. P. Mackessy. 1999. Discrimination between envenomated and nonenvenomated prey by western diamondback rattlesnakes (Crotalus atrox): Chemosensory consequences of venom. Copeia 1999:640–648.

Christman, S. P. 1975. The status of the extinct rattlesnake Crotalus giganteus. Copeia 1975:43–47.

———. 1980. Patterns of geographic variation in Florida snakes. Bull. Florida St. Mus. Biol. Sci. 25:157–256.

———. 1982. Storeria dekayi. Cat. Am. Amphib. Rept. 306:1–4.

Churchill, T. A., and K. B. Storey. 1991. Metabolic responses to freezing by garter snakes. Cryo-Lett. 12:359–366.

———. 1992. Freezing survival of the garter snake Thamnophis sirtalis parietalis. Can. J. Zool. 70:99–105.

Cieslak, E. S. 1945. Relations between the reproductive cycle and pituitary gland in the snake Thamnophis radix. Physiol. Zool. 18:299–329.

Cink, C. L. 1977. Snake predation on Bell's vireo nestlings. Wilson Bull. 89:347–350.

———. 1990. Snake predation on chimney swift nestlings. J. Field Ornithol. 61:288–289.

———. 1991. Snake predation on nestling eastern phoebes followed by turtle predation on snake. Kansas Orinthol. Soc. Bull. 42(3): 29.

Clamp, H. J. 1990. A snake story. Bull. South Carolina Herpetol. Soc. Sept. 1990:1–12.

Clark, A. 1998. Reptile sheds yield high quality DNA. Herpetol. Rev. 29:17–18.

Clark, D. R., Jr. 1964a. The structures of the hemipenis as systematic characters in the genus *Virginia* Baird and Girard. Herpetologica 20:33–37.

———. 1964b. Reproduction and sexual dimorphism in a population of the rough earth snake, *Virginia striatula* (Linnaeus). Texas J. Sci. 16:265–295.

———. 1967a. Notes on sexual dimorphism in tail-length in American snakes. Trans. Kansas Acad. Sci. 69:226–232.

———. 1967b. Experiments into selection of soil type, soil moisture level, and temperature by five species of small snakes. Trans. Kansas Acad. Sci. 70:490–496.

———. 1968. A proposal of specific status for the western worm snake, *Carphophis vermis* (Kennicott). Herpetologica 24:104–112.

———. 1970a. Ecological study of the worm snake *Carphophis vermis* (Kennicott). Univ. Kansas Publ. Mus. Nat. Hist. 19:85–194.

———. 1970b. Age specific "reproductive effort" in the worm snake *Carphophis vermis* (Kennicott). Trans. Kansas Acad. Sci. 73:20–24.

———. 1970c. Loss of the left oviduct in the colubrid snake genus *Tantilla*. Herpetologica 26:130–133.

———. 1974. The western ribbon snake *(Thamnophis proximus)*: Ecology of a Texas population. Herpetologica 30:372–379.

Clark, D. R., Jr., C. M. Bunck, and R. J. Hall. 1997. Female reproductive dynamics in a Maryland population of ringneck snakes *(Diadophis punctatus)*. J. Herpetol. 31:476–483.

Clark, D. R., Jr., and R. R. Fleet. 1976. The rough earth snake *(Virginia striatula)*: Ecology of a Texas population. Southwest. Nat. 20:467–478.

Clark, D. R., Jr., and C. S. Lieb. 1973. Notes on reproduction in the night snake *(Hypsiglena torquata)*. Southwest. Nat. 18:248–252.

Clark, D. R., Jr., and G. W. Pendleton. 1995. Texas rat snake *(Elaphe obsoleta lindheimeri)* eggs and hatchlings from a communal nest. Southwest. Nat. 40:203–207.

Clark, H. 1953. Eggs, egg-laying and incubation of the snake *Elaphe emoryi* (Baird and Girard). Copeia 1953:90–92.

Clark, H., B. Florio, and R. Hurowitz. 1955. Embryonic growth of *Thamnophis s. sirtalis* in relation to fertilization and placental function. Copeia 1955:9–13.

Clark, R. F. 1949. Snakes of the hill parishes of Louisiana. J. Tennessee Acad. Sci. 24:244–261.

———. 1954. Eggs and egg-laying of *Lampropeltis c. calligaster* (Harlan). Herpetologica 10:15–16.

Clarke, G. K. 1961. Report on a bite by a red diamond rattlesnake, *Crotalus ruber ruber*. Copeia 1961:418–422.

Clarke, J. A., J. T. Chopko, and S. J. Mackessy. 1996. The effect of moonlight on activity patterns of adult and juvenile prairie rattlesnakes *(Crotalus viridis viridis)*. J. Herpetol. 30:192–197.

Clarke, R. F. 1958. An ecological study of reptiles and amphibians in Osage County, Kansas. Emporia State Res. Stud. 7:1–52.

Clarkson, R. W., and J. C. deVos, Jr. 1986. The bullfrog, *Rana catesbeiana* Shaw, in the Lower Colorado River, Arizona-California. J. Herpetol. 20:42–49.

Clausen, H. J. 1936a. The effect of aggregation on the respiratory metabolism of the brown snake, *Storeria dekayi*. J. Cell. Comp. Physiol. 8:367–386.

———. 1936b. Observations on the brown snake, *Storeria dekayi* (Holbrook), with especial reference to the habits and birth of the young. Copeia 1936:98–102.

Cleveland, E. D. 1986. County record for Graham's crawfish snake *(Regina grahami)*. Trans. Kansas Acad. Sci. 89:9.

Cliburn, J. W. 1956. The taxonomic relations of the water snakes *Natrix taxispilota* and *rhombifera*. Herpetologica 12:198–200.

———. 1962. Further notes on the behavior of a captive black pine snake *(Pituophis melanoleucus lodingi* Blanchard). Herpetologica 18:34–37.

———. 1975. The hemipenis of *Pituophis melanoleucus*. J. Herpetol. 9:254–255.

Cliff, F. S. 1954. Snakes of the islands in the Gulf of California, Mexico. Trans. San Diego Soc. Nat. Hist. 12:67–98.

Cobb, V. A. 1990. Reproductive notes on the eggs and offspring of *Tantilla gracilis* (Serpentes: Colubridae), with evidence of communal nesting. Southwest. Nat. 35:222–224.

Cobb, V. A., and C. R. Peterson. 1999. *Crotalus viridus lutosus* (Great Basin rattlesnake). Mortality. Herpetol. Rev. 30:45–46.

Cochran, P. A. 1987. *Opheodrys vernalis* (smooth green snake). Behavior. Herpetol. Rev. 18:36–37.

Cohen, A. C., and B. C. Myers. 1970. A function of the horns (suprocular scales) in the sidewinder rattlesnake, *Crotalus cerastes*, with comments on other horned snakes. Copeia 1970:574–575.

Cohen, E. 1948a. Emergence of *Coluber c. constrictor* from hibernation. Copeia 1948:137–138.

———. 1948b. Delayed parturition of *Storeria occipitomaculata* (Storer) in captivity. Herpetologica 4:227.

Cohen, H. J. 1978. An observation of double clutch production by *Elaphe obsoleta* in captivity. Herpetol. Rev. 9:140–141.

Cole, C. J., and L. M. Hardy. 1981. Systematics of North American colubrid snakes related to *Tantilla planiceps* (Blainville). Bull. Am. Mus. Nat. Hist. 171:201–284.

———. 1983a. *Tantilla atriceps*. Cat. Am. Amphib. Rept. 317:1–2.

———. 1983b. *Tantilla hobartsmithi*. Cat. Am. Amphib. Rept. 318:1–2.

———. 1983c. *Tantilla planiceps*. Cat. Am. Amphib. Rept. 319:1–2.

Collins, J. T. 1990. Standard common and current scientific names for North American amphibians and reptiles. 3rd ed. Soc. Stud. Amphib. Rept. Herpetol. Circ. 19:1–41.

———. 1991. Viewpoint: A new taxonomic arrangement for some North American amphibians and reptiles. Herpetol. Rev. 22:42–43.

———. 1992. Reply to Grobman on variation in *Opheodrys aestivus*. Herpetol. Rev. 23:15–16.

———. 1993. Amphibians and reptiles in Kansas. 3rd ed., revised. Univ. Kansas Mus. Nat. Hist. Publ. Ed. Ser. 13:1–397.

Collins, J. T., and S. L. Collins. 1993. Reptiles and amphibians of Cheyenne Bottoms. Hillsboro, Kansas: Hirth Publishing.

Collins, J. T., and J. L. Knight. 1980. *Crotalus horridus*. Cat. Am. Amphib. Rept. 253:1–2.

Collins, R. F. 1980. Stomach contents of some snakes from eastern and central North Carolina. Brimleyana 4:157–159.

Collins, R. F., and C. C. Carpenter. 1970. Organ position-ventral scute relationship in the water moccasin (*Agkistrodon piscivorus leucostoma*), with notes on food habits and distribution. Proc. Oklahoma Acad. Sci. 498:15–18.

Conant, R. 1938. On the seasonal occurrence of reptiles in Lucas County, Ohio. Herpetologica 1:137–144.

———. 1940. A new species of fox snake, *Elaphe vulpina* Baird and Girard. Herpetologica 2:1–14.

———. 1942. Notes on the young of three recently described snakes, with comments upon their relationships. Bull. Chicago Acad. Sci. 6:193–200.

———. 1943a. *Natrix erythrogaster erythrogaster* in the northeastern part of its range. Herpetologica 2:83–86.

———. 1943b. Studies on North American water snakes—I: *Natrix kirtlandii* (Kennicott). Am. Midl. Nat. 29:313–341.

———. 1949. Two new races of *Natrix erythrogaster*. Copeia 1949:1–15.

———. 1950. On the taxonomic status of *Thamnophis butleri* (Cope). Bull. Chicago Acad. Sci. 9:71–77.

———. 1951. The reptiles of Ohio. 2nd ed. Notre Dame, Indiana: Notre Dame Press.

———. 1955. Notes on three Texas reptiles, including an addition to the fauna of the state. Am. Mus. Novitates 1726:1–6.

———. 1960. The queen snake, *Natrix septemvittata*, in the interior highlands of Arkansas and Missouri, with comments upon similar disjunct distributions. Proc. Acad. Nat. Sci. Philadelphia 112:25–40.

———. 1963. Evidence for the specific status of the water snake *Natrix fasciata*. Am. Mus. Novitates 2122:1–38.

———. 1965a. Miscellaneous notes and comments on toads, lizards, and snakes from Mexico. Am. Mus. Novitates 2205:1–38.

———. 1965b. Notes on reproduction in two natricine snakes from Mexico. Herpetologica 21:140–144.

———. 1969. A review of the water snakes of the genus *Natrix* in Mexico. Bull. Am. Mus. Nat. Hist. 142:1–140.

Conant, R., and R. M. Bailey. 1936. Some herpetological records from Monmouth and Ocean counties, New Jersey. Occ. Pap. Mus. Zool. Univ. Michigan 328:1–10.

Conant, R., and W. M. Clay. 1937. A new subspecies of water snake from islands in Lake Erie. Occ. Pap. Mus. Zool. Univ. Michigan 346:1–9.

Conant, R., and J. T. Collins. 1998. A field guide to reptiles and amphibians: Eastern and central North America. 3rd ed., expanded. Houghton Mifflin, Boston.

Conant, R., and A. Downs, Jr. 1940. Miscellaneous notes on the eggs and young of reptiles. Zoologica (New York) 25:33–48.

Conant, R., and J. D. Lazell, Jr. 1973. The Carolina salt marsh snake: A distinct form of *Natrix sipedon*. Breviora 400:1–13.

Conant, R., E. S. Thomas, and R. L. Rausch. 1945. The plains garter snake, *Thamnophis radix*, in Ohio. Copeia 1945:61–68.

Congdon, J. D., A. E. Dunham, and D. W. Tinkle. 1982. Energy budgets and life histories of reptiles, 233–271. In: C. Gans and F. H. Pough (eds.), Biology of the Reptilia. Vol. 13. Physiology D, physiological ecology. New York: Academic Press,.

Contreras-B, A. J., and C. H. Treviño-S. 1987. Notas sobre predacion de aves en reptiles. Southwest. Nat. 32:505–506.

Conway, C. H., and W. R. Flemming. 1960. Placental transmission of Na^{22} and I^{131} in *Natrix*. Copeia 1960:53–55.

Cook, D. G., and F. J. Aldridge. 1984. *Coluber constrictor priapus* (southern black racer). Food. Herpetol. Rev. 15:49.

Cook, F. A. 1945. Intergradation of *Lampropeltis calligaster* and *Lampropeltis rhombomaculata* in Mississippi. Copeia 1945:47–48.

———. 1954. Snakes of Mississippi. Jackson: Mississippi Game Fish. Comm.

Cook, P. M., M. P. Rowe, and R. W. Van Devender. 1994. Allometric scaling and interspecific differences in the rattling sounds of rattlesnakes. Herpetologica 50:358–368.

Cook, S. F., Jr. 1955. Rattlesnake hybrids: *Crotalus viridis* × *Crotalus scutulatus*. Copeia 1955:139–141.

———. 1960. On the occurrence and life history of *Contia tenuis*. Herpetologica 16:163–173.

Cooper, J. E. 1958. The snake *Haldea valeriae pulchra* in Maryland. Herpetologica 14:121–122.

Cooper, J. G. 1870. The fauna of California and its geographical distribution. Proc. California Acad. Sci. 4:61–81.

Cooper, W., A. Ohmart, and D. L. Dahlsten. 1978. Predation by a rubber boa on chestnut-backed chicadees in an artificial nesting site. Western Birds 9:41–42.

Cooper, W. E., Jr. 1992. Post-bite elevation in tongue-flick rate by neonatal garter snakes (*Thamnophis radix*). Ethology 91:339–345.

Cooper, W. E., Jr., and K. J. Alfieri. 1993. Caudal autumy in the eastern garter snake, *Thamnophis s. sirtalis*. Amphibia-Reptilia 4:86–89.

Cooper, W. E., Jr., G. M. Burghardt, and W. S. Brown. 2000. Behavioural responses by hatchling racers (*Coluber constrictor*) from two geographically distinct populations to chemical stimuli from potential prey and predators. Amphibia-Reptilia 21:103–115.

Cooper, W. E., Jr., D. G. Buth, and L. J. Vitt. 1990. Prey odor discrimination by ingestively naive coachwhip snakes (*Masticophis flagellum*). Chemoecology 1:86–91.

Cooper, W. E., Jr., S. G. McDowell, and J Ruffer. 1989. Strike-induced chemosensory searching in the colubrid snakes *Elaphe g. guttata* and *Thamnophis sirtalis*. Ethology 81:19–28.

Cope, E. D. 1861a [1860]. Catalogue of the Colubridae in the Museum of the Academy of Natural Sciences of Philadelphia, with notes and descriptions of new species. Part 2. Proc. Acad. Nat. Sci. Philadelphia 12:74–79, 241–266.

———. 1861b [1860]. Notes and descriptions of new and little known species of American reptiles. Proc. Acad. Nat. Sci. Philadelphia 12:339–345.

———. 1861c. Contributions to the ophiology of Lower California, Mexico, and Central America. Proc. Acad. Nat. Sci. Philadelphia 13:292–306.

———. 1862. Notes upon some reptiles of the Old World. Proc. Acad. Nat. Sci. Philadelphia 14:337–344.

———. 1866. Fourth contribution to the herpetology of tropical America. Proc. Acad. Nat. Sci. Philadelphia 2:123–132.

———. 1867 [1866]. On the Reptilia and Batrachia of the Sonoran Province of the Nearctic Region. Proc. Acad. Nat. Sci. Philadelphia 18:300–315.

———. 1868. Observations on some specimens of Vertebrata presented by Wm. M. Gabb, of San Francisco, which were procured by him in western Nevada and the northern part of Lower California. Proc. Acad. Nat. Sci. Philadelphia 20:2.

———. 1869 [1868]. Sixth Contribution to the herpetology of tropical America. Proc. Acad. Nat. Sci. Philadelphia 20:305–313.

———. 1871. Ninth contribution to the herpetology of tropical America. Proc. Acad. Nat. Sci. Philadelphia 23:200–223.

———. 1876. On the Batrachia and Reptilia of Costa Rica. J. Acad. Nat. Sci. Philadelphia ,ser. 2, 8:93–154.

———. 1880. On the zoological position in Texas. U.S. Natl. Mus. Bull. 17:1–51.

———. 1883. Notes on the geographical distribution of Batrachia and Reptilia in western North America. Proc. Acad. Nat. Sci. Philadelphia 35:10–35.

———. 1886 [1885]. Thirteenth contribution to the herpetology of tropical America. Proc. Am. Phil. Soc. 23:271–287.

———. 1888. On the snakes of Florida. Proc. U.S. Natl. Mus. 11:381–401.

———. 1889. On the *Eutaenia* of southeastern Indiana. Proc. U.S. Natl. Mus. 11:399–401.

———. 1892a. A new species of *Eutaenia* from western Pennsylvania. Am. Nat. 26:964–965.

———. 1892b. A critical review of the characters and variations of snakes of North America. Proc. U.S. Natl. Mus. 14:589–694.

———. 1893. The color variation of the milk snake. Am. Nat. 27:1066–1071.

———. 1895. On some new North American snakes. Am. Nat. 29:676–680.

———. 1896. On a new *Glauconia* from New Mexico. Am. Nat. 30:753.

———. 1900. The crocodilians, lizards, and snakes of North America. Ann. Rept. U.S. Natl. Mus. 1898, 153–1294.

Corgan, J. X. 1976. Vertebrate fossils of Tennessee. Tennessee Div. Geol. Bull. 77:1–100.

Corgan, J. X., and E. Breitburg. 1996. Tennessee's prehistoric vertebrates. Tennessee Div. Geol. Bull. 84:1–170.

Cornett, J. W. 1982. *Masticophis lateralis* (California striped racer). Food. Herpetol. Rev. 13:96.

Costanzo, J. P. 1985. The bioenergetics of hibernation in the eastern garter snake, *Thamnophis sirtalis sirtalis.* Physiol. Zool. 58:682.692.

——. 1986. Influences of hibernaculum microenvironment on the winter life history of the garter snake (*Thamnophis sirtalis*). Ohio J. Sci. 86:199–204.

——. 1989a. A physiological basis for prolonged submergence in hibernating garter snakes *Thamnophis sirtalis*: Evidence for an energy-sparing adaptation. Physiol. Zool. 62:580–592.

——. 1989b. Conspecific scent trailing by garter snakes (*Thamnophis sirtalis*) during autumn. J. Chem. Ecol. 15:2531–2538.

——. 1989c. Effects of humidity, temperature, and submergence behavior on survivorship and energy use in hibernating garter snakes, *Thamnophis sirtalis*. Can. J. Zool. 67:2486–2492.

Costanzo, J. P., and D. L. Claussen. 1988. Natural freeze tolerance in a reptile. Cryo-Lett. 9:380–385.

Costanzo, J. P., D. L. Claussen, and R. E. Lee. 1990. Adaptations to cold in eastern garter snakes (*Thamnophis sirtalis*): Critical thermal minima, supercooling, and freeze tolerance. Cryobiology 26:679–680.

Cottam, C., W. C. Glazener, and G. G. Raun. 1959. Notes on food of moccasins and rattlesnakes from the Welder Wildlife Refuge, Sinton, Texas. Welder Wildl. Found. Contr. 45:1–12.

Coues, E. 1875. Synopsis of the reptiles and batrachians of Arizona, 585–663. In: Report upon United States geographical surveys west of the one hundredth meridian (Wheeler Report). Vol. 5. Zoology. Washington, D.C.: U.S. Government Printing Office.

Coulson, D. P., and J. G. Peluch. 1984. *Thamnophis butleri* new to Wellington County. Ontario Field Biol.38:44.

Cowles, R. B. 1938. Unusual defense postures assumed by rattlesnakes. Copeia 1938:13–16.

——. 1941a. Evidence of venom in *Hypsiglena ochrorhynchus*. Copeia 1941:4–6.

——. 1941b. Observations on the winter activities of desert reptiles. Ecology 22:125–140.

——. 1945. Some of the activities of the sidewinder. Copeia 1945:220–222.

Cowles, R. B., and C. M. Bogert. 1935. Observations on the California lyre snake, *Trimorphodon vandenburghi* Klauber, with notes on the effectiveness of its venom. Copeia 1935:80–85.

——. 1944. A preliminary study of the thermal requirements of desert reptiles. Bull. Am. Mus. Nat. Hist. 83:261–296.

Cowles, R. B., and R.L. Phelan. 1958. Olfaction in rattlesnakes. Copeia 1958:77–83.

Cox, T. M. 1986. More on the bird-eating activities of the black rat snake, *Elaphe obsoleta obsoleta* (Say). Notes From NOAH 14(1): 18–19.

Cranston, T. 1989a. Natural history and captive husbandry of the western green rat snake. Vivarium 2(1): 8–11, 23.

——. 1989b. Captive propagation and husbandry of the western green rat snake (*Senticolis triaspis intermedia*): The untold story, 81–85. In: R. Gowen (ed.), Captive propagation and husbandry of reptiles and amphibians. Proceedings of the fourth Northern California Herpetological Society conference on captive propagation and husbandry of reptiles and amphibians.

——. 1991. Notes on the natural history, husbandry, and breeding of the gray-banded kingsnake (*Lampropeltis alterna*). Vivarium 3(2): 7–10.

——. 1992. The natural history and captive husbandry of the Trans-Pecos rat snake (*Bogertophis subocularis*). Vivarium 4(5): 18–21.

——. 1994. Natural history of the Sierra Mountain kingsnake (*Lampropeltis zonata multicincta*). Vivarium 6(3): 38–47.

Crews, D. 1980. Studies in squamate sexuality. Bioscience 30:835–838.

——. 1983. Alternative reproductive tactics in reptiles. Bioscience 33:562–566.

——. 1991. Trans-seasonal action of androgen in the control of spring courtship behavior in male red-sided garter snakes. Proc. Natl. Acad. Sci. 88:3545–3548.

Crews, D., B. Camazine, M. Diamond, R. Mason, R. R. Tokarz, and W. R. Garstka. 1984. Hormonal independence of courtship behavior in the male garter snake. Horm. Behav. 18:29–41.

Crews, D., and W. R. Garstka. 1982. The ecological physiology of a garter snake. Sci. Am. 247(5): 159–168.

Crews, D., M. Grassman, W. R. Garstka, A. Halpert, and B. Camazine. 1987. Sex and seasonal differences in metabolism in the red-sided garter snake, *Thamnophis sirtalis parietalis*. Can. J. Zool. 65:2362–2368.

Criddle, S. 1937. Snakes from an ant hill. Copeia 1937:142.

Crimmins, M. L. 1927. Prevalence of poisonous snakes in the El Paso and San Antonio Districts in Texas. Bull. Antivenin Inst. Am. 1:23–24.

——. 1931. Rattlesnakes and their enemies in the Southwest. Bull. Antivenin Inst. Am. 5:46–47.

——. 1937. A case of *Oxybelis* poisoning in man. Copeia 1937:233.

Cromwell, W. R. 1982. Underground desert toads. Pacific Discovery 35:10–17.

Cross, C. L., and C. Marshall. 1998. *Agkistrodon piscivorus piscivorus* (eastern cottonmouth). Predation. Herpetol. Rev. 29:43.

Cross, J. K. 1970. The shovel-nosed snake *(Chionactis occipitalis)* in Baja California. Herpetologica 26:134–140.

———. 1979. Multivariate and univariate character geography in *Chionactis* (Reptilia: Serpentes). Ph.D. Dissertation, University of Arizona, Tempe.

Cruz, E., S. Gibson, K. Kandler, G. Sanchez, and D. Chiszar. 1987. Strike-induced chemosensory searching in rattlesnakes: A rodent specialist *(Crotalis viridis)* differs from a lizard specialist *(Crotalus pricei)*. Bull Psychon. Soc. 25:136–138.

Cunningham, G. R., S. M. Hickey, and C. M. Gowen. 1996. *Crotalus viridis viridis* (prairie rattlesnake). Behavior. Herpetol. Rev. 27:24.

Cunningham, J. D. 1955. Arboreal habits of certain reptiles and amphibians in southern California. Herpetologica 11:217–220.

———. 1959. Reproduction and food of some California snakes. Herpetologica 15:17–19.

———. 1966a. Additional observations on the body temperatures of reptiles. Herpetologica 22:184–189.

———. 1966b. Observations on the taxonomy and natural history of the rubber boa, *Charina bottae*. Southwest. Nat. 11:298–299.

Curtis, L. 1949. The snakes of Dallas County, Texas. Field and Lab. (So. Methodist Univ.) 17:1–13.

———. 1952. Cannibalism in the Texas coral snake. Herpetologica 8:27.

Czaplicki, J. 1975. Habituation of the chemically elicited prey-attack response in the diamond-backed water snake, *Natrix rhombifera rhombifera*. Herpetologica 31:403–409.

Czaplicki, J., and R. H. Porter. 1974. Visual cues mediating the selection of goldfish *(Carassius auratus)* by two species of Natrix. J. Herpetol. 8:129–134.

Dalrymple, G. H. 1994. Non-indigenous amphibians and reptiles in Florida, 67–78. In: D. C. Schmitz, and T. C. Brown (eds.), An assessment of invasive non-indigenous species in Florida's public lands. Tech. Rep. Florida Dept. Environ. Protect. TSS-94-100.

Dalrymple, G. H., F. S. Bernardino, Jr., T. M. Steiner, and R. J. Nodell. 1991. Patterns of species diversity of snake community assemblages, with data on two Everglades snake assemblages. Copeia 1991:517–521.

Dalrymple, G. H., and N. G. Reichenbach. 1981. Interactions between the prairie garter snake *(Thamnophis radix)* and common garter snake *(T. sirtalis)* in Killdeer Plains, Wyandot County, Ohio. Ohio Biol. Surv. Biol. Notes 14:244–250.

———. 1984. Management of an endangered species of snake in Ohio, U.S.A. Biol. Conserv. 30:195–200.

Dalrymple, G. H., T. M. Steiner, R. J. Nodell, and F. S.

Bernardino, Jr. 1991. Seasonal activity of the snakes of Long Pine Key, Everglades National Park. Copeia 1991:294–302.

Daniel, J. C. 1983. The book of Indian reptiles. Bombay Nat. Hist. Soc.

Darling, D. 1947. Northwestern herpetology contributions. Herpetologica 4:28.

Darlington, P. J., Jr. 1957. Zoogeography: The geographical distribution of animals. New York: John Wiley and Sons

Dart, R. C., J. T. McNally, D. W. Spaite, and R. Gustafson. 1992. The sequelae of pitviper poisoning in the United States, 395–404. In: J. A. Campbell, and E. D. Brodie, Jr. (eds.), Biology of the pitvipers. Tyler, Texas: Selva.

Dathe, F., and K. Dedekind. 1985. Pflege und Zucht von Bairds Erdnattern *(Elaphe obsoleta bairdi* Yarrow, 1880) im Tierpark Berlin. Milu (Berlin) 6:11–17.

Daudin, F. M. 1801–1803. Historie naturelle, générale et particuliére des reptiles. 7 vols. Paris: F. Dufart.

Davis, D. D. 1936. Courtship and mating behavior in snakes. Field Mus. Nat. Hist. Zool. Ser. 20:257–290.

———. 1946. Observations on the burrowing behavior of the hog-nosed snake. Copeia 1946:75–78.

———. 1948. Flash display of aposematic colors in *Farancia* and other snakes. Copeia 1948:208–211.

Davis, W. B. 1951. Food of the black-banded snake, *Coniophanes imperialis imperialis* Baird. Copeia 1951:314.

Davis, W. F. 1969. Robin kills snake. Wilson Bull. 81:470–471.

Davison, W. B., and E. Bollinger. 2000. Predation rates on real and artificial nests of grassland birds. Auk 117:147–153.

Dean, B. 1938. Note on the sea-snakes, *Pelamis platurus* (Linnaeus). Science (New York) 88:144–145.

Deckert, R. F. 1918. A list of reptiles from Jacksonville, Florida. Copeia 1918(54): 30–33.

Degenhardt, W. G. 1986. The discovery of *Aponomma elaphensis* larvae (Acarina: Ixodidae) on *Elaphe subocularis* (Reptilia: Colubridae). Southwest. Nat. 31:111.

Degenhardt, W. G., T. L. Brown, and D. A. Easterla. 1976. The taxonomic status of *Tantilla cucullata* and *Tantilla diabola*. Texas J. Sci. 27:225–234.

Degenhardt, W. G., and P. B. Degenhardt. 1965. The host-parasite relationship between *Elaphe subocularis* (Reptilia: Colubridae) and *Aponomma* elaphensis (Acarina: Ixodidae). Southwest. Nat. 10:167–178.

Degenhardt, W. G., C. W. Painter, and A. H. Price. 1996. Amphibians and reptiles of New Mexico. Albuquerque: University of New Mexico Press.

Delgadillo Espinosa, J., E. Godinez Cano, F. Correa Sanchez, and A. Gonzalez Ruiz. 1999. *Crotalus willardi silus* (ridge-nosed rattlesnake). Reproduction. Herpetol. Rev. 30:168–168.

De Lisle, H. F. 1982. Venomous colubrid snakes. Bull. Chicago Herpetol. Soc. 17:1–17.

Denman, N. S., and I. S. Lapper. 1964. The herpetology of Mont St. Hilairie, Rouville County, Quebec, Canada. Herpetologica 20:25–30.

Densmore, L. D., III, F. L. Rose, and S. J. Kain. 1992. Mitochondrial DNA evolution and speciation in water snakes (genus *Nerodia*) with special reference to *Nerodia harteri*. Herpetologica 48:60–68.

de Porben-Platón, A., and R. C. Feuer. 1975. Sexual precocity and growth rate in a male *Constrictor constrictor imperator*. Bull. Philadelphia Herpetol. Soc. 23:9–12.

de Queiroz, A. 1984. Effects of prey type on the prey-handling behavior of the bullsnake, *Pituophis melanoleucus*. J. Herpetol. 18:333–336.

de Queiroz, A., and R. Lawson. 1994. Phylogenetic relationships of the garter snakes based on DNA sequence and allozyme variation. Biol. J. Linn. Soc. 53:209–229.

de Rageot, R. 1992. Observations on the mammals of Mackay Island National Wildlife Refuge, Virginia and North Carolina. Banisteria 1:11–13.

Dessauer, H. C. 1967. Molecular approach to the taxonomy of colubrid snakes. Herpetologica 23:148–155.

Dessauer, H. C., J. E. Cadle, and R. Lawson. 1987. Patterns of snake evolution suggested by their proteins. Fieldiana: Zool. 34:1–34.

Dessauer, H. C., and F. H. Pough. 1975. Geographic variation of blood proteins and the systematics of kingsnakes *(Lampropeltis getulus)*. Comp. Biochem. Physiol. 50B:9–12.

Devine, M. C. 1975. Copulatory plugs in snakes: Enforced chastity. Science (New York) 187:844–845.

———. 1977. Copulatory plugs, restricted mating opportunities and reproductive competition among male garter snakes. Nature (London) 267:345–346.

Dial, B. E. 1965. Pattern and coloration in juveniles of two West Texas *Elaphe*. Herpetologica 21:75–78.

Dial, B. E., P. J. Weldon, and B. Curtis. 1989. Chemosensory identification of snake predators *(Phyllorhynchus descurtatus)* by banded geckos *(Coleonyx variegatus)*. J. Herpetol. 23:224–229.

Dibble, C. 2000. [Letter to J. Kevin Bowler]. Herpetology 30(23): 9–10.

Dickman, J. D., J. S. Colton, D. Chiszar, and C. A. Colton. 1987. Trigeminal responses to thermal stimulation of the oral cavity in rattlesnakes *(Crotalus viridis)* before and after bilateral anesthetization of the facial pit organs. Brain Res. 400:365–370.

Dickson, J. D. 1948. Observations on the feeding habits of the scarlet snake. Copeia 1948:216–217.

Diemer, J. E., and D. W. Speake. 1983. The distribution of the eastern indigo snake, *Drymarchon corais couperi* in Georgia. J. Herpetol. 17:256–264.

Diener, R. A. 1957a. A western hognose eats a collard lizard. Herpetologica 13:122.

———. 1957b. An ecological study of the plain-bellied water snake. Herpetologica 13:203–211.

———. 1961. Notes on the bite of the broadbanded copperhead, *Ancistrodon contortrix laticinctus* Gloyd and Conant. Herpetologica 17:143–144.

Dill, C. D. 1972. Reptilian core temperatures: Variation within individuals. Copeia 1972:577–579.

Diller, L. V. 1990. A field observation on the feeding behavior of *Crotalus viridis lutosus*. J. Herpetol. 24:95–97.

Diller, L. V., and D. R. Johnson. 1988. Food habits, consumption rates, and predation rates of western rattlesnakes and gopher snakes in southwestern Idaho. Herpetologica 44:228–233.

Diller, L. V., and R. L. Wallace. 1981. Additional distribution records and abundance of three species of snakes in southwestern Idaho. Great Basin Nat. 41:154–157.

———. 1984. Reproductive biology of the Northern Pacific rattlesnake *(Crotalus viridis oreganus)* in northern Idaho. Herpetologica 40:182–193.

———. 1986. Aspects of the life history and ecology of the desert night snake, *Hypsiglena torquata deserticola*: Colubridae, in southwestern Idaho. Southwest. Nat. 31:55–64.

———. 1996. Comparative ecology of two snake species *(Crotalus viridis* and *Pituophis melanoleucus)* in southwestern Idaho. Herpetologica 52:343–360.

Ditmars, R. L. 1931a. The reptile book. Garden City, New York: Doubleday, Doron and Co.

———. 1931b. Snakes of the world. New York: McMillan.

———. 1936. The reptiles of North America. Garden City, New York: Doubleday, Doran and Co.

———. 1939. A field book of North American snakes. Garden City, New York: Doubleday, Doran and Co.

Dix, M. W. 1968. Snake food preference: Innate intraspecific geographic variation. Science (New York) 159:1478–1479.

Dixon, J. R. 1960. A new name for the snake, *Arizona elegans arizonae*. Southwest. Nat. 5:226.

———. 1967. Amphibians and reptiles of Los Angeles County, California. Los Angeles Co. Mus. Nat. Hist. Sci. Ser. 23 10:1–64.

———. 1987. Amphibians and reptiles of Texas with keys, taxonomic synopses, bibliography, and distribution maps. College Station: Texas A&M University Press.

Dixon, J. R., and R. H. Dean. 1986. Status of the southern populations of the night snake (*Hypsiglena*: Colubridae) exclusive of California and Baja California. Southwest. Nat. 31:307–318.

Dixon, J. R., and R. R. Fleet. 1976. *Arizona, A. elegans.* Cat. Am. Amphib. Rept. 179:1–4.

Dixon, J. R., R. K. Vaughan, and L. D. Wilson. 2000. The taxonomy of *Tantilla rubra* and allied taxa (Serpentes: Colubridae). Southwest. Nat. 45:141–153.

Dobie, J. L., C. J. Leary, and J. A. Holman. 1996. A Pleistocene indigo snake, *Drymarchon corais*, from Bogue Chitto Creek, Dallas County, Alabama. J. Alabama Acad. Sci. 67:1–4.

Dodd, C. K., Jr. 1993. Population structure, body mass, activity, and orientation of an aquatic snake (*Seminatrix pygaea*) during a drought. Can. J. Zool. 71:1281–1288.

Dodd, C. K., Jr., and R. Franz. 1995. Seasonal abundance and habitat use of selected snakes trapped in xeric and mesic communities of north-central Florida. Bull. Florida Mus. Nat. Hist. 38:43–67.

Dodge, C. H., and G. E. Folk, Jr. 1960. A case of rattlesnake poisoning in Iowa with a description of early symptoms. Proc. Iowa Acad. Sci. 67:622–624.

Dolley, J. S. 1939. An anomalous pregnancy in the copperhead. Copeia 1939:170.

Donahue, M. W. 1995. *Storeria dekayi dekayi* (northern brown snake). Catesbeiana 15:50.

Dongarra, T. 1998. A case for *Lampropeltis triangulum temporalis*: The coastal milk snake. Reptile & Amphibian Mag. 52:64–67.

Doody, J. S., R. J. Brauman, J. E. Young, and R. A. Fiorillo. 1996. *Farancia abacura* (mud snake). Death feigning. Herpetol. Rev. 27:82–83.

Dorcas, M. E. 1992. Relationships among montane populations of *Crotalus lepidus* and *Crotalus triseriatus*, 71–87. In: J. A. Campbell and E. D. Brodie, Jr. (eds.), Biology of the pit vipers. Tyler, Texas: Selva.

Dorcas, M. E., J. W. Gibbons, and H. G. Dowling. 1998. *Seminatrix, S. pygaea.* Cat. Am. Amphib. Rept. 679:1–5.

Dorcas, M. E., and C. R. Peterson. 1997. Head-body temperature differences in free-ranging rubber boas. J. Herpetol. 31:87–93.

———. 1998. Daily body temperature variation in free-ranging rubber boas. Herpetologica 54:88–103.

Dorcas, M. E., C. R. Peterson, and M. E. T. Flint. 1997. The thermal biology of digestion in rubber boas (*Charina bottae*): Physiology, behavior, and environmental constraints. Physiol. Zool. 70:292–300.

Doughty, P. 1994. Critical thermal minima of garter

snakes (*Thamnophis*) depend on species and body size. Copeia 1994:537–540.

Dove, L. B., D. A. Baeyens, and M. V. Plummer. 1982. Evaporative water loss in *Opheodrys aestivus* (Colubridae). Southwest. Nat. 27:228–230.

Dowling, H. G. 1950. Studies of the black swamp snake, *Seminatrix pygaea* (Cope), with descriptions of two new subspecies. Misc. Publ. Mus. Zool. Univ. Michigan 76:1–38.

———. 1952. A taxonomic study of the rat snakes, genus *Elaphe* Fitzinger. IV. A check of American forms. Occ. Pap. Mus. Zool. Univ. Michigan 541:1–12.

———. 1957a. A taxonomic study of the ratsnakes, genus *Elaphe* Fitzinger. V. The *rosalie* section. Occ. Pap. Mus. Zool. Univ. Michigan 583:1–22.

———. 1957b. A review of the amphibians and reptiles of Arkansas. Univ. Arkansas Mus. Occ. Pap. 3:1–51.

———. 1958a. A taxonomic study of the ratsnakes. VI. Validation of the genera *Gonysoma* Wagler and *Elaphe* Fitzinger. Copeia 1958:29–40.

———. 1958b. Pleistocene snakes of the Ozark Plateau. Am. Mus. Novitates 1882:1–9.

———. 1960. A taxonomic study of ratsnakes, genus *Elaphe* Fitzinger. VII. The *triaspis* section. Zoologica (New York) 45:53–80.

———. 1975. Yearbook of herpetology. New York: HISS.

Dowling, H. G., and I. Fries. 1987. A taxonomic study of the ratsnakes. VIII. A proposed new genus for *Elaphe triaspis* (Cope). Herpetologica 43:200–207.

Dowling, H. G., C. A. Hass, S. B. Hedges, and R. Highton. 1996. Snake relationships revealed by slow-moving proteins: A preliminary survey. J. Zool. (London) 240:1–28.

Dowling, H. G., R. Highton, G. C. Maha, and L. R. Maxson. 1983. Biochemical evaluation of colubrid snake phylogeny. J. Zool. (London) 201:309–329.

Dowling, H. G., and L. R. Maxson. 1990. Genetic and taxonomic relations of the short-tailed snakes, genus *Stilosoma*. J. Zool. (London) 221:77–85.

Dowling, H. G., and R. M. Price. 1988. A proposed new genus for *Elaphe subocularis* and *Elaphe rosaliae*. Snake 20:52–63.

Drda, W. J. 1968. A study of snakes wintering in a small cave. J. Herpetol. 1:64–70.

Drummond, H. 1979. Stimulus control of amphibious predation in the northern water snake (*Nerodia s. sipedon*). Zeit. Tierpsychol. 50:18–44.

———. 1983. Aquatic foraging in garter snakes: A comparison of specialists and generalists. Behaviour 86:1–30.

———. 1985. The role of vision in the predatory behaviour of natricine snakes. Anim. Behav. 33:206–215.

Drummond, H., and G. M. Burghardt. 1983. Geographic variation in the foraging behavior of the garter snake, *Thamnophis elegans*. Behav. Ecol. Sociobiol. 12:43–48.

Duellman, W. E. 1948. *Thamnophis s. sauritus* eats own young. Herpetologica 4:210.

———. 1955. Notes on reptiles and amphibians from Arizona. Occ. Pap. Mus. Zool. Univ. Michigan 569:1–14.

———. 1958a. A monographic study of the colubrid snake genus *Leptodeira*. Bull. Am. Mus. Nat. Hist. 114:1–152.

———. 1958b. A preliminary analysis of the herpetofauna of Colima, Mexico. Occ. Pap. Mus. Zool. Univ. Michigan 589:1–22.

———. 1961. The amphibians and reptiles of Michoacán, México. Univ. Kansas Publ. Mus. Nat. Hist. 15(1): 1–148.

———. 1963. Amphibians and reptiles of the rainforests of southern El Petén, Guatemala. Univ. Kansas Publ. Mus. Nat. Hist. 15(1): 205–249.

Duellman, W. E., and A. Schwartz. 1958. Amphibians and reptiles of southern Florida. Bull. Florida St. Mus. Biol. Sci. 3:181–324.

Dugès, A. 1865. Du *Liophis jani*. Mem. Acad. Sci. Lett. Montpellier 6:32–33.

Duméril, A. M. C., G. Bibron, and A. Duméril. 1854. Erpétologie générale ou histoire naturelle complète des reptiles, vol. 7, part 2. Paris: Librairie Encyclopedique de Roret.

Dunbar, G. L. 1979. Effects of early feeding experience on chemical preference of the northern water snake, *Natrix s. sipedon* (Reptilia, Serpentes, Colubridae). J. Herpetol. 13:165–169.

Duncan, R. B. 1992. *Lampropeltis pyromelana* (Sonoran mountain kingsnake). Predation. Herpetol. Rev. 23:81.

Dundee, H. A. 1950. Additional records of *Hypsiglena* from Oklahoma, with notes on the behavior and the eggs. Herpetologica 6:28–30.

Dundee, H. A., and M. C. Miller. 1968. Aggregative behavior and habitat conditioning by the prairie ringneck snake, *Diadophis punctatus arnyi*. Tulane Stud. Zool. Bot. 15:41–58.

Dundee, H. A., and D. A. Rossman. 1989. The amphibians and reptiles of Louisiana. Baton Rouge: Louisiana State University Press.

Dunlap, K. D., and J. W. Lang. 1990. Offspring sex ratio varies with maternal size in the common garter snake, *Thamnophis sirtalis*. Copeia 1990:568–570.

Dunn, E. R. 1949. Relative abundance of some Panamanian snakes. Ecology 30:39–57.

Dunn, E. R., and G. C. Wood. 1939. Notes on eastern snakes of the genus *Coluber*. Notulae Naturae (Acad. Nat. Sci. Philadelphia) 5:1–4.

Dunson, M. K., and W. A. Dunson. 1975. The relation between plasma Na concentration and salt gland Na-K ATPase content in the diamondback terrapin and yellow-bellied sea snake. J. Comp. Physiol. 101:89–97.

Dunson, W. A. 1971. The sea snakes are coming. Nat. Hist. 80:52–60.

———, ed. 1975. The biology of sea snakes. Baltimore, Maryland: University Park Press.

———. 1978. Role of skin in sodium and water exchange of aquatic snakes placed in seawater. Am. J. Physiol. 235:R151–R159.

———. 1979. Occurrence of partially striped forms of the mangrove snake *Nerodia fasciata compressicauda* Kennicott and comments on the status of *N. f. taeniata* Cope. Florida Sci. 49:94–102.

———. 1980. The relation of sodium and water balance to survival in sea water of estuarine and freshwater races of the snakes *Nerodia fasciata, N. sipedon*, and *N. vallida*. Copeia 1980:268–280.

———. 1982. Salinity relations of crocodiles in Florida Bay. Copeia 1982:374–385.

Dunson, W. A., and G. W. Ehlert. 1971. Effects of temperature, salinity, and surface water flow on distribution of the sea snake *Pelamis*. Limnol. Oceangr. 16:845–853.

Dunson, W. A., and J. Freda. 1985. Water permeability of the skin of the amphibious snake, *Agkistrodon piscivorus*. J. Herpetol. 19:93–98.

Dunson, W. A., R. K. Packer, and M. K. Dunson. 1971. Sea snakes: An unusual salt gland under the tongue. Science (New York) 173:437–441.

Dunson, W. A., and G. D. Robinson. 1976. Sea snake skin: Permeable to water but not to sodium. J. Comp. Physiol. 108:303–311.

Dunson, W. A., and G. D. Stokes. 1983. Asymmetrical diffusion of sodium and water through the skin of sea snakes. Physiol. Zool. 56:106–111.

Durner, G. M., and J. E. Gates. 1993. Spatial ecology of black rat snakes on Remmington Farms, Maryland. J. Wildl. Mgt. 57:812–826.

Duvall, D. 1986. Shake, rattle, and roll. Nat. Hist. 95:66–73.

Duvall, D., S. J. Arnold, and G. W. Schuett. 1992. Pitviper mating systems: Ecological potential, sexual selection, and microevolution, 321–336. In: J. A. Campbell and E. D. Brodie, Jr. (eds.), Biology of the pitvipers. Tyler, Texas: Selva.

Duvall, D., and S. J. Beaupre. 1998. Sexual strategy and size dimorphism in rattlesnakes: Integrating proximate and ultimate causation. Am. Zool. 38:152–165.

Duvall, D., D. Chiszar, W. K. Hayes, J. K. Leonhardt, and M. J. Goode. 1990. Chemical and behavioral ecology of foraging in prairie rattlesnakes *(Crotalus viridis viridis)*. J. Chem. Ecol. 16:87–101.

Duvall, D., M. J. Goode, W. K. Hayes, J. K. Leonhardt, and D. G. Brown. 1990. Prairie rattlesnake vernal migration: Field experimental analyses and survival value. Natl. Geogr. Res. 6:457–469.

Duvall, D., M. B. King, and K. J. Gutzwiller. 1985. Behavioral ecology and ethology of the prairie rattlesnake. Natl. Geogr. Res. 1:80–111.

Duvall, D., M. B. King, and R. Miller. 1983. Rattler. Wyoming Wild Life 47(10): 26–30.

Duvall, D., and G. W. Schuett. 1997. Straight-line movement and competitive mate searching in prairie rattlesnakes, *Crotalus viridis viridis*. Anim. Behav. 54:329–334.

Duvall, D., K. M. Scudder, and D. Chiszar. 1980. Rattlesnake predatory behavior: Mediation of prey discrimination and release of swallowing cues arising from envenomated mice. Anim. Behav. 28:674–683.

Dwyer, C. M., and H. Kaiser. 1997. Relationship between skull form and prey selection in the thamnophiine snake genera *Nerodia* and *Regina*. J. Herpetol. 31:463–475.

Dymond, J. R., and F. E. J. Fry. 1932. Notes on the breeding habits of the green snake *(Liopeltis vernalis)*. Copeia 1932:102.

Dyrkacz, S. 1977. The natural history of the eastern milk snake (Reptilia, Serpentes, Colubridae) in a disturbed environment. J. Herpetol. 11:155–159.

Dyrkacz, S., and M. J. Corn. 1974. Response of naive, neonate bullsnakes to water extracts of potential prey items. Herpetol. Rev. 5:74.

Easterla, D. A. 1967. Black rat snake preys upon gray *Myotis* and winter observations of red bats. Am. Midl. Nat. 77:527–528.

———. 1975a. Reproduction and ecological observations on *Tantilla rubra cucullata* from Big Bend National Park, Texas (Serpentes: Colubridae). Herpetologica 31:234–236.

———. 1975b. Giant desert centipede preys upon snake. Southwest. Nat. 20:411.

Eberle, W. G. 1972. Comparative chromosomal morphology of the New World Natricine snake genera *Natrix* and *Regina*. Herpetologica 28:98–105.

Eckle, W. L., and T. G. Grubb. 1986. Prey remains from golden eagle nests in central Arizona. Western Birds 17:87–89.

Edgren, R. A., Jr. 1948. Notes on a litter of young timber rattlesnakes. Copeia 1948:132.

———. 1952. A synopsis of the snakes of the genus *Heterodon*, with the diagnosis of a new race of *Heterodon*

nasicus Baird and Girard. Chicago Acad Sci. Nat. Hist. Misc. 112:1–4.

———. 1953. Copulatory adjustment in snakes and its evolutionary implication. Copeia 1953:162–164.

———. 1955. The natural history of the hog-nosed snakes, genus *Heterodon*: A review. Herpetologica 11:105–117.

———. 2000. Kirtland's snake in Edison Park: An historical vignette. Bull. Chicago Herpetol. Soc. 35(6): 141.

Ehrlich, P. R., and J. H. Camin. 1960. Natural selection in Middle Island water snakes *(Natrix sipedon* L.). Evolution 14:136.

Eichholz, M. W., and W. D. Koenig. 1992. Gopher snake attraction to bird's nests. Southwest. Nat. 37:293–298.

Elick, G. E., and J. A. Sealander. 1972. Comparative water loss in relation to habitat selection in small colubrid snakes. Am. Midl. Nat. 88:429–439.

Ellis, D. E., and S. Brunson. 1993. "Tool" use by the red-tailed hawk *(Buteo jamaicensis)*. J. Raptor Res. 27:128.

Elvin, D. W. 1963. Variation and distribution of the shovel-nosed snakes *(Chionactis occipitalis)* in the northern Mojave Desert, California and Nevada. Herpetologica 19:73–76.

Ely, E. 1997. *Tantilla planiceps* (California black-headed snake). Predation. Herpetol. Rev. 28:154–155.

Emmerson, F. H. 1982. Western diamondback rattlesnake in southern Nevada: A correction and comments. Great Basin Nat. 42:350.

Emsley, M. 1977. Snakes of Trinidad and Tobago. Bull. Maryland Herpetol. Soc. 13:201–304.

Enge, K. M. 1998. *Amphiuma means* (two-toed amphiuma). Diet. Herpetol. Rev. 29:162.

Enge, K. M., and J. D. Sullivan. 2000. Seasonal activity of the scarlet snake, *Cemophora coccinea*, in Florida. Herpetol. Rev. 31:82–84.

Engeman, R. M., and J. J. Delutes, III. 1994. *Pituophis melanoleucus deserticola* (Great Basin gopher snake). Behavior. Herpetol. Rev. 25:125.

Englstoft, C., and K. E. Ovaska. 2000. Artificial cover-objects as a method for sampling snakes *(Contia tenuis* and *Thamnophis* spp.) in British Columbia. Northwest. Nat. 81:35–43.

Englstoft, C., K. E. Ovaska, and N. Honkanen. 1999. The harmonic direction finder: A new method for tracking movements of small snakes. Herpetol. Rev. 30:84–87.

Enkerlin-Hoeflich, E. C., M. J. Whiting, and L. Coronado-Limon. 1993. Attempted predation on chicks of the threatened green-cheeked Amazon parrot by an indigo snake. Snake 25:141–143.

Ernst, C. H. 1964. Sexual dimorphism in American *Agkistrodon* fang lengths. Herpetologica 20:214.

————. 1965. Fang length comparisons of American *Agkistrodon*. Trans. Kentucky Acad. Sci. 26:12–18.

————. 1974. Taxonomic status of the red-bellied snake, *Storeria occipitomaculata*, in Minnesota. J. Herpetol. 8:347–350.

————. 1982. A study of fangs of snakes belonging to the *Agkistrodon*-complex. J. Herpetol. 16:72–80.

————. 1992. Venomous reptiles of North America. Washington, D.C.: Smithsonian Institution Press.

————. 2002. *Storeria occipitomaculata*. Cat. Am. Amphib. Rept. 759:1–8.

Ernst, C. H., and R. W. Barbour. 1989. Snakes of eastern North America. Fairfax, Virginia: George Mason University Press.

Ernst, C. H., S. C. Belfit, S. W. Sekscienski, and A. F. Laemmerzahl. 1997. The amphibians and reptiles of Ft. Belvoir and Northern Virginia. Bull. Maryland Herpetol. Soc. 33:1–62.

Ernst, C. H., and C. W. Brown. 2000. *Ramphotyphlops braminus* (Brahminy blind snake): Florida. Herpetol. Rev. 31:256.

Ernst, C. H., and S. W. Gotte. 1986. Notes on the reproduction of the shortheaded garter snake, *Thamnophis brachystoma*. Bull. Maryland Herpetol. Soc. 22:6–9.

Ernst, C. H., S. W. Gotte, and J. E. Lovich. 1985. Reproduction in the mole kingsnake, *Lampropeltis calligaster rhombomaculata*. Bull. Maryland Herpetol. Soc. 21:16–22.

Ernst, C. H., and A. F. Lammerzahl. 1989. Eastern hognose snake eats spotted salamander. Bull. Maryland Herpetol. Soc. 25:25–26.

Ernst, C. H., and G. R. Zug. 1996. Snakes in question. Washington, D.C.: Smithsonian Institution Press.

Ernst, S. G. 1945. The food of the red-shouldered hawk in New York state. Auk 62:452–453.

————. 1962. Notes on the life history of the eastern ringneck snake. Turtox News 40:266–267.

Erwin, D. B. 1964. Some findings on newborn rubber boas, *Charina b. bottae*. Copeia 1964:222–223.

————. 1974. Taxonomic status of the southern rubber boa, *Charina bottae umbratica*. Copeia 1974:996–997.

Eshelman, R. E. 1975. Geology and paleontology of the early Pleistocene (late Blancan) White Rock fauna from north-central Kansas. Univ. Michigan Mus. Paleontol. Pap. 13:1–60.

Esponda, P., and J. M. Bedford. 1987. Post-testicular change in the reptile sperm surface with particular reference to the snake, *Natrix fasciata*. J. Exp. Zool. 241:123–132.

Essex, H. E. 1932. The physiologic action of the venom of the water moccasin *(Agkistrodon piscivorus)*. Bull. Antivenin Inst. Am. 5:81.

Evans, H. E., and R. M. Roecker. 1951. Notes on the herpetology of Ontario, Canada. Herpetologica 7:69–71.

Evans, P. D. 1942. A method of fishing used by water snakes. Chicago Nat. 5:53–55.

Even, E. 1995. The "multi-mammae mouse" as an ideal prey for *Lampropeltis pyromelana*. Litt. Serpent. Engl. Ed. 15:21–22.

Facemire, C. F., and S. D. Fretwell. 1980. Nest predation by the speckled king snake. Wilson Bull. 92:249–250.

Falck, H. S. 1940. Food of the eastern rock rattlesnake in captivity. Copeia 1940:135.

Fann, E. C. 1997. Population density and present habitat range of the western pygmy rattlesnake *(Sistrurus miliarius streckeri)* in Tennessee. Am. Zoo Aqua. Reg. Conf. Proc. 1997:34–35.

Farr, D. R. 1988. The ecology of garter snakes, *Thamnophis sirtalis* and *T. elegans* in southeastern British Columbia. Master's Thesis, University of Victoria, British Columbia.

Farr, D. R., and P. T. Gregory. 1991. Sources of variation in estimating litter characteristics of snakes. J. Herpetol. 25:261–267.

Farrell, T. M., P. G. May, and M. A. Pilgrim. 1995. Reproduction in the rattlesnake, *Sistrurus miliarius barbouri*, in central Florida. J. Herpetol. 29:21–27.

Fay, L. P. 1988. Late Wisconsinan Applachian herpetofaunas: Relative stability in the midst of change. Ann. Carnegie Mus. 57:189–220.

Feaver, P. E. 1976. A population study of the northern watersnake, *Natrix sipedon*, in southeastern Michigan. Herpetol. Rev. 7:81.

Feder, M. E., and S. J. Arnold. 1982. Anaerobic metabolism and behavior during predatory encounters between snakes *(Thamnophis elegans)* and salamanders *(Plethodon jordani)*. Oecologia (Berlin) 53:93–97.

Feldman, C. R., and J. A. Wilkinson. 2000a. *Rana mucosa* (mountain yellow-legged frog). Predation. Herpetol. Rev. 31:102.

————. 2000b. *Thamnophis sirtalis fitchi* (valley garter snake). Diet. Herpetol. Rev. 31:248.

Fendley, T. T. 1980. Incubating wood duck and hooded merganser hens killed by black rat snakes. Wilson Bull. 92:526–527.

Fenton, M. B., and L. E. Licht. 1990. Why rattle snake? J. Herpetol. 24:274–279.

Ferguson, D. E. 1963. Notes concerning the effects of heptachlor on certain poikilotherms. Copeia 1963:441–443.

Ferguson, J. H., and R. M. Thornton. 1984. Oxygen storage capacity and tolerance of submergence of a nonaquatic reptile and an aquatic reptile. Comp. Biochem. Physiol. 77A:183–187.

Fetterolf, P. M. 1979. Common garter snake predation on ring-billed gull chicks. Can. Field-Nat. 93:317–318.

Fiero, M. K., M. W. Seifert, T. J. Weaver, and C. A. Bonilla. 1972. Comparative study of juvenile and adult prairie rattlesnake (Crotalus viridis viridis) venoms. Toxicon 10:81–82.

Finch, D. M. 1981. Nest predation on Abert's towhees by coachwhips and roadrunners. Condor 83:389.

Finkler, M. S., and D. L. Claussen. 1999. Influence of temperature, body size, and inter-individual variation on forced and voluntary swimming and crawling speeds in Nerodia sipedon and Regina septemvittata. J. Herpetol. 33:62–71.

Finley, R. B., Jr., D. Chiszar, and H. M. Smith. 1994. Field observations of salivary digestion of rodent tissue by the wandering garter snake, Thamnophis elegans vagrans. Bull. Chicago Herpetol. Soc. 29:5–6.

Finneran, L. C. 1948. Reptiles at Branford County, Connecticut. Herpetologica 4:123–126.

———. 1949. A sexual aggregation of the garter snake Thamnophis butleri Cope. Copeia 1949:141–144.

Fischer, R. U., D. E. Scott, J. D. Congdon, and S. A. Busa. 1994. Mass dynamics during embryonic development and parental investment in cottonmouth neonates. J. Herpetol. 28:364–369.

Fischman, H. K., J. Mitra, and H. Dowling. 1972. Chromosome characteristics of 13 species in the order Serpentes. Mammal Chromosome Newsl. 13:72–73.

Fisher, C. B. 1973. Status of the flat-headed snake, Tantilla gracilis Baird and Girard, in Louisiana. J. Herpetol. 7:136–137.

Fitch, H. S. 1936. Amphibians and reptiles of the Rogue River Basin, Oregon. Am. Midl. Nat. 17:634–652.

———. 1940. A biogeographical study of the ordinoides artenkreis of garter snakes (genus Thamnophis). Univ. California Publ. Zool. 44:1–150.

———. 1941. The feeding habits of California garter snakes. California Fish Game 27:1–32.

———. 1949. Study of snake populations in central California. Am. Midl. Nat. 41:513–579.

———. 1956. Temperature responses in free-living amphibians and reptiles in northeastern Kansas. Univ. Kansas Publ. Mus. Nat. Hist. 8:417–476.

———. 1958. Home ranges, territories, and seasonal movements of vertebrates of the Natural History Reservation. Univ. Kansas Publ. Mus. Nat Hist. 11:63–326.

———. 1960a. Criteria for determining sex and breeding maturity in snakes. Herpetologica 16:49–51.

———. 1960b. Autecology of the copperhead. Univ. Kansas Publ. Mus. Nat. Hist. 13:85–288.

———. 1961. Longevity and age-size groups in some common snakes, 396–414. In: W.F. Blair (ed.), Vertebrate speciation. Austin: University of Texas Press.

———. 1963a. Natural history of the racer Coluber constrictor. Univ. Kansas Publ. Mus. Nat. Hist. 15:351–468.

———. 1963b. Natural history of the black rat snake (Elaphe o. obsoleta) in Kansas. Copeia 1963:649–658.

———. 1965. An ecological study of the garter snake Thamnophis sirtalis. Univ. Kansas Publ. Mus. Nat. Hist. 15:493–564.

———. 1970. Reproductive cycles in lizards and snakes. Univ. Kansas Mus. Nat. Hist. Misc. Publ. 52:1–247.

———. 1975. A demographic study of the ringneck snake (Diadophis punctatus) in Kansas. Univ. Kansas. Mus. Nat. Hist. Misc. Publ. 62:1–53.

———. 1978. A field study of the prairie kingsnake (Lampropeltis calligaster). Trans. Kansas Acad. Sci. 81:354–362.

———. 1980a. Remarks concerning certain western garter snakes of the Thamnophis elegans complex. Trans. Kansas Acad. Sci. 83:106–113.

———. 1980b. Thamnophis sirtalis. Cat. Am. Amphib. Rept. 270:1–4.

———. 1981. Sexual size differences in reptiles. Univ. Kansas Mus. Nat. Hist. Misc. Publ. 70:1–72.

———. 1982. Resources of a snake community in prairie-woodland habitat of northeastern Kansas, 93–97. In: N. J. Scott, Jr. (ed.), Herpetological communities. U.S. Fish Wildl. Serv. Wildl. Res. Rep. 13.

———. 1983a. Thamnophis elegans. Cat. Am. Amphib. Rept. 320:1–4.

———. 1984. Thamnophis couchii. Cat. Am. Amphib. Rept. 351:1–3.

———. 1985a. Variation in clutch and litter size in New World reptiles. Univ. Kansas Mus. Nat. Hist. Misc. Publ. 76:1–76.

———. 1985b. Observation on rattle size and demography of prairie rattlesnakes (Crotalus viridis) and timber rattlesnakes (Crotalus horridus) in Kansas. Occ. Pap. Mus. Nat. Hist. Univ. Kansas 118:1–11.

———. 1992. Methods of sampling snake populations and their relative success. Herpetol. Rev. 23:17–19.

———. 1993. Relative abundance of snakes in Kansas. Trans. Kansas Acad. Sci. 96:213–224.

———. 1998. The Sharon Springs Roundup and prairie rattlesnake demography. Trans. Kansas Acad. Sci. 101:101–113.

———. 1999. A Kansas snake community: Composition and changes over 50 years. Malabar, Florida: Krieger Publishing Co.

Fitch, H. S., W. S. Brown, and W. S. Parker. 1981. Coluber

mormon, a species distinct from *C. constrictor*. Trans. Kansas Acad. Sci. 84:196–203.

Fitch, H. S., and R. R. Fleet. 1970. Natural history of the milk snake *(Lampropeltis triangulum)* in northeastern Kansas. Herpetologica 26:387–396.

Fitch, H. S., and B. Glading. 1947. A field study of a rattlesnake population. California Fish Game 33:103–123.

Fitch, H. S., and T. P. Maslin. 1961. Occurrence of the garter snake, *Thamnophis sirtalis*, in the Great Plains and Rocky Mountains. Univ. Kansas Publ. Mus. Nat. Hist. 13:289–308.

Fitch, H. S., and G. R. Pisani. 1993. Life history traits of the western diamondback rattlesnake *(Crotalus atrox)* studied from roundup samples in Oklahoma. Occ. Pap. Mus. Nat. Hist. Univ. Kansas 156:1–24.

Fitch, H. S., and H. W. Shirer. 1971. A radiotelemetric study of spatial relationships in some common snakes. Copeia 1971:118–128.

Fitch, H. S., and H. Twining. 1946. Feeding habits of the Pacific rattlesnake. Copeia 1946:64–71.

Fitzinger, L. 1833. *Elaphe parreyssii*—Parreyss's *Elaphe*. In: J. Wagler (ed.), Descriptiones et icones Amphibiorum . Part 3. München, Stuttgart, Tübingen, Germany: J. G. Cotta'sche.

———. 1843. Systema reptilium. Fasciculus primus. Amblyglossae. Vienna: Vindobonae, Apud Braumüller et Seidel.

Fix, J. D., and S. A. Minton, Jr. 1976. Venom extraction and yields from the North American coral snake, *Micrurius fulvius*. Toxicon 14:143–145.

Flanigan, A. B. 1971. Predation on snakes by eastern bluebird and brown thrasher. Wilson Bull. 83:441.

Flank, L. 2000. Salt marsh snake. Rept. Amphib. Hobbyist 6(1): 44–48.

Fleet, R. R., and J. C. Kroll. 1978. Litter size and parturition behavior in *Sistrurus miliarius streckeri*. Herpetol. Rev. 9:11.

Fleharty, E. D. 1963. Oxygen consumption and Q_{10} for two species of garter snakes (genus *Thamnophis*). Trans. Kansas Acad. Sci. 66:482–487.

———. 1967. Comparative ecology of *Thamnophis elegans*, *T. crytopsis*, and *T. rufipunctatus* in New Mexico. Southwest. Nat. 12:207–229.

Fleishman, L. J. 1985. Cryptic movement in the vine snake *Oxybelis aeneus*, Copeia 1985:242–245.

Foekema, G. M. M. 1972. Ontwikkeling en voortplanting van *Boa constrictor* Linnaeus in een huiskamerterrarium. Lacerta 31:131–144.

Fogleman, B., W. Byrd, and E. Hanebrink. 1986. Observations of the male combat dance in the cottonmouth *(Agkistrodon piscivorus)*. Bull. Chicago Herpetol. Soc. 21:26–28.

Foley, G. W. 1971. Perennial communal nesting in the black racer *(Coluber constrictor)*. Herpetol. Rev. 3:41.

Fontenot, L. W., G. P. Noblet, and S. G. Platt. 1994. Rotenone hazards to amphibians and reptiles. Herpetol. Rev. 25:150–156.

Fontenot, L. W., G. P. Noblet, and S. G. Platt. 1996. A survey of herpetofauna inhabiting polychlorinated biphenyl contaminated and reference watersheds in Pickens County, South Carolina. J. Elisha Mitchell Sci. Soc. 112:20–30.

Fontenot, L. W., and S. G. Platt. 1993. Observations on crayfish predation by water snakes, *Nerodia* (Reptilia: Colubridae). Brimleyana 19:95–99.

———. 1996. *Regina septemvittata* (queen snake). Reproduction. Herpetol. Rev. 27:205.

Foote, R., and J. A. MacMahon. 1977. Electrophoretic studies on rattlesnake *(Crotalus and Sistrurus)* venom: Taxonomic implications. J. Biochem. Physiol. 57B:235–241.

Force, E. R. 1931. Habits and birth of young of the lined snake, *Tropidoclonion lineatum* (Hallowell). Copeia 1931:51–53.

———. 1935. A local study of the opisthoglyph snake *Tantilla gracilis* Baird and Girard. Pap. Michigan Acad. Sci., Arts, Lett. (1934) 20:645–659.

———. 1936a. Notes on the blind snake, *Leptotyphlops dulcis* (Baird and Girard) in northeastern Oklahoma. Proc. Oklahoma Acad. Sci. 16:24–26.

———. 1936b. The relation of the knobbed anal keels to age and sex in the lined snake *Tropidoclonion lineatum* (Hallowell). Pap. Michigan Acad. Sci., Arts, Lett. 21:613–617.

Ford, K. M., III. 1992. Herpetofauna of the Albert Ahrens local fauna (Pleistocene: Irvingtonian), Nebraska. Master's Thesis, Michigan State University, East Lansing.

Ford, N. B. 1978. Evidence for species specificity of pheromone trails in two sympatric garter snakes, *Thamnophis*. Herpetol. Rev. 9:10.

———. 1981. Seasonality of pheromone trailing behavior in two species of garter snake, *Thamnophis* (Colubridae). Southwest. Nat. 26:385–388.

———. 1982a. Species specificity of sex pheromone trails of sympatric and allopatric garter snakes *(Thamnophis)*. Copeia 1982:10–13.

———. 1982b. Courtship behavior of the queen snake, *Regina septemvittata*. Herpetol. Rev. 13:72.

Ford, N. B., and V. Cobb. 1992. Timing of courtship in two colubrid snakes of the southern United States. Copeia 1992:573–577.

Ford, N. B., V. Cobb, and W. W. Lamar. 1990. Reproductive data on snakes from northeastern Texas. Texas J. Sci. 42:355–368.

Ford, N. B., V. Cobb, and J. Stout. 1991. Species diversity and seasonal abundance of snakes in a mixed pine-hardwood forest in eastern Texas. Southwest. Nat. 36:171–177.

Ford, N. B., and D. Holland. 1990. The role of pheromones in the spacing behaviour of snakes, 465–472. In: D. W. McDonald, D. Müller-Schwarze, and S. E. Navynczuk (eds.), Chemical signals in vertebrates 5. New York: Oxford University Press.

Ford, N. B., and J. P. Karges. 1987. Reproduction in the checkered garter snake, *Thamnophis marcianus*, from southern Texas and northeastern Mexico: Seasonality and evidence for multiple clutches. Southwest. Nat. 32:93–101.

Ford, N. B., and D. W. Killebrew. 1983. Reproductive tactics and female body size in Butler's garter snake, *Thamnophis butleri*. J. Herpetol. 17:271–275.

Ford, N. B., and J. R. Low, Jr. 1984. Sex pheromone source location by garter snakes: A mechanism for detection of direction in nonvolatile trails. J. Chem. Ecol. 10:1193–1199.

Ford, N. B., and M. L. O'Bleness. 1986. Species and sexual specificity of pheromone trails of the garter snake, *Thamnophis marcianus*. J. Herpetol. 20:259–262.

Ford, N. B., and C. W. Schofield. 1984. Species specificity of sex pheromone trails in the plains garter snake, *Thamnophis radix*. Herpetologica 40:51–55.

Ford, N. B., and R. A. Seigel. 1989a. Relationships among body size, clutch size, and egg size in three species of oviparous snakes. Herpetologica 45:75–83.

———. 1989b. Phenotypic plasticity in reproductive traits: Evidence from a viviparous snake. Ecology 70:1768–1774.

———. 1994a. Phenotypic plasticity: Implications for captive-breeding and conservation programs, 175–182. In: J. B. Murphy, K. Adler and J. T. Collins (eds.), Captive management and conservation of amphibians and reptiles. Soc. Stud. Amphib. Rept. Herpetol. Circ. 11.

———. 1994b. An experimental study of the trade-offs between age and size at maturity effects of energy availabilty. Funct. Ecol. 8:91–96.

Ford, N. B., and G. A. Shuttlesworth. 1986. Effects of variation to food intake on locomotory performance of juvenile garter snakes. Copeia 1986:999–1001.

Forks, T. 1979. Kingsnake "lays turtle eggs." Bull. Chicago Herpetol. Soc. 14:119.

Forster, J. R. 1771. A catalogue of the animals of North America. In: J. B. Bossu (ed.), Travels through that part of North America formerly called Louisiana. London.

Forstner, M. R. J., R. A. Hilsenbeck, and J. F. Scudday. 1997. Geographic variation in whole venom profiles from the mottled rock rattlesnake *(Crotalus lepidus lepidus)* in Texas. J. Herpetol. 31:277–287.

Fouquette, M. J., Jr. 1954. Food competition among four sympatric species of garter snakes, genus *Thamnophis*. Texas J. Sci. 6:172–189.

Fouquette, M. J., Jr., and H. L. Lindsay, Jr. 1955. An ecological survey of reptiles in parts of northwestern Texas. Texas J. Sci. 7:402–421.

Fouquette, M. J., Jr., and F. E. Potter, Jr. 1961. A new black-headed snake *(Tantilla)* from southwestern Texas. Copeia 1961:144–148.

Fouquette, M. J., Jr., and D. A. Rossman. 1963. Noteworthy records of Mexican amphibians and reptiles in the Florida State Museum and the Texas Natural History Collection. Herpetologica 19:185–201.

Fowler, J. A. 1947. Snakes eating bats. Copeia 1947:210.

Fowlie, J. A. 1965. The snakes of Arizona. Fallbrook, California: Azul Quinta.

Fox, W. 1948a. The relationships of the garter snake, *Thamnophis ordinoides*. Copeia 1948:113–126.

———. 1948b. Effect of temperature on development of scutellation in the garter snake, *Thamnophis elegans atratus*. Copeia 1948:252–262.

———. 1951. Relationships among the garter snakes of the *Thamnophis elegans* Rassenkreis. Univ. California Publ. Zool. 50:485–530.

———. 1952. Seasonal variation in the male reproductive system of Pacific Coast garter snakes. J. Morph. 90:481–554.

———. 1954. Genetic and environmental variation in the timing of the reproductive cycles of male garter snakes. J. Morph. 95:415–450.

———. 1956. Seminal receptacles of snakes. Anat. Rec. 124:519–540.

———. 1965. A comparison of the male urogenital systems of blind snakes, Leptotyphlopidae and Typhlopidae. Herpetologica 21:241–256.

Fox, W., and H. C. Dessauer. 1962. The single right oviduct and other urogenital structures of female *Typhlops* and *Leptotyphlops*. Copeia 1962:590–597.

———. 1964. Collection of garter snakes for blood studies. Year Book. Am. Phil. Soc. 1964:263–266.

Fox, W., C. Gordon, and M. H. Fox. 1961. Morphological effects of low temperatures during the embryonic development of the garter snake, *Thamnophis elegans*. Zoologica (New York) 46:57–71.

Fraker, M. A. 1970. Home range and homing in the water-snake, *Natrix sipedon sipedon*. Copeia 1970:665–673.

Franklin, M. A. 1944. Notes on the young of the brown water snake. Copeia 1944:250.

Franz, R. 1976. Feeding behavior in the snakes, *Regina alleni* and *Regina rigida*. Herpetol. Rev. 7:82–83.

———. 1977. Observations on the food, feeding behavior, and parasites of the striped swamp snake, *Regina alleni*. Herpetologica 33:91–94.

———. 1992. Florida pine snake, 254–258. In: P. E. Moler (ed.), Rare and endangered biota of Florida. Vol 3. Amphibians and reptiles. Gainesville: University Press of Florida.

Freed, P. S., and K. Neitman. 1988. Notes on predation on the endangered Houston toad, *Bufo houstonensis*. Texas J. Sci. 40:454–456.

Freedman, W., and P. M. Catling. 1978. Population size and structure of four sympatric species of snakes at Amherstburg, Ontario. Can. Field-Nat. 92:167–173.

———. 1979. Movements of sympatric species of snakes at Amherstburg, Ontario. Can. Field-Nat. 93:399–404.

Frey, J. K. 1996. *Crotalus lepidus* (rock rattlesnake). Aquatic behavior. Herpetol. Rev. 27:145.

Fritts, T. H. 1984. Does the brown tree snake pose a threat to Florida and its tourist industry? 71–72. In: D. C. Schmitz and T. C. Brown (eds.), An assessment of invasive non-indigenous species in Florida's Public Lands. Tech. Rep. Florida Dept. Environ. Protect. TSS-94-100.

Frost, D. R. 1983. *Sonora semiannulata*. Cat. Am. Amphib. Rept. 333:1–4.

Frost, D. R., and J. T. Collins. 1988. Nomenclatural notes on reptiles of the United States. Herpetol. Rev. 19:73–74.

Frost, D. R., and T. R. Van Devender. 1979. The relationship of the groundsnakes *Sonora semiannulata* and *S. episcopa*. Occ. Pap. Mus. Zool. Louisiana St. Univ. 52:1–9.

Funderburg, J. B. 1958. The yellow-lipped snake, *Rhadinaea flavilata* Cope, in North Carolina. J. Elisha Mitchell Sci. Soc. 74:135–136.

———. 1968. Eastern diamondback rattlesnake feeding on carrion. J. Herpetol. 2:161–162.

Funderburg, J. B., and D. S. Lee. 1968. The amphibian and reptile fauna of pocket gopher *(Geomys)* mounds in central Florida. J. Herpetol. 1:99–100.

Funk, R. S. 1964a. On the food of *Crotalus m. molossus*. Herpetologica 20:134.

———. 1964b. Birth of a brood of western cottonmouths, *Agkistrodon piscivorus leucostoma*. Trans. Kansas Acad. Sci. 67:199.

———. 1964c. On the reproduction of *Micruroides euryxanthus* (Kennicott). Copeia 1964:219.

———. 1964d. Fifth *Ficimia quadrangularis desertorum* Taylor in United States. Southwest. Nat. 9:105.

———. 1965a. Food of *Crotalus cerastes laterorepens* in Yuma County, Arizona. Herpetologica 21:15–17.

———. 1965b. Albino glossy snake, *Arizona elegans*, from northern Sonora. Southwest. Nat. 10:316–317.

———. 1967. A new colubrid snake of the genus *Chionactis* from Arizona. Southwest. Nat. 12:180–188.

Funk, R. S., and J. K. Tucker. 1978. Variation in a large brood of lined snakes, *Tropidoclonion lineatum* (Reptilia, Serpentes, Colubridae). J. Herpetol. 12:115–117.

Furry, K., T. Swain, and D. Chiszar. 1991. Strike-induced chemosensory searching and trail following by prairie rattlesnakes *(Crotalus viridis)* preying upon deer mice *(Peromyscus maniculatus):* Chemical discrimination among individual mice. Herpetologica 47:69–78.

Gadd, J. P. 1983 (1982). Observations on the sexual behaviour of the boa constrictor, *Constrictor constrictor*, in captivity, with notes on an unsuccessful parturition. British Herpetol. Soc. Bull. 6:39–41.

Galligan, J. H., and W. A. Dunson. 1979. Biology and status of timber rattlesnake *(Crotalus horridus)* populations in Pennsylvania. Biol. Conserv. 15:13–58.

Gannon, V., and D. M. Secoy. 1984. Growth and reproductive rates of a northern population of the prairie rattlesnake, *Crotalus v. viridis*. J. Herpetol. 18:13–19.

———. 1985. Seasonal and daily activity patterns in a Canadian population of the prairie rattlesnake, *Crotalus viridis viridis*. Can. J. Zool. 63:86–91.

Garcia, C. M., and H. Drummond. 1988. Seasonal and sexual ontogenetic variation in the diet of the Mexican garter snake, *Thamnophis eques*, in Lake Tecocomulco, Hildalgo. J. Herpetol. 22:129–134.

Garland, T., Jr. 1988. Genetic basis of activity metabolism. I. Inheritance of speed, stamina, and antipredator displays in the garter snake *Thamnophis sirtalis*. Evolution 42:335–350.

Garland, T., Jr., and S. J. Arnold. 1983. Effects of a full stomach on locomotory performance of juvenile garter snakes *(Thamnophis elegans)*. Copeia 1983:1092–1096.

Garman, S. W. 1874. Description of a new species of North American serpent. Proc. Boston Soc. Nat. Hist. 17:92–94.

———. 1884 [1883]. North American Reptilia. Part I. Ophidia. Mem. Mus. Comp. Zool. 8(3): 1–185.

Garstka, W. R. 1982. Systematics of the *mexicana* species group of the colubrid genus *Lampropeltis*, with an hypothesis mimicry. Breviora 466:1–35.

Garstka, W. R., B. Camazine, and D. Crews. 1982. Interactions of behavior and physiology during the annual reproductive cycle of the red-sided garter snake

(*Thamnophis sirtalis parietalis*), Herpetologica 38:104–123.

Garton, J. S., and R. W. Dimmick. 1969. Food habits of the copperhead in middle Tennessee. J. Tennessee Acad. Sci. 44:113–117.

Garton, J. S., E. W. Harris, and R. A. Brandon. 1970. Descriptive and ecological notes on *Natrix cyclopion* in Illinois. Herpetologica 26:454–461.

Gartside, D. F., J. S. Rogers, and H. C. Dessauer. 1977. Speciation with little genic and morphologic differentiation in the ribbon snakes *Thamnophis proximus* and *T. sauritus* (Colubridae). Copeia 1977:697–705.

Gates, G. O. 1957. A study of the herpetofauna in the vicinity of Wickenburg, Maricopa County, Arizona. Trans. Kansas Acad. Sci. 60:403–418.

Gehlbach, F. R. 1956. Annotated records of southwestern amphibians and reptiles. Trans. Kansas Acad. Sci. 59:364–372.

———. 1965. Herpetology of the Zuni Mountains region, northwestern New Mexico. Proc. U.S. Natl. Mus. 116:243–332.

———. 1967. *Lampropeltis mexicana*. Cat. Am. Amphib. Rept. 55:1–2.

———. 1970. Death-feigning and erratic behavior in leptotyphlopid, colubrid, and elapid snakes. Herpetologica 26:25–34.

———. 1971. Lyre snakes of the *Trimorphodon biscutatus* complex. Herpetologica 27:200–211.

———. 1972. Coral snake mimicry reconsidered: The strategy of self-mimicry. Forma Functio 5:311–320.

———. 1974. Evolutionary relations of southwestern ringneck snakes (*Diadophis punctatus*). Herpetologica 30:140–148.

Gehlbach, F. R., and J. K. Baker. 1962. Kingsnakes allied with *Lampropeltis mexicana*: Taxonomy and natural history. Copeia 1962:291–300.

Gehlbach, F. R., and R. S. Baldridge. 1987. Live blind snakes (*Leptotyphlops dulcis*) in eastern screech owl (*Otus asio*) nests: A novel commensalism. Oecologia (Berlin) 71:560–563.

Gehlbach, F. R., and B. B. Collette. 1959. Distributional and biological notes on the Nebraska herpetofauna. Herpetologica 15:141–143.

Gehlbach, F. R., and J. A. Holman. 1974. Paleoecology of amphibians and reptiles from Pratt Cave, Guadalupe Mountains National Park, Texas. Southwest. Nat. 19:191–197.

Gehlbach, F. R., and C. J. McCoy. 1965. Additional observations on variation and distribution of the gray-banded kingsnake, *Lampropeltis mexicana* (Garman). Herpetologica 21:35–38.

Gehlbach, F. R., J. F. Watkins II, and J. C. Kroll. 1972. Pheromone trail following studies of typhlopid, leptotyphlopid, and colubrid snakes. Behaviour 40:282–294.

Gehlbach, F. R., J. F. Watkins II, and H. W. Reno. 1968. Blind snake defensive behavior elicited by ant attacks. Bioscience 18:784–785.

Genter, D. L. 1984. *Crotalus viridis* (prairie rattlesnake). Food. Herpetol. Rev. 15:49–50.

Gervais, F. L .P. 1843. p. 191. In: C.D. d'Orbigny (ed.), Dictionnaire universel d'historie naturelle . . ., vol. 3. Paris: C. Renard.

Gibbons, J. W. 1972. Reproduction, growth, and sexual dimorphism in the canebrake rattlesnake (*Crotalus horridus atricaudatus*). Copeia 1972:222–226.

Gibbons, J. W., J. W. Coker, and T. M. Murphy, Jr. 1977. Selected aspects of the life history of rainbow snake (*Farancia erytrogramma*). Herpetologica 33:276–281.

Gibbons, J. W., and R. D. Semlitsch. 1991. Guide to the reptiles and amphibians of the Savannah River Site. Athens: University of Georgia Press.

Gibson, A. R., and J. B. Falls. 1975. Evidence for multiple insemination in the common garter snake, *Thamnophis sirtalis*. Can. J. Zool. 53:1362–1368.

———. 1979a. Thermal biology of the common garter snake *Thamnophis sirtalis* (L.). I. Temporal variation, environmental effects, and sex differences. Oecologia (Berlin) 43:79–97.

———. 1979b. Thermal biology of the common garter snake *Thamnophis sirtalis* (L.). II. The effects of melanism. Oecologia (Berlin) 43:99–109.

———. 1988. Melanism in the common garter snake: A Lake Erie phenomenon, 233–245. In: J. F. Downhower (ed.), The biogeography of the Island Region of western Lake Erie. Columbus: Ohio St. Univeristy Press.

Gibson, A. R., D. A. Smucny, and J. Kollar. 1989. The effects of feeding and ecdysis on temperature selection by young garter snakes in a simple thermal mosaic. Can. J. Zool. 67:19–23.

Gier, P. J., R. L. Wallace, and R. L. Ingermann. 1989. Influence of pregnancy on behavioral thermoregulation in the northern Pacific rattlesnake *Crotalus viridis oreganus*. J. Exp. Biol. 145:465–469.

Giles, L. W. 1940. Food habits of the raccoon in eastern Iowa. J. Wildl. Mgt. 4:375–382.

Gilhen, J. 1970. An unusual Nova Scotia population of the northern ringneck snake, *Diadophis punctatus edwardsi* (Merrem). Occ. Pap. Nova Scotia Mus. 9:1–12.

Gillingham, J. C. 1974. Reproductive behavior of the western fox snake, *Elaphe v. vulpina* (Baird and Girard). Herpetologica 30:309–313.

———. 1976. Early egg deposition by the southern black racer, *Coluber constrictor priapus*. Herpetol. Rev. 7:115.

———. 1979. Reproductive behavior of the rat snakes of eastern North America, genus *Elaphe*. Copeia 1979:319–331.

———. 1980. Communication and combat behavior in the black rat snake (*Elaphe obsoleta*). Herpetologica 36:120–127.

Gillingham, J. C., and R. E. Baker. 1981. Evidence for scavenging behavior in the western diamondback rattlesnake (*Crotalus atrox*). Zeit. Tierpsychol. 55:217–227.

Gillingham, J. C., C. C. Carpenter, B. J. Brecke, and J. B. Murphy. 1977. Courtship and copulatory behavior of the Mexican milk snake, *Lampropeltis triangulum sinaloae* (Colubridae). Southwest. Nat. 22:187–194.

Gillingham, J. C., and J. A. Chambers. 1980. Observations on the reproductive behaviour of the eastern indigo snake, *Drymarchon corais couperi*, in captivity. British J. Herpetol. 6:99–100.

Gillingham, J. C., and D. L. Clark. 1981. An analysis of prey-searching behavior in the western diamondback rattlesnake, *Crotalus atrox*. Behav. Neurol. Biol. 32:235–240.

Gillingham, J. C., and J. A. Dickinson. 1980. Postural orientation during courtship in the eastern garter snake, *Thamnophis s. sirtalis*. Behav. Neurol. Biol. 28:211–217.

Gillingham, J. C., J. Rowe, and M. A. Weins. 1990. Chemosensory orientation and earthworm location by foraging eastern garter snakes, *Thamnophis s. sirtalis*, 522–532. In: D. W. MacDonald, D. Müller-Schwarze, and S. E. Natynczuk (eds.), Chemical signals in vertebrates 5. New York: Oxford University Press.

Gillingham, J. C., and T. Rush. 1974. Notes on the fishing behavior of water snakes. J. Herpetol. 8:384–385.

Gilmore, C. W. 1938. Fossil snakes of North America. Geol. Soc. Am. Spec. Pap. 9:1–93.

Githens, T. S., and I. D. George. 1931. Comparative studies of the venoms of certain rattlesnakes. Bull. Antivenin Inst. Am. 5:31–35.

Githens, T. S., and N. O. Wolff. 1939. The polyvalency of crotalidic antivenins. J. Immunol. 37:33–51.

Glaser, R. 1955. A rock in the intestinal tract of the snake *Hypsiglena*. Copeia 1955:248.

Glass, J. K. 1972. Feeding behavior of the western shovel-nosed snake, *Chionactis occipitalis klauberi*, with special reference to scorpions. Southwest. Nat. 16:445–447.

Glenn, J. L., and H. E. Lawler. 1987. *Crotalus scutulatus salvini* (Huamantlan rattlesnake). Behavior. Herpetol. Rev. 18:15–16.

Glenn, J. L., and R. C. Straight. 1977. The midget faded rattlesnake (*Crotalus viridis concolor*) venom: Lethal toxicity and individual variability. Toxicon 15:129–133.

———. 1985. Venom properties of the rattlesnakes (*Crotalus*) inhabiting the Baja California region of Mexico. Toxicon 23:769–775.

———. 1989. Intergradation of two different venom populations of the Mojave rattlesnake (*Crotalus scutulatus scutulatus*) in Arizona. Toxicon 27:411–418.

———. 1990. Venom characteristics as an indicator of hybridization between *Crotalus viridis viridis* and *Crotalus scutulatus scutulatus* in New Mexico. Toxicon 28:857–862.

Glenn, J. L., R. C. Straight, M. C. Wolfe, and D. L. Hardy. 1983. Geographical variation in *Crotalus scutulatus scutulatus* (Mojave rattlesnake) venom properties. Toxicon 21:119–130.

Glissmeyer, H. R. 1951. Egg production of the Great Basin rattlesnake. Herpetologica 7:24–27.

Gloyd, H. K. 1928. The amphibians and reptiles of Franklin County, Kansas. Trans. Kansas Acad. Sci. 31:115–141.

———. 1934. Studies on the breeding habits and young of the copperhead, *Agkistrodon mokasen* Beauvois. Pap. Michigan Acad. Sci., Arts, Lett. 19:587–604.

———. 1935. The subspecies of *Sistrurus miliarius*. Occ. Pap. Mus. Zool. Univ. Michigan 322:1–7.

———. 1936. The subspecies of *Crotalus lepidus*. Occ. Pap. Mus. Zool. Univ. Michigan 337:1–5.

———. 1940. The rattlesnakes, genera *Sistrurus* and *Crotalus*. Chicago Acad. Sci. Spec. Publ. 4:1–266.

———. 1947. Notes on the courtship and mating behavior of certain snakes. Chicago Acad. Sci. Nat. Hist. Misc. 12:1–4.

———. 1969. Two additional subspecies of North American snakes, genus *Agkistrodon*. Proc. Biol. Soc. Washington 82:219–232.

Gloyd, H. K., and R. Conant. 1934a. The broad-banded copperhead: A new subspecies of *Agkistrodon mokasen*. Occ. Pap. Mus. Zool. Univ. Michigan 283:1–5.

———. 1934b. The taxonomic status, range, and natural history of Schott's racer. Occ. Pap. Mus. Zool. Univ. Michigan 287:1–17.

———. 1943. A synopsis of the American forms of *Agkistrodon* (copperheads and moccasins). Bull. Chicago Acad. Sci. 7:147–170.

———. 1990. Snakes of the *Agkistrodon* complex: A monographic review. Soc. Stud. Amphib. Rept. Contr. Herpetol. 6:1–614.

Godley, J. S. 1980. Foraging ecology of the striped swamp snake, *Regina alleni*, in southern Florida. Ecol. Monogr. 50:411–436.

———. 1982. Predation and defensive behavior of the

striped swamp snake *(Regina alleni)*. Florida Field Nat. 10:31–36.

Godley, J. S., R. W. McDiarmid, and N. N. Rojas. 1984. Estimating prey size and number in crayfish-eating snakes, genus *Regina*. Herpetologica 40:82–88.

Godwin, J. C. 1992. *Regina alleni* (striped crayfish snake). Predation. Herpetol. Rev. 23:82.

Goff, C. C. 1936. Distribution and variation of a new subspecies of water snake, *Natrix cyclopion floridana*, with a discussion of its relationships. Occ. Pap. Mus. Zool. Univ. Michigan 327:1–9.

Goin, C. J. 1947. A note on the food of *Heterodon simus*. Copeia 1947:275.

Golan, L., C. Radcliffe, T. Miller, B. O'Connell, and D. Chiszar. 1982. Trailing behavior in prairie rattlesnakes *(Crotalus viridis)*. J. Herpetol. 16:287–293.

Goldberg, S. R. 1975. Reproduction in the striped racer, *Masticophis lateralis* (Colubridae). J. Herpetol. 9:361–363.

———. 1995a. Reproduction in the western patchnose snake, *Salvadora hexalepis*, and the mountain patchnose snake, *Salvadora grahamiae* (Colubridae), from Arizona. Southwest. Nat. 40:119–120.

———. 1995b. Reproduction in the lyre snake, *Trimorphodon biscutatus* (Colubridae), from Arizona. Southwest. Nat. 40:334–335.

———. 1995c. Reproduction in the banded sand snake, *Chilomeniscus cinctus* (Colubridae), from Arizona. Great Basin Nat. 55:372–373.

———. 1995d. Reproduction in the California mountain kingsnake, *Lampropeltis zonata* (Colubridae), in Southern California. Bull. So. California Acad. Sci. 94:218–221.

———. 1996. Reproduction in the saddled leafnose snake, *Phyllorhynchus browni* and the spotted leafnose snake, *Phyllorhynchus decurtatus*, from Arizona. J. Herpetol. 30:280–282.

———. 1997a. Reproduction in the western shovelnose snake, *Chionactis occipitalis* (Colubridae), from California. Great Basin Nat. 57:85–87.

———. 1997b. Reproduction in the Sonoran mountain kingsnake *Lampropeltis pyromelana* (Serpentes: Colubridae). Texas J. Sci. 49:219–222.

———. 1997c. Reproduction in the western coral snake, *Micruroides euryxanthus* (Elapidae), from Arizona and Sonora, México. Great Basin Nat. 57:363–365.

———. 1998a. Reproduction in the Mexican vine snake *Oxybelis aeneus* (Serpentes: Colubridae). Texas J. Sci. 50:51–56.

———. 1998b. Reproduction in the blackneck garter snake, *Thamnophis cyrtopsis* (Serpentes: Colubridae). Texas J. Sci. 50:229–234.

———. 1999a. Reproduction in the tiger rattlesnake, *Crotalus tigris* (Serpentes: Viperidae). Texas J. Sci. 51:31–36.

———. 1999b. Reproduction in the red diamond rattlesnake in California. California Fish Game 85:177–180.

———. 1999c. Reproduction in the blacktail rattlesnake, *Crotalus molossus* (Serpentes: Viperidae). Texas J. Sci. 51:323–328.

———. 2000a. Reproduction in the rock rattlesnake, *Crotalus lepidus* (Serpentes: Viperidae). Herpetol. Nat. Hist. 7:83–86.

———. 2000b. Reproduction in the twin-spotted rattlesnake, *Crotalus pricei* (Serpentes: Viperidae). Western N. Am. Nat. 60:98–100.

Goldberg, S. R., and A. T. Holycross. 1999. Reproduction in the desert massasauga, *Sistrurus catenatus edwardsii*, in Arizona and Colorado. Southwest. Nat. 44:531–535.

Goldberg, S. R., and W. S. Parker. 1975. Seasonal testicular histology of the colubrid snakes, *Masticophis taeniatus* and *Pituophis melanoleucus*. Herpetologica 31:317–322.

Goldberg, S. R., and P. C. Rosen. 1999. Reproduction in the Sonoran shovelnose snake *(Chionactis palarostris)* and the western shovelnose snake *(Chionactis occipitalis)* (Serpentes: Colubridae). Texas J. Sci. 51:153–158.

———. 2000. Reproduction in the Mojave rattlesnake, *Crotalus scutulatus* (Serpentes: Viperidae). Texas J. Sci. 52:101–109.

Golder, F. 1981. Anomalien bei der Fortpflanzung von *Elaphe g. guttata*. Salamandra 17:71–77.

Goldsmith, S. K. 1984. Aspects of the natural history of the rough green snake, *Opheodrys aestivus* (Colubridae). Southwest. Nat. 29:445–452.

———. 1986. Feeding behavior of an arboreal, insectivorous snake *(Opheodrys aestivus)* (Colubridae). Southwest. Nat. 31:246–249.

———. 1988. Courtship behavior of the rough green snake, *Opheodrys aestivus* (Colubridae: Serpentes). Southwest. Nat. 33:473–477.

Goldstein, R. C. 1941. Notes on the mud snake in Florida. Copeia 1941:49–50.

Goode, M. J., and G. W. Schuett. 1994. Male combat in the western shovelnose snake *(Chionactis occipitalis)*. Herpetol. Nat. Hist. 2:115–117.

Goodman, J. D. 1953. Further evidence of the venomous nature of the saliva of *Hypsiglena ochrorhyncha*. Herpetologica 9:174–175.

Goodman, J. D., and J. M. Goodman. 1976. Contrasting color and pattern as enticement display in snakes. Herpetologica 32:145–148.

Goodman, R. H., and D. Tate. 1997. *Diadophis punctatus*

vandenburghi (Monterey ringneck snake). Diet. Herpetol. Rev. 28:90.

Goodman, R. H., Jr., G. L. Stewart, and T. J. Moisi. 1997. *Crotalus cerastes cerastes* (Mojave Desert sidewinder). Longevity. Herpetol. Rev. 28:89.

Gordon, D. M., and F. R. Cook. 1980. An aggregation of gravid snakes in the Quebec Laurentians. Can. Field-Nat. 94:456–457.

Gorman, G. C., and F. Gress. 1970. Chromosome cytology of four boid snakes and a varanid lizard, with comments on the cytosystematics of primitive snakes. Herpetologica 26:308–316.

Gorzula, S. J. 1973. Defensive behaviour of a captive colubrid, *Rhinocheilus lecontei*. British J. Herpetol. 4:333–334.

Gove, D., and G. M. Burghardt. 1975. Responses of ecologically dissimilar populations of the water snake *Natrix s. sipedon* to chemical cues from prey. J. Chem. Ecol. 1:25–40.

———. 1983. Context-correlated parameters of snake and lizard tongue-flicking. Anim. Behav. 31:718–723.

Graham, G. L. 1977. The karyotype of the Texas coral snake, *Micrurus fulvius tenere*. Herpetologica 33:345–348.

Graham, J. B. 1974a. Aquatic respiration in the sea snake *Pelamis platurus*. Respir. Physiol. 21:1–7.

———. 1974b. Body temperature of the sea snake *Pelamis platurus*. Copeia 1974:531–533.

Graham, J. B., J. H. Gee, J. Motta, and I. Rubinoff. 1987. Subsurface buoyance regulation by the sea snake *Pelamis platurus*. Physiol. Zool. 60:251–261.

Graham, J. B., J. H. Gee, and F. S. Robison. 1975. Hydrostatic and gas exchange functions of the lung of the sea snake *Pelamis platurus*. Comp. Biochem. Physiol. 50A:477–482.

Graham, J. B., W. R. Lowell, I. Rubinoff, and J. Motta. 1987. Surface and subsurface swimming of the sea snake *Pelamis platurus*. J. Exp. Biol. 127:27–44.

Graham, J. B., I. Rubinoff, and M. K. Hecht. 1971. Temperature physiology of the sea snake *Pelamis platurus*: An index of its colonization potential in the Atlantic Ocean. Proc. Natl. Acad. Sci. 68:1360–1363.

Granger, A. M. 1982. Notes on the captive breeding of the desert rosy boa *(Lichanura trivirgata gracia)*. British Herpetol. Soc Bull. 5:33–34.

Grant, G. S. 1970. Rattlesnake predation on the clapper rail. Chat 34:20–21.

Grant, J. 1969. Early emergence from hibernation of the rubber boa. Can. Field-Nat. 83:281.

Gratz, R. K., and V. H. Hutchison. 1977. Energetics for activity in the diamondback water snake, *Natrix rhombifera*. Physiol. Zool. 50:99–114.

Graves, B. M. 1989. Defensive behavior of female prairie rattlesnakes *(Crotalus viridis)* changes after parturition. Copeia 1989:793–794.

———. 1991. Consumption of an adult mouse by a free-ranging neonate prairie rattlesnake. Southwest. Nat. 36:143.

Graves, B. M., and D. Duvall. 1983. Occurrence and function of prairie rattlesnake mouth gaping in a nonfeeding context. J. Exp. Zool. 227:471–474.

———. 1985a. Avomic prairie rattlesnakes *(Crotalus viridis)* fail to attack rodent prey. Zeit. Tierpsychol. 67:161–166.

———. 1985b. Mouth gaping and head shaking by prairie rattlesnakes are associated with vomeronasal organ olfaction. Copeia 1985:496–497.

———. 1987. An experimental study of aggregation and thermoregulation in prairie rattlesnakes *(Crotalus viridis viridis)*. Herpetologica 43:259–264.

———. 1988. Evidence of an alarm pheromone from the cloacal sacs of prairie rattlesnakes. Southwest. Nat. 33:339–345.

———. 1990. Spring emergence patterns of wandering garter snakes and prairie rattlesnakes in Wyoming. J. Herpetol. 24:351–356.

———. 1993. Reproduction, rookery use, and thermoregulation in free-ranging, pregnant *Crotalus v. viridis*. J. Herpetol. 27:33–41.

Graves, B. M., and M. Halpern. 1988. Neonate plains garter snakes *(Thamnophis radix)* are attracted to conspecific skin extracts. J. Comp. Psychol. 102:251–253.

Graves, B. M., M. Halpern, and J. L. Friesen. 1991. Snake aggregation pheromones: Source and chemosensory mediation in western ribbon snakes *(Thamnophis proximus)*. J. Comp. Psychol. 105:140–144.

Graves, B. M., M. Halpern, and J. C. Gillingham. 1993. Effects of vomeronasal system deafferentation on home range use in a natural population of eastern garter snakes, *Thamnophis sirtalis*. Anim. Behav. 45:307–311.

Gray, J. E. 1842. Zoological miscellaney. To be continued occasionally. Part II: 41–48. London: Trusteees of the British Museum (Natural History).

———. 1849. Catalogue of specimens of snakes in the collection of the British Museum. London: Trustees of the British Museum (Natural History).

Gray, L. J., and M. E. Douglas. 1989. Predation by terrestrial vertebrates on stranded fish and crayfish in a tallgrass prairie stream. Pap. 121st Ann. Meet. Kansas Acad. Sci. 8:11.

Greatwood, J. H. 1978. Breeding of the snake, *Lampropeltis mexicana blairi*, in captivity. British J. Herpetol. 5:745–746.

Greding, E. J., Jr. 1964. Food of *Ancistrodon contortrix* in

Houston and Trinity counties, Texas. Southwest. Nat. 9:105.

Green, M., and J. A. Holman. 1977. A late Tertiary stream channel fauna from South Bijou Hill, South Dakota. J. Paleontol. 51:543–547.

Green, N. B., and T. K. Pauley. 1987. Amphibians and reptiles of West Virginia. University of Pittsburgh Press.

Greenberg, C. H., D. G. Neary, and L. D. Harris. 1994. A comparison of herpetofaunal sampling effectiveness of pitfall, single-ended, and double-ended funnel traps used with drift fences. J. Herpetol. 28:319–324.

Greene, B. D., J. R. Dixon, J. M. Mueller, M. J. Whiting, and O. W. Thornton, Jr. 1994. Feeding ecology of the Concho water snake, *Nerodia harteri paucimaculata.* J. Herpetol. 28:165–172.

Greene, B. D., J. R. Dixon, M. J. Whiting, and J. M. Mueller. 1999. Reproductive ecology of the Concho water snake, *Nerodia harteri paucimaculata.* Copeia 1999:701–709.

Greene, H. W. 1973. Defensive tail display by snakes and amphisbaenians. J. Herpetol. 7:143–161.

———. 1976. Scale overlap, a directional sign stimulus for prey ingestion by ophiophagous snakes. Zeit. Tierpsychol. 41:113–120.

———. 1983. *Boa constrictor* (boa, béquer, boa constrictor), 380–382. In: D. H. Janzen (ed.), Costa Rican natural history. University of Chicago Press.

———. 1984. Feeding behavior and diet of the eastern coral snake, *Micrurus fulvius.* In: R.A. Seigel et al. (eds.), Vertebrate eccology and systematics: A tribute to Henry Stitch, 147–162. Univ. Kansas Mus. Nat. Hist. Spec. Publ. 10.

———. 1990. A sound defense of the rattlesnake. Pacific Discovery 43(4): 10–19.

———. 1994. Systematics and natural history, foundations for understanding and conserving biodiversity. Am. Zool. 34:48–56.

———. 1997. Snakes: The evolution of mystery in nature. Berkeley: University of California Press.

Greene, H. W., and G. M. Burghardt. 1978. Behavior and phylogeny: Constriction in ancient and modern snakes. Science (New York) 200:74–77.

Greene, H. W., and D. Cundall. 2000. Limbless tetrapods and snakes with legs. Science (New York) 287:1939–1941.

Greene, H. W., and R. W. McDiarmid. 1981. Coral snake mimicry: Does it occur? Science (New York) 213:1207–1212.

Greene, H. W., and G. V. Oliver, Jr. 1965. Notes on the natural history of the western massasauga. Herpetologica 21:225–228.

Greene, H. W., and W. F. Pyburn. 1973. Comments on aposematism and mimicry among coral snakes. Biologist 55:144–148.

Greenhall, A. M. 1936. A cannibalistic hog-nose snake. Copeia 1936:171.

Greer, A. E. 1966. Viviparity and oviparity in the snake genera *Conophis, Toluca, Gyalopion,* and *Ficimia,* with comments in *Tomodon* and *Helicops.* Copeia 1966:371–373.

Gregory, P. T. 1974. Patterns of spring emergence of the red-sided garter snake *(Thamnophis sirtalis parietalis)* in the Interlake region of Manitoba. Can. J. Zool. 52:1063–1069.

———. 1975a. Aggregations of gravid snakes in Manitoba, Canada. Copeia 1975:185–186.

———. 1975b. Arboreal mating behavior in the red-sided garter snake. Can. Field-Nat. 89:461–462.

———. 1977a. Life history observations of three species of snakes in Manitoba. Can. Field-Nat. 91:19–27.

———. 1977b. Life-history parameters of the red-sided garter snake *(Thamnophis sirtalis parietalis)* in one extreme environment, the Interlake Region of Manitoba. Natl. Mus. Natural Sci. Ottawa Publ. Zool. 13:1–44.

———. 1978. Feeding habits and diet overlap of three species of garter snakes *(Thamnophis)* on Vancouver Island. Can. J. Zool. 56:1967–1974.

———. 1982. Reptilian hibernation, 53–154. In: C. Gans and F. H. Poughs (eds.), Biology of the Reptilia. Vol. 13. Physiology D, physiological ecology. London: Academic Press.

———. 1983. Habitat, diet, and composition of assemblages of garter snakes *(Thamnophis)* on Vancouver Island. Can. J. Zool. 56:1967–1974.

———. 1984a. Habitat, diet, and composition of assemblages of garter snakes *(Thamnophis)* at eight sites on Vancouver Island. Can. J. Zool. 62:2013–2022.

———. 1984b. Correlations between body temperature and environmental factors and their variations with activity in garter snakes *(Thamnophis).* Can. J. Zool. 62:2244–2249.

———. 1990. Temperature differences between head and body in garter snakes *(Thamnophis)* at a den in central British Columbia. J. Herpetol. 24:241–245.

Gregory, P. T., L. H. Crampton, and K. M. Skebo. 1999. Conflicts and interactions among reproduction, thermoregulation and feeding in viviparous reptiles: Are gravid snakes anorexic? J. Zool. (London) 248:231–241.

Gregory, P. T., and K. W. Larsen. 1993. Geographic variation in reproductive characteristics among Canadian populations of the common garter snake *(Thamnophis sirtalis).* Copeia 1993:946–958.

Gregory, P. T., K. W. Larsen, and D. R. Farr. 1992. Snake litter size = live young + dead young + yolks. Herpetol. J. 2:145–146.

Gregory, P. T., J. M. Macartney, and D. H. Rivard. 1980. Small mammal predation and prey handling behavior by the garter snake *Thamnophis elegans*. Herpetologica 36:87–93.

Gregory, P. T., and A. G. D. McIntosh. 1980. Thermal niche overlap in garter snakes *(Thamnophis)* on Vancouver Island. Can. J. Zool. 58:351–355.

Gregory, P. T., and K. J. Nelson. 1991. Predation on fish and intersite variation in the diet of common garter snakes, *Thamnophis sirtalis*, on Vancouver Island. Can. J. Zool. 69:988–994.

Gregory, P. T., and C. J. Prelypchan. 1994. Analysis of variance of first-year growth in captive garter snakes *(Thamnophis elegans)* by family and sex. J. Zool. (London) 232:313–322.

Gregory, P. T., and K. M. Skebo. 1998. Trade-offs between reproductive traits and the influence of food intake during pregnancy in the garter snake, *Thamnophis elegans*. Am. Nat. 151:477–486.

Gregory, P. T., and K. W. Stewart. 1975. Long-distance dispersal and feeding strategy of the red-sided garter snake *(Thamnophis sirtalis parietalis)* in the Interlake of Manitoba. Can. J. Zool. 53:238–245.

Grenard, S. 1994. Snakebite: Are "non-poisonous" colubrids really harmless. Reptile & Amphibian Mag. Sept./Oct. 1994:51–63.

Griffin, P. R., and S. D. Aird. 1990. A new small myotoxin from the venom of the prairie rattlesnake *(Crotalus viridis viridis)*. FEBS Letters 274:43–47.

Grismer, J. L. 1994. Food observations on the endemic Sierra San Pedro Mártir garter snake *(Thamnophis elegans hueyi)* from Baja California, México. Herpetol. Nat. Hist. 2:107–108.

Grismer, L. L. 1990. A new long-nosed snake *(Rhinocheilus lecontei)* from Isla Cerralvo, Baja California Sur, México. Proc. San Diego Soc. Nat. Hist. 4:1–7.

Grismer, L. L., and J. A. McGuire. 1993. The oasis of central Baja California, México. Part I. A preliminary account of the relict mesophilic herpetofauna and status of oases. Bull. So. California Acad. Sci. 92:2–24.

Grismer, L. L., J. A. McGuire, and B. D. Hollingsworth. 1994. A report on the herpetofauna of the Vizcaíno Peninsula, Baja California, México, with a discussion of its biogeographic and taxonomic implications. Bull. So. California Acad. Sci. 93:45–80.

Gritis, P. 1993. The rough green snake: Aspects of its natural history and life in captivity. Reptile & Amphibian Mag. Mar./Apr. 1993:55–57.

Grizzell, R. A., Jr. 1949. The hibernation site of three snakes and a salamander. Copeia 1949:231–232.

Grobman, A. B. 1941. A contribution to the knowledge of variation of *Opheodrys vernalis* (Harlan), with the description of a new subspecies. Misc. Publ. Mus. Zool. Univ. Michigan 50:1–38.

———. 1978. An alternative solution to the coral snake mimic problem (Reptilia, Serpentes, Elapidae). J. Herpetol. 12:1–11.

———. 1984. Scutellation variation in *Opheodrys aestivus*. Bull. Florida St. Mus. Biol. Sci. 29:153–170.

———. 1992a. Metamerism in the snake *Opheodrys vernalis*, with a description of a new subspecies. J. Herpetol. 26:175–186.

———. 1992b. On races, clines, and common names in *Opheodrys*. Herpetol. Rev. 23:14–15.

Grogan, W. L., Jr. 1974. Effects of accidental envenomation from the saliva of the eastern hognose snake, *Heterodon platyrhinos*. Herpetologica 30:248–249.

Grogan, W. L., Jr., and D. C. Forester. 1998. New records of the milk snake, *Lampropeltis triangulum*, from the coastal plain of the Delmarva Peninsula, with comments on the status of *L. t. temporalis*. Maryland Nat. 42:5–14.

Groschupf, K. 1982. *Cnemidophorus uniparens* (desert grassland whiptail). Behavior. Herpetol. Rev. 13:46.

Groschupf, K., and S. Lower. 1988. *Oxybelis aeneus* (brown vine snake). Behavior. Herpetol. Rev. 19:85.

Groves, F. 1957. Eggs and young of the corn snake in Maryland. Herpetologica 13:79–80.

———. 1960. The eggs and young of *Drymarchon corais couperi*. Copeia 1960:51–53.

———. 1961. Notes on two large broods of *Haldea v. valeriae* (Baird and Girard). Herpetologica 17:71.

Groves, J. D. 1978. Spider predation on amphibians and reptiles. Bull. Maryland Herpetol. Soc. 14:44–46.

Groves, J. D., and R. J. Assetto. 1976. *Lampropeltis triangulum elapsoides*. Herpetol. Rev. 7:114.

Grudzien, T. A., B. J. Huebner, A. Cvetkovic, and G. R. Joswiak. 1992. Multivariate analysis of head shape in *Thamnophis s. sirtalis* (Serpentes: Colubridae) among island and mainland populations from northern Lake Michigan. Am. Midl. Nat. 127:339–347.

Grudzien, T. A., and P. J. Owens. 1991. Genic similarity in the gray and brown color morphs of the snake *Storeria occipitomaculata*. J. Herpetol. 25:90–92.

Guidry, E. V. 1953. Herpetological notes from southeastern Texas. Herpetologica 9:49–56.

Guilday, J. E. 1962. The Pleistocene local fauna of the Natural Chimneys, Augusta County, Virginia. Ann. Carnegie Mus. 36:87–122.

Guilday, J. E., H. W. Hamilton, and A. D. McCrady. 1966. The bone breccia of Bootlegger Sink, York County, Pa. Ann. Carnegie Mus. 8:145–163.

Guilday, J. E., P. S. Martin, and A. D. McCrady. 1964. New Paris 4: A Pleistocene cave deposit in Bedford County, Pennsylvania. Natl. Speleol. Soc. Bull. 26:121–194.

Guillén, F. C., and H. Drummond. 1989. Ataques anfibios en culebras semiácuticas: Manejo del problema de la refracción por parte de especialistas y generalistas. Acta Zool. Mexicana, n.ser. 35:3–18.

Guitiérrez, J. M., and R. Bolaños. 1980. Karyotype of the yellow-bellied sea snake, *Pelamis platurus*. J. Herpetol. 14:161–165.

Guitiérrez, J. M., A. Solórzano, and L. Cerdas. 1985. Estudioscariológicos de cinco especies de serpientes costarricenses de la familia Colubridae. Rev. Biol. Trop. 32:263–267.

Gumbart, T. C., and K. A. Sullivan. 1990. Predation on yellow-eyed junco nestlings by twin-spotted rattlesnakes. Southwest. Nat. 35:367–368.

Günther, A. C. L. G. 1860. Description of *Leptodeira torquata*, a new snake from Central America. Ann. Mag. Nat. Hist. (London), ser. 3, 5:169–171.

Günther, A. C. L. G. 1885–1902. Reptilia and Batrachia, xx, 326. In: F. D. Godman and O. Salvin. Biologia Centrali-Americana. London: Dulau and Co.

Gurrola-Hidalgo, M. A., and N. Chavez C. 1996. *Lampropeltis triangulum nelsoni* (milk snake). Predation. Herpetol. Rev. 27:83.

Gut, H. J., and C. E. Ray. 1963. The Pleistocene vertebrate fauna of Reddick, Florida. Quart. J. Florida Acad. Sci. 26:315–328.

Guthrie, J. E. 1932. Snakes versus birds; birds versus snakes. Wilson Bull. 44:88–101.

Gutzke, W. H. N., G. L. Paukstis, and L. L. McDaniel. 1985. Skewed sex ratios for adult and hatchling bullsnakes, *Pituophis melanoleucus*, in Nebraska. Copeia 1985:649–652.

Gutzke, W. H. N., C. Tucker, and R. T. Mason. 1993. Chemical recognition of kingsnakes by crotalines: Effects of size on the ophiophage defensive response. Brain Behav. Evol. 41:234–238.

Guyer, C., and M. S. Laska. 1996. *Coluber* (= *Masticophis*) *mentovarius* (tropical racer). Predation. Herpetol. Rev. 27:203.

Haggerty, T. 1981. Rat snake preys on nestlings of roughwinged swallow and common grackle. Chat 45:77.

Hahn, D. E. 1979a. Leptotyphlopidae, *Leptotyphlops*. Cat. Am. Amphib. Rept. 230:1–4.

———. 1979b. *Leptotyphlops dulcis*. Cat. Am. Amphib. Rept. 231:1–2.

———. 1979c. *Leptotyphlops humilis*. Cat. Am. Amphib. Rept. 232:1–4.

———. 1980. Liste der rezenten Amphibien und Reptilien. Anomalepididae, Leptotyphlopidae, Typhlopidae. Das Tierreich 101:1–93.

Haines, T. P. 1940. Delayed fertilization in *Leptodeira annulata polysticta*. Copeia 1940:116–118.

Hall, P. M., and A. J. Meier. 1993. Reproduction and behavior of western mud snakes *(Farancia abacura reinwardtii)* in American alligator nests. Copeia 1993:219–222.

Hall, R. J. 1969. Ecological observations on Graham's watersnake *(Regina grahami* Baird and Girard). Am. Midl. Nat. 81:156–163.

Hallowell, E. 1852. Descriptions of new species of reptiles inhabiting North America. Proc. Acad. Nat. Sci. Philadelphia 6:177–182.

———. 1853. On some new reptiles from California. Proc. Acad. Nat. Sci. Philadelphia 6:236–238.

———. 1854. Descriptions of reptiles from California. Proc. Acad. Nat. Sci. Philadelphia 7:91–97.

———. 1857 [1856]. Notice of a collection of reptiles from Kansas and Nebraska, presented to the Academy of Natural Sciences by Dr. Hammond, U.S.A. Proc. Acad. Nat. Sci. Philadelphia 1856:241.

Halloy, M., and G. M. Burghardt. 1990. Ontogeny of fish capture and ingestion in four species of garter snakes *(Thamnophis)*. Behaviour 112:299–318.

Halpern, M., and N. Frumin. 1979. Roles of the vomeronasal and olfactory systems in prey attack and feeding in adult garter snakes. Physiol. Behav. 22:1183–1189.

Halpert, A. P., W. R. Garstka, and D. Crews. 1982. Sperm transport and storage and its relation to the annual sexual cycle of the female red-sided garter snake, *Thamnophis sirtalis parietalis*. J. Morph. 174:149–159.

Halpin, Z. T. 1990. Responses of juvenile eastern garter snakes *(Thamnophis sirtalis sirtalis)* to own, conspecific, and clean odors. Copeia 1990:1157–1160.

Hamel, P. B. 1996. *Agkistrodon piscivorus leucostoma* (western cottonmouth). Carrion feeding. Herpetol. Rev. 27:143.

Hamilton, W. J., Jr. 1947. Hibernation of the lined snake. Copeia 1947:209–210.

———. 1950. Food of the prairie rattlesnake *(Crotalus v. viridis* Rafinesque). Herpetologica 6:34.

———. 1951a. Notes on the food and reproduction of the Pelee Island water snake, *Natrix sipedon insularum* Conant and Clay. Can. Field-Nat. 65:64–65.

———. 1951b. The food and feeding behavior of the garter snake in New York state. Am. Midl. Nat. 46:385–390.

Hamilton, W. J., Jr., and J. A. Pollack. 1955. The food of some crotalid snakes from Fort Benning, Georgia. Chicago Acad. Sci. Nat. Hist. Misc. 140:1–4.

———. 1956. The food of some colubrid snakes from Fort Benning, Georgia. Ecology 37:519–526.

Hammack, S. H. 1991. *Heterodon nasicus kennerlyi* (Mexican hognose snake). Oophagy. Herpetol. Rev. 22:132.

Hammerson, G. A. 1977. Head-body temperature differences monitored by telemetry in the snake *Masticophis flagellum piceus*. Comp. Biochem. Physiol. 57A:399–402.

———. 1978. Observations on the reproduction, courtship, and aggressive behavior of the striped racer, *Masticophis lateralis euryxanthus* (Reptilia, Serpentes, Colubridae). J. Herpetol. 12:253–255.

———. 1979. Thermal ecology of the striped racer, *Masticophis lateralis*. Herpetologica 35:267–273.

———. 1981. Opportunistic scavenging by *Crotalus ruber* not field-proven. J. Herpetol. 15:125.

———. 1986. Amphibians and reptiles in Colorado. Denver: Colorado Div. Wildl., Dept. Nat. Res.,.

———. 1987. Thermal behaviour of the snake *Coluber constrictor* in west-central California. J. Therm. Biol. 12:195–197.

———. 1988. *Opheodrys aestivus* (rough green snake). Antipredator behavior. Herpetol. Rev. 19:85.

———. 1989. Effects of weather and feeding on body temperature and activity in the snake *Masticophis flagellum*. J. Therm. Biol. 14:219–224.

Hammerson, G. A., and A. D. Benedict. 1998. *Tantilla hobartsmithi* (southwestern blackhead snake). Utah. Herpetol. Rev. 29:55.

Hammock, M. W. 1984. Reproduction and breeding behavior in captive black pine snakes. Bull. Chicago Herpetol. Soc. 19:125–130.

Hanebrink, E., and W. Byrd. 1986. Species composition and diversity of water snake (*Nerodia* sp.) populations in northeastern Arkansas. Bull. Chicago Herpetol. Soc. 21:72–78.

Hansen, R. W., and J. M. Brode. 1980. Status of the giant garter snake, *Thamnophis couchi gigas* (Fitch). California Dept. Fish Game, Inland Fish. Endang. Spec. Progr. Spec. Publ. 80-5:1–14.

Hansen, R. W., and G. E. Hansen. 1990. *Thamnophis gigas* (giant garter snake). Reproduction. Herpetol. Rev. 21:93–94.

Hansen, R. W., and B. Thomason. 1991. *Contia tenuis* (sharp-tailed shrew). Predation. Herpetol. Rev. 22:60–61.

Hansknecht, K. A., T. R. Creque, and C. H. Ernst. 1999. *Thamnophis sauritus sauritus*. Hibernaculum. Herpetol. Rev. 30:104.

Harding, J. H. 1997. Amphibians and reptiles of the Great Lakes Region. Ann Arbor: University of Michigan Press.

Hardy, D. L. 1983. Envenomation by the Mojave rattlesnake (*Crotalus scutulatus scutulatus*) in southern Arizona, U.S.A. Toxicon 21:111–118.

———. 1986. Fatal rattlesnake envenomation in Arizona: 1969–1984. Clinical Toxicol. 24:1–10.

Hardy, D. L., M. Jeter, and J. J. Corrigan, Jr. 1982. Envenomation by the northern blacktail rattlesnake (*Crotalus molossus molossus):* Report of two cases and the *in vitro* effects of the venom on fibrinolysis and platelet aggregation. Toxicon 20:487–492.

Hardy, L. M. 1971. A comparison of karyotypes of the snake genera *Virginia* Baird and Girard and *Storeria* Baird and Girard from northeastern Louisiana. Swanews 971:12.

———. 1975a. A systematic revision of the colubrid snake genus *Gyalopion*. J. Herpetol. 9:107–132.

———. 1975b. A systematic revision of the colubrid snake genus *Ficimia*. J. Herpetol. 9:133–168.

———. 1975c. Comparative morphology and evolutionary relationships of the colubrid snake genera *Pseudoficimia, Ficimia,* and *Gyalopion*. J. Herpetol. 9:323–336.

———. 1976a. *Ficimia streckeri*. Cat. Am. Amphib. Rept. 181:1–2.

———. 1976b. *Gyalopion, G. canum, G. quadrangularis*. Cat. Am. Amphib. Rept. 182:1–4.

———. 1990. *Ficimia*. Cat. Am. Amphib. Rept. 471:1–5.

———. 1995. Checklist of the amphibians and reptiles of the Caddo Lake watershed in Texas and Louisiana. Louisiana State Univ. Shreveport, Bull. Mus. Life Sciences 10:1–31.

Hardy, L. M., and C. J. Cole. 1968. Morphological variation in a population of the snake *Tantilla gracilis* Baird and Girard. Univ. Kansas Publ. Mus. Nat. Hist. 17:613–629.

Hardy, L. M., and R. W. McDiarmid. 1969. The amphibians and reptiles of Sinaloa, Mexico. Univ. Kansas Publ. Mus. Nat. Hist. 18:39–252.

Harlan, R. 1827. Genera of North American Reptilia and a synopsis of the species. J. Acad. Nat. Sci. Philadelphia 5:317–372.

Harrington, J. W. 1953. A fossil Pleistocene snake from Denton County, Texas. Field and Lab. (So. Methodist Univ.) 21:20.

Harriot, S. C. 1940. Chipmunk eating a red-bellied snake. J. Mammal. 21:92.

Harris, A. H. 1959. Second record of the Arizona lyre snake in New Mexico. Southwest. Nat. 4:42–43.

Harris, H. H., Jr. 1965. Case reports of two dusky pigmy

rattlesnake bites *(Sistrurus miliarius barbouri)*. Bull. Maryland Herpetol. Soc. 2:8–10.

Harris, H. H., Jr., and R. S. Simmons. 1972. An April birth record for *Crotalus lepidus* with a summary of annual broods of rattlesnakes. Bull. Maryland Herpetol. Soc. 8:54–56.

———. 1974. The New Mexican ridge-nosed rattlesnake. Natl. Parks Conserv. Mag. 48(3): 22–24.

———. 1976. The paleogeography and evolution of *Crotalus willardi*, with a formal description of a new subspecies from New Mexico, United States. Bull. Maryland Herpetol. Soc. 12:1–22.

———. 1977. Additional notes concerning cannibalism in pit vipers. Bull. Maryland Herpetol. Soc. 13:121–122.

Harris, L. H., Jr. 1999. A comparison between the black racer and the black ratsnake with observations of the feeding behavior of the black ratsnake. Herpetology 29(2): 1–5.

Harrison, M. B. 1933. The significance of knobbed anal keels in the garter snake, *Thamnophis sirtalis sirtalis* (Linnaeus). Copeia 1933:1–3.

Hart, D. R. 1979. Niche relationships of *Thamnophis radix haydeni* and *Thamnophis sirtalis parietalis* in the Interlake District of Manitoba. Tulane Stud. Zool. Bot. 21:125–140.

Harwig, S. H. 1966. Rattlesnakes are where and when you find them. J. Ohio Herpetol. Soc. 5:163.

Harwood, P. D. 1945. The behavior and growth of young Dekay's snakes *(Storeria dekayi dekayi)* in captivity. Am. Midl. Nat. 34:523–525.

Haverly, J. E., and K. V. Kardong. 1996. Sensory deprivation effects on the predatory behavior of the rattlesnake, *Crotalus viridis oreganus*. Copeia 1996:419–428.

Hawley, A. W. L., and M. Aleksiuk. 1975. Thermal regulation of spring mating behavior in the red-sided garter snake *(Thamnophis sirtalis parietalis)*. Can. J. Zool. 53:768–776.

———. 1976a. The influence of photoperiod and temperature on seasonal testicular recrudescence in the red-sided garter snake *(Thamnophis sirtalis parietalis)*. Comp. Biochem. Physiol. 53A:215–221.

———. 1976b. Sexual receptivity in the female red-sided garter snake *(Thamnophis sirtalis parietalis)*. Copeia 1976:401–404.

Hay, O. P. 1892. Descriptions of a supposed new species of *Storeria* from Florida. Science (New York) 19:199.

———. 1917. Vertebrates mostly from Stratum no. 3 at Vero, Florida; together with descriptions of a new species. Ann. Rept. Florida Geol. Surv. 9:43–68.

Hayes, F. E. 1985b. *Hypsiglena torquata deserticola* (desert night snake). Behavior. Herpetol. Rev. 16:79,81.

———. 1986. *Thamnophis couchi hammondi* (two-striped garter snake). Behavior. Herpetol. Rev. 17:22–23.

———. 1987. *Storeria dekayi dekayi* (northern brown snake). Behavior. Herpetol. Rev. 18:16–17.

Hayes, F. E., and W. S. Baker. 1986. *Thamnophis couchi hammondi* (two-striped garter snake). Behavior. Herpetol. Rev. 17:22–23.

Hayes, M. P. 1985a. *Coluber constrictor priapus* (southern black racer). Food. Herpetol. Rev. 16:78.

Hayes, W. K. 1986. Observations of courtship in the rattlesnake, *Crotalus viridis oreganus*. J. Herpetol. 20:246–249.

———. 1991. Ontogeny of striking, prey-handling and envenomation behavior of prairie rattlesnakes *(Crotalus v. viridis)*. Toxicon 29:867–875.

———. 1992. Factors associated with the mass of venom expended by prairie rattlesnakes *(Crotalus v. viridis)* feeding on mice. Toxicon 30:449–460.

———. 1993. Effects of hunger on striking, prey-handling, and venom expenditure of prairie rattlesnakes *(Crotalus v. viridis)*. Herpetologica 49:305–310.

Hayes, W. K., and D. Duvall. 1991. A field study of prairie rattlesnake predatory strikes. Herpetologica 47:78–81.

Hayes, W. K., D. Duvall, and G. W. Schuett. 1992. A preliminary report on the courtship behavior of free-ranging prairie rattlesnakes, *Crotalus viridis viridis* (Rafinesque), in south-central Wyoming, 45–48. In: P. Strimple and J. Strimple (eds.), Contributions in Herpetology. Cincinnati, Ohio: Greater Cincinnati Herpetological Society.

Hayes, W. K., and D. M. Hayes. 1993. Stimuli influencing the release and aim of predatory strikes of the northern Pacific rattlesnake *(Crotalus viridis oreganus)*. Northwest. Nat. 74:1–9.

Hayes, W. K., and F. E. Hayes. 1985. Human envenomation from the bite of the eastern garter snake, *Thamnophis s. sirtalis* (Serpentes: Colubridae). Toxicon 23:719–721.

Hayes, W. K., I. I. Kaiser, and D. Duvall. 1992. The Mass of venom expended by prairie rattlesnakes when feeding on rodent prey, 383–388. In: J. A. Campbell and E. D. Brodie, Jr. (eds.), Biology of the pit vipers. Tyler, Texas: Selva.

Hayes, W. K., E. A. Verde, and F. E. Hayes. 1994. Cardiac responses during courtship, male-male fighting, and other activities in rattlesnakes. J. Tennessee Acad. Aci. 69:7–9.

Haywood, C. A., and R. W. Harris. 1972. Fight between rock squirrel and bullsnake. Texas J. Sci. 22:427.

Heatwole, H. 1987. Sea snakes. Sydney, Australia: New South Wales University Press.

Heatwole, H., and E. P. Finnie. 1980. Seal predation on a sea snake. Herpetofauna 11:24.

Hebard, W. B. 1950. Adimorphic color pattern of the garter snake, *Thamnophis elegans vagrans,* in the Puget Sound region. Copeia 1950:217–219.

———. 1951a. Notes on the ecology of gartersnakes in the Puget Sound region. Herpetologica 7:61–62.

———. 1951b. Notes on the life history of the Puget Sound garter snake, *Thamnophis ordinoides.* Herpetologica 7:177–179.

Hebrard, J. J., and R. C. Lee. 1981. A large collection of brackish water snakes from the central Atlantic Coast of Florida. Copeia 1981:886–889.

Hecht, M. K., C. Kropach, and B. M. Hecht. 1974. Distribution of the yellow-bellied sea snake, *Pelamis platurus,* and its significance in relation to the fossil record. Herpetologica 30:387–396.

Hecht, M. K., and D. Marien. 1956. The coral snake mimic problem: A reinterpretation. J. Morph. 98:335–366.

Heckrotte, C. 1962. The effect of the environmental factors in the locomotory activity of the plains garter snake *(Thamnophis radix radix).* Anim. Behav. 10:193–207.

———. 1967. Relations of body temperature, size, and crawling speed of the common garter snake, *Thamnophis s. sirtalis.* Copeia 1967:759–763.

———. 1975. Temperature and light effects on the circadean rhythm and locomotory activity of the plains garter snake *(Thamnophis radix haydeni).* J. Interdiscipl. Cycle Res. 6:279–290.

Heinrich, G. 1996. *Micrurus fulvius fulvius* (eastern coral snake). Diet. Herpetol. Rev. 27:25.

Heinrich, G., and K. R. Studenroth, Jr. 1996. *Agkistrodon piscivorus conanti* (Florida cottonmouth). Diet. Herpetol. Rev. 27:22.

Heinrich, M. L., and D. W. Kaufman. 1985. Herpetofauna of the Konza Prairie Research Natural Area, Kansas. Prairie Nat. 17:101–112.

Heinrich, M. L., and H. E. Klaassen. 1985. Side dominance in constricting snakes. J. Herpetol. 19:531–533.

Heller, S., and M. Halpern. 1981. Laboratory observations on conspecific and congeneric scent trailing in garter snakes *(Thamnophis).* Behav. Neural Biol. 33:372–377.

Hellman, R. E., and S. R. Telford, Jr. 1956. Notes on a large number of red-bellied mudsnakes, *Farancia a. abacura,* from north-central Florida. Copeia 1956:257–258.

Henderson, R. W. 1970. Feeding behavior, digestion, and water requirements of *Diadophis punctatus arnyi* Kennicott. Herpetologica 26:520–526.

———. 1974a. Resource partitioning among snakes of the University of Kansas Natural History Reservation: A preliminary analysis. Milwaukee Public Mus. Contr. Biol. Geol. 1:1–11.

———. 1974b. Aspects of the ecology of the neotropical vine snake, *Oxybelis aeneus* (Wagler). Herpetologica 30:19–24.

———. 1982. Trophic relationships and foraging strategies of some New World tree snakes *(Leptophis, Oxybelis, Uromacer).* Amphibia-Reptilia 3:71–80.

Henderson, R. W., and M. H. Binder. 1980. The ecology and behavior of vine snakes *(Ahaetulla, Oxybelis, Thelotornis, Uromacer):* A review. Milwaukee Public Mus. Contr. Biol. Geol. 37:1–38.

Henderson, R. W., M. H. Binder, R. A. Sajdak, and J. A. Buday. 1980. Aggregating behavior and exploitation of subterranean habitat by gravid eastern milksnakes *(Lampropeltis triangulum).* Milwaukee Public Mus. Contr. Biol. Geol. 32:1–9.

Henderson, R. W., T. W. P. Micucci, G. Puorto, and R. W. Bourgeois. 1995. Ecological correlates and patterns in the distribution of Neotropical biomes (Serpentes: Boidae): A preliminary assessment. Herpetol. Nat. Hist. 3:15–27.

Henderson, R. W., and M. A. Nickerson. 1977. Observations on the feeding behaviour and movements of the snakes *Oxybelis aeneus* and *O. fulgidus.* British J. Herpetol. 5:63–667.

Hendricks, P. 1996. *Thamnophis elegans vagrans* (wandering garter snake). U.S.A.: Wyoming. Herpetol. Rev. 27:89.

Hensley, M. M. 1950. Results of a herpetological reconnaissance in extreme southwestern Arizona and adjacent Sonora, with a description of a new subspecies of the Sonoran whipsnake, *Masticophis bilineatus.* Trans. Kansas Acad. Sci. 53:270–288.

———. 1962. Another snake recorded in the diet of the bullfrog. Herpetologica 18:141.

Hensley, R. C., and K. G. Smith. 1986. Eastern bluebird responses to nocturnal black rat snake nest predation. Wilson Bull. 98:602–603.

Herald, E. S. 1949. Effects of DDT-oil solutions upon amphibians and reptiles. Herpetologica 5:117–120.

Herman, D. W. 1979. Captive reproduction in the scarlet kingsnake, *Lampropeltis triangulum elapsoides* (Holbrook). Herpetol. Rev. 10:115.

———. 1983. *Cemophora coccinea copei* (northern scarlet snake). Coloration and reproduction. Herpetol. Rev. 14:119.

Hermann, J. A. 1950. Mammals of the Stockton Plateau of northeastern Terrell County, Texas. Texas J. Sci. 2:368–393.

Herreid, C. F., II. 1961. Snakes as predators of bats. Herpetologica 17:271–272.

Herrington, R. E. 1989. Reproductive biology of the brown water snake, *Nerodia taxispilota*, in central Georgia. Brimleyana 15:103–110.

Hersek, M. J., D. H. Owings, and D. F. Hennessy. 1992. Combat between rattlesnakes *(Crotalus viridis oreganus)* in the field. J. Herpetol. 26:105–107.

Herzog, H. A., and G. M. Burghardt. 1986. Development of antipredator responses in snakes: I. Defensive and open-field behaviors in newborns and adults of three species of garter snakes *(Thamnophis melanogaster, T. sirtalis, T. butleri)*. J. Comp. Psychol. 100:372–379.

Herzog, H. A., and J. M. Schwartz. 1990. Geographical variation in the anti-predator behaviour of neonate garter snakes, *Thamnophis sirtalis*. Anim. Behav. 40:597–598.

Herzog, H. A., Jr., B. B. Bowers, and G. M. Burghardt. 1989a. Development of antipredator responses in snakes: IV. Interspecific and intraspecific differences in habituation of defensive behavior. Develop. Psychobiol. 22:489–508.

———. 1989b. Stimulus control of antipredator behavior in newborn and juvenile garter snakes *(Thamnophis)*. J. Comp. Psychol. 103:233–242.

———. 1992. Development of antipredator responses in snakes: V. Species differences in ontogenetic trajectories. Develop. Psychobiol. 25:199–211.

Hess, J. B., and W. D. Klimstra. 1975. Summer foods of the diamond-backed water snake *(Natrix rhombifera)*, from Reelfoot Lake, Tennessee. Trans. Illinois St. Acad. Sci. 68:285–288.

Heyrend, F. L., and A. Call. 1951. Growth and age in western striped racer and Great Basin rattlesnake. Herpetologica 7:28–40.

Hibbard, C. W. 1934. Notes on some cave bats of Kansas. Trans. Kansas Acad. Sci. 37:235–238.

———. 1937. *Hypsiglena ochrorhynchus* in Kansas and additional notes on *Leptotyphlops dulcis*. Copeia 1937:74.

———. 1964. A brooding colony of the blind snake, *Leptotyphlops dulcis dissecta* Cope. Copeia 1964:222.

Highfill, D. R., and R. A. Mead. 1975. Sources and levels of progesterone during pregnancy in the garter snake, *Thamnophis elegans*. Gen. Comp. Endocrinol. 27:389–400.

Highton, R. 1956. Systematics and variation of the endemic Florida snake genus *Stilosoma*. Bull. Florida St. Mus. Biol. Sci. 1:73–96.

———. 1976. *Stilosoma, S. extenuatum*. Cat. Am. Amphib. Rept. 183:1–2.

Hilken, G., and R. Schlepper. 1998. Der *Lampropeltis mexicana*-Komplex (Serpentes, Colubridae): Naturgeschichte und Terrarienhaltung. Salamandra 34:97–124.

Hill, R. E., and S. P. Mackessy. 1997. Venom yields from several species of colubrid snakes and differential effects of ketamine. Toxicon 35:671–678.

Hill, W. H. 1971. Pleistocene snakes from a cave in Kendall County, Texas. Texas J. Sci. 22:209–216.

Hillis, D. M. 1974. A note on cannibalism in corn snakes. Bull. Maryland Herpetol. Soc. 10:31–32.

———. 1977. An incident of death-feigning in *Sonora semiannulata blanchardi*. Bull. Maryland Herpetol. Soc. 13:116–117.

Hillis, D. M., and S. L. Campbell. 1982. New localities for *Tantilla rubra cucullata* (Colubridae) and the distribution of its two morphotypes. Southwest. Nat. 27:220–221.

Hingley, K. J. 1988. The maintenance and reproduction of the western fox snake, *Elaphe vulpina vulpina*, in captivity. Litt. Serpent. Engl. Ed. 8:111–122.

Hirschfeld, S. E. 1968. Vertebrate fauna of Nichol's Hammock, a natural trap. Quart. J. Florida Acad. Sci. 31:177–189.

Hirth, H. F. 1966a. Weight changes and mortality of three species of snakes during hibernation. Herpetologica 22:8–12.

———. 1966b. The ability of two species of snakes to return to a hibernaculum after displacement. Southwest. Nat. 11:49–53.

———. 1969. Body temperatures of snakes in different seasons. J. Herpetol. 3:99–100.

Hirth, H. F., and A. C. King. 1968. Biomass densities of snakes in the cold desert of Utah. Herpetologica 24:333–335.

Hirth, H. F., R. C. Pendleton, A. C. King, and T. R. Downard. 1969. Dispersal of snakes from a hibernaculum in northwestern Utah. Ecology 50:332–339.

Hjertaas, D. G., and P. Hjertaas. 1990. Predation at bank swallow colonies near Katepwa Lake. Blue Jay 48:163–165.

Hoffman, L. H. 1970a. Placentation in the garter snake *Thamnophis sirtalis*. J. Morph. 131:57–88.

———. 1970b. Observation on gestation in the garter snake, *Thamnophis sirtalis sirtalis*. Copeia 1970:770–780.

Hoffman, R. L. 1945. Notes on the herpetological fauna of Alleghany County, Virginia. Herpetologica 2:109–205.

Hoffman, R. L. 2000. *Elaphe guttata guttata* (corn snake). Catesbeiana 20:39–40.

Hoge, A. R. 1947. Notas Erpetológicas. 2. Dimorfismo sexual nos boides. Mem. Inst. Butantan 20:181–187.

Holbrook, J. E. 1836–1842. North American herpetology; or, a description of the reptiles inhabiting the United States. Vols. 1–33. Philadelphia: J. Dobson.

Holfort, T. 1996. Zur Fortpflanzung der Rauhen Grasnatter, *Opheodrys aestivus* (Linnaeus, 1766). Sauria (Berlin) 18(4): 19–22.

Hollingsworth, B. D., and E. Mellink. 1996. *Crotalus exsul lorenzoensis* (San Lorenzo Island rattlesnake). Arboreal behavior. Herpetol. Rev. 27:143–144.

Hollingsworth, B. D., and T. R. Prosser. 1997. Geographic distribution. *Thamnophis marcianus marcianus* (checkered garter snake). U.S.A.: California. Herpetol. Rev. 28:211.

Holman, J. A. 1958a. Notes on reptiles and amphibians from Florida caves. Herpetologica 14:179–180.

———. 1958b. The Pleistocene herpetofauna of Sabertooth Cave, Citrus County, Florida. Copeia 1958:276–280.

———. 1959a. Amphibians and reptiles from the Pleistocene (Illinoian) of Williston, Florida. Copeia 1959:96–102.

———. 1959b. A Pleistocene herpetofauna near Orange Lake, Florida. Herpetologica 15:121–124.

———. 1962a. Additional records of Florida Pleistocene amphibians and reptiles. Herpetologica 18:115–119.

———. 1962b. A Texas Pleistocene herpetofauna. Copeia 1962:255–261.

———. 1963. Late Pleistocene amphibians and reptiles of the Clear Creek and Ben Franklin local faunas of Texas. J. Grad. Res. Center So. Methodist Univ. 31:152–167.

———. 1964. Pleistocene amphibians and reptiles from Texas. Herpetologica 20:73–83.

———. 1965a. Pleistocene snakes from the Seymour Formation of Texas. Copeia 1965:102–104.

———. 1965b. A late Pleistocene herpetofauna from Missouri. Trans. Illinois St. Acad. Sci. 58:190–194.

———. 1965c. A small Pleistocene herpetofauna from Houston, Texas. Texas J. Sci. 27:418–423.

———. 1966. The Pleistocene herpetofauna of Miller's Cave, Texas. Texas J. Sci. 18:372–377.

———. 1967. A Pleistocene herpetofauna from Ladd's Georgia. Bull. Georgia Acad. Sci. 25:154–166.

———. 1968a. A Pleistocene herpetofauna from Kendall County, Texas. Quart. J. Florida Acad. Sci. 31:165–172.

———. 1968b. Upper Pliocene snakes from Idaho. Copeia 1968:152–158.

———. 1969a. The Pleistocene amphibians and reptiles of Texas. Publ. Mus., Michigan St. Univ., Biol. Ser. 4:161–192.

———. 1969b. Herpetofauna of the Slaton local fauna of Texas. Southwest. Nat. 14:203–212.

———. 1970. A Pleistocene herpetofauna from Eddy County, New Mexico. Texas J. Sci. 22:29–39.

———. 1971. Herpetofauna of the Sundahl local fauna (Pleistocene: Illinoian) of Kansas. Contr. Mus. Paleontol. Univ. Michigan 23:349–355.

———. 1972a. Amphibians and reptiles, 55–71. In: M. F. Skinner et al. (eds.), Early Pleistocene preglacial and glacial rocks and faunas of north-central Nebraska. Bull. Am. Mus. Nat. Hist. 148.

———. 1972b. Herpetofauna of the Kanapolis local fauna (Pleistocene: Yarmouth) of Kansas. Michigan Acad. 5:87–98.

———. 1974. Late Pleistocene herpetofauna from southwestern Missouri. J. Herpetol. 8:343–346.

———. 1975. Herpetofauna of the WaKeeney local fauna (Lower Pliocene: Clapendonian) of Trego County, Kansas. Univ. Michigan Mus. Paleontol. Pap. Paleontol. 12:49–66.

———. 1976. Paleoclimatic implications of "ecologically incompatible" herpetological species (late Pleistocene: southeastern United States). Herpetologica 32:290–295.

———. 1977a. America's northernmost Pleistocene herpetofauna (Java, northcentral South Dakota). Copeia 1977:191–193.

———. 1977b. The Pleistocene (Kansan) herpetofauna of Cumberland Cave, Maryland. Ann. Carnegie Mus. 46:157–172.

———. 1978. The late Pleistocene herpetofauna of Devil's Den Sinkhole, Levy County, Florida. Herpetologica 34:228–237.

———. 1979a. A review of North American tertiary snakes. Publ. Mus., Michigan St. Univ., Paleontol. Ser. 1:201–260.

———. 1979b. Herpetofauna of the Nash Local Fauna (Pleistocene: Aftonian) of Kansas. Copeia 1979:747–749.

———. 1980. Paleoclimatic implications of Pleistocene herpetofauanas of eastern and central North America. Trans. Nebraska Acad. Sci. 8:131–140.

———. 1981. A review of North American Pleistocene snakes. Publ. Mus. Michigan St. Univ. Paleontol. Ser. 1:261–306.

———. 1982a. A fossil snake (*Elaphe vulpina*) from a Pliocene ash bed in Nebraska. Trans. Nebraska Acad. Sci. 10:37–42.

———. 1982b. The Pleistocene (Kansas) herpetofauna of Trout Cave, West Virginia. Ann. Carnegie Mus. 51:391–404.

———. 1984. Herpetofauna of the Duck Creek and Williams local faunas (Pleistocene: Illinoian) of Kansas, 20–28. In: H. H. Genoways and M. R. Dawson (eds.),

Contributions in Quatenary vertebrate paleontology, a volune in memorial to John E. Guilday. Carnegie Mus. Nat. Hist. Spec. Publ. 8.

———. 1985. Herpetofauna of Ladds Quarry. Natl. Geogr. Res. 1:423–436.

———. 1986a. The known herpetofauna of the Late Quaternary of Virginia poses a dilemma, 36–42. In: J. N. McDonald and S. O. Bird (eds.), The Quarternary of Virginia—a symposium volume. Charlottesville: Commonwealth of Virginia, Dept. of Mines, Minerals, and Energy, Division of Mineral Resources.

———. 1986b. Snakes of the Berends local fauna Pleistocene: Early Illinoian of Oklahoma. Copeia 1986:811–812.

———. 1986c. Butler Springs herpetofauna of Kansas (Pleistocene: Illinoian) and its climatic significance. J. Herpetol. 20:568–570.

———. 1987a. Climatic significance of a late Illinoian herpetofauna from southwestern Kansas. Contr. Mus. Paleontol. Univ. Michigan 27:129–141.

———. 1987b. Snakes from the Robert local fauna (late Wisconsin) of Meade County, Kansas. Contr. Mus. Paleontol. Univ. Michigan 27:143–150.

———. 1987c. Herpetofauna of New Trout Cave. Natl. Geogr. Res. 3:305–317.

———. 1995. Pleistocene amphibians and reptiles in North America. New York: Oxford University Press.

———. 1996. The large Pleistocene (Sangamonian) herpetofauna of the Williston IIIA Site, North-central Florida. Herpetol. Nat. Hist. 4:35–47.

———. 1997. Amphibians and reptiles from the Pleistocene (Late Wisconsinan) of Sheriden Pit Cave, northwestern Ohio. Michigan Acad. 29:1–20.

———. 2000. Fossil snakes of North America. Bloomington: Indiana University Press.

Holman, J. A., G. Bell, and J. Lamb. 1990. A Late Pleistocene herpetofauna from Bell Cave, Alabama. Herpetol. J. 1:521–529.

Holman, J. A., and C. J. Clausen. 1984. Fossil vertebrates associated with paleo-Indian artifact at Little Salt Spring, Florida. J. Vert. Paleontol. 4:146–154.

Holman, J. A., and L. P. Fay. 1998. Racers (Coluber constrictor) from a Quaternary fissure near Rockton, Illinois—An ancient hibernaculum? Bull. Chicago Herpetol. Soc. 33:9–10.

Holman, J. A., and F. Grady. 1987. Herpetofauna of New Trout Cave. Natl. Geogr. Res. 3:305–317.

———. 1989. The fossil herpetofauna (Pleistocene: Irvingtonian) of Hamilton Cave, Pendelton County, West Virginia. Natl. Speleol. Soc. Bull. 51:34–41.

———. 1994. A Pleistocene herpetofauna from Worm Hole Cave, Pendleton County, West Virginia. Natl. Speleol. Soc. Bull. 56:46–49.

Holman, J. A., and W. H. Hill. 1961. A mass unidirectional movement of Natrix sipedon pictiventris. Copeia 1961:498–499.

Holman, J. A., and J. N. McDonald. 1986. A late Quaternary herpetofauna from Saltville, Virginia. Brimleyana 12:85–100.

Holman, J. A., and R. L. Richards. 1981. Late Pleistocene occurrence in southern Indiana of the smooth green snake, Opheodrys vernalis. J. Herpetol. 15:123–124.

Holman, J. A., and M. E. Schloeder. 1991. Fossil herpetofauna of the Lisco C Quarries (Pliocene: early Blancan) of Nebraska. Trans. Nebraska Acad. Sci. 18:19–29.

Holman, J. A., and A. J. Winkler. 1987. A mid-Pleistocene (Irvingtonian) herpetofauna from a cave in southcentral Texas. Texas Mem. Mus., Pearce-Sellards Ser. 44:1–17.

Holt, E. G. 1919. Coluber swallowing a stone. Copeia 76:99–100.

Holtzman, D. A. 1993. The ontogeny of nasal chemical senses in garter snakes. Brain Behav. Ecol. 41:163–170.

Holtzman, D. A., and M. Halpern. 1990. Embryonic and neonatal development of the vomeronasal and olfactory systems in garter snakes (Thamnophis spp.). J. Morph. 203:123–140.

Holtzman, D. A., G. R. ten Eyck, and D. Begun. 1989. Artificial hibernation of garter (Thamnophis sp.) and corn (Elaphe guttata guttata) snakes. Herpetol. Rev. 20:67–69.

Holycross, A. T. 1995. Crotalus viridis (western rattlesnake). Phenology. Herpetol. Rev. 26:37–38.

———. 2000a. Crotalus atrox (western diamondback rattlesnake). Morphology. Herpetol. Rev. 31:177–178.

———. 2000b. Crotalus viridis viridis (prairie rattlesnake). Morphology. Herpetol. Rev. 31:178.

———. 2000c. Crotalus willardi obscurus (New Mexico ridgenose rattlesnake). Caudal dichromotism. Herpetol. Rev. 31:246.

Holycross, A. T., and R. Simonson. 1998. Lampropeltis triangulum (milk snake). U.S.A.: Arizona. Herpetol. Rev. 29:113.

Hood, C. H., and O. Hawksley. 1975. A Pleistocene fauna from Zoo Cave, Taney County, Missouri. Missouri Speleol. 15:1–42.

Hopkins, M. N., Jr. 1981. Belted kingfisher nesting in sawdust pile. Oriole 45(1):22.

Hopkins, W. A., C. L. Rowe, and J. D. Congdon. 1999. Elevated trace element concentrations and standard metabolic rate in banded water snakes (Nerodia fasciata) exposed to coal combustion waste. Exp. Toxicol. Chem. 18:1258–1263.

Horwarth, B. 1974. Sperm storage: As a function of the

female reproductive system, 237–270. In: A. D. Johnson and C. W. Foley (eds.), The oviduct and its functions. New York: Academic Press.

Howell, C. T., and S. F. Wood. 1957. The prairie rattlesnake at Gran Quivara National Monument, New Mexico. Bull. So. California Acad. Sci. 56:97–98.

Howitz, J. L. 1986. Bullsnake predation on black-capped chickadee nest. Loon 58:132.

Hoyer, R. F. 1974. Description of a rubber boa (Charina bottae) population from western Oregon. Herpetologica 30:275–283.

Hoyer, R. F., R. T. Mason, M. P. LeMaster, and I. T. Moore. 2000. Observations of sharp-tailed snakes (Contia tenuis) in Oregon. Northwest. Sci. 81:77.

Hoyer, R. F., and G. R. Stewart. 2000a. Biology of the rubber boa (Charina bottae), with emphasis on C. b. umbratica. Part I: Capture, size, sexual dimorphism, and reproduction. J. Herpetol. 34:348–354.

———. 2000b. Biology of the rubber boa (Charina bottae), with emphasis on C. b. umbratica. Part II: Diet, antagonists, and predators. J. Herpetol. 34:354–360.

Hoyer, R. F., and R. M. Storm. 1991. Reproductive biology of the rubber boa Charina bottae, 109–118. In: M. Urichek (ed.), Proceedings of the 15th International Herpetological Symposium on Captive Propagation and Husbandry. Seattle, Washington: Herpetological Symposium, Inc.

Huang, S. Y., J. C. Perez, E. D. Rael, C. Lieb. M. Martinez, and S. A. Smith. 1992. Variation in the antigenic characteristics of venom from the Mojave rattlesnake (Crotalus scutulatus scutulatus). Toxicon 30:387–396.

Huang, W.-S. 1996. Sexual size dimorphism of sea snakes in Taiwan. Bull. Natl. Mus. Sci. (Taichung) 7:113–120.

Hubble, D. A. 1971. A comparison of karyotypes of Storeria dekayi (Holbrook) and Storeria occipitomaculata (Storer) from northwestern Louisiana. Swanews 971(2): 11.

Hudnall, J. A. 1979. Surface activity and horizontal movements in a marked population of Sistrurus miliarius barbouri. Bull. Maryland Herpetol. Soc. 15:134–138.

Hudson, D. M., and B. H. Brattstrom. 1977. A small herpetofauna from the Late Pleistocene of Newport Beach Mesa, Orange County, California. Bull. So. California Acad. Sci. 76:16–20.

Hudson, G. E. 1957. Late parturition in the rubber boa. Copeia 1957:51–52.

Hudson, R. G. 1947. Ophiophagous young black snakes. Herpetologica 3:178.

———. 1954. An annotated list of the reptiles and amphibians of the Unami Valley, Pa. Herpetologica 10:67–72.

Huheey, J. E. 1958. Some feeding habits of the eastern hog-nosed snake. Herpetologica 14:68.

———. 1959. Distribution and variation in the glossy water snake, Natrix rigida (Say). Copeia 1959:303–311.

———. 1970. Behavioral notes on mockingbirds and black rat snake. Chat 34:23.

Huheey, J. E., and W. M. Palmer. 1962. The eastern glossy watersnake, Regina rigida rigida, in North Carolina. Herpetologica 18:140–141.

Huheey, J. E., and A. Stupka. 1967. Amphibians and reptiles of Great Smoky Mountains National Park. Knoxville: University of Tennessee Press.

Hulme, J. H. 1952. Observation of a snake bite by a cottonmouth moccasin. Herpetologica 8:51.

Hulse, A. C. 1971. Fluorescence in Leptotyphlops humilis (Serpentes: Leptotyphlopidae). Southwest. Nat. 16:123–124.

———. 1973. Herpetofauna of the Fort Apache Indian Reservation, east central Arizona. J. Herpetol. 7:275–282.

Hulse, A. C., and K. L. Hulse. 1992. New county records for amphibians and reptiles from Pennsylvania. Herpetol. Rev. 23(2): 62–64.

Hunsaker, D., II. 1965. The ratsnake Elaphe rosalie in Baja California. Herpetologica 21:71–72.

Hurter, J. 1911. Herpetology of Missouri. Trans. St. Louis Acad. Sci. 20:59–274.

Hutchison, R. H. 1929. On the incidence of snake bite poisoning in the United States. Bull. Antivenin Inst. Am. 3:43–57.

Imler, R. H. 1945. Bullsnakes and their control on a Nebraska wildlife refuge. J. Wildl. Mgt. 9:265–273.

Ingermann, R. L., N. J. Berner, and F. R. Ragsdale. 1991a. Effect of pregnancy and temperature on red cell oxygen-affinity in the viviparous snake Thamnophis elegans. J. Exp. Biol. 156:399–406.

———. 1991b. Changes in red cell ATP concentration and oxygen-affinity following birth in the neonatal garter snake Thamnophis elegans. J. Exp. Biol. 157:579–584.

International Commission on Zoologial Nomenclature. 2000. Opinion 1960. Crotalus ruber Cope, 1892 (Reptilia, Serpentes): Specific name given precedence over that of Crotalus exsul Garman, 1884. Bull. Zool. Nomencl. 57:189–190.

Ippoliti, S. 1980. Cannibalism in a corn snake hatchling (Elaphe guttata). Bull. Philadelphia Herpetol. Soc. 28:14.

Iraha, T., and H. Kakazu. 1995. A case of predation on Ramphotyphlops braminus by Dinodon rufozonatus walli from Ishigakijima Island, Yaeyama Group. Akamata 12:21–22.

Irwin, K. J. 1995. Observations on amphibians and reptiles

in the Lower Rio Grande Valley, Texas. Kansas Herpetol. Soc. Newsl. 100:7–17.

Iverson, J. B. 1975. Notes on Nebraska reptiles. Trans. Kansas Acad. Sci. 78:51–62.

———. 1978. Reproductive notes on Florida snakes. Florida Scientist 41:201–207.

———. 1990. Sex ratios in snakes: A cautionary note. Copeia 1990:571–573.

———. 1995. *Heterodon nasicus* (western hognose snake). Reproduction. Herpetol. Rev. 26:206.

Jackson, D. L., and R. Franz. 1981. Ecology of the eastern coral snake *(Micrurus fulvius)* in northern peninsular Florida. Herpetologica 37:213–228.

Jackson, J. A. 1970. Predation of a black rat snake on yellow-shafted flicker nestlings. Wilson Bull. 82:329–330.

———. 1974. Gray rat snakes vs. red cockaded woodpecker: Predator-prey adaptation. Auk 91:342–347.

———. 1977. Notes on the behavior of the gray rat snake *(Elaphe obsoleta spiloides)*. J. Mississippi Acad. Sci. 22:94–96.

———. 1978. Predation by a gray rat snake on red-cockaded woodpecker nestlings. Bird-Banding 49:187–188.

Jackson, J. A., and O. H. Dakin. 1982. An encounter between a nesting barn owl and a gray rat snake. Raptor Res. 16:60–61.

Jackson, J. F. 1971. Intraspecific predation in *Coluber constrictor*. J. Herpetol. 5:196.

Jackson, J. F., and D. L. Martin. 1980. Caudal luring in the dusky pygmy rattlesnake, *Sistrurus miliarius barbouri*. Copeia 1980:926–927.

Jackson, M. K. 1977. Histology and distribution of cutaneous touch corpuscles in some leptotyphlopid and colubrid snakes (Reptilia, Serpentes). J. Herpetol. 11:7–15.

Jackson, M. K., and H. W. Reno. 1975. Comparative skin structure of some fossorial and subfossorial leptotyphlopid and colubrid snakes. Herpetologica 31:350–359.

Jacob, J. S. 1977. An evaluation of the possibility of hybridization between the rattlesnakes *Crotalus atrox* and *C. scutulatus* in the southwestern United States. Southwest. Nat. 22:469–485.

Jacob, J. S., and J. S. Altenbach. 1977. Sexual color dimorphism in *Crotalus lepidus klauberi* Gloyd (Reptilia, Serpentes, Viperidae). J. Herpetol. 11:81–84.

Jacob, J. S., and H. S. McDonald. 1975. Temperature preference and electrocardiography of *Elaphe obsoleta* (Serpentes). Comp. Biochem. Physiol. 52A:591–594.

———. 1976. Diving bradycardia in four species of North American aquatic snakes. Comp. Biochem. Physiol. 53A:69–72.

Jacob, J. S., and C. W. Painter. 1980. Overwinter thermal

ecology of *Crotalus viridis* in the north-central plains of New Mexico. Copeia 1980:799–805.

Jacob, J. S., S. R. Williams, and R. P. Reynolds. 1987. Reproductive activity of male *Crotalus atrox* and *C. scutulatus* (Reptilia: Viperidae) in northeastern Chihuahua, Mexico. Southwest Nat. 32:273–276.

Jacobson, E., H. Calderwood, and C. Spencer. 1980. Gastrotomy in a gulf hammock rat snake *(Elaphe obsoleta williamsi)*. Vet. Med. Sm. Anim. Clin. 75:877–880.

Jacobson, E., and W. G. Whitford. 1970. The effect of acclimation on physiological responses to temperature in the snakes *Thamnophis proximus* and *Natrix rhombifera*. Comp. Biochem. Physiol. 35A:439–449.

———. 1971. Physiological responses to temperature in the patch-nosed snake, *Salvadora hexalepis*. Herpetologica 27:289–295.

Jaksic, F. M., and H. W. Greene. 1984. Empirical evidence of non-correlation between tail loss frequency and predation intensity on lizards. Oikos 42:407–411.

James, E. 1823. Account of an expedition from Pittsburgh to the Rocky Mountains, performed in the years 1819, 1820, vol. 1. London: Longman, Hurst, Rees, Ovme, and Brown.

Jameson, D. L., and A. M. Jameson, Jr. 1956. Food habits and toxicity of the venom of the night snake. Herpetologica 12:240.

Jan, G. 1862. Enumerazione sistematica delle specie d'ofidi del grupo Calamaridae. Archiv. Zool. Anat. Fisiol. 2(1): 1–76.

———. 1863. Elenco sistematico degli ofidi descritti e disegnati per l'iconografia generale. Lombardi, Milano: Tipographia Di A.

Jansen, D. W. 1987. The myonecrotic effect of Duvernoy's gland secretion of the snake *Thamnophis elegans vagrans*. J. Herpetol. 21:81–83.

Janzen, D. H. 1970. Altruism by coatis in the face of predation by *Boa constrictor*. J. Mammal. 51:387–389.

Jayne, B. C. 1985. Swimming in constricting *(Elaphe g. guttata)* and nonconstricting *(Nerodia fasciata pictiventris)* colubrid snakes. Copeia 1985:195–208.

———. 1986. Kinematics of terrestrial snake locomotion. Copeia 1986:915–927.

Jemison, S. C., L. A. Bishop, P. G. May, and T. M. Farrell. 1995. The impact of pit-tags on growth and movement of the rattlesnake, *Sistrurus miliarius*. J. Herpetol. 29:129–132.

Jennings, M. R. 1983. *Masticophis lateralis*. Cat. Am. Amphib. Rept. 343:1–2.

———. 1997. *Pituophis melanoleucus annectans* (San Diego gopher snake) and *Masticophis lateralis lateralis* (California striped racer). Predation. Herpetol. Rev. 28:205–206.

Jennings, M. R., G. R. Rathbun, and C. A. Langtimm. 1996. *Pituophis melanoleucus catenifer* (Pacific gopher snake). Prey. Herpetol. Rev. 27:26.

Jennings, W. B., D. F. Bradford, and D. F. Johnson. 1992. Dependence of the garter snake *Thamnophis elegans* on amphibians in the Sierra Nevada of California. J. Herpetol. 26:503–505.

Jensen, J. B. 1996. *Heterodon simus* (southern hognose snake). Hatchling size. Herpetol. Rev. 27:25.

———. 2000. *Rana capito* (gopher frog). Predation. Herpetol. Rev. 31:42.

Johnson, B. D., H. L. Stahnke, and J. A. Hoppe. 1968. Variations of *Crotalus scutulatus* raw venom concentrations. J. Arizona Acad. Sci. 5:41–42.

Johnson, E. 1974. Zoogeography of the Lubbock Lake site. Mus. Bull. West Texas Mus. Assoc. 15:107–122.

———. 1987. Vertebrate remains, 49–89. In: E. Johnson (ed.), Late Quaternary studies on the Southern High Plains. College Station: Texas A&M University Press.

Johnson, E. K. 1987. Stability of venoms from the northern Pacific rattlesnake *(Crotalus viridis oreganus)*. Northwest. Sci. 61:110–113.

Johnson, E. K., K. V. Kardong, and C. L. Ownby. 1987. Observations on white and yellow venoms from an individual southern Pacific rattlesnake *(Crotalus viridis helleri)*. Toxicon 25:1169–1180.

Johnson, E. K., and C. L. Ownby. 1993. Isolation of a myotoxin from the venom of *Agkistrodon contortrix laticinctus* (broad-banded copperhead) and pathogenesis of myonecrosis induced by it in mice. Toxicon 31:243–255.

Johnson, G. 1992. Swamp rattler. Conservationist (Albany, New York) 47(2): 26–33.

———. 2000. Spatial ecology of the eastern massasauga *(Sistrurus c. catenatus)* in a New York peatland. J. Herpetol. 34:186–192.

Johnson, L. F., J. S. Jacob, and P. Torrence. 1982. Annual testicular and androgenic cycles of the cottonmouth *(Agkistrodon piscivorus)* in Alabama. Herpetologica 38:16–25.

Johnson, R. M. 1950. Mating activities between two subspecies of *Elaphe obsoleta*. Herpetologica 6:42–44.

Johnson, T. B. 1983. Status Report: *Crotalus willardi willardi* (Meek, 1905). U.S. Fish Wildl. Serv. Contr. 14-16-0002-81-224.

Johnson, T. B., and G. S. Mills. 1982. A preliminary report on the status of *Crotalus lepidus, C. pricei,* and *C. willardi* in southeastern Arizona. U.S. Fish Wildl. Serv. Contr. 14-16-0002-81-224.

Johnson, T. R. 1987. The amphibians and reptiles of Missouri. Jefferson City: Missouri Department of Conservation.

Jones, G. S., L. A. Thomas, and K. Wong. 1995. *Ramphotyphlops braminus* (Braminy blind snake). Massachusetts: Suffolk County: Boston. Herpetol. Rev. 26:210–211.

Jones, J. M. 1976. Variations of venom proteins in *Agkistrodon* snakes from North America. Copeia 1976:558–562.

Jones, K. B. 1988. Influence of prey on the feeding behavior of *Trimorphodon biscutatus lambda* (Colubridae). Southwest. Nat. 33:488–490.

———. 1990. Habitat use and predatory behavior of *Thamnophis cyrtopsis* (Serpentes: Colubridae) in a seasonally variable aquatic environment. Southwest. Nat. 35:115–122.

Jones, K. B., and W. G. Whitford. 1989. Feeding behavior of free-roaming *Masticophis flagellum*: An efficient ambush predator. Southwest. Nat. 34:460–467.

Jones, L. 1976. Field data on *Heterodon p. platyrhinos* in Prince George's County, Maryland. Bull. Maryland Herpetol. Soc. 12:29–32.

Jordan, R., Jr. 1970. Death-feigning in a captive red-bellied snake, *Storeria occipitomaculata* (Storer). Herpetologica 26:466–468.

Joy, J. E., and D. Crews. 1987. Hibernation in garter snakes *(Thamnophis sirtalis parietalis)*: Seasonal cycles of cold tolerance. Comp. Biochem. Physiol. 87A:1097–1101.

Joy, W. D. 1992. World record boa constrictor "rediscovered." Notes from NOAH 28(10): 21.

Judd, F. W., and M. Bray. 1996. Date of birth, litter, and neonate size of a diamondback water snake, *Nerodia rhombifer*, from southernmost Texas. Texas J. Sci. 48:85–86.

Judd, W. W. 1954. Observations on the food of the little brown snake *Storeria dekayi* at London, Ontario. Copeia 1954:62–64.

———. 1955. Observations on the habitat and food of the queen snake, *Natrix septemvittata*, at London, Ontario. Can. Field-Nat. 69:167–168.

Julian, G. 1951. Sex ratios of the winter population. Herpetologica 6:21–24.

Justy, G. M., and F. F. Mallory. 1985. Thermoregulatory behaviour in the northern water snake, *Nerodia s. sipedon*, and the eastern garter snake, *Thamnophis s. sirtalis*. Can. Field-Nat. 99:246–249.

Kamb, A. H. 1978. Unusual feeding behavior of the red milk snake, *Lampropeltis triangulum syspila* (Lacepede). Trans. Kansas Acad. Sci. 81:273.

Kamel, S., and R. E. Gatten, Jr. 1983. Aerobic and anaerobic activity metabolism of limbless and fossorial reptiles. Physiol. Zool. 56:419–429.

Kamosawa, M., and H. Ota. 1996. Reproductive biology of the Brahminy blind snake *(Ramphotyphlops braminus)* from the Ryukyu Archipelago, Japan. J. Herpetol. 30:9–14.

Kapus, E. J. 1964. Anatomical evidence for *Heterodon* being poisonous. Herpetologica 20:137–138.

Kardong, K. V. 1974. Kinesis of the jaw apparatus during the strike in the cottonmouth snake, *Agkistrodon piscivorus*. Forma Functio 7:327–354.

———. 1979. "Protovipers" and the evolution of snake fangs. Evolution 33:433–443.

———. 1980. Gopher snakes and rattlesnakes: Presumptive Batesian mimicry. Northwest. Sci. 54:1–4.

———. 1986a. Predatory strike behavior of the rattlesnake, *Crotalus viridis oreganus*. J. Comp. Psychol. 100:304–314.

———. 1986b. The predatory strike of the rattlesnake: When things go amiss. Copeia 1986:816–820.

———. 1996. Mechanical damage inflicted by fangs on prey during predatory strikes by rattlesnakes, *Crotalus viridis oreganus*. Bull. Maryland Herpetol. Soc. 32:113–118.

Kardong, K. V., and V. L. Bels. 1998. Rattlesnake strike behavior: Kinematics. J. Exp. Biol. 201:837–850.

Kardong, K. V., and D. L. Luchtel. 1986. Ultrastructure of Duvernoy's gland from the wandering garter snake, *Thamnophis elegans vagrans* (Serpentes, Colubridae). J. Morph. 188:1–13.

Kasper, S., and S. N. Kasper. 1997. *Thamnophis elegans vagrans* (wandering garter snake). Paralysis. Herpetol. Rev. 28:46.

Kasper, S., and D. Parmley. 1990. A late Pleistocene herpetofauna from the lower Texas Panhandle. Texas J. Sci. 42:289–294.

Kassay, E. 1957. Evidence of ophiophagy in the night snake. Herpetologica 13:172.

Kassing, E. F. 1961. A life history study of the Great Plains ground snake, *Sonora episcopa episcopa* (Kennicott). Texas J. Sci. 13:185–203.

Kats, L. B. 1986. *Nerodia sipedon* (northern water snake). Feeding. Herpetol. Rev. 17:61, 64.

Kats, L. B., J. A. Goodsell, N. Matthews, C. Bahn, and A. R. Blaustein. 1998. *Taricha torosa* (California newt). Predation. Herpetol. Rev. 29:230.

Kauffeld, C. F. 1943a. Field notes on some Arizona reptiles and amphibians. Am. Midl. Nat. 29:342–359.

———. 1943b. Growth and feeding of new-born Price's and green rock rattlesnakes. Am. Midl. Nat. 29:607–614.

———. 1948. Notes on a hook-nosed snake from Texas. Copeia 1948:301.

———. 1957. Snakes and snake hunting. Garden City, New York: Hanover House.

———. 1969. Snakes: The keeper and the kept. Garden City, New York: Doubleday.

Kay, F. R. 1970. *Leptotyphlops humilis* in Death Valley, California. Great Basin Nat. 30:91–93.

Kean, C. A., and T. D. Tuberville. 1995. *Seminatrix pygaea* (black swamp snake). Size. Herpetol. Rev. 26:103.

Keck, M. B. 1994. A new technique for sampling semi-aquatic snake populations. Herpetol. Nat. Hist. 2:101–103.

———. 1998. Habitat use by semi-aquatic snakes at ponds on a reclaimed strip mine. Southwest. Nat. 43:13–19.

Keegan, H. L. 1944. Indigo snakes feeding upon poisonous snakes. Copeia 1944:59.

Keenlyne, K. D. 1972. Sexual differences in feeding habits of *Crotalus horridus horridus*. J. Herpetol. 6:234–237.

———. 1978. Reproductive cycles in two rattlesnakes. Am. Midl. Nat. 100:368–375.

Keenlyne, K. D., and J. R. Beer. 1973. Food habits of *Sistrurus catenatus catenatus*. J. Herpetol. 7:382–384.

Keiser, E. D., Jr. 1970. Sexual dimorphism and ontogenetic variation in the haemapophyses of ophidian postcloacal vertebrae. Herpetologica 26:331–334.

———. 1974. A systematic study of the neotropical vine snake, *Oxybelis aeneus* (Wagler). Texas Mem. Mus. Bull. 22:1–51.

———. 1975. Observations on tongue extension of vine snakes (genus *Oxybelis*) with suggested behavioral hypotheses. Herpetologica 31:131–133.

———. 1982. *Oxybelis aeneus*. Cat. Am. Amphib. Rept. 305:1–4.

———. 1993. *Agkistrodon piscivorus leucostoma* (western cottonmouth). Behavior. Herpetol. Rev. 24:34.

Keller, W. L., and E. J. Heske. 2000. Habitat use by three species of snakes at the Middle Fork Fish and Wildlife Area, Illinois. J. Herpetol. 34:558–564.

Kennedy, J. L. 1978. Field observations on courtship and copulation in the eastern king snake and the four-lined rat snake. Herpetologica 34:51–52.

Kennedy, J. P. 1959. A minimum egg complement for the western mud snake, *Farancia abacura reinwardti*. Copeia 1959:71.

———. 1964. Natural history notes on some snakes of eastern Texas. Texas J. Sci. 16:210–215.

———. 1965a. Notes on the behavior of a snake, *Oxybelis aeneus* Wagler, in Veracruz. Southwest. Nat. 10:136–144.

———. 1965b. Territorial behavior in the eastern coachwhip, *Masticophis flagellum*. Anat. Rec. 151:499.

Kennicott, R. 1856. Description of a new snake from Illinois. Proc. Acad. Nat. Sci. Philadelphia 8:95–96.

———. 1859a. Notes on *Coluber calligaster* of Say, and a description of new species of serpents in the collection of the North Western University of Evanston, Ill. Proc. Acad. Nat. Sci. Philadelphia 11:98–100.

———. 1859b. In: S. F. Baird (ed.), Report upon reptiles collected on the survey. Zoological Report part 4, no. 4, 9–13. In: Report of Henry L. Abbot upon explorations and surveys for a railroad route from the Sacramento Valley to the Columbia River, vol. 10. In: Reports of explorations and surveys, to ascertain the most practicable and economical route from the Mississippi River to the Pacific Ocean. Senate Exec. Doc. 78.

———. 1860a. Descriptions of new species of North American Serpentes in the Museum of the Smithsonian Institution, Washington. Proc. Acad. Nat. Sci. Philadelphia 12:328–338.

———. 1860b. [Descriptions of snakes] In: J. G. Cooper, Report upon reptiles collected on the survey, 292–396. [In] Reports of explorations and surveys, to ascertain the most practicable and economical route for a railroad from the Mississippi River to the Pacific Ocean, vol. 12. Washington, D.C.

———. 1861. On three new forms of rattlesnakes. Proc. Acad. Nat. Sci. Philadelphia 13:206–208.

Keogh, J. S. 1996. Evolution of the colubrid snake tribe Lampropeltini: A morphological perspective. Herpetologica 52:406–416.

——— 1998. Molecular phylogeny of elapid snakes and a consideration of their biogeographic history. Biol. J. Linn. Soc. 63:177–203.

Keogh, J. S., and F. P. DeSerto. 1994. Temperature dependent defensive behavior in three species of North American colubrid snakes. J. Herpetol. 28:258–261.

Kephart, D. G. 1981. Population ecology and population structure of Thamnophis elegans and Thamnophis sirtalis. Ph.D. Dissertation, University of Chicago.

———. 1982. Microgeographic variation in the diets of garter snakes. Oecologia (Berlin) 52:287–291.

Kephart, D. G., and S. J. Arnold. 1982. Garter snake diets in a fluctuating environment: A seven year study. Ecology 63:1232–1236.

Kern, G. W. 1956. A shrew eaten by a king snake, Lampropeltis c. calligaster (Harlan). Herpetologica 12:135.

Kilpatrick, C. W., and E. G. Zimmerman. 1973. Karyology of North American natricine snakes (family Colubridae) of the genera Natrix and Regina. Can. J. Genet. Cytol. 15:355–361.

King, K. A. 1975. Unusual food item of the western diamondback rattlesnake (Crotalus atrox). Southwest. Nat. 20:416–417.

King, M., and D. Duvall. 1990. Prairie rattlesnake seasonal migrations: Episodes of movement, vernal foraging and sex differences. Anim. Behav. 39:924–935.

King, M., D. McCarron, D. Duvall, G. Baxter, and W. Gern. 1983. Group avoidance of conspecific but not interspecific chemical cues by prairie rattlesnakes (Crotalus viridis). J. Herpetol. 17:196–198.

King, R. B. 1986. Population ecology of the lake Erie water snake, Nerodia sipedon insularum. Copeia 1986:757–772.

———. 1989. Body size variation among island and mainland snake populations. Herpetologica 45:84–88.

———. 1992. Lake Erie water snakes revisited: Morph- and age-specific variation in relative crypsis. Evol. Ecol. 6:115–124.

———. 1993a. Microgeographic, historical, and size-correlated variation in water snake diet composition. J. Herpetol. 27:90–94.

———. 1993b. Color-pattern variation in Lake Erie water snakes: Prediction and measurement of natural selection. Evolution 47:1819–1833.

———. 1993c. Color pattern in lake Erie water snakes: Inheritance. Can. J. Zool. 71:1985–1990.

———. 1993d. Determinants of offspring number and size in the brown snake, Storeria dekayi. J. Herpetol. 27:175–185.

———. 1997. Variation in brown snake (Storeria dekayi) morphology and scalation: Sex, family, and microgeographic differences. J. Herpetol. 31:335–346.

King, R. B., T. D. Bittner, A. Queral-Regil, and J. H. Cline. 1999. Sexual dimorphism in neonate and adult snakes. J. Zool. (London) 247:19–28.

King, R. B., J. H. Cline, and C. J. Hubbard. 2000. Age and litter effects on testosterone levels in young water snakes. Copeia 2000:593–596.

King, R. B., and R. Lawson. 1997. Microevolution in island water snakes. Bioscience 47:279–286.

King, R. B., A. Qureal-Regil, T. D. Bittner, J. M. Kerfin, and J. Hageman. 1999. Nerodia sipedon insularum (Lake Erie water snake). Diet. Herpetol. Rev. 30:169–170.

King, R. S. 1999. Habitat use and movement patterns of the eastern massasauga in Wisconsin, 80. In: B. Johnson and M. Wright (eds.), Second international symposium and workshop on conservation of the eastern massasauga rattlesnake, Sistrurus catenatus catenatus: Population and habitat management issues in urban, bog, prairie, and forested ecosystems. Scarborough, Ontario, Canada: Toronto Zoo.

Kingery, H. E., and U. C. Kingery. 1995. Gopher snake as predator at long-billed curlew and rough-winged swallow nests. Cent. Field Orinithol. J. 29:18–19.

Kinghorn, J. R. 1956. The snakes of Australia. London: Angus and Robertson.

Kingsbury, B. A. 1996. Status of the eastern massasauga, *Sistrurus c. catenatus*, in Indiana with management recommendations for recovery. Proc. Indiana Acad. Sci. 105:195–205.

Kingsbury, B. A., and C. J. Coppola. 2000. Hibernacula of the copperbelly water snake *(Nerodia erythrogaster neglecta)* in southern Indiana and Kentucky. J. Herpetol. 34:294–298.

Kirk, J. J. 1979. *Thamnophis ordinoides.* Cat. Am. Amphib. Rept. 233:1–2.

———. 1983. *Thamnophis ordinoides* (northwestern garter snake). Behavior. Herpetol. Rev. 14:22.

Kirk, V. M. 1969. An observation of a predator-escape technique practiced by a worm snake *Potamophis striatulus* (L.). Turtox News 47:44.

Kirkwood, J. K., and C. Gili. 1994. Food consumption in relation to bodyweight in captive snakes. Res. Vet. Sci. 57:35–38.

Kissner, K. J., G. Blouin-Demers, and P. J. Weatherhead. 2000. Sexual dimorphism in malodorousness of musk secretions of snakes. J. Herpetol. 34:491–493.

Kissner, K. J., D. M. Secoy, and M. R. Forbes. 1998. Sexual dimorphism in size of cloacal glands of the garter snake, *Thamnophis radix haydeni.* J. Herpetol. 32:268–270.

Kitchell, J. F. 1969. Thermophilic and thermophobic responses of snakes in a thermal gradient. Copeia 1969:189–191.

Kitchens, C. S., S. Hunter, and L. H. S. Van Mierop. 1987. Severe myonecrosis in a fatal case of envenomation by the canebrake rattlesnake *(Crotalus horridus atricaudatus).* Toxicon 25:455–458.

Kitchens, C. S., and L. H. S. Van Mierop. 1983. Mechanism of defibrination in humans after envenomantion by the eastern diamondback rattlesnake. Am. J. Hemotol. 14:345–354.

Klauber, L. M. 1924. Notes on the distribution of snakes in San Diego County, California. Bull. Zool. Soc. San Diego 1:1–23.

———. 1928. A list of the amphibians and reptiles of San Diego County, California. Bull. Zool. Soc. San Diego 4:1–8.

———. 1930. New and renamed subspecies of *Crotalus confluentis* Say, with remarks on related species. Trans. San Diego Soc. Nat. Hist. 6:95–144.

———. 1931a. A new subspecies of the California boa, with notes on the genus *Lichanura.* Trans. San Diego Soc. Nat. Hist. 6:305–318.

———. 1931b. A statistical survey of the snakes of the southern border of California. Bull. Zool. Soc. San Diego 8:1–93.

———. 1931c. Notes on the worm snakes of the Southwest, with descriptions of two new subspecies. Trans. San Diego Soc. Nat. Hist. 6:333–352.

———. 1933. Notes on *Lichanura.* Copeia 1933:214–215.

———. 1935a. *Phyllorhynchus,* the leaf-nosed snake. Bull. Zool. Soc. San Diego 12:1–31.

———. 1935b. A new subspecies of *Crotalus confluentus,* the prairie rattlesnake. Trans. San Diego Soc. Nat. Hist. 8:75–90.

———. 1936. A statistical study of the rattlesnakes: I. Introduction. II. Sex ratio. III. Birth rate. Occ. Pap. San Diego Soc. Nat. Hist. 1:1–24.

———. 1937. A new snake of the genus *Sonora* from Mexico. Trans. San Diego Soc. Nat. Hist. 8:363–366.

———. 1939a. Studies of reptile life in the arid Southwest. Bull. Zool. Soc. San Diego 14:1–100.

———. 1939b. A new subspecies of the western worm snake. Trans. San Diego Soc. Nat. Hist. 9:67–68.

———. 1939c. A statistical study of the rattlesnakes. VI. Fangs. Occ. Pap. San Diego Soc. Nat. Hist. 5:1–61.

———. 1940a. The worm snakes of the genus *Leptotyphlops* in the United States and northern Mexico. Trans. San Diego Soc. Nat. Hist. 9:87–162.

———. 1940b. The lyre snakes (genus *Trimorphodon*) of the United States. Trans. San Diego Soc. Nat. Hist. 9:163–194.

———. 1940c. Two new subspecies of *Phyllorhynchus,* the leaf-nosed snake, with notes on the genus. Trans. San Diego Soc. Nat. Hist. 9:195–214.

———. 1941. The long-nosed snakes of the genus *Rhinocheilus.* Trans. San Diego Soc. Nat. Hist. 9:289–332.

———. 1943a. Tail-length differences in snakes with notes on sexual dimorphism and the coefficient of divergence. Bull. Zool. Soc. San Diego 18:1–60.

———. 1943b. The subspecies of the rubber boa, *Charina.* Trans. San Diego Soc. Nat. Hist. 10:83–90.

———. 1944. The sidewinder, *Crotalus cerastes,* with description of a new subspecies. Trans. San Diego Soc. Nat. Hist. 10:91–126.

———. 1946a. The glossy snake, *Arizona,* with descriptions of new subspecies. Trans. San Diego Soc. Nat. Hist. 10:311–398.

———. 1946b. A new gopher snake *(Pituophis)* from Santa Cruz Island, California. Trans. San Diego Soc. Nat. Hist. 11:41–48.

———. 1949a. Some new and revised rattlesnakes. Trans. San Diego Soc. Nat. Hist. 11:61–116.

———. 1949b. The subspecies of the ridge-nosed rattle-snake, *Crotalus willardi*. Trans. San Diego Soc. Nat. Hist. 11:121–140.

———. 1951. The shovel-nosed snake, *Chionactis*, with descriptions of two new subspecies. Trans. San Diego Soc. Nat. Hist. 11:141–204.

———. 1972. Rattlesnakes: Their habits, life histories, and influence on mankind. 2nd ed. Berkeley: University of California Press.

Klawe, W. L. 1964. Food of the black-and-yellow sea snake, *Pelamis platurus*, from Ecuadorian coastal waters. Copeia 1964:712–713.

Klemens, M. W. 1993. Amphibians and reptiles of Connecticut and adjacent regions. Bull. Connecticut St. Geol. Nat. Hist. Surv. 112:1–318.

Kley, N. J., and E. L. Brainerd. 1999. Feeding by mandibular raking in a snake. Nature (London) 402:369–370.

Klimstra, W. D. 1959a. Food habits of the cottonmouth in southern Illinois. Chicago Acad. Sci. Nat. Hist. Misc. 168:1–8.

———. 1959b. Food habits of the yellow-bellied king snake in southern Illinois. Herpetologica 15:1–5.

———. 1959c. Foods of the racer, *Coluber constrictor*, in southern Illinois. Copeia 1959:210–214.

Klingener, D. 1957. A marking study of the shortheaded garter snake in Pennsylvania. Herpetologica 13:100.

Klippel, W. E., and P. W. Parmalee. 1982. The paleontology of Cheek Bend Cave, Phase II. Report to the Tennessee Valley Authority.

Kluge, A. G. 1993. *Calabaria* and the phylogeny of erycine snakes. Zool. J. Linn. Soc. 107:293–351.

Klynstra, F. B. 1959. Pas op met "Ongevaarlijke" slangen. Lacerta 17:31.

Knable, A. E. 1970. Food habits of the red fox *(Vulpes fulva)* in Union County, Illinois. Trans. Illinois St. Acad. Sci. 63:359–365.

Knapik, P. G., and J. R. Hodgson. 1986. *Storeria occipitomaculata* (redbelly snake). Predation. Herpetol. Rev. 17:22.

Kneeland, M. C., J. L. Koprowski, and M. C. Corse. 1995. Potential predators of Chiricahua fox squirrels *(Sciurus nayaritensis chiricahuae)*. Southwest. Nat. 40:340–342.

Knepton, J. C., Jr. 1951. Reproduction by a king snake *Lampropeltis getulus getulus* Linnaeus. Herpetologica 7:85–89.

Knight, A., L. D. Densmore III, and E. D. Rael. 1992. Molecular systematics of the *Agkistrodon* complex, 49–70. In: J. A. Campbell and E. D. Brodie, Jr. (eds.), Biology of the pitvipers. Tyler, Texas: Selva.

Knight, J. L. 1986. Variation in snout morphology in the North American snake *Pituophis melanoleucus* (Serpentes: Colubridae). J. Herpetol. 20:77–79.

Knight, J. L., and R. K. Loraine. 1986. Notes on turtle egg predation by *Lampropeltis getulus* (Linnaeus) (Reptilia: Colubridae) on the Savannah River Plant, South Carolina. Brimleyana 12:1–4.

Koch, E. D., and C. R. Peterson. 1995. Amphibians and reptiles of Yellowstone and Grand Teton National Parks. Salt Lake City: University of Utah Press.

Kochman, H. I., and S. P. Christman. 1992. Atlantic salt marsh snake *Nerodia clarkii taeniata* (Cope), 111–116. In: P.E. Moler (ed.), Rare and endangered biota of Florida. Vol. 3. Amphibians and reptiles. Gainesville: University Press of Florida.

Kofron, C. P. 1978. Foods and habitats of aquatic snakes (Reptilia, Serpentes) in a Louisiana swamp. J. Herpetol. 12:543–554.

———. 1979a. Reproduction in aquatic snakes in south-central Louisiana. Herpetologica 35:44–50.

———. 1979b. Female reproductive biology of the brown snake, *Storeria dekayi*, in Louisiana. Copeia 1979:463–466.

Kofron, C. P., and J. R. Dixon. 1980. Observations on aquatic colubrid snakes in Texas. Southwest. Nat. 25:107–109.

Kolbe, J. J. 1999. Size and demographic structure of an isolated population of the western hognose snake, *Heterodon nasicus*, in northwestern Illinois. Bull. Chicago Herpetol. Soc. 34:149–152.

Kolbe, J. J., L. J. Harmon, and D. A. Warner. 1999. New state record lengths and associated natural history notes for some Illinois snakes. Trans. Illinois St. Acad. Sci. 92:133–135.

Koob, T. J., and I. P. Callard. 1982. Relaxin: Speculations on its physiological importance in some nonmammalian species, 163–173. In: B. G. Steinetz, C. Schwalbe, and G. Weiss (eds.), Relaxin: Structure, function, and evolution. Ann. New York Acad. Sci. 380.

Korschgen, L. J. 1970. Soil-food-chain-pesticide wildlife relationships in aldrin-treated fields. J. Wildl. Mgt. 34:186–199.

Koster, W. J. 1940. The first record of the snake, *Hypsiglena*, from New Mexico. Herpetologica 2:30.

Kraus, F., D. G. Mink, and W. M. Brown. 1996. Crotaline intergeneric relationships based on mitochondrial DNA sequence data. Copeia 1996:763–773.

Krempels, D. M. 1984. Near infrared reflectance by coral snakes: Aposematic coloration? Progr. 6th Ann. Meet. Am. Soc. Ichthyol. Herpetol., p. 142.

Krevosky, G. E., and T. E. Graham. 1987. Large trout prey of the northern water snake. Bull. Chicago Herpetol. Soc. 22:133.

Krivda, W. 1993. Road kills of migrating garter snakes at the Pas, Manitoba. Blue Jay 51:197–198.

Krohmer, R. W. 1986. Effects of mammalian go-nadotropins (oFSH and oLH) on testicular develop-ment in the immature water snake, *Nerodia sipedon*. Gen. Comp. Endocrinol. 64:330–338.

———. 1989. Body temperature relationships in the lined snake, *Tropidoclonion lineatum*. Comp. Biochem. Physiol. 92A:541–543.

Krohmer, R. W., and R. D. Aldridge. 1985a. Male repro-ductive cycle of the lined snake *(Tropidoclonion linea-tum)*. Herpetologica 41:33–38.

———. 1985b. Female reproductive cycle of the lined snake *(Tropidoclonion lineatum)*. Herpetologica 41:39–44.

Krohmer, R. W., and D. Crews. 1987. Facilitation of courtship behavior in the male red-sided garter snake *(Thamnophis sirtalis parietalis)* following lesions of the septum or nucleus sphericus. Physiol. Behav. 40:759–765.

———. 1989a. Temperature activation of courtship be-havior in the male red-sided garter snake *(Thamnophis sirtalis parietalis)*: Role of the anterior hypothalamus-preoptic area. Behav. Neurosci. 101:228–236.

———. 1989b. Control of length of the courtship season in the red-sided garter snake, *Thamnophis sirtalis parietalis*: The role of temperature. Can. J. Zool. 67:987–993.

Krohmer, R. W., M. Grassman, and D. Crews. 1987. An-nual reproductive cycle in the male red-sided garter snake, *Thamnophis sirtalis parietalis*: Field and labora-tory studies. Gen. Comp. Endocrinol. 68:64–75.

Kroll, J. C. 1971. Combat behavior in male Great Plains ground snakes *(Sonora episcopa episcopa)*. Texas J. Sci. 23:300.

———. 1973. Taste buds in the oral epithelium of the blind snake, *Leptotyphlops dulcis* (Reptilia: Leptotyph-lopidae). Southwest. Nat. 17:365–370.

———. 1976. Feeding adaptations of hognose snakes. Southwest. Nat. 20:537–557.

Kroll, J. C., D. G. Zahradnik, and R. Ford. 1973. Thermo-genic cycles in *Opheodrys vernalis* and *Elaphe obsoleta* (Serpentes: Colubridae). Proc. West Virginia Acad. Sci. 45:77–81.

Kronen, D. 1980. Notes on the eggs and hatchlings of the longnose snake, *Rhinocheilus lecontei*, including the oc-currence of a semi-striped pattern. Bull. Chicago Her-petol. Soc. 15:54–56.

Kropach, C. 1971a. Sea snake *(Pelamis platurus)* aggrega-tions on slicks in Panama. Herpetologica 27:131–135.

———. 1971b. Another color variety of of the sea snake *Pelamis platurus* from Panama Bay. Herpetologica 27:326–327.

———. 1972. *Pelamis platurus* as a potential colonizer of the Caribbean Sea. Bull. Biol. Soc. Washington 2:267–269.

———. 1975. The yellow-bellied sea snake, *Pelamis*, in the eastern Pacific, 185–213. In: W. A. Dunson (ed.), The bi-ology of sea snakes. Baltimore, Maryland: University Park Press.

Kropach, C., and J. D. Soule. 1973. An unusual association between an ectoproct and a sea snake. Herpetologica 29:17–19.

Krutzch, P. H. 1944. California lyre snake feeding on the pocketed bat. J. Mammal. 25:410–411.

Krysko, K. L., and J. Decker. 1996. *Tantilla oolitica* (rim rock crowned snake). U.S.A.: Florida. Herpetol. Rev. 27:215.

Krysko, K. L., L. E. Krysko, and B. Dierking. 1998. *Lam-propeltis getula floridana* (Florida kingsnake). Combat ritual. Herpetol. Rev. 29:104.

Krysko, K. L., L. E. Krysko, and C. Hurt. 2000. Reproduc-tion and distribution of the South Florida mole kingsnake *(Lampropeltis calligaster occipitolineata)* from central peninsular Florida. J. Elisha Mitchell Sci. Soc. 116:344–347.

Kubie, J. L., J. Cohen, and M. Halpern. 1978. Shedding en-hances the sexual attractiveness of oestrodiol treated garter snakes and their untreated penmates. Anim. Behav. 26:562–570.

Kubie, J. L., and M. Halpern. 1975. Laboratory observa-tion of trailing behavior in garter snakes. J. Comp. Physiol. Psychol. 89:667–674.

———. 1978. Garter snake trailing behavior: Effects of varying prey-extract concentration and mode of prey-extract presentation. J. Comp. Physiol. Psychol. 92:362–373.

———. 1979. Chemical senses involved in garter snake prey trailing. J. Comp. Physiol. Psychol. 93:648–667.

Kumazawa, Y., H. Ota, M. Nishida, and T. Ozawa. 1996. Gene rearrangements in snake mitochondrial genomes: Highly concerted evolution of control-region-like se-quences duplicated and inserted into a tRNA gene clus-ter. Mol. Biol. Evol. 13:1242–1254.

Kupferberg, S. J. 1994. Exotic larval bullfrogs *(Rana cates-beiana)* as prey for native garter snakes. Functional and conservation implications. Herpetol. Rev. 25:95–97.

Kurfess, J. F. 1967. Mating, gestation, and growth rate in *Lichanura r. roseofusca*. Copeia 1967:477–479.

Lacépède, B. G. E. 1788–1789. Histoirie naturelle des quadrupèdes ovipares et des serpens. 2 vols. Paris: Académie Royal des Sciences.

Lacey, H., C. H. Shewchuk, P. T. Gregory, M. J. Sarell, and L. A. Gregory. 1996. The occurrence of the night snake,

Hypsiglena torquata, in British Columbia, with comments on its body size and diet. Can. Field-Nat. 110:620–625.

Lachner, E. A. 1942. An aggregation of snakes and salamanders during hibernation. Copeia 1942:262–263.

Lacki, M. J., J. W. Hummer, and J. L. Fitzgerald. 1994. Application of line transects for estimating population density of the endangered copperbelly water snake in southern Indiana. J. Herpetol. 28:241–245.

LaDuc, T. J., D. I. Lannutti, M. K. Ross, and D. Beamer. 1996. *Lampropeltis getula splendida* (desert kingsnake). Diet. Herpetol. Rev. 27:25.

LaDuke, T. C. 1991. The fossil snakes of Pit 91, Rancho La Brea, California. Contrib. Sci., Nat. Hist. Mus. Los Angeles Co. 424:1–28.

Lagesse, L. A., and N. B. Ford. 1996. Ontogenetic variation in the diet of the southern copperhead, *Agkistrodon contortrix*, in northeastern Texas. Texas J. Sci. 48:48–54.

Lagler, K. R., and J. C. Salyer, II. 1945. Influence of availability on the feeding habits of the common garter snake. Copeia 1945:159–162.

———. 1947 [1945]. Food and habits of the common watersnake, *Natrix s. sipedon*, in Michigan. Pap. Michigan Acad. Sci., Arts, Lett. 31:169–180.

Lamb, T., R. W. Gaul, Jr., M. L. Tripp, J. M. Horton, and B. W. Grant. 1998. A herpetofaunal inventory of the lower Roanoke River floodplain. J. Elisha Mitchell Sci. Soc. 114:43–55.

Lancaster, D. L., and S. E. Wise. 1996. Differential response by the ringneck snake, *Diadophis punctatus*, to odors of tail-autotomizing prey. Herpetologica 52:98–108.

Landreth, H. F. 1972. Physiological responses of *Elaphe obsoleta* and *Pituophis melanoleucus* to lowered ambient temperatures. Herpetologica 28:376–380.

———. 1973. Orientation and behavior of the rattlesnake, *Crotalus atrox*. Copeia 1973:26–31.

Landy, M. J., D. A. Langebartel, E. O. Moll, and H. M. Smith. 1966. A collection of snakes from Volcán Tacaná, Chiapas, Mexico. J. Ohio Herpetol. Soc. 5:93–101.

Lang, J. W. 1969. Hibernation and movements of *Storeria occipitomaculata* in northern Minnesota. J. Herpetol. 3:196–197.

Langebartel, D. A. 1953. The reptiles and amphibians, 97–108. In: R. T. Hatt (ed.), Faunal and archeological researches in Yucatan caves. Cranbrook Inst. Sci. Bull. 33.

Langebartel, D. A., and H. M. Smith. 1954. Summary of the Norris Collection of reptiles and amphibians from Sonora, Mexico. Herpetologica 10:125–136.

Langlois, T. H. 1924. Notes on some Michigan snakes. Pap. Michigan Acad. Sci., Arts, Lett. 4:605–610.

———. 1964. Amphibians and reptiles of the Erie Islands. Ohio J. Sci. 64:11–25.

LaPointe, J. 1953. Case report of a bite from the massasauga, *Sistrurus catenatus catenatus*. Copeia 1953:128–129.

Laposha, N. A., J. S. Parmerlee, Jr., R. Powell, and D. D. Smith. 1985. *Nerodia erythrogaster transversa* (blotched water snake). Reproduction. Herpetol. Rev. 16:81.

Lardie, G. E. 1976. Eastern hognose snake lays infertile eggs. Bull. Oklahoma Herpetol. Soc. 1:21.

Lardie, R. L. 1961. Ejection of a secretion from the vent of *Rhinocheilus lecontei*. Bull. Philadelphia Herpetol. Soc. 9(6): 18.

———. 1965. Eggs and young of *Rhinocheilus lecontei tessellatus*. Copeia 1965:366.

———. 1976a. Eggs of the Great Plains ground snake *Sonora episcopa episcopa* from Texas and Oklahoma. Bull. Oklahoma Herpetol. Soc. 1:19.

———. 1976b. Large centipede eaten by a western massasauga. Bull. Oklahoma Herpetol. Soc. 1:40.

———. 1976c. Distributional notes on the checkered garter snake and other *Thamnophis* in north-central Oklahoma. Bull. Oklahoma Herpetol. Soc. 1:56–57.

———. 1976d. Record-sized brood of checkered garter snakes. Bull. Oklahoma Herpetol. Soc. 1:67.

Larsen, K. W. 1987. Movements and behavior of migratory garter snakes, *Thamnophis sirtalis*. Can. J. Zool. 65:2241–2247.

Larsen, K. W., and P. T. Gregory. 1989. Population size and survivorship of the common garter snake, *Thamnophis sirtalis*, near the northern limit of its distribution. Holarctic Ecol. 12:81–86.

Larsen, K. W., P. T. Gregory, and R. Antoniak. 1993. Reproductive ecology of the common garter snake *Thamnophis sirtalis* at the northern limit of the range. Am. Midl. Nat. 129:336–345.

Laughlin, H. E. 1959. Stomach contents of some aquatic snakes from Lake McAlester, Pittsbourgh County, Oklahoma. Texas J. Sci. 11:83–85.

Laughlin, H. E., and B. J. Wilks. 1962. The use of sodium pentobarbital in population studies of poisonous snakes. Texas J. Sci. 14:188–191.

Lavín-Murcio, P. A., and K. V. Kardong. 1995. Scents related to venom and prey as cues in the poststrike trailing behavior of rattlesnakes, *Crotalus viridis oreganus*. Herpetologica 51:39–44.

Lawler, H. E. 1977. The status of *Drymarchon corais couperi* (Holbrook), the eastern indigo snake, in the southeastern United States. Herpetol. Rev. 8:76–79.

Lawson, P. A. 1989. Orientation abilities and mechanisms in a northern migratory population of the common garter snake *(Thamnophis sirtalis)*. Musk-Ox 37:110–115.

———. 1994. Orientation abilities and mechanisms in nonmigratory populations of garter snakes (*Thamnophis sirtalis* and *T. ordinoides*). Copeia 1994:263–274.

Lawson, P. A., and D. M. Secoy. 1991. The use of solar cues as migratory orientation guides by the plains garter snake, *Thamnophis radix*. Can. J. Zool. 69:2700–2702.

Lawson, R. 1987. Molecular studies of thamnophiine snakes: 1. The phylogeny of the genus *Nerodia*. J. Herpetol. 21:140–157.

———. 1996. Gene flow and melanism in Lake Erie garter snake populations. Biol. J. Linn. Soc. 59:1–19.

Lawson, R., and H. C. Dessauer. 1979. Biochemical genetics and systematics of garter snakes of the *Thamnophis elegans-couchii-ordinoides* complex. Occ. Pap. Mus. Zool. Louisiana St. Univ. 56:1–24.

Lawson, R., and C. S. Lieb. 1990. Variation and hybridization in *Elaphe bairdi* (Serpentes: Colubridae). J. Herpetol. 24:280–292.

Lawson, R., A. J. Meier, P. G. Frank and P. E. Moler. 1991. Allozyme variation and systematics of the *Nerodia fasciata-Nerodia clarkii* complex of water snakes (Serpentes: Colubridae). Copeia 1991:638–659.

Layne, J. N., and T. M. Steiner. 1984. Sexual dimorphism in occurrence of keeled dorsal scales in the eastern indigo snake (*Drymarchon corais couperi*). Copeia 1984:776–778.

Layne, J. R., and N. B. Ford. 1984. Flight distance of the queen snake, *Regina septemvittata*. J. Herpetol. 18:496–498.

Lazell, J. D. 1964. The Lesser Antillean representatives of *Bothrops* and *Constrictor*. Bull. Mus. Comp. Zool. 132:245–273.

———. 1988. *Typhlops braminus* (Brahminy blind snake). Rattling. Herpetol. Rev. 19:85.

———. 1993. *Heterodon platirhinos* (eastern hognose snake). Melanism heredity. Herpetol. Rev. 24:35.

Lazell, J. D., and J. A. Musick. 1981. Status of the Outer Banks kingsnake, *Lampropeltis getulus sticticeps*. Herpetol. Rev. 12:7.

Lazell, J. D., and J. C. T. Nisbet. 1972. Snake-eating terns. Man and Nature 1972(June): 27–29.

Leary, C. J., and V. R. Razafindratsita. 1998. Attempted predation on a hylid frog, *Phrynohyas venulosa*, by an indigo snake, *Drymarchon corais*, and the response of conspecific frogs to distress calls. Amphibia-Reptilia 19:442–446.

LeBuff, C. R., Jr. 1953. Observations on the eggs and young of *Drymarchon corais couperi*. Herpetologica 9:166.

Lee, D. S. 1968a. Herpetofauna associated with Central Florida mammals. Herpetologica 24:83–84.

———. 1968b. Springs as hibernation sites for Maryland's herpetofauna. Bull. Maryland Herpetol. Soc. 4:82–83.

Lee, R. K. K., D. A. Chiszar, and H. M. Smith. 1988. Poststrike orientation of the prairie rattlesnake facilitates location of envenomated prey. J. Ethology 6:129–134.

Lee, R. K. K., D. A. Chiszar, H. M. Smith, and K. Kandler. 1992. Chemical and orientational cues mediate selection of prey trails by prairie rattlesnakes (*Crotalus viridis*). J. Herpetol. 26:95–98.

Leonard, W. P., D. M. Darda, and K. R. McAllister. 1996. Aggregations of sharptail snakes (*Contia tenuis*) on the east slope of the Cascade Range in Washington State. Northwest. Nat. 77:47–49.

Leonard, W. P., and M. A. Leonard. 1998. Occurrence of the sharptail snake (*Contia tenuis*) at Trout Lake, Klickitat County, Washington. Northwest. Nat. 79:75–76.

Leonard, W. P., and K. Ovaska. 1998. *Contia, Contia tenuis*. Cat. Am. Amphib. Rept. 677:1–7.

Leonard, W. P., and R. C. Stebbins. 1999. Observations of antipredator tactics of the sharp-tailed snake (*Contia tenuis*). Northwest. Nat. 80:74–77.

Lewis, T. H. 1946. Notes on reptiles from the state of Washington. Copeia 1946:155–159.

———. 1949. Dark coloration in the reptiles of the Tularosa Malpais, New Mexico. Copeia 1949:181–184.

Lewis, T. H., and M. L. Johnson. 1956. Notes on a herpetological collection from Sinaloa, Mexico. Herpetologica 12:277–280.

Lewke, R. E. 1979. Neck-biting and other aspects of reproductive biology of the Yuma kingsnake (*Lampropeltis getulus*). Herpetologica 35:154–157.

———. 1982. *Lampropeltis getulus holbrooki* (speckled kingsnake). Food. Herpetol. Rev. 13:18.

Li, Q., T. R. Colberg, and C. L. Ownby. 1993. Purification and characterization of two high molecular weight hemorrhagic toxins from *Crotalus viridis viridis* venom using monoclonal antibodies. Toxicon 31:711–722.

Licht, E. L. 1985. *Thamnophis elegans vagrans* (gray garter snake), longevity. Bull. Maryland Herpetol. Soc. 21:150.

Licht, L. E. 1968. Unpalatability and toxicity of toad eggs. Herpetologica 24:93–98.

Licht, L. E., and B. Low. 1968. Cardiac responses of snakes after ingestion of toad parotoid venom. Copeia 1968:547–551.

Licht, P., and F. R. Gehlbach. 1961. *Ficimia cana* and *Tropidodipsas fasciata* (Reptilia: Serpentes) in San Luis Potosi, Mexico. Southwest. Nat. 6:197–198.

Lillywhite, H. B. 1982. Cannibalistic carrion ingestion by the rattlesnake, *Crotalus viridis*. J. Herpetol. 16:95.

————. 1985. Trailing movements and sexual behavior in *Coluber constrictor*. J. Herpetol. 19:306–308.

Lind, A. J., and H. H. Welsh, Jr. 1990. Predation by *Thamnophis couchii* on *Dicamptodon ensatus*. J. Herpetol. 24:104–106.

————. 1994. Ontogenetic changes in foraging behaviour and habitat use by the Oregon garter snake, *Thamnophis atratus hydrophilus*. Anim. Behav. 48:1261–1273.

Linder, A. D. 1963. Ophiophagy by the rubber boa. Herpetologica 19:143.

Lindner, D. 1962a. Feeding observations on *Micuroides*. Bull. Philadelphia Herpetol. Soc. 10(2–3): 31.

————. 1962b [1963]. Observations on the natural food preferences of the Mexican black-headed snake, *Tantilla atriceps*. Bull. Philadelphia Herpetol. Soc. 10(4): 32.

Lindsey, P. 1979. Combat behavior in the dusky pygmy rattlesnake, *Sistrurus miliarius barbouri*, in captivity. Herpetol. Rev. 10:93.

Liner, E. A. 1954. The herpetofauna of Lafayette, Terebonne, and Vermilion parishes, Louisiana. Proc. Louisiana Acad. Sci. 17:65–85.

————. 1977. Letisimulation in *Storeria dekayi limnetes* Anderson. Trans. Kansas Acad. Sci. 80:81–82.

————. 1983. *Tantilla wilcoxi*. Cat. Am. Amphib. Rept. 345:1–2.

————. 1990. A long lived record of an *Elaphe obsoleta obsoleta*. Bull. Chicago Herpetol. Soc. 25:50.

————. 1997. *Elaphe obsoleta lindheimeri* (Texas rat snake). Prey. Herpetol. Rev. 28:90.

Liner, E. A., and A. H. Chaney. 1990. *Tantilla rubra rubra* (red blackhead snake). Arborealty. Herpetol. Rev. 21:20.

Linnaeus, C. 1758. Systema naturae . . . 10th ed. Vol. 1. Sweden: Stockholm.

————. 1766. Systema naturae . . . 12th ed. Sweden: Stockholm.

Linsdale, J. M. 1940. Amphibians and reptiles in Nevada. Proc. Am. Acad. Arts Sci. 73:197–257.

Linzey, D. W. 1979. Snakes of Alabama. Huntsville, Alabama: Strode Publishers.

Linzey, D. W., and and M. J. Clifford. 1981. Snakes of Virginia. Charlottesville: University Press of Virginia.

List, J. C. 1950. Observations on the courtship behavior of *Thamnophis sirtalis sirtalis*. Herpetologica 6:71–74.

————. 1958. Notes on the skeleton of the blind snake, *Typhlops braminus*. Spolia Zeylan. 28:169–174.

Little, E. L., Jr. 1940. Amphibians and reptiles of the Roosevelt Reservoir area, Arizona. Copeia 1940:260–265.

Littlefield, C. D. 1971. An unusual encounter between an American bittern and common garter snake. Murrelet 52:27–28.

Liu, C.-S., C.-L. Wang, and R. Q. Blackwell. 1975. Isolation and partial characterization of pelamitoxin A from *Pelamis platurus* venom. Toxicon 13:31–36.

Loafman, P., and L. Jones. 1996. *Dicampeton copei* (Cope's giant salamander). Metamorphosis and predation. Herpetol. Rev. 27:136.

Lockington, W. N. 1876. Description of a new genus and species of colubrine snake. Proc. California Acad. Sci. 7:52–53.

Lockwood, R. A. 1954. Food habits of the mole snake. Herpetologica 10:110.

Logan, L. E., and C. C. Black. 1979. The Quarternary vertebrate fauna of Upper Sloth Cave, Guadalupe Mountains National Park, Texas. U.S. Natl. Park Serv. Trans. Proc. Ser. 4:141–158.

Lohrer, F. E. 1980. Eastern coachwhip predation on nestling blue jays. Florida Field Nat. 8:28–29.

Lopez, T. J., and L. R. Maxson. 1995. Mitochondrial DNA sequence variation and genetic differentiation among colubrine snakes (Reptilia: Colubridae: Colubrinae). Biochem. System. Ecol. 23:487–505.

————. 1996. Albumin and mitochondrial DNA evolution: Phylogenetic implications for colubrine snakes (Colubridae: Colubrinae). Amphibia-Reptilia 17:247–259.

Love, W. B. 1978. Observations on the herpetofauna of Key West, Florida, with special emphasis on the rosy rat snake. Bull. Georgia Herpetol. Soc. 4:3–8.

————. 1995. *Osteopilus septentrionalis* (Cuban treefrog). Predation. Herpetol. Rev. 26:201–202.

————. 2000. *Gekko gekko* (Tokay gekko). Predation. Herpetol. Rev. 31:174.

Loveridge, A. 1938. Food of *Micrurus fulvius fulvius*. Copeia 1938:201–202.

————. 1944. Cannibalism in the common coral snake. Copeia 1944:254.

Lowe, C. H. 1942. Notes on mating of desert rattlesnakes. Copeia 1942:261–262.

————. 1948a. Territorial behavior in snakes and the so-called courtship dance. Herpetologica 4:129–135.

————. 1948b. Effect of venom of *Micruroides* upon *Xantusia vigilis*. Herpetologica 4:136.

————. 1955. Generic status of the aquatic snake *Thamnophis angustirostris*. Copeia 1955:307–309.

————. 1964. The vertebrates of Arizona. Tucson: University of Arizona Press.

————. 1967. The amphibians and reptiles of Arizona, 153–174. In: C.H. Lowe (ed.), The vertebrates of Arizona. Tucson: University of Arizona Press.

Lowe, C. H., and K. S. Norris, Jr. 1950. Aggressive behavior in male sidewinders, *Crotalus cerastes*, with a discussion of aggressive behavior and territoriality in snakes. Chicago Acad. Sci. Nat. Hist. Misc. 66:1–13.

———. 1955. Analysis of the herpetofauna of Baja California, Mexico. III. New and revived reptilian subspecies of Isla de San Esteban, Gulf of California, Sonora, Mexico, with notes on other satellite islands of Isla Tiburón. Herpetologica 11:89–96.

Lowe, C. H., C. R. Schwalbe, and T. B. Johnson. 1986. The venomous reptiles of Arizona. Phoenix: Arizona Game and Fish Department.

Lowe, C. H., and W. H. Woodin III. 1954. A new racer (genus *Masticophis*) from Arizona and Sonora, Mexico. Proc. Biol. Soc. Washington 67:247–250.

Lowell, J. A. 1957. A bite by a sidewinder rattlesnake. Herpetologica 13:135–136.

Lucas, S. G., A. B. Heckert, and P. L. Sealey. 1995. A fossil specimen of the long-nosed snake *Rhinocheilus* from the Pliocene of southern New Mexico. Texas J. Sci. 47:9–12.

Luckydoo, A. K., and C. R. Blem. 1993. High temperature triggers circadian activity rhythms of brown water snakes *(Nerodia taxispilota)*. Virginia J. Sci. 44:111.

Ludlow, M. E. 1981. Observations on *Crotalus v. viridis* (Rafinesque) and the herpetofauna of the Ken-Caryl Ranch, Jefferson County, Colorado. Herpetol. Rev. 12:50–52.

Lueth, F. X. 1941. Effects of temperature on snakes. Copeia 1941:125–132.

Lundelius, E. L., Jr., R. W. Graham, E. Anderson, J. Guilday, J. A. Holman, D. W. Steadman, and S. D. Webb. 1983. Terrestrial vertebrate faunas, 311–353. In: S. Porter (ed.), The Late Pleistocene. Minneapolis: University of Minnesota Press, Minneapolis.

Lutterschmidt, W. I., J. J. Lutterschmidt, and H. K. Reinert. 1996. An improved timing device for monitoring pulse frequency of temperature-sensing transmitters in free-ranging animals. Am. Midl. Nat. 136:172–180.

Lutterschmidt, W. I., R. L. Nydam, and H. W. Greene. 1996. County record for the woodland vole, *Microtus pinetorum* (Rodentia: Muridae), LeFlore County, OK, with natural history notes on a predatory snake. Proc. Oklahoma Acad. Sci. 76:93–94.

Lutterschmidt, W. I., and L. A. Rayburn. 1993. Observations of feeding behavior in *Thamnophis marcianus* after surgical procedures. J. Herpetol. 27:95–96.

Lutterschmidt, W. I., and H. K. Reinert. 1990. The effect of ingested transmitters upon the temperature preference of the northern water snake, *Nerodia s. sipedon*. Herpetologica 46:39–42.

Lyman-Henley, L. P., and G. M. Burghardt. 1994. Opposites attract: Effects of social and dietary experience on snake aggregation behaviour. Anim. Behav. 47:980–982.

———. 1995. Diet, litter, and sex effects on chemical prey preference, growth, and site selection in two sympatric species of *Thamnophis*. Herpetol. Monogr. 9:140–160.

Lynch, J. D. 1965. The Pleistocene amphibians of Pit II, Arredondo, Florida. Copeia 1965:72–77.

———. 1966a. Additional treefrogs (Hylidae) from the North American Pleistocene. Ann. Carnegie Mus. 38:265–271.

———. 1966b. Communal egg laying in the pilot blacksnake, *Elaphe obsoleta obsoleta*. Herpetologica 22:305.

Lynch, W. 1978. Death-feigning in the eastern yellow-bellied racer. Blue Jay 36:92–93.

Lyon, M. W., and C. Bishop. 1936. Bite of the prairie rattlesnake *Sistrurus catenatus*. Raf. Proc. Indiana Acad. Sci. 45:253–256.

Lyons, W. J. 1971. Profound thrombocytopena associated with *Crotalus ruber* envenomation: A clinical case. Toxicon 9:237–240.

MacArtney, J. M. 1985. The ecology of the northern Pacific rattlesnake, *Crotalus viridis oreganus*, in British Columbia. Master's Thesis, University of Victoria, British Columbia.

———. 1989. Diet of the northern Pacific rattlesnake, *Crotalus viridis oreganus*, in British Columbia. Herpetologica 45:299–304.

MacArtney, J. M., and P. T. Gregory. 1981. Differential susceptibility of sympatric garter snake species to amphibian skin secretions. Am. Midl. Nat. 106:271–281.

———. 1988. Reproductive biology of female rattlesnakes *(Crotalus viridis)* in British Columbia. Copeia 1988:47–57.

MacArtney, J. M., P. T. Gregory, and M. B. Charland. 1990. Growth and sexual maturity of the western rattlesnake, *Crotalus viridis*, in British Columbia. Copeia 1990:528–542.

MacArtney, J. M., K. W. Larson, and P. T. Gregory. 1989. Body temperatures and movements of hibernating snakes *(Crotalus and Thamnophis)* and thermal gradients of natural hibernacula. Can. J. Zool. 67:108–114.

MacArtney, J. M., and B. Weichel. 1993. Status of the prairie rattlesnake and the eastern yellow-bellied racer in Saskatchewan. Prov. Mus. Alberta Nat. Hist. Occ. Pap. 19:291–299.

MacDonald, L. 1973. Attack latency of *Constrictor constrictor* as a function of prey activity. Herpetologica 29:45–48.

Macey, R. J. 1983. *Charina bottae* (Pacific rubber boa). Food. Herpetol. Rev. 14:19.

Macht, D. I. 1937. Comparative toxicity of sixteen specimens of *Crotalus* venom. Proc. Soc. Exp. Biol. Med. 36:499–501.

Mackessy, S. P. 1985. Fractionation of red diamond rattlesnake *(Crotalus ruber ruber)* venom: Protease, phosphodiesterase, L-amino acid oxidase activities and effects of metal ions and inhibitors on protease activity. Toxicon 23:337–340.

———. 1988. Venom ontogeny in the Pacific rattlesnake *Crotalus viridis helleri* and *C. v. oreganus.* Copeia 1988:92–101.

———. 1991. Morphology and ultrastructure of the venom glands of the northern Pacific rattlesnake *Crotalus viridis oreganus.* J. Morph. 208:109–128.

Mahaney, P. A. 1997. *Crotalus pricei* (twin-spotted rattlesnake). Reproduction. Herpetol. Rev. 28:205.

Mahrdt, C. R., and B. H. Banta. 1996. *Chionactis occipitalis annulata* (Colorado desert shovelnose snake). Predation and diurnal activity. Herpetol. Rev. 27:81.

———. 1997. *Aneides lugubris* (arboreal salamander). Predation. Herpetol. Rev. 28:81.

Malnate, E. 1939. A study of the yellow-lipped snake, *Rhadinaea flavilata* (Cope). Zoologica (New York) 24:359–366.

Manion, S. 1968. *Crotalus willardi*—The Arizona ridge-nosed rattlesnake. Herpetology 2(3): 27–30.

Manjarrez, J., and C. Macias Garcia. 1991. Feeding ecology of *Nerodia rhombifera* in a Veracruz swamp. J. Herpetol. 25:499–502.

———. 1992. *Thamnophis proximus rutiloris* (western ribbon snake). Herpetol. Rev. 23:61–62.

Mankins, J. V., J. R. Meyer, and G. Jarrell. 1965. Rat snake preys on bat in total darkness. J. Mammal. 46:496.

Mansueti, R. 1946. Mating of the pilot blacksnake. Herpetologica 3:998–100.

Mao, S.-H., B.-Y. Chen, F.-Yi Yin, and Y.-W. Guo. 1983. Immunotaxonomic relationships of sea snakes to terrestrial elapids. Comp. Biochem. Physiol. 74A:869–872.

Maple, W. T., and L. P. Orr. 1968. Overwintering adaptations of *Sistrurus catenatus* in northeastern Ohio. J. Herpetol. 2:179–180.

Mara, W. P. 1994. The scarlet snake. Reptile and Amphibian Mag. Mar./Apr. 1994:17–20.

———. 1995a. Salt marsh snakes. Reptile and Amphibian Mag. Mar./Apr. 1995:20–24.

———. 1995b. Observations on scarlet snakes, *Cemophora coccinea.* Trop. Fish Hobbyist 43:128, 130, 132, 134–137.

Marion, K. R., and O. J. Sexton. 1984. Body temperatures and behavioral activities of hibernating prairie rattlesnakes, *Crotalus viridis*, in artificial dens. Prairie Nat. 16:11–116.

Markel, R. G. 1990. Kingsnakes and milk snakes. Neptune, New Jersey: T. F. H. Publishing, Inc.

Markezich, A. 1962. Ophiophagy in western fox snakes, *Elaphe v. vulpina.* Bull. Philadelphia Herpetol. Soc. 10(4): 5.

Markx, A. 1986. De verzorging en de kweek van de Californische roze boa, *Lichanura trivirgata roseofusca.* Lacerta 44:77–81.

Marr, J. C. 1944. Notes on amphibians and reptiles from the central United States. Am. Midl. Nat. 32:478–490.

Marr, W. V. 1985. Gopher snake preys on northern oriole nestlings. Murrelet 66:95–97.

Martin, B. E. 1974. Distribution and habitat adaptations in rattlesnakes of Arizona. HERP: Bull. New York Herpetol. Soc. 10(3–4): 3–12.

———. 1975a. Notes on a brood of the Arizona ridge-nosed rattlesnake *Crotalus willardi willardi.* Bull. Maryland Herpetol. Soc. 11:64–65.

———. 1975b. An occurrence of the Arizona ridge-nosed rattlesnake, *Crotalus willardi willardi*, observed feeding in nature. Bull. Maryland Herpetol. Soc. 11:66–67.

———. 1975c. A brood of Arizona ridge-nosed rattlesnakes *(Crotalus willardi willardi)* bred and born in captivity. Bull. Maryland Herpetol. Soc. 12:187–189.

———. 1976a. Notes on the breeding behavior in a captive pair of Sonora mountain kingsnakes *(Lampropeltis pyromelana).* Bull. Maryland Herpetol. Soc. 12:23–24.

———. 1976b. A reproductive record for the New Mexican ridge-nosed rattlesnake *(Crotalus willardi obscurus).* Bull. Maryland Herpetol. Soc. 12:126–128.

Martin, D. L. 1984. An instance of sexual defense in the cottonmouth, *Agkistrodon piscivorus.* Copeia 1984:772–774.

Martin, K. 1979. Common garter snake predation on robin nestlings. Can. Field-Nat. 93:772–774.

Martin, P. J. 1930. Snake hunt nets large catch. Bull. Antivenin Inst. Am. 4:77–78.

Martin, P. S. 1958. A biogeography of reptiles and amphibians in the Gomez Frias Region, Tamaulipas, Mexico. Misc. Publ. Mus. Zool. Univ. Michigan 101:1–102.

Martin, R. A. 1974. Fossil vertebrates from the Haile XIVA fauna, Alachua County, Florida, 100–113. In: S. D. Webb (ed.), Pleistocene mammals of Florida. Gainesville: University Press of Florida.

Martin, W. F., and R. B. Huey. 1971. The function of the epiglottis in sound production (hissing) of *Pituophis melanoleucus.* Copeia 1971:752–754.

Martin, W. H. 1988. Life history of the timber rattlesnake. Catesbeiana 8:9–12.

———. 1990. The timber rattlesnake, *Crotalus horridus*, in the Appalachian Mountains of eastern North America. Catesbeiana 10:49.

———. 1993. Reproduction of the timber rattlesnake (*Crotalus horridus*) in the Appalachian Mountains. J. Herpetol. 27:133–143.

———. 1996. *Crotalus horridus* (timber rattlesnake). Reproductive phenology. Herpetol. Rev. 27:144–145.

Martin, W. H., and D. B. Means. 2000. Distribution and habitat relationships of the eastern diamondback rattlesnake (*Crotalus adamanteus*). Herpetol. Nat. Hist. 7:9–34.

Martof, B. 1955. Some records of reptiles in Georgia. Copeia 1955:302–305.

Martof, B., W. M. Palmer, J. R. Bailey, J. R. Harrison III, and J. Dermid. 1980. Amphibians and reptiles of the Carolinas and Virginia. Chapel Hill: University of North Carolina Press.

Marvel, B. 1972. A feeding observation on the yellow-bellied water snake, *Natrix erythrogaster flavigaster*. Bull. Maryland Herpetol. Soc. 8:52.

Mason, R. T. 1993. Chemical ecology of the red-sided garter snake, *Thamnophis sirtalis parietalis*. Brain Behav. Evol. 41:261–268.

Mason, R. T., and D. Crews. 1985. Female mimicry in garter snakes. Nature (London) 316:59–60.

Mathews, A. E. 1989. Conflict, controversy, and compromise: The Concho water snake (*Nerodia harteri paucimaculata*) versus the Stacy Dam and Reservoir. Environ. Mgt. 13:297–307.

Matity, J. G., D. P. Chivers, and R. J. F. Smith. 1994. Population and sex differences in antipredator responses of breeding fathead minnows (*Pimephales promelas*) to chemical stimuli from garter snakes (*Thamnophis radix* and *T. sirtalis*). J. Chem. Ecol. 20(8): 2111–2121.

Mattison, C. 1989. Notes on shovel-nosed snakes and sand snakes, *Chionactis* and *Chilomeniscus*. British Herpetol. Soc. Bull. 28:25–30.

Mattlin, R. H. 1946. Snake devours its own slough. Herpetologica 3:122.

———. 1948. Observations on the eggs and young of the eastern fox snake. Herpetologica 4:115–116.

Mauger, D., and T. P. Wilson. 1999. Population characteristics and seasonal activity of *Sistrurus catenatus catenatus* in Will County, Illinois: Implications for management and monitoring, 110–1124. In: B. Johnson and M. Wright (eds.), Second international symposium and workshop on the conservation of the eastern massasauga rattlesnake, *Sistrurus catenatus catenatus*: Population and habitat management issues in urban, bog, prairie, and forested ecosystems. Scarborough, Ontario, Canada: Toronto Zoo.

May, P. G., T. M. Farrell, S. T. Heulett, M. A. Pilgrim, L. A. Bishop, D. J. Spence, A. M. Rabatsky, M. G. Campbell, A. D. Aycrigg, and W. E. Richardson II. 1996. Seasonal abundance and activity of a rattlesnake (*Sistrurus miliarius barbouri*) in central Florida. Copeia 1996:389–401.

May, P. G., S. T. Heulett, T. M. Farrell, and M. A. Pilgrim. 1997. Live fast, love hard, and die young: The ecology of pigmy rattlesnakes. Reptile & Amphibian Mag. Jan./Feb. 1997:36–49.

Mazzarella, D. 1974. Growth rate of *Lichanura r. roseofusca* in captivity. Bull. Maryland Herpetol. Soc. 10:115–117.

McAllister, A. J. 1995. Wetland use by the black rat snake, *Elaphe obsoleta*, in eastern Ontario. Can. Field-Nat. 109:449–451.

McAllister, C. T. 1985. *Nerodia rhombifera*. Cat. Am. Amphib. Rept. 376:1–4.

McAllister, W. H. 1963. Evidence of mild toxicity in the saliva of the hognose snake (*Heterodon*). Herpetologica 19:132–137.

McCallion, J. 1944. Notes on *Natrix harteri* in captivity. Copeia 1944:63.

McCauley, R. H., Jr. 1945. The reptiles of Maryland and the District of Columbia. Hagerstown, Maryland: Privately published.

McCleary, R. J. R., and R. W. McDiarmid. 1993. *Phyllorhynchus descurtatus*. Cat. Am. Amphib. Rept. 580:1–5.

McCoid, M. J., T. H. Fritts, and E. W. Campbell, III. 1994. A brown tree snake (Colubridae: *Boiga irregularis*) sighting in Texas. Texas J. Sci. 46:365–368.

McComb, W. C., and R. E. Noble. 1981. Herpetofaunal use of natural tree cavities and nest boxes. Wildl. Soc. Bull. 9:262–267.

McCoy, C. J. 1960. An unusually large aggregation of *Leptotyphlops*. Copeia 1960:368.

———. 1961a. Birth season and young of *Crotalus scutulatus* and *Agkistrodon contortrix lacticinctus*. Herpetologica 17:140.

———. 1961b. Additional records of *Ficimia cana* from Mexico and Texas. Herpetologica 17:215.

———. 1961c. A technique for collecting in urban areas. J. Ohio Herpetol. Soc. 3:4.

———. 1975. Cave-associated snakes, *Elaphe guttata*, in Oklahoma. Natl. Speleol. Soc. Bull. 37:41.

———. 1982. Amphibians and reptiles in Pennsylvania. Spec. Publ. Carnegie Mus. Nat. Hist. 6:1–91.

McCoy, C. J., and F. R. Gehlbach. 1967. Cloacal hemorrhage and the defense display of the colubrid snake *Rhinocheilus lecontei*. Texas J. Sci. 19:349–352.

McCoy, C. J., and D. E. Hahn. 1979. The yellow-bellied sea snake, *Pelamis platurus* (Reptilia: Hydrophiidae), in the Philippines. Ann. Carnegie Mus. 48:231–234.

McCranie, J. R. 1980a. *Crotalus adamanteus*. Cat. Am. Amphib. Rept. 252:1–2.

———. 1980b. *Crotalus pricei*. Cat. Am. Amphib. Rept. 266:1–2.

———. 1980c. *Drymarchon, D. corais*. Cat. Am. Amphib. Rept. 267:1–4.

———. 1983. *Nerodia taxispilota*. Cat. Am. Amphib. Rept. 331:1–2.

———. 1990. *Nerodia erythrogaster*. Cat. Am. Amphib. Rept. 500:1–8.

McCrystal, H. K. 1982. *Elaphe guttata emoryi* (Great Plains rat snake). Food. Herpetol. Rev. 13:46–47.

McCrystal, H. K., and J. R. Dixon. 1983. Eggs and young of Schott's whipsnake, *Masticophis taeniatus schotti*. Texas J. Sci. 35:161–163.

McCrystal, H. K., and R. J. Green. 1986. *Agkistrodon contortrix pictigaster* (Trans-Pecos copperhead). Feeding. Herpetol. Rev. 17:61.

McCrystal, H. K., and M. J. McCord. 1986. *Crotalus mitchellii*. Cat. Am. Amphib. Rept. 388:1–4.

McDaniel, V. R., and J. P. Karges. 1983. *Farancia abacura*. Cat. Am. Amphib. Rept. 314:1–2.

McDiarmid, R. W. 1968. Variation, distribution, and systematic status of the black-headed snake *Tantilla yaquia* Smith. Bull. So. California Acad. Sci. 67:159–177.

———. 1977. *Tantilla yaquia*. Cat. Am. Amphib. Rept. 198:1–2.

McDiarmid, R. W., J. A. Campbell, and T'S. A. Touré. 1999. Snake species of the world: A taxonomic and geographic reference, vol. 1. Washington, D.C.: Herpetologists' League.

McDiarmid, R. W., J. F. Copp, and D. E. Breedlove. 1976. Notes on the herpetofauna of western Mexico: New records from Sinaloa and the Tres Marias Islands. Contr. Sci., Nat. Hist. Mus. Los Angeles Co. 275:1–17.

McDiarmid, R. W., and R. J. R. McCleary. 1993. *Phyllorhynchus*. Cat. Am. Amphib. Rept. 579:1–5.

McDonald, H. C., and E. Anderson. 1975. A Late Pleistocene vertebrate fauna from southeastern Idaho. Tebiwa 18:20–37.

McDowell, A. 1051. Bull snake active in December. Herpetologica 7:142.

McDowell, S. B. 1972. The genera of sea-snakes of the *Hydrophis* group (Serpentes: Elapidae). Trans. Zool. Soc. London 32:195–247.

McDuffie, G. T. 1961. Notes on the ecology of the copperhead in Ohio. J. Ohio Herpetol. Soc. 3:26–27.

McEachern, M. H. 1991. A color guide to corn snakes captive bred in the United States. Herpetocultural Library Ser. 400:1–49.

McGinnis, S. M., and R. G. Moore. 1969. Thermoregulation in the boa constrictor, *Boa constrictor*. Herpetologica 25:38–45.

McGurty, B. M. 1988. Natural history of the California mountain kingsnake *Lampropeltis zonata*, 73–88. In: H. F. DeLisle, P. R. Brown, B. Kaufman, and B. M. McGurty (eds.), Proceedings of the Conference on California Herpetology. Southwest. Herpetol. Soc. Spec. Publ. 4.

McIntosh, A. G. D., and P. T. Gregory. 1976. Predation on a bat by a western yellow-bellied racer. Can. Field-Nat. 90:73.

McIntyre, D. C. 1977. Reproductive habits of captive Trans-Pecos rat snakes, *Elaphe subocularis*. J. No. Ohio Assoc. Herpetol. 3(1): 20–22.

McKeever, J. L. 1958. Chipmunk and garter snake. Can. Field-Nat. 72:170.

McKeown, S. 1996. A field guide to reptiles and amphibians in the Hawaiian Islands. Los Osos, California: Diamond Head Publishing Co.

McKinney, C. O., and R. E. Ballinger. 1966. Snake predators of lizards in western Texas. Southwest. Nat. 11:410–412.

McKinstry, D. M. 1978. Evidence of toxic saliva in some colubrid snakes of the United States. Toxicon 16:523–534.

Mead, J. I. 1985. Paleontology of Hidden Cave: Amphibians and reptiles, 162–170. In: D. H. Thomas (ed.), The archaeology of Hidden Cave, Nevada. Anthropol. Pap. Am. Mus. Nat. Hist. 61.

———. 1988. Herpetofauna from Danger Cave, Last Supper Cave, and Hanging Rock Shelter, 116–120. In: D. K. Grayson (ed.), Danger Cave, Last Supper Cave, and Hanging Rock Shelter: The faunas. Anthropol. Pap. Am. Mus. Nat. Hist. 66.

Mead, J. I., and C. J. Bell. 1994. Late Pleistocene and Holocene herpetofaunas of the Great Basin and Colorado Plateau, 255–275. In: K. T. Harper, L. L. St. Clair, K. H. Thorne, and W. M. Hess (eds.), Natural history of the Colorado Plateau and Great Basin. Niwot: University Press of Colorado.

Mead, J. I., T. H. Heaton, and E. M. Mead. 1989. Lake Quaternary reptiles from two caves in the east-central Great Basin. J. Herpetol. 23:186–189.

Mead, J. I., E. L. Roth, T. R. Van Devender, and D. W. Steadman. 1984. The late Wisconsin vertebrate fauna from Deadman Cave, southern Arizona. Trans. San Diego Soc. Nat. Hist. 20:247–276.

Mead, J. I., R. S. Thompson, and T. R. Van Devender. 1982. Late Wisconsinan and Holocene fauna from Smith Creek Canyon, Snake Range, Nevada. Trans. San Diego Soc. Nat. Hist. 20:1–16.

Mead, J. I., and T. R. Van Devender. 1981. Late Holocene diet of *Bassariscus astutus* in the Grand Canyon, Arizona. J. Mammal. 62:439–442.

Mead, R. A., V. P. Eroschenko, and D. R. Highfill. 1981. Effects of progesterone and estrogen on the histology of the oviduct of the garter snake, *Thamnophis elegans*. Gen. Comp. Endocrinol. 45:345–354.

Meade, G. P. 1934a. Some observations on captive snakes. Copeia 1934:4–5.

———. 1934b. Feeding *Farancia abacura* in captivity. Copeia 1934b. 1934:91–92.

———. 1935. Hibernation of *Farancia abacura* in captivity. Copeia 1935:99.

———. 1937. Breeding habits of *Farancia abacura* in captivity. Copeia 1937:12–15.

———. 1940. Maternal care of eggs of Farancia. Herpetologica 2:15–20.

Means, D. B. 1985. Radio-tracking the eastern diamondback rattlesnake. Natl. Geogr. Soc. Res. Rep. 18:529–536.

———. 1986. Life history and ecology of the eastern diamondback rattlesnake *(Crotalus adamanteus)*. Final Project Rept. Tallahasse: Florida Game Fresh Water Fish Commission.

Means, L. L., and J. W. Goertz. 1983. Nesting activities of northern mockingbirds in northern Louisiana. Southwest. Nat. 28:61–70.

Mecham, J. S. 1959. Some Pleistocene amphibians and reptiles from Friesenhahn Cave, Texas. Southwest. Nat. 3:17–27.

———. 1983. *Nerodia harteri*. Cat. Am. Amphib. Rept. 330:1–2.

Mecham, J. S., and W. W. Milstead. 1949. *Lampropeltis alterna* from Pecos County, Texas. Herpetologica 5:140.

Medica, P. A. 1975. *Rhinocheilus, Rhinocheilus lecontei*. Cat. Am. Amphib. Rept. 175:1–4.

Medonca, M. T., and D. Crews. 1989. Effect of fall mating on ovarian development in the red-sided garter snake. Am. J. Physiol. 257:R1548–R1550.

Medonca, M. T., A. T. Tousignant, and D. Crews. 1996. Pinealectomy, melatonin, and courtship behavior in male red-sided garter snakes *(Thamnophis sirtalis parietalis)*. J. Exp. Zool. 274:63–74.

Medsger, O. P. 1922. Milk snake and red-bellied snake. Copeia 111:79–80.

Meek, S. E. 1906 [1905]. An annotated list of a collection of reptiles from southern California and northern Lower California. Field Columbian Mus. Publ. Zool. Ser. 7:3–19.

Megonigal, J. P. 1985. *Agkistrodon contortrix mokeson* (northern copperhead) and *Lampropeltis getulus getulus* (eastern kingsnake). Catesbeiana 5(1): 16.

Mehrtens, J. M. 1987. Living snakes of the world in color. New York: Sterling Publishing.

Mellink, E. 1990. *Crotalus scutulatus* (Mojave rattlesnake). Reproduction. Herpetol. Rev. 21:93.

Mendelson, J. R., and W. B. Jennings. 1992. Shifts in the relative abundance of snakes in a desert grassland. J. Herpetol. 26:38–45.

Menne, H. A. L. 1959. Lets over het voorkomen van ratelslangen in Canada. Lacerta 18:4–6.

Merli, J. 1992. Nesting habits of the northern pine snake *(Pituophis m. melanoleucus)*. Vivarium 4(1): 16–19.

Merrem, B. 1820. Tentamen systematis amphibiorum. Marburg: Krieger.

Mertens, R. 1956a. Uber reptilien bastarde, II. Senckenbergiana Biol. 37:383–394.

———. 1956b. Das Problem der Mimikry bei Korallenschlangen. Zool. Jahrb., System. 84:541–576.

———. 1957. Gibt es ein Mimikry bei Korallenschlangen? Natur u. Volk 87:56–66.

Meshaka, W. E., Jr. 1994. Clutch parameters of *Storeria dekayi* Holbrook (Serpentes: Colubridae) from south-central Florida. Brimleyana 21:73–76.

Meshaka, W. E., Jr., and K. P. Jansen. 1997. *Osteopilis septentrionalis* (Cuban treefrog). Predation. Herpetol. Rev. 28:147–148.

Meshaka, W. E., Jr., S. E. Trauth, and C. Files. 1988. *Elaphe obsoleta obsoleta* (black rat snake). Antipredator behavior. Herpetol. Rev. 19:84.

Metrolis, A. P. 1971. A feeding observation on the rainbow snake *(Farancia erytrogramma erythrogramma)*. Bull. Maryland Herpetol. Soc. 7:41.

Metter, D. E. 1963. A rattlesnake that encountered a porcupine. Copeia 1963:161.

Meylan, P. A. 1982. The squamate reptiles of the Ingles IA Fauna (Irvingtonian: Citrus County, Florida). Bull. Florida St. Mus. Biol. Sci. 27:1–85.

———. 1985. *Heterodon simus*. Cat. Am. Amphib. Rept. 375:1–2.

———. 1995. Pleistocene amphibians and reptiles from the Leisey Shell Pit, Hillsborough County, Florida. Bull. Florida St. Mus. Nat. Hist. 37:273–297.

Michaels, S. J. 1985a. Ophiophagy in two captive boids, *Eunectes murinus* and *Candoia carinata paulsoni*. Bull. Chicago Herpetol. Soc. 20:25–26.

———. 1985b. *Candoia carinata* (Soloman Island boa). Ophiophagy. Herpetol. Rev. 16:54.

Miller, D. E. 1985. Rain water drinking by the mangrove

water snake, *Nerodia fasciata compressicauda*. Herpetol. Rev. 16:71.

Miller, D. E., and H. R. Mushinsky. 1990. Foraging ecology and prey size in the mangrove water snake *Nerodia fasciata compressicauda*. Copeia 1990:1099–1106.

Miller, D. J. 1979. A life history study of the gray-banded kingsnake, *Lampropeltis mexicana alterna*, in Texas. Chihuahuan Desert Res. Inst. Contr. 87:1–48.

Miller, L. 1942. A Pleistocene tortoise from the McKittrick Asphalt. Trans. San Diego Soc. Nat. Hist. 9:439–442.

Miller. R. 1976. Aquatic behavior in the eastern garter snake, *Thamnophis s. sirtalis*. Bull. Maryland Herpetol. Soc. 12:122.

Miller, W. D. 1971. Pleistocene vertebrates of the Los Angeles Basin and vicinity (exclusive of Rancho La Brea). Nat. Hist. Mus. Los Angeles Co., Sci. Bull. 10:1–24.

Mills, M. S., and C. J. Hudson. 1995. *Nerodia taxispilota* (brown water snake). Diet. Herpetol. Rev. 26:149.

Mills, M. S., C. J. Hudson, and H. J. Berna. 1995. Spatial ecology and movements of the brown water snake (*Nerodia taxispilota*). Herpetologica 51:412–423.

Mills, M. S., S. M. Poppy, A. M. Mills, T. J. Ryan, and M. E. Dorcas. 2000. *Seminatrix pygaea* (black swamp snake). Diet. Herpetol. Rev. 31:47.

Mills, M. S., and S. R. Yeomans. 1993. *Heterodon platirhinus* (eastern hognose snake). Diet. Herpetol. Rev. 24:62.

Mills, T. 1995. Natural history of the scarlet kingsnake *Lampropeltis triangulum elapsoides* in South Carolina. Vivarium 7(2): 24–29.

Milstead, W. W. 1953. Geographic variation in the garter snake, *Thamnophis cyrtopsis*. Texas J. Sci. 5:348–379.

Milstead, W. W., J. S. Mecham, and H. McClintock. 1950. The amphibians and reptiles of the Stockton Plateau in northern Terrell County, Texas. Texas J. Sci. 1950:543–562.

Minesky, J. J., and R. D. Aldridge. 1982. The male reproductive cycle of the queen snake (*Regina septemvittata*) in western Pennsylvania. Progr. Ann. Jt. Meet. Soc. Stud. Amphib. Rept./Herpetol. League 1982, p. 114.

Minton, S. A., Jr. 1949a. The black-headed snake in southern Indiana. Copeia 1949:146–147.

———. 1949b. Coral snake preyed upon by a bullfrog. Copeia 1949:288.

———. 1953. Variation in venom samples from copperheads (*Agkistrodon contortrix mokeson*) and timber rattlesnakes (*Crotalus horridus horridus*). Copeia 1953:212–215.

———. 1956a. Some properties of North American pit viper venoms and their correlation with phylogeny, 145–151. In: E. Buckley and N. Porges (eds.), Venoms. Washington, D.C.: American Association for the Adancement of Science.

———. 1956b. A new snake of the genus *Tantilla* from West Texas. Fieldiana: Zool. 34:449–452.

———. 1959 [1958]. Observations on amphibians and reptiles of the Big Bend Region of Texas. Southwest. Nat. 3:28–54.

———. 1966. A contribution to the herpetology of West Pakistan. Bull. Am. Mus. Nat. Hist. 134:27–184.

———. 1967. Observations on toxicity and antigenic makeup of venoms from juvenile snakes. Toxicon 4:294.

———. 1968. The fate of amphibians and reptiles in a suburban area. J. Herpetol. 2:113–116.

———. 1972. Amphibians and reptiles of Indiana. Indiana Acad. Sci., Monogr. 3:1–346.

———. 1974. Venom diseases. Springfield, Illinois: Charles C. Thomas Publishing.

———. 1976. Serological relationships among some congeneric North American and Eurasian colubrid snakes. Copeia 1976:672–678.

———. 1980. *Thamnophis butleri*. Cat. Am. Amphib. Rept. 258:1–2.

———. 1983. *Sistrurus catenatus*. Cat. Am. Amphib. Rept. 332:1–2.

———. 1986. Non-poisonous snake bite. Herpetology 16:14.

———. 1990. Venomous bites by nonvenomous snakes: An annotated bibliography of colubrid envenomation. J. Wilderness Med. 1:119–127.

Minton, S. A., Jr., and A. B. Bechtel. 1958. Another Indiana record of *Cemophora coccinea* and a note on egg eating. Copeia 1958:47.

Minton, S. A., Jr., J. M. Cisneros, and B. M. de Cervantes. 1997. Ophiophagy by an arthropod-eating snake. Bull. Chicago Herpetol. Soc. 32:253.

Minton, S. A., Jr., and M. R. Minton. 1969. Venomous reptiles. New York: Scribner's.

Minton, S. A., Jr., and S. A. Weinstein. 1984. Protease activity and lethal toxicity of venoms from some little known rattlesnakes. Toxicon 22:828–830.

Mirarchi, R. E., and R. R. Hitchcock. 1982. Radio-instrumented mourning dove preyed upon by gray rat snake. Auk 99:583.

Mitchell, J. C. 1976. Notes on reproduction in *Storeria dekayi* and *Virginia striatula* from Virginia and North Carolina. Bull. Maryland Herpetol. Soc. 12:133–135.

———. 1977a. Geographic variation of *Elaphe guttata* (Reptilia: Serpentes) in the Atlantic Coastal Plain. Copeia 1977:33–41.

———. 1977b. An instance of cannibalism in *Agkistrodon*

contortrix (Serpentes: Viperidae). Bull. Maryland Herpetol. Soc. 13:119.

———. 1978. Balling behavior in *Chionactis occipitalis* (Reptilia, Serpentes, Colubridae). J. Herpetol. 12:435–436.

———. 1981. Notes on male combat in two Virginia snakes, *Agkistrodon contortrix* and *Elaphe obsoleta*. Catesbeiana 1(1): 7–9.

———. 1982a. *Farancia*. Cat. Am. Amphib. Rept. 292:1–2.

———. 1982b. *Farancia erytrogramma*. Cat. Am. Amphib. Rept. 293:1–2.

———. 1986. Cannibalism in reptiles: A worldwide review. Soc. Stud. Amphib. Rept. Herpetol. Circ. 15:1–37.

———. 1994. The reptiles of Virginia. Washington, D.C.: Smithsonian Institution Press.

Mitchell, J. C., and R. A. Beck. 1992. Free-ranging domestic cat predation on native vertebrates in rural and urban Virginia. Virginia J. Sci. 43:197–207.

Mitchell, J. C., and J. D. Groves. 1993. Intraspecific oophagy in reptiles. Herpetol. Rev. 24:126–130.

Mitchell, J. C., C. A. Pague, and D. L. Early. 1982. *Elaphe obsoleta* (black rat snake). Autophagy. Herpetol. Rev. 13:47.

Mitchell, J. C., and G. R. Zug. 1984. Spermatogenic cycle of *Nerodia taxispilota* (Serpentes: Colubridae) in south-central Virginia. Herpetologica 40:200–204.

Mitchell, M. C., L. B. Best, and J. P. Gionfriddo. 1996. Avian nest-site selection and nesting success in two Florida citrus groves. Wilson Bull. 108:573–583.

Mittleman, M. B. 1949. Geographic variation in Marcy's garter snake, *Thamnophis marcianus* (Baird and Girard). Bull. Chicago Acad. Sci. 8:235–249.

Mocquard, M. F. 1899. Contribution à la faune herpétologique de la Basse-Californie. Nouv. Arch. Mus. d'Hist Nat. Paris, ser. 4, 1:297–344.

Moehn, L. D. 1967. A combat dance between two prairie kingsnakes. Copeia 1967:480–481.

Mole, R. R., and F. W. Urich. 1894. Biological notes upon some of the Ophidia of Trinidad, B.W. I, with a preliminary list of the species recorded from the island. Proc. Zool. Soc. London 1894:499–518.

Moler, P. E., ed. 1992. Rare and endangered biota of Florida. Vol. III. Amphibians and reptiles. Gainesville: University Press of Florida.

Moll, E. O. 1962. Recent herpetological records for Illinois. Herpetologica 18:207–209.

Monroe, E. A., and S. E. Monroe. 1968. Origin of iridescent colors on the indigo snake. Science (New York) 159:97–98.

Montgomery, G. G., and A. S. Rand. 1978. Movements, body temperature, and hunting strategy of a *Boa constrictor*. Copeia 1978:532–533.

Montgomery, W. B., and G. W. Shuett. 1989. Autumnal mating with subsequent production of offspring in the rattlesnake *Sistrurus miliarius streckeri*. Bull. Chicago Herpetol. Soc. 24:205–207.

Moon, B. R., and T. Candy. 1997. Coelomic and muscular cross-sectional areas in three families of snakes. J. Herpetol. 31:37–44.

Moore, I. T., M. P. Lemaster, and R. T. Mason. 2000. Behavioural and hormonal responses to capture stress in the male red-sided garter snake, *Thamnophis sirtalis parietalis*. Anim. Behav. 59:529–534.

Moore, I. T., J. P. Lerner, D. T. Lerner, and R. T. Mason. 2000. Relationships between annual cyces of testosterone, corticosterone, and body condition in male red-spotted garter snakes, *Thamnophis sirtalis concinnus*. Physiol. Biochem. Zool. 73:307–312.

Moore, R. G. 1978. Seasonal and daily activity patterns and thermoregulation in the southwestern speckled rattlesnake *(Crotalus mitchelli pyrrhus)* and the Colorado Desert sidewinder *(Crotalus cerastes laterorepens)*. Copeia 1978:439–442.

Mori, N., H. Ishizaki, and A. T. Tu. 1989. Isolation and characterization of *Pelamis platurus* (yellow-bellied sea snake) postsynaptic neurotoxin. J. Pharm. Pharmacol. 41:331–334.

Mori, N., T. Nikai, H. Sugihara, and A. T. Tu. 1987. Biochemical characterization of hemorrhagic toxins with fibrinogenase activity isolated from *Crotalus ruber ruber* venom. Arch. Biochem. Physiol. 253:108–121.

Moriarty, J. J., and M. Linck. 1997. Reintroduction of bullsnakes into a recreated prairie. In: J.J. Moriarty and D. Jones (eds.), Minnesota's amphibians and reptiles: Their conservation and status. Proc. Symp. Excelsior, Minnesota: Serpent's Tale.

Morris, M. A. 1974a. Notes on parturition in the Midland brown snake, *Storeria dekayi*. Trans. Illinois St. Acad. Sci. 67:3–4.

———. 1974b. Observations on a large litter of the snake *Storeria dekayi*. Trans. Illinois St. Acad. Sci. 67:359–360.

———. 1978. Temperature elevation as a releaser of mating behavior in some North American colubrid snakes. Bull. Chicago Herpetol. Soc. 13:9–12.

———. 1982. Activity, reproduction, and growth of *Opheodrys aestivus* in Illinois (Serpentes: Colubridae). Chicago Acad. Sci. Nat. Hist. Misc. 214:1–10.

———. 1984. *Elaphe obsoleta* (black rat snake). Autophagy. Herpetol. Rev. 15:19.

———. 1985. Envenomation from the bite of *Heterodon nasicus* (Serpentes: Colubridae). Herpetologica 41:361–585.

Morris, M. A., and K. Vail. 1991. Courtship and mating of

captive rough green snakes, *Opheodrys aestivus*, from Illinois. Bull. Chicago Herpetol. Soc. 26:34.

Mosauer, W. 1932a. Adaptive convergence in the sand reptiles of the Sahara and of California: A study of structure and behavior. Copeia 1932:72–78.

———. 1932b. The amphibians and reptiles of the Guadalupe Mountains of New Mexico and Texas. Occ. Pap. Mus. Zool. Univ. Michigan 246:1–18.

———. 1932c. On the locomotion of snakes. Science (New York) 76:583–585.

———. 1933. Locomotion and diurnal range of *Sonora occipitalis, Crotalus cerastes,* and *Crotalus atrox* as seen from their tracks. Copeia 1933:14–16.

———. 1935a. The reptiles of a sand dune area and its surroundings in the Colorado Desert, California: A study in habitat preference. Ecology 16:13–27.

———. 1935b. How fast can snakes travel? Copeia 1935:6–9.

———. 1936. The reptilian fauna of sand dune areas of the Vizcano Desert and of north-western Lower California. Occ. Pap. Mus. Zool. Univ. Michigan 329:1–26.

Mosauer, W., and E. L. Lazier. 1933. Death from insolation in desert snakes. Copeia 1933:149.

Mosimann, J. E., and G. B. Rabb. 1952. The herpetology of Tiber Reservoir area, Montana. Copeia 1952:23–27.

Moulis, R. 1976. Autecology of the eastern indigo snake, *Drymarchon corais couperi.* HERP: Bull. New York Herpetol. Soc. 12(3–4): 14–23.

Moulis, R., and G. K. Williamson. 1996. *Regina rigida* (glossy crayfish snake). Behavior. Herpetol. Rev. 27:146–147.

Mount, R. H. 1975. Reptiles and amphibians of Alabama. Auburn: Alabama Agricultural Experiment Station, Auburn University.

———. 1981. The red imported fire ant, *Solenopsis invicta* (Hymenoptera: Formicidae) as a possible serious predator on some native southeastern vertebrates: Direct observations and subjective impressions. J. Alabama Acad. Sci. 52:71–78.

Mount, R. H., and J. Cecil. 1982. *Agkistrodon piscivorus* (cottonmouth). Hybridization. Herpetol. Rev. 13:95–96.

Mount, R. H., and T. D. Schwaner. 1970. Taxonomic and distributional relationships between the water snakes *Natrix taxispilota* (Holbrook) and *Natrix rhombifera* (Hallowell). Herpetologica 26:76–82.

Mueller, J. M., and M. J. Whiting. 1989. *Masticophis flagellum testaceus* (western coachwhip). Predation. Herpetol. Rev. 20:72–73.

Mulaik, S., and D. Mulaik. 1941. *Elaphe bairdi* from Kerr County, Texas. Copeia 1941:263–264.

———. 1943. Observations on *Ficimia streckeri* Taylor. Am. Midl. Nat. 29:796–797.

Mullin, S. J. 1994. Life history characteristics of *Nerodia clarkii compressicauda* at Placido Bayou, Florida. J. Herpetol. 28:371–374.

———. 1996. Adaptations facilitating faculative oophagy in the gray rat snake, *Elaphe obsoleta spiloides.* Amphibia-Reptilia 17:387–394.

———. 1999. *Elaphe obsoleta spiloides* (gray rat snake). Reproduction. Herpetol. Rev. 30:100–101.

Mullin, S. J., and R. J. Cooper. 1998. The foraging ecology of the gray rat snake *(Elaphe obsoleta spiloides)*—Visual stimuli facilitate location of arboreal prey. Am. Midl. Nat. 140:397–401.

———. 2000. The foraging ecology of the gray rat snake *(Elaphe obsoleta spiloides).* II. Influence of habitat structural complexity when searching for arboreal avian prey. Amphibia-Reptilia 21:211–222.

Mullin, S. J., and W. H. N. Gutzke. 1999. The foraging ecology of the gray rat snake *(Elaphe obsoleta spiloides).* I. Influence of habitat structural complexity when searching for mammalian prey. Herpetologica 55:18–28.

Mullin, S. J., W. H. N. Gutzke, G. D. Zenitsky, and R. J. Cooper. 2000. Home ranges of rat snakes (Colubridae: *Elaphe*) in different habitats. Herpetol. Rev. 31:20–22.

Mullin, S. J., and H. R. Mushinsky. 1995. Foraging ecology of the mangrove salt marsh snake, *Nerodia clarkii compressicauda*: Effects of vegetational density. Amphibia-Reptilia 16:167–175.

———. 1997. Use of experimental enclosures to examine foraging success in water snakes: A case study. J. Herpetol. 31:565–569.

Mulvany, P. S. 1983. Tarantula preys on a western ribbon snake with notes on the relationship between narrowmouth toads and tarantulas. Bull. Oklahoma Herpetol. Soc. 8:92–99.

Mumme, R. L. 1987. Eastern indigo snake preys on juvenile Florida scrub jay. Florida Field Nat. 15:53–54.

Munro, D. F. 1949a. Excretia of a blue racer with reference to diet. Herpetologica 5:74.

———. 1949b. Food of *Heterodon nasicus nasicus.* Herpetologica 5:133.

———. 1949c. Gain in size and weight of *Heterodon* eggs during incubation. Herpetologica 5:133–134.

———. 1949d. Hatching of a clutch of *Heterodon* eggs. Herpetologica 5:134–136.

Murdaugh, H. V., Jr., and J. E. Jackson. 1962. Heart rate and blood lactic acid concentration during experimental diving of some snakes. Am. J. Physiol. 202:1163–1165.

Murphy, J. B., and J. A. Shadduck. 1978. Reproduction in the eastern diamondback rattlesnake, *Crotalus adamanteus*, in captivity, with comments regarding taratoid birth anomaly. British J. Herpetol. 5:727–733.

Murphy, J. C. 1980. The lyre snakes. Bull. Chicago Herpetol. Soc. 15:24–28.

———. 1997. Book review: *Snakes in question: The Smithsonian answer book* by Carl H. Ernst and George R. Zug. 1996. Bull. Chicago Herpetol. Soc. 32:170.

Murphy, J. C., and R. M. Curry. 2000a. A case of parthenogenesis in the plains garter snake, *Thamnophis radix*. Bull. Chicago Herpetol. Soc. 35:17–19.

———. 2000b. Erratum: A case of parthenogenesis in the plains garter snake, *Thamnophis radix*. Bull. Chicago Herpetol. Soc. 35:49

Murphy, J. C., and M. Dloogatch. 1980. An additional note on the egg-eating habits of the western hognose snake in Illinois. Bull. Chicago Herpetol. Soc. 15:98.

Murphy, J. C., B. W. Tryon, and B. J. Brecke. 1978. An inventory of reproduction and social behavior in captive gray-banded kingsnakes, *Lampropeltis mexicana alterna* (Brown). Herpetologica 34:84–93.

Murphy, R. W. 1988. The problematic phylogenetic analysis of interlocus heteropolymer isozyme characters: A case study from sea snakes and cobras. Can. J. Zool. 66:2628–2633.

Murphy, R. W., and C. B. Crabtree. 1985. Evolutionary aspects of isozyme patterns, number of loci, and tissue-specific gene expression in the prairie rattlesnake, *Crotalus viridis viridis*. Herpetologica 41:451–470.

———. 1988. Genetic identification of a natural hybrid rattlesnake: *Crotalus scutulatus scutulatus* × *C. viridis viridis*. Herpetologica 44:119–123.

Murphy, R. W., V. Kovac, O. Haddrath, G. S. Allen, A. Fishbein, and N. E. Mandrak. 1994. mtDNA gene sequence, allozyme, and morphological uniformity among red diamond rattlesnakes, *Crotalus ruber* and *Crotalus exsul*. Can. J. Zool. 73:270–281.

Murphy, T. D. 1964. Box turtle, *Terrapene carolina*, in stomach of copperhead, *Agkistrodon contortrix*. Copeia 1964:221.

Murray, L. T. 1939. Annotated list of amphibians and reptiles from the Chisos Mountains. Contr. Baylor Univ. Mus. 24:4–16.

Mushinsky, H. R. 1979. Mating behavior of the common water snake, *Nerodia sipedon sipedon*, in eastern Pennsylvania (Reptilia, Serpentes, Colubridae). J. Herpetol. 13:127–129.

———. 1984. Observations of the feeding habits of the short-tailed snake, *Stilosoma extenuatum* in captivity. Herpetol. Rev. 15:67–68.

Mushinsky, H. R., and J. J. Hebrard. 1977a. Food partitioning by five species of water snakes in Louisiana. Herpetologica 33:162–166.

———. 1977b. The use of time by sympatric water snakes. Can. J. Zool. 55:1545–1550.

Mushinsky, H. R., J. J. Hebrard, and D. S. Vodopich. 1982. Ontogeny of water snake foraging ecology. Ecology 63:1624–1629.

Mushinsky, H. R., J. J. Hebrard, and M. S. Walley. 1980. The role of temperature on the behavioral and ecological associations of sympatric watersnakes. Copeia 1980:744–754.

Mushinsky, H. R., and K. H. Lotz. 1980. Chemoreceptive responses of two sympatric water snakes to extracts of commonly ingested prey species. Ontogenetic and ecological considerations. J. Chem. Ecol. 6:523–535.

Mushinsky, H. R., and D. E. Miller. 1993. Predation on water snakes: Ontogenetic and interspecific considerations. Copeia 1993:660–665.

Mushinsky, H. R., and B. W. Witz. 1993. Notes on the peninsula crowned snake, *Tantilla relicta,* in periodically burned habitat. J. Herpetol. 27:468–470.

Mutschmann, F. 1999. Observations on the natural history of the Mexican ribbon snake *Thamnophis proximus alpinus* Rossman, 1963. Sauria (Berlin) 21(4): 13–18.

Myer, J. S., and A. P. Kowell. 1973. Effects of feeding schedule and food deprivation on the growth of neonate garter snakes *(Thamnophis sirtalis)*. J. Herpetol. 7:225–229.

Myer, P. A. 1987. Feeding behavior of the glossy crayfish snake, *Regina rigida*. Bull. Maryland Herpetol. Soc. 23:168–170.

Myers, C. W. 1956. An unrecorded food item of the timber rattlesnake. Herpetologica 12:326.

———. 1965. Biology of the ringneck snake, *Diadophis punctatus*, in Florida. Bull. Florida St. Mus. Biol. Sci. 10:43–90.

———. 1967. The pine woods snake, *Rhadinaea flavilata* (Cope). Bull. Florida St. Mus. Biol. Sci. 11:47–97.

———. 1974. The systematics of *Rhadinaea* (Colubridae), a genus of New World snakes. Bull. Am. Mus. Nat. Hist. 153:1–262.

Myers, C. W., and A. A. Arata. 1961. Remarks on "defensive" behavior in the hognose snake *Heterodon simus* (Linnaeus). Quart. J. Florida Acad. Sci. 24:108–110.

Myers, G. S. 1945. Nocturnal observations on sea snakes in Bahia Honda, Panama. Herpetologica 3:22–23.

Myres, B. C., and M. M. Eells. 1968. Thermal aggregation in *Boa constrictor*. Herpetologica 24:61–66.

Neal, J. C., W. G. Montague, and D. A. James. 1993.

Climbing by black rat snakes on cavity trees of red-cockaded woodpeckers. Wildl. Soc. Bull. 21:160–165.

Nealen, P. M., and R. Breitwisch. 1997. Northern cardinal sexes defend nests equally. Wilson Bull. 109:269–278.

Neill, W. T. 1947. Size and habits of the cottonmouth moccasin. Herpetologica 3:203–205.

———. 1948a. Hibernation of amphibians and reptiles in Richmond County, Georgia. Herpetologica 4:107–114.

———. 1948b. Spiders preying on reptiles and amphibians. Herpetologica 4:158.

———. 1948c. Extra-uterine embryos in snakes. Copeia 1948:139.

———. 1948d. Unusual behavior of *Storeria dekayi dekayi* in Georgia. Herpetologica 4:163.

———. 1949a. Head bobbing, a widespread habit of snakes. Herpetologica 5:114–115.

———. 1949b. A new subspecies of rat snake (genus *Elaphe*), and notes on related forms. Herpetologica 5(suppl. 2): 12.

———. 1950. Ontogenetic changes in the coloration of the snake *Cemophora coccinea*. Copeia 1950:62.

———. 1951. Notes on the natural history of certain North American snakes. Publ. Res. Div. Ross Allen's Rept. Inst. 1:47–60.

———. 1954. Evidence of venom in snakes of the genera *Alsophis* and *Rhadinaea*. Copeia 1954:59–69.

———. 1957. Some misconceptions regarding the eastern coral snake, *Micrurus fulvius*. Herpetologica 13:111–118.

———. 1958. The occurrence of amphibians and reptiles in saltwater areas, and a bibliography. Bull. Mar. Sci., Gulf Caribbean 8:1–97.

———. 1960. The caudal lure of various juvenile snakes. Quart. J. Florida Acad. Sci. 23:173–200.

———. 1961a. Snakes swallowing irregurgitable objects. Bull. Philadelphia Herpetol. Soc. 9(1): 17.

———. 1961b. River frog swallows eastern diamondback rattlesnake. Bull. Philadelphia Herpetol. Soc. 9(1): 19.

———. 1962. The reproductive cycle of snakes in a tropical region, British Honduras. Quart. J. Florida Acad. Sci. 25:234–253.

———. 1964. Taxonomy, natural history, and zoogeography of the rainbow snake, *Farancia erytrogramma* (Palisot de Beauvois). Am. Midl. Nat. 71:257–295.

———. 1965. Notes on aquatic snakes, *Natrix* and *Tretanorhinus* in Cuba. Herpetologica 21:62–67.

Neill, W. T., and E. R. Allen. 1956. Secondarily ingested food items in snakes. Herpetologica 12:172–174.

———. 1959. Studies on the amphibians and reptiles of British Honduras. Publ. Res. Div. Ross Allen's Rept. Inst. 2(1): 1–76.

Neill, W. T., and J. M. Boyles. 1957. The eggs of the crowned snake, *Tantilla coronata*. Herpetologica 13:77–78.

Nelson, D. H., and J. W. Gibbons. 1972. Ecology, abundance, and seasonal activity of the scarlet snake, *Cemophora coccinea*. Copeia 1972:582–584.

Nelson, K. J., and P. T. Gregory. 2000. Activity patterns of garter snakes, *Thamnophis sirtalis*, in relation to weather conditions at a fish hatchery on Vancouver Island, British Columbia. J. Herpetol. 34:32–40.

Nelson, R. J., R. T. Mason, R. W. Krohmer, and D. Crews. 1987. Pinealectomy blocks vernal courtship behavior in red-sided garter snakes. Physiol. Behav. 39:231–233.

Nelson, W. F. 1969. Notes on parturition and brood sizes in *Storeria occipitomaculata*. J. Tennessee Acad. Sci. 44:20–21.

Netting, M. G. 1969. Does robin eat Dekay's snake? Wilson Bull. 81:470–471.

Newcomer, R. T., D. H. Taylor, and S. I. Guttman. 1974. Celestial orientation in two species of water snakes (*Natrix sipedon* and *Regina septemvittata*). Herpetologica 30:194–200.

Newman, E. A., and P. N. Hartline. 1981. Integration of visual and infrared information in bimodal neurons of the rattlesnake optic tectum. Science (New York) 213:789–791.

Newton, M. S., and R. Smith. 1975. The snake that lost its habitat. Nat. Hist. (New York) 84:72–77

Nichols, T. J. 1982. Courtship and copulatory behavior of captive eastern hognose snakes, *Heterodon platyrhinos*. Herpetol. Rev. 13:16–17.

Nickerson, M. A., and C. E. Mays. 1970 [1969]. A preliminary herpetofaunal analysis of the Graham (Pinaleno) Mountain region, Graham Co., Arizona, with ecological comments. Trans. Kansas Acad. Sci. 72:492–505.

Nicoletto, P. 1985. Some reptiles from Sinking Creek and Gap Mountains, Montgomery County, Virginia, April-June 1983. Catesbeiana 5:13–15.

Noble, G. K. 1937. The sense organs involved in the courtship of *Storeria, Thamnophis* and other snakes. Bull. Am. Mus. Nat. Hist. 73:673–725.

Noble, G. K., and H. J. Clausen. 1936. The aggregation behavior of *Storeria dekayi* and other snakes with especial reference to the sense organs involved. Ecol. Monogr. 6:269–316.

Norman, B. R. 1977. Notes on the embryonic development of the wandering garter snake in western Washington. Bull. Chicago Herpetol. Soc. 12:103–107.

———. 1978. Hybridization in the *Thamnophis* of western Washington. Bull. Chicago Herpetol. Soc. 13:82–84.

Norrie, S. 1986. Reproduction of the rosy boa, *Lichanura trivirgata*. British Herpetol. Soc. Bull. 16:33–35.

Norris, K. S., and J. L. Kavanau. 1966. The burrowing of the western shovel-nosed snake, *Chionactis occipitalis* Hallowell, and the undersand environment. Copeia 1966:650–664.

Novotny, F. J. 1990. *Thamnophis brachystoma*. Herpetol. Rev. 21:42.

Nugent, P. E., J. Escobar, E. Conradi, and C. E. Walters. 1989. Swallow-tailed kites capture bat and rough green snakes. Chat 54:91–92.

Nussbaum, R. A. 1980. The Brahminy blind snake *(Ramphotyphlops braminus)* in the Seychelles Archipelago: Distribution, variation, and further evidence of parthenogenesis. Herpetologica 36:215–221.

Nussbaum, R. A., E. D. Brodie, Jr., and R. M. Storm. 1983. Amphibians and reptiles of the Pacific Northwest. Moscow: University of Idaho Press.

Nussbaum, R. A., and R. F. Hoyer. 1974. Geographic variation and the validity of subspecies in the rubber boa, *Charina bottae* (Blainville). Northwest. Sci. 48:219–229.

Obrecht, C. B. 1946. Notes on South Carolina reptiles and amphibians. Copeia 1946:71–74.

O'Brien, C. J. 1998. *Regina alleni* (striped crayfish snake). Antipredator behavior. Herpetol. Rev. 29:46–47.

O'Conner, P. F. 1991. Captive propagation and post-copulatory plugs of the eastern indigo snake, *Drymarchon corais couperi*. Vivarium 3(3): 32–35.

Odum, R. A. 1979. The distribution and status of the New Jersey timber rattlesnake including an analysis of Pine Barren populations. HERP: Bull. New York Herpetol. Soc. 15:27–35.

Oguma, K., and S. Makino. 1932. A revised check-list of the chromosome number in vertebrata. J. Genetics 26:239–254.

Oldak, P. D. 1976. Comparison of the scent gland secretion lipids of twenty-five snakes: Implications for biochemical systematics. Copeia 1976:320–326.

Oldfield, B. L., and D. E. Keyler. 1989. Survey of timber rattlesnake *(Crotalus horridus)* distribution along the Mississippi River in western Wisconsin. Trans. Wisconsin Acad. Sci., Arts, Lett. 77:27–34.

Oldham, J. C., and H. M. Smith. 1991. The generic status of the smooth green snake, *Opheodrys vernalis*. Bull. Maryland Herpetol. Soc. 27:201–215.

Olson, R. E. 1967. Peripheral range extensions and some new records of Texas amphibians and reptiles. Texas J. Sci. 19:99–106.

———. 1977. Evidence for the species status of Baird's ratsnake. Texas J. Sci. 29:79–84.

Olson, U. 1987. The corn snake *(Elaphe guttata guttata)* in the wild and in the terrarium, part I. Litt. Serpent. Engl. Ed. 7:17–33.

Orejas-Miranda, B., G. R. Zug, D. Y. E. Garcia, and F. Achaval. 1977. Scale organs on the head of *Leptotyphlops* (Reptilia: Serpentes): A variational study. Proc. Biol. Soc. Washington 90:209–213.

Ortenburger, A. I. 1923. A note on the genera *Coluber* and *Masticophis*, and a description of a new species of *Masticophis*. Occ. Pap. Mus. Zool. Univ. Michigan 139:1–14.

———. 1928. The whip snakes and racers, genera *Masticophis* and *Coluber*. Univ. Michigan Stud., Mem. Univ. Michigan Mus. 1:1–247.

Ortenburger, A. I., and B. Freeman. 1930. Notes on some reptiles and amphibians from western Oklahoma. Publ. Univ. Oklahoma Biol. Surv. 2:175–188.

Ortenburter, A. I., and R. D. Ortenburger. 1926. Field observations on some amphibians and reptiles of Pima County, Arizona. Proc. Oklahoma Acad. Sci. 6:101–121.

Orth, J. C. 1939. Moth larvae in a copperhead's stomach. Copeia 1939:54–55.

Osborne, S. T. 1984. *Rhinocheilus lecontei antonii* (Mexican long-nosed snake). Behavior. Herpetol. Rev. 15:50.

Osgood, D. W. 1970. Thermoregulation in water snakes studied by telemetry. Copeia 1970:568–571.

———. 1978. Effects of temperature on the development of meristic characters in *Natrix fasciata*. Copeia 1978:33–47.

Osypka, N. M., and S. J. Arnold. 2000. The developmental effect of sex ratio on a sexually dimorphic scale count in the garter snake *Thamnophis elegans*. J. Herpetol. 34:1–5.

Ota, H., T. Hikada, M. Matsui, A. Mori, and A. H. Wynn. 1991. Morphological variation, karyotype and reproduction of the parthenogenetic blind snake, *Ramphotyphlops braminus*, from the insular region of East Asia and Saipan. Amphibia-Reptilia 12:181–193.

———. 1993. Data on numerical characters of the blind snake, *Ramphotyphlops braminus*, from the insular region of East Asia and Saipan. Akamata 8:5–10.

Ottley, J. R., and E. E. Jacobsen. 1983. Pattern and coloration of juvenile *Elaphe rosaliae* with notes on natural history. J. Herpetol. 17:189–191.

Ottley, J. R., R. W. Murphy, and G. V. Smith. 1980. The taxonomic status of the rosy boa *Lichanura roseofusca* (Serpentes: Boidae). Great Basin Nat. 40:59–62.

Ovaska, K., and C. Engelstoft. 1999. *Contia tenuis* (Sharp-tailed snake). Defensive behavior. Herpetol. Rev. 30:168.

Over, W. H. 1923. Amphibians and reptiles of South Dakota. South Dakota Geol. Nat. Hist. Surv. Bull. 12:1–34.

———. 1928. A personal experience with rattlesnake bite. Bull. Antivenin Inst. Am. 2:8–10.

Owens, V. 1949a. An overwintering colony of *Coluber c. constrictor* (Say) and *Elaphe o. obsoleta* (Say). Herpetologica 5:90.

———. 1949b. Snakes eaten by the tarantula, *Eurypelma californica*. Herpetologica 5:148.

Pack, H. J. 1930. Snakes of Utah. Utah Agric. Exp. Stat. Bull. 221:1–32.

Padgett, T. M. 1987. Observations of courtship behavior in *Elaphe obsoleta* (black rat snake). Catesbeiana 7:27–28.

Painter, C. W., and T. L. Brown. 1991. *Leptotyphlops dulcis dissectus* (New Mexico blind snake). U.S.A.: New Mexico. Herpetol. Rev. 22:67.

Painter, C. W., L. A. Fitzgerald, and M. L. Heinrich. 1999. *Crotalus atrox* (western diamondback rattlesnake). Morphology. Herpetol. Rev. 30:44.

Painter, C. W., and T. J. Hibbitts. 1996. *Thamnophis rufipunctatus* (narrow-headed garter snake). Maximum size. Herpetol. Rev. 27:147.

Painter, C. W., P. W. Hyder, and G. Swinford. 1992. Three species new to the herpetofauna of New Mexico. Herpetol. Rev. 23:62.

Painter, C. W., N. J. Scott, Jr., and M. J. Altenbach. 1999. *Thamnophis elegans vagrans* (wandering garter snake). Diet. Herpetol. Rev. 30:48.

Palis, J. G. 1993. *Agkistrodon piscivorus conanti* (Florida cottonmouth). Prey. Herpetol. Rev. 24:59, 62.

———. 2000. *Scaphiopus holbrookii* (eastern spadefoot). Predation. Herpetol. Rev. 31:42–43.

Palisot de Beauvois, A. M. F. J. 1799. Memoir on Amphibia. Serpents. Trans. Am. Philos. Soc. 4:362–381.

Palmer, W. M. 1978. *Sistrurus miliarius*. Cat. Am. Amphib. Rept. 220:1–2.

Palmer, W. M., and A. L. Braswell. 1976. Communal egg laying and hatchlings of the rough green snake, *Opheodrys aestivus* (Linnaeus) (Reptilia, Serpentes, Colubridae). J. Herpetol. 10:257–259.

———. 1995. Reptiles of North Carolina. Chapel Hill: University of North Carolina Press.

Palmer, W. M., and G. Tregembo. 1970. Notes on the natural history of the scarlet snake *Cemophora coccinea copei* Jan in North Carolina. Herpetologica 26:300–302.

Palmer, W. M., and G. M. Williamson. 1971. Observations on the natural history of the Carolina pigmy rattlesnake, *Sistrurus miliarius miliarius* Linnaeus. J. Elisha Mitchell Sci. Soc. 87:20–25.

Parent, C., and P. J. Weatherhead. 2000. Behavioral and life history responses of eastern massasauga rattlesnakes *(Sistrurus catenatus catenatus)* to human disturbance. Oecologia (Berlin) 125:170–178.

Parker, S. A., and D. Stotz. 1977. An observation on the foraging behavior of the Arizona ridge-nosed rattle-snake, *Crotalus willardi willardi* (Serpentes: Crotalidae). Bull. Maryland Herpetol. Soc. 13:123.

Parker, W. S. 1976. Population estimates, age structure, and denning habits of the whipsnakes, *Masticophis t. taeniatus*, in a northern Utah Atriplex-Sarcobatus community. Herpetologica 32:53–57.

———. 1982. *Masticophis taeniatus*. Cat. Am. Amphib. Rept. 304:1–4.

Parker, W. S., and W. S. Brown. 1972. Telemetric study of movements and oviposition of two female *Masticophis t. taeniatus*. Copeia 1972:892–895.

———. 1973. Species composition and population changes in two complexes of snake hibernacula in northern Utah. Herpetologica 28:319–326.

———. 1974. Mortality and weight changes of Great Basin rattlesnakes *(Crotalus viridis)* at a hibernaculum in northern Utah. Herpetologica 30:234–239.

———. 1980. Comparative ecology of two colubrid snakes, *Masticophis t. taeniatus* and *Pituophis melanoleucus deserticola*, in northern Utah. Milwaukee Public Mus. Publ. Biol. Geol. 7:1–104.

Parkinson, C. L., K. R. Zamudio, and H. W. Greene. 2000. Phylogeny of the pitviper clade *Agkistrodon*: Historical ecology, species status, and conservation of cantils. Mol. Ecol. 9:411–420.

Parks, L. H. 1973. An active bull snake in near-freezing temperature. Trans. Kansas Acad. Sci. 72:266.

Parmalee, P. W., R. D. Oesch, and J. E. Guilday. 1969. Pleistocene and Recent vertebrate faunas from Crankshaft Cave, Missouri. Illinois St. Mus., Rep. Invest. 14:1–37.

Parmley, D. 1982. Food items of roadrunners from Palo Pinto County, northcentral Texas. Texas J. Sci. 34:94–95.

———. 1986. An annotated key to isolated trunk vertebrae of *Elaphe* (Colubridae) species occurring in Texas. Texas J. Sci. 38:41–44.

———. 1988a. Additional Pleistocene amphibians and reptiles from the Seymour Formation, Texas. J. Herpetol. 22:82–87.

———. 1988b. Middle Holocene herpetofauna of Klein Cave, Kerr County, Texas. Southwest. Nat. 33:378–382.

———. 1988c. Early Hemphillian (Late Miocene) snakes from the Higgins Local Fauna of Lipscomb County, Texas. J. Vert. Paleontol. 8:322–327.

———. 1990a. Late Pleistocene snakes from Fowlkes Cave, Culberson County, Texas. J. Herpetol. 24:266–274.

———. 1990b. A late Holocene herpetofauna fom Montague County, Texas. Texas J. Sci. 42:412–415.

———. 1994. Reevaluation of the extinct kingsnake *Lampropeltis intermedius* Brattstrom (Colubridae) with comments on the ancestry of *Lampropeltis triangulum*. Herpetol. Nat. Hist. 2:83–88.

Parmley, D., and J. A. Holman. 1995. Hemphillian (late Miocene) snakes from Nebraska, with comments on Arikareean through Blancan snakes of midcontinental North America. J. Vert. Paleontol. 15:79–95.

Parmley, D., and G. B. Lacy. 1997. Holocene herpetofauna of the Box Elder Creek local fauna, Caddo County, Oklahoma. J. Herpetol. 31:624–625.

Parmley, D., and C. Mulford. 1985. An instance of a largemouth bass, *Micropterus salmoides*, feeding on a water snake, *Nerodia erythrogaster transversa*. Texas J. Sci. 37:389.

Parmley, D., and R. S. Pfau. 1997. Amphibians and reptiles of the Late Pleistocene Tonk Creek Local Fauna, Stonewall County, Texas. Texas J. Sci. 49:151–158.

Parmley, D., and D. Walker. 1998. *Elaphe vulpina* (Colubridae) from the Blancan of Washington, with a review of the species' paleodistribution. Herpetol. Nat. Hist. 6:41–46.

Parrish, H. M., and M. S. Kahn. 1967. Bites by coral snakes: Reports of 11 representative cases. Am. J. Med. Sci. 81:561–568.

Parrish, H. M., and R. E. Thompson. 1958. Human envenomation from bites of recently milked rattlesnakes: A report of three cases. Copeia 1958:83–86.

Passek, K. M., and J. C. Gillingham. 1997. Thermal influence on defensive behaviours of the eastern garter snake, *Thamnophis sirtalis*. Anim. Behav. 54:629–633.

Patch, C. L. 1919. A rattlesnake, melano garter snakes and other reptiles from Point Pelee, Ontario. Can. Field-Nat. 33:60–61.

Patten, R. B. 1981. Author's reply. J. Herpetol. 15:126.

Patten, R. B., and B. H. Banta. 1980. A rattlesnake, *Crotalus ruber*, feeds on a road-killed animal. J. Herpetol. 14:111–112.

Patton, T. H. 1963. Fossil vertebrates from Miller's Cave, Llano County, Texas. Texas Mem. Mus. Bull. 7:1–41.

Pauley, T. K. 1973. The status of the genus *Carphophis* in Ohio and West Virginia. Proc. West Virginia Acad. Sci. 45:64–70.

Paulson, D. R. 1966. Variation in some snakes from the Florida Keys. Quart. J. Florida Acad. Sci. 29:295–308.

Peabody, R. B., J. A. Johnson, and E. D. Brodie, Jr. 1975. Intraspecific escape from ingestion of the rubber boa, *Charina bottae*. J. Herpetol. 9:247.

Pearson, D. D. 1966. Serological and immunoelectrophoretic comparisons among species of snakes. Bull. Serol. Mus. 36:8.

Pendlebury G. B. 1976. The western hognose snake, *Heterodon nasicus nasicus*, in Alberta. Can. Field-Nat. 90:416–422.

Penn, G. H., Jr. 1943. Herpetological notes from Cameron Parish, Louisiana. Copeia 1943:58–59.

———. 1950. Utilization of crawfishes by cold-blooded vertebrates in the eastern United States. Am. Midl. Nat. 44:643–658.

Perkins, C. B. 1938. The snakes of San Diego County with descriptions and key. Bull. Zool. Soc. San Diego 13:1–66.

———. 1940. A key to the snakes of the United States. Bull. Zool. Soc. San Diego 16:1–63.

———. 1943. Notes on captive bred snakes. Copeia 1943:108–112.

———. 1951. Hybrid rattlesnakes. Herpetologica 7:146.

———. 1952. Incubation period of snake eggs. Herpetologica 8:79.

Perkins, M. J., and B. D. Palmer. 1996. Histology and functional morphology of the oviduct of an oviparous snake, *Diadophis punctatus*. J. Morph. 227:67–79.

Perry, A. 1920. The mating of water snakes. Copeia 83:49–50.

Perry, J. 1978. An observation of "dance" behavior in the western cottonmouth, *Agkistrodon piscivorus leucostoma* (Reptilia, Serpentes, Viperidae). J. Herpetol. 12:428–429.

Perry, T. W., and G. Hauer. 1996. *Tantilla nigriceps* (plains black-headed snake). Maximum size and size variation. Herpetol. Rev. 27:205–206.

Perry-Richardson, J. J., C. W. Schofield, and N. B. Ford. 1990. Courtship of the garter snake, *Thamnophis marcianus*, with a description of female behavior for coitus interruption. J. Herpetol. 24:76–78.

Peters, J. 1953. A fossil snake of the genus *Heterodon* from the Pliocene of Kansas. J. Paleontol. 27:328–331.

Peterson, A. 1990. Ecology and management of a timber rattlesnake (*Crotalus horridus* L.) population in south-central New York state, 255–261. In: R. S. Mitchell, C. J. Sheviak, and D. J. Leopold (eds.), Ecosystem management: Rare species and significant habitats. Proc. 15th Ann. Nat. Areas Conf., New York St. Mus. Bull. 471.

Peterson, C. C., B. M. Walton, and A. F. Bennett. 1998. Intrapopulation variation in ecological energetics of the garter snake *Thamnophis sirtalis*, with analysis of the precision of doubly labled water measurements. Physiol. Zool. 71:333–349.

Peterson, C. R. 1987. Daily variation in the body temperature of free-ranging garter snakes. Ecology 68:160–169.

Peterson, H. W. 1956. A record of viviparity in a normally oviparous snake. Herpetologica 12:152.

Peterson, K. H. 1983. Reproduction of captive *Crotalus mitchelli* and *Crotalus durissus* at the Houston Zoological Gardens. Proc. Rept. Symp. Capt. Prop. Husb. 6:323–327.

————. 1990. Conspecific and self-envenomation in snakes. Bull. Chicago Herpetol. Soc. 25:26–28.

Peterson, R. L. 1950. Amphibians and reptiles of Brazos County, Texas. Am. Midl. Nat. 43:157–164.

Petrides, G. A. 1941. The coral king snake a predator upon the russet-backed thrush. Yosemite Nat. Notes 20:36.

Pettus, D. 1958. Water relationships in *Natrix sipedon*. Copeia 1958:207–211.

————. 1963. Salinity and subspeciation in *Natrix sipedon*. Copeia 1963:499–504.

Petzold, H.-G. 1969. Observations on the reproductive biology of the American ringed snake *Leptodeira annulata*. Int. Zoo Yrbk. 9:54–56.

Phillips, C. 1939. The flat tailed snake. Proc. Florida Acad. Sci. 4:210–211.

Pickwell, G. V. 1971. Knotting and coiling behavior in the pelagic sea snake *Pelamis platurus* (L.). Copeia 1971:348–350.

Pickwell, G. V., R. L. Bezy, and J. E. Fitch. 1983. Northern occurrences of the sea snake, *Pelamis platurus*, in the eastern Pacific, with a record of predation on the species. California Fish Game 69:172–177.

Pickwell, G. V., and W. A. Culotta. 1980. *Pelamis, Pelamis platurus*. Cat. Am. Amphib. Rept. 255:1–4 .

Pickwell, G. V., J. A. Vick, W. H. Shipman, and M. M. Grenan. 1972. Production, toxicity, and preliminary pharmacology of venom from the sea snake, *Pelamis platurus*, 247–265. In: L. R. Worthen (ed.), Proc. Third Food-drugs from the sea conference. Washington, D.C.: Marine Technical Society.

Pierce, P. E., and D. A. Ross. 1989. Bald eagles prey on snakes. Passenger Pigeon 51:155–156.

Pimentel, R. A. 1958. Southern occurrence of the sharp-tailed snake in a unique community. Herpetologica 14:169–170.

Pinder, M. J. 1996. *Regina septemvittata* (queen snake). Catesbeiana 16:9.

Pinney, R. 1994. Sea snakes. Reptile & Amphibian Mag. Jan./Feb. 1994:21–28, 30–32, 34–35.

Pinou, T., C. A. Hass, and L. R. Maxson. 1995. Geographic variation of serum albumin in the monotypic snake genus *Diadophis* (Colubridae: Xenodontinae). J. Herpetol. 29:105–110.

Pisani, G. R. 1967. Notes on the courtship and mating behavior of *Thamnophis brachystoma* (Cope). Herpetologica 23:112–115.

————. 1971. An unusually large litter of *Virginia valeriae pulchra*. J. Herpetol. 5:207–208.

Pisani, G. R., and R. C. Bothner. 1970. The annual reproductive cycle of *Thamnophis brachystoma*. Sci. Stud., St. Bonaventure Univ. 26:15–34.

Pisani, G. R., J. T. Collins, and S. R. Edwards. 1973. A re-evaluation of the subspecies of *Crotalus horridus*. Trans. Kansas Acad. Sci. 75:255–263.

Pisani, G. R., and B. R. Stephenson. 1991. Food habits in Oklahoma *Crotalus atrox* in fall and early spring. Trans. Kansas Acad. Sci. 94:137–141.

Platt, D. R. 1969. Natural history of the hognose snakes *Heterodon platyrhinos* and *Heterodon nasicus*. Univ. Kansas Publ. Mus. Nat. Hist. 18:253–420.

————. 1983. *Heterodon*. Cat. Am. Amphib. Rept. 315:1–2.

————. 1984. Growth of bullsnakes (*Pituophis melanoleucus sayi*) on a sand prairie in south central Kansas. Univ. Kansas Publ. Mus. Nat. Hist. Spec. Publ. 10:41–55.

————. 1985. History and spelling of the name *Heterodon platirhinos*. J. Herpetol. 19:417–418.

Platt, D. R., and T. R. Rainwater. 2000. *Agkistrodon piscivorus* (cottonmouth). Diet. Herpetol. Rev. 31:244.

Platt, D. R., and C. H. Rousell. 1963. County records of snakes from southcentral Kansas. Trans. Kansas Acad. Sci. 66:551.

Plummer, M. V. 1977. Predation by black rat snakes in bank swallow colonies. Southwest. Nat. 22:147–148.

————. 1981a. Communal nesting of *Opheodrys aestivus* in the laboratory. Copeia 1981:243–246.

————. 1981b. Habitat utilization, diet, and movements of a temporate arboreal snake (*Opheodrys aestivus*). J. Herpetol. 15:425–432.

————. 1983. Annual variation in stored lipids and reproduction in green snakes (*Opheodrys aestivus*). Copeia 1983:741–745.

————. 1984. Female reproduction in an Arkansas population of rough green snakes (*Opheodrys aestivus*). Univ. Kansas Mus. Nat. Hist. Spec. Publ. 10:105–113.

————. 1985a. Growth and maturity in green snakes (*Opheodrys aestivus*). Herpetologica 41:28–33.

————. 1985b. Demography of green snakes (*Opheodrys aestivus*). Herpetologica 41:373–381.

————. 1987. Geographic variation in body size of green snakes (*Opheodrys aestivus*). Copeia 1987:483–485.

————. 1989. Observations on the nesting ecology of green snakes (*Opheodrys aestivus*). Herpetol. Rev. 20:87–89.

————. 1990a. Nesting movements, nesting behavior, and nest sites of green snakes (*Opheodrys aestivus*) revealed by radiotelemetry. Herpetologica 46:190–195.

————. 1990b. High predation on green snakes, *Opheodrys aestivus*. J. Herpetol. 24:327–328.

————. 1991. Patterns of feces production in free-living green snakes, *Opheodrys aestivus*. J. Herpetol. 25:222–226.

————. 1992. Relationships among mothers, litters, and

neonates in diamondback water snakes *(Nerodia rhombifer)*. Copeia 1992:1096–1098.

———. 1993. Thermal ecology of arboreal green snakes *(Opheodrys aestivus)*. J. Herpetol. 27:254–260.

———. 1997a. Speed and endurance of gravid and nongravid green snakes, *Opheodrys aestivus*. Copeia 1997:191–194.

———. 1997b. Population ecology of green snakes *(Opheodrys aestivus)* revisited. Herpetol. Monogr. 11:102–123.

———. 1999–2000. Ecological aspects of shedding in free-ranging hognose snakes *(Heterodon platirhinos)*. Herpetol. Nat. Hist. 7:91–94.

———. 2000. *Crotalus scutulatus* (Mojave rattlesnake). Thermal stress. Herpetol. Rev. 31:104–105.

Plummer, M. V., and J. D. Congdon. 1992. *Coluber constrictor* (black racer). Predation. Herpetol. Rev. 23:80–81.

———. 1994. Radiotelemetric study of activity and movements of racers *(Coluber constrictor)* associated with a Carolina Bay in South Carolina. Copeia 1994:20–26.

———. 1996. Rates of metabolism and water flux in free-ranging racers, *Coluber constrictor*. Copeia 1996:8–14.

Plummer, M. W., and J. M. Goy. 1984. Ontogenetic dietary shift of water snakes *(Nerodia rhombifera)* in a fish hatchery. Copeia 1984:550–552.

Plummer, M. W., and N. E. Mills. 1996. Observations on trailing and mating behaviors in hognose snakes *(Heterodon platirhinos)*. J. Herpetol. 30:80–82.

Plummer, M. W., and H. L. Snell. 2000. Spatial ecology and survivorship of resident and translocated hognose snakes *(Heterodon platirhinos)*. J. Herpetol. 34:565–574.

———. 1988. Nest site selection and water relations of eggs in the snake, *Opheodrys aestivus*. Copeia 1988:58–64.

Polis, G. A., and C. A. Myers. 1985. A survey of intraspecific predation among reptiles and amphibians. J. Herpetol. 19:99–107.

Pook, C. E., W. Wuster, and R. S. Thorpe. 2000. Historical biogeography of the western rattlesnake (Serpentes: Viperidae: *Crotalus viridis*), inferred from mitochondrial DNA sequence information. Mol. Phylogenetics Evol. 15:269–282.

Pope, C. H. 1944. Amphibians and reptiles of the Chicago area. Chicago: Chicago Natural History Museum Press.

———. 1961. The giant snakes. The natural history of the boa constrictor, the anaconda, and the largest pythons, including comparative facts about other snakes and basic information on reptiles in general. New York: Alfred A. Knopf.

Poran, N. S., and R. G. Coss. 1990. Development of anti-snake defenses in California ground squirrels *(Sper-*

mophilus beecheyi): I. Behavioral and immunological relationships. Behaviour 112:222–245.

Porchuk, B. D., and R. J. Brooks. 1995. *Coluber constrictor* (blue racer), *Elaphe vulpina* (eastern fox snake), and *Chelydra serpentina* (snapping turtle). Reproduction. Herpetol. Rev. 26:148.

Porras, L., and L. D. Wilson. 1979. New distributional records for *Tantilla oolitica* Telford (Reptilia, Serpentes, Colubridae) from the Florida Keys. J. Herpetol. 13:218–220.

Porter, C. A. 1994. Organization and chromosomal location of repetitive DNA sequences in three species of squamate reptiles. Chromosome Res. 2:263–272.

Porter, R. H., and J. A. Czaplicki. 1977. Evidence for a specific searching immage in hunting water snakes *(Natrix sipedon)* (Reptilia, Serpentes, Colubridae). J. Herpetol. 11:213–216.

Porter, T. 1983. Induced cannibalism in *Crotalus mitchelli*. Bull. Chicago Herpetol. Soc. 18:48.

Posey, C. R. 1973. An observation on the feeding habits of the eastern king snake. Bull. Maryland Herpetol. Soc. 9:105.

Poteet, M. F., and C. J. Bell. 1999. *Thamnophis sirtalis concinnus* (red-spotted garter snake). Diet. Herpetol. Rev. 30:170–171.

Pough, F. H. 1966. Ecological relationships in southeastern Arizona with notes on other species. Copeia 1966:676–683.

———. 1976. Multiple cryptic effects of crossbanded and ringed patterns of snakes. Copeia 1976:834–836.

———. 1978. Ontogenetic changes in endurance in water snakes *(Natrix sipedon)*: Physiological correlates and ecological consequences. Copeia 1978:69–75.

———. 1988. Mimicry and related problems, 153–234. In: C. Gans and R. B. Huey (eds.), Biology of the Reptilia. Vol. 16. Defense and life history. New York: Alan R. Liss.

Pough, F. H., G. Kwiecinski, and W. Bemis. 1978. Melanin deposits associated with the venom glands of snakes. J. Morph. 155:63–71.

Pough, F. H., and H. B. Lillywhite. 1984. Blood volume and blood oxygen capacity of sea snakes. Physiol. Zool. 57:32–39.

Powell, R. 1982. *Thamnophis proximus* (western ribbon snake). Reproduction. Herpetol. Rev. 13:48.

———. 1990. *Elaphe vulpina*. Cat. Am. Amphib. Rept. 470:1–3.

Powell, R., J. T. Collins, and L. D. Fish. 1992. *Virginia valeriae*. Cat. Am. Amphib. Rept. 552:1–6.

———. 1994. *Virginia striatula*. Cat. Am. Amphib. Rept. 599:1–6.

Powell, R., J. T. Collins, and E. D. Hooper, Jr. 1998. A key to amphibians and reptiles of the continental United States and Canada. Lawrence: University of Kansas Press.

Powell, R., M. Inboden, and D. D. Smith. 1990. Erstnachweis von Hybriden zwischen den Klapperschlagen *Crotalus cerastes laterorepens* Klauber, 1944 und *Crotalus scutulatus scutulatus* (Kennicott, 1861). Salamandra 26:319–329.

Powell, R., and J. S. Parmerlee. 1991. Notes on reproduction in *Clonophis kirtlandii* (Serpentes: Colubridae). Bull. Chicago Herpetol. Soc. 26(2): 32.

Powers, A. 1972. An instance of cannibalism in captive *Crotalus viridis helleri* with a brief review of cannibalism in rattlesnakes. Bull. Maryland Herpetol. Soc. 8:60–61.

Prange, H. D., and S. P. Christman. 1976. The allometrics of rattlesnake skeletons. Copeia 1976: 542–545.

Prange, H. D., and K. Schmidt-Nielsen. 1969. Evaporative water loss in snakes. Comp. Biochem. Physiol. 28:973–975.

Prentiss, D. J. 1994. *Coluber constrictor priapus* (southern black racer). Prey. Herpetol. Rev. 25:70.

Preston, R. E. 1966. Turtles of the Gilliland Faunule from the Pleistocene of Know County, Texas. Pap. Michigan Acad. Sci., Arts, Lett. 71:221–239.

———. 1979. Late Pleistocene cold-blooded vertebrate fauna from the mid-continental United States. I. Reptilia; Testudines, Crocodilia. Univ. Michigan Mus. Paleontol. Pap. Paleontol. 19:1–53.

Price, A. H. 1978. New locality records and range extensions for *Thamnophis brachystoma* (Reptilia: Serpentes) in Pennsylvania. Bull. Maryland Herpetol. Soc. 14:260–263.

———. 1980. *Crotalus molossus.* Cat. Am. Amphib. Rept. 242:1–2.

———. 1982. *Crotalus scutulatus.* Cat. Am. Amphib. Rept. 291:1–2.

———. 1987. *Hypsiglena torquata jani* (Texas night snake). Behavior. Herpetol. Rev. 18:16.

———. 1988. Observations on maternal behavior and neonate aggregation in the western diamondback rattlesnake, *Crotalus atrox* (Crotalidae). Southwest. Nat. 33:370–374.

———. 1998. Poisonous snakes of Texas. Austin: University of Texas Press.

Price, A. H., and J. L. LaPointe. 1990. Activity patterns of a Chihuahuan Desert snake community. Ann. Carnegie Mus. 59:15–23.

Price, R. 1987. Disjunct occurrence of mole snakes in peninsular Florida, and the description of a new subspecies of *Lampropeltis calligaster.* Bull. Chicago Herpetol. Soc. 22:148.

Price, R. M. 1982. Dorsal scale microdermatoglyphics:

Ecological indicator or taxonomic tool? J. Herpetol. 16:294–306.

———. 1990a. *Bogertophis.* Cat. Am. Amphib. Rept. 497:1–2.

———. 1990b. *Bogertophis rosaliae.* Cat. Am. Amphib. Rept. 498:1–3.

———. 1991. *Senticolis, S. triaspis.* Cat. Am. Amphib. Rept. 525:1–4.

Price, W. H., and L. G. Carr. 1943. Eggs of *Heterodon simus.* Copeia 1943:193.

Priede, M. 1990. The sea snakes are coming. New Scientist 128(1742): 29–33.

Prieto, A. A., and E. R. Jacobson. 1968. A new locality for melanistic *Crotalus molossus molossus* in southern New Mexico. Herpetologica 24:339–340.

Printiss, D. J. 1994. *Coluber constrictor priapus* (southern black racer). Prey. Herpetol. Rev. 25:70.

Prior, K. A., H. L. Gibbs, and P. J. Weatherhead. 1996. Population genetic structure in the black rat snake: Implications for management. Conserv. Biol. 11:1147–1158.

Prior, K. A., and C. M. Shilton. 1996. Post-hibernation mortality in black rat snakes, *Elaphe o. obsoleta.* J. Herpetol. 30:275–278.

Prior, K. A., and P. J. Weatherhead. 1994. Response of free-ranging eastern massasauga rattlesnakes to human disturbance. J. Herpetol. 28:255–257.

———. 1996. Habitat features of black rat snake hibernacula in Ontario. J. Herpetol. 30:211–218.

Pritchett, C. L., and J. M. Alfonzo. 1988. Red-tailed hawk "captured" by a striped whipsnake. J. Raptor Res. 22:89.

Prosser, M. R., H. L. Gibbs, and P. J. Weatherhead. 1999. Microgeographic population genetic structure in the northern water snake, *Nerodia sipedon sipedon,* detected using microcatellite DNA loci. Mol. Ecol. 8:329–333.

Puckette, B. G. 1962. Ophiophagy in *Hyla versicolor.* Herpetologia 18:143.

Punzo, F. 1974. Comparative analysis of the feeding habits of two species of Arizona blind snakes, *Leptotyphlops h. humilis* and *Leptotyphlops d. dulcis.* J. Herpetol. 8:153–156.

———. 2000. Reproduction, growth, survivorship and activity patterns in the southwestern earless lizard (*Cophosaurus texanus scitulus*) (Phrynosomatidae) from the Big Bend region of Texas. Texas J. Sci. 52:179–194.

Queiroz, A. de., and R. Lawson. 1994. Phylogenetic relationships of the garter snakes based on DNA sequence and allozyme variation. Biol. J. Linn. Soc. 53:209–229.

Queral-Regil, A., and R. B. King. 1998. Evidence of phenotypic plasticity in snake body size and relative head dimensions in response to amount and size of prey. Copeia 1998:423–429.

Quesnel, V. C., and L. Wehekind. 1969. Observations on the constrictive phase of feeding behavior in *Boa constrictor*. J. Trinidad Field Nat. Club 1969:12–13.

Quinn, H. R. 1977. Further notes on reproduction in *Crotalus willardi* (Reptilia, Serpentes, Crotalidae). Bull. Maryland Herpetol. Soc. 13:111.

———. 1979a. Sexual dimorphism in tail pattern of Oklahoma snakes. Texas J. Sci. 31:157–160.

———. 1979b. Reproduction and growth of the Texas coral snake *Micrurus fulvius tenere*. Copeia 1979:453–463.

Quinn, J. S. 1985. Caspian terns respond to rattlesnake predation on colony. Wilson Bull. 97:233–234.

Rabatsky, A. M., and T. M. Farrell. 1996. The effects of age and light level on foraging posture and frequency of caudal luring in the rattlesnake, *Sistrurus miliarius barbouri*. J. Herpetol. 30:558–561.

Radcliffe, C. W., D. Chiszar, and B. O'Connell. 1980. Effects of prey size on poststrike behavior in rattlesnakes *(Crotalus durissus, C. enyo, and C. viridis)*. Bull. Psychon. Soc. 16:449–450.

Radcliffe, C. W., D. Chiszar, and H. M. Smith. 1980. Prey-induced caudal movements in *Boa constrictor* with comments on the evolution of caudal luring. Bull. Maryland Herpetol. Soc. 16:19–22.

Rael, E. D., J. D. Johnson, O. Molina, and H. K. McCrystal. 1992. Distribution of Mojave toxin-like protein in rock rattlesnake *(Crotalus lepidus)* venom, 163–168. In: J. A. Campbell and E. D. Brodie, Jr. (eds.), Biology of the pit vipers. Tyler, Texas: Selva.

Rael, E. D., R. A. Knight, and H. Zepeda. 1984. Electrophoretic variants of Mojave rattlesnake *(Crotalus scutulatus scutulatus)* venoms and migration differences of Mojave toxin. Toxicon 22:980–985.

Rafinesque, C. S. 1818. Further account of discoveries in natural history in the western states. Am. Month. Mag. Crit. Rev. 4:39–42.

Ragsdale, F. R., K. M. Imel, E. E. Nilsson, and R. L. Ingermann. 1993. Pregnancy-associated factors affecting organic phosphate levels and oxygen affinity of garter snake red cells. Gen. Comp. Endocrinol. 91:181–188.

Rahn, H. 1940. Sperm viability in the uterus of the garter snake, *Thamnophis*. Copeia 1940:109–115.

———. 1942a. Effect of temperature on color change in the rattlesnake. Copeia 1942:178.

———. 1942b. The reproductive cycle of the prairie rattler. Copeia 1942:233–240.

Ramírez-Bautista, A., G. Gutiérrez-Mayén, and A. Gonzalez-Romero. 1995. Clutch sizes in a community of snakes from the mountains of the valley of México. Herpetol. Rev. 26:12–13.

Ramirez-Bautista, A., X. Hernández-Ibarra, and R. Torres-Cervantes. 2000a. *Elaphe guttata emoryi* (Great Plains rat snake). Diet. Herpetol. Rev. 25:178.

———. 2000b. *Salvadora grahamiae lineata* (Texas patch-nose snake). Diet. Herpetol. Rev. 25:180.

Ramirez-Bautista, A., and Z. Uribe. 1992. *Trimorphodon biscutatus* (lyre snake). Predation fatality. Herpetol. Rev. 23:82.

Ramsey, L. W. 1946. Captive specimens of *Tropidoclonion lineatum*. Herpetologica 3:112.

———. 1948. Combat dance and range extension of *Agkistrodon piscivorus leucostoma*. Herpetologica 4:228.

———. 1953. The lined snake, *Tropidoclonion lineatum* (Hallowell). Herpetologica 9:7–23.

Randall, J. A., S. M. Hatch, and E. R. Hekkala. 1995. Interspecific variation in anti-predator behavior in sympatric species of kangaroo rat. Behav. Ecol. Sociobiol. 36:243–250.

Randall, P. E. 1940. Seasonal food habits of the marsh hawk in Pennsylvania. Wilson Bull. 52:165–172.

Raney, E. C., and R. M. Roecker. 1947. Food and growth of two species of watersnakes from western New York. Copeia 1947:171–174.

Raun, G. G. 1962. Observations on behavior of newborn hog-nosed snakes, *Heterodon p. platyrhinos*. Texas J. Sci. 14:3–6.

———. 1965. A guide to Texas snakes. Texas Mem. Mus., Mus. Notes 9:1–85.

Reams, R. D., C. J. Franklin, and J. M. Davis. 1999. *Micrurus fulvius tener* (Texas coral snake). Diet. Herpetol. Rev. 30:228–229.

———. 2000a. *Sceloporus olivaceus* (Texas spiny lizard). Predation. Herpetol. Rev. 31:176.

———. 2000b. *Masticophis flagellum* (western coachwhip). Secondary ingestion. Herpetol. Rev. 31:247.

Reams, R. D., and A. M. Stevens. 1999. *Nerodia taxispilota* (brown water snake). Feeding behavior. Herpetol. Rev. 30:103.

Reaser, J. K., and R. E. Dexter. 1996. *Rana pretiosa* (spotted frog). Predation. Herpetol. Rev. 27:75.

Redmer, M. 1988. Two instances of reptile prey discarded by avian predators. Bull. Chicago Herpetol. Soc. 23:28.

Redmer, M., and J. P. Zaworski. 1987. Notes on two red plains garter snakes, *Thamnophis radix radix,* from Illinois. Bull. Chicago Herpetol. Soc. 22:179.

Redmond, R. L., and D. A. Jenni. 1986. Population ecology of the long-billed curlew *(Numenius americanus)* in western Idaho. Auk 103:755–767.

Reed, R. N. 1997. *Trimorphodon biscutatus quadruplex* (lyre snake). Diet. Herpetol. Rev. 28:206.

Regal, P. J. 1966. Thermophilic response following feeding in certain reptiles. Copeia 1966:588–590.

Reichenbach, N. G. 1983. An aggregation of female garter snakes under corrugated metal sheets. J. Herpetol. 17:412–413.

Reichenbach, N. G., and G. H. Dalrymple. 1986. Energy use, life histories, and the evaluation of potential competition in two species of garter snakes. J. Herpetol. 20:133–153.

Reichling, S. 1982. Reproduction in captive black pine snakes *Pituophis melanoleucus lodingi*. Herpetol. Rev. 13:41.

———. 1988. Reproduction in captive Louisiana pine snakes, *Pituophis melanoleucus ruthveni*. Herpetol. Rev. 19:77–78.

———. 1990. Reproductive traits of the Louisiana pine snake *Pituophis melanoleucus ruthveni* (Serpentes: Colubridae). Southwest. Nat. 35:221–222.

———. 1995. The taxonomic status of the Louisiana pine snake *(Pituophis melanoleucus ruthveni)* and its relevance to the evolutionary species concept. J. Herpetol. 29:186–198.

Reid, J. R., and T. E. Lott. 1963. Feeding of *Leptotyphlops dulcis dulcis* (Baird and Girard). Herpetologica 19:141–142.

Reinert, H. K. 1975. Another winter record of a snake *(Natrix septemvittata)*. Bull. Philadelphia Herpetol. Soc. 23:7.

———. 1978. The ecology and morphological variation of the massasauga rattlesnake *(Sistrurus catenatus)*. M.S. Thesis, Clarion State College, Clarion, Pennsylvania.

———. 1981. Reproduction by the massasauga *(Sistrurus catenatus catenatus)*. Am. Midl. Nat. 105:393–395.

———. 1984a. Habitat separation between sympatric snake populations. Ecology 65:478–486.

———. 1984b. Habitat variation within sympatric snake populations. Ecology 65:1673–1682.

———. 1990. A profile and impact assessment of organized rattlesnake hunts in Pennsylvania. J. Pennsylvania Acad. Sci. 64:136–144.

———. 1991. The spatial ecology of timber rattlesnakes *(Crotalus horridus)*. Progr. Jt. Ann. Meet. Soc. Stud. Amphib. Rept./Herpetol. League, Pennsylvania State University (Abstract).

Reinert, H. K., D. Cundall, and L. M. Bushar. 1984. Foraging behavior of the timber rattlesnake, *Crotalus horridus*. Copeia 1984:976–981.

Reinert, H. K., and W. R. Kodrich. 1982. Movements and habitat utilization by the massasauga, *Sistrurus catenatus catenatus*. J. Herpetol. 16:162–171.

Reinert, H. K., and R. R. Rupert, Jr. 1999. Impacts of translocation on behavior and survival of timber rattlesnakes, *Crotalus horridus*. J. Herpetol. 33:45–61.

Reinert, H. K., and R. T. Zappalorti. 1988a. Timber rattlesnakes *(Crotalus horridus)* of the Pine Barrens: Their movement patterns and habitat preference. Copeia 1988:964–978.

———. 1988b. Field observation of the association of adult and neonatal timber rattlesnakes, *Crotalus horridus*, with possible evidence for conspecific trailing. Copeia 1988:1057–1059.

Repp, R. 1998. Wintertime observations on five species of reptiles in the Tucson area: Sheltersite selections/ fidelity to sheltersites/notes on behavior. Bull. Chicago Herpetol. Soc. 33:49–56.

Resetarits, W. J., Jr. 1983. *Thamnophis proximus proximus* (western ribbon snake). Food. Herpetol. Rev. 14:75

Reuss, T. 1834. Zoologische miscellen, reptilien, ophidier. Senckenberg Mus., Frankfurt am Main 1(2): 127–162.

Reynolds, H. C. 1945. Some aspects of the life history and ecology of the opposum in central Missouri. J. Mammal. 26:361–379.

Reynolds, J. H. 1980. A mark-recapture study of the scarlet snake, *Cemophora coccinea*, in a coastal plain sandhill community. Master's Thesis, North Carolina State University, Raleigh.

Reynolds, R. P. 1982. Seasonal incidence of snakes in northeastern Chihuahua, Mexico. Southwest. Nat. 27:161–166.

Reynolds, R. P., and G. V. Pickwell. 1984. Records of the yellow-bellied sea snake, *Pelamis platurus*, from the Galápagos Islands. Copeia 1984:786–789.

Reynolds, R. P., and N. J. Scott, Jr. 1982. Use of a mammalian resource by a Chihuahuan snake community, 99–118. In: N. J. Scott, Jr. (ed.), Herpetological communities. U.S. Fish Wildl. Serv. Wildl. Res. Rep. 13.

Richards, R. L. 1990. Quaternary distribution of the timber rattlesnake *(Crotalus horridus)* in southern Indiana. Proc. Indiana Acad. Sci. 99:113–122.

Riches, R. J. 1962. Notes on the garter snake *(Thamnophis sirtalis)* with particular reference to growth and breeding. British J. Herpetol. 3:31–32.

———. 1967. Early maturity in garter snakes *(Thamnophis elegans elegans)*. British J. Herpetol. 4:16–17.

Richmond, N. D. 1944. How *Natrix taxispilota* eats the channel catfish. Copeia 1944:254.

———. 1945. The habits of the rainbow snake in Virginia. Copeia 1945:28–30.

———. 1952. *Opheodrys aestivus* in aquatic habitats in Virginia. Herpetologica 8:38.

———. 1954a. Variation and sexual dimorphism in hatchlings of the rainbow snake, *Abastor erythrogrammus*. Copeia 1954:87–92.

———. 1954b. The ground snake, *Haldea valeriae*, in Pennsylvania and West Virginia with description of a new subspecies. Ann. Carnegie Mus. 33:251–260.

———. 1956. Autumn mating of the rough green snake. Herpetologica 12:325.

———. 1964. Fossil amphibians and reptiles of Frankstown Cave, Pennsylvania. Ann. Carnegie Mus. 36:225–228.

Ridlehuber, K. T., and N. J. Silvy. 1981. Texas rat snake feeds on Mexican freetail bat and wood duck eggs. Southwest. Nat. 26:70–71.

Riemer, W. J. 1954. A new subspecies of the snake *Masticophis lateralis* from California. Copeia 1954:45–48.

———. 1957. The snake *Farancia abacura*: An attended nest. Herpetologica 13:31–32.

Rigley, L. 1971. "Combat dance" of the black rat snake, *Elaphe o. obsoleta*. J. Herpetol. 5:65–66.

Riley, D., and I. P. Gallard. 1988. An estrogen receptor in the liver of the viviparous watersnake, *Nerodia*; characterization and seasonal changes in binding capacity. Endocrinology 123:753–761.

Robertson, I. C., and P. J. Weatherhead. 1992. The role of temperature in microhabitat selection by northern water snakes *(Nerodia sipedon)*. Can. J. Zool. 70:417–422.

Robinette, J. W., and S. E. Trauth. 1992. Reproduction in the western mud snake, *Farancia abacura reinwardtii* (Serpentes: Colubridae), in Arkansas. Proc. Arkansas Acad. Sci. 46:61–64.

Rodgers, R. B. 1985. *Heterodon platyrinos* (eastern hognose snake). Behavior. Herpetol. Rev. 16:111.

Rodman, G. B., Jr. 1939. Habits of *Trimorphodon vandenburghi* in captivity. Copeia 1939:50.

Rodríguez, M. C., and H. Drummond. 2000. Exploitation of avian nestlings and lizards by insular milksnakes, *Lampropeltis triangulum*. J. Herpetol. 34:139–142.

Rodríguez-Robles, J. A. 1994. Are Duvernoy's gland secretions of colubrid snakes venoms? J. Herpetol. 28:388–390.

———. 1998. Alternative perspectives on the diet of gopher snakes *(Pituophis catenifer*, Colubridae): Literature records versus stomach contents of wild and museum specimens. Copeia 1998:463–466.

Rodríguez-Robles, J. A., C. J. Bell, and H. W. Greene. 1999a. Food habits of the glossy snake, *Arizona elegans*, with comparisons to the diet of sympatric long-nosed snakes, *Rhinocheilus lecontei*. J. Herpetol. 33:87–92.

———. 1999b. Gape size and evolution of diet on snakes: Feeding ecology of erycine boas. J. Zool. (London) 248:49–58.

Rodríguez-Robles, J. A., D. F. Denardo, and R. E. Staub. 1999c. Phylogeography of the California mountain kingsnake, *Lampropeltis zonata* (Colubridae). Mol. Ecol. 8:1923–1934.

Rodríguez-Robles, J. A., and H. W. Greene. 1999. Food habits of the long-nosed snake *(Rhinocheilus lecontei)*, a 'specialist' predator? J. Zool. (London) 248:489–499.

Rodríguez-Robles, J. A., and J. M. de Jesús-Escobar. 1999. Molecular systematics of New World lampropeltinine snakes (Colubridae): Implications for biogeography and evolution of food habits. Biol. J. Linn. Soc. 68:355–385.

———. 2000. Molecular systematics of New World gopher, bull, and pinesnakes *(Pituophis:* Colubridae), a transcontinental species complex. Mol. Phylogenetics Evol. 14:35–50.

Rodríguez-Robles, J. A., D. G. Mulcahy, and H. W. Greene. 1999d. Feeding ecology of the desert nightsnake, *Hypsiglena torquata* (Colubridae) Copeia 1999:93–100.

Rodríguez-Robles, J. A., G. R. Stewart, and T. J. Papenfuss. 2001. Mitochrondrial DNA-based phylogeography of North American rubber boas, *Charina bottae* (Serpentes: Boidae). Mol. Phylogenetics Evol. 18:227–237.

Rogers, K. L. 1976. Herpetofauna of the Beck Ranch local fauna (upper Pliocene: Blancan) of Texas. Publ. Mus., Michigan St. Univ., Paleontol. Ser. 1:167–200.

———. 1982. Herpetofaunas of Courland Canal and Hall Ash local faunas (Pleistocene: early Kansas) of Jewell Co., Kansas. J. Herpetol. 16:174–177.

———. 1984. Herpetofauna of the Big Springs and Hornet's Nest quarries (northeastern Nebraska, Pleistocene: late Blancan). Trans. Nebraska Acad. Sci. 12:81–94.

Rogers, K. L., C. A. Repenning, R. M. Forester, E. E. Larson, S. A. Hall, G. R. Smith, E. Anderson, and T. J. Brown. 1985. Middle Pleistocene (Late Irvingtonian) climatic changes in south-central Colorado. Natl. Geogr. Res. 1:535–563.

Rose, F. L. 1989. Aspects of the biology of the Concho water snake *(Nerodia harteri paucimaculata)*. Texas J. Sci. 41:115–131.

Rose, F. L., and K. W. Selcer. 1989. Genetic divergence off allopatric populations of *Nerodia harteri*. J. Herpetol. 23:261–267.

Rose, W. 1950. The reptiles and amphibians of southern Africa. Cape Town, South Africa: Maskew Miller.

Rosen, P. C. 1991a. Comparative field study of thermal preferenda in garter snakes *(Thamnophis)*. J. Herpetol. 25:301–312.

———. 1991b. Comparative ecology and life history of the racer *(Coluber constrictor)* in Michigan. Copeia 1991:897–909.

Rosen, P. C., and C. H. Lowe. 1994. Highway mortality of snakes in the Sonoran Desert of southern Arizona. Biol. Conserv. 68:143–148.

Rosen, P. C., and C. R. Schwalbe. 1988. Status of the Mexican and narrow-headed garter snakes *(Thamnophis eques megalops* and *Thamnophis rufipunctatus)* in Arizona. U.S. Fish Wildl. Serv., Unpublished Report.

Rosenberg, H. I., A. Bdolah, and E. Kochva. 1985. Lethal factors and enzymes in the secretion from Duvernoy's gland of three colubrid snakes. J. Exp. Zool. 233:5–14.

Ross, D. A. 1989. Amphibians and reptiles in the diets of North American raptors. Wisconsin Dept. Nat. Resour., Endang. Resour. Rep. 59:1–33.

Ross, P., Jr., and D. Crews. 1977. Influence of the seminal plug on mating behavior in the garter snake. Nature (London) 267:344–345.

Rossi, J. V. 1992. Snakes of the United States and Canada. Vol. 1. Eastern area. Malabar, Florida: Krieger Publishing Co.

Rossi, J. V., and J. J. Feldner. 1993. *Crotalus willardi* (Arizona ridgenose rattlesnake) and *Crotalus lepidus klauberi* (banded rock rattlesnake). Arboreal behavior. Herpetol. Rev. 24:35.

Rossi, J. V., and R. Lewis. 1994. *Drymarchon corais couperi* (eastern indigo snake). Prey. Herpetol. Rev. 25:123–124.

Rossi, J. V., and R. Rossi. 1991. Notes on the captive reproduction of the southern hognose snake, *Heterodon simus.* Bull. Chicago Herpetol. Soc. 26:265–266.

———. 1992. Notes on the natural history, husbandry, and breeding of the southern hognose snake *(Heterodon simus).* Vivarium 3(6): 16–18, 27.

———. 1993. Notes on the captive maintenance and feeding behavior of a juvenile short-tailed snake *(Stilosoma extenuatum).* Herpetol. Rev. 24:100–101.

———. 1994. *Diadophis punctatus punctatus* (southern ringneck snake). Anti-ophiophagous behavior. Herpetol. Rev. 25:123.

———. 1995. Snakes of the United States and Canada. Vol. 2. Western area. Malabar, Florida: Krieger Publishing Co.

———. 1999a. Notes on a nearly successful captive breeding and parasite-related death of a narrow-headed garter snake, *Thamnophis rufipunctatus.* Bull. Chicago Herpetol. Soc. 34:210.

———. 1999b. Notes on reproduction of the black-striped snake, *Coniophanes imperialis imperialis,* from Texas. Bull. Chicago Herpetol. Soc. 34:227.

———. 2000. Comparison of growth, behavior, parasites, and oral bacteria of Brazos water snakes, *Nerodia harteri harteri,* raised in an outdoor enclosure with related specimens raised indoors. Bull. Chicago Herpetol. Soc. 35:221–228.

Rossman, D. A. 1956. Notes on food of a captive black swamp snake, *Seminatrix pygaea pygaea* (Cope). Herpetologica 12:154–155.

———. 1960. Herpetofaunal survey of the Pine Hills area of southern Illinois. Quart. J. Florida Acad. Sci. 22:207–225.

———. 1962. *Thamnophis proximus* (Say), a valid species of garter snake. Copeia 1962:741–48.

———. 1963a. Relationships and taxonomic status of the North American natricine snake genera *Liodytes, Regina,* and *Clonophis.* Occ. Pap. Mus. Zool. Louisiana St. Univ. 29:1–29.

———. 1963b. The colubrid snake genus *Thamnophis:* A revision of the *sauritus* group. Bull. Florida St. Mus. Biol. Sci. 7:99–178.

———. 1965. A new subspecies of the common garter snake, *Thamnophis sirtalis,* from the Florida Gulf Coast. Proc. Louisiana Acad. Sci. 27:67–73.

———. 1970a. *Thamnophis proximus.* Cat. Am. Amphib. Rept. 98:1–3.

———. 1970b. *Thamnophis sauritus.* Cat. Am. Amphib. Rept. 99:1–2.

———. 1971. Systematics of the neotropical populations of *Thamnophis marcianus* (Serpentes: Colubridae). Occ. Pap. Mus. Zool. Louisiana St. Univ. 41:1–13.

———. 1973. Evidence of the conspecificity of *Carphophis amoenus* (Say) and *Carphophis vermis* (Kennicott). J. Herpetol. 7:140–141.

———. 1979. Morphological evidence for taxonomic partitioning of the *Thamnophis elegans complex* (Serpentes: Colubridae). Occ. Pap. Mus. Zool. Louisiana St. Univ. 55:1–12.

———. 1985. *Liodytes* resurrected, reexamined, and reinterred. J. Herpetol. 19:169–171.

———. 1995. A second external character for distinguishing garter snakes *(Thamnophis)* from water snakes *(Nerodia).* Herpetol. Rev. 26:182–183.

Rossman, D. A., and W. G. Eberle. 1977. Partition of the genus *Natrix,* with preliminary observations on evolutionary trends in natricine snakes. Herpetologica 33:34–43.

Rossman, D. A., and R. L. Erwin. 1980. Geographic variation in the snake *Storeria occipitomaculata* (Storer) (Serpentes: Colubridae) in southeastern United States. Brimleyana 4:95–102.

Rossman, D. A., N. B. Ford, and R. A. Seigel. 1996. The garter snake: Evolution and ecology. Norman: University of Oklahoma Press.

Rossman, D. A., and P. A. Myer. 1990. Behavioral and morphological adaptations for snail extraction in the North American brown snakes (genus *Storeria).* J. Herpetol. 24:434–438.

Rossman, D. A., and R. Powell. 1985. *Clonophis, C. kirtlandii.* Cat. Am. Amphib. Rept. 364:1–2.

Rossman, D. A., and G. R. Stewart. 1987. Taxonomic reevaluation of *Thamnophis couchii* (Serpentes: Colubridae). Occ. Pap. Mus. Zool. Lousiana St. Univ. 63:1–25.

Rossman, D. A., and V. Wallach. 1991. *Virginia*. Cat. Am. Amphib. Rept. 529:1–4.

Rossman, N. J., D. A. Rossman, and N. K. Keith. 1982. Comparative visceral topography of New World snake tribe Thamnophiini (Colubridae, Natricinae). Tulane Stud. Zool. Bot. 23:123–164.

Roth, E. D., P. G. May, and T. M. Farrell. 1999. Pigmy rattlesnakes use frog-derived chemical cues to select foraging sites. Copeia 1999:772–774.

Rothman, N. 1961. Mud, rainbow, and black swamp snakes in captivity. Bull. Philadelphia Herpetol. Soc. 9(3): 17–20.

Rowe, M. P., R. G. Coss, and D. H. Owings. 1986. Rattlesnake rattles and burrowing owl hisses: A case of acoustic Batesian mimicry. Ethology 72:53–71.

Roze, J. A. 1974. *Micuroides, M. euryxanthus*. Cat. Am. Amphib. Rept. 163:1–4.

———. 1996. Coral snakes of the Americas: Biology, identification, and venoms. Malabar, Florida: Kreiger Publishing Co.

Roze, J. A., and G. M. Tilger. 1983. *Micrurus fulvius*. Cat. Am. Amphib. Rept. 316:1–4.

Ruben, J. A. 1977. Some correlates of cranial and cervical morphology with predatory modes in snakes. J. Morph. 152:89–100.

———. 1979. Blood physiology during activity in the snakes *Masticophis flagellum* (Colubridae) and *Crotalus viridis* (Crotalidae). Comp. Biochem. Physiol. 64A:577–580.

———. 1983. Mineralized tissues and excercise physiology of snakes. Am. Zool. 23:377–381.

Ruben, J. A., and C. Geddes. 1983. Some morphological correlates of striking in snakes. Copeia 1983:221–225.

Rubinoff, I., J. B. Graham, and J. Motta. 1986. Diving of the sea snake *Pelamis platurus* in the Gulf of Panama. I. Dive depth and duration. Marine Biol. 91:181–191.

Rubinoff, I., and C. Kropach. 1970. Differential reactions of Atlantic and Pacific predators to sea snake. Nature (London) 228:1288–1290.

Rubio, M. 1998. Rattlesnake: Portrait of a predator. Washington, D.C.: Smithsonian Institution Press.

Ruick, J. D., Jr., 1948. Collecting coral snakes, *Micrurus fulvius tenere*, in Texas. Herpetologica 4:215–216.

Rundquist, E. M. 1997. Bullsnake combat in Sedgwick County, Kansas. Kansas Herpetol. Soc. Newsl. 108:19.

Russell, A. P., and A. M. Bauer. 1993. The amphibians and reptiles of Alberta. Alberta, Canada: University of Calgary Press.

Russell, F. E. 1960. Snake venom poisoning in southern California. California Med. 93:347–350.

———. 1967a. Bites by the Sonoran coral snake, *Micruroides euryxanthus*. Toxicon 5:39–42.

———. 1967b. Gel diffusion study of human sera following rattlesnake venom poisoning. Toxicon 5:147–148.

———. 1983. Snake venom poisoning. Great Neck, New York: Scholium International.

Russell, F. E., J. A. Emery, and T. E. Long. 1960. Some properties of rattlesnake venom following 26 years storage. Proc. Soc. Exp. Biol. Med. 103:737–739.

Russell, F. E., and B. A. Michaelis. 1960. Zootoxicologic effects of *Crotalus* venoms. Physiologist 3:135.

Russell, K. R., and H. G. Hanlin. 1999. Aspects of the ecology of worm snakes *(Carphophis amoenus)* associated with small isolated wetlands in South Carolina. J. Herpetol. 33:339–344.

Russell, M. J., M. Ample, and A. Strieby. 1999a. *(Scinax elaeochroa)*. Predation. Herpetol. Rev. 30:38.

———. 1999b. *Clelia clelia* (mussurana). Attempted predation. Herpetol. Rev. 30:43.

Ruthven, A. G. 1908. Variations and genetic relationships of the garter snakes. Bull. U.S. Natl. Mus. 61:1–201.

Rutledge, A. 1936. Birds and serpents. Nature Mag. 27:137–139.

Sabath, M., and R. Worthington. 1959. Eggs and young of certain Texas reptiles. Herpetologica 15:31–32.

Sabath, M. D., and L. E. Sabath. 1969. Morphological intergradation in Gulf coastal brown snakes, *Storeria dekayi* and *Storeria tropica*. Am. Midl. Nat. 81:148–155.

Saenz, D., S. J. Burgdorf, D. C. Rudolph, and C. M. Duran. 1996. *Crotalus horridus* (timber rattlesnake). Climbing. Herpetol. Rev. 27:145.

Saiff, E. 1975. Preglottal structures in the snake family Colubridae. Copeia 1975:589–592.

Sajdak, R. A., and S. L. Sajdak. 1999. *Thamnophis sirtalis sirtalis* (eastern garter snake). Carrion feeding. Herpetol. Rev. 30:229.

Salmon, G. T., W. F. Holmstrom, Jr., B. W. Tryon, and G. P. Merker. 1997. Longevity records for the gray-banded kingsnake, *Lampropeltis alterna*. Bull. Chicago Herpetol. Soc. 32:152–153.

Samejima, Y., Y. Aoki, and D. Mebs. 1991. Amino acid sequence of a myotoxin from venom of the eastern diamond back rattlesnake *(Crotalus adamanteus)*. Toxicon 29:461–468.

Sanchez, F. C., A. Gonzalez Ruiz, E. Godinez Cano, and J. F. Delgadillo Espinosa. 1999. *Crotalus lepidus morulus* (rock rattlesnake). Reproduction. Herpetol. Rev. 30:168.

Sánchez-Hernández, C., and A. Ramírez-Bautista. 1992.

Trimorphodon biscutatus (lyre snake). Prey. Herpetol. Rev. 23:121.

Sanders, J. S., and J. S. Jacob. 1981. Thermal ecology of the copperhead *(Agkistrodon contortrix)*. Herpetologica 37:264–270.

Sanderson, W. E. 1993. Additional evidence for the specific status of *Nerodia cyclopion* and *Nerodia floridana* (Reptilia: Colubridae). Brimleyana 19:83–94.

Sandidge, L. L. 1953. Food and dens of the opossum *(Didelphis virginiana)* in northeastern Kansas. Trans. Kansas Acad. Sci. 56:97–106.

Sankey, J. T. 1996. Vertebrate paleontology and magnetostratigraphy of the Upper Glens Ferry (latest Pliocene) and Lower Bruneau (Pliocene-Pleistocene) formations near Murphy, southwestern Idaho. J. Idaho Acad. Sci. 32:71–88.

Sattler, P. W., and S. I. Guttman. 1976. An electrophoretic analysis of *Thamnophis sirtalis* from western Ohio. Copeia 1976:352–356.

Saul, D. W. 1968. An unusual hognose snake from Blount Island, Duval County, Florida. Bull. Maryland Herpetol. Soc. 4:21–22.

Saunders, J. J. 1977. Late Pleistocene vertebrates of the Western Ozark Highlands. Illinois St. Mus., Rep. Invest., 33:1–118.

Savage, J. M., and F. S. Cliff. 1953. A new subspecies of sidewinder, *Crotalus cerastes*, from Arizona. Chicago Acad. Sci. Nat. Hist. Misc. 119:1–7.

Savage, J. M., and J. B. Slowinski. 1990. A simple consistent terminology for the basic colour patterns of the venomous coral snakes and their mimics. Herpetol. J. 1:530–532.

———. 1992. The colouration of the venomous coral snakes (family Elapidae) and their mimics (families Aniliidae and Colubridae). Biol. J. Linn. Soc. 45:235–254.

Savary, W. 1999. *Crotalus molossus molossus* (northern blacktail rattlesnake). Brood defense. Herpetol. Rev. 30:45.

Savitzky, B. A., and G. M. Burghardt. 2000. Ontogeny of predatory behavior in the aquatic specialist snake, *Nerodia rhombifer*, during the first year of life. Herpetol. Monogr. 14:401–419.

Sawyer, M. W., and J. T. Baccus. 1996. Movement ecology and thermal biology of *Bogertophis subocularis* from Texas (Serpentes: Colubridae). Southwest. Nat. 41:182–186.

Say, T. 1823. In: E. James, An account of an expedition from Pittsburgh to the Rocky Mountains, performed in the years 1819, 1820, vol. 2, 339. Philadelphia: H. C. Peary and I. Lea.

———. 1825. Descriptions of three new species of *Coluber* inhabiting the United States. J. Acad. Nat. Sci. Philadelphia, ser. 1, 4:237–241.

Scarborough, R. M., J. W. Rose, M. A. Hsu, D. R. Phillips, V. A. Fried, A. M. Campbell, L. Nannizzi, and I. F. Charo. 1991. Barbourin: A GPHb-IIIa-specific integrin antagonist from the venom of *Sistrurus m. barbouri*. J. Biol. Chem. 266:9359–9362.

Schaeffel, F., and A. de Queiroz. 1990. Alternative mechanisms of enhanced underwater vision in the garter snakes *Thamnophis melanogaster* and *T. couchii*. Copeia 1990:50–58.

Schaeffer, R. C., Jr., R. W. Carlson, H. Whigham, F. E. Russell, and M. H. Weil. 1973. Some hemodynamic effects of rattlesnake *(Crotalus viridis helleri)* venom. Proc. West. Pharmacol. Soc. 16:58–62.

Schlauch, F. C. 1975. Agonistic behavior in a suburban Long Island population of the smooth green snake, *Opheodrys vernalis*. Engelhardtia 6:25–26.

Schlegel, H. 1837. Essai sur la physionomie des serpens, vol. 2. La Haye: J. Kips, J. Hz, and W. P. van Stockum.

Schlieffelin, C. D., and A. de Queiroz. 1991. Temperature and defense in the common garter snake: Warm snakes are more aggressive than cold snakes. Herpetologica 47:230–237.

Schmidt, D. F., W. K. Hayes, and F. E. Hayes. 1993. Influence of prey movement on the aim of predatory strikes of the western rattlesnake *(Crotalus viridis)*. Great Basin Nat. 53:203–206.

Schmidt, K. P. 1919. Rediscovery of *Amphiardis inornatus* (Garman), with notes on other specimens from Oklahoma. Copeia 73:71–73.

———. 1928. Notes on American coral snakes. Bull. Antivenin Inst. Am. 2:63–64.

———. 1932. Stomach contents of some American coral snakes, with the description of a new species of *Geophis*. Copeia 1932:6–9.

———. 1940. Notes on Texan snakes of the genus *Salvadora*. Field Mus. Nat. Hist. Zool. Ser. 24:143–150.

Schmidt, K. P., and D. D. Davis. 1941. Field book of snakes of the United States and Canada. New York: G. P. Putnam's Sons.

Schmidt, K. P., and R. F. Inger. 1957. Living reptiles of the world. Garden City, New York: Hanover House.

Schmidt-Nielsen, K., and R. Fange. 1958. Salt glands in marine reptiles. Nature (London) 182:783–785.

Schoener, T. W. 1977. Competition and the niche, 35–136. In: C. Gans and D. W. Tinkle (eds.), Biology of the Reptilia, vol. 7. New York: Academic Press.

Schroder, R. C. 1950. Hibernation of blue racers and bull

snakes in western Illinois. Chicago Acad. Sci. Nat. Hist. Misc. 75:1–2.

Schueler, F. W. 1975. Notes on garter snake *(Thamnophis sirtalis)* spring mortality and behaviour at Long Point. Ontario Field. Biol. 29:45–49.

Schuett, G. W. 1982. A copperhead *(Agkistrodon contortrix)* brood produced from autumn copulations. Copeia 1982:700–702.

———. 1986. Selected topics on reproduction of the copperhead, *Agkistrodon contortrix* (Reptilia, Serpentes, Viperidae). Master's Thesis, Central Michigan University, Mt. Pleasant.

———. 1992. Is long term sperm storage an important component of the reproductive biology of temperate pit vipers? pp. 169–184. In: J. A. Campbell and E. D. Brode, Jr. (eds.), Biology of the pit vipers. Tyler, Texas: Selva.

———. 1998. Current research on male aggression and parthenogenesis in snakes. Sonoran Herpetologist 11:98–101.

Schuett, G. W., D. L. Clark, and F. Kraus. 1984. Feeding mimicry in the rattlesnake *Sistrurus catenatus*, with comments on the evolution of the rattle. Anim. Behav. 32:625–626.

Schuett, G. W., and D. Duvall. 1996. Head lifting by female copperheads, *Agkistrodon contortrix*, during courtship: Potential mate choices. Anim. Behav. 51:367–373.

Schuett, G. W., P. J. Fernandez, D. Chiszar, and H. M. Smith. 1998. Fatherless reproduction: A new type of parthenogenesis in snakes. Fauna 1:20–25.

Schuett, G. W., P. J. Fernandez, W. F. Gergits, N. J. Casna, D. Chiszar, H. M. Smith, J. B. Mitton, S. P. Mackessey, R. A. Odum, and M. J. Demlong. 1997. Production of offspring in the absence of males: Evidence for facultative parthenogenesis in bisexual snakes. Herpetol. Nat. Hist. 5:1–10.

Schuett, G. W., and J. C. Gillingham. 1986. Sperm storage and multiple paternity in the copperhead, *Agkistrodon contortrix*. Copeia 1986:807–811.

———. 1988. Courtship and mating of the copperhead, *Agkistrodon contortrix*. Copeia 1988:374–381.

Schuett, G. W., H. J. Harlow, J. D. Rose, E. A. Van Kirk, and W. J. Murdoch. 1996. Levels of plasma corticosterone and testosterone in male copperheads *(Agkistrodon contortrix)* following staged fights. Horm. Behav. 30:60–68.

———. 1997. Annual cycle of plasma testosterone in male copperheads, *Agkistrodon contortrix* (Serpentes, Viperidae): Relationship to timing of spermatogenesis, mating, and agonistic behavior. Gen. Comp. Endocrinol. 105:417–424.

Schulz, K.-D. 1992a. Variation, distribution, and biology of *Elaphe triaspis* (Cope, 1866), Part 1, with remarks on the husbandry and breeding of the southern subspecies *Elaphe triaspis mutabilis* (Cope, 1885). Litt. Serpent. Engl. Ed. 12:32–41.

———. 1992b. Variation, distribution, and biology of *Elaphe triaspis* (Cope, 1866), Part 2, with remarks about care and breeding of the southern subspecies *Elaphe triaspis mutabilis* (Cope, 1885). Litt. Serpent. Engl. Ed. 12:54–68.

———. 1996. A monograph of the colubrid snakes of the genus *Elaphe* Fitzinger. Havlickuv Brod, Czech Republic: Koeltz Scientific Books.

Schulz, K.-D., and H.-D. Philippen. 1991. The systematic-taxonomic position of *Elaphe bairdi* (Yarrow, 1880). Litt. Serpent. Engl. Ed. 11:138–141.

Schwab, D. 1988. Growth and rattle development in a captive timber rattlesnake, *Crotalus horridus*. Bull. Chicago Herpetol. Soc. 23:26–27.

Schwalbe, C. R., and P. C. Rosen. 1988. Preliminary report on effect of bullfrogs on wetland herpetofauna in southeastern Arizona, 166–173. In: R. C. Szaro, K. E. Severson, and D. R. Patton (eds.), Management of amphibians, reptiles, and small mammals in North America. USDA Forest Serv., Rocky Mountain Forest and Range Exp. Sta., Gen. Tech. Rep. RM-166.

Schwammer, H. 1983. Herpetologische Beobachtungen aus Colorado/U.S.A. Aquaria (St. Gallen) 30(6): 90–93.

Schwaner, T. D., and H. C. Dessauer. 1982. Comparative immunodiffusion survey of snake transferrins focused on the relationships of the natricines. Copeia 1982:541–549.

Schwartz, A. 1953. A new subspecies of crowned snake *(Tantilla coronata)* from the southern Appalachian Mountains. Herpetologica 9:153–157.

Schwartz, J. M., G. F. McCracken, and G. M. Burghardt. 1989. Multiple paternity in wild populations of the garter snake, *Thamnophis sirtalis*. Behav. Ecol. Sociobiol. 25:269–273.

Schwenkmeyer, R. C. 1949. Hibernation of the California striped racer. Herpetologica 5:84.

Scott, D. 1986. Notes on the eastern hognose snake, *Heterodon platyrhinos* Latreille (Squamata: Colubridae), on a Virginia barrier island. Brimleyana 12:51–55.

Scott, D. E., R. U. Fischer, J. D. Congdon, and S. A. Busa. 1995. Whole body lipid dynamics and reproduction in the eastern cottonmouth, *Agkistrodon piscivorus*. Herpetologica 51:472–487.

Scott, J. R., and D. Pettus. 1979. Effects of seasonal acclimation on the preferred body temperature of
Thamnophis elegans vagrans. J. Therm. Biol. 4:307–309.

Scott, J. R., C. R. Tracy, and D. Pettus. 1982. A biophysical
analysis of daily and seasonal utilization of climate
space by a montane snake. Ecology 63:482–493.

Scott, N. J. 1969. A zoogeographic analysis of the snakes
of Costa Rica. Ph.D. Dissertation, University of Southern California, Los Angeles.

Scott, N. J., T. C. Maxwell, O. W. Thornton, Jr., L. A.
Fitzgerald, and J. W. Flury. 1989. Distribution, habitat,
and future of Harter's water snake, *Nerodia harteri*, in
Texas. J. Herpetol. 23:373–389.

Scott, N. J., and R. W. McDiarmid. 1984a. *Trimorphodon*.
Cat. Am. Amphib. Rept. 352:1–2.

———. 1984b. *Trimorphodon biscutatus*. Cat. Am. Amphib.
Rept. 353:1–4.

Scribner, S. J., and P. J. Weatherhead. 1994. Locomotion
and antipredator behaviour in three species of semi-
aquatic snakes. Can. J. Zool. 73:321–329.

Scudder, K. M., and D. Chiszar. 1977. Effects of six visual
stimulus conditions on defensive and exploratory behavior in two species of rattlesnakes. Psychol. Rec.
3:519–526.

Scudder, K. M., D. Chiszar, and H. M. Smith. 1992. Strike-
induced chemosensory searching and trailing behaviour in neonatal rattlesnakes. Anim. Behav. 44:574–576.

Scudder, K. M., D. Chiszar, H. M. Smith, and T. Melcer.
1988. Response of neonatal prairie rattlesnakes *(Crotalus viridis)* to conspecific and heterospecific chemical
cues. Psychol. Rec. 38:459–471.

Scudder, K. M., N. J. Stewart, and H. M. Smith. 1980. Response of neonate water snakes *(Nerodia sipedon
sipedon)* to conspecific chemical cues. J. Herpetol.
14:196–198.

Scudder, R. M., and G. M. Burghardt. 1983. A comparative
study of defensive behavior in three sympatric
species of water snakes *(Nerodia)*. Zeit. Tierpsychol.
63:17–26.

———. 1985. The role of feeding regimens in the growth
of neonate broad-banded water snakes, *Nerodia fasciata
confluens*, and possible effects on reproduction. Develop.
Psychobiol. 18:203–214.

Scudder, S. 1972. Observations on snakes in the burrows
of mole crickets. Bull. Maryland Herpetol. Soc. 8:95.

Scudder-Davis, R. M., and G. M. Burghardt. 1996. Ontogenetic changes in growth efficiency in laboratory-reared
water snakes of the genus *Nerodia*. Snake 27:75–84.

Sealy, J. B. 1996. *Crotalus horridus* (timber rattlesnake).
Mating. Herpetol. Rev. 27:23–24.

Secor, S. M. 1987. Courtship and mating behavior of the
speckled kingsnake, *Lampropeltis getulus holbrooki*. Herpetologica 43:15–28.

———. 1992. A preliminary analysis of the movement
and home range size of the sidewinder, *Crotalus
cerastes*, 389–393. In: J. A. Campbell and E. D. Brodie, Jr.
(eds.), Biology of the pit vipers. Tyler, Texas: Selva.

———. 1994. Natural history of the sidewinder, *Crotalus
cerastes*, 281–301. In: P. R. Brown and J. W. Wright
(eds.), Herpetology of North American deserts: Proceedings of a symposium. Southwest. Herpetol. Soc.
Spec. Publ. 5.

———. 1995. Ecological aspects of foraging mode for the
snakes *Crotalus cerastes* and *Masticophis flagellum*. Herpetol. Monogr. 9:169–186.

Secor, S. M., and J. M. Diamond. 2000. Evolution of regu-
latory responses to feeding in snakes. Physiol. Biochem.
Zool. 73:123–141.

Secor, S. M., B. C. Jayne, and A. F. Bennett. 1992. Locomotor performance and energetic cost of sidewinding by
the snake *Crotalus cerastes*. J. Exp. Biol. 163:1–14.

Secor, S. M., and K. A. Nagy. 1994. Bioenergetic correlates
of foraging mode for the snakes *Crotalus cerastes* and
Masticophis flagellum. Ecology 75:1600–1614.

Secoy, D. M. 1979. Investigatory behaviour of plains garter
snakes, *Thamnophis radix* (Reptilia: Colubridae), in tests
of repellant chemicals. Can. J. Zool. 57:691–693.

Seib, R. L. 1984. Prey use in three syntopic neotropical
racers. J. Herpetol. 18:412–420.

Seibert, H. C. 1950. Population density of snakes in an
area near Chicago. Copeia 1950:229–230.

———. 1951. Population density of snakes on Penikese Island, Massachusetts. Copeia 1951:314.

———. 1965. A snake hibernaculum uncovered in mid-
winter. J. Ohio Herpetol. Soc. 5:29.

Seibert, H. C., and C. W. Hagen. 1947. Studies on a population of snakes in Illinois. Copeia 1947:6–22.

Seidel, M. E., and R. G. Lindeborg. 1973. Lags in metabolic response to temperature of two garter snakes,
Thamnophis elegans and *Thamnophis radix*. Herpetologica 29:358–360.

Seigel, R. A. 1986. Ecology and conservation of an endangered rattlesnake, *Sistrurus catenatus*, in Missouri, U.S.A.
Biol. Conserv. 35:333–346.

———. 1992. Ecology of a specialized predator: *Regina
grahami* in Missouri. J. Herpetol. 26:32–37.

Seigel, R. A., and H. S. Fitch. 1984. Ecological patterns of
relative clutch mass in snakes. Oecologia (Berlin)
61:293–301.

———. 1985. Annual variation in reproduction in snakes
in a fluctuating environment. J. Anim. Ecol. 54:497–505.

Seigel, R. A., H. S. Fitch, and N. B. Ford. 1986. Variation in relative clutch mass in snakes among and within species. Herpetologica 42:179–185

Seigel, R. A., and N. B. Ford. 1991. Phenotypic plasticity in the reproductive characteristics of an oviparous snake, *Elaphe guttata*: Implications for life history studies. Herpetologica 47:301–307.

———. 1992. Effect of energy input on variation in clutch size and offspring size in a viviparous reptile. Funct. Ecol. 6:382–385.

Seigel, R. A., N. B. Ford, and L. A. Mahrt. 2000. Ecology of an aquatic snake *(Thamnophis marcianus)* in a desert environment: Implications of early timing of birth and geographic variation in reproduction. Am. Midl. Nat. 143:453–462.

Seigel, R. A., J. W. Gibbons, and T. K. Lynch. 1995b. Temporal changes in reptile populations: Effects of a severe drought on aquatic snakes. Herpetologica 51:424–434.

Seigel, R. A., M. M. Huggins, and N. B. Ford. 1987. Reduction in locomotor ability as a cost of reproduction. Oecologia (Berlin) 73:481–485.

Seigel, R. A., R. K. Loraine, and J. W. Gibbons. 1995a. Reproductive cycles and temporal variation in fecundity in the black swamp snake, *Seminatrix pygaea*. Am. Midl. Nat. 134:371–377.

Seigel, R. A., C. A. Sheil, and J. S. Doody. 1998. Changes in a population of an endangered rattlesnake *Sistrurus catenatus* following a severe flood. Biol. Conserv. 83:127–131.

Semlitsch, R. D. 1979. The influence of temperature in ecdysis rates in snakes (genus *Natrix*) (Reptilia, Serpentes, Colubridae). J. Herpetol. 13:212–214.

———. 1988. Annual emergence of juvenile mud snakes *(Farancia abacura)* at aquatic habitats. Copeia 1988:243–245.

Semlitsch, R. D., K. L. Brown, and J. P. Caldwell. 1981. Habitat utilization, seasonal activity, and population size structure of the southeastern crowned snake *Tantilla coronata*. Herpetologica 37:40–46.

Semlitsch, R. D., and J. W. Gibbons. 1978. Reproductive allocations in the brown water snake, *Natrix taxispilota*. Copeia 1978:721–723.

———. 1982. Body size dimorphism and sexual selection in two species of water snakes. Copeia 1982:974–976.

Semlitsch, R. D., and G. B. Moran. 1984. Ecology of the redbelly snake *(Storeria occipitomaculata)* using mesic habitats in South Carolina. Am. Midl. Nat. 111:33–40.

Sever, D. M., and T. J. Ryan. 1999. Ultrastructure of the reproductive system of the black swamp snake *(Seminatrix pygaea)*: Part 1. Evidence for oviducal sperm storage. J. Morph. 241:1–18.

Sever, D. M., T. J. Ryan, T. Morris, D. Patton, and S. Swafford. 2000. Ultrastructure of the reproductive system of the black swamp snake *(Seminatrix pygaea)*. II. Annual oviducal cycle. J. Morph. 245:146–160.

Sexton, O. J. 1979. Remarks on defensive behavior of hognose snakes, *Heterodon*. Herpetol. Rev. 10:86–87.

Sexton, O. J., and J. E. Bramble. 1994. Post-hibernation behavior of a population of garter snakes *(Thamnophis sirtalis)*. Amphibia-Reptilia 15:9–20.

Sexton, O. J., and H. Heatwole. 1965. Life history notes on some Panamanian snakes. Caribbean J. Sci. 5:39–43.

Sexton, O. J., and S. R. Hunt. 1980. Temperature relationships and movements of snakes *(Elaphe obsoleta, Coluber constrictor)* in a cave hibernaculum. Herpetologica 36:20–26.

Sexton, O. J., and K. R. Marion. 1981. Experimental analysis of movements by prairie rattlesnakes, *Crotalus viridis*, during hibernation. Oecologia (Berlin) 51:37–41.

Shannon, F. A., and F. L. Humphrey. 1963. Analysis of color pattern polymorphism in the snake *Rhinocheilus lecontei*. Herpetologica 19:153–160.

Sharma, R. C., and T. G. Vazirani. 1977. Food and feeding habits of some reptiles of Rajasthan. Rec. Zool. Surv. India 73:77–93.

Shaw, C. E. 1948. The male combat "dance" of some crotalid snakes. Herpetologica 4:137–145.

———. 1951. Male combat in American colubrid snakes with remarks on combat in other colubrid and elapid snakes. Herpetologica 7:149–168.

———. 1953. A hibernating *Chionactis occipitalis annulatus*. Herpetologica 9:72.

———. 1959. Observations on the feeding behavior of a captive rosy boa, *Lichanura roseofusca*. Copeia 1959:336.

———. 1961. Snakes of the sea. Zoo Nooz 34(7): 3–5.

———. 1966. Southern Pacific rattlesnake. Zoo Nooz 39:19.

———. 1971. The coral snakes, genera *Micrurus* and *Micruroides* of the United States and northern Mexico, 157–172. In: W. Bücherl and E. E. Buckley (eds.), Venomous animals and their venoms. Vol. 2. Venomous vertebrates. New York: Academic Press.

Shaw, C. E., and S. Campbell. 1974. Snakes of the American West. New York: A. E. Knopf.

Shaw, G. 1802. General zoology, or systematic natural history, vol. 3, part 2. London: G. Kearsley.

Shine, R., P. S. Harlow, M. J. Elphick, M. M. Olsson, and R. T. Mason. 2000. Conflicts between courtship and thermoregulation: The thermal ecology of amorous male garter snakes *(Thamnophis sirtalis parietalis*, Colubridae). Physiol. Biochem. Zool. 73:508–516.

Shine, R., D. O'Conner, and R. T. Mason. 2000a. Sexual conflict in the snake den. Behav. Ecol. Sociobiol. 48:392–401.

————. 2000b. Female mimicry in garter snakes: Behavioural tactics of "she-males" and the males that court them. Can. J. Zool. 78:1391–1396.

Shine, R., and R. A. Seigel. 1996. A neglected life-history trait: Clutch-size variance in snakes. J. Zool. (London) 239:209–223.

Shively, S. H., and J. C. Mitchell. 1994. Male combat in copperheads *(Agkistrodon contortrix)* from northern Virginia. Banisteria 3:29–30.

Sibley, H. 1951. Snakes are scared of you! Field and Stream 55(9): 46–48.

Sievert, L. M., and P. Andreadis. 1999. Specific dynamic action and postprandial thermophily in juvenile northern water snakes, *Nerodia sipedon.* J. Therm. Biol. 24:51–55.

Silver, J. 1928. Pilot black-snake feeding on big brown bat. J. Mammal. 9:149.

Simons, L. H. 1986. *Crotalus atrox* (western diamondback rattlesnake). Pattern. Herpetol. Rev. 17:20, 22.

————. 1989. Vertebrates killed by desert fire. Southwest. Nat. 34:144–145.

Simonson, W. E. 1951. Courtship and mating of the fox-snake, *Elaphe vulpina vulpina.* Copeia 1951:309.

Sinclair, R. M. 1951. Notes on Tennessee snakes of the genus *Haldea.* Herpetologica 7:145.

Singh, L., T. Sharma, and S. P. Ray-Chaudhuri. 1968. Chromosomes and the classification of the snakes of the family Boidae. Cytogenetics 7:161–168.

Sironi, M., M. Chiaraviglio, R. Cervantes, M. Bertona, and M. Río. 2000. Dietary habits of *Boa constrictor occidentalis,* in the Cordoba Province, Argentina. Amphibia-Reptilia 21:226–232.

Sisk, M. E., and C. J. McCoy. 1963. Stomach contents of *Natrix r. rhombifera* (Reptilia: Serpentes) from an Oklahoma lake. Proc. Oklahoma Acad. Sci. 44:68–71.

Sisk, N. R., and J. F. Jackson. 1997. Tests of two hypotheses for the origin of the crotaline rattle. Copeia 1997:485–495.

Skalka, P., and P. Vozenilek. 1986. Case of parthenogenesis in water snake, *Nerodia sipedon.* Fauna Bohemiae Septentrionalis 11:81–82.

Skehan, P., Jr. 1960. Feeding notes on captive reptiles. Herpetologica 16:32.

Slaughter, B. H. 1966. The Moore Pit local fauna: Pleistocene of Texas. J. Paleontol. 40:78–91.

Slavens, F. L., and K. Slavens. 1991. Reptiles and amphibians in captivity. Breeding, longevity, and inventory. Seattle, Washington: Slaveware.

Sleijpen, F. 1991. Breeding *Nerodia fasciata.* Litt. Serpent. Engl. Ed. 11:39–43.

Slevin, J. R. 1950. A remarkable concentration of desert snakes. Herpetologica 6:12–13.

————. 1951. A high birth rate for *Natrix sipedon sipedon* (Linne). Herpetologica 7:132.

Slowinski, J. B. 1995. A phylogenetic analysis of the New World coral snakes (Elapidae: *Leptomicrurus, Micruroides,* and *Micrurus*) based on allozymic and morphological characters. J. Herpetol. 29:325–338.

Small, M. F., S. P. Tabor, and C. Fazzari. 1994. *Masticophis flagellum* (western coachwhip). Foraging. Herpetol. Rev. 25:28.

Smetsers, P. 1990. Care and breeding of *Sistrurus miliarius barbouri,* the Barbour's pygmy rattlesnake. Litt. Serpent. Engl. Ed. 10:181–189.

Smith, A. G. 1945. The status of *Thamnophis butleri* Cope, and a redescription of *Thamnophis brachystoma* Cope. Proc. Biol. Soc. Washington 58:147–154.

————. 1946. Notes on the secondary sex characters of *Thamnophis ruthveni.* Copeia 1946:106.

————. 1947. Navel closure time and age in the young of *Thamnophis radix.* Herpetologica 3:153–154.

————. 1948. Intergradation in worm snakes *(Carphophis)* from Kentucky. Chicago Acad. Sci. Nat. Hist. Misc. 18:1–3.

Smith, A. K. 1975. Incidence of tail coiling in a population of ringneck snakes *(Diadophis punctatus).* Trans. Kansas Acad. Sci. 77:237–238.

Smith, C. 1992. *Crotalus adamanteus* (eastern diamondback rattlesnake). Behavior. Herpetol. Rev. 23:118.

————. 1997. *Agkistrodon contortrix contortrix* (southern copperhead). Diet. Herpetol. Rev. 28:153.

Smith, C. R. 1982. Food resource partitioning of fossorial Florida reptiles, 173–178. In: N. J. Scott, Jr. (ed.). Herpetological communities. U.S. Fish Wildl. Serv. Wildl. Res. Rep. 13.

Smith, D. D. 1975. Death feigning by the western coachwhip snake. Herpetol. Rev. 6:126.

Smith, D. D., D. J. Pflanz, and R. Powell. 1993. Observations of autohemorrhaging in *Tropidophis haetianus, Rhinocheilus lecontei, Heterodon platyrhinos,* and *Nerodia erythrogaster.* Herpetol. Rev. 24:130–131.

Smith, G. C. 1976. Ecological energetics of three species of ectothermic vertebrates. Ecology 57:252–264.

Smith, G. C., and D. Watson. 1972. Selection patterns of corn snakes, *Elaphe guttata,* of different phenotypes of the house mouse. Copeia 1972:529–532.

Smith, G. R., and J. B. Iverson. 1993. Reactions to odor trails in bullsnakes. J. Herpetol. 27:333–335.

Smith, H. M. 1941a. A new genus of Central American snakes related to *Tantilla.* J. Washington Acad. Sci. 31:115–117.

————. 1941b. Notes on Mexican snakes of the genus *Masticophis.* J. Washington Acad. Sci. 31:388–398.

———. 1942. A resume of Mexican snakes of the genus *Tantilla*. Zoologica (New York) 27:33–42.

———. 1956. Handbook of amphibians and reptiles of Kansas. 2nd ed. Univ. Kansas Mus. Nat. Hist. Misc. Publ. 9:1–356.

———. 1963. The identity of the Black Hills population of *Storeria occipitomaculata*, the red-bellied snake. Herpetologica 19:17–21.

———. 1990. Signs and symptoms following human envenomation by the Mojave rattlesnake, *Crotalus scutulatus*, treated without use of antivenom. Bull. Maryland Herpetol. Soc. 26:105–110.

Smith, H. M., and E. D. Brodie, Jr. 1982. Reptiles of North America: A guide to field identification. New York: Golden Press.

Smith, H. M., and D. Chiszar. 1993. Apparent intergradation in Texas between the subspecies of the Texas blind snake *(Leptotyphlops dulcis)*. Bull. Maryland Herpetol. Soc. 29:143–155.

———. 1994. Variation in the lined snake *(Tropidoclonion lineatum)* in northern Texas. Bull. Maryland Herpetol. Soc. 30:6–14.

Smith, H. M., D. Chiszar, J. R. Staley II, and K. Tepedelen. 1994. Populational relationships in the corn snake *Elaphe guttata* (Reptilia: Serpentes). Texas J. Sci. 46:259–292.

Smith, H. M., D. Chiszar, and K. Tepedelen. 1999. Behavioral resourcefulness in a striped whipsnake, *Masticophis t. taeniatus*. Bull. Maryland Herpetol. Soc. 35:1–3.

Smith, H. M., C. A. Pague, and D. Chiszar. 1996. A brood of lined snakes *(Tropidoclonion lineatum)* from southeastern Colorado. Bull. Maryland Herpetol. Soc. 32:24–27.

Smith, H. M., and O. Sanders. 1952. Distributional data on Texan amphibians and reptiles. Texas J. Sci. 4:204–219.

Smith, H. M., and F. N. White. 1955. Adrenal enlargement and its significance in the hognose snakes *(Heterodon)*. Herpetologica 11:137–144.

Smith, H. M., F. van Breukelen, D. L. Auth, and D. Chiszar. 1998. A subspecies of the Texas blind snake *(Leptotyphlops dulcis)* without supraoculars. Southwest. Nat. 43:437–440.

Smith, K. S., and R. L. Cifelli. 2000. A synopsis of the Pleistocene vertebrates of Oklahoma. Oklahoma Geol. Surv. Bull. 147:1–36.

Smith, L. L., and R. Franz. 1994. Use of Florida round-tailed muskrat houses by amphibians and reptiles. Florida Field Nat. 22:69–74.

Smith, M. A. 1926. Monograph of the sea snakes. London: British Museum (Natural History).

Smith, P. W. 1961. The amphibians and reptiles of Illinois. Illinois Nat. Hist. Surv. Bull. 28:1–298.

Smith, P. W., and M. M. Hensley. 1958. Notes on a small collection of amphibians and reptiles from the vicinity of the Pinacate Lava Cap in northwestern Sonora, Mexico. Trans. Kansas Acad. Sci. 61:64–76.

Smith, P. W., and S. A. Minton. 1957. A distributional summary of the herpetofauna of Illinois and Indiana. Am. Midl. Nat. 58:341–351.

Smith, S. M. 1975. Innate recognition of coral snake pattern by a possible avian predator. Science (New York) 187:759–760.

Smith, S. M., and A. M. Mostrom. 1985. "Coral snake" rings: Are they helpful in foraging? Copeia 1985:384–387.

Smith, T. L., and K. V. Kardong. 2000. Absence of polarity perception by rattlesnakes of envenomated prey trails. J. Herpetol. 34:621–624.

Smits, A. W., and H. B. Lillywhite. 1985. Maintenance of blood volume in snakes: Transcapillary shifts of extravascular fluids during acute hemorrhage. J. Comp. Physiol. B 155:305–310.

Smyth, T. 1949. Notes on the timber rattlesnake at Mountain Lake, Virginia. Copeia 1949:78–79.

Snelling, E., Jr., and J. T. Collins. 1996. *Sistrurus miliarius barbouri* (dusky pigmy rattlesnake). Maximum size. Herpetol. Rev. 27:84.

Snider, A. T., and J. K. Bowler. 1992. Longevity of reptiles and amphibians in North American collections. Soc. Stud. Amphib. Rept. Herpetol. Circ. 21:1–40.

Solórzano, A., and L. Cerdas. 1987. *Drymobius margaritiferus* (speckled racer). Reproduction. Herpetol. Rev. 18:75–76.

Somma L. A. 1989. *Elaphe bairdi* (Baird's Rat Snake). Drinking. Herpetol. Rev. 20:72.

Sonnini de Manoncourt, C. N. S., and P. A. Latreille. 1801. Histoire naturelle des reptiles, avec figures dessinees d'apres nature, vol. 3. Paris: Chez Deterville.

Soto, J. G., J. C. Perez, M. M. Lopez, M. Martinez, T. B. Quintanilla-Hernandez, M. S. Santa-Hernandez, K. Turner, J. L. Glenn, R. C. Straight, and S. A. Minton. 1989. Comparative enzymatic study of HPLC-fractionated *Crotalus* venom. Comp. Biochem. Physiol. 93B:847–855.

Spaur, R. C., and H. M. Smith. 1971. Adrenal enlargement in the hog-nosed snake *Heterodon platyrhinos*. J. Herpetol. 5:197–199.

Speake, D. W., and R. H. Mount. 1973. Some possible ecological effects of "Rattlesnake Roundups" in the southeastern coastal plain, 267–277. In: Proc. 27th Ann. Conf. South East Assoc. Game Fish Comm. 1973.

Spiess, P., and M. Smith. 1998. The rubber boa *Charina bottae*. Reptile & Amphibian Mag. 56:26–29.

Spiteri, D. E. 1988. The geographic variability of the species *Lichanura trivirgata* and a description of a new subspecies, 113–130. In: H. F. De Lisle, P. R. Brown, B. Kaufman, and B. M. McCurty (eds.), Proceedings of the Conference on California herpetology. Southwest. Herpetol. Soc. Spec. Publ. 4.

———. 1991. The subspecies of *Lichanura trivirgata*: Why the confusion? Bull. Chicago Herpetol. Soc. 26:153–156.

Stabler, R. M. 1948. Prairie rattlesnake eats spadefoot toad. Herpetologica 4:168.

Staedeli, J. H. 1964. Eggs and young of the vermilion-lined ground snake *Sonora semiannulata linearis*. Copeia 1964:581–582.

———. 1972. The mysterious rear-fanged snakes. Zoo Nooz 45(10): 18–19.

Stafford, P. 2000. Snakes. Washington, D.C.: Smithsonian Institution Press.

Stanford, J. S. 1942. Reptiles eaten by birds. Copeia 1942:186.

Starrett, B. L., and A. T. Holycross. 2000. *Crotalus lepidus klauberi* (banded rock rattlesnake). Caudal luring. Herpetol. Rev. 31:245.

Staszko, R., and J. G. Walls. 1994. Rat snakes: A hobbyist's guide to *Elaphe* and kin. Neptune, New Jersey: T. F. H. Publ., Inc.

Steadman, D. W., and L. J. Craig. 1993. Late Pleistocene and Holocene vertebrates from Jora Lemon's (Fish Club) Cave, Albany County, New York. Bull. New York St. Archaeol. Assoc. 105:9–15.

Steadman, D. W., L. J. Craig, and J. Bopp. 1993 [1992]. Didly Cave: A new late Quaternary vertebrate fauna from New York state. Current Res. Pleistocene 9:110–112.

Stebbins, R. C. 1954. Amphibians and reptiles of western North America. New York: McGraw-Hill.

———. 1985. A field guide to western reptiles and amphibians. Boston: Houghton Mifflin.

Steehouder, A. M. 1983. *Thamnophis radix butleri* × *Thamnophis sirtalis parietalis*. Litt. Serpent. Engl. Ed. 3:169–170.

Stegall, T. D., D. H. Sifford, and B. D. Johnson. 1994. Proteinase BAEEase, and TAMEase activities of selected crotalid venoms. SAAS Bull. Biochem. Biotech. 7:7–13.

Stejneger, L. 1890. On a new genus of colubrinae snakes from North America. Proc. U.S. Natl. Mus. 13:151–155.

———. 1893. Annotated list of reptiles and batrachians collected by the Death Valley expedition in 1891, with descriptions of new species. N. Am. Fauna 7:159–228.

———. 1895 [1893]. The poisonous snakes of North America, 337–487. In: Annual Report of the U.S. National Museum. Washington, D.C.: Smithsonian Institution.

———. 1903. The reptiles of the Huachuca Mountains, Arizona. Proc. U.S. Natl. Mus. 25:149–158.

Stejneger, L., and T. Barbour. 1917. A check list of North American amphibians and reptiles. Cambridge, Massachusetts: Harvard University Press.

Stevenson, R. D., C. R. Peterson, and J. S. Tsuji. 1985. The thermal dependence of locomotion, tongue flicking, digestion, and oxygen consumption in the wandering garter snake. Physiol. Zool. 58:46–57.

Stewart, G. R. 1965. Thermal ecology of the garter snakes *Thamnophis sirtalis concinnus* (Hallowell) and *Thamnophis ordinoides* (Baird and Girard). Herpetologica 21:81–102.

———. 1968. Some observations on the natural history of two Oregon garter snakes (genus *Thamnophis*). J. Herpetol. 2:71–86.

———. 1972. An unusual record of sperm storage in a female garter snake (genus *Thamnophis*). Herpetologica 28:346–347.

———. 1977. *Charina, C. bottae*. Cat. Am. Amphib. Rept. 205:1–2.

———. 1987. The rubber boa (*Charina bottae*) in California, with particular reference to the southern subspecies, *C. b. umbratica*, 131–138. In: H. F. DeLisle, P. R. Brown, B. Kaufman, and B. M. McCurty (eds.), Proceedings of the Conference on California Herpetology. Southwest. Herpetol. Soc. Spec. Publ. 4.

Stewart, G. R., D. G. Blackburn, D. C. Baxter, and L. H. Hoffman. 1990. Nutritional provision to embryos in a predominantly lecithotrophic placental reptile, *Thamnophis ordinoides* (Squamata: Serpentes). Physiol. Zool. 63:722–734.

Stewart, J. R. 1989. Faculative placentotrophy and the evolution of squamate placentation: Quality of eggs and neonates in *Virginia striatula*. Am. Nat. 133:111–117.

———. 1990. Development of the extraembryonic membranes and histology of the placentae in *Virginia striatula* (Squamata. Serpentes). J. Morph. 205:33–43.

Stewart, J. R., and R. E. Castillo. 1984. Nutritional provision of the yolk of two species of viviparous reptiles. Physiol. Zool. 57:377–383.

Stewart, M. M. 1961. Biology of the Allegheny Indian Reservation and vicinity. Part 3. The amphibians, reptiles, and mammals. New York St. Mus. Sci. Serv. Bull. 383:63–88.

Stewart, M. M., G. E. Larson, and T. H. Mathews. 1960. Morphological variation in a litter of timber rattlesnakes. Copeia 1960:366–367.

Stewart, P. A. 1981. Female wood duck apparently killed by black rat snake. Chat 45:97.

Stickel, L. F., W. H. Stickel, and F. C. Schmid. 1980. Ecology of a Maryland population of black rat snakes *(Elaphe o. obsoleta)*. Am. Midl. Nat. 103:1–14.

Stickel, W. H. 1941. The subspecies of the spade-nosed snake, *Sonora occipitalis*. Bull. Chicago Acad. Sci. 6:135–140.

———. 1943. The Mexican snakes of the genera *Sonora* and *Chionactis* with notes on the status of other colubrid genera. Proc. Biol. Soc. Washington 56:109–127.

———. 1951. Distinctions between the snake genera *Contia* and *Eirenis*. Herpetologica 7:125–131.

Stickel, W. H., and J. B. Cope. 1947. The home ranges and wanderings of snakes. Copeia 1947:127–136.

Stille, B. 1987. Dorsal scale microdermatoglyphics and rattlesnake *(Crotalus* and *Sistrurus)* phylogeny (Reptilia: Viperidae: Crotalinae). Herpetologica 43:98–104.

Stimson, A. C., and H. T. Engelhardt. 1960. The treatment of snakebite. J. Occup. Med. 2:163–168.

Stoddard, H. L. 1942. The bobwhite quail: Its habits, preservation, and increase. New York: Charles Scribner's Sons.

Stokes, G. D., and W. A. Dunson. 1982. Permeability and channel structure of reptilian skin. Am. J. Physiol. 242:F681–F689.

Stone, A., and D. A. Holtzman. 1996. Feeding responses in young boa constrictors are mediated by the vomeronasal system. Anim. Behav. 52:949–955.

Storer, D. H. 1839. Reptiles of Massachusetts, 203–253. In: Reports—on the fishes, reptiles, and birds; the herbaceous plants and quadrupeds; the insects injurious to vegatation; and the invertebrate aminals—of Massachusetts. Commissioners on the Zoological and Botanical Survey of Massachusetts.

Storey, K. B. 1990. Life in a frozen state: Adaptive strategies for natural freeze tolerance in amphibians and reptiles. Am. J. Physiol. 258:R559–R568.

———. 1996. Metabolic adaptations supporting anoxia tolerance in reptiles: Recent advances. Comp. Biochem. Physiol. 113B:23–35.

Storm, R. M. 1947. *Sonora semiannulata* in Oregon. Copeia 1947:68.

———. 1955. A possible snake hibernaculum. Herpetologica 11:160.

Storm, R. M., and P. L. Leonard, eds. 1995. Reptiles of Washington and Oregon. Seattle, Washington: Seattle Audubon Society.

Storment, D. 1990. Field observations of sexual dimorphism in head pattern (markings) in timber rattlesnakes *(Crotalus horridus)*. Bull. Chicago Herpetol. Soc. 25:160–162.

Stovall, R. H. 1976. Observations on the micro- and ultrastructure of the visual cells of certain snakes (Reptilia, Serpentes, Colubridae). J. Herpetol. 10:269–275.

Straight, R. C., and J. L. Glenn. 1993. Human fatalities caused by venomous animals in Utah, 1900–90. Great Basin Nat. 53:390–394.

Straight, R. C., J. L. Glenn, T. B. Wolt, and M. C. Wolfe. 1991. Regional differences in content of small basic peptide toxins in the venoms of *Crotalus adamanteus* and *Crotalus horridus*. Comp. Biochem. Physiol. 100B:51–58.

———. 1992. North-south regional variation in phospholipase A activity in the venom of *Crotalus ruber*. Comp. Biochem. Physiol. 103B:635–639.

Strathemann, U. 1995. Remarks on the outdoor keeping of North American water snakes of the genera *Thamnophis* and *Nerodia*. Part II. Experiences made with *Thamnophis* and *Nerodia*. Sauria (Berlin) 17(2): 15–23.

Strecker, J. K. 1926. On the habits of southern snakes. Contr. Baylor Univ. Mus. 4:1–11.

———. 1927. Observations on the food habits of Texas amphibians and reptiles. Copeia 162:6–9.

———. 1930. A catalogue of the amphibians and reptiles of Travis County, Texas. Contr. Baylor Univ. Mus. 23:1–16.

Strimple, P. 1992a. *Crotalus mitchelli*, the speckled rattlesnake. Litt. Serpent. Engl. Ed. 12:26–31.

———. 1992b. Report on the maintenance and growth of a juvenile eastern diamondback rattlesnake, *Crotalus adamanteus*, during its first year in captivity. Litt. Serpent. Engl. Ed. 12:85–88.

———. 1993a. Report on the feeding and growth of a juvenile mottled rock rattlesnake, *Crotalus lepidus lepidus*, during three years in captivity. Litt. Serpent. Engl. Ed. 13:89–94.

———. 1993b. Captive birth of Mojave rattlesnakes, *Crotalus scutulatus scutulatus*. Litt. Serpent. Engl. Ed. 13:166–168.

Stuart, J. N. 1988. *Hypsiglena torquata jani* (Texas night snake). Behavior. Herpetol. Rev. 19:84–85.

———. 1991. A note on defensive behavior in the New Mexico garter snake. Bull. Maryland Herpetol. Soc. 27:31–32.

Stuart, J. N., and C. W. Painter. 1993. Notes on hibernation of the smooth green snake, *Opheodrys vernalis*, in New Mexico. Bull. Maryland Herpetol. Soc. 29:140–142.

Stuart, L. C. 1954. Herpetofauna of the southwestern highlands of Guatemala. Contr. Lab. Vert. Biol., Univ. Michigan 68:1–65.

Stull, O. G. 1929. The description of a new subspecies of

Pituophis melanoleucus from Louisiana. Occ. Pap. Mus. Zool. Univ. Michigan 205:1–3.

———. 1940. Variations and relationships in the snakes of the genus *Pituophis*. Bull. U.S. Natl. Mus. 175:1–225.

Stumpel, A. H. P. 1995. *Masticophis taeniatus taeniatus* (desert striped whipsnake). Elevation record. Herpetol. Rev. 26:102.

Sullivan, B. K. 1981a. Observed differences in body temperature and associated behavior in four snake species. J. Herpetol. 15:245–246.

———. 1981b. Distribution and relative abundance of snakes along a transect in California. J. Herpetol. 15:247–248.

Surface, H. A. 1906. The serpents of Pennsylvania. Bull. Pennsylvania St. Dept. Agric. Div. Zool. 4:113–208.

Sutherland, I. D. W. 1958. The "combat dance" of the timber rattlesnake. Herpetologica 14:23–24.

Swain, T. A., and H. M. Smith. 1978. Communal nesting in *Coluber constrictor* in Colorado (Reptilia: Serpentes). Herpetologica 34:175–177.

Swanson, P. 1948. *Natrix sipedon compressicauda* at Key West, Florida. Herpetologica 4:105–106.

———. 1952. The reptiles of Venango County, Pennsylvania. Am. Midl. Nat. 47:161–182.

Sweeney, R. 1992. Garter snakes: Their natural history and care in captivity. London: Blandford.

Sweet, S. S. 1985. Geographic variation, convergent crypsis and mimicry in gopher snakes *(Pituophis melanoleucus)* and western rattlesnakes *(Crotalus viridis)*. J. Herpetol. 19:55–67.

Sweet, S. S., and W. S. Parker. 1990. *Pituophis melanoleucus*. Cat. Am. Amphib. Rept. 474:1–8.

Swenson, L. E. 1950. Food of captive western hog-nosed snakes. J. Colorado-Wyoming Acad. Sci. 4:74–75.

Swinford, G. W. 1989. Captive reproduction of the banded rock rattlesnake *Crotalus lepidus klauberi*, 99–110. In: M. J. Uricheck (ed.), 13th International Herpetological Symposium on Captive Propagation and Husbandry. Stanford, California: International Herpetological Symposiums.

Switak, K. H. 1976. Sand Swimmer. Pacific Discovery 29(3): 10–11.

———. 1978. Leben in der Wüste: *Chilomeniscus* und *Chionactis*, die Nattern, die im Sand schwimmen. Aquar. Aqua Terra 12:355–359.

———. 1982. Leben in der Wüste: Die Langnasen-Natter, *Rhinocheilus lecontei*. Aquar. Aqua Terra 16:657–659.

———. 1985. Leben in der Wüste: Die Trans-Pecos-Natter, *Elaphe subocularis*. Aquar. Aqua Terra 19:313–316.

Szaro, R. C., S. C. Belfit, J. K. Altkin, and R. D. Babb. 1988. The use of timed fixed-area plots and a mark-recapture technique in assessing riparian garter snake populations, 239–246. In: R. C. Szaro, K. E. Severson, and D. R. Patton (eds.), Management of amphibians, reptiles, and small mammals in North America. USDA Forest Serv. Tech. Rep. RM-166.

Szelistowski, W. A., and P. A. Meylan. 1996. *Regina alleni* (striped crayfish snake). Predation. Herpetol. Rev. 27:204–205.

Tabor, S. P., and D. J. Germano. 1997. *Masticophis flagellum* (coachwhip). Prey. Herpetol. Rev. 28:90.

Taggart, T. W. 1992. Observations on Kansas amphibians and reptiles. Kansas Herpetol. Soc. Newsl. 88:13–15.

Takeya, H., S. Nishida, N. Nishino, Y. Makinori, T. Omorisatoh, T. Nikai, H. Sugihara, and S. Iwanaga. 1993. Primary structures of platelet aggregation inhibitors (Disintegrins) autoproteolytically released from snake venom hemorrhagic metalloproteinases and new flavogenic peptide substrates for these enzymes. J. Biochem. (Tokyo) 113:473–483.

Takeya, H., A. Onikura, T. Nikai, H. Sugihara, and S. Iwanaga. 1990. Primary structure of a hemorrhagic metalloproteinase, HT-2, isolated from the venom of *Crotalus ruber ruber*. J. Biochem. (Tokyo) 108:711–719.

Tan, N.-H., and G. Ponnudurai. 1990. A comparative study of the biological activities of venoms from snakes of the genus *Agkistrodon* (moccasins and copperheads). Comp. Biochem. Physiol. 95B:577–582.

———. 1991. A comparative study of the biological activities of rattlesnake (genera *Crotalus* and *Sistrurus*) venom. Comp. Biochem. Physiol. 98C:455–461.

Tanner, V. M. 1938. A new subspecies of worm snake from Utah. Proc. Utah Acad. Sci. 15:149–150.

Tanner, W. W. 1943. Two new species of *Hypsiglena* from western North America. Great Basin Nat. 4:49–54.

———. 1944. A taxonomic study of the genus *Hypsiglena*. Great Basin Nat. 5:25–92.

———. 1949. Food of the wandering garter snake, *Thamnophis elegans vagrans* (Baird and Girard), in Utah. Herpetologica 5:85–86.

———. 1953. A study of taxonomy and phylogeny of *Lampropeltis pyromelana* Cope. Great Basin Nat. 13:47–66.

———. 1954. Herpetological notes concerning some reptiles of Utah and Arizona. Herpetologica 10:92–96.

———. 1966a. A re-evaluation of the genus *Tantilla* in the southwestern United States and northwestern Mexico. Herpetologica 22:134–152.

———. 1966b. An albino wandering garter snake. Proc. Utah Acad. Sci. 43:163.

———. 1967. *Contia tenuis* Baird and Girard in continental British Columbia. Herpetologica 23:323.

———. 1983. *Lampropeltis pyromelana*. Cat. Amer. Amphib. Rept. 342:1–2.

———. 1985. Snakes of western Chihuahua. Great Basin Nat. 45:615–676.

———. 1990. *Thamnophis rufipunctatus*. Cat. Amer. Amphib. Rept. 505:1–2.

Tanner, W. W., and D. Cox. 1981. Reproduction in the snake *Lampropeltis pyromelana*. Great Basin Nat. 41:314–316.

Tanner, W. W., and R. B. Loomis. 1957. A taxonomic and distributional study of the western subspecies of milk snake *Lampropeltis doliata*. Trans. Kansas Acad. Sci. 60:12–42.

Tanner, W. W., and C. H. Lowe. 1989. Variations in *Thamnophis elegans* with descriptions of new subspecies. Great Basin Nat. 49:511–516.

Tanner, W. W., and J. R. Ottley. 1981. Reproduction in *Hypsiglena*. Great Basin Nat. 41:310.

Tanzer, E. C. 1970. Polymorphism in the *mexicana*-complex of kingsnakes, with notes on their natural history. Herpetologica 26:419–428.

Taub, A. M. 1967. Comparative histological studies on Duvernoy's gland of colubrid snakes. Bull. Am. Mus. Nat. Hist. 138:1–50.

Taub, A. M., and W. A. Dunson. 1967. The salt gland in a sea snake *(Laticauda)*. Nature (London) 215:995–996.

Taylor, E. H. 1931. Notes on two specimens of the rare snake *Ficimia cana* and the description of a new species of *Ficimia* from Texas. Copeia 1931:4–7.

———. 1937 [1936]. Notes and comments on certain American and Mexican snakes of the genus *Tantilla*, with descriptions of new species. Trans. Kansas Acad. Sci. 39:335–338.

———. 1939a [1938]. Notes on the Mexican snakes of the genus *Leptodeira*, with a proposal of a new snake genus, *Pseudoleptodeira*. Univ. Kansas Sci. Bull. 25:315–355.

———. 1939b [1938]. On Mexican snakes of the genera *Trimorphodon* and *Hypsiglena*. Univ. Kansas Sci. Bull. 25:357–383.

———. 1939c. On North American snakes of the genus *Leptotyphlops*. Copeia 1939:1–7.

———. 1949. A preliminary account of the herpetology of the state of San Luis Potosi, Mexico. Univ. Kansas Sci. Bull. 33, part 1, no. 2, 169–215.

———. 1953. Early records of the seasnake, *Pelamis platurus* in Latin America. Copeia 1953:124.

Taylor, W. P. 1935. Notes on *Crotalus atrox* near Tucson, Arizona, with a special reference to its breeding habits. Copeia 1935:154–155.

Tchernov, E., O. Rieppel, H. Zaher, M. J. Polcyn, and L. L. Jacobs. 2000. A fossil snake with limbs. Science (New York) 287:2010–2012.

Teather, K. L. 1991. The relative importance of visual and chemical cues for foraging in newborn blue-striped garter snakes *(Thamnophis sirtalis similis)*. Behaviour 117:255–261.

Telford, S. R., Jr. 1948. A large litter of *Natrix* in Florida. Herpetologica 4:184.

———. 1952. A herpetological survey in the vicinity of Lake Shipp, Polk County, Florida. Quart. J. Florida Acad. Sci. 15:175–185.

———. 1966. Variation among the southeastern crowned snakes, genus *Tantilla*. Bull. Florida St. Mus. Biol. Sci. 10:261–304.

———. 1980a. *Tantilla oolitica*. Cat. Am. Amphib. Rept. 256:1.

———. 1980b. *Tantilla relicta*. Cat. Am. Amphib. Rept. 257:1–2.

———. 1982. *Tantilla coronata*. Cat. Am. Amphib. Rept. 308:1–2.

Tennant, A. 1984. The snakes of Texas. Austin: Texas Monthly Press.

———. 1985. A field guide to Texas snakes. Austin: Texas Monthly Press.

———. 1997. A field guide to snakes of Florida. Houston, Texas: Gulf Publishing Co.

Termeer, M. 1987. *Natrix rhombifera*. Litt. Serpent. Engl. Ed. 7:255.

Terrick, T. D., R. L. Mumme, and G. M. Burghardt. 1995. Aposematic coloration enhances chemosensory recognition of noxious prey in the garter snake *Thamnophis radix*. Anim. Behav. 49:859–866.

Test, F. H. 1958. Butler's garter snake eats amphibians. Copeia 1958:151.

Tevis, L. 1943. Field notes on a red rattlesnake in Lower California. Copeia 1943:241–245.

Theodoratus, D. H., and D. Chiszar. 2000. Habitat selection and prey odor in the foraging behavior of western rattlesnakes *(Crotalus viridis)*. Behaviour 137:119–135.

Thomas, M. E. 1974. Bats as food source for *Boa constrictor*. J. Herpetol. 8:188.

Thomas, R. A. 1994. *Ramphotyphlops braminus* (Braminy blind snake). U.S.A.: Louisiana. Herpetol. Rev. 25:34.

Thomas, R. A., and F. S. Hendricks. 1976. Letisimulation in *Virginia striatula* (Linnaeus). Southwest. Nat. 21:123–124.

Thompson, F. G. 1957. A new Mexican gartersnake (genus *Thamnophis*) with notes on related forms. Occ. Pap. Mus. Zool. Univ. Michigan 584: 1–10.

Thompson, J. S., and B. I. Crother. 1998. Allozyme variation among disjunct populations of the Florida green watersnake *(Nerodia floridana)*. Copeia 1998:715–719.

Thorne, E. T. 1977. Sybille Creek snake dance. Wyoming Wild Life 41(6): 14.

Thornton, O. W., Jr., and J. R. Smith. 1995a. *Regina grahamii* (Graham's crayfish snake). Reproduction. Herpetol. Rev. 26:102.

———. 1995b. Late prehistoric snakes of E. V. Spence and O. H. Ivie reservoir basins of Coke, Coleman, Concho, and Runnels counties, Texas. Texas J. Sci. 47:295–307.

———. 1996a. *Nerodia erythrogaster transversa* (blotched water snake). Reproduction. Herpetol. Rev. 27:83.

———. 1996b. *Thamnophis proximus rubrilineatus* (redstripe ribbon snake). Reproduction. Herpetol. Rev. 27:206.

Thurow, G. R. 1993. *Clonophis kirtlandi* (Kirtland's snake). Diet. Herpetol. Rev. 24:34–35.

Tiebout, H. M., III. 1997. Caudal luring by a temperate colubrid snake, *Elaphe obsoleta*, and its implications for the evolution of the rattle among rattlesnakes. J. Herpetol. 31:290–292.

Tiebout, H. M., III, and J. R. Cary. 1987. Dynamic spatial ecology of the water snake, *Nerodia sipedon*. Copeia 1987:1–18.

Tiersch, J. R., and C. R. Figul, Jr. 1991. A triplod snake. Copeia 1991:838–841.

Tihen, J. A. 1938 [1937]. Additional distributional records of amphibians and reptiles in Kansas counties. Trans. Kansas Acad. Sci. 40:401–409.

———. 1962. A review of New World fossil bufonids. Am. Midl. Nat. 68:1–50.

Tilden, A. R., and V. H. Hutchison. 1993. Influence of photoperiod and temperature on serum melatonin in the diamondback water snake, *Nerodia rhombifera*. Gen. Comp. Endocrinol. 92:347–354.

Timmerman, W. W. 1995. Home range, habitat use, and behavior of the eastern diamondback rattlesnake *(Crotalus adamanteus)* on the Ordway Preserve. Bull. Florida Mus. Nat. Hist. 38:127–158.

Tinkle, D. W. 1951. Peculiar behavior of indigo snakes in captivity. Copeia 1951:77–78.

———. 1957. Ecology, maturation, and reproduction of *Thamnophis sauritus proximus*. Ecology 38:69–77

———. 1959. Observations of reptiles and amphibians in a Louisiana swamp. Am. Midl. Nat. 62:189–205.

———. 1960. A population of *Opheodrys aestivus* (Reptilia: Squamata). Copeia 1960:29–34.

———. 1962. Reproductive potential and cycles in female *Crotalus atrox* from northwestern Texas. Copeia 1962:306–313.

———. 1967. The life and demography of the side-

blotched lizard, *Uta stansburiana*. Misc. Publ. Mus. Zool. Univ. Michigan 132:1–182.

Tinkle, D. W., and R. Conant. 1961. The rediscovery of the water snake, *Natrix harteri*, in western Texas, with the description of a new subspecies. Southwest. Nat. 6:33–44.

Tinkle, D. W., and J. W. Gibbons. 1977. The distribution and evolution of viviparity in reptiles. Misc. Publ. Mus. Zool. Univ. Michigan 154:1–55.

Tinkle, D. W., and E. A. Liner. 1955. Behavior of *Natrix* in aggregations. Field and Lab. (So. Methodist Univ.) 23:84–87.

Tolson, P. J., and R. W. Henderson. 1993. The natural history of West Indian boas. Excelsior, Minnesota: Serpent's Tale.

Tomkins, J. R. 1965. Swallow-tailed kite and snake: An unusual encounter. Wilson Bull. 77:294.

Touzeau, T., and M. Sievert. 1993. Postprandial thermophily in rough green snakes *(Opheodrys aestivus)*. Copeia 1993:1174–1176.

Toweill, D. E. 1982. Winter foods of eastern Oregon bobcats. Northwest. Sci. 56:310–315.

Trapido, H. 1940. Mating time and sperm viability in *Storeria*. Copeia 1940:107–109.

———. 1941. A new species of *Natrix* from Texas. Am. Midl. Nat. 25:673–680.

———. 1944. The snakes of the genus *Storeria*. Am. Midl. Nat. 31:1–84.

Trauth, S. E. 1982a. *Cemophora coccinea* (scarlet snake). Reproduction. Herpetol. Rev. 13:126.

———. 1982b. *Ambystoma maculatum* (Ambystomidae) in the diet of *Heterodon platirhinos* (Colubridae) from northern Arkansas. Southwest. Nat. 27:230.

———. 1983. *Lampropeltis calligaster* (prairie kingsnake). Predation. Herpetol. Rev. 14:74.

———. 1990. Flooding as a factor in the decemination of a population of green water snakes *(Nerodia cyclopion cyclopion)* from Arkansas. Bull. Chicago Herpetol. Soc. 25:1–3.

———. 1991a. Distribution, scutellation, and reproduction in the queen snake, *Regina septemvittata* (Serpentes: Colubridae), from Arkansas. Proc. Arkansas Acad. Sci. 45:103–106.

———. 1991b. Posterior maxillary fangs of the flathead snake, *Tantilla gracilis* (Serpentes: Colubridae), using scanning electron microscopy. Proc. Arkansas Acad. Sci. 45:133–136.

———. 1993. Enlarged posterior maxillary teeth in the scarlet snake, *Cemophora coccinea* (Serpentes: Colubridae), using scanning electron microscopy. Proc. Arkansas Acad. Sci. 47:157–160.

Trauth, S. E., and B. G. Cochran. 1992. In search of western diamondback rattlesnakes (Crotalus atrox) in Arkansas. Bull. Chicago Herpetol. Soc. 27:89–94.

Treadwell, R. W. 1962. Time and sequence of appearance of certain gross structures in Pituophis melanoleucus sayi embryos. Herpetologica 18:120–124.

Treadwell, R. W., and T. Hibbitts. 1968. Tantilla diabola from Val Verde County, Texas. Texas J. Sci. 20:281–282.

Trinco, L. A., and H. M. Smith. 1972 [1971]. The karyology of ophidians: A review. Trans. Kansas Acad. Sci. 74:138–146.

Troost, G. 1836. On a new genus of serpents, and new species of the genus Heterodon, inhabiting Tennessee. Ann. Lyc. Nat. Hist. New York 3:174–190.

Trutnau, L. 1986. Nonvenomous snakes: A comprehensive guide to care and breeding of over 100 species. Stuttgart, Germany: Eugen Ulmer.

Tryon, B. 1976. Second generation reproduction and courtship behavior in the Trans-Pecos ratsnake Elaphe subocularis. Herpetol. Rev. 7:156–157.

———. 1978. Reproduction in a pair of captive Arizona ridge-nosed rattlesnakes, Crotalus willardi willardi (Reptilia, Serpentes, Crotalidae). Bull. Maryland Herpetol. Soc. 14:83–88.

———. 1984. Additional instances of multiple egg-clutch production in snakes. Trans. Kansas Acad. Sci. 87:98–104.

———. 1985. Snake hibernation and breeding: In and out of the zoo, 19–31. In: S. Townson and K. Lawrence (eds.), Reptiles: Breeding, behaviour, and veterinary aspects. London: British Herpetological Society.

Tryon, B., and G. Carl. 1980. Reproduction in the male kingsnake, Lampropeltis calligaster rhombomaculata (Serpentes, Colubridae). Trans. Kansas Acad. Sci. 83:66–73.

Tryon, B., and R. K. Guese. 1984. Death-feigning in the gray-banded kingsnake Lampropeltis alterna. Herpetol. Rev. 15:108–109.

Tryon, B., and H. K. McCrystal. 1982. Micrurus fulvius tenere reproduction. Herpetol. Rev. 13:47–48.

Tryon, B., and J. B. Murphy. 1982. Miscellaneous notes on the reproductive biology of reptiles. 5. Thirteen varieties of the genus Lampropeltis, species mexicana, triangulum and zonata. Trans. Kansas Acad. Sci. 85:96–119.

Tschambers, B. 1950. Number of young of Liodytes alleni. Herpetologica 6:48.

Tu, A. T. 1976. Investigation of the sea snake, Pelamis platurus (Reptilia, Serpentes, Hydrophiidae), on the Pacific Coast of Costa Rica, Central America. J. Herpetol. 10:13–18.

———. 1977. Venoms: Chemistry and molecular biology. New York: Wiley-Interscience.

———. 1991. Primary structure of the sea-snake neurotoxins and their modes of attachment to acetylcholine receptor, 87–95. In: M.-F. Thompson, R. Sarojini, and R. Nagabhushanam (eds.), Bioactive compounds from marine organisms with emphasis on the Indian ocean. An Indo-United States Symposium. New Delhi: Oxford and IBH Publishers.

———, ed. 1982. Rattlesnake venoms: Their actions and treatment. New York: Mercel Dekker.

Tu, A. T., T. S. Lin, and A. L. Bieber. 1975. Purification and chemical characterization of the major neurotoxin from the venom of Pelamis platurus. Biochemistry 14:3408–3413.

Tu, M.-C., and V. H. Hutchison. 1994. Influence of pregnancy on thermoregulation of water snakes, Nerodia rhombifera. J. Therm. Biol. 19:255–259.

———. 1995a. Lack of postprandial thermophily in diamondback water snakes, Nerodia rhombifera. Comp. Biochem. Physiol. 110A:21–25.

———. 1995b. Thermoregulatory behavior is not influenced by sex or ecdysis in the diamondback water snake, Nerodia rhombifera. J. Herpetol. 29:146–148.

———. 1995c. Interaction of photoperiod, temperature, season, and diel cycles on thermoregulation of water snakes (Nerodia rhombifera). Copeia 1995:289–293.

Tucker, J. K. 1976. Observations on the birth of a brood of Kirtland's water snake, Clonophis kirtlandi (Kennicott) (Reptilia, Serpentes, Colubridae). J. Herpetol. 10:53–54.

———. 1977. Notes on the food habits of Kirtland's water snake, Clonophis kirtlandi. Bull. Maryland Herpetol. Soc. 13:193–195.

———. 1994a. Laboratory investigation of fossorial behavior in Kirtland's snake, Clonophis kirtlandii (Kennicott) (Serpentes: Colubridae), with some comments on management of the species. Bull. Chicago Herpetol. Soc. 29(5): 93–94

———. 1994b. Clonophis kirtlandii (Kirtland's Snake). Subterranean prey capture. Herpetol. Rev. 25(3): 122–123.

———. 1995a. Notes on the road-killed snakes and their implications on habitat modification due to summer flooding on the Mississippi River in west central Illinois. Trans. Illinois St. Acad. Sci. 88:61–71.

———. 1995b. Flood-associated activities of some reptiles and amphibians at Carlyle Lake, Fayette County, Illinois. Trans. Illinois St. Acad. Sci. 88:73–81.

———. 2000. Illinois snakes. Young-of-year morphology and food habits. Herpetol. Rev. 31:106–107.

Tucker, J. K., and J. B. Camerer. 1994. Nerodia rhombifer rhombifer (diamnondback water snake). Reproduction. Herpetol. Rev. 25:28–29.

Turner, F. B. 1955. Reptiles and amphibians of Yellow-stone National Park. Yellowstone Interp. Ser. 5:1–40.

Turner, F. B., and R. H. Wauer. 1963. A survey of the herpetofauna of the Death Valley area. Great Basin Nat. 23:119–128.

Twente, J. W. 1955. Aspects of a population study of cavern-dwelling bats. J. Mammal. 36:379–390.

Tyler, J. D. 1977. Coachwhip preys on horned lizard. Southwest. Nat. 22:146.

———. 1991. Vertebrate prey of the loggerhead shrike in Oklahoma. Proc. Oklahoma Acad. Sci. 71:17–20.

Tyning, T. 1987. In the path of progress. Sanctuary (Lincoln) 26(9): 3–5.

Uhler, F. M., C. Cottam, and T. E. Clarke. 1939. Food of snakes of the George Washington National Forest, Virginia. Trans. N. Am. Wildl. Conf. 4:605–622.

Underwood, G. 1967. A contribution to the classification of snakes. British Mus. Nat. Hist. Publ. 653:1–179.

Vaeth, R. H. 1980. Observation of ophiophagy in the western hooknose snake, *Gyalopion canum*. Bull. Maryland Herpetol. Soc. 16:94–96.

———. 1984. A note on courtship and copulatory behavior in *Micrurus fulvius*. Bull. Chicago Herpetol. Soc. 18:86–88.

Vagvolgyi, A., and M. Halpern. 1983. Courtship behavior in garter snakes: Effects of artificial hibernation. Can. J. Zool. 61:1171–1174.

Vallarino, O., and P. J. Weldon. 1996. Reproduction in the yellow-bellied sea snake *(Pelamis platurus)* from Panama: Field and laboratory observations. Zoo Biol. 15:309–314.

Van Dam, G. H. 1978. Amphibians and reptiles, 19–25. In: J. E. Guilday (ed.), The Baker Bluff Cave deposit, Tennessee, and the Late Pleistocene faunal gradient. Bull. Carnegie Mus. Nat. Hist. 11.

van Dam, R., and M. K. Hecht. 1954. Fossil rattlesnakes of the genus *Crotalus* from northern Massachusetts. Copeia 1954:158–159.

Van Denburgh, J. 1895. Description of a new rattlesnake *(Crotalus pricei)* from Arizona. Proc. California Acad. Sci., ser. 2, 5:856–857.

———. 1897. The reptiles of the Pacific Coast and Great Basin. Occ. Pap. California Acad. Sci. 5:1–236.

———. 1920. Description of a new subspecies of boa *(Charina bottae utahensis)* from Utah. Proc. California Acad. Sci., ser. 4, 10:31–32.

———. 1922. The reptiles of western North America. Vol. 2. Snakes and turtles. Occ. Pap. California Acad. Sci. 10:617–1028.

Van Denburgh, J., and J. R. Slevin. 1913. A list of the amphibians and reptiles of Arizona, with notes on the species in the collection of the Academy. Proc. California Acad. Sci., ser. 4, 3:391–454.

———. 1918. The garter snakes of western North America. Proc. California Acad. Sci., ser. 4, 8:181–270.

van der Eerden, H. 1985. Breeding *Elaphe guttata guttata* in the terrarium. Litt. Serpent. Engl. Ed. 5:199–202.

Vandermast, D. B. 1999. *Elaphe obsoleta* (black rat snake). Antipredator behavior. Herpetol. Rev. 30:169.

van der Pols, J. 1986. The husbandry and breeding of the rosy boa *Lichanura trivirgata roseofusca* (Cope, 1861). Litt. Serpent. Engl. Ed. 6:98–106.

———. 1988. Care, breeding, and other things worth knowing about the rubber boa, *Charina bottae bottae* (Blainville). Litt. Serpent. Engl. Ed. 8:244–254.

Van Devender, T. R., and G. L. Bradley. 1994. Late Quaternary amphibians and reptiles from Maravillas Canyon Cave, Texas, with discussion of the biogeography and evolution of the Chihuahuan Desert herpetofauna, 23–53. In: P. R. Brown and J. W. Wright (eds.), Herpetology of the North American Deserts. Proceedings of a Symposium. Southwest. Herpetol. Soc. Spec. Publ. 5.

Van Devender, T. R., and C. H. Lowe, Jr. 1977. Amphibians and reptiles of Yepómera, Chihuahua, Mexico. J. Herpetol. 11:41–50.

Van Devender, T. R., C. H. Lowe, and H. E. Lawler. 1994. Factors influencing the distribution of the neotropical vine snake *(Oxybelis aeneus)* in Arizona and Sonora, México. Herpetol. Nat. Hist. 2:25–42.

Van Devender, T. R., and J. I. Mead. 1978. Early Holocene and late Pleistocene amphibians and reptiles in Sonoran Desert packrat midens. Copeia 1978:464–475.

Van Devender, T. R., J. I. Mead, and A. M. Rea. 1991. Late Quaternary plants and vertebrates from Picacho Peak, Arizona. Southwest. Nat. 36:302–314.

Van Devender, T. R., K. B. Moodie, and A. H. Harris. 1976. The desert tortoise *(Gopherus agassizii)* in the Pleistocene of the northern Chihuahuan Desert. Herpetologica 32:298–304.

Van Devender, T. R., A. M. Phillips III, and J. I. Mead. 1977. Late Pleistocene reptiles and small mammals from the Lower Grand Canyon of Arizona. Southwest. Nat. 22:49–66.

Van Devender, T. R., A. M. Rea, and W. E. Hall. 1991. Faunal analysis of late Quaternary vertebrates from Organ Pipe Cactus National Monument, southwestern Arizona. Southwest. Nat. 36:94–106.

Van Devender, T. R., A. M. Rea, and M. L. Smith. 1985. The Sangamon interglacial vertebrate fauna from Rancho la Brisca, Sonora, Mexico. Trans. San Diego Soc. Nat. Hist. 21:23–55.

Van Devender, T. R., and R. D. Worthington. 1977. The herpetofauna of Howell's Ridge Cave and the paleoecology of the northwestern Chihuahua Desert, 85–106. In: R. H. Wauer and D. H. Riskind (eds.), Trans. Symp. Biological Resources of the Chihuahua Desert Region, United States and Mexico. Natl. Park Serv. Trans. Proc. Ser. 13.

Van Duyn, G. 1937. Snakes that "play possum." Nature Mag. 29:215–217.

Van Frank, R., and M. K. Hecht. 1954. Fossil rattlesnakes of the genus *Crotalus* from northern Massachusetts. Copeia 1954:158–159.

Van Heest, R. W., and J. A. Hay. 2000. *Charina bottae* (rubber boa). Antipredator behavior. Herpetol. Rev. 31:177.

van het Meer, J. 1989. The genus *Thamnophis,* Part V: *Thamnophis (radix) butleri*. Litt. Serpent. Engl. Ed. 9:4–8.

———. 1996. *Thamnophis marcianus marcianus*. Litt. Serpent. Engl. Ed. 16:23.

Van Hyning, O. C. 1931. Reproduction of some Florida snakes. Copeia 1931:59–60.

———. 1932. Food of some Florida snakes. Copeia 1932:37.

Varkey, A. 1979. Comparative cranial myology of North American natricine snakes. Milwaukee Publ. Mus. Publ. Biol. Geol. 4:1–70.

Vaughan, R. K., J. R. Dixon, and R. A. Thomas. 1996. A reevaluation of populations of the corn snake *Elaphe guttata* (Reptilia: Serpentes: Colubridae) in Texas. Texas J. Sci. 48:175–190.

Veer, V., D. Chiszar, and H. M. Smith. 1997. *Sonora semiannulata* (ground snake). Antipredation. Herpetol. Rev. 28:91.

Velhagen, W. A., Jr., and A. H. Savitzky. 1998. Evolution of embryonic growth in thamnophiine snakes. Copeia 1998:549–558.

Verkerk, J. W. 1987. Enkele aanvullende opmerkingen over het gedrag van de dwerggratelslang *(Sistrurus miliarius barbouri)*. Lacerta 45:142–143.

Vermersch, T. G., and R. E. Kuntz. 1986. Snakes of south-central Texas. Austin, Texas: Eakin Press.

Vest, D. K. 1981a. Envenomation following the bite of a wandering garter snake *(Thamnophis elegans vagrans)*. Clinical Toxicol. 18:573–575.

———. 1981b. The toxic Duvernoy's secretion of the wandering garter snake, *Thamnophis elegans vagrans*. Toxicon 19:831–839.

———. 1988. Some effects and properties of Duvernoy's gland secretion from *Hypsiglena torquata texana* (Texas night snake). Toxicon 26:417–419.

Vetas, B. 1951. Temperatures of entrance and emergence. Herpetologica 7:15–19.

Vial, J. L., T. L. Berger, and W. T. McWilliams, Jr. 1977. Quantitative demography of copperheads, *Agkistrodon contortrix* (Serpentes: Viperidae). Res. Popul. Ecol. (Kyoto) 18:223–234.

Viets, B. E. 1993. An annotated list of the herpetofauna of the F. B. and Rena G. Ross Natural History Reservation. Trans. Kansas Acad. Sci. 96:103–113.

Villa, J. D. 1993. *Trimorphodon biscutatus quadruplex* (Zorcuata). Size. Herpetol. Rev. 24:106–107.

Vincent, J. W. 1982a. Color pattern variation in *Crotalus lepidus lepidus* (Viperidae) in southwestern Texas. Southwest. Nat. 27:263–272.

———. 1982b. Phenotypic variation in *Crotalus lepidus lepidus* (Kennicott). J. Herpetol. 16:189–191.

Vincent, T. 1975. Body temperatures of *Thamnophis sirtalis parietalis* at the den site. J. Herpetol. 9:252–254.

Vincent, T., and D. M. Secoy. 1978. The effects of annual variation in temperature and cold resistance in a northern population of the red-sided garter snake, *Thamnophis sirtalis parietalis* (Reptilia, Serpentes, Colubridae). J. Herpetol. 12:291–294.

Viosca, P., Jr. 1926. A snake tragedy. Copeia 151:109.

Visser, J. 1967. Color varieties, brood size, and food of South African *Pelamis platurus* (Ophidia: Hydrophiidae). Copeia 1967:219.

Vitt, L. J. 1974. Body temperatures of high latitude reptiles. Copeia 1974:225–256.

———. 1975. Observations on reproduction in five species of Arizona snakes. Herpetologica 31:83–84.

———. 1978. Caloric content of lizard and snake (Reptilia) eggs and bodies and the conversion of weight to caloric data. J. Herpetol. 12:65–72.

Vitt, L. J., and A. C. Hulse. 1973. Observations on feeding habits and tail display of the Sonoran coral snake, *Micruroides euryxanthus*. Herpetologica 29:302–304.

Vitt, L. J., and R. D. Ohmart. 1978. Herpetofauna of the Lower Colorado River: Davis Dam to the Mexican Border. Proc. West. Found. Vert. Zool. 2:33–72.

Vogt, R. C. 1981. Natural history of amphibians and reptiles of Wisconsin. Milwaukee, Wisconsin: Milwaukee Public Museum.

Vorhies, C. T. 1926. Notes on some uncommon snakes of southern Arizona. Copeia 157:158–160.

———. 1929. Feeding of *Micruroides euryxanthus*, the Sonoran coral snake. Bull. Antivenin Inst. Am. 2:98.

———. 1948. Food items of rattlesnakes. Copeia 1948:302–303.

Vorhies, C. T., and W. P. Taylor. 1940. Life history and ecology of the white-throated wood rat, *Neotoma albigula albigula*, in relation to grazing in Arizona. Univ. Arizona, Agric. Tech. Bull. 86:453–529.

Voris, H. K. 1977. A phylogeny of the sea snakes (Hydrophiidae). Fieldiana: Zool. 70:79–166.

Voss, G. 1991. Virginia-Uhu, *Bubo virginianus*, Verzeht Strumpfbandnatter, *Thamnophis sirtalis*. Beitr. Vogel 37:348–349.

Wagler, J. 1824. Serpentum brasiliensium species novae ou historie naturelle des espèces nouvelles de serpens, recueillies et observées pendent le voyage dans l'intérieuer du Brésil dans les annees 1817, 1818, 1819, 1820. . . . Publiée par Jean de Spix. Monachii: Typis Francisci Seraphici Hübschmanni.

———. 1830. Natürliches System der Amphibien, mit voranfehender Classification der Säugthiere und Vogel. München, Stuttgart, und Tubingen.

———. 1833. Descriptiones et icons amphibiorum. Pars. tertia, plate 27. Leipzig: Isis von Oken.

Wagner, R. T. 1962. Notes on the combat dance in *Crotalus adamanteus*. Bull. Philadelphia Herpetol. Soc. 10(1): 7–8.

Waide, R. B., and R. Thomas. 1984. Aggression between two *Drymarchon corais melanurus* in Campeche, Mexico. Herpetol. Rev. 15:10.

Walker, M. V. 1946. Reptiles and amphibians of Yosemite National Park. Yosemite Nat. Notes 25(1): 1–48.

Wall, F. 1921. Snakes of Ceylon. Columbo: Government Printer.

Wallace, R. L., and L. V. Diller. 1990. Feeding ecology of the rattlesnake, *Crotalus viridis oreganus*, in northern Idaho. J. Herpetol. 24:246–253.

Wallach, V., G. S. Jones, and R. R. Kunkel. 1991. *Ramphotyphlops braminus* (Braminy blind snake). U.S.A.: Massachusetts. Herpetol. Rev. 22:68.

Walley, H. D. 1999. *Rhadinaea flavilata*. Cat. Am. Amphib. Rept. 699:1–5.

Walley, H. D., and C. M. Eckerman. 1999. *Heterodon nasicus*. Cat. Am. Amphib. Rept. 698:1–10.

Walley, H. D., and M. V. Plummer. 2000. *Opheodrys aestivus*. Cat. Am. Amphib. Rept. 718:1–14.

Walls, G. L. 1934. The reptilian retina. I. A new concept of visual-cell evolution. Am. J. Ophtholmol. 17:892–915.

Walters, A. C., and W. Card. 1996. *Agkistrodon piscivorus conanti* (Florida cottonmouth). Herpetol. Rev. 27:203.

Walters, A. C., D. T. Roberts, and C. V. Covell, Jr. 1996. *Agkistrodon contortrix contortrix* (southern copperhead). Prey. Herpetol. Rev. 27:202.

Warkentin, K. M. 1995. Adaptive plasticity in hatching age: A response to predation risk trade-offs. Proc. Natl. Acad. Sci. 92:3507–3510.

Warren, J. W. 1953. Notes on the behavior of *Chionactis occipitalis*. Herpetologica 9:121–124.

Wasser, J. S. 1990. Seasonal variations in plasma and tissue chemistry in water snakes, *Nerodia sipedon*. Copeia 1990:399–408.

Watermolen, D. J. 1991. *Storeria occipitimaculata occipitomaculata* (northern redbelly snake). Behavior. Herpetol. Rev. 22:61.

———. 1992. *Elaphe vulpina* (fox snake). Predation. Herpetol. Rev. 23:120.

Watkins, J. F., II, F. R. Gehlbach, and R. S. Baldridge. 1967. Ability of the blind snake, *Leptotyphlops dulcis,* to follow pheromone trails of army ants, *Neivamyrmex nigrescens* and *N. opacithorax*. Southwest. Nat. 12:455–462.

Watkins, J. F., II, F. R. Gehlbach, and J. C. Kroll. 1969. Attractant-repellent secretions of blind snakes *(Leptotyphlops dulcis)* and their army ant prey *(Neivamyrmex nigrescens)*. Ecology 50:1098–1102.

Watkins, J. F., II, F. R. Gehlbach, and R. W. Plsek. 1972. Behavior of blind snakes *(Leptotyphlops dulcis)* in response to army ant *(Neivamyrmex nigrescens)* raiding columns. Texas J. Sci. 23:556–557.

Wattiez, R., C. Remy, P. Falmagne, and G. Toubeau. 1994. Purification and preliminary characterization of a frog-derived proteinaceous chemoattractant eliciting prey attack by checkered garter snakes *(Thamnophis marcianus)*. J. Chem. Ecol. 20:1143–1160.

Wauer, R. H. 1999. The American robin. Austin: University of Texas Press.

Waye, H. L. 1999. Size and age structure of a population of western terrestrial garter snakes *(Thamnophis elegans)*. Copeia 1999:819–823.

Waye, H. L., and P. T. Gregory. 1993. Choices of neonate *Thamnophis elegans vagrans* between conspecific, congeneric, and heterogeneric odors. J. Herpetol. 27:435–4441.

Weatherhead, P. J. 1989. Temporal and thermal aspects of hibernation of black rat snakes *(Elaphe obsoleta)* in Ontario. Can. J. Zool. 67:2332–2335.

Weatherhead, P. J., G. P. Brown, M. R. Prosser, and K. J. Kissner. 1998. Variation in offspring sex ratios in the northern water snake *(Nerodia sipedon)*. Can. J. Zool. 76:2200–2206.

———. 1999. Factors affecting neonate size variation in northern water snakes, *Nerodia sipedon*. J. Herpetol. 33:577–589.

Weatherhead, P. J., and M. B. Charland. 1985. Habitat selection in an Ontario population of the snake, *Elaphe obsoleta*. J. Herpetol. 19:12–19.

Weatherhead, P. J., and D. J. Hoysak. 1989. Spatial and activity patterns of black rat snakes *(Elaphe obsoleta)* from radiotelemetry and recapture data. Can. J. Zool. 67:463–468.

Weatherhead, P. J., and K. A. Prior. 1992. Preliminary observations of habitat use and movements of the eastern massasauga rattlesnake *(Sistrurus c. catenatus)*. J. Herpetol. 26:447–452.

Weatherhead, P. J., and I. C. Robertson. 1992. Thermal constraints on swimming performance and escape response of northern water snakes *(Nerodia sipedon)*. Can. J. Zool. 70:94–98.

Weaver, W. G. 1965. The cranial anatomy of the hognosed snakes *(Heterodon)*. Bull. Florida St. Mus. Biol. Sci. 9:275–304.

Webb, R. G. 1960. Notes on some amphibians and reptiles from northern Mexico. Trans. Kansas Acad. Sci. 63:289–298.

———. 1970. Reptiles of Oklahoma. Norman: University of Oklahoma Press.

———. 1976. A review of the garter snake *Thamnophis elegans* in Mexico. Contr. Sci., Nat. Hist. Mus. Los Angeles Co. 284:1–13.

———. 1980. *Thamnophis cyrtopsis*. Cat. Am. Amphib. Rept. 245:1–4.

Webb, R. G., and M. Hensley. 1959. Notes on reptiles from the Mexican state of Durango. Publ. Mus., Michigan State Univ., Biol. Ser. 1(6): 251–258.

Webber, T. A. 1980. Eastern coachwhip predation on juvenile scrub jays. Florida Field Nat. 8:29–30.

Wehekind, L. 1955. Notes on foods of the Trinidad snakes. British J. Herpetol. 2:9–13.

Weigel, R. D. 1962. Fossil vertebrates of Vero, Florida. Florida Geol. Surv. Spec. Publ. 10:1–59.

Weil, M. R. 1985. Comparison of plasma and testicular testosterone levels during the active season in the common garter snake, *Thamnophis sirtalis* (L.). Comp. Biochem. Physiol. 81A:585–587.

Weil, M. R., and R. D. Aldridge. 1979. The effect of temperature on the male reproductive system of the common water snake *(Nerodia sipedon)*. J. Exp. Zool. 210:327–332.

———. 1981. Seasonal androgenesis in the male water snake, *Nerodia sipedon*. Gen. Comp. Endocrinol. 44:44–53.

Weinstein, S. A., C. F. DeWitt, and L. A. Smith. 1992. Variability of venom-neutralizing properties of serum from snakes of the colubrid genus *Lampropeltis*. J. Herpetol. 26:452–461.

Weinstein, S. A., and L. A. Smith. 1990. Preliminary fractionation of tiger rattlesnake *(Crotalus tigris)* venom. Toxicon 28:1447–1455.

Weitzel, N. H., and H. R. Panik. 1993. Long-term fluctuations of an isolated population of the Pacific chorus frog *(Pseudacris regilla)* in northwestern Nevada. Great Basin Nat. 53:379–384.

Weldon, P. J. 1982. Responses to ophiophagous snakes by snakes of the genus *Thamnophis*. Copeia 1982:788–794.

———. 1988. Feeding responses of Pacific snappers (genus *Lutjanus*) to the yellow-bellied sea snake *(Pelamis platurus)*. Zool. Sci. (Tokyo) 5:443–448.

Weldon, P. J., and G. M. Burghardt. 1979. The ophiophage defensive response in crotaline snakes: Extension to new taxa. J. Chem. Ecol. 5:141–151.

Weldon, P. J., N. B. Ford, and J. J. Perry-Richardson. 1990. Responses by corn snakes *(Elaphe guttata)* to chemicals from herteospecific snakes. J. Chem. Ecol. 16:37–43.

Weldon, P. J., and T. L. Leto. 1995. A comparative analysis of proteins in the scent gland secretions of snakes. J. Herpetol. 29:474–476.

Weldon, P. J., H. A. Lloyd, and M. S. Blum. 1990. Glycerol monoethers in the scent gland secretions of the western diamondback rattlesnake *(Crotalus atrox)*. Experentia 46:774–775.

Weldon, P. J., R. Ortiz, and T. R. Sharp. 1992. The chemical ecology of crotaline snakes, 309–319. In: J. A. Campbell and E. D. Brodie, Jr. (eds.), Biology of the pitvipers. Tyler, Texas: Selva.

Weldon, P. J., H. W. Sampson, L. Wong, and H. A. Lloyd. 1991. Histology and biochemistry of the scent glands of the yellow-bellied sea sanke *(Pelamis platurus:* Hydrophiidae). J. Herpetol. 25:367–370.

Weldon, P. J., and F. M. Schell. 1984. Responses of king snakes *(Lampropeltis getulus getulus)* to chemicals from colubrid and crotaline snakes. J. Chem. Ecol. 10:1509–1520.

Weldon, P. J., and O. Vallarino. 1988. Wounds on the yellow-bellied sea snake *(Pelamis platurus)* from Panama: Evidence of would-be predators? Biotropica 20:174–176.

Wellstead, C. F. 1981. Behavioral observation in bullsnakes. Herpetol. Rev. 12:6.

Welsh, H. H., Jr., and A. J. Lind. 2000. Evidence of lingual-luring by an aquatic snake. J. Herpetol. 34:67–74.

Wendelken, P. W. 1978. On prey-specific hunting behavior in the western ribbon snake, *Thamnophis proximus*. (Reptilia, Serpentes, Colubridae). J. Herpetol. 12:577–578.

Wentz, C. M. 1953. Experimenting with a coral king snake. Yosemite Nat. Notes 32:80.

Wenzel, D. E. 1990. Observations of captive breeding behavior, matings, and oviposition in the eastern hognose snake *(Heterodon platirhinos)*. Bull. Chicago Herpetol. Soc. 25:86.

Werler, J. E. 1949. Eggs and young of several Texas and Mexican snakes. Herpetologica 5:59–60.

———. 1951. Miscellaneous notes on the eggs and young

of Texan and Mexican reptiles. Zoologica (New York) 36:37–48.

Werler, J. E., and D. M. Darling. 1950. A case of poisoning from a bite of a coral snake, *Micrurus f. tenere* Baird and Girard. Herpetologica 6:197–199.

Werler, J. E., and J. R. Dixon. 2000. Texas snakes: Identification, distribution, and natural history. Austin: University of Texas Press.

Wetmore, A. 1965. The birds of the Republic of Panama. Part 1. Tinamidae (Tinamous) to Rynchopidae (Skimmers). Smithsonian Misc. Coll. 150:1–483.

Wharton, C. H. 1960. Birth and behavior of a brood of cottonmouths, *Agkistrodon piscivorus piscivorus*, with notes on tail-luring. Herpetologica 16:124–129.

———. 1966. Reproduction and growth in the cottonmouths, *Agkistrodon piscivorus* Lacépède, of Cedar Keys, Florida. Copeia 1966:149–161.

———. 1969. The cottonmouth moccasin on Sea Horse Key, Florida. Bull. Florida St. Mus. Biol. Sci. 14:227–272.

Wheeler, D. G. 1994. An unusual incidence of venom squirting by a captive western diamondback rattlesnake, *Crotalus atrox*. Bull. Chicago Herpetol. Soc. 29:199.

Wheeler, G. C. 1947. The amphibians and reptiles of North Dakota. Am. Midl. Nat. 38:162–190.

Wheeler, W. E. 1984. Duck egg predation by fox snakes in Wisconsin. Wildl. Soc. Bull. 12:77–78.

White, A. M. 1979. An unusually large brood of northern copperheads *(Agkistrodon contortrix mokeson)* from Ohio. Ohio J. Sci. 79:78.

White, D. R., J. C. Mitchell, and W. S. Woolcott. 1982. Reproductive cycle and embryonic development of *Nerodia taxispilota* (Serpentes: Colubridae) at the northeastern edge of its range. Copeia 1982:646–652.

White, F. N., and R. C. Lasiewski. 1971. Rattlesnake denning: Theoretical considerations on winter temperatures. J. Theor. Biol. 30:553–557.

White, M., and J. A. Kolb. 1974. A preliminary study of *Thamnophis* near Sagehen Creek, California. Copeia 1974:126–136.

Whitecar, T. L. 1973. Florida 1st protected snake, the indigo. Florida Nat. Mag. 1973(April): 23–25.

Whiting, M. J., J. R. Dixon, and B. D. Greene. 1996. Measuring snake activity patterns: The influence of habitat herterogeneity on catchability. Amphibia-Reptilia 17:47–54.

———. 1997. Spatial ecology of the Concho water snake *(Nerodia harteri paucimaculata)* in a large lake system. J. Herpetol. 31:327–335.

———. 1998. Notes on the spatial ecology and habitat use of three sympatric *Nerodia* (Serpentes: Colubridae). Snake 28:44–50.

Whiting, M. J., B. D. Greene, J. R. Dixon, A. L. Mercer, and C. C. Eckerman. 1992. Observations on the foraging ecology of the western coachwhip snake, *Masticophis flagellum testaceus*. Snake 24:157–160.

Whiteman, H. H., T. M. Mills, and J. W. Gibbons. 1995. Confirmation of a range extension for the pine woods snake *(Rhadinaea flavilata)*. Herpetol. Rev. 26:158.

Whittier, J. M., and D. Crews. 1990. Body mass and reproduction in female red-sided garter snakes *(Thamnophis sirtalis parietalis)*. Herpetologica 46:219–226.

Wickler, W. 1968. Mimicry in plants and animals. New York: McGraw Hill.

Wilkinson, J. A., J. L. Glenn, R. C. Straight, and J. W. Sites, Jr. 1991. Distribution and genetic variation in venom A and B poppulations of the Mojave rattlesnake *(Crotalus scutulatus scutulatus)* in Arizona. Herpetologica 47:54–68.

Willard, D. E. 1967. Evidence for toxic saliva in *Rhadinaea flavilata* (the yellow lipped snake). Herpetologica 23:238.

———. 1977. Constricting methods of snakes. Copeia 1977:379–382.

Williams, K. L. 1985. *Cemophora, C. coccinea*. Cat. Am. Amphib. Rept. 374:1–4.

———. 1988. Systematics and natural history of the American milk snake, *Lampropeltis triangulum*. 2nd ed. Milwaukee, Wisconsin: Milwaukee Public Museum.

———. 1994. *Lampropeltis triangulum*. Cat. Am. Amphib. Rept. 594:1–9.

Williams, K. L., B. C. Brown, and L. D. Wilson. 1966. A new subspecies of the colubrid snake *Cemophora coccinea* (Blumenbach) from southern Texas. Texas J. Sci. 18:85–88.

Williams, K. L., and L. D. Wilson. 1967. A review of the colubrid snake genus *Cemophora* Cope. Tulane Stud. Zool. 13:104–124.

Williams, R. R., Jr., and I. L. Brisbin, Jr. 1978. Responses of captive-reared eastern kingsnakes *(Lampropeltis getulus)* to several prey odor stimuli. Herpetologica 34:79–83.

Williamson, G. K., and R. A. Moulis. 1979. Survey of reptiles and amphibians on Fort Stewart and Hunter Army Airfield. Savannah, Georgia: Savannah Science Museum.

Williamson, G. M., and S. M. Roble. 1999. Noteworthy snake records from False Cape State Park, City of Virginia Beach, Virginia. Catesbeiana 19:61–64.

Williamson, M. A. 1971. An instance of cannibalism in *Crotalus lepidus* (Serpentes: Crotalidae). Herpetol. Rev. 3:18.

Willis, L., S. T. Threlkeld, and C. C. Carpenter. 1982. Tail loss patterns in *Thamnophis* (Reptilia: Colubridae) and the probable fate of injured individuals. Copeia 1982:98–101.

Wills, C. A., and S. J. Beaupre. 2000. An application of randomization for detecting evidence of thermoregulation in timber rattlesnakes *(Crotalus horridus)* from Northwest Arkansas. Physiol. Biochem. Zool. 73:325–334.

Wilson, A. G., and E. M. Wilson. 1996. *Plethodon idahoensis* (Coeur d'Alene Salamander). Snake predation. Herpetol. Rev. 27:138.

Wilson, L. D. 1970a. The coachwhip snake, *Masticophis flagellum* (Shaw): Taxonomy and distribution. Tulane Stud. Zool. Bot. 16:31–99.

———. 1970b. The racer *Coluber constrictor* (Serpentes: Colubridae) in Louisiana and eastern Texas. Texas J. Sci. 22:67–85.

———. 1973a. *Masticophis*. Cat. Am. Amphib. Rept. 144:1–2.

———. 1973b. *Masticophis flagellum*. Cat. Am. Amphib. Rept. 145:1–4.

———. 1975a. *Drymobius*. Cat. Am. Amphib. Rept. 170:1–2.

———. 1975b [1974]. *Drymobius margaritiferus*. Cat. Am. Amphib. Rept. 172:1–2.

———. 1978. *Coluber constrictor*. Cat. Am. Amphib. Rept. 218:1–4.

———. 1982. *Tantilla*. Cat. Am. Amphib. Rept. 307:1–4.

———. 1986. *Coluber*. Cat. Am. Amphib. Rept. 399:1–4.

———. 1999. Checklist and key to the species of the genus *Tantilla* (Serpentes: Colubridae), with some commentary on distribution. Smithsonian Herpetol. Inform. Serv. 122:1–36.

Wilson, L. D., and S. B. Friddle. 1946. Notes on the king snake in West Virginia. Copeia 1946:47–48.

Wilson, L. D., and J. R. Meyer. 1982. The snakes of Honduras. Milwaukee Public Mus. Publ. Biol. Geol. 6:1–159.

Wilson, L. D., and L. Porras. 1983. The ecologial impact of man on the South Florida herpetofauna. Univ. Kansas Mus. Nat. Hist. Spec. Publ. 9:1–89.

Wilson, L. D., R. K. Vaughan, and J. R. Dixon. 2000. *Tantilla cucullata*. Cat. Am. Amphib. Rept. 719:1–2.

Wilson, R. 1985. Yellow warbler nestling predation by eastern fox snake. Ontario Birds 3:73–75.

Wilson, R. L. 1968. Systematics and faunal analysis of a Lower Pliocene vertebrate assemblage from Trago County, Kansas. Contr. Mus. Paleontol. Univ. Michigan 22:75–126.

Wilson, S. C. 1954. Snake fight. Texas Fish and Game 12(5):16–17.

Wilson, T. P., and D. Mauger. 1999. Home range and habitat use of *Sistrurus catenatus catenatus* in eastern Will County, Illinois, 125–134. In: B. Johnson and M. Wright (eds.), Second international symposium and workshop on the conservation of the eastern massasauga rattlesnake, *Sistrurus catenatus catenatus*: Population and habitat management issues in urban, bog, prairie, and forested ecosystems. Scarborough, Ontario, Canada: Toronto Zoo.

Wilson, V. 1951. Some notes on a captive scarlet snake. Herpetologica 7:172.

Wistrand, H. E. 1972. Predation on a snake by *Spermophilus tridecemlineatus*. Am. Midl. Nat. 88:511–512.

Withgott, J. H. 1996. Post-prandial chemosensory searching in black rat snakes. Anim. Behav. 52:775–781.

Withgott, J. H., and C. J. Amlaner. 1996. *Elaphe obsoleta obsoleta* (black rat snake). Foraging. Herpetol. Rev. 27:81–82.

Witmer, M. T. 1994. *Heterodon* and other not-so-harmless "harmless" snakes. J. No. Ohio Assoc. Herpetol. 16:12–20.

Witmer, M. T., and A. M. Bauer. 1995. Early breeding in a captive corn snake *(Elaphe guttata guttata)*. Herpetol. Rev. 26:141.

Wood, J. T. 1949. Observations on *Natrix septemvittata* (Say) in southeastern Ohio. Am. Midl Nat. 42:744–750.

———. 1954. The distribution of poisonous snakes in Virginia. Virginia J. Sci. 5:152–167.

Wood, J. T., and W. E. Duellman. 1950. Size and scutellation in *Natrix septemvittata* (Say) in southeastern Ohio. Am. Midl. Nat. 42:173–178.

Wood, W. F. 1945. Local populations of lizards and snakes. Copeia 1945:177.

Wood, W. F., J. M. Parker, and P. J. Weldon. 1995. Volatile components in scent gland secretions of garter snakes (*Thamnophis* sp.). J. Chem. Ecol. 21:213–219.

Woodbury, A. M. 1929. A new rattlesnake from Utah. Bull. Univ. Utah (Biol. Ser.) 20:106.

———. 1933. Biotic relationships of Zion Canyon, Utah, with special reference to succession. Ecol. Monogr. 3:147–246.

———. 1951. Symposium: A snake den in Toole County, Utah. Introduction—a ten year study. Herpetologica 7:4–14.

———. 1952. Amphibians and reptiles of the Great Salt Lake Valley. Herpetologica 8:42–50.

Woodbury, A. M., and R. M. Hansen. 1950. A snake den in Tintic Mountains, Utah. Herpetologica 6:66–70.

Woodin, W. H., III. 1950. Notes on Arizona species of *Thamnophis*. Herpetologica 6:39–41.

———. 1953. Notes on some reptiles from the Huachuca area of southeastern Arizona. Bull. Chicago Acad. Sci. 9:285–296.

——. 1962. *Ficimia quadrangularis*, a snake new to the fauna of the United States. Herpetologica 18:52–53.

Woodward, B. D., and S. Mitchell. 1990. Predation on frogs in breeding choruses. Southwest. Nat. 35:449–450.

Woolfenden, G. E. 1962. A range extension and subspecific relations of the short-tailed snake, *Stilosoma extenuatum*. Copeia 1962:648–649.

Worley, M. 1970. In search of *Natrix harteri*. Bull. Chicago Herpetol. Soc. 5:41–43.

Worthington, R. D. 1980. *Elaphe subocularis*. Cat. Am. Amphib. Rept. 268:1–2.

Wozniak, E. M., and R. C. Bothner. 1966. Some ecological comparisons between *Thamnophis brachystoma* and *Thamnophis sirtalis* on the Allegheny High Plateau. J. Ohio Herpetol. Soc. 5:164–165.

Wray, K. P., and F. M. Morrissiey. 1999. *Nerodia floridana* (Florida green watersnake). Reproduction. Herpetol. Rev. 30:47.

Wright, A. 1986. Notes on defensive postures observed in captive specimens of the western worm snake *Carphophis amoenus vermis* (Kennicott). Litt. Serpent. Engl. Ed. 6:167–170.

Wright, A. H., and S. C. Bishop. 1915. A biological reconnaissance of the Okefinokee Swamp in Georgia. II. Snakes. Proc. Acad. Nat. Sci. Philadelphia 67:139–192.

Wright, A. H., and A. A. Wright. 1957. Handbook of snakes of the United States and Canada, vols. 1 and 2. Ithaca, New York: Comstock Pubishing Associates, Cornell University Press.

——. 1962. Handbook of snakes of the United States and Canada, vol. 3. Bibliography. Ann Arbor, Michigan: Edwards Brothers, Inc.

Wright, B. A. 1941. Habit and habitat studies of the massasauga rattlesnake (*Sistrurus catenatus catenatus* Raf.) in northeastern Illinois. Am. Midl. Nat. 25:659–672.

Wright, D. L., K. V. Kardong, and D. L. Bentley. 1979. The functional anatomy of the teeth of the western terrestrial garter snake, *Thamnophis elegans*. Herpetologica 35:223–228.

Wright, R. A. S. 1988. *Lampropeltis getulus getulus*. Catesbeiana 8:14.

Wynn, A. H., C. J. Cole, and A. L. Gardner. 1987. Apparent triploidy in the unisexual Brahminy blind snake, *Ramphotyphlops braminus*. Am. Mus. Novitates 2868:1–7.

Yarrow, H. C. 1875. Report upon the collections of batrachians and reptiles made in portions of Nevada, Utah, California, Colorado, New Mexico, and Arizona during the years 1871, 1872, 1873, and 1874, 509–633. In: Report upon United States geographical surveys west of the one hundredth meridian (Wheeler Report). Vol. 5. Zoology. Washington, D.C.: U.S. Government Printing Office.

——. 1882. Descriptions of new species of reptiles and amphibians in the United States National Museum. Proc. U.S. Natl. Mus. 299:438–443.

Yeager, C. P., and G. M. Burghardt. 1991. Effect of food competition on aggregation: Evidence for social recognition in the plains garter snake (*Thamnophis radix*). J. Comp. Psychol. 105(4): 380–386.

Yeatman, H. C. 1983. *Virginia valeriae* (eastern smooth snake). Defense. Herpetol. Rev. 14:22.

Yerger, R. W. 1953. Yellow bullhead preyed upon by cottonmouth moccasin. Copeia 1953:115.

Yingling, R. P. 1982. *Lichanura, L. trivirgata*. Cat. Am. Amphib. Rept. 294:1–2.

Young, B. A. 1989. Ontogenetic changes in the feeding system of the red-sided garter snake, *Thamnophis sirtalis parietalis*. I. Allometric analysis. J. Zool. (London) 218:365–381.

——. 1991. The influences of the aquatic medium on the prey capture system of snakes. J. Nat. Hist. 25:519–531.

——. 1997. A review of sound production and hearing in snakes with a discussion of intraspecific acoustic communication in snakes. J. Pennsylvania Acad. Sci. 71:39–46.

Young, B. A., and I. P. Brown. 1993. On the acoustic profile of the rattlesnake rattle. Amphibia-Reptilia 14:373–380

Young, B. A., J. Lalor, and J. Solomon. 1999. The comparative biomechanics of an ophidian defensive behaviour: Head triangulation in hognose snake (*Heterodon*) and an egg-eating snake (*Dasypeltis*). J. Zool. (London) 248:169–177.

Young, B. A., K. Meltzer, C. Marsit, and G. Abishahin. 1999. Cloacal popping in snakes. J. Herpetol. 33:557–566.

Young, B. A., S. Sheft, and W. Yost. 1995. Sound production in *Pituophis melanoleucus* (Serpentes: Colubridae) with the first description of a vocal cord in snakes. J. Exp. Zool. 273:472–481.

Young, R. A. 1973. Anthills as hibernating sites for *Opheodrys vernalis blanchardi*. Bull. Chicago Herpetol. Soc. 8:7.

——. 1977. Notes on the Graham's water snake, *Regina grahami* Baird and Girard in DuPage County, Illinois. Bull. Chicago Herpetol. Soc. 8:4–5.

Young, R. A., and D. M. Miller. 1980. Notes on the natural history of the Grand Canyon rattlesnake, *Crotalus viridis abyssus* Klauber. Bull. Chicago Herpetol. Soc. 15:1–5.

Young, R. A., D. M. Miller, and D. C. Ochsner. 1980. The Grand Canyon rattlesnake (*Crotalus viridis abyssus*):

Comparison of venom protein profiles with other *viridis* subspecies. Comp. Biochem. Physiol. 66B:601–603.

Young, R. A., and T. L. Vandeventer. 1988. Recent observations of the Louisiana pine snake, *Pituophis melanoleucus ruthveni* Stull. Bull. Chicago Herpetol. Soc. 23:203–207.

Young, T. S., and J. Laerm. 1993. A Late Pleistocene vertebrate assemblage from the St. Marks River, Wakulla County, Florida. Brimleyana 18:15–57.

Zann, L. P., R. J. Cuffey, and C. Kropach. 1975. Fouling organisms and parasites associated with the skin of sea snakes, 251–265. In: W. A. Dunson (ed.), The biology of sea snakes. Baltimore, Maryland: University Park Press.

Zappalorti, R. T., and J. Burger. 1985. On the importance of disturbed sites to habitat selection by pine snakes in the pine barrens of New Jersey. Environ. Conserv. 12:358–361.

Zappalorti, R. T., E. W. Johnson, and Z. Leszczynski. 1983. The ecology of the northern pine snake, *Pituophis melanoleucus melanoleucus* (Daudin) (Reptilia, Serpentes, Colubridae) in southern New Jersey, with special notes on habitat and nesting behavior. Bull. Chicago Herpetol. Soc. 18:57–72.

Zaremba, T. 1978. A fox snake hibernaculum. Bull. Chicago Herpetol. Soc. 13:87–90.

Zaworski, J. P. 1990. Ophiophagy in *Pituophis melanoleucus deserticola*. Bull. Chicago Herpetol. Soc. 25:100.

Zegel, J. C. 1975. Notes on collecting and breeding the eastern coral snake, *Micrurus fulvius fulvius*. Bull. Southwest. Herpetol. Soc. 1:9–10.

Zelnick, G. E. 1966. Midsummer feeding habits of the midland water snake. Southwest. Nat. 11:311–312.

Zimmerman, E. G., and C. W. Kilpatrick. 1973. Karyology of North American crotaline snakes (family Viperidae) of the genera *Agkistrodon, Sistrurus,* and *Crotalus*. Can. J. Genet. Cytol. 15:389–395.

Ziolkowski, C., H. A. Murchison, and A. L. Bieber. 1992.

Effects of myotoxin a on fusion and contractile activity in myoblast-myotube cell cultures. Toxicon 30:397–409.

Zippel, K. C., and L. Kirkland. 1998. *Opheodrys aestivus* (rough green snake). Spider-web entrapment. Herpetol. Rev. 29:46.

Zorichak, J. L. 1953. The ruffed grouse as a snake eater. Flicker 25:2–3.

Zug, D. A., and W. A. Dunson. 1979. Salinity preference in fresh water and estuarine snakes *(Nerodia sipedon* and *N. fasciata)*. Florida Scientist 42:1–8.

Zug, G. R. 1993. Herpetology: An introductory biology of amphibians and reptiles. New York: Academic Press.

Zweifel, R. G. 1952. Pattern variation and evolution of the mountain kingsnake, *Lampropeltis zonata*. Copeia 1952:152–168.

———. 1954. Adaptation to feeding in the snake *Contia tenuis*. Copeia 1954:299–300.

———. 1975. *Lampropeltis zonata*. Cat. Am. Amphib. Rept. 174:1–4.

———. 1980. Aspects of the biolgy of a laboratory population of kingsnakes, 141–152. In: J. B. Murphy and J. T. Collins (eds.), Reproductive biology and diseases of captive reptiles. Soc. Stud. Amphib. Rept. Contr. Herpetol. 1.

———. 1997. Alternating use of hemipenes in the kingsnake, *Lampropeltis getula*. J. Herpetol. 31:459–461.

———. 1998. Apparent non-Mendelian inheritance of melanism in the garter snake, *Thamnophis sirtalis*. Herpetologica 54:83–87.

Zweifel, R. G., and H. C. Dessauer. 1983. Multiple insemination demonstrated experimentally in the kingsnake *(Lampropeltis getulus)*. Experientia 39:317–319.

Zweifel, R. G., and K. S. Norris. 1955. Contribution to the herpetology of Sonora, Mexico: Descriptions of new subspecies of snakes *(Micuroides euryxanthus* and *Lampropeltis getulus)* and miscellaneous collecting notes. Am. Midl. Nat. 54:230–249.

Index to Scientific and Common Names